BUTTERWORTHS BUSINESS LANDLORD AND TENANT HANDBOOK

Fourth edition

KATIE BRADFORD, LLM, *Solicitor*
Property and Finance Litigation Partner, Linklaters

PAUL MATTHEWS, BCL, LLD,
Solicitor-Advocate, Withers LLP
HM Coroner for the City of London
Visiting Professor, King's College London

LexisNexis
® Butterworths

Members of the LexisNexis Group worldwide

United Kingdom	LexisNexis Butterworths, a Division of Reed Elsevier (UK) Ltd, Halsbury House, 35 Chancery Lane, London, WC2A 1EL, and London House, 20–22 East London Street, Edinburgh EH7 4BQ
Argentina	LexisNexis Argentina, Buenos Aires
Australia	LexisNexis Butterworths, Chatswood, New South Wales
Austria	LexisNexis Verlag ARD Orac GmbH & Co KG, Vienna
Benelux	LexisNexis Benelux, Amsterdam
Canada	LexisNexis Canada, Markham, Ontario
Chile	LexisNexis Chile Ltda, Santiago
China	LexisNexis China, Beijing and Shanghai
France	LexisNexis SA, Paris
Germany	LexisNexis Deutschland GmbH, Munster
Hong Kong	LexisNexis Hong Kong, Hong Kong
India	LexisNexis India, New Delhi
Italy	Giuffrè Editore, Milan
Japan	LexisNexis Japan, Tokyo
Malaysia	Malayan Law Journal Sdn Bhd, Kuala Lumpur
Mexico	LexisNexis Mexico, Mexico
New Zealand	LexisNexis NZ Ltd, Wellington
Poland	Wydawnictwo Prawnicze LexisNexis Sp, Warsaw
Singapore	LexisNexis Singapore, Singapore
South Africa	LexisNexis Butterworths, Durban
USA	LexisNexis, Dayton, Ohio

© Reed Elsevier (UK) Ltd 2007
Published by LexisNexis Butterworths

A CIP Catalogue record for this book is available from the British Library.

ISBN 978 1 4057 2590 3

Typeset by Columns Design Ltd, Reading, England.

Printed and bound in Great Britain by William Clowes Limited, Beccles, Suffolk.

Visit LexisNexis UK at www.lexisnexis.co.uk

PREFACE TO THE FOURTH EDITION

Nearly three years have elapsed since the third edition of this handbook. As with the earlier editions, the aim remains that of providing the current text of statutory materials (primary and secondary) relating to the relationship of landlord and tenant in the business context.

In the last edition, the most significant changes were those caused by the then recent overhaul of Part II of the Landlord and Tenant Act 1954. This time there is nothing so dramatic. We have taken the opportunity to update the statutory texts generally. Perhaps the most extensive revision is the addition in 2005 of new ss 24A–24M to the Disability Discrimination Act 1995. Other changes are reflected in the Regulatory Reform (Fire Safety) Order 2005, Control of Asbestos Regulations 2006, and the Energy Performance of Buildings (Certificates and Inspections) (England and Wales) Regulations 2007.

As with the third edition, in the preparation of this edition we have been much assisted by Frances Richardson, Associate in the Litigation Department of Linklaters. We are very grateful to her, and indeed to the editorial staff at the publishers who have overseen the handbook on its way to the press. Suggestions for improvement in future editions are welcomed from users. Indeed, in this edition we have included s 136 of the Law of Property Act 1925 at the suggestion of one of our readers.

The handbook includes materials available to us as at 22 June 2007, which is also the date up to which all the statutes and statutory instruments included are printed as subsequently amended.

Katie Bradford
Paul Matthews

Clerkenwell EC1

August 2007

PREFACE TO THE THIRD EDITION

Some six years have elapsed since the second edition of this handbook. The aim remains that of the first and second editions, namely, to provide the current text of statutory materials (primary and secondary) relating to the relationship of landlord and tenant in the business context.

The changes since the second edition are many and varied. Relevant sections from new legislation such as the Human Rights Act 1998, the Contracts (Rights of Third Parties) Act 1999, the Terrorism Act 2000 and the Commonhold and Leasehold Reform Act 2002 have been included. At the same time the opportunity has been taken to include further provisions from existing legislation (including the Insolvency Act 1986 and the Disability Discrimination Act 1995) that we consider would be particularly helpful to practitioners in this area. On the other hand the provisions of the Land Registration Act 1925 and the Rules of the Supreme Court 1965 have been omitted following their repeal, but not replaced by their modern counterparts, as we considered that these were of less importance in landlord and tenant than in other contexts, and in any case were better dealt with in other works.

However, without any doubt the most significant changes are those caused by the recent overhaul of Part II of the Landlord and Tenant Act 1954. This overhaul took rather longer to materialise than was originally anticipated, and this in itself contributed to the length of time between editions, as we could not produce a new one so long as these important changes were promised to be "just around the corner".

In the preparation of this edition we have been much assisted by the efforts of Frances Richardson, Associate in the Litigation Department of Linklaters. We are very grateful to her, and indeed to the editorial staff at Butterworths who have overseen the handbook on its way to a new edition.

The handbook includes materials available to us as at 17th August 2004, which is also the date up to which all the statutes and statutory instruments included are printed as subsequently amended.

Katie Bradford
Paul Matthews

Clerkenwell EC1

14th November 2004

PREFACE TO THE SECOND EDITION

In the second edition we have included those provisions from the Disability Discrimination Act 1995 which directly relate to the landlord and tenant relationship. In addition the amendments made by the Trusts of Land and Appointment of Trustees Act 1996 have been incorporated.

We have also taken the opportunity to include material which falls into a fifth category in addition to those listed in the preface to the first edition. This material does not have a direct landlord and tenant reference but is used by practitioners in the field so extensively that we thought it would be useful to have the statutory provisions readily to hand. The principal example is the provisions on bona vacantia contained in the Companies Act 1985. Statutes and statutory instruments are listed alphabetically and chronologically in the contents list to help readers locate materials more easily.

As before, prescribed forms and relevant statutory instruments have also been updated.

The handbook includes materials available as at 30 October 1998.

Katie Bradford
Paul Matthews

Clerkenwell EC1

October 1998

PREFACE TO THE FIRST EDITION

This handbook and its companion volume *Butterworths Residential Landlord and Tenant Handbook* are the successors to *Butterworths Landlord and Tenant Handbook* (1992). The statutory materials relating to the law of landlord and tenant are now too extensive to fit comfortably in one volume. The division between residential landlord and tenant on the one hand, and business landlord and tenant on the other, whilst easy to state, has proved more difficult to operate in practice. Users may wonder why certain statutes or statutory instruments have been included, whilst others have been omitted. The principles upon which we have relied in selecting material for inclusion are set out below.

First, we include statutes which relate exclusively to the letting of premises on which a business is to be conducted, the prime example being the Landlord and Tenant Act 1954, Part II. Secondly, we take the view that tenancies for agricultural purposes fall within this first category, since agriculture is itself a business, although for historical and other reasons agricultural tenancies have been subject to a different régime from those relating to other kinds of business. Thus the Agricultural Holdings Act 1986, the Agricultural Tenancies Act 1995 and the many statutory instruments bearing upon agricultural tenancies are incorporated. Thirdly, we include some landlord and tenant materials which mainly or only apply in a business context, for example, the rules on distress for rent and on double rent.

Fourthly, there are some materials of equal application in both a residential and a business context, the importance of which in the latter context mean that they cannot be omitted from this volume. Examples are the landlord and tenant provisions of the Law of Property Act 1925, and the Protection from Eviction Act 1977. There is, therefore, an overlap with the companion volume, but we take the view that the overlap is small, whilst the benefit to the user of having these provisions in this volume will be significant.

Omitted material includes certain landlord and tenant materials which, though concerned with residential lettings, might nonetheless be useful to a person carrying on or advising a business. An obvious case would be one where the business concerned consisted of or included the letting of residential premises for profit. This is a matter for regret, but a line has to be drawn somewhere.

Prescribed forms

Given the importance of using prescribed forms in modern landlord and tenant law, we have proceeded on the basis that where a statute or statutory instrument prescribes a form, it should be included in this work at the appropriate point in the statutory material itself. There are one or two exceptional cases where we have sought to make a modest space saving by omitting something which everyone has access to in a different context, for example the form of an originating summons prescribed by the Rules of the Supreme Court 1965, Appendix A.

The Landlord and Tenant (Covenants) Act 1995 (Notices) Regulations 1995 prescribe the forms of notices to be used for the purposes of the 1995 Act. These Regulations came into force on 1 January 1996 and are reproduced in full.

The nature of a handbook of this kind is such that it cannot be more than a freeze-frame, a snapshot of the statute book at a given moment in time. This means that no account can be taken of draft and proposed legislation, such as the Trusts of

Land and Appointment of Trustees Bill introduced into the House of Lords in November 1995, but whose ultimate fate is not yet known.

The contents of the Handbook take into account materials available as at 1 January 1996.

Katie Bradford
Paul Matthews

Clerkenwell EC1

January 1996

CONTENTS

Alphabetical list

PART II STATUTORY INSTRUMENTS

Chronological list

PART I
STATUTES

DISTRESS FOR RENT ACT 1689

(2 Will & Mar c 5)

An Act for enabling the Sale of Goods distrained for Rent in case the Rent be not paid in a reasonable time

NOTES

The short title was given to this Act by the Statute Law Revision Act 1948.

1 Goods, distrained for rent may be appraised and sold, if not replevied with sufficient security

Whereas the most ordinary and ready way for recovery of arrears of rent is by distresse yet such distresses not being to be sold but onely detained as pledges for inforceing the payment of such rent the persons distraining have little benefit thereby. For the remedying whereof bee it enacted and ordained by the King and Queens most excellent Majestyes by and with the advice and consent of the lords spirituall and temporall and commons in this present Parlyament assembled and by authoritie of the same that ... that where any goods or chattells shall be distrained for any rent reserved and due upon any demise lease or contract whatsoever and the tenant or owner of the goods soe distrained shall not within five dayes [next] after such distresse taken and notice thereof (with the cause of such takeing) left at the chiefe mansion house or other most notorious place on the premises charged with the rent distrained for replevy the same with sufficient security to be given to the sheriffe according to law that then in such case after such distresse and notice as aforesaid and expiration of the said five dayes the person distraining shall and may with the sheriffe or undersheriffe of the county or with the constable of the hundred parish or place where such distresse shall be taken (who are hereby required to be aiding and assisting therein) cause the goods and chattells soe distrained to be appraized by two sworne appraizers (whome such sheriffe under sheriffe or constable are hereby impowred to sweare) to appraize the same truely according to the best of their understandings and after such appraisment shall and may lawfully sell the goods and chattells soe distrained for the best price can be gotten for the same towards satisfaction of the rent for which the said goods and chattells shall be distrained and of the charges of such distresse appraisment and sale leaving the overplus (if any) in the hands of the said sheriffe under sheriffe or constable for the owners use.

[1]

NOTES

Repealed, so far as requiring any sheriff or under sheriff or constable to be aiding and assisting at any distress for rent or to swear any appraiser thereat, by the Parish Constables Act 1872, s 13.

Words omitted repealed by the Statute Law Revision Act 1948.

The word "next" in square brackets was interlined on the roll.

2 Sheaves or cocks of corn loose, etc, or hay, in any barn, etc, may be detained, and if not replevied, sold

And whereas noe sheaves or cocks of corne loose or in the straw or hay in any barne or granary or on any hovell stack or rick can by the law be distrained or otherwise secured for rent whereby landlords are oftentimes cousened and deceived by their tenants who sell their corne graine and hay to strangers and remove the same from the premises chargeable with such rent and thereby avoid the payment of the same. Bee it further enacted by the authoritie aforesaid that for remedying the said practice and deceit it shall and may ... be lawfull to and for any person or persons haveing rent arreare and due upon any such demise lease or contract as aforesaid to seize and secure any sheaves or cocks of corne or corne loose or in the straw or hay lying or being in any barne or granary or upon any hovell stack or rick or otherwise upon any part of the land or ground charged with such rent and to locke up or detaine the same in the place where the same shall be found for or in the nature of a distresse untill the same shall be replevyed upon such security to be given as aforesaid and in default of replevying the same as aforesaid within the time aforesaid to sell the same after such appraisment thereof to be made soe as neverthelesse such corne graine or hay soe distrained as aforesaid be not removed by the person or persons distraineing to the damage of the owner thereof out of the place where the same shall be found and seized but be kept there (as impounded) untill the same shall be replevyed or sold in default of replevying the same within the time aforesaid.

[2]

NOTES
Words omitted repealed by the Statute Law Revision Act 1948.

3 Pound-breach or rescous, treble damages ...

And ... upon any pound breach or rescous of goods or chattells distrained for rent the person or persons grieved thereby shall in a speciall action upon the case for the wrong thereby sustained recover his and their treble damages ... against the offender or offenders in any such rescous or pound-breach any or either of them or against the owners of the goods distrained in case the same be afterwards found to have come to his use or possession.

[3]

NOTES
Section heading: words repealed by virtue of the Administration of Justice Act 1965, s 34(1), Sch 2.
Words omitted in the first place repealed by the Statute Law Revision Act 1888; words omitted in the second place repealed by the Administration of Justice Act 1965, s 34(1), Sch 2.

4 Wrongful distress, double damages and full costs

Provided alwayes ... that in case any such distresse and sale as aforesaid shall be made by vertue or colour of this present Act for rent pretended to be arreare and due where in truth noe rent is arreare or due to the person or persons distraining or to him or them in whose name or names or right such distresse shall be taken as aforesaid that then the owner of such goods or chattells distrained and sold as aforesaid his executors or administrators shall and may by action of trespasse or upon the case to be brought against the person or persons soe distraining any or either of them his or their executors or administrators recover double of the value of the goods or chattells soe distrained and sold ...

[4]

NOTES
Words omitted in the first place repealed by the Statute Law Revision Act 1888; words omitted in the second place repealed by the Administration of Justice Act 1965, s 34(1), Sch 2.

LANDLORD AND TENANT ACT 1709

(8 Anne c 18)

ARRANGEMENT OF SECTIONS

An Act for the better Security of Rents and to prevent Frauds committed by Tenants

NOTES
The short title was given to this Act by the Short Titles Act 1896.

1 Goods taken in execution not removed unless party taking pay rent due

... no goods or chattels whatsoever lying or being in or upon any messuage lands or tenements which are or shall be leased for life or lives term of years at will or otherwise shall be liable to be taken by virtue of any execution on any pretence whatsoever unless the party at whose suit the said execution is sued out shall before the removal of such goods from off the said premises by virtue of such execution or extent pay to the landlord of the said premises or his bailiff all such sum or sums of money as are or shall be due for rent for the said premises at the time of the taking such goods or chattels by virtue of such execution

Provided the said arrears of rent do not amount to more than one year's rent and in case the said arrears shall exceed one year's rent then the said party at whose suit such execution is sued out paying the said landlord or his bailiff one year's rent may proceed to execute his judgment as he might have done before the making of this Act and the sheriff or other officer is hereby impowered and required to levy and pay to the plaintiff as well the money so paid for rent as the execution money.

[5]

NOTES

Words omitted repealed by the Statute Law Revision Act 1948.

2, 3   *(Repealed by the Statute Law Revision Act 1867.)*

4   Action for arrears of rent against tenant for life

And whereas no action ... lies against a tenant for life or lives for any arrears of rent during the continuance of such estate for life or lives ... it shall and may be lawful for any person or persons having any rent in arrear or due upon any lease or demise for life or lives to bring an action or actions ... for such arrears of rent in the same manner as they might have done in case such rent were due and reserved upon a lease for years.

[6]

NOTES

Words omitted repealed by or by virtue of the Statute Law Revision Act 1948.

5   *(Repealed by the Statute Law Revision Act 1867.)*

6   Distress for arrears on leases determined

And whereas tenants per auter vie and lessees for years or at will frequently hold over the tenements to them demised after the determination of such leases. And whereas after the determination of such or any other leases no distress can by law be made for any arrears of rent that grew due on such respective leases before the determination thereof ... it shall and may be lawful for any person or persons having any rent in arrear or due upon any lease for life or lives or for years or at will ended or determined to distrain for such arrears after the determination of the said respective leases in the same manner as they might have done if such lease or leases had not been ended or determined.

[7]

NOTES

Words omitted repealed by or by virtue of the Statute Law Revision Act 1948.

7   Limitation of such distress

Provided that such distress be made within the space of six calendar months after the determination of such lease [and] during the continuance of such landlords title or interest and during the possession of the tenant from whom such arrears became due.

[8]

NOTES

The word "and" in square brackets was interlined on the roll.

8   Proviso for the crown

Provided always and it is hereby enacted and declared by the authority aforesaid that nothing in this Act contained shall extend or be construed to extend to let hinder or prejudice her Majesty her heirs or successors in the levying recovering or seizing any debts fines penalties or forfeitures that are or shall be due payable or answerable to her Majesty her heirs or successors but that it shall and may be lawful for her Majesty her heirs and successors to levy recover and seize such debts fines penalties and forfeitures in the same manner as if this Act had never been made any thing in this Act contained to the contrary thereof in any wise notwithstanding.

[9]

LANDLORD AND TENANT ACT 1730

(4 Geo 2 c 28)

*An Act for the more effectual preventing Frauds committed by Tenants, and for the more easy
Recovery of Rents and Renewal of Leases*

NOTES

The short title was given to this Act by the Short Titles Act 1896.

1 Persons holding over lands, etc, after expiration of leases, to pay double the yearly value

In case any tenant or tenants for any term for life, lives, or years, or other person or persons
who are or shall come into possession of any lands, tenements, or hereditaments by, from, or
under, or by collusion with such tenant or tenants, shall wilfully hold over any lands,
tenements, or hereditaments after the determination of such term or terms, and after demand
made and notice in writing given for delivering the possession thereof by his or their landlords
or lessors or the person or persons to whom the remainder or reversion of such lands,
tenements, or hereditaments shall belong, his or their agent or agents thereunto lawfully
authorized, then and in such case, such person or persons so holding over shall, for and during
the time he, she, and they shall so hold over or keep the person or persons entitled out of
possession of the said lands, tenements and hereditaments as aforesaid, pay to the person or
persons so kept out of possession, their executors, administrators, or assigns, at the rate of
double the yearly value of the lands, tenements, and hereditaments so detained, for so long
time as the same are detained, to be recovered in any of his Majesty's courts of record by
action ...

[10]

NOTES

Words omitted repealed by the Statute Law Revision Act 1948.

2–4 *(Repealed by the Statute Law Revision Act 1867.)*

5 Method of recovering seck rents, etc

And whereas the remedy for recovering rents seck, rents of assize, and chief rents are tedious
and difficult: ... from and after the twenty-fourth day of June, one thousand seven hundred
and thirty one, all and every person or persons, bodies politick and corporate, shall and may
have the like remedy by distress and by impounding and selling the same, in cases of rents
seck, rents of assize, and chief rents, which have been duly answered or paid for the space of
three years, within the space of twenty years before the first day of this present session of
Parliament, or shall be hereafter created, as in case of rent reserved upon lease, any law or
usage to the contrary notwithstanding.

[11]

NOTES

Words omitted repealed by virtue of the Statute Law Revision Act 1948.

6 *(Repealed by the Law of Property Act 1925, s 207, Sch 7.)*

7 Not to extend to Scotland

Provided always, that nothing in this Act contained shall extend to ... Scotland.

[12]

NOTES

Words omitted repealed by the Statute Law Revision Act 1948.

DISTRESS FOR RENT ACT 1737

(11 Geo 2 c 19)

ARRANGEMENT OF SECTIONS

An Act for the more effectual securing the Payment of Rents, and preventing Frauds by Tenants

___

NOTES

The short title was given to this Act by the Short Titles Act 1896.

___

Preamble

Whereas the several laws heretofore made for the better security of rents, and to prevent frauds committed by tenants, have not proved sufficient to obtain the good ends and purposes designed thereby, but rather the fraudulent practices of tenants, and the mischief intended by the said Acts to be prevented have of late years increased, to the great loss and damage of their lessors or landlords: For remedy whereof, may it please your most excellent Majesty that it may be enacted, and be it enacted by the King's most excellent Majesty, by and with the advice and consent of the lords spiritual and temporal, and commons, in this present Parliament assembled, and by the authority of the same, that

1 Landlords may distrain and sell goods fraudulently carried off the premises

From and after the twenty-fourth day of June in the year of our Lord one thousand seven hundred and thirty eight, in case any tenant or tenants, lessee or lessees for life or lives, term of years, at will, sufferance, or otherwise, of any messuages, lands, tenements, or hereditaments, upon the demise or holding whereof any rent is or shall be reserved, due, or made payable, shall fraudulently or clandestinely convey away, or carry off or from such premises, his, her, or their goods or chattels, to prevent the landlord or lessor, landlords or lessors, from distraining the same for arrears of rent so reserved, due, or made payable, it shall and may be lawful to and for every landlord or lessor, landlords or lessors, within ... England, dominion of Wales, or the town of Berwick upon Tweed, or any person or persons by him, her, or them for that purpose lawfully impowered, within the space of thirty days next ensuing such conveying away or carrying off such goods or chattels as aforesaid, to take and seize such goods and chattels wherever the same shall be found, as a distress for the said arrears of rent, and the same to sell or otherwise dispose of in such manner as if the said goods and chattels had actually been distrained by such lessor or landlord, lessors or landlords, in and upon such premises for such arrears of rent, any law, custom, or usage to the contrary in any wise notwithstanding.

[13]

___

NOTES

Words omitted repealed by the Statute Law Revision Act 1948.

___

2 Unless sold to any person not privy to the fraud

Provided always, that no landlord or lessor or other person intitled to such arrears of rent shall take or seize any such goods or chattels as a distress for the same which shall be sold bona fide and for a valuable consideration before such seizure made to any person or persons not privy to such fraud as aforesaid, any thing herein contained to the contrary notwithstanding.

[14]

3 Penalty on the said fraud, or assisting thereto

And to deter tenants from such fraudulent conveying away their goods and chattels, and others from wilfully aiding or assisting therein or concealing the same, be it further enacted by the authority aforesaid, that from and after the said twenty fourth day of June, if any such tenant or lessee shall fraudulently remove and convey away his or her goods or chattels as aforesaid, or if any person or persons shall wilfully and knowingly aid or assist any such tenant or lessee in such fraudulent conveying away or carrying off of any part of his or her goods or chattels, or in concealing the same, all and every person and persons so offending shall forfeit and pay to the landlord or landlords, lessor or lessors from whose estate such goods and chattels were fraudulently carried off as aforesaid, double the value of the goods by him, her, or them respectively carried off or concealed as aforesaid, to be recovered by action of debt in [the High Court], or in the courts of session in the counties palatine of Chester, Lancaster, or Durham respectively, ...

[15]

NOTES

Words in square brackets substituted by virtue of the Supreme Court of Judicature (Consolidation) Act 1925, ss 1, 18, 224(1); words omitted repealed by the Statute Law Revision Act 1948.

4 If the goods exceed not the value of £50, landlords to have recourse to two justices

Provided always, ... that where the goods and chattels so fraudulently carried off or concealed shall not exceed the value of fifty pounds, it shall and may be lawful for the landlord or landlords from whose estate such goods or chattels were removed, his, her, or their bailiff, servant, or agent in his, her, or their behalf, to exhibit a complaint in writing against such offender or offenders before two or more justices of the peace ..., not being interested in the lands or tenements whence such goods were removed, who may summon the parties concerned, examine the fact, and all proper witnesses upon oath, ... and in a summary way determine whether such person or persons be guilty of the offence with which he or they are charged; and to enquire in like manner of the value of the goods and chattels by him, her, or them respectively so fraudulently carried off or concealed as aforesaid; and, upon full proof of the offence, by order under their hands and seals, the said justices of peace may and shall adjudge the offender or offenders to pay double the value of the said goods and chattels ... , at such time as the said justices shall appoint; ...

[16]

NOTES

Words omitted in the first place repealed by the Statute Law Repeals Act 1888; words omitted in the second place repealed by the Courts Act 2003, s 109(1), (3), Sch 8, para 2, Sch 10 and the Statute Law Revision Act 1948; words omitted in the third place repealed by the Statute Law Revision Act 1948; words omitted in the fourth place repealed by the Justices of the Peace Act 1949, s 46(2), Sch 7, Pt III; words omitted in the fifth place repealed by the Statute Law Revision Act 1948 and the Summary Jurisdiction Act 1884, s 4, Schedule.

5 Appeal from them to the [Crown Court]

Provided also, that it shall and may be lawful for any person who thinks himself aggrieved by such order of the said two justices to appeal to the [Crown Court] ...

[17]

NOTES

Section heading: words in square brackets substituted by virtue of the Courts Act 1971, s 56(1), Sch 8, Pt I, para 2.

Words in square brackets substituted by virtue of the Courts Act 1971, s 56(1), Sch 8, Pt I, para 2; words omitted repealed by the Summary Jurisdiction Act 1884, s 4, Schedule.

6 The two justices order, on such appeal, not to be executed

Provided also, that, where the party appealing shall enter into a recognizance with one or two sufficient surety or sureties in double the sum so ordered to be paid, with condition to appear at [the Crown Court], the order of the said two justices shall not be executed against him in the mean time.

[18]

NOTES

Words in square brackets substituted by virtue of the Courts Act 1971, s 56(1), Sch 8, Pt I, para 2.

7 Landlords may break open houses to seize goods fraudulently secured therein

And ... where any goods or chattels fraudulently or clandestinely conveyed or carried away by any tenant or tenants, lessee or lessees, his, her, or their servant or servants, agent or agents, or other person or persons aiding or assisting therein, shall be put, placed, or kept in any house, barn, stable, out-house, yard, close, or place, locked up, fastened, or otherwise secured, so as to prevent such goods or chattels from being taken and seized as a distress for arrears of rent, it shall and may be lawful for the landlord or landlords, lessor or lessors, his, her, or their steward, bailiff, receiver, or other person or persons impowered, to take and seize, as a distress for rent, such goods and chattels (first calling to his, her, or their assistance the constable, head-borough, borsholder, or other peace-officer of the hundred, borough, parish, district, or place where the same shall be suspected to be concealed, who are hereby required to aid and assist therein; and in case of a dwelling-house, oath being also first made before some justice of the peace of a reasonable ground to suspect that such goods or chattels are therein), in the daytime, to break open and enter into such house, barn, stable, out-house, yard, close, and place, and to take and seize such goods and chattels for the said arrears of rent, as he, she, or they might have done by virtue of this or any former Act if such goods and chattels had been put in any open field or place.

[19]

NOTES

Words omitted repealed by the Statute Law Revision Act 1888.

8 And may distrain stock or cattle on the premises, for arrears of rent

And ... from and after the said twenty fourth day of June, which shall be in the year of our Lord one thousand seven hundred and thirty eight, it shall and may be lawful to and for every lessor or landlord, lessors or landlords, or his, her, or their steward, bailiff, receiver, or other person or persons impowered by him, her, or them, to take and seize, as a distress for arrears of rent, any cattle or stock of their respective tenant or tenants feeding or depasturing upon any common, appendent or appurtenant, or any ways belonging to all or any part of the premises demised or holden; and also to take and seize all sorts of corn and grass, hops, roots, fruits, pulse, or other product whatsoever which shall be growing on any part of the estates so demised or holden, as a distress for arrears of rent; and the same to cut, gather, make, cure, carry, and lay up, when ripe, in the barns or other proper place on the premises so demised or holden; and in case there shall be no barn or proper place on the premises so demised or holden, then in any other barn or proper place which such lessor or landlord, lessors or landlords, shall hire or otherwise procure for that purpose, and as near as may be to the premises, and in convenient time to appraise, sell, or otherwise dispose of the same, towards satisfaction of the rent for which such distress shall have been taken, and of the charges of such distress, appraisement, and sale, in the same manner as other goods and chattels may be seized, distrained, and disposed of; and the appraisement thereof to be taken when cut, gathered, cured, and made, and not before.

[20]

NOTES

Words omitted repealed by the Statute Law Revision Act 1888.

9 Tenants to have notice of the place where the distress is lodged. Distress of corn, etc, to cease, if rent be paid before it be cut

Provided always, that notice of the place where the goods and chattels so distrained shall be lodged or deposited shall, within the space of one week after the lodging or depositing thereof in such place, be given to such lessee or tenant, or left at the last place of his or her abode; and that if after any distress for arrears of rent so taken, of corn, grass, hops, roots, fruits, pulse, or other product which shall be growing as aforesaid and at any time before the same shall be ripe and cut, cured, or gathered, the tenant or lessee, his or her executors, administrators, or assigns, shall pay or cause to be paid to the lessor or landlord, lessors or landlords, for whom such distress shall be taken, or to the steward or other person, usually imployed to receive the rents of such lessor or lessors, landlord or landlords, the whole rent which shall be then in arrear, together with the full costs and charges of making such distress and which shall have been occasioned thereby, that then and upon such payment or lawful tender thereof actually made, whereby the end of such distress will be fully answered, the same, and every part thereof shall cease, and the corn, grass, hops, roots, fruits, pulse, or other product so distrained, shall be delivered up to the lessee or tenant, his or her executors, administrators, or assigns, any thing herein before contained to the contrary notwithstanding.

[21]

10 Distresses may be secured, and sold on the premisses

And whereas great difficulties and inconveniences frequently arise to landlords and lessors and other persons taking distresses for rent, in removing the goods and chattels or stock distrained off the premisses, in cases where by law they may not be impounded and secured thereupon, and also to the tenants themselves many times, by the damage unavoidably done to such goods and chattels or stock in the removal thereof: Be it enacted by the authority aforesaid, that from and after the said twenty fourth day of June one thousand seven hundred and thirty eight, it shall and may be lawful to and for any person or persons lawfully taking any distress for any kind of rent, to impound or otherwise secure the distress so made, of what nature or kind soever it may be, in such place or on such part of the premisses chargeable with the rent as shall be most fit and convenient for the impounding and securing such distress, and to appraise, sell, and dispose of the same upon the premisses in like manner and under the like directions and restraints to all intents and purposes as any person taking a distress for rent may now do off the premisses by virtue of an Act made in the second year of the reign of King William and Queen Mary, intituled "An Act for enabling the sale of goods distrained for rent, in case the rent be not paid in a reasonable time," or of one other Act made in the fourth year of his present Majesty, intituled "An Act for the more effectual preventing frauds committed by tenants, and for the more easy recovery of rents and renewal of leases"; and that it shall and may be lawful to and for any person or persons whatsoever to come and go to and from such place or part of the said premisses where any distress for rent shall be impounded and secured as aforesaid, in order to view, appraise, and buy, and also in order to carry off or remove the same on account of the purchaser thereof, and that if any pound-breach or rescous shall be made of any goods and chattels, or stock distrained for rent and impounded or otherwise secured by virtue of this Act, the person or persons aggrieved thereby shall have the like remedy as in cases of pound-breach or rescous is given and provided by the said Statute.

[22]

NOTES

An Act for enabling the sale of goods distrained for rent, in the case of rent be not paid in a reasonable time: see the Distress for Rent Act 1689, at [1].

An Act for the more effectual preventing frauds committed by tenants, and for the more easy recovery of rents and renewal of leases: see the Landlord and Tenant Act 1730, at [10].

11–15 (*S 11 repealed by the Law of Property Act 1925, s 207, Sch 7; ss 12, 13 repealed by the Statute Law Revision Act 1867; s 14 repealed by the Statute Law (Repeals) Act 1989; s 15 repealed by the Statute Law (Repeals) Act 1977.*)

16 Provision for landlords, where tenants desert the premisses

And whereas landlords are often great sufferers by tenants running away in arrear, and not only suffering the demised premisses to lie uncultivated without any distress thereon, whereby their landlords or lessors might be satisfied for the rent-arrear, but also refusing to deliver up the possession of the demised premisses, whereby the landlords are put to the expence and delay of recovering in ejectment: Be it further enacted by the authority aforesaid, that from and after the said twenty fourth day of June one thousand seven hundred and thirty eight, if any tenant holding any lands, tenements, or hereditaments at a rack-rent, or where the rent reserved shall be full three fourths of the yearly value of the demised premisses, who shall be in arrear for one year's rent, shall desert the demised premisses and leave the same uncultivated or unoccupied, so as no sufficient distress can be had to countervail the arrears of rent, it shall and may be lawful to and for two or more justices of the peace ... (having no interest in the demised premises), at the request of the lessor or landlord, lessors or landlords, or his, her, or their bailiff or receiver, to go upon and view the same, and to affix or cause to be affixed on the most notorious part of the premisses, notice in writing what day (at the distance of fourteen days at least) they will return to take a second view thereof; and if upon such second view the tenant, or some person on his or her behalf, shall not appear and pay the rent in arrear, or there shall not be sufficient distress upon the premisses, then the said justices may put the landlord or landlords, lessor or lessors into the possession of the said demised premisses, and the lease thereof to such tenant, as to any demise therein contained only, shall from thenceforth become void.

[23]

NOTES

Words omitted repealed by the Courts Act 2003, s 109(1), (3), Sch 8, para 3, Sch 10.

One year's rent: the period of one year was reduced to six months by the Deserted Tenements Act 1817.

17 Tenants may appeal from the justices

Provided always, that such proceedings of the said justices shall be examinable into in a summary way by the next justice or justices of assize of the respective counties in which such lands or premisses lie; and if they lie in the city of London or county of Middlesex, by the judges of the courts of King's Bench or Common Pleas; and if in the counties palatine of Chester, Lancaster, or Durham, then before the judges thereof; and if in Wales, then before the courts of grand-sessions respectively, who are hereby respectively impowered to order restitution to be made to such tenant, together with his or her expences and costs, to be paid by the lessor or landlord, lessors or landlords, if they shall see cause for the same; and in case they shall affirm the act of the said justices, to award costs not exceeding five pounds for the frivolous appeal.

[24]

18 Tenants holding premisses after the time they notify for quitting them, to pay double rent from such time

And whereas great inconveniences have happened and may happen to landlords whose tenants have power to determine their leases, by giving notice to quit the premisses by them holden, and yet refusing to deliver up the possession when the landlord hath agreed with another tenant for the same: Be it further enacted by the authority aforesaid, that from and after the said twenty fourth day of June one thousand seven hundred and thirty eight, in case any tenant or tenants shall give notice of his, her, or their intention to quit the premisses by him, her, or them holden, at a time mentioned in such notice, and shall not accordingly deliver up the possession thereof at the time in such notice contained, that then the said tenant or tenants, his, her, or their executors or administrators, shall from thenceforward pay to the landlord or landlords, lessor or lessors, double the rent or sum which he, she, or they should otherwise have paid, to be levied, sued for, and recovered at the same times and in the same manner as the single rent or sum, before the giving such notice, could be levied, sued for, or recovered; and such double rent or sum shall continue to be paid during all the time such tenant or tenants shall continue in possession as aforesaid.

[25]

19 Distresses for rent not unlawful, etc, for any irregularity in the disposition of them

And whereas it hath sometimes happened that upon a distress made for rent justly due, the directions of the Statute made in the second year of the reign of King William and Queen Mary, intituled "An Act for enabling the sale of goods distrained for rent, in case the rent be not paid in a reasonable time," have not been strictly pursued, but through the mistake or inadvertency of the landlord or other person intituled to such rent, and distraining for the same, or of the bailiff or agent of such landlord or other person, some irregularity or tortious act hath been afterwards done in the disposition of the distress so seized or taken as aforesaid, for which irregularity or tortious act the party distraining hath been deemed a trespasser ab initio, and in an action brought against him as such, the plaintiff hath been intituled to recover, and has actually recovered the full value of the rent for which such distress was taken: And whereas it is a very great hardship upon landlords and other persons intituled to rents, that a distress duly made should be thus in effect avoided for any subsequent irregularity: Be it enacted by the authority aforesaid, that from and after the said twenty fourth day of June in the year of our Lord one thousand seven hundred and thirty eight, where any distress shall be made for any kind of rent justly due, and any irregularity or unlawful act shall be afterwards done by the party or parties distraining, or by his, her, or their agents, the distress itself shall not be therefore deemed to be unlawful, nor the party or parties making it be deemed a trespasser or trespassers ab initio; but the party or parties aggrieved by such unlawful act or irregularity shall or may recover full satisfaction for the special damage he, she or they shall have sustained thereby, and no more, in an action of trespass or on the case, at the election of the plaintiff or plaintiffs: Provided always, that where the plaintiff or plaintiffs shall recover in such action, he, she, or they shall be paid his, her, or their full costs of suit, and have all the like remedies for the same as in other cases of costs.

[26]

NOTES

An Act for enabling the sale of goods distrained for rent, in case the rent be not paid in a reasonable time: see the Distress for Rent Act 1689, at [1].

20–23 *(S 20 repealed by the Statute Law (Repeals) Act 1986; s 21 repealed by the Statute Law Revision Act 1958; s 22 repealed by the Statute Law Revision and Civil Procedure Act 1883, s 4; s 23 repealed by the Statute Law Revision and Civil Procedure Act 1881, s 3, Schedule.)*

FIRES PREVENTION (METROPOLIS) ACT 1774

(14 Geo 3 c 78)

An Act ... for the more effectually preventing Mischiefs by Fire within the Cities of London and Westminster and the Liberties thereof, and other the Parishes, Precincts, and Places within the Weekly Bills of Mortality, the Parishes of Saint Mary-le-bon, Paddington, Saint Pancras and Saint Luke at Chelsea, in the County of Middlesex ...

NOTES

The short title was given to this Act by the Short Titles Act 1896; words omitted repealed by the Statute Law Revision Act 1887.

(Whole Act except ss 83, 86, repealed by the Metropolitan Fire Brigade Act 1865, s 34.)

83 Money insured on houses burnt how to be applied

And in order to deter and hinder ill-minded persons from wilfully setting their house or houses or other buildings on fire with a view of gaining to themselves the insurance money, whereby the lives and fortunes of many families may be lost or endangered: Be it further enacted by the authority aforesaid, that it shall and may be lawful to and for the respective governors or directors of the several insurance offices for insuring houses or other buildings against loss by fire, and they are hereby authorised and required, upon the request of any person or persons interested in or intitled unto any house or houses or other buildings which may hereafter be burnt down, demolished or damaged by fire, or upon any grounds of suspicion that the owner or owners, occupier or occupiers, or other person or persons who shall have insured such house or houses or other buildings have been guilty of fraud, or of wilfully setting their house or houses or other buildings on fire, to cause the insurance money to be laid out and expended, as far as the same will go, towards rebuilding, reinstating or repairing such house or houses or other buildings so burnt down, demolished or damaged by fire, unless the party or parties claiming such insurance money shall, within sixty days next after his, her or their claim is adjusted, give a sufficient security to the governors or directors of the insurance office where such house or houses or other buildings are insured, that the same insurance money shall be laid out and expended as aforesaid, or unless the said insurance money shall be in that time settled and disposed of to and amongst all the contending parties, to the satisfaction and approbation of such governors or directors of such insurance office respectively.

[27]

86 No action to lie against a person where the fire accidentally begins

And ... no action, suit or process whatever shall be had, maintained or prosecuted against any person in whose house, chamber, stable, barn or other building, or on whose estate any fire shall ... accidentally begin, nor shall any recompence be made by such person for any damage suffered thereby, any law, usage or custom to the contrary notwithstanding: ... provided that no contract or agreement made between landlord and tenant shall be hereby defeated or made void.

[28]

NOTES

Words omitted in the first place repealed by the Statute Law Revision Act 1888; words omitted in the second place repealed by the Statute Law Revision Act 1948; words omitted in the third place repealed by the Statute Law Revision Act 1958 and by virtue of the Statute Law Revision Act 1861.

SALE OF FARMING STOCK ACT 1816

(56 Geo 3 c 50)

ARRANGEMENT OF SECTIONS

An Act to regulate the Sale of Farming Stock taken in Execution

[20 June 1816]

NOTES

The short title was given to this Act by the Short Titles Act 1896.

1 No sheriff or other officer shall carry off or sell from any lands any straw, chaff, etc, in any case; nor any hay or other produce, where covenant against removal

No sheriff or other officer in England or Wales shall, by virtue of any process of any court of law, carry off, or sell or dispose of for the purpose of being carried off, from any lands let to farm any straw threshed or unthreshed, or any straw of crops growing, or any chaff, colder, or any turnips, or any manure, compost, ashes, or seaweed, in any case whatsoever; nor any hay, grass or grasses, whether natural or artificial, nor any tares or vetches, nor any roots or vegetables, being produce of such lands, in any case where, according to any covenant or written agreement entered into and made for the benefit of the owner or landlord of any farm, such hay, grass or grasses, tares and vetches, roots or vegetables, ought not to be taken off or withholden from such lands, or which by the tenor or effect of such covenants or agreements ought to be used or expended thereon, and of which covenants or agreements such sheriff or other officer shall have received a written notice before he shall have proceeded to sale.

[29]

2 Tenant to give notice to sheriff of the existence of covenants and name, etc, of landlord; and sheriff to give notice to landlord of taking possession of produce

... the tenant or occupier of any lands let to farm, against whose goods any process of law shall issue, whereby such goods may be taken and sold, shall, on having knowledge of such process, give a written notice to the sheriff or other officer executing the same of such covenants or agreements whereof he or she shall have knowledge, and which may relate to and regulate or are intended to regulate the use and expenditure of the crops or produce grown or growing thereon, and also of the name and residence of the owner or landlord of such lands; and such sheriff or other officer shall forthwith on executing such process, and before any sale shall have been proceeded in, send a notice by the general post to the owner or landlord of such lands, in all cases where such owner or landlord shall be resident in any part of this United Kingdom, and shall have been made known to and ascertained by such sheriff or other officer, and also to the known steward or agent of such landlord or owner in respect of such lands, stating to such owner, landlord, and agent the fact of possession having been taken of any crops or produce herein-before mentioned; and such sheriff or other officer shall, in all cases of the absence or silence of such landlord or owner, or his or her agent, postpone and delay the sale of such crops or produce until the latest day he lawfully can or may appoint for such sale.

[30]

NOTES
Words omitted repealed by the Statute Law Revision Act 1888.

3 Sheriff may dispose of produce subject to an agreement to expend it on the land

Provided always ... that such sheriff or other officer executing such process may dispose of any crops or produce hereinbefore mentioned to any person or persons who shall agree in writing with such sheriff or other officer, in cases where no covenant or written agreement shall be shown, to use and expend the same on such lands in such manner as shall accord with the custom of the country, and in cases where any covenant or written agreement shall be shown then according to such covenant or written agreement; and after such sale or disposal so qualified it shall be lawful for such person or persons to use all such necessary barns, stables, buildings, outhouses, yards, and fields, for the purpose of consuming such crops or produce, as such sheriff or other officer shall allot or assign to them for that purpose, and which such tenant or occupier would have been entitled to and ought to have used for the like purpose on such lands.

[31]

NOTES
Words omitted repealed by the Statute Law Revision Act 1888.

4 Sheriff may permit landlord to bring action on such agreement in his name

... such sheriff or other officer shall, on the request of any landlord or owner who shall be aggrieved by any breach of such agreement, permit such landlord or owner to bring any action or actions in the name of such sheriff or other officer for the recovery of damages in respect of such breach; such landlord or owner having nevertheless fully indemnified such sheriff or other officer against all costs whatsoever and all loss and damage, before any such action shall be commenced.

[32]

NOTES
Words omitted repealed by the Statute Law Revision Act 1888.

5 Sheriff to inquire as to the name and residence of the landlord

... such sheriff or other officer shall, before any sale of any crops or produce of any lands let to farm shall be proceeded in, make by all ways and means due inquiry within the parish where such lands shall be situate as to the name and residence of the landlord or owner of such lands.

[33]

NOTES
Words omitted repealed by the Statute Law Revision Act 1888.

6 Landlord not to distrain for rent on purchaser of produce severed from the soil or other things sold subject to agreement

... in all cases where any purchaser or purchasers of any crop or produce herein-before mentioned shall have entered into any agreement with such sheriff or other officer touching the use and expenditure thereof on lands let to farm, it shall not be lawful for the owner or landlord of such lands to distrain for any rent on any corn, hay, straw, or other produce thereof, which, at the time of such sale and the execution of such agreement entered into under the provisions of this Act, shall have been severed from the soil and sold subject to such agreement by such sheriff or other officer, nor on any turnips whether drawn or growing, if sold according to the provisions of this Act, nor on any horses, sheep, or other cattle, nor on any beasts whatsoever, nor on any waggons, carts, or other implements of husbandry which any person or persons shall employ, keep, or use on such lands, for the purpose of threshing out, carrying, or consuming any such corn, hay, straw, turnips, or other produce, under the provisions of the Act and the agreement or agreements directed to be entered into between the sheriff or other officer and the purchaser or purchasers of such crops and produce as herein-before are mentioned.

[34]

NOTES
Words omitted repealed by the Statute Law Revision Act 1888.

7   Sheriff not to sell any clover, etc, growing with corn

... no sheriff or other officer shall, by virtue of any process whatsoever, sell or dispose of any clover, rye-grass, or any artificial grass or grasses whatsoever, which shall be newly sown and be growing under any crop of standing corn.

[35]

NOTES
Words omitted repealed by the Statute Law Revision Act 1888.

8   Act not to extend to straw, etc, removeable under contract

Provided always ... that this Act shall not extend to any straw, turnips, or other articles which the tenant may remove from the farm consistently with some contract in writing.

[36]

NOTES
Words omitted repealed by the Statute Law Revision Act 1888.

9   Sheriff not to be liable for damages, unless for wilful omission

... in every case where any action shall be brought against such sheriff or other officer for any breach of or omission of compliance with the provisions of this Act, no plaintiff shall be entitled to recover any damages against such sheriff or other officer, unless it shall be proved on the trial of such action that such breach or omission was wilful on the part of such sheriff or other officer.

[37]

NOTES
Words omitted repealed by the Statute Law Revision Act 1888.

10   Indemnity to sheriff and others acting under the provisions of this Act

... no sheriff[, under sheriff or other officer] nor any or either of their deputies, agents, bailiffs, or servants, nor any person or persons who shall purchase any hay, straw, chaff, turnips, grass or grasses, or other produce and things herein-before mentioned, under the provisions of this Act, nor his, her, or their servant or servants, shall be deemed or taken to be a trespasser by reason of his, her, or their coming upon or remaining in possession of any barns or other buildings, yards or fields, for the purpose of threshing out or consuming any straw, hay, turnips, or other produce herein-before mentioned, under the provisions of this Act, or for doing any matter or thing whatsoever fit and necessary to be done for the purpose of executing the same, and carrying into effect all stipulations contained in any agreement made under such provisions, though such Acts shall have been done by such sheriff or other officer, and by such person or persons, his, her, or their servants, after the return of the process under which such sheriff or other officer shall have acted.

[38]

NOTES

Words omitted repealed by the Statute Law Revision Act 1888; words in square brackets substituted by the Courts Act 2003, s 109(1), Sch 8, para 5.

11 Assignee of bankrupt, etc, not to take any produce, etc, in any other way than the bankrupt, etc, would have been entitled to do

... no assignee of any bankrupt, ... nor any assignee under any bill of sale, nor any purchaser of the goods, chattels, stock, or crop of any person or persons engaged or employed in husbandry on any lands let to farm, shall take, use, or dispose of any hay, straw, grass or grasses, turnips, or other roots, or any other produce of such lands, or any manure, compost, ashes, seaweed, or other dressings intended for such lands, and being thereon, in any other manner and for any other purpose than such bankrupt, ... or other person so employed in husbandry ought to have taken, used, or disposed of the same, if no commission of bankruptcy had issued, or no such assignment or assignments had been executed, or sale made.

[39]

NOTES

Words omitted in the first place repealed by the Statute Law Revision Act 1888; words omitted in the second and third places repealed by the Statute Law Revision Act 1873.

LANDLORD AND TENANT ACT 1851

(14 & 15 Vict c 25)

An Act to improve the Law of Landlord and Tenant in relation to Emblements, to growing Crops seized in Execution, and to Agricultural Tenants Fixtures

[24 July 1851]

NOTES

The short title was given to this Act by the Short Titles Act 1896.

1 *(Repealed by the Statute Law (Repeals) Act 1971.)*

2 Growing crops seized and sold under execution to be liable for accruing rent

In case all or any part of the growing crops of the tenant of any farm or lands shall be seized and sold by any sheriff or other officer by virtue of any writ of fieri facias or other writ of execution, such crops, so long as the same shall remain on the farms or lands, shall, in default of sufficient distress of the goods and chattels of the tenant, be liable to the rent which may accrue and become due to the landlord after any such seizure and sale, and to the remedies by distress for recovery of such rent, and that notwithstanding any bargain and sale or assignment which may have been made or executed of such growing crops by any such sheriff or other officer.

[40]

3–5 *(S 3 repealed by the Statute Law (Repeals) Act 1971; s 4 repealed by the Tithe Act 1936, s 48, Sch 9; s 5 outside the scope of this work.)*

COMMON LAW PROCEDURE ACT 1852

(15 & 16 Vict c 76)

ARRANGEMENT OF SECTIONS

An Act to amend the Process, Practice, and Mode of Pleading in the Superior Courts of Common Law at Westminster, and in the Superior Courts of the Counties Palatine of Lancaster and Durham

[30 June 1852]

(*Preamble repealed by the Statute Law Revision Act 1892.*)

1–167   (*Ss 1, 10, 24, 26, 92, 100, 104 repealed by the Statute Law Revision Act 1875; ss 2–9, 11–22, 25, 27–91, 93–99, 101–103, 109, 111, 116–125, 128–131, 133–167 repealed by the Statute Law Revision and Civil Procedure Act 1883, s 3, Schedule; s 23 repealed by the Commissioners for Oaths Act 1889, s 12, Schedule; ss 105–108, 112–115 repealed by the Courts Act 1971, s 56, Sch 11, Pt 1; ss 110, 132 repealed by the Statute Law Revision Act 1950; s 126 repealed by the Supreme Court Act 1981, s 152(4), Sch 7; s 127 repealed by the Administration of Justice Act 1965, s 34(1), Sch 2.*)

Ejectment

And with respect to the action of ejectment:

168–209   (*Ss 168–207 repealed by the Statute Law Revision and Civil Law Procedure Act 1883, s 3, Schedule; s 208 repealed by the Statute Law Revision Act 1892; s 209 repealed by the Law of Property Act 1925, s 207, Sch 7.*)

210   Proceedings in ejectment by landlord for non-payment of rent

In all cases between landlord and tenant, as often as it shall happen that one half year's rent shall be in arrear, and the landlord or lessor, to whom the same is due, hath right by law to re-enter for the non-payment thereof, such landlord or lessor shall and may, without any formal demand, or re-entry, serve a writ in ejectment for the recovery of the demised premises; ... which service ... shall stand in the place and stead of a demand and re-entry; and in case of judgment against the defendant for nonappearance, if it shall be made appear to the court where the said action is depending, by affidavit, or be proved upon the trial in case the defendant appears, that half a year's rent was due before the said writ was served, and that no sufficient distress was to be found on the demised premises, countervailing the arrears then due, and that the lessor had power to re-enter, then and in every such case the lessor shall recover judgment and execution, in the same manner as if the rent in arrear had been legally demanded, and a re-entry made; and in case the lessee or his assignee, or other person claiming or deriving under the said lease, shall permit and suffer judgment to be had and recovered on such trial in ejectment, and execution to be executed thereon, without paying the rent and arrears, together with full costs, and without proceeding for relief in equity within six months after such execution executed, then and in such case the said lessee, his assignee, and all other persons claiming and deriving under the said lease, shall be barred and foreclosed from all relief or remedy in law or equity, other than by bringing error for reversal of such judgment, in case the same shall be erroneous, and the said landlord or lessor shall from thenceforth hold the said demised premises discharged from such lease; ... provided that nothing herein contained shall extend to bar the right of any mortgagee of such lease, or any part thereof, who shall not be in possession, so as such mortgagee shall and do, within six months after such judgment obtained and execution executed pay all rent in arrear, and all costs and damages sustained by such lessor or person entitled to the remainder or reversion as aforesaid, and perform all the covenants and agreements which, on the part and behalf of the first lessee, are and ought to be performed.

[41]

211 Lessee proceeding in equity not to have injunction or relief without payment of rent and costs

In case the said lessee, his assignee, or other person claiming any right, title, or interest, in law or equity, of, in, or to the said lease, shall, within the time aforesaid, proceed for relief in any court of equity, such person shall not have or continue any injunction against the proceedings at law on such ejectment, unless he does or shall, within forty days next after a full and perfect answer shall be made by the claimant in such ejectment, bring into court, and lodge with the proper officer such sum and sums of money as the lessor or landlord shall in his answer swear to be due and in arrear over and above all just allowances, and also the costs taxed in the said suit, there to remain till the hearing of the cause, or to be paid out to the lessor or landlord on good security, subject to the decree of the court; and in case such proceedings for relief in equity shall be taken within the time aforesaid, and after execution is executed, the lessor or landlord shall be accountable only for so much and no more as he shall really and bona fide, without fraud, deceit, or wilful neglect, make of the demised premises from the time of his entering into the actual possession thereof; and if what shall be so made by the lessor or landlord happen to be less than the rent reserved on the said lease, then the said lessee or his assignee, before he shall be restored to his possession, shall pay such lessor or landlord, what the money so by him made fell short of the reserved rent for the time such lessor or landlord held the said lands.

[42]

212 Tenant paying all rent with costs, proceedings to cease

If the tenant or his assignee do or shall, at any time before the trial in such ejectment, pay or tender to the lessor or landlord, his executors or administrators, or his or their attorney in that cause, or pay into the court where the same cause is depending, all the rent and arrears, together with the costs, then and in such case all further proceedings on the said ejectment shall cease and be discontinued; and if such lessee, his executors, administrators, or assigns, shall, upon such proceedings as aforesaid, be relieved in equity, he and they shall have, hold, and enjoy the demised lands, according to the lease thereof made, without any new lease.

[43]

213   (*Repealed by the Administration of Justice Act 1965, s 34(1), Sch 2.*)

214 On trial of any ejectment between landlord and tenant, juries to give damages for mesne profits down to the verdict, or to a day specified therein

Wherever it shall appear on the trial of any ejectment at the suit of a landlord against a tenant, that such tenant or his attorney hath been served with due notice of trial, the judge before whom such cause shall come on to be tried shall, whether the defendant shall appear upon such trial or not, permit the claimant on the trial, after proof of his right to recover possession of the whole or of any part of the premises mentioned in the writ in ejectment, to go into evidence of the mesne profits thereof which shall or might have accrued from the day of the expiration or determination of the tenant's interest in the same down to the time of the verdict given in the cause, or to some preceding day to be specially mentioned therein; and the jury on the trial finding for the claimant shall in such case give their verdict upon the whole matter, both as to the recovery of the whole or any part of the premises, and also as to the amount of the damages to be paid for such mesne profits; and in such case the landlord shall have judgment within the time herein-before provided, not only for the recovery of possession and costs, but also for the mesne profits found by the jury: Provided always, that nothing herein-before contained shall be construed to bar any such landlord from bringing any action for the mesne profits which shall accrue from the verdict, or the day so specified therein down to the day of the delivery of possession of the premises recovered in the ejectment.

[44]

215–217   (*Ss 215, 216 repealed by the Statute Law Revision Act 1892; s 217 repealed by the Administration of Justice Act 1965, s 34(1), Sch 2.*)

218 Saving of former remedies

Nothing herein contained shall be construed to prejudice or affect any other right of action or remedy which landlords may possess in any of the cases herein-before provided for, otherwise than herein-before expressly enacted.

[45]

219, 220 *(Repealed by the Administration of Justice Act 1965, s 34(1), Sch 2.)*

221 Jurisdiction of courts and judges

The several courts and the judges thereof respectively shall and may exercise over the proceedings the like jurisdiction as heretofore exercised in the action of ejectment, so as to ensure a trial of the title, and of actual ouster, when necessary, only, and for all other purposes for which such jurisdiction may at present be exercised; and the provisions of all statutes not inconsistent with the provisions of this Act, and which may be applicable to the altered mode of proceeding, shall remain in force and be applied thereto.

[46]

NOTES
Repealed, except in relation to any jurisdiction conferred by this enactment, by the Statute Law Revision and Civil Procedure Act 1883, ss 3, 5, Schedule.

222–226 *(S 222 repealed by the Statute Law Revision and Civil Procedure Act 1883, s 3, Schedule; s 223 repealed by the Statute Law Revision Act 1875; ss 224, 225 repealed by the Supreme Court of Judicature (Officers) Act 1879, s 29, Sch 2; s 226 repealed by the Statute Law Revision Act 1892.)*

227 Interpretation of terms

In the construction of this Act the word "court" shall be understood to mean any one of the Superior Courts of Common Law at Westminster in which any action is brought; and the word "judge" shall be understood to mean a judge or baron of any of the said courts; and the word "master" shall be understood to mean a master of any of the said courts; and the word "action" shall be understood to mean any personal action brought by writ of summons in any of the said courts; and no part of the United Kingdom of Great Britain and Ireland, nor the Islands of Man, Guernsey, Jersey, Alderney, or Sark, nor any Islands adjacent to any of them, being part of the Dominions of Her Majesty, shall be deemed to be "beyond the seas," within the meaning of this Act: And wherever in this Act, in describing or referring to any person or party, matter or thing, any word importing the singular number or masculine gender is used, the same shall be understood to include and shall be applicable to several persons and parties as well as one person or party, and females as well as males, and bodies corporate as well as individuals, and several matters and things as well as one matter or thing, unless it otherwise be provided, or there be something in the subject or context repugnant to such construction.

[47]

NOTES
Repealed, except in relation to any jurisdiction conferred by this enactment, by the Statute Law Revision and Civil Procedure Act 1883, ss 3, 5, Schedule.

228–234 *(Repealed by the Statute Law Revision and Civil Law Procedure Act 1883, s 3, Schedule.)*

235 Short title of Act

In citing this Act in any instrument, document, or proceeding, it shall be sufficient to use the expression "The Common Law Procedure Act 1852."

[48]

236 Act not to extend to Ireland or Scotland

Nothing in this Act shall extend to Ireland or Scotland ...

[49]

NOTES
Words omitted repealed by the Statute Law Revision Act 1892.

APPORTIONMENT ACT 1870

(33 & 34 Vict c 35)

ARRANGEMENT OF SECTIONS

An Act for the better Apportionment of Rents and other periodical Payments

[1 August 1870]

(Preamble repealed by the Statute Law Revision Act 1893.)

1 Short title

This Act may be cited for all purposes as "The Apportionment Act 1870."

[50]

2 Rents, etc to be apportionable in respect of time

... all rents, annuities, dividends, and other periodical payments in the nature of income (whether reserved or made payable under an instrument in writing or otherwise) shall, like interest on money lent, be considered as accruing from day to day, and shall be apportionable in respect of time accordingly.

[51]

NOTES

Words omitted repealed by the Statute Law Revision (No 2) Act 1893.

---

3 Apportioned part of rent, etc to be payable when the next entire portion shall have become due

The apportioned part of any such rent, annuity, dividend, or other payment shall be payable or recoverable in the case of a continuing rent, annuity, or other such payment when the entire portion of which such apportioned part shall form part shall become due and payable, and not before, and in the case of a rent, annuity, or other such payment determined by re-entry, death, or otherwise when the next entire portion of the same would have been payable if the same had not so determined, and not before.

[52]

4 Persons shall have the same remedies for recovering apportioned parts as for entire portions—Proviso as to rents reserved in certain cases

All persons and their respective heirs, executors, administrators, and assigns, and also the executors, administrators, and assigns respectively of persons whose interests determine with their own deaths, shall have such or the same remedies at law and in equity for recovering such apportioned parts as aforesaid when payable (allowing proportionate parts of all just allowances) as they respectively would have had for recovering such entire portions as aforesaid if entitled thereto respectively; provided that persons liable to pay rents reserved out of or charged on lands or other hereditaments of any tenure, and the same lands or other hereditaments, shall not be resorted to for any such apportioned part forming part of an entire or continuing rent as aforesaid specifically, but the entire or continuing rent, including such apportioned part, shall be recovered and received by the heir or other person who, if the rent had not been apportionable under this Act, or otherwise, would have been entitled to such entire or continuing rent, and such apportioned part shall be recoverable from such heir or other person by the executors or other parties entitled under this Act to the same by action at law or suit in equity.

[53]

5 Interpretation

In the construction of this Act—

The word "rents" includes rent service, rentcharge, and rent seck, and also tithes and all periodical payments or renderings in lieu of or in the nature of rent or tithe.

The word "annuities" includes salaries and pensions.

The word "dividends" includes (besides dividends strictly so called) all payments made by the name of dividend, bonus, or otherwise out of the revenue of trading or other public companies, divisible between all or any of the members of such respective companies, whether such payments shall be usually made or declared, at any fixed times or otherwise; and all such divisible revenue shall, for the purposes of this Act, be deemed to have accrued by equal daily increment during and within the period for or in respect of which the payment of the same revenue shall be declared or expressed to be made, but the said word "dividend" does not include payments in the nature of a return or reimbursement of capital.

[54]

6 Act not to apply to policies of assurance

Nothing in this Act contained shall render apportionable any annual sums made payable in policies of assurance of any description.

[55]

7 Nor where stipulation made to the contrary

The provisions of this Act shall not extend to any case in which it is or shall be expressly stipulated that no apportionment shall take place.

[56]

GROUND GAME ACT 1880

(43 & 44 Vict c 47)

ARRANGEMENT OF SECTIONS

An Act for the better protection of Occupiers of Land against injury to their Crops from Ground Game

[7 September 1880]

1 Occupier to have a right inseparable from his occupation to kill ground game concurrently with any other person entitled to kill the same on land in his occupation

Every occupier of land shall have, as incident to and inseparable from his occupation of the land, the right to kill and take ground game thereon, concurrently with any other person who may be entitled to kill and take ground game on the same land: Provided that the right conferred on the occupier by this section shall be subject to the following limitations:

(1) The occupier shall kill and take ground game only by himself or by persons duly authorised by him in writing:

(a)   The occupier himself and one other person authorised in writing by such occupier shall be the only persons entitled under this Act to kill ground game with firearms;

(b)   No person shall be authorised by the occupier to kill or take ground game, except members of his household resident on the land in his occupation, persons in his ordinary service on such land, and any one other person bona fide employed by him for reward in the taking and destruction of ground game;

(c)   Every person so authorised by the occupier, on demand by any person having a concurrent right to take and kill the ground game on the land or any person authorised by him in writing to make such demand, shall produce to the person so demanding the document by which he is authorised, and in default he shall not be deemed to be an authorised person.

(2)   A person shall not be deemed to be an occupier of land for the purposes of this Act by reason of his having a right of common over such lands; or by reason of an occupation for the purpose of grazing or pasturage of sheep, cattle, or horses for not more than nine months.

(3)   In the case of moorlands, and unenclosed lands (not being arable lands), the occupier and the persons authorised by him shall exercise the rights conferred by this section only from the eleventh day of December in one year until the thirty-first day of March in the next year, both inclusive; but this provision shall not apply to detached portions of moorlands or unenclosed lands adjoining arable lands, where such detached portions of moorlands or unenclosed lands are less than twenty-five acres in extent.

[57]

2   Occupier entitled to kill ground game on land in his occupation not to divest himself wholly of such right

Where the occupier of land is entitled otherwise than in pursuance of this Act to kill and take ground game thereon, if he shall give to any other person a title to kill and take such ground game, he shall nevertheless retain and have, as incident to and inseparable from such occupation, the same right to kill and take ground game as is declared by section one of this Act. Save as aforesaid, but subject as in section six hereafter mentioned, the occupier may exercise any other or more extensive right which he may possess in respect of ground game or other game, in the same manner and to the same extent as if this Act had not passed.

[58]

3   All agreements in contravention of right of occupier to destroy ground game void

Every agreement, condition, or arrangement which purports to divest or alienate the right of the occupier as declared, given, and reserved to him by this Act, or which gives to such occupier any advantage in consideration of his forbearing to exercise such right, or imposes upon him any disadvantage in consequence of his exercising such right, shall be void.

[59]

4   Exemption from game licences

The occupier and the persons duly authorised by him as aforesaid shall not be required to obtain a licence to kill game for the purpose of killing and taking ground game on land in the occupation of such occupier, and the occupier shall have the same power of selling any ground game so killed by him, or the persons authorised by him, as if he had a licence to kill game: …

[60]

NOTES

Words omitted repealed by the Local Government Act 1966, s 43(2)(a), Sch 6, Pt I.

---

5   Saving clause

Where at the date of the passing of this Act the right to kill and take ground game on any land is vested by lease, contract of tenancy, or other contract bona fide made for valuable consideration in some person other than the occupier, the occupier shall not be entitled under this Act, until the determination of that contract, to kill and take ground game on such land …

Nothing in this Act shall affect any special right of killing or taking ground game to which any person other than the landlord, lessor, or occupier may have become entitled before the passing of this Act by virtue of any franchise, charter, or Act of Parliament.

[61]

PART I
STATUTES

NOTES

Words omitted repealed by the Statute Law Revision Act 1894.

6 Prohibition of night shooting, spring traps above ground or poison

No person having a right of killing ground game under this Act or otherwise shall use any firearms for the purpose of killing ground game between the expiration of the first hour after sunset and the commencement of the last hour before sunrise; *and no such person shall, for the purpose of killing ground game ... employ poison,* and any person acting in contravention of this section shall, on summary conviction, be liable to a penalty not exceeding [level 1 on the standard scale].

[62]

NOTES

Words in italics repealed, except as to Greater London, by the Prevention of Damage by Rabbits Act 1939, ss 5(2), 6(3); words omitted repealed by the Pests Act 1954, s 15(2), Schedule; reference to level 1 on the standard scale substituted by virtue of the Criminal Justice Act 1982, ss 38, 46.

7 As to non-occupier having right of killing game

Where a person who is not in occupation of land has the sole right of killing game thereon (with the exception of such right of killing and taking ground game as is by this Act conferred on the occupier as incident to and inseparable from his occupation), such person shall, for the purpose of any Act authorising the institution of legal proceedings by the owner of an exclusive right to game, have the same authority to institute such proceedings as if he were such exclusive owner, without prejudice nevertheless to the right of the occupier conferred by this Act.

[63]

8 Interpretation clause

For the purposes of this Act—
The words "ground game" mean hares and rabbits.

[64]

9 Exemption from penalties

A person acting in accordance with this Act shall not thereby be subject to any proceedings or penalties in pursuance of any law or statute.

[65]

10 Saving of existing prohibitions

Nothing in this Act shall authorise the killing or taking of ground game on any days or seasons, or by any methods, prohibited by any Act of Parliament in force at the time of the passing of this Act.

[66]

11 Short title

This Act may be cited for all purposes as the Ground Game Act 1880.

[67]

LAW OF DISTRESS AMENDMENT ACT 1888

(51 & 52 Vict c 21)

ARRANGEMENT OF SECTIONS

An Act to amend the Law of Distress for Rent

[7 August 1888]

1   Short title

This Act may be cited as the Law of Distress Amendment Act 1888.

[68]

2   Extent

This Act shall not apply to Scotland or Ireland.

[69]

3   *(Repealed by the Statute Law Revision Act 1908.)*

4   Certain goods exempted from distress as under 9 & 10 Vict c 95, s 96

... the following goods and chattels shall be exempt from distress for rent; namely, any goods or chattels of the tenant or his family which would be protected from seizure in execution under section ninety-six of the County Courts Act 1846, or any enactment amending or substituted for the same.

Provided that this enactment shall not extend to any case where the lease, term, or interest of the tenant has expired, and where possession of the premises in respect of which the rent is claimed has been demanded and where the distress is made not earlier than seven days after such demand.

[70]

NOTES

Words omitted repealed by the Statute Law Revision Act 1908.
County Courts Act 1846, s 96: see now the County Courts Act 1984, s 89.

5   Repeal of 2 W & M c 5, s 1, except where appraisement is required in writing

So much of an Act passed in the second year of the reign of their Majesties King William the Third and Mary, chapter five, as requires appraisement before sale of goods distrained is hereby repealed, except in cases where the tenant or owner of the goods and chattels by writing requires such appraisement to be made, and the landlord or other person levying a distress may, except as aforesaid, sell the goods and chattels distrained without causing them to be previously appraised; and for the purposes of sale the goods and chattels distrained shall, at the request in writing of the tenant or owner of such goods and chattels, be removed to a public auction room or to some other fit and proper place specified in such request and be there sold. The costs and expenses of appraisement when required by the tenant or owner shall be borne and paid by him; and the cost and expenses attending any such removal, and any damage to the goods and chattels arising therefrom, shall be borne and paid by the person requesting the removal.

[71]

NOTES

Act of 2 W & M c 5: Distress for Rent Act 1689 at **[1]**.

6   Extension of time to replevy at request of tenant

The period of five days provided in the said Act of William and Mary, chapter five, within which the tenant or owner of goods and chattels distrained may replevy the same, shall be extended to a period of not more than fifteen days if the tenant or such owner make a request in writing in that behalf to the landlord or other person levying the distress, and also give security for any additional cost that may be occasioned by such extension of time: Provided that the landlord or person levying the distress may, at the written request, or with the written consent, of the tenant or such owner as aforesaid, sell the goods and chattels distrained, or part of them, at any time before the expiration of such extended period as aforesaid.

[72]

PART I
STATUTES

NOTES

Said Act of William and Mary: Distress for Rent Act 1689, at **[1]**.

7   Distress to be levied by certified bailiffs

... no person shall act as a bailiff to levy any distress for rent unless he shall be authorised to act as a bailiff by a certificate in writing under the hand of a [judge assigned to a county court district, or acting as a judge so assigned]; and such certificate may be general or apply to a particular distress or distresses, and may be granted at any time after the passing of this Act in such manner as may be prescribed by rules under this Act ...

A [district judge] may exercise the power of granting certificates hereby conferred upon a [judge assigned to a county court district, or acting as a judge so assigned] in cases in which he may be authorised to do so by rules made under this Act.

If any person not holding a certificate under this section shall levy a distress contrary to the provisions of this Act, the person so levying, and any person who has authorised him so to levy, shall be deemed to have committed a trespass.

[73]

NOTES

Words omitted repealed by the Statute Law Revision Act 1908 and words in first and third pairs of square brackets substituted by virtue of the Courts Act 1971, s 56(1), Sch 8, Pt I, para 2; words in second pair of square brackets substituted by the Courts and Legal Services Act 1990, s 74(1)(a), (3).

Prescribed by rules: the Distress for Rent Rules 1988, SI 1988/2050, at **[1192]**.

8   Power to make rules

... the Lord Chancellor may from time to time make, alter, and revoke rules—

    (1)   For regulating the security (if any) to be required from bailiffs;

    (2)   For regulating the fees, charges, and expenses in and incidental to distresses; and

    (3)   For carrying into effect the objects of this Act.

[74]

NOTES

Words omitted repealed by the Statute Law Revision Act 1908.

Extension: the power to make rules was extended by the Law of Distress Amendment Act 1895, s 3, at **[77]**.

Rules: the Distress for Rent Rules 1988, SI 1988/2050, at **[1192]**.

9   *(Repealed by the Statute Law Revision Act 1908.)*

LAW OF DISTRESS AMENDMENT ACT 1895

(58 & 59 Vict c 24)

An Act to amend the Law of Distress Amendment Act 1888

[6 July 1895]

1   Power to cancel bailiff certificates

A certificate granted to a bailiff by the judge of a county court under the Law of Distress Amendment Act 1888, may at any time be cancelled or declared void by a judge of that county court, ...

[75]

NOTES

Words omitted repealed by the Statute Law Revision Act 1908.

Judge of a county court: by virtue of the Courts Act 1971, s 56(1), Sch 8, Pt I, para 2, this is now to be construed as a reference to a judge assigned to a county court district, or acting as a judge so assigned.

2 Penalty for acting without certificate

If any person not holding a certificate for the time being in force under the Law of Distress Amendment Act 1888, levies a distress contrary to the provisions of that Act, he shall without prejudice to any civil liability be liable on summary conviction to a fine not exceeding [level 1 on the standard scale].

[76]

NOTES

Reference to level 1 on the standard scale substituted by virtue of the Criminal Justice Act 1982, ss 38, 46.

3 Duration of certificates

The power to make rules under the Law of Distress Amendment Act 1888 shall extend to making provision for fixing the duration of certificates granted, or to be hereafter granted, to bailiffs.

[77]

4 Unlawful distress

A court of summary jurisdiction, on complaint that goods or chattels exempt under section four of the Law of Distress Amendment Act 1888 from distress for rent, have been taken under such distress, may, by summary order, direct that the goods and chattels so taken, if not sold, be restored; or, if they have been sold, that such sum as the court may determine to be the value thereof shall be paid to the complainant by the person who levied the distress or directed it to be levied.

[78]

5   *(Repealed by the Police and Criminal Evidence Act 1984, s 119(2), Sch 7, Pt V.)*

6 Short title

This Act may be cited as the Law of Distress Amendment Act 1895.

[79]

SMALL HOLDINGS AND ALLOTMENTS ACT 1908

(8 Edw 7 c 36)

ARRANGEMENT OF SECTIONS

PART II
ALLOTMENTS

Provision of Allotments

PART III
GENERAL

Provisions affecting Land acquired

Supplemental

An Act to consolidate the enactments with respect to Small Holdings and Allotments in England and Wales

[1 August 1908]

1–22   ((*Pt I) Repealed by the Small Holdings and Allotments Act 1926, s 22, Sch 2.*)

PART II
ALLOTMENTS

Provision of Allotments

23   Duty of certain councils to provide allotments

(1)   If the council of any borough, urban district, or parish are of opinion that there is a demand for allotments ... in the borough, urban district, or parish, ... the council shall provide a sufficient number of allotments, and shall let such allotments to persons ... resident in the borough, district, or parish, and desiring to take the same.

(2)   On a representation in writing to the council of any borough, urban district, or parish, by any six registered parliamentary electors or [persons who are liable to pay an amount in respect of council tax] resident in the borough, urban district, or parish, that the circumstances of the borough, urban district, or parish are such that it is the duty of the council to take proceedings under this Part of this Act therein, the council shall take such representation into consideration.

(3), (4)   ...

[80]

NOTES
Sub-s (1): words omitted repealed by the Land Settlement (Facilities) Act 1919, ss 25, 33, Schs 2, 3.
Sub-s (2): words in square brackets substituted by the Local Government Finance Act 1992, s 117(1), Sch 13, para 4.
Sub-s (3): repealed by the Land Settlement (Facilities) Act 1919, ss 25, 33, Schs 2, 3.
Sub-s (4): repealed by the Allotments Act 1950, s 15(3), Schedule.

24–29   (*S 24 repealed by the Local Government Act 1972, s 272(1), Sch 30; ss 25–29 outside the scope of this work.*)

30   Recovery of rent and possession of allotments

(1)   The rent for an allotment let by a council in pursuance of this Act, and the possession of such an allotment in the case of any notice to quit, or failure to deliver up possession thereof as required by law, may be recovered by the council as landlords, in the like manner as in any other case of landlord and tenant.

(2)   If the rent for any allotment is in arrear for not less than forty days, or if it appears to the council that the tenant of an allotment not less than three months after the commencement of the tenancy thereof has not duly observed the rules affecting the allotment made by or in pursuance of this Act, or is resident more than one mile out of the borough, district, or parish for which the allotments are provided, the council may serve upon the tenant, or, if he is residing out of the borough, district or parish, leave at his last known place of abode in the borough, district, or parish, or fix in some conspicuous manner on the allotment, a written notice determining the tenancy at the expiration of one month after the notice has been so served or affixed, and thereupon the tenancy shall be determined accordingly: ...

(3)   Upon the recovery of an allotment from any tenant, the court directing the recovery may stay delivery of possession until payment of the compensation (if any) due to the outgoing tenant has been made or secured to the satisfaction of the court.

[81]

NOTES
Sub-s (2): words omitted repealed by the Allotments Act 1922, s 23, Schedule.

31–37   *(S 31 repealed by the Land Settlement Facilities Act 1919, s 33, Sch 3; ss 32–35 outside the scope of this work; s 36 repealed by the London Government Act 1963, s 93(1), Sch 18, Pt II; s 37 repealed by the Local Government Act 1972, s 272(1), Sch 30.)*

PART III
GENERAL

38–43   *(Outside the scope of this work.)*

Provisions affecting Land acquired

44–46   *(Outside the scope of this work.)*

47   Compensation for improvements

(1)   *Where a council has let a small holding or allotment to any tenant [otherwise than under a farm business tenancy], the tenant shall as against the council have the same rights with respect to compensation for the improvements mentioned in Part I of the Second Schedule to this Act as he would have had if the holding had been a holding to which [subsections (2) to (5) of section 79 of the Agricultural Holdings Act 1986] applied:*

Provided that the tenant shall not be entitled to compensation in respect of any such improvement if executed contrary to an express prohibition in writing by the council affecting either the whole or any part of the holding or allotment; …

(2)   *Where land has been hired by a council for small holdings or allotments [otherwise than under a farm business tenancy], the council shall ([subject to any provision to the contrary in the agreement or order for hiring]) be entitled at the determination of the tenancy on quitting the land to compensation under the [Agricultural Holdings Act 1986] for any improvement mentioned in Part I of the Second Schedule to this Act, and for any improvement mentioned in Part II of that Schedule which was necessary or proper to adapt the land for small holdings or allotments, as if the land were a holding to which [subsections (2) to (5) of section 79 of the Agricultural Holdings Act 1986] applied, and the improvements mentioned in Part II of the said Schedule were improvements mentioned in [Schedule 8 to the Agricultural Holdings Act 1986]:*

Provided that, in the case of land hired compulsorily, the amount of the compensation payable to the council for those improvements shall be such sum as fairly represents the increase (if any) in the value to the landlord and his successors in title of the holding due to those improvements.

(3)   *The tenant of an allotment to which Part II of this Act applies may, if [he is not a tenant under a farm business tenancy and] he so elects, claim compensation for improvements under [section 3 of the Allotments Act 1922] instead of under the [Agricultural Holdings Act 1986] as amended by this section, notwithstanding that the allotment exceeds two acres in extent.*

(4)   *A tenant of any small holding or allotment [who is not a tenant under a farm business tenancy] may, before the expiration of his tenancy, remove any fruit and other trees and bushes planted or acquired by him for which he has no claim for compensation, and may remove any toolhouse, shed, greenhouse, fowl-house, or pigsty built or acquired by him for which he has no claim for compensation.*

[(5)   In this section, "farm business tenancy" has the same meaning as in the Agricultural Tenancies Act 1995.]

[82]

NOTES
  Repealed, in relation to small holdings, by the Agriculture Act 1947, s 67(2).
  Sub-s (1): words in first pair of square brackets inserted by the Agricultural Tenancies Act 1995, s 40, Schedule, para 1(2); words in second pair of square brackets substituted by the Agricultural Holdings Act 1986, s 100, Sch 14, para 1; words omitted repealed by the Local Government, Planning and Land Act 1980, ss 1(5), 194, Sch 5, para 1(c), Sch 34, Pt V.
  Sub-s (2): words in first pair of square brackets inserted by the Agricultural Tenancies Act 1995, s 40, Schedule, para 1(3); words in second pair of square brackets substituted by the Land Settlement (Facilities) Act 1919, s 25, Sch 2; remaining words in square brackets substituted by the Agricultural Holdings Act 1986, s 100, Sch 14, para 1.

Sub-s (3): words in first pair of square brackets inserted by the Agricultural Tenancies Act 1995, s 40, Schedule, para 1(4); words in second pair of square brackets substituted by the Statute Law (Repeals) Act 1993; words in third square brackets substituted by the Agricultural Holdings Act 1986, s 100, Sch 14, para 1.

Sub-s (4): words in square brackets inserted by the Agricultural Tenancies Act 1995, s 40, Schedule, para 1(5).

Sub-s (5): added by the Agricultural Tenancies Act 1995, s 40, Schedule, para 1(6).

48–60 (*S 48 repealed by the Endowments and Glebe Measure 1976, s 47(4), Sch 8; ss 49, 52, 53, 57, 58 outside the scope of this work; s 50 repealed by the Agriculture Act 1947, ss 61, 110, Sch 13; s 51 repealed by the Statute Law (Repeals) Act 1973; ss 54, 59 repealed by the Local Government, Planning and Land Act 1980, s 194, Sch 34, Pt V; ss 55, 56 repealed by the Small Holdings and Allotments Act 1926, s 22, Sch 2; s 60 repealed by the Statute Law (Repeals) Act 1993.*)

Supplemental

61   Interpretation

(*1*)   *For the purposes of this Act—*

The expression "small holding" means an agricultural holding which exceeds one acre and either does not exceed fifty acres, or, if exceeding fifty acres, is at the date of sale or letting of an annual value for the purposes of income tax not exceeding [one hundred pounds]:

The expression "allotment" includes a field garden:

The expressions "agriculture" and "cultivation" shall include horticulture and the use of land for any purpose of husbandry, inclusive of the keeping or breeding of live stock, poultry, or bees, and the growth of fruit, vegetables, and the like:

.....

The expression "prescribed" means prescribed by regulations made by the Board:

The expression "landlord", in relation to any land compulsorily hired by a council, means the person for the time being entitled to receive the rent of the land from the council.

(2)   In this Act and in the enactments incorporated with this Act the expression "land" shall include any right or easement in or over land.

(3)   For the purposes of this Act, any expenses incurred by a council ... in the purchase or redemption of ... any quit rent, chief rent, tithe, or other rentcharge, or other perpetual annual sum issuing out of land so acquired, shall be deemed to have been incurred in the purchase of the land.

(4)   In this Act references to a parish council shall, in the case of a rural parish not having a parish council, include references to the parish meeting.

(5)   Any notice required by this Act to be served or given may be sent by registered post.

[83]

NOTES

Repealed, in relation to small holdings, by the Agriculture Act 1947, s 67(2).

Sub-s (1): words in square brackets in definition "small holding" substituted by the Small Holdings and Allotments Act 1926, s 16; definitions omitted repealed by the Local Government Act 1985, s 102(2), Sch 17 and the Local Government Act 1972, s 272(1), Sch 30.

Sub-s (3): words omitted in the first place repealed by the Statute Law (Repeals) Act 1993; words omitted in the second place repealed by the Statute Law Revision Act 1964.

Transfer of functions: functions of the Board under this Act relating to allotments, so far as it applies to England, now exercised by the Secretary of State for the Environment by virtue of the Secretary of State for the Environment Order 1970, SI 1970/1681, art 2(1), and so far as it applies to Wales, now exercised by the National Assembly for Wales by virtue of the National Assembly for Wales (Transfer of Functions) Order 1999, SI 1999/672, art 2, Sch 1. Functions previously transferred by the combined effect of s 2(1) of this Act, the Ministry of Agriculture and Fisheries Act 1919, s 1(1), the Transfer of Functions (Ministry of Food) Order 1955, SI 1955/554 and the Minister of Land and Natural Resources Order 1965, SI 1965/143, the Ministry of Land and Natural Resources (Dissolution) Order 1967, SI 1967/156.

62   (*Repealed by the Statute Law (Repeals) Act 1993.*)

63 Short title and extent

(1)   This Act may be cited as the Small Holdings and Allotments Act 1908.

(2)   ...

(3)   This Act shall not extend to Scotland or Ireland.

[84]

NOTES

Sub-s (2): repealed by the Statute Law Revision Act 1927.

(*First and Second Schedules outside the scope of this work; Third Schedule repealed by the Statute Law Revision Act 1927.*)

LAW OF DISTRESS AMENDMENT ACT 1908

(8 Edw 7 c 53)

ARRANGEMENT OF SECTIONS

An Act to amend the Law as regards a Landlord's right of Distress for Rent

[21 December 1908]

1   Under tenant or lodger, if distress levied, to make declaration that immediate tenant has no property in goods distrained

If any superior landlord shall levy, or authorise to be levied, a distress on any furniture, goods, or chattels of—

(a)   any under tenant liable to pay by equal instalments not less often than every actual or customary quarter of a year a rent which would return in any whole year the full annual value of the premises or of such part thereof as is comprised in the under tenancy, or

(b)   any lodger, or

(c)   any other person whatsoever not being a tenant of the premises or of any part thereof, and not having any beneficial interest in any tenancy of the premises or of any part thereof,

for arrears of rent due to such superior landlord by his immediate tenant, such under tenant, lodger, or other person aforesaid may serve such superior landlord, or the bailiff or other agent employed by him to levy such distress, with a declaration in writing made by such under tenant, lodger, or other person aforesaid, setting forth that such immediate tenant has no right of property or beneficial interest in the furniture, goods, or chattels so distrained or threatened to be distrained upon, and that such furniture, goods, or chattels are the property or in the lawful possession of such under tenant, lodger, or other person aforesaid, and are not goods or live stock to which this Act is expressed not to apply; and also, in the case of an under tenant or lodger, setting forth the amount of rent (if any) then due to his immediate landlord, and the times at which future instalments of rent will become due, and the amount thereof, and containing an undertaking to pay to the superior landlord any rent so due or to become due to his immediate landlord, until the arrears of rent in respect of which the distress was levied or authorised to be levied have been paid off, and to such declaration shall be annexed a correct inventory, subscribed by the under tenant, lodger, or other person aforesaid, of the furniture, goods and chattels referred to in the declaration; ...

[85]

NOTES
Words omitted repealed by the Perjury Act 1911, s 17, Schedule.

2 Penalty

If any superior landlord, or any bailiff or other agent employed by him, shall, after being served with the before-mentioned declaration and inventory, and in the case of an under tenant or lodger after such undertaking as aforesaid has been given, and the amount of rent (if any) then due has been paid or tendered in accordance with that undertaking, levy or proceed with a distress on the furniture, goods, or chattels of the under tenant, lodger, or other person aforesaid, such superior landlord, bailiff, or other agent shall be deemed guilty of an illegal distress, and the under tenant, lodger, or other person aforesaid, may apply to a justice of the peace for an order for the restoration to him of such goods, and such application shall be heard before [two justices who] shall inquire into the truth of such declaration and inventory, and shall make such order for the recovery of the goods or otherwise as to him or them may seem just, and the superior landlord shall also be liable to an action at law at the suit of the under tenant, lodger, or other person aforesaid, in which action the truth of the declaration and inventory may likewise be inquired into.

[86]

NOTES
Words in square brackets substituted by the Access to Justice Act 1999, s 78(2), Sch 11, para 11.

3 Payments by under tenant or lodger to superior landlord

For the purposes of the recovery of any sums payable by an under tenant or lodger to a superior landlord under such an undertaking as aforesaid, or under a notice served in accordance with section six of this Act, the under tenant or lodger shall be deemed to be the immediate tenant of the superior landlord, and the sums payable shall be deemed to be rent; but, where the under tenant or lodger has, in pursuance of any such undertaking or notice as aforesaid, paid any sums to the superior landlord, he may deduct the amount thereof from any rent due or which may become due from him to his immediate landlord, and any person (other than the tenant for whose rent the distress is levied or authorised to be levied) from whose rent a deduction has been made in respect of such a payment may make the like deductions from any rent due or which may become due from him to his immediate landlord.

[87]

4 Exclusion of certain goods

This Act shall not apply—

(1) to goods belonging to the husband or wife [or civil partner] of the tenant whose rent is in arrear, nor to goods comprised in any ... settlement made by such tenant, nor to goods in the possession, order, or disposition of such tenant by the consent and permission of the true owner under such circumstances that such tenant is the reputed owner thereof, not to any [agisted livestock within the meaning of section 18 of the Agricultural Holdings Act 1986 [on land comprised in a tenancy to which that Act applies]];

(2)

    (a)   to goods of a partner of the immediate tenant;

    (b)   to goods (not being goods of a lodger) upon premises where any trade or business is carried on in which both the immediate tenant and the under tenant have an interest;

    (c)   to goods (not being goods of a lodger) on premises used as offices or warehouses where the owner of the goods neglects for one calendar month after notice (which shall be given in like manner as a notice to quit) to remove the goods and vacate the premises;

    (d)   to goods belonging to and in the offices of any company or corporation on premises the immediate tenant whereof is a director or officer, or in the employment of such company or corporation:

Provided that it shall be competent for ... two justices, upon application by the superior landlord or any under tenant or other such person as aforesaid, upon hearing the parties to determine whether any goods are in fact goods covered by subsection (2) of this section.

[88]

NOTES

Sub-s (1): words in first pair of square brackets inserted by the Civil Partnership Act 2004, s 261(1), Sch 27, para 3; words omitted repealed by the Consumer Credit Act 1974, s 192(3)(b), Sch 5, Pt I; words in second (outer) pair of square brackets substituted by the Agricultural Holdings Act 1986, s 100, Sch 14, para 4; words in third (inner) pair of square brackets substituted by the Agricultural Tenancies Act 1995, s 40, Schedule, para 2.

Proviso: words omitted repealed by the Access to Justice Act 1999, s 106, Sch 15, Pt V, Table (3).

[4A   Hire purchase etc agreements

(1)   Goods—
  (a)   bailed under a hire-purchase agreement or a consumer hire agreement, or
  (b)   agreed to be sold under a conditional sale agreement,

are, where the relevant agreement has not been terminated, excluded from the application of this Act except during the period between the service of a default notice under the Consumer Credit Act 1974 in respect of the goods and the date on which the notice expires or is earlier complied with.

(2)   Goods comprised in a bill of sale are excluded from the application of this Act except during the period between service of a default notice under the Consumer Credit Act 1974 in respect of goods subject to a regulated agreement under which a bill of sale is given by way of security and the date on which the notice expires or is earlier complied with.

(3)   In this section—
  "conditional sale agreement" means an agreement for the sale of goods under which the purchase price or part of it is payable by instalments, and the property in the goods is to remain in the seller (notwithstanding that the buyer is to be in possession of the goods) until such conditions as to the payment of instalments or otherwise as may be specified in the agreement are fulfilled;
  "consumer hire agreement" has the meaning given by section 15 of the Consumer Credit Act 1974;
  "hire-purchase agreement" means an agreement, other than a conditional sale agreement, under which—
    (a)   goods are bailed in return for periodical payments by the person to whom they are bailed, and
    (b)   the property in the goods will pass to that person if the terms of the agreement are complied with and one or more of the following occurs—
      (i)   the exercise of an option to purchase by that person,
      (ii)   the doing of any other specified act by any party to the agreement,
      (iii)   the happening of any other specified event; and
  "regulated agreement" has the meaning given by section 189(1) of the Consumer Credit Act 1974.]

[89]

NOTES

Inserted by the Consumer Credit Act 1974, s 192(3)(a), Sch 4, Pt I, para 5, except in relation to consumer hire agreements.

5   Exclusion of certain under tenants

This Act shall not apply to any under tenant where the under tenancy has been created in breach of any covenant or agreement in writing between the landlord and his immediate tenant, or where the under tenancy has been created under a lease existing at the date of the passing of this Act contrary to the wish of the landlord in that behalf, expressed in writing and delivered at the premises within a reasonable time after the circumstances have come, or with due diligence would have come, to his knowledge.

[90]

6   To avoid distress

In cases where the rent of the immediate tenant of the superior landlord is in arrear it shall be lawful for such superior landlord to serve upon any under tenant or lodger a notice (by registered post addressed to such under tenant or lodger upon the premises) stating the amount of such arrears of rent, and requiring all future payments of rent, whether the same has already accrued due or not, by such under tenant or lodger to be made direct to the superior landlord giving such notice until such arrears shall have been duly paid, and such notice shall operate to transfer to the superior landlord the right to recover, receive, and give a discharge for such rent.

[91]

7   (*Repealed by the Statute Law Revision Act 1927.*)

8   Repeal of 34 & 35 Vict c 79

The Lodgers' Goods Protection Act 1871 shall, wherever and so far as this Act applies, be repealed …

[92]

NOTES
Words omitted repealed by the Statute Law Revision Act 1927.

9   Definitions

In this Act the words "superior landlord" shall be deemed to include a landlord in cases where the goods seized are not those of an under tenant or lodger; and the words "tenant" and "under tenant" do not include a lodger.

[93]

10   Act not to extend to Scotland

This Act shall not extend to Scotland and shall only apply in Ireland to a rent issuing out of lands or tenements situate wholly within the boundaries of a municipality or of a township having town commissioners.

[94]

11   Short title

This Act may be cited as the Law of Distress Amendment Act 1908.

[95]

STATEMENT OF RATES ACT 1919

(9 & 10 Geo 5 c 31)

An Act to provide for the information to occupiers of the amount of the rates payable for the houses which they occupy

[22 July 1919]

1   Provisions with respect to demands and receipts for rent in which any sum for rates is included

(1)   … every document containing a demand for rent or receipt for rent, which includes any sum for rates paid or payable under any statutory enactment by the owner instead of the occupier, shall state either the annual, half yearly, quarterly, monthly, or weekly amount of such rates paid or payable in accordance with the last demands received by the owner from the rating authorities at the time of making his demand or giving his receipt in respect of the hereditament in question: Provided that, where such a statement as is required by this section has been furnished in connection with a demand for rent or receipt for rent in respect of a particular period, it shall not be necessary to furnish the statement upon any subsequent demand for rent or receipt for rent in respect of that period.

(2)   This Act shall not apply to weekly lettings at inclusive rentals in any market established under or controlled by statute.

[96]

NOTES

Words omitted repealed by the Statute Law Revision Act 1927.

2 Definition

The expressions "demand for rent" and "receipt for rent" shall include a rent-book, rent-card and any document used for the notification or collection of rent due or for the acknowledgment of the receipt of the same.

[97]

3 Penalty

If any person makes a demand for rent or gives a receipt for rent in contravention of this Act, he shall, in respect of each offence, be liable on summary conviction to a fine of not exceeding [level 1 on the standard scale].

[98]

NOTES

Reference to level 1 on the standard scale substituted by virtue of the Criminal Justice Act 1982, ss 38, 46.

4 Short title, commencement and extent

(1) This Act may be cited as the Statement of Rates Act 1919.

(2) ...

(3) This Act shall not extend to Scotland or Ireland.

[99]

NOTES

Sub-s (2): repealed by the Statute Law Revision Act 1927.

LAW OF PROPERTY ACT 1922

(12 & 13 Geo 5 c 16)

An Act to assimilate and amend the law of Real and Personal Estate, to abolish copyhold and other special tenures, to amend the law relating to commonable lands and of intestacy, and to amend the Wills Act 1837, the Settled Land Acts 1882 to 1890, the Conveyancing Acts 1881 to 1911, the Trustee Act 1893, and the Land Transfer Acts 1875 and 1897

[29 June 1922]

1–144A *(Ss 1–3, 5–9, 11, 15, 17–25, 27, 29–34, 43, 72–82, 84, 85, 87, 89–108 repealed by the Law of Property Act 1925, s 207, Sch 7; ss 4, 10, 13, 28 repealed by the Settled Land Act 1925, s 119, Sch 5, and the Law of Property Act 1925, s 207, Sch 7; ss 12, 26, 86 repealed by the Settled Land Act 1925, s 119, Sch 5; ss 14, 16 repealed by the Land Charges Act 1925 s 24, Schedule; ss 35–42, 44–71 repealed by the Settled Land Act 1925, s 119, Sch 5, and the Universities and College Estates Act 1925, s 44, Sch 2; ss 83, 113, 123 repealed by the Trustee Act 1925, s 70, Sch 2, and the Law of Property Act 1925, s 207, Sch 7; ss 88, 109, 111, 112, 114–122, 124–127 repealed by the Trustee Act 1925, s 70, Sch 2; s 110 repealed by the Trustee Act 1925, s 70, Sch 2, and the Administration of Estates Act 1925, s 56, Sch 2, Pt II; ss 128–136, 138–143 repealed by the Statute Law (Repeals) Act 1969; for ss 137, 144, 144A.)*

PART VII
PROVISIONS RESPECTING LEASEHOLDS

Conversion of Perpetually Renewable Leaseholds into Long Terms

145 Conversion of perpetually renewable leaseholds

For the purpose of converting perpetually renewable leases and underleases (not being an interest in perpetually renewable copyhold land enfranchised by Part V of this Act, but including a perpetually renewable underlease derived out of an interest in perpetually renewable copyhold land) into long terms, for preventing the creation of perpetually renewable leasehold interests and for providing for the interests of the persons affected, the provisions contained in the Fifteenth Schedule to this Act shall have effect.

[100]

146–187   (*Ss 146, 152 repealed by the Law of Property Act 1925, s 207, Sch 7; ss 147–151, 153–155, 157–163 repealed by the Administration of Estates Act 1925, s 56, Sch 2, Pt II; s 156 repealed by the Law of Property Act 1925, s 207, Sch 7 and the Administration of Estates Act 1925, s 56, Sch 2, Pt II; ss 164–187 repealed by the Land Registration Act 1925, s 147, Schedule.*)

PART XI
GENERAL PROVISIONS

188   General definitions and jurisdiction of the court

In this Act unless a contrary intention appears—

(1)   "Land" includes land of any tenure, and mines and minerals, buildings or parts (whether the division is horizontal, vertical or otherwise) of buildings and other corporeal hereditaments; also a manor, an advowson, and a rent and other incorporeal hereditaments, and an easement, right, privilege, or benefit in, over, or derived from land; *but not an undivided share in land;* and "mines and minerals" include any strata or seam of minerals or substances in or under any land, and powers of working and getting the same *but not an undivided share thereof*;

(2)–(5)   …

(6)   "Court" means the High Court of Justice, … or the county court, … ; and all matters within the jurisdiction of the High Court under this Act shall, subject to the Acts regulating the court, be assigned to the Chancery Division of the court; and every application to the court under this Act shall, except where it is otherwise expressed and subject to any rules of court to the contrary, be by summons at chambers, and the court shall have full power and discretion to make such order as it thinks fit respecting the costs, charges and expenses of all or any of the parties to any application;

(7), (8)   …

(9)   "The Land Transfer Acts" means the Land Transfer Acts 1875 and 1897, and includes any Act consolidating or amending the same, including this Act; and "Land Registrar" means the registrar under those Acts;

(10)–(22)   …

(23)   "Settled land" has the same meaning as in the Settled Land Acts, and where the settlement consists of more than one instrument, or where any estate, interest, power or charge is by this Act made to take effect as if limited or protected by the settlement, it includes every estate or interest comprised in such compound settlement;

(24)–(29)   …

(*30*)   *"Trust for sale", in relation to land, means an immediate binding trust for sale, with or without a power at discretion to postpone the sale … ;*

(31), (32)   …

[101]

NOTES

Sub-s (1): words in italics in both places repealed by the Trusts of Land and Appointment of Trustees Act 1996, s 25(2), Sch 4; the original wording is reproduced here for reasons of historical interest or in view of the savings contained in ss 3, 18(3), 25(5) of the 1996 Act.

Sub-ss (2)–(5), (7), (8), (10)–(18), (20)–(22), (24)–(29), (32): repealed by the Statute Law (Repeals) Act 1969.

Sub-s (6): words omitted repealed by the Courts Act 1971, s 56(4), Sch 11, Pt II.

Sub-s (19): repealed by the Mental Health Act 1959, s 149(2), Sch 8, Pt I.

Sub-s (30): repealed by the Trusts of Land and Appointment of Trustees Act 1996, s 25(2), Sch 4; the original wording is reproduced here for reasons of historical interest or in view of the savings contained in ss 3, 18(3), 25(5) of the 1996 Act; words omitted repealed by the Statute Law (Repeals) Act 1969.

Sub-s (31): repealed by the Ministry of Agriculture, Fisheries and Food (Dissolution) Order 2002, SI 2002/794, art 5(2), Sch 2.

189   *(Repealed by the Statute Law (Repeals) Act 1969.)*

190   Special definitions applicable to Part VII

In Part VII of this Act—

  (i)   "Lessor" means the person for the time being entitled in reversion expectant on the interest demised, or, where the reversion is encumbered, the person having power to accept a surrender of the lease, or underlease;

  (ii)   "Lessee" and "underlessee" include the persons respectively deriving title under them;

  (iii)   "A perpetually renewable lease or underlease" means a lease or underlease the holder of which is entitled to enforce (whether or not subject to the fulfilment of any condition) the perpetual renewal thereof, and includes a lease or underlease for a life or lives or for a term of years, whether determinable with life or lives or not, which is perpetually renewable as aforesaid, but does not include copyhold land held for a life or lives or for years, whether or not determinable with life, where the tenant had before the commencement of this Act a right of perpetual renewal subject or not to the fulfilment of any condition;

  (iv)   "Underlease", unless the context otherwise requires, includes a subterm created out of a derivative leasehold interest.

[102]

191   Short title, commencement and extent

  (1)   This Act may be cited as the Law of Property Act 1922.

  (2)   ...

  (3)   This Act (including the repeals therein) shall not extend to Scotland or Ireland.

[103]

NOTES
Sub-s (2): repealed by the Statute Law Revision Act 1950.

SCHEDULES

(First, Third and Ninth Schedules repealed by the Settled Land Act 1925, s 119, Sch 5, and the Law of Property Act 1925, s 207, Sch 7; Second, Fourth, Eighth and Eleventh Schedules repealed by the Law of Property Act 1925, s 207, Sch 7; Fifth Schedule repealed by the Settled Land Act 1925, s 119, Sch 5; Sixth Schedule repealed by the Settled Land Act 1925, s 119, Sch 5, the Law of Property Act 1925, s 207, Sch 7, and the Administration of Estates Act 1925, s 56, Sch 2, Pt II; Seventh Schedule repealed by the Land Charges Act 1925, s 24, Schedule; Tenth Schedule repealed by the Settled Land Act 1925, s 119, Sch 5, and the Universities and College Estates Act 1925, s 44, Sch 2; Twelfth, Thirteenth and Fourteenth Schedules repealed by the Statute Law (Repeals) Act 1969.)

FIFTEENTH SCHEDULE
PROVISIONS RELATING TO PERPETUALLY RENEWABLE LEASES
AND UNDERLEASES

Section 145

1   Conversion of perpetually renewable leases into long terms

  (1)   Land comprised in a perpetually renewable lease which was subsisting at the commencement of this Act shall, by virtue of this Act, vest in the person who at such commencement was entitled to such lease, for a term of two thousand years, to be calculated from the date at which the existing term or interest commenced, at the rent and subject to the lessees' covenants and conditions (if any) which under the lease would have been payable or enforceable during the subsistence of such term or interest.

  (2)   The rent, covenants and conditions (if any) shall (subject to the express provisions of this Act to the contrary) be payable and enforceable during the subsistence of the term created by this Act; and that term shall take effect in substitution for the term or interest created by the

lease, and be subject to the like power of re-entry (if any) and other provisions which affected the term or interest created by the lease, but without any right of renewal.

2 Conversion of perpetually renewable underleases into long terms

(1)   Land comprised in any underlease, which at the commencement of this Act was perpetually renewable and was derived out of a head term affected by this Act, shall, by virtue of this Act, vest in the person who at such commencement was entitled to the subterm or interest for a term of two thousand years less one day, to be calculated from the date at which the head term created by this Act commenced, at the rent and subject to the underlessee's covenants and conditions (if any) which under the underlease would have been payable or enforceable during the subsistence of such subterm or interest.

(2)   The rent, covenants and conditions (if any) shall (subject to the express provisions of this Act to the contrary) be payable and enforceable during the subsistence of the subterm created by this Act; and that subterm shall take effect in substitution for the subterm or interest created by the underlease, and be subject to the like power of re-entry (if any) and other provisions which affected the subterm or interest created by the underlease, but without any right of renewal.

(3)   The foregoing provisions of this section shall also apply to any perpetually renewable subterm or interest which, at the commencement of this Act, was derived out of any other subterm or interest, but so that in every case the subterm created by this Act shall be one day less in duration than the derivative term created by this Act, out of which it takes effect.

3 Incidence of equities, incumbrances, and subterms

(1)   Every term or subterm created by this Part of this Act shall be subject to all the same trusts, powers, executory limitations over, rights and equities (if any), and to all the same incumbrances and obligations of every kind, as the term, subterm, or other interest which it replaces would have been subject to if this Part of this Act had not been passed, but without prejudice to the provisions of Part I of this Act, and where an infant is entitled, the person, of full age, who by virtue of that Part of this Act, becomes entitled to the legal estate of the infant shall be deemed to have been entitled to the said lease, subterm or interest at the commencement of this Act.

(2)   Where any subterm or interest, subsisting at the commencement of this Act, was derived out of a lease or underlease affected by this Act, but was not perpetually renewable, the same shall be deemed to take effect out of the term created by this Act or out of any derivative subterm so created, as the case may require.

4 Title acquired and stamps

(1)   This Part of this Act shall not operate to confer any better title to any term or subterm hereby created than the title to the perpetually renewable term, subterm, or interest which it replaces.

(2)   This Act shall not render any lease or instrument which has been duly stamped according to the law in force at its date, liable to be further stamped, nor shall any stamp duty be payable by reason only of the creation by this Act of any term or subterm.

5 Dispositions purporting to create perpetually renewable leaseholds

[(1)]   A grant, after the commencement of this Act, of a term, subterm, or other leasehold interest with a covenant or obligation for perpetual renewal, which would have been valid if this Part of this Act had not been passed, shall (subject to the express provisions of this Act) take effect as a demise for a term of two thousand years or in the case of a subdemise for a term less in duration by one day than the term out of which it is derived, to commence from the date fixed for the commencement of the term, subterm, or other interest, and in every case free from any obligation for renewal or for payment of any fines, fees, costs, or other money in respect of renewal.

[(2)   Sub-paragraph (3) applies where a grant—
    (a)   relates to commonhold land, and
    (b)   would take effect by virtue of sub-paragraph (1) as a demise for a term of two thousand years or a subdemise for a fixed term.

(3)   The grant shall be treated as if it purported to be a grant of the term referred to in sub-paragraph (2)(b) (and sections 17 and 18 of the Commonhold and Leasehold Reform Act 2002 (residential and non-residential leases) shall apply accordingly).]

6 Satisfaction of existing contracts to grant perpetually renewable interests

(1)   Any obligation in force at the commencement of this Act for the grant (otherwise than by way of renewal) of a lease, subterm, or other leasehold interest with a covenant or obligation for perpetual renewal shall be deemed to be an obligation for the grant of a lease for a term of two thousand years, or, in the case of an underlease, for a term less in duration by one day than the term out of which it is to be derived, but the amount of the rent to be paid shall, if necessary, be adjusted, having regard to the loss of fines and other payments (if any) which would have been payable on renewal.

(2)   In case any dispute arises respecting the adjustment of the rent, the matter shall be submitted to the [Secretary of State] for determination, in the manner provided by this Act.

7 Future contracts for renewal and as to leases for lives

(1)   Any contract entered into after the commencement of this Act, for the grant of a lease, subterm, or other leasehold interest with a covenant or obligation for perpetual renewal shall (subject to the express provisions of this Part of this Act) operate as an agreement for a demise for a term of two thousand years, or in the case of a contract for a subdemise, for a term less in duration by one day than the term out of which it is derived, to commence from the date agreed for the commencement of the term, subterm or other interest, and in every case free from the obligation for renewal or for payment of any fines, fees, costs or other money in respect of renewal.

(2)   Any contract entered into after such commencement for the renewal of a lease or underlease for a term exceeding sixty years from the termination of the lease or underlease, and whether or not contained in the lease or underlease, shall (subject to the express provisions of this Part of this Act) be void.

(3)   ...

8 Effect of powers to grant renewable leases

(1)   Every power conferred by custom or contained in a statute (except as hereinafter mentioned) or other instrument authorising a tenant for life of full age, statutory owner, trustee, or other person to grant a lease or underlease with a covenant or obligation for perpetual renewal, shall have effect, in regard to any grant made after the commencement of this Act, as if the same authorised the grant of a lease or underlease for a term not exceeding two thousand years at the best rent that can be reasonably obtained, having regard to any fine which may be taken and to all the circumstances of the case, or, if the power authorises a grant at a peppercorn rent or other rent less then the best rent, then at any rent so authorised.

(2)   Every power to grant a lease or underlease at a rent or in consideration of a fine for life or lives, or for any term of years determinable with life or lives or on the marriage of any person, shall have effect in regard to any grant made after the commencement of this Act, as if the same authorised the grant of a lease or underlease for a term not exceeding ninety years determinable after the death or marriage (as the case may be) of the original lessee or of the survivor of the original lessees by at least one month's notice in writing given to determine the same on one of the usual quarter days, either by the lessor or the persons deriving title under him to the person entitled to the leasehold interest, or by the lessee or other persons in whom the leasehold interest is vested to the lessor or the persons deriving title under him.

9 Saving of rights and powers under 8 Edw 7 c 36

Nothing in this Act shall prejudicially affect any right of renewal conferred by section forty-four of the Small Holdings and Allotments Act 1908, or the power conferred by section forty of that Act, to grant leases for the purposes of that Act, with a similar right of renewal.

10 Powers and covenants implied in leases and underleases affected

(1)   Every lease or underlease which, by virtue of this Part of this Act, takes effect for a term of two thousand years or for a derivative term of two thousand years less one or more days (as the case may require) shall be deemed to contain—

    (i)   A power (exerciseable only with the consent of the persons, if any, interested in any derivative interest which might be prejudicially affected) for the lessee or underlessee by giving notice in writing to the lessor at least ten days before the lease or underlease would (but for this Act) have expired if it had not been renewed after the commencement of this Act, to determine the lease or underlease at the date on which (but for this Act) it would have expired if it had not been renewed as aforesaid;

Also a like power (exerciseable with the like consent if any) to determine subsequently by notice as aforesaid the lease or underlease at the time at which, if this Act had not been passed and all renewals had in the meantime been made in due course, the lease or underlease would have expired if it had not been further renewed after the date of the notice:

Provided that if any such notice be given all uncommuted additional rent attributable to a fine or other money which, if this Act had not been passed, would have been payable on a renewal made after the date of the notice, shall [cease or] not become payable:

(ii) A covenant by the lessee or underlessee to register every assignment or devolution of the term or subterm, including all probates or letters of administration affecting the same, with the lessor or his solicitor or agent, within six months from the date of the assignment, devolution, or grant of probate or letters of administration, and to pay a fee of [one guinea] (which shall be accepted in satisfaction of all costs) in respect of each registration; and the covenant so deemed to be contained shall be in substitution for any express covenant to register with the lessor or his solicitor or agent, assignments or devolutions of the term or subterm, and to pay fees or costs in respect of such registration:

(iii) A covenant by the lessee or underlessee within one year from the commencement of this Act to produce his lease or underlease or sufficient evidence thereof (including an assignment of part of the land comprised in the lease or underlease) with any particulars required to show that a perpetual right of renewal was subsisting at the commencement of this Act, to the lessor or his solicitor or agent, who shall, subject to the payment of his costs, if the right of renewal is admitted or proved, endorse notice of that fact on the lease, underlease, assignment, or copy thereof, at the expense of the lessee or underlessee; and such endorsement signed by or on behalf of the lessor shall, in favour of a purchaser, be sufficient evidence that the right of renewal was subsisting as aforesaid, either in respect of the whole or part of the land as the case may require:

and the power of re-entry (if any) contained in the lease or underlease shall apply and extend to the breach of every covenant deemed to be contained as aforesaid.

(2) If any dispute arises respecting the date on which a notice is authorised to be served by this section, or whether or not a lease or underlease or assignment or a copy thereof ought to be endorsed as aforesaid, the matter shall be submitted to the [Secretary of State] for determination in the manner provided by this Act.

11 Liability of lessees and underlessees

(1) In the case of every term or subterm created by this Act or under any power conferred by this Part of this Act, each lessee or underlessee, although he may be the original lessee or underlessee, and notwithstanding any stipulation to the contrary, shall be liable only for rent accruing and for breaches of covenants or conditions occurring while he or his personal representatives shall have the term or subterm vested in him or them, and in like manner, as respects an original lessee or underlessee, as if the term or subterm had, immediately after its creation, been assigned to him.

(2) Nothing in this Part of this Act shall affect the liability of any person in respect of rent accruing or the breach of any covenant or condition occurring before the commencement of this Act.

12 Conversion of fines into additional rent

(1) Where, under the lease, underlease, or otherwise, any fine or other money, including a heriot, is payable by the lessee or underlessee on renewal, then and in every such case [an amount to be ascertained as hereinafter provided] shall, save as in this Act provided and unless commuted, become payable to the lessor as additional rent, during the subsistence of the term or subterm created by this Act, by as nearly as may be equal yearly instalments the first instalment to be paid at the end of one year from the commencement of this Act; but no sums payable for costs of examination of the lessee's or underlessee's title or of granting a new lease or underlease or of any other work which is rendered unnecessary by this Act shall be taken into account in ascertaining the additional rent.

[(2) In default of agreement and unless the [Secretary of State], having regard to the practice and other circumstances of the case, otherwise directs, the following provisions shall have effect for the purpose of ascertaining the annual instalments of additional rent:—

(a) the additional rent shall be ascertained on the basis of the fines and other payments which would have been payable on the occasion of the first renewal after the commencement of this Act, if this Act had not been passed;

(b) where the lessee or underlessee has a right to renew at different times, the occasion of the first renewal shall be such date as he may, by notice in writing given to the lessor within one year after the commencement of this Act, select from among the dates at which he would have been entitled to renew his lease or underlease had it remained renewable, or, in default of such notice, the last day on which he would have been entitled to renew, regard being had to the date of the last renewal.]

(3)   But where the time at or within which the said fine or other money must be paid is not definitely fixed by or ascertainable from the lease or underlease the same shall, for the purpose of ascertaining the amount of the annual instalments of additional rent, be deemed to have been payable on such date as may, within one year from the commencement of this Act, be agreed between the lessor and the lessee or underlessee [or in default] of such agreement, as may be fixed by the [Secretary of State].

(4)   The additional rent shall be deemed part of the rent reserved by the lease or underlease for all purposes, including any covenant for payment of rent or proviso for re-entry contained in the lease or underlease.

(5)   Subject to any order by the [Secretary of State] or the court to the contrary, and in default of agreement, the amount of each annual instalment of additional rent shall be ascertained by [an actuary, regard being had to the interval or average interval occurring between the dates of renewal and to any circumstances affecting the amount payable on renewal].

(6)   If the lessee or underlessee is liable to forfeit his right of renewal if he makes default in payment of a fine or other money or in doing any other act or thing within a time ascertainable by the dropping of a life, but not otherwise, then [such percentage as the [Secretary of State] may generally or in any particular instance with a view to maintaining any existing practice, prescribe] of the annual value of the land (ascertained as provided by this Act in the case of enfranchised land for the extinguishment of manorial incidents) shall be treated as added to the fines and other money payable by the lessee or underlessee on renewal for the purpose of ascertaining the amount of the annual instalment of additional rent, and as compensation to the lessor for loss of his right of re-entry (present or future) which would have accrued by reason of any failure to exercise the right of renewal

13   Interest on fines

(1)   Where, under the lease or underlease any unpaid fine or other money payable on a renewal carries interest, then any annual instalment of additional rent payable in lieu thereof shall, until paid, carry interest from the date on which the instalment becomes payable, and at the same rate at which such interest would have been payable if this Act had not been passed.

(2)   Where the lease or underlease does not provide for payment of such interest, then each annual instalment of additional rent shall, until paid, carry interest at the current rate from the time when demand in writing is made claiming the money.

14   Provisions respecting commutation of additional rent and other matters

(1)   The lessor and lessee or underlessee may agree—

(a) For the commutation or discharge of any claims in respect of additional rent [or any part thereof];

(b) The amount (if any) of the annual instalments of additional rent payable;

(c) The dates for payment of additional rent;

(d) The interval or average interval between dates of renewal;

(e) The dates on which the lessee or underlessee has power under this Act to determine the lease or underlease;

(f) The amount of the rent (including the annual instalments of additional rent) to be apportioned in respect of any part of the land comprised in the lease or underlease, and thereupon the lessee's or underlessee's covenants shall be apportioned in regard to the land to which the apportionment relates.

(2)   A statement in writing respecting any such agreement, which is endorsed on any such lease or underlease, or the counterpart or assignment, and signed by the lessor and lessee or underlessee, shall be conclusive evidence of the matters stated, and the costs of and incidental to the agreement and any negotiations therefor shall be borne be the lessee or underlessee.

(3)   The additional rent may, by such endorsement, be made payable by instalments at the times at which the original rent is made payable or otherwise.

15   Compensation of lessor's agents

Any claims for compensation by any officer, solicitor, or other agent of the lessor in respect of fees or remuneration (not being remuneration attributable to work rendered unnecessary by this Act) which would have been payable by the lessee or underlessee on any renewal, if this Act had not been passed, shall be treated as part of the fines or other money payable to the lessor and be discharged out of the additional rent or commutation money or otherwise by the lessor, and the lessee or underlessee shall not otherwise be concerned therewith.

16   Disputes to be submitted to the [Secretary of State]

(1)   If the lessor and lessee or underlessee or the lessor's agent (as the case may require) do not agree, or any dispute arises as to the amount or date for payment of any annual instalment of additional rent, or the amount for which the same ought to be commuted, or the amount at which any rent ought to be adjusted, or apportioned, or the amount of compensation (if any) payable by the lessor to his officer, solicitor or other agent, [or the appointment of or instructions to be given to an actuary under paragraph 12(5) of this Schedule] the question or dispute shall be submitted to the [Secretary of State] for determination, when the parties may be represented by solicitors or counsel, and the award of the [Secretary of State] shall (subject only to such appeal to the court as may be prescribed by rules of court) be final.

(2)   The [Secretary of State] may issue regulations in respect of any of the matters aforesaid, and determine by whom and in what proportions the cost of any application to the [Secretary of State] shall be paid.

(3)   If a dispute as to the amount for which any annual instalment of additional rent ought to be commuted is submitted to the [Secretary of State], and if the lessor would (under the lease or underlease subsisting at the commencement of this Act, or any lease or underlease which would have been subsisting if this Act had not been passed and the successive renewable leases or underleases had been renewed in the ordinary course) have had a right to refuse renewal by reason of a default in payment of a fine, then the [Secretary of State] shall, in the arbitration, have regard to the value of such right (unless compensation has been given for the loss of the right) in like manner as if a corresponding absolute right to determine the term or subterm created by this Act had, by reason of a corresponding default, been made exercisable by the lessor at the time at which the renewable lease or underlease would have expired if the lessor had lawfully refused to renew it. [For the purposes of this sub-paragraph the compensation to be given for the loss of the said right shall be regulated by the practice (if any) which obtained, before the commencement of this Act, in assessing the value of the said right, unless the [Secretary of State] otherwise directs.]

17   Power to raise and apply capital for commuting additional rent

(1)   A power authorising a tenant for life of full age, statutory owner, trustee, or other person to apply or direct the application of or raise any money for or in the discharge of the costs, fines, and other sums payable on the renewal of any such lease or underlease shall be deemed to authorise the payment, application, or raising of money for the commutation of any additional rent made payable by this Act.

(2)   Out of the money so applicable or raiseable, the lessor may discharge any compensation payable to his officer, solicitor, or other agent.

(3)   If the reversion is settled land, or [subject to a trust of land], any commutation money shall be treated as capital money or proceeds of sale arising from such land (as the case may require).

(4)   If the land comprised in the lease or underlease is settled land or [subject to a trust of land], the commutation money may be paid out of capital money or personal estate (not being chattels real) held on the same trusts as the land.

18   Notices

The provisions of section sixty-seven of the Conveyancing Act 1881 shall apply to any notice required or authorised to be given under this Part of this Act or under any provision implied by this Part of this Act.

19 Registered leases and underleases

Where any lease or underlease to which this Part of this Act applies is registered under the Land Transfer Acts, effect shall be given to the provisions of this Act by making such alterations in the register as may be prescribed under those Acts.

20 Office copies and searches

(1)   The original or counterpart of any lease or underlease or assignment to which this Part of this Act applies may be deposited at the Central Office of the *Supreme Court.*

(2)   A separate file of instruments so deposited shall be kept, and any person who furnishes the prescribed evidence to show that he has a sufficient interest in the lease or underlease or reversion expectant thereon may search that file and inspect the lease or underlease or counterpart or assignment, and an office copy thereof shall be delivered to him at his request.

(3)   A copy of an instrument so deposited, with any plan or endorsements thereon, may be presented at any time at the Central Office, and, if found correct, may be stamped as an office copy, and when so stamped shall become and be an office copy.

(4)   An office copy of the instrument so deposited with the plan and endorsements (if any) shall without further proof be sufficient evidence of the contents of the instrument, plan, and endorsements (if any), and of the deposit thereof at the Central Office.

(5)   Where an instrument so deposited has perished or become undecipherable, an office copy thereof may be similarly deposited, and office copies thereof may be issued in lieu of office copies of the original, and the provisions of this section shall apply thereto as if office copies so issued were office copies of the original instrument.

(6)   General rules may be made for the purposes of this section prescribing the evidence to be furnished before a search is authorised, regulating the practice of the Central Office, and prescribing, with the concurrence of the Treasury, the fees to be taken therein.

[104]

NOTES

Para 5: sub-para (1) numbered as such, and sub-paras (2), (3) added, by the Commonhold and Leasehold Reform Act 2002, s 68, Sch 5, para 1.

Para 6: words in square brackets in sub-para (2) substituted by the Ministry of Agriculture, Fisheries and Food (Dissolution) Order 2002, SI 2002/794, art 5(1), Sch 1, para 1(a).

Para 7: sub-para (3) repealed by the Law of Property Act 1925, s 207, Sch 7.

Para 10: words in square brackets in sub-para (1)(i) inserted by the Law of Property (Amendment) Act 1924, s 2, Sch 2, para 5(1); words in square brackets in sub-para (2) substituted by SI 2002/794, art 5(1), Sch 1, para 1(b).

Para 12: words in square brackets in sub-para (1) substituted by the Law of Property (Amendment) Act 1924, s 2, Sch 2, para 5(2); sub-para (2) substituted by the 1924 Act, s 2, Sch 2, para 5(3) and words in square brackets substituted by SI 2002/794, art 5(1), Sch 1, para 1(c); words in first pair of square brackets in sub-para (3) substituted by the 1924 Act, s 2, Sch 2, para 5(4) and words in second pair of square brackets substituted by SI 2002/794, art 5(1), Sch 1, para 1(c); words in first pair of square brackets in sub-para (5) substituted by SI 2002/794, art 5(1), Sch 1, para 1(c) and words in second pair of square brackets substituted by the 1924 Act s 2, Sch 2, para 5(5); words in first (outer) pair of square brackets in sub-para (6) substituted by the 1924 Act s 2, Sch 2, para 5(6) and words in second (inner) pair of square brackets substituted by SI 2002/794, art 5(1), Sch 1, para 1(c).

Para 14: words in square brackets in sub-para (1)(a) added by the Law of Property (Amendment) Act 1924, s 2, Sch 2, para 5(7).

Para 16: words in square brackets in heading substituted by SI 2002/794, art 5(1), Sch 1, para 1(d); words in first pair of square brackets in sub-para (1) inserted by the Law of Property (Amendment) Act 1924, s 2, Sch 2, para 5(8) and words in second and third pair of square brackets substituted by SI 2002/794, art 5(1), Sch 1; words in both pairs of square brackets in sub-para (2) substituted by SI 2002/794, art 5(1), Sch 1, para 1(d); words in first, second and fourth (inner) pair of square brackets substituted by SI 2002/794, art 5(1), Sch 1, para 1(d); words in third (outer) pair of square brackets added by the 1924 Act, s 2, Sch 2, para 5(9).

Para 17: words in square brackets in sub-paras (3), (4) substituted for original words "held on trust for sale" by the Trusts of Land and Appointment of Trustees Act 1996, s 25(1), Sch 3, para 1; the original wording is reproduced here for reasons of historical interest or in view of the savings contained in ss 3, 18(3), 25(5) of the 1996 Act.

Para 20: for the words in italics in sub-para (1) there are substituted the words "Senior Courts" by the Constitutional Reform Act 2005, s 59(5), Sch 11, Pt 2, para 4(1), (3), as from a day to be appointed.

Modification: any reference to solicitor(s) etc modified to include references to bodies recognised under the Administration of Justice Act 1985, s 9, by virtue of the Solicitors' Incorporated Practices Order 1991, SI 1991/2684, arts 4, 5, Sch 1.

Conveyancing Act 1881, s 67: see now the Law of Property Act 1925, s 196.

Prescribed percentage: the percentage prescribed as generally applicable, except where the Minister prescribes in any other particular instance any other percentage, for the purposes of para 12, is five per cent by virtue of the Renewable Leaseholds Regulations 1925, SR & O 1925/857, at **[1001]**.

Regulations: Renewable Leaseholds Regulations 1925, SR & O 1925/857, at **[1001]**.

Rules: Filing of Leases Rules 1925, SR & O 1925/1128, at **[1003]**; the Filing of Leases Fee Order 1925, SR & O 1925/1149.

(Sixteenth Schedule repealed by the Land Registration Act 1925, s 147, Schedule.)

ALLOTMENTS ACT 1922

(12 & 13 Geo 5 c 51)

ARRANGEMENT OF SECTIONS

An Act to amend the law relating to Allotments

[4 August 1922]

1 Determination of tenancies of allotment gardens

(1)   Where land is let on a tenancy for use by the tenant as an allotment garden or is let to any local authority or association for the purpose of being sub-let for such use the tenancy of the land or any part shall not (except as hereinafter provided) be terminable by the landlord by notice to quit or re-entry, notwithstanding any agreement to the contrary, except by—

    (a)   [twelve months'] or longer notice to quit expiring on or before the sixth day of April or on or after the twenty-ninth day of September in any year; or

    (b)   re-entry, after three months' previous notice in writing to the tenant, under a power of re-entry contained in or affecting the contract of tenancy on account of the land being required for building, mining, or any other industrial purpose or for roads or sewers necessary in connection with any of those purposes; or

    (c)   re-entry under a power in that behalf contained in or affecting the contract of tenancy in the case of land let by a corporation or company being the owners or lessees of a railway, dock, canal, water, or other public undertaking on account of the land being required by the corporation, or company, for any purpose (not being the use of the land for agriculture) for which it was acquired or held by the corporation, or company, or has been appropriated under any statutory provision, but so that, except in a case of emergency, three months' notice in writing of the intended re-entry shall be given to the tenant; or

    (d)   re-entry under a power in that behalf contained in or affecting the contract of tenancy, in the case of land let by a local authority ... , after three months' previous notice in writing to the tenant on account of the land being required by the local authority for a purpose (not being the use of land for agriculture) for which it was acquired by the local authority, or has been appropriated under any statutory provision; or

    (e)   re-entry for non-payment of rent or breach of any term or condition of the tenancy or on account of the tenant becoming bankrupt or compounding with his creditors, or where the tenant is an association, on account of its liquidation.

(2), (3)   ...

(4)   This section shall not apply to land held by or on behalf of the [Secretary of State for Defence or Minister of Supply], and so let as aforesaid when possession of the land is required for naval, military, or air force purposes [or for purposes of the Ministry of Supply as the case may be].

[105]

NOTES

Sub-s (1): words in square brackets substituted by the Allotments Act 1950, s 1; words omitted repealed by the Statute Law (Repeals) Act 1993.

Sub-ss (2), (3): repealed by the Statute Law (Repeals) Act 1993.

Sub-s (4): words in first pair of square brackets substituted by the Allotments Act 1950, s 8, and the Defence (Transfer of Functions) (No 1) Order 1964, SI 1964/488, art 2 Sch 1, Pt I; words in second pair of square brackets added by the Allotments Act 1950, s 8.

Transfer of functions: transfer of certain functions under this section: for functions see SI 1953/1673, SI 1957/561, SI 1959/1768, SI 1964/490, SI 1964/2048, SI 1966/741, SI 1966/1015, SI 1970/1536, SI 1970/1537, SI 1971/719, SI 1974/692, SI 1983/1127, SI 1992/1296, SI 1995/2986, SI 1997/2971, SI 2001/2568.

2   Compensation on quitting allotment gardens

(1)   Where under any contract of tenancy land is, before or after the passing of this Act, let for use by the tenant as an allotment garden, the tenant shall, subject to the provisions of this section and notwithstanding any agreement to the contrary, be entitled at the termination of the tenancy, on quitting the land, to obtain from the landlord compensation as provided by this section.

[(2)   Subject to the provisions of this section, compensation shall be recoverable under this section only if the tenancy is terminated by the landlord by notice to quit or by re-entry under paragraph (b), (c) or (d) of subsection (1) of the last preceding section.]

(3)   The compensation recoverable from the landlord under this section shall be for crops growing upon the land in the ordinary course of the cultivation of the land as an allotment garden or allotment gardens, and for manure applied to the land.

(4)   A tenant whose tenancy is terminated by the termination of the tenancy of his landlord shall be entitled to recover from his landlord such compensation (if any) as would have been recoverable if his tenancy had been terminated by notice to quit given by his landlord.

(5)   ...

(6)   This section shall also apply to any contract of tenancy made after the passing of this Act by which land is let to any local authority or association for the purpose of being sub-let for use by the tenants as allotment gardens and, notwithstanding that the crops have been grown and the manure applied by the tenants of the local authority or association. Section twenty-three of the Land Settlement (Facilities) Act 1919 shall not apply to land let after the passing of this Act to any local authority or association for the purpose of being sub-let for use by the tenants as allotment gardens.

(7)   This section shall apply to the termination of the tenancy of the whole or any part of the land the subject of a contract of tenancy.

(8)   Except as provided by this section or by the contract of tenancy, the tenant of land under a contract of tenancy to which this section applies shall not be entitled to recover compensation from the landlord at the termination of the tenancy.

(9)   If the tenancy of the tenant is terminated on the twenty-ninth day of September or the eleventh day of October, or at any date between those days, either by notice to quit given by the landlord or by the termination of the tenancy of the landlord, the tenant whose tenancy is so terminated shall be entitled at any time within twenty-one days after the termination of the tenancy to remove any crops growing on the land.

(10)   ...

[106]

NOTES

Sub-s (2): substituted by the Allotments Act 1950, s 2, except in relation to a tenancy terminated by notice to quit given before 26 October 1950.

Sub-s (5): repealed by the Allotments Act 1950, s 15, Schedule.

Sub-s (10): repealed by the Statute Law (Repeals) Act 1973.

3 Provision as to cottage holdings and certain allotments

(1)   The foregoing provisions of this Act as to determination of tenancies of allotment gardens and compensation to a tenant on quitting the same shall not apply to any parcel of land attached to a cottage.

(2)   In the case of any allotment within the meaning of this section (not being an allotment garden), the tenant shall, on the termination of his tenancy by effluxion of time, or from any other cause, be entitled, notwithstanding any agreement to the contrary, to obtain from the landlord compensation for the following matters:—

(a)   For crops, including fruit, growing upon the land in the ordinary course of cultivation and for labour expended upon and manure applied to the land; and

(b)   For fruit trees or bushes provided and planted by the tenant with the previous consent in writing of the landlord, and for drains, outbuildings, pigsties, fowl-houses, or other structural improvements made or erected by and at the expense of the tenant on the land with such consent.

(3)   Any sum due to the landlord from the tenant in respect of rent or of any breach of the contract of tenancy under which the land is held, or wilful or negligent damage committed or permitted by the tenant, shall be taken into account in reduction of the compensation.

(4)   The amount of the compensation shall, in default of agreement, be determined and recovered in the same manner as compensation is, under this Act, to be determined and recovered in the case of an allotment garden.

(5)   The [Agricultural Holdings Act 1986] shall, in the case of an allotment within the meaning of this section [which is an agricultural holding within the meaning of that Act], have effect as if the provisions of this section as to the determination and recovery of compensation were substituted for the provisions of [that Act] as to the determination and recovery of compensation, and a claim for compensation for any matter or thing for which a claim for compensation can be made under this section, may be made either under [that Act] or under this section, but not under both.

(6)   ...

(7)   In this section the expression "allotment" means any parcel of land, whether attached to a cottage or not, of not more than two acres in extent, held by a tenant under a landlord [otherwise than under a farm business tenancy (within the meaning of the Agricultural Tenancies Act 1995)] and cultivated as a farm or a garden, or partly as a garden and partly as a farm.

[107]

NOTES

Sub-s (5): words in square brackets substituted by the Agricultural Holdings Act 1986, s 100, Sch 14, para 9.

Sub-s (6): repealed by the Statute Law (Repeals) Act 1993.

Sub-s (7): words in square brackets inserted by the Agricultural Tenancies Act 1995, s 40, Schedule, para 3.

Transfer of functions: functions of the Minister of Agriculture, Fisheries and Food under this Act, in relation to cottage holdings, so far as they relate to Wales, now exercised by the Secretary of State for Wales by virtue of the Transfer of Functions (Wales) (No 1) Order 1978, SI 1978/272, art 2, Sch 1; all functions of a Minister of the Crown under this Act (except s 1(4)), and so far as they relate to Wales, now exercised by the National Assembly for Wales by virtue of the National Assembly for Wales (Transfer of Functions) Order 1999, SI 1999/672, art 2, Sch 1.

4 Further provision as to allotment gardens and allotments

(1)   A tenant of land held under a contract of tenancy to which any of the foregoing provisions of this Act apply may, before the termination of the tenancy, remove any fruit trees or bushes provided and planted by the tenant and any erection, fencing or other improvement erected or made by and at the expense of the tenant, making good any injury caused by such removal.

(2)   A tenant of land held under a contract of tenancy to which any of the foregoing provisions of this Act apply and which is made with a mortgagor but is not binding on the mortgagee, shall, on being deprived of possession by the mortgagee, be entitled to recover compensation from him as if he were the landlord and had then terminated the tenancy, but subject to the deduction from such compensation of any rent or other sum due from the tenant in respect of the land.

[108]

5 Rights of tenant who has paid compensation to outgoing tenant

Where a tenant of an allotment has paid compensation to an outgoing tenant for any fruit trees or bushes or other improvement, he shall have the same rights as to compensation or removal as he would have had under this Act if the fruit trees or bushes had been provided and planted or the improvement had been made by him and at his expense.

[109]

6 Assessment and recovery of compensation

(1) The compensation under the foregoing provisions of this Act, and such further compensation (if any) as is recoverable under the contract of tenancy [(not being a farm business tenancy within the meaning of the Agricultural Tenancies Act 1995)] shall, in default of agreement, be determined by a valuation made by a person appointed in default of agreement by the judge of the county court having jurisdiction in the place where the land is situated, on an application in writing being made for the purpose by the landlord or tenant, and, if not paid within fourteen days after the amount is agreed or determined, shall be recoverable upon order made by the county court as money ordered to be paid by a county court under its ordinary jurisdiction, is recoverable.

(2) The proper charges of the valuer for the valuation shall be borne by the landlord and tenant in such proportion as the valuer shall direct, but be recoverable by the valuer from either of the parties and any amount paid by either of the parties in excess of the amount (if any) directed by the valuer to be borne by him shall be recoverable from the other party and may be deducted from any compensation payable to such party.

[110]

NOTES

Sub-s (1): words in square brackets inserted by the Agricultural Tenancies Act 1995, s 40, Schedule, para 4.

Modification: sub-s (2) modified by the Opencast Coal Act 1958, s 41(1), Sch 8, para 8.

7–9 (*Ss 7, 8 outside the scope of this work; s 9 repealed by the Rentcharges Act 1977, s 17(2), Sch 2.*)

10 Powers of entry on unoccupied land

(1) The council of a borough or urban district ... may, after giving such notice of intention to enter as is hereinafter provided—

(a) enter upon any land to which this section applies for the purpose of providing allotment gardens thereon;

(b) adapt any such land for use for such purpose;

(c) let any such land for use by the tenant as an allotment garden or to any association (being an association to which land may be let by the council under the Small Holdings and Allotments Acts 1908 to 1919) for the purpose of sub-letting for such use, but so that any tenancy created by the council shall terminate at the date when the right of occupation of the council is terminated under this section;

(d) on the termination of such occupation remove any erection or work of adaptation making good any injury to the land caused by such removal.

(2) Before entry under this section, the council shall give not less than fourteen days' notice in writing to the owner of the land, in such manner as notices may be given to an owner under the regulations for the time being applicable to compulsory hiring of land under the Allotments Acts.

(3) The right of occupation of the council may be terminated—

(a) by not less than six months' notice in writing to that effect given by the council to the owner in manner aforesaid, and expiring on or before the sixth day of April, or on or after the twenty-ninth day of September in any year; or

[(b) by not less than three months' notice in writing given by the owner to the council in any case where the land is required for any purpose other than the use of the land for agriculture, sport, or recreation, and by not less than six months' notice in writing so given and expiring on or before the sixth day of April, or on or after the twenty-ninth day of September, where the land is required for use for sport or recreation].

(4) A tenant to whom land is let by a council under this section and whose tenancy is terminated by the termination of the right of occupation of the council shall, unless otherwise

agreed in the contract of tenancy, be entitled to recover from the council such compensation (if any) as would have been recoverable if his tenancy had been terminated by notice to quit given by the council, and have the same right to remove his crops as if the tenancy had been so terminated.

(5)   Any person who is interested in any land on which entry is made by the council under this section, and who suffers any loss by reason of the exercise of the powers conferred by this section shall, if he makes a claim not later than one year after the termination of the right of occupation, be entitled to be paid by the council such amount or amounts by way of periodical payments or otherwise as may represent the loss, and such amount or amounts shall in default of agreement be determined by a valuation made by a person appointed, in default of agreement, by the Minister:

Provided that a periodical payment of compensation in the nature of rent shall not exceed the rental value of the land as defined by this section.

(6)   This section applies to—
    (a)   land which at the date of the notice of intended entry is not the subject of a rateable occupation; ...
    (b)   ...

except land being the property of a local authority or land which has been acquired by any corporation or company for the purposes of a railway, dock, canal, water, or other public undertaking, or forming part of any metropolitan common within the meaning of the Metropolitan Commons Act 1866 or any land which is subject, or might be made subject, to regulation under an order or scheme made in pursuance of the Inclosure Acts 1845 to 1899 or under any local Act or otherwise, or land which is or forms part of any town or village green, or any area dedicated or appropriated as a public park, garden, or pleasure ground, or for use for the purposes of public recreation, or land forming part of the New Forest (as defined in the New Forest Act 1877), or of the trust property to which the National Trust Act 1907 applies.

(7)   For the purposes of this section—
The expression "rental value" means the annual rent which a tenant might reasonably be expected to pay for the land if the land had continued in the same condition as at the date when entry was made under this section, or at the date when possession thereof was so first taken as aforesaid, as the case may be.
The expression "rateable occupation" means such occupation as would involve liability to payment of the poor rate or any rate leviable in like manner as the poor rate.
The expression "owner" includes the person who, but for the occupation of the council, would be entitled to the possession of the land.

[111]

NOTES
Sub-ss (1), (6): words omitted repealed by the Statute Law (Repeals) Act 1993.
Sub-s (3): para (b) substituted by the Allotments Act 1925, s 6.
Transfer of functions: functions of the Minister under this Act relating to allotments, so far as it applies to England, now exercised by the Secretary of State for the Environment by virtue of the Secretary of State for the Environment Order 1970, SI 1970/1681, art 2(1), and so far as it applies to Wales, now exercised the National Assembly for Wales by virtue of the National Assembly for Wales (Transfer of Functions) Order 1999, SI 1999/672, art 2, Sch 1. Functions previously transferred by the combined effect of s 2(1) of this Act, the Ministry of Agriculture and Fisheries Act 1919, s 1(1), the Transfer of Functions (Ministry of Food) Order 1955, SI 1955/554, the Minister of Land and Natural Resources Order 1965, SI 1965/143 and the Ministry of Land and Natural Resources (Dissolution) Order 1967, SI 1967/156.
Regulations as to compulsory hiring: the Small Holdings and Allotments (Compulsory Hiring) Regulations 1936, SR & O 1936/196.

---

11   Determination of questions arising on resumption of land

(1)   Where land has been let to a local authority or to an association for the purpose of being sub-let for use as allotment gardens, or is occupied by a council under the powers of entry conferred by this Act, and the landlord, or the person who but for such occupation would be entitled to the possession of the land, proposes to resume possession of the land in accordance with the provisions of this Act for any particular purpose, notice in writing of the purpose for which resumption is required shall be given to the local authority or association.

(2)   The local authority or association may, by a counter notice served within [twenty-one] days after receipt of such notice on the person requiring possession, demand that the question as to whether resumption of possession is required in good faith for the purpose

specified in the notice shall be determined by arbitration under and in accordance with the provisions of the [Agricultural Holdings Act 1986].

(3)   Possession of the land shall not be resumed until after the expiration of the said period of [twenty-one] days or the determination of such question as aforesaid where such determination is demanded under this section.

(4)   This section shall not apply to any case where resumption of possession is required by a corporation or company being the owners or lessees of a railway, dock, canal, water, or other public undertaking.

[112]

NOTES

Sub-s (2): words in first pair of square brackets substituted by the Allotments Act 1925, s 9; words in second pair of square brackets substituted by the Agricultural Holdings Act 1986, s 100, Sch 14, para 10.
Sub-s (3): words in square brackets substituted by the Allotments Act 1925, s 9.

12–21   (*Ss 12, 15, 21 outside the scope of this work; s 13 repealed by the Allotments Act 1950, s 15, Schedule; s 14 repealed by the Local Government Act 1972, s 272(1), Sch 30; s 16(1), (2) repealed by the Local Government Finance (Repeals, Savings and Consequential Amendments) Order 1990, SI 1990/776, art 3(1), Sch 1; s 16(3) repealed by the Allotments Act 1950, s 15(3), Schedule; ss 17, 19 repealed by the Statute Law (Repeals) Act 1993; s 18(1) repealed by the National Loans Act 1968, s 24(2), (3), Sch 6, Pt II, except in relation to any loans made before 1 April 1968; s 18(2) repealed by the Local Government Act 1933, s 307, Sch 11, Pt IV, and the Local Government Act 1939, s 207, Sch 8; s 20 repealed by the Local Government, Planning and Land Act 1980, ss 1(5), 194, Sch 5, para 4, Sch 34, Pt V.*)

22   Interpretation

(1)   For the purposes of this Act, where the context permits—
The expression "allotment garden" means an allotment not exceeding forty poles in extent which is wholly or mainly cultivated by the occupier for the production of vegetable or fruit crops for consumption by himself or his family;
The expression "landlord" means in relation to any land the person for the time being entitled to receive the rents and profits of the land;
The designations of landlord and tenant shall continue to apply to the parties until the conclusion of any proceedings taken under this Act in respect of compensation and shall include the legal personal representative of either party;
The expression "council" shall, in the case of a rural parish not having a parish council, mean the parish meeting;
The expression "industrial purpose" shall not include use for agriculture or sport, and the expression "agriculture" includes forestry, horticulture, or the keeping and breeding of livestock;
The expression "the Allotments Acts" means the provisions of the Small Holdings and Allotments Acts 1908 to 1919, which relate to allotments and this Act;

.....

(2)   ...

(3)   Compensation recoverable by a tenant under this Act for crops or other things shall be based on the value thereof to an incoming tenant.

(4)   Where land is used by the tenant thereof as an allotment garden, then, for the purposes of this Act, unless the contrary is proved—
(a)   the land shall be deemed to have been let to him to be used by him as an allotment garden; and
(b)   where the land has been sublet to him by a local authority or association which holds the land under a contract of tenancy, the land shall be deemed to have been let to that authority or association for the purpose of being sub-let for such use as aforesaid.

(5), (6)   ...

[113]

NOTES

Sub-s (1): definitions omitted repealed by the London Government Act 1963, s 93(1), Sch 18, Pt II and the Statute Law (Repeals) Act 1993.

Sub-s (2): repealed by the Statute Law (Repeals) Act 1993.
Sub-s (5): repealed by the London Government Act 1963, s 93(1), Sch 18, Pt II.
Sub-s (6): repealed by the Agricultural Holdings Act 1923, s 58, Sch 4.

23 Short title, commencement, and repeal

(1)   This Act may be cited as the Allotments Act 1922 and the provisions of the Small Holdings and Allotments Acts 1908 to 1919 which relate to allotments and this Act may be cited together as the Allotments Acts 1908 to 1922.

(2)   ...

(3)   This Act shall not apply to Scotland or Ireland.

[114]

NOTES

Sub-s (2): repealed by the Statute Law Revision Act 1950.

(Schedule repealed by the Statute Law Revision Act 1950.)

SETTLED LAND ACT 1925

(15 & 16 Geo 5 c 18)

ARRANGEMENT OF SECTIONS

PART II
POWERS OF A TENANT FOR LIFE

Leasing powers

Provisions as to building, mining and forestry leases

PART IX
SUPPLEMENTARY PROVISIONS

An Act to consolidate the enactments relating to Settled Land in England and Wales
[9 April 1925]

1–40   (*Ss 1–27, 29–40 outside the scope of this work; s 28 repealed by the Mental Health Act 1959, s 149(2), Sch 8, Pt I.*)

PART II
POWERS OF A TENANT FOR LIFE

Leasing Powers

41 Power to lease for ordinary or building or mining or forestry purposes

A tenant for life may lease the settled land, or any part thereof, or any easement, right, or privilege of any kind over or in relation to the land, for any purpose whatever, whether involving waste or not, for any term not exceeding—

(i) In case of a building lease, nine hundred and ninety-nine years;

(ii) In case of a mining lease, one hundred years;

(iii) In case of a forestry lease, nine hundred and ninety-nine years;

(iv) In case of any other lease, fifty years.

[115]

42 Regulations respecting leases generally

(1) Save as hereinafter provided, every lease—

(i) shall be by deed, and be made to take effect in possession not later than twelve months after its date, or in reversion after an existing lease having not more than seven years to run at the date of the new lease;

(ii) shall reserve the best rent that can reasonably be obtained, regard being had to any fine taken, and to any money laid out or to be laid out for the benefit of the settled land, and generally to the circumstances of the case;

(iii) shall contain a covenant by the lessee for payment of the rent, and a condition of re-entry on the rent not being paid within a time therein specified not exceeding thirty days.

(2) A counterpart of every lease shall be executed by the lessee and delivered to the tenant for life or statutory owner, of which execution and delivery the execution of the lease by the tenant for life or statutory owner shall be sufficient evidence.

(3) A statement, contained in a lease or in an indorsement thereon, signed by the tenant for life or statutory owner, respecting any matter of fact or of calculation under this Act in relation to the lease, shall, in favour of the lessee and of those claiming under him, be sufficient evidence of the matter stated.

(4) A fine received on the grant of a lease under any power conferred by this Act shall be deemed to be capital money arising under this Act.

(5) A lease at the best rent that can be reasonably obtained without fine, and whereby the lessee is not exempted from punishment for waste, may be made—

(i) Where the term does not exceed twenty-one years—
  (a) without any notice of an intention to make the lease having been given under this Act; and
  (b) notwithstanding that there are no trustees of the settlement; and

(ii) Where the term does not extend beyond three years from the date of the writing, by any writing under hand only containing an agreement instead of a covenant by the lessee for payment of rent.

[116]

43 Leasing powers for special objects

The leasing power of a tenant for life extends to the making of—

(i) a lease for giving effect (in such manner and so far as the law permits) to a covenant of renewal, performance whereof could be enforced against the owner for the time being of the settled land; and

(ii) a lease for confirming, as far as may be, a previous lease being void or voidable, but so that every lease, as and when confirmed, shall be such a lease as might at the date of the original lease have been lawfully granted under this Act or otherwise, as the case may require.

[117]

Provisions as to building, mining and forestry leases

44   Regulations respecting building leases

(1)   Every building lease shall be made partly in consideration of the lessee, or some person by whose direction the lease is granted, or some other person, having erected or agreeing to erect buildings, new or additional, or having improved or repaired or agreeing to improve or repair buildings, or having executed or agreeing to execute on the land leased, an improvement authorised by this Act for or in connexion with building purposes.

(2)   A peppercorn rent or a nominal or other rent less than the rent ultimately payable, may be made payable for the first five years or any less part of the term.

(3)   Where the land is contracted to be leased in lots, the entire amount of rent to be ultimately payable may be apportioned among the lots in any manner:

Provided that—
   (i)   the annual rent reserved by any lease shall not be less than [50p]; and
   (ii)   the total amount of the rents reserved on all leases for the time being granted shall not be less than the total amount of the rents which, in order that the leases may be in conformity with this Act, ought to be reserved in respect of the whole land for the time being leased; and
   (iii)   the rent reserved by any lease shall not exceed one-fifth part of the full annual value of the land comprised in that lease with the buildings thereon when completed.

[118]

NOTES

Sub-s (3): sum in square brackets substituted by virtue of the Decimal Currency Act 1969, s 10(1).

45   Regulations respecting mining leases

(1)   In a mining lease—
   (i)   the rent may be made to be ascertainable by or to vary according to the acreage worked, or by or according to the quantities of any mineral or substance gotten, made merchantable, converted, carried away, or disposed of, in or from the settled land, or any other land, or by or according to any facilities given in that behalf; and
   (ii)   the rent may also be made to vary according to the price of the minerals or substances gotten, or any of them, and such price may be the saleable value, or the price or value appearing in any trade or market or other price list or return from time to time, or may be the marketable value as ascertained in any manner prescribed by the lease (including a reference to arbitration), or may be an average of any such prices of values taken during a specified period; and
   (iii)   a fixed or minimum rent may be made payable, with or without power for the lessees, in case the rent, according to acreage or quantity or otherwise, in any specified period does not produce an amount equal to the fixed or minimum rent, to make up the deficiency in any subsequent specified period, free of rent other than the fixed or minimum rent.

(2)   A lease may be made partly in consideration of the lessee having executed, or agreeing to execute, on the land leased an improvement authorised by this Act, for or in connexion with mining purposes.

[119]

46   Variation of building or mining lease according to circumstances of district

(1)   Where it is shown to the court with respect to the district in which any settled land is situate, either—
   (i)   that it is the custom for land therein to be leased for building or mining purposes for a longer term or on other conditions than the term or conditions specified in that behalf in this Act; or
   (ii)   that it is difficult to make leases for building or mining purposes of land therein, except for a longer term or on other conditions than the term and conditions specified in that behalf in this Act;

the court may, if it thinks fit, authorise generally the tenant for life or statutory owner to make from time to time leases of or affecting the settled land in that district, or parts thereof for any term or on any conditions as in the order of the court expressed, or may, if it thinks fit, authorise the tenant for life or statutory owner to make any such lease in any particular case.

(2)   Thereupon the tenant for life or statutory owner, and, subject to any direction in the order of the court to the contrary, each of his successors in title being a tenant for life or statutory owner, may make in any case, or in the particular case, a lease of the settled land, or part thereof, in conformity with the order.

[120]

47   Capitalisation of part of mining rent

Under a mining lease, whether the mines or minerals leased are already opened or in work or not, unless a contrary intention is expressed in the settlement there shall be from time to time set aside, as capital money arising under this Act, part of the rent as follows, namely—where the tenant for life or statutory owner is impeachable for waste in respect of minerals, three fourth parts of the rent, and otherwise one fourth part thereof, and in every such case the residue of the rent shall go as rents and profits.

[121]

48   Regulations respecting forestry leases

(1)   In the case of a forestry lease—
   (i)   a peppercorn rent or a nominal or other rent less than the rent ultimately payable, may be made payable for the first ten years or any less part of the term;
  (ii)   the rent may be made to be ascertainable by, or to vary according to the value of the timber on the land comprised in the lease, or the produce thereof, which may during any year be cut, converted carried away, or otherwise disposed of;
 (iii)   a fixed or minimum rent may be made payable, with or without power for the lessee, in case the rent according to value in any specified period does not produce an amount equal to the fixed or minimum rent, to make up the deficiency in any subsequent specified period, free of rent other than the fixed or minimum rent; and
 (iv)   any other provisions may be made for the sharing of the proceeds or profits of the user of the land between the reversioner and the Forestry Commissioners.

(2)   In this expression "timber" includes all forest products.

[122]

NOTES

Forestry Commissioners: by the Forestry Act 1967, s 50, Sch 6, para 5, reference to the Forestry Commissioners in sub-s (1) above is to be construed as a reference to the Minister who is, by s 49(1) of that Act, the Secretary of State as respects England and the Secretary of State as respects Wales.

49–116   (*Outside the scope of this work.*)

PART IX
SUPPLEMENTARY PROVISIONS

117   Definitions

(1)   In this Act, unless the context otherwise requires, the following expressions have the meanings hereby assigned to them respectively, that is to say:—
   (i)   "Building purposes" include the erecting and the improving of, and the adding to, and the repairing of buildings; and a "building lease" is a lease for any building purposes or purposes connected therewith;
  (ii)   "Capital money arising under this Act" means capital money arising under the powers and provisions of this Act or the Acts replaced by this Act, and receivable for the trusts and purposes of the settlement and includes securities representing capital money;
 (iii)   "Death duty" means estate duty ... and every other duty leviable or payable on death;
 (iv)   "Determinable fee" means a fee determinable whether by limitation or condition;
  (v)   "Disposition" and "conveyance" include a mortgage, charge by way of legal mortgage, lease, assent, vesting declaration, vesting instrument, disclaimer,

release and every other assurance of property or of an interest therein by any instrument, except a will, and "dispose of" and "convey" have corresponding meanings;

(vi) "Dower" includes "freebench";

(vii) "Hereditaments" mean real property which on an intestacy might before the commencement of this Act have devolved on an heir;

(viii) "Instrument" does not include a statute unless the statute creates a settlement;

(ix) "Land" includes land of any tenure, and mines and minerals whether or not held apart from the surface, buildings or parts of buildings (whether the division is horizontal, vertical or made in any other way) and other corporeal hereditaments; also a manor, an advowson, and a rent and other incorporeal hereditaments, and an easement, right, privilege, or benefit in, over, or derived from land, and any estate or interest in land[, but does not (except in the phrase "trust of land") include] an undivided share in land;

(x) "Lease" includes an agreement for a lease, and "forestry lease" means a lease to the Forestry Commissioners for any purpose for which they are authorised to acquire land by the Forestry Act 1919;

(xi) "Legal mortgage" means a mortgage by demise or sub-demise or a charge by way of legal mortgage, and "legal mortgagee" has a corresponding meaning; "legal estate" means an estate interest or charge in or over land (subsisting or created at law) which is by statute authorised to subsist or to be created at law; and "equitable interests" mean all other interests and charges in or over land or in the proceeds of sale thereof; an equitable interest "capable of subsisting at law" means such an equitable interest as could validly subsist at law, if clothed with the legal estate; and "estate owner" means the owner of a legal estate;

(xii) "Limitation" includes a trust, and "trust" includes an implied or constructive trust;

(xiii) ...

(xiv) "Manor" includes lordship, and reputed manor or lordship; and "manorial incident" has the same meaning as in the Law of Property Act 1922;

(xv) "Mines and minerals" mean mines and minerals whether already opened or in work or not, and include all minerals and substances in, on, or under the land, obtainable by underground or by surface working; and "mining purposes" include the sinking and searching for, winning, working, getting, making merchantable, smelting or otherwise converting or working for the purposes of any manufacture, carrying away, and disposing of mines and minerals, in or under the settled land, or any other land, and the erection of buildings, and the execution of engineering and other works suitable for those purposes; and a "mining lease" is a lease for any mining purposes or purposes connected therewith, and includes a grant or licence for any mining purposes;

(xvi) ...

(xvii) "Notice" includes constructive notice;

(xviii) "Personal representative" means the executor, original or by representation, or administrator, for the time being of a deceased person, and where there are special personal representatives for the purposes of settled land means those personal representatives;

(xix) "Possession" includes receipt of rents and profits, or the right to receive the same, if any; and "income" includes rents and profits;

(xx) "Property" includes any thing in action, and any interest in real or personal property;

(xxi) "Purchaser" means a purchaser in good faith for value, and includes a lessee, mortgagee or other person who in good faith acquires an interest in settled land for value; and in reference to a legal estate includes a chargee by way of legal mortgage;

(xxii) "Rent" includes yearly or other rent, and toll, duty, royalty, or other reservation, by the acre, or the ton, or otherwise; and in relation to rent, "payment" includes delivery; and "fine" includes premium or fore-gift, and any payment, consideration, or benefit in the nature of a fine, premium, or fore-gift;

(xxiii) "Securities" include stocks, funds, and shares;

(xxiv) "Settled land" includes land which is deemed to be settled land; "settlement" includes an instrument or instruments which under this Act or the Acts which it replaces is or are deemed to be or which together constitute a settlement, and a settlement which is deemed to have been made by any person or to be subsisting for the purposes of this Act; "a settlement subsisting at the commencement of this Act" includes a settlement created by virtue of this Act

PART I
STATUTES

immediately on the commencement thereof; and "trustees of the settlement" mean the trustees thereof for the purposes of this Act howsoever appointed or constituted;

(xxv) "Small dwellings" mean dwelling-houses of a rateable value not exceeding one hundred pounds per annum;

(xxvi) "Statutory owner" means the trustees of the settlement or other persons who, during a minority, or at any other time when there is no tenant for life, have the powers of a tenant for life under this Act, but does not include the trustees of the settlement, where by virtue of an order of the court or otherwise the trustees have power to convey the settled land in the name of the tenant for life;

(xxvii) "Steward" includes deputy steward, or other proper officer, of a manor;

(xxviii) "Tenant for life" includes a person (not being a statutory owner) who has the powers of a tenant for life under this Act, and also (where the context requires) one of two or more persons who together constitute the tenant for life, or have the powers of a tenant for life; and "tenant in tail" includes a person entitled to an entailed interest in any property; and "entailed interest" has the same meaning as in the Law of Property Act 1925;

(xxix) A "term of years absolute" means a term of years, taking effect either in possession or in reversion, with or without impeachment for waste, whether at a rent or not and whether subject or not to another legal estate, and whether certain or liable to determination by notice, re-entry, operation of law, or by a provision for cesser on redemption, or in any other event (other than the dropping of a life, or the determination of a determinable life interest), but does not include any term of years determinable with life or lives or with the cesser of a determinable life interest, nor, if created after the commencement of this Act, a term of years which is not expressed to take effect in possession within twenty-one years after the creation thereof where required by statute to take effect within that period; and in this definition the expression "term of years" includes a term for less than a year, or for a year or years and a fraction of a year or from year to year;

(xxx) "Trust corporation" means the Public Trustee or a corporation either appointed by the court in any particular case to be a trustee or entitled by rules made under subsection (3) of section four of the Public Trustee Act 1906, to act as custodian trustee, and "trust for sale" [has the same meaning] as in the Law of Property Act 1925;

(xxxi) In relation to settled land "vesting deed" or "vesting order" means the instrument whereby settled land is conveyed to or vested or declared to be vested in a tenant for life or statutory owner; "vesting assent" means the instrument whereby a personal representative, after the death of a tenant for life or statutory owner, or the survivor of two or more tenants for life or statutory owners, vests settled land in a person entitled as tenant for life or statutory owner; "vesting instrument" means a vesting deed, a vesting assent or, where the land affected remains settled land, a vesting order; "principal vesting instrument" includes any vesting instrument other than a subsidiary vesting deed; and "trust instrument" means the instrument whereby the trusts of the settled land are declared, and includes any two or more such instruments and a settlement or instrument which is deemed to be a trust instrument;

(xxxii) "United Kingdom" means Great Britain and Northern Ireland;

(xxxiii) "Will" includes codicil.

[(1A) Any reference in this Act to money, securities or proceeds of sale being paid or transferred into court shall be construed as referring to the money, securities or proceeds being paid or transferred into the *Supreme Court* or any other court that has jurisdiction, and any reference in this Act to the court, in a context referring to the investment or application of money, securities or proceeds of sale paid or transferred into court, shall be construed, in the case of money, securities or proceeds paid or transferred into the *Supreme Court*, as referring to the High Court, and, in the case of money, securities or proceeds paid or transferred into another court, as referring to that other court.]

(2) Where an equitable interest in or power over property arises by statute or operation of law, references to the "creation" of an interest or power include any interest or power so arising.

(3)   References to registration under the Land Charges Act 1925, apply to any registration made under any statute which is by the Land Charges Act 1925, to have effect as if the registration had been made under that Act.

[123]

PART I
STATUTES

NOTES
Sub-s (1): in para (iii) words omitted repealed by the Finance Act 1949, s 52, Sch 11, Pt IV; words in square brackets in para (ix) substituted for original words "not being" and words in square brackets in para (xxx) substituted for original words ""trustees for sale" and "power to postpone a sale" have the same meanings" by the Trusts of Land and Appointment of Trustees Act 1996, s 25(1), Sch 3, para 2(1), (13), the original wording is reproduced here for reasons of historical interest or in view of the savings contained in ss 3, 18(3), 25(5) of the 1996 Act; para (xiii) repealed by the Mental Health Act 1959, s 149(2), Sch 8, Pt I; para (xvi) repealed by the Ministry of Agriculture, Fisheries and Food (Dissolution) Order 2002, SI 2002/794, art 5(2), Sch 2.
Sub-s (1A): inserted by the Administration of Justice Act 1965, s 17(1), Sch 1; for the words in italics in both places they occur there are substituted the words "Senior Courts" by the Constitutional Reform Act 2005, s 59(5), Sch 11, Pt 2, para 4(1), (3), as from a day to be appointed.
Forestry Commissioners: by the Forestry Act 1967, s 50, Sch 6, para 5, reference to the Forestry Commissioners in sub-s (1) above is to be construed as a reference to the Minister who is, by s 49(1) of that Act, the Secretary of State as respects England and the Secretary of State as respects Wales.
Modification: definition "Trust corporation" modified in relation to charities by the Charities Act 1993, s 35.
Forestry Act 1919: see now the Forestry Act 1967.
Land Charges Act 1925: see now the Land Charges Act 1972.

118, 119   (*Outside the scope of this work.*)

120   Short title, commencement and extent

(1)   This Act may be cited as the Settled Land Act 1925.

(2)   …

(3)   This Act extends to England and Wales only.

[124]

NOTES
Sub-s (2): repealed by the Statute Law Revision Act 1950.

(*First and Fourth Schedules repealed by the Statute Law (Repeals) Act 2004; Second and Third Schedules outside the scope of this work; Fifth Schedule repealed by the Statute Law Revision Act 1950.*)

TRUSTEE ACT 1925

(15 & 16 Geo 5 c 19)

An Act to consolidate certain enactments relating to trustees in England and Wales
[9 April 1925]

1–11   ((*Pt I*) *s 1 repealed by the Trustee Investments Act 1961, s 16(2), Sch 5; ss 2–11 repealed by the Trustee Act 2000, s 40(1), (3), Sch 2, Pt II, para 18, Sch 4, Pt II.*)

PART II
GENERAL POWERS OF TRUSTEE AND PERSONAL REPRESENTATIVE

12–25   (*Ss 12–20, 22, 24, 25 outside the scope of this work; ss 21, 23 repealed by the Trustee Act 2000, s 40(1), (3), Sch 2, Pt II, paras 21, 23, Sch 4, Pt II.*)

Indemnities

26   Protection against liability in respect of rents and covenants

(1)   Where a personal representative or trustee liable as such for

(a)   any rent, covenant, or agreement reserved by or contained in any lease; or

(b)   any rent, covenant or agreement payable under or contained in any grant made in consideration of a rentcharge; or

(c)   any indemnity given in respect of any rent, covenant or agreement referred to in either of the foregoing paragraphs;

satisfies all liabilities under the lease or grant [which may have accrued and been claimed] up to the date of the conveyance hereinafter mentioned, and, where necessary, sets apart a sufficient fund to answer any future claim that may be made in respect of any fixed and ascertained sum which the lessee or grantee agreed to lay out on the property demised or granted, although the period for laying out the same may not have arrived, then and in any such case the personal representative or trustee may convey the property demised or granted to a purchaser, legatee, devisee, or other person entitled to call for a conveyance thereof and thereafter

(i)   he may distribute the residuary real and personal estate of the deceased testator or intestate, or, as the case may be, the trust estate (other than the fund, if any, set apart as aforesaid) to or amongst the persons entitled thereto, without appropriating any part, or any further part, as the case may be, of the estate of the deceased or of the trust estate to meet any future liability under the said lease or grant;

(ii)   notwithstanding such distribution, he shall not be personally liable in respect of any subsequent claim under the said lease or grant.

[(1A)   Where a personal representative or trustee has as such entered into, or may as such be required to enter into, an authorised guarantee agreement with respect to any lease comprised in the estate of a deceased testator or intestate or a trust estate (and, in a case where he has entered into such an agreement, he has satisfied all liabilities under it which may have accrued and been claimed up to the date of distribution)—

(a)   he may distribute the residuary real and personal estate of the deceased testator or intestate, or the trust estate, to or amongst the persons entitled thereto—
  (i)   without appropriating any part of the estate of the deceased, or the trust estate, to meet any future liability (or, as the case may be, any liability) under any such agreement, and
  (ii)   notwithstanding any potential liability of his to enter into any such agreement; and

(b)   notwithstanding such distribution, he shall not be personally liable in respect of any subsequent claim (or, as the case may be, any claim) under any such agreement.

In this subsection "authorised guarantee agreement" has the same meaning as in the Landlord and Tenant (Covenants) Act 1995.]

(2)   This section operates without prejudice to the right of the lessor or grantor, or the persons deriving title under the lessor or grantor, to follow the assets of the deceased or the trust property into the hands of the persons amongst whom the same may have been respectively distributed, and applies notwithstanding anything to the contrary in the will or other instrument, if any, creating the trust.

(3)   In this section lease includes an underlease and an agreement for a lease or underlease and any instrument giving any such indemnity as aforesaid or varying the liabilities under the lease; grant applies to a grant whether the rent is created by limitation, grant, reservation, or otherwise, and includes an agreement for a grant and any instrument giving any such indemnity as aforesaid or varying the liabilities under the grant; lessee and grantee include persons respectively deriving title under them.

[125]

NOTES
  Sub-s (1): words in square brackets substituted with retrospective effect by the Law of Property (Amendment) Act 1926, ss 7, 8(2), Schedule.
  Sub-s (1A): inserted by the Landlord and Tenant (Covenants) Act 1995, s 30(1), Sch 1, para 1.

27–33   (*Ss 27, 28, 31–33 outside the scope of this work; s 29 repealed by the Powers of Attorney Act 1971, s 11(2), (4), Sch 2; s 30 repealed by the Trustee Act 2000, s 40(1), (3), Sch 2, Pt II, para 24, Sch 4, Pt II.*)

PART III
APPOINTMENT AND DISCHARGE OF TRUSTEES

34–39   (*Outside the scope of this work.*)

40   Vesting of trust property in new or continuing trustees

(1)   Where by a deed a new trustee is appointed to perform any trust, then

   (a)   if the deed contains a declaration by the appointor to the effect that any estate or interest in any land subject to the trust, or in any chattel so subject, or right to recover or receive any debt or other thing in action so subject, shall vest in the persons who by virtue of the deed become or are the trustees for performing the trust, the deed shall operate, without any conveyance or assignment, to vest in those persons as joint tenants and for the purposes of the trust the estate interest or right to which the declaration relates; and

   (b)   if the deed is made after the commencement of this Act and does not contain such a declaration, the deed shall, subject to any express provision to the contrary therein contained, operate as if it had contained such a declaration by the appointor extending to all the estates interests and rights with respect to which a declaration could have been made.

(2)   Where by a deed a retiring trustee is discharged under [section 39 of this Act or section 19 of the Trusts of Land and Appointment of Trustees Act 1996] without a new trustee being appointed, then

   (a)   if the deed contains such a declaration as aforesaid by the retiring and continuing trustees, and by the other person, if any, empowered to appoint trustees, the deed shall, without any conveyance or assignment, operate to vest in the continuing trustees alone, as joint tenants, and for the purposes of the trust, the estate, interest, or right to which the declaration relates; and

   (b)   if the deed is made after the commencement of this Act and does not contain such a declaration, the deed shall, subject to any express provision to the contrary therein contained, operate as if it had contained such a declaration by such persons as aforesaid extending to all the estates, interests and rights with respect to which a declaration could have been made.

(3)   An express vesting declaration, whether made before or after the commencement of this Act, shall, notwithstanding that the estate, interest or right to be vested is not expressly referred to, and provided that the other statutory requirements were or are complied with, operate and be deemed always to have operated (but without prejudice to any express provision to the contrary contained in the deed of appointment or discharge) to vest in the persons respectively referred to in subsections (1) and (2) of this section, as the case may require, such estates, interests and rights as are capable of being and ought to be vested in those persons.

(4)   This section does not extend

   (a)   to land conveyed by way of mortgage for securing money subject to the trust, except land conveyed on trust for securing debentures or debenture stock;

   (b)   to land held under a lease which contains any covenant, condition or agreement against assignment or disposing of the land without licence or consent, unless, prior to the execution of the deed containing expressly or impliedly the vesting declaration, the requisite licence or consent has been obtained, or unless, by virtue of any statute or rule of law, the vesting declaration, express or implied, would not operate as a breach of covenant or give rise to a forfeiture;

   (c)   to any share, stock, annuity or property which is only transferable in books kept by a company or other body, or in manner directed by or under an Act of Parliament.

In this subsection lease includes an underlease and an agreement for a lease or underlease.

(5)   For purposes of registration of the deed in any registry, the person or persons making the declaration expressly or impliedly, shall be deemed the conveying party or parties, and the conveyance shall be deemed to be made by him or them under a power conferred by this Act.

(6)   This section applies to deeds of appointment or discharge executed on or after the first day of January, eighteen hundred and eighty-two.

[126]

NOTES

Sub-s (2): words in square brackets substituted for original words "the statutory power" by the Trusts of Land and Appointment of Trustees Act 1996, s 25(1), Sch 3, para 3(1), (14); the original wording is reproduced here for reasons of historical interest or in view of the savings contained in ss 3, 18(3), 25(5) of the 1996 Act.

Modification: this section is modified, in relation to trust property of trade unions and unincorporated employers' associations, by the Trade Union and Labour Relations (Consolidation) Act 1992, s 13.

41–63, 63A　　*((Pt IV) Outside the scope of this work.)*

PART V

GENERAL PROVISIONS

64–67　　*(Ss 64, 66, 67 outside the scope of this work; s 65 repealed by the Criminal Law Act 1967, s 10, Sch 3, Pt I.)*

68　Definitions

[(1)]　　In this Act, unless the context otherwise requires, the following expressions have the meanings hereby assigned to them respectively, that is to say:—

(1)　"Authorised investments" mean investments authorised by the instrument, if any, creating the trust for the investment of money subject to the trust, or by law;

(2)　"Contingent right" as applied to land includes a contingent or executory interest, a possibility coupled with an interest, whether the object of the gift or limitation of the interest, or possibility is or is not ascertained, also a right of entry, whether immediate or future, and whether vested or contingent;

(3)　"Convey" and "conveyance" as applied to any person include the execution by that person of every necessary or suitable assurance (including an assent) for conveying, assigning, appointing, surrendering, or otherwise transferring or disposing of land whereof he is seised or possessed, or wherein he is entitled to a contingent right, either for his whole estate or for any less estate, together with the performance of all formalities required by law for the validity of the conveyance; "sale" includes an exchange;

(4)　"Gazette" means the London Gazette;

(5)　"Instrument" includes Act of Parliament;

(6)　"Land" includes land of any tenure, and mines and minerals, whether or not severed from the surface, buildings or parts of buildings, whether the division is horizontal, vertical or made in any other way, and other corporeal hereditaments; also a manor, an advowson, and a rent and other incorporeal hereditaments, and an easement, right, privilege, or benefit in, over, or derived from land, … ; and in this definition "mines and minerals" include any strata or seam of minerals or substances in or under any land, and powers of working and getting the same, …; and "hereditaments" mean real property which under an intestacy occurring before the commencement of this Act might have devolved on an heir;

(7)　"Mortgage" and "mortgagee" include a charge or chargee by way of legal mortgage, and relate to every estate and interest regarded in equity as merely a security for money, and every person deriving title under the original mortgagee;

(8)　…

(9)　"Personal representative" means the executor, original or by representation, or administrator for the time being of a deceased person;

(10)　"Possession" includes receipt of rents and profits or the right to receive the same, if any; "income" includes rents and profits; and "possessed" applies to receipt of income of and to any vested estate less than a life interest in possession or in expectancy in any land;

(11)　"Property" includes real and personal property, and any estate share and interest in any property, real or personal, and any debt, and any thing in action, and any other right or interest, whether in possession or not;

(12)　"Rights" include estates and interests;

(13)　"Securities" include stocks, funds, and shares; … and "securities payable to bearer" include securities transferable by delivery or by delivery and endorsement;

(14)　"Stock" includes fully paid up shares, and so far as relates to vesting orders made by the court under this Act, includes any fund, annuity, or security transferable in books kept by any company or society, or by instrument of transfer either alone or accompanied by other formalities, and any share or interest therein;

(15) "Tenant for life," "statutory owner," "settled land," "settlement," "trust instrument," "trustees of the settlement" ... "term of years absolute" and "vesting instrument" have the same meanings as in the Settled Land Act 1925, and "entailed interest" has the same meaning as in the Law of Property Act 1925;

(16) "Transfer" in relation to stock or securities, includes the performance and execution of every deed, power of attorney, act, and thing on the part of the transferor to effect and complete the title in the transferee;

(17) "Trust" does not include the duties incident to an estate conveyed by way of mortgage, but with this exception the expressions "trust" and "trustee" extend to implied and constructive trusts, and to cases where the trustee has a beneficial interest in the trust property, and to the duties incident to the office of a personal representative, and "trustee" where the context admits, includes a personal representative, and "new trustee" includes an additional trustee;

(18) "Trust corporation" means the Public Trustee or a corporation either appointed by the court in any particular case to be a trustee, or entitled by rules made under subsection (3) of section four of the Public Trustee Act 1906, to act as custodian trustee;

(19) "Trust for sale" in relation to land means an immediate ... trust for sale, whether or not exercisable at the request or with the consent of any person ...;

(20) "United Kingdom" means Great Britain and Northern Ireland.

[(2)   Any reference in this Act to paying money or securities into court shall be construed as referring to paying the money or transferring or depositing the securities into or in the *Supreme Court* or into or in any other court that has jurisdiction, and any reference in this Act to payment of money or securities into court shall be construed—

(a)   with reference to an order of the High Court, as referring to payment of the money or transfer or deposit of the securities into or in the *Supreme Court*; and

(b)   with reference to an order of any other court, as referring to payment of the money or transfer or deposit of the securities into or in that court.]

[(3)   Any reference in this Act to a person who lacks capacity in relation to a matter is to a person—

(a)   who lacks capacity within the meaning of the Mental Capacity Act 2005 in relation to that matter, or

(b)   in respect of whom the powers conferred by section 48 of that Act are exercisable and have been exercised in relation to that matter.]

[127]

NOTES

Sub-s (1): numbered as such, para (8), and words omitted from para (13) repealed, by or by virtue of the Administration of Justice Act 1965, s 17(1), Sch 1; words in italics in paras (6), (19) repealed by the Trusts of Land and Appointment of Trustees Act 1996, s 25(2), Sch 4; the original wording is reproduced here for reasons of historical interest or in view of the savings contained in ss 3, 18(3), 25(5) of the 1996 Act; words omitted from para (15) repealed by the Mental Health Act 1959, s 149(2), Sch 8, Pt I.

Sub-s (2): added by the Administration of Justice Act 1965, s 17(1), Sch 1; for the words in italics in both places they occur there are substituted the words "Senior Courts" by the Constitutional Reform Act 2005, s 59(5), Sch 11, Pt 2, para 4(1), (3), as from a day to be appointed.

Sub-s (3): added by the Mental Capacity Act 2005, Sch 6, para 3(1), (6), as from a day to be appointed.

Modification: definition "Trust corporation" modified in relation to charities by the Charities Act 1993, s 35.

---

69   Application of Act

(1)   This Act, except where otherwise expressly provided, applies to trusts including, so far as this Act applies thereto, executorships and administratorships constituted or created either before or after the commencement of this Act.

(2)   The powers conferred by this Act on trustees are in addition to the powers conferred by the instrument, if any, creating the trust, but those powers, unless otherwise stated, apply if and so far only as a contrary intention is not expressed in the instrument, if any, creating the trust, and have effect subject to the terms of that instrument.

(3)   ...

[128]

NOTES
Sub-s (3): repealed by the Statute Law (Repeals) Act 1978.

---

70 (*Outside the scope of this work.*)

71 Short title, commencement, extent

(1) This Act may be cited as the Trustee Act 1925.

(2) ...

(3) This Act, except where otherwise expressly provided, extends to England and Wales only.

(4) The provisions of this Act bind the Crown.

[129]

NOTES
Sub-s (2): repealed by the Statute Law Revision Act 1950.

(*Sch 1 repealed by the Statute Law (Repeals) Act 1978; Sch 2 repealed by the Statute Law Revision Act 1950.*)

LAW OF PROPERTY ACT 1925

(15 & 16 Geo 5 c 20)

ARRANGEMENT OF SECTIONS

PART I
GENERAL PRINCIPLES AS TO LEGAL ESTATES,
EQUITABLE INTERESTS AND POWERS

PART II
CONTRACTS, CONVEYANCES AND OTHER INSTRUMENTS

Contracts

Conveyances and other Instruments

Covenants

PART IV
EQUITABLE INTERESTS AND THINGS IN ACTION

PART V
LEASES AND TENANCIES

PART XI
MISCELLANEOUS

Miscellaneous

Redemption and Apportionment of Rents, etc

Notices

PART XII
CONSTRUCTION, JURISDICTION, AND GENERAL PROVISIONS

An Act to consolidate the enactments relating to Conveyancing and the Law of Property in England and Wales

[9 April 1925]

PART I
GENERAL PRINCIPLES AS TO LEGAL ESTATES, EQUITABLE INTERESTS AND POWERS

1 Legal estates and equitable interests

(1)   The only estates in land which are capable of subsisting or of being conveyed or created at law are—

(a)   An estate in fee simple absolute in possession;

(b)   A term of years absolute.

(2)   The only interests or charges in or over land which are capable of subsisting or of being conveyed or created at law are—

(a)   An easement, right, or privilege in or over land for an interest equivalent to an estate in fee simple absolute in possession or a term of years absolute;

(b)   A rentcharge in possession issuing out of or charged on land being either perpetual or for a term of years absolute;

(c)   A charge by way of legal mortgage;

(d)   ... and any other similar charge on land which is not created by an instrument;

(e)   Rights of entry exercisable over or in respect of a legal term of years absolute, or annexed, for any purpose, to a legal rentcharge.

(3)   All other estates, interests, and charges in or over land take effect as equitable interests.

(4)   The estates, interests, and charges which under this section are authorised to subsist or to be conveyed or created at law are (when subsisting or conveyed or created at law) in this Act referred to as "legal estates", and have the same incidents as legal estates subsisting at the commencement of this Act; and the owner of a legal estate is referred to as "an estate owner" and his legal estate is referred to as his estate.

(5)   A legal estate may subsist concurrently with or subject to any other legal estate in the same land in like manner as it could have done before the commencement of this Act.

(6)   A legal estate is not capable of subsisting or of being created in an undivided share in land or of being held by an infant.

(7)   Every power of appointment over, or power to convey or charge land or any interest therein, whether created by a statute or other instrument or implied by law, and whether created before or after the commencement of this Act (not being a power vested in a legal mortgagee or an estate owner in right of his estate and exercisable by him or by another person in his name and on his behalf), operates only in equity.

(8)   Estates, interests, and charges in or over land which are not legal estates are in this Act referred to as "equitable interests", and powers which by this Act are to operate in equity only are in this Act referred to as "equitable powers".

(9)   The provisions in any statute or other instrument requiring land to be conveyed to uses shall take effect as directions that the land shall (subject to creating or reserving thereout any legal estate authorised by this Act which may be required) be conveyed to a person of full age upon the requisite trusts.

(10)   The repeal of the Statute of Uses (as amended) does not affect the operation thereof in regard to dealings taking effect before the commencement of this Act.

[130]

NOTES

Sub-s (2): words omitted repealed by the Finance Act 1963, s 73(8)(b), Sch 14, Pt IV, and the Tithe Act 1936, s 48(3), Sch 9.

Statute of Uses Act (1535): repealed by the Law of Property Act 1922 and, in relation to transactions after 1926, by s 207 of, and Sch 7 to, this Act.

2–4   (*Outside the scope of this work.*)

5   Satisfied terms, whether created out of freehold or leasehold land to cease

(1)   Where the purposes of a term of years created or limited at any time out of freehold land, become satisfied either before or after the commencement of this Act (whether or not that term either by express declaration or by construction of law becomes attendant upon the freehold reversion) it shall merge in the reversion expectant thereon and shall cease accordingly.

(2)   Where the purposes of a term of years created or limited, at any time, out of leasehold land, become satisfied after the commencement of this Act, that term shall merge in the reversion expectant thereon and shall cease accordingly.

(3)   Where the purposes are satisfied only as respects part of the land comprised in a term, this section shall have effect as if a separate term had been created in regard to that part of the land.

[131]

6   Saving of lessors' and lessees' covenants

(1)   Nothing in this Part of this Act affects prejudicially the right to enforce any lessor's or lessee's covenants, agreements or conditions (including a valid option to purchase or right of pre-emption over the reversion), contained in any such instrument as is in this section mentioned, the benefit or burden of which runs with the reversion or the term.

(2)   This section applies where the covenant, agreement or condition is contained in any instrument—

(a)   creating a term of years absolute, or

(b)   varying the rights of the lessor or lessee under the instrument creating the term.

[132]

7   (*Outside the scope of this work.*)

8   Saving of certain legal powers to lease

(1)   All leases or tenancies at a rent for a term of years absolute authorised to be granted by a mortgagor or mortgagee or by the Settled Land Act 1925, or any other statute (whether or not extended by any instrument) may be granted in the name and on behalf of the estate owner by the person empowered to grant the same, whether being an estate owner or not, with the same effect and priority as if this Part of this Act had not been passed; but this section does not (except as respects the usual qualified covenant for quiet enjoyment) authorise any person granting a lease in the name of an estate owner to impose any personal liability on him.

(2)   Where a rentcharge is held for a legal estate, the owner thereof may under the statutory power or under any corresponding power, create a legal term of years absolute for securing or compelling payment of the same; but in other cases terms created under any such power shall, unless and until the estate owner of the land charged gives legal effect to the transaction, take effect only as equitable interests.

[133]

9–39   (*Ss 9, 10, 12–15, 20–22, 24, 27, 31, 33, 34, 36–39 outside the scope of this work; s 11 repealed by the Law of Property Act 1969, s 16, Sch 2, Pt I; ss 16–18 repealed with savings by* *the Finance Act 1975, ss 50, 52(2), (3), 59(5), Sch 13, Pt I; ss 19, 23, 25, 26, 28–30, 32, 35 repealed by the Trusts of Land and Appointment of Trustees Act 1996, ss 5(1), 25(2), Sch 2, para 2, Sch 4.)*

PART II
CONTRACTS, CONVEYANCES AND OTHER INSTRUMENTS

Contracts

40–43   (*S 40 repealed by the Law of Property (Miscellaneous Provisions) Act 1989, ss 2(8), 4, Sch 2; ss 41–43 outside the scope of this work.*)

44   Statutory commencements of title

(1)   After the commencement of this Act [fifteen years] shall be substituted for forty years as the period of commencement of title which a purchaser of land may require; nevertheless earlier title than [fifteen years] may be required in cases similar to those in which earlier title than forty years might immediately before the commencement of this Act be required.

(2)   Under a contract to grant or assign a term of years, whether derived or to be derived out of freehold or leasehold land, the intended lessee or assign shall not be entitled to call for the title to the freehold.

(3)   Under a contract to sell and assign a term of years derived out of a leasehold interest in land, the intended assign shall not have the right to call for the title to the leasehold reversion.

(4)   On a contract to grant a lease for a term of years to be derived out of a leasehold interest, with a leasehold reversion, the intended lessee shall not have the right to call for the title to that reversion.

[(4A)   Subsections (2) and (4) of this section do not apply to a contract to grant a term of years if the grant will be an event within section 4(1) of the Land Registration Act 2002 (events which trigger compulsory first registration of title).]

(5)   Where by reason of any of [subsections (2) to (4) of this section], an intending lessee or assign is not entitled to call for the title to the freehold or to a leasehold reversion, as the case may be, he shall not, where the contract is made after the commencement of this Act, be deemed to be affected with notice of any matter or thing of which, if he had contracted that such title should be furnished, he might have had notice.

(6)   Where land of copyhold or customary tenure has been converted into freehold by enfranchisement, then, under a contract to sell and convey the freehold, the purchaser shall not have the right to call for the title to make the enfranchisement.

(7)   Where the manorial incidents formerly affecting any land have been extinguished, then, under a contract to sell and convey the freehold, the purchaser shall not have the right to call for the title of the person entering into any compensation agreement or giving a receipt for the compensation money to enter into such agreement or to give such receipt, and shall not be deemed to be affected with notice of any matter or thing of which, if he had contracted that such title should be furnished, he might have had notice.

(8)   A purchaser shall not be deemed to be or ever to have been affected with notice of any matter or thing of which, if he had investigated the title or made enquiries in regard to matters prior to the period of commencement of title fixed by this Act, or by any other statute, or by any rule of law, he might have had notice, unless he actually makes such investigation or enquiries.

(9)   Where a lease whether made before or after the commencement of this Act, is made under a power contained in a settlement, will, Act of Parliament, or other instrument, any preliminary contract for or relating to the lease shall not, for the purpose of the deduction of title to an intended assign, form part of the title, or evidence of the title, to the lease.

(10)   This section, save where otherwise expressly provided, applies to contracts for sale whether made before or after the commencement of this Act, and applies to contracts for exchange in like manner as to contracts for sale, save that it applies only to contracts for exchange made after such commencement.

(11) This section applies only if and so far as a contrary intention is not expressed in the contract.

[(12) Nothing in this section applies in relation to registered land or to a term of years to be derived out of registered land.]

[134]

NOTES

Sub-s (1): words in square brackets substituted, in relation to contracts made after 1969, by the Law of Property Act 1969, s 23.

Sub-s (4A): inserted by the Land Registration Act 2002, s 133, Sch 11, para 2(1), (2).

Sub-s (5): words in square brackets substituted by the Land Registration Act 2002, s 133, Sch 11, para 2(1), (3).

Sub-s (12): added by the Land Registration Act 2002, s 133, Sch 11, para 2(1), (4).

45–47 (*Outside the scope of this work.*)

48 Stipulations preventing a purchaser, lessee, or underlessee from employing his own solicitor to be void

(1) Any stipulation made on the sale of any interest in land after the commencement of this Act to the effect that the conveyance to, or the registration of the title of, the purchaser shall be prepared or carried out at the expense of the purchaser by a solicitor appointed by or acting for the vendor, and any stipulation which might restrict a purchaser in the selection of a solicitor to act on his behalf in relation to any interest in land agreed to be purchased, shall be void; and, if a sale is effected by demise or subdemise, then, for the purposes of this subsection, the instrument required for giving effect to the transaction shall be deemed to be a conveyance:

Provided that nothing in this subsection shall affect any right reserved to a vendor to furnish a form of conveyance to a purchaser from which the draft can be prepared, or to charge a reasonable fee therefor, or, where a perpetual rentcharge is to be reserved as the only consideration in money or money's worth, the right of a vendor to stipulate that the draft conveyance is to be prepared by his solicitor at the expense of the purchaser.

(2) Any covenant or stipulation contained in, or entered into with reference to any lease or underlease made before or after the commencement of this Act—

    (a) whereby the right of preparing, at the expense of a purchaser, any conveyance of the estate or interest of the lessee or underlessee in the demised premises or in any part thereof, or of otherwise carrying out, at the expense of the purchaser, any dealing with such estate or interest, is expressed to be reserved to or vested in the lessor or underlessor or his solicitor; or

    (b) which in any way restricts the right of the purchaser to have such conveyance carried out on his behalf by a solicitor appointed by him;

shall be void:

Provided that, where any covenant or stipulation is rendered void by this subsection, there shall be implied in lieu thereof a covenant or stipulation that the lessee or underlessee shall register with the lessor or his solicitor within six months from the date thereof, or as soon after the expiration of that period as may be practicable, all conveyances and devolutions (including probates or letters of administration) affecting the lease or underlease and pay a fee of one guinea in respect of each registration, and the power of entry (if any) on breach of any covenant contained in the lease or underlease shall apply and extend to the breach of any covenant so to be implied.

(3) Save where a sale is effected by demise or subdemise, this section does not affect the law relating to the preparation of a lease or underlease or the draft thereof.

(4) In this section "lease" and "underlease" include any agreement therefor or other tenancy, and "lessee" and "underlessee" and "lessor" and "underlessor" have corresponding meanings.

[135]

NOTES

Modifications: in this section any reference to a solicitor is to be construed as including a reference to a licensed conveyancer or to a body corporate for the time being recognised under the Administration of Justice Act 1985, s 32, see s 34(2) thereof; any reference to a solicitor is also to be construed as including a reference to a body corporate for the time being recognised under the Administration of Justice

Act 1985, s 9, see Sch 2, para 37 thereto; any reference to a solicitor is also to be construed as including a reference to an institution or practitioner recognised under the Building Societies Act 1986 as suitable to provide conveyancing services, see s 124, Sch 21, paras 9(c), 12(2) thereof (but note the relevant provisions of the 1986 Act have not yet been brought into force and are in any case repealed by the Courts and Legal Services Act 1990, s 125(7), Sch 20, as from a day to be appointed, when they will then be superseded by s 36 et seq of that Act).

49, 50   (*Outside the scope of this work.*)

Conveyances and other Instruments

51 Lands lie in grant only

(1)   All lands and all interests therein lie in grant and are incapable of being conveyed by livery or livery and seisin, or by feoffment, or by bargain and sale; and a conveyance of an interest in land may operate to pass the possession or right to possession thereof, without actual entry, but subject to all prior rights thereto.

(2)   The use of the word grant is not necessary to convey land or to create any interest therein.

[136]

52 Conveyances to be by deed

(1)   All conveyances of land or of any interest therein are void for the purpose of conveying or creating a legal estate unless made by deed.

(2)   This section does not apply to—
    (a)   assents by a personal representative;
    (b)   disclaimers made in accordance with [sections 178 to 180 or sections 315 to 319 of the Insolvency Act 1986] or not required to be evidenced in writing;
    (c)   surrenders by operation of law, including surrenders which may, by law, be effected without writing;
    (d)   leases or tenancies or other assurances not required by law to be made in writing;
    (e)   receipts [other than those falling within section 115 below];
    (f)   vesting orders of the court or other competent authority;
    (g)   conveyances taking effect by operation of law.

[137]

NOTES
Sub-s (2): words in first pair of square brackets substituted by the Insolvency Act 1986, s 439(2), Sch 14; words in second pair of square brackets substituted by the Law of Property (Miscellaneous Provisions) Act 1989, s 1(8), Sch 1, para 2, except in relation to instruments delivered as deeds before 31 July 1990.

53 Instruments required to be in writing

(1)   Subject to the provisions hereinafter contained with respect to the creation of interests in land by parol—
    (a)   no interest in land can be created or disposed of except by writing signed by the person creating or conveying the same, or by his agent thereunto lawfully authorised in writing, or by will, or by operation of law;
    (b)   a declaration of trust respecting any land or any interest therein must be manifested and proved by some writing signed by some person who is able to declare such trust or by his will;
    (c)   a disposition of an equitable interest or trust subsisting at the time of the disposition, must be in writing signed by the person disposing of the same, or by his agent thereunto lawfully authorised in writing or by will.

(2)   This section does not affect the creation or operation of resulting, implied or constructive trusts.

[138]

NOTES
Application: sub-s (1)(c) does not apply to any transfer of title to uncertificated units of a security by means of a relevant system and any disposition or assignment of an interest in uncertificated units of a

security title to which is held by a relevant nominee: see the Uncertificated Securities Regulations 2001, SI 2001/3755, reg 38(5), (6). See also, in relation to financial collateral arrangements: the Financial Collateral Arrangements (No 2) Regulations 2003, SI 2003/3226, reg 4(2).

54   Creation of interests in land by parol

(1)   All interests in land created by parol and not put in writing and signed by the persons so creating the same, or by their agents thereunto lawfully authorised in writing, have, notwithstanding any consideration having been given for the same, the force and effect of interests at will only.

(2)   Nothing in the foregoing provisions of this Part of this Act shall affect the creation by parol of leases taking effect in possession for a term not exceeding three years (whether or not the lessee is given power to extend the term) at the best rent which can be reasonably obtained without taking a fine.

[139]

55   Savings in regard to last two sections

Nothing in the last two foregoing sections shall—
   (a)   invalidate dispositions by will; or
   (b)   affect any interest validly created before the commencement of this Act; or
   (c)   affect the right to acquire an interest in land by virtue of taking possession; or
   (d)   affect the operation of the law relating to part performance.

[140]

56   Persons taking who are not parties and as to indentures

(1)   A person may take an immediate or other interest in land or other property, or the benefit of any condition, right of entry, covenant or agreement over or respecting land or other property, although he may not be named as a party to the conveyance or other instrument.

(2)   A deed between parties, to effect its objects, has the effect of an indenture though not indented or expressed to be an indenture.

[141]

57   Description of deeds

Any deed, whether or not being an indenture, may be described (at the commencement thereof or otherwise) as a deed simply, or as a conveyance, deed of exchange, vesting deed, trust instrument, settlement, mortgage, charge, transfer of mortgage, appointment, lease or otherwise according to the nature of the transaction intended to be effected.

[142]

58   Provisions as to supplemental instruments

Any instrument (whether executed before or after the commencement of this Act) expressed to be supplemental to a previous instrument, shall, as far as may be, be read and have effect as if the supplemental instrument contained a full recital of the previous instrument, but this section does not operate to give any right to an abstract or production of any such previous instrument, and a purchaser may accept the same evidence that the previous instrument does not affect the title as if it had merely been mentioned in the supplemental instrument.

[143]

59, 60   (*Outside the scope of this work.*)

61   Construction of expressions used in deeds and other instruments

In all deeds, contracts, wills, orders and other instruments executed, made or coming into operation after the commencement of this Act, unless the context otherwise requires—
   (a)   "Month" means calendar month;
   (b)   "Person" includes a corporation;
   (c)   The singular includes the plural and vice versa;
   (d)   The masculine includes the feminine and vice versa.

[144]

62 General words implied in conveyances

(1) A conveyance of land shall be deemed to include and shall by virtue of this Act operate to convey, with the land, all buildings, erections, fixtures, commons, hedges, ditches, fences, ways, waters, watercourses, liberties, privileges, easements, rights, and advantages whatsoever, appertaining or reputed to appertain to the land, or any part thereof, or, at the time of conveyance, demised, occupied, or enjoyed with or reputed or known as part or parcel of or appurtenant to the land or any part thereof.

(2) A conveyance of land, having houses or other buildings thereon, shall be deemed to include and shall by virtue of this Act operate to convey, with the land, houses, or other buildings, all outhouses, erections, fixtures, cellars, areas, courts, courtyards, cisterns, sewers, gutters, drains, ways, passages, lights, watercourses, liberties, privileges, easements, rights, and advantages whatsoever, appertaining or reputed to appertain to the land, houses, or other buildings conveyed, or any of them, or any part thereof, or, at the time of conveyance, demised, occupied, or enjoyed with, or reputed or known as part or parcel of or appurtenant to, the land, houses, other buildings conveyed, or any of them, or any part thereof.

(3) A conveyance of a manor shall be deemed to include and shall by virtue of this Act operate to convey, with the manor, all pastures, feedings, wastes, warrens, commons, mines, minerals, quarries, furzes, trees, woods, underwoods, coppices, and the ground and soil thereof, fishings, fisheries, fowlings, courts leet, courts baron, and other courts, view of frankpledge and all that to view of frankpledge doth belong, mills, multcures, customs, tolls, duties, reliefs, heriots, fines, sums of money, amerciaments, waifs, estrays, chief-rents, quitrents, rentscharge, rents seck, rents of assize, fee farm rents, services, royalties, jurisdictions, franchises, liberties, privileges, easements, profits, advantages, rights, emoluments, and hereditaments whatsoever, to the manor appertaining or reputed to appertain, or, at the time of conveyance, demised, occupied, or enjoyed with the same, or reputed or known as part, parcel, or member thereof.

For the purposes of this subsection the right to compensation for manorial incidents on the extinguishment thereof shall be deemed to be a right appertaining to the manor.

(4) This section applies only if and as far as a contrary intention is not expressed in the conveyance, and has effect subject to the terms of the conveyance and to the provisions therein contained.

(5) This section shall not be construed as giving to any person a better title to any property, right, or thing in this section mentioned than the title which the conveyance gives to him to the land or manor expressed to be conveyed, or as conveying to him any property, right, or thing in this section mentioned, further or otherwise than as the same could have been conveyed to him by the conveying parties.

(6) This section applies to conveyances made after the thirty-first day of December, eighteen hundred and eighty-one.

[145]

63 All estate clause implied

(1) Every conveyance is effectual to pass all the estate, right, title, interest, claim, and demand which the conveying parties respectively have, in, to, or on the property conveyed, or expressed or intended so to be, or which they respectively have power to convey in, to, or on the same.

(2) This section applies only if and as far as a contrary intention is not expressed in the conveyance, and has effect subject to the terms of the conveyance and to the provisions therein contained.

(3) This section applies to conveyances made after the thirty-first day of December, eighteen hundred and eighty-one.

[146]

64 Production and safe custody of documents

(1) Where a person retains possession of documents, and gives to another an acknowledgment in writing of the right of that other to production of those documents, and to delivery of copies thereof (in this section called an acknowledgment), that acknowledgment shall have effect as in this section provided.

(2) An acknowledgment shall bind the documents to which it relates in the possession or under the control of the person who retains them, and in the possession or under the control of

every other person having possession or control thereof from time to time, but shall bind each individual possessor or person as long only as he has possession or control thereof; and every person so having possession or control from time to time shall be bound specifically to perform the obligations imposed under this section by an acknowledgment, unless prevented from so doing by fire or other inevitable accident.

(3)   The obligations imposed under this section by an acknowledgment are to be performed from time to time at the request in writing of the person to whom an acknowledgment is given, or of any person, not being a lessee at a rent, having or claiming any estate, interest, or right through or under that person, or otherwise becoming through or under that person interested in or affected by the terms of any document to which the acknowledgment relates.

(4)   The obligations imposed under this section by an acknowledgment are—

  (i)   An obligation to produce the documents or any of them at all reasonable times for the purpose of inspection, and of comparison with abstracts or copies thereof, by the person entitled to request production or by any person by him authorised in writing; and

  (ii)   An obligation to produce the documents or any of them at any trial, hearing, or examination in any court, or in the execution of any commission, or elsewhere in the United Kingdom, on any occasion on which production may properly be required, for proving or supporting the title or claim of the person entitled to request production, or for any other purpose relative to that title or claim; and

  (iii)   An obligation to deliver to the person entitled to request the same true copies or extracts, attested or unattested, of or from the documents or any of them.

(5)   All costs and expenses of or incidental to the specific performance of any obligation imposed under this section by an acknowledgment shall be paid by the person requesting performance.

(6)   An acknowledgment shall not confer any right to damages for loss or destruction of, or injury to, the documents to which it relates, from whatever cause arising.

(7)   Any person claiming to be entitled to the benefit of an acknowledgment may apply to the court for an order directing the production of the documents to which it relates, or any of them, or the delivery of copies of or extracts from those documents or any of them to him, or some person on his behalf; and the court may, if it thinks fit, order production, or production and delivery, accordingly, and may give directions respecting the time, place, terms, and mode of production or delivery, and may make such order as it thinks fit respecting the costs of the application, or any other matter connected with the application.

(8)   An acknowledgment shall by virtue of this Act satisfy any liability to give a covenant for production and delivery of copies of or extracts from documents.

(9)   Where a person retains possession of documents and gives to another an undertaking in writing for safe custody thereof, that undertaking shall impose on the person giving it, and on every person having possession or control of the documents from time to time, but on each individual possessor or person as long only as he has possession or control thereof, an obligation to keep the document safe, whole, uncancelled, and undefaced, unless prevented from so doing by fire or other inevitable accident.

(10)   Any person claiming to be entitled to the benefit of such an undertaking may apply to the court to assess damages for any loss or destruction of, or injury to, the documents or any of them, and the court may, if it thinks fit, direct an inquiry respecting the amount of damages, and order payment thereof by the person liable, and may make such order as it thinks fit respecting the costs of the application, or any other matter connected with the application.

(11)   An undertaking for safe custody of documents shall by virtue of this Act satisfy any liability to give a covenant for safe custody of documents.

(12)   The rights conferred by an acknowledgment or an undertaking under this section shall be in addition to all such other rights relative to the production, or inspection, or the obtaining of copies of documents, as are not, by virtue of this Act, satisfied by the giving of the acknowledgment or undertaking, and shall have effect subject to the terms of the acknowledgment or undertaking, and to any provisions therein contained.

(13)   This section applies only if and as far as a contrary intention is not expressed in the acknowledgment or undertaking.

(14)   This section applies to an acknowledgment or undertaking given, or a liability respecting documents incurred, after the thirty-first day of December, eighteen hundred and eighty-one.

[147]

NOTES
   See further, the Energy Act 2004, s 159(2), Sch 21, para 7(6)(b), which provides that where a person is entitled, in consequence of an energy transfer scheme, to possession of a document relating in part to the title to land or other property in England and Wales, or to the management of such land or other property this section shall have effect accordingly, and on the basis that the acknowledgement did not contain an expression of contrary intention.

65   Reservation of legal estates

(1)   A reservation of a legal estate shall operate at law without any execution of the conveyance by the grantee of the legal estate out of which the reservation is made, or any regrant by him, so as to create the legal estate reserved, and so as to vest the same in possession in the person (whether being the grantor or not) for whose benefit the reservation is made.

(2)   A conveyance of a legal estate expressed to be made subject to another legal estate not in existence immediately before the date of the conveyance, shall operate as a reservation unless a contrary intention appears.

(3)   This section applies only to reservations made after the commencement of this Act.

[148]

66–71   (*Outside the scope of this work.*)

72   Conveyances by a person to himself, etc

(1)   In conveyances made after the twelfth day of August, eighteen hundred and fifty-nine, personal property, including chattels real, may be conveyed by a person to himself jointly with another person by the like means by which it might be conveyed by him to another person.

(2)   In conveyances made after the thirty-first day of December, eighteen hundred and eighty-one, freehold land, or a thing in action, may be conveyed by a person to himself jointly with another person, by the like means by which it might be conveyed by him to another person; and may, in like manner, be conveyed by a husband to his wife, and by a wife to her husband, alone or jointly with another person.

(3)   After the commencement of this Act a person may convey land to or vest land in himself.

(4)   Two or more persons (whether or not being trustees or personal representatives) may convey, and shall be deemed always to have been capable of conveying, any property vested in them to any one or more of themselves in like manner as they could have conveyed such property to a third party; provided that if the persons in whose favour the conveyance is made are, by reason of any fiduciary relationship or otherwise, precluded from validly carrying out the transaction, the conveyance shall be liable to be set aside.

[149]

73–75   (*S 73 repealed by the Law of Property (Miscellaneous Provisions) Act 1989, s 4, Sch 2; ss 74, 75 outside the scope of this work.*)

Covenants

76   Covenants for title

(1)   In a conveyance there shall, in the several cases in this section mentioned, be deemed to be included, and there shall in those several cases, by virtue of this Act, be implied, a covenant to the effect in this section stated, by the person or by each person who conveys, as far as regards the subject-matter or share of subject-matter expressed to be conveyed by him, with the person, if one, to whom the conveyance is made, or with the persons jointly, if more than one, to whom the conveyance is made as joint tenants, or with each of the persons, if more than one, to whom the conveyance is (when the law permits) made as tenants in common, that is to say:

(A)   *In a conveyance for valuable consideration, other than a mortgage, a covenant by a person who conveys and is expressed to convey as beneficial owner in the terms set out in Part I of the Second Schedule to this Act;*

(B)   *In a conveyance of leasehold property for valuable consideration, other than a mortgage, a further covenant by a person who conveys and is expressed to convey as beneficial owner in the terms set out in Part II of the Second Schedule to this Act;*

(C)   *In a conveyance by way of mortgage (including a charge) a covenant by a person who conveys or charges and is expressed to convey or charge as beneficial owner in the terms set out in Part III of the Second Schedule to this Act;*

(D)   *In a conveyance by way of mortgage (including a charge) of freehold property subject to a rent or of leasehold property, a further covenant by a person who conveys or charges and is expressed to convey or charge as beneficial owner in the terms set out in Part IV of the Second Schedule to this Act;*

(E)   *In a conveyance by way of settlement, a covenant by a person who conveys and is expressed to convey as settlor in the terms set out in Part V of the Second Schedule to this Act;*

(F)   *In any conveyance, a covenant by every person who conveys and is expressed to convey as trustee or mortgagee, or as personal representative of a deceased person, ... or under an order of the court, in the terms set out in Part VI of the Second Schedule to this Act, which covenant shall be deemed to extend to every such person's own acts only, and may be implied in an assent by a personal representative in like manner as in a conveyance by deed.*

(2)   *Where in a conveyance it is expressed that by direction of a person expressed to direct as beneficial owner another person conveys, then, for the purposes of this section, the person giving the direction, whether he conveys and is expressed to convey as beneficial owner or not, shall be deemed to convey and to be expressed to convey as beneficial owner the subject-matter so conveyed by his direction; and a covenant on his part shall be implied accordingly.*

(3)   *Where a wife conveys and is expressed to convey as beneficial owner, and the husband also conveys and is expressed to convey as beneficial owner, then, for the purposes of this section, the wife shall be deemed to convey and to be expressed to convey by direction of the husband, as beneficial owner; and, in addition to the covenant implied on the part of the wife, there shall also be implied, first, a covenant on the part of the husband as the person giving that direction, and secondly, a covenant on the part of the husband in the same terms as the covenant implied on the part of the wife.*

(4)   *Where in a conveyance a person conveying is not expressed to convey as beneficial owner, or as settlor, or as trustee, or as mortgagee, or as personal representative of a deceased person, ... or under an order of the court, or by direction of a person as beneficial owner, no covenant on the part of the person conveying shall be, by virtue of this section, implied in the conveyance.*

(5)   *In this section a conveyance does not include a demise by way of lease at a rent, but does include a charge and "convey" has a corresponding meaning.*

(6)   *The benefit of a covenant implied as aforesaid shall be annexed and incident to, and shall go with, the estate or interest of the implied covenantee, and shall be capable of being enforced by every person in whom that estate or interest is, for the whole or any part thereof, from time to time vested.*

(7)   *A covenant implied as aforesaid may be varied or extended by a deed or an assent, and, as so varied or extended, shall, as far as may be, operate in the like manner, and with all the like incidents, effects, and consequences, as if such variations or extensions were directed in this section to be implied.*

(8)   *This section applies to conveyances made after the thirty-first day of December, eighteen hundred and eighty-one, but only to assents by a personal representative made after the commencement of this Act.*

[150]

71

77   Implied covenants in conveyance subject to rents

(1)   In addition to the covenants implied under [Part I of the Law of Property (Miscellaneous Provisions) Act 1994], there shall in the several cases in this section mentioned, be deemed to be included and implied, a covenant to the effect in this section stated, by and with such persons as are hereinafter mentioned, that is to say:—

(A)   In a conveyance for valuable consideration, other than a mortgage, of the entirety of the land affected by a rentcharge, a covenant by the grantee or joint and several covenants by the grantees, if more than one, with the conveying parties and with each of them, if more than one, in the terms set out in Part VII of the Second Schedule to this Act. Where a rentcharge has been apportioned in respect of any land, with the consent of the owner of the rentcharge, the covenants in this paragraph shall be implied in the conveyance of that land in like manner as if the apportioned rentcharge were the rentcharge referred to, and the document creating the rentcharge related solely to that land:

(B)   In a conveyance for valuable consideration, other than a mortgage, of part of land affected by a rentcharge, subject to a part of that rentcharge which has been or is by that conveyance apportioned (but in either case without the consent of the owner of the rentcharge) in respect of the land conveyed:—

   (i)   A covenant by the grantee of the land or joint and several covenants by the grantees, if more than one, with the conveying parties and with each of them, if more than one, in the terms set out in paragraph (i) of Part VIII of the Second Schedule to this Act;

   (ii)   A covenant by a person who conveys or is expressed to convey as beneficial owner, or joint and several covenants by the persons who so convey or are expressed to so convey, if at the date of the conveyance any part of the land affected by such rentcharge is retained, with the grantees of the land and with each of them (if more than one) in the terms set out in paragraph (ii) of Part VIII of the Second Schedule to this Act:

(C)   *In a conveyance for valuable consideration, other than a mortgage, of the entirety of the land comprised in a lease, for the residue of the term or interest created by the lease, a covenant by the assignee or joint and several covenants by the assignees (if more than one) with the conveying parties and with each of them (if more than one) in the terms set out in Part IX of the Second Schedule to this Act. Where a rent has been apportioned in respect of any land, with the consent of the lessor, the covenants in this paragraph shall be implied in the conveyance of that land in like manner as if the apportioned rent were the original rent reserved, and the lease related solely to that land:*

(D)   *In a conveyance for valuable consideration, other than a mortgage, of part of the land comprised in a lease, for the residue of the term or interest created by the lease, subject to a part of the rent which has been or is by the conveyance apportioned (but in either case without the consent of the lessor) in respect of the land conveyed:—*

   (i)   *A covenant by the assignee of the land, or joint and several covenants by the assignees, if more than one, with the conveying parties and with each of them, if more than one, in the terms set out in paragraph (i) of Part X of the Second Schedule to this Act;*

   (ii)   *A covenant by a person who conveys or is expressed to convey as beneficial owner, or joint and several covenants by the persons who so convey or are expressed to so convey, if at the date of the conveyance any part of the land comprised in the lease is retained, with the assignees of the land and with each of them (if more than one) in the terms set out in paragraph (ii) of Part X of the Second Schedule to this Act.*

[(2)   Where in a conveyance for valuable consideration, other than a mortgage, part of land affected by a rentcharge is, without the consent of the owner of the rentcharge, expressed to be conveyed subject to or charged with the entire rent, paragraph (B)(i) of subsection (1) of this section shall apply as if, in paragraph (i) of Part VIII of the Second Schedule to this Act—

(a) any reference to the apportioned rent were to the entire rent; and

(b) the words "(other than the covenant to pay the entire rent)" were omitted.

(2A) Where in a conveyance for valuable consideration, other than a mortgage, part of land affected by a rentcharge is, without the consent of the owner of the rentcharge, expressed to be conveyed discharged or exonerated from the entire rent, paragraph (B)(ii) of subsection (1) of this section shall apply as if, in paragraph (ii) of Part VIII of the Second Schedule to this Act—

(a) any reference to the balance of the rent were to the entire rent; and

(b) the words ", other than the covenant to pay the entire rent," were omitted.]

(3) In this section "conveyance" does not include a demise by way of lease at a rent.

(4) Any covenant which would be implied under this section by reason of a person conveying or being expressed to convey as beneficial owner may, by express reference to this section, be implied, with or without variation, in a conveyance, whether or not for valuable consideration, by a person who conveys or is expressed to convey as settlor, or as trustee, or as mortgagee, or as personal representative of a deceased person, … or under an order of the court.

(5) The benefit of a covenant implied as aforesaid shall be annexed and incident to, and shall go with, the estate or interest of the implied covenantee, and shall be capable of being enforced by every person in whom that estate or interest is, for the whole or any part thereof, from time to time vested.

(6) A covenant implied as aforesaid may be varied or extended by deed, and, as so varied or extended, shall, as far as may be, operate in the like manner, and with all the like incidents, effects and consequences, as if such variations or extensions were directed in this section to be implied.

(7) In particular any covenant implied under this section may be extended by providing that—

(a) the land conveyed; or

(b) the part of the land affected by the rentcharge which remains vested in the covenantor; *or*

(c) *the part of the land demised which remains vested in the covenantor;*

shall, as the case may require, stand charged with the payment of all money which may become payable under the implied covenant.

(8) This section applies only to conveyances made after the commencement of this Act.

[151]

NOTES

Sub-s (1): words in square brackets substituted for original words "the last preceding section", except in relation to any disposition of property to which s 76 of this Act, or the Land Registration Act 1925, s 24(1)(a) at continues to apply, by the Law of Property (Miscellaneous Provisions) Act 1994, s 21(1), (4), Sch 1, para 1 at **[632]**; words in italics repealed by the Landlord and Tenant (Covenants) Act 1995, ss 14, 30(2), Sch 2, as from 1 January 1996, subject to savings specified in s 30(3) thereof, at **[702]**.

Sub-ss (2), (2A): substituted for original sub-s (2) by the Landlord and Tenant (Covenants) Act 1995, s 30(1), Sch 1, para 2, as from 1 January 1996, subject to savings specified in s 30(3) thereof at **[702]**; the original sub-s (2) read as follows—

"(2) Where in a conveyance for valuable consideration, other than a mortgage, part of land affected by a rentcharge, or part of land comprised in a lease is, without the consent of the owner of the rentcharge or of the lessor, as the case may be, expressed to be conveyed—

(i) subject to or charged with the entire rent—
then paragraph (B)(ii) or (D)(i) of the last subsection, as the case may require, shall have effect as if the entire rent were the apportioned rent; or

(ii) discharged or exonerated from the entire rent—
then paragraph (B)(ii) or (D)(ii) of the last subsection, as the case may require, shall have effect as if the entire rent were the balance of the rent, and the words "other than the covenant to pay the entire rent" had been omitted.".

Sub-s (4): words omitted repealed by the Mental Health Act 1959, s 149(2), Sch 8, Pt I.

Sub-s (7): para (c) and word "or" preceding it repealed by the Landlord and Tenant (Covenants) Act 1995, s 30(2), Sch 2, except in relation to tenancies which are not new tenancies (as defined by ss 1, 28(1) of that Act, at **[675]** and **[700]**).

78   Benefit of covenants relating to land

(1)   A covenant relating to any land of the covenantee shall be deemed to be made with the covenantee and his successors in title and the persons deriving title under him or them, and shall have effect as if such successors and other persons were expressed.

For the purposes of this subsection in connexion with covenants restrictive of the user of land "successors in title" shall be deemed to include the owners and occupiers for the time being of the land of the covenantee intended to be benefited.

(2)   This section applies to covenants made after the commencement of this Act, but the repeal of section fifty-eight of the Conveyancing Act 1881 does not affect the operation of covenants to which that section applied.

[152]

NOTES
Modification: by virtue of the Landlord and Tenant (Covenants) Act 1995, s 30(4)(b), at **[702]**, this section is disapplied in relation to new tenancies (as defined by ss 1, 28(1) of that Act, at **[675]** and **[700]**).

79   Burden of covenants relating to land

(1)   A covenant relating to any land of a covenantor or capable of being bound by him, shall, unless a contrary intention is expressed, be deemed to be made by the covenantor on behalf of himself his successors in title and the persons deriving title under him or them, and, subject as aforesaid, shall have effect as if such successors and other persons were expressed.

This subsection extends to a covenant to do some act relating to the land, notwithstanding that the subject-matter may not be in existence when the covenant is made.

(2)   For the purposes of this section in connexion with covenants restrictive of the user of land "successors in title" shall be deemed to include the owners and occupiers for the time being of such land.

(3)   This section applies only to covenants made after the commencement of this Act.

[153]

NOTES
Modification: by virtue of the Landlord and Tenant (Covenants) Act 1995, s 30(4)(a), at **[702]**, this section is disapplied in relation to new tenancies (as defined by ss 1, 28(1) of that Act, at **[675]** and **[700]**).

80–83   (*Outside the scope of this work.*)

84   Power to discharge or modify restrictive covenants affecting land

[(1)   The Lands Tribunal shall (without prejudice to any concurrent jurisdiction of the court) have power from time to time, on the application of any person interested in any freehold land affected by any restriction arising under covenant or otherwise as to the user thereof or the building thereon, by order wholly or partially to discharge or modify any such restriction on being satisfied—

    (a)   that by reason of changes in the character of the property or the neighbourhood or other circumstances of the case which the Lands Tribunal may deem material, the restriction ought to be deemed obsolete; or

    (aa)   that (in a case falling within subsection (1A) below) the continued existence thereof would impede some reasonable user of the land for public or private purposes or, as the case may be, would unless modified so impede such user; or

    (b)   that the persons of full age and capacity for the time being or from time to time entitled to the benefit of the restriction, whether in respect of estates in fee simple or any lesser estates or interests in the property to which the benefit of the restriction is annexed, have agreed, either expressly or by implication, by their acts or omissions, to the same being discharged or modified; or

    (c)   that the proposed discharge or modification will not injure the persons entitled to the benefit of the restriction;

and an order discharging or modifying a restriction under this subsection may direct the applicant to pay to any person entitled to the benefit of the restriction such sum by way of consideration as the Tribunal may think it just to award under one, but not both, of the following heads, that is to say, either—

    (i)   a sum to make up for any loss or disadvantage suffered by that person in consequence of the discharge or modification; or

    (ii)   a sum to make up for any effect which the restriction had, at the time when it was imposed, in reducing the consideration then received for the land affected by it.

(1A)   Subsection (1)(aa) above authorises the discharge or modification of a restriction by reference to its impeding some reasonable user of land in any case in which the Lands Tribunal is satisfied that the restriction, in impeding that user, either—

    (a)   does not secure to persons entitled to the benefit of it any practical benefits of substantial value or advantage to them; or

    (b)   is contrary to the public interest;

and that money will be an adequate compensation for the loss or disadvantage (if any) which any such person will suffer from the discharge or modification.

(1B)   In determining whether a case is one falling within subsection (1A) above, and in determining whether (in any such case or otherwise) a restriction ought to be discharged or modified, the Lands Tribunal shall take into account the development plan and any declared or ascertainable pattern for the grant or refusal of planning permissions in the relevant areas, as well as the period at which and context in which the restriction was created or imposed and any other material circumstances.

(1C)   It is hereby declared that the power conferred by this section to modify a restriction includes power to add such further provisions restricting the user of or the building on the land affected as appear to the Lands Tribunal to be reasonable in view of the relaxation of the existing provisions, and as may be accepted by the applicant; and the Lands Tribunal may accordingly refuse to modify a restriction without some such addition.

(2)   The court shall have power on the application of any person interested—

    (a)   to declare whether or not in any particular case any freehold land is, or would in any given event be, affected by a restriction imposed by any instrument; or

    (b)   to declare what, upon the true construction of any instrument purporting to impose a restriction, is the nature and extent of the restriction thereby imposed and whether the same is, or would in any given event be, enforceable and if so by whom.

Neither subsections (7) and (11) of this section nor, unless the contrary is expressed, any later enactment providing for this section not to apply to any restrictions shall affect the operation of this subsection or the operation for purposes of this subsection of any other provisions of this section.

(3)   The Lands Tribunal shall, before making any order under this section, direct such enquiries, if any, to be made of any government department or local authority, and such notices, if any, whether by way of advertisement or otherwise, to be given to such of the persons who appear to be entitled to the benefit of the restriction intended to be discharged, modified, or dealt with as, having regard to any enquiries, notices or other proceedings previously made, given or taken, the Lands Tribunal may think fit.

(3A)   On an application to the Lands Tribunal under this section the Lands Tribunal shall give any necessary directions as to the persons who are or are not to be admitted (as appearing to be entitled to the benefit of the restriction) to oppose the application, and no appeal shall lie against any such direction; but rules under the Lands Tribunal Act 1949 shall make provision whereby, in cases in which there arises on such an application (whether or not in connection with the admission of persons to oppose) any such question as is referred to in subsection (2)(a) or (b) of this section, the proceedings on the application can and, if the rules so provide, shall be suspended to enable the decision of the court to be obtained on that question by an application under that subsection, or by means of a case stated by the Lands Tribunal, or otherwise, as may be provided by those rules or by rules of court.

(5)   Any order made under this section shall be binding on all persons, whether ascertained or of full age or capacity or not, then entitled or thereafter capable of becoming entitled to the benefit of any restriction, which is thereby discharged, modified or dealt with, and whether such persons are parties to the proceedings or have been served with notice or not.

(6)   An order may be made under this section notwithstanding that any instrument which is alleged to impose the restriction intended to be discharged, modified, or dealt with, may not have been produced to the court or the Lands Tribunal, and the court or the Lands Tribunal may act on such evidence of that instrument as it may think sufficient.

(7)   This section applies to restrictions whether subsisting at the commencement of this Act or imposed thereafter, but this section does not apply where the restriction was imposed on the occasion of a disposition made gratuitously or for a nominal consideration for public purposes.

(8)   This section applies whether the land affected by the restrictions is registered or not …

(9)   Where any proceedings by action or otherwise are taken to enforce a restrictive covenant, any person against whom the proceedings are taken, may in such proceedings apply to the court for an order giving leave to apply to the Lands Tribunal under this section, and staying the proceedings in the meantime.

(11)   This section does not apply to restrictions imposed by the Commissioners of Works under any statutory power for the protection of any Royal Park or Garden or to restrictions of a like character imposed upon the occasion of any enfranchisement effected before the commencement of this Act in any manor vested in His Majesty in right of the Crown or the Duchy of Lancaster, nor (subject to subsection (11A) below) to restrictions created or imposed—

    (a)   for naval, military or air force purposes,

    [(b)   for civil aviation purposes under the powers of the Air Navigation Act 1920, of section 19 or 23 of the Civil Aviation Act 1949 or of section 30 or 41 of the Civil Aviation Act 1982.]

(11A)   Subsection (11) of this section—

    (a)   shall exclude the application of this section to a restriction falling within subsection (11)(a), and not created or imposed in connection with the use of any land as an aerodrome, only so long as the restriction is enforceable by or on behalf of the Crown; and

    (b)   shall exclude the application of this section to a restriction falling within subsection (11)(b), or created or imposed in connection with the use of any land as an aerodrome, only so long as the restriction is enforceable by or on behalf of the Crown or any public or international authority.

(12)   Where a term of more than forty years is created in land (whether before or after the commencement of this Act) this section shall, after the expiration of twenty-five years of the term, apply to restrictions, affecting such leasehold land in like manner as it would have applied had the land been freehold:

Provided that this subsection shall not apply to mining leases.]

[154]

NOTES

By virtue of the Law of Property Act 1969, s 28(1), this section has effect as set out in Sch 3 to that Act, incorporating the amendments made by the Landlord and Tenant Act 1954, s 52(1) and by s 28(1)–(9) of the 1969 Act (and the omission of repealed provisions), subject, however, to any other enactments affecting this section and to s 28(11) of the 1969 Act.

Sub-s (8): words omitted repealed by the Land Registration Act 2002, ss 133, 135, Sch 11, para 2(1), (5), Sch 13.

Sub-s (11): para (b) substituted by the Civil Aviation Act 1982, s 109, Sch 15, para 1.

85–129   *((Pt III, IV) Ss 85–111, 113–122, 125 outside the scope of this work; s 112 spent; ss 123, 124, 126–129 repealed by the Powers of Attorney Act 1971, ss 8, 11(2), Sch 2.)*

PART IV
EQUITABLE INTERESTS AND THINGS IN ACTION

130–135   *(Ss 130–132, 134, 135 outside the scope of this work; s 133 repealed by the Statute Law (Repeals) Act 1969, s 1, Schedule, Pt III.)*

136   Legal assignments of things in action

(1)   Any absolute assignment by writing under the hand of the assignor (not purporting to be by way of charge only) of any debt or other legal thing in action, of which express notice in writing has been given to the debtor, trustee or other person from whom the assignor would

have been entitled to claim such debt or thing in action, is effectual in law (subject to equities having priority over the right of the assignee) to pass and transfer from the date of such notice—

(a) the legal right to such debt or thing in action;

(b) all legal and other remedies for the same; and

(c) the power to give a good discharge for the same without the concurrence of the assignor:

Provided that, if the debtor, trustee or other person liable in respect of such debt or thing in action has notice—

(a) that the assignment is disputed by the assignor or any person claiming under him; or

(b) of any other opposing or conflicting claims to such debt or thing in action;

he may, if he thinks fit, either call upon the persons making claim thereto to interplead concerning the same, or pay the debt or other thing in action into court under the provisions of the Trustee Act 1925.

(2) This section does not affect the provisions of the Policies of Assurance Act 1867.

[(3) The county court has jurisdiction (including power to receive payment of money or securities into court) under the proviso to subsection (1) of this section where the amount or value of the debt or thing in action does not exceed [£30,000].]

[154A]

NOTES

Sub-s (3): added by the County Courts Act 1984, s 148(1), Sch 2, para 4; sum in square brackets substituted by the High Court and County Courts Jurisdiction Order 1991, SI 1991/724, art 2(5), (8), Schedule, Part I.

137, 138 *(Outside the scope of this work.)*

PART V
LEASES AND TENANCIES

139 Effect of extinguishment of reversion

(1) Where a reversion expectant on a lease of land is surrendered or merged, the estate or interest which as against the lessee for the time being confers the next vested right to the land, shall be deemed the reversion for the purpose of preserving the same incidents and obligations as would have affected the original reversion had there been no surrender or merger thereof.

(2) This section applies to surrenders or mergers effected after the first day of October, eighteen hundred and forty-five.

[155]

140 Apportionment of conditions on severance

(1) Notwithstanding the severance by conveyance, surrender, or otherwise of the reversionary estate in any land comprised in a lease, and notwithstanding the avoidance or cesser in any other manner of the term granted by a lease as to part only of the land comprised therein, every condition or right of re-entry, and every other condition contained in the lease, shall be apportioned, and shall remain annexed to the severed parts of the reversionary estate as severed, and shall be in force with respect to the term whereon each severed part is reversionary, or the term in the part of the land as to which the term has not been surrendered, or has not been avoided or has not otherwise ceased, in like manner as if the land comprised in each severed part, or the land as to which the term remains subsisting, as the case may be, had alone originally been comprised in the lease.

(2) In this section "right of re-entry" includes a right to determine the lease by notice to quit or otherwise; but where the notice is served by a person entitled to a severed part of the reversion so that it extends to part only of the land demised, the lessee may within one month determine the lease in regard to the rest of the land by giving to the owner of the reversionary estate therein a counter notice expiring at the same time as the original notice ...

(3) This section applies to leases made before or after the commencement of this Act and whether the severance of the reversionary estate or the partial avoidance or cesser of the term was effected before or after such commencement:

Provided that, where the lease was made before the first day of January eighteen hundred and eighty-two nothing in this section shall affect the operation of a severance of the reversionary estate or partial avoidance or cesser of the term which was effected before the commencement of this Act.

[156]

NOTES

Sub-s (2): words omitted added by the Law of Property (Amendment) Act 1926, s 2, and repealed by the Agricultural Holdings Act 1948, ss 98, 100(1), Sch 8.

141 Rent and benefit of lessee's covenants to run with the reversion

(1)   Rent reserved by a lease, and the benefit of every covenant or provision therein contained, having reference to the subject-matter thereof, and on the lessee's part to be observed or performed, and every condition of re-entry and other condition therein contained, shall be annexed and incident to and shall go with the reversionary estate in the land, or in any part thereof, immediately expectant on the term granted by the lease, notwithstanding severance of that reversionary estate, and without prejudice to any liability affecting a covenantor or his estate.

(2)   Any such rent, covenant or provision shall be capable of being recovered, received, enforced, and taken advantage of, by the person from time to time entitled, subject to the term, to the income of the whole or any part, as the case may require, of the land leased.

(3)   Where that person becomes entitled by conveyance or otherwise, such rent, covenant or provision may be recovered, received, enforced or taken advantage of by him notwithstanding that he becomes so entitled after the condition of re-entry or forfeiture has become enforceable, but this subsection does not render enforceable any condition of re-entry or other condition waived or released before such person becomes entitled as aforesaid.

(4)   This section applies to leases made before or after the commencement of this Act, but does not affect the operation of—

(a)   any severance of the reversionary estate; or

(b)   any acquisition by conveyance or otherwise of the right to receive or enforce any rent covenant or provision;

effected before the commencement of this Act.

[157]

NOTES

Modification: by virtue of the Landlord and Tenant (Covenants) Act 1995, s 30(4)(b) at **[702]**, this section is disapplied in relation to new tenancies (as defined by ss 1, 28(1) of that Act at **[675]** and **[700]**).

142 Obligation of lessor's covenants to run with reversion

(1)   The obligation under a condition or of a covenant entered into by a lessor with reference to the subject-matter of the lease shall, if and as far as the lessor has power to bind the reversionary estate immediately expectant on the term granted by the lease, be annexed and incident to and shall go with that reversionary estate, or the several parts thereof, notwithstanding severance of that reversionary estate, and may be taken advantage of and enforced by the person in whom the term is from time to time vested by conveyance, devolution in law, or otherwise; and, if and as far as the lessor has power to bind the person from time to time entitled to that reversionary estate, the obligation aforesaid may be taken advantage of and entered against any person so entitled.

(2)   This section applies to leases made before or after the commencement of this Act, whether the severance of the reversionary estate was effected before or after such commencement:

Provided that, where the lease was made before the first day of January eighteen hundred and eighty-two, nothing in this section shall affect the operation of any severance of the reversionary estate effected before such commencement.

This section takes effect without prejudice to any liability affecting a covenantor or his estate.

[158]

NOTES

Modification: by virtue of the Landlord and Tenant (Covenants) Act 1995, s 30(4)(b) at **[702]**, this section is disapplied in relation to new tenancies (as defined by ss 1, 28(1) of that Act at **[675]** and **[700]**).

143 Effect of licences granted to lessees

(1)   Where a licence is granted to a lessee to do any act, the licence, unless otherwise expressed, extends only—

    (a)   to the permission actually given; or

    (b)   to the specific breach of any provision or covenant referred to; or

    (c)   to any other matter thereby specifically authorised to be done;

and the licence does not prevent any proceeding for any subsequent breach unless otherwise specified in the licence.

(2)   Notwithstanding any such licence—

    (a)   All rights under covenants and powers of re-entry contained in the lease remain in full force and are available as against any subsequent breach of covenant, condition or other matter not specifically authorised or waived, in the same manner as if no licence had been granted; and

    (b)   The condition or right of entry remains in force in all respects as if the licence had not been granted, save in respect of the particular matter authorised to be done.

(3)   Where in any lease there is a power or condition of re-entry on the lessee assigning, subletting or doing any other specified act without a licence, and a licence is granted—

    (a)   to any one of two or more lessees to do any act, or to deal with his equitable share or interest; or

    (b)   to any lessee, or to any one of two or more lessees to assign or underlet part only of the property, or to do any act in respect of part only of the property;

the licence does not operate to extinguish the right of entry in case of any breach of covenant or condition by the co-lessees of the other shares or interests in the property, or by the lessee or lessees of the rest of the property (as the case may be) in respect of such shares or interests or remaining property, but the right of entry remains in force in respect of the shares, interests or property not the subject of the licence.

This subsection does not authorise the grant after the commencement of this Act of a licence to create an undivided share in a legal estate.

(4)   This section applies to licences granted after the thirteenth day of August, eighteen hundred and fifty-nine.

[159]

144 No fine to be exacted for licence to assign

In all leases containing a covenant, condition, or agreement against assigning, underletting, or parting with the possession, or disposing of the land or property leased without licence or consent, such covenant, condition, or agreement shall, unless the lease contains an express provision to the contrary, be deemed to be subject to a proviso to the effect that no fine or sum of money in the nature of a fine shall be payable for or in respect of such licence or consent; but this proviso does not preclude the right to require the payment of a reasonable sum in respect of any legal or other expense incurred in relation to such licence or consent.

[160]

145 Lessee to give notice of ejectment to lessor

Every lessee to whom there is delivered any writ for the recovery of premises demised to or held by him, or to whose knowledge any such writ comes, shall forthwith give notice thereof to his lessor or his bailiff or receiver, and, if he fails so to do, he shall be liable to forfeit to the person of whom he holds the premises an amount equal to the value of three years' improved or rack rent of the premises, to be recovered by action in any court having jurisdiction in respect of claims for such an amount.

[161]

146 Restrictions on and relief against forfeiture of leases and underleases

(1)   A right of re-entry or forfeiture under any proviso or stipulation in a lease for a breach of any covenant or condition in the lease shall not be enforceable, by action or otherwise, unless and until the lessor serves on the lessee a notice—

    (a)   specifying the particular breach complained of; and

    (b)   if the breach is capable of remedy, requiring the lessee to remedy the breach; and

    (c)   in any case, requiring the lessee to make compensation in money for the breach;

and the lessee fails, within a reasonable time thereafter, to remedy the breach, if it is capable of remedy, and to make reasonable compensation in money, to the satisfaction of the lessor, for the breach.

(2)   Where a lessor is proceeding, by action or otherwise, to enforce such a right of re-entry or forfeiture, the lessee may, in the lessor's action, if any, or in any action brought by himself, apply to the court for relief; and the court may grant or refuse relief, as the court, having regard to the proceedings and conduct of the parties under the foregoing provisions of this section, and to all the other circumstances, thinks fit; and in case of relief may grant it on such terms, if any, as to costs, expenses, damages, compensation, penalty, or otherwise, including the granting of an injunction to restrain any like breach in the future, as the court, in the circumstances of each case, thinks fit.

(3)   A lessor shall be entitled to recover as a debt due to him from a lessee, and in addition to damages (if any), all reasonable costs and expenses properly incurred by the lessor in the employment of a solicitor and surveyor or valuer, or otherwise, in reference to any breach giving rise to a right of re-entry or forfeiture which, at the request of the lessee, is waived by the lessor, or from which the lessee is relieved, under the provisions of this Act.

(4)   Where a lessor is proceeding by action or otherwise to enforce a right of re-entry or forfeiture under any covenant, proviso, or stipulation in a lease, or for non-payment of rent, the court may, on application by any person claiming as under-lessee any estate or interest in the property comprised in the lease or any part thereof, either in the lessor's action (if any) or in any action brought by such person for that purpose, make an order vesting, for the whole term of the lease or any less term, the property comprised in the lease or any part thereof in any person entitled as under-lessee to any estate or interest in such property upon such conditions as to execution of any deed or other document, payment of rent, costs, expenses, damages, compensation, giving security, or otherwise, as the court in the circumstances of each case may think fit, but in no case shall any such under-lessee be entitled to require a lease to be granted to him for any longer term than he had under his original sub-lease.

(5)   For the purposes of this section—

    (a)   "Lease" includes an original or derivative under-lease; also an agreement for a lease where the lessee has become entitled to have his lease granted; also a grant at a fee farm rent, or securing a rent by condition;

    (b)   "Lessee" includes an original or derivative under-lessee, and the persons deriving title under a lessee; also a grantee under any such grant as aforesaid and the persons deriving title under him;

    (c)   "Lessor" includes an original or derivative under-lessor, and the persons deriving title under a lessor; also a person making such grant as aforesaid and the persons deriving title under him;

    (d)   "Under-lease" includes an agreement for an underlease where the underlessee has become entitled to have his underlease granted;

    (e)   "Underlessee" includes any person deriving title under an underlessee.

(6)   This section applies although the proviso or stipulation under which the right of re-entry or forfeiture accrues is inserted in the lease in pursuance of the directions of any Act of Parliament.

(7)   For the purposes of this section a lease limited to continue as long only as the lessee abstains from committing a breach of covenant shall be and take effect as a lease to continue for any longer term for which it could subsist, but determinable by a proviso for re-entry on such a breach.

(8)   This section does not extend—

    (i)   To a covenant or condition against assigning, underletting, parting with the possession, or disposing of the land leased where the breach occurred before the commencement of this Act; or

    (ii)   In the case of a mining lease, to a covenant or condition for allowing the lessor to have access to or inspect books, accounts, records, weighing machines or other things, or to enter or inspect the mine or the workings thereof.

(9)   This section does not apply to a condition for forfeiture on the bankruptcy of the lessee or on taking in execution of the lessee's interest if contained in a lease of—

    (a)   Agricultural or pastoral land;

(b)   Mines or minerals;

(c)   A house used or intended to be used as a public-house or beershop;

(d)   A house let as a dwelling-house, with the use of any furniture, books, works of art, or other chattels not being in the nature of fixtures;

(e)   Any property with respect to which the personal qualifications of the tenant are of importance for the preservation of the value or character of the property, or on the ground of neighbourhood to the lessor, or to any person holding under him.

(10)   Where a condition of forfeiture on the bankruptcy of the lessee or on taking in execution of the lessee's interest is contained in any lease, other than a lease of any of the classes mentioned in the last subsection, then—

(a)   if the lessee's interest is sold within one year from the bankruptcy or taking in execution, this section applies to the forfeiture condition aforesaid;

(b)   if the lessee's interest is not sold before the expiration of that year, this section only applies to the forfeiture condition aforesaid during the first year from the date of the bankruptcy or taking in execution.

(11)   This section does not, save as otherwise mentioned, affect the law relating to re-entry or forfeiture or relief in case of non-payment of rent.

(12)   This section has effect notwithstanding any stipulation to the contrary.

[(13)   The county court has jurisdiction under this section ...]

[162]

NOTES

Sub-s (13): added by the County Courts Act 1984, s 148(1), Sch 2, para 5; words omitted repealed by the High Court and County Courts Jurisdiction Order 1991, SI 1991/724, art 2(1)(a), (8), Schedule, Pt I.

Modification: the reference to a solicitor is deemed to include a reference to bodies recognised under the Administration of Justice Act 1985, s 9, by virtue of the Solicitors' Incorporated Practices Order 1991, SI 1991/2684, arts 4, 5, Sch 1.

---

147   Relief against notice to effect decorative repairs

(1)   After a notice is served on a lessee relating to the internal decorative repairs to a house or other building, he may apply to the court for relief, and if, having regard to all the circumstances of the case (including in particular the length of the lessee's term or interest remaining unexpired), the court is satisfied that the notice is unreasonable, it may, by order, wholly or partially relieve the lessee from liability for such repairs.

(2)   This section does not apply:—

(i)   where the liability arises under an express covenant or agreement to put the property in a decorative state of repair and the covenant or agreement has never been performed;

(ii)   to any matter necessary or proper—

(a)   for putting or keeping the property in a sanitary condition, or

(b)   for the maintenance or preservation of the structure;

(iii)   to any statutory liability to keep a house in all respects reasonably fit for human habitation;

(iv)   to any covenant or stipulation to yield up the house or other building in a specified state of repair at the end of the term.

(3)   In this section "lease" includes an underlease and an agreement for a lease, and "lessee" has a corresponding meaning and includes any person liable to effect the repairs.

(4)   This section applies whether the notice is served before or after the commencement of this Act, and has effect notwithstanding any stipulation to the contrary.

[(5)   The county court has jurisdiction under this section ...]

[163]

NOTES

Sub-s (5): added by the County Courts Act 1984, s 148(1), Sch 2, para 6; words omitted repealed by the High Court and County Courts Jurisdiction Order 1991, SI 1991/724, art 2(1)(a), (8), Schedule, Pt I.

---

148   Waiver of a covenant in a lease

(1)   Where any actual waiver by a lessor or the persons deriving title under him of the benefit of any covenant or condition in any lease is proved to have taken place in any

particular instance, such waiver shall not be deemed to extend to any instance, or to any breach of covenant or condition save that to which such waiver specially relates, nor operate as a general waiver of the benefit of any such covenant or condition.

(2)   This section applies unless a contrary intention appears and extends to waivers effected after the twenty-third day of July, eighteen hundred and sixty.

[164]

149   Abolition of interesse termini, and as to reversionary leases and leases for lives

(1)   The doctrine of interesse termini is hereby abolished.

(2)   As from the commencement of this Act all terms of years absolute shall, whether the interest is created before or after such commencement, be capable of taking effect at law or in equity, according to the estate interest or powers of the grantor, from the date fixed for commencement of the term, without actual entry.

(3)   A term, at a rent or granted in consideration of a fine, limited after the commencement of this Act to take effect more than twenty-one years from the date of the instrument purporting to create it, shall be void, and any contract made after such commencement to create such a term shall likewise be void; but this subsection does not apply to any term taking effect in equity under a settlement, or created out of an equitable interest under a settlement, or under an equitable power for mortgage, indemnity or other like purposes.

(4)   Nothing in subsections (1) and (2) of this section prejudicially affects the right of any person to recover any rent or to enforce or take advantage of any covenants or conditions or, as respects terms or interests created before the commencement of this Act, operates to vary any statutory or other obligations imposed in respect of such terms or interests.

(5)   Nothing in this Act affects the rule of law that a legal term, whether or not being a mortgage term, may be created to take effect in reversion expectant on a longer term, which rule is hereby confirmed.

(6)   Any lease or underlease, at a rent, or in consideration of a fine, for life or lives or for any term of years determinable with life or lives, or on the marriage of the lessee, [or on the formation of a civil partnership between the lessee and another person,] or any contract therefor, made before or after the commencement of this Act, or created by virtue of Part V of the Law of Property Act 1922, shall take effect as a lease, underlease or contract therefor, for a term of ninety years determinable [after (as the case may be) the death or marriage of, or the formation of a civil partnership by, the original lessee or the survivor of the original lessees,] by at least one month's notice in writing given to determine the same on one of the quarter days applicable to the tenancy, either by the lessor or the persons deriving title under him, to the person entitled to the leasehold interest, or if no such person is in existence by affixing the same to the premises, or by the lessee or other persons in whom the leasehold interest is vested to the lessor or the persons deriving title under him:

Provided that—

(a)   this subsection shall not apply to any term taking effect in equity under a settlement or created out of an equitable interest under a settlement for mortgage, indemnity, or other like purposes;

(b)   the person in whom the leasehold interest is vested by virtue of Part V of the Law of Property Act 1922 shall, for the purposes of this subsection, be deemed an original lessee;

(c)   if the lease, underlease, or contract therefor is made determinable on the dropping of the lives of persons other than or besides the lessees, then the notice shall be capable of being served after the death of any person or of the survivor of any persons (whether or not including the lessees) on the cesser of whose life or lives the lease, underlease, or contract is made determinable, instead of after the death of the original lessee or of the survivor of the original lessees;

(d)   if there are no quarter days specially applicable to the tenancy, notice may be given to determine the tenancy on one of the usual quarter days.

[(7)   Subsection (8) applies where a lease, underlease or contract—

(a)   relates to commonhold land, and

(b)   would take effect by virtue of subsection (6) as a lease, underlease or contract of the kind mentioned in that subsection.

(8) The lease, underlease or contract shall be treated as if it purported to be a lease, underlease or contract of the kind referred to in subsection (7)(b) (and sections 17 and 18 of the Commonhold and Leasehold Reform Act 2002 (residential and non-residential leases) shall apply accordingly).]

[165]

NOTES

Sub-s (6): words in first pair of square brackets inserted and words in second pair of square brackets substituted by the Civil Partnership Act 2004, s 81, Sch 8, para 1.
Sub-ss (7), (8): added by the Commonhold and Leasehold Reform Act 2002, s 68, Sch 5, para 3.

---

150 Surrender of a lease, without prejudice to underleases with a view to the grant of a new lease

(1) A lease may be surrendered with a view to the acceptance of a new lease in place thereof, without a surrender of any under-lease derived thereout.

(2) A new lease may be granted and accepted, in place of any lease so surrendered, without any such surrender of an under-lease as aforesaid, and the new lease operates as if all under-leases derived out of the surrendered lease had been surrendered before the surrender of that lease was effected.

(3) The lessee under the new lease and any person deriving title under him is entitled to the same rights and remedies in respect of the rent reserved by and the covenants, agreements and conditions contained in any under-lease as if the original lease had not been surrendered but was or remained vested in him.

(4) Each under-lessee and any person deriving title under him is entitled to hold and enjoy the land comprised in his under-lease (subject to the payment of any rent reserved by and to the observance of the covenants agreements and conditions contained in the under-lease) as if the lease out of which the under-lease was derived had not been surrendered.

(5) The lessor granting the new lease and any person deriving title under him is entitled to the same remedies, by distress or entry in and upon the land comprised in any such under-lease for rent reserved by or for breach of any covenant, agreement or condition contained in the new lease (so far only as the rents reserved by or the covenants, agreements or conditions contained in the new lease do not exceed or impose greater burdens than those reserved by or contained in the original lease out of which the under-lease is derived) as he would have had—

    (a) If the original lease had remained on foot; or
    (b) If a new under-lease derived out of the new lease had been granted to the under-lessee or a person deriving title under him;

as the case may require.

(6) This section does not affect the powers of the court to give relief against forfeiture.

[166]

151 Provision as to attornments by tenants

(1) Where land is subject to a lease—

    (a) the conveyance of a reversion in the land expectant on the determination of the lease; or
    (b) the creation or conveyance of a rentcharge to issue or issuing out of the land;

shall be valid without any attornment of the lessee:

Nothing in this subsection—

    (i) affects the validity of any payment of rent by the lessee to the person making the conveyance or grant before notice of the conveyance or grant is given to him by the person entitled thereunder; or
    (ii) renders the lessee liable for any breach of covenant to pay rent, on account of his failure to pay rent to the person entitled under the conveyance or grant before such notice is given to the lessee.

(2) An attornment by the lessee in respect of any land to a person claiming to be entitled to the interest in the land of the lessor, if made without the consent of the lessor, shall be void.

This subsection does not apply to an attornment—

    (a) made pursuant to a judgment of a court of competent jurisdiction; or

(b)   to a mortgagee, by a lessee holding under a lease from the mortgagor where the right of redemption is barred; or

(c)   to any other person rightfully deriving title under the lessor.

[167]

152   Leases invalidated by reason of non-compliance with terms of powers under which they are granted

(1)   Where in the intended exercise of any power of leasing, whether conferred by an Act of Parliament or any other instrument, a lease (in this section referred to as an invalid lease) is granted, which by reason of any failure to comply with the terms of the power is invalid, then—

(a)   as against the person entitled after the determination of the interest of the grantor to the reversion; or

(b)   as against any other person who, subject to any lease properly granted under the power, would have been entitled to the land comprised in the lease;

the lease, if it was made in good faith, and the lessee has entered thereunder, shall take effect in equity as a contract for the grant, at the request of the lessee, of a valid lease under the power, of like effect as the invalid lease, subject to such variations as may be necessary in order to comply with the terms of the power:

Provided that a lessee under an invalid lease shall not, by virtue of any such implied contract, be entitled to obtain a variation of the lease if the other persons who would have been bound by the contract are willing and able to confirm the lease without variation.

(2)   Where a lease granted in the intended exercise of such a power is invalid by reason of the grantor not having power to grant the lease at the date thereof, but the grantor's interest in the land comprised therein continues after the time when he might, in the exercise of the power, have properly granted a lease in the like terms, the lease shall take effect as a valid lease in like manner as if it had been granted at that time.

(3)   Where during the continuance of the possession taken under an invalid lease the person for the time being entitled, subject to such possession, to the land comprised therein or to the rents and profits thereof, is able to confirm the lease without variation, the lessee, or other person who would have been bound by the lease had it been valid, shall, at the request of the person so able to confirm the lease, be bound to accept a confirmation thereof, and thereupon the lease shall have effect and be deemed to have had effect as a valid lease from the grant thereof.

Confirmation under this subsection may be by a memorandum in writing signed by or on behalf of the persons respectively confirming and accepting the confirmation of the lease.

(4)   Where a receipt or a memorandum in writing confirming an invalid lease is, upon or before the acceptance of rent thereunder, signed by or on behalf of the person accepting the rent, that acceptance shall, as against that person, be deemed to be a confirmation of the lease.

(5)   The foregoing provisions of this section do not affect prejudicially—

(a)   any right of action or other right or remedy to which, but for those provisions or any enactment replaced by those provisions, the lessee named in an invalid lease would or might have been entitled under any covenant on the part of the grantor for title or quiet enjoyment contained therein or implied thereby; or

(b)   any right of re-entry or other right or remedy to which, but for those provisions or any enactment replaced thereby, the grantor or other person for the time being entitled to the reversion expectant on the termination of the lease, would or might have been entitled by reason of any breach of the covenants, conditions or provisions contained in the lease and binding on the lessee.

(6)   Where a valid power of leasing is vested in or may be exercised by a person who grants a lease which, by reason of the determination of the interest of the grantor or otherwise, cannot have effect and continuance according to the terms thereof independently of the power, the lease shall for the purposes of this section be deemed to have been granted in the intended exercise of the power although the power is not referred to in the lease.

(7)   This section does not apply to a lease of land held on charitable, ecclesiastical or public trusts.

(8)   This section takes effect without prejudice to the provision in this Act for the grant of leases in the name and on behalf of the estate owner of the land affected.

[168]

153 Enlargement of residue of long terms into fee simple estates

(1)   Where a residue unexpired of not less than two hundred years of a term, which, as originally created, was for not less than three hundred years, is subsisting in land, whether being the whole land originally comprised in the term, or part only thereof,—

(a)   without any trust or right of redemption affecting the term in favour of the freeholder, or other person entitled in reversion expectant on the term; and

(b)   without any rent, or with merely a peppercorn rent or other rent having no money value, incident to the reversion, or having had a rent, not being merely a peppercorn rent or other rent having no money value, originally so incident, which subsequently has been released or has become barred by lapse of time, or has in any other way ceased to be payable;

the term may be enlarged into a fee simple in the manner, and subject to the restrictions in this section provided.

(2)   This section applies to and includes every such term as aforesaid whenever created, whether or not having the freehold as the immediate reversion thereon; but does not apply to—

(i)   Any term liable to be determined by re-entry for condition broken; or

(ii)   Any term created by subdemise out of a superior term, itself incapable of being enlarged into fee simple.

(3)   This section extends to mortgage terms, where the right of redemption is barred.

(4)   A rent not exceeding the yearly sum of one pound which has not been collected or paid for a continuous period of twenty years or upwards shall, for the purposes of this section, be deemed to have ceased to be payable:

...

(5)   Where a rent incident to a reversion expectant on a term to which this section applies is deemed to have ceased to be payable for the purposes aforesaid, no claim for such rent or for any arrears thereof shall be capable of being enforced.

(6)   Each of the following persons, namely—

(i)   Any person beneficially entitled in right of the term, whether subject to any incumbrance or not, to possession of any land comprised in the term, and, in the case of a married woman without the concurrence of her husband, whether or not she is entitled for her separate use or as her separate property, ... ;

(ii)   Any person being in receipt of income as trustee, in right of the term, or having the term vested in him [as a trustee of land], whether subject to any incumbrance or not;

(iii)   Any person in whom, as personal representative of any deceased person, the term is vested, whether subject to any incumbrance or not;

shall, so far as regards the land to which he is entitled, or in which he is interested in right of the term, in any such character as aforesaid, have power by deed to declare to the effect that, from and after the execution of the deed, the term shall be enlarged into a fee simple.

(7)   Thereupon, by virtue of the deed and of this Act, the term shall become and be enlarged accordingly, and the person in whom the term was previously vested shall acquire and have in the land a fee simple instead of the term.

(8)   The estate in fee simple so acquired by enlargement shall be subject to all the same trusts, powers, executory limitations over, rights and equities, and to all the same covenants and provisions relating to user and enjoyment, and to all the same obligations of every kind, as the term would have been subject to if it had not been so enlarged.

(9)   But where—

(a)   any land so held for the residue of a term has been settled in trust by reference to other land, being freehold land, so as to go along with that other land, or, in the case of settlements coming into operation before the commencement of this Act, so as to go along with that other land as far as the law permits; and

(b)   at the time of enlargement, the ultimate beneficial interest in the term, whether subject to any subsisting particular estate or not, has not become absolutely and indefeasibly vested in any person, free from charges or powers of charging created by a settlement;

the estate in fee simple acquired as aforesaid shall, without prejudice to any conveyance for value previously made by a person having a contingent or defeasible interest in the term, be liable to be, and shall be, conveyed by means of a subsidiary vesting instrument and settled in like manner as the other land, being freehold land, aforesaid, and until so conveyed and settled shall devolve beneficially as if it had been so conveyed and settled.

(10) The estate in fee simple so acquired shall, whether the term was originally created without impeachment of waste or not, include the fee simple in all mines and minerals which at the time of enlargement have not been severed in right or in fact, or have not been severed or reserved by an inclosure Act or award.

[169]

NOTES

Sub-s (4): words omitted repealed by the Statute Law (Repeals) Act 2004.

Sub-s (6): words omitted repealed by the Married Women (Restraint upon Anticipation) Act 1949, s 1, Sch 2; words in square brackets in para (ii) substituted for original words "in trust for sale" by the Trusts of Land and Appointment of Trustees Act 1996, s 25(1), Sch 3, para 4(1), (16), the original wording is reproduced here for reasons of historical interest or in view of the savings contained in ss 3, 18(3), 25(5) of the 1996 Act.

---

154 Application of Part V to existing leases

This part of this Act, except where otherwise expressly provided, applies to leases created before or after the commencement of this Act, and "lease" includes an under-lease or other tenancy.

[170]

155–179 (*Ss 155–162, 164–166, 173–176, 179 outside the scope of this work; s 163 repealed by the Perpetuities and Accumulations Act 1964, ss 4(6), 15(5); ss 167–170, 178 repealed by the Statute Law (Repeals) Act 1969; s 171 repealed by the Mental Health Act 1959, s 149(2), Sch 8, Pt I; s 172 repealed by the Insolvency Act 1985, s 235(3), Sch 10, Pt IV; s 177 repealed by the Administration of Justice Act 1982, s 75, Sch 9, Pt I.*)

PART XI
MISCELLANEOUS

Miscellaneous

180–184 (*Outside the scope of this work.*)

185 Merger

There is no merger by operation of law only of any estate the beneficial interest in which would not be deemed to be merged or extinguished in equity.

[171]

186–188 (*Outside the scope of this work.*)

189 Indemnities against rents

(1) A power of distress given by way of indemnity against a rent or any part thereof payable in respect of any land, or against the breach of any covenant or condition in relation to land, is not and shall not be deemed ever to have been a bill of sale, within the meaning of the Bills of Sale Acts 1878 and 1882, as amended by any subsequent enactment.

(2) The benefit of all covenants and powers given by way of indemnity against a rent or any part thereof payable in respect of land, or against the breach of any covenant or condition in relation to land, is and shall be deemed always to have been annexed to the land to which the indemnity is intended to relate, and may be enforced by the estate owner for the time being of the whole or any part of that land, notwithstanding that the benefit may not have been expressly apportioned or assigned to him or to any of his predecessors in title.

[172]

Redemption and Apportionment of Rents, etc

190 Equitable apportionment of rents and remedies for non-payment or breach of covenant

(1)   Where in a conveyance for valuable consideration, other than a mortgage, of part of land which is affected by a rentcharge, such rentcharge or a part thereof is, without the consent of the owner thereof, expressed to be—

    (a)   charged exclusively on the land conveyed or any part thereof in exoneration of the land retained or other land; or

    (b)   charged exclusively on the land retained or any part thereof in exoneration of the land conveyed or other land; or

    (c)   apportioned between the land conveyed or any part thereof, and the land retained by the grantor or any part thereof;

then, without prejudice to the rights of the owner of the rentcharge, such charge or apportionment shall be binding as between the grantor and the grantee under the conveyance and their respective successors in title.

(2)   Where—

    (a)   any default is made in payment of the whole or part of a rentcharge by the person who, by reason of such charge or apportionment as aforesaid, is liable to pay the same; or

    (b)   any breach occurs of any of the covenants (other than in the case of an apportionment the covenant to pay the entire rentcharge) or conditions contained in the deed or other document creating the rentcharge, so far as the same relate to the land retained or conveyed, as the case may be;

the owner for the time being of any other land affected by the entire rentcharge who—

    (i)   pays or is required to pay the whole or part of the rentcharge which ought to have been paid by the defaulter aforesaid; or

    (ii)   incurs any costs, damages or expenses by reason of the breach of covenant or condition aforesaid;

may enter into and distrain on the land in respect of which the default or breach is made or occurs, or any part of that land, and dispose according to law of any distress found, and may also take possession of the income of the same land until, by means of such distress and receipt of income or otherwise the whole or part of the rentcharge (charged or apportioned as aforesaid) so unpaid and all costs, damages and expenses incurred by reason of the non-payment thereof or of the breach of the said covenants and conditions, are fully paid or satisfied.

(3)   Where in a conveyance for valuable consideration, other than a mortgage, of part of land comprised in a lease, for the residue of the term or interest created by the lease, the rent reserved by such lease or a part thereof is, without the consent of the lessor, expressed to be—

    (a)   charged exclusively on the land conveyed or any part thereof in exoneration of the land retained by the assignor or other land; or

    (b)   charged exclusively on the land retained by the assignor or any part thereof in exoneration of the land conveyed or other land; or

    (c)   apportioned between the land conveyed or any part thereof and the land retained by the assignor or any part thereof;

then, without prejudice to the rights of the lessor, such charge or apportionment shall be binding as between the assignor and the assignee under the conveyance and their respective successors in title.

(4)   Where—

    (a)   any default is made in payment of the whole or part of a rent by the person who, by reason of such charge or apportionment as aforesaid, is liable to pay the same; or

    (b)   any breach occurs of any of the lessee's covenants (other than in the case of an apportionment the covenant to pay the entire rent) or conditions contained in the lease, so far as the same relate to the land retained or conveyed, as the case may be;

the lessee for the time being of any other land comprised in the lease, in whom, as respects that land, the residue of the term or interest created by the lease is vested, who—

    (i)   pays or is required to pay the whole or part of the rent which ought to have been paid by the defaulter aforesaid; or

(ii)   incurs any costs, damages or expenses by reason of the breach of covenant or condition aforesaid;

may enter into and distrain on the land comprised in the lease in respect of which the default or breach is made or occurs, or any part of that land, and dispose according to law of any distress found, and may also take possession of the income of the same land until (so long as the term or interest created by the lease is subsisting) by means of such distress and receipt of income or otherwise, the whole or part of the rent (charged or apportioned as aforesaid) so unpaid and all costs, damages and expenses incurred by reason of the non-payment thereof or of the breach of the said covenants and conditions, are fully paid or satisfied.

(5)   The remedies conferred by this section take effect so far only as they might have been conferred by the conveyance whereby the rent or any part thereof is expressed to be charged or apportioned as aforesaid, but a trustee, personal representative, mortgagee or other person in a fiduciary position has, and shall be deemed always to have had, power to confer the same or like remedies.

(6)   This section applies only if and so far as a contrary intention is not expressed in the conveyance whereby the rent or any part thereof is expressed to be charged or apportioned as aforesaid, and takes effect subject to the terms of that conveyance and to the provisions therein contained.

(7)   The remedies conferred by this section apply only where the conveyance whereby the rent or any part thereof is expressed to be charged or apportioned is made after the commencement of this Act, and do not apply where the rent is charged exclusively as aforesaid or legally apportioned with the consent of the owner or lessor.

(8)   The rule of law relating to perpetuities does not affect the powers or remedies conferred by this section or any like powers or remedies expressly conferred, before or after the commencement of this Act, by an instrument.

[173]

191–195   (*S 191 repealed by the Rentcharges Act 1977, s 17(2), Sch 2; ss 192–195 outside the scope of this work.*)

Notices

196   Regulations respecting notices

(1)   Any notice required or authorised to be served or given by this Act shall be in writing.

(2)   Any notice required or authorised by this Act to be served on a lessee or mortgagor shall be sufficient, although only addressed to the lessee or mortgagor by that designation, without his name, or generally to the persons interested, without any name, and notwithstanding that any person to be affected by the notice is absent, under disability, unborn, or unascertained.

(3)   Any notice required or authorised by this Act to be served shall be sufficiently served if it is left at the last-known place of abode or business in the United Kingdom of the lessee, lessor, mortgagee, mortgagor, or other person to be served, or, in case of a notice required or authorised to be served on a lessee or mortgagor, is affixed or left for him on the land or any house or building comprised in the lease or mortgage, or, in case of a mining lease, is left for the lessee at the office or counting-house of the mine.

(4)   Any notice required or authorised by this Act to be served shall also be sufficiently served, if it is sent by post in a registered letter addressed to the lessee, lessor, mortgagee, mortgagor, or other person to be served, by name, at the aforesaid place of abode or business, office, or counting-house, and if that letter is not returned [by the postal operator (within the meaning of the Postal Services Act 2000) concerned] undelivered; and that service shall be deemed to be made at the time at which the registered letter would in the ordinary course be delivered.

(5)   The provisions of this section shall extend to notices required to be served by any instrument affecting property executed or coming into operation after the commencement of this Act unless a contrary intention appears.

(6)   This section does not apply to notices served in proceedings in the court.

[174]

NOTES

Sub-s (4): words in square brackets substituted by the Postal Services Act 2000 (Consequential Modifications No 1) Order 2001, SI 2001/1149, art 3(1), Sch 1, para 7.

Modification: the reference to last known place of abode or business in this section is modified in its application to notices served by a tenant on a landlord of premises to which the Landlord and Tenant Act 1987, Pt VI applies, by virtue of s 49 of that Act.

197–200 (*S 197 spent for certain purposes and repealed for certain purposes by the Law of Property Act 1969, s 16, Sch 2, Pt I; ss 198–200 outside the scope of this work.*)

PART XII
CONSTRUCTION, JURISDICTION, AND GENERAL PROVISIONS

201–204 (*Outside the scope of this work.*)

205 General definitions

(1)   In this Act unless the context otherwise requires, the following expressions have the meanings hereby assigned to them respectively, that is to say:—

(i) "Bankruptcy" includes liquidation by arrangement; also in relation to a corporation means the winding up thereof;

(ii) "Conveyance" includes a mortgage, charge, lease, assent, vesting declaration, vesting instrument, disclaimer, release and every other assurance of property or of an interest therein by any instrument, except a will; "convey" has a corresponding meaning; and "disposition" includes a conveyance and also a devise, bequest, or an appointment of property contained in a will; and "dispose of" has a corresponding meaning;

(iii) "Building purposes" include the erecting and improving of, and the adding to, and the repairing of buildings; and a "building lease" is a lease for building purposes or purposes connected therewith;

[(iiiA)   ...]

(iv) "Death duty" means estate duty, ... and every other duty leviable or payable on a death;

(v) "Estate owner" means the owner of a legal estate, but an infant is not capable of being an estate owner;

(vi) "Gazette" means the London Gazette;

(vii) "Incumbrance" includes a legal or equitable mortgage and a trust for securing money, and a lien, and a charge of a portion, annuity, or other capital or annual sum; and "incumbrancer" has a meaning corresponding with that of incumbrance, and includes every person entitled to the benefit of an incumbrance, or to require payment or discharge thereof;

(viii) "Instrument" does not include a statute, unless the statute creates a settlement;

(ix) "Land" includes land of any tenure, and mines and minerals, whether or not held apart from the surface, buildings or parts of buildings (whether the division is horizontal, vertical or made in any other way) and other corporeal hereditaments; also a manor, an advowson, and a rent and other incorporeal hereditaments, and an easement, right, privilege, or benefit in, over, or derived from land; *but not an undivided share in land*; and "mines and minerals" include any strata or seam of minerals or substances in or under any land, and powers of working and getting the same *but not an undivided share thereof*; and "manor" includes a lordship, and reputed manor or lordship; and "hereditament" means any real property which on an intestacy occurring before the commencement of this Act might have devolved upon an heir;

(x) "Legal estates" mean the estates, interests and charges, in or over land (subsisting or created at law) which are by this Act authorised to subsist or to be created as legal estates; "equitable interests" mean all the other interests and charges in or over land *or in the proceeds of sale thereof*; an equitable interest "capable of subsisting as a legal estate" means such as could validly subsist or be created as a legal estate under this Act;

(xi) "Legal powers" include the powers vested in a chargee by way of legal mortgage or in an estate owner under which a legal estate can be transferred or created; and "equitable powers" mean all the powers in or over land under which equitable interests or powers only can be transferred or created;

(xii) "Limitation Acts" means the Real Property Limitation Acts 1833, 1837 and 1874, and "limitation" includes a trust;

[*(xiii)* *"Mental disorder" has the meaning assigned to it by [section 1 of the Mental Health Act 1983] and "receiver" in relation to a person suffering from mental disorder, means a receiver appointed for that person under [Part VIII of the Mental Health Act 1959 or Part VII of the said Act of 1983].*]

(xiv) a "mining lease" means a lease for mining purposes, that is, the searching for, winning, working, getting, making merchantable, carrying away, or disposing of mines and minerals, or purposes connected therewith, and includes a grant or licence for mining purposes;

(xv) "Minister" means [the Minister of Agriculture, Fisheries and Food];

(xvi) "Mortgage" includes any charge or lien on any property for securing money or money's worth; "legal mortgage" means a mortgage by demise or subdemise or a charge by way of legal mortgage and "legal mortgagee" has a corresponding meaning; "mortgage money" means money or money's worth secured by a mortgage; "mortgagor" includes any person from time to time deriving title under the original mortgagor or entitled to redeem a mortgage according to his estate interest or right in the mortgaged property; "mortgagee" includes a chargee by way of legal mortgage and any person from time to time deriving title under the original mortgagee; and "mortgagee in possession" is, for the purposes of this Act, a mortgagee who, in right of the mortgage, has entered into and is in possession of the mortgaged property; and "right of redemption" includes an option to repurchase only if the option in effect creates a right of redemption;

(xvii) "Notice" includes constructive notice;

(xviii) "Personal representative" means the executor, original or by representation, or administrator for the time being of a deceased person, and as regards any liability for the payment of death duties includes any person who takes possession of or intermeddles with the property of a deceased person without the authority of the personal representatives or the court;

(xix) "Possession" includes receipt of rents and profits or the right to receive the same, if any; and "income" includes rents and profits;

(xx) "Property" includes any thing in action, and any interest in real or personal property;

(xxi) "Purchaser" means a purchaser in good faith for valuable consideration and includes a lessee, mortgagee or other person who for valuable consideration acquires an interest in property except that in Part I of this Act and elsewhere where so expressly provided "purchaser" only means a person who acquires an interest in or charge on property for money or money's worth; and in reference to a legal estate includes a chargee by way of legal mortgage; and where the context so requires "purchaser" includes an intending purchaser; "purchase" has a meaning corresponding with that of "purchaser"; and "valuable consideration" includes marriage[, and formation of a civil partnership,] but does not include a nominal consideration in money;

(xxii) "Registered land" has the same meaning as in the [Land Registration Act 2002;]
    ...

(xxiii) "Rent" includes a rent service or a rentcharge, or other rent, toll, duty, royalty, or annual or periodical payment in money or money's worth, reserved or issuing out of or charged upon land, but does not include mortgage interest; "rentcharge" includes a fee farm rent; "fine" includes a premium or foregift and any payment, consideration, or benefit in the nature of a fine, premium or foregift; "lessor" includes an underlessor and a person deriving title under a lessor or underlessor; and "lessee" includes an underlessee and a person deriving title under a lessee or underlessee, and "lease" includes an underlease or other tenancy;

(xxiv) "Sale" includes an extinguishment of manorial incidents, but in other respects means a sale properly so called;

(xxv) "Securities" include stocks, funds and shares

(xxvi) "Tenant for life", "statutory owner", "settled land", "settlement", "vesting deed", "subsidiary vesting deed", "vesting order", "vesting instrument", "trust instrument", "capital money" and "trustees of the settlement" have the same meanings as in the Settled Land Act 1925;

(xxvii) "Term of years absolute" means a term of years (taking effect either in possession or in reversion whether or not at a rent) with or without impeachment for waste, subject or not to another legal estate, and either certain or liable to determination by notice, re-entry, operation of law, or by a provision for cesser on redemption, or in any other event (other than the dropping of a life, or the determination of a determinable life interest); but does not include any term of years determinable with life or lives or with the cesser of a determinable life interest, nor, if created after the commencement of this Act, a term of years which is not expressed to take effect in possession within twenty-one years after the creation thereof where required by this Act to take effect within that period; and in this definition the expression "term of years" includes a term for less than a year, or for a year or years and a fraction of a year or from year to year;

(xxviii) "Trust Corporation" means the Public Trustee or a corporation either appointed by the court in any particular case to be a trustee or entitled by rules made under subsection (3) of section four of the Public Trustee Act 1906 to act as custodian trustee;

(xxix) "Trust for sale", in relation to land, means an immediate *binding* trust for sale, whether or not exercisable at the request or with the consent of any person, *and with or without a power at discretion to postpone the sale*; "trustees for sale" mean the persons (including a personal representative) holding land on trust for sale; *and "power to postpone a sale" means power to postpone in the exercise of a discretion;*

(xxx) "United Kingdom" means Great Britain and Northern Ireland;

(xxxi) "Will" includes codicil.

[(1A) Any reference in this Act to money being paid into court shall be construed as referring to the money being paid into the *Supreme Court* or any other court that has jurisdiction, and any reference in this Act to the court, in a context referring to the investment or application of money paid into court, shall be construed, in the case of money paid into the *Supreme Court*, as referring to the High Court, and in the case of money paid into another court, as referring to that other court.]

(2) Where an equitable interest in or power over property arises by statute or operation of law, references to the creation of an interest or power include references to any interest or power so arising.

(3) References to registration under the Land Charges Act 1925 apply to any registration made under any other statute which is by the Land Charges Act 1925 to have effect as if the registration had been made under that Act.

[175]

NOTES

Sub-s (1): para (iiiA) inserted by the County Courts Act 1984, s 148(1), Sch 2, para 9, repealed by the High Court and County Courts Jurisdiction Order 1991, SI 1991/724, art 2(8), Schedule, Pt I; in para (iv) words omitted repealed by the Finance Act 1949, s 52(9), (10), Sch 11, Pt IV; in paras (ix) (x), (xxix) words in italics repealed by the Trusts of Land and Appointment of Trustees Act 1996, s 25(2), Sch 4; the original wording is reproduced here for reasons of historical interest or in view of the savings contained in ss 3, 18(3), 25(5) of the 1996 Act; para (xiii) substituted by the Mental Health Act 1959, s 149(1), Sch 7, Pt I, repealed by the Mental Capacity Act 2005, s 67(1), (2), Sch 6, para 4(1), (3), Sch 7, as from a day to be appointed, words in square brackets substituted by the Mental Health Act 1983, s 148, Sch 4, para 5(b); in para (xv) words in square brackets substituted by virtue of the Transfer of Functions (Ministry of Food) Order 1955, SI 1955/554; in para (xxi) words in square brackets inserted by the Civil Partnership Act 2004, s 261(1), Sch 27, para 7; in para (xxii) words in square brackets substituted and words omitted repealed by the Land Registration Act 2002, s 133, Sch 11, para 2(1), (13), Sch 13.

Sub-s (1A): inserted by the Administration of Justice Act 1965, ss 17, 18, Sch 1; for the words in italics in both places they occur there are substituted the words "Senior Courts" by the Constitutional Reform Act 2005, s 59(5), Sch 11, Pt 2, para 4(1), (3), as from a day to be appointed.

Modification: definition "Trust corporation" modified in relation to charities by the Charities Act 1993, s 35.

Real Property Limitation Acts 1833, 1837, 1874: see now the Limitation Act 1980.

Mental Health Act 1959, Pt VIII: repealed by (with the exception of s 120), and replaced by the Mental Health Act 1983.

Minister of Agriculture, Fisheries and Food: the Ministry of Agriculture, Fisheries and Food was dissolved by the Ministry of Agriculture, Fisheries and Food (Dissolution) Order 2002, SI 2002/794. Subject to specific provision to the contrary, the functions of the Minister were transferred to the Secretary of State, and the property, rights and liabilities of the Minister were transferred to the Secretary of State for Environment, Food and Rural Affairs.

Land Charges Act 1925: see now the Land Charges Act 1972, and the Local Land Charges Act 1975.

206, 207   (*S 206 repealed by the Statute Law (Repeals) Act 2004; s 207 outside the scope of this work.*)

208   Application to the Crown

(1)   Nothing in this Act shall be construed as rendering any property of the Crown subject to distress, or liable to be taken or disposed of by means of any distress.

(2)   This Act shall not in any manner (save as otherwise expressly provided and except so far as it relates to undivided shares, joint ownership, leases for lives or leases for years terminable with life or marriage) affect or alter the descent, devolution or tenure or the nature of the estates and interests of or in any land for the time being vested in His Majesty either in right of the Crown or of the Duchy of Lancaster or of or in any land for the time being belonging to the Duchy of Cornwall and held in right or in respect of the said Duchy, but so nevertheless that after the commencement of this Act, no estates, interests or charges in or over any such lands as aforesaid shall be conveyed or created, except such estates, interests or charges as are capable under this Act of subsisting or of being conveyed or created.

(3)   Subject as aforesaid the provisions of this Act bind the Crown.

[176]

209   Short title, commencement, extent

(1)   This Act may be cited as the Law of Property Act 1925.

(2)   ...

(3)   This Act extends to England and Wales only.

[177]

NOTES
Sub-s (2): repealed by the Statute Law Revision Act 1950.

SCHEDULES

(*First Schedule outside the scope of this work.*)

SECOND SCHEDULE
IMPLIED COVENANTS

Sections 76, 77

(*Pts I–VI repealed by the Law of Property (Miscellaneous Provisions) Act 1994, s 21(2), Sch 2.*)

PART VII
COVENANT IMPLIED IN A CONVEYANCE FOR VALUABLE CONSIDERATION, OTHER THAN A MORTGAGE, OF THE ENTIRETY OF LAND AFFECTED BY A RENTCHARGE

That the grantees or the persons deriving title under them will at all times, from the date of the conveyance or other date therein stated, duly pay the said rentcharge and observe and perform all the covenants, agreements and conditions contained in the deed or other document creating the rentcharge, and thenceforth on the part of the owner of the land to be observed and performed:

And also will at all times, from the date aforesaid, save harmless and keep indemnified the conveying parties and their respective estates and effects, from and against all proceedings, costs, claims and expenses on account of any omission to pay the said rentcharge or any part thereof, or any breach of any of the said covenants, agreements and conditions.

[178]

PART VIII
COVENANTS IMPLIED IN A CONVEYANCE FOR VALUABLE CONSIDERATION, OTHER THAN A MORTGAGE, OF PART OF LAND AFFECTED BY A RENTCHARGE, SUBJECT TO A PART (NOT LEGALLY APPORTIONED) OF THAT RENTCHARGE

(i)   That the grantees, or the persons deriving title under them, will at all times, from the date of the conveyance or other date therein stated, pay the apportioned rent and observe and perform all the covenants (other than the covenant to pay the entire rent) and conditions contained in the deed or other document creating the rentcharge, so far as the same relate to the land conveyed:

And also will at all times, from the date aforesaid, save harmless and keep indemnified the conveying parties and their respective estates and effects, from and against all proceedings, costs, claims and expenses on account of any omission to pay the said apportioned rent, or any breach of any of the said covenants and conditions, so far as the same relate as aforesaid.

(ii)   That the conveying parties, or the persons deriving title under them, will at all times, from the date of the conveyance or other date therein stated, pay the balance of the rentcharge (after deducting the apportioned rent aforesaid, and any other rents similarly apportioned in respect of land not retained), and observe and perform all the covenants, other than the covenant to pay the entire rent, and conditions contained in the deed or other document creating the rentcharge, so far as the same relate to the land not included in the conveyance and remaining vested in the covenantors:

And also will at all times, from the date aforesaid, save harmless and keep indemnified the grantees and their estates and effects, from and against all proceedings, costs, claims and expenses on account of any omission to pay the aforesaid balance of the rentcharge, or any breach of any of the said covenants and conditions so far as they relate aforesaid.

[179]

PART IX
COVENANT IN A CONVEYANCE FOR VALUABLE CONSIDERATION, OTHER THAN A MORTGAGE, OF THE ENTIRETY OF THE LAND COMPRISED IN A LEASE FOR THE RESIDUE OF THE TERM OR INTEREST CREATED BY THE LEASE

That the assignees, or the persons deriving title under them, will at all times, from the date of the conveyance or other date therein stated, duly pay all rent becoming due under the lease creating the term or interest for which the land is conveyed, and observe and perform all the covenants, agreements and conditions therein contained and thenceforth on the part of the lessees to be observed and performed:

And also will at all times, from the date aforesaid, save harmless and keep indemnified the conveying parties and their estates and effects, from and against all proceedings, costs, claims and expenses on account of any omission to pay the said rent or any breach of any of the said covenants, agreements and conditions.

[180]

NOTES
Repealed by the Landlord and Tenant (Covenants) Act 1995, s 30(2), (3), Sch 2, except in relation to tenancies which are not new tenancies (as defined by ss 1, 28(1) of that Act, at **[675]** and **[700]**).

PART X
COVENANTS IMPLIED IN A CONVEYANCE FOR VALUABLE CONSIDERATION, OTHER THAN A MORTGAGE, OF PART OF THE LAND COMPRISED IN A LEASE, FOR THE RESIDUE OF THE TERM OR INTEREST CREATED BY THE LEASE, SUBJECT TO A PART (NOT LEGALLY APPORTIONED) OF THAT RENT

(i)   That the assignees, or the persons deriving title under them, will at all times, from the date of the conveyance or other date therein stated, pay the apportioned rent and observe and perform all the covenants, other than the covenant to pay the entire rent, agreements and conditions contained in the lease creating the term or interest for which the land is conveyed, and thenceforth on the part of the lessees to be observed and performed, so far as the same relate to the land conveyed:

And also will at all times from the date aforesaid save harmless and keep indemnified, the conveying parties and their respective estates and effects, from and against all proceedings, costs, claims and expenses on account of any omission to pay the said apportioned rent or any breach of any of the said covenants, agreements and conditions, so far as the same relate as aforesaid.

(ii)   That the conveying parties, or the persons deriving title under them, will at all times, from the date of the conveyance, or other date therein stated, pay the balance of the rent (after deducting the apportioned rent aforesaid and any other rents similarly apportioned in respect of land not retained) and observe and perform all the covenants, other than the covenant to

pay the entire rent, agreements and conditions contained in the lease and on the part of the lessees to be observed and performed so far as the same relate to the land demised (other than the land comprised in the conveyance) and remaining vested in the covenantors:

And also will at all times, from the date aforesaid, save harmless and keep indemnified, the assignees and their estates and effects, from and against all proceedings, costs, claims and expenses on account of any omission to pay the aforesaid balance of the rent or any breach of any of the said covenants, agreements and conditions so far as they relate as aforesaid.

[181]

NOTES

Repealed as noted to Pt IX at **[180]**.

(*Third and Fourth Schedules outside the scope of this work; Fifth and Sixth Schedules repealed by the Statute Law (Repeals) Act 2004; Seventh Schedule repealed by the Statute Law Revision Act 1950.*)

ADMINISTRATION OF ESTATES ACT 1925

(15 & 16 Geo 5 c 23)

An Act to consolidate Enactments relating to the Administration of the Estates of Deceased Persons

[9 April 1925]

1–3   ((*Pt I*) *Outside the scope of this work.*)

PART II
EXECUTORS AND ADMINISTRATORS

General Provisions

4–8   (*S 4 repealed by the Supreme Court of Judicature (Consolidation) Act 1925, s 226, Sch 6; ss 5–8 outside the scope of this work.*)

[9   Vesting of estate in Public Trustee where intestacy or lack of executors

(1)   Where a person dies intestate, his real and personal estate shall vest in the Public Trustee until the grant of administration.

(2)   Where a testator dies and—
  (a)   at the time of his death there is no executor with power to obtain probate of the will, or
  (b)   at any time before probate of the will is granted there ceases to be any executor with power to obtain probate,
the real and personal estate of which he disposes by the will shall vest in the Public Trustee until the grant of representation.

(3)   The vesting of real or personal estate in the Public Trustee by virtue of this section does not confer on him any beneficial interest in, or impose on him any duty, obligation or liability in respect of, the property.]

[182]

NOTES

Substituted by the Law of Property (Miscellaneous Provisions) Act 1994, s 14(1), subject to transitional provisions contained in s 14(2)–(6) thereof.

10–52   (*Ss 10–14, 16, 18–20 repealed by the Supreme Court of Judicature (Consolidation) Act 1925, s 226, Sch 6; s 15, 17, 21–52 outside the scope of this work.*)

PART V
SUPPLEMENTAL

53 (*Outside the scope of this work.*)

54 Application of Act

Save as otherwise expressly provided, this Act does not apply in any case where the death occurred before the commencement of this Act.

[183]

55 Definitions

In this Act, unless the context otherwise requires, the following expressions have the meanings hereby assigned to them respectively, that is to say:—

(1)

    (i) "Administration" means, with reference to the real and personal estate of a deceased person, letters of administration whether general or limited, or with the will annexed or otherwise:

    (ii) "Administrator" means a person to whom administration is granted:

    (iii) "Conveyance" includes a mortgage, charge by way of legal mortgage, lease, assent, vesting, declaration, vesting instrument, disclaimer, release and every other assurance of property or of an interest therein by any instrument, except a will, and "convey" has a corresponding meaning, and "disposition" includes a "conveyance" also a devise bequest and an appointment of property contained in a will, and "dispose of" has a corresponding meaning:

    [(iiiA) "the County Court limit", in relation to any enactment contained in this Act, means the amount for the time being specified by an Order in Council under section 145 of the County Courts Act 1984 as the county court limit for the purposes of that enactment (or, where no such Order in Council has been made, the corresponding limit specified by Order in Council under section 192 of the County Courts Act 1959):]

    (iv) "the Court" means the High Court and also the county court, where that court has jurisdiction ...

    (v) "Income" includes rents and profits:

    (vi) "Intestate" includes a person who leaves a will but dies intestate as to some beneficial interest in his real or personal estate:

    [(via) "Land" has the same meaning as in the Law of Property Act 1925;]

    (vii) "Legal estates" mean the estates charges and interests in or over land (subsisting or created at law) which are by statute authorised to subsist or to be created at law; and "equitable interests" mean all other interests and charges in or over land *or in the proceeds of sale thereof*:

    (viii) *"[Person of unsound mind]" includes a [person of unsound mind] whether so found or not, and in relation to a [person of unsound mind] not so found; ... and "defective" includes every person affected by the provisions of section one hundred and sixteen of the Lunacy Act 1890, as extended by section sixty-four of the Mental Deficiency Act 1913, and for whose benefit a receiver has been appointed:*

    (ix) "Pecuniary legacy" includes an annuity, a general legacy, a demonstrative legacy so far as it is not discharged out of the designated property, and any other general direction by a testator for the payment of money, including all death duties free from which any devise, bequest, or payment is made to take effect:

    (x) "Personal chattels" mean carriages, horses, stable furniture and effects (not used for business purposes), motor cars and accessories (not used for business purposes), garden effects, domestic animals, plate, plated articles, linen, china, glass, books, pictures, prints, furniture, jewellery, articles of household or personal use or ornament, musical and scientific instruments and apparatus, wines, liquors and consumable stores, but do not include any chattels used at the death of the intestate for business purposes nor money or securities for money:

    (xi) "Personal representative" means the executor, original or by representation, or administrator for the time being of a deceased person, and as regards any liability for the payment of death duties includes any person who takes possession of or intermeddles with the property of a deceased person without

95

the authority of the personal representatives or the court, and "executor" includes a person deemed to be appointed executor as respects settled land:

(xii) "Possession" includes the receipt of rents and profits or the right to receive the same, if any:

(xiii) "Prescribed" means prescribed by rules of court ... :

(xiv) "Probate" means the probate of a will:

(xv), (xvi)

(xvii) "Property" includes a thing in action and any interest in real or personal property:

(xviii) "Purchaser" means a lessee, mortgagee, or other person who in good faith acquires an interest in property for valuable consideration, also an intending purchaser and "valuable consideration" includes marriage, [and formation of a civil partnership,] but does not include a nominal consideration in money:

(xix) "Real estate" save as provided in Part IV of this Act means real estate, including chattels real, which by virtue of Part I of this Act devolves on the personal representative of a deceased person:

(xx) "Representation" means the probate of a will and administration, and the expression "taking out representation" refers to the obtaining of the probate of a will or of the grant of administration:

(xxi) "Rent" includes a rent service or a rentcharge, or other rent, toll, duty, or annual or periodical payment in money or money's worth, issuing out of or charged upon land, but does not include mortgage interest; and "rentcharge" includes a fee farm rent:

(xxii) ...

(xxiii) "Securities" include stocks, funds, or shares:

(xxiv) "Tenant for life," "statutory owner,", *"land"* "settled land," "settlement," "trustees of the settlement," "term of years absolute," "death duties," and "legal mortgage," have the same meanings as in the Settled Land Act 1925, and "entailed interest" and "charge by way of legal mortgage" have the same meanings as in the Law of Property Act 1925:

(xxv) "Treasury solicitor" means the solicitor for the affairs of His Majesty's Treasury, and includes the solicitor for the affairs of the Duchy of Lancaster:

(xxvi) "Trust corporation" means the public trustee or a corporation either appointed by the court in any particular case to be a trustee or entitled by rules made under subsection (3) of section four of the Public Trustee Act 1906, to act as custodian trustee:

(xxvii) "Trust for sale," in relation to land, means an immediate binding trust for sale, whether or not exercisable at the request or with the consent of any person, and with or without a power at discretion to postpone the sale; and "power to postpone a sale" means power to postpone in the exercise of a discretion:

(xxviii) "Will" includes codicil.

(2) References to a child or issue living at the death of any person include child or issue en ventre sa mere at the death.

(3) References to the estate of a deceased person include property over which the deceased exercises a general power of appointment (including the statutory power to dispose of entailed interests) by his will.

[184]

NOTES

Sub-s (1): para (iiiA) inserted by the County Courts Act 1984, s 148(1), Sch 2, Pt II, para 15; in para (iv) words omitted repealed by the Courts Act 1971, s 56(4), Sch 11, Pt II; para (via) inserted, in paras (vii), (xxiv) words in italics repealed, and para (xxvii) repealed, by the Trusts of Land and Appointment of Trustees Act 1996, s 25(1), (2), Sch 3, para 6(1), (5), Sch 4, the original wording is reproduced here for reasons of historical interest or in view of the savings contained in ss 3, 18(3), 25(5) of the 1996 Act; para (viii) repealed by the Mental Capacity Act 2005, s 67(1), Sch 6, para 5(1), (3), Sch 7, as from a day to be appointed, words omitted repealed by the Mental Health Act 1959, s 149(2), Sch 8, Pt I, and words in square brackets substituted by the Mental Treatment Act 1930, s 20(5); in para (xiii) words omitted repealed by the Supreme Court Act 1981, s 152(4), Sch 7; para (xv) repealed by the Law of Property (Miscellaneous Provisions) Act 1994, s 21(2), Sch 2; paras (xvi), (xxii) repealed by the Supreme Court Act 1981, s 152(4), Sch 7; in para (xviii) words in square brackets inserted by the Civil Partnership Act 2004, s 71, Sch 4, Pt 2, para 12.

Modification: definition "Trust corporation" modified in relation to charities by the Charities Act 1993, s 35.

County Courts Act 1959, s 192: repealed by the County Courts Act 1984, s 148(3), Sch 4 and replaced by s 145 of the 1984 Act.

Lunacy Act 1890, s 116, Mental Deficiency Act 1913, s 64: repealed by the Mental Health Act 1959, s 1; see now the Mental Health Act 1984, ss 94(2), 95.

56 (*Spent on the repeal of Sch 2 by the Statute Law Revision Act 1950.*)

57 Application to Crown

(1)   The provisions of this Act bind the Crown and the Duchy of Lancaster, and the Duke of Cornwall for the time being as respects the estates of persons dying after the commencement of this Act, but not so as to affect the time within which proceedings for the recovery of real or personal estate vesting in or devolving on His Majesty in right of His Crown, or His Duchy of Lancaster, or on the Duke of Cornwall, may be instituted.

(2)   Nothing in this Act in any manner affects or alters the descent or devolution of any property for the time being vested in His Majesty either in right of the Crown or of the Duchy of Lancaster or of any property for the time being belonging to the Duchy of Cornwall.

[185]

58 Short title, commencement and extent

(1)   This Act may be cited as the Administration of Estates Act 1925.

(2)   …

(3)   This Act extends to England and Wales only.

[186]

NOTES

Sub-s (2): repealed by the Statute Law Revision Act 1950.

(*First Schedule, Pt I repealed by the Insolvency Act 1985, s 235(3), Sch 10, Pt III, Pt II outside the scope of this work; Second Schedule repealed by the Statute Law Revision Act 1950.*)

ALLOTMENTS ACT 1925

(15 & 16 Geo 5 c 61)

An Act to facilitate the acquisition and maintenance of allotments, and to make further provision for the security of tenure of tenants of allotments

[7 August 1925]

1 Interpretation

In this Act, unless the context otherwise requires,—

"Allotment" means an allotment garden as defined by the Allotments Act 1922, or any parcel of land not more than five acres in extent cultivated or intended to be cultivated as a garden or farm, or partly as a garden and partly as a farm;

.....

"The Act of 1922" means the Allotments Act 1922.

[187]

NOTES

Definition omitted repealed by the Statute Law (Repeals) Act 1993.

2–6   (*S 2 repealed by the National Loans Act 1968, s 24(2), (3), Sch 6, Pt II, except in relation to any loans made before 1 April 1968; s 3 repealed by the Statute Law (Repeals) Act 1993; s 4 repealed by the Allotments Act 1950, s 15, Schedule; s 5 outside the scope of this work; s 6 amends the Allotments Act 1922, s 10(3) at* **[111]**.)

7 Amendment of section 10(4) of the Act of 1922

The right of a tenant to claim compensation under subsection (4) of section 10 of the Act of 1922 shall be exercisable notwithstanding that it is otherwise agreed in the contract of tenancy in any case where the rent payable by the tenant under his contract of tenancy for the land exceeds [1p] per pole ...

[188]

NOTES

Sum in square brackets substituted by virtue of the Decimal Currency Act 1969, s 10(1); words omitted repealed by the Statute Law (Repeals) Act 1993.

8–13   *(S 8 outside the scope of this work; s 9 amends the Allotments Act 1922, s 11 at* **[112]***; ss 10, 11 repealed by the Statute Law (Repeals) Act 1993; s 12 repealed by the Local Government Act 1972, s 272(1), Sch 30; s 13 repealed by the Local Government, Planning and Land Act 1980, ss 1(5), 194, Sch 5, para 5, Sch 34, Pt V.)*

14   Short title

(1)   This Act may be cited as the Allotments Act 1925, and the Allotments Acts 1908 to 1922 and this Act may be cited together as the Allotments Acts 1908 to 1925.

(2)   This Act shall not apply to Scotland or Northern Ireland.

[189]

LANDLORD AND TENANT ACT 1927

(17 & 18 Geo 5 c 36)

ARRANGEMENT OF SECTIONS

PART I
COMPENSATION FOR IMPROVEMENTS AND GOODWILL ON THE TERMINATION OF TENANCIES OF BUSINESS PREMISES

PART II
GENERAL AMENDMENTS OF THE LAW OF LANDLORD AND TENANT

PART III
GENERAL

PART I
STATUTES

An Act to provide for the payment of compensation for improvements and goodwill to tenants of premises used for business purposes, or the grant of a new lease in lieu thereof; and to amend the law of landlord and tenant

[22 December 1927]

PART I
COMPENSATION FOR IMPROVEMENTS AND GOODWILL ON THE TERMINATION
OF TENANCIES OF BUSINESS PREMISES

1   Tenant's right to compensation for improvements

(1)   Subject to the provisions of this Part of this Act, a tenant of a holding to which this Part of this Act applies shall, if a claim for the purpose is made in the prescribed manner [and within the time limited by section forty-seven of the Landlord and Tenant Act 1954] be entitled, at the termination of the tenancy, on quitting his holding, to be paid by his landlord compensation in respect of any improvement (including the erection of any building) on his holding made by him or his predecessors in title, not being a trade or other fixture which the tenant is by law entitled to remove, which at the termination of the tenancy adds to the letting value of the holding:

Provided that the sum to be paid as compensation for any improvement shall not exceed—

(a)   the net addition to the value of the holding as a whole which may be determined to be the direct result of the improvement; or

(b)   the reasonable cost of carrying out the improvement at the termination of the tenancy, subject to a deduction of an amount equal to the cost (if any) of putting the works constituting the improvement into a reasonable state of repair, except so far as such cost is covered by the liability of the tenant under any covenant or agreement as to the repair of the premises.

(2)   In determining the amount of such net addition as aforesaid, regard shall be had to the purposes for which it is intended that the premises shall be used after the termination of the tenancy, and if it is shown that it is intended to demolish or to make structural alterations in the premises or any part thereof or to use the premises for a different purpose, regard shall be had to the effect of such demolition, alteration or change of user on the additional value attributable to the improvement, and to the length of time likely to elapse between the termination of the tenancy and the demolition, alteration or change of user.

(3)   In the absence of agreement between the parties, all questions as to the right to compensation under this section, or as to the amount thereof, shall be determined by the tribunal hereinafter mentioned, and if the tribunal determines that, on account of the intention to demolish or alter or to change the user of the premises, no compensation or a reduced amount of compensation shall be paid, the tribunal may authorise a further application for compensation to be made by the tenant if effect is not given to the intention within such time as may be fixed by the tribunal.

[190]

NOTES

Sub-s (1): words in square brackets substituted by the Landlord and Tenant Act 1954, s 47(5).

2   Limitation on tenant's right to compensation in certain cases

(1)   A tenant shall not be entitled to compensation under this Part of this Act—

(a)   in respect of any improvement made before the commencement of this Act; or

(b)   in respect of any improvement made in pursuance of a statutory obligation, or of any improvement which the tenant or his predecessors in title were under an obligation to make in pursuance of a contract entered into, whether before or after the passing of this Act, for valuable consideration, including a building lease; or

(c) in respect of any improvement made less than three years before the termination of the tenancy; or

(d) if within two months after the making of the claim under section one, subsection (1), of this Act the landlord serves on the tenant notice that he is willing and able to grant to the tenant, or obtain the grant to him of, a renewal of the tenancy at such rent and for such term as, failing agreement, the tribunal may consider reasonable; and, where such a notice is so served and the tenant does not within one month from the service of the notice send to the landlord an acceptance in writing of the offer, the tenant shall be deemed to have declined the offer.

(2)   Where an offer of the renewal of a tenancy by the landlord under this section is accepted by the tenant, the rent fixed by the tribunal shall be the rent which in the opinion of the tribunal a willing lessee other than the tenant would agree to give and a willing lessor would agree to accept for the premises, having regard to the terms of the lease, but irrespective of the value attributable to the improvement in respect of which compensation would have been payable.

(3)   The tribunal in determining the compensation for an improvement shall in reduction of the tenant's claim take into consideration any benefits which the tenant or his predecessors in title may have received from the landlord or his predecessors in title in consideration expressly or impliedly of the improvement.

[191]

NOTES

Sub-s (2): spent in view of the provision made by the Landlord and Tenant Act 1954, s 48(3) at **[278]**.

---

3 Landlord's right to object

(1)   Where a tenant of a holding to which this Part of this Act applies proposes to make an improvement on his holding, he shall serve on his landlord notice of his intention to make such improvement, together with a specification and plan showing the proposed improvement and the part of the existing premises affected thereby, and if the landlord, within three months after the service of the notice, serves on the tenant notice of objection, the tenant may, in the prescribed manner, apply to the tribunal, and the tribunal may, after ascertaining that notice of such intention has been served upon any superior landlords interested and after giving such persons an opportunity of being heard, if satisfied that the improvement—

(a) is of such a nature as to be calculated to add to the letting value of the holding at the termination of the tenancy; and

(b) is reasonable and suitable to the character thereof; and

(c) will not diminish the value of any other property belonging to the same landlord, or to any superior landlord from whom the immediate landlord of the tenant directly or indirectly holds;

and after making such modifications (if any) in the specification or plan as the tribunal thinks fit, or imposing such other conditions as the tribunal may think reasonable, certify in the prescribed manner that the improvement is a proper improvement:

Provided that, if the landlord proves that he has offered to execute the improvement himself in consideration of a reasonable increase of rent, or of such increase of rent as the tribunal may determine, the tribunal shall not give a certificate under this section unless it is subsequently shown to the satisfaction of the tribunal that the landlord has failed to carry out his undertaking.

(2)   In considering whether the improvement is reasonable and suitable to the character of the holding, the tribunal shall have regard to any evidence brought before it by the landlord or any superior landlord (but not any other person) that the improvement is calculated to injure the amenity or convenience of the neighbourhood.

(3)   The tenant shall, at the request of any superior landlord or at the request of the tribunal, supply such copies of the plans and specifications of the proposed improvement as may be required.

(4)   Where no such notice of objection as aforesaid to a proposed improvement has been served within the time allowed by this section, or where the tribunal has certified an improvement to be a proper improvement, it shall be lawful for the tenant as against the immediate and any superior landlord to execute the improvement according to the plan and

specification served on the landlord, or according to such plan and specification as modified by the tribunal or by agreement between the tenant and the landlord or landlords affected, anything in any lease of the premises to the contrary notwithstanding:

Provided that nothing in this subsection shall authorise a tenant to execute an improvement in contravention of any restriction created or imposed—
  (a)   for naval, military or air force purposes;
  (b)   for civil aviation purposes under the powers of the Air Navigation Act 1920;
  (c)   for securing any rights of the public over the foreshore or bed of the sea.

(5)   A tenant shall not be entitled to claim compensation under this Part of this Act in respect of any improvement unless he has, or his predecessors in title have, served notice of the proposal to make the improvement under this section, and (in case the landlord has served notice of objection thereto) the improvement has been certified by the tribunal to be a proper improvement and the tenant has complied with the conditions, if any, imposed by the tribunal, nor unless the improvement is completed within such time after the service on the landlord of the notice of the proposed improvement as may be agreed between the tenant and the landlord or may be fixed by the tribunal, and where proceedings have been taken before the tribunal, the tribunal may defer making any order as to costs until the expiration of the time so fixed for the completion of the improvement.

(6)   Where a tenant has executed an improvement of which he has served notice in accordance with this section and with respect to which either no notice of objection has been served by the landlord or a certificate that it is a proper improvement has been obtained from the tribunal, the tenant may require the landlord to furnish to him a certificate that the improvement has been duly executed; and if the landlord refuses or fails within one month after the service of the requisition to do so, the tenant may apply to the tribunal who, if satisfied that the improvement has been duly executed, shall give a certificate to that effect.

Where the landlord furnishes such a certificate, the tenant shall be liable to pay any reasonable expenses incurred for the purpose by the landlord, and if any question arises as to the reasonableness of such expenses, it shall be determined by the tribunal.

[192]

4–7   (*Repealed by the Landlord and Tenant Act 1954, s 45, Sch 7, Pt I.*)

8   Rights of mesne landlords

(1)   Where, in the case of any holding, there are several persons standing in the relation to each other of lessor and lessee, the following provisions shall apply:—
  Any mesne landlord who has paid or is liable to pay compensation under this Part of this Act shall, at the end of his term, be entitled to compensation from his immediate landlord in like manner and on the same conditions as if he had himself made the improvement ... in question, except that it shall be sufficient if the claim for compensation is made at least two months before the expiration of his term:
  A mesne landlord shall not be entitled to make a claim under this section unless he has, within the time and in the manner prescribed, served on his immediate superior landlord copies of all documents relating to proposed improvements and claims which have been sent to him in pursuance of this Part of this Act:
  Where such copies are so served, the said superior landlord shall have, in addition to the mesne landlord, the powers conferred by or in pursuance of this Part of this Act in like manner as if he were the immediate landlord of the occupying tenant, and shall, in the manner and to the extent prescribed, be at liberty to appear before the tribunal and shall be bound by the proceedings:
  ...

(2)   In this section, references to a landlord shall include references to his predecessors in title.

[193]

NOTES
Sub-s (1): words omitted repealed by the Landlord and Tenant Act 1954, ss 45, 68(1), Sch 7.

9   Restriction on contracting out

This Part of this Act shall apply notwithstanding any contract to the contrary, being a contract made at any time after the eighth day of February, nineteen hundred and twenty-seven:

Provided that, if on the hearing of a claim or application under this Part of this Act it appears to the tribunal that a contract made after such date as aforesaid, so far as it deprives any person of any right under this Part of this Act, was made for adequate consideration, the tribunal shall in determining the matter give effect thereto.

[194]

NOTES
Words in italics repealed, except in relation to a contract made before 10 December 1953, by the Landlord and Tenant Act 1954, s 49 at **[279]**.

10 Right of entry

The landlord of a holding to which this Part of this Act applies, or any person authorised by him may at all reasonable times enter on the holding or any part of it, for the purpose of executing any improvement he has undertaken to execute and of making any inspection of the premises which may reasonably be required for the purposes of this Part of this Act.

[195]

11 Right to make deductions

(1)   Out of any money payable to a tenant by way of compensation under this Part of this Act, the landlord shall be entitled to deduct any sum due to him from the tenant under or in respect of the tenancy.

(2)   Out of any money due to the landlord from the tenant under or in respect of the tenancy, the tenant shall be entitled to deduct any sum payable to him by the landlord by way of compensation under this Part of this Act.

[196]

12 Application of 13 and 14 Geo 5 c 9, s 20

Section twenty of the Agricultural Holdings Act 1923 (which relates to charges in respect of money paid for compensation), as set out and modified in the First Schedule to this Act, shall apply to the case of money paid for compensation under this Part of this Act, including any proper costs, charges, or expenses incurred by a landlord in opposing any proposal by a tenant to execute an improvement, or in contesting a claim for compensation, and to money expended by a landlord in executing an improvement the notice of a proposal to execute which has been served on him by a tenant under this Part of this Act.

[197]

NOTES
Agricultural Holdings Act 1923, s 20: see now the Agricultural Holdings Act 1986, ss 86, 87 at **[493]**, **[494]**.

13 Power to apply and raise capital money

(1)   Capital money arising under the Settled Land Act 1925 (*either as originally enacted or as applied in relation to trusts for sale by section twenty-eight of the Law of Property Act 1925*), or under the University and College Estates Act 1925, may be applied—
  (a)   in payment as for an improvement authorised by the Act of any money expended and costs incurred by a landlord under or in pursuance of this Part of this Act in or about the execution of any improvement;
  (b)   in payment of any sum due to a tenant under this Part of this Act in respect of compensation for an improvement … and any costs, charges, and expenses incidental thereto;
  (c)   in payment of the costs, charges, and expenses of opposing any proposal by a tenant to execute an improvement.

(2)   The satisfaction of a claim for such compensation as aforesaid shall be included amongst the purposes for which a tenant for life, statutory owner, *trustee for sale, or personal representative* may raise money under section seventy-one of the Settled Land Act 1925.

(3)   Where the landlord liable to pay compensation for an improvement … is a tenant for life or in a fiduciary position, he may require the sum payable as compensation and any costs, charges, and expenses incidental thereto, to be paid out of any capital money held on the same trusts as the settled land.

In this subsection "capital money" includes any personal estate held on the same trusts as the land, *and "settled land" includes land held on trust for sale or vested in a personal representative.*

[198]

NOTES
Sub-s (1): words in italics repealed by the Trusts of Land and Appointment of Trustees Act 1996, s 25(2), Sch 4, the original wording is reproduced here for reasons of historical interest or in view of the savings contained in ss 3, 18(3), 25(5) of the 1996 Act; words omitted repealed by the Landlord and Tenant Act 1954, s 45, Sch 7, Part I.

Sub-s (2): words in italics repealed by the Trusts of Land and Appointment of Trustees Act 1996, s 25(2), Sch 4; the original wording is reproduced here for reasons of historical interest or in view of the savings contained in ss 3, 18(3), 25(5) of the 1996 Act.

Sub-s (3): words omitted repealed by the Landlord and Tenant Act 1954, s 45, Sch 7, Part I; words in italics repealed by the Trusts of Land and Appointment of Trustees Act 1996, s 25(2), Sch 4, the original wording is reproduced here for reasons of historical interest or in view of the savings contained in ss 3, 18(3), 25(5) of the 1996 Act.

14 Power to sell or grant leases notwithstanding restrictions

Where the powers of a landlord to sell or grant leases are subject to any statutory or other restrictions, he shall, notwithstanding any such restrictions or any rule of law to the contrary, be entitled to offer to sell or grant any such reversion or lease as would under this Part of this Act relieve him from liability to pay compensation thereunder, and to convey and grant the same, and to execute any lease which he may be ordered to grant under this Part of this Act.

[199]

15 Provisions as to reversionary leases

(1) Where the amount which a landlord is liable to pay as compensation for an improvement under this Part of this Act has been determined by agreement or by an award of the tribunal, and the landlord had before the passing of this Act granted or agreed to grant a reversionary lease commencing on or after the termination of the then existing tenancy, the rent payable under the reversionary lease shall, if the tribunal so directs, be increased by such amount as, failing agreement, may be determined by the tribunal having regard to the addition to the letting value of the holding attributable to the improvement:

Provided that no such increase shall be permissible unless the landlord has served or caused to be served on the reversionary lessee copies of all documents relating to the improvement when proposed which were sent to the landlord in pursuance of this Part of this Act.

(2) The reversionary lessee shall have the same right of objection to the proposed improvement and of appearing and being heard at any proceedings before the tribunal relative to the proposed improvement as if he were a superior landlord, and if the amount of compensation for the improvement is determined by the tribunal, any question as to the increase of rent under the reversionary lease shall, where practicable, be settled in the course of the same proceedings.

(3) ...

[200]

NOTES
Sub-s (3): repealed by the Landlord and Tenant Act 1954, s 45, Sch 7, Pt I.

16 Landlord's right to reimbursement of increased taxes, rates or insurance premiums

Where the landlord is liable to pay any ... rates (including water rate) in respect of any premises comprised in a holding, or has undertaken to pay the premiums on any fire insurance policy on any such premises, and in consequence of any improvement executed by the tenant on the premises under this Act the assessment of the premises or the rate of premium on the policy is increased, the tenant shall be liable to pay to the landlord sums equal to the amount by which—

    (a)   the ... rates payable by the landlord are increased by reason of the increase of such assessment;

    (b)   the fire premium payable by the landlord is increased by reason of the increase in the rate of premium;

and the sums so payable by the tenant shall be deemed to be in the nature of rent and shall be recoverable as such from the tenant, ...

[201]

17 Holdings to which Part I applies

(1) The holdings to which this Part of this Act applies are any premises held under a lease, other than a mining lease, made whether before or after the commencement of this Act, and used wholly or partly for carrying on thereat any trade or business, and [not being—

(a) agricultural holdings within the meaning of the Agricultural Holdings Act 1986 held under leases in relation to which that Act applies, or

(b) holdings held under farm business tenancies within the meaning of the Agricultural Tenancies Act 1995.]

(2) This Part of this Act shall not apply to any holding let to a tenant as the holder of any office, appointment or employment, from the landlord, and continuing so long as the tenant holds such office, appointment or employment, but in the case of a tenancy created after the commencement of this Act, only if the contract is in writing and expresses the purpose for which the tenancy is created.

(3) For the purposes of this section, premises shall not be deemed to be premises used for carrying on thereat a trade or business—

(a) by reason of their being used for the purpose of carrying on thereat any profession;

(b) by reason that the tenant thereof carries on the business of subletting the premises as residential flats, whether or not the provision of meals or any other service for the occupants of the flats is undertaken by the tenant:

Provided that, so far as this Part of this Act relates to improvements, premises regularly used for carrying on a profession shall be deemed to be premises used for carrying on a trade or business.

(4) In the case of premises used partly for purposes of a trade or business and partly for other purposes, this Part of this Act shall apply to improvements only if and so far as they are improvements in relation to the trade or business.

[202]

PART II
GENERAL AMENDMENTS OF THE LAW OF LANDLORD AND TENANT

18 Provisions as to covenants to repair

(1) Damages for a breach of a covenant or agreement to keep or put premises in repair during the currency of a lease, or to leave or put premises in repair at the termination of a lease, whether such covenant or agreement is expressed or implied, and whether general or specific, shall in no case exceed the amount (if any) by which the value of the reversion (whether immediate or not) in the premises is diminished owing to the breach of such covenant or agreement as aforesaid; and in particular no damage shall be recovered for a breach of any such covenant or agreement to leave or put premises in repair at the termination of a lease, if it is shown that the premises, in whatever state of repair they might be, would at or shortly after the termination of the tenancy have been or be pulled down, or such structural alterations made therein as would render valueless the repairs covered by the covenant or agreement.

(2) A right of re-entry or forfeiture for a breach of any such covenant or agreement as aforesaid shall not be enforceable, by action or otherwise, unless the lessor proves that the fact that such a notice as is required by section one hundred and forty-six of the Law of Property Act 1925, had been served on the lessee was known either—

(a)   to the lessee; or

(b)   to an under-lessee holding under an under-lease which reserved a nominal reversion only to the lessee; or

(c)   to the person who last paid the rent due under the lease either on his own behalf or as agent for the lessee or under-lessee;

and that a time reasonably sufficient to enable the repairs to be executed had elapsed since the time when the fact of the service of the notice came to the knowledge of any such person.

Where a notice has been sent by registered post addressed to a person at his last known place of abode in the United Kingdom, then, for the purposes of this subsection, that person shall be deemed, unless the contrary is proved, to have had knowledge of the fact that the notice had been served as from the time at which the letter would have been delivered in the ordinary course of post.

This subsection shall be construed as one with section one hundred and forty-six of the Law of Property Act 1925.

(3)   This section applies whether the lease was created before or after the commencement of this Act.

[203]

19   Provisions as to covenants not to assign, etc, without licence or consent

(1)   In all leases whether made before or after the commencement of this Act containing a covenant condition or agreement against assigning, under-letting, charging or parting with the possession of demised premises or any part thereof without licence or consent, such covenant condition or agreement shall, notwithstanding any express provision to the contrary, be deemed to be subject—

(a)   to a proviso to the effect that such licence or consent is not to be unreasonably withheld, but this proviso does not preclude the right of the landlord to require payment of a reasonable sum in respect of any legal or other expenses incurred in connection with such licence or consent; and

(b)   (if the lease is for more than forty years, and is made in consideration wholly or partially of the erection, or the substantial improvement, addition or alteration of buildings, and the lessor is not a Government department or local or public authority, or a statutory or public utility company) to a proviso to the effect that in the case of any assignment, under-letting, charging or parting with the possession (whether by the holders of the lease or any under-tenant whether immediate or not) effected more than seven years before the end of the term no consent or licence shall be required, if notice in writing of the transaction is given to the lessor within six months after the transaction is effected.

[(1A)   Where the landlord and the tenant under a qualifying lease have entered into an agreement specifying for the purposes of this subsection—

(a)   any circumstances in which the landlord may withhold his licence or consent to an assignment of the demised premises or any part of them, or

(b)   any conditions subject to which any such licence or consent may be granted,

then the landlord—

(i)   shall not be regarded as unreasonably withholding his licence or consent to any such assignment if he withholds it on the ground (and it is the case) that any such circumstances exist, and

(ii)   if he gives any such licence or consent subject to any such conditions, shall not be regarded as giving it subject to unreasonable conditions;

and section 1 of the Landlord and Tenant Act 1988 (qualified duty to consent to assignment etc) shall have effect subject to the provisions of this subsection.

(1B)   Subsection (1A) of this section applies to such an agreement as is mentioned in that subsection—

(a)   whether it is contained in the lease or not, and

(b)   whether it is made at the time when the lease is granted or at any other time falling before the application for the landlord's licence or consent is made.

(1C)   Subsection (1A) shall not, however, apply to any such agreement to the extent that any circumstances or conditions specified in it are framed by reference to any matter falling to be determined by the landlord or by any other person for the purposes of the agreement, unless under the terms of the agreement—

(a) that person's power to determine that matter is required to be exercised reasonably, or

(b) the tenant is given an unrestricted right to have any such determination reviewed by a person independent of both landlord and tenant whose identity is ascertainable by reference to the agreement,

and in the latter case the agreement provides for the determination made by any such independent person on the review to be conclusive as to the matter in question.

(1D) In its application to a qualifying lease, subsection (1)(b) of this section shall not have effect in relation to any assignment of the lease.

(1E) In subsections (1A) and (1D) of this section—

(a) "qualifying lease" means any lease which is a new tenancy for the purposes of section 1 of the Landlord and Tenant (Covenants) Act 1995 other than a residential lease, namely a lease by which a building or part of a building is let wholly or mainly as a single private residence; and

(b) references to assignment include parting with possession on assignment.]

(2) In all leases whether made before or after the commencement of this Act containing a covenant condition or agreement against the making of improvements without licence or consent, such covenant condition or agreement shall be deemed, notwithstanding any express provision to the contrary, to be subject to a proviso that such licence or consent is not to be unreasonably withheld; but this proviso does not preclude the right to require as a condition of such licence or consent the payment of a reasonable sum in respect of any damage to or diminution in the value of the premises or any neighbouring premises belonging to the landlord, and of any legal or other expenses properly incurred in connection with such licence or consent nor, in the case of an improvement which does not add to the letting value of the holding, does it preclude the right to require as a condition of such licence or consent, where such a requirement would be reasonable, an undertaking on the part of the tenant to reinstate the premises in the condition in which they were before the improvement was executed.

(3) In all leases whether made before or after the commencement of this Act containing a covenant condition or agreement against the alteration of the user of the demised premises, without licence or consent, such covenant condition or agreement shall, if the alteration does not involve any structural alteration of the premises, be deemed, notwithstanding any express provision to the contrary, to be subject to a proviso that no fine or sum of money in the nature of a fine, whether by way of increase of rent or otherwise, shall be payable for or in respect of such licence or consent; but this proviso does not preclude the right of the landlord to require payment of a reasonable sum in respect of any damage to or diminution in the value of the premises or any neighbouring premises belonging to him and of any legal or other expenses incurred in connection with such licence or consent.

Where a dispute as to the reasonableness of any such sum has been determined by a court of competent jurisdiction, the landlord shall be bound to grant the licence or consent on payment of the sum so determined to be reasonable.

(4) This section shall not apply to leases of agricultural holdings within the meaning of the [Agricultural Holdings Act 1986] [which are leases in relation to which that Act applies, or to farm business tenancies within the meaning of the Agricultural Tenancies Act 1995], and paragraph (b) of subsection (1), subsection (2) and subsection (3) of this section shall not apply to mining leases.

[204]

NOTES

Sub-ss (1A)–(1E): inserted by the Landlord and Tenant (Covenants) Act 1995, s 22.

Sub-s (4): words in first pair of square brackets substituted by the Agricultural Holdings Act 1986, s 100, Sch 14, para 15; words in second pair of square brackets inserted by the Agricultural Tenancies Act 1995, s 40, Schedule, para 6.

Modification: sub-ss (1)–(3) are modified, where the RTM company has acquired the right to manage, by the Commonhold and Leasehold Reform Act 2002, s 102, Sch 7, para 1.

20 Apportionment of rents

(1) An order of apportionment of a rent reserved by a lease or any such other rent or payment as is mentioned in section ten of the Inclosure Act 1854, may be made by the [Secretary of State] under sections ten to fourteen of that Act, on the application of any person interested in the rent or payment, or any part thereof, or in the land in respect of which such rent or payment is payable, without the concurrence of any other person:

Provided that the Minister may in any such case, on the application of any person entitled to the rent or payment or any part thereof, require as a condition of making the order that any apportioned part of the rent or payment which does not exceed the yearly sum of [£5] shall be redeemed forthwith [in accordance with sections 8 to 10 of the Rentcharges Act 1977 (which, for the purposes of this section, shall have effect with the necessary modifications)].

[(1A) An order of apportionment under sections 10 to 14 of the said Act of 1854 may provide for the amount apportioned to any part of the land in respect of which the rent or payment is payable to be nil.]

(2) Where the reason for the application was due to any action taken by a person other than the applicant, the Minister shall, notwithstanding anything in section fourteen of the Inclosure Act 1854, have power to direct by whom and in what manner the expenses of the application or any part thereof are to be paid.

[205]

NOTES

Sub-s (1): words in first pair of square brackets substituted by virtue of the Secretary of State for the Environment Order 1970, SI 1970/1681; sum in second pair of square brackets substituted by the Housing Act 1980, s 143(1); words in third pair of square brackets substituted by the Rentcharges Act 1977, s 17(1), (4), Sch 1, para 3.

Sub-s (1A): inserted by the Housing Act 1980, s 143(3).

Transfer of functions: functions of the Secretary of State, so far as exercisable in relation to Wales, are transferred to the National Assembly for Wales, by the National Assembly for Wales (Transfer of Functions) Order 1999, SI 1999/672, art 2, Sch 1.

PART III
GENERAL

[21 The tribunal

The tribunal for the purposes of Part I of this Act shall be the court exercising jurisdiction in accordance with the provisions of section sixty-three of the Landlord and Tenant Act 1954.]

[206]

NOTES

Substituted by the Landlord and Tenant Act 1954, s 63(10).

22 *(Repealed by the Landlord and Tenant Act 1954, s 68(1), Sch 7, Pt II.)*

23 Service of notices

(1) Any notice, request, demand or other instrument under this Act shall be in writing and may be served on the person on whom it is to be served either personally, or by leaving it for him at his last known place of abode in England or Wales, or by sending it through the post in a registered letter addressed to him there, or, in the case of a local or public authority or a statutory or a public utility company, to the secretary or other proper officer at the principal office of such authority or company, and in the case of a notice to a landlord, the person on whom it is to be served shall include any agent of the landlord duly authorised in that behalf.

(2) Unless or until a tenant of a holding shall have received notice that the person theretofore entitled to the rents and profits of the holding (hereinafter referred to as "the original landlord") has ceased to be so entitled, and also notice of the name and address of the person who has become entitled to such rents and profits, any claim, notice, request, demand, or other instrument, which the tenant shall serve upon or deliver to the original landlord shall be deemed to have been served upon or delivered to the landlord of such holding.

[207]

24 Application to Crown, Duchy, ecclesiastical and charity lands

(1) This Act shall apply to land belonging to His Majesty in right of the Crown or the Duchy of Lancaster and to land belonging to the Duchy of Cornwall, and to land belonging to any Government department, and for that purpose the provisions of the Agricultural Holdings Act 1923, relating to Crown and Duchy Lands, as set out and adapted in Part I of the Second Schedule to this Act, shall have effect.

(2)   The provisions of the Agricultural Holdings Act 1923, with respect to the application of that Act to ecclesiastical and charity lands, as set out and adapted in Part II of the Second Schedule to this Act, shall apply for the purposes of this Act.

(3)   ...

(4)   Where any land is vested in the [official custodian for charities] in trust for any charity, the trustees of the charity and not the [custodian] shall be deemed to be the landlord for the purposes of this Act.

[208]

NOTES

Sub-s (3): repealed by the Endowments and Glebe Measure 1976, s 47(4), Sch 8.
Sub-s (4): words in square brackets substituted by the Charities Act 1960, s 48(1), Sch 6.
Agricultural Holdings Act 1923: see now the Agricultural Holdings Act 1986, ss 86(4), 95 at **[493]**, **[503]**.

25   Interpretation

(1)   For the purposes of this Act, unless the context otherwise requires—

The expression "tenant" means any person entitled in possession to the holding under any contract of tenancy, whether the interest of such tenant was acquired by original contract, assignment, operation of law or otherwise;

The expression "landlord" means any person who under a lease is, as between himself and the tenant or other lessee, for the time being entitled to the rents and profits of the demised premises payable under the lease;

The expression "predecessor in title" in relation to a tenant or landlord means any person through whom the tenant or landlord has derived title, whether by assignment, by will, by intestacy, or by operation of law;

The expression "lease" means a lease, under-lease or other tenancy, assignment operating as a lease or under-lease, or an agreement for such lease, under-lease tenancy, or assignment;

The expression "mining lease" means a lease for any mining purpose or purposes connected therewith, and "mining purposes" include the sinking and searching for, winning, working, getting, making merchantable, smelting or otherwise converting or working for the purposes of any manufacture, carrying away, and disposing of mines and minerals, in or under land, and the erection of buildings, and the execution of engineering and other works suitable for those purposes;

The expression "term of years absolute" has the same meaning as in the Law of Property Act 1925;

The expression "statutory company" means any company constituted by or under an Act of Parliament to construct, work or carry on any ... , tramway, hydraulic power, dock, canal or railway undertaking; and the expression "public utility company" means any company within the meaning of the Companies (Consolidation) Act 1908, or a society registered under the Industrial and Provident Societies Acts 1893 to 1913, carrying on any such undertaking;

The expression "prescribed" means [prescribed by rules of court or by a practice direction].

(2)   The designation of landlord and tenant shall continue to apply to the parties until the conclusion of any proceedings taken under or in pursuance of this Act in respect of compensation.

[209]

NOTES

Sub-s (1): in definition "statutory company" words omitted repealed by the Gas Act 1986, s 67(4), Sch 9, Pt I, the Water Act 1989, s 109, Sch 27, Pt I and the Electricity Act 1989, s 112(4), Sch 18; in definition "prescribed" words in square brackets substituted by the Civil Procedure (Modification of Enactments) Order 2001, SI 2001/2717, art 3.
Industrial and Provident Societies Act 1893 to 1913: repealed and replaced by the Industrial and Provident Societies Act 1965.

26   Short title, commencement and extent

(1)   This Act may be cited as the Landlord and Tenant Act 1927.

(2) ...

(3) This Act shall extend to England and Wales only.

[210]

NOTES

Sub-s (2): repealed by the Statute Law Revision Act 1950.

SCHEDULES

FIRST SCHEDULE
PROVISIONS AS TO CHARGES

Section 12

(1) A landlord, on paying to the tenant the amount due to him under Part I of this Act, in respect of compensation for an improvement ... under that Part, or on expending after notice given in accordance with that Part such amount as may be necessary to execute an improvement, shall be entitled to obtain from [the Minister of Agriculture, Fisheries and Food] (hereinafter referred to as the Minister) an order in favour of himself and the persons deriving title under him charging the holding, or any part thereof, with repayment of the amount paid or expended, including any proper costs, charges or expenses incurred by a landlord in opposing any proposal by a tenant to execute an improvement or in contesting a claim for compensation, and of all costs properly incurred by him in obtaining the charge, with such interest, and by such instalments, and with such directions for giving effect to the charge, as the Minister thinks fit.

(2) Where the landlord obtaining the charge is not an absolute owner of the holding for his own benefit, no instalment or interest shall be made payable after the time when the improvement ... in respect whereof compensation is paid will, in the opinion of the Minister, have become exhausted.

(3) Where the estate or interest of a landlord is determinable or liable to forfeiture by reason of his creating or suffering any charge thereon, that estate or interest shall not be determined or forfeited by reason of his obtaining such a charge, anything in any deed, will or other instrument to the contrary thereof notwithstanding.

(4) The sum charged shall be a charge on the holding, or the part thereof charged, for the landlord's interest therein and for interests in the reversion immediately expectant on the termination of the lease; but so that, in any case where the landlord's interest is an interest in a leasehold, the charge shall not extend beyond that leasehold interest.

(5) Any company now or hereafter incorporated by Parliament, and having power to advance money for the improvement of land, may take an assignment of any charge made under this Schedule, upon such terms and conditions as may be agreed upon between the company and the person entitled to the charge, and may assign any charge so acquired by them.

(6) Where a charge may be made under this Schedule for compensation due under an award, the tribunal making the award shall, at the request and cost of the person entitled to obtain the charge, certify the amount to be charged and the term for which the charge may properly be made, having regard to the time at which each improvement ... in respect of which compensation is awarded is to be deemed to be exhausted.

(7) A charge under this Schedule may be registered under section ten of the Land Charges Act 1925 as a land charge of Class A.

[211]

NOTES

Para (1): words omitted repealed by the Landlord and Tenant Act 1954, s 45, Sch 7, Pt I; words in square brackets substituted by virtue of the Transfer of Functions (Ministry of Food) Order 1955, SI 1955/554.

Paras (2), (6): words omitted repealed by the Landlord and Tenant Act 1954, s 45, Sch 7, Pt I.

Minister of Agriculture, Fisheries and Food: the Ministry of Agriculture, Fisheries and Food was dissolved by the Ministry of Agriculture, Fisheries and Food (Dissolution) Order 2002, SI 2002/794. Subject to specific provision to the contrary, the functions of the Minister were transferred to the Secretary of State, and the property, rights and liabilities of the Minister were transferred to the Secretary of State for Environment, Food and Rural Affairs.

Land Charges Act 1925, s 10: repealed, see now the Land Charges Act 1972, Sch 2.

SECOND SCHEDULE

Section 24

PART I
APPLICATION TO CROWN AND DUCHY LAND

1.—(a) With respect to any land belonging to His Majesty in right of the Crown, or to a Government department, for the purposes of this Act, the Commissioners of Crown Lands, or other the proper officer or body having charge of the land for the time being, or, in case there is no such officer or body, then such person as His Majesty may appoint in writing under the Royal Sign Manual, shall represent His Majesty, and shall be deemed to be the landlord.

(b) ...

2.—(a) With respect to land belonging to His Majesty in right of the Duchy of Lancaster, for the purposes of this Act, the Chancellor of the Duchy shall represent His Majesty, and shall be deemed to be the landlord.

(b) The amount of any compensation under Part I of this Act payable by the Chancellor of the Duchy shall be raised and paid as an expense incurred in improvement of land belonging to His Majesty in right of the Duchy within section twenty-five of the Act of the fifty-seventh year of King George the Third, chapter ninety-seven.

3.—(a) With respect to land belonging to the Duchy of Cornwall, for the purposes of this Act, such person as the Duke of Cornwall, or the possessor for the time being of the Duchy of Cornwall appoints, shall represent the Duke of Cornwall or other the possessor aforesaid, and be deemed to be the landlord, and may do any act or thing under this Act which a landlord is authorised or required to do thereunder.

(b) Any compensation under Part I of this Act payable by the Duke of Cornwall, or other the possessor aforesaid, shall be paid, and advances therefor made, in the manner and subject to the provisions of section eight of the Duchy of Cornwall Management Act 1863, with respect to improvements of land mentioned in that section.

[212]

NOTES

Para 1: sub-para (b) repealed by the Crown Estate Act 1961, s 9(4), Sch 3, Pt II.

Section twenty-five of the Act of the fifty-seventh year of King George the Third, chapter ninety-seven: see the Land Revenues of the Crown Act 1817, s 25.

PART II
APPLICATION TO ECCLESIASTICAL AND CHARITY LAND

1.—(a) Where lands are assigned or secured as the endowment of a see, the powers by this Act conferred on a landlord in respect of charging land shall not be exercised by the bishop in respect of those lands, except with the previous approval in writing of the Estates Committee of the Ecclesiastical Commissioners.

(b) ...

(c) The Ecclesiastical Commissioners may, if they think fit, on behalf of an ecclesiastical corporation, out of any money in their hands, pay to the tenant the amount of compensation due to him under Part I of this Act, and thereupon they may, instead of the corporation obtain from the minister a charge on the holding in respect thereof in favour of themselves, ...

2. The powers by this Act conferred on a landlord in respect of charging land shall not be exercised by trustees for ecclesiastical or charitable purposes, except with the approval in writing of the [Charity Commission] or the Board of Education, as the case may require.

[213]

NOTES

Para 1: words omitted repealed by the Endowments and Glebe Measure 1976, s 47(4), Sch 8.

Para 2: words in square brackets substituted by the Charities Act 2006, s 75(1), Sch 8, para 20.

LAW OF PROPERTY (AMENDMENT) ACT 1929

(19 & 20 Geo 5 c 9)

An Act to amend the provisions of the Law of Property Act, 1925, relating to relief against forfeiture of under-leases

[5 February 1929]

1 Relief of under-lessees against breach of covenant

Nothing in subsection (8), subsection (9) or subsection (10) of section one hundred and forty-six of the Law of Property Act 1925 (which relates to restrictions on and relief against forfeiture of leases and under-leases), shall affect the provisions of subsection (4) of the said section.

[214]

2 Short title

This Act may be cited as the Law of Property (Amendment) Act 1929, and the Law of Property Act 1925, the Law of Property (Amendment) Act 1926, so far as it amends that Act, and this Act may be cited together as the Law of Property Acts 1925 to 1929.

[215]

LEASEHOLD PROPERTY (REPAIRS) ACT 1938

(1 & 2 Geo 6 c 34)

ARRANGEMENT OF SECTIONS

An Act to amend the law as to the enforcement by landlords of obligations to repair and similar obligations arising under leases

[23 June 1938]

1 Restriction on enforcement of repairing covenants in long leases of small houses

(1)   Where a lessor serves on a lessee under sub-section (1) of section one hundred and forty-six of the Law of Property Act 1925, a notice that relates to a breach of a covenant or agreement to keep or put in repair during the currency of the lease [all or any of the property comprised in the lease], and at the date of the service of the notice [three] years or more of the term of the lease remain unexpired, the lessee may within twenty-eight days from that date serve on the lessor a counter-notice to the effect that he claims the benefit of this Act.

(2)   A right to damages for a breach of such a covenant as aforesaid shall not be enforceable by action commenced at any time at which [three] years or more of the term of the lease remain unexpired unless the lessor has served on the lessee not less than one month before the commencement of the action such a notice as is specified in subsection (1) of section one hundred and forty-six of the Law of Property Act 1925, and where a notice is served under this subsection, the lessee may, within twenty-eight days from the date of the service thereof, serve on the lessor a counter-notice to the effect that he claims the benefit of this Act.

(3)   Where a counter-notice is served by a lessee under this section, then, notwithstanding anything in any enactment or rule of law, no proceedings, by action or otherwise, shall be taken by the lessor for the enforcement of any right of re-entry or forfeiture under any proviso

or stipulation in the lease for breach of the covenant or agreement in question, or for damages for breach thereof, otherwise than with the leave of the court.

(4)   A notice served under subsection (1) of section one hundred and forty-six of the Law of Property Act 1925, in the circumstances specified in subsection (1) of this section, and a notice served under subsection (2) of this section shall not be valid unless it contains a statement, in characters not less conspicuous than those used in any other part of the notice, to the effect that the lessee is entitled under this Act to serve on the lessor a counter-notice claiming the benefit of this Act, and a statement in the like characters specifying the time within which, and the manner in which, under this Act a counter-notice may be served and specifying the name and address for service of the lessor.

(5)   Leave for the purposes of this section shall not be given unless the lessor proves—
   (a)   that the immediate remedying of the breach in question is requisite for preventing substantial diminution in the value of his reversion, or that the value thereof has been substantially diminished by the breach;
   (b)   that the immediate remedying of the breach is required for giving effect in relation to the [premises] to the purposes of any enactment, or of any byelaw or other provision having effect under an enactment, [or for giving effect to any order of a court or requirement of any authority under any enactment or any such byelaw or other provision as aforesaid];
   (c)   in a case in which the lessee is not in occupation of the whole of the [premises as respects which the covenant or agreement is proposed to be enforced], that the immediate remedying of the breach is required in the interests of the occupier of [those premises] or of part thereof;
   (d)   that the breach can be immediately remedied at an expense that is relatively small in comparison with the much greater expense that would probably be occasioned by postponement of the necessary work; or
   (e)   special circumstances which in the opinion of the court, render it just and equitable that leave should be given.

(6)   The court may, in granting or in refusing leave for the purposes of this section impose such terms and conditions on the lessor or on the lessee as it may think fit.

[216]

NOTES

Sub-ss (1), (2), (5): words in square brackets substituted by the Landlord and Tenant Act 1954, s 51(2), (5).

2 Restriction on right to recover expenses of survey, etc

A lessor on whom a counter-notice is served under the preceding section shall not be entitled to the benefit of subsection (3) of section one hundred and forty-six of the Law of Property Act 1925, (which relates to costs and expenses incurred by a lessor in reference to breaches of covenant), so far as regards any costs or expenses incurred in reference to the breach in question, unless he makes an application for leave for the purposes of the preceding section, and on such an application the court shall have power to direct whether and to what extent the lessor is to be entitled to the benefit thereof.

[217]

3 Saving for obligation to repair on taking possession

This Act shall not apply to a breach of a covenant or agreement in so far as it imposes on the lessee an obligation to put [premises] in repair that is to be performed upon the lessee taking possession of the premises or within a reasonable time thereafter.

[218]

NOTES

Word in square brackets substituted by the Landlord and Tenant Act 1954, s 51(2).

4   *(Repealed by the Landlord and Tenant Act 1954, s 51(2).)*

5 Application to past breaches

This Act applies to leases created, and to breaches occurring, before or after the commencement of this Act.

[219]

6 Court having jurisdiction under this Act

(1)   In this Act the expression "the court" means the county court, except in a case which any proceedings by action for which leave may be given would have to be taken in a court other than the county court, and means in the said excepted case that other court.

(2)   …

[220]

PART I
STATUTES

NOTES
Sub-s (2): repealed by the County Courts Act 1959, s 204, Sch 3.

7 Application of certain provisions of 15 and 16 Geo 5 c 20

(1)   In this Act the expressions "lessor", "lessee" and "lease" have the meanings assigned to them respectively by sections one hundred and forty-six and one hundred and fifty-four of the Law of Property Act 1925, except that they do not include any reference to such a grant as is mentioned in the said section one hundred and forty-six, or to the person making, or to the grantee under such a grant, or to persons deriving title under such a person; and "lease" means a lease for a term of [seven years or more, not being a lease of an agricultural holding within the meaning of the [Agricultural Holdings Act 1986]] [which is a lease in relation to which that Act applies and not being a farm business tenancy within the meaning of the Agricultural Tenancies Act 1995].

(2)   The provisions of section one hundred and ninety-six of the said Act (which relate to the service of notices) shall extend to notices and counter-notices required or authorised by this Act.

[221]

NOTES
Sub-s (1): words in first (outer) pair of square brackets substituted by the Landlord and Tenant Act 1954, s 51(2), words in second (inner) pair of square brackets substituted by the Agricultural Holdings Act 1986, s 100, Sch 14, para 17; words in third pair of square brackets added by the Agricultural Tenancies Act 1995, s 40, Schedule, para 8.

8 Short title and extent

(1)   This Act may be cited as the Leasehold Property (Repairs) Act 1938.

(2)   This Act shall not extend to Scotland or to Northern Ireland.

[222]

AGRICULTURE ACT 1947

(10 & 11 Geo 6 c 48)

ARRANGEMENT OF SECTIONS

PART II
GOOD ESTATE MANAGEMENT AND GOOD HUSBANDRY

Rules of good estate management and good husbandry

PART V
ADMINISTRATIVE AND GENERAL

Agricultural Land Tribunals

Supplementary

An Act to make further provision for agriculture

[6 August 1947]

1–8   *((Pt I) Repealed by the Agriculture Act 1993, s 64(1), Sch 5 (ss 3–7 previously repealed subject to savings by the Agriculture Act 1957, s 36(1)(a), (3), Sch 4, Pt I).)*

PART II
GOOD ESTATE MANAGEMENT AND GOOD HUSBANDRY

9   *(Repealed by the Agriculture Act 1958, s 10(1), Sch 2, Pt I.)*

Rules of good estate management and good husbandry

10 Good estate management

(1)   For the purposes of this Act, an owner of agricultural land shall be deemed to fulfil his responsibilities to manage it in accordance with the rules of good estate management in so far as his management of the land and (so far as it affects the management of that land) of other land managed by him is such as to be reasonably adequate, having regard to the character and situation of the land and other relevant circumstances, to enable an occupier of the land reasonably skilled in husbandry to maintain efficient production as respects both the kind of produce and the quality and quantity thereof.

(2)   In determining whether the management of land is such as aforesaid, regard shall be had, but without prejudice to the generality of the provisions of the last foregoing subsection, to the extent to which the owner is providing, improving, maintaining and repairing fixed equipment on the land in so far as is necessary to enable an occupier of the land reasonably skilled in husbandry to maintain efficient production as aforesaid.

(3)   The responsibilities under the rules of good estate management of an owner of land in the occupation of another person shall not in relation to the maintenance and repair of fixed equipment include an obligation to do anything which that other person is under an obligation to do by virtue of any agreement.

[223]

11 Good husbandry

(1)   For the purposes of this Act, the occupier of an agricultural unit shall be deemed to fulfil his responsibilities to farm it in accordance with the rules of good husbandry in so far as the extent to which and the manner in which the unit is being farmed (as respects both the kind of operations carried out and the way in which they are carried out) is such that, having regard to the character and situation of the unit, the standard of management thereof by the owner and other relevant circumstances, the occupier is maintaining a reasonable standard of efficient production, as respects both the kind of produce and the quality and quantity thereof, while keeping the unit in a condition to enable such a standard to be maintained in the future.

(2)   In determining whether the manner in which a unit is being farmed is such as aforesaid, regard shall be had, but without prejudice to the generality of the provisions of the last foregoing subsection, to the extent to which—

    (a)   permanent pasture is being properly mown or grazed and maintained in a good state of cultivation and fertility and in good condition;

   (b)   the manner in which arable land is being cropped is such as to maintain that land clean and in a good state of cultivation and fertility and in good condition;

   (c)   the unit is properly stocked where the system of farming practised requires the keeping of livestock, and an efficient standard of management of livestock is maintained where livestock are kept and of breeding where the breeding of livestock is carried out;

   (d)   the necessary steps are being taken to secure and maintain crops and livestock free from disease and from infestation by insects and other pests;

   (e)   the necessary steps are being taken for the protection and preservation of crops harvested or lifted, or in course of being harvested or lifted;

   (f)   the necessary work of maintenance and repair is being carried out.

(3)   The responsibilities under the rules of good husbandry of an occupier of an agricultural unit which is not owned by him shall not include an obligation to carry out any work of maintenance or repair which the owner of the unit or any part thereof is under an obligation to carry out in order to fulfil his responsibilities to manage in accordance with the rules of good estate management.

[224]

12–67   (*Ss 12, 13, 14(1)–(4), 15–19, 53 repealed by the Agriculture Act 1958, ss 1(1), 10(1), Sch 2, Pt I; ss 14(5)–(8), 20 repealed with savings by the Agriculture Act 1958, ss 1(1), 10(1), (2), Sch 2, Pt I; s 21 repealed with a saving by the Agriculture Act 1958, s 10(1), (3), Sch 2, Pt I; ss 22–46 repealed by the Agricultural Holdings Act 1948, ss 98–100, Sch 8; ss 47–52, 54–56, 60–66 repealed with savings by the Agriculture Act 1970, ss 64(1), 113(3), Sch 3, Sch 5, Pt III; ss 57–59 repealed by the Statute Law (Repeals) Act 2004; s 67 outside the scope of this work.*)

PART V
ADMINISTRATIVE AND GENERAL

68–72   (*Ss 68–70 repealed by the Agriculture (Miscellaneous Provisions) Act 1963, s 18(2), Schedule, Pt I; ss 71, 72 repealed by the Agriculture (Miscellaneous Provisions) Act 1972, ss 21(1), 26(3), Sch 6.*)

Agricultural Land Tribunals

73 Establishment, constitution and procedure of Agricultural Land Tribunals

(1)   [For the purposes of this section the Lord Chancellor shall, after consulting the Chairman of the Agricultural Land Tribunals,] by order constitute such number of areas, together comprising the whole of England and Wales, as he may consider expedient, and for each area so constituted there shall be established an Agricultural Land Tribunal, which shall be charged with the duty of [hearing and determining references and applications made to them under any enactment].

(2)   The provisions in that behalf of the Ninth Schedule to this Act shall have effect as to the constitution of Agricultural Land Tribunals and otherwise in relation thereto.

(3)   [The Lord Chancellor] may by order make provision for the procedure of Agricultural Land Tribunals, and in particular—

   [(aa) as to the manner in which applications are to be made to the Tribunals and the time within which they are to be made;]

   (a)   for the taking of evidence on oath, affirmation or otherwise, the cross-examination of witnesses, and for the summoning of witnesses in like manner as for the purposes of an arbitration under the [Agricultural Holdings Act 1986];

   (b)   for the recording and proof of the decisions of the Tribunals, and for enabling the Tribunals to decide by a majority;

   (c)   ...

(4)   An order under the last foregoing subsection may make different provision for the procedure on different classes of reference [or application] to the Tribunals.

[(5)   An Agricultural Land Tribunal may, for the purpose of hearing and determining applications and references made to them under any enactment, sit in two or more divisions, and, in relation to the hearing and determination of any such application or reference by such a division, that division shall be deemed to be the Tribunal.]

[225]

NOTES

Sub-s (1): words in first pair of square brackets substituted by the Constitutional Reform Act 2005, s 15(1), Sch 4, Pt 1, paras 29, 30; words in second pair of square brackets substituted by the Agriculture Act 1958, s 8(1), Sch 1, Pt I, para 3.

Sub-s (3): words in first pair of square brackets substituted, para (aa) inserted, and para (c) repealed, by the Agriculture Act 1958, s 8(1), Sch 1, Pt I, para 3; in para (a) words in square brackets substituted by the Agricultural Holdings Act 1986, s 100, Sch 14, para 18.

Sub-s (4): words in square brackets inserted by the Agriculture Act 1958, s 8(1), Sch 1, Pt I, para 3.

Sub-s (5): added by the Agriculture Act 1958, s 8(1), Sch 1, Pt I, para 3.

Transfer of functions: functions conferred on the Minister of Agriculture, Fisheries and Food in relation to Agricultural Land Tribunals by this section were transferred to the Lord Chancellor, though certain duties remained with the Minister, by the Agriculture Act 1958, s 5. The Ministry of Agriculture, Fisheries and Food was dissolved by the Ministry of Agriculture, Fisheries and Food (Dissolution) Order 2002, SI 2002/794, and subject to specific provision to the contrary, the functions of the Minister were transferred to the Secretary of State, and the property, rights and liabilities of the Minister were transferred to the Secretary of State for Environment, Food and Rural Affairs.

Orders: the Agricultural Lands Tribunal (Rules) Order 1978, SI 1978/259 at **[1044]**; the Agricultural Lands Tribunals (Succession to Agricultural Tenancies) Order 1984, SI 1984/1301 at **[1083]**.

74 Proceedings before Agricultural Land Tribunal on reference of Minister's proposals

(1) In any case where by any of the provisions of this Act a person is empowered to require that a proposal of the Minister to take any action shall be referred to the Agricultural Land Tribunal, then if within the prescribed time and in the prescribed manner the said person so requires, the proposal shall be referred accordingly.

(2) On any such reference the Tribunal shall determine—
  (a) whether the conditions as to which the Minister must be satisfied before taking the action are fulfilled, and
  (b) whether, having regard to their determination under the foregoing paragraph and to all the circumstances of the case, the Minister should or should not take the action proposed,

and shall report to the Minister accordingly; and the Minister shall forward a copy of the report to any person who availed himself of an opportunity to make representations to the Minister afforded to him under the provisions in question of this Act.

(3) In any such case as is mentioned in subsection (1) of this section the Minister shall not give effect to the proposal until the expiration of the period within which a reference to the Tribunal may be required.

(4) Where such a reference is duly required the Minister shall act in accordance with the report of the Tribunal and not otherwise.

(5) Forthwith after taking action in any such case as is mentioned in subsection (1) of this section the Minister shall serve notice thereof in writing on any person who under the provisions in question of this Act was entitled to be afforded an opportunity to make representations to the Minister.

[226]

NOTES

Transfer of functions: functions of the Minister, so far as exercisable in relation to Wales, are transferred to the National Assembly for Wales, by the National Assembly for Wales (Transfer of Functions) Order 1999, SI 1999/672, art 2, Sch 1. The Ministry of Agriculture, Fisheries and Food was dissolved by the Ministry of Agriculture, Fisheries and Food (Dissolution) Order 2002, SI 2002/794, and subject to specific provision to the contrary, the functions of the Minister were transferred to the Secretary of State, and the property, rights and liabilities of the Minister were transferred to the Secretary of State for Environment, Food and Rural Affairs.

75–102 (*Ss 75, 82, 90, 98–101 outside the scope of this work; ss 76(1), (3), s 91 repealed by the Agriculture Act 1958, s 10(6), Sch 3; ss 76(2), 102 repealed by the Weeds Act 1959, s 10, Schedule; s 77 repealed by the Agriculture (Miscellaneous Provisions) Act 1972, ss 18, 26(3), Sch 6; ss 78–81 repealed by the Agricultural Statistics Act 1979, s 7(2), Sch 2; ss 83, 84, 86, 88, 89, 92–95 repealed by the Statute Law (Repeals) Act 2004; s 85 repealed by the Statute Law (Repeals) Act 1973; s 87 repealed by the Agriculture (Miscellaneous Provisions)*

Act 1963, s 18(2), Schedule, Pt I; s 96 repealed by Statute Law (Repeals) Act 1993; s 97 repealed by the Statute Law (Repeals) Act 1986.)

Supplementary

103–108   (*S 103 repealed by the Agriculture Act 1986, s 24(5), Sch 4; ss 104–108 outside the scope of this work.*)

109   Interpretation

(1)   In this Act the expression "agricultural land" means land used for agriculture which is so used for the purposes of a trade or business, or which is designated by the Minister for the purposes of this subsection, and includes any land so designated as land which in the opinion of the Minister ought to be brought into use for agriculture:

Provided that no designation under this subsection shall extend—
  (a)   to land used as pleasure grounds, private gardens or allotment gardens, or
  (b)   to land kept or preserved mainly or exclusively for the purposes of sport or recreation, except where the Minister is satisfied that its use for agriculture would not be inconsistent with its use for the said purposes and it is so stated in the designation.

(2)   In this Act the expression "agricultural unit" means land which is occupied as a unit for agricultural purposes, including—
  (a)   any dwelling-house or other building occupied by the same person for the purpose of farming the land, and
  (b)   any other land falling within the definition in this Act of the expression "agricultural land" which is in the occupation of the same person, being land as to which the Minister is satisfied that having regard to the character and situation thereof and other relevant circumstances it ought in the interests of full and efficient production to be farmed in conjunction with the agricultural unit, and directs accordingly:

Provided that the Minister shall not give a direction under this subsection as respects any land unless it is for the time being not in use for any purpose which appears to him to be substantial having regard to the use to which it might be put for agriculture.

(3)   In this Act the following expressions have the meanings hereby respectively assigned to them, that is to say:—
  "agriculture" includes horticulture, fruit growing, seed growing, dairy farming and livestock breeding and keeping, the use of land as grazing land, meadow land, osier land, market gardens and nursery grounds, and the use of land for woodlands where that use is ancillary to the farming of land for other agricultural purposes, and "agricultural" shall be construed accordingly;
  "allotment garden" means an allotment not exceeding [0.10 hectare] in extent which is wholly or mainly cultivated by the occupier for the production of vegetables or fruit for consumption by himself or his family;
  "fixed equipment" includes any building or structure affixed to land and any works on, in, over or under land, and also includes anything grown on land for a purpose other than use after severance from the land, consumption of the thing grown or of produce thereof, or amenity, and references to fixed equipment on land shall be construed accordingly;
  "functions" includes powers and duties;
  "livestock" includes any creature kept for the production of food, wool, skins or fur, or for the purpose of its use in the farming of land;
  "pasture" includes meadow;
  "prescribed" has the meaning assigned to it by the last foregoing section;
  "produce" includes anything (whether live or dead) produced in the course of agriculture;
  "relevant circumstances", in relation to an owner or occupier, includes all circumstances affecting management or farming other than the personal circumstances of the owner or occupier.

(4)   References in this Act to any enactment shall be construed, except where the context otherwise requires, as references to that enactment as amended by or under any other enactment, including this Act.

(5)   References in this Act to the farming of land include references to the carrying on in relation to the land of any agricultural activity; and in relation to any agricultural activity the person having the right to carry it on shall be deemed to be the occupier of the land.

(6)   References in this Act to the use of land for agriculture include, in relation to land forming part of an agricultural unit, references to any use of the land in connection with the farming of the unit.

[227]

NOTES

Sub-s (3): in definition "allotment garden" words in square brackets substituted by the Agriculture Act 1947 (Amendment) Regulations 1978, SI 1978/446, reg 2(1).

Transfer of functions: functions of the Minister, so far as exercisable in relation to Wales, are transferred to the National Assembly for Wales, by the National Assembly for Wales (Transfer of Functions) Order 1999, SI 1999/672, art 2, Sch 1. The Ministry of Agriculture, Fisheries and Food was dissolved by the Ministry of Agriculture, Fisheries and Food (Dissolution) Order 2002, SI 2002/794, and subject to specific provision to the contrary, the functions of the Minister were transferred to the Secretary of State, and the property, rights and liabilities of the Minister were transferred to the Secretary of State for Environment, Food and Rural Affairs.

110   (*Repealed by the Agriculture Act 1958, s 10(6), Sch 3.*)

111   Short title, commencement and extent

(1)   This Act may be cited as the Agriculture Act 1947.

(2)   ...

(3)   This Act, except in so far as is expressly provided therein, shall not extend to Scotland or Northern Ireland.

[228]

NOTES

Sub-s (2): repealed by the Agriculture Act 1958, s 10(6), Sch 3.

(*First Schedule repealed by the Agriculture Act 1957, s 36(1), Sch 4, Pt I; Second and Eleventh Schedules repealed by the Statute Law (Repeals) Act 2004; Eighth Schedule, Pt II and Ninth Schedule outside the scope of this work; Third, Fourth, Fifth, Sixth and Seventh Schedules repealed by the Agricultural Holdings Act 1948, ss 98–100, Sch 8; Eighth Schedule, Pt I repealed by the Agriculture Act 1970, s 113(3), Sch 5, Pt III; Tenth Schedule repealed by the Agriculture (Miscellaneous Provisions) Act 1972, s 26(3), Sch 6; Twelfth Schedule repealed by the Agriculture (Miscellaneous Provisions) Act 1963, s 18(2), Schedule, Pt I; Thirteenth Schedule repealed by the Agriculture Act 1958, s 10(6), Sch 3.*)

ALLOTMENTS ACT 1950

(14 Geo 6 c 31)

ARRANGEMENT OF SECTIONS

Allotments

Abolition of contractual restrictions on keeping hens and rabbits

Supplementary

An Act to amend the law relating to allotments and to abolish restrictions on the keeping of hens and rabbits

[26 October 1950]

Allotments

1, 2   (*S 1(1) amends the Allotments Act 1922, s 1(1)(a) at* **[105]**; *s 1(2) repealed by the Statute Law (Repeals) Act 1973; s 2(1) substitutes the Allotments Act 1922, s 2(2) at* **[106]**; *s 2(2) repealed by the Statute Law (Repeals) Act 1973.*)

3 Compensation to tenant of an allotment garden for disturbance

(1)   Where a tenancy under which land let, whether before or after the passing of this Act, for use by the tenant as an allotment garden or to a local authority or association for the purpose of being sub-let for such use is terminated, as to the whole or any part of the land comprised in the tenancy—

    (a)   by re-entry under paragraph (b), (c) or (d) of subsection (1) of section one of the Allotments Act 1922; or

    (b)   where the landlord is himself a tenant, by the termination of his tenancy; or

    (c)   where the landlord is a local authority who have let the land under section ten of the Allotments Act 1922 by the termination of the right of occupation of the authority;

the tenant shall, notwithstanding any agreement to the contrary, be entitled, on quitting the land or that part thereof, as the case may be, to recover from the landlord compensation for the disturbance of an amount determined in accordance with subsection (2) of this section.

(2)   The amount of any compensation recoverable under this section shall be—

    (a)   where the tenancy terminates as to the whole of the land, an amount equal to one year's rent of the land at the rate at which rent was payable immediately before the termination of the tenancy;

    (b)   where the tenancy terminates as to part of the land, an amount bearing to the amount mentioned in the foregoing paragraph the same proportion that the area of that part bears to the area of the whole of the land.

(3)   Compensation under this section shall be in addition to any compensation to which the tenant may be entitled under the Allotments Act 1922.

(4)   Subsection (2) of section four of the Allotments Act 1922 (which enables the tenant of an allotment garden to recover compensation from a mortgagee who deprives him of possession) shall apply to compensation under this section as it applies to compensation under that Act.

(5)   ...

[229]

NOTES

Sub-s (5): repealed by the Statute Law (Repeals) Act 1973.

4 Right of landlord of an allotment garden to compensation for deterioration

(1)   Where the tenant of land let, whether before or after the passing of this Act, on a tenancy for use by the tenant as an allotment garden quits the land on the termination of the tenancy, the landlord shall, notwithstanding any agreement to the contrary, be entitled to recover from the tenant compensation in respect of any deterioration of the land caused by failure of the tenant to maintain it clean and in a good state of cultivation and fertility.

(2)   The amount of any compensation recoverable under this section shall be the cost, as at the date of the tenant's quitting the land, of making good the deterioration.

(3)   Where the tenant of land let on a tenancy for use by him as an allotment garden has remained therein during two or more tenancies, his landlord shall not be deprived of his right

to compensation under this section in respect of deterioration of the land by reason only that the tenancy during which an act or omission occurred which in whole or in part caused the deterioration was a tenancy other than the tenancy at the termination of which the tenant quits the land.

(4)   ...

[230]

___

NOTES

Sub-s (4): repealed by the Statute Law (Repeals) Act 1993.

___

5   Set-off of compensation against rent, etc

(1)   Out of any money payable to a tenant by way of compensation under section two of the Allotments Act 1922 or section three of this Act, the landlord shall be entitled to deduct any sum due to him from the tenant under or in respect of the tenancy (including any sum due by way of compensation under section four of this Act).

(2)   Out of any money due to the landlord from the tenant under or in respect of the tenancy (including any money due by way of compensation under section four of this Act), the tenant shall be entitled to deduct any sum payable to him by the landlord by way of compensation under section two of the Allotments Act 1922 or section three of this Act.

[231]

6   Exclusion of cottage holdings, and provisions as to war-time allotments

The foregoing provisions of this Act shall not apply to any parcel of land attached to a cottage, and the said provisions, other than those of section two, shall not apply to land let by a local authority under Regulation sixty-two A of the Defence (General) Regulations 1939; ... .

[232]

___

NOTES

Words omitted repealed by the Statute Law (Repeals) Act 2004.

Modification: modified to have effect as if the reference to the Defence (General) Regulations 1939, SR & O 1939/927, reg 62A included a reference to the Emergency Laws (Miscellaneous Provisions) Act 1953, s 5, by virtue of the Emergency Laws (Miscellaneous Provisions) Act 1953, s 5(3).

___

7   Application of provisions of the Allotments Act 1922 for purposes of preceding sections

Section six of the Allotments Act 1922 (which relates to the determination and recovery of compensation under the foregoing provisions of that Act) and section seven of that Act (which provides for the application of those provisions to Crown lands) shall have effect as if the references to those provisions included references to the foregoing provisions of this Act, and subsection (4) of section twenty-two of that Act (which provides, amongst other things, that, for the purposes of that Act, where land is used by the tenant thereof as an allotment garden, it shall, unless the contrary is proved, be deemed to have been let to him to be used as an allotment garden) shall have effect as if the reference to that Act included a reference to this Act.

[233]

8–11   (*S 8 amends the Allotments Act 1922, s 1(4) at* **[105]***; ss 9, 10 outside the scope of this work; s 11(1) repealed by the Decimal Currency Act 1969, s 17(2), Sch 4; s 11(2) repealed by the Parish Councils Act 1957, s 15(1), Sch 2.*)

Abolition of contractual restrictions on keeping hens and rabbits

12   Abolition of contractual restrictions on keeping hens and rabbits

(1)   Notwithstanding any provision to the contrary in any lease or tenancy or in any covenant, contract or undertaking relating to the use to be made of any land, it shall be lawful for the occupier of any land to keep, otherwise than by way of trade or business, hens or rabbits in any place on the land and to erect or place and maintain such buildings or structures on the land as are reasonably necessary for that purpose:

Provided that nothing in this subsection shall authorise any hens or rabbits to be kept in such a place or in such a manner as to be prejudicial to health or a nuisance or affect the operation of any enactment.

(2)   …

[234]

NOTES
Sub-s (2): repealed by the Statute Law (Repeals) Act 1973.

Supplementary

13   (*Outside the scope of this work.*)

14 Interpretation

(1)   In this Act the expressions "allotment garden" and "landlord" have the same meanings as they have for the purposes of the Allotments Act 1922 and the provisions of subsection (1) of section twenty-two of that Act relating to the continued application to parties of the designations of landlord and tenant shall apply for the purposes of this Act as they apply for the purposes of that Act.

(2)   References in this Act to any other enactment shall, except so far as the context otherwise requires, be construed as references to that enactment as amended by any subsequent enactment, including this Act.

[235]

15 Short title, citation, extent and repeal

(1)   This Act may be cited as the Allotments Act 1950 and the Allotments Acts 1908 to 1931 and this Act may be cited together as the Allotments Acts 1908 to 1950.

(2)   This Act shall not extend to Scotland or Northern Ireland.

(3)   …

[236]

NOTES
Sub-s (3): repealed by the Statute Law (Repeals) Act 1973.

(*Schedule repealed by the Statute Law (Repeals) Act 1973.*)

AGRICULTURE (MISCELLANEOUS PROVISIONS) ACT 1954

(2 & 3 Eliz 2 c 39)

An Act to continue the power to make grants or contributions in respect of field drainage, liming and other matters; to amend Part IV of the Agriculture Act 1947 with respect to the holdings to be treated as smallholdings, and to the contributions to losses of smallholdings authorities; to alter the manner of appointing nominated members of Agricultural Land Tribunals, and enable those Tribunals to award costs and to refer questions of law to the High Court; to amend the Agricultural Holdings Act 1948 with respect to the operation of certain notices to quit; to make further provision with respect to research and education in sugar beet growing, to the collection of waste for use as animal feedings stuffs, to preventing the spread of pests and diseases by imported bees and to the application of the Diseases of Animals Act 1950 to air transport; to amend the Seeds Act 1920 with respect to the consequences of contraventions of that Act, and to the delivery and effect of particulars given thereunder; to amend the law as to agricultural wages of holiday workers in Scotland; and to extend the Corn Returns Act 1882 to Scotland

[4 June 1954]

1–4 (*S 1 repealed by the Statute Law (Repeals) Act 1993; s 2 repealed by the Statute Law (Repeals) Act 1986; s 3 repealed by the Statute Law (Repeals) Act 2004; s 4 repealed by the Agriculture Act 1958, s 10(1), Sch 2, Pt I.*)

5 Power of Agricultural Land Tribunal to award costs

(1)   An Agricultural Land Tribunal, where it appears to them that any person concerned in a reference [or application] to them (including any Minister of the Crown or Government department so concerned) has acted frivolously, vexatiously or oppressively in applying for or in connection with the reference [or application] may order that person to pay to any other person either a specified sum in respect of the costs incurred by him at or with a view to the hearing or the taxed amount of those costs; and an order may be made under this subsection whether or not the reference [or application] proceeds to a hearing.

(2)   Any costs required by an order under this section to be taxed may be taxed in the county court according to such of the scales prescribed by county court rules for proceedings in the county court as may be directed by the order or, if the order gives no direction, by the county court.

(3)   Any sum payable by virtue of an order of an Agricultural Land Tribunal under this section shall, if the county court so orders, be recoverable by execution issued from the county court or otherwise as if payable under an order of that court; and, subject to county court rules, an application for an order of the county court under this subsection may be made *ex parte*.

(4)   The powers of the county court under this section may be exercised by the registrar.

[237]

NOTES

Sub-s (1): words in square brackets inserted by the Agriculture Act 1958, s 8(1), Sch 1, Pt I, para 26.

---

6 Power of Agricultural Land Tribunal to refer questions of Law to High Court

(1)   Any question of law arising in the course of proceedings before an Agricultural Land Tribunal may, at the request of any party to the proceedings, be referred by the Tribunal to the High Court for decision, whether before or after the Tribunal have given their decision in the proceedings.

(2)   Subject to the following provisions of this section, if an Agricultural Land Tribunal, after giving their decision in any proceedings, refuse any such request to refer a question to the High Court under this section, any person aggrieved by the refusal may apply to the High Court for an order directing them to do so.

(3)   ...

(4)   Provision shall be made by order under subsection (3) of section seventy-three of the Agriculture Act 1947 (which relates to the procedure of Agricultural Land Tribunals), for limiting the time for requesting a Tribunal to refer a question to the High Court under this section, and for requiring notice to be given to a Tribunal within a time limited by the order of any intended application to the High Court under this section; and provision shall be made by rules of court for limiting the time for instituting proceedings in the High Court under subsection (2) of this section.

(5)   Where, after an Agricultural Land Tribunal have given their decision in any proceedings, they refer a question to the High Court under this section, or receive notice of an intended application to the High Court for an order directing them to do so, effect shall not be given to the Tribunal's decision unless and until the Tribunal otherwise order after the proceedings in the High Court and any proceedings arising therefrom have been concluded (or the right to take or continue any such proceedings has lapsed); and any such order of the Tribunal shall, where necessary, modify their decision so as to give effect to the decision on any reference to the High Court and, in a case relating to a notice to quit, may postpone (or further postpone) the date at which the tenancy is to be terminated by the notice, if it has effect.

(6)   [The Lord Chancellor] may, by order under subsection (3) of section seventy-three of the Agriculture Act 1947, make such provision as he thinks necessary or expedient for enabling the chairman of an Agricultural Land Tribunal to exercise all or any of the Tribunal's powers under the last foregoing subsection, and for regulating any proceedings before an Agricultural Land Tribunal which are consequent on the reference of any question to the High

Court under this section or on the decision on such a reference, and enabling any such proceedings to be dealt with by an Agricultural Land Tribunal constituted for the purpose, where they cannot conveniently be dealt with by the Tribunal originally constituted for the purpose of the proceedings in the course of which the question arose.

(7)   ...

[238]

PART I
STATUTES

NOTES

Sub-s (3): repealed by the Agriculture Act 1958, ss 8(1), 10(1), Sch 1, Pt I, para 27, Sch 2, Pt I.
Sub-s (6): words in square brackets substituted by the Agriculture Act 1958, s 8(1), Sch 1, Pt I, para 27.
Sub-s (7): repealed by the Statute Law (Repeals) Act 2004.
Order: the Agriculture (Miscellaneous Provisions) Act 1954 (Commencement) Order 1954, SI 1954/1137.

7–14   (*S 7 repealed by the Agriculture (Miscellaneous Provisions) Act 1976, s 26(3), Sch 4, Pt II; s 8 repealed by the Sugar Act 1956, s 32(2); s 9 outside the scope of this work; s 10 repealed by the Bees Act 1980, s 5(3); s 11 repealed by the Animal Health Act 1981, s 96, Sch 6; s 12 repealed by the Plant Varieties and Seeds Act 1964, s 31(1), Sch 6; s 13 repealed by the Statute Law (Repeals) Act 1973; s 14 applies to Scotland only.*)

15   Construction of references to enactments

Any reference in this Act to any previous enactment shall, except in so far as the contrary intention appears, be construed as a reference to that enactment as amended, extended or applied by any subsequent enactment, including this Act.

[239]

16   (*Outside the scope of this work.*)

17   Short title and repeal

(1)   This Act may be cited as the Agriculture (Miscellaneous Provisions) Act 1954.

(2)   ...

[240]

NOTES

Sub-s (2): repealed by the Statute Law (Repeals) Act 1973.

(*First Schedule repealed by the Agriculture Act 1958, s 10(1), Sch 2, Pt I; Second Schedule repealed by the Animal Health Act 1981, s 96, Sch 6; Third Schedule repealed by the Statute Law (Repeals) Act 1973.*)

LANDLORD AND TENANT ACT 1954

(2 & 3 Eliz 2 c 56)

ARRANGEMENT OF SECTIONS

PART II
SECURITY OF TENURE FOR BUSINESS, PROFESSIONAL AND OTHER TENANTS

Tenancies to which Part II applies

Continuation and renewal of tenancies

Applications to court

General and supplementary provisions

PART III
COMPENSATION FOR IMPROVEMENTS

PART IV
MISCELLANEOUS AND SUPPLEMENTARY

An Act to provide security of tenure for occupying tenants under certain leases of residential property at low rents and for occupying sub-tenants of tenants under such leases; to enable tenants occupying property for business, professional or certain other purposes to obtain new tenancies in certain cases; to amend and extend the Landlord and Tenant Act 1927, the Leasehold Property (Repairs) Act 1938; and section eighty-four of the Law of Property Act 1925; to confer jurisdiction on the County Court in certain disputes between landlords and tenants; to make provision for the termination of tenancies of derelict land; and for purposes connected with the matters aforesaid.

[30 July 1954]

1–22   ((*Pt I) Ss 1–10, 12–14, 14A, 16–22 outside the scope of this work; s 11 repealed by the Rent Act 1957, s 26(3), Sch 8, Pt I; s 15 repealed by the Rent Act 1968, s 117(5), Sch 17.*)

PART II
SECURITY OF TENURE FOR BUSINESS, PROFESSIONAL AND OTHER TENANTS

NOTES
As to the exclusion of Part II (ss 23–46) of this Act in relation to leases or tenancies granted to contractors in respect of the running of any removal centre or part of a removal centre, see the Immigration and Asylum Act 1999, s 149(3).

Tenancies to which Part II applies

23   Tenancies to which Part II applies

(1)   Subject to the provisions of this Act, this Part of this Act applies to any tenancy where the property comprised in the tenancy is or includes premises which are occupied by the tenant and are so occupied for the purposes of a business carried on by him or for those and other purposes.

[(1A)   Occupation or the carrying on of a business—
  (a)   by a company in which the tenant has a controlling interest; or
  (b)   where the tenant is a company, by a person with a controlling interest in the company,
shall be treated for the purposes of this section as equivalent to occupation or, as the case may be, the carrying on of a business by the tenant.

(1B)   Accordingly references (however expressed) in this Part of this Act to the business of, or to use, occupation or enjoyment by, the tenant shall be construed as including references to the business of, or to use, occupation or enjoyment by, a company falling within subsection (1A)(a) above or a person falling within subsection (1A)(b) above.]

(2)   In this Part of this Act the expression "business" includes a trade, profession or employment and includes any activity carried on by a body of persons, whether corporate or unincorporate.

(3)   In the following provisions of this Part of this Act the expression "the holding", in relation to a tenancy to which this Part of this Act applies, means the property comprised in

the tenancy, there being excluded any part thereof which is occupied neither by the tenant nor by a person employed by the tenant and so employed for the purposes of a business by reason of which the tenancy is one to which this Part of this Act applies.

(4)   Where the tenant is carrying on a business, in all or any part of the property comprised in a tenancy, in breach of a prohibition (however expressed) of use for business purposes which subsists under the terms of the tenancy and extends to the whole of that property, this Part of this Act shall not apply to the tenancy unless the immediate landlord or his predecessor in title has consented to the breach or the immediate landlord has acquiesced therein.

In this subsection the reference to a prohibition of use for business purposes does not include a prohibition of use for the purposes of a specified business, or of use for purposes of any but a specified business, but save as aforesaid includes a prohibition of use for the purposes of some one or more only of the classes of business specified in the definition of that expression in subsection (2) of this section.

[241]

NOTES

Sub-ss (1A), (1B): inserted by the Regulatory Reform (Business Tenancies) (England and Wales) Order 2003, SI 2003/3096, arts 2, 13.

Continuation and renewal of tenancies

24   Continuation of tenancies to which Part II applies and grant of new tenancies

(1)   A tenancy to which this Part of this Act applies shall not come to an end unless terminated in accordance with the provisions of this Part of this Act; and, subject to the [following provisions of this Act either the tenant or the landlord under such a tenancy may apply to the court for an order for the grant of] a new tenancy—

(a)   if the landlord has given notice under [section 25 of this Act] to terminate the tenancy, or

(b)   if the tenant has made a request for a new tenancy in accordance with section twenty-six of this Act.

(2)   The last foregoing subsection shall not prevent the coming to an end of a tenancy by notice to quit given by the tenant, by surrender or forfeiture, or by the forfeiture of a superior tenancy [unless—

(a)   in the case of a notice to quit, the notice was given before the tenant had been in occupation in right of the tenancy for one month; ...

(b)   ...].

[(2A)   Neither the tenant nor the landlord may make an application under subsection (1) above if the other has made such an application and the application has been served.

(2B)   Neither the tenant nor the landlord may make such an application if the landlord has made an application under section 29(2) of this Act and the application has been served.

(2C)   The landlord may not withdraw an application under subsection (1) above unless the tenant consents to its withdrawal.]

(3)   Notwithstanding anything in subsection (1) of this section,—

(a)   where a tenancy to which this Part of this Act applies ceases to be such a tenancy, it shall not come to an end by reason only of the cesser, but if it was granted for a term of years certain and has been continued by subsection (1) of this section then (without prejudice to the termination thereof in accordance with any terms of the tenancy) it may be terminated by not less than three nor more than six months' notice in writing given by the landlord to the tenant;

(b)   where, at a time when a tenancy is not one to which this Part of this Act applies, the landlord gives notice to quit, the operation of the notice shall not be affected by reason that the tenancy becomes one to which this Part of this Act applies after the giving of the notice.

[242]

NOTES

Sub-s (1): words in first pair of square brackets substituted by the Regulatory Reform (Business Tenancies) (England and Wales) Order 2003, SI 2003/3096, arts 2, 3(1); words in second pair of square brackets substituted by the Law of Property Act 1969, s 3(2).

Sub-s (2): words in square brackets added by the Law of Property Act 1969, s 4(1); words omitted repealed by SI 2003/3096, art 28(2), Sch 6, subject to transitional provisions in art 29(2) thereof at **[1309]**.

Sub-ss (2A)–(2C): inserted by SI 2003/3096, arts 2, 3(2).

[24A Applications for determination of interim rent while tenancy continues

(1)   Subject to subsection (2) below, if—

  (a)   the landlord of a tenancy to which this Part of this Act applies has given notice under section 25 of this Act to terminate the tenancy; or

  (b)   the tenant of such a tenancy has made a request for a new tenancy in accordance with section 26 of this Act,

either of them may make an application to the court to determine a rent (an "interim rent") which the tenant is to pay while the tenancy ("the relevant tenancy") continues by virtue of section 24 of this Act and the court may order payment of an interim rent in accordance with section 24C or 24D of this Act.

(2)   Neither the tenant nor the landlord may make an application under subsection (1) above if the other has made such an application and has not withdrawn it.

(3)   No application shall be entertained under subsection (1) above if it is made more than six months after the termination of the relevant tenancy.]

[243]

NOTES

Commencement: 1 June 2004.

Substituted, together with ss 24B, 24C, 24D, for s 24A (as originally inserted by the Law of Property Act 1969, s 3(1)), by the Regulatory Reform (Business Tenancies) (England and Wales) Order 2003, SI 2003/3096, arts 2, 18.

[24B Date from which interim rent is payable

(1)   The interim rent determined on an application under section 24A(1) of this Act shall be payable from the appropriate date.

(2)   If an application under section 24A(1) of this Act is made in a case where the landlord has given a notice under section 25 of this Act, the appropriate date is the earliest date of termination that could have been specified in the landlord's notice.

(3)   If an application under section 24A(1) of this Act is made in a case where the tenant has made a request for a new tenancy under section 26 of this Act, the appropriate date is the earliest date that could have been specified in the tenant's request as the date from which the new tenancy is to begin.]

[244]

NOTES

Commencement: 1 June 2004.

Substituted as noted to s 24A at **[243]**.

[24C Amount of interim rent where new tenancy of whole premises granted and landlord not opposed

(1)   This section applies where—

  (a)   the landlord gave a notice under section 25 of this Act at a time when the tenant was in occupation of the whole of the property comprised in the relevant tenancy for purposes such as are mentioned in section 23(1) of this Act and stated in the notice that he was not opposed to the grant of a new tenancy; or

  (b)   the tenant made a request for a new tenancy under section 26 of this Act at a time when he was in occupation of the whole of that property for such purposes and the landlord did not give notice under subsection (6) of that section, and the landlord grants a new tenancy of the whole of the property comprised in the relevant tenancy to the tenant (whether as a result of an order for the grant of a new tenancy or otherwise).

(2)   Subject to the following provisions of this section, the rent payable under and at the commencement of the new tenancy shall also be the interim rent.

(3)   Subsection (2) above does not apply where—

    (a)   the landlord or the tenant shows to the satisfaction of the court that the interim rent under that subsection differs substantially from the relevant rent; or

    (b)   the landlord or the tenant shows to the satisfaction of the court that the terms of the new tenancy differ from the terms of the relevant tenancy to such an extent that the interim rent under that subsection is substantially different from the rent which (in default of such agreement) the court would have determined under section 34 of this Act to be payable under a tenancy which commenced on the same day as the new tenancy and whose other terms were the same as the relevant tenancy.

(4)   In this section "the relevant rent" means the rent which (in default of agreement between the landlord and the tenant) the court would have determined under section 34 of this Act to be payable under the new tenancy if the new tenancy had commenced on the appropriate date (within the meaning of section 24B of this Act).

(5)   The interim rent in a case where subsection (2) above does not apply by virtue only of subsection (3)(a) above is the relevant rent.

(6)   The interim rent in a case where subsection (2) above does not apply by virtue only of subsection (3)(b) above, or by virtue of subsection (3)(a) and (b) above, is the rent which it is reasonable for the tenant to pay while the relevant tenancy continues by virtue of section 24 of this Act.

(7)   In determining the interim rent under subsection (6) above the court shall have regard—

    (a)   to the rent payable under the terms of the relevant tenancy; and

    (b)   to the rent payable under any sub-tenancy of part of the property comprised in the relevant tenancy,

but otherwise subsections (1) and (2) of section 34 of this Act shall apply to the determination as they would apply to the determination of a rent under that section if a new tenancy of the whole of the property comprised in the relevant tenancy were granted to the tenant by order of the court and the duration of that new tenancy were the same as the duration of the new tenancy which is actually granted to the tenant.

(8)   In this section and section 24D of this Act "the relevant tenancy" has the same meaning as in section 24A of this Act.]

[245]

NOTES
Commencement: 1 June 2004.
Substituted as noted to s 24A at **[243]**.

[24D   Amount of interim rent in any other case

(1)   The interim rent in a case where section 24C of this Act does not apply is the rent which it is reasonable for the tenant to pay while the relevant tenancy continues by virtue of section 24 of this Act.

(2)   In determining the interim rent under subsection (1) above the court shall have regard—

    (a)   to the rent payable under the terms of the relevant tenancy; and

    (b)   to the rent payable under any sub-tenancy of part of the property comprised in the relevant tenancy,

but otherwise subsections (1) and (2) of section 34 of this Act shall apply to the determination as they would apply to the determination of a rent under that section if a new tenancy from year to year of the whole of the property comprised in the relevant tenancy were granted to the tenant by order of the court.

(3)   If the court—

    (a)   has made an order for the grant of a new tenancy and has ordered payment of interim rent in accordance with section 24C of this Act, but

    (b)   either—

        (i)   it subsequently revokes under section 36(2) of this Act the order for the grant of a new tenancy; or

        (ii)   the landlord and tenant agree not to act on the order,

the court on the application of the landlord or the tenant shall determine a new interim rent in accordance with subsections (1) and (2) above without a further application under section 24A(1) of this Act.]

[246]

NOTES

Commencement: 1 June 2004.

Substituted as noted to s 24A at **[243]**.

---

25 Termination of tenancy by the landlord

(1)   The landlord may terminate a tenancy to which this Part of this Act applies by a notice given to the tenant in the prescribed form specifying the date at which the tenancy is to come to an end (hereinafter referred to as "the date of termination"):

Provided that this subsection has effect subject to [the provisions of section 29B(4) of this Act and] the provisions of Part IV of this Act as to the interim continuation of tenancies pending the disposal of applications to the court.

(2)   Subject to the provisions of the next following subsection, a notice under this section shall not have effect unless it is given not more than twelve nor less than six months before the date of termination specified therein.

(3)   In the case of a tenancy which apart from this Act could have been brought to an end by notice to quit given by the landlord—

    (a)   the date of termination specified in a notice under this section shall not be earlier than the earliest date on which apart from this Part of this Act the tenancy could have been brought to an end by notice to quit given by the landlord on the date of the giving of the notice under this section; and

    (b)   where apart from this Part of this Act more than six months' notice to quit would have been required to bring the tenancy to an end, the last foregoing subsection shall have effect with the substitution for twelve months of a period six months longer than the length of notice to quit which would have been required as aforesaid.

(4)   In the case of any other tenancy, a notice under this section shall not specify a date of termination earlier than the date on which apart from this Part of this Act the tenancy would have come to an end by effluxion of time.

(5)   ...

[(6)   A notice under this section shall not have effect unless it states whether the landlord is opposed to the grant of a new tenancy to the tenant.

(7)   A notice under this section which states that the landlord is opposed to the grant of a new tenancy to the tenant shall not have effect unless it also specifies one or more of the grounds specified in section 30(1) of this Act as the ground or grounds for his opposition.

(8)   A notice under this section which states that the landlord is not opposed to the grant of a new tenancy to the tenant shall not have effect unless it sets out the landlord's proposals as to—

    (a)   the property to be comprised in the new tenancy (being either the whole or part of the property comprised in the current tenancy);

    (b)   the rent to be payable under the new tenancy; and

    (c)   the other terms of the new tenancy.]

[247]

NOTES

Sub-s (1): words in square brackets inserted by the Regulatory Reform (Business Tenancies) (England and Wales) Order 2003, SI 2003/3096, arts 2, 11, subject to transitional provisions in art 29(1) thereof at **[1309]**.

Sub-s (5): repealed by SI 2003/3096, arts 2, 4(1), 28(2), Sch 6, subject to transitional provisions in art 29(1) thereof at **[1309]**.

Sub-ss (6)–(8): substituted for original sub-s (6) by SI 2003/3096, arts 2, 4(2), subject to transitional provisions in art 29(1) thereof at **[1309]**.

Modification: where compulsory rights orders in respect of opencast coal operations are in existence, s 30(1)(f), (g) at **[254]** is modified for certain purposes of sub-s (6) above and ss 26(6), 31, at **[248]**, **[254]**, by the Opencast Coal Act 1958, s 37, Sch 7, para 21.

Notice ... in the prescribed form: the Forms are set out in the Landlord and Tenant Act 1954, Part 2 (Notices) Regulations 2004, SI 2004/1005, Sch 2 at **[1327]**–**[1343]**.

---

26 Tenant's request for a new tenancy

(1)   A tenant's request for a new tenancy may be made where the [current tenancy] is a tenancy granted for a term of years certain exceeding one year, whether or not continued by section twenty-four of this Act, or granted for a term of years certain and thereafter from year to year.

(2)   A tenant's request for a new tenancy shall be for a tenancy beginning with such date, not more than twelve nor less than six months after the making of the request, as may be specified therein:

Provided that the said date shall not be earlier than the date on which apart from this Act the current tenancy would come to an end by effluxion of time or could be brought to an end by notice to quit given by the tenant.

(3)   A tenant's request for a new tenancy shall not have effect unless it is made by notice in the prescribed form given to the landlord and sets out the tenant's proposals as to the property to be comprised in the new tenancy (being either the whole or part of the property comprised in the current tenancy), as to the rent to be payable under the new tenancy and as to the other terms of the new tenancy.

(4)   A tenant's request for a new tenancy shall not be made if the landlord has already given notice under the last foregoing section to terminate the current tenancy, or if the tenant has already given notice to quit or notice under the next following section; and no such notice shall be given by the landlord or the tenant after the making by the tenant of a request for a new tenancy.

(5)   Where the tenant makes a request for a new tenancy in accordance with the foregoing provisions of this section, the current tenancy shall, subject to the provisions of [sections 29B(4) and 36(2)] of this Act and the provisions of Part IV of this Act as to the interim continuation of tenancies, terminate immediately before the date specified in the request for the beginning of the new tenancy.

(6)   Within two months of the making of a tenant's request for a new tenancy the landlord may give notice to the tenant that he will oppose an application to the court for the grant of a new tenancy, and any such notice shall state on which of the grounds mentioned in section thirty of this Act the landlord will oppose the application.

[248]

NOTES

Sub-s (1): words in square brackets substituted by the Regulatory Reform (Business Tenancies) (England and Wales) Order 2003, SI 2003/3096, art 28(1), Sch 5, paras 1, 3, subject to transitional provisions in art 29(1) thereof at **[1309]**.

Sub-s (5): words in square brackets substituted by SI 2003/3096, arts 2, 12, subject to transitional provisions in art 29(1) thereof at **[1309]**.

Modification: modified as noted to s 25 at **[247]**.

Notice in the prescribed form: the Forms are set out in the Landlord and Tenant Act 1954, Part 2 (Notices) Regulations 2004, SI 2004/1005, Sch 2 at **[1327]**–**[1343]**.

---

27 Termination by tenant of tenancy for fixed term

(1)   Where the tenant under a tenancy to which this Part of this Act applies, being a tenancy granted for a term of years certain, gives to the immediate landlord, not later than three months before the date on which apart from this Act the tenancy would come to an end by effluxion of time, a notice in writing that the tenant does not desire the tenancy to be continued, section twenty-four of this Act shall not have effect in relation to the tenancy [unless the notice is given before the tenant has been in occupation in right of the tenancy for one month].

[(1A)   Section 24 of this Act shall not have effect in relation to a tenancy for a term of years certain where the tenant is not in occupation of the property comprised in the tenancy at the time when, apart from this Act, the tenancy would come to an end by effluxion of time.]

(2)   A tenancy granted for a term of years certain which is continuing by virtue of section twenty-four of this Act [shall not come to an end by reason only of the tenant ceasing to occupy the property comprised in the tenancy but] may be brought to an end on any ... day by not less than three months' notice in writing given by the tenant to the immediate landlord, whether the notice is given ... after the date on which apart from this Act the tenancy would have come to an end [or before that date, but not before the tenant has been in occupation in right of the tenancy for one month].

[(3)   Where a tenancy is terminated under subsection (2) above, any rent payable in respect of a period which begins before, and ends after, the tenancy is terminated shall be apportioned, and any rent paid by the tenant in excess of the amount apportioned to the period before termination shall be recoverable by him.]

[249]

NOTES
Sub-s (1): words in square brackets added by the Law of Property Act 1969, s 4(2)(a).
Sub-s (1A): inserted by the Regulatory Reform (Business Tenancies) (England and Wales) Order 2003, SI 2003/3096, arts 2, 25(1).
Sub-s (2): words in first pair of square brackets inserted and words omitted in first place repealed by SI 2003/2096, arts 2, 25(2), 28(2), Sch 6, subject to transitional provisions in art 29(2) thereof at **[1309]**; words omitted in second place repealed, and words in second pair of square brackets added, by the Law of Property Act 1969, s 4(2)(b).
Sub-s (3): added by SI 2003/3096, arts 2, 25(3).

28   Renewal of tenancies by agreement

Where the landlord and tenant agree for the grant to the tenant of a future tenancy of the holding, or of the holding with other land, on terms and from a date specified in the agreement, the current tenancy shall continue until that date but no longer, and shall not be a tenancy to which this Part of this Act applies.

[250]

[Applications to court

29   Order by court for grant of new tenancy or termination of current tenancy

(1)   Subject to the provisions of this Act, on an application under section 24(1) of this Act, the court shall make an order for the grant of a new tenancy and accordingly for the termination of the current tenancy immediately before the commencement of the new tenancy.

(2)   Subject to the following provisions of this Act, a landlord may apply to the court for an order for the termination of a tenancy to which this Part of this Act applies without the grant of a new tenancy—
    (a)   if he has given notice under section 25 of this Act that he is opposed to the grant of a new tenancy to the tenant; or
    (b)   if the tenant has made a request for a new tenancy in accordance with section 26 of this Act and the landlord has given notice under subsection (6) of that section.

(3)   The landlord may not make an application under subsection (2) above if either the tenant or the landlord has made an application under section 24(1) of this Act.

(4)   Subject to the provisions of this Act, where the landlord makes an application under subsection (2) above—
    (a)   if he establishes, to the satisfaction of the court, any of the grounds on which he is entitled to make the application in accordance with section 30 of this Act, the court shall make an order for the termination of the current tenancy in accordance with section 64 of this Act without the grant of a new tenancy; and
    (b)   if not, it shall make an order for the grant of a new tenancy and accordingly for the termination of the current tenancy immediately before the commencement of the new tenancy.

(5)   The court shall dismiss an application by the landlord under section 24(1) of this Act if the tenant informs the court that he does not want a new tenancy.

(6)   The landlord may not withdraw an application under subsection (2) above unless the tenant consents to its withdrawal.]

[251]

NOTES
Commencement: 1 June 2004.
Substituted, together with the preceding cross-heading, by the Regulatory Reform (Business Tenancies) (England and Wales) Order 2003, SI 2003/3096, arts 2, 5.

[29A   Time limits for applications to court

(1)   Subject to section 29B of this Act, the court shall not entertain an application—

(a)   by the tenant or the landlord under section 24(1) of this Act; or

(b)   by the landlord under section 29(2) of this Act,

if it is made after the end of the statutory period.

(2)In this section and section 29B of this Act "the statutory period" means a period ending—

(a)   where the landlord gave a notice under section 25 of this Act, on the date specified in his notice; and

(b)   where the tenant made a request for a new tenancy under section 26 of this Act, immediately before the date specified in his request.

(3)   Where the tenant has made a request for a new tenancy under section 26 of this Act, the court shall not entertain an application under section 24(1) of this Act which is made before the end of the period of two months beginning with the date of the making of the request, unless the application is made after the landlord has given a notice under section 26(6) of this Act.]

[252]

NOTES
Commencement: 1 June 2004.
Inserted, together with s 29B, by the Regulatory Reform (Business Tenancies) (England and Wales) Order 2003, SI 2003/3096, arts 2, 10.

[29B   Agreements extending time limits

(1)   After the landlord has given a notice under section 25 of this Act, or the tenant has made a request under section 26 of this Act, but before the end of the statutory period, the landlord and tenant may agree that an application such as is mentioned in section 29A(1) of this Act, may be made before the end of a period specified in the agreement which will expire after the end of the statutory period.

(2)   The landlord and tenant may from time to time by agreement further extend the period for making such an application, but any such agreement must be made before the end of the period specified in the current agreement.

(3)   Where an agreement is made under this section, the court may entertain an application such as is mentioned in section 29A(1) of this Act if it is made before the end of the period specified in the agreement.

(4)   Where an agreement is made under this section, or two or more agreements are made under this section, the landlord's notice under section 25 of this Act or tenant's request under section 26 of this Act shall be treated as terminating the tenancy at the end of the period specified in the agreement or, as the case may be, at the end of the period specified in the last of those agreements.]

[253]

NOTES
Commencement: 1 June 2004.
Inserted as noted to s 29A at **[252]**.

30   Opposition by landlord to application for new tenancy

(1)   The grounds on which a landlord may oppose an application under [section 24(1) of this Act, or make an application under section 29(2) of this Act,] are such of the following

grounds as may be stated in the landlord's notice under section twenty-five of this Act or, as the case may be, under subsection (6) of section twenty-six thereof, that is to say—

(a)   where under the current tenancy the tenant has any obligations as respects the repair and maintenance of the holding, that the tenant ought not to be granted a new tenancy in view of the state of repair of the holding, being a state resulting from the tenant's failure to comply with the said obligations;

(b)   that the tenant ought not to be granted a new tenancy in view of his persistent delay in paying rent which has become due;

(c)   that the tenant ought not to be granted a new tenancy in view of other substantial breaches by him of his obligations under the current tenancy, or for any other reason connected with the tenant's use or management of the holding;

(d)   that the landlord has offered and is willing to provide or secure the provision of alternative accommodation for the tenant, that the terms on which the alternative accommodation is available are reasonable having regard to the terms of the current tenancy and to all other relevant circumstances, and that the accommodation and the time at which it will be available are suitable for the tenant's requirements (including the requirement to preserve goodwill) having regard to the nature and class of his business and to the situation and extent of, and facilities afforded by, the holding;

(e)   where the current tenancy was created by the sub-letting of part only of the property comprised in a superior tenancy and the landlord is the owner of an interest in reversion expectant on the termination of that superior tenancy, that the aggregate of the rents reasonably obtainable on separate lettings of the holding and the remainder of that property would be substantially less than the rent reasonably obtainable on a letting of that property as a whole, that on the termination of the current tenancy the landlord requires possession of the holding for the purpose of letting or otherwise disposing of the said property as a whole, and that in view thereof the tenant ought not to be granted a new tenancy;

(f)   that on the termination of the current tenancy the landlord intends to demolish or reconstruct the premises comprised in the holding or a substantial part of those premises or to carry out substantial work of construction on the holding or part thereof and that he could not reasonably do so without obtaining possession of the holding;

(g)   subject as hereinafter provided, that on the termination of the current tenancy the landlord intends to occupy the holding for the purposes, or partly for the purposes, of a business to be carried on by him therein, or as his residence.

[(1A)   Where the landlord has a controlling interest in a company, the reference in subsection (1)(g) above to the landlord shall be construed as a reference to the landlord or that company.

(1B)   Subject to subsection (2A) below, where the landlord is a company and a person has a controlling interest in the company, the reference in subsection (1)(g) above to the landlord shall be construed as a reference to the landlord or that person.]

(2)   The landlord shall not be entitled to oppose an application [under section 24(1) of this Act, or make an application under section 29(2) of this Act,] on the ground specified in paragraph (g) of the last foregoing subsection if the interest of the landlord, or an interest which has merged in that interest and but for the merger would be the interest of the landlord, was purchased or created after the beginning of the period of five years which ends with the termination of the current tenancy, and at all times since the purchase or creation thereof the holding has been comprised in a tenancy or successive tenancies of the description specified in subsection (1) of section twenty-three of this Act.

[(2A)   Subsection (1B) above shall not apply if the controlling interest was acquired after the beginning of the period of five years which ends with the termination of the current tenancy, and at all times since the acquisition of the controlling interest the holding has been comprised in a tenancy or successive tenancies of the description specified in section 23(1) of this Act.]

[(3)   ...]

[254]

NOTES

Sub-s (1): words in square brackets substituted by the Regulatory Reform (Business Tenancies) (England and Wales) Order 2003, SI 2003/3096, arts 2, 6(1).

Sub-ss (1A), (1B): inserted by SI 2003/3096, arts 2, 14(1).

Sub-s (2): words in square brackets inserted by SI 2003/3096, arts 2, 6(2).
Sub-s (2A): inserted by SI 2003/3096, arts 2, 14(2).
Sub-s (3): added by the Law of Property Act 1969, s 6, and repealed by SI 2003/3096, art 28(2), Sch 6.
Modification: modified as noted to s 25 at **[247]**.

31 Dismissal of application for new tenancy where landlord successfully opposes

(1) If the landlord opposes an application under subsection (1) of section twenty-four of this Act on grounds on which he is entitled to oppose it in accordance with the last foregoing section and establishes any of those grounds to the satisfaction of the court, the court shall not make an order for the grant of a new tenancy.

(2) [Where the landlord opposes an application under section 24(1) of this Act, or makes an application under section 29(2) of this Act, on one or more of the grounds specified in section 30(1)(d) to (f) of this Act but establishes none of those grounds, and none of the other grounds specified in section 30(1) of this Act, to the satisfaction of the court, then if the court would have been satisfied on any of the grounds specified in section 30(1)(d) to (f) of this Act] if the date of termination specified in the landlord's notice or, as the case may be, the date specified in the tenant's request for a new tenancy as the date from which the new tenancy is to begin, had been such later date as the court may determine, being a date not more than one year later than the date so specified,—

    (a)   the court shall make a declaration to that effect, stating of which of the said grounds the court would have been satisfied as aforesaid and specifying the date determined by the court as aforesaid, but shall not make an order for the grant of a new tenancy;

    (b)   if, within fourteen days after the making of the declaration, the tenant so requires the court shall make an order substituting the said date for the date specified in the said landlord's notice or tenant's request, and thereupon that notice or request shall have effect accordingly.

[255]

NOTES
Sub-s (2): words in square brackets substituted by the Regulatory Reform (Business Tenancies) (England and Wales) Order 2003, SI 2003/3096, arts 2, 7.
Modification: modified as noted to s 25 at **[247]**.

[31A Grant of new tenancy in some cases where section 30(1)(f) applies

(1) Where the landlord opposes an application under section 24(1) of this Act on the ground specified in paragraph (f) of section 30(1) of this Act[, or makes an application under section 29(2) of this Act on that ground,] the court shall not hold that the landlord could not reasonably carry out the demolition, reconstruction or work of construction intended without obtaining possession of the holding if—

    (a)   the tenant agrees to the inclusion in the terms of the new tenancy of terms giving the landlord access and other facilities for carrying out the work intended and, given that access and those facilities, the landlord could reasonably carry out the work without obtaining possession of the holding and without interfering to a substantial extent or for a substantial time with the use of the holding for the purposes of the business carried on by the tenant; or

    (b)   the tenant is willing to accept a tenancy of an economically separable part of the holding and either paragraph (a) of this section is satisfied with respect to that part or possession of the remainder of the holding would be reasonably sufficient to enable the landlord to carry out the intended work.

(2) For the purposes of subsection (1)(b) of this section a part of a holding shall be deemed to be an economically separable part if, and only if, the aggregate of the rents which, after the completion of the intended work, would be reasonably obtainable on separate lettings of that part and the remainder of the premises affected by or resulting from the work would not be substantially less than the rent which would then be reasonably obtainable on a letting of those premises as a whole.]

[256]

NOTES
Inserted by the Law of Property Act 1969, s 7(1).
Sub-s (1): words in square brackets inserted by the Regulatory Reform (Business Tenancies) (England and Wales) Order 2003, SI 2003/3096, arts 2, 8.

32 Property to be comprised in new tenancy

(1) [Subject to the following provisions of this section], an order under section twenty-nine of this Act for the grant of a new tenancy shall be an order for the grant of a new tenancy of the holding; and in the absence of agreement between the landlord and the tenant as to the property which constitutes the holding the court shall in the order designate that property by reference to the circumstances existing at the date of the order.

[(1A) Where the court, by virtue of paragraph (b) of section 31A(1) of this Act, makes an order under section 29 of this Act for the grant of a new tenancy in a case where the tenant is willing to accept a tenancy of part of the holding, the order shall be an order for the grant of a new tenancy of that part only.]

(2) The foregoing provisions of this section shall not apply in a case where the property comprised in the current tenancy includes other property besides the holding and the landlord requires any new tenancy ordered to be granted under section twenty-nine of this Act to be a tenancy of the whole of the property comprised in the current tenancy; but in any such case—
- (a) any order under the said section twenty-nine for the grant of a new tenancy shall be an order for the grant of a new tenancy of the whole of the property comprised in the current tenancy, and
- (b) references in the following provisions of this Part of this Act to the holding shall be construed as references to the whole of that property.

(3) Where the current tenancy includes rights enjoyed by the tenant in connection with the holding, those rights shall be included in a tenancy ordered to be granted under section twenty-nine of this Act [except as otherwise agreed between the landlord and the tenant or, in default of such agreement, determined by the court].

[257]

NOTES
Sub-s (1): words in square brackets substituted by the Law of Property Act 1969, s 7(2).
Sub-s (1A): inserted by the Law of Property Act 1969, s 7(2).
Sub-s (3): words in square brackets added by the Law of Property Act 1969, s 8.

33 Duration of new tenancy

Where on an application under this Part of this Act the court makes an order for the grant of a new tenancy, the new tenancy shall be such tenancy as may be agreed between the landlord and the tenant, or, in default of such an agreement, shall be such a tenancy as may be determined by the court to be reasonable in all the circumstances, being, if it is a tenancy for a term of years certain, a tenancy for a term not exceeding [fifteen] years, and shall begin on the coming to an end of the current tenancy.

[258]

NOTES
Word in square brackets substituted by the Regulatory Reform (Business Tenancies) (England and Wales) Order 2003, SI 2003/3096, arts 2, 26.

34 Rent under new tenancy

[(1)] The rent payable under a tenancy granted by order of the court under this Part of this Act shall be such as may be agreed between the landlord and the tenant or as, in default of such agreement, may be determined by the court to be that at which, having regard to the terms of the tenancy (other than those relating to rent), the holding might reasonably be expected to be let in the open market by a willing lessor, there being disregarded—
- (a) any effect on rent of the fact that the tenant has or his predecessors in title have been in occupation of the holding,
- (b) any goodwill attached to the holding by reason of the carrying on thereat of the business of the tenant (whether by him or by a predecessor of his in that business),
- [(c) any effect on rent of an improvement to which this paragraph applies],
- (d) in the case of a holding comprising licensed premises, any addition to its value attributable to the licence, if it appears to the court that having regard to the terms of the current tenancy and any other relevant circumstances the benefit of the licence belongs to the tenant.

[(2) Paragraph (c) of the foregoing subsection applies to any improvement carried out by a person who at the time it was carried out was the tenant, but only if it was carried out otherwise than in pursuance of an obligation to his immediate landlord, and either it was carried out during the current tenancy or the following conditions are satisfied, that is to say,—

    (a)   that it was completed not more than twenty-one years before the application [to the court] was made; and

    (b)   that the holding or any part of it affected by the improvement has at all times since the completion of the improvement been comprised in tenancies of the description specified in section 23(1) of this Act; and

    (c)   that at the termination of each of those tenancies the tenant did not quit.]

[(2A)   If this Part of this Act applies by virtue of section 23(1A) of this Act, the reference in subsection (1)(d) above to the tenant shall be construed as including—

    (a)   a company in which the tenant has a controlling interest, or

    (b)   where the tenant is a company, a person with a controlling interest in the company.]

[(3)   Where the rent is determined by the court the court may, if it thinks fit, further determine that the terms of the tenancy shall include such provision for varying the rent as may be specified in the determination.]

[(4)   It is hereby determined that the matters which are to be taken into account by the court in determining the rent include any effect on rent of the operation of the provisions of the Landlord and Tenant (Covenants) Act 1995.]

[259]

NOTES

Sub-s (1): numbered as such, and para (c) substituted, by the Law of Property Act 1969, s 1(1).

Sub-s (2): added by the Law of Property Act 1969, s 1(1); words in square brackets substituted by the Regulatory Reform (Business Tenancies) (England and Wales) Order 2003, SI 2003/3096, arts 2, 9.

Sub-s (2A): inserted by SI 2003/3096, arts 2, 15.

Sub-s (3): added by the Law of Property Act 1969, s 2.

Sub-s (4): added by the Landlord and Tenant (Covenants) Act 1995, s 30(1), Sch 1, para 3.

---

35 Other terms of new tenancy

[(1)]   The terms of a tenancy granted by order of the court under this Part of this Act (other than terms as to the duration thereof and as to the rent payable thereunder)[, including, where different persons own interests which fulfil the conditions specified in section 44(1) of this Act in different parts of it, terms as to the apportionment of the rent,] shall be such as may be agreed between the landlord and the tenant or as, in default of such agreement, may be determined by the court; and in determining those terms the court shall have regard to the terms of the current tenancy and to all relevant circumstances.

[(2)   In subsection (1) of this section the reference to all relevant circumstances includes (without prejudice to the generality of that reference) a reference to the operation of the provisions of the Landlord and Tenant (Covenants) Act 1995.]

[260]

NOTES

Sub-s (1): numbered as such by the Landlord and Tenant (Covenants) Act 1995, s 30(1), Sch 1, para 4(1); words in square brackets inserted by the Regulatory Reform (Business Tenancies) (England and Wales) Order 2003, SI 2003/3096, arts 2, 27(3).

Sub-s (2): added by the Landlord and Tenant (Covenants) Act 1995, s 30(1), Sch 1, para 4(2).

---

36 Carrying out of order for new tenancy

(1)   Where under this Part of this Act the court makes an order for the grant of a new tenancy, then, unless the order is revoked under the next following subsection or the landlord and the tenant agree not to act upon the order, the landlord shall be bound to execute or make in favour of the tenant, and the tenant shall be bound to accept, a lease or agreement for a tenancy of the holding embodying the terms agreed between the landlord and the tenant or determined by the court in accordance with the foregoing provisions of this Part of this Act; and where the landlord executes or makes such a lease or agreement the tenant shall be bound, if so required by the landlord, to execute a counterpart or duplicate thereof.

(2)   If the tenant, within fourteen days after the making of an order under this Part of this Act for the grant of a new tenancy, applies to the court for the revocation of the order the court

shall revoke the order; and where the order is so revoked, then, if it is so agreed between the landlord and the tenant or determined by the court, the current tenancy shall continue, beyond the date at which it would have come to an end apart from this subsection, for such period as may be so agreed or determined to be necessary to afford to the landlord a reasonable opportunity for reletting or otherwise disposing of the premises which would have been comprised in the new tenancy; and while the current tenancy continues by virtue of this subsection it shall not be a tenancy to which this Part of this Act applies.

(3)   Where an order is revoked under the last foregoing subsection any provision thereof as to payment of costs shall not cease to have effect by reason only of the revocation; but the court may, if it thinks fit, revoke or vary any such provision or, where no costs have been awarded in the proceedings for the revoked order, award such costs.

(4)   A lease executed or agreement made under this section, in a case where the interest of the lessor is subject to a mortgage, shall be deemed to be one authorised by section ninety-nine of the Law of Property Act 1925 (which confers certain powers of leasing on mortgagors in possession), and subsection (13) of that section (which allows those powers to be restricted or excluded by agreement) shall not have effect in relation to such a lease or agreement.

[261]

37   Compensation where order for new tenancy precluded on certain grounds

[(1)   Subject to the provisions of this Act, in a case specified in subsection (1A), (1B) or (1C) below (a "compensation case") the tenant shall be entitled on quitting the holding to recover from the landlord by way of compensation an amount determined in accordance with this section.

(1A)   The first compensation case is where on the making of an application by the tenant under section 24(1) of this Act the court is precluded (whether by subsection (1) or subsection (2) of section 31 of this Act) from making an order for the grant of a new tenancy by reason of any of the grounds specified in paragraphs (e), (f) and (g) of section 30(1) of this Act (the "compensation grounds") and not of any grounds specified in any other paragraph of section 30(1).

(1B)   The second compensation case is where on the making of an application under section 29(2) of this Act the court is precluded (whether by section 29(4)(a) or section 31(2) of this Act) from making an order for the grant of a new tenancy by reason of any of the compensation grounds and not of any other grounds specified in section 30(1) of this Act.

(1C)   The third compensation case is where—

(a)   the landlord's notice under section 25 of this Act or, as the case may be, under section 26(6) of this Act, states his opposition to the grant of a new tenancy on any of the compensation grounds and not on any other grounds specified in section 30(1) of this Act; and

(b)   either—
   (i)   no application is made by the tenant under section 24(1) of this Act or by the landlord under section 29(2) of this Act; or
   (ii)   such an application is made but is subsequently withdrawn.]

(2)   [Subject to] [the following provisions of this section, compensation under this section] shall be as follows, that is to say,—

(a)   where the conditions specified in the next following subsection are satisfied [in relation to the whole of the holding] it shall be [the product of the appropriate multiplier and] twice the rateable value of the holding,

(b)   in any other case it shall be [the product of the appropriate multiplier and] the rateable value of the holding.

(3)   The said conditions are—

(a)   that, during the whole of the fourteen years immediately preceding the termination of the current tenancy, premises being or comprised in the holding have been occupied for the purposes of a business carried on by the occupier or for those and other purposes;

(b)   that, if during those fourteen years there was a change in the occupier of the premises, the person who was the occupier immediately after the change was the successor to the business carried on by the person who was the occupier immediately before the change.

137

[(3A)   If the conditions specified in subsection (3) above are satisfied in relation to part of the holding but not in relation to the other part, the amount of compensation shall be the aggregate of sums calculated separately as compensation in respect of each part, and accordingly, for the purpose of calculating compensation in respect of a part any reference in this section to the holding shall be construed as a reference to that part.

(3B)   Where section 44(1A) of this Act applies, the compensation shall be determined separately for each part and compensation determined for any part shall be recoverable only from the person who is the owner of an interest in that part which fulfils the conditions specified in section 44(1) of this Act.]

(4)   Where the court is precluded from making an order for the grant of a new tenancy under this Part of this Act in [a compensation case], the court shall on the application of the tenant certify that fact.

(5)   For the purposes of subsection (2) of this section the rateable value of the holding shall be determined as follows—

    (a)   where in the valuation list in force at the date on which the landlord's notice under section twenty-five or, as the case may be, subsection (6) of section twenty-six of this Act is given a value is then shown as the annual value (as hereinafter defined) of the holding, the rateable value of the holding shall be taken to be that value;

    (b)   where no such value is so shown with respect to the holding but such a value or such values is or are so shown with respect to premises comprised in or comprising the holding or part of it, the rateable value of the holding shall be taken to be such value as is found by a proper apportionment or aggregation of the value or values so shown;

    (c)   where the rateable value of the holding cannot be ascertained in accordance with the foregoing paragraphs of this subsection, it shall be taken to be the value which, apart from any exemption from assessment to rates, would on a proper assessment be the value to be entered in the said valuation list as the annual value of the holding;

and any dispute arising, whether in proceedings before the court or otherwise, as to the determination for those purposes of the rateable value of the holding shall be referred to the Commissioners of Inland Revenue for decision by a valuation officer.

An appeal shall lie to the Lands Tribunal from any decision of a valuation officer under this subsection, but subject thereto any such decision shall be final.

[(5A)   If part of the holding is domestic property, as defined in section [66 of the Local Government Finance Act 1988,—

    (a)   the domestic property shall be disregarded in determining the rateable value of the holding under subsection (5) of this section; and

    (b)   if, on the date specified in subsection (5)(a) of this section, the tenant occupied the whole or any part of the domestic property, the amount of compensation to which he is entitled under subsection (1) of this section shall be increased by the addition of a sum equal to his reasonable expenses in removing from the domestic property.

(5B)   Any question as to the amount of the sum referred to in paragraph (b) of subsection (5A) of this section shall be determined by agreement between the landlord and the tenant or, in default of agreement, by the court.

(5C)   If the whole of the holding is domestic property, as defined in section 66 of the Local Government Finance Act 1988, for the purposes of subsection (2) of this section the rateable value of the holding shall be taken to be an amount equal to the rent at which it is estimated the holding might reasonably be expected to let from year to year if the tenant undertook to pay all usual tenant's rates and taxes and to bear the cost of the repairs and insurance and the other expenses (if any) necessary to maintain the holding in a state to command that rent.

(5D)   The following provisions shall have effect as regards a determination of an amount mentioned in subsection (5C) of this section—

    (a)   the date by reference to which such a determination is to be made is the date on which the landlord's notice under section 25 or, as the case may be, subsection (6) of section 26 of this Act is given;

    (b)   any dispute arising, whether in proceedings before the court or otherwise, as to such a determination shall be referred to the Commissioners of Inland Revenue for decision by a valuation officer;

(c)   an appeal shall lie to the Lands Tribunal from such a decision but, subject to that, such a decision shall be final.]

[(5E)   Any deduction made under paragraph 2A of Schedule 6 to the Local Government Finance Act 1988 (deduction from valuation of hereditaments used for breeding horses etc) shall be disregarded, to the extent that it relates to the holding, in determining the rateable value of the holding under subsection (5) of this section.]

(6)   The Commissioners of Inland Revenue may by statutory instrument make rules prescribing the procedure in connection with references under this section.

(7)   In this section—

the reference to the termination of the current tenancy is a reference to the date of termination specified in the landlord's notice under section twenty-five of this Act or, as the case may be, the date specified in the tenant's request for a new tenancy as the date from which the new tenancy is to begin;

the expression "annual value" means rateable value except that where the rateable value differs from the net annual value the said expression means net annual value;

the expression "valuation officer" means any officer of the Commissioners of Inland Revenue for the time being authorised by a certificate of the Commissioners to act in relation to a valuation list.

[(8)   In subsection (2) of this section "the appropriate multiplier" means such multiplier as the Secretary of State may by order made by statutory instrument prescribe [and different multipliers may be so prescribed in relation to different cases].

(9)   A statutory instrument containing an order under subsection (8) of this section shall be subject to annulment in pursuance of a resolution of either House of Parliament.]

[262]

NOTES

Sub-ss (1), (1A), (1B), (1C): substituted for original sub-s (1) by the Regulatory Reform (Business Tenancies) (England and Wales) Order 2003, SI 2003/3096, arts 2, 19(1).

Sub-s (2): words in first pair of square brackets inserted with savings by the Local Government and Housing Act 1989, s 149(6), Sch 7, paras 2–5 at **[597]**, **[602]**; words in second pair of square brackets substituted and words in third pair of square brackets inserted by SI 2003/3096, arts 2, 19(2); words in fourth and fifth pairs of square brackets inserted by the Local Government, Planning and Land Act 1980, s 193, Sch 33, para 4(1).

Sub-ss (3A), (3B): inserted by SI 2003/3096, arts 2, 19(3).

Sub-s (4): words in square brackets substituted by SI 2003/3096, arts 2, 19(4).

Sub-ss (5A)–(5D): inserted with savings by the Local Government and Housing Act 1989, s 149(6), Sch 7, paras 2–5 at **[597]**, **[602]**.

Sub-s (5E): inserted by the Local Government Finance (Miscellaneous Amendments and Repeal) Order 1990, SI 1990/1285, art 2, Schedule, Pt I, para 4(b).

Sub-s (8): added by the Local Government, Planning and Land Act 1980, s 193, Sch 33, para 4(2); words in square brackets inserted with savings by the Local Government and Housing Act 1989, s 149(6), Sch 7, paras 2–5 at **[597]**, **[602]**.

Sub-s (9): added by the Local Government, Planning and Land Act 1980, s 193, Sch 33, para 4(2).

Transfer of Functions: functions of the Secretary of State, so far as exercisable in relation to Wales, are transferred to the National Assembly for Wales, by the National Assembly for Wales (Transfer of Functions) Order 1999, SI 1999/672, art 2, Sch 1.

Rules: the Landlord and Tenant (Determination of Rateable Value Procedure) Rules 1954, SI 1954/1255 at **[1012]**.

Orders: the Landlord and Tenant Act 1954 (Appropriate Multiplier) Order 1990, SI 1990/363 at **[1218]**.

[37A   Compensation for possession obtained by misrepresentation

(1)   Where the court—

(a)   makes an order for the termination of the current tenancy but does not make an order for the grant of a new tenancy, or

(b)   refuses an order for the grant of a new tenancy,

and it subsequently made to appear to the court that the order was obtained, or the court was induced to refuse the grant, by misrepresentation or the concealment of material facts, the court may order the landlord to pay to the tenant such sum as appears sufficient as compensation for damage or loss sustained by the tenant as the result of the order or refusal.

(2)   Where—

(a)   the tenant has quit the holding—

(i)   after making but withdrawing an application under section 24(1) of this Act; or

      (ii)   without making such an application; and
    (b)   it is made to appear to the court that he did so by reason of misrepresentation or the concealment of material facts,

the court may order the landlord to pay to the tenant such sum as appears sufficient as compensation for damage or loss sustained by the tenant as the result of quitting the holding.]

             [263]

NOTES

Commencement: 1 June 2004.
Inserted by the Regulatory Reform (Business Tenancies) (England and Wales) Order 2003, SI 2003/3096, arts 2, 20, subject to transitional provisions in art 29(5) thereof at **[1309]**.

38 Restriction on agreements excluding provisions of Part II

(1)   Any agreement relating to a tenancy to which this Part of this Act applies (whether contained in the instrument creating the tenancy or not) shall be void [(except as provided by [section 38A of this Act])] in so far as it purports to preclude the tenant from making an application or request under this Part of this Act or provides for the termination or the surrender of the tenancy in the event of his making such an application or request or for the imposition of any penalty or disability on the tenant in that event.

(2)   Where—
    (a)   during the whole of the five years immediately preceding the date on which the tenant under a tenancy to which this Part of this Act applies is to quit the holding, premises being or comprised in the holding have been occupied for the purposes of a business carried on by the occupier or for those and other purposes, and
    (b)   if during those five years there was a change in the occupier of the premises, the person who was the occupier immediately after the change was the successor to the business carried on by the person who was the occupier immediately before the change,

any agreement (whether contained in the instrument creating the tenancy or not and whether made before or after the termination of that tenancy) which purports to exclude or reduce compensation under [section 37 of this Act] shall to that extent be void, so however that this subsection shall not affect any agreement as to the amount of any such compensation which is made after the right to compensation has accrued.

(3)   In a case not falling within the last foregoing subsection the right to compensation conferred by [section 37 of this Act] may be excluded or modified by agreement.

  [(4)   ...]

             [264]

NOTES

Sub-s (1): words in first (outer) pair of square brackets inserted by the Law of Property Act 1969, s 5; words in second (inner) pair of square brackets substituted by the Regulatory Reform (Business Tenancies) (England and Wales) Order 2003, SI 2003/3096, arts 2, 21(1).
Sub-ss (2), (3): words in square brackets substituted by SI 2003/3096, art 28(1), Sch 5, paras 1, 4.
Sub-s (4): added by the Law of Property Act 1969, s 5, and repealed by SI 2003/3096, arts 2, 21(2), 28(2), Sch 6, subject to transitional provisions in art 29(2)–(4) thereof at **[1309]**.

[38A Agreements to exclude provisions of Part 2

(1)   The persons who will be the landlord and the tenant in relation to a tenancy to be granted for a term of years certain which will be a tenancy to which this Part of this Act applies may agree that the provisions of sections 24 to 28 of this Act shall be excluded in relation to that tenancy.

(2)   The persons who are the landlord and the tenant in relation to a tenancy to which this Part of this Act applies may agree that the tenancy shall be surrendered on such date or in such circumstances as may be specified in the agreement and on such terms (if any) as may be so specified.

(3)   An agreement under subsection (1) above shall be void unless—
    (a)   the landlord has served on the tenant a notice in the form, or substantially in the form, set out in Schedule 1 to the Regulatory Reform (Business Tenancies) (England and Wales) Order 2003 ("the 2003 Order"); and
    (b)   the requirements specified in Schedule 2 to that Order are met.

(4)   An agreement under subsection (2) above shall be void unless—
   (a)   the landlord has served on the tenant a notice in the form, or substantially in the form, set out in Schedule 3 to the 2003 Order; and
   (b)   the requirements specified in Schedule 4 to that Order are met.]

[265]

NOTES
Commencement: 1 June 2004.
Inserted by the Regulatory Reform (Business Tenancies) (England and Wales) Order 2003, SI 2003/3096, arts 2, 22(1).

General and supplementary provisions

39   Saving for compulsory acquisitions

(1)   ...

(2)   If the amount of the compensation which would have been payable under section thirty-seven of this Act if the tenancy had come to an end in circumstances giving rise to compensation under that section and the date at which the acquiring authority obtained possession had been the termination of the current tenancy exceeds the amount of [the compensation payable under section 121 of the Lands Clauses Consolidation Act 1845 or section 20 of the Compulsory Purchase Act 1965 in the case of a tenancy to which this Part of this Act applies], that compensation shall be increased by the amount of the excess.

(3)   Nothing in section twenty-four of this Act shall affect the operation of the said section one hundred and twenty-one.

[266]

NOTES
Sub-s (1): repealed by the Land Compensation Act 1973, ss 47(2), 86, Sch 3.
Sub-s (2): words in square brackets substituted by the Land Compensation Act 1973, s 47(3).

[40   Duties of tenants and landlords of business premises to give information to each other

(1)   Where a person who is an owner of an interest in reversion expectant (whether immediately or not) on a tenancy of any business premises has served on the tenant a notice in the prescribed form requiring him to do so, it shall be the duty of the tenant to give the appropriate person in writing the information specified in subsection (2) below.

(2)   That information is—
   (a)   whether the tenant occupies the premises or any part of them wholly or partly for the purposes of a business carried on by him;
   (b)   whether his tenancy has effect subject to any sub-tenancy on which his tenancy is immediately expectant and, if so—
      (i)   what premises are comprised in the sub-tenancy;
      (ii)   for what term it has effect (or, if it is terminable by notice, by what notice it can be terminated);
      (iii)   what is the rent payable under it;
      (iv)   who is the sub-tenant;
      (v)   (to the best of his knowledge and belief) whether the sub-tenant is in occupation of the premises or of part of the premises comprised in the sub-tenancy and, if not, what is the sub-tenant's address;
      (vi)   whether an agreement is in force excluding in relation to the sub-tenancy the provisions of sections 24 to 28 of this Act; and
      (vii)   whether a notice has been given under section 25 or 26(6) of this Act, or a request has been made under section 26 of this Act, in relation to the sub-tenancy and, if so, details of the notice or request; and
   (c)   (to the best of his knowledge and belief) the name and address of any other person who owns an interest in reversion in any part of the premises.

(3)   Where the tenant of any business premises who is a tenant under such a tenancy as is mentioned in section 26(1) of this Act has served on a reversioner or a reversioner's

mortgagee in possession a notice in the prescribed form requiring him to do so, it shall be the duty of the person on whom the notice is served to give the appropriate person in writing the information specified in subsection (4) below.

(4)   That information is—

(a)   whether he is the owner of the fee simple in respect of the premises or any part of them or the mortgagee in possession of such an owner,

(b)   if he is not, then (to the best of his knowledge and belief)—

(i)   the name and address of the person who is his or, as the case may be, his mortgagor's immediate landlord in respect of those premises or of the part in respect of which he or his mortgagor is not the owner in fee simple;

(ii)   for what term his or his mortgagor's tenancy has effect and what is the earliest date (if any) at which that tenancy is terminable by notice to quit given by the landlord; and

(iii)   whether a notice has been given under section 25 or 26(6) of this Act, or a request has been made under section 26 of this Act, in relation to the tenancy and, if so, details of the notice or request;

(c)   (to the best of his knowledge and belief) the name and address of any other person who owns an interest in reversion in any part of the premises; and

(d)   if he is a reversioner, whether there is a mortgagee in possession of his interest in the premises and, if so, (to the best of his knowledge and belief) what is the name and address of the mortgagee.

(5)   A duty imposed on a person by this section is a duty—

(a)   to give the information concerned within the period of one month beginning with the date of service of the notice; and

(b)   if within the period of six months beginning with the date of service of the notice that person becomes aware that any information which has been given in pursuance of the notice is not, or is no longer, correct, to give the appropriate person correct information within the period of one month beginning with the date on which he becomes aware.

(6)   This section shall not apply to a notice served by or on the tenant more than two years before the date on which apart from this Act his tenancy would come to an end by effluxion of time or could be brought to an end by notice to quit given by the landlord.

(7)   Except as provided by section 40A of this Act, the appropriate person for the purposes of this section and section 40A(1) of this Act is the person who served the notice under subsection (1) or (3) above.

(8)   In this section—

"business premises" means premises used wholly or partly for the purposes of a business;

"mortgagee in possession" includes a receiver appointed by the mortgagee or by the court who is in receipt of the rents and profits, and "his mortgagor" shall be construed accordingly;

"reversioner" means any person having an interest in the premises, being an interest in reversion expectant (whether immediately or not) on the tenancy;

"reversioner's mortgagee in possession" means any person being a mortgagee in possession in respect of such an interest; and

"sub-tenant" includes a person retaining possession of any premises by virtue of the Rent (Agriculture) Act 1976 or the Rent Act 1977 after the coming to an end of a sub-tenancy, and "sub-tenancy" includes a right so to retain possession.]

[267]

NOTES

Commencement: 1 June 2004.

Substituted by the Regulatory Reform (Business Tenancies) (England and Wales) Order 2003, SI 2003/3096, arts 2, 23, 29(6), except in relation to a notice served before 1 June 2004.

[40A   Duties in transfer cases

(1)   If a person on whom a notice under section 40(1) or (3) of this Act has been served has transferred his interest in the premises or any part of them to some other person and gives the appropriate person notice in writing—

(a)   of the transfer of his interest; and

(b)   of the name and address of the person to whom he transferred it, on giving the notice he ceases in relation to the premises or (as the case may be) to that part to be under any duty imposed by section 40 of this Act.

(2) If—

(a) the person who served the notice under section 40(1) or (3) of this Act ("the transferor") has transferred his interest in the premises to some other person ("the transferee"); and

(b) the transferor or the transferee has given the person required to give the information notice in writing—

(i) of the transfer; and

(ii) of the transferee's name and address,

the appropriate person for the purposes of section 40 of this Act and subsection (1) above is the transferee.

(3) If—

(a) a transfer such as is mentioned in paragraph (a) of subsection (2) above has taken place; but

(b) neither the transferor nor the transferee has given a notice such as is mentioned in paragraph (b) of that subsection,

any duty imposed by section 40 of this Act may be performed by giving the information either to the transferor or to the transferee.]

[268]

NOTES

Commencement: 1 June 2004.

Inserted, together with s 40B, by the Regulatory Reform (Business Tenancies) (England and Wales) Order 2003, SI 2003/3096, arts 2, 24, 29(6), except in relation to a notice served under s 40 at **[267]** before 1 June 2004.

[40B Proceedings for breach of duties to give information

A claim that a person has broken any duty imposed by section 40 of this Act may be made the subject of civil proceedings for breach of statutory duty; and in any such proceedings a court may order that person to comply with that duty and may make an award of damages.]

[269]

NOTES

Commencement: 1 June 2004.

Inserted as noted to s 40A at **[268]**.

41 Trusts

(1) Where a tenancy is held on trust, occupation by all or any of the beneficiaries under the trust, and the carrying on of a business by all or any of the beneficiaries, shall be treated for the purposes of section twenty-three of this Act as equivalent to occupation or the carrying on of a business by the tenant; and in relation to a tenancy to which this Part of this Act applies by virtue of the foregoing provisions of this subsection—

(a) references (however expressed) in this Part of this Act and in the Ninth Schedule to this Act to the business of, or to carrying on of business, use, occupation or enjoyment by, the tenant shall be construed as including references to the business of, or to carrying on of business, use, occupation or enjoyment by, the beneficiaries or beneficiary;

(b) the reference in paragraph (d) of [subsection (1) of] section thirty-four of this Act to the tenant shall be construed as including the beneficiaries or beneficiary; and

(c) a change in the persons of the trustees shall not be treated as a change in the person of the tenant.

(2) Where the landlord's interest is held on trust the references in paragraph (g) of subsection (1) of section thirty of this Act to the landlord shall be construed as including references to the beneficiaries under the trust or any of them; but, except in the case of a trust arising under a will or on the intestacy of any person, the reference in subsection (2) of that section to the creation of the interest therein mentioned shall be construed as including the creation of the trust.

[270]

143

NOTES
Sub-s (1): words in square brackets in para (b) inserted by the Law of Property Act 1969, s 1(2).

[41A Partnerships

(1)   The following provisions of this section shall apply where—

    (a)   a tenancy is held jointly by two or more persons (in this section referred to as the joint tenants); and

    (b)   the property comprised in the tenancy is or includes premises occupied for the purposes of a business; and

    (c)   the business (or some other business) was at some time during the existence of the tenancy carried on in partnership by all the persons who were then the joint tenants or by those and other persons and the joint tenants' interest in the premises was then partnership property; and

    (d)   the business is carried on (whether alone or in partnership with other persons) by one or some only of the joint tenants and no part of the property comprised in the tenancy is occupied, in right of the tenancy, for the purposes of a business carried on (whether alone or in partnership with other persons) by the other or others.

(2)   In the following provisions of this section those of the joint tenants who for the time being carry on the business are referred to as the business tenants and the others as the other joint tenants.

(3)   Any notice given by the business tenants which, had it been given by all the joint tenants, would have been—

    (a)   a tenant's request for a new tenancy made in accordance with section 26 of this Act; or

    (b)   a notice under subsection (1) or subsection (2) of section 27 of this Act;

shall be treated as such if it states that it is given by virtue of this section and sets out the facts by virtue of which the persons giving it are the business tenants; and references in those sections and in section 24A of this Act to the tenant shall be construed accordingly.

(4)   A notice given by the landlord to the business tenants which, had it been given to all the joint tenants, would have been a notice under section 25 of this Act shall be treated as such a notice, and references in that section to the tenant shall be construed accordingly.

(5)   An application under section 24(1) of this Act for a new tenancy may, instead of being made by all the joint tenants, be made by the business tenants alone; and where it is so made—

    (a)   this Part of this Act shall have effect, in relation to it, as if the references therein to the tenant included references to the business tenants alone; and

    (b)   the business tenants shall be liable, to the exclusion of the other joint tenants, for the payment of rent and the discharge of any other obligation under the current tenancy for any rental period beginning after the date specified in the landlord's notice under section 25 of this Act or, as the case may be, beginning on or after the date specified in their request for a new tenancy.

(6)   Where the court makes an order under [section 29 of this Act for the grant of a new tenancy it may order the grant to be made to the business tenants or to them jointly] with the persons carrying on the business in partnership with them, and may order the grant to be made subject to the satisfaction, within a time specified by the order, of such conditions as to guarantors, sureties or otherwise as appear to the court equitable, having regard to the omission of the other joint tenants from the persons who will be the tenant under the new tenancy.

(7)   The business tenants shall be entitled to recover any amount payable by way of compensation under section 37 or section 59 of this Act.]

[271]

NOTES
Inserted by the Law of Property Act 1969, s 9.
Sub-s (6): words in square brackets substituted by the Regulatory Reform (Business Tenancies) (England and Wales) Order 2003, SI 2003/3096, art 28(1), Sch 5, paras 1, 5.

42 Groups of companies

(1)   For the purposes of this section two bodies corporate shall be taken to be members of a group if and only if one is a subsidiary of the other or both are subsidiaries of a third body corporate [or the same person has a controlling interest in both].

...

(2)   Where a tenancy is held by a member of a group, occupation by another member of the group, and the carrying on of a business by another member of the group, shall be treated for the purposes of section twenty-three of this Act as equivalent to occupation or the carrying on of a business by the member of the group holding the tenancy; and in relation to a tenancy to which this Part of this Act applies by virtue of the foregoing provisions of this subsection—
  (a)   references (however expressed) in this Part of this Act and in the Ninth Schedule to this Act to the business of or to use occupation or enjoyment by the tenant shall be construed as including references to the business of or to use occupation or enjoyment by the said other member;
  (b)   the reference in paragraph (d) of [subsection (1) of] section thirty-four of this Act to the tenant shall be construed as including the said other member; and
  (c)   an assignment of the tenancy from one member of the group to another shall not be treated as a change in the person of the tenant.

[(3)   Where the landlord's interest is held by a member of a group—
  (a)   the reference in paragraph (g) of subsection (1) of section 30 of this Act to intended occupation by the landlord for the purposes of a business to be carried on by him shall be construed as including intended occupation by any member of the group for the purposes of a business to be carried on by that member; and
  (b)   the reference in subsection (2) of that section to the purchase or creation of any interest shall be construed as a reference to a purchase from or creation by a person other than a member of the group.]

[272]

NOTES

Sub-s (1): words in square brackets inserted and words omitted repealed by the Regulatory Reform (Business Tenancies) (England and Wales) Order 2003, SI 2003/3096, arts 2, 16, 28(2), Sch 6.

Sub-s (2): words in square brackets in para (b) inserted by the Law of Property Act 1969, s 1(2).

Sub-s (3): substituted by the Law of Property Act 1969, s 10.

43 Tenancies excluded from Part II

(1)   This Part of this Act does not apply—
  (a)   to a tenancy of an agricultural holding [[[which is a tenancy in relation to which the Agricultural Holdings Act 1986 applies or a tenancy which would be a tenancy of an agricultural holding in relation to which that Act applied if subsection (3) of section 2 of that Act] did not have effect or, in a case where approval was given under subsection (1) of that section], if that approval had not been given];
  [(aa) to a farm business tenancy;]
  (b)   to a tenancy created by a mining lease;
  (c), (d)   ...

(2)   This Part of this Act does not apply to a tenancy granted by reason that the tenant was the holder of an office, appointment or employment from the grantor thereof and continuing only so long as the tenant holds the office, appointment or employment, or terminable by the grantor on the tenant's ceasing to hold it, or coming to an end at a time fixed by reference to the time at which the tenant ceases to hold it:

Provided that this subsection shall not have effect in relation to a tenancy granted after the commencement of this Act unless the tenancy was granted by an instrument in writing which expressed the purpose for which the tenancy was granted.

(3)   This Part of this Act does not apply to a tenancy granted for a term certain not exceeding [six months] unless—
  (a)   the tenancy contains provision for renewing the term or for extending it beyond [six months] from its beginning; or
  (b)   the tenant has been in occupation for a period which, together with any period during which any predecessor in the carrying on of the business carried on by the tenant was in occupation, exceeds [twelve months].

[273]

PART I
STATUTES

NOTES

Sub-s (1): words in first (outer) pair of square brackets in para (a) inserted retrospectively by the Agriculture Act 1958, s 8(1), Sch 1, Pt I, para 29; words in second (inner) pair of square brackets substituted by the Agricultural Holdings Act 1986, s 100, Sch 14, para 21; words in third (inner) pair of square brackets substituted by the Agricultural Tenancies Act 1995, s 40, Schedule, para 10(a); para (aa) inserted by the Agricultural Tenancies Act 1995, s 40, Schedule, para 10(b); para (c) repealed by the Housing Act 1980, s 152, Sch 26; para (d) repealed by the Landlord and Tenant (Licensed Premises) Act 1990, ss 1, 2(a).

Sub-s (3): words in square brackets substituted by the Law of Property Act 1969, s 12.

[43A   Jurisdiction of county court to make declaration

Where the rateable value of the holding is such that the jurisdiction conferred on the court by any other provision of this Part of this Act is, by virtue of section 63 of this Act, exercisable by the county court, the county court shall have jurisdiction (but without prejudice to the jurisdiction of the High Court) to make any declaration as to any matter arising under this Part of this Act, whether or not any other relief is sought in the proceedings.]

[274]

NOTES

Inserted by the Law of Property Act 1969, s 13.

44   Meaning of "the landlord" in Part II, and provisions as to mesne landlords, etc

(1)   Subject to [subsections (1A) and (2) below,] in this Part of this Act the expression "the landlord", in relation to a tenancy (in this section referred to as "the relevant tenancy"), means the person (whether or not he is the immediate landlord) who is the owner of that interest in the property comprised in the relevant tenancy which for the time being fulfils the following conditions, that is to say—

    (a)   that it is an interest in reversion expectant (whether immediately or not) on the termination of the relevant tenancy, and

    [(b)   that it is either the fee simple or a tenancy which will not come to an end within fourteen months by effluxion of time and, if it is such a tenancy, that no notice has been given by virtue of which it will come to an end within fourteen months or any further time by which it may be continued under section 36(2) or section 64 of this Act],

and is not itself in reversion expectant (whether immediately or not) on an interest which fulfils those conditions.

[(1A)   The reference in subsection (1) above to a person who is the owner of an interest such as is mentioned in that subsection is to be construed, where different persons own such interests in different parts of the property, as a reference to all those persons collectively.]

(2)   References in this Part of this Act to a notice to quit given by the landlord are references to a notice to quit given by the immediate landlord.

(3)   The provisions of the Sixth Schedule to this Act shall have effect for the application of this Part of this Act to cases where the immediate landlord of the tenant is not the owner of the fee simple in respect of the holding.

[275]

NOTES

Sub-s (1): words in first pair of square brackets substituted by the Regulatory Reform (Business Tenancies) (England and Wales) Order 2003, SI 2003/3096, arts 2, 27(1); para (b) substituted by the Law of Property Act 1969, s 14(1).

Sub-s (1A): inserted by SI 2003/3096, arts 2, 27(2).

45   (*Repealed by the Statute Law (Repeals) Act 1974.*)

46   Interpretation of Part II

[(1)]   In this Part of this Act—

    "business" has the meaning assigned to it by subsection (2) of section twenty-three of this Act;

    ["current tenancy" means the tenancy under which the tenant holds for the time being;]

"date of termination" has the meaning assigned to it by subsection (1) of section twenty-five of this Act;

subject to the provisions of section thirty-two of this Act, "the holding" has the meaning assigned to it by subsection (3) of section twenty-three of this Act;

["interim rent" has the meaning given by section 24A(1) of this Act;]

"mining lease" has the same meaning as in the Landlord and Tenant Act 1927.

[(2)   For the purposes of this Part of this Act, a person has a controlling interest in a company, if, had he been a company, the other company would have been its subsidiary; and in this Part—

"company" has the meaning given by section 735 of the Companies Act 1985; and

"subsidiary" has the meaning given by section 736 of that Act.]

[276]

NOTES

Sub-s (1): numbered as such, definition "current tenancy" substituted and definition "interim rent" inserted, by the Regulatory Reform (Business Tenancies) (England and Wales) Order 2003, SI 2003/3096, arts 2, 17(1), 28(1), Sch 5, paras 1, 6.

Sub-s (2): added by SI 2003/3096, arts 2, 17(2).

PART III
COMPENSATION FOR IMPROVEMENTS

47   Time for making claims for compensation for improvements

(1)   Where a tenancy is terminated by notice to quit, whether given by the landlord or by the tenant, or by a notice given by any person under Part I or Part II of this Act, the time for making a claim for compensation at the termination of the tenancy shall be a time falling within the period of three months beginning on the date on which the notice is given:

Provided that where the tenancy is terminated by a tenant's request for a new tenancy under section twenty-six of this Act, the said time shall be a time falling within the period of three months beginning on the date on which the landlord gives notice, or (if he has not given such a notice) the latest date on which he could have given notice, under subsection (6) of the said section twenty-six or, as the case may be, paragraph (a) of subsection (4) of section fifty-seven or paragraph (b) of subsection (1) of section fifty-eight of this Act.

(2)   Where a tenancy comes to an end by effluxion of time, the time for making such a claim shall be a time not earlier than six nor later than three months before the coming to an end of the tenancy.

(3)   Where a tenancy is terminated by forfeiture or re-entry, the time for making such a claim shall be a time falling within the period of three months beginning with the effective date of the order of the court for the recovery of possession of the land comprised in the tenancy or, if the tenancy is terminated by re-entry without such an order, the period of three months beginning with the date of the re-entry.

(4)   In the last foregoing subsection the reference to the effective date of an order is a reference to the date on which the order is to take effect according to the terms thereof or the date on which it ceases to be subject to appeal, whichever is the later.

(5)   ...

[277]

NOTES

Sub-s (5): amends the Landlord and Tenant Act 1927, s 1(1) at **[190]**.

48   Amendments as to limitations on tenant's right to compensation

(1)   So much of paragraph (b) of subsection (1) of section two of the Act of 1927 as provides that a tenant shall not be entitled to compensation in respect of any improvement made in pursuance of a statutory obligation shall not apply to any improvement begun after the commencement of this Act, but section three of the Act of 1927 (which enables a landlord to object to a proposed improvement) shall not have effect in relation to an improvement made in pursuance of a statutory obligation except so much thereof as—

(a)   requires the tenant to serve on the landlord notice of his intention to make the improvement together with such a plan and specification as are mentioned in that section and to supply copies of the plan and specification at the request of any superior landlord; and

(b)   enables the tenant to obtain at his expense a certificate from the landlord or the tribunal that the improvement has been duly executed.

(2)   Paragraph (c) of the said subsection (1) (which provides that a tenant shall not be entitled to compensation in respect of any improvement made less than three years before the termination of the tenancy) shall not apply to any improvement begun after the commencement of this Act.

(3)   No notice shall be served after the commencement of this Act under paragraph (d) of the said subsection (1) (which excludes rights to compensation where the landlord serves on the tenant notice offering a renewal of the tenancy on reasonable terms).

[278]

49   Restrictions on contracting out

In section nine of the Act of 1927 (which provides that Part I of that Act shall apply notwithstanding any contract to the contrary made after the date specified in that section) the proviso (which requires effect to be given to such a contract where it appears to the tribunal that the contract was made for adequate consideration) shall cease to have effect except as respects a contract made before the tenth day of December, nineteen hundred and fifty-three.

[279]

50   Interpretation of Part III

In this Part of this Act the expression "Act of 1927" means the Landlord and Tenant Act 1927, the expression "compensation" means compensation under Part I of that Act in respect of an improvement, and other expressions used in this Part of this Act and in the Act of 1927 have the same meanings in this Part of this Act as in that Act.

[280]

PART IV
MISCELLANEOUS AND SUPPLEMENTARY

51   Extension of Leasehold Property (Repairs) Act 1938

(1)   The Leasehold Property (Repairs) Act 1938 (which restricts the enforcement of repairing covenants in long leases of small houses) shall extend to every tenancy (whether of a house or of other property, and without regard to rateable value) where the following conditions are fulfilled, that is to say,—

(a)   that the tenancy was granted for a term of years certain of not less than seven years;

(b)   that three years or more of the term remain unexpired at the date of the service of the notice of dilapidations or, as the case may be, at the date of commencement of the action for damages; and

[(c)   that the tenancy is neither a tenancy of an agricultural holding in relation to which the Agricultural Holdings Act 1986 applies nor a farm business tenancy].

(2)   ...

(3)   The said Act of 1938 shall apply where there is an interest belonging to Her Majesty in right of the Crown or to a Government department, or held on behalf of Her Majesty for the purposes of a Government department, in like manner as if that interest were an interest not so belonging or held.

(4)   Subsection (2) of section twenty-three of the Landlord and Tenant Act 1927 (which authorises a tenant to serve documents on the person to whom he has been paying rent) shall apply in relation to any counter-notice to be served under the said Act of 1938.

(5)   This section shall apply to tenancies granted, and to breaches occurring, before or after the commencement of this Act, except that it shall not apply where the notice of dilapidations was served, or the action for damages begun, before the commencement of this Act.

(6)   In this section the expression "notice of dilapidations" means a notice under subsection (1) of section one hundred and forty-six of the Law of Property Act 1925.

[281]

PART I
STATUTES

NOTES

Sub-s (1): para (c) substituted by the Agricultural Tenancies Act 1995, s 40, Schedule, para 11.

Sub-s (2): amends the Leasehold Property (Repairs) Act 1938, ss 1, 3, 7 at **[216]**, **[218]**, **[221]** and repeals s 4 thereof.

52   (*Amends the Law of Property Act 1925, s 84(12) at* **[154]**.)

53   Jurisdiction of county court where lessor refuses licence or consent

(1)   Where a landlord withholds his licence or consent—

(a)   to an assignment of the tenancy or a subletting, charging or parting with the possession of the demised property or any part thereof, or

(b)   to the making of an improvement on the demised property or any part thereof, or

(c)   to a change in the use of the demised property or any part thereof, or to the making of a specified use of that property,

and the High Court has jurisdiction to make a declaration that the licence or consent was unreasonably withheld, then without prejudice to the jurisdiction of the High Court the county court shall have [the like jurisdiction whatever the net annual value for rating of the demised property is to be taken to be for the purposes of the County Courts Act 1984] and notwithstanding that the tenant does not seek any relief other than the declaration.

(2)   Where on the making of an application to the county court for such a declaration the court is satisfied that the licence or consent was unreasonably withheld, the court shall make a declaration accordingly.

(3)   The foregoing provisions of this section shall have effect whether the tenancy in question was created before or after the commencement of this Act and whether the refusal of the licence or consent occurred before or after the commencement of this Act.

(4)   Nothing in this section shall be construed as conferring jurisdiction on the county court to grant any relief other than such a declaration as aforesaid.

[282]

NOTES

Sub-s (1): words in square brackets substituted by the County Courts Act 1984, s 148(1), Sch 2, Pt V, para 23.

54   Determination of tenancies of derelict land

Where a landlord, having power to serve a notice to quit, on an application to the county court satisfies the court—

(a)   that he has taken all reasonable steps to communicate with the person last known to him to be the tenant, and has failed to do so,

(b)   that during the period of six months ending with the date of the application neither the tenant nor any person claiming under him has been in occupation of the property comprised in the tenancy or any part thereof, and

(c)   that during the said period either no rent was payable by the tenant or the rent payable has not been paid,

the court may if it thinks fit by order determine the tenancy as from the date of the order.

[283]

55   (*Repealed by the Regulatory Reform (Business Tenancies) (England and Wales) Order 2003, SI 2003/3096, art 28(2), Sch 6, subject to transitional provisions in art 29(1), (2) thereof at* **[1309]**.)

56   Application to Crown

(1)   Subject to the provisions of this and the four next following sections, Part II of this Act shall apply where there is an interest belonging to Her Majesty in right of the Crown or the Duchy of Lancaster or belonging to the Duchy of Cornwall, or belonging to a Government department or held on behalf of Her Majesty for the purposes of a Government department, in like manner as if that interest were an interest not so belonging or held.

(2)   The provisions of the Eighth Schedule to this Act shall have effect as respects the application of Part II of this Act to cases where the interest of the landlord belongs to Her Majesty in right of the Crown or the Duchy of Lancaster or to the Duchy of Cornwall.

(3)   Where a tenancy is held by or on behalf of a Government department and the property comprised therein is or includes premises occupied for any purposes of a Government department, the tenancy shall be one to which Part II of this Act applies; and for the purposes of any provision of the said Part II or the Ninth Schedule to this Act which is applicable only if either or both of the following conditions are satisfied, that is to say—

(a)   that any premises have during any period been occupied for the purposes of the tenant's business;

(b)   that on any change of occupier of any premises the new occupier succeeded to the business of the former occupier,

the said conditions shall be deemed to be satisfied respectively, in relation to such a tenancy, if during that period or, as the case may be, immediately before and immediately after the change, the premises were occupied for the purposes of a Government department.

(4)   The last foregoing subsection shall apply in relation to any premises provided by a Government department without any rent being payable to the department therefor as if the premises were occupied for the purposes of a Government department.

(5)   The provisions of Parts III and IV of this Act amending any other enactment which binds the Crown or applies to land belonging to Her Majesty in right of the Crown or the Duchy of Lancaster, or land belonging to the Duchy of Cornwall, or to land belonging to any Government department, shall bind the Crown or apply to such land.

(6)   Sections fifty-three and fifty-four of this Act shall apply where the interest of the landlord, or any other interest in the land in question, belongs to Her Majesty in right of the Crown or the Duchy of Lancaster or to the Duchy of Cornwall, or belongs to a Government department or is held on behalf of Her Majesty for the purposes of a Government department, in like manner as if that interest were an interest not so belonging or held.

[(7)   Part I of this Act shall apply where—

(a)   there is an interest belonging to Her Majesty in right of the Crown and that interest is under the management of the Crown Estate Commissioners; or

(b)   there is an interest belonging to Her Majesty in right of the Duchy of Lancaster or belonging to the Duchy of Cornwall;

as if it were an interest not so belonging.]

[284]

NOTES

Sub-s (7): added by the Housing Act 1980, s 73(4)(a).

57   Modification on grounds of public interest of rights under Part II

(1)   Where the interest of the landlord or any superior landlord in the property comprised in any tenancy belongs to or is held for the purposes of a Government department or is held by a local authority, statutory undertakers or a development corporation, the Minister or Board in charge of any Government department may certify that it is requisite for the purposes of the first-mentioned department, or, as the case may be, of the authority, undertakers or corporation, that the use or occupation of the property or a part thereof shall be changed by a specified date.

(2)   A certificate under the last foregoing subsection shall not be given unless the owner of the interest belonging or held as mentioned in the last foregoing subsection has given to the tenant a notice stating—

(a)   that the question of the giving of such a certificate is under consideration by the Minister or Board specified in the notice, and

(b)   that if within twenty-one days of the giving of the notice the tenant makes to that Minister or Board representations in writing with respect to that question, they will be considered before the question is determined,

and if the tenant makes any such representations within the said twenty-one days the Minister or Board shall consider them before determining whether to give the certificate.

(3)   Where a certificate has been given under subsection (1) of this section in relation to any tenancy, then,—

(a)   if a notice given under subsection (1) of section twenty-five of this Act specifies as the date of termination a date not earlier than the date specified in the certificate and contains a copy of the certificate [subsection] (6) of that section shall not apply to the notice and no application for a new tenancy shall be made by the tenant under [subsection (1) of] section twenty-four of this Act;

(b) if such a notice specifies an earlier date as the date of termination and contains a copy of the certificate, then if the court makes an order under Part II of this Act for the grant of a new tenancy the new tenancy shall be for a term expiring not later than the date specified in the certificate and shall not be a tenancy to which Part II of this Act applies.

(4) Where a tenant makes a request for a new tenancy under section twenty-six of this Act, and the interest of the landlord or any superior landlord in the property comprised in the current tenancy belongs or is held as mentioned in subsection (1) of this section, the following provisions shall have effect:—

(a) if a certificate has been given under the said subsection (1) in relation to the current tenancy, and within two months after the making of the request the landlord gives notice to the tenant that the certificate has been given and the notice contains a copy of the certificate, then,—

    (i) if the date specified in the certificate is not later than that specified in the tenant's request for a new tenancy, the tenant shall not make an application under section twenty-four of this Act for the grant of a new tenancy;

    (ii) if, in any other case, the court makes an order under Part II of this Act for the grant of a new tenancy the new tenancy shall be for a term expiring not later than the date specified in the certificate and shall not be a tenancy to which Part II of this Act applies;

(b) if no such certificate has been given but notice under subsection (2) of this section has been given before the making of the request or within two months thereafter, the request shall not have effect, without prejudice however to the making of a new request when the Minister or Board has determined whether to give a certificate.

(5) Where application is made to the court under Part II of this Act for the grant of a new tenancy and the landlord's interest in the property comprised in the tenancy belongs or is held as mentioned in subsection (1) of this section, the Minister or Board in charge of any Government department may certify that it is necessary in the public interest that if the landlord makes an application in that behalf the court shall determine as a term of the new tenancy that it shall be terminable by six months' notice to quit given by the landlord.

Subsection (2) of this section shall apply in relation to a certificate under this subsection, and if notice under the said subsection (2) has been given to the tenant—

(a) the court shall not determine the application for the grant of a new tenancy until the Minister or Board has determined whether to give a certificate,

(b) if a certificate is given, the court shall on the application of the landlord determine as a term of the new tenancy that it shall be terminable as aforesaid, and section twenty-five of this Act shall apply accordingly.

(6) The foregoing provisions of this section shall apply to an interest held by a [[Local Health Board] or Special Health Authority], as they apply to an interest held by a local authority but with the substitution, for the reference to the purposes of the authority, of a reference to the purposes of [the National Health Service Act 2006 or the National Health Service (Wales) Act 2006].

(7) Where the interest of the landlord or any superior landlord in the property comprised in any tenancy belongs to the National Trust the Minister of Works may certify that it is requisite, for the purpose of securing that the property will as from a specified date be used or occupied in a manner better suited to the nature thereof, that the use or occupation of the property should be changed; and subsections (2) to (4) of this section shall apply in relation to certificates under this subsection, and to cases where the interest of the landlord or any superior landlord belongs to the National Trust, as those subsections apply in relation to certificates under subsection (1) of this section and to cases where the interest of the landlord or any superior landlord belongs or is held as mentioned in that subsection.

(8) In this and the next following section the expression "Government department" does not include the Commissioners of Crown Lands and the expression "landlord" has the same meaning as in Part II of this Act; and in the last foregoing subsection the expression "National Trust" means the National Trust for Places of Historic Interest or Natural Beauty.

[285]

NOTES

Sub-s (3): word in first pair of square brackets substituted and words in second pair of square brackets inserted by the Regulatory Reform (Business Tenancies) (England and Wales) Order 2003, SI 2003/3096, art 28(1), Sch 5, paras 1, 7.

Sub-s (6): words in first (outer) pair of square brackets substituted by the Health Authorities Act 1995, s 2(1), Sch 1, para 89; words in second (inner) pair of square brackets substituted by the References to Health Authorities Order 2007, SI 2007/961, art 3, Schedule, para 3; words in third pair of square brackets substituted by the National Health Service (Consequential Provisions) Act 2006, s 2, Sch 1, paras 14, 15.

Transfer of functions: the title of the Minister of Works was changed to "the Minister of Public Buildings and Works" by the Minister of Works (Change of Style and Title) Order 1962, SI 1962/1549. The Ministry of Public Buildings and Works was dissolved by the Secretary of State for the Environment Order 1970, SI 1970/1681 and the functions of the Minister under this Act were transferred to the Secretary of State. The functions of the Secretary of State, so far as exercisable in relation to Wales, are exercised concurrently with the National Assembly for Wales, by the National Assembly for Wales (Transfer of Functions) Order 1999, SI 1999/672, art 2, Sch 1.

58   Termination on special grounds of tenancies to which Part II applies

(1)   Where the landlord's interest in the property comprised in any tenancy belongs to or is held for the purposes of a Government department, and the Minister or Board in charge of any Government department certifies that for reasons of national security it is necessary that the use or occupation of the property should be discontinued or changed, then—

(a)   if the landlord gives a notice under subsection (1) of section twenty-five of this Act containing a copy of the certificate, [subsection] (6) of that section shall not apply to the notice and no application for a new tenancy shall be made by the tenant under [subsection (1) of] section twenty-four of this Act;

(b)   if (whether before or after the giving of the certificate) the tenant makes a request for a new tenancy under section twenty-six of this Act, and within two months after the making of the request the landlord gives notice to the tenant that the certificate has been given and the notice contains a copy of the certificate,—

(i)   the tenant shall not make an application under section twenty-four of this Act for the grant of a new tenancy, and

(ii)   if the notice specifies as the date on which the tenancy is to terminate a date earlier than that specified in the tenant's request as the date on which the new tenancy is to begin but neither earlier than six months from the giving of the notice nor earlier than the earliest date at which apart from this Act the tenancy would come to an end or could be brought to an end, the tenancy shall terminate on the date specified in the notice instead of that specified in the request.

(2)   Where the landlord's interest in the property comprised in any tenancy belongs to or is held for the purposes of a Government department, nothing in this Act shall invalidate an agreement to the effect—

(a)   that on the giving of such a certificate as is mentioned in the last foregoing subsection the tenancy may be terminated by notice to quit given by the landlord of such length as may be specified in the agreement, if the notice contains a copy of the certificate; and

(b)   that after the giving of such a notice containing such a copy the tenancy shall not be one to which Part II of this Act applies.

(3)   Where the landlord's interest in the property comprised in any tenancy is held by statutory undertakers, nothing in this Act shall invalidate an agreement to the effect—

(a)   that where the Minister or Board in charge of a Government department certifies that possession of the property comprised in the tenancy or a part thereof is urgently required for carrying out repairs (whether on that property or elsewhere) which are needed for the proper operation of the landlord's undertaking, the tenancy may be terminated by notice to quit given by the landlord of such length as may be specified in the agreement, if the notice contains a copy of the certificate; and

(b)   that after the giving of such a notice containing such a copy, the tenancy shall not be one to which Part II of this Act applies.

(4)   Where the court makes an order under Part II of this Act for the grant of a new tenancy and the Minister or Board in charge of any Government department certifies that the public interest requires the tenancy to be subject to such a term as is mentioned in paragraph (a) or (b) of this subsection, as the case may be, then—

(a)   if the landlord's interest in the property comprised in the tenancy belongs to or is held for the purposes of a Government department, the court shall on the application of the landlord determine as a term of the new tenancy that such an

agreement as is mentioned in subsection (2) of this section and specifying such length of notice as is mentioned in the certificate shall be embodied in the new tenancy;
    (b)   if the landlord's interest in that property is held by statutory undertakers, the court shall on the application of the landlord determine as a term of the new tenancy that such an agreement as is mentioned in subsection (3) of this section and specifying such length of notice as is mentioned in the certificate shall be embodied in the new tenancy.

[286]

NOTES

Sub-s (1): word in first pair of square brackets substituted and words in second pair of square brackets inserted by the Regulatory Reform (Business Tenancies) (England and Wales) Order 2003, SI 2003/3096, art 28(1), Sch 5, paras 1, 7.

Transfer of functions: the functions of the Secretary of State, so far as exercisable in relation to Wales, are exercised concurrently with the National Assembly for Wales, by the National Assembly for Wales (Transfer of Functions) Order 1999, SI 1999/672, art 2, Sch 1.

59 Compensation for exercise of powers under ss 57 and 58

(1)   Where by virtue of any certificate given for the purposes of either of the two last foregoing sections [or, subject to subsection (1A) below, section 60A below] the tenant is precluded from obtaining an order for the grant of a new tenancy, or of a new tenancy for a term expiring later than a specified date, the tenant shall be entitled on quitting the premises to recover from the owner of the interest by virtue of which the certificate was given an amount by way of compensation, and subsections (2), (3) [to (3B)] and (5) to (7) of section thirty-seven of this Act shall with the necessary modifications apply for the purposes of ascertaining the amount.

[(1A)   No compensation shall be recoverable under subsection (1) above where the certificate was given under section 60A below and either—
    (a)   the premises vested in the Welsh Development Agency under section 7 (property of Welsh Industrial Estates Corporation) or 8 (land held under Local Employment Act 1972) of the Welsh Development Agency Act 1975, [and were transferred to the National Assembly for Wales by virtue of the Welsh Development Agency (Transfer of Functions to the National Assembly for Wales and Abolition) Order 2005], or
    [(b)   the tenant was not the tenant of the premises when the interest by virtue of which the certificate was given was acquired by the Welsh Development Agency or, if the interest was acquired on or after 1 April 2006, by the National Assembly for Wales in exercise of functions transferred to it by the Welsh Development Agency (Transfer of Functions to the National Assembly for Wales and Abolition) Order 2005].]

[(1B) ...]

(2)   Subsections (2) and (3) of section thirty-eight of this Act shall apply to compensation under this section as they apply to compensation under section thirty-seven of this Act.

[287]

NOTES

Sub-s (1): words in first pair of square brackets inserted by the Welsh Development Agency Act 1975, s 11(2)(a) and substituted, subject to transitional provisions, by the Government of Wales Act 1998, s 129(2), Sch 15, para 1; words in second pair of square brackets inserted by the Regulatory Reform (Business Tenancies) (England and Wales) Order 2003, SI 2003/3096, art 28(1), Sch 5, paras 1, 8.

Sub-s (1A): inserted by the Welsh Development Agency Act 1975, s 11(2)(b); words in square brackets added and para (b) substituted by the Welsh Development Agency (Transfer of Functions to the National Assembly for Wales and Abolition) Order 2005, SI 2005/3226, art 7(1), Sch 2, Pt 1, para 1(1), (2), subject to transitional provisions in art 3 thereof.

Sub-s (1B): inserted by the Development of Rural Wales Act 1976, s 27, Sch 7, para 1(2), and repealed, subject to transitional provisions, by the Government of Wales Act 1998, s 152, Sch 18, Pt IV.

60 Special provisions as to premises provided under Distribution of Industry Acts 1945 and 1950, etc

(1)   [Where the property comprised in a tenancy consists of premises of which the Minister of Technology or *[the English Industrial Estates Corporation]* is the landlord, being premises situated in a locality which is either—

   (a)   a development area ... or

   (b)   an intermediate area ...

and the Minister of Technology certifies that it is necessary or expedient for achieving [the purpose mentioned in section 2(1) of the said Act of 1972]] that the use or occupation of the property should be changed, paragraphs (a) and (b) of subsection (1) of section fifty-eight of this Act shall apply as they apply where such a certificate is given as is mentioned in that subsection.

(2)   Where the court makes an order under Part II of this Act for the grant of a new tenancy of [any such premises] as aforesaid, and [the Minister of Technology certifies] that it is necessary or expedient as aforesaid that the tenancy should be subject to a term, specified in the certificate, prohibiting or restricting the tenant from assigning the tenancy or sub-letting, charging or parting with possession of the premises or any part thereof or changing the use of the premises or any part thereof, the court shall determine that the terms of the tenancy shall include the terms specified in the certificate.

[(3)   In this section "development area" and "intermediate area" mean an area for the time being specified as a development area or, as the case may be, as an intermediate area by an order made, or having effect as if made, under section 1 of the Industrial Development Act 1982.]

[288]

NOTES

Sub-s (1): words in first (outer) pair of square brackets substituted by the Local Employment Act 1970, s 5, Schedule; words in second (inner) pair of square brackets substituted by the English Industrial Estates Corporation Act 1981, s 9(1) and substituted further by the words "the Urban Regeneration Agency" by the Leasehold Reform, Housing and Urban Development Act 1993, s 187(1), Sch 21, para 2, as from a day to be appointed; words omitted repealed by the Industry Act 1972, s 19(3), Sch 4, Pt I; words in final (inner) pair of square brackets substituted by the Local Employment Act 1972, s 22(1), Sch 3.

Sub-s (2): words in square brackets substituted by the Local Employment Act 1970, s 5, Schedule.

Sub-s (3): substituted by the Industrial Development Act 1982, s 19, Sch 2, Pt II, para 2(b).

This section, as amended, now applies to premises specified as development areas or intermediate areas in accordance with the Industrial Development Act 1982, s 1, and the section heading should be read accordingly.

Transfer of functions: functions of the Minister of Technology under this section were transferred to the Secretary of State by the Secretary of State for Trade and Industry Order 1970, SI 1970/1537, art 2(2). The functions of the Secretary of State, so far as exercisable in relation to Wales, are transferred to the National Assembly for Wales, by the National Assembly for Wales (Transfer of Functions) Order 1999, SI 1999/672, art 2, Sch 1.

[60A   Welsh Development Agency premises

(1)   Where the property comprised in a tenancy consists of premises of which the [National Assembly for Wales is the landlord by virtue of the Welsh Development Agency (Transfer of Functions to the National Assembly for Wales and Abolition) Order 2005 or by virtue of the Assembly exercising its functions under that Order, and the Assembly] certifies that it is necessary or expedient, for the purpose of providing employment appropriate to the needs of the area in which the premises are situated, that the use or occupation of the property should be changed, paragraphs (a) and (b) of section 58(1) above shall apply as they apply where such a certificate is given as is mentioned in that subsection.

(2)   Where the court makes an order under Part II of this Act for the grant of a new tenancy of any such premises as aforesaid, and the [National Assembly for Wales] certifies that it is necessary or expedient as aforesaid that the tenancy should be subject to a term, specified in the certificate, prohibiting or restricting the tenant from assigning the tenancy or sub-letting, charging or parting with possession of the premises or any part of the premises or changing the use of the premises or any part of the premises, the court shall determine that the terms of the tenancy shall include the terms specified in the certificate.]

[289]

NOTES

Inserted by the Welsh Development Agency Act 1975, s 11(1).

Words in square brackets substituted by the Welsh Development Agency (Transfer of Functions to the National Assembly for Wales and Abolition) Order 2005, SI 2005/3226, art 7(1)(b), Sch 2, Pt 1, para 1(3), (4).

Transfer of functions: the functions of the Secretary of State, so far as exercisable in relation to Wales, are transferred to the National Assembly for Wales, by the National Assembly for Wales (Transfer of Functions) Order 1999, SI 1999/672, art 2, Sch 1.

60B, 61, 62   (*S 60B inserted by the Development of Rural Wales Act 1976, s 27, Sch 7, para 1(1) and repealed, subject to transitional provisions, by the Government of Wales Act 1998, s 152, Sch 18, Pt IV; s 61 repealed by the Endowments and Glebe Measure Act 1976, s 47(4), Sch 8; s 62 repealed by the House of Commons Disqualification Act 1957, s 14(1), Sch 4, Pt I and the Industrial Expansion Act 1968, s 18(2), Sch 4.*)

63   Jurisdiction of court for purposes of Parts I and II and of Part I of Landlord and Tenant Act 1927

(1)   Any jurisdiction conferred on the court by any provision of Part I of this Act shall be exercised by the county court.

(2)   Any jurisdiction conferred on the court by any provision of Part II of this Act or conferred on the tribunal by Part I of the Landlord and Tenant Act 1927, shall, subject to the provisions of this section, be exercised [by the High Court or a county court].

(3)   ...

(4)   The following provisions shall have effect as respects transfer of proceedings from or to the High Court or the county court, that is to say—

    (a)   where an application is made to the one but by virtue of [an Order under section 1 of the Courts and Legal Services Act 1990] cannot be entertained except by the other, the application shall not be treated as improperly made but any proceedings thereon shall be transferred to the other court;

    (b)   any proceedings under the provisions of Part II of this Act or of Part I of the Landlord and Tenant Act 1927, which are pending before one of those courts may by order of that court made on the application of any person interested be transferred to the other court, if it appears to the court making the order that it is desirable that the proceedings and any proceedings before the other court should both be entertained by the other court.

(5)   In any proceedings where in accordance with the foregoing provisions of this section the county court exercises jurisdiction the powers of the judge of summoning one or more assessors under subsection (1) of section eighty-eight of the County Courts Act 1934, may be exercised notwithstanding that no application is made in that behalf by any party to the proceedings.

(6)   Where in any such proceedings an assessor is summoned by a judge under the said subsection (1),—

    (a)   he may, if so directed by the judge, inspect the land to which the proceedings relate without the judge and report to the judge in writing thereon;

    (b)   the judge may on consideration of the report and any observations of the parties thereon give such judgment or make such order in the proceedings as may be just;

    (c)   the remuneration of the assessor shall be at such rate as may be determined by the Lord Chancellor with the approval of the Treasury and shall be defrayed out of moneys provided by Parliament.

(7)   In this section the expression "the holding"—

    (a)   in relation to proceedings under Part II of this Act, has the meaning assigned to it by subsection (3) of section twenty-three of this Act,

    (b)   in relation to proceedings under Part I of the Landlord and Tenant Act 1927, has the same meaning as in the said Part I.

(8)   ...

(9)   Nothing in this section shall prejudice the operation of [section 41 of the County Courts Act 1984] (which relates to the removal into the High Court of proceedings commenced in a county court).

(10)   ...

[290]

NOTES

Sub-ss (2), (4), (9): words in square brackets substituted by the High Court and County Courts Jurisdiction Order 1991, SI 1991/724, art 2(1)(d), (8), Schedule, Pt I, subject to transitional provisions and savings contained in arts 11, 12 thereof at **[1237]**, **[1238]**.

Sub-ss (3), (8): repealed by SI 1991/724, art 2(1)(d), (8), Schedule, Pt I, subject to transitional provisions and savings contained in arts 11, 12 thereof at **[1237]**, **[1238]**.

Sub-s (10): substitutes the Landlord and Tenant Act 1927, s 21 at **[206]**.
County Courts Act 1934, s 88(1): see now County Courts Act 1984, s 63(1).

64 Interim continuation of tenancies pending determination by court

(1)   In any case where—
    (a)   a notice to terminate a tenancy has been given under Part I or Part II of this Act or a request for a new tenancy has been made under Part II thereof, and
    (b)   an application to the court has been made under the said Part I or [under section 24(1) or 29(2) of this Act], as the case may be, and
    (c)   apart from this section the effect of the notice or request would be to terminate the tenancy before the expiration of the period of three months beginning with the date on which the application is finally disposed of,

the effect of the notice or request shall be to terminate the tenancy at the expiration of the said period of three months and not at any other time.

(2)   The reference in paragraph (c) of subsection (1) of this section to the date on which an application is finally disposed of shall be construed as a reference to the earliest date by which the proceedings on the application (including any proceedings on or in consequence of an appeal) have been determined and any time for appealing or further appealing has expired, except that if the application is withdrawn or any appeal is abandoned the reference shall be construed as a reference to the date of the withdrawal or abandonment.

[291]

NOTES

Sub-s (1): words in square brackets substituted by the Regulatory Reform (Business Tenancies) (England and Wales) Order 2003, SI 2003/3096, art 28(1), Sch 5, paras 1, 9.

65 Provisions as to reversions

(1)   Where by virtue of any provision of this Act a tenancy (in this subsection referred to as "the inferior tenancy") is continued for a period such as to extend to or beyond the end of the term of a superior tenancy, the superior tenancy shall, for the purposes of this Act and of any other enactment and of any rule of law, be deemed so long as it subsists to be an interest in reversion expectant upon the termination of the inferior tenancy and, if there is no intermediate tenancy, to be the interest in reversion immediately expectant upon the termination thereof.

(2)   In the case of a tenancy continuing by virtue of any provision of this Act after the coming to an end of the interest in reversion immediately expectant upon the termination thereof, subsection (1) of section one hundred and thirty-nine of the Law of Property Act 1925 (which relates to the effect of the extinguishment of a reversion) shall apply as if references in the said subsection (1) to the surrender or merger of the reversion included references to the coming to an end of the reversion for any reason other than surrender or merger.

(3)   Where by virtue of any provision of this Act a tenancy (in this subsection referred to as "the continuing tenancy") is continued beyond the beginning of a reversionary tenancy which was granted (whether before or after the commencement of this Act) so as to begin on or after the date on which apart from this Act the continuing tenancy would have come to an end, the reversionary tenancy shall have effect as if it had been granted subject to the continuing tenancy.

(4)   Where by virtue of any provision of this Act a tenancy (in this subsection referred to as "the new tenancy") is granted for a period beginning on the same date as a reversionary tenancy or for a period such as to extend beyond the beginning of the term of a reversionary tenancy, whether the reversionary tenancy in question was granted before or after the commencement of this Act, the reversionary tenancy shall have effect as if it had been granted subject to the new tenancy.

[292]

NOTES

Modification: modified by the Local Government and Housing Act 1989, s 186, Sch 10, para 20(4).

66 Provisions as to notices

(1)   Any form of notice required by this Act to be prescribed shall be prescribed by regulations made by [the Secretary of State] by statutory instrument.

(2)   Where the form of a notice to be served on persons of any description is to be prescribed for any of the purposes of this Act, the form to be prescribed shall include such an explanation of the relevant provisions of this Act as appears to [the Secretary of State] requisite for informing persons of that description of their rights and obligations under those provisions.

(3)   Different forms of notice may be prescribed for the purposes of the operation of any provision of this Act in relation to different cases.

(4)   Section twenty-three of the Landlord and Tenant Act 1927 (which relates to the service of notices) shall apply for the purposes of this Act.

(5)   Any statutory instrument under this section shall be subject to annulment in pursuance of a resolution of either House of Parliament.

[293]

NOTES

Sub-ss (1), (2): words in square brackets substituted by the Transfer of Functions (Lord Chancellor and Secretary of State) Order SI 1974/1896, arts 2, 3(2).

Transfer of functions: the functions of the Secretary of State, so far as exercisable in relation to Wales, are transferred to the National Assembly for Wales, by the National Assembly for Wales (Transfer of Functions) Order 1999, SI 1999/672, art 2, Sch 1.

Regulations: the Landlord and Tenant (Notices) Regulations 1957, SI 1957/1157; the Landlord and Tenant Act 1954, Part II (Assured Tenancies) (Notices) Regulations 1986, SI 1986/2181; the Leasehold Reform (Notices) Regulations 1997, SI 1997/640; the Long Residential Tenancies (Supplemental Forms) Regulations 1997, SI 1997/3005; the Landlord and Tenant Act 1954, Part 2 (Notices) Regulations 2004, SI 2004/1005 at **[1322]**.

67   Provisions as to mortgagees in possession

Anything authorised or required by the provisions of this Act, other than subsection ... (3) of section forty, to be done at any time by, to or with the landlord, or a landlord of a specified description, shall, if at that time the interest of the landlord in question is subject to a mortgage and the mortgagee is in possession or a receiver appointed by the mortgagee or by the court is in receipt of the rents and profits, be deemed to be authorised or required to be done by, to or with the mortgagee instead of that landlord.

[294]

NOTES

Words omitted repealed by the Regulatory Reform (Business Tenancies) (England and Wales) Order 2003, SI 2003/3096, art 28(2), Sch 6, subject to transitional provisions in art 29(6) thereof at **[1309]**.

Modification: modified by the Local Government and Housing Act 1989, s 186, Sch 10, para 19(2).

68   Repeal of enactments and transitional provisions

(1)   ...

(2)   The transitional provisions set out in the Ninth Schedule to this Act shall have effect.

[295]

NOTES

Sub-s (1): repealed by the Statute Law (Repeals) Act 1974.

69   Interpretation

(1)   In this Act the following expressions have the meanings hereby assigned to them respectively, that is to say—

"agricultural holding" has the same meaning as in the [Agricultural Holdings Act 1986];

"development corporation" has the same meaning as in the New Towns Act 1946;

["farm business tenancy" has the same meaning as in the Agricultural Tenancies Act 1995;]

"local authority" [[means any local authority within the meaning of the Town and Country Planning Act 1990, any National Park authority, the Broads Authority[, the London Fire and Emergency Planning Authority] or] ... a joint authority established by Part IV of the Local Government Act 1985];

"mortgage" includes a charge or lien and "mortgagor" and "mortgagee" shall be construed accordingly;

"notice to quit" means a notice to terminate a tenancy (whether a periodical tenancy or a tenancy for a term of years certain) given in accordance with the provisions (whether express or implied) of that tenancy;

"repairs" includes any work of maintenance, decoration or restoration, and references to repairing, to keeping or yielding up in repair and to state of repair shall be construed accordingly;

"statutory undertakers" has the same meaning as in the Town and Country Planning Act 1947 ... ;

"tenancy" means a tenancy created either immediately or derivatively out of the freehold, whether by a lease or underlease, by an agreement for a lease or underlease or by a tenancy agreement or in pursuance of any enactment (including this Act), but does not include a mortgage term or any interest arising in favour of a mortgagor by his attorning tenant to his mortgagee, and references to the granting of a tenancy and to demised property shall be construed accordingly;

"terms", in relation to a tenancy, includes conditions.

(2)   References in this Act to an agreement between the landlord and the tenant (except in section seventeen and subsections (1) and (2) of section thirty-eight thereof) shall be construed as references to an agreement in writing between them.

(3)   References in this Act to an action for any relief shall be construed as including references to a claim for that relief by way of counterclaim in any proceedings.

[296]

NOTES

Sub-s (1): in definition "agricultural holding" words in square brackets substituted by the Agricultural Holdings Act 1986, s 100, Sch 14, para 22; definition "farm business tenancy" inserted by the Agricultural Tenancies Act 1995, s 40, Schedule, para 12; in definition "local authority" words in first (outer) pair of square brackets substituted by the Environment Act 1995, s 78, Sch 10, para 3, words in second (inner) pair of square brackets inserted by the Local Government Act 1985, s 84, Sch 14, Pt II, para 36, words in third (inner) pair of square brackets inserted by the Greater London Authority Act 1999, s 328, Sch 29, Pt I, para 1, and words omitted repealed by the Education Reform Act 1988, s 237(2), Sch 13, Pt I; in definition "statutory undertakers" words omitted repealed by the Coal Industry Act 1994, s 67(1), (8), Sch 9, para 5, Sch 11, Pt II.

Modification: modified by the Waste Regulation and Disposal (Authorities) Order 1985, SI 1985/1884, art 10, Sch 3, para 4.

70   Short title and citation, commencement and extent

(1)   This Act may be cited as the Landlord and Tenant Act 1954, and the Landlord and Tenant Act 1927, and this Act may be cited together as the Landlord and Tenant Acts 1927 and 1954.

(2)   This Act shall come into operation on the first day of October, nineteen hundred and fifty-four.

(3)   This Act shall not extend to Scotland or to Northern Ireland.

[297]

SCHEDULES

(*First, Second, Third, Fourth and Fifth Schedules outside the scope of this work.*)

SIXTH SCHEDULE
PROVISIONS FOR PURPOSES OF PART II WHERE IMMEDIATE LANDLORD IS NOT THE FREEHOLDER

Section 44

Definitions

1.   In this Schedule the following expressions have the meanings hereby assigned to them in relation to a tenancy (in this Schedule referred to as "the relevant tenancy"), that is to say:—

"the competent landlord" means the person who in relation to the tenancy is for the time being the landlord (as defined by section forty-four of this Act) for the purposes of Part II of this Act;

"mesne landlord" means a tenant whose interest is intermediate between the relevant tenancy and the interest of the competent landlord; and

"superior landlord" means a person (whether the owner of the fee simple or a tenant) whose interest is superior to the interest of the competent landlord.

Power of court to order reversionary tenancies

2.   Where the period for which in accordance with the provisions of Part II of this Act it is agreed or determined by the court that a new tenancy should be granted thereunder will extend beyond the date on which the interest of the immediate landlord will come to an end, the power of the court under Part II of this Act to order such a grant shall include power to order the grant of a new tenancy until the expiration of that interest and also to order the grant of such a reversionary tenancy or reversionary tenancies as may be required to secure that the combined effects of those grants will be equivalent to the grant of a tenancy for that period; and the provisions of Part II of this Act shall, subject to the necessary modifications, apply in relation to the grant of a tenancy together with one or more reversionary tenancies as they apply in relation to the grant of one new tenancy.

Acts of competent landlord binding on other landlords

3.—(1)   Any notice given by the competent landlord under Part II of this Act to terminate the relevant tenancy, and any agreement made between that landlord and the tenant as to the granting, duration, or terms of a future tenancy, being an agreement made for the purposes of the said Part II, shall bind the interest of any mesne landlord notwithstanding that he has not consented to the giving of the notice or was not a party to the agreement.

(2)   The competent landlord shall have power for the purposes of Part II of this Act to give effect to any agreement with the tenant for the grant of a new tenancy beginning with the coming to an end of the relevant tenancy, notwithstanding that the competent landlord will not be the immediate landlord at the commencement of the new tenancy, and any instrument made in the exercise of the power conferred by this sub-paragraph shall have effect as if the mesne landlord had been a party thereto.

(3)   Nothing in the foregoing provisions of this paragraph shall prejudice the provisions of the next following paragraph.

Provisions as to consent of mesne landlord to acts of competent landlord

4.—(1)   If the competent landlord, not being the immediate landlord, gives any such notice or makes any such agreement as is mentioned in sub-paragraph (1) of the last foregoing paragraph without the consent of every mesne landlord, any mesne landlord whose consent has not been given thereto shall be entitled to compensation from the competent landlord for any loss arising in consequence of the giving of the notice or the making of the agreement.

(2)   If the competent landlord applies to any mesne landlord for his consent to such a notice or agreement, that consent shall not be unreasonably withheld, but may be given subject to any conditions which may be reasonable (including conditions as to the modification of the proposed notice or agreement or as to the payment of compensation by the competent landlord).

(3)   Any question arising under this paragraph whether consent has been unreasonably withheld or whether any conditions imposed on the giving of consent are unreasonable shall be determined by the court.

Consent of superior landlord required for agreements affecting his interest

5.   An agreement between the competent landlord and the tenant made for the purposes of Part II of this Act in a case where—

(a)   the competent landlord is himself a tenant, and

(b)   the agreement would apart from this paragraph operate as respects any period after the coming to an end of the interest of the competent landlord,

shall not have effect unless every superior landlord who will be the immediate landlord of the tenant during any part of that period is a party to the agreement.

[Withdrawal by competent landlord of notice given by mesne landlord

6.   Where the competent landlord has given a notice under section 25 of this Act to terminate the relevant tenancy and, within two months after the giving of the notice, a superior landlord—

(a)   becomes the competent landlord; and

(b)   gives to the tenant notice in the prescribed form that he withdraws the notice previously given,

the notice under section 25 of this Act shall cease to have effect, but without prejudice to the giving of a further notice under that section by the competent landlord.

Duty to inform superior landlords

7.   If the competent landlord's interest in the property comprised in the relevant tenancy is a tenancy which will come or can be brought to an end within sixteen months (or any further time by which it may be continued under section 36(2) or section 64 of this Act) and he gives to the tenant under the relevant tenancy a notice under section 25 of this Act to terminate the tenancy or is given by him a notice under section 26(3) of this Act:—

(a)   the competent landlord shall forthwith send a copy of the notice to his immediate landlord; and

(b)   any superior landlord whose interest in the property is a tenancy shall forthwith send to his immediate landlord any copy which has been sent to him in pursuance of the preceding sub-paragraph or this sub-paragraph.]

[298]

NOTES

Paras 6, 7: added, together with the preceding cross-heading, by the Law of Property Act 1969, s 14(2).

Notice in the prescribed form: the Forms are set out in the Landlord and Tenant Act 1954, Part 2 (Notices) Regulations 2004, SI 2004/1005, Sch 2 at **[1327]**–**[1343]**.

(Seventh Schedule repealed by the Statute Law (Repeals) Act 1974.)

EIGHTH SCHEDULE
APPLICATION OF PART II TO LAND BELONGING TO CROWN AND DUCHIES OF
LANCASTER AND CORNWALL

Section 56

1.   Where an interest in any property comprised in a tenancy belongs to Her Majesty in right of the Duchy of Lancaster, then for the purposes of Part II of this Act the Chancellor of the Duchy shall represent Her Majesty and shall be deemed to be the owner of the interest.

2.   Where an interest in any property comprised in a tenancy belongs to the Duchy of Cornwall, then for the purposes of Part II of this Act such person as the Duke of Cornwall, or other the possessor for the time being of the Duchy of Cornwall, appoints shall represent the Duke of Cornwall or other the possessor aforesaid, and shall be deemed to be the owner of the interest and may do any act or thing under the said Part II which the owner of that interest is authorised or required to do thereunder.

3.   ...

4.   The amount of any compensation payable under section thirty-seven of this Act by the Chancellor of the Duchy of Lancaster shall be raised and paid as an expense incurred in improvement of land belonging to Her Majesty in right of the Duchy within section twenty-five of the Act of the fifty-seventh year of King George the Third, Chapter ninety-seven.

5.   Any compensation payable under section thirty-seven of this Act by the person representing the Duke of Cornwall or other the possessor for the time being of the Duchy of Cornwall shall be paid, and advances therefor made, in the manner and subject to the provisions of section eight of the Duchy of Cornwall Management Act 1863 with respect to improvements of land mentioned in that section.

[299]

NOTES

Para 3: repealed by the Crown Estate Act 1961, s 9(4), Sch 3, Pt II.

NINTH SCHEDULE
TRANSITIONAL PROVISIONS

Sections 41, 42, 56, 68

1, 2. ...

3. Where immediately before the commencement of this Act a person was protected by section seven of the Leasehold Property (Temporary Provisions) Act 1951, against the making of an order or giving of a judgment for possession or ejectment, the Rent Acts shall apply in relation to the dwelling-house to which that person's protection extended immediately before the commencement of this Act as if section fifteen of this Act had always had effect.

4. For the purposes of section twenty-six and subsection (2) of section forty of this Act a tenancy which is not such a tenancy as is mentioned in subsection (1) of the said section twenty-six but is a tenancy to which Part II of this Act applies and in respect of which the following conditions are satisfied, that is to say—

(a) that it took effect before the commencement of this Act at the coming to an end by effluxion of time or notice to quit of a tenancy which is such a tenancy as is mentioned in subsection (1) of the said section twenty-six or is by virtue of this paragraph deemed to be such a tenancy; and

(b) that if this Act had then been in force the tenancy at the coming to an end of which it took effect would have been one to which Part II of this Act applies; and

(c) that the tenant is either the tenant under the tenancy at the coming to an end of which it took effect or a successor to his business,

shall be deemed to be such a tenancy as is mentioned in subsection (1) of the said section twenty-six.

5.—(1) A tenant under a tenancy which was current at the commencement of this Act shall not in any case be entitled to compensation under section thirty-seven or fifty-nine of this Act unless at the date on which he is to quit the holding the holding or part thereof has continuously been occupied for the purposes of the carrying on of the tenant's business (whether by him or by any other person) for at least five years.

(2) Where a tenant under a tenancy which was current at the commencement of this Act would but for this sub-paragraph be entitled both to—

(a) compensation under section thirty-seven or section fifty-nine of this Act; and

(b) compensation payable, under the provisions creating the tenancy, on the termination of the tenancy,

he shall be entitled, at his option, to the one or the other, but not to both.

6.—(1) Where the landlord's interest in the property comprised in a tenancy which, immediately before the commencement of this Act, was terminable by less than six months' notice to quit given by the landlord belongs to or is held for the purposes of a Government Department or is held by statutory undertakers, the tenancy shall have effect as if that shorter length of notice were specified in such an agreement as is mentioned in subsection (2) or (3) of section fifty-eight of this Act, as the case may be, and the agreement were embodied in the tenancy.

(2) The last foregoing sub-paragraph shall apply in relation to a tenancy where the landlord's interest belongs or is held as aforesaid and which, immediately before the commencement of this Act, was terminable by the landlord without notice as if the tenancy had then been terminable by one month's notice to quit given by the landlord.

7. ...

8. Where at the commencement of this Act any proceedings are pending on an application made before the commencement of this Act to the tribunal under section five of the Landlord and Tenant Act 1927, no further step shall be taken in the proceedings except for the purposes of an order as to costs; and where the tribunal has made an interim order in the proceedings under subsection (13) of section five of that Act authorising the tenant to remain in possession

of the property comprised in his tenancy for any period, the tenancy shall be deemed not to have come to an end before the expiration of that period, and section twenty-four of this Act shall have effect in relation to it accordingly.

9, 10.   ...

11.   Notwithstanding the repeal of Part II of the Leasehold Property (Temporary Provisions) Act 1951, where immediately before the commencement of this Act a tenancy was being continued by subsection (3) of section eleven of that Act it shall not come to an end at the commencement of this Act, and section twenty-four of this Act shall have effect in relation to it accordingly.

[300]

NOTES
Paras 1, 2, 7, 9, 10: repealed by the Statute Law (Repeals) Act 1976.

COSTS OF LEASES ACT 1958

(6 & 7 Eliz c 52)

An Act to make provision for the incidence of the costs of leases

[23 July 1958]

1 Costs of leases

Notwithstanding any custom to the contrary, a party to a lease shall, unless the parties thereto agree otherwise in writing, be under no obligation to pay the whole or any part of any other party's solicitor's costs of the lease.

[301]

NOTES
Modification: the reference to a solicitor is modified to include a reference to bodies recognised under the Administration of Justice Act 1985, s 9, by virtue of the Solicitors' Incorporated Practices Order 1991, SI 1991/2684, arts 4, 5, Sch 1.

2 Interpretation

In this Act—
- (a)   "lease" includes an underlease and an agreement for a lease or underlease or for a tenancy or sub-tenancy;
- (b)   "costs" includes fees, charges, disbursements (including stamp duty), expenses and remuneration.

[302]

3 Short Title

This Act may be cited as the Costs of Leases Act 1958.

[303]

RECORDED DELIVERY SERVICE ACT 1962

(10 & 11 Eliz 2 c 27)

An Act to authorise the sending by the recorded delivery service of certain documents and other things required or authorised to be sent by registered post; and for purposes connected therewith

[3 July 1962]

1 Recorded delivery service to be an alternative to registered post

(1) Any enactment which requires or authorises a document or other thing to be sent by registered post (whether or not it makes any other provision in relation thereto) shall have effect as if it required or, as the case may be, authorised that thing to be sent by registered post or the recorded delivery service; and any enactment which makes any other provision in relation to the sending of a document or other thing by registered post or to a thing so sent shall have effect as if it made the like provision in relation to the sending of that thing by the recorded delivery service or, as the case may be, to a thing sent by that service.

(2) The Schedule to this Act shall have effect for the purpose of making consequential adaptations of the enactments therein mentioned.

(3) Subject to the following subsection [the Secretary of State] may by order make such amendments of any enactment contained in a local or private Act (being an enactment to which this Act applies) as appear to him to be necessary or expedient in consequence of subsection (1) of this section.

(4) Before making an order under this section, [the Secretary of State] shall, unless it appears to him to be impracticable to do so, consult with the person who promoted the Bill for the Act to which the order relates, or where it appears to [the Secretary of State] that some other person has succeeded to the promoter's interest in that Act, that other person.

(5) Any order under this section may be varied or revoked by a subsequent order thereunder, and the power to make any such order shall be exercisable by statutory instrument which shall be subject to annulment in pursuance of a resolution of either House of Parliament.

(6) This section shall not be construed as authorising the sending by the recorded delivery service of anything which [by virtue of the Postal Services Act 2000 or the terms and conditions of the service concerned] is not allowed to be sent by that service.

[304]

NOTES
Sub-ss (3), (4): words in square brackets substituted by virtue of the Post Office Act 1969, s 5, and the Ministry of Posts and Telecommunications (Dissolution) Order 1974, SI 1974/691, arts 2, 3(3).

Sub-s (6): words in square brackets substituted by the Postal Services Act 2000 (Consequential Modifications No 1) Order 2001, SI 2001/1149, art 3(1), Sch 1, para 19.

2 Application and interpretation

(1) Subject to the next following subsection, this Act applies to the following enactments, that is to say,—

(a) the provisions of any Act (whether public general, local or private) passed before or in the same Session as this Act;

(b) the provisions of any Church Assembly Measure so passed;

(c) the provisions of any agricultural marketing scheme made under the Agricultural Marketing Act 1958, before the passing of this Act or having effect as if made under that Act;

and, in the case of a provision which has been applied by or under any other enactment passed, or any instrument made under any enactment passed, before or in the same Session as this Act, applies to that provision as so applied, subject, however, in the case of an instrument made after the passing of this Act to any contrary intention appearing therein; and references in this Act (except this section) to any enactment shall be construed accordingly.

(2) This Act does not apply—

(a) to subsection (2) of section nine of the Crown Proceedings Act 1947 (which enables proceedings to be brought against the Crown for loss of or damage to registered inland postal packets);

(b) to any enactment which, either as originally enacted or as amended by any subsequent enactment, requires or authorises a thing to be sent by the recorded delivery service as an alternative to registered post or makes provision in relation to a thing sent by that service;

(c) to the provisions of any Act of the Parliament of Northern Ireland or of any local or private Act which extends only to Northern Ireland.

(3) In this Act—

references to sending a document or other thing include references to serving, executing, giving or delivering it or doing any similar thing;

references to sending any thing by registered post include references to sending it by or in a registered letter or packet, whether the references are expressed in those terms or terms having the like effect and whether or not there is any mention of the post or prepayment;

references to any thing sent by registered post or the recorded delivery service shall be construed accordingly; and

references to a local Act include references to any Act confirming a provisional order or scheme.

[305]

3 Extent

(1) It is hereby declared that (subject to subsection (2) of the foregoing section) this Act extends to Northern Ireland.

(2) ...

(3) This Act, so far as it amends any enactment which extends to the Isle of Man or to any of the Channel Islands, or which applies in relation to persons of or belonging to any such island, shall extend to that island or, as the case may be, shall apply in like manner in relation to those persons.

[306]

NOTES

Sub-s (2): repealed by the Northern Ireland Constitution Act 1973, s 41(1), Sch 6, Pt I.

4 Short title

This Act may be cited as the Recorded Delivery Service Act 1962.

[307]

SCHEDULE
ADAPTATION OF ENACTMENTS

Section 1

1. Any reference, however worded,—
   (a) in any enactment the provisions of which apply to, or operate in consequence of the operation of, any enactment amended by section one of this Act; or
   (b) in any enactment relating to the sending of documents or other things otherwise than by registered post or to documents or other things so sent;

to the registered post or to a registered letter or packet, shall be construed as including a reference to the recorded delivery service or to a letter or packet sent by that service; and any reference, however worded, in any such enactment to a Post Office receipt for a registered letter or to an acknowledgment of or certificate of delivery of a registered letter shall be construed accordingly.

2. The foregoing paragraph shall not be taken to prejudice the generality of subsection (1) of section one of this Act.

3, 4. ...

5. The requirement imposed by subsection (4) of section nine of the Agricultural Marketing Act 1958 that every scheme under that Act shall be so framed as to secure that the notice mentioned in paragraph (b) of that subsection shall be served by registered post shall have effect as a requirement that that notice shall be served by registered post or by the recorded delivery service.

[308]

NOTES

Para 3: applies to Scotland only.
Para 4: repealed by the Supreme Court Act 1981, ss 152(4), 153(4)(c), Sch 7.

PERPETUITIES AND ACCUMULATIONS ACT 1964

(1964 c 55)

An Act to modify the law of England and Wales relating to the avoidance of future interests in property on grounds of remoteness and governing accumulations of income from property
[16 July 1964]

PART I
STATUTES

Perpetuities

1 Power to specify perpetuity period

(1)   Subject to section 9(2) of this Act and subsection (2) below, where the instrument by which any disposition is made so provides, the perpetuity period applicable to the disposition under the rule against perpetuities, instead of being of any other duration, shall be of a duration equal to such number of years not exceeding eighty as is specified in that behalf in the instrument.

(2)   Subsection (1) above shall not have effect where the disposition is made in exercise of a special power of appointment, but where a period is specified under that subsection in the instrument creating such a power the period shall apply in relation to any disposition under the power as it applies in relation to the power itself.

[309]

2–8   (*Outside the scope of this work.*)

9 Options relating to land

(1)   The rule against perpetuities shall not apply to a disposition consisting of the conferring of an option to acquire for valuable consideration an interest reversionary (whether directly or indirectly) on the term of a lease if—

   (a)   the option is exercisable only by the lessee or his successors in title, and
   (b)   it ceases to be exercisable at or before the expiration of one year following the determination of the lease.

This subsection shall apply in relation to an agreement for a lease as it applies in relation to a lease, and "lessee" shall be construed accordingly.

(2)   In the case of a disposition consisting of the conferring of an option to acquire for valuable consideration any interest in land, the perpetuity period under the rule against perpetuities shall be twenty-one years, and section 1 of this Act shall not apply:

Provided that this subsection shall not apply to a right of pre-emption conferred on a public or local authority in respect of land used or to be used for religious purposes where the right becomes exercisable only if the land ceases to be used for such purposes.

[310]

10–14   (*Outside the scope of this work.*)

Supplemental

15 Short title, interpretation and extent

(1)   This Act may be cited as the Perpetuities and Accumulations Act 1964.

(2)   In this Act—
   "disposition" includes the conferring of a power of appointment and any other disposition of an interest in or right over property, and references to the interest disposed of shall be construed accordingly;
   "in being" means living or en ventre sa mere;
   "power of appointment" includes any discretionary power to transfer a beneficial interest in property without the furnishing of valuable consideration;
   "will" includes a codicil;
and for the purposes of this Act a disposition contained in a will shall be deemed to be made at the death of the testator.

(3)   For the purposes of this Act a person shall be treated as a member of a class if in his case all the conditions identifying a member of the class are satisfied, and shall be treated as a potential member if in his case some only of those conditions are satisfied but there is a possibility that the remainder will in time be satisfied.

(4)   Nothing in this Act shall affect the operation of the rule of law rendering void for remoteness certain dispositions under which property is limited to be applied for purposes other than the benefit of any person or class of persons in cases where the property may be so applied after the end of the perpetuity period.

(5)   The foregoing sections of this Act shall apply (except as provided in section 8(2) above) only in relation to instruments taking effect after the commencement of this Act, and in the case of an instrument made in the exercise of a special power of appointment shall apply only where the instrument creating the power takes effect after that commencement;

Provided that section 7 above shall apply in all cases for construing the foregoing reference to a special power of appointment.

(6)   This Act shall apply in relation to a disposition made otherwise than by an instrument as if the disposition had been contained in an instrument taking effect when the disposition was made.

(7)   This Act binds the Crown.

(8)   Except in so far as the contrary intention appears, any enactment of the Parliament of Northern Ireland passed for purposes similar to the purposes of this Act shall bind the Crown.

(9)   This Act shall not extend to Scotland or (apart from subsection (8) above) to Northern Ireland.

[311]

AGRICULTURE ACT 1970

(1970 c 40)

ARRANGEMENT OF SECTIONS

PART III
SMALLHOLDINGS IN ENGLAND AND WALES

Preliminary

Reorganisation of smallholdings

Management of smallholdings

PART VIII
GENERAL

An Act to make provision with respect to agriculture and related matters and with respect to flood warning systems; and to amend the Diseases of Animals Act 1950

[29 May 1970]

NOTES

Neither the Agricultural Holdings Act 1986, s 36(1) (right of any eligible person to apply for new tenancy on death of tenant) at **[443]** nor s 41 of that Act (application by not fully eligible person to be treated as eligible) at **[448]** apply if the holding consists of land held by a smallholdings authority or the Minister for the purposes of smallholdings within the meaning of Pt III of this Act.

1–36   *((Pts I, II) Ss 1–27 repealed by the Agriculture Act 1986, ss 9, 10, 24(5), Sch 4; ss 28–30, 32, 33 outside the scope of this work; s 31 repealed by the Statute Law (Repeals) Act 1993; s 34 repealed by the Statute Law (Repeals) Act 2004; ss 35, 36 repealed by the Statute Law (Repeals) Act 1986.)*

PART III
SMALLHOLDINGS IN ENGLAND AND WALES

Preliminary

37 Interpretation of Part III

(1)   In this Part of this Act, except in so far as the context otherwise requires, the following expressions have the following meanings respectively, that is to say—

"existing smallholding" means a unit of land which, being held by a smallholdings authority or (as the case may be) by the Minister for the purposes of smallholdings, is for the time being let as a smallholding (whether under this Act or under the previous enactments relating to smallholdings) or, if it is not for the time being in use, was so let when it was last in use;

"the Minister" (subject to section 62 of this Act) means the Minister of Agriculture, Fisheries and Food;

"the Ministers" means the Minister and the Secretary of State for Wales and, in the case of anything falling to be done by the Ministers, means those Ministers acting jointly;

"smallholdings estate", in relation to anything falling to be done by a smallholdings authority, means the aggregate of the land which is for the time being held by the authority for the purposes of smallholdings;

"the previous enactments relating to smallholdings" means any of the following, that is to say, the Small Holdings and Allotments Acts 1908 to 1931 and Part IV of the Agriculture Act 1947;

"working capital", in relation to a smallholding, includes any sum paid or payable by an incoming tenant (whether to the landlord or to the outgoing tenant) in respect of compensation paid or payable to an outgoing tenant.

(2)   In this Part of this Act—

(a)   any reference to land held by a smallholdings authority for the purposes of smallholdings shall be construed as including a reference to any land in which an interest is so held by the authority, other than a right to take possession arising under the provisions of the Small Holdings and Allotments Acts 1908 to 1931;

(b)   any reference to smallholdings provided by a smallholdings authority is a reference to any land which is for the time being held by the authority for the purposes of smallholdings and let as a smallholding, whether under this Part of this Act or under the previous enactments relating to smallholdings;

(c)   any reference to the purposes of smallholdings, in relation to any time before the commencement of this Part of this Act, shall be construed as a reference to the purposes which were the purposes of smallholdings in accordance with Part IV of the Agriculture Act 1947.

(3)   Any reference in this Part of this Act to the creation of a new smallholding shall be construed as a reference to any letting of land by a smallholdings authority or by the Minister where—

(a)   the land is for the time being held by the authority or the Minister for the purposes of smallholdings and the letting is a letting of the land as a smallholding;

(b)   immediately before it is so let, the land or part of it is being used (or, if it is not then in use, is land which was last used) otherwise than as land held and let as mentioned in the preceding paragraph; and

(c)   the land so let is not a holding resulting from such an enlargement or amalgamation as is mentioned in section 40(2)(a) of this Act or resulting from a similar enlargement or amalgamation effected by the Minister.

(4)   Subsections (1), (3) and (5) of section 109 of the Agriculture Act 1947 (interpretation) shall have effect for the purposes of this Part of this Act as they have effect for the purposes of that Act.

(5)   It is hereby declared that the provisions of sections 46 and 47 of this Act with respect to the powers of smallholdings authorities relate only to their capacity as corporations; and nothing in those provisions shall be construed as authorising, on the part of any smallholdings authority, any act or omission which apart from those provisions would be actionable at the suit of any person on any grounds other than a limitation imposed by law on the capacity of the authority as a corporation.

[312]

NOTES

Minister of Agriculture, Fisheries and Food: the Ministry of Agriculture, Fisheries and Food was dissolved by the Ministry of Agriculture, Fisheries and Food (Dissolution) Order 2002, SI 2002/794, and subject to specific provision to the contrary, the functions of the Minister were transferred to the Secretary of State, and the property, rights and liabilities of the Minister were transferred to the Secretary of State for Environment, Food and Rural Affairs.

Transfer of functions: the functions of the Secretary of State under the provisions of this Act printed in this title, so far as exercisable in relation to Wales, are transferred to the National Assembly for Wales, by the National Assembly for Wales (Transfer of Functions) Order 1999, SI 1999/672, art 2, Sch 1.

Reorganisation of smallholdings

38   Smallholdings authorities

The following councils shall be smallholdings authorities, that is to say—

(a)   ...

(b)   the council of every county in England ... ;

[(bb) the council of every county or county borough in Wales;]

(c), (d)..

[313]

NOTES

Para (a) repealed by the Local Government Act 1985, s 102(2), Sch 17; words omitted from para (b) repealed, and para (bb) inserted, by the Local Government (Wales) Act 1994, s 66(6), (8), Sch 16, para 38(1), Sch 18; paras (c), (d) repealed by the Local Government Act 1972, s 272(1), Sch 30.

39 General aim of statutory smallholdings

(1) In the performance of their functions under this Part of this Act smallholdings authorities, having regard to the general interests of agriculture and of good estate management, shall make it their general aim to provide opportunities for persons to be farmers on their own account by letting holdings to them being persons who satisfy the requirements of subsection (2) and of any regulations made under subsection (6) of section 44 of this Act and holdings which, unless let in accordance with proposals approved by virtue of section 41(4) of this Act, fall within the upper limit for a smallholding.

(2) For the purposes of the foregoing subsection and section 41(3) and (4) of this Act, a holding shall be treated as falling within the upper limit for a smallholding if in the opinion of the Minister it is capable, when farmed under reasonably skilled management, of providing full-time employment for not more than two men (including the person to whom it is let) with or without additional part-time employment for another man, and in any other case shall be treated as exceeding that upper limit, the number of men for whom it is capable of providing full-time employment being estimated in such manner as the Ministers may by regulations prescribe.

[314]

NOTES

Transfer of functions: see the note to s 37 at [312].
Regulations: the Smallholdings (Full-Time Employment) Regulations 1970, SI 1970/1050 at [1031].

40 Reorganisation of smallholdings estates

(1) Every smallholdings authority who immediately before the commencement of this Part of this Act hold any land for the purposes of smallholdings shall review the authority's smallholdings estate and (subject to any direction given under subsection (4) of this section) shall, before the end of the period of eighteen months beginning with the commencement of this Part of this Act or such extended period as in any particular case the Minister may allow, submit to the Minister proposals with respect to the future management of that estate.

(2) For the purposes of this section each smallholdings authority shall in particular consider to what extent (if any), with a view to giving effect to the general aim specified in section 39(1) of this Act and having regard to the general interests of agriculture and of good estate management, the authority's smallholdings estate should be reorganised—

(a) by enlarging one or more existing smallholdings or amalgamating the whole or part of one or more existing smallholdings with other land (whether that other land is or forms part of an existing smallholding, or is otherwise comprised in the authority's smallholdings estate, or not) with or without the carrying out of improvements in connection with any such enlargement or amalgamation, or

(b) by improving one or more existing smallholdings without any enlargement or amalgamation, or

(c) by creating one or more new smallholdings, with or without the carrying out of improvements in connection therewith.

(3) Any proposals of a smallholdings authority under this section shall be formulated so as to comply with any general directions given by the Ministers, or with any special directions given to the authority by the Minister, as to the form of the proposals or as to the particulars to be contained in them.

(4) If, on the application of a smallholdings authority, the Minister is satisfied that the authority's smallholdings estate is not suitable to be reorganised as mentioned in subsection (2) of this section, he may give a direction exempting the authority from the duty to submit proposals under this section.

[315]

NOTES

Transfer of functions: see the note to s 37 at [312].

41 Approval by Minister of proposals for reorganisation

(1) Where any proposals have been submitted to the Minister by a smallholdings authority under section 40 of this Act, the Minister, subject to the following provisions of this section, may approve the proposals, or may reject them and direct the authority to submit to him new proposals under that section within such time as may be specified in the direction.

(2)   Where the Minister approves any such proposals, he may approve them either as submitted or with such modifications as he considers appropriate, and may approve them (with or without such modifications) either unconditionally or subject to conditions; and in the following provisions of this Part of this Act any reference to the approval of any such proposals by the Minister is a reference to his approving them in any way authorised by the preceding provisions of this subsection.

(3)   Subject to subsection (4) of this section, the Minister shall not approve any proposals of a smallholdings authority under section 40 of this Act in so far as it appears to him that an existing smallholding as enlarged or improved in accordance with the proposals, or a holding resulting from a proposed amalgamation, or a new smallholding proposed to be created, would exceed the upper limit for a smallholding.

(4)   The Minister may approve any such proposals of a smallholdings authority notwithstanding that it appears to him that, in the case of one or more holdings, the upper limit for a smallholding would be exceeded, if it is represented to him by the authority, and he is satisfied—

(a)   that the holdings are to be let as smallholdings in accordance with section 44 of this Act, and

(b)   that, by reason of the nature or extent of fixed equipment on the holding or holdings, or of the special qualities of the soil, or of other exceptional circumstances, it is necessary or expedient for them to exceed that limit.

(5)   Subject to subsections (3) and (4) of this section, in determining whether to approve any proposals of a smallholdings authority submitted under section 40 of this Act the Minister shall have regard to the considerations specified in subsection (2) of that section.

(6)   Where any proposals of a smallholdings authority under section 40 of this Act have been approved by the Minister, then, until those proposals are amended or superseded by subsequent proposals so approved, it shall be the duty of the smallholdings authority—

(a)   to perform their functions under the following provisions of this Part of this Act in such a way as to give effect to those proposals as so approved, and

(b)   if the approval of the Minister is given subject to conditions, to comply with those conditions.

[316]

NOTES

Transfer of functions: see the note to s 37 at **[312]**.

42   Subsequent reviews and proposals for further reorganisation

(1)   Where proposals have been submitted to the Minister by a smallholdings authority under section 40 of this Act, and the Minister has approved those proposals, the Minister, at any time after the end of the period of five years beginning with the date of approval, may direct the smallholdings authority to carry out a further review of their smallholdings estate and to submit to him further proposals with respect to the future management of that estate.

(2)   A smallholdings authority to whom the Minister has given a direction under subsection (1) of this section shall comply with that direction within such period as may be specified in the direction or such extended period as the Minister may allow; and any proposals submitted in compliance with such a direction shall indicate how far the authority's previous proposals, as approved by the Minister, are intended to remain unaltered and how far they are to be amended or superseded by the new proposals.

(3)   Subsections (2) and (3) of section 40 and subsections (1) to (5) of section 41 of this Act shall have effect (subject to the necessary modifications) in relation to proposals submitted to the Minister under this section as they have effect in relation to proposals submitted to him under the said section 40.

(4)   The power of the Minister under subsection (1) of this section to direct a further review shall include power to direct subsequent reviews where proposals have been approved by him by virtue of this section, but with intervals of not less than five years between the date of approval and any direction requiring a further review; and accordingly—

(a)   in subsection (1) of this section the reference to proposals submitted to the Minister under section 40 of this Act shall be construed as including a reference to proposals submitted to him in accordance with subsections (1) and (2) of this section, and

(b)   in subsection (2) of this section the reference to a direction given by the Minister under subsection (1) of this section shall be construed accordingly.

(5)   Where by virtue of this section the Minister has approved proposals amending or superseding proposals previously approved by him, then, until further proposals amending or superseding the proposals for the time being in force are approved by the Minister, it shall be the duty of the smallholdings authority—

(a)   to perform their functions under the subsequent provisions of this Part of this Act in such a way as to give effect to the proposals as approved by the Minister and for the time being in force, and

(b)   if the approval of the Minister to the proposals for the time being in force has been given subject to conditions, to comply with those conditions.

(6)   Where under subsection (4) of section 40 of this Act the Minister has given a direction exempting a smallholdings authority from the duty to submit proposals under that section, the Minister may revoke that direction at any time after the end of the period of five years beginning with the date on which it was given; and where such a direction is revoked the provisions of sections 40 and 41 of this Act shall have effect in relation to that authority as if, in subsection (1) of the said section 40, the reference to the commencement of this Part of this Act were a reference to the date of the revocation, and any reference in this Part of this Act to proposals submitted under the said section 40 or approved under the said section 41 shall be construed accordingly.

(7)   In relation to proposals of which different parts are approved by the Minister on different dates, any reference in this section to the date of approval shall be construed as a reference to the latest of those dates.

[317]

NOTES

Transfer of functions: see the note to s 37 at **[312]**.

43   Submission and approval of proposals otherwise than in connection with reviews

(1)   Where a smallholdings authority, other than an exempt smallholdings authority, propose to carry out any such transaction as is mentioned in paragraph (a), paragraph (b) or paragraph (c) of section 40(2) of this Act, and the transaction—

(a)   would be inconsistent with any previous proposals of the authority as approved by the Minister and for the time being in force under the preceding provisions of this Part of this Act, and has not been provided for by any proposals previously approved under this section, and

(b)   is intended to be carried out at a time when no review of the authority's smallholdings estate is required to be carried out by a direction given by the Minister under those provisions,

the authority shall submit to the Minister proposals under this section for carrying out that transaction.

(2)   Any proposals submitted by a smallholdings authority under subsection (1) of this section shall be by way of amending the previous proposals of the authority approved by the Minister under the preceding provisions of this Part of this Act, in the form in which (whether as originally approved or as subsequently amended) those proposals are for the time being in force.

(3)   Where an exempt smallholdings authority propose to carry out any such transaction as is mentioned in paragraph (a) or paragraph (c) of section 40(2) of this Act, and the transaction has not been provided for by any proposals of the authority previously approved by the Minister under this section, the authority shall submit to the Minister proposals under this section for carrying out that transaction.

(4)   An exempt smallholdings authority proposing to carry out any such transaction as is mentioned in paragraph (b) of section 40(2) of this Act may, if (having regard to the provisions of section 51 of this Act) it appears to the authority to be expedient to do so, submit to the Minister proposals under this section for carrying out that transaction.

(5)   Subsection (3) of section 40 and subsections (1) to (5) of section 41 of this Act shall have effect (subject to the necessary modifications) in relation to proposals submitted to the Minister under this section as they have effect in relation to proposals submitted to him under the said section 40.

171

(6)   Subject to subsection (7) of this section, where the Minister has approved any proposals under this section, subsection (5) of section 42 of this Act shall have effect as if those proposals had been approved under that section.

(7)   In the case of proposals submitted by an exempt smallholdings authority and approved by the Minister under this section, subsection (6) of section 41 of this Act shall have effect as if those proposals had been approved under that section.

(8)   In this section "exempt smallholdings authority" means a smallholdings authority in respect of which a direction given under section 40(4) of this Act is for the time being in force.

[318]

NOTES

Transfer of functions: see the note to s 37 at **[312]**.

Management of smallholdings

44   Letting of smallholdings

(1)   Any land held by a smallholdings authority for the purposes of smallholdings may be let by them as a smallholding in accordance with the following provisions of this section.

(2)   Subject to subsection (3) of this section, no land shall be so let except to a person who is to farm the holding and either—

(a)   is regarded by the authority as being qualified by reason of his agricultural experience to farm the holding on his own account, or

(b)   is a person in respect to whom the authority are satisfied that within a reasonably short time he will become eligible to be so regarded.

(3)   Notwithstanding anything in subsection (2) of this section, a smallholdings authority may let land under this section as a smallholding, or as part of a group of two or more smallholdings, to two or more persons proposing to farm the land together on a co-operative system if, having regard to the aggregate agricultural experience of those persons, the authority are satisfied that they are, or will within a reasonably short time become, qualified to farm the land together on such a system on their own account.

(4)   Subject to subsection (5) of this section, a smallholdings authority shall not under this section—

(a)   let any holding resulting from such an enlargement or amalgamation as is mentioned in section 40(2)(a) of this Act, or

(b)   create any new smallholding,

unless the enlargement or amalgamation, or the creation of a new smallholding, as the case may be, is in accordance with proposals which have been approved by the Minister and are for the time being in force under the preceding provisions of this Part of this Act.

(5)   Subsection (4) of this section shall not apply to the letting of any holding, or the creation of a new smallholding, if—

(a)   the letting or creation is effected by the smallholdings authority with the consent in writing of the Minister, and

(b)   that consent is given before any proposals have been submitted by the authority under section 40 of this Act or before any proposals so submitted by the authority have been approved by the Minister.

(6)   Regulations made by the Ministers may make provision as to the selection of tenants to whom land may be let under this section, and in particular—

(a)   may specify requirements (whether as to agricultural experience or otherwise) to be fulfilled by persons to whom land is to be let under this section, and

(b)   may require smallholdings authorities, before letting land under this section, to take such preparatory steps as may be prescribed by the regulations.

[319]

NOTES

Transfer of functions: see the note to s 37 at **[312]**.
Regulations: the Smallholdings (Selection of Tenants) Regulations 1970, SI 1970/1049.

45   Rent to be charged for smallholdings

(1)   A smallholdings authority in determining the rent at which any land is to be let by them under section 44 of this Act, shall have regard to the rent which, in their opinion, might reasonably be expected to be determined to be the rent properly payable if—

(a)   the land were already let as an agricultural holding;

(b)   the terms of that letting (other than terms relating to rent) were those on which the smallholdings authority propose to let the land in question; and

(c)   the question what rent should be payable in respect of that agricultural holding had been referred to arbitration under the enactments relating to agricultural holdings which are for the time being in force.

(2)   For the purposes of the foregoing subsection it shall be assumed that, on any such arbitration as is mentioned in paragraph (c) of that subsection, there would be no improvements, or matters treated as equivalent to improvements, and no dilapidation, deterioration or damage, of which, in accordance with the enactments referred to in that paragraph, special account (whether by way of reducing or increasing the rent determined) would fall to be taken in determining what rent should be payable.

(3)   Subsection (1) of this section (but without the assumptions specified in subsection (2) thereof) shall have effect in relation to any revision by agreement of the rent at which any land has been let by a smallholdings authority as a smallholding (whether under section 44 of this Act or under the previous enactments relating to smallholdings) as it has effect in relation to determining the rent at which any land is to be let under the said section 44.

[320]

46   Equipment of smallholdings

(1)   A smallholdings authority shall have power to provide, improve, maintain and repair fixed equipment on land held by the authority for the purposes of smallholdings, and to carry out any other improvements on or for the benefit of any such land.

(2)   The power conferred by the foregoing subsection shall include power to enter into an agreement with a tenant of any such land for—

(a)   the provision, improvement, maintenance or repair by the tenant of fixed equipment on the land, or

(b)   the carrying out by the tenant of other improvements on or for the benefit of the land,

on such terms as may be specified in the agreement.

[321]

47   General powers of management

(1)   Subject to the provisions of this Part of this Act, a smallholdings authority shall have all such powers as are required by the authority for the management of land held by them for the purposes of smallholdings.

(2)   A smallholdings authority shall have power, for the benefit of the occupiers of smallholdings provided by the authority, to further the formation of bodies of persons, whether corporate or unincorporate, having for their object or one of their objects the promotion of efficiency in the conduct of smallholdings through co-operative methods, and in particular through co-operative purchase and hiring of requisites for the smallholdings or the co-operative sale, marketing or preparation for marketing of the produce of the smallholdings, and to assist the carrying on and extension of the activities of such bodies.

(3)   To such extent as appears to a smallholdings authority to be expedient for the purpose of assisting the conduct of smallholdings provided by the authority, or of promoting co-operative schemes for the conduct of such smallholdings, the authority shall have power—

(a)   to acquire by purchase or hiring machinery and other equipment, live or dead stock, seeds, fertilisers and any other requisites and to sell or let them on such terms as may be decided by the authority, and

(b)   to provide services on such terms as may be so decided.

(4)   A smallholdings authority shall have power to carry out arrangements made by the authority for the disposal by the authority of the produce of smallholdings provided by them.

[322]

48–53   (*Outside the scope of this work.*)

Additional powers of Minister in relation to smallholdings

54 Land held by Minister for purposes of smallholdings

(1)   This section applies to any land which is for the time being held by the Minister for the purposes of smallholdings.

(2)   Subject to the following provisions of this section, in relation to land to which this section applies the Minister shall have the like duties and powers as smallholdings authorities have under the provisions of sections 44 to 47 and 49(1) and (2) of this Act in relation to land held by them for the purposes of smallholdings, as if in those provisions any reference to smallholdings provided by a smallholdings authority were a reference to smallholdings on land to which this section applies.

(3)   Where for the purpose of assisting the conduct of smallholdings on land to which this section applies the Minister has (whether before or after the commencement of this Part of this Act) acquired by purchase or hiring machinery or other equipment, live or dead stock, seeds, fertilisers or other requisites, or provides any services, the powers of the Minister under section 47(3) of this Act, as applied by subsection (2) of this section, shall include power to sell or let them to, or (as the case may be) to provide the services for, any persons, whether they are tenants of smallholdings or not.

(4)   Where any arrangements are made by the Minister under section 47(4) of this Act, as applied by subsection (2) of this section, and it appears to the Minister that any facilities provided in accordance with the arrangements are not required to be reserved exclusively for disposing of the produce of smallholdings on land to which this section applies, the arrangements may include provision for the use of those facilities for disposing of the produce of other agricultural holdings.

(5)   Subject to subsection (6) of this section, the Minister may, in accordance with arrangements made by him with the approval of the Treasury, make loans for the purpose of providing working capital for a tenant of a smallholding on land to which this section applies, or for a person intending to become such a tenant.

(6)   A loan made by the Minister under subsection (5) of this section in respect of a smallholding (or, if two or more loans are so made, the aggregate amount of those loans) shall not exceed three-quarters of the aggregate working capital which in the opinion of the Minister is required for the proper working of the smallholding.

(7)   The Minister may designate any land for the time being vested in him as being land held by him for the purposes of smallholdings, and may at any time revoke any such designation; and—

    (a)   any land comprised in such a designation which is for the time being in force shall for the purposes of this section be taken to be land held by the Minister for the purposes of smallholdings, whether apart from the designation it would be taken to be so held or not, and

    (b)   any land in respect of which such a designation has been revoked under this subsection shall be conclusively presumed to be land not held by the Minister for those purposes.

[323]

NOTES

Transfer of functions: see the note to s 37 at **[312]**.

55, 56   (*Outside the scope of this work.*)

General and supplementary provisions

57–60   (*S 57 repealed by the Local Government Act 1972, s 272(1), Sch 30; ss 58–60 outside the scope of this work.*)

61 Special classes of land

(1)   Land forming part of the possessions … of the Duchy of Cornwall may be leased to a smallholdings authority or to the Minister for the purposes of smallholdings for a term not exceeding 35 years, with or without a right of renewal for a further term not exceeding 35 years.

(2)   The powers of leasing conferred by subsection (1) of this section shall be exercisable—

    (a)   ...

    (b)   in the case of land forming part of the possessions of the Duchy of Cornwall, by the Duke of Cornwall or such other persons as for the time being have power to dispose of land belonging to the Duchy.

(3)   In the case of glebe land—

    (a)   the like powers of leasing may be exercised by the [Diocesan Board of Finance in which the land is vested], but shall not be so exercised except with the consent of the Church Commissioners [in a case where their consent would be required if the transaction were carried out under the Endowments and Glebe Measure 1976];

    (b)   the consent of any person, other than the Church Commissioners, shall not be required to enable the land to be sold to a smallholdings authority or to the Minister for the purposes of smallholdings.

(4), (5)   ...

(6)   Where, in any case not falling within any of the preceding subsections, a person, by virtue of the Settled Land Act 1925, the Universities and College Estates Act 1925 or any other enactment, has power, whether subject to any consent or conditions or not, to lease any land for agricultural purposes for a term not exceeding that specified in the enactment, he shall (without prejudice to that power) have power by virtue of this subsection, subject to the like consent and conditions (if any), to lease the land to a smallholdings authority or to the Minister for the purposes of smallholdings for a term not exceeding 35 years, with or without a right of renewal for a further term not exceeding 35 years.

[324]

NOTES

Sub-ss (1), (2): words omitted repealed by the Duchy of Lancaster Act 1988, s 1(4), Schedule.

Sub-s (3): words in first pair of square brackets substituted and words in second pair of square brackets inserted by the Church of England (Miscellaneous Provisions) Measure 2006, s 14, Sch 5, para 17(a).

Sub-ss (4), (5): repealed by the Church of England (Miscellaneous Provisions) Measure 2006, s 14, Sch 5, para 17(b).

Transfer of functions: see the note to s 37 at **[312]**.

---

62   Provisions as to Wales (including Monmouthshire)

(1)   Where by or under any provision to which this section applies (including any enactment as applied by such a provision) anything is authorised or required to be done—

    (a)   by the Minister in relation to the council of a county [or county borough] ... in Wales, or

    (b)   by such a council in relation to the Minister,

whether (in either case) the council fall within that provision in their capacity as a smallholdings authority or otherwise, any reference in that provision to the Minister shall, for the purposes of the application of that provision in relation to that council, be construed as a reference to the Ministers.

(2)   This section applies to the following provisions, that is to say—

    (a)   all the provisions of this Part of this Act except section 37, 52(1), 54, 55, 56(2) and (4), 59(2) and 61 and Schedule 3;

    (b)   section 2(7) and the proviso to section 6(1) of the Small Holdings and Allotments Act 1926, as those provisions have effect (in relation to certain matters in existence before 1st October 1949) by virtue of paragraph (a) of the proviso to section 67(2) of the Agriculture Act 1947; and

    (c)   the provisions of the Small Holdings and Allotments Acts 1908 to 1926, as applied to cottage holdings by section 12 of the Agricultural Land (Utilisation) Act 1931, with the exception of section 2(2) of the Small Holdings and Allotments Act 1926 as so applied.

(3)   In this section any reference to Wales includes Monmouthshire.

[325]

NOTES

Sub-s (1): words in square brackets inserted by the Local Government (Wales) Act 1994, s 66(6), Sch 16, para 38(4); words omitted repealed by the Local Government Act 1972, s 272(1), Sch 30.

Transfer of functions: see the note to s 37 at **[312]**.
Regulations: the Smallholdings (Contributions Towards Losses) Regulations 1970, SI 1970/1051.

63, 64   (*Outside the scope of this work.*)

65   Commencement and extent of Part III

(1)   This Part of this Act shall come into operation on such day as the Ministers may by order made by statutory instrument appoint, …

(2)   This Part of this Act extends to England and Wales only.

[326]

NOTES
Sub-s (1): words omitted repealed by the Statute Law (Repeals) Act 1993.
Orders: the Agriculture Act 1970 (Commencement No 2) Order 1970, SI 1970/1048.

66–109   (*In so far as unrepealed, outside the scope of this work.*)

PART VIII
GENERAL

110–112   (*Ss 110, 111 outside the scope of this work; s 112 repealed by the Northern Ireland Constitution Act 1973, s 41(1), Sch 6, Pt I.*)

113   Short title, construction of references and repeals

(1)   This Act may be cited as the Agriculture Act 1970.

(2)   Except in so far as the context otherwise requires, any reference in this Act to any enactment shall be construed as a reference to that enactment as amended, extended or applied by or under any other enactment, including any enactment contained in this Act.

(3)   …

(4)   The inclusion in this Act of any express saving, transitional provision or amendment shall not be taken as affecting the operation in relation to this Act of section 38 of the Interpretation Act 1889 (which relates to the effect of repeals).

[327]

NOTES
Sub-s (3): repealed by the Statute Law (Repeals) Act 1989.

SCHEDULES

(*Sch 1 repealed by the Agriculture Act 1986, ss 9, 10, 24(5), Sch 4; Sch 2 sets out the Agriculture Act 1967, s 26, as amended.*)

SCHEDULE 3
TRANSITIONAL PROVISIONS FOR PART III
Section 64(1)

1.   In this Schedule "the repeal" means the repeal by this Act of the enactments specified in Part III of Schedule 5 thereto, and "the repealed enactments" means the enactments so specified.

2.   Any land which immediately before the commencement of Part III of this Act is held by a smallholdings authority for the purposes of smallholdings shall, notwithstanding the repeal, continue to be held by that authority for the purposes of smallholdings, subject to any power exercisable by the authority by virtue of any enactment to appropriate or dispose of it for other purposes.

3.   The repeal shall not affect the validity of any letting effected before the commencement of Part III of this Act.

4.   The repeal shall not affect the operation of any of the repealed enactments in relation to allotments or in relation to allotment committees.

5.   The repeal, in so far as it relates to section 48 of the Small Holdings and Allotments Act 1908, shall not affect the operation of that section in relation to cottage holdings.

6.   ...

7.   The repeal shall not affect any duty of the Minister to give effect to any trust on which any land is held by the Minister or to any scheme established under the Charitable Trusts Acts 1853 to 1939, or any of those Acts, and subsisting immediately before the commencement of Part III of this Act in accordance with section 48(4) of the Charities Act 1960.

8.   ...

9.   Without prejudice to the preceding provisions of this Schedule, in so far as any agreement made, record, map or plan compiled and kept, or other thing done by virtue of any of the repealed enactments could have been made, compiled and kept or done by virtue of a corresponding provision of Part III of this Act, it shall not be invalidated by the repeal but shall have effect as if made, compiled and kept or done by virtue of that corresponding provision.

[328]

NOTES

Para 6: repealed by the Statute Law (Repeals) Act 1993.
Para 8: repealed by the Statute Law (Repeals) Act 2004.
Transfer of functions: see the note to s 37 at **[312]**.

(Sch 4 repealed in part by the Agriculture (Miscellaneous Provisions) Act 1972, s 26(3), Sch 6, the Agricultural Holdings (Notices to Quit) Act 1977, s 13(2), Sch 2, and the Agricultural Holdings Act 1986, s 101(1), Sch 15, Pt I; remainder amends the Agricultural Land (Utilisation) Act 1931, s 12, and the Agriculture Act 1947, s 58, Sch 8, Pt II; Sch 5 repealed by the Statute Law (Repeals) Act 1989.)

DEFECTIVE PREMISES ACT 1972

(1972 c 35)

An Act to impose duties in connection with the provision of dwellings and otherwise to amend the law of England and Wales as to liability for injury or damage caused to persons through defects in the state of premises

[29 June 1972]

1–3   *(Outside the scope of this work.)*

4   Landlord's duty of care in virtue of obligation or right to repair premises demised

(1)   Where premises are let under a tenancy which puts on the landlord an obligation to the tenant for the maintenance or repair of the premises, the landlord owes to all persons who might reasonably be expected to be affected by defects in the state of the premises a duty to take such care as is reasonable in all the circumstances to see that they are reasonably safe from personal injury or from damage to their property caused by a relevant defect.

(2)   The said duty is owed if the landlord knows (whether as the result of being notified by the tenant or otherwise) or if he ought in all the circumstances to have known of the relevant defect.

(3)   In this section "relevant defect" means a defect in the state of the premises existing at or after the material time and arising from, or continuing because of, an act or omission by the landlord which constitutes or would if he had had notice of the defect, have constituted a failure by him to carry out his obligation to the tenant for the maintenance or repair of the premises; and for the purposes of the foregoing provision "the material time" means—

(a)   where the tenancy commenced before this Act, the commencement of this Act; and

(b)   in all other cases, the earliest of the following times, that is to say—
   (i)   the time when the tenancy commences;
   (ii)   the time when the tenancy agreement is entered into;
   (iii)   the time when possession is taken of the premises in contemplation of the letting.

(4)   Where premises are let under a tenancy which expressly or impliedly gives the landlord the right to enter the premises to carry out any description of maintenance or repair of the premises, then, as from the time when he first is, or by notice or otherwise can put himself, in a position to exercise the right and so long as he is or can put himself in that position, he shall be treated for the purposes of subsections (1) to (3) above (but for no other purpose) as if he were under an obligation to the tenant for that description of maintenance or repair of the premises; but the landlord shall not owe the tenant any duty by virtue of this subsection in respect of any defect in the state of the premises arising from, or continuing because of, a failure to carry out an obligation expressly imposed on the tenant by the tenancy.

(5)   For the purposes of this section obligations imposed or rights given by any enactment in virtue of a tenancy shall be treated as imposed or given by the tenancy.

(6)   This section applies to a right of occupation given by contract or any enactment and not amounting to a tenancy as if the right were a tenancy, and "tenancy" and cognate expressions shall be construed accordingly.

[329]

NOTES
   Modification: this section is modified where a RTM company has acquired the right to manage, by the Commonhold and Leasehold Reform Act 2002, s 102, Sch 7, para 2.

5   (*Outside the scope of this work.*)

6 Supplemental

(1)   In this Act—

   "disposal", in relation to premises, includes a letting, and an assignment or surrender of a tenancy, of the premises and the creation by contract of any other right to occupy the premises, and "dispose" shall be construed accordingly;

   "personal injury" includes any disease and any impairment of a person's physical or mental condition;

   "tenancy" means—
      (a)   a tenancy created either immediately or derivatively out of the freehold, whether by a lease or underlease, by an agreement for a lease or underlease or by a tenancy agreement, but not including a mortgage term or any interest arising in favour of a mortgagor by his attorning tenant to his mortgagee; or
      (b)   a tenancy at will or a tenancy on sufferance; or
      (c)   a tenancy, whether or not constituting a tenancy at common law, created by or in pursuance of any enactment;
   and cognate expressions shall be construed accordingly.

(2)   Any duty imposed by or enforceable by virtue of any provision of this Act is in addition to any duty a person may owe apart from that provision.

(3)   Any term of an agreement which purports to exclude or restrict, or has the effect of excluding or restricting, the operation of any of the provisions of this Act, or any liability arising by virtue of any such provision, shall be void.

(4)   ...

[330]

NOTES
   Sub-s (4): repeals the Occupiers' Liability Act 1957, s 4.

7 Short title, commencement and extent

(1) This Act may be cited as the Defective Premises Act 1972.

(2) This Act shall come into force on 1st January 1974.

(3) This Act does not extend to Scotland or Northern Ireland.

[331]

SEX DISCRIMINATION ACT 1975

(1975 c 65)

ARRANGEMENT OF SECTIONS

PART I
DISCRIMINATION TO WHICH ACT APPLIES

PART III
DISCRIMINATION IN OTHER FIELDS

Goods, facilities, services and premises

PART VIII
SUPPLEMENTAL

An Act to render unlawful certain kinds of sex discrimination and discrimination on the ground of marriage, and establish a Commission with the function of working towards the elimination of such discrimination and promoting equality of opportunity between men and women generally; and for related purposes

[12 November 1975]

PART I
DISCRIMINATION TO WHICH ACT APPLIES

[1 Direct and indirect discrimination against women

(1) In any circumstances relevant for the purposes of any provision of this Act, other than a provision to which subsection (2) applies, a person discriminates against a woman if—

    (a) on the ground of her sex he treats her less favourably than he treats or would treat a man, or

    (b) he applies to her a requirement or condition which he applies or would apply equally to a man but—

      (i)   which is such that the proportion of women who can comply with it is considerably smaller than the proportion of men who can comply with it, and

     (ii)   which he cannot show to be justifiable irrespective of the sex of the person to whom it is applied, and

    (iii)   which is to her detriment because she cannot comply with it.

(2)   In any circumstances relevant for the purposes of a provision to which this subsection applies, a person discriminates against a woman if—

    (a)   on the ground of her sex, he treats her less favourably than he treats or would treat a man, or

  [(b)   he applies to her a provision, criterion or practice which he applies or would apply equally to a man, but—

      (i)   which puts or would put women at a particular disadvantage when compared with men,

     (ii)   which puts her at that disadvantage, and

    (iii)   which he cannot show to be a proportionate means of achieving a legitimate aim.]

(3)   Subsection (2) applies to—

    (a)   any provision of Part 2,

    (b)   sections 35A and 35B, and

    (c)   any other provision of Part 3, so far as it applies to vocational training.

(4)   ...]

                                                         [332]

NOTES

Substituted by the Sex Discrimination (Indirect Discrimination and Burden of Proof) Regulations 2001, SI 2001/2660, reg 3.

Sub-s (2): para (b) substituted by the Employment Equality (Sex Discrimination) Regulations 2005, SI 2005/2467, reg 3(1).

Sub-s (4): repealed by the Civil Partnership Act 2004, ss 251(1), (3), 261(4), Sch 30.

Transfer of functions: functions of the Secretary of State for Trade and Industry transferred to the Secretary of State for Communities and Local Government, by the Secretary of State for Communities and Local Government Order 2006, SI 2006/1926, arts 7(1), (2), (3)(b), 8.

2 Sex discrimination against men

(1)   Section 1, and the provisions of Parts II and III relating to sex discrimination against women, are to be read as applying equally to the treatment of men, and for that purpose shall have effect with such modifications as are requisite.

(2)   In the application of subsection (1) no account shall be taken of special treatment afforded to women in connection with pregnancy or childbirth.

                                                         [333]

NOTES

Transfer of functions: functions of the Secretary of State for Trade and Industry transferred to the Secretary of State for Communities and Local Government, by the Secretary of State for Communities and Local Government Order 2006, SI 2006/1926, arts 7(1), (2), (3)(b), 8.

[2A Discrimination on the grounds of gender reassignment

(1)   A person ("A") discriminates against another person ("B") in any circumstances relevant for the purposes of—

    (a)   any provision of Part II,

    (b)   section 35A or 35B, or

    (c)   any other provision of Part III, so far as it applies to vocational training,

if he treats B less favourably than he treats or would treat other persons, and does so on the ground that B intends to undergo, is undergoing or has undergone gender reassignment.

(2)   Subsection (3) applies to arrangements made by any person in relation to another's absence from work or from vocational training.

(3)   For the purposes of subsection (1), B is treated less favourably than others under such arrangements if, in the application of the arrangements to any absence due to B undergoing gender reassignment—

    (a)   he is treated less favourably than he would be if the absence was due to sickness or injury, or

    (b)   he is treated less favourably than he would be if the absence was due to some other cause and, having regard to the circumstances of the case, it is reasonable for him to be treated no less favourably.

(4)   In subsections (2) and (3) "arrangements" includes terms, conditions or arrangements on which employment, a pupillage or tenancy or vocational training is offered.

(5)   For the purposes of subsection (1), a provision mentioned in that subsection framed with reference to discrimination against women shall be treated as applying equally to the treatment of men with such modifications as are requisite.]

[334]

NOTES

Inserted by the Sex Discrimination (Gender Reassignment) Regulations 1999, SI 1999/1102, reg 2(1).

Transfer of functions: functions of the Secretary of State for Trade and Industry transferred to the Secretary of State for Communities and Local Government, by the Secretary of State for Communities and Local Government Order 2006, SI 2006/1926, arts 7(1), (2), (3)(b), 8.

3   (*Outside the scope of this work.*)

[3A   Discrimination on the ground of pregnancy or maternity leave

(1)   In any circumstances relevant for the purposes of a provision to which this subsection applies, a person discriminates against a woman if—

    (a)   at a time in a protected period, and on the ground of the woman's pregnancy, the person treats her less favourably than he would treat her had she not become pregnant; or

    (b)   on the ground that the woman is exercising or seeking to exercise, or has exercised or sought to exercise, a statutory right to maternity leave, the person treats her less favourably than he would treat her if she were neither exercising nor seeking to exercise, and had neither exercised nor sought to exercise, such a right.

(2)   In any circumstances relevant for the purposes of a provision to which this subsection applies, a person discriminates against a woman if, on the ground that section 72(1) of the Employment Rights Act 1996 (compulsory maternity leave) has to be complied with in respect of the woman, he treats her less favourably than he would treat her if that provision did not have to be complied with in respect of her.

(3)   For the purposes of subsection (1)—

    (a)   in relation to a woman, a protected period begins each time she becomes pregnant, and the protected period associated with any particular pregnancy of hers ends in accordance with the following rules—

        (i)   if she is entitled to ordinary but not additional maternity leave in connection with the pregnancy, the protected period ends at the end of her period of ordinary maternity leave connected with the pregnancy or, if earlier, when she returns to work after the end of her pregnancy;

        (ii)   if she is entitled to ordinary and additional maternity leave in connection with the pregnancy, the protected period ends at the end of her period of additional maternity leave connected with the pregnancy or, if earlier, when she returns to work after the end of her pregnancy;

        (iii)   if she is not entitled to ordinary maternity leave in respect of the pregnancy, the protected period ends at the end of the 2 weeks beginning with the end of the pregnancy;

    (b)   where a person's treatment of a woman is on grounds of illness suffered by the woman as a consequence of a pregnancy of hers, that treatment is to be taken to be on the ground of the pregnancy;

    (c)   a "statutory right to maternity leave" means a right conferred by section 71(1) or 73(1) of the Employment Rights Act 1996 (ordinary and additional maternity leave).

(4)   In subsection (3) "ordinary maternity leave" and "additional maternity leave" shall be construed in accordance with sections 71 and 73 of the Employment Rights Act 1996.

(5)   Subsections (1) and (2) apply to—

    (a)   any provision of Part 2,

(b)   sections 35A and 35B, and

(c)   any other provision of Part 3, so far as it applies to vocational training.]

[334A]

NOTES

Commencement: 1 October 2005.

Inserted by the Employment Equality (Sex Discrimination) Regulations 2005, SI 2005/2467, reg 4.

Transfer of functions: functions of the Secretary of State for Trade and Industry transferred to the Secretary of State for Communities and Local Government, by the Secretary of State for Communities and Local Government Order 2006, SI 2006/1926, arts 7(1), (2), (3)(b), 8.

4   Discrimination by way of victimisation

(1)   A person ("the discriminator") discriminates against another person ("the person victimised") in any circumstances relevant for the purposes of any provision of this Act if he treats the person victimised less favourably than in those circumstances he treats or would treat other persons, and does so by reason that the person victimised has—

(a)   brought proceedings against the discriminator or any other person under this Act or the Equal Pay Act 1970 [or sections 62 to 65 of the Pensions Act 1995] [or Part I of Schedule 5 to the Social Security Act 1989], or

(b)   given evidence or information in connection with proceedings brought by any person against the discriminator or any other person under this Act or the Equal Pay Act 1970 [or sections 62 to 65 of the Pensions Act 1995] [or Part I of Schedule 5 to the Social Security Act 1989], or

(c)   otherwise done anything under or by reference to this Act or the Equal Pay Act 1970 [or sections 62 to 65 of the Pensions Act 1995] [or Part I of Schedule 5 to the Social Security Act 1989] in relation to the discriminator or any other person, or

(d)   alleged that the discriminator or any other person has committed an act which (whether or not the allegation so states) would amount to a contravention of this Act or give rise to a claim under the Equal Pay Act 1970 [or proceedings under Part I of Schedule 5 to the Social Security Act 1989] [or sections 62 to 65 of the Pensions Act 1995],

or by reason that the discriminator knows the person victimised intends to do any of those things, or suspects the person victimised has done, or intends to do, any of them.

(2)   Subsection (1) does not apply to treatment of a person by reason of any allegation made by him if the allegation was false and not made in good faith.

(3)   For the purposes of subsection (1), a provision of Part II or III framed with reference to discrimination against women shall be treated as applying equally to the treatment of men and for that purpose shall have effect with such modifications as are requisite.

[335]

NOTES

Sub-s (1): words in first, third, fifth and eighth pairs of square brackets inserted by the Pensions Act 1995, s 66(2); words in second, fourth, sixth and seventh pairs of square brackets inserted by the Social Security Act 1989, s 23, Sch 5, Pt II, para 14(1).

Transfer of functions: functions of the Secretary of State for Trade and Industry transferred to the Secretary of State for Communities and Local Government, by the Secretary of State for Communities and Local Government Order 2006, SI 2006/1926, arts 7(1), (2), (3)(b), 8.

[4A   Harassment, including sexual harassment

(1)   For the purposes of this Act, a person subjects a woman to harassment if—

(a)   on the ground of her sex, he engages in unwanted conduct that has the purpose or effect—

(i)   of violating her dignity, or

(ii)   of creating an intimidating, hostile, degrading, humiliating or offensive environment for her,

(b)   he engages in any form of unwanted verbal, non-verbal or physical conduct of a sexual nature that has the purpose or effect—

(i)   of violating her dignity, or

(ii)   of creating an intimidating, hostile, degrading, humiliating or offensive environment for her, or

    (c)   on the ground of her rejection of or submission to unwanted conduct of a kind mentioned in paragraph (a) or (b), he treats her less favourably than he would treat her had she not rejected, or submitted to, the conduct.

(2)   Conduct shall be regarded as having the effect mentioned in sub-paragraph (i) or (ii) of subsection (1)(a) or (b) only if, having regard to all the circumstances, including in particular the perception of the woman, it should reasonably be considered as having that effect.

(3)   For the purposes of this Act, a person ("A") subjects another person ("B") to harassment if—

    (a)   A, on the ground that B intends to undergo, is undergoing or has undergone gender reassignment, engages in unwanted conduct that has the purpose or effect—
        (i)   of violating B's dignity, or
        (ii)   of creating an intimidating, hostile, degrading, humiliating or offensive environment for B, or

    (b)   A, on the ground of B's rejection of or submission to unwanted conduct of a kind mentioned in paragraph (a), treats B less favourably than A would treat B had B not rejected, or submitted to, the conduct.

(4)   Conduct shall be regarded as having the effect mentioned in sub-paragraph (i) or (ii) of subsection (3)(a) only if, having regard to all the circumstances, including in particular the perception of B, it should reasonably be considered as having that effect.

(5)   Subsection (1) is to be read as applying equally to the harassment of men, and for that purpose shall have effect with such modifications as are requisite.

(6)   For the purposes of subsections (1) and (3), a provision of Part 2 or 3 framed with reference to harassment of women shall be treated as applying equally to the harassment of men, and for that purpose will have effect with such modifications as are requisite.]

[335A]

NOTES

Commencement: 1 October 2005.

Inserted by the Employment Equality (Sex Discrimination) Regulations 2005, SI 2005/2467, reg 5.

5 Interpretation

(1)   In this Act—
    (a)   references to discrimination refer to any discrimination falling within sections 1 to 4; and
    (b)   references to sex discrimination refer to any discrimination falling within [section 1, 2 or 3A],

and related expressions shall be construed accordingly.

(2)   In this Act—

"woman" includes a female of any age, and

"man" includes a male of any age.

[(3)   Each of the following comparisons, that is—
    (a)   a comparison of the cases of persons of different sex under section 1(1) or (2),
    (b)   a comparison of the cases of persons required for the purposes of section 2A, and
    (c)   a comparison of the cases of persons who do and who do not fulfil the condition in section 3(2),

must be such that the relevant circumstances in the one case are the same, or not materially different, in the other.]

[336]

NOTES

Sub-s (1): words in square brackets substituted by the Employment Equality (Sex Discrimination) Regulations 2005, SI 2005/2467, reg 6.

Sub-s (3): substituted by the Civil Partnership Act 2004, s 251(1), (3).

Transfer of functions: functions of the Secretary of State for Trade and Industry transferred to the Secretary of State for Communities and Local Government, by the Secretary of State for Communities and Local Government Order 2006, SI 2006/1926, arts 7(1), (2), (3)(b), 8.

6–21   (*(Pt II) Outside the scope of this work.*)

PART III
DISCRIMINATION IN OTHER FIELDS

NOTES

As to the effect of legislation made before this Act which imposes a requirement to do an act which would otherwise be unlawful by Pt III of this Act, see ss 51, 51A of this Act and the Employment Act 1989, s 1; see also for exemptions from Pt III of this Act, ss 4–6 of the 1989 Act.

21A, 22–28   (*Ss 21A (as inserted by the Equality Act 2006, s 83(1)), 22–27 outside the scope of this work; s 28 repealed by the Employment Equality (Sex Discrimination) Regulations 2005, SI 2005/2467, reg 23(1)(a).*)

Goods, facilities, services and premises

29   Discrimination in provision of goods, facilities or services

(1)   It is unlawful for any person concerned with the provision (for payment or not) of goods, facilities or services to the public or a section of the public to discriminate against a woman who seeks to obtain or use those goods, facilities or services—

(a)   by refusing or deliberately omitting to provide her with any of them, or

(b)   by refusing or deliberately omitting to provide her with goods, facilities or services of the like quality, in the like manner and on the like terms as are normal in his case in relation to male members of the public or (where she belongs to a section of the public) to male members of that section.

(2)   The following are examples of the facilities and services mentioned in subsection (1)—

(a)   access to and use of any place which members of the public or a section of the public are permitted to enter;

(b)   accommodation in a hotel, boarding house or other similar establishment;

(c)   facilities by way of banking or insurance or for grants, loans, credit or finance;

(d)   facilities for education;

(e)   facilities for entertainment, recreation or refreshment;

(f)   facilities for transport or travel;

(g)   the services of any profession or trade, or any local or other public authority.

(3)   For the avoidance of doubt it is hereby declared that where a particular skill is commonly exercised in a different way for men and for women it does not contravene subsection (1) for a person who does not normally exercise it for women to insist on exercising it for a woman only in accordance with his normal practice or, if he reasonably considers it impracticable to do that in her case, to refuse or deliberately omit to exercise it.

[(4)   In its application in relation to vocational training to discrimination falling within section 2A, subsection (1)(b) shall have effect as if references to male members of the public, or of a section of the public, were references to members of the public, or of a section of the public, who do not intend to undergo, are not undergoing and have not undergone gender reassignment.]

[337]

NOTES

Sub-s (4): added by the Sex Discrimination (Gender Reassignment) Regulations 1999, SI 1999/1102, reg 6.

Transfer of functions: functions of the Secretary of State for Trade and Industry transferred to the Secretary of State for Communities and Local Government, by the Secretary of State for Communities and Local Government Order 2006, SI 2006/1926, arts 7(1), (2), (3)(b), 8.

30   Discrimination in disposal or management of premises

(1)   It is unlawful for a person, in relation to premises in Great Britain of which he has power to dispose, to discriminate against a women—

(a)   in the terms on which he offers her those premises, or

(b)   by refusing her application for those premises, or

(c)   in his treatment of her in relation to any list of persons in need of premises of that description.

(2)   It is unlawful for a person, in relation to premises managed by him, to discriminate against a woman occupying the premises—

(a)   in the way he affords her access to any benefits or facilities, or by refusing or deliberately omitting to afford her access to them, or

(b)   by evicting her, or subjecting her to any other detriment.

(3)   Subsection (1) does not apply to a person who owns an estate or interest in the premises and wholly occupies them unless he uses the services of an estate agent for the purposes of the disposal of the premises, or publishes or causes to be published an advertisement in connection with the disposal.

[338]

NOTES

Transfer of functions: functions of the Secretary of State for Trade and Industry transferred to the Secretary of State for Communities and Local Government, by the Secretary of State for Communities and Local Government Order 2006, SI 2006/1926, arts 7(1), (2), (3)(b), 8.

31 Discrimination: consent for assignment or sub-letting

(1)   Where the licence or consent of the landlord or of any other person is required for the disposal to any person of premises in Great Britain comprised in a tenancy, it is unlawful for the landlord or other person to discriminate against a woman by withholding the licence or consent for disposal of the premises to her.

(2)   Subsection (1) does not apply if—

(a)   the person withholding a licence or consent, or a near relative of his ("the relevant occupier") resides, and intends to continue to reside, on the premises, and

(b)   there is on the premises, in addition to the accommodation occupied by the relevant occupier, accommodation (not being storage accommodation or means of access) shared by the relevant occupier with other persons residing on the premises who are not members of his household, and

(c)   the premises are small premises as defined in section 32(2).

(3)   In this section "tenancy" means a tenancy created by a lease or sub-lease, by an agreement for a lease or sub-lease or by a tenancy agreement or in pursuance of any enactment; and "disposal", in relation to premises comprised in a tenancy, includes assignment or assignation of the tenancy and sub-letting or parting with possession of the premises or any part of the premises.

(4)   This section applies to tenancies created before the passing of this Act, as well as to others.

[339]

NOTES

Transfer of functions: functions of the Secretary of State for Trade and Industry transferred to the Secretary of State for Communities and Local Government, by the Secretary of State for Communities and Local Government Order 2006, SI 2006/1926, arts 7(1), (2), (3)(b), 8.

32 Exception for small dwellings

(1)   Sections 29(1) and 30 do not apply to the provision by a person of accommodation in any premises, or the disposal of premises by him, if—

(a)   that person or a near relative of his ("the relevant occupier") resides, and intends to continue to reside, on the premises, and

(b)   there is on the premises, in addition to the accommodation occupied by the relevant occupier, accommodation (not being storage accommodation or means of access) shared by the relevant occupier with other persons residing on the premises who are not members of his household, and

(c)   the premises are small premises.

(2)   Premises shall be treated for the purposes of subsection (1) as small premises if—

(a)   in the case of premises comprising residential accommodation for one or more households (under separate letting or similar agreements) in addition to the accommodation occupied by the relevant occupier, there is not normally residential accommodation for more than two such households and only the relevant occupier and any member of his household reside in the accommodation occupied by him;

(b)   in the case of premises not falling within paragraph (a), there is not normally residential accommodation on the premises for more than six persons in addition to the relevant occupier and any members of his household.

[340]

NOTES

Transfer of functions: functions of the Secretary of State for Trade and Industry transferred to the Secretary of State for Communities and Local Government, by the Secretary of State for Communities and Local Government Order 2006, SI 2006/1926, arts 7(1), (2), (3)(b), 8.

33   (*Outside the scope of this work.*)

34 **Exception for voluntary bodies**

(1)   This section applies to a body—
    (a)   the activities of which are carried on otherwise than for profit, and
    (b)   which was not set up by any enactment.

(2)   Sections 29(1) and 30 shall not be construed as rendering unlawful—
    (a)   the restriction of membership of any such body to persons of one sex (disregarding any minor exceptions), or
    (b)   the provision of benefits, facilities or services to members of any such body where the membership is so restricted,

even though membership of the body is open to the public, or to a section of the public.

(3)   Nothing in section 29 or 30 shall—
    (a)   be construed as affecting a provision to which this subsection applies, or
    (b)   render unlawful an act which is done in order to give effect to such a provision.

(4)   Subsection (3) applies to a provision for conferring benefits on persons of one sex only (disregarding any benefits to persons to the opposite sex which are exceptional or are relatively insignificant), being a provision which constitutes the main object of a body within subsection (1).

[341]

NOTES

Transfer of functions: functions of the Secretary of State for Trade and Industry transferred to the Secretary of State for Communities and Local Government, by the Secretary of State for Communities and Local Government Order 2006, SI 2006/1926, arts 7(1), (2), (3)(b), 8.

35 **Further exceptions from ss 29(1) and 30**

(1), (2)   ...

(3)   Sections 29(1) and 30 do not apply—
    (a)   to discrimination which is rendered unlawful by any provision in column 1 of the table below, or
    (b)   to discrimination which would be so unlawful but for any provision in column 2 of that table, or
    (c)   to discrimination which contravenes a term modified or included by virtue of an equality clause.

TABLE

Provision creating illegality	*Exception*
Part II	Sections 6(3), 7(1)(b), 15(4), 19 and 20.
	Schedule 4 paragraphs 1 and 2.
Section 22 or 23	[Sections 26 and 27].
	Schedule 4 paragraph 4.

[342]

NOTES
Sub-ss (1), (2): outside the scope of this work.
Sub-s (3): in the Table, words in square brackets substituted by the Employment Equality (Sex Discrimination) Regulations 2005, SI 2005/2467, reg 23(1)(b).
Transfer of functions: functions of the Secretary of State for Trade and Industry transferred to the Secretary of State for Communities and Local Government, by the Secretary of State for Communities and Local Government Order 2006, SI 2006/1926, arts 7(1), (2), (3)(b), 8.

35A–76   (*Outside the scope of this work.*)

PART VIII
SUPPLEMENTAL

77–81   (*Outside the scope of this work.*)

82   General interpretation provisions

(1)   In this Act, unless the context otherwise requires—
"access" shall be construed in accordance with section 50;
"act" includes a deliberate omission;
"advertisement" includes every form of advertisement, whether to the public or not, and whether in a newspaper or other publication, by television or radio, by display of notices, signs, labels, showcards or goods, by distribution of samples, circulars, catalogues, price lists or other material by exhibition of pictures, models or films, or in any other way, and references to the publishing of advertisements shall be construed accordingly;
"associated employer" shall be construed in accordance with subsection (2);

.....

"the Commission" means the *Equal Opportunities Commission*;
"Commissioner" means a member of the Commission;

.....

"designate" shall be construed in accordance with subsection (3);
[references in Parts 2 and 3 to subjecting a person to a detriment do not include subjecting a person to harassment;]
"discrimination" and related terms shall be construed in accordance with section 5(1);
"dispose", in relation to premises, includes granting a right to occupy the premises, and any reference to acquiring premises shall be construed accordingly;
"education" includes any form of training or instruction;
["the Education Acts" has the meaning given by section 578 of the Education Act 1996;]

.....

"employment" means employment under a contract of service or of apprenticeship or a contract personally to execute any work or labour, and related expressions shall be construed accordingly;
"employment agency" means a person who, for profit or not, provides services for the purpose of finding employment for workers or supplying employers with workers;

.....

"equality clause" has the meaning given in section 1(2) of the Equal Pay Act 1970 (as set out in section 8(1) of this Act);
"estate agent" means a person who, by way of profession or trade, provides services for the purpose of finding premises for persons seeking to acquire them or assisting in the disposal of premises;
"final" shall be construed in accordance with subsection (4);
"firm" has the meaning given by section 4 of the Partnership Act 1890;
"formal investigation" means an investigation under section 57;
"further education" has the meaning given by [section 2 of the Education Act 1996] ... ;
["gender reassignment" means a process which is undertaken under medical supervision for the purpose of reassigning a person's sex by changing physiological or other characteristics of sex, and includes any part of such a process;]
"general notice", in relation to any person, means a notice published by him at a time and a manner appearing to him suitable for securing that the notice is seen within a reasonable time by persons likely to be affected by it;

"genuine occupational qualification" shall be construed in accordance with section 7(2)[, except in the expression "supplementary genuine occupational qualification", which shall be construed in accordance with section 7B(2)];

"Great Britain" includes such of the territorial waters of the United Kingdom as are adjacent to Great Britain;

[references to subjecting a person to harassment, and to acts of harassment, shall be construed in accordance with section 4A;]

"independent school" has the meaning given by [section 463 of the Education Act 1996] ... ;

.....

"man" includes a male of any age;

.....

"near relative" shall be construed in accordance with subsection (5);

"non-discrimination notice" means a notice under section 67;

"notice" means a notice in writing;

"prescribed" means prescribed by regulations made by the Secretary of State by statutory instrument;

"profession" includes any vocation or occupation;

"proprietor", in relation to any school, has the meaning given by [section 579 of the Education Act 1996] ... ;

["provision, criterion or practice" includes "requirement or condition";]

.....

"retirement" includes retirement (whether voluntary or not) on grounds of age, length of service or incapacity;

.....

"school" has the meaning given by [section 4 of the Education Act 1996], ... ;

.....

"trade" includes any business;

"training" includes any form of education or instruction;

"university" includes a university college and the college, school or hall of a university;

.....

["vocational training"—
- (a) means all types, and all levels, of—
  - (i) vocational training, advanced vocational training and retraining, and
  - (ii) vocational guidance, and
- (b) includes practical work experience undertaken for a limited period for the purposes of a person's vocational training (as defined by paragraph (a));]

"woman" includes a female of any age.

[(1A) References in this Act to the dismissal of a person from employment or to the expulsion of a person from a position as partner include references—
- (a) to the termination of that person's employment or partnership by the expiration of any period (including a period expiring by reference to an event or circumstance), not being a termination immediately after which the employment or partnership is renewed on the same terms; and
- (b) to the termination of that person's employment or partnership by any act of his (including the giving of notice) in circumstances such that he is entitled to terminate it without notice by reason of the conduct of the employer or, as the case may be, the conduct of the other partners.]

(2) For the purposes of this Act two employers are to be treated as associated if one is a company of which the other (directly or indirectly) has control or if both are companies of which a third person (directly or indirectly) has control.

(3) Any power conferred by this Act to designate establishments or persons may be exercised either by naming them or by identifying them by reference to a class or other description.

(4) For the purposes of this Act *a non-discrimination notice or* a finding by a court or tribunal becomes final when an appeal against the *notice or* finding is dismissed, withdrawn or abandoned or when the time for appealing expires without an appeal having been brought; *and for this purpose an appeal against a non-discrimination notice shall be taken to be dismissed if, notwithstanding that a requirement of the notice is quashed on appeal, a direction is given in respect of it under section 68(3).*

(5) For the purposes of this Act a person is a near relative of another if that person is the wife or husband [or civil partner], or parent or child, a grandparent or grandchild, or a brother

or sister of the other (whether of full blood or half-blood or [by marriage or civil partnership)], and "child" includes an illegitimate child and the wife or husband [or civil partner] of an illegitimate child.

(6)   Except so far as the context otherwise requires, any reference in this Act to an enactment shall be construed as a reference to that enactment as amended by or under any other enactment including this Act.

(7)   In this Act, except where otherwise indicated—

(a)   a reference to a numbered Part, section or Schedule is a reference to the Part or section of, or the Schedule to, this Act so numbered, and

(b)   a reference in a section to a numbered subsection is a reference to the subsection of that section so numbered, and

(c)   a reference in a section, subsection or Schedule to a numbered paragraph is a reference to the paragraph of that section, subsection or Schedule so numbered, and

(d)   a reference to any provision of an Act (including this Act) includes a Schedule incorporated in the Act by that provision.

[343]

NOTES

Sub-s (1): in definition "the Commission" for the words in italics there are substituted the words "Commission for Equality and Human Rights" and definitions "formal investigation" and "non-discrimination notice" repealed by the Equality Act 2006, ss 40, 91, Sch 3, paras 6, 18(a), Sch 4, as from a day to be appointed; definition relating to "detriment" and "harassment" inserted and definition "vocational training" inserted by the Employment Equality (Sex Discrimination) Regulations 2005, SI 2005/2467, reg 33; definition "the Education Acts" inserted, and words in square brackets in definitions "further education", "independent school", "proprietor" and "school" substituted by the Education Act 1996, s 582(1), Sch 37, Pt I, para 36; definition omitted in the third place repealed by the Employment Protection Act 1975, s 125(3), Sch 18; definition "gender reassignment" and words in square brackets in definition "genuine occupational qualification" inserted by the Sex Discrimination (Gender Reassignment) Regulations 1999, SI 1999/1102, regs 2(3), 4(6); definition "provision, criterion or practice" inserted by the Sex Discrimination (Indirect Discrimination and Burden of Proof) Regulations 2001, SI 2001/2660, reg 8(4); definition omitted in the seventh place repealed by the Industrial Training Act 1982, s 20, Sch 3, para 5(b), Sch 4; definition omitted in the ninth place repealed by the Education Act 1996, s 582(2), Sch 38, Pt II; words omitted from definitions "further education", "independent school", "proprietor" and "school", and other definitions omitted, apply to Scotland only.

Sub-s (1A): inserted by the Sex Discrimination Act 1986, s 2(3).

Sub-s (4): words in italics repealed by the Equality Act 2006, ss 40, 91, Sch 3, paras 6, 18(b), Sch 4, as from a day to be appointed.

Sub-s (5): words in first and third pairs of square brackets inserted and words in second pair of square brackets substituted by the Civil Partnership Act 2004, s 261(1), Sch 27, para 54.

Modification: sub-s (1A) is modified, in relation to governing bodies with delegated budgets, by the Education (Modification of Enactments Relating to Employment) (England) Order 2003, SI 2003/1964, art 3, Schedule and the Education (Modification of Enactments Relating to Employment) (Wales) Order 2006, SI 2006/1073, art 3, Schedule.

Transfer of functions: functions of the Secretary of State for Trade and Industry transferred to the Secretary of State for Communities and Local Government, by the Secretary of State for Communities and Local Government Order 2006, SI 2006/1926, arts 7(1), (2), (3)(b), 8.

83–86   (*Outside the scope of this work.*)

87   Short title and extent

(1)   This Act may be cited as the Sex Discrimination Act 1975.

(2)   This Act (except paragraph 16 of Schedule 3) does not extend to Northern Ireland.

[344]

(*Sch 1, Pt I repealed in part by the Sex Discrimination Act 1986, s 9(2), Schedule, Pt II, remainder amends the Equal Pay Act 1970; Sch 1, Pt II contains the text of the Equal Pay Act 1970 as so amended; Schs 2–4, 6 outside the scope of this work; Sch 5 repealed in part by the Employment Protection Act 1975, s 125(3), Sch 18, and the Sex Discrimination Act 1986, s 9, Schedule, Pt II, remainder applies to Scotland only or amends the Factories Act 1961, s 15(2).*)

RACE RELATIONS ACT 1976

(1976 c 74)

ARRANGEMENT OF SECTIONS

PART I
DISCRIMINATION TO WHICH ACT APPLIES

PART III
DISCRIMINATION IN OTHER FIELDS

Goods, facilities, services and premises

PART X
SUPPLEMENTAL

An Act to make fresh provision with respect to discrimination on racial grounds and relations between people of different racial groups; and to make in the Sex Discrimination Act 1975 amendments for bringing provisions in that Act relating to its administration and enforcement into conformity with the corresponding provisions in this Act

[22 November 1976]

PART I
DISCRIMINATION TO WHICH ACT APPLIES

1 Racial discrimination

(1)   A person discriminates against another in any circumstances relevant for the purposes of any provision of this Act if—

(a)   on racial grounds he treats that other less favourably than he treats or would treat other persons; or

(b)   he applies to that other a requirement or condition which he applies or would apply equally to persons not of the same racial group as that other but—
   (i)   which is such that the proportion of persons of the same racial group as that other who can comply with it is considerably smaller than the proportion of persons not of that racial group who can comply with it; and
   (ii)   which he cannot show to be justifiable irrespective of the colour, race, nationality or ethnic or national origins of the person to whom it is applied; and
   (iii)   which is to the detriment of that other because he cannot comply with it.

[(1A)   A person also discriminates against another if, in any circumstances relevant for the purposes of any provision referred to in subsection (1B), he applies to that other a provision, criterion or practice which he applies or would apply equally to persons not of the same race or ethnic or national origins as that other, but—

(a)   which puts or would put persons of the same race or ethnic or national origins as that other at a particular disadvantage when compared with other persons,

(b)   which puts that other at that disadvantage, and

(c)   which he cannot show to be a proportionate means of achieving a legitimate aim.

(1B)   The provisions mentioned in subsection (1A) are—

(a)   Part II;

(b)   sections 17 to 18D;

(c)   section 19B, so far as relating to—
    (i)   any form of social security;
    (ii)   health care;
    (iii)   any other form of social protection; and
    (iv)   any form of social advantage;
which does not fall within section 20;

(d)   sections 20 to 24;

(e)   sections 26A and 26B;

(f)   sections 76 and 76ZA; and

(g)   Part IV, in its application to the provisions referred to in paragraphs (a) to (f).

(1C)   Where, by virtue of subsection (1A), a person discriminates against another, subsection (1)(b) does not apply to him.]

(2)   It is hereby declared that, for the purposes of this Act, segregating a person from other persons on racial grounds is treating him less favourably than they are treated.

[345]

NOTES

Sub-ss (1A)–(1C): inserted by the Race Relations Act 1976 (Amendment) Regulations 2003, SI 2003/1626, reg 3.

---

2   Discrimination by way of victimisation

(1)   A person ("the discriminator") discriminates against another person ("the person victimised") in any circumstances relevant for the purposes of any provision of this Act if he treats the person victimised less favourably than in those circumstances he treats or would treat other persons, and does so by reason that the person victimised has—

(a)   brought proceedings against the discriminator or any other person under this Act; or

(b)   given evidence or information in connection with proceedings brought by any person against the discriminator or any other person under this Act; or

(c)   otherwise done anything under or by reference to this Act in relation to the discriminator or any other person; or

(d)   alleged that the discriminator or any other person has committed an act which (whether or not the allegation so states) would amount to a contravention of this Act,

or by reason that the discriminator knows that the person victimised intends to do any of those things, or suspects that the person victimised has done, or intends to do, any of them.

(2)   Subsection (1) does not apply to treatment of a person by reason of any allegation made by him if the allegation was false and not made in good faith.

[346]

3   Meaning of "racial grounds", "racial group" etc

(1)   In this Act, unless the context otherwise requires—

"racial grounds" means any of the following grounds, namely colour, race nationality or ethnic or national origins;

"racial group" means a group of persons defined by reference to colour, race, nationality or ethnic or national origins, and references to a person's racial group refer to any racial group into which he falls.

(2)   The fact that a racial group comprises two or more distinct racial groups does not prevent it from constituting a particular racial group for the purposes of this Act.

(3)   In this Act—

(a)   references to discrimination refer to any discrimination falling within section 1 or 2; and

    (b)   references to racial discrimination refer to any discrimination falling within section 1,

and related expressions shall be construed accordingly.

(4)   A comparison of the case of a person of a particular racial group with that of a person not of that group under section 1(1) [or (1A)] must be such that the relevant circumstances in the one case are the same, or not materially different, in the other.

[347]

NOTES

Sub-s (4): words in square brackets inserted by the Race Relations Act 1976 (Amendment) Regulations 2003, SI 2003/1626, reg 4.

[3A Harassment

(1)   A person subjects another to harassment in any circumstances relevant for the purposes of any provision referred to in section 1(1B) where, on grounds of race or ethnic or national origins, he engages in unwanted conduct which has the purpose or effect of—

    (a)   violating that other person's dignity, or

    (b)   creating an intimidating, hostile, degrading, humiliating or offensive environment for him.

(2)   Conduct shall be regarded as having the effect specified in paragraph (a) or (b) of subsection (1) only if, having regard to all the circumstances, including in particular the perception of that other person, it should reasonably be considered as having that effect.]

[348]

NOTES

Commencement: 19 July 2003.

Inserted by the Race Relations Act 1976 (Amendment) Regulations 2003, SI 2003/1626, reg 5.

4–16   *((Pt II) ss 4–15 outside the scope of this work; s 16 repealed by the Race Relations (Amendment) Act 2000, s 9(2), Sch 3.)*

PART III
DISCRIMINATION IN OTHER FIELDS

17–19F   *(Outside the scope of this work.)*

Goods, facilities, services and premises

20   ... provision of goods, facilities or services

(1)   It is unlawful for any person concerned with the provision (for payment or not) of goods, facilities or services to the public or a section of the public to discriminate against a person who seeks to obtain or use those goods, facilities or services—

    (a)   by refusing or deliberately omitting to provide him with any of them; or

    (b)   by refusing or deliberately omitting to provide him with goods, facilities or services of the like quality, in the like manner and on the like terms as are normal in the first-mentioned person's case in relation to other members of the public or (where the person so seeking belongs to a section of the public) to other members of that section.

(2)   The following are examples of the facilities and services mentioned in subsection (1)—

    (a)   access to and use of any place which members of the public are permitted to enter;

    (b)   accommodation in a hotel, boarding house or other similar establishment;

    (c)   facilities by way of banking or insurance or for grants, loans, credit or finance;

    (d)   facilities for education;

    (e)   facilities for entertainment, recreation or refreshment;

    (f)   facilities for transport or travel;

    (g)   the services of any profession or trade, or any local or other public authority.

[(3) It is unlawful for any person concerned with the provision of goods, facilities or services as mentioned in subsection (1), in relation to such provision, to subject to harassment—

    (a)   a person who seeks to obtain or use those goods, facilities or services, or

    (b)   a person to whom he provides those goods, facilities or services.]

[349]

NOTES

Section heading: words omitted repealed by the Race Relations Act 1976 (Amendment) Regulations 2003, SI 2003/1626, reg 22(1).

Sub-s (3): added by SI 2003/1626, reg 22(2).

21 ... disposal or management of premises

(1) It is unlawful for a person, in relation to premises in Great Britain of which he has power to dispose, to discriminate against another—

    (a)   in the terms on which he offers him those premises; or

    (b)   by refusing his application for those premises; or

    (c)   in his treatment of him in relation to any list of persons in need of premises of that description.

(2) It is unlawful for a person, in relation to premises managed by him, to discriminate against a person occupying the premises—

    (a)   in the way he affords him access to any benefits or facilities, or by refusing or deliberately omitting to afford him access to them; or

    (b)   by evicting him, or subjecting him to any other detriment.

[(2A) It is unlawful for a person, in relation to such premises as are referred to in subsection (1) or (2), to subject to harassment a person who applies for or, as the case may be, occupies such premises.]

(3) Subsection (1) does not apply to [discrimination, on grounds other than those of race or ethnic or national origins, by] a person who owns an estate or interest in the premises and wholly occupies them unless he uses the services of an estate agent for the purposes of the disposal of the premises, or publishes or causes to be published an advertisement in connection with the disposal.

[350]

NOTES

Section heading: words omitted repealed by the Race Relations Act 1976 (Amendment) Regulations 2003, SI 2003/1626, reg 23(1).

Sub-s (2A): inserted by SI 2003/1626, reg 23(2)(a).

Sub-s (3): words in square brackets inserted by SI 2003/1626, reg 23(2)(b).

22 Exception from ss 20(1) and 21: small dwellings

(1) Sections 20(1) and 21 do not apply to [discrimination on grounds other than those of race or ethnic or national origins in either] the provision by a person of accommodation in any premises, or the disposal of premises by him, if—

    (a)   that person or a near relative of his ("the relevant occupier") resides, and intends to continue to reside, on the premises; and

    (b)   there is on the premises, in addition to the accommodation occupied by the relevant occupier, accommodation (not being storage accommodation or means of access) shared by the relevant occupier with other persons residing on the premises who are not members of his household; and

    (c)   the premises are small premises.

(2) Premises shall be treated for the purposes of this section as small premises if—

    (a)   in the case of premises comprising residential accommodation for one or more households (under separate letting or similar agreements) in addition to the accommodation occupied by the relevant occupier, there is not normally residential accommodation for more than two such households and only the relevant occupier and any member of his household reside in the accommodation occupied by him;

    (b)   in the case of premises not falling within paragraph (a), there is not normally residential accommodation on the premises for more than six persons in addition to the relevant occupier and any members of his household.

[351]

NOTES

Sub-s (1): words in square brackets inserted by the Race Relations Act 1976 (Amendment) Regulations 2003, SI 2003/1626, reg 24.

23 Further exceptions from [ss 20] and 21

(1) Sections [20] and 21 do not apply—
  (a) to discrimination [or harassment] which is rendered unlawful by any provision of Part II or section 17 or 18; or
  (b) to discrimination which would be rendered unlawful by any provision of Part II but for any of the following provisions, namely sections 4(3)[, 4A(1)(b)], 5(1)(b), 6, 7(4), 9 and 14(4).

(2) Section 20(1) does not apply to anything done by a person as a participant in arrangements under which he (for reward or not) takes into his home, and treats as if they were members of his family, children, elderly persons, or persons requiring a special degree of care and attention.

[352]

NOTES

Section heading: words in square brackets substituted by the Race Relations Act 1976 (Amendment) Regulations 2003, SI 2003/1626, reg 25(1).
Sub-s (1): number in square brackets substituted and words in square brackets inserted by SI 2003/1626, reg 25(2).

24 ... consent for assignment or sub-letting

(1) Where the licence or consent of the landlord or of any other person is required for the disposal to any person of premises in Great Britain comprised in a tenancy, it is unlawful for the landlord or other person[—
  (a) to discriminate against a person by withholding the licence or consent for disposal of the premises to him, or
  (b) in relation to such a licence or consent, to subject to harassment a person who applies for the licence or consent, or from whom the licence or consent is withheld].

(2) Subsection (1) does not apply [to discrimination on grounds other than those of race or ethnic or national origins] if—
  (a) the person withholding a licence or consent, or a near relative of his ("the relevant occupier") resides, and intends to continue to reside, on the premises; and
  (b) there is on the premises, in addition to the accommodation occupied by the relevant occupier, accommodation (not being storage accommodation or means of access) shared by the relevant occupier with other persons residing on the premises who are not members of his household; and
  (c) the premises are small premises.

(3) Section 22(2) (meaning of "small premises") shall apply for the purposes of this as well as of that section.

(4) In this section "tenancy" means a tenancy created by a lease or sub-lease, by an agreement for a lease or sub-lease or by a tenancy agreement or in pursuance of any enactment; and "disposal", in relation to premises comprised in a tenancy, includes assignment or assignation of the tenancy and sub-letting or parting with possession of the premises or any part of the premises.

(5) This section applies to tenancies created before the passing of this Act, as well as to others.

[353]

NOTES

Section heading: words omitted repealed by the Race Relations Act 1976 (Amendment) Regulations 2003, SI 2003/1626, reg 26(1).

Sub-s (1): words in square brackets substituted by SI 2003/1626, reg 26(2)(a).
Sub-s (2): words in square brackets inserted by SI 2003/1626, reg 26(2)(b).

25–70 (*Outside the scope of this work.*)

PART X
SUPPLEMENTAL

71–77 (*Outside the scope of this work.*)

78 General interpretation provisions

(1) In this Act, unless the context otherwise requires—
"access" shall be construed in accordance with section 40;
"act" includes a deliberate omission;
"advertisement" includes every form of advertisement or notice, whether to the public or
   not, and whether in a newspaper or other publication, by television or radio, by
   display of notices, signs, labels, showcards or goods, by distribution of samples,
   circulars, catalogues, price lists or other material, by exhibition of pictures, models or
   films, or in any other way, and references to the publishing of advertisements shall be
   construed accordingly;

.....

["body" includes an unincorporated association;]
"the Commission" means the *Commission for Racial Equality*;
"Commissioner" means a member of the Commission;
["criminal investigation" has the meaning given by section 57(4B);]
["criminal proceedings" includes—
   (*a*) *proceedings on dealing summarily with a charge under the Army Act 1955
        or the Air Force Act 1955 or on summary trial under the Naval Discipline
        Act 1957;*
   (*b*) *proceedings before a summary appeal court constituted under any of those
        Acts;*
   (*c*) *proceedings before a court-martial constituted under any of those Acts or a
        disciplinary court constituted under section 52G of the Act of 1957;*
   (*d*) *proceedings before the Courts-Martial Appeal Court; and*
   (*e*) *proceedings before a Standing Civilian Court;]*
"designated county court" has the meaning given by section 67(1);
["detriment" does not include conduct of a nature such as to constitute harassment under
   section 3A;]
"discrimination" and related terms shall be construed in accordance with section 3(3);
"dispose", in relation to premises, includes granting a right to occupy the premises, and
   any reference to acquiring premises shall be construed accordingly;
"education" includes any form of training or instruction;
["the Education Acts" has the meaning given by section 578 of the Education Act 1996;]

.....

"employment" means employment under a contract of service or of apprenticeship or a
   contract personally to execute any work or labour, and related expressions shall be
   construed accordingly;
"employment agency" means a person who, for profit or not, provides services for the
   purpose of finding employment for workers or supplying employers with workers;

.....

"estate agent" means a person who, by way of profession or trade, provides services for
   the purpose of finding premises for persons seeking to acquire them or assisting in
   the disposal of premises;
"final" shall be construed in accordance with subsection (4);
"firm" has the meaning given by section 4 of the Partnership Act 1890;
"formal investigation" means an investigation under section 48;

.....

"general notice", in relation to any person, means a notice published by him at a time
   and in a manner appearing to him suitable for securing that the notice is seen within
   a reasonable time by persons likely to be affected by it;
"genuine occupational qualification" shall be construed in accordance with section 5;

195

"Great Britain" includes such of the territorial waters of the United Kingdom as are adjacent to Great Britain;

"independent school" has for England and Wales the meaning given by [section 463 of the Education Act 1996], ...;

.....

.....

"Minister of the Crown" includes the Treasury and the Defence Council;

"nationality" includes citizenship;

"near relative" shall be construed in accordance with subsection (5);

"non-discrimination notice" means a notice under section 58;

"notice" means a notice in writing;

"prescribed" means prescribed by regulations made by the Secretary of State;

"profession" includes any vocation or occupation;

"proprietor", in relation to a school, has for England and Wales the meaning given by [section 579 of the Education Act 1996], ...;

.....

"racial grounds" and "racial group" have the meaning given by section 3(1);

"school" has for England and Wales the meaning given by [section 4 of the Education Act 1996], ...;

.....

["social protection" and "social advantage" have the same meaning as in Article 3 of Council Directive 2000/43/EC;]

"trade" includes any business;

"training" includes any form of education or instruction;

"university" includes a university college and the college, school or hall of a university;

.....

(2) It is hereby declared that in this Act "premises", unless the context otherwise requires, includes land of any description.

(3) Any power conferred by this Act to designate establishments or persons may be exercised either by naming them or by identifying them by reference to a class or other description.

(4) For the purposes of this Act *a non-discrimination notice or* a finding by a court or tribunal becomes final when an appeal against the *notice or* finding is dismissed, withdrawn or abandoned or when the time for appealing expires without an appeal having been brought; *and for this purpose an appeal against a non-discrimination notice shall be taken to be dismissed if, notwithstanding that a requirement of the notice is quashed on appeal, a direction is given in respect of it under section 59(3).*

(5) For the purposes of this Act a person is a near relative of another if that person is the wife or husband, a parent or child [or civil partner], a grandparent or grandchild, or a brother or sister of the other (whether of full blood or half-blood or [by marriage or civil partnership)], and "child" includes an illegitimate child and the wife or husband [or civil partner] of an illegitimate child.

(6) Except so far as the context otherwise requires, any reference in this Act to an enactment shall be construed as a reference to that enactment as amended by or under any other enactment, including this Act.

(7) In this Act, except where otherwise indicated—
  (a) a reference to a numbered Part, section or Schedule is a reference to the Part or section of, or the Schedule to, this Act so numbered; and
  (b) a reference in a section to a numbered subsection is a reference to the subsection of that section so numbered; and
  (c) a reference in a section, subsection or Schedule to a numbered paragraph is a reference to the paragraph of that section, subsection or Schedule so numbered; and
  (d) a reference to any provision of an Act (including this Act) includes a Schedule incorporated in the Act by that provision.

[354]

NOTES

Sub-s (1): definitions "body", "criminal investigation" and "criminal proceedings" inserted by the Race Relations (Amendment) Act 2000, s 9(1), Sch 2, para 19; in definition "the Commission" for the words in italics there are substituted the words "Commission for Equality and Human Rights" and definitions "formal investigation" and "non-discrimination notice" repealed by the Equality Act 2006, s 40, Sch 3,

paras 21, 33(a), as from a day to be appointed; definition "criminal proceedings" substituted by definition
""criminal proceedings" includes service law proceedings (as defined by section 324(5) of the Armed
Forces Act 2006);" by the Armed Forces Act 2006, s 378(1), Sch 16, para 81, as from a day to be
appointed; definitions "detriment", "social protection" and "social advantage" inserted by the Race
Relations Act 1976 (Amendment) Regulations 2003, SI 2003/1626, reg 52; definition "the Education
Acts" inserted, and words in square brackets in definitions "independent school", "proprietor" and
"school" substituted by the Education Act 1996, s 582(1), Sch 37, Pt I, para 43; definition omitted in the
fifth place repealed by the Industrial Training Act 1982, s 20, Sch 3, para 7(b), Sch 4; definition omitted
in the ninth place repealed by the Education Act 1996, s 582(2), Sch 38, Pt II; words omitted from
definitions "independent school", "proprietor" and "school", and other definitions omitted, apply to
Scotland only.

Sub-s (4): words in italics repealed by the Equality Act 2006, ss 40, 91, Sch 3, paras 21, 33(b), Sch 4,
as from a day to be appointed.

Sub-s (5): words in first and third pairs of square brackets inserted and words in second pair of square
brackets substituted by the Civil Partnership Act 2004, s 261(1), Sch 27, para 55.

79 (*Outside the scope of this work.*)

80 Short title and extent

(1)   This Act may be cited as the Race Relations Act 1976.

(2)   This Act, except so far as it amends or repeals any provision of the House of
Commons Disqualification Act 1975 or the Northern Ireland Assembly Disqualification
Act 1975, does not extend to Northern Ireland.

[355]

(*Schs 1, 1A, 2, 5 outside the scope of this work; Sch 3 repealed by the Trade Union and
Labour Relations (Consolidation) Act 1992, s 300(1), Sch 1; Sch 4, in so far as unrepealed, in
part amends the Sex Discrimination Act 1975 and in part applies to Scotland only.*)

TORTS (INTERFERENCE WITH GOODS) ACT 1977

(1977 c 32)

An Act to amend the law concerning conversion and other torts affecting goods
[22 July 1977]

1–11   (*Outside the scope of this work.*)

Uncollected goods

12 Bailee's power of sale

(1)   This section applies to goods in the possession or under the control of a bailee
where—

(a)   the bailor is in breach of an obligation to take delivery of the goods or, if the terms
of the bailment so provide, to give directions as to their delivery, or

(b)   the bailee could impose such an obligation by giving notice to the bailor, but is
unable to trace or communicate with the bailor, or

(c)   the bailee can reasonably expect to be relieved of any duty to safeguard the goods
on giving notice to the bailor, but is unable to trace or communicate with the
bailor.

(2)   In the cases in Part I of Schedule 1 to this Act a bailee may, for the purposes of
subsection (1), impose an obligation on the bailor to take delivery of the goods, or as the case
may be to give directions as to their delivery, and in those cases the said Part I sets out the
methods of notification.

(3)   If the bailee—

(a)   has in accordance with Part II of Schedule 1 to this Act given notice to the bailor
of his intention to sell the goods under this subsection, or

(b)   has failed to trace or communicate with the bailor with a view to giving him such
a notice, after having taken reasonable steps for the purpose,

and is reasonably satisfied that the bailor owns the goods, he shall be entitled, as against the bailor, to sell the goods.

(4)   Where subsection (3) applies but the bailor did not in fact own the goods, a sale under this section, or under section 13, shall not give a good title as against the owner, or as against a person claiming under the owner.

(5)   A bailee exercising his powers under subsection (3) shall be liable to account to the bailor for the proceeds of sale, less any costs of sale, and—

(a)   the account shall be taken on the footing that the bailee should have adopted the best method of sale reasonably available in the circumstances, and

(b)   where subsection (3)(a) applies, any sum payable in respect of the goods by the bailor to the bailee which accrued due before the bailee gave notice of intention to sell the goods shall be deductible from the proceeds of sale.

(6)   A sale duly made under this section gives a good title to the purchaser as against the bailor.

(7)   In this section, section 13, and Schedule 1 to this Act,

(a)   "bailor" and "bailee" include their respective successors in title, and

(b)   references to what is payable, paid or due to the bailee in respect of the goods include references to what would be payable by the bailor to the bailee as a condition of delivery of the goods at the relevant time.

(8)   This section, and Schedule 1 to this Act, have effect subject to the terms of the bailment.

(9)   This section shall not apply where the goods were bailed before the commencement of this Act.

[356]

13   Sale authorised by the court

(1)   If a bailee of the goods to which section 12 applies satisfies the court that he is entitled to sell the goods under section 12, or that he would be so entitled if he had given any notice required in accordance with Schedule 1 to this Act, the court—

(a)   may authorise the sale of the goods subject to such terms and conditions, if any, as may be specified in the order, and

(b)   may authorise the bailee to deduct from the proceeds of sale any costs of sale and any amount due from the bailor to the bailee in respect of the goods, and

(c)   may direct the payment into court of the net proceeds of sale, less any amount deducted under paragraph (b), to be held to the credit of the bailor.

(2)   A decision of the court authorising a sale under this section shall, subject to any right of appeal, be conclusive, as against the bailor, of the bailee's entitlement to sell the goods, and gives a good title to the purchaser as against the bailor.

(3)   In this section "the court" means the High Court or a county court, [and a county court shall have jurisdiction in the proceedings save that, in Northern Ireland, a county court shall only have jurisdiction in proceedings if the value of the goods does not exceed the county court limit mentioned in Article 10(1) of the County Courts (Northern Ireland) Order 1980.]

[357]

NOTES

Sub-s (3): words in square brackets substituted by the High Court and County Courts Jurisdiction Order 1991, SI 1991/724, art 2(1)(i), (8), Schedule, Pt I, subject to transitional provisions and savings contained in arts 11, 12 thereof at **[1237]**, **[1238]**.

Supplemental

14   Interpretation

(1)   In this Act, unless the context otherwise requires—

.....

"enactment" includes an enactment contained in an Act of the Parliament of Northern Ireland or an Order in Council made under the Northern Ireland (Temporary Provisions) Act 1972, or in a Measure of the Northern Ireland Assembly,

"goods" includes all chattels personal other than things in action and money,
"High Court" includes the High Court of Justice in Northern Ireland.

(2) References in this Act to any enactment include references to that enactment as amended, extended or applied by or under that or any other enactment.

[358]

NOTES

Sub-s (1): definition "county court limit" repealed by the High Court and County Courts Jurisdiction Order 1991, SI 1991/724, art 2(8), Schedule, Pt I, subject to transitional provisions and savings contained in arts 11, 12 thereof at **[1237]**, **[1238]**.

15, 16 (*Outside the scope of this work.*)

17 Short title, etc

(1) This Act may be cited as the Torts (Interference with Goods) Act 1977.

(2) This Act shall come into force on such day as the Lord Chancellor may by order contained in a statutory instrument appoint, and such an order may appoint different dates for different provisions or for different purposes.

(3) …

[359]

NOTES

Sub-s (3): outside the scope of this work.

Orders: the Torts (Interference with Goods) Act 1977 (Commencement No 1) Order 1977, SI 1977/1910; the Torts (Interference with Goods) Act 1977 (Commencement No 2) Order 1978, SI 1978/627; the Torts (Interference with Goods) Act 1977 (Commencement No 3) Order 1980, SI 1980/2024.

SCHEDULES

SCHEDULE 1
UNCOLLECTED GOODS

Section 12

PART I
POWER TO IMPOSE OBLIGATION TO COLLECT GOODS

1.—(1) For the purposes of section 12(1) a bailee may, in the circumstances specified in this Part of this Schedule, by notice given to the bailor impose on him an obligation to take delivery of the goods.

(2) The notice shall be in writing, and may be given either—
   (a) by delivering it to the bailor, or
   (b) by leaving it at his proper address, or
   (c) by post.

(3) The notice shall—
   (a) specify the name and address of the bailee, and give sufficient particulars of the goods and the address or place where they are held, and
   (b) state that the goods are ready for delivery to the bailor, or where combined with a notice terminating the contract of bailment, will be ready for delivery when the contract is terminated, and
   (c) specify the amount, if any, which is payable by the bailor to the bailee in respect of the goods and which became due before the giving of the notice.

(4) Where the notice is sent by post it may be combined with a notice under Part II of this Schedule if the notice is sent by post in a way complying with paragraph 6(4).

(5) References in this Part of this Schedule to taking delivery of the goods include, where the terms of the bailment admit, references to giving directions as to their delivery.

(6) This Part of this Schedule is without prejudice to the provisions of any contract requiring the bailor to take delivery of the goods.

Goods accepted for repair or other treatment

2.   If a bailee has accepted goods for repair or other treatment on the terms (expressed or implied) that they will be re-delivered to the bailor when the repair or other treatment has been carried out, the notice may be given at any time after the repair or other treatment has been carried out.

Goods accepted for valuation or appraisal

3.   If a bailee has accepted goods in order to value or appraise them, the notice may be given at any time after the bailee has carried out the valuation or appraisal.

Storage, warehousing, etc

4.—(1)   If a bailee is in possession of goods which he has held as custodian, and his obligation as custodian has come to an end, the notice may be given at any time after the ending of the obligation, or may be combined with any notice terminating his obligation as custodian.

(2)   This paragraph shall not apply to goods held by a person as mercantile agent, that is to say by a person having in the customary course of his business as a mercantile agent authority either to sell goods or to consign goods for the purpose of sale, or to buy goods, or to raise money on the security of goods.

Supplemental

5.   Paragraphs 2, 3 and 4 apply whether or not the bailor has paid any amount due to the bailee in respect of the goods, and whether or not the bailment is for reward, or in the course of business, or gratuitous.

[360]

PART II
NOTICE OF INTENTION TO SELL GOODS

6.—(1)   A notice under section 12(3) shall—

   (a)   specify the name and address of the bailee, and give sufficient particulars of the goods and the address or place where they are held, and

   (b)   specify the date on or after which the bailee proposes to sell the goods, and

   (c)   specify the amount, if any, which is payable by the bailor to the bailee in respect of the goods, and which became due before the giving of the notice.

(2)   The period between giving of the notice and the date specified in the notice as that on or after which the bailee proposes to exercise the power of sale shall be such as will afford the bailor a reasonable opportunity of taking delivery of the goods.

(3)   If any amount is payable in respect of the goods by the bailor to the bailee, and became due before giving of the notice, the said period shall be not less than three months.

(4)   The notice shall be in writing and shall be sent by post in a registered letter, or by the recorded delivery service.

7.—(1)   The bailee shall not give a notice under section 12(3), or exercise his right to sell the goods pursuant to such a notice, at a time when he has notice that, because of a dispute concerning the goods, the bailor is questioning or refusing to pay all or any part of what the bailee claims to be due to him in respect of the goods.

(2)   This paragraph shall be left out of account in determining under section 13(1) whether a bailee of goods is entitled to sell the goods under section 12, or would be so entitled if he had given any notice required in accordance with this Schedule.

Supplemental

8.   For the purposes of this Schedule, and of section 26 of the Interpretation Act 1889 in its application to this Schedule, the proper address of the person to whom a notice is to be given shall be—

(a)   in the case of a body corporate, a registered or principal office of the body corporate, and

(b)   in any other case, the last known address of the person.

[361]

(Sch 2 outside the scope of this work.)

PROTECTION FROM EVICTION ACT 1977

(1977 c 43)

ARRANGEMENT OF SECTIONS

PART I
UNLAWFUL EVICTION AND HARASSMENT

PART III
SUPPLEMENTAL PROVISIONS

An Act to consolidate section 16 of the Rent Act 1957 and Part III of the Rent Act 1965, and related enactments.

[29 July 1977]

PART I
UNLAWFUL EVICTION AND HARASSMENT

1   Unlawful eviction and harassment of occupier

(1)   In this section "residential occupier", in relation to any premises, means a person occupying the premises as a residence, whether under a contract or by virtue of any enactment or rule of law giving him the right to remain in occupation or restricting the right of any other person to recover possession of the premises.

(2)   If any person unlawfully deprives the residential occupier of any premises of his occupation of the premises or any part thereof, or attempts to do so, he shall be guilty of an offence unless he proves that he believed, and had reasonable cause to believe, that the residential occupier had ceased to reside in the premises.

(3)   If any person with intent to cause the residential occupier of any premises—

(a)   to give up the occupation of the premises or any part thereof; or

(b)   to refrain from exercising any right or pursuing any remedy in respect of the premises or part thereof;

does acts [likely] to interfere with the peace or comfort of the residential occupier or members of his household, or persistently withdraws or withholds services reasonably required for the occupation of the premises as a residence, he shall be guilty of an offence.

[(3A)   Subject to subsection (3B) below, the landlord of a residential occupier or an agent of the landlord shall be guilty of an offence if—

    (a)   he does acts likely to interfere with the peace or comfort of the residential occupier or members of his household, or

    (b)   he persistently withdraws or withholds services reasonably required for the occupation of the premises in question as a residence,

and (in either case) he knows, or has reasonable cause to believe, that that conduct is likely to cause the residential occupier to give up the occupation of the whole or part of the premises or to refrain from exercising any right or pursuing any remedy in respect of the whole or part of the premises.

(3B)   A person shall not be guilty of an offence under subsection (3A) above if he proves that he had reasonable grounds for doing the acts or withdrawing or withholding the services in question.

(3C)   In subsection (3A) above "landlord", in relation to a residential occupier of any premises, means the person who, but for—

    (a)   the residential occupier's right to remain in occupation of the premises, or

    (b)   a restriction on the person's right to recover possession of the premises,

would be entitled to occupation of the premises and any superior landlord under whom that person derives title.]

(4)   A person guilty of an offence under this section shall be liable—

    (a)   on summary conviction, to a fine not exceeding [the prescribed sum] or to imprisonment for a term not exceeding 6 months or to both;

    (b)   on conviction on indictment, to a fine or to imprisonment for a term not exceeding 2 years or to both.

(5)   Nothing in this section shall be taken to prejudice any liability or remedy to which a person guilty of an offence thereunder may be subject in civil proceedings.

(6)   Where an offence under this section committed by a body corporate is proved to have been committed with the consent or connivance of, or to be attributable to any neglect on the part of, any director, manager or secretary or other similar officer of the body corporate or any person who was purporting to act in any such capacity, he as well as the body corporate shall be guilty of that offence and shall be liable to be proceeded against and punished accordingly.

[362]

NOTES
Sub-s (3): word in square brackets substituted by the Housing Act 1988, s 29(1).
Sub-ss (3A)–(3C): inserted by the Housing Act 1988, s 29(2).
Sub-s (4): words in square brackets substituted by virtue of the Magistrates' Court Act 1980, s 32(2).

2   Restriction on re-entry without due process of law

Where any premises are let as a dwelling on a lease which is subject to a right of re-entry or forfeiture it shall not be lawful to enforce that right otherwise than by proceedings in the court while any person is lawfully residing in the premises or part of them.

[363]

3   Prohibition of eviction without due process of law

(1)   Where any premises have been let as a dwelling under a tenancy which is [neither a statutorily protected tenancy nor an excluded tenancy] and—

    (a)   the tenancy (in this section referred to as the former tenancy) has come to an end, but

    (b)   the occupier continues to reside in the premises or part of them,

it shall not be lawful for the owner to enforce against the occupier, otherwise than by proceedings in the court, his right to recover possession of the premises.

(2)   In this section "the occupier", in relation to any premises, means any person lawfully residing in the premises or part of them at the termination of the former tenancy.

[(2A)   Subsections (1) and (2) above apply in relation to any restricted contract (within the meaning of the Rent Act 1977) which—
  (a)   creates a licence; and
  (b)   is entered into after the commencement of section 69 of the Housing Act 1980;
as they apply in relation to a restricted contract which creates a tenancy.]

[(2B)   Subsections (1) and (2) above apply in relation to any premises occupied as a dwelling under a licence, other than an excluded licence, as they apply in relation to premises let as a dwelling under a tenancy, and in those subsections the expressions "let" and "tenancy" shall be construed accordingly.

(2C)   References in the preceding provisions of this section and section 4(2A) below to an excluded tenancy do not apply to—
  (a)   a tenancy entered into before the date on which the Housing Act 1988 came into force, or
  (b)   a tenancy entered into on or after that date but pursuant to a contract made before that date,
but, subject to that, "excluded tenancy" and "excluded licence" shall be construed in accordance with section 3A below.]

(3)   This section shall, with the necessary modifications, apply where the owner's right to recover possession arises on the death of the tenant under a statutory tenancy within the meaning of the Rent Act 1977 or the Rent (Agriculture) Act 1976.

[364]

NOTES

Sub-s (1): words in square brackets substituted by the Housing Act 1988, s 30(1).
Sub-s (2A): inserted by the Housing Act 1980, s 69(1).
Sub-ss (2B), (2C): inserted by the Housing Act 1988, s 30(2).

[3A   Excluded tenancies and licences

(1)   Any reference in this Act to an excluded tenancy or an excluded licence is a reference to a tenancy or licence which is excluded by virtue of any of the following provisions of this section.

(2)   A tenancy or licence is excluded if—
  (a)   under its terms the occupier shares any accommodation with the landlord or licensor; and
  (b)   immediately before the tenancy or licence was granted and also at the time it comes to an end, the landlord or licensor occupied as his only or principal home premises of which the whole or part of the shared accommodation formed part.

(3)   A tenancy or licence is also excluded if—
  (a)   under its terms the occupier shares any accommodation with a member of the family of the landlord or licensor;
  (b)   immediately before the tenancy or licence was granted and also at the time it comes to an end, the member of the family of the landlord or licensor occupied as his only or principal home premises of which the whole or part of the shared accommodation formed part; and
  (c)   immediately before the tenancy or licence was granted and also at the time it comes to an end, the landlord or licensor occupied as his only or principal home premises in the same building as the shared accommodation and that building is not a purpose-built block of flats.

(4)   For the purposes of subsections (2) and (3) above, an occupier shares accommodation with another person if he has the use of it in common with that person (whether or not also in common with others) and any reference in those subsections to shared accommodation shall be construed accordingly, and if, in relation to any tenancy or licence, there is at any time more than one person who is the landlord or licensor, any reference in those subsections to the landlord or licensor shall be construed as a reference to any one of those persons.

(5)   In subsections (2) to (4) above—
  (a)   "accommodation" includes neither an area used for storage nor a staircase, passage, corridor or other means of access;
  (b)   "occupier" means, in relation to a tenancy, the tenant and, in relation to a licence, the licensee; and

    (c)   "purpose-built block of flats" has the same meaning as in Part III of Schedule 1 to the Housing Act 1988;

and section 113 of the Housing Act 1985 shall apply to determine whether a person is for the purposes of subsection (3) above a member of another's family as it applies for the purposes of Part IV of that Act.

(6)   A tenancy or licence is excluded if it was granted as a temporary expedient to a person who entered the premises in question or any other premises as a trespasser (whether or not, before the beginning of that tenancy or licence, another tenancy or licence to occupy the premises or any other premises had been granted to him).

(7)   A tenancy or licence is excluded if—
    (a)   it confers on the tenant or licensee the right to occupy the premises for a holiday only; or
    (b)   it is granted otherwise than for money or money's worth.

[(7A)   A tenancy or licence is excluded if it is granted in order to provide accommodation [under section 4 or Part VI of the Immigration and Asylum Act 1999].]

[(7B)   Section 32 of the Nationality, Immigration and Asylum Act 2002 (accommodation centre: tenure) provides for a resident's licence to occupy an accommodation centre to be an excluded licence.]

[(7C)   A tenancy or licence is excluded if it is granted in order to provide accommodation under the Displaced Persons (Temporary Protection) Regulations 2005.]

(8)   A licence is excluded if it confers rights of occupation in a hostel, within the meaning of the Housing Act 1985, which is provided by—
    (a)   the council of a county, [county borough,] district or London Borough, the Common Council of the City of London, the Council of the Isle of Scilly, the Inner London Education Authority, [the London Fire and Emergency Planning Authority,] a joint authority within the meaning of the Local Government Act 1985 or a residuary body within the meaning of that Act;
    (b)   a development corporation within the meaning of the New Towns Act 1981;
    (c)   the Commission for the New Towns;
    (d)   an urban development corporation established by an order under section 135 of the Local Government, Planning and Land Act 1980;
    (e)   a housing action trust established under Part III of the Housing Act 1988;
    (f)   ... ;
    (g)   the Housing Corporation ... ;
    [(ga) the Secretary of State under section 89 of the Housing Associations Act 1985;]
    [(h)   a housing trust (within the meaning of the Housing Associations Act 1985) which is a charity or a registered social landlord (within the meaning of the Housing Act 1985); or]
    (i)   any other person who is, or who belongs to a class of person which is, specified in an order made by the Secretary of State.

(9)   The power to make an order under subsection (8)(i) above shall be exercisable by statutory instrument which shall be subject to annulment in pursuance of a resolution of either House of Parliament.]

                                                            [365]

NOTES

Inserted by the Housing Act 1988, s 31.

Sub-s (7A): inserted by the Immigration and Asylum Act 1999, s 169(1), Sch 14, para 73; words in square brackets substituted by the Immigration, Asylum and Nationality Act 2006, s 43(4)(a).

Sub-s (7B): inserted by the Nationality, Immigration and Asylum Act 2002, s 32(5), as from a day to be appointed.

Sub-s (7C): inserted by the Displaced Persons (Temporary Protection) Regulations 2005, SI 2005/1379, Schedule, para 1.

Sub-s (8): words in first pair of square brackets in para (a) inserted by the Local Government (Wales) Act 1994, s 22(2), Sch 8, para 4(1); words in second pair of square brackets in para (a) inserted by the Greater London Authority Act 1999, s 328, Sch 29, Pt I, para 27; para (f) and words omitted from para (g) repealed, and para (ga) inserted, subject to transitional provisions, by the Government of Wales Act 1998, ss 131, 140, 152, Sch 16, para 2, Sch 18, Pts IV, VI; para (h) substituted by the Housing Act 1996 (Consequential Provisions) Order 1996, SI 1996/2325, art 5, Sch 2, para 7.

Transfer of functions: the functions of the Secretary of State, so far as exercisable in relation to Wales, are transferred to the National Assembly for Wales, by the National Assembly for Wales (Transfer of Functions) Order 1999, SI 1999/672, art 2, Sch 1.

Orders: the Protection from Eviction (Excluded Licences) Order 1991, SI 1991/1943; the Protection from Eviction (Excluded Licences) (The Shaftesbury Society) Order 1999, SI 1999/1758; the Protection from Eviction (Excluded Licences) (Royal British Legion Industries Ltd) (England) Order 2003, SI 2003/2436.

4 Special provisions for agricultural employees

(1) This section shall apply where the tenant under the former tenancy (within the meaning of section 3 of this Act) occupied the premises under the terms of his employment as a person employed in agriculture, as defined in section 1 of the Rent (Agriculture) Act 1976, but is not a statutory tenant as defined in that Act.

(2) In this section "the occupier", in relation to any premises, means—
    (a)   the tenant under the former tenancy; or
    (b)   the [surviving spouse or surviving civil partner] of the tenant under the former tenancy residing with him at his death or, if the former tenant leaves no such [surviving spouse or surviving civil partner], any member of his family residing with him at his death.

[(2A) In accordance with section 3(2B) above, any reference in subsections (1) and (2) above to the tenant under the former tenancy includes a reference to the licensee under a licence (other than an excluded licence) which has come to an end (being a licence to occupy premises as a dwelling); and in the following provisions of this section the expressions "tenancy" and "rent" and any other expressions referable to a tenancy shall be construed accordingly.]

(3) Without prejudice to any power of the court apart from this section to postpone the operation or suspend the execution of an order for possession, if in proceedings by the owner against the occupier the court makes an order for the possession of the premises the court may suspend the execution of the order on such terms and conditions, including conditions as to the payment by the occupier of arrears of rent, mesne profits and otherwise as the court thinks reasonable.

(4) Where the order for possession is made within the period of 6 months beginning with the date when the former tenancy came to an end, then, without prejudice to any powers of the court under the preceding provisions of this section or apart from this section to postpone the operation or suspend the execution of the order for a longer period, the court shall suspend the execution of the order for the remainder of the said period of 6 months unless the court—
    (a)   is satisfied either—
        (i)   that other suitable accommodation is, or will within that period be made, available to the occupier; or
        (ii)   that the efficient management of any agricultural land or the efficient carrying on of any agricultural operations would be seriously prejudiced unless the premises are available for occupation by a person employed or to be employed by the owner; or
        (iii)   that greater hardship (being hardship in respect of matters other than the carrying on of such a business as aforesaid) would be caused by the suspension of the order until the end of that period than by its execution within that period; or
        (iv)   that the occupier, or any person residing or lodging with the occupier, has been causing damage to the premises or has been guilty of conduct which is a nuisance or annoyance to persons occupying other premises; and
    (b)   considers that it would be reasonable not to suspend the execution of the order for the remainder of that period.

(5) Where the court suspends the execution of an order for possession under subsection (4) above it shall do so on such terms and conditions, including conditions as to the payment by the occupier of arrears of rent, mesne profits and otherwise as the court thinks reasonable.

(6) A decision of the court not to suspend the execution of the order under subsection (4) above shall not prejudice any other power of the court to postpone the operation or suspend the execution of the order for the whole or part of the period of 6 months mentioned in that subsection.

(7) Where the court has, under the preceding provisions of this section, suspended the execution of an order for possession, it may from time to time vary the period of suspension or terminate it and may vary any terms or conditions imposed by virtue of this section.

(8)   In considering whether or how to exercise its powers under subsection (3) above, the court shall have regard to all the circumstances and, in particular, to—
- (a)   whether other suitable accommodation is or can be made available to the occupier;
- (b)   whether the efficient management of any agricultural land or the efficient carrying on of any agricultural operations would be seriously prejudiced unless the premises were available for occupation by a person employed or to be employed by the owner; and
- (c)   whether greater hardship would be caused by the suspension of the execution of the order than by its execution without suspension or further suspension.

(9)   Where in proceedings for the recovery of possession of the premises the court makes an order for possession but suspends the execution of the order under this section, it shall make no order for costs, unless it appears to the court, having regard to the conduct of the owner or of the occupier, that there are special reasons for making such an order.

(10)   Where, in the case of an order for possession of the premises to which subsection (4) above applies, the execution of the order is not suspended under that subsection or, the execution of the order having been so suspended, the suspension is terminated, then, if it is subsequently made to appear to the court that the failure to suspend the execution of the order or, as the case may be, the termination of the suspension was—
- (a)   attributable to the provisions of paragraph (a)(ii) of subsection (4), and
- (b)   due to misrepresentation or concealment of material facts by the owner of the premises,

the court may order the owner to pay to the occupier such sum as appears sufficient as compensation for damage or loss sustained by the occupier as a result of that failure or termination.

[366]

NOTES
Sub-s (2): words in square brackets substituted by the Civil Partnership Act 2004, s 81, Sch 8, para 15.
Sub-s (2A): inserted by the Housing Act 1988, s 30(3).

---

5   ((*Pt II*) *Outside the scope of this work.*)

PART III
SUPPLEMENTAL PROVISIONS

6   (*Outside the scope of this work.*)

7 Service of notices

(1)   If for the purpose of any proceedings (whether civil or criminal) brought or intended to be brought under this Act, any person serves upon—
- (a)   any agent of the landlord named as such in the rent book or other similar document, or
- (b)   the person who receives the rent of the dwelling,

a notice in writing requiring the agent or other person to disclose to him the full name and place of abode or place of business of the landlord, that agent or other person shall forthwith comply with the notice.

(2)   If any such agent or other person as is referred to in subsection (1) above fails or refuses forthwith to comply with a notice served on him under that subsection, he shall be liable on summary conviction to a fine not exceeding [level 4 on the standard scale] unless he shows to the satisfaction of the court that he did not know, and could not with reasonable diligence have ascertained, such of the facts required by the notice to be disclosed as were not disclosed by him.

(3)   In this section "landlord" includes—
- (a)   any person from time to time deriving title under the original landlord,
- (b)   in relation to any dwelling-house, any person other than the tenant who is or, but for Part VII of the Rent Act 1977 would be, entitled to possession of the dwelling-house, and

(c) any person who, ... grants to another the right to occupy the dwelling in question as a residence and any person directly or indirectly deriving title from the grantor.
[367]

NOTES
Sub-s (2): reference to level 4 on the standard scale substituted by virtue of the Criminal Justice Act 1982, ss 39, 46, Sch 3.
Sub-s (3): words omitted from para (c) repealed by the Housing Act 1988, s 140, Sch 17, Pt I, para 26, Sch 18.

8 Interpretation

(1) In this Act "statutorily protected tenancy" means—

(a) a protected tenancy within the meaning of the Rent Act 1977 or a tenancy to which Part I of the Landlord and Tenant Act 1954 applies;

(b) a protected occupancy or statutory tenancy as defined in the Rent (Agriculture) Act 1976;

(c) a tenancy to which Part II of the Landlord and Tenant Act 1954 applies;

(d) a tenancy of an agricultural holding within the meaning of the [Agricultural Holdings Act 1986] [which is a tenancy in relation to which that Act applies];

[(e) an assured tenancy or assured agricultural occupancy under Part I of the Housing Act 1988];

[(f) a tenancy to which Schedule 10 to the Local Government and Housing Act 1989 applies];

[(g) a farm business tenancy within the meaning of the Agricultural Tenancies Act 1995.]

(2) For the purposes of Part I of this Act a person who, under the terms of his employment, had exclusive possession of any premises other than as a tenant shall be deemed to have been a tenant and the expressions "let" and "tenancy" shall be construed accordingly.

(3) In Part I of this Act "the owner", in relation to any premises, means the person who, as against the occupier, is entitled to possession thereof.

[(4) In this Act "excluded tenancy" and "excluded licence" have the meaning assigned by section 3A of this Act.

(5) If, on or after the date on which the Housing Act 1988 came into force, the terms of an excluded tenancy or excluded licence entered into before that date are varied, then—

(a) if the variation affects the amount of the rent which is payable under the tenancy or licence, the tenancy or licence shall be treated for the purposes of sections 3(2C) and 5(1B) above as a new tenancy or licence entered into at the time of the variation; and

(b) if the variation does not affect the amount of the rent which is so payable, nothing in this Act shall affect the determination of the question whether the variation is such as to give rise to a new tenancy or licence.

(6) Any reference in subsection (5) above to a variation affecting the amount of the rent which is payable under a tenancy or licence does not include a reference to—

(a) a reduction or increase effected under Part III or Part VI of the Rent Act 1977 (rents under regulated tenancies and housing association tenancies), section 78 of that Act (power of rent tribunal in relation to restricted contracts) or sections 11 to 14 of the Rent (Agriculture) Act 1976; or

(b) a variation which is made by the parties and has the effect of making the rent expressed to be payable under the tenancy or licence the same as a rent for the dwelling which is entered in the register under Part IV or section 79 of the Rent Act 1977.]
[368]

NOTES
Sub-s (1): words in first pair of square brackets in para (d) substituted by the Agricultural Holdings Act 1986, s 100, Sch 14, para 61; words in second pair of square brackets and para (g) added by the Agricultural Tenancies Act 1995, s 40, Schedule, para 29; para (e) added by the Housing Act 1988, s 33(2); para (f) added by the Local Government and Housing Act 1989, s 194, Sch 11, para 54.
Sub-ss (4)–(6): added by the Housing Act 1988, s 33(3).

9 The court for purposes of Part I

(1)   The court for the purposes of Part I of this Act shall, subject to this section, be—

(a)   the county court, in relation to premises with respect to which the county court has for the time being jurisdiction in actions for the recovery of land; and

(b)   the High Court, in relation to other premises.

(2)   Any powers of a county court in proceedings for the recovery of possession of any premises in the circumstances mentioned in section 3(1) of this Act may be exercised with the leave of the judge by any registrar of the court, except in so far as rules of court otherwise provide.

(3)   Nothing in this Act shall affect the jurisdiction of the High Court in proceedings to enforce a lessor's right of re-entry or forfeiture or to enforce a mortgagee's right of possession in a case where the former tenancy was not binding on the mortgagee.

(4)   Nothing in this Act shall affect the operation of—

(a)   section 59 of the Pluralities Act 1838;

(b)   section 19 of the Defence Act 1842;

(c)   section 6 of the Lecturers and Parish Clerks Act 1844;

(d)   paragraph 3 of Schedule 1 to the Sexual Offences Act 1956; or

(e)   section 13 of the Compulsory Purchase Act 1965.

[369]

10   Application to Crown

In so far as this Act requires the taking of proceedings in the court for the recovery of possession or confers any powers on the court it shall (except in the case of section 4(10)) be binding on the Crown.

[370]

11   Application to Isles of Scilly

(1)   In its application to the Isles of Scilly, this Act (except in the case of section 5) shall have effect subject to such exceptions, adaptations and modifications as the Secretary of State may by order direct.

(2)   The power to make an order under this section shall be exercisable by statutory instrument which shall be subject to annulment, in pursuance of a resolution of either House of Parliament.

(3)   An order under this section may be varied or revoked by a subsequent order.

[371]

12   *(Outside the scope of this work.)*

13   Short title, etc

(1)   This Act may be cited as the Protection from Eviction Act 1977.

(2)   This Act shall come into force on the expiry of the period of one month beginning with the date on which it is passed.

(3)   This Act does not extend to Scotland or Northern Ireland.

(4)   References in this Act to any enactment are references to that enactment as amended, and include references thereto as applied by any other enactment including, except where the context otherwise requires, this Act.

[372]

(Sch 1, paras 1, 3, 4 amend legislation outside the scope of this work; para 2 repealed by the County Courts Act 1984, s 148(3), Sch 4; Schs 2, 3 outside the scope of this work.)

CRIMINAL LAW ACT 1977

(1977 c 45)

An Act to amend the law of England and Wales with respect to criminal conspiracy; to make new provision in that law, in place of the provisions of the common law and the Statutes of

Forcible Entry, for restricting the use or threat of violence for securing entry into any premises and for penalising unauthorised entry or remaining on premises. in certain circumstances; otherwise to amend the criminal law, including the law with respect to the administration of criminal justice; to provide for the alteration of certain pecuniary and other limits; to amend section 9(4) of the Administration of Justice Act 1973, the Legal Aid Act 1974, the Rabies Act 1974 and the Diseases of Animals (Northern Ireland) Order 1975 and the law about juries and coroners' inquests; and for connected purposes

[29 July 1977]

1–5   *((Pt I) Outside the scope of this work.)*

PART II
OFFENCES RELATING TO ENTERING AND REMAINING ON PROPERTY

6   Violence for securing entry

(1)   Subject to the following provisions of this section, any person who, without lawful authority, uses or threatens violence for the purpose of securing entry into any premises for himself or for any other person is guilty of an offence, provided that—

(a)   there is someone present on those premises at the time who is opposed to the entry which the violence is intended to secure; and

(b)   the person using or threatening the violence knows that that is the case.

[(1A)   Subsection (1) above does not apply to a person who is a displaced residential occupier or a protected intending occupier of the premises in question or who is acting on behalf of such an occupier; and if the accused adduces sufficient evidence that he was, or was acting on behalf of, such an occupier he shall be presumed to be, or to be acting on behalf of, such an occupier unless the contrary is proved by the prosecution.]

(2)   [Subject to subsection (1A) above,] the fact that a person has any interest in or right to possession or occupation of any premises shall not for the purposes of subsection (1) above constitute lawful authority for the use or threat of violence by him or anyone else for the purpose of securing his entry into those premises.

(3)   ...

(4)   It is immaterial for the purposes of this section—

(a)   whether the violence in question is directed against the person or against property; and

(b)   whether the entry which the violence is intended to secure is for the purpose of acquiring possession of the premises in question or for any other purpose.

(5)   A person guilty of an offence under this section shall be liable on summary conviction to imprisonment for a term not exceeding six months or to a fine not exceeding [level 5 on the standard scale] or to both.

(6)   ...

(7)   Section 12 below contains provisions which apply for determining when any person is to be regarded for the purposes of this Part of this Act as a displaced residential occupier of any premises or of any access to any premises [and section 12A below contains provisions which apply for determining when any person is to be regarded for the purposes of this Part of this Act as a protected intending occupier of any premises or of any access to any premises.]

[373]

NOTES

Sub-s (1A): inserted by the Criminal Justice and Public Order Act 1994, s 72(1), (2).

Sub-s (2): words in square brackets inserted by the Criminal Justice and Public Order Act 1994, s 72(1), (3).

Sub-s (3): repealed by the Criminal Justice and Public Order Act 1994, ss 72(1), (4), 168(3), Sch 11.

Sub-s (5): maximum fine converted to level 5 on the standard scale by virtue of the Criminal Justice Act 1982, ss 38, 46.

Sub-s (6): repealed by the Serious Organised Crime and Police Act 2005, ss 111, 174(2), Sch 7, Pt 1, para 19(1), (2), Sch 17, Pt 2.

Sub-s (7): words in square brackets added by the Criminal Justice and Public Order Act 1994, s 72(1), (5).

7–11   (*Ss 7–10 outside the scope of this work; s 11 repealed by the Police and Criminal Evidence Act 1984, ss 7(2), 119(2), Sch 7, Pt I.*)

12   Supplementary provisions

(1)   In this Part of this Act—
  (a)   "premises" means any building, any part of a building under separate occupation, any land ancillary to a building, the site comprising any building or buildings together with any land ancillary thereto, and (for the purposes only of sections 10 and 11 above) any other place; and
  (b)   "access" means, in relation to any premises, any part of any site or building within which those premises are situated which constitutes an ordinary means of access to those premises (whether or not that is its sole or primary use).

(2)   References in this section to a building shall apply also to any structure other than a movable one, and to any movable structure, vehicle or vessel designed or adapted for use for residential purposes; and for the purposes of subsection (1) above—
  (a)   part of a building is under separate occupation if anyone is in occupation or entitled to occupation of that part as distinct from the whole; and
  (b)   land is ancillary to a building if it is adjacent to it and used (or intended for use) in connection with the occupation of that building or any part of it.

(3)   Subject to subsection (4) below, any person who was occupying any premises as a residence immediately before being excluded from occupation by anyone who entered those premises, or any access to those premises, as a trespasser is a displaced residential occupier of the premises for the purposes of this Part of this Act so long as he continues to be excluded from occupation of the premises by the original trespasser or by any subsequent trespasser.

(4)   A person who was himself occupying the premises in question as a trespasser immediately before being excluded from occupation shall not by virtue of subsection (3) above be a displaced residential occupier of the premises for the purposes of this Part of this Act.

(5)   A person who by virtue of subsection (3) above is a displaced residential occupier of any premises shall be regarded for the purposes of this Part of this Act as a displaced residential occupier also of any access to those premises.

(6)   Anyone who enters or is on or in occupation of any premises by virtue of—
  (a)   any title derived from a trespasser; or
  (b)   any licence or consent given by a trespasser or by a person deriving title from a trespasser,
shall himself be treated as a trespasser for the purposes of this Part of this Act (without prejudice to whether or not he would be a trespasser apart from this provision); and references in this Part of this Act to a person's entering or being on or occupying any premises as a trespasser shall be construed accordingly.

(7)   Anyone who is on any premises as a trespasser shall not cease to be a trespasser for the purposes of this Part of this Act by virtue of being allowed time to leave the premises, nor shall anyone cease to be a displaced residential occupier of any premises by virtue of any such allowance of time to a trespasser.

(8)   No rule of law ousting the jurisdiction of magistrates' courts to try offences where a dispute of title to property is involved shall preclude magistrates' courts from trying offences under this Part of this Act.

[374]

12A–64   (*In so far as unrepealed outside the scope of this work.*)

65   Citation, etc

(1)   This Act may be cited as the Criminal Law Act 1977.

(2)   The provisions of sections [15] to 32 and 48 above, so far as they relate to proceedings before magistrates' courts, shall be construed as one with the [Magistrates' Courts Act 1980] except that in those provisions "fine" shall include any pecuniary penalty.

(3)   Except where the context otherwise requires, any reference in this Act to any enactment is a reference to it as amended, and includes a reference to it as extended or applied, by or under any other enactment, including this Act.

(4) The enactments specified in Schedule 12 to this Act shall have effect subject to the amendments there specified, being minor amendments and amendments consequential on the provisions of this Act.

(5) Subject to the transitional provisions contained in this Act, the enactments specified in Schedule 13 to this Act (which include certain spent provisions) are hereby repealed to the extent specified in the third column of that Schedule.

(6) There shall be defrayed out of money provided by Parliament any increase attributable to the provisions of this Act in the sums payable out of such money under any other Act.

(7) This Act shall come into force on such day as the Secretary of State may appoint by order made by statutory instrument, and different days may be so appointed for different purposes.

(8) Without prejudice to any other transitional provision contained in this Act, the transitional provisions contained in Schedule 14 to this Act shall have effect.

(9) Without prejudice to Schedule 14 or any other transitional provision contained in this Act, an order under subsection (7) above may make such transitional provision as appears to the Secretary of State to be necessary or expedient in connection with the provisions thereby brought into force.

(10) In this Act—
    (a) ...
    (b) the following provisions extend to Northern Ireland namely—
        sections 38 to 40,

        ...
        section 52,

        ...
        subsections (1), (3) and (6) to (10) of this section,
        Schedule 7,
        in Schedule 14, paragraph 5;
    (c) section 31 and Schedule 6, so far as they amend any enactment which extends to the Channel Islands or the Isle of Man, extend to the Channel Islands or the Isle of Man, as the case may be;
    (d) subsections (4) and (5) above and Schedules 12 and 13, so far as they relate to—
        (i) section 45 of the Prison Act 1952 (in its application to persons for the time being in Northern Ireland or in the Channel Islands or the Isle of Man);
        (ii) Part III and section 39(1) of the Criminal Justice Act 1961; and
        (iii) sections 60 and 63 of the Criminal Justice Act 1967 (in their application to persons for the time being in Northern Ireland or in the Channel Islands or the Isle of Man),
    extend to Northern Ireland, the Channel Islands and the Isle of Man (as well as, by virtue of paragraph (a) above, to Scotland);
    (e) section 32(3) extends to all places (except Scotland) to which section 2 of the European Communities Act 1972 extends (as well as, by virtue of paragraph (a) above, to Scotland) ...
but save as aforesaid, this Act extends to England and Wales only.

[375]

NOTES

Sub-s (2): number and words in square brackets substituted by the Magistrates' Courts Act 1980, s 154(1), Sch 7, para 153.

Sub-s (10): para (a) applies to Scotland only; in para (b), words omitted in the first place repealed by the Criminal Appeal (Northern Ireland) Act 1980, s 51(2), Sch 5 and words omitted in the second place repealed by the Diseases of Animals (Northern Ireland) Order 1981, SI 1981/1115; words omitted from para (e) repealed by the Magistrates' Courts Act 1980, s 154(3), Sch 9.

Orders: the commencement orders made under this section which are relevant to the provisions of this Act printed in this title are the Criminal Law Act 1977 (Commencement No 1) Order 1977, SI 1977/1365 and the Criminal Law Act 1977 (Commencement No 3) Order 1977, SI 1977/1682.

(Schs 1–14 in so far as unrepealed outside the scope of this work.)

INTERPRETATION ACT 1978

(1978 c 30)

An Act to consolidate the Interpretation Act 1889 and certain other enactments relating to the construction and operation of Acts of Parliament and other instruments, with amendments to give effect to recommendations of the Law Commission and the Scottish Law Commission

[20 July 1978]

1–4   (*Outside the scope of this work.*)

Interpretation and construction

5, 6   (*Outside the scope of this work.*)

7   References to service by post

Where an Act authorises or requires any document to be served by post (whether the expression "serve" or the expression "give" or "send" or any other expression is used) then, unless the contrary intention appears, the service is deemed to be effected by properly addressing, pre-paying and posting a letter containing the document and, unless the contrary is proved, to have been effected at the time at which the letter would be delivered in the ordinary course of post.

[376]

8   (*Outside the scope of this work.*)

9   References to time of day

Subject to section 3 of the Summer Time Act 1972 (construction of references to points of time during the period of summer time), whenever an expression of time occurs in an Act, the time referred to shall, unless it is otherwise specifically stated, be held to be Greenwich mean time.

[377]

10–17   (*Outside the scope of this work.*)

Miscellaneous

18   (*Outside the scope of this work.*)

19   Citation of other Acts

(1)   Where an Act cites another Act by year, statute, session or chapter, or a section or other portion of another Act by number or letter, the reference shall, unless the contrary intention appears, be read as referring—
(a)   in the case of Acts included in any revised edition of the statutes printed by authority, to that edition;
(b)   in the case of Acts not so included but included in the edition prepared under the direction of the Record Commission, to that edition;
(c)   in any other case, to the Acts printed by the Queen's Printer, or under the superintendence or authority of Her Majesty's Stationery Office.

(2)   An Act may continue to be cited by the short title authorised by any enactment notwithstanding the repeal of that enactment.

[378]

20   (*Outside the scope of this work.*)

Supplementary

21, 22   (*Outside the scope of this work.*)

23 Application to other instruments

(1), (2) ...

(3) Sections 9 and 19(1) also apply to deeds and other instruments and documents as they apply to Acts and subordinate legislation; and in the application of section 17(2)(a) to Acts passed or subordinate legislation made after the commencement of this Act, the reference to any other enactment includes any deed or other instrument or document.

(4) ...

[379]

NOTES
Sub-ss (1), (2), (4): outside the scope of this work.
See further, the Companies Act 2006, s 1160(4), in relation to the disapplication of so much of sub-s (3) above as applies s 17(2)(a) hereof to deeds, instruments and documents other than enactments, in respect of any repeal and re-enactment effected by regulations under the Companies Act 2006, s 1160.

24, 25 *(Outside the scope of this work.)*

26 Commencement

This Act shall come into force on 1st January 1979.

[380]

27 Short title

This Act may be cited as the Interpretation Act 1978.

[381]

(Schs 1–3 outside the scope of this work.)

LIMITATION ACT 1980

(1980 c 58)

PART I
ORDINARY TIME LIMITS FOR DIFFERENT CLASSES OF ACTION

1–14B *(Outside the scope of this work.)*

Actions to recover land and rent

15–18 *(Outside the scope of this work.)*

19 Time limit for actions to recover rent

No action shall be brought, or distress made, to recover arrears of rent, or damages in respect of arrears of rent, after the expiration of six years from the date on which the arrears became due.

[382]

[Commonhold

19A Actions for breach of commonhold duty

An action in respect of a right or duty of a kind referred to in section 37(1) of the Commonhold and Leasehold Reform Act 2002 (enforcement) shall not be brought after the expiration of six years from the date on which the cause of action accrued.]

[383]

NOTES
Commencement: 27 September 2004.

Inserted, together with preceding cross-heading, by the Commonhold and Leasehold Reform Act 2002, s 68, Sch 5, para 4.

20–33 (*Outside the scope of this work.*)

PART III
MISCELLANEOUS AND GENERAL

34–40 (*Outside the scope of this work.*)

41 Short title, commencement and extent

(1) This Act may be cited as the Limitation Act 1980.

(2) This Act, except section 35, shall come into force on 1st May 1981.

(3), (4) ...

[384]

NOTES
Sub-ss (3), (4): outside the scope of this work.

(*Schs 1–4 outside the scope of this work.*)

SUPREME COURT ACT 1981

(1981 c 54)

NOTES
Title substituted by the title "Senior Courts Act 1981" by the Constitutional Reform Act 2005, s 59(5), Sch 11, Pt 1, para 1, as from a day to be appointed.

An Act to consolidate with amendments the Supreme Court of Judicature (Consolidation) Act 1925 and other enactments relating to the Supreme Court in England and Wales and the administration of justice therein; to repeal certain obsolete or unnecessary enactments so relating; to amend Part VIII of the Mental Health Act 1959, the Courts-Martial (Appeals) Act 1968, the Arbitration Act 1979 and the law relating to county courts; and for connected purposes

[28 July 1981]

1–14 ((*Pt I) Outside the scope of this work.*)

PART II
JURISDICTION

15–18 (*Outside the scope of this work.*)

THE HIGH COURT

19–31 (*Outside the scope of this work.*)

Powers

32–37 (*Outside the scope of this work.*)

38 Relief against forfeiture for non-payment of rent

(1) In any action in the High Court for the forfeiture of a lease for non-payment of rent, the court shall have power to grant relief against forfeiture in a summary manner, and may do

so subject to the same terms and conditions as to the payment of rent, costs or otherwise as could have been imposed by it in such an action immediately before the commencement of this Act.

(2)　Where the lessee or a person deriving title under him is granted relief under this section, he shall hold the demised premises in accordance with the terms of the lease without the necessity for a new lease.

[385]

39–128　　(*In so far as unrepealed outside the scope of this work.*)

PART VI
MISCELLANEOUS AND SUPPLEMENTARY

129–149　　(*In so far as unrepealed outside the scope of this work.*)

Supplementary

150　　(*Outside the scope of this work.*)

151　Interpretation of this Act, and rules of construction for other Acts and documents

(1)　In this Act, unless the context otherwise requires—

"action" means any civil proceedings commenced by writ or in any other manner prescribed by rules of court;

"appeal", in the context of appeals to the civil division of the Court of Appeal, includes—

(a)　an application for a new trial, and

(b)　an application to set aside a verdict, finding or judgment in any cause or matter in the High Court which has been tried, or in which any issue has been tried, by a jury;

["arbitration agreement" has the same meaning as it has in [Part I of the Arbitration Act 1996;]]

"cause" means any action or any criminal proceedings;

"Division", where it appears with a capital letter, means a division of the High Court;

"judgment" includes a decree;

"jurisdiction" includes powers;

"matter" means any proceedings in court not in a cause;

"party", in relation to any proceedings, includes any person who pursuant to or by virtue of rules of court or any other statutory provision has been served with notice of, or has intervened in, those proceedings;

"prescribed" means—

(a)　except in relation to fees, prescribed by rules of court; ...

(b)　...

["senior judge", where the reference is to the senior judge of a Division, means the president of that Division;]

"solicitor" means a solicitor of the *Supreme Court*;

"statutory provision" means any enactment, whenever passed, or any provision contained in subordinate legislation (as defined in section 21(1) of the Interpretation Act 1978), whenever made;

"this or any other Act" includes an Act passed after this Act.

(2)　Section 128 contains definitions of expressions used in Part V and in the other provisions of this Act relating to probate causes and matters.

(3)　Any reference in this Act to rules of court under section 84 includes a reference to rules of court [in relation to the *Supreme Court*] under any provision of this or any other Act which confers on the [Civil Procedure Rule Committee] or the Crown Court Rule Committee power to make rules of court.

(4)　Except where the context otherwise requires, in this or any other Act—

.....

"divisional court" (with or without capital letters) means a divisional court constituted under section 66;

"judge of the *Supreme Court*" means—

215

(a)   a judge of the Court of Appeal other than an ex-officio judge within paragraph (b) or (c) of section 2(2), or

(b)   a judge of the High Court,

and accordingly does not include, as such, a judge of the Crown Court;

"official referees' business" has the meaning given by section 68(6);

.....

(5)   The provisions of Schedule 4 (construction of references to superseded courts and officers) shall have effect.

[386]

NOTES

Sub-s (1): definition "arbitration agreement" inserted by the Courts and Legal Services Act 1990, s 125(3), Sch 18, para 41 and words in square brackets therein substituted by the Arbitration Act 1996, s 107(1), Sch 3, para 37(1), (3); in definition "prescribed", words omitted repealed by the Courts Act 2003, s 109(1), (3), Sch 8, para 265, Sch 10; definition "senior judge" substituted by the Constitutional Reform Act 2005, s 15(1), Sch 4, Pt 1, paras 114, 146; in definition "solicitor" for the words in italics there are substituted the words "Senior Courts" by the Constitutional Reform Act 2005, s 59(5), Sch 11, Pt 4, para 26(1), (2), as from a day to be appointed.

Sub-s (3): words in first pair of square brackets inserted and words in second pair of square brackets substituted by the Civil Procedure Act 1997, s 10, Sch 2, para 1(1), (7)(a); for the words in italics there are substituted the words "Senior Courts" by the Constitutional Reform Act 2005, s 59(5), Sch 11, Pt 4, para 26(1), (2), as from a day to be appointed.

Sub-s (4): definitions "Criminal Appeal Rules" and "Crown Court Rules" (omitted) repealed by the Courts Act 2003 (Consequential Amendments) Order 2004, SI 2004/2035, art 3, Schedule, paras 11, 18; in the definition "judge of the Supreme Court" for the words in italics there are substituted the words "Senior Courts" by the Constitutional Reform Act 2005, s 59(5), Sch 11, Pt 4, para 26(1), (2), as from a day to be appointed; definition "Rules of the Supreme Court" repealed by the Civil Procedure Act 1997, s 10, Sch 2, para 1(1), (7)(b).

---

152   (*Outside the scope of this work.*)

153 **Citation, commencement and extent**

(1)   This Act may be cited as the *Supreme Court Act 1981*.

(2)   This Act, except the provisions mentioned in subsection (3), shall come into force on 1st January 1982; and references to the commencement of this Act shall be construed as references to the beginning of that day.

(3)   Sections 72, 143 and 152(2) and this section shall come into force on the passing of this Act.

(4)   In this Act—

(a)–(c)..

(d)   section 145 extends to any place to which the Courts-Martial (Appeals) Act 1968 extends, and section 152(1) and (4) and Schedules 5 and 7, so far as they relate to any of the following enactments, namely—

Army Act 1955,

Air Force Act 1955,

section 9(2) of, and Part II of Schedule 1 to, the Criminal Appeal Act 1966,

Courts-Martial (Appeals) Act 1968,

Hovercraft Act 1968,

...

extend to any place to which that enactment extends;

but, save as aforesaid, the provisions of this Act, other than those mentioned in subsection (5), extend to England and Wales only.

(5)   The provisions of this Act whose extent is not restricted by subsection (4) are—

section 27;

section 150;

section 151(1);

section 152(4) and Schedule 7 as far as they relate to the Naval Prize Act 1864, the Prize Courts Act 1915 and section 56 of the Administration of Justice Act 1956;

this section;

paragraph 1 of Schedule 4.

[387]

NOTES

Sub-s (1): for the words in italics there are substituted the words "Senior Courts Act 1981" by the Constitutional Reform Act 2005, s 59(5), Sch 11, Pt 1, para 1(2), as from a day to be appointed.

Sub-s (4): paras (a)–(c) apply to Scotland and Northern Ireland only; words omitted from para (d) repealed by the Merchant Shipping Act 1995, s 314(1), Sch 12.

(Schs 1, 2, 4–7 outside the scope of this work; Sch 3 repealed by the County Courts Act 1984, s 148(3), Sch 4.)

COUNTY COURTS ACT 1984

(1984 c 28)

ARRANGEMENT OF SECTIONS

PART V
ENFORCEMENT OF JUDGMENTS AND ORDERS

Claims in respect of goods seized

PART VI
ADMINISTRATION ORDERS

PART IX
MISCELLANEOUS AND GENERAL

Forfeiture for non-payment of rent

Replevin

General

An Act to consolidate certain enactments relating to county courts

[26 June 1984]

1–84   *(In so far as unrepealed outside the scope of this work.)*

PART V
ENFORCEMENT OF JUDGMENTS AND ORDERS

85–98   (*Outside the scope of this work.*)

Claims in respect of goods seized

99–101   (*Outside the scope of this work.*)

102   Claims for rent where goods seized in execution

(1)   Section 1 of the Landlord and Tenant Act 1709 shall not apply to goods seized in execution under process of a county court, but the following provisions of this section shall apply in substitution.

(2)   The landlord of any tenement in which any goods are seized may claim the rent of the tenement in arrear at the date of the seizure, at any time within the 5 days next following that date, or before the removal of the goods, by delivering to the bailiff or officer making the levy a claim in writing, signed by himself or his agent, stating—

(a)   the amount of rent claimed to be in arrear; and

(b)   the period in respect of which the rent is due.

(3)   Where such a claim is made, the bailiff or officer making the levy shall in addition distrain for the rent so claimed and the cost of the distress, and shall not, within 5 days next after the distress, sell any part of the goods seized, unless—

(a)   the goods are of a perishable nature; or

(b)   the person whose goods have been seized so requests in writing.

(4)   The bailiff shall afterwards sell under the execution and distress such of the goods as will satisfy—

(a)   first, the costs of and incidental to the sale;

(b)   next, the claim of the landlord not exceeding—
     (i)   in a case where the tenement is let by the week, 4 weeks' rent;
     (ii)   in a case where the tenement is let for any other term less than a year, the rent of two terms of payment;
     (iii)   in any other case, one year's rent; and

(c)   lastly, the amount for which the warrant of execution issued.

(5)   If any replevin is made of the goods seized, the bailiff shall nevertheless sell such portion of them as will satisfy the costs of and incidental to the sale under the execution and the amount for which the warrant of execution issued.

(6)   In any event the surplus of the sale, if any, and the residue of the goods shall be returned to the execution debtor.

(7)   The fees of the [district judge] and broker for keeping possession, appraisement and sale under any such distress shall be the same as would have been payable if the distress had been an execution of the court, and no other fees shall be demanded or taken in respect thereof.

[(8)   Nothing in this section affects section 346 of the Insolvency Act 1986.]

[388]

NOTES
   Sub-s (7): words in square brackets substituted by virtue of the Courts and Legal Services Act 1990, s 74(1), (3).
   Sub-s (8): substituted by the Insolvency Act 1986, s 439(2), Sch 14.

103–111   (*Outside the scope of this work.*)

PART VI
ADMINISTRATION ORDERS

112–115   (*Outside the scope of this work.*)

116 Right of landlord to distrain notwithstanding order

A landlord or other person to whom any rent is due from a debtor in respect of whom an administration order is made, may at any time, either before or after the date of the order, distrain upon the goods or effects of the debtor for the rent due to him from the debtor, with this limitation, that if the distress for rent is levied after the date of the order, it shall be available only for six months' rent accrued due prior to the date of the order and shall not be available for rent payable in respect of any period subsequent to the date when the distress was levied, but the landlord or other person to whom the rent may be due from the debtor may prove under the order for the surplus due for which the distress may not have been available.

[389]

117–127   (*Outside the scope of this work.*)

PART IX
MISCELLANEOUS AND GENERAL

128–137   (*Outside the scope of this work.*)

Forfeiture for non-payment of rent

138   Provisions as to forfeiture for non-payment of rent

(1)   This section has effect where a lessor is proceeding by action in a county court (being an action in which the county court has jurisdiction) to enforce against a lessee a right of re-entry or forfeiture in respect of any land for non-payment of rent.

(2)   If the lessee pays into court [or to the lessor] not less than 5 clear days before the return day all the rent in arrear and the costs of the action, the action shall cease, and the lessee shall hold the land according to the lease without any new lease.

(3)   If—
    (a)   the action does not cease under subsection (2); and
    (b)   the court at the trial is satisfied that the lessor is entitled to enforce the right of re-entry or forfeiture,
the court shall order possession of the land to be given to the lessor at the expiration of such period, not being less than 4 weeks from the date of the order, as the court thinks fit, unless within that period the lessee pays into court [or to the lessor] all the rent in arrear and the costs of the action.

(4)   The court may extend the period specified under subsection (3) at any time before possession of the land is recovered in pursuance of the order under that subsection.

(5)   ... if—
    (a)   within the period specified in the order; or
    (b)   within that period as extended under subsection (4),
the lessee pays into court [or to the lessor]—
      (i)   all the rent in arrear; and
      (ii)   the costs of the action,
he shall hold the land according to the lease without any new lease.

(6)   Subsection (2) shall not apply where the lessor is proceeding in the same action to enforce a right of re-entry or forfeiture on any other ground as well as for non-payment of rent, or to enforce any other claim as well as the right of re-entry or forfeiture and the claim for arrears of rent.

(7)   If the lessee does not—
    (a)   within the period specified in the order; or
    (b)   within that period as extended under subsection (4), pay into court [or to the lessor]—
      (i)   all the rent in arrear; and
      (ii)   the costs of the action,
the order shall be [enforceable] in the prescribed manner and so long as the order remains unreversed the lessee shall[, subject to subsections (8) and (9A),] be barred from all relief.

(8)   The extension under subsection (4) of a period fixed by a court shall not be treated as relief from which the lessee is barred by subsection (7) if he fails to pay into court [or to the lessor] all the rent in arrear and the costs of the action within that period.

(9)   Where the court extends a period under subsection (4) at a time when—

(a)   that period has expired; and

(b)   a warrant has been issued for the possession of the land, the court shall suspend the warrant for the extended period; and, if, before the expiration period, the lessee pays into court [or to the lessor] all the rent in arrear and all the costs of the action, the court shall cancel the warrant.

[(9A)   Where the lessor recovers possession of the land at any time after the making of the order under subsection (3) (whether as a result of the enforcement of the order or otherwise) the lessee may, at any time within six months from the date on which the lessor recovers possession, apply to the court for relief; and on any such application the court may, if it thinks fit, grant to the lessee such relief, subject to such terms and conditions, as it thinks fit.

(9B)   Where the lessee is granted relief on an application under subsection (9A) he shall hold the land according to the lease without any new lease.

(9C)   An application under subsection (9A) may be made by a person with an interest under a lease of the land derived (whether immediately or otherwise) from the lessee's interest therein in like manner as if he were the lessee; and on any such application the court may make an order which (subject to such terms and conditions as the court thinks fit) vests the land in such a person, as lessee of the lessor, for the remainder of the term of the lease under which he has any such interest as aforesaid, or for any lesser term.

In this subsection any reference to the land includes a reference to a part of the land.]

(10)   Nothing in this section or section 139 shall be taken to affect—

(a)   the power of the court to make any order which it would otherwise have power to make as respects a right of re-entry or forfeiture on any ground other than non-payment of rent; or

(b)   section 146(4) of the Law of Property Act 1925 (relief against forfeiture).

[390]

NOTES

Sub-ss (2), (3), (8), (9): words in square brackets inserted by the Courts and Legal Services Act 1990, s 125(2), Sch 17, para 17.

Sub-s (5): words omitted repealed by the Administration of Justice Act 1985, ss 55(1), (2), 67(2), Sch 8, Pt III; words in square brackets inserted by the Courts and Legal Services Act 1990, s 125(2), Sch 17, para 17.

Sub-s (7): words in first pair of square brackets inserted by the Courts and Legal Services Act 1990, s 125(2), Sch 17, para 17; words in second pair of square brackets substituted, and words in third pair of square brackets inserted, by the Administration of Justice Act 1985, s 55(1), (3).

Sub-ss (9A)–(9C): inserted by the Administration of Justice Act 1985, s 55(1), (4).

139   Service of summons and re-entry

(1)   In a case where section 138 has effect, if—

(a)   one-half-year's rent is in arrear at the time of the commencement of the action; and

(b)   the lessor has a right to re-enter for non-payment of that rent; and

(c)   no sufficient distress is to be found on the premises countervailing the arrears then due,

the service of the summons in the action in the prescribed manner shall stand in lieu of a demand and re-entry.

(2)   Where a lessor has enforced against a lessee, by re-entry without action, a right of re-entry or forfeiture as respects any land for non-payment of rent, the lessee may ... at any time within six months from the date on which the lessor re-entered apply to the county court for relief, and on any such application the court may, if it thinks fit, grant to the lessee such relief as the High Court could have granted.

[(3)   Subsections (9B) and (9C) of section 138 shall have effect in relation to an application under subsection (2) of this section as they have effect in relation to an application under subsection (9A) of that section.]

[391]

NOTES

Sub-s (2): words omitted repealed by the High Court and County Courts Jurisdiction Order 1991, SI 1991/724, art 2(1), (8), Schedule, Pt I, subject to transitional provisions and savings contained in arts 11, 12 thereof at **[1237]**, **[1238]**.

Sub-s (3): added by the Administration of Justice Act 1985, s 55(5).

140 Interpretation of sections 138 and 139

For the purposes of sections 138 and 139—

"lease" includes—

(a)   an original or derivative under-lease;
(b)   an agreement for a lease where the lessee has become entitled to have his lease granted; and
(c)   a grant at a fee farm rent, or under a grant securing a rent by condition;

"lessee" includes—

(a)   an original or derivative under-lessee;
(b)   the persons deriving title under a lessee;
(c)   a grantee under a grant at a fee farm rent, or under a grant securing a rent by condition; and
(d)   the persons deriving title under such a grantee;

"lessor" includes—

(a)   an original or derivative under-lessor;
(b)   the persons deriving title under a lessor;
(c)   a person making a grant at a fee farm rent, or a grant securing a rent by condition; and
(d)   the persons deriving title under such a grantor;

"under-lease" includes an agreement for an under-lease where the under-lessee has become entitled to have his underlease granted; and

"under-lessee" includes any person deriving title under an under-lessee.

[392]

141–143   (*S 141 repealed by the Statute Law (Repeals) Act 1986; ss 142, 143 outside the scope of this work.*)

Replevin

144 Replevin

Schedule 1 to this Act shall have effect.

[393]

145   (*Outside the scope of this work.*)

General

146   (*Outside the scope of this work.*)

147 Interpretation

(1)   In this Act, unless the context otherwise requires—

"action" means any proceedings in a county court which may be commenced as prescribed by plaint;

"Admiralty county court" means a county court appointed to have Admiralty jurisdiction by order under this Act;

"Admiralty proceedings" means proceedings in which the claim would not be within the jurisdiction of a county court but for sections 26 and 27;

"bailiff" includes a [district judge];

"the county court limit" means—

(a)   in relation to any enactment contained in this Act for which a limit is for the time being specified by an Order under section 145, that limit,
(b)   ...
(c)   in relation to any enactment contained in this Act and not within

221

paragraph (a) ... , the county court limit for the time being specified by any other Order in Council or order defining the limit of county court jurisdiction for the purposes of that enactment;

.....

"court" and "county court" mean a court held for a district under this Act;

["deposit-taking institution" means a person who may, in the course of his business, lawfully accept deposits in the United Kingdom;]

"district" and "county district" mean a district for which a court is to be held under section 2;

.....

"hearing" includes trial, and "hear" and "heard" shall be construed accordingly;

"hereditament" includes both a corporeal and an incorporeal hereditament;

"judge", in relation to a county court, means a judge assigned to the district of that court under subsection (1) of section 5 and any person sitting as a judge for that district under subsection (3) or (4) of that section;

"judgment summons" means a summons issued on the application of a person entitled to enforce a judgment or order under section 5 of the Debtors Act 1869 requiring a person, or, where two or more persons are liable under the judgment or order, requiring any one or more of them, [to attend court];

"landlord", in relation to any land, means the person entitled to the immediate reversion or, if the property therein is held in joint tenancy, any of the persons entitled to the immediate reversion;

["legal representative" means an authorised advocate or authorised litigator, as defined by section 119(1) of the Courts and Legal Services Act 1990;]

.....

"matter" means every proceeding in a county court which may be commenced as prescribed otherwise than by plaint;

"officer", in relation to a court, means any [district judge], [deputy district judge] or [assistant district judge] of that court, and any clerk, bailiff, usher or messenger in the service of that court;

"part-time [district judge]" and "part-time [assistant district judge]" have the meaning assigned to them by section 10(3);

"party" includes every person served with notice of, or attending, any proceeding, whether named as a party to that proceeding or not;

"prescribed" means prescribed by [rules of court];

"probate proceedings" means proceedings brought in a county court by virtue of section 32 or transferred to that court under section 40;

"proceedings" includes both actions and matters;

"[district judge]" and "[district judge] of a county court" mean a [district judge] appointed for a district under this Act, or, in a case where two or more [district judges] are appointed jointly, either or any of those [district judges];

"return day" means the day appointed in any summons or proceeding for the appearance of the defendant or any other day fixed for the hearing of any proceedings;

.....

"ship" includes any description of vessel used in navigation;

"solicitor" means solicitor of the *Supreme Court*;

.....

[(1A) The definition of "deposit-taking institution" in subsection (1) must be read with—

(a) section 22 of the Financial Services and Markets Act 2000;

(b) any relevant order under that section; and

(c) Schedule 2 to that Act.]

(2), (3) ...

[394]

NOTES

Sub-s (1): in definitions "bailiff", "officer", "part-time district judge" and "part-time assistant district judge" and "district judge" and "district judge of a county court" words in square brackets substituted by virtue of the Courts and Legal Services Act 1990, s 74(1), (3); in definition "the county court limit" words omitted repealed by the High Court and County Courts Jurisdiction Order 1991, SI 1991/724, art 2(8), Schedule; definitions "county court rules" and "the rule committee" (omitted) repealed by the Civil Procedure Act 1997, s 10, Sch 2, para 2(1), (9); definition "deposit-taking institution" substituted by the Financial Services and Markets Act 2000 (Consequential Amendments and Repeals) Order 2001, SI 2001/3649, art 296(1), (2); definition "fees orders" (omitted) repealed by the Courts Act 2003, s 109(1), (3), Sch 8, para 277, Sch 10; in definition "judgment summons" words in square brackets substituted by the Civil Procedure (Modification of Enactments) Order 2002, SI 2002/439, arts 2, 9;

definition "legal representative" inserted by the Courts and Legal Services Act 1990, s 125(3), Sch 18, para 49(1); definition "matrimonial cause" (omitted) repealed by the Matrimonial and Family Proceedings Act 1984, s 46(3), Sch 3; in definition "prescribed" words in square brackets substituted by the Civil Procedure Act 1997, s 10, Sch 2, para 2(2); in definition "solicitor" for the words in italics there are substituted the words "Senior Courts" by the Constitutional Reform Act 2005, s 59(5), Sch 11, Pt 2, para 4(1), (3), as from a day to be appointed; definitions "standard scale" and "statutory maximum" (omitted) repealed by the Statute Law (Repeals) Act 1993.

Sub-s (1A): inserted by SI 2001/3649, art 296(1), (3).

Sub-ss (2), (3): repealed by the Local Government Finance (Repeals, Savings and Consequential Amendments) 1990, SI 1990/776, art 3(1), Sch 1.

148, 149   (*Outside the scope of this work.*)

150   Commencement

This Act shall come into force on 1st August 1984.

[395]

151   Short title

This Act may be cited as the County Courts Act 1984.

[396]

SCHEDULES

SCHEDULE 1
REPLEVIN

Section 144

1.—(1)   The sheriff shall have no power or responsibility with respect to replevin bonds or replevins.

(2)   The [district judge] for the district in which any goods subject to replevin are taken shall have power, subject to the provisions of this Schedule, to approve of replevin bonds and to grant replevins and to issue all necessary process in relation to them, and any such process shall be executed by a bailiff of the court.

(3)   The [district judge] shall, at the instance of the party whose goods have been seized, cause the goods to be replevied to that party on his giving such security as is provided in this Schedule.

2.—(1)   It shall be a condition of any security given under paragraph 1 that the replevisor will—

   (a)   commence an action of replevin against the seizor in the High Court within one week from the date when the security is given; or

   (b)   commence such an action in a county court within one month from that date.

(2)   In either case—

   (a)   the replevisor shall give security, to be approved by the [district judge] having power in the matter, for such an amount as the [district judge] thinks sufficient to cover both the probable costs of the action and either—
      (i)   the alleged rent or damage in respect of which the distress has been made; or
      (ii)   in a case where the goods replevied have been seized otherwise than under colour of distress, the value of the goods; and

   (b)   it shall be a further condition of the security that the replevisor will—
      (i)   prosecute the action with effect and without delay; and
      (ii)   make a return of the goods, if a return of them is ordered in the action.

(3)   …

3.   …

[397]

NOTES

Para 1: words in square brackets substituted by virtue of the Courts and Legal Services Act 1990, s 74(1), (3).

Para 2: in sub-para (2)(a) words in square brackets substituted by virtue of the Courts and Legal Services Act 1990, s 74(1), (3); sub-para (3) repealed by the Courts and Legal Services Act, s 125(2), (7), Sch 17, para 18, Sch 20.
Para 3: repealed by the Courts and Legal Services Act 1990, s 125(2), (7), Sch 17, para 18, Sch 20.

(*Schs 2–4 in so far as unrepealed are outside the scope of this work.*)

COMPANIES ACT 1985

(1985 c 6)

ARRANGEMENT OF SECTIONS

PART XX
WINDING UP OF COMPANIES REGISTERED UNDER THIS ACT
OR THE FORMER COMPANIES ACTS

CHAPTER VI
MATTERS ARISING SUBSEQUENT TO WINDING UP

PART XXV
MISCELLANEOUS AND SUPPLEMENTARY PROVISIONS

PART XXVI
INTERPRETATION

PART XXVII
FINAL PROVISIONS

An Act to consolidate the greater part of the Companies Acts

[11 March 1985]

1–500   ((*Pts I–XIX*) *outside the scope of this work.*)

PART XX
WINDING UP OF COMPANIES REGISTERED UNDER THIS ACT OR THE FORMER
COMPANIES ACTS

501–650   (*Ss 501–650 (Chs I–V) repealed by the Insolvency Act 1986, ss 437, 438, Schs 11, 12.*)

CHAPTER VI
MATTERS ARISING SUBSEQUENT TO WINDING UP

651–653   (*Outside the scope of this work.*)

654   Property of dissolved company to be bona vacantia

(*1*)   *When a company is dissolved, all property and rights whatsoever vested in or held on trust for the company immediately before its dissolution (including leasehold property, but not including property held by the company on trust for any other person) are deemed to be bona vacantia and—*

    (*a*)   *accordingly belong to the Crown, or to the Duchy of Lancaster or to the Duke of Cornwall for the time being (as the case may be), and*

    (*b*)   *vest and may be dealt with in the same manner as other bona vacantia accruing to the Crown, to the Duchy of Lancaster or to the Duke of Cornwall.*

(*2*)   *Except as provided by the section next following, the above has effect subject and without prejudice to any order made by the court under section 651 or 653.*

[398]

NOTES
Whole Act repealed by the Companies Act 2006, s 1295, Sch 16, as from a day to be appointed.

655   Effect on s 654 of company's revival after dissolution

(*1*)   *The person in whom any property or right is vested by section 654 may dispose of, or of an interest in, that property or right notwithstanding that an order may be made under section 651 or 653.*

(*2*)   *Where such an order is made—*

    (*a*)   *it does not affect the disposition (but without prejudice to the order so far as it relates to any other property or right previously vested in or held on trust for the company), and*

    (*b*)   *the Crown or, as the case may be, the Duke of Cornwall shall pay to the company amount of any consideration received for the property or right, or interest therein, or*

        (*i*)   *the amount of any consideration received for the property or right, or interest therein, or*

        (*ii*)   *the value of any such consideration at the time of the disposition,*

or, if no consideration was received, an amount equal to the value of the property, right or interest disposed of, as at the date of the disposition.

(*3*)   *Where a liability accrues under subsection (2) in respect of any property or right which, before the order under section 651 or 653 was made, had accrued as bona vacantia to the Duchy of Lancaster, the Attorney General of the Duchy shall represent Her Majesty in any proceedings arising in connection with that liability.*

(*4*)   *Where a liability accrues under subsection (2) in respect of any property or right which, before the order under section 651 or 653 was made, had accrued as bona vacantia to the Duchy of Cornwall, such persons as the Duke of Cornwall (or other possessor for the time being of the Duchy) may appoint shall represent the Duke (or other possessor) in any proceedings arising out of that liability.*

(*5*)   *This section applies in relation to the disposition of any property, right or interest on or after 22nd December 1981, whether the company concerned was dissolved before, on or after that day.*

[399]

NOTES
Repealed as noted to s 654 at **[398]**.

656   Crown disclaimer of property vesting as bona vacantia

(*1*)   *Where property vests in the Crown under section 654, the Crown's title to it under that section may be disclaimed by a notice signed by the Crown representative, that is to say the Treasury Solicitor, or, in relation to property in Scotland, the Queen's and Lord Treasurer's Remembrancer.*

(2)   The right to execute a notice of disclaimer under this section may be waived by or on behalf of the Crown either expressly or by taking possession or other act evincing that intention.

(3)   A notice of disclaimer under this section is of no effect unless it is executed—

    (a)   within 12 months of the date on which the vesting of the property under section 654 came to the notice of the Crown representative, or

    (b)   if an application in writing is made to the Crown representative by any person interested in the property requiring him to decide whether he will or will not disclaim, within a period of 3 months after the receipt of the application or such further period as may be allowed by the court which would have had jurisdiction to wind up the company if it had not been dissolved.

(4)   A statement in a notice of disclaimer of any property under this section that the vesting of it came to the notice of the Crown representative on a specified date, or that no such application as above mentioned was received by him with respect to the property before a specified date, is sufficient evidence of the fact stated, until the contrary is proved.

(5)   A notice of disclaimer under this section shall be delivered to the registrar of companies and retained and registered by him; and copies of it shall be published in the Gazette and sent to any persons who have given the Crown representative notice that they claim to be interested in the property.

(6)   This section applies to property vested in the Duchy of Lancaster or the Duke of Cornwall under section 654 as if for references to the Crown and the Crown representative there were respectively substituted references to the Duchy of Lancaster and to the Solicitor to that Duchy, or to the Duke of Cornwall and to the Solicitor to the Duchy of Cornwall, as the case may be.

[400]

NOTES
Repealed as noted to s 654 at **[398]**.

657   Effect of Crown disclaimer under s 656

(1)   Where notice of disclaimer is executed under section 656 as respects any property, that property is deemed not to have vested in the Crown under section 654.

[(2)   As regards property in England and Wales, [section 178(4) and sections 179 to 182 of the Insolvency Act] shall apply as if the property had been disclaimed by the liquidator under the said section 91 immediately before the dissolution of the company.]

(3)   As regards property in Scotland, the following 4 subsections apply.

(4)   The Crown's disclaimer operates to determine, as from the date of the disclaimer, the rights, interests and liabilities of the company, and the property of the company, in or in respect of the property disclaimed; but it does not (except so far as is necessary for the purpose of releasing the company and its property from liability) affect the rights or liabilities of any other person.

(5)   The court may, on application by a person who either claims an interest in disclaimed property or is under a liability not discharged by this Act in respect of disclaimed property, and on hearing such persons as it thinks fit, make an order for the vesting of the property in or its delivery to any persons entitled to it, or to whom it may seem just that the property should be delivered by way of compensation for such liability, or a trustee for him, and on such terms as the court thinks just.

(6)   On such a vesting order being made, the property comprised in it vests accordingly in the person named in that behalf in the order, without conveyance or assignation for that purpose.

(7)   Part II of Schedule 20 has effect for the protection of third parties where the property disclaimed is held under a lease.

[401]

NOTES
Repealed as noted to s 654 at **[398]**.
Sub-s (2): substituted by the Insolvency Act 1985, s 109(1), Sch 6, para 46; words in square brackets substituted by the Insolvency Act 1986, s 439(1), Sch 13, Pt I.

The said section 91: i e the Insolvency Act 1985, s 91 (repealed). It is thought that this reference should also have been altered by the Insolvency Act 1986 to a reference to ss 178–180 of that Act.

658–715A   (*Outside the scope of this work.*)

PART XXV
MISCELLANEOUS AND SUPPLEMENTARY PROVISIONS

716–724   (*Outside the scope of this work.*)

725   Service of documents

   (*1*)   *A document may be served on a company by leaving it at, or sending it by post to, the company's registered office.*

   (*2*)   *Where a company registered in Scotland carries on business in England and Wales, the process of any court in England and Wales may be served on the company by leaving it at, or sending it by post to, the company's principal place of business in England and Wales, addressed to the manager or other head officer in England and Wales of the company.*

   (*3*)   *Where process is served on a company under subsection (2), the person issuing out the process shall send a copy of it by post to the company's registered office.*

[402]

NOTES
Repealed as noted to s 654 at **[398]**.

726–734   (*Outside the scope of this work.*)

PART XXVI
INTERPRETATION

735   "Company", etc

   (*1*)   *In this Act—*
   (*a*)   *"company" means a company formed and registered under this Act, or an existing company;*
   (*b*)   *"existing company" means a company formed and registered under the former Companies Acts, but does not include a company registered under the Joint Stock Companies Acts, the Companies Act 1862 or the Companies (Consolidation) Act 1908 in what was then Ireland;*
   (*c*)   *"the former Companies Acts" means the Joint Stock Companies Acts, the Companies Act 1862, the Companies (Consolidation) Act 1908, the Companies Act 1929 and the Companies Acts 1948 to 1983.*

   (*2*)   *"Public company" and "private company" have the meanings given by section 1(3).*

   (*3*)   *"The Joint Stock Companies Acts" means the Joint Stock Companies Act 1856, the Joint Stock Companies Acts 1856, 1857, the Joint Stock Banking Companies Act 1857 and the Act to enable Joint Stock Banking Companies to be formed on the principle of limited liability, or any one or more of those Acts (as the case may require), but does not include the Joint Stock Companies Act 1844.*

   (*4*)   *The definitions in this section apply unless the contrary intention appears.*

[403]

NOTES
Repealed as noted to s 654 at **[398]**.

735A, 735B   (*Outside the scope of this work.*)

[736   "Subsidiary", "holding company" and "wholly-owned subsidiary"

   (*1*)   *A company is a "subsidiary" of another company, its "holding company", if that other company—*

(a)   holds a majority of the voting rights in it, or
(b)   is a member of it and has the right to appoint or remove a majority of its board of directors, or
(c)   is a member of it and controls alone, pursuant to an agreement with other shareholders or members, a majority of the voting rights in it,
or if it is a subsidiary of a company which is itself a subsidiary of that other company.

(2)   A company is a "wholly-owned subsidiary" of another company if it has no members except that other and that other's wholly-owned subsidiaries or persons acting on behalf of that other or its wholly-owned subsidiaries.

(3)   In this section "company" includes any body corporate.]

[404]

NOTES
Repealed as noted to s 654 at **[398]**.
Substituted, together with s 736A, for original s 736, by the Companies Act 1989, s 144(1), subject to transitional provisions.
The original s 736 is reproduced here because of its continuing application for certain purposes—

"736   "Holding company", "subsidiary" and "wholly-owned subsidiary"

(1)   For the purposes of this Act, a company is deemed to be a subsidiary of another if (but only if)—
(a)   that other either—
  (i)   is a member of it and controls the composition of its board of directors, or
  (ii)   holds more than half in nominal value of its equity share capital, or
(b)   the first-mentioned company is a subsidiary of any company which is that other's subsidiary.
The above is subject to subsection (4) below in this section.

(2)   For purposes of subsection (1), the composition of a company's board of directors is deemed to be controlled by another company if (but only if) that other company by the exercise of some power exercisable by it without the consent or concurrence of any other person can appoint or remove the holders of all or a majority of the directorships.

(3)   For purposes of this last provision, the other company is deemed to have power to appoint to a directorship with respect to which any of the following conditions is satisfied—
(a)   that a person cannot be appointed to it without the exercise in his favour by the other company of such a power as is mentioned above, or
(b)   that a person's appointment to the directorship follows necessarily from his appointment as director of the other company, or
(c)   that the directorship is held by the other company itself or by a subsidiary of it.

(4)   In determining whether one company is a subsidiary of another—
(a)   any shares held or power exercisable by the other in a fiduciary capacity are to be treated as not held or exercisable by it,
(b)   subject to the two following paragraphs, any shares held or power exercisable—
  (i)   by any person as nominee for the other (except where the other is concerned only in a fiduciary capacity), or
  (ii)   by, or by a nominee for, a subsidiary of the other (not being a subsidiary which is concerned only in a fiduciary capacity),
are to be treated as held or exercisable by the other,
(c)   any shares held or power exercisable by any person by virtue of the provisions of any debentures of the first-mentioned company or of a trust deed for securing any issue of such debentures are to be disregarded,
(d)   any shares held or power exercisable by, or by a nominee for, the other or its subsidiary (not being held or exercisable as mentioned in paragraph (c)) are to be treated as not held or exercisable by the other if the ordinary business of the other or its subsidiary (as the case may be) includes the lending of money and the shares are held or the power is exercisable as above mentioned by way of security only for the purposes of a transaction entered into in the ordinary course of that business.

(5)   For purposes of this Act—
(a)   a company is deemed to be another's holding company if (but only if) the other is its subsidiary, and
(b)   a body corporate is deemed the wholly-owned subsidiary of another if it has no members except that other and that other's wholly-owned subsidiaries and its or their nominees.

(6)   In this section "company" includes any body corporate.".

[736A   Provisions supplementing s 736

(1)   The provisions of this section explain expressions used in section 736 and otherwise supplement that section.

(2)   In section 736(1)(a) and (c) the references to the voting rights in a company are to the rights conferred on shareholders in respect of their shares or, in the case of a company not having a share capital, on members, to vote at general meetings of the company on all, or substantially all, matters.

(3)   In section 736(1)(b) the reference to the right to appoint or remove a majority of the board of directors is to the right to appoint or remove directors holding a majority of the voting rights at meetings of the board on all, or substantially all, matters; and for the purposes of that provision—

    (a)   a company shall be treated as having the right to appoint to a directorship if—
        (i)   a person's appointment to it follows necessarily from his appointment as director of the company, or
        (ii)   the directorship is held by the company itself; and
    (b)   a right to appoint or remove which is exercisable only with the consent or concurrence of another person shall be left out of account unless no other person has a right to appoint or, as the case may be, remove in relation to that directorship.

(4)   Rights which are exercisable only in certain circumstances shall be taken into account only—

    (a)   when the circumstances have arisen, and for so long as they continue to obtain, or
    (b)   when the circumstances are within the control of the person having the rights;

and rights which are normally exercisable but are temporarily incapable of exercise shall continue to be taken into account.

(5)   Rights held by a person in a fiduciary capacity shall be treated as not held by him.

(6)   Rights held by a person as nominee for another shall be treated as held by the other; and rights shall be regarded as held as nominee for another if they are exercisable only on his instructions or with his consent or concurrence.

(7)   Rights attached to shares held by way of security shall be treated as held by the person providing the security—

    (a)   where apart from the right to exercise them for the purpose of preserving the value of the security, or of realising it, the rights are exercisable only in accordance with his instructions;
    (b)   where the shares are held in connection with the granting of loans as part of normal business activities and apart from the right to exercise them for the purpose of preserving the value of the security, or of realising it, the rights are exercisable only in his interests.

(8)   Rights shall be treated as held by a company if they are held by any of its subsidiaries; and nothing in subsection (6) or (7) shall be construed as requiring rights held by a company to be treated as held by any of its subsidiaries.

(9)   For the purposes of subsection (7) rights shall be treated as being exercisable in accordance with the instructions or in the interests of a company if they are exercisable in accordance with the instructions of or, as the case may be, in the interests of—

    (a)   any subsidiary or holding company of that company, or
    (b)   any subsidiary of a holding company of that company.

(10)   The voting rights in a company shall be reduced by any rights held by the company itself.

(11)   References in any provision of subsections (5) to (10) to rights held by a person include rights falling to be treated as held by him by virtue of any other provision of those subsections but not rights which by virtue of any such provision are to be treated as not held by him.

(12)   In this section "company" includes any body corporate.]

[405]

NOTES
Repealed as noted to s 654 at **[398]**.
Substituted as noted to s 736, at **[404]**.

736B–744A   (Outside the scope of this work.)

PART XXVII
FINAL PROVISIONS

745 (*Outside the scope of this work.*)

746 Commencement

... *this Act comes into force on 1st July 1985.*

[406]

NOTES
Repealed as noted to s 654 at **[398]**.
Words omitted repealed by the Companies Act 1989, s 212, Sch 24.

---

747 Citation

This Act may be cited as the Companies Act 1985.

[407]

(*Schs 1–25 outside the scope of this work.*)

AGRICULTURAL HOLDINGS ACT 1986

(1986 c 5)

ARRANGEMENT OF SECTIONS

PART I
INTRODUCTORY

PART II
PROVISIONS AFFECTING TENANCY DURING ITS CONTINUANCE

Written tenancy agreements

Fixed equipment

Variation of rent

PART III
NOTICES TO QUIT

PART IV
SUCCESSION ON DEATH OR RETIREMENT OF TENANT

Succession on retirement of tenant

Interpretation

PART V
COMPENSATION ON TERMINATION OF TENANCY

Compensation to tenant for disturbance

Compensation to tenant for improvements and tenant-right matters

Compensation to tenant for adoption of special system of farming

Compensation to landlord for deterioration of holding

Supplementary provisions with respect to compensation

PART VI
MARKET GARDENS AND SMALLHOLDINGS

PART VII
MISCELLANEOUS AND SUPPLEMENTAL

An Act to consolidate certain enactments relating to agricultural holdings, with amendments to give effect to recommendations of the Law Commission

[18 March 1986]

NOTES

Transfer of functions: functions of the Minister under this Act (except those contained in Sch 12, para 4(1)(a) at **[526]**) so far as exercisable in relation to Wales are transferred to the National Assembly for Wales, by the National Assembly for Wales (Transfer of Functions) Order 1999, SI 1999/672, art 2, Sch 1.

As to the application of this Act in relation to any tenancy beginning on or after 1 September 1995, see the Agricultural Tenancies Act 1995, s 4 at **[639]**.

As to the exclusion of this Act in relation to leases or tenancies granted to contractors in respect of the running of any removal centre or part of a removal centre, see the Immigration and Asylum Act 1999, s 149(3).

PART I
INTRODUCTORY

1 Principal definitions

(1) In this Act "agricultural holding" means the aggregate of the land (whether agricultural land or not) comprised in a contract of tenancy which is a contract for an agricultural tenancy, not being a contract under which the land is let to the tenant during his continuance in any office, appointment or employment held under the landlord.

(2) For the purposes of this section, a contract of tenancy relating to any land is a contract for an agricultural tenancy if, having regard to—

    (a)   the terms of the tenancy,

    (b)   the actual or contemplated use of the land at the time of the conclusion of the contract and subsequently, and

    (c)   any other relevant circumstances,

the whole of the land comprised in the contract, subject to such exceptions only as do not substantially affect the character of the tenancy, is let for use as agricultural land.

(3) A change in user of the land concerned subsequent to the conclusion of a contract of tenancy which involves any breach of the terms of the tenancy shall be disregarded for the purpose of determining whether a contract which was not originally a contract for an agricultural tenancy has subsequently become one unless it is effected with the landlord's permission, consent or acquiescence.

(4) In this Act "agricultural land" means—

    (a)   land used for agriculture which is so used for the purposes of a trade or business, and

    (b)   any other land which, by virtue of a designation under section 109(1) of the Agriculture Act 1947, is agricultural land within the meaning of that Act.

(5) In this Act "contract of tenancy" means a letting of land, or agreement for letting land, for a term of years or from year to year; and for the purposes of this definition a letting of land, or an agreement for letting land, which, by virtue of subsection (6) of section 149 of the Law of Property Act 1925, takes effect as such a letting of land or agreement for letting land as is mentioned in that subsection shall be deemed to be a letting of land or, as the case may be, an agreement for letting land, for a term of years.

[408]

2 Restriction on letting agricultural land for less than from year to year

(1) An agreement to which this section applies shall take effect, with the necessary modifications, as if it were an agreement for the letting of land for a tenancy from year to year unless the agreement was approved by the Minister before it was entered into.

(2) Subject to subsection (3) below, this section applies to an agreement under which—

    (a)   any land is let to a person for use as agricultural land for an interest less than a tenancy from year to year, or

    (b)   a person is granted a licence to occupy land for use as agricultural land,

if the circumstances are such that if his interest were a tenancy from year to year he would in respect of that land be the tenant of an agricultural holding.

(3) This section does not apply to an agreement for the letting of land, or the granting of a licence to occupy land—

    (a)   made (whether or not it expressly so provides) in contemplation of the use of the land only for grazing or mowing (or both) during some specified period of the year, or

    (b)   by a person whose interest in the land is less than a tenancy from year to year and has not taken effect as such a tenancy by virtue of this section.

(4)   Any dispute arising as to the operation of this section in relation to any agreement shall be determined by arbitration under this Act.

[409]

NOTES

Transfer of functions: see the note at the beginning of this Act.

3 Tenancies for two years or more to continue from year to year unless terminated by notice

(1)   Subject to section 5 below, a tenancy of an agricultural holding for a term of two years or more shall, instead of terminating on the term date, continue (as from that date) as a tenancy from year to year, but otherwise on the terms of the original tenancy so far as applicable, unless—

    (a)   not less than one year nor more than two years before the term date a written notice has been given by either party to the other of his intention to terminate the tenancy, or

    (b)   section 4 below applies.

(2)   A notice given under subsection (1) above shall be deemed, for the purposes of this Act, to be a notice to quit.

(3)   This section does not apply to a tenancy which, by virtue of subsection (6) of section 149 of the Law of Property Act 1925, takes effect as such a term of years as is mentioned in that subsection.

(4)   In this section "term date", in relation to a tenancy granted for a term of years, means the date fixed for the expiry of that term.

[410]

4 Death of tenant before term date

(1)   This section applies where—

    (a)   a tenancy such as is mentioned in subsection (1) of section 3 above is granted on or after 12th September 1984 to any person or persons,

    (b)   the person, or the survivor of the persons, dies before the term date, and

    (c)   no notice effective to terminate the tenancy on the term date has been given under that subsection.

(2)   Where this section applies, the tenancy, instead of continuing as mentioned in section 3(1) above—

    (a)   shall, if the death is one year or more before the term date, terminate on that date, or

    (b)   shall, if the death is at any other time, continue (as from the term date) for a further period of twelve months, but otherwise on the terms of the tenancy so far as applicable, and shall accordingly terminate on the first anniversary of the term date.

(3)   For the purposes of the provisions of this Act with respect to compensation any tenancy terminating in accordance with this section shall be deemed to terminate by reason of a notice to quit given by the landlord of the holding.

(4)   In this section "term date" has the same meaning as in section 3 above.

[411]

5 Restriction on agreements excluding effect of section 3

(1)   Except as provided in this section, section 3 above shall have effect notwithstanding any agreement to the contrary.

(2)   Where before the grant of a tenancy of an agricultural holding for a term of not less than two, and not more than five, years—

    (a)   the persons who will be the landlord and the tenant in relation to the tenancy agree that section 3 above shall not apply to the tenancy, and

    (b)   those persons make a joint application in writing to the Minister for his approval of that agreement, and

    (c)   the Minister notifies them of his approval,

section 3 shall not apply to the tenancy if it satisfies the requirements of subsection (3) below.

(3)   A tenancy satisfies the requirements of this subsection if the contract of tenancy is in writing and it, or a statement endorsed upon it, indicates (in whatever terms) that section 3 does not apply to the tenancy.

[412]

NOTES

Transfer of functions: see the note at the beginning of this Act.

PART II
PROVISIONS AFFECTING TENANCY DURING ITS CONTINUANCE

Written tenancy agreements

6 Right to written tenancy agreement

(1)   Where in respect of a tenancy of an agricultural holding—

    (a)   there is not in force an agreement in writing embodying all the terms of the tenancy (including any model clauses incorporated in the contract of tenancy by virtue of section 7 below), or

    (b)   such an agreement in writing is in force but the terms of the tenancy do not make provision for one or more of the matters specified in Schedule 1 to this Act,

the landlord or tenant of the holding may, if he has requested the other to enter into an agreement in writing embodying all the terms of the tenancy and containing provision for all of the said matters but no such agreement has been concluded, refer the terms of the tenancy to arbitration under this Act.

(2)   On any such reference the arbitrator in his award—

    (a)   shall specify the existing terms of the tenancy, subject to any variations agreed between the landlord and the tenant,

    (b)   in so far as those terms as so varied neither make provision for, nor make provision inconsistent with, the matters specified in Schedule 1 to this Act, shall make provision for all of the said matters having such effect as may be agreed between the landlord and the tenant or, in default of agreement, as appears to the arbitrator to be reasonable and just between them, and

    (c)   may include any further provisions relating to the tenancy which may be agreed between the landlord and the tenant.

(3)   Where it appears to the aribitrator on a reference under this section that, by reason of any provision which he is required to include in his award, it is equitable that the rent of the holding should be varied, he may vary the rent accordingly.

(4)   The award of an arbitrator under this section shall have effect as if the terms and provisions specified and made in the award were contained in an agreement in writing entered into by the landlord and the tenant and having effect (by way of variation of the agreement previously in force in respect of the tenancy) as from the making of the award or, if the award so provides, from such later date as may be specified in it.

(5)   Where in respect of a tenancy of an agricultural holding—

    (a)   the terms of the tenancy neither make provision for, nor make provision inconsistent with, the matter specified in paragraph 9 of Schedule 1 to this Act, and

    (b)   the landlord requests the tenant in writing to enter into such an agreement as is mentioned in subsection (1) above containing provision for all of the matters specified in that Schedule,

the tenant may not without the landlord's consent in writing assign, sub-let or part with possession of the holding or any part of it during the period while the determination of the terms of the tenancy is pending; and any transaction entered into in contravention of this subsection shall be void.

(6)   The period mentioned in subsection (5) above is the period beginning with the date of service of the landlord's request on the tenant and ending with the date on which an agreement is concluded in accordance with that request or (as the case may be) with the date on which the award of an arbitrator on a reference under this section relating to the tenancy takes effect.

[413]

Fixed equipment

7   The model clauses

(1)   The Minister may, after consultation with such bodies of persons as appear to him to represent the interests of landlords and tenants of agricultural holdings, make regulations prescribing terms as to the maintenance, repair and insurance of fixed equipment (in this Act referred to as "the model clauses").

(2)   Regulations under this section may make provision for any matter arising under them to be determined by arbitration under this Act.

(3)   The model clauses shall be deemed to be incorporated in every contract of tenancy of an agricultural holding except in so far as they would impose on one of the parties to an agreement in writing a liability which under the agreement is imposed on the other.

[414]

NOTES

Transfer of functions: see the note at the beginning of this Act.
Regulations: the Agriculture (Maintenance, Repair and Insurance of Fixed Equipment) Regulations 1973, SI 1973/1473, (taking effect as if made hereunder by virtue of the Interpretation Act 1978, s 17(2)(b)), at **[1035]**.

---

8   Arbitration where terms of written agreement are inconsistent with the model clauses

(1)   This section applies where an agreement in writing relating to a tenancy of an agricultural holding effects substantial modifications in the operation of regulations under section 7 above.

(2)   Where this section applies, then, subject to subsection (6) below, the landlord or tenant of the holding may, if he has requested the other to vary the terms of the tenancy as to the maintenance, repair and insurance of fixed equipment so as to bring them into conformity with the model clauses but no agreement has been reached on the request, refer those terms of the tenancy to arbitration under this Act.

(3)   On any reference under this section the arbitrator shall consider whether (disregarding the rent payable for the holding) the terms referred to arbitration are justifiable having regard to the circumstances of the holding and of the landlord and the tenant, and, if he determines that they are not so justifiable, he may by his award vary them in such manner as appears to him reasonable and just between the landlord and tenant.

(4)   Where it appears to the arbitrator on any reference under this section that by reason of any provision included in his award it is equitable that the rent of the holding should be varied, he may vary the rent accordingly.

(5)   The award of an arbitrator under this section shall have effect as if the terms and provisions specified and made in the award were contained in an agreement in writing entered into by the landlord and the tenant and having effect (by way of variation of the agreement previously in force in respect of the tenancy) as from the making of the award or, if the award so provides, from such later date as may be specified in it.

(6)   Where there has been a reference under this section relating to a tenancy, no further such reference relating to that tenancy shall be made before the expiry of three years from the coming into effect of the award of the arbitrator on the previous reference.

[415]

9   Transitional arrangements where liability in respect of fixed equipment transferred

(1)   Where by virtue of section 6, 7 or 8 above the liability for the maintenance or repair of any item of fixed equipment is transferred from the tenant to the landlord, the landlord may

within the prescribed period beginning with the date on which the transfer takes effect require that there shall be determined by arbitration under this Act and paid by the tenant the amount of any relevant compensation.

(2) In subsection (1) above "relevant compensation" means compensation which would have been payable either under subsection (1) of section 71 below or in accordance with subsection (3) of that section, in respect of any previous failure by the tenant to discharge the liability mentioned in subsection (1) above, if the tenant had quitted the holding on the termination of his tenancy at the date on which the transfer takes effect.

(3) Where by virtue of section 6, 7 or 8 above the liability for the maintenance or repair of any item of fixed equipment is transferred from the landlord to the tenant, any claim by the tenant in respect of any previous failure by the landlord to discharge the said liability shall, if the tenant within the prescribed period beginning with the date on which the transfer takes effect so requires, be determined by arbitration under this Act.

(4) Where the terms of a tenancy of an agricultural holding as to the maintenance, repair or insurance of fixed equipment (whether established by the operation of regulations under section 7 above or by agreement) are varied by new regulations made under that section, then, if a reference is made under section 6 above within the prescribed period after the coming into operation of the new regulations, the arbitrator shall, for the purposes of subsection (2) of the said section 6, disregard the variation.

[416]

NOTES

Prescribed period: the Agriculture (Miscellaneous Time Limits) Regulations 1959, SI 1959/171, reg 2(2), (3) at **[1030]** (having effect for the purposes of this section by virtue of the Interpretation Act 1978, s 17(2)(b)); the Agriculture (Time Limit) Regulations 1988, SI 1988/282 at **[1168]**.

10 Tenant's right to remove fixtures and buildings

(1) Subject to the provisions of this section—
   (a) any engine, machinery, fencing or other fixture (of whatever description) affixed, whether for the purposes of agriculture or not, to an agricultural holding by the tenant, and
   (b) any building erected by him on the holding,
shall be removable by the tenant at any time during the continuance of the tenancy or before the expiry of two months from its termination, and shall remain his property so long as he may remove it by virtue of this subsection.

(2) Subsection (1) above shall not apply—
   (a) to a fixture affixed or a building erected in pursuance of some obligation,
   (b) to a fixture affixed or a building erected instead of some fixture or building belonging to the landlord,
   (c) to a building in respect of which the tenant is entitled to compensation under this Act or otherwise, or
   (d) to a fixture affixed or a building erected before 1st January 1884.

(3) The right conferred by subsection (1) above shall not be exercisable in relation to a fixture or building unless the tenant—
   (a) has paid all rent owing by him and has performed or satisfied all his other obligations to the landlord in respect of the holding, and
   (b) has, at least one month before both the exercise of the right and the termination of the tenancy, given to the landlord notice in writing of his intention to remove the fixture or building.

(4) If, before the expiry of the notice mentioned in subsection (3) above, the landlord gives to the tenant a counter-notice in writing electing to purchase a fixture or building comprised in the notice, subsection (1) above shall cease to apply to that fixture or building, but the landlord shall be liable to pay to the tenant the fair value of that fixture or building to an incoming tenant of the holding.

(5) In the removal of a fixture or building by virtue of subsection (1) above, the tenant shall not do any avoidable damage to any other building or other part of the holding, and immediately after the removal shall make good all damage so done that is occasioned by the removal.

(6)   Any dispute between the landlord and the tenant with respect to the amount payable by the landlord under subsection (4) above in respect of any fixture or building shall be determined by arbitration under this Act.

(7)   This section shall apply to a fixture or building acquired by a tenant as it applies to a fixture or building affixed or erected by him.

(8)   This section shall not be taken as prejudicing any right to remove a fixture that subsists otherwise than by virtue of this section.

[417]

11   Provision of fixed equipment necessary to comply with statutory requirements

(1)   Where, on an application by the tenant of an agricultural holding, the Tribunal are satisfied that it is reasonable, having regard to the tenant's responsibilities to farm the holding in accordance with the rules of good husbandry, that he should carry on on the holding an agricultural activity specified in the application to the extent and in the manner so specified and—

(a)   that, unless fixed equipment is provided on the holding, the tenant, in carrying on that activity to that extent and in that manner, will contravene requirements imposed by or under any enactment, or

(b)   that it is reasonable that the tenant should use, for purposes connected with that activity, fixed equipment already provided on the holding, but that, unless that equipment is altered or repaired, the tenant, in using the equipment for those purposes, will contravene such requirements,

the Tribunal may direct the landlord to carry out, within a period specified in the direction, such work for the provision or, as the case may be, the alteration or repair of that fixed equipment as will enable the tenant to comply with the said requirements.

(2)   Where it appears to the Tribunal that an agricultural activity specified in the tenant's application has not been carried on on the holding continuously for a period of at least three years immediately preceding the making of the application the Tribunal shall not direct the landlord to carry out work in connection with that activity unless they are satisfied that the starting of the activity did not or, where the activity has not yet been started, will not constitute or form part of a substantial alteration of the type of farming carried on on the holding.

(3)   The Tribunal shall not direct the landlord to carry out work under this section unless they are satisfied—

(a)   that it is reasonable to do so having regard to the landlord's responsibilities to manage the land comprised in the holding in accordance with the rules of good estate management and also to the period for which the holding may be expected to remain a separate holding and to any other material consideration, and

(b)   that the landlord has refused to carry out that work on being requested in writing to do so by the tenant or has not agreed to carry it out within a reasonable time after being so requested.

(4)   The Tribunal shall not direct the landlord to carry out work under this section if he is under a duty to carry out the work in order to comply with a requirement imposed on him by or under any enactment or if provision is made by the contract of tenancy, or by any other agreement between the landlord and the tenant, for the carrying out of work by one of them.

(5)   If the landlord fails to comply with a direction under this section the tenant shall have the same remedies as if the contract of tenancy had contained an undertaking by the landlord to carry out the work required by the direction within the period allowed by the Tribunal.

(6)   Notwithstanding any term in the contract of tenancy restricting the carrying out by the tenant of alterations to the holding, the remedies referred to in subsection (5) above shall include the right of the tenant to carry out the work himself and recover the reasonable cost of the work from the landlord.

(7)   The Tribunal, on an application by the landlord, may extend or further extend the period specified in a direction under this section if it is shown to their satisfaction that the period so specified, or that period as previously extended under this subsection, as the case may be, will not allow sufficient time both for the completion of preliminary arrangements necessary or desirable in connection with the work required by the direction (including, in appropriate cases, the determination of an application by the landlord for a grant out of money provided by Parliament in respect of that work) and for the carrying out of the said work.

(8)   The reference in subsection (6) above to the reasonable cost of work carried out by a tenant shall, where the tenant has received a grant in respect of the work out of money provided by Parliament, be construed as a reference to the reasonable cost reduced by the amount of the grant.

[418]

Variation of rent

12   Arbitration of rent

(1)   Subject to the provisions of Schedule 2 to this Act, the landlord or tenant of an agricultural holding may by notice in writing served on the other demand that the rent to be payable in respect of the holding as from the next termination date shall be referred to arbitration under this Act.

(2)   On a reference under this section the arbitrator shall determine what rent should be properly payable in respect of the holding at the [next termination date following the date of the demand for arbitration and accordingly shall, with effect from that next termination date], increase or reduce the rent previously payable or direct that it shall continue unchanged.

(3)   A demand for arbitration under this section shall cease to be effective for the purposes of this section on the next termination date following the date of the demand unless before the said termination date—

(a)   an arbitrator has been appointed by agreement between the parties, or

(b)   an application has been made to the President of the Royal Institution of Chartered Surveyors for the appointment of an arbitrator by him.

(4)   References in this section (and in Schedule 2 to this Act) in relation to a demand for arbitration with respect to the rent of any holding, to the next termination date following the date of the demand are references to the next day following the date of the demand on which the tenancy of the holding could have been determined by notice to quit given at the date of the demand.

(5)   Schedule 2 to this Act shall have effect for supplementing this section.

[419]

NOTES

Sub-s (2): words in square brackets substituted by the Regulatory Reform (Agricultural Tenancies) (England and Wales) Order 2006, SI 2006/2805, arts 2, 3, subject to transitional provisions in art 10 thereof.

President of the Royal Institution of Chartered Surveyors: by virtue of s 99 of, and Sch 13, para 5 to, this Act at **[506]**, **[527]**, the reference to the President of the Royal Institution of Chartered Surveyors has effect, in relation to applications for the appointment of an arbitrator made before 1 January 1986, as if it included a reference to the Minister. See further the "Transfer of functions" note at the beginning of this Act.

See further, as to the exclusion of this Act in relation to leases or tenancies granted to contractors in respect of the running of any removal centre or part of a removal centre: the Immigration and Asylum Act 1999, s 149(3).

13   Increases of rent for landlord's improvements

(1)   Where the landlord of an agricultural holding has carried out on the holding any improvement to which this section applies he may by notice in writing served on the tenant within six months from the completion of the improvement increase the rent of the holding as from the completion of the improvement by an amount equal to the increase in the rental value of the holding attributable to the carrying out of the improvement.

(2)   This section applies to—

(a)   an improvement carried out at the request of, or in agreement with, the tenant,

(b)   an improvement carried out in compliance with a direction given by the Tribunal under section 11 above,

(c)   an improvement carried out in pursuance of a notice served by the landlord under section 67(5) below,

(d)   an improvement carried out in compliance with a direction given by the Minister under powers conferred on him by or under any enactment,

(e)   works executed on the holding for the purpose of complying with the requirements of a notice under section 3 of the Agriculture (Safety, Health and Welfare Provisions) Act 1956 (provision of sanitary conveniences and washing facilities),

(f) an improvement carried out in compliance with an improvement notice served, or an undertaking accepted, under Part VII of the Housing Act 1985 or Part VIII of the Housing Act 1974.

(3) No increase of rent shall be made under subsection (1) above in respect of an improvement within paragraph (a), (b) or (f) of subsection (2) above if within six months from its completion the landlord and tenant agree on any increase of rent or other benefit to the landlord in respect of the improvement.

(4) The increase in rent provided for by subsection (1) above shall be reduced proportionately—

(a) in the case of an improvement within paragraph (b) of subsection (2) above, where a grant has been made to the landlord in respect of the improvement out of money provided by Parliament,

(b) in the case of an improvement within any other paragraph of that subsection, where a grant has been made to the landlord in respect of the improvement out of money provided by Parliament or local government funds, and

(c) in the case of an improvement within paragraph (f) of that subsection, where the tenant has contributed to the cost incurred by his landlord in carrying out the improvement.

(5) Where, on the failure of a landlord to carry out an improvement specified in such a direction as is referred to in subsection (2)(b) above, the tenant has himself carried out the improvement, the provisions of this section shall apply as if the improvement had been carried out by the landlord and as if any grant made to the tenant in respect of the improvement out of money provided by Parliament had been made to the landlord.

(6) No increase in rent shall take effect by virtue of subsection (5) above until the tenant has recovered from the landlord the reasonable cost of the improvement reduced by the amount of any grant made to the tenant in respect of the improvement out of money provided by Parliament.

(7) Any dispute arising between the landlord and the tenant of the holding under this section shall be determined by arbitration under this Act.

(8) This section applies to an improvement whether or not it is one for the carrying out of which compensation is provided under Part V or VI of this Act.

[420]

NOTES

Transfer of functions: see the note at the beginning of this Act.

Cultivation of land and disposal of produce

14 Variation of terms of tenancies as to permanent pasture

(1) This section applies where a contract for a tenancy of an agricultural holding provides for the maintenance of specified land, or a specified proportion of the holding, as permanent pasture.

(2) Where this section applies, the landlord or tenant may, by notice in writing served on the other, demand a reference to arbitration under this Act of the question whether it is expedient in order to secure the full and efficient farming of the holding that the area of land required to be maintained as permanent pasture should be reduced.

(3) On a reference under subsection (2) above the arbitrator may by his award direct that the provisions of the contract of tenancy as to land which is to be maintained as permanent pasture or is to be treated as arable land and as to cropping shall have effect subject to such modifications as may be specified in the direction.

(4) If, on a reference under subsection (2) above, the arbitrator gives a direction reducing the area of land which under the contract of tenancy is to be maintained as permanent pasture, he may order that the contract of tenancy shall have effect as if it provided that on quitting the holding on the termination of the tenancy the tenant should leave—

(a)   as permanent pasture, or

(b)   as temporary pasture sown with seeds mixture of such kind as may be specified in the order,

such area of land (in addition to the area of land required by the contract of tenancy, as modified by the direction, to be maintained as permanent pasture) as may be so specified.

(5)   The area of land specified in an order made under subsection (4) above shall not exceed the area by which the land required by the contract of tenancy to be maintained as permanent pasture has been reduced by virtue of the direction.

[421]

15   Disposal of produce and cropping

(1)   Subject to the provisions of this section and to section 82 below, the tenant of an agricultural holding shall notwithstanding any custom of the country or the provisions of the contract of tenancy or of any agreement respecting the disposal of crops or the method of cropping of arable land) have, without incurring any penalty, forfeiture or liability, the following rights, namely—

(a)   to dispose of the produce of the holding, other than manure produced on the holding, and

(b)   to practise any system of cropping of the arable land on the holding.

(2)   Subsection (1) above shall not apply—

(a)   in the case of a tenancy from year to year, as respects the year before the tenant quits the holding or any period after he has given or received notice to quit which results in his quitting the holding, or

(b)   in the case of any other tenancy, as respects the year before its termination.

(3)   Subject to any agreement in writing to the contrary, the tenant of an agricultural holding shall not at any time after he has given or received notice to quit the holding sell or remove from the holding any manure or compost or any hay or straw or roots grown in the last year of the tenancy unless the landlord's written consent has been obtained before the sale or removal.

(4)   Before, or as soon as possible after, exercising his rights under subsection (1) above, a tenant shall make suitable and adequate provision—

(a)   in the case of an exercise of the right to dispose of produce, to return to the holding the full equivalent manurial value of all crops sold off or removed from the holding in contravention of the custom, contract or agreement, and

(b)   in the case of an exercise of the right to practise any system of cropping, to protect the holding from injury or deterioration.

(5)   If the tenant of an agricultural holding exercises his rights under subsection (1) above in such manner as to, or to be likely to, injure or deteriorate the holding, the landlord shall have the following remedies, but no other, namely—

(a)   the right to obtain, if the case so requires, an injunction to restrain the exercise of those rights in that manner, and

(b)   the right in any case, on the tenant's quitting the holding on the termination of the tenancy, to recover damages for any injury to or deterioration of the holding attributable to the exercise by the tenant of those rights.

(6)   For the purposes of any proceedings for an injunction brought under paragraph (a) of subsection (5) above, the question whether the tenant is exercising, or has exercised, his rights under subsection (1) above in such a manner as to, or to be likely to, injure or deteriorate his holding shall be determined by arbitration under this Act; and the award of the arbitrator shall, for the purposes of any proceedings brought under subsection (5) (including an arbitration under paragraph (b)) be conclusive proof of the facts stated in the award.

(7)   In this section—

"arable land" does not include land in grass which, by the terms of a contract of tenancy, is to be retained in the same condition throughout the tenancy; and

"roots" means the produce of any root crop of a kind normally grown for consumption on the holding.

[422]

Distress

16 No distress for rent due more than a year previously

(1)   Subject to subsection (2) below, the landlord of an agricultural holding shall not be entitled to distrain for rent which became due in respect of that holding more than one year before the making of the distress.

(2)   Where it appears that, according to the ordinary course of dealing between the landlord and the tenant of the holding, the payment of rent has been deferred until the expiry of a quarter or half-year after the date at which the rent legally became due, the rent shall, for the purposes of subsection (1) above, be deemed to have become due at the expiry of that quarter or half-year and not at the date at which it became legally due.

[423]

17 Compensation to be set off against rent for purposes of distress

Where the amount of any compensation due to the tenant of an agricultural holding, whether under this Act or under custom or agreement, has been ascertained before the landlord distrains for rent, that amount may be set off against the rent and the landlord shall not be entitled to distrain for more than the balance.

[424]

18 Restrictions on distraining on property of third party

(1)   Property belonging to a person other than the tenant of an agricultural holding shall not be distrained for rent if—
  (a)   the property is agricultural or other machinery and is on the holding under an agreement with the tenant for its hire or use in the conduct of his business, or
  (b)   the property is livestock and is on the holding solely for breeding purposes.

(2)   Agisted livestock shall not be distrained by the landlord of an agricultural holding for rent where there is other sufficient distress to be found; and if such livestock is distrained by him by reason of other sufficient distress not being found, there shall not be recovered by that distress a sum exceeding the amount of the price agreed to be paid for the feeding, or any part of the price which remains unpaid.

(3)   The owner of the agisted livestock may, at any time before it is sold, redeem it by paying to the distrainer a sum equal to the amount mentioned in subsection (2) above, and payment of that sum to the distrainer shall be in full discharge as against the tenant of any sum of that amount which would otherwise be due from the owner of the livestock to the tenant in respect of the price of feeding.

(4)   Any portion of the agisted livestock shall, so long as it remains on the holding, continue liable to be distrained for the amount for which the whole of the livestock is distrainable.

(5)   In this section "livestock" includes any animal capable of being distrained; and "agisted livestock" means livestock belonging to another person which has been taken in by the tenant of an agricultural holding to be fed at a fair price.

[425]

19 Settlement of disputes as to distress

(1)   Where a dispute arises—
  (a)   in respect of any distress having been levied on an agricultural holding contrary to the provisions of this Act,
  (b)   as to the ownership of any livestock distrained or as to the price to be paid for the feeding of that stock, or
  (c)   as to any other matter or thing relating to a distress on an agricultural holding,
the dispute may be determined by the county court or on complaint by a magistrates' court, and the court may make an order for restoration of any livestock or things unlawfully distrained, may declare the price agreed to be paid for feeding or may make any other order that justice requires.

(2)   Any person aggrieved by a decision of a magistrates' court under this section may appeal to the Crown Court.

(3)   In this section "livestock" includes any animal capable of being distrained.

[426]

Miscellaneous

20 Compensation for damage by game

(1)   Where the tenant of an agricultural holding has sustained damage to his crops from any wild animals or birds the right to kill and take which is vested in the landlord or anyone (other than the tenant himself) claiming under the landlord, being animals or birds which the tenant has not permission in writing to kill, he shall, if he complies with the requirements of subsection (2) below, be entitled to compensation from his landlord for the damage.

(2)   The requirements of this subsection are that the tenant shall give his landlord—
  (a)   notice in writing within one month after the tenant first became, or ought reasonably to have become, aware of the occurrence of the damage,
  (b)   a reasonable opportunity to inspect the damage—
    (i)   in the case of damage to a growing crop, before the crop is begun to be reaped, raised or consumed, and
    (ii)   in the case of damage to a crop which has been reaped or raised, before the crop is begun to be removed from the land, and
  (c)   notice in writing of the claim, together with particulars of it, within one month after the expiry of the year in respect of which the claim is made.

(3)   For the purposes of subsection (2) above—
  (a)   seed once sown shall be treated as a growing crop whether or not it has germinated, and
  (b)   "year" means any period of twelve months ending, in any year, with 29th September or with such other date as may by agreement between the landlord and tenant be substituted for that date.

(4)   The amount of compensation under this section shall, in default or agreement made after the damage has been suffered, be determined by arbitration under this Act.

(5)   Where the right to kill and take the wild animals or birds that did the damage is vested in some person other than the landlord, the landlord shall be entitled to be indemnified by that other person against all claims for compensation under this section; and any question arising under this subsection shall be determined by arbitration under this Act.

[427]

21   Extension of tenancies in lieu of claims to emblements

(1)   Where the tenancy of an agricultural holding held by a tenant at a rackrent determines by the death or cesser of the estate of any landlord entitled for his life, or for any other uncertain interest, instead of claims to emblements the tenant shall continue to hold and occupy the holding until the occupation is determined by a twelve months' notice to quit expiring at the end of a year of the tenancy, and shall then quit upon the terms of his tenancy in the same manner as if the tenancy were then determined by effluxion of time or other lawful means during the continuance of his landlord's estate.

(2)   The succeeding landlord shall be entitled to recover from the tenant, in the same manner as his predecessor could have done, a fair proportion of the rent for the period which may have elapsed from the date of the death or cesser of the estate of his predecessor to the time of the tenant so quitting.

(3)   The succeeding landlord and the tenant respectively shall as between themselves and as against each other be entitled to all the benefits and advantages and be subject to the terms, conditions and restrictions to which the preceding landlord and the tenant respectively would have been entitled and subject if the tenancy had determined in manner aforesaid at the expiry of the said twelve months' notice.

[428]

22   Rights to require certain records to be made

(1)   At any time during the tenancy of an agricultural holding—
  (a)   the landlord or the tenant may require the making of a record of the condition of the fixed equipment on the holding and of the general condition of the holding itself (including any parts not under cultivation), and
  (b)   the tenant may require the making of a record of any fixtures or buildings which, under section 10 above, he is entitled to remove and of existing improvements executed by him or in respect of the execution of which he, with the written consent of the landlord, paid compensation to an outgoing tenant.

(2)   Any such record shall be made by a person appointed, in default of agreement between the landlord and tenant, by the President of the Royal Institution of Chartered Surveyors (referred to in this section as "the President"); and any person so appointed may, on production of evidence of his appointment, enter the holding at all reasonable times for the purpose of making any such record.

(3)   The cost of making any such record shall, in default of agreement between the landlord and tenant, be borne by them in equal shares.

(4)   No application may be made to the President for a person to be appointed by him under subsection (2) above unless the application is accompanied by such fee as may be prescribed as the fee for such an application.

(5)   Any instrument of appointment purporting to be made by the President by virtue of subsection (2) above and to be signed by or on behalf of the President shall be taken to be such an instrument unless the contrary is shown.

[429]

NOTES

President of the Royal Institution of Chartered Surveyors: by virtue of s 99 of, and Sch 13, para 6 to, this Act at **[506]**, **[527]**, references to the President of the Royal Institution of Chartered Surveyors have effect in relation to the appointment of a person in pursuance of an application made before 1 January 1986 as if for references to the President of the Royal Institution of Chartered Surveyors there were substituted references to the Minister, and as if sub-ss (4), (5) of this section were omitted. See further the "Transfer of functions" note at the beginning of this Act.

Regulations: the Agricultural Holdings (Fee) Regulations 1996, SI 1996/337 at **[1255]**.

23   Landlord's power of entry

The landlord of an agricultural holding or any person authorised by him may at all reasonable times enter on the holding for any of the following purposes, namely—

(a)   viewing the state of the holding,

(b)   fulfilling the landlord's responsibilities to manage the holding in accordance with the rules of good estate management,

(c)   providing or improving fixed equipment on the holding otherwise than in fulfilment of those responsibilities.

[430]

24   Restriction of landlord's remedies for breach of contract of tenancy

Notwithstanding any provision in a contract of tenancy of an agricultural holding making the tenant liable to pay a higher rent or other liquidated damages in the event of a breach or non-fulfilment of a term or condition of the contract, the landlord shall not be entitled to recover in consequence of any such breach or non-fulfilment, by distress or otherwise, any sum in excess of the damage actually suffered by him in consequence of the breach or non-fulfilment.

[431]

PART III
NOTICES TO QUIT

Notices to quit whole or part of agricultural holding

25   Length of notice to quit

(1)   A notice to quit an agricultural holding or part of an agricultural holding shall (notwithstanding any provision to the contrary in the contract of tenancy of the holding) be invalid if it purports to terminate the tenancy before the expiry of twelve months from the end of the then current year of tenancy.

(2)   Subsection (1) above shall not apply—

(a)   where the tenant is insolvent,

(b)   to a notice given in pursuance of a provision in the contract of tenancy authorising the resumption of possession of the holding or some part of it for some specified purpose other than the use of the land for agriculture,

(c)   to a notice given by a tenant to a sub-tenant,

(d)   where the tenancy is one which, by virtue of subsection (6) of section 149 of the Law of Property Act 1925, has taken effect as such a term of years as is mentioned in that subsection.

(3)   Where on a reference under section 12 above with respect to an agricultural holding the arbitrator determines that the rent payable in respect of the holding shall be increased, a notice to quit the holding given by the tenant at least six months before it purports to take effect shall not be invalid by virtue of subsection (1) above if it purports to terminate the tenancy at the end of the year of the tenancy beginning with the date as from which the increase of rent is effective.

(4)   On an application made to the Tribunal with respect to an agricultural holding under paragraph 9 of Part II of Schedule 3 to this Act, the Tribunal may, if they grant a certificate in accordance with the application—

(a)   specify in the certificate a minimum period of notice for termination of the tenancy (not being a period of less than two months), and

(b)   direct that that period shall apply instead of the period of notice required in accordance with subsection (1) above;

and in any such case a notice to quit the holding which states that the Tribunal have given a direction under this subsection shall not be invalid by virtue of subsection (1) above if the notice given is not less than the minimum notice specified in the certificate.

(5)   A notice to quit within subsection (3) or (4) above shall not be invalid by virtue of any term of the contract of tenancy requiring a longer period of notice to terminate the tenancy, and a notice to quit within subsection (4) above shall not be invalid by reason of its terminating at a date other than the end of a year of the tenancy.

[432]

26   Restriction on operation of notices to quit

(1)   Where—

(a)   notice to quit an agricultural holding or part of an agricultural holding is given to the tenant, and

(b)   not later than one month from the giving of the notice to quit the tenant serves on the landlord a counter-notice in writing requiring that this subsection shall apply to the notice to quit,

then, subject to subsection (2) below, the notice to quit shall not have effect unless, on an application by the landlord, the Tribunal consent to its operation.

(2)   Subsection (1) above shall not apply in any of the Cases set out in Part I of Schedule 3 to this Act; and in this Act "Case A", "Case B" (and so on) refer severally to the Cases set out and so named in that Part of that Schedule.

(3)   Part II of that Schedule shall have effect in relation to the Cases there specified.

[433]

27   Tribunal's consent to operation of notice to quit

(1)   Subject to subsection (2) below, the Tribunal shall consent under section 26 above to the operation of a notice to quit an agricultural holding or part of an agricultural holding if, but only if, they are satisfied as to one or more of the matters mentioned in subsection (3) below, being a matter or matters specified by the landlord in his application for their consent.

(2)   Even if they are satisfied as mentioned in subsection (1) above, the Tribunal shall withhold consent under section 26 above to the operation of the notice to quit if in all the circumstances it appears to them that a fair and reasonable landlord would not insist on possession.

(3)   The matters referred to in subsection (1) above are—

(a)   that the carrying out of the purpose for which the landlord proposes to terminate the tenancy is desirable in the interests of good husbandry as respects the land to which the notice relates, treated as a separate unit;

(b)   that the carrying out of the purpose is desirable in the interests of sound management of the estate of which the land to which the notice relates forms part or which that land constitutes;

(c)   that the carrying out of the purpose is desirable for the purposes of agricultural research, education, experiment or demonstration, or for the purposes of the enactments relating to smallholdings;

(d) that the carrying out of the purpose is desirable for the purposes of the enactments relating to allotments;

(e) that greater hardship would be caused by withholding than by giving consent to the operation of the notice;

(f) that the landlord proposes to terminate the tenancy for the purpose of the land's being used for a use, other than for agriculture, not falling within Case B.

(4) Where the Tribunal consent under section 26 above to the operation of a notice to quit, they may impose such conditions as appear to them requisite for securing that the land to which the notice relates will be used for the purpose for which the landlord proposes to terminate the tenancy.

(5) Where, on an application by the landlord, the Tribunal are satisfied that, by reason of any change of circumstances or otherwise, any condition imposed under subsection (4) above ought to be varied or revoked, they shall vary or revoke the condition accordingly.

(6) Where—

(a) on giving consent under section 26 above to the operation of a notice to quit the Tribunal imposed a condition under subsection (4) above, and

(b) it is proved on an application to the Tribunal on behalf of the Crown that the landlord has acted in contravention of the condition or has failed within the time allowed by the condition to comply with it,

the Tribunal may by order impose on the landlord a penalty of an amount not exceeding two years' rent of the holding at the rate at which rent was payable immediately before the termination of the tenancy, or, where the notice to quit related to a part only of the holding, of an amount not exceeding the proportion of the said two years' rent which it appears to the Tribunal is attributable to that part.

(7) The Tribunal may, in proceedings under this section, by order provide for the payment by any party of such sum as the Tribunal consider a reasonable contribution towards costs.

(8) A penalty imposed under subsection (6) above shall be a debt due to the Crown and shall, when recovered, be paid into the Consolidated Fund.

(9) An order under subsection (6) or (7) above shall be enforceable in the same manner as a judgment or order of the county court to the like effect.

[434]

28 Additional restrictions on operation of notice to quit given under Case D

(1) This section applies where—

(a) notice to quit an agricultural holding or part of an agricultural holding is given to the tenant, and

(b) the notice includes a statement in accordance with Case D to the effect that it is given by reason of the tenant's failure to comply with a notice to do work.

(2) If the tenant serves on the landlord a counter-notice in writing in accordance with subsection (3) or (4) below requiring that this subsection shall apply to the notice to quit, the notice to quit shall not have effect (whether as a notice to which section 26(1) above does or does not apply) unless, on an application by the landlord, the Tribunal consent to its operation.

(3) Subject to subsection (4) below, a counter-notice under subsection (2) above shall be served not later than one month from the giving of the notice to quit.

(4) Where the tenant not later than one month from the giving of the notice to quit serves on the landlord an effective notice requiring the validity of the reason stated in the notice to quit to be determined by arbitration under this Act—

(a) any counter-notice already served under subsection (2) above shall be of no effect, but

(b) if the notice to quit would, apart from this subsection, have effect in consequence of the arbitration, the tenant may serve a counter-notice under subsection (2) not later than one month from the date on which the arbitrator's award is delivered to him.

(5) The Tribunal shall consent under subsection (2) above to the operation of the notice to quit unless it appears to them, having regard—

(a) to the extent to which the tenant has failed to comply with the notice to do work,

(b) to the consequences of his failure to comply with it in any respect, and

(c)   to the circumstances surrounding any such failure,

that a fair and reasonable landlord would not insist on possession.

(6)   In this section "notice to do work" means a notice served on a tenant of an agricultural holding for the purposes of paragraph (b) of Case D, being a notice requiring the doing of any work of repair, maintenance or replacement.

[435]

29   Power to make supplementary provision

The Lord Chancellor may by order provide for any of the matters specified in Schedule 4 to this Act.

[436]

NOTES

Orders: the Agricultural Holdings (Arbitration on Notices) Order 1987, SI 1987/710 at **[1142]**.

30   Notice to quit where tenant is a service man

Schedule 5 to this Act, which makes provision as to notices to quit in cases where the tenant of an agricultural holding is a service man, shall have effect.

[437]

Notices to quit part of agricultural holding

31   Notice to quit part of holding valid in certain cases

(1)   A notice to quit part of an agricultural holding held on a tenancy from year to year given by the landlord of the holding shall not be invalid on the ground that it relates to part only of the holding if it is given—

(a)   for the purpose of adjusting the boundaries between agricultural units or amalgamating agricultural units or parts of such units, or

(b)   with a view to the use of the land to which the notice relates for any of the objects mentioned in subsection (2) below,

and the notice states that it is given for that purpose or with a view to any such use, as the case may be.

(2)   The objects referred to in subsection (1) above are—

(a)   the erection of cottages or other houses for farm labourers, whether with or without gardens;

(b)   the provision of gardens for cottages or other houses for farm labourers;

(c)   the provision of allotments;

(d)   the letting of land (with or without other land) as a smallholding under Part III of the Agriculture Act 1970;

(e)   the planting of trees;

(f)   the opening or working of a deposit of coal, ironstone, limestone, brick-earth or other mineral, or a stone quarry or a clay, sand or gravel pit, or the construction of any works or buildings to be used in connection therewith;

(g)   the making of a watercourse or reservoir;

(h)   the making of a road, railway, tramroad, siding, canal or basin, or a wharf, pier, or other work connected therewith.

[438]

32   Right to treat notice to quit part of holding as notice to quit entire holding

(1)   Where there is given to the tenant of an agricultural holding a notice to quit part of the holding, being either—

(a)   such a notice as is rendered valid by section 31 above, or

(b)   a notice given by a person entitled to a severed part of the reversionary estate in the holding,

subsection (2) below shall apply.

(2)   If—

(a)   within twenty-eight days after the giving of the notice, or

(b)   where the operation of the notice depends on any proceedings under this Part of this Act, within twenty-eight days after the time at which it is determined that the notice has effect,

the tenant gives to the landlord or (as the case may be) to the persons severally entitled to the severed parts of the reversion a counter-notice in writing to the effect that he accepts the notice to quit as a notice to quit the entire holding given by the landlord or (as the case may be) those persons, to take effect at the same time as the original notice, the notice to quit shall have effect accordingly.

[439]

NOTES

Counter-notice: in relation to a counter-notice see the Land Compensation Act 1973, s 59(6).

33   Reduction of rent where notice is given to quit part of holding

(1)   Where the landlord of an agricultural holding resumes possession of part of the holding either—

(a)   by virtue of section 31(1) above, or

(b)   in pursuance of a provision in that behalf contained in the contract of tenancy,

the tenant shall be entitled to a reduction of rent proportionate to that part of the holding and in respect of any depreciation of the value to him of the residue of the holding caused by the severance or by the use to be made of the part severed.

(2)   The amount of any reduction of rent under this section shall, in default of agreement made after the landlord resumes possession of the part of the holding concerned, be determined by arbitration under this Act.

(3)   In a case falling within subsection (1)(b) above that falls to be determined by arbitration under this Act the arbitrator, in assessing the amount of the reduction, shall take into consideration any benefit or relief allowed to the tenant under the contract of tenancy in respect of the land possession of which is resumed by the landlord.

[440]

PART IV
SUCCESSION ON DEATH OR RETIREMENT OF TENANT

Tenancies to which Part IV applies

34   Tenancies to which Part IV applies

(1)   The provisions of this Part of this Act shall have effect with respect to—

(a)   any tenancy of an agricultural holding granted before 12th July 1984, and

(b)   a tenancy granted on or after that date if (but only if)—
   (i)   the tenancy was obtained by virtue of a direction of the Tribunal under section 39 or 53 below,
   (ii)   the tenancy was granted (following a direction under section 39 below) in circumstances within section 45(6) below,
   (iii)   the tenancy was granted by a written contract of tenancy indicating (in whatever terms) that this Part of this Act is to apply in relation to the tenancy, or
   (iv)   the tenancy was granted otherwise than as mentioned in the preceding provisions of this subsection to a person who, immediately before that date, was a tenant of the holding or of any agricultural holding which comprised the whole or a substantial part of the land comprised in the holding.

(2)   In this section "tenant" does not include an executor, administrator, trustee in bankruptcy or other person deriving title from a tenant by operation of law.

[(3)   Where this Act applies in relation to a tenancy by virtue of section 4(1)(g) of the Agricultural Tenancies Act 1995, the reference in subsection (1)(b)(iv) above to a substantial part of the land comprised in the holding means a substantial part determined by reference to either area or value.]

[441]

NOTES
Sub-s (3): added by the Regulatory Reform (Agricultural Tenancies) (England and Wales) Order 2006, SI 2006/2805, arts 2, 4(1).

Succession on death of tenant

35 Application of sections 36 to 48

(1)   Sections 36 to 48 below (except sections 40(5), 42 and 45(8) which are of general application) shall apply where—

    (a)   an agricultural holding is held under a tenancy which falls within paragraph (a) or (b) of section 34(1) above, and

    (b)   the sole (or sole surviving) tenant (within the meaning of that section) dies and is survived by a close relative of his.

(2)   In sections 36 to 48 below (and in Part I of Schedule 6 to this Act)—

"close relative" of a deceased tenant means—

    (a)   the wife[, husband or civil partner] of the deceased;

    (b)   a brother or sister of the deceased;

    (c)   a child of the deceased;

    (d)   any person (not within (b) or (c) above) who, in the case of any marriage [or civil partnership] to which the deceased was at any time a party, was treated by the deceased as a child of the family in relation to that marriage [or civil partnership];

"the date of death" means the date of the death of the deceased;

"the deceased" means the deceased tenant of the holding;

"the holding" (except where the context otherwise requires) means the agricultural holding mentioned in subsection (1) above;

"related holding" means, in relation to the holding, any agricultural holding comprising the whole or a substantial part of the land comprised in the holding;

"the tenancy" means the tenancy of the holding.

[(3)   Where this Act applies in relation to a tenancy by virtue of section 4(1)(g) of the Agricultural Tenancies Act 1995, the reference in subsection (2) above (in the definition of "related holding") to a substantial part of the land comprised in the holding means a substantial part determined by reference to either area or value.]

[442]

NOTES
Sub-s (2): in definition "close relative" words in square brackets in para (a) substituted and words in square brackets in para (d) inserted by the Civil Partnership Act 2004, s 81, Sch 8, para 36.
Sub-s (3): added by the Regulatory Reform (Agricultural Tenancies) (England and Wales) Order 2006, SI 2006/2805, arts 2, 4(2).

36 Right of any eligible person to apply for new tenancy on death of tenant

(1)   Any eligible person may apply under section 39 below to the Tribunal for a direction entitling him to a tenancy of the holding unless excluded by subsection (2) or section 37 or 38 below.

(2)   Subsection (1) above (and section 41 below) shall not apply if on the date of death the holding was held by the deceased under—

    (a)   a tenancy for a fixed term of years of which more than twenty-seven months remained unexpired, or

    (b)   a tenancy for a fixed term of more than one but less than two years.

(3)   For the purposes of this section and sections 37 to 48 below, "eligible person" means (subject to the provisions of Part I of Schedule 6 to this Act and without prejudice to section 41 below) any surviving close relative of the deceased in whose case the following conditions are satisfied—

    (a)   in the seven years ending with the date of death his only or principal source of livelihood throughout a continuous period of not less than five years, or two or more discontinuous periods together amounting to not less than five years, derived from his agricultural work on the holding or on an agricultural unit of which the holding forms part, and

(b) he is not the occupier of a commercial unit of agricultural land.

(4) In the case of the deceased's wife the reference in subsection (3)(a) above to the relative's agricultural work shall be read as a reference to agricultural work carried out by either the wife or the deceased (or both of them).

[(4A) In the case of the deceased's civil partner the reference in subsection (3)(a) above to the relative's agricultural work shall be read as a reference to agricultural work carried out by either the civil partner or the deceased (or both of them).]

(5) Part I of Schedule 6 to this Act, which supplements subsection (3) above and makes provision with respect to the assessment of the productive capacity of agricultural land for the purposes of paragraph (b) of that subsection, shall have effect.

[(6) The reference in subsection (3)(a) above to agricultural work carried out by a person on the holding or on an agricultural unit of which the holding forms part includes—

(a) agricultural work carried out by him from the holding or an agricultural unit of which the holding forms part, and

(b) other work carried out by him on or from the holding or an agricultural unit of which the holding forms part,

which is of a description approved in writing by the landlord after the commencement of this subsection.]

[443]

NOTES

Sub-s (4A): inserted by the Civil Partnership Act 2004, s 81, Sch 8, para 37.
Sub-s (6): added by the Regulatory Reform (Agricultural Tenancies) (England and Wales) Order 2006, SI 2006/2805, arts 2, 5(1).

37 Exclusion of statutory succession where two successions have already occurred

(1) Section 36(1) above (and section 41 below) shall not apply if on each of the last two occasions when there died a sole (or sole surviving) tenant of the holding or of a related holding there occurred one or other of the following things, namely—

(a) a tenancy of the holding or of a related holding was obtained by virtue of a direction of the Tribunal under section 39 below, or such a tenancy was granted (following such a direction) in circumstances within section 45(6) below, or

(b) a tenancy of the holding or of a related holding was granted by the landlord to a person who, being a close relative of the tenant who died on that occasion, was or had become the sole or sole remaining applicant for such a direction.

(2) If on any occasion prior to the date of death, as a result of an agreement between the landlord and the tenant for the time being of the holding or of a related holding, the holding or a related holding became let—

(a) under a tenancy granted by the landlord, or

(b) by virtue of an assignment of the current tenancy,

to a person who, if the said tenant had died immediately before the grant or assignment would have been his close relative, that occasion shall for the purposes of subsection (1) above be deemed to be an occasion such as is mentioned in that subsection on which a tenancy of the holding or a related holding was obtained by virtue of a direction of the Tribunal under section 39 below.

(3) If any such tenancy was granted as mentioned in subsection (2) above for a term commencing later than the date of the grant, the holding under that tenancy shall for the purposes of that subsection not be taken to have become let under that tenancy until the commencement of the term.

(4) Subsections (1) and (2) above—

(a) shall apply whether or not any tenancy granted or obtained (otherwise than by virtue of an assignment) as mentioned in those provisions related to the whole of the land held by the tenant on the occasion of whose death, or with whose agreement, the tenancy was so granted or obtained, as the case may be, and

(b) shall apply where a joint tenancy is granted by the landlord to persons one of whom is a person such as is mentioned in either of those subsections as they apply where a tenancy is granted by the landlord to any such person alone.

(5)   Subsection (2) above shall apply where a tenancy is assigned to joint tenants one of whom is a person such as is mentioned in that subsection as it applies where a tenancy is assigned to any such person alone.

(6)   Where a tenancy of the holding or of a related holding was obtained by virtue of a direction of the Tribunal under section 53(7) below, that occasion shall for the purposes of subsection (1) above be deemed to be an occasion such as is mentioned in that subsection on which a tenancy of the holding or a related holding was obtained by virtue of a direction of the Tribunal under section 39 below.

(7)   Subsection (2) above shall, in relation to any time before 12th September 1984, have effect with the substitution for the words from "as a result" to "grant or assignment" of the words "the holding or a related holding became let under a new tenancy granted by the landlord, with the agreement of the outgoing tenant, to a person who, if the outgoing tenant had died immediately before the grant".

(8)   Subsections (4) and (5) above shall not apply in relation to any tenancy if—

(a)   it was granted before 12th September 1984,

(b)   it was obtained by virtue of any direction given in any proceedings arising out of an application made under Part II of the Agriculture (Miscellaneous Provisions) Act 1976 before 12th September 1984, or

(c)   it was granted (following such a direction) in circumstances within section 23(6) of the said Act of 1976.

(9)   In this section "tenant" has the same meaning as in section 34 above.

[444]

38   Other excluded cases

(1)   Section 36(1) above (and section 41 below) shall not apply if on the date of death the tenancy is the subject of a valid notice to quit to which subsection (1) of section 26 above applies, being a notice given before that date in the case of which—

(a)   the month allowed by that subsection for serving a counter-notice under that subsection expired before that date without such a counter-notice having been served, or

(b)   the Tribunal consented before that date to its operation.

(2)   Section 36(1) (and section 41) shall not apply if on the date of death the tenancy is the subject of a valid notice to quit given before that date and falling within Case C or F.

(3)   Those sections shall not apply if on the date of death the tenancy is the subject of a valid notice to quit given before that date and falling within Case B, D or E, and

(a)   the time within which the tenant, could have required any question arising in connection with the notice to be determined by arbitration under this Act expired before that date without such a requirement having been made by the tenant, and the month allowed for serving any counter-notice in respect of the notice expired before that date without any such counter-notice having been served, or

(b)   questions arising in connection with the notice were referred to arbitration under this Act before that date and were determined before that date in such a way as to uphold the operation of the notice and (where applicable) the month allowed for serving any counter-notice in respect of the notice expired before that date without a counter-notice having been served, or

(c)   the Tribunal consented before that date to the operation of the notice.

(4)   Those sections shall not apply if the holding consists of land held by a smallholdings authority or the Minister for the purposes of smallholdings within the meaning of Part III of the Agriculture Act 1970 (whether the tenancy was granted before or after the commencement of the said Part III).

(5)   Those sections shall not apply if the tenancy was granted by trustees in whom the land is vested on charitable trusts the sole or principal object of which is the settlement or employment in agriculture of persons who have served in any of Her Majesty's naval, military or air forces.

[445]

NOTES
Transfer of functions: see the note at the beginning of this Act.

39 Applications for tenancy of holding

(1) An application under this section by an eligible person to the Tribunal for a direction entitling him to a tenancy of the holding shall be made within the period of three months beginning with the day after the date of death.

(2) Where only one application is made under this section the Tribunal, if satisfied—

    (a) that the applicant was an eligible person at the date of death, and

    (b) that he has not subsequently ceased to be such a person,

shall determine whether he is in their opinion a suitable person to become the tenant of the holding.

(3) Where two or more applications are made under this section, then, subject to subsection (4) below, subsection (2) above shall apply to each of the applicants as if he were the only applicant.

(4) If the applicants under this section include a person validly designated by the deceased in his will as the person he wished to succeed him as tenant of the holding, the Tribunal shall first make a determination under subsection (2) above as regards that person, and shall do so as regards the other applicant or each of the other applicants only if the Tribunal determine that the person so designated is not in their opinion a suitable person to become the tenant of the holding.

(5) If under the preceding provisions of this section only one applicant is determined by the Tribunal to be in their opinion a suitable person to become the tenant of the holding, the Tribunal shall, subject to subsection (10) and section 44 below, give a direction entitling him to a tenancy of the holding.

(6) If under the preceding provisions of this section each of two or more applicants is determined by the Tribunal to be in their opinion a suitable person to become the tenant of the holding, the Tribunal—

    (a) shall, subject to subsection (9) below, determine which of those applicants is in their opinion the more or most suitable person to become the tenant of the holding, and

    (b) shall, subject to subsection (10) and section 44 below, give a direction entitling that applicant to a tenancy of the holding.

(7) Before making a determination under subsection (2) above in the case of any applicant the Tribunal shall afford the landlord an opportunity of stating his views on the suitability of that applicant.

(8) In making a determination under subsection (2) above in the case of a particular applicant, or a determination under subsection (6) above as between two or more applicants, the Tribunal shall have regard to all relevant matters including—

    (a) the extent to which the applicant or each of those applicants has been trained in, or has had practical experience of, agriculture,

    (b) the age, physical health and financial standing of the applicant or each of those applicants, and

    (c) the views (if any) stated by the landlord on the suitability of the applicant or any of those applicants.

(9) Where subsection (6) above would apply apart from this subsection, the Tribunal may, with the consent of the landlord, give instead a direction specifying any two, any three or any four of the applicants within that subsection, and entitling the specified applicants to a joint tenancy of the holding.

(10) Where the person or persons who would, subject to section 44 below, be entitled to a direction under this section entitling him or them to a tenancy or (as the case may be) to a joint tenancy of the holding agree to accept instead a tenancy or joint tenancy of a part of the holding, any direction given by the Tribunal under subsection (5), (6) or (9) above shall relate to that part of the holding only.

[446]

40 Provisions supplementary to section 39

(1) In section 39 above "will" includes codicil, and for the purposes of that section a person shall be taken to be validly designated by the deceased in his will as the person he wishes to succeed him as tenant of the holding if, but only if, a will of the deceased which is the subject of a grant of probate or administration—

(a) contains an effective specific bequest to that person of the deceased's tenancy of the holding, or

(b) does not contain an effective specific bequest of that tenancy, but does contain a statement specifically mentioning the holding or the deceased's tenancy of the holding and exclusively designating that person (in whatever words, and whether by name or description) as the person whom the deceased wishes to succeed him as tenant of the holding.

(2) For the purposes of subsection (1) above a statement which is framed so as to designate as mentioned in paragraph (b) of that subsection different persons in different circumstances shall be taken to satisfy that paragraph if, in the events which have happened, the statement exclusively designates a particular person.

(3) A direction under section 39 above given in favour of a person by reason of his being a person validly designated by the deceased as mentioned in subsection (4) of that section shall be valid even if the probate or administration by virtue of which he was such a person at the giving of the direction is subsequently revoked or varied.

(4) For the purposes of this Part of this Act an application under section 39 above which is withdrawn or abandoned shall be treated as if it had never been made.

(5) Provision shall be made by order under section 73(3) of the Agriculture Act 1947 (procedure of Agricultural Land Tribunals) for requiring any person making an application to the Tribunal under section 39 above or section 41 below to give notice of the application to the landlord of the agricultural holding to which the application relates and to take such steps as the order may require for bringing the application to the notice of other persons interested in the outcome of the application.

[447]

41 Application by not fully eligible person to be treated as eligible

(1) This section applies to any surviving close relative of the deceased who for some part of the seven years ending with the date of death engaged (whether full-time or part-time) in agricultural work on the holding, being a person in whose case—

(a) the condition specified in paragraph (b) of the definition of "eligible person" in section 36(3) above is satisfied, and

(b) the condition specified in paragraph (a) of that definition, though not fully satisfied, is satisfied to a material extent.

(2) A person to whom this section applies may within the period of three months beginning with the day after the date of death apply to the Tribunal for a determination that he is to be treated as an eligible person for the purposes of sections 36 to 48 of this Act.

(3) If on an application under this section—

(a) the Tribunal are satisfied that the applicant is a person to whom this section applies, and

(b) it appears to the Tribunal that in all the circumstances it would be fair and reasonable for the applicant to be able to apply under section 39 above for a direction entitling him to a tenancy of the holding,

the Tribunal shall determine that he is to be treated as an eligible person for the purposes of sections 36 to 48 of this Act, but shall otherwise dismiss the application.

(4) In relation to a person in respect of whom the Tribunal have determined as mentioned in subsection (3) above sections 36 to 48 of this Act shall apply as if he were an eligible person.

(5) A person to whom this section applies may make an application under section 39 above as well as an application under this section; and if the Tribunal determine as mentioned in subsection (3) above in respect of a person who has made an application under that section, the application under that section shall (without prejudice to subsection (4) above) be treated as made by an eligible person.

(6) Without prejudice to the generality of paragraph (b) of subsection (1) above, cases where the condition mentioned in that paragraph might be less than fully satisfied include

cases where the close relative's agricultural work on the holding fell short of providing him with his principal source of livelihood because the holding was too small.

[(7)   The references in subsections (1) and (6) above to agricultural work carried out by a person on the holding include—
  (a)   agricultural work carried out by him from the holding, and
  (b)   other work carried out by him on or from the holding,

which is of a description approved in writing by the landlord after the commencement of this subsection.]

[448]

NOTES
  Sub-s (7): added by the Regulatory Reform (Agricultural Tenancies) (England and Wales) Order 2006, SI 2006/2805, arts 2, 5(2).

42   Procedure where deceased held more than one holding

(1)   Subsections (2) and (3) below shall have effect where at the expiry of the period of three months beginning with the day after the date of death of a tenant there are pending before the Tribunal separate applications made under section 39 above by any person, or (as the case may be) by each one of a number of persons, in respect of more than one agricultural holding held by the tenant at that date.

(2)   The applications referred to in subsection (1) above (together with, in each case, any associated application made under section 41 above) shall, subject to and in accordance with the provisions of any such order as is referred to in section 40(5) above, be heard and determined by the Tribunal in such order as may be decided—
  (a)   where the applications were made by one person, by that person,
  (b)   where the applications were made by two or more persons, by agreement between those persons or, in default of agreement, by the chairman of the Tribunal.

(3)   Any decision made by the chairman under subsection (2)(b) above shall be made according to the respective sizes of the holdings concerned so that any application in respect of any holding which is larger than any other of those holdings shall be heard and determined by the Tribunal before any application in respect of that other holding.

[449]

43   Restriction on operation of notice to quit given by reason of death of tenant

(1)   A notice to quit the holding given to the tenant of the holding by reason of the death of the deceased and falling within Case G shall not have effect unless—
  (a)   no application to become the tenant of the holding is made (or has already at the time of the notice to quit been made) under section 39 above within the period mentioned in subsection (1) of that section, or
  (b)   one or more such applications having been made within that period—
    (i)   none of the applicants is determined by the Tribunal to be in their opinion a suitable person to become the tenant of the holding, or
    (ii)   the Tribunal consent under section 44 below to the operation of the notice to quit in relation to the whole or part of the holding.

(2)   Where the Tribunal consent under section 44 below to the operation of a notice to quit to which subsection (1) above applies in relation to part only of the holding, the notice shall have effect accordingly as a notice to quit that part and shall not be invalid by reason that it relates only to part of the holding.

[450]

44   Opportunity for landlord to obtain Tribunal's consent to operation of notice to quit

(1)   Before giving a direction under section 39(5) or (6) above in a case where a notice to quit to which section 43(1) above applies has been given the Tribunal shall afford the landlord an opportunity of applying for their consent under this section to the operation of the notice.

(2)   Subject to subsection (5) below, section 27 above shall apply in relation to an application for, or the giving of, the Tribunal's consent under this section as it applies in relation to an application for, or the giving of, their consent under section 26 above.

(3)   The Tribunal shall not entertain an application for their consent to the operation of a notice to quit to which section 43(1) above applies unless it is made in pursuance of subsection (1) above.

(4)   Subject to subsection (5) below, if the Tribunal give their consent on an application made in pursuance of subsection (1) above, they shall dismiss the application or each of the applications made under section 39 above.

(5)   Where in any case—
    (a)   a notice to quit to which section 43(1) above applies has been given, and
    (b)   section 39(10) above applies,
the Tribunal shall give their consent to the operation of the notice to quit in relation to the part of the holding which would, in accordance with section 39(10), be excluded from any direction given by the Tribunal with respect to the holding under section 39; and subsections (2) and (4) above shall not apply.

(6)   If on an application made in pursuance of subsection (1) above the Tribunal give their consent to the operation of a notice to quit—
    (a)   within the period of three months ending with the date on which the notice purports to terminate the tenancy ("the original operative date"), or
    (b)   at any time after that date,
the Tribunal may, on the application of the tenant, direct that the notice shall have effect from a later date ("the new operative date").

(7)   The new operative date, in the case of a notice to quit, must be a date not later than the end of the period of three months beginning with—
    (a)   the original operative date, or
    (b)   the date on which the Tribunal give their consent to the operation of the notice,
whichever last occurs.

[451]

45   Effect of direction under section 39

(1)   A direction by the Tribunal—
    (a)   under section 39(5) or (6) above entitling an applicant to a tenancy of the holding, or
    (b)   under section 39(9) above entitling two or more applicants to a joint tenancy of the holding,
shall entitle him or them to a tenancy or joint tenancy of the holding as from the relevant time on the terms provided by sections 47 and 48 below; and accordingly such a tenancy or joint tenancy shall be deemed to be at that time granted by the landlord to, and accepted by, the person or persons so entitled.

(2)   Where the deceased's tenancy was not derived from the interest held by the landlord at the relevant time, the tenancy or joint tenancy deemed by virtue of subsection (1) above to be granted to, and accepted by, the person or persons so entitled shall be deemed to be granted by the person for the time being entitled to the interest from which the deceased's tenancy was derived, instead of by the landlord, with like effect as if the landlord's interest and any other supervening interest were not subsisting at the relevant time.

(3)   The reference in subsection (2) above to a supervening interest is a reference to any interest in the land comprised in the deceased's tenancy, being an interest created subsequently to that tenancy and derived (whether immediately or otherwise) from the interest from which that tenancy was derived and still subsisting at the relevant time.

(4)   Subsection (2) above shall not be read as affecting the rights and liabilities of the landlord under this Part of this Act.

(5)   Any tenancy of the holding inconsistent with the tenancy to which a direction such as is mentioned in subsection (1) above entitles the person or persons concerned shall, if it would not cease at the relevant time apart from this subsection, cease at that time as if terminated at that time by a valid notice to quit given by the tenant.

(6)   If the person or persons whom such a direction entitles to a tenancy or joint tenancy of the holding as from the relevant time becomes or become the tenant or joint tenants of the holding before that time under a tenancy granted by the landlord to, and accepted by, the person or persons concerned, the direction shall cease to have effect and section 48 below shall not apply.

(7)   The rights conferred on any person by such a direction (as distinct from his rights under his tenancy of the holding after he has become the tenant or joint tenant of the holding) shall not be capable of assignment.

(8)   The Lord Chancellor may by regulations provide for all or any of the provisions of sections 36 to 48 of this Act (except this subsection) to apply, with such exceptions, additions or other modifications as may be specified in the regulations, in cases where the person or any of the persons whom such a direction entitles to a tenancy or joint tenancy of the holding dies before the relevant time.

[452]

NOTES

Regulations: the Agriculture (Miscellaneous Provisions) Act 1976 (Application of Provisions) Regulations 1977, SI 1977/1215 at **[1041]** (having effect as if made hereunder by virtue of the Interpretation Act 1978, s 17(2)(b)).

46   Interpretation of section 45

(1)   Subject to subsection (2) below, in sections 45 above and 48 below "the relevant time"—

(a)   except where the following paragraph applies, means the end of the twelve months immediately following the end of the year of tenancy in which the deceased died,

(b)   if a notice to quit the holding was given to the tenant by reason of the death of the deceased, being a notice falling within Case G which, apart from section 43 above, would have terminated the tenancy at a time after the end of those twelve months, means that time.

(2)   Where the Tribunal give a direction under section 39(5), (6) or (9) above in relation to the holding at any time after the beginning of the period of three months ending with the relevant time apart from this subsection ("the original relevant time"), then—

(a)   if the direction is given within that period, the Tribunal may, on the application of the tenant, specify in the direction, as the relevant time for the purposes of this section and section 48 below, such a time falling within the period of three months immediately following the original relevant time as they think fit,

(b)   if the direction is given at any time after the original relevant time the Tribunal shall specify in the direction, as the relevant time for those purposes, such a time falling within the period of three months immediately following the date of the giving of the direction as they think fit,

and any time so specified shall be the relevant time for those purposes accordingly.

(3)   Where in accordance with section 39(10) above, the tenancy to which a direction under that section entitles the person or persons concerned is a tenancy of part of the deceased's holding, references in sections 45 above and 48 below to the holding shall be read as references to the whole of the deceased's holding or to the part of that holding to which the direction relates, as the context requires.

[453]

47   Terms of new tenancy unless varied by arbitration

(1)   Subject to the provisions of this section and section 48 below, the terms of the tenancy or joint tenancy to which a direction under section 39(5), (6) or (9) above entitles the person or persons concerned shall be the same as the terms on which the holding was let immediately before it ceased to be let under the contract of tenancy under which it was let at the date of death.

(2)   If on the date of death the holding was held by the deceased under a tenancy for a fixed term of years, subsection (1) above shall have effect as if the tenancy under which the holding was let at the date of death had before that date become a tenancy from year to year on (with that exception) the terms of the actual tenancy as far as applicable.

(3)   If the terms of the tenancy to which such a direction entitles the person or persons concerned would not, apart from this subsection, include a covenant by the tenant or each of the tenants not to assign, sub-let or part with possession of the holding or any part of it without the landlord's consent in writing, subsection (1) above shall have effect as if those terms included such a covenant.

[454]

48   Arbitration on terms of new tenancy

(1)   Where the Tribunal give a direction such as is mentioned in subsection (1) of section 45 above, the provisions of this section shall apply unless excluded by subsection (6) of that section.

(2)   In the following provisions of this section—
"the landlord" means the landlord of the holding;
"the prescribed period" means the period between the giving of the direction and—
  (a)   the end of the three months immediately following the relevant time, or
  (b)   the end of the three months immediately following the date of the giving of the direction,
whichever last occurs;
"the relevant time" has the meaning given by subsection (1) or (as the case may require) subsection (2) of section 46 above;
"the tenant" means the person or persons entitled to a tenancy or joint tenancy of the holding by virtue of the direction;
and references to the holding shall be read in accordance with section 46(3) above.

(3)   At any time within the prescribed period the landlord or the tenant may by notice in writing served on the other demand a reference to arbitration under this Act of one or both of the questions specified in subsection (4) below.

(4)   Those questions (referred to in the following provisions of this section as "question (a)" and "question (b)" respectively) are—
  (a)   what variations in the terms of the tenancy which the tenant is entitled to or has obtained by virtue of the direction are justifiable having regard to the circumstances of the holding and the length of time since the holding was first let on those terms;
  (b)   what rent should be or should have been properly payable in respect of the holding at the relevant time.

(5)   Where question (a) is referred to arbitration under subsection (3) above (with or without question (b)), the arbitrator—
  (a)   shall determine what variations, if any, in the terms mentioned in that question are justifiable as there mentioned, and
  (b)   without prejudice to the preceding paragraph, shall include in his award such provisions, if any, as are necessary—
    (i)   for entitling the landlord to recover from the tenant under those terms a sum equal to so much as is in all the circumstances fair and reasonable of the aggregate amount of the compensation mentioned in subsection (8)(a) below, and
    (ii)   for entitling the tenant to recover from the landlord under those terms a sum equal to so much as is in all the circumstances fair and reasonable of the aggregate amount of the compensation mentioned in subsection (8)(b) below,
and shall accordingly, with effect from the relevant time, vary those terms in accordance with his determination or direct that that they are to remain unchanged.

(6)   Where question (a) but not question (b) is referred to arbitration under subsection (3) above and it appears to the arbitrator that by reason of any provision included in his award under subsection (5) above (not being a provision of a kind mentioned in paragraph (b) of that subsection) it is equitable that the rent of the holding should be varied, he may vary the rent accordingly with effect from the relevant time.

(7)   Where question (b) is referred to arbitration under subsection (3) above (with or without question (a)), the arbitrator shall determine what rent should be or should have been properly payable in respect of the holding at the relevant time and accordingly shall, with effect from that time, increase or reduce the rent which would otherwise be or have been payable or direct that it shall remain unchanged.

(8)   The compensation referred to in subsection (5)(b) above is—
  (a)   the compensation paid or payable by the landlord, whether under this Act or under agreement or custom, on the termination of the deceased's tenancy of the holding,
  (b)   the compensation paid or payable to the landlord, whether under this Act or under agreement, on that termination in respect of any such dilapidation or deterioration of, or damage to, any part of the holding or anything in or on the holding as the tenant is or will be liable to make good under the terms of his tenancy.

(9)   For the purposes of this section the rent properly payable in respect of the holding shall be the rent at which the holding might reasonably be expected to be let by a prudent and willing landlord to a prudent and willing tenant, taking into account all relevant factors, including (in every case) the terms of the tenancy or prospective tenancy (including those relating to rent) and any such other matters as are specifically mentioned in sub-paragraph (1) of paragraph 1 of Schedule 2 to this Act (read with sub-paragraphs (2) and (3) of that paragraph).

(10)   On any reference under subsection (3) above the arbitrator may include in his award such further provisions, if any, relating to the tenancy which the tenant is entitled to or has obtained by virtue of the direction as may be agreed between the landlord and the tenant.

(11)   If the award of an arbitrator under this section is made before the relevant time, section 47(1) above shall have effect subject to, and in accordance with, the award.

(12)   If the award of an arbitrator under this section is made after the relevant time, it shall have effect as if the terms of the award were contained in an agreement in writing entered into by the landlord and the tenant and having effect as from the relevant time.

[455]

Succession on retirement of tenant

49   Application of sections 50 to 58

(1)   Sections 50 to 58 below (except sections 53(11) and 55(7) which are of general application) shall apply where—
- (a)   an agricultural holding is held under a tenancy from year to year, being a tenancy which falls within paragraph (a) or (b) of section 34(1) above, and
- (b)   a notice is given to the landlord by the tenant, or (in the case of a joint tenancy) by all the tenants, of the holding indicating (in whatever terms) that he or they wish a single eligible person named in the notice to succeed him or them as tenant of the holding as from a date specified in the notice, being a date on which the tenancy of the holding could have been determined by notice to quit given at the date of the notice and which falls not less than one year, but not more than two years, after the date of the notice.

(2)   In subsection (1) above "tenant" has the same meaning as in section 34 above.

(3)   In this section and sections 50 to 58 below (and in Part I of Schedule 6 to this Act as applied by section 50(4))—
"close relative" of the retiring tenant means—
- (a)   the wife[, husband or civil partner] of the retiring tenant;
- (b)   a brother or sister of the retiring tenant;
- (c)   a child of the retiring tenant;
- (d)   any person (not within (b) or (c) above) who, in the case of any marriage [or civil partnership] to which the retiring tenant has been at any time a party, has been treated by the latter as a child of the family in relation to that marriage;

"eligible person" has the meaning given by section 50 below;
"the holding" means the holding in respect of which the retirement notice is given;
"the nominated successor" means the eligible person named in the retirement notice;
"related holding" means, in relation to the holding, any agricultural holding comprising the whole or a substantial part of the land comprised in the holding;
"the retirement date" means the date specified in the retirement notice as the date as from which the proposed succession is to take place;
"the retirement notice" means the notice mentioned in subsection (1) above;
"the retiring tenant" means the tenant by whom the retirement notice was given, or, where it was given by joint tenants (and the context so permits), any one of those tenants, and "the retiring tenants" accordingly means those tenants;
"the tenancy" means the tenancy of the holding.

[(4)   Where this Act applies in relation to a tenancy by virtue of section 4(1)(g) of the Agricultural Tenancies Act 1995, the reference in subsection (3) above (in the definition of "related holding") to a substantial part of the land comprised in the holding means a substantial part determined by reference to either area or value.]

[456]

NOTES
Sub-s (3): in definition "close relative" words in square brackets in para (a) substituted and words in square brackets in para (d) inserted by the Civil Partnership Act 2004, s 81, Sch 8, para 36.
Sub-s (4): added by the Regulatory Reform (Agricultural Tenancies) (England and Wales) Order 2006, SI 2006/2805, arts 2, 4(3).

50 Right to apply for new tenancy on retirement of tenant

(1) The eligible person named in the retirement notice may (subject to section 57(2) below) apply under section 53 below to the Tribunal for a direction entitling him to a tenancy of the holding unless excluded by section 51 below.

(2) For the purposes of sections 49 to 58 of this Act, "eligible person" means (subject to the provisions of Part I of Schedule 6 to this Act as applied by subsection (4) below) a close relative of the retiring tenant in whose case the following conditions are satisfied—
  (a) in the last seven years his only or principal source of livelihood throughout a continuous period of not less than five years, or two or more discontinuous periods together amounting to not less than five years, derived from his agricultural work on the holding or on an agricultural unit of which the holding forms part, and
  (b) he is not the occupier of a commercial unit of agricultural land.

(3) In the case of the wife of the retiring tenant the reference in subsection (2)(a) above to the relative's agricultural work shall be read as a reference to agricultural work carried out by either the wife or the retiring tenant (or both of them).

[(3A) In the case of the civil partner of the retiring tenant the reference in subsection (2)(a) above to the relative's agricultural work shall be read as a reference to agricultural work carried out by either the civil partner or the retiring tenant (or both of them).]

(4) Part I of Schedule 6 to this Act shall apply for the purposes of supplementing subsection (2) above and making provision with respect to the assessment of the productive capacity of agricultural land for the purposes of paragraph (b) of that subsection, but subject to the modifications set out in Part II of that Schedule.

[(5) The reference in subsection (2)(a) above to agricultural work carried out by a person on the holding or on an agricultural unit of which the holding forms part includes—
  (a) agricultural work carried out by him from the holding or an agricultural unit of which the holding forms part, and
  (b) other work carried out by him on or from the holding or an agricultural unit of which the holding forms part,
which is of a description approved in writing by the landlord after the commencement of this subsection.]

[457]

NOTES
Sub-s (3A): inserted by the Civil Partnership Act 2004, s 81, Sch 8, para 38.
Sub-s (5): added by the Regulatory Reform (Agricultural Tenancies) (England and Wales) Order 2006, SI 2006/2805, arts 2, 5(3).

51 Excluded cases

(1) Sections 37 and 38 above shall apply for the purpose of excluding the application of section 50(1) above, but subject to the following modifications—
  (a) references to sections 36(1) and 41 above shall be read as references to section 50(1),
  (b) references to the holding, a related holding and the tenancy shall be read in accordance with section 49(3) above, and
  (c) references to the date of death shall be read as references to the date of the giving of the retirement notice.

(2) Section 50(1) shall not apply if the retiring tenant has at any time given any other notice under section 49(1) above in respect of the holding or a related holding and an application to become the tenant of the holding or a related holding has been duly made by any person under section 53 below in respect of that notice.

(3)   Section 50(1) shall not apply if at the retirement date the retiring tenant will be under sixty-five, unless the retirement notice is given on the grounds that—

(a)   the retiring tenant or (where the notice is given by joint tenants) each of the retiring tenants is or will at the retirement date be incapable, by reason of bodily or mental infirmity, of conducting the farming of the holding in such a way as to secure the fulfilment of the responsibilities of the tenant to farm in accordance with the rules of good husbandry, and

(b)   any such incapacity is likely to be permanent,

and that fact is stated in the notice.

(4)   If on the date of the giving of the retirement notice the tenancy is the subject of a valid notice to quit given before that date and including a statement that it is given for any such reason as is referred to in Case B, D or E (not being a notice to quit falling within section 38(3) above as applied by subsection (1) above), section 50(1) shall not apply unless one of the events mentioned in subsection (5) below occurs.

(5)   Those events are as follows—

(a)   it is determined by arbitration under this Act that the notice to quit is ineffective for the purposes of section 26(2) above on account of the invalidity of any such reason as aforesaid, or

(b)   where a counter-notice is duly served under section 28(2) above—

(i)   the Tribunal withhold consent to the operation of the notice to quit, or

(ii)   the period for making an application to the Tribunal for such consent expires without such an application having been made.

(6)   Where one of the events mentioned in subsection (5) above occurs the relevant period shall for the purposes of sections 53(1) and 54(2) below be the period of one month beginning with the date on which the arbitrator's award is delivered to the tenant, with the date of the Tribunal's decision to withhold consent, or with the expiry of the said period for making an application (as the case may be).

[458]

52   Notices to quit restricting operation of section 53

(1)   If the tenancy becomes the subject of a valid notice to quit given on or after the date of the giving of the retirement notice (but before the Tribunal have begun to hear any application by the nominated successor under section 53 below in respect of the retirement notice) and the notice to quit—

(a)   falls within Case C and is founded on a certificate granted under paragraph 9 of Part II of Schedule 3 to this Act in accordance with an application made before that date, or

(b)   falls within Case F,

the retirement notice shall be of no effect and no proceedings, or (as the case may be) no further proceedings, shall be taken under this Part of this Act in respect of it.

(2)   If the tenancy becomes the subject of a valid notice to quit given on or after the date of the giving of the retirement notice (but before the Tribunal have begun to hear any application by the nominated successor under section 53 below in respect of the retirement notice) and the notice to quit—

(a)   includes a statement that it is given for any such reason as is referred to in Case B, or

(b)   includes a statement that it is given for any such reason as is referred to in Case D and is founded on a notice given for the purposes of that Case before that date,

the retirement notice shall be of no effect and no proceedings, or (as the case may be) no further proceedings, shall be taken under this Part of this Act in respect of it unless one of the events mentioned in subsection (3) below occurs.

(3)   Those events are as follows—

(a)   it is determined by arbitration under this Act that the notice to quit is ineffective for the purposes of section 26(2) above on account of the invalidity of any such reason as aforesaid, or

(b)   where a counter-notice is duly served under section 28(2) above—

(i)   the Tribunal withhold consent to the operation of the notice to quit, or

(ii)   the period for making an application to the Tribunal for such consent expires without such an application having been made.

(4)   Where—

(a)   one of the events mentioned in subsection (3) above occurs, and

(b)   the notice to quit was given before the time when the relevant period for the purposes of sections 53(1) and 54(2) would expire apart from this subsection,

that period shall for those purposes expire at the end of the period of one month beginning with the date on which the arbitrator's award is delivered to the tenant, with the date of the Tribunal's decision to withhold consent, or with the expiry of the said period for making an application (as the case may be).

(5)   For the purposes of this Part of this Act an application by the nominated successor under section 53 below which is invalidated by subsection (1) or (2) above shall be treated as if it had never been made.

[459]

53   Application for tenancy of holding by nominated successor

(1)   An application under this section by the nominated successor to the Tribunal for a direction entitling him to a tenancy of the holding shall be made within the relevant period.

(2)   In subsection (1) above "the relevant period" means (subject to sections 51(6) and 52(4) above) the period of one month beginning with the day after the date of the giving of the retirement notice.

(3)   Any such application—
  (a)   must be accompanied by a copy of the retirement notice, and
  (b)   must be signed by both the nominated successor and the retiring tenant or, where the notice was given by joint tenants, by each of the retiring tenants.

(4)   If the retirement notice includes a statement in accordance with section 51(3) above that it is given on the grounds mentioned in that provision, then, before the nominated successor's application is further proceeded with under this section, the Tribunal must be satisfied—
  (a)   that the retiring tenant or (as the case may be) each of the retiring tenants either is or will at the retirement date be incapable, by reason of bodily or mental infirmity, of conducting the farming of the holding in such a way as to secure the fulfilment of the responsibilities of the tenant to farm in accordance with the rules of good husbandry, and
  (b)   that any such incapacity is likely to be permanent.

(5)   If the Tribunal are satisfied—
  (a)   that the nominated successor was an eligible person at the date of the giving of the retirement notice, and
  (b)   that he has not subsequently ceased to be such a person,
the Tribunal shall determine whether he is in their opinion a suitable person to become the tenant of the holding.

(6)   Before making a determination under subsection (5) above the Tribunal shall afford the landlord an opportunity of stating his views on the suitability of the nominated successor; and in making any such determination the Tribunal shall have regard to all relevant matters, including—
  (a)   the extent to which the nominated successor has been trained in, or has had practical experience of, agriculture,
  (b)   his age, physical health and financial standing,
  (c)   the views (if any) stated by the landlord on his suitability.

(7)   If the nominated successor is determined under that subsection to be in their opinion a suitable person to become the tenant of the holding, the Tribunal shall, subject to subsection (8) below, give a direction entitling him to a tenancy of the holding.

(8)   The Tribunal shall not give such a direction if, on an application made by the landlord, it appears to the Tribunal that greater hardship would be caused by giving the direction than by refusing the nominated successor's application under this section.

(9)   If the Tribunal dispose of the nominated successor's application otherwise than by the giving of a direction under subsection (7) above the retirement notice shall be of no effect (but without prejudice to section 51(2) above).

(10)   For the purposes of this Part of this Act, an application by the nominated successor under this section which is withdrawn or abandoned shall be treated as if it had never been made.

(11)   Provision shall be made by order under section 73(3) of the Agriculture Act 1947 (procedure of Agricultural Land Tribunals) for requiring any person making an application to the Tribunal for a direction under this section to give notice of the application to the landlord of the agricultural holding to which the application relates.

[460]

54   Restriction on operation of certain notices to quit

(1)   This section applies to any notice to quit the holding or part of it given to the tenant of the holding (whether before or on or after the date of the giving of the retirement notice), not being a notice to quit falling within any provision of section 38 above (as applied by section 51(1) above) or section 51 or 52 above.

(2)   A notice to quit to which this section applies shall not, if it would otherwise be capable of so having effect, have effect—

   (a)   at any time during the relevant period, or
   (b)   where an application to become the tenant of the holding is made by the nominated successor under section 53 above within that period, at any time before the application has been finally disposed of by the Tribunal or withdrawn or abandoned,

and shall in any event not have effect if any such application is disposed of by the Tribunal by the giving of a direction under section 53(7) above.

(3)   In subsection (2) above "the relevant period" means (subject to sections 51(6) and 52(4) above) the period of one month beginning with the day after the date of the giving of the retirement notice.

[461]

55   Effect of direction under section 53

(1)   A direction by the Tribunal under section 53(7) above entitling the nominated successor to a tenancy of the holding shall entitle him to a tenancy of the holding as from the relevant time on the terms provided by section 56 below; and accordingly such a tenancy shall be deemed to be at that time granted by the landlord to, and accepted by, the nominated successor.

(2)   Where the tenancy of the retiring tenant or (as the case may be) of the retiring tenants was not derived from the interest held by the landlord at the relevant time, the tenancy deemed by virtue of subsection (1) above to be granted to, and accepted by, the nominated successor shall be deemed to be granted by the person for the time being entitled to the interest from which the tenancy of the retiring tenant or tenants was derived, instead of by the landlord, with like effect as if the landlord's interest and any other supervening interest were not subsisting at the relevant time.

(3)   The reference in subsection (2) above to a supervening interest is a reference to any interest in the land comprised in the tenancy of the retiring tenant or tenants, being an interest created subsequently to that tenancy and derived (whether immediately or otherwise) from the interest from which that tenancy was derived and still subsisting at the relevant time.

(4)   Subsection (2) above shall not be read as affecting the rights and liabilities of the landlord under this Part of this Act.

(5)   Any tenancy of the holding inconsistent with the tenancy to which the nominated successor is entitled by virtue of a direction under section 53(7) above shall, if it would not cease at the relevant time apart from this subsection, cease at that time as if terminated at that time by a valid notice to quit given by the tenant.

(6)   The rights conferred on any person by such a direction (as distinct from his rights under his tenancy of the holding after he has become the tenant) shall not be capable of assignment.

(7)   The Lord Chancellor may by regulations provide for all or any of the provisions of sections 37(6) and 50 to 58 of this Act (except this subsection) to apply, with such exceptions, additions or other modifications as may be specified in the regulations, in cases where the nominated successor, being entitled to a tenancy of the holding by virtue of such a direction, dies before the relevant time.

(8)   In this section "the relevant time" means the retirement date, except that—

   (a)   where such a direction is given within the period of three months ending with the retirement date, the Tribunal may, on the application of the tenant, specify in the direction, as the relevant time for the purposes of this section, such a time falling within the period of three months immediately following the retirement date as they think fit,

(b) where such a direction is given at any time after the retirement date, the Tribunal shall specify in the direction, as the relevant time for those purposes, such a time falling within the period of three months immediately following the date of the giving of the direction as they think fit,

and any time so specified shall be the relevant time for those purposes accordingly.

[462]

56 Terms of new tenancy

(1) Subject to subsections (2) and (3) below, the terms of the tenancy to which a direction under section 53(7) above entitles the nominated successor shall be the same as the terms on which the holding was let immediately before it ceased to be let under the contract of tenancy under which it was let at the date of the giving of the retirement notice.

(2) If the terms of the tenancy to which the nominated successor is entitled as mentioned in subsection (1) above would not, apart from this subsection, include a covenant by the tenant not to assign, sub-let or part with possession of the holding or any part of it without the landlord's consent in writing, subsection (1) above shall have effect as if those terms included that covenant.

(3) Where the Tribunal give a direction under section 53(7) above, subsections (3) to (12) of section 48 above shall have effect in relation to the tenancy which the nominated successor is entitled to or has obtained by virtue of the direction, but with the substitution—

(a) in subsection (8)(a) of a reference to the tenancy of the retiring tenant or (as the case may be) tenants for the reference to the deceased's tenancy,

(b) in subsection (11) of a reference to subsection (1) above for the reference to section 47(1).

(4) In those provisions, as extended by subsection (3) above—

"the landlord" means the landlord of the holding;

"the prescribed period" means the period between the giving of the direction and—
(a) the end of the three months immediately following the relevant time, or
(b) the end of the three months immediately following the date of the giving of the direction,
whichever last occurs;

"the relevant time" has the meaning given by section 55(8) above;

"the tenant" means the nominated successor.

[463]

57 Effect of death of retiring tenant on succession to the holding

(1) Subsections (2) to (4) below apply where the retiring tenant, being the sole (or sole surviving) tenant of the holding, dies after giving the retirement notice.

(2) If the tenant's death occurs at a time when no application by the nominated successor has been made under section 53 above or such an application has not been finally disposed of by the Tribunal, the retirement notice shall be of no effect and no proceedings, or (as the case may be) no further proceedings, shall be taken under section 53 above in respect of it; and accordingly sections 36 to 48 above shall apply on the tenant's death in relation to the holding.

(3) If the tenant's death occurs at a time when any such application has been so disposed of by the giving of a direction such as is mentioned in subsection (1) of section 55 above, but before the relevant time (within the meaning of that section), that section and section 56 above shall continue to have effect in relation to the holding; and accordingly sections 36 to 48 above shall not apply on the tenant's death in relation to the holding.

(4) If the tenant's death occurs at a time when any such application has been so disposed of otherwise than by the giving of any such direction, sections 36 to 48 above shall apply on the tenant's death in relation to the holding, but no application under section 39 (or 41) above may be made on that occasion by the nominated successor in relation to the holding.

(5)   Where the retirement notice was given by joint tenants and one of those tenants, not being the sole surviving tenant of the holding, dies, his death shall not affect any rights of the nominated successor under sections 50 to 56 above.

[464]

58   Effect of direction under section 53 on succession to other holdings

Where—
(a)   the retiring tenant, being the sole (or sole surviving) tenant of the holding, dies, and
(b)   the nominated successor is for the time being entitled to a tenancy of the holding by virtue of a direction under section 53(7) above,

then for the purpose of determining whether, in relation to any other agricultural holding held by the retiring tenant at the date of his death, the nominated successor is a person in whose case the condition specified in paragraph (b) of section 36(3) above is satisfied, the nominated successor shall be deemed to be in occupation of the holding.

[465]

Interpretation

59   Interpretation of Part IV

(1)   In sections 36 to 48 above (and in Part I of Schedule 6 to this Act)—
"close relative" of a deceased tenant,
"the date of death",
"the deceased",
"the holding",
"related holding", and
"the tenancy",

have the meanings given by section 35(2) above; and in those sections "eligible person" has the meaning given by section 36(3) above.

(2)   In sections 49 to 58 above (and in Part I of Schedule 6 to this Act as applied by section 50(4) above)—
"close relative" of the retiring tenant,
"the holding",
"the nominated successor",
"related holding",
"the retirement date",
"the retirement notice",
"the retiring tenant",
"the retiring tenants", and
"the tenancy",

have the meanings given by section 49(3) above; and in those sections "eligible person" has the meaning given by section 50(2) above.

[466]

PART V
COMPENSATION ON TERMINATION OF TENANCY

Compensation to tenant for disturbance

60   Right to, and measure of, compensation for disturbance

(1)   This section applies where the tenancy of an agricultural holding terminates by reason—
(a)   of a notice to quit the holding given by the landlord, or
(b)   of a counter-notice given by the tenant under section 32 above after the giving to him of such a notice to quit part of the holding as is mentioned in that section,
and the tenant quits the holding in consequence of the notice or counter-notice.

(2)   Subject to section 61 below, where this section applies there shall be payable by the landlord to the tenant by way of compensation for disturbance—

(a)   a sum computed under subsection (3) below (in this section referred to as "basic compensation"), and

(b)   a sum computed under subsection (4) below (in this section referred to as "additional compensation").

(3)   The amount of basic compensation shall be—

(a)   an amount equal to one year's rent of the holding at the rate at which rent was payable immediately before the termination of the tenancy, or

(b)   where the tenant has complied with the requirements of subsection (6) below, a greater amount equal to either the amount of the tenant's actual loss or two years' rent of the holding whichever is the smaller.

(4)   The amount of additional compensation shall be an amount equal to four years' rent of the holding at the rate at which rent was payable immediately before the termination of the tenancy of the holding.

(5)   In subsection (3) above "the amount of the tenant's actual loss" means the amount of the loss or expense directly attributable to the quitting of the holding which is unavoidably incurred by the tenant upon or in connection with the sale or removal of his household goods, implements of husbandry, fixtures, farm produce or farm stock on or used in connection with the holding, and includes any expenses reasonably incurred by him in the preparation of his claim for basic compensation (not being costs of an arbitration to determine any question arising under this section or section 61 below).

(6)   The requirements of this subsection are—

(a)   that the tenant has not less than one month before the termination of the tenancy given to the landlord notice in writing of his intention to make a claim for an amount under subsection (3)(b) above, and

(b)   that the tenant has, before their sale, given to the landlord a reasonable opportunity of making a valuation of any such goods, implements, fixtures, produce or stock as are mentioned in subsection (5) above.

(7)   Compensation payable under this section shall be in addition to any compensation to which the tenant may be entitled apart from this section.

[467]

NOTES

This section, together with ss 61–70, is excluded in relation to the termination of a tenancy if the person served with the notice to quit elects that the Land Compensation Act 1973, s 59(2), shall apply to the notice and gives up possession of the holding on or before the date on which his tenancy terminates in accordance with the notice; see s 59(2)(b) of that Act.

---

61   Cases where compensation under section 60 is not payable

(1)   Neither basic compensation nor additional compensation shall be payable under section 60 above where the operation of section 26(1) above in relation to the relevant notice is excluded by virtue of Case C, D, E, F or G.

(2)   Additional compensation shall not be so payable where the operation of section 26(1) above in relation to the relevant notice is excluded by virtue of Case A or H.

(3)   Except as provided by subsection (4) below, additional compensation shall not be payable under section 60 above where—

(a)   the relevant notice contains a statement either that the carrying out of the purpose for which the landlord proposes to terminate the tenancy is desirable on any of the grounds mentioned in paragraphs (a) to (c) of section 27(3) above or that the landlord will suffer hardship unless the notice has effect, and

(b)   if an application for consent in respect of the notice is made to the Tribunal in pursuance of section 26(1) above, the Tribunal consent to its operation and state in the reasons for their decision that they are satisfied as to any of the matters mentioned in paragraphs (a), (b), (c) and (e) of section 27(3).

(4)   Additional compensation shall be payable in a case falling within subsection (3) above where such an application as is mentioned in paragraph (b) of that subsection is made and—

(a)   the reasons given by the Tribunal also include the reason that they are satisfied as to the matter mentioned in paragraph (f) of section 27(3) above, or

(b)   the Tribunal include in their decision a statement under subsection (5) below.

(5)   Where such an application as is mentioned in subsection (3)(b) above is made in respect of the relevant notice and the application specifies the matter mentioned in paragraph (b) of section 27(3) above (but not that mentioned in paragraph (f) of that subsection), the Tribunal shall if they are satisfied as to the matter mentioned in paragraph (b) but would, if it had been specified in the application, have been satisfied also as to the matter mentioned in paragraph (f) include a statement to that effect in their decision.

(6)   In this section—
"basic compensation" and "additional compensation" have the same meanings as in section 60 above;
"the relevant notice" means the notice to quit the holding or part of the holding, as the case may be, mentioned in section 60(1) above.

[468]

NOTES
Exclusion: excluded as noted to s 60 at **[467]**.

62   Compensation on termination in pursuance of early resumption clause

(1)   Where—
   (a)   the tenancy of an agricultural holding terminates by reason of a notice to quit the holding given in pursuance of a provision in the contract of tenancy authorising the resumption of possession of the holding for some specified purpose other than the use of the land for agriculture, and
   (b)   the tenant quits the holding in consequence of the notice,
compensation shall be payable by the landlord to the tenant, in addition to any other compensation so payable apart from this section in respect of the holding.

(2)   The amount of compensation payable under this section shall be equal to the value of the additional benefit (if any) which would have accrued to the tenant if the tenancy had, instead of being terminated as provided by the notice, been terminated by it on the expiration of twelve months from the end of the year of tenancy current when the notice was given.

(3)   For the purposes of subsection (2) above, the current year of a tenancy for a term of two years or more is the year beginning with such day in the period of twelve months ending with the date on which the notice is served as corresponds to the day on which the term would expire by the effluxion of time.

[469]

NOTES
Exclusion: excluded as noted to s 60 at **[467]**.

63   Compensation for disturbance: supplementary provisions

(1)   Where—
   (a)   the tenant of an agricultural holding has sub-let the holding, and
   (b)   the sub-tenancy terminates by operation of law in consequence of the termination of the tenancy by reason of any such notice or counter-notice as is referred to in section 60(1)(a) or (b) above,
section 60 shall apply if the sub-tenant quits the holding in consequence of the termination of the sub-tenancy as mentioned in paragraph (b) above as it applies where a tenant quits a holding in consequence of any such notice or counter-notice.

(2)   Where the tenant of an agricultural holding has sub-let the holding and in consequence of a notice to quit given by his landlord becomes liable to pay compensation under section 60 or 62 above to the sub-tenant, the tenant shall not be debarred from recovering compensation under that section by reason only that, owing to not being in occupation of the holding, on the termination of his tenancy he does not quit the holding.

(3)   Where the tenancy of an agricultural holding terminates by virtue of such a counter-notice as is mentioned in section 60(1)(b) above, and—
   (a)   the part of the holding affected by the notice to quit together with any part of the holding affected by any relevant previous notice rendered valid by section 31 above is less than one-fourth of the original holding, and
   (b)   the holding as proposed to be diminished is reasonably capable of being farmed as a separate holding,

compensation shall not be payable under section 60 above except in respect of the part of the holding to which the notice to quit relates.

(4)   In subsection (3) above "relevant previous notice" means any notice to quit given by the same person who gave the current notice to quit or, where that person is a person entitled to a severed part of the reversionary estate in the holding, by that person or by any other person so entitled.

[470]

NOTES

Exclusion: excluded as noted to s 60 at [467].

Compensation to tenant for improvements and tenant-right matters

64   Tenant's right to compensation for improvements

(1)   The tenant of an agricultural holding shall, subject to the provisions of this Act, be entitled on the termination of the tenancy, on quitting the holding, to obtain from his landlord compensation for an improvement specified in Schedule 7 or Part I of Schedule 8 to this Act carried out on the holding by the tenant, being an improvement begun on or after 1st March 1948.

(2)   In this Act "relevant improvement" means an improvement falling within subsection (1) above.

(3)   Subsection (1) above shall have effect as well where the tenant entered into occupation of the holding before 1st March 1948 as where he entered into occupation on or after that date.

(4)   The provisions of Part I of Schedule 9 to this Act shall have effect with respect to the rights of the tenant of an agricultural holding with respect to compensation for improvements specified in Part II of that Schedule carried out on the holding, being improvements begun before 1st March 1948.

[471]

NOTES

Exclusion: excluded as noted to s 60 at [467].

65   Tenant's right to compensation for tenant-right matters

(1)   The tenant of an agricultural holding shall, subject to the provisions of this Act, be entitled on the termination of the tenancy, on quitting the holding, to obtain from his landlord compensation for any such matter as is specified in Part II of Schedule 8 to this Act.

(2)   The tenant shall not be entitled to compensation under subsection (1) above for crops or produce grown, seeds sown, cultivations, fallows or acts of husbandry performed, or pasture laid down, in contravention of the terms of a written contract of tenancy unless—

    (a)   the growing of the crops or produce, the sowing of the seeds, the performance of the cultivations, fallows or acts of husbandry, or the laying down of the pasture was reasonably necessary in consequence of the giving of a direction under the Agriculture Act 1947, or

    (b)   the tenant shows that the term of the contract contravened was inconsistent with the fulfilment of his responsibilities to farm the holding in accordance with the rules of good husbandry.

(3)   Subject to paragraphs 6 and 7 of Schedule 12 to this Act, subsection (1) above shall apply to a tenant on whatever date he entered into occupation of the holding.

[472]

NOTES

Exclusion: excluded as noted to s 60 at [467].

66   Measure of compensation

(1)   The amount of any compensation under this Act for a relevant improvement specified in Schedule 7 to this Act shall be an amount equal to the increase attributable to the

improvement in the value of the agricultural holding as a holding, having regard to the character and situation of the holding and the average requirements of tenants reasonably skilled in husbandry.

(2)   The amount of any compensation under this Act for a relevant improvement specified in Part I of Schedule 8 to this Act, or for any matter falling within Part II of that Schedule, shall be the value of the improvement or matter to an incoming tenant calculated in accordance with such method, if any, as may be prescribed.

(3)   Where the landlord and the tenant of an agricultural holding have entered into an agreement in writing whereby any benefit is given or allowed to the tenant in consideration of his carrying out an improvement specified in Part I of Schedule 8 to this Act, the benefit shall be taken into account in assessing compensation under this Act for the improvement.

(4)   Nothing in this Act shall prevent the substitution, in the case of matters falling within Part II of Schedule 8 to this Act, for the measure of compensation specified in subsection (2) above, of such measure of compensation, to be calculated according to such method, if any, as may be specified in a written contract of tenancy.

(5)   Where a grant out of money provided by Parliament or local government funds has been or will be made to the tenant of an agricultural holding in respect of a relevant improvement, the grant shall be taken into account in assessing compensation under this Act for the improvement.

[473]

NOTES
   Exclusion: excluded as noted to s 60 at **[467]**.
   Regulations: the Agriculture (Calculation of Value for Compensation) Regulations 1978, SI 1978/809 at **[1072]** (having effect as if made hereunder by virtue of Interpretation Act 1978, s 17(2)(b)).

67   Compensation for long-term improvements: consent required

(1)   The tenant of an agricultural holding shall not be entitled to compensation for a relevant improvement specified in Schedule 7 to this Act unless the landlord has given his consent in writing to the carrying out of the improvement.

(2)   Any such consent may be given by the landlord unconditionally or upon such terms as to compensation or otherwise as may be agreed upon in writing between the landlord and the tenant; and the provisions of section 66(1) above shall have effect subject to the provisions of any such agreement as is made.

(3)   Where, in the case of an improvement specified in Part II of Schedule 7 to this Act, a tenant is aggrieved by the refusal of his landlord to give his consent under subsection (1) above, or is unwilling to agree to any terms subject to which the landlord is prepared to give his consent, the tenant may apply to the Tribunal for approval of the carrying out of the improvement, and the following provisions of this section shall have effect with respect to the application.

(4)   The Tribunal may approve the carrying out of the improvement, either unconditionally or upon such terms, whether as to reduction of the compensation which would be payable if the Tribunal approved unconditionally or as to other matters, as appear to them to be just, or may withhold their approval.

(5)   If the Tribunal grant their approval, the landlord may, within the prescribed period from receiving notification of the Tribunal's decision, serve notice in writing on the Tribunal and the tenant that the landlord proposes himself to carry out the improvement.

(6)   Where the Tribunal grant their approval, then if—

   (a)   no notice is duly served by the landlord under subsection (5) above, or

   (b)   such a notice is duly served, but on an application made by the tenant the Tribunal determines that the landlord has failed to carry out the improvement within a reasonable time,

the approval of the Tribunal shall have effect for the purposes of subsection (1) above as if it were the consent of the landlord, and any terms subject to which the approval was given shall have effect as if they were contained in an agreement in writing between the landlord and the tenant.

(7)   In subsection (5) above, "the prescribed period" means the period prescribed by the Lord Chancellor by order.

[474]

68 Improvements: special cases

(1)   The tenant of an agricultural holding shall not be entitled to compensation for a relevant improvement specified in paragraph 1 of Schedule 8 to this Act unless, not later than one month before the improvement was begun, he gave notice in writing to the landlord of his intention to carry out the improvement.

(2)   Where, on an application of the sub-tenant of an agricultural holding, the Tribunal have directed the immediate landlord of the sub-tenant to carry out work under section 11 above being work which constitutes an improvement specified in Schedule 7 to this Act—
   (a)   section 67 above shall not apply as respects a claim by the immediate landlord against his superior landlord for compensation in respect of that work, and
   (b)   if, on the failure of the immediate landlord to comply with the direction of the Tribunal, the sub-tenant has himself carried out the work, sections 64 and 66 above shall have effect for the purposes of a claim for compensation by the immediate landlord against his superior landlord as if the work had been carried out by the immediate landlord and as if any grant made to the sub-tenant in respect of the work out of money provided by Parliament had been made to the immediate landlord.

(3)   Where the tenant of an agricultural holding has carried out on the holding an improvement specified in Schedule 7 to this Act in accordance with provision for the making of the improvement and for the tenant's being responsible for doing the work in a hill farming land improvement scheme approved under section 1 of the Hill Farming Act 1946, being provision included in the scheme at the instance or with the consent of the landlord—
   (a)   the landlord shall be deemed to have consented as mentioned in subsection (1) of section 67 above,
   (b)   any agreement as to compensation or otherwise made between the landlord and the tenant in relation to the improvement shall have effect as if it had been such an agreement on terms as is mentioned in subsection (2) of that section, and
   (c)   the provisions of subsections (5) and (6) of that section as to the carrying out of improvements by the landlord shall not apply.

(4)   In assessing the amount of any compensation payable under custom or agreement to the tenant of an agricultural holding, if it is shown to the satisfaction of the person assessing the compensation that the cultivations in respect of which the compensation is claimed were wholly or in part the result of or incidental to work in respect of the cost of which an improvement grant has been paid under section 1 of the Hill Farming Act 1946, the amount of the grant shall be taken into account as if it had been a benefit allowed to the tenant in consideration of his executing the cultivations and the compensation shall be reduced to such extent as that person considers appropriate.

(5)   Where the tenant of an agricultural holding claims compensation in respect of works carried out in compliance with an improvement notice served, or an undertaking accepted, under Part VII of the Housing Act 1985 or Part VIII of the Housing Act 1974—
   (a)   section 67 above shall not apply as respects the works, and
   (b)   if a person other than the tenant has contributed to the cost of carrying out the works, compensation in respect of the works as assessed under section 66 above shall be reduced proportionately.

[475]

69 Improvements: successive tenancies

(1)   Where the tenant of an agricultural holding has remained in the holding[, or in any agricultural holding which comprised the whole or a substantial part of the land comprised in

the holding,] during two or more tenancies, he shall not be deprived of his right to compensation under this Act in respect of relevant improvements by reason only that the improvements were made during a tenancy other than the one at the termination of which he quits the holding.

[(1A)   Where this Act applies in relation to any tenancy referred to in subsection (1) above by virtue of section 4(1)(g) of the Agricultural Tenancies Act 1995, the reference in that subsection to a substantial part of the land comprised in the holding means a substantial part determined by reference to either area or value.]

(2)   Where, on entering into occupation of an agricultural holding, the tenant—
   (a)   with the consent in writing of his landlord paid to an outgoing tenant any compensation payable by the landlord under or in pursuance of this Act (or the Agricultural Holdings Act 1948 or Part III of the Agriculture Act 1947) in respect of the whole or part of a relevant improvement, or
   (b)   has paid tó the landlord the amount of any such compensation payable to an outgoing tenant,

the tenant shall be entitled, on quitting the holding, to claim compensation in respect of the improvement or part in the same manner, if at all, as the outgoing tenant would have been entitled if the outgoing tenant had remained tenant of the holding and quitted it at the time at which the tenant quits it.

(3)   Where, in a case not falling within subsection (2) above, the tenant, on entering into occupation of an agricultural holding, paid to his landlord any amount in respect of the whole or part of a relevant improvement, he shall, subject to any agreement in writing between the landlord and the tenant, be entitled on quitting the holding to claim compensation in respect of the improvement or part in the same manner, if at all, as he would have been entitled if he had been tenant of the holding at the time when the improvement was carried out and the improvement or part had been carried out by him.

[476]

NOTES

Sub-s (1): words in square brackets inserted, except in relation to compensation payable on termination of a tenancy where that tenancy was granted before 19 October 2006, by the Regulatory Reform (Agricultural Tenancies) (England and Wales) Order 2006, SI 2006/2805, arts 2, 6(1), (8).

Sub-s (1A): inserted, except in relation to compensation payable on termination of a tenancy where that tenancy was granted before 19 October 2006, by SI 2006/2805, arts 2, 6(2), (8).

Exclusion: excluded as noted to s 60 at **[467]**.

Compensation to tenant for adoption of special system of farming

70   Compensation for special system of farming

(1)   Where the tenant of an agricultural holding shows that, by the continuous adoption of a system of farming which has been more beneficial to the holding—
   (a)   than the system of farming required by the contract of tenancy, or
   (b)   in so far as no system of farming is so required, than the system of farming normally practised on comparable agricultural holdings,

the value of the holding as a holding has been increased during the tenancy, having regard to the character and situation of the holding and the average requirements of tenants reasonably skilled in husbandry, the tenant shall be entitled, on quitting the holding on the termination of the tenancy, to obtain from the landlord compensation of an amount equal to the increase.

(2)   Compensation shall not be recoverable under this section unless—
   (a)   the tenant has, not later than one month before the termination of the tenancy, given to the landlord notice in writing of his intention to claim compensation under this section, and
   (b)   a record has been made under section 22 above of the condition of the fixed equipment on the holding and of the general condition of the holding.

(3)   Compensation shall not be recoverable under this section in respect of any matter arising before the date of the making of the record referred to in subsection (2) above or, if more than one such record has been made, the first of them.

(4)   In assessing the value of an agricultural holding for the purposes of this section due allowance shall be made for any compensation agreed or awarded to be paid to the tenant for

an improvement falling within section 64(1) or (4) above or (subject to paragraph 8 of Schedule 12 to this Act) for any such matter as is specified in Part II of Schedule 8 to this Act, being an improvement or matter which has caused, or contributed to, the benefit.

(5)   Nothing in this section shall entitle a tenant to recover for an improvement falling within section 64(1) or (4) above or an improvement to which the provisions of this Act relating to market gardens apply or (subject to the said paragraph 8) for any such matter as is specified in Part II of Schedule 8 to this Act, any compensation which he is not entitled to recover apart from this section.

[477]

NOTES
Exclusion: excluded as noted to s 60 at **[467]**.

Compensation to landlord for deterioration of holding

71 Compensation for deterioration of particular parts of holding

(1)   The landlord of an agricultural holding shall be entitled to recover from a tenant of the holding, on the tenant's quitting the holding on the termination of the tenancy, compensation in respect of the dilapidation or deterioration of, or damage to, any part of the holding or anything in or on the holding caused by non-fulfilment by the tenant of his responsibilities to farm in accordance with the rules of good husbandry.

(2)   Subject to subsection (5) below, the amount of the compensation payable under subsection (1) above shall be the cost, as at the date of the tenant's quitting the holding, of making good the dilapidation, deterioration or damage.

(3)   Notwithstanding anything in this Act, the landlord may, in lieu of claiming compensation under subsection (1) above, claim compensation in respect of matters specified in that subsection under and in accordance with a written contract of tenancy.

(4)   Where the landlord claims compensation in accordance with subsection (3) above—
   (a)   compensation shall be so claimed only on the tenant's quitting the holding on the termination of the tenancy, and
   (b)   compensation shall not be claimed in respect of any one holding both under such a contract as is mentioned in that subsection and under subsection (1) above;

and for the purposes of paragraph (b) above any claim under section 9(1) above shall be disregarded.

(5)   The amount of the compensation payable under subsection (1) above, or in accordance with subsection (3) above, shall in no case exceed the amount (if any) by which the value of the landlord's reversion in the holding is diminished owing to the dilapidation, deterioration or damage in question.

[478]

72 Compensation for general deterioration of holding

(1)   This section applies where, on the quitting of an agricultural holding by the tenant on the termination of the tenancy, the landlord shows that the value of the holding generally has been reduced by reason of any such dilapidation, deterioration or damage as is mentioned in section 71(1) above or otherwise by non-fulfilment by the tenant of his responsibilities to farm in accordance with the rules of good husbandry.

(2)   Where this section applies, the landlord shall be entitled to recover from the tenant compensation for the matter in question, in so far as the landlord is not compensated for it under subsection (1), or in accordance with subsection (3), of section 71 above.

(3)   The amount of the compensation payable under this section shall be equal to the decrease attributable to the matter in question in the value of the holding as a holding, having regard to the character and situation of the holding and the average requirements of tenants reasonably skilled in husbandry.

(4)   Compensation shall not be recoverable under this section unless the landlord has, not later than one month before the termination of the tenancy, given notice in writing to the tenant of his intention to claim such compensation.

[479]

NOTES
 Modification: modified, in relation to tenancies terminated by virtue of the Land Compensation Act 1973, s 56(3)(c), by s 56(4) of that Act.

73 Deterioration of holding: successive tenancies

 [(1)] Where the tenant of an agricultural holding has remained on the holding[, or on any agricultural holding which comprised the whole or a substantial part of the land comprised in the holding,] during two or more tenancies his landlord shall not be deprived of his right to compensation under section 71 or 72 above in respect of any dilapidation, deterioration or damage by reason only that the tenancy during which an act or omission occurred which in whole or in part caused the dilapidation, deterioration or damage was a tenancy other than the tenancy at the termination of which the tenant quits the holding.

 [(2) Where this Act applies in relation to any tenancy referred to in subsection (1) above by virtue of section 4(1)(g) of the Agricultural Tenancies Act 1995, the reference in that subsection to a substantial part of the land comprised in the holding means a substantial part determined by reference to either area or value.]

[480]

NOTES
 Sub-s (1): numbered as such and words in square brackets inserted, except in relation to compensation payable on termination of a tenancy where that tenancy was granted before 19 October 2006, by the Regulatory Reform (Agricultural Tenancies) (England and Wales) Order 2006, SI 2006/2805, arts 2, 6(3), (4), (8).
 Sub-s (2): added, except in relation to compensation payable on termination of a tenancy where that tenancy was granted before 19 October 2006, by SI 2006/2805, arts 2, 6(5), (8).

Supplementary provisions with respect to compensation

74 Termination of tenancy of part of holding

 (1) Where the landlord of an agricultural holding resumes possession of part of the holding by virtue of section 31 or 43(2) above, the provisions of this Act with respect to compensation shall apply to that part of the holding as if it were a separate holding which the tenant had quitted in consequence of a notice to quit.

 (2) Where the landlord of an agricultural holding resumes possession of part of the holding in pursuance of a provision in that behalf contained in the contract of tenancy—

　(a)　the provisions of this Act with respect to compensation shall apply to that part of the holding as if it were a separate holding which the tenant had quitted in consequence of a notice to quit, but

　(b)　the arbitrator in assessing the amount of compensation payable to the tenant, except the amount of compensation under section 60(2)(b) above, shall take into consideration any benefit or relief allowed to the tenant under the contract of tenancy in respect of the land possession of which is resumed by the landlord.

 (3) Where a person entitled to a severed part of the reversionary estate in an agricultural holding resumes possession of part of the holding by virtue of a notice to quit that part given to the tenant by virtue of section 140 of the Law of Property Act 1925 the provisions of this Act with respect to compensation shall apply to that part of the holding as if—

　(a)　it were a separate holding which the tenant had quitted in consequence of the notice to quit, and

　(b)　the person resuming possession were the landlord of that separate holding.

 (4) References in this Act to the termination of the tenancy of, or (as the case may be) of part of, an agricultural holding include references to the resumption of possession of part of an agricultural holding in circumstances within subsection (1), (2) or (3) above.

[481]

75 Compensation where reversionary estate in holding is severed

 (1) Where the reversionary estate in an agricultural holding is for the time being vested in more than one person in several parts, the tenant shall be entitled, on quitting the entire

273

holding, to require that any compensation payable to him under this Act shall be determined as if the reversionary estate were not so severed.

(2)   Where subsection (1) above applies, the arbitrator shall, where necessary, apportion the amount awarded between the persons who for the purposes of this Act together constitute the landlord of the holding, and any additional costs of the award caused by the apportionment shall be directed by the arbitrator to be paid by those persons in such proportions as he shall determine.

[482]

76   Restrictions on compensation for things done in compliance with this Act

(1)   Notwithstanding anything in this Act or any custom or agreement—
   (a)   no compensation shall be payable to the tenant of an agricultural holding in respect of anything done in pursuance of an order under section 14(4) above,
   (b)   in assessing compensation to an outgoing tenant of an agricultural holding where land has been ploughed up in pursuance of a direction under that section, the value per hectare of any tenant's pasture comprised in the holding shall be taken not to exceed the average value per hectare of the whole of the tenant's pasture comprised in the holding on the termination of the tenancy.

(2)   In subsection (1) above "tenant's pasture" means pasture laid down at the expense of the tenant or paid for by the tenant on entering on the holding.

(3)   The tenant of an agricultural holding shall not be entitled to any compensation for a relevant improvement specified in Part I of Schedule 8 to this Act or (subject to paragraph 8 of Schedule 12 to this Act) for any such matter as is specified in Part II of Schedule 8 if it is an improvement or matter made or effected for the purposes of section 15(4) above.

[483]

77   No compensation under custom for improvement or tenant-right matter

(1)   A landlord or tenant of an agricultural holding shall not be entitled under custom to any compensation from the other for any improvement, whether or not one in respect of the carrying out of which compensation is provided under this Act, or (subject to paragraph 8 of Schedule 12 to this Act) for any matter specified in Part II of Schedule 8 to this Act or otherwise.

(2)   Subsection (1) above shall not apply to compensation for an improvement of a kind specified in Schedule 7 or Part I of Schedule 8 to this Act begun before 1st March 1948.

[484]

78   Extent to which compensation recoverable under agreements

(1)   Save as expressly provided in this Act, in any case for which apart from this section the provisions of this Act provide for compensation, a tenant or landlord shall be entitled to compensation in accordance with those provisions and not otherwise, and shall be so entitled notwithstanding any agreement to the contrary.

(2)   Where the landlord and tenant of an agricultural holding enter into an agreement in writing for any such variation of the terms of the contract of tenancy as could be made by direction or order under section 14 above, the agreement may provide for the exclusion of compensation in the same manner as under section 76(1) above.

(3)   Nothing in the provisions of this Act, apart from this section, shall be construed as disentitling a tenant or landlord to compensation in any case for which the said provisions do not provide for compensation, but (subject to paragraph 8 of Schedule 12 to this Act) a claim for compensation in any such case shall not be enforceable except under an agreement in writing.

[485]

PART VI
MARKET GARDENS AND SMALLHOLDINGS

79   Additional rights with respect to improvements for tenants of market gardens

(1)   Subsections (2) to (5) below apply in the case of an agricultural holding in respect of which it is agreed by an agreement in writing that the holding shall be let or treated as a

market garden; and where the land to which such agreement relates consists of part of an agricultural holding only, those subsections shall apply as if that part were a separate holding.

(2)   The provisions of this Act shall apply as if improvements of a kind specified in Schedule 10 to this Act begun on or after 1st March 1948 were included amongst the improvements specified in Part I of Schedule 8 to this Act and as if improvements begun before that day consisting of the erection or enlargement of buildings for the purpose of the trade or business of a market gardener were included amongst the improvements specified in Part II of Schedule 9 to this Act.

(3)   In section 10 above—
  (a)   subsection (2)(c) shall not exclude that section from applying to any building erected by the tenant on the holding or acquired by him for the purposes of his trade or business as a market gardener, and
  (b)   subsection (2)(d) shall not exclude that section from applying to any building acquired by him for those purposes (whenever erected).

(4)   It shall be lawful for the tenant to remove all fruit trees and fruit bushes planted by him on the holding and not permanently set out, but if the tenant does not remove them before the termination of his tenancy they shall remain the property of the landlord and the tenant shall not be entitled to any compensation in respect of them.

(5)   The right of an incoming tenant to claim compensation in respect of the whole or part of an improvement which he has purchased may be exercised although his landlord has not consented in writing to the purchase.

[486]

80   Power of Tribunal to direct holding to be treated as market garden

(1)   Where the tenant of an agricultural holding desires to make on the holding or any part of it an improvement specified in Schedule 10 to this Act and the landlord refuses, or fails within a reasonable time, to agree in writing that the holding or that part of it, as the case may be, shall be treated as a market garden, the tenant may apply to the Tribunal for a direction under subsection (2) below.

(2)   On such an application, the Tribunal may, after being satisfied that the holding or part is suitable for the purposes of market gardening, direct that subsections (2) to (5) of section 79 above shall, either in respect of all the improvements specified in the said Schedule 10 or in respect of some only of those improvements, apply to the holding or to that part of it; and the said subsections shall apply accordingly as respects any improvements executed after the date on which the direction is given.

(3)   Where a direction is given under subsection (2) above, then, if the tenancy is terminated by notice to quit given by the tenant or by reason of the tenant becoming insolvent, the tenant shall not be entitled to compensation in respect of improvements specified in the direction unless the conditions mentioned in subsection (4) below are satisfied.

(4)   Those conditions are that—
  (a)   the tenant not later than one month after the date on which the notice to quit is given or the date of the insolvency, as the case may be, or such later date as may be agreed, produces to the landlord an offer in writing by a substantial and otherwise suitable person (being an offer which is to hold good for a period of three months from the date on which it is produced)—
    (i)   to accept a tenancy of the holding from the termination of the existing tenancy, and on the terms and conditions of that tenancy so far as applicable, and,
    (ii)   subject as hereinafter provided, to pay to the outgoing tenant all compensation payable under this Act or under the contract of tenancy, and
  (b)   the landlord fails to accept the offer within three months after it has been produced.

(5)   If the landlord accepts any such offer as is mentioned in subsection (4) above, the incoming tenant shall pay to the landlord on demand all sums payable to him by the outgoing tenant on the termination of the tenancy in respect of rent or breach of contract or otherwise in respect of the holding, and any amount so paid may, subject to any agreement between the outgoing tenant and incoming tenant, be deducted by the incoming tenant from any compensation payable by him to the outgoing tenant.

(6)   A direction under subsection (2) above may be given subject to such conditions (if any) for the protection of the landlord as the Tribunal think fit.

(7) Without prejudice to the generality of subsection (6) above, where a direction relates to part only of an agricultural holding, it may, on the application of the landlord, be given subject to the condition that it shall become operative only in the event of the tenant's consenting to the division of the holding into two parts, of which one shall be that to which the direction relates, to be held at rents settled, in default of agreement, by arbitration under this Act, but otherwise on the same terms and conditions (so far as applicable) as those on which the holding is held.

(8) A new tenancy created by the acceptance of a tenant in accordance with the provisions of this section on the terms and conditions of the existing tenancy shall be deemed for the purposes of Schedule 2 to this Act not to be a new tenancy.

(9) For the purposes of subsection (3) above a person has become insolvent if any of the events mentioned in section 96(2)(a) or (b) below has occurred; and the reference in subsection (4) above to the date of the insolvency is a reference to the date of the occurrence of the event in question.

[487]

81 Agreements as to compensation relating to market gardens

(1) Where an agreement in writing secures to the tenant of an agricultural holding, for an improvement for which compensation is payable by virtue of section 79 or section 80 above, fair and reasonable compensation having regard to the circumstances existing when the agreement was made, the compensation so secured shall, as respects that improvement, be substituted for compensation under this Act.

(2) The landlord and tenant of an agricultural holding who have agreed that the holding shall be let or treated as a market garden may by agreement in writing substitute, for the provisions as to compensation which would otherwise be applicable to the holding, the provisions as to compensation known as the "Evesham custom", and set out in subsections (3) to (5) of section 80 above.

[488]

82 Application of section 15 to smallholdings

(1) Section 15(1) above shall not apply to a tenancy of land let as a smallholding by a smallholdings authority or by the Minister in pursuance of a scheme, approved by the Minister for the purposes of this section, which—
   (a) provides for the farming of such holdings on a co-operative basis,
   (b) provides for the disposal of the produce of such holdings, or
   (c) provides other centralised services for the use of the tenants of such holdings.

(2) Where it appears to the Minister that the provisions of any scheme approved by him for the purposes of this section are not being satisfactorily carried out, he may, in accordance with subsection (3) below, withdraw his approval to the scheme.

(3) Before withdrawing his approval to a scheme the Minister shall—
   (a) serve a notice on the persons responsible for the management of the scheme specifying a date (not being earlier than one month after the service of the notice) and stating that on that date his approval to the scheme will cease to have effect and that, accordingly, section 15(1) will then apply to the tenancies granted in pursuance of the scheme,
   (b) give to those persons an opportunity of making representations to him;
and, if the said notice is not withdrawn by the Minister before the said date, section 15(1) shall as from that date apply to the said tenancies.

[489]

NOTES

Transfer of functions: see the note at the beginning of this Act.

PART VII
MISCELLANEOUS AND SUPPLEMENTAL

83 Settlement of claims on termination of tenancy

(1) Without prejudice to any other provision of this Act, any claim of whatever nature by the tenant or landlord of an agricultural holding against the other, being a claim which arises—

(a)   under this Act or any custom or agreement, and

(b)   on or out of the termination of the tenancy of the holding or part of it,

shall, subject to the provisions of this section, be determined by arbitration under this Act.

(2)   No such claim as is mentioned in subsection (1) above shall be enforceable unless before the expiry of two months from the termination of the tenancy the claimant has served notice in writing on his landlord or tenant, as the case may be, of his intention to make the claim.

(3)   A notice under subsection (2) above shall specify the nature of the claim; but it shall be sufficient if the notice refers to the statutory provision, custom or term of an agreement under which the claim is made.

(4)   The landlord and tenant may, within the period of eight months from the termination of the tenancy, by agreement in writing settle any such claim as is mentioned in subsection (1) above.

(5)   Where by the expiry of the said period any such claim as is mentioned in subsection (1) above has not been settled, it shall be determined by arbitration under this Act.

(6)   Where a tenant lawfully remains in occupation of part of an agricultural holding after the termination of a tenancy, references in subsections (2) and (4) above to the termination of the tenancy shall, in the case of a claim relating to that part of the holding, be construed as references to the termination of the occupation.

[490]

NOTES

This section is applied, with modifications to sub-s (4), by the Opencast Coal Act 1958, s 24(2), (6).

84   Arbitrations

(1)   Any matter which by or by virtue of this Act or regulations made under this Act is required to be determined by arbitration under this Act shall, notwithstanding any agreement (under a contract of tenancy or otherwise) providing for a different method of arbitration, be determined by the arbitration of a single arbitrator …

[(2)   The arbitrator shall be a person appointed by agreement between the parties or, in default of agreement, a person appointed on the application of either of the parties by the President of the RICS.

(3)   If the arbitrator dies, or is incapable of acting, a new arbitrator may be appointed as if no arbitrator had been appointed.

(4)   No application may be made to the President of the RICS for an arbitrator to be appointed by him under this section unless the application is accompanied by such fee as may be prescribed as the fee for such an application; but once the fee has been paid in connection with any such application no further fee shall be payable in connection with any subsequent application for the appointment by him of a new arbitrator in relation to that arbitration.

(5)   Where by virtue of this Act compensation under an agreement is to be substituted for compensation under this Act for improvements or for any such matters as are specified in Part II of Schedule 8 to this Act, the arbitrator shall award compensation in accordance with the agreement instead of in accordance with this Act.

(6)   In this section "the RICS" means the Royal Institution of Chartered Surveyors.]

[491]

NOTES

Sub-s (1): words omitted repealed by the Regulatory Reform (Agricultural Tenancies) (England and Wales) Order 2006, SI 2006/2805, arts 2, 7(1), 18, Sch 2, subject to transitional provisions in art 10 thereof.

Sub-ss (2)–(6): substituted for sub-ss (2)–(5) as originally enacted by SI 2006/2805, arts 2, 7(2), subject to transitional provisions in art 10 thereof.

85   Enforcement

(1)   Subject to subsection (3) below, where a sum agreed or awarded under this Act to be paid for compensation, costs or otherwise by a landlord or tenant of an agricultural holding is not paid within fourteen days after the time when the payment becomes due, it shall be recoverable, if the county court so orders, as if it were payable under an order of that court.

(2)   Where a sum becomes due to a tenant of an agricultural holding in respect of compensation from the landlord, and the landlord fails to discharge his liability within the period of one month from the date on which the sum becomes due, the tenant shall be entitled to obtain from the Minister an order charging the holding with payment of the amount due.

(3)   Where the landlord of an agricultural holding is entitled to receive the rents and profits of the holding otherwise than for his own benefit (whether as trustee or in any other character)—

(a)   he shall not be under any liability to pay any sum agreed or awarded under this Act to be paid to the tenant or awarded under this Act to be paid by the landlord, and it shall not be recoverable against him personally, but

(b)   if he fails to pay any such sum to the tenant for one month after it becomes due, the tenant shall be entitled to obtain from the Minister an order charging the holding with payment of the sum.

[492]

NOTES

Transfer of functions: see the note at the beginning of this Act.
See further, in relation to charges created pursuant to applications under this section, the Land Charges Act 1972, s 2(2), Sch 2, para 1.

86   Power of landlord to obtain charge on holding

(1)   Where the landlord of an agricultural holding—

(a)   has paid to the tenant of the holding an amount due to him under this Act, or under custom or agreement, or otherwise, in respect of compensation for an improvement falling within section 64(1) or (4) above, for any such matter as is specified in Part II of Schedule 8 to this Act or for disturbance, or

(b)   has defrayed the cost of the execution by him, in pursuance of a notice served under section 67(5) above, of an improvement specified in Part II of Schedule 7 to this Act,

he shall be entitled to obtain from the Minister an order charging the holding or any part of it with repayment of the amount of the compensation or the amount of the cost, as the case may be.

(2)   Where there falls to be determined by arbitration under this Act the amount of compensation for an improvement falling within 64(1) or (4) above or for any such matter as is specified in Part II of Schedule 8 to this Act payment of which entitles the landlord to obtain a charge under subsection (1) above, the arbitrator shall, at the request and cost of the landlord, certify—

(a)   the amount of the compensation, and

(b)   the term for which the charge may properly be made having regard to the time at which each improvement or matter in respect of which compensation is awarded is to be deemed to be exhausted.

(3)   Where the landlord of an agricultural holding is entitled to receive the rents and profits of the holding otherwise than for his own benefit (whether as trustee or in any other character) he shall, either before or after paying to the tenant of the holding any sum agreed or awarded under this Act to be paid to the tenant for compensation or awarded under this Act to be paid by the landlord, be entitled to obtain from the Minister an order charging the holding with repayment of that sum.

(4)   The rights conferred by this section on a landlord of an agricultural holding to obtain an order charging land shall not be exercised by trustees for ecclesiastical or charitable purposes except with the approval in writing of the [Charity Commission].

[493]

NOTES

Sub-s (4): words in square brackets substituted by the Charities Act 2006, s 75(1), Sch 8, para 79.
Transfer of functions: see the note at the beginning of this Act.
See further, in relation to charges created pursuant to applications under this section, the Land Charges Act 1972, s 2(2), Sch 2, para 1.

87   General provisions as to charges under this Act on holdings

(1)   An order of the Minister under this Act charging an agricultural holding or any part of an agricultural holding with payment or repayment of a sum shall charge it, in addition, with payment of all costs properly incurred in obtaining the charge.

(2)   Any such order shall be made in favour of the person obtaining the charge and of his executors, administrators and assigns, and the order shall make such provision as to the payment of interest and the payment of the sum charged by instalments, and shall contain such directions for giving effect to the charge, as the Minister thinks fit.

(3)   In the case of a charge under section 86 above the sum charged shall be a charge on the holding or the part of the holding charged, as the case may be, for the landlord's interest in the holding and for all interests in the holding subsequent to that of the landlord, but so that in any case where the landlord's interest is an interest in a leasehold, the charge shall not extend beyond the interest of the landlord, his executors, administrators and assigns.

(4)   In the case of a charge under section 86 above where the landlord is not absolute owner of the holding for his own benefit, no instalment or interest shall be made payable after the time when the improvement in respect of which compensation is paid will, in the opinion of the Minister, have become exhausted.

(5)   Notwithstanding anything in any deed, will or other instrument to the contrary, where the estate or interest in an agricultural holding of the landlord is determinable or liable to forfeiture by reason of his creating or suffering any charge on it, that estate or interest shall not be determined or forfeited by reason that the tenant obtains a charge on the holding under section 85(2) above or that the landlord obtains a charge on the holding under section 86 above.

(6)   A charge created under section 85 above or section 74 of the Agricultural Holdings Act 1948 shall rank in priority to any other charge, however and whenever created or arising; and charges created under those sections shall, as between themselves, rank in the order of their creation.

(7)   Any company now or hereafter incorporated by Parliament, and having power to advance money for the improvement of land, may take an assignment of any charge created under section 85(2) or 86(1) above upon such terms and conditions as may be agreed upon between the company and the person entitled to the charge, and may assign any charge of which they have taken an assignment under this subsection.

(8)   Subsection (6) above shall bind the Crown.

[494]

NOTES

Transfer of functions: see the note at the beginning of this Act.

88   Power of limited owners to give consents etc

The landlord of an agricultural holding, whatever his estate or interest in it, may, for the purposes of this Act, give any consent, make any agreement or do or have done to him any other act which he might give, make, do or have done to him if he were owner in fee simple or, if his interest is an interest in a leasehold, were absolutely entitled to that leasehold.

[495]

89   Power of limited owners to apply capital for improvements

(1)   Where under powers conferred by the Settled Land Act 1925 *or the Law of Property Act 1925* capital money is applied in or about the execution of any improvement specified in Schedule 7 to this Act no provision shall be made for requiring the money or any part of it to be replaced out of income, and accordingly any such improvement shall be deemed to be an improvement authorised by Part I of Schedule 3 to the Settled Land Act 1925.

(2)   Where under powers conferred by the Universities and College Estates Act 1925 capital money is applied in payment for any improvement specified in Schedule 7 to this Act no provision shall be made for replacing the money out of income unless the Minister requires such provision to be made under section 26(5) of that Act or, in the case of a university or college to which section 2 of the Universities and College Estates Act 1964 applies, it appears to the university or college to be necessary to make such provision under the said section 26(5) as modified by Schedule 1 to the said Act of 1964.

[496]

NOTES

Sub-s (1): words in italics repealed by the Trusts of Land and Appointment of Trustees Act 1996, s 25(2), Sch 4; the original wording is reproduced here for reasons of historical interest or in view of the savings contained in ss 3, 18(3), 25(5) of the 1996 Act.

Transfer of functions: see the note at the beginning of this Act.

90 Estimation of best rent for purposes of Acts and other instruments

In estimating the best rent or reservation in the nature of rent of an agricultural holding for the purposes of any Act of Parliament, deed or other instrument, authorising a lease to be made provided that the best rent, or reservation in the nature of rent, is reserved, it shall not be necessary to take into account against the tenant any increase in the value of the holding arising from any improvements made or paid for by him.

[497]

91 Power of Minister to vary Schedules 7, 8 and 10

(1)   The Minister may, after consultation with such bodies of persons as appear to him to represent the interests of landlords and tenants of agricultural holdings, by order vary the provisions of Schedules 7, 8 and 10 to this Act.

(2)   An order under this section may make such provision as to the operation of this Act in relation to tenancies current when the order takes effect as appears to the Minister to be just having regard to the variation of the said Schedules effected by the order.

[498]

NOTES

Transfer of functions: see the note at the beginning of this Act.

92 Advisory committee on valuation of improvements and tenant-right matters

(1)   The Minister shall appoint a committee to advise him as to the provisions to be included in regulations under section 66(2) above, consisting of such number of persons, having such qualifications, as the Minister thinks expedient, including persons appointed by the Minister as having experience in land agency, farming, estate management and the valuation of tenant-right.

(2)   The Minister may pay to the members of the committee such travelling and other allowances as he may with the consent of the Treasury determine.

[499]

NOTES

Transfer of functions: see the note at the beginning of this Act.

93 Service of notices

(1)   Any notice, request, demand or other instrument under this Act shall be duly given to or served on the person to or on whom it is to be given or served if it is delivered to him, or left at his proper address, or sent to him by post in a registered letter or by the recorded delivery service.

(2)   Any such instrument shall be duly given to or served on an incorporated company or body if it is given or served on the secretary or clerk of the company or body.

(3)   Any such instrument to be given to or served on a landlord or tenant shall, where an agent or servant is responsible for the control of the management or farming, as the case may be, of the agricultural holding, be duly given or served if given to or served on that agent or servant.

(4)   For the purposes of this section and of section 7 of the Interpretation Act 1978 (service by post), the proper address of any person to or on whom any such instrument is to be given or served shall, in the case of the secretary or clerk of an incorporated company or body, be that of the registered or principal office of the company or body, and in any other case be the last known address of the person in question.

(5)   Unless or until the tenant of an agricultural holding has received—

(a) notice that the person who before that time was entitled to receive the rents and profits of the holding ("the original landlord") has ceased to be so entitled, and

(b) notice of the name and address of the person who has become entitled to receive the rents and profits,

any notice or other document served upon or delivered to the original landlord by the tenant shall be deemed for the purposes of this Act to have been served upon or delivered to the landlord of the holding.

[500]

94 Orders and regulations

(1) Any power to make an order or regulations conferred on the Minister or the Lord Chancellor by any provision of this Act (except section 85 or 86) shall be exercisable by statutory instrument.

(2) Any statutory instrument containing an order or regulations made under any provision of this Act (except section 22(4)[, 84(4)] or 91 …) shall be subject to annulment in pursuance of a resolution of either House of Parliament.

(3) No regulations shall be made under section 22(4) above or [section 84(4) above] to this Act unless a draft of the regulations has been laid before and approved by a resolution of each House of Parliament.

(4) An order made under section 91 above shall be of no effect unless approved by a resolution of each House of Parliament.

[501]

NOTES

Sub-s (2): number in square brackets inserted and words omitted repealed by the Regulatory Reform (Agricultural Tenancies) (England and Wales) Order 2006, SI 2006/2805, arts 2, 7(3), 18, Sch 2, subject to transitional provisions in art 10 thereof.

Sub-s (3): words in square brackets substituted by SI 2006/2805, arts 2, 7(4), subject to transitional provisions in art 10 thereof.

Transfer of functions: see the note at the beginning of this Act.

95 Crown land

(1) The provisions of this Act, except section 11 above, shall apply to land belonging to Her Majesty in right of the Crown or the Duchy of Lancaster and to land belonging to the Duchy of Cornwall, subject in either case to such modifications as may be prescribed.

(2) For the purposes of this Act—

(a) as respects land belonging to Her Majesty in right of the Crown, the Crown Estate Commissioners or other the proper officer or body having charge of the land for the time being, or, if there is no such officer or body, such person as Her Majesty may appoint in writing under the Royal Sign Manual, shall represent Her Majesty and shall be deemed to be the landlord,

(b) as respects land belonging to Her Majesty in right of the Duchy of Lancaster, the Chancellor of the Duchy shall represent Her Majesty and shall be deemed to be the landlord,

(c) as respects land belonging to the Duchy of Cornwall, such person as the Duke of Cornwall or other the possessor for the time being of the Duchy of Cornwall appoints shall represent the Duke of Cornwall or other the possessor aforesaid, and shall be deemed to be the landlord and may do any act or thing which a landlord is authorised or required to do under this Act.

(3) Without prejudice to subsection (1) above it is hereby declared that the provisions of this Act, except section 11 above, apply to land notwithstanding that the interest of the landlord or tenant is held on behalf of Her Majesty for the purposes of any government department; but those provisions shall, in their application to any land in which an interest is so held, have effect subject to such modifications as may be prescribed.

(4) Any compensation payable under this Act by the Chancellor of the Duchy of Lancaster for long-term improvements shall, and any compensation so payable under section 60(2)(b) or 62 above may, be raised and paid as an expense incurred in improvement of land belonging to Her Majesty in right of the Duchy within section 25 of the Duchy of Lancaster Act 1817; and any compensation so payable under this Act for short-term improvements and tenant-right matters shall be paid out of the annual revenues of the Duchy.

(5)　Any compensation payable under this Act by the Duke of Cornwall or other the possessor for the time being of the Duchy of Cornwall for long-term improvements shall, and any compensation so payable under section 60(2)(b) or 62 above may, be paid and advances therefor made in the manner and subject to the provisions of section 8 of the Duchy of Cornwall Management Act 1863 with respect to improvements of land mentioned in that section.

(6)　Nothing in subsection (5) above shall be taken as prejudicing the operation of the Duchy of Cornwall Management Act 1982.

(7)　In this section—

"long-term improvements" means relevant improvements specified in Schedule 7 to this Act, improvements falling within section 64(4) above and improvements specified in Schedule 10 to this Act;

"short-term improvements and tenant-right matters" means relevant improvements specified in Part I of Schedule 8 to this Act and such matters as are specified in Part II of that Schedule.

[502]

96　Interpretation

(1)　In this Act, unless the context otherwise requires—

"agreement" includes an agreement arrived at by means of valuation or otherwise, and "agreed" has a corresponding meaning;

"agricultural holding" has the meaning given by section 1 above;

"agricultural land" has the meaning given by section 1 above;

"agricultural unit" means land which is an agricultural unit for the purposes of the Agriculture Act 1947;

"agriculture" includes horticulture, fruit growing, seed growing, dairy farming and livestock breeding and keeping, the use of land as grazing land, meadow land, osier land, market gardens and nursery grounds, and the use of land for woodlands where that use is ancillary to the farming of land for other agricultural purposes and "agricultural" shall be construed accordingly;

"building" includes any part of a building;

"Case A", "Case B" (and so on) refer severally to the Cases set out and so named in Part I of Schedule 3 to this Act;

"contract of tenancy" has the meaning given by section 1 above;

"county court", in relation to an agricultural holding, means the county court within the district in which the holding or the larger part of the holding is situated;

"fixed equipment" includes any building or structure affixed to land and any works on, in, over or under land, and also includes anything grown on land for a purpose other than use after severance from the land, consumption of the thing grown or of its produce, or amenity, and any reference to fixed equipment on land shall be construed accordingly;

"landlord" means any person for the time being entitled to receive the rents and profits of any land;

"livestock" includes any creature kept for the production of food, wool, skins, or fur or for the purpose of its use in the farming of land or the carrying on in relation to land of any agricultural activity;

"local government funds" means, in relation to any grant in respect of an improvement executed by the landlord or tenant of an agricultural holding, the funds of any body which, under or by virtue of any enactment, has power to make grants in respect of improvements of the description in question within any particular area (whether or not it is a local authority for that area);

"the Minister" means—

    (a)　in relation to England, the [Secretary of State], and

    (b)　in relation to Wales, the Secretary of State;

"the model clauses" has the meaning given by section 7 above;

"pasture" includes meadow;

"prescribed" means prescribed by the Minister by regulations;

"relevant improvement" has the meaning given by section 64(2) above;

"tenant" means the holder of land under a contract of tenancy, and includes the executors, administrators, assigns, or trustee in bankruptcy of a tenant, or other person deriving title from a tenant;

"termination", in relation to a tenancy, means the cesser of the contract of tenancy by reason of effluxion of time or from any other cause;

"the Tribunal" means an Agricultural Land Tribunal established under Part V of the Agriculture Act 1947.

(2)   For the purposes of this Act, a tenant is insolvent if—

(a)   he has been adjudged bankrupt or has made a composition or arrangement with his creditors, or

(b)   where the tenant is a body corporate, a winding-up order has been made with respect to it or a resolution for voluntary winding-up has been passed with respect to it (other than a resolution passed solely for the purposes of its reconstruction or of its amalgamation with another body corporate).

(3)   Sections 10 and 11 of the Agriculture Act 1947 (which specify the circumstances in which an owner of agricultural land is deemed for the purposes of that Act to fulfil his responsibilities to manage the land in accordance with the rules of good estate management and an occupier of such land is deemed for those purposes to fulfil his responsibilities to farm it in accordance with the rules of good husbandry) shall apply for the purposes of this Act.

(4)   References in this Act to the farming of land include references to the carrying on in relation to the land of any agricultural activity.

(5)   References in this Act to the use of land for agriculture include, in relation to land forming part of an agricultural unit, references to any use of the land in connection with the farming of the unit.

(6)   The designations of landlord and tenant shall continue to apply to the parties until the conclusion of any proceedings taken under or in pursuance of this Act in respect of compensation.

[503]

NOTES

Sub-s (1): in definition "the Minister" words in square brackets substituted by the Ministry of Agriculture, Fisheries and Food (Dissolution) Order 2002, SI 2002/794, art 5(1), Sch 1, para 27.

Transfer of functions: see the note at the beginning of this Act.

---

97   Saving for other rights etc

Subject to sections 15(5) and 83(1) above in particular, and to any other provision of this Act which otherwise expressly provides, nothing in this Act shall prejudicially affect any power, right or remedy of a landlord, tenant or other person vested in or exercisable by him by virtue of any other Act or law or under any custom of the country or otherwise, in respect of a contract of tenancy or other contract, or of any improvements, deteriorations, waste, emblements, tillages, away-going crops, fixtures, tax, rate, tithe rentcharge, rent or other thing.

[504]

98   Application of Act to old tenancies etc

(1)   Subject to sections 4 and 34 above, to the provisions of Schedule 12 to this Act and to any other provision to the contrary, this Act applies in relation to tenancies of agricultural holdings whenever created, agreements whenever made and other things whenever done.

(2)   The provisions of this Act shall apply in relation to tenancies of agricultural holdings granted or agreed to be granted, agreements made and things done before the dates specified in paragraphs 1 to 5 and 10 of Schedule 12 to this Act (being dates no later than 1st March 1948) subject to the modifications there specified.

(3)   Paragraphs 6 to 9 of Schedule 12 to this Act, which make provision with respect to compensation for tenant-right matters in relation to tenants of agricultural holdings who entered into occupation before the dates specified in those paragraphs (being dates no later than 31st December 1951), shall have effect.

[505]

99   Transitional provisions and savings

(1)   Schedule 13 to this Act, which excepts from the operation of this Act certain cases current at the commencement of this Act and contains other transitional provisions and savings, shall have effect.

(2)   The re-enactment in paragraphs 6 to 8 of Schedule 12 to this Act of provisions contained in the Agricultural Holdings Act (Variation of Fourth Schedule) Order 1951 shall be

without prejudice to the validity of those provisions; and any question as to the validity of any of those provisions shall be determined as if the re-enacting provisions of this Act were contained in a statutory instrument made under the powers under which the original provision was made.

(3)   Nothing in this Act (except paragraph 8 of Schedule 13) shall be taken as prejudicing the operation of sections 16 and 17 of the Interpretation Act 1978 (which relate to the effect of repeals).

[506]

100   Consequential amendments

Schedule 14 to this Act shall have effect.

[507]

101   Repeals and revocations

(1)   The enactments specified in Part I of Schedule 15 to this Act are hereby repealed to the extent specified in the third column of that Schedule.

(2)   The instruments specified in Part II of Schedule 15 to this Act are hereby revoked to the extent specified in the third column of that Schedule.

[508]

102   Citation, commencement and extent

(1)   This Act may be cited as the Agricultural Holdings Act 1986.

(2)   This Act shall come into force at the end of the period of three months beginning with the day on which it is passed.

(3)   Subject to subsection (4) below, this Act extends to England and Wales only.

(4)   Subject to subsection (5) below and to paragraph 26(6) of Schedule 14 to this Act, the amendment or repeal by this Act of an enactment which extends to Scotland or Northern Ireland shall also extend there.

(5)   Subsection (4) above does not apply to the amendment or repeal by this Act of section 9 of the Hill Farming Act 1946, section 48(4) of the Agriculture Act 1967 or an enactment contained in the Agriculture (Miscellaneous Provisions) Act 1968.

[509]

SCHEDULES

SCHEDULE 1
MATTERS FOR WHICH PROVISION IS TO BE MADE IN WRITTEN
TENANCY AGREEMENTS

Section 6

1.   The names of the parties.

2.   Particulars of the holding with sufficient description, by reference to a map or plan, of the fields and other parcels of land comprised in the holding to identify its extent.

3.   The term or terms for which the holding or different parts of it is or are agreed to be let.

4.   The rent reserved and the dates on which it is payable.

5.   The incidence of the liability for rates (including drainage rates).

6.   A covenant by the tenant in the event of the destruction by fire of harvested crops grown on the holding for consumption on it to return to the holding the full equivalent manurial value of the crops destroyed, in so far as the return of the value is required for the fulfilment of his responsibilities to farm in accordance with the rules of good husbandry.

7.   A covenant by the tenant (except where the interest of the tenant is held for the purposes of a government department or where the tenant has made provision approved by the Minister in lieu of such insurance) to insure against damage by fire all dead stock on the holding and all harvested crops grown on the holding for consumption on it.

8. A power for the landlord to re-enter on the holding in the event of the tenant not performing his obligations under the agreement.

9. A covenant by the tenant not to assign, sub-let or part with possession of the holding or any part of it without the landlord's consent in writing.

[510]

NOTES
Transfer of functions: see the note at the beginning of this Act.

SCHEDULE 2
ARBITRATION OF RENT: PROVISIONS SUPPLEMENTARY TO SECTION 12
Section 12

Amount of rent

1.—(1) For the purposes of section 12 of this Act, the rent properly payable in respect of a holding shall be the rent at which the holding might reasonably be expected to be let by a prudent and willing landlord to a prudent and willing tenant, taking into account (subject to sub-paragraph (3) and paragraphs 2 and 3 below) all relevant factors, including (in every case) the terms of the tenancy (including those relating to rent), the character and situation of the holding (including the locality in which it is situated), the productive capacity of the holding and its related earning capacity, and the current level of rents for comparable lettings, as determined in accordance with sub-paragraph (3) below.

(2) In sub-paragraph (1) above, in relation to the holding—
    (a) "productive capacity" means the productive capacity of the holding (taking into account fixed equipment and any other available facilities on the holding) on the assumption that is in the occupation of a competent tenant practising a system of farming suitable to the holding, and
    (b) "related earning capacity" means the extent to which, in the light of that productive capacity, a competent tenant practising such a system of farming could reasonably be expected to profit from farming the holding.

(3) In determining for the purposes of that sub-paragraph the current level of rents for comparable lettings, the arbitrator shall take into account any available evidence with respect to the rents (whether fixed by agreement between the parties or by arbitration under this Act) which are, or (in view of rents currently being tendered) are likely to become, payable in respect of tenancies of comparable agricultural holdings on terms (other than terms fixing the rent payable) similar to those of the tenancy under consideration, but shall disregard—
    (a) any element of the rents in question which is due to an appreciable scarcity of comparable holdings available for letting on such terms compared with the number of persons seeking to become tenants of such holdings on such terms,
    (b) any element of those rents which is due to the fact that the tenant of, or a person tendering for, any comparable holding is in occupation of other land in the vicinity of that holding that may conveniently be occupied together with that holding, and
    (c) any effect on those rents which is due to any allowances or reductions made in consideration of the charging of premiums.

2.—(1) On a reference under section 12 of this Act, the arbitrator shall disregard any increase in the rental value of the holding which is due to—
    (a) tenant's improvements or fixed equipment other than improvements executed or equipment provided under an obligation imposed on the tenant by the terms of his contract of tenancy, and
    (b) landlord's improvements, in so far as the landlord has received or will receive grants out of money provided by Parliament or local government funds in respect of the execution of those improvements.

(2) In this paragraph—
    (a) "tenant's improvements" means any improvements which have been executed on the holding, in so far as they were executed wholly or partly at the expense of the tenant (whether or not that expense has been or will be reimbursed by a grant out of money provided by Parliament or local government funds) without any equivalent allowance or benefit made or given by the landlord in consideration of their execution,

    (b)   "tenant's fixed equipment" means fixed equipment provided by the tenant, and

    (c)   "landlord's improvements" means improvements executed on the holding by the landlord.

  (3)   Where the tenant has held a previous tenancy of the holding, then—

    (a)   in the definition of "tenant's improvements" in sub-paragraph (2)(a) above, the reference to any such improvements as are there mentioned shall extend to improvements executed during that tenancy, and

    (b)   in the definition of "tenant's fixed equipment" in sub-paragraph (2)(b), the reference to such equipment as is there mentioned shall extend to equipment provided during that tenancy,

excluding, however, any improvement or fixed equipment so executed or provided in respect of which the tenant received any compensation on the termination of that (or any other) tenancy.

  (4)   For the purposes of sub-paragraph (2)(a) above, the continuous adoption by the tenant of a system of farming more beneficial to the holding—

    (a)   than the system of farming required by the contract of tenancy, or

    (b)   in so far as no system is so required, than the system of farming normally practised on comparable agricultural holdings,

shall be treated as an improvement executed at his expense.

3.   On a reference under section 12 of this Act the arbitrator—

    (a)   shall disregard any effect on the rent of the fact that the tenant who is a party to the arbitration is in occupation of the holding, and

    (b)   shall not fix the rent at a lower amount by reason of any dilapidation or deterioration of, or damage to, buildings or land caused or permitted by the tenant.

Frequency of arbitrations under section 12

4.—(1)   Subject to the following provisions of this Schedule, a demand for arbitration shall not be effective for the purposes of section 12 of this Act if the next termination date following the date of the demand falls earlier than the end of three years from any of the following dates, that is to say—

    (a)   the commencement of the tenancy, or

    (b)   the date as from which there took effect a previous increase or reduction of rent (whether made under that section or otherwise), or

    (c)   the date as from which there took effect a previous direction of an arbitrator under that section that the rent should continue unchanged.

  (2)   The following shall be disregarded for the purposes of sub-paragraph (1)(b) above—

    (a)   an increase or reduction of rent under section 6(3) or 8(4) of this Act;

    (b)   an increase of rent under subsection (1) of section 13 of this Act or such an increase as is referred to in subsection (3) of that section, or any reduction of rent agreed between the landlord and the tenant of the holding in consequence of any change in the fixed equipment provided on the holding by the landlord;

    (c)   a reduction of rent under section 33 of this Act.

5.—(1)   This paragraph applies in any case where a tenancy of an agricultural holding ("the new holding") commences under a contract of tenancy between—

    (a)   a person who immediately before the date of the commencement of the tenancy was entitled to a severed part of the reversionary estate in an agricultural holding ("the original holding") in which the new holding was then comprised, and

    (b)   the person who immediately before that date was the tenant of the original holding,

and where the rent payable in respect of the new holding at the commencement of the tenancy of that holding represents merely the appropriate portion of the rent payable in respect of the original holding immediately before the commencement of that tenancy.

  (2)   In any case to which this paragraph applies—

    (a)   paragraph (a) of sub-paragraph (1) of paragraph 4 above shall be read as referring to the commencement of the tenancy of the original holding, and

    (b)   references to rent in paragraphs (b) and (c) of that sub-paragraph shall be read as references to the rent payable in respect of the original holding, until the first occasion following the commencement of the tenancy of the new holding on which any such increase or reduction of, or direction with respect to, the rent of the new holding as is mentioned in paragraph (b) or (c) takes effect.

6.   Where under an agreement between the landlord and the tenant of the holding (not being an agreement expressed to take effect as a new contract of tenancy between the parties) provision is made for adjustment of the boundaries of the holding or for any other variation of the terms of the tenancy, exclusive of those relating to rent, then, unless the agreement otherwise provides—

    (a)   that provision shall for the purposes of sub-paragraph (1) of paragraph 4 above be treated as not operating to terminate the tenancy, and accordingly as not resulting in the commencement of a new contract of tenancy between the parties, and

    (b)   any increase or reduction of rent solely attributable to any such adjustment or variation as aforesaid shall be disregarded for the purposes of paragraph (b) of that sub-paragraph.

[7.—(1)   This paragraph applies in any case where—

    (a)   a tenancy of an agricultural holding ("the new tenancy") is granted to a person who, immediately before the grant of the new tenancy, was the tenant of the holding, or of any agricultural holding which comprised the whole or a substantial part of the land comprised in the holding, under a contract of tenancy ("the previous tenancy"),

    (b)   this Act applies in relation to the new tenancy by virtue of section 4(1)(g) of the Agricultural Tenancies Act 1995, and

    (c)   the rent payable under the new tenancy is unchanged from that payable under the previous tenancy, disregarding any increase or reduction in rent solely attributable to an adjustment of the boundaries of the holding.

(2)   The reference in sub-paragraph (1) above to a substantial part of the land comprised in the holding means a substantial part determined by reference to either area or value.

(3)   In any case to which this paragraph applies—

    (a)   paragraph (a) of sub-paragraph (1) of paragraph 4 above shall be read as referring to the commencement of the previous tenancy, and

    (b)   references to rent in paragraphs (b) and (c) of that sub-paragraph shall be read as references to the rent payable under the previous tenancy,

until the first occasion following the commencement of the new tenancy on which any such increase or reduction of, or direction with respect to, the rent payable under the new tenancy as is mentioned in paragraph (b) or (c) takes effect.]

[511]

NOTES

    Para 7: added by the Regulatory Reform (Agricultural Tenancies) (England and Wales) Order 2006, SI 2006/2805, arts 2, 8, subject to transitional provisions in art 10 thereof.

SCHEDULE 3
CASES WHERE CONSENT OF TRIBUNAL TO OPERATION OF NOTICE TO QUIT IS
NOT REQUIRED
Section 26

PART I
THE CASES

CASE A

The holding is let as a smallholding by a smallholdings authority or the Minister in pursuance of Part III of the Agriculture Act 1970 and was so let on or after 12th September 1984, and

    (a)   the tenant has attained the age of sixty-five, and

    (b)   if the result of the notice to quit taking effect would be to deprive the tenant of living accommodation occupied by him under the tenancy, suitable alternative accommodation is available for him, or will be available for him when the notice takes effect, and

    (c)   the instrument under which the tenancy was granted contains an acknowledgment signed by the tenant that the tenancy is subject to the provisions of this Case (or to those of Case I in section 2(3) of the Agricultural Holdings (Notices to Quit) Act 1977),

and it is stated in the notice to quit that it is given by reason of the said matter.

CASE B

[The notice to quit is given on the ground that the land is required for a use, other than for agriculture—

- (a) for which permission has been granted on an application made under the enactments relating to town and country planning,
- (b) for which permission under those enactments is granted by a general development order by reason only of the fact that the use is authorised by—
    - (i) a private or local Act,
    - (ii) an order approved by both Houses of Parliament, or
    - (iii) an order made under section 14 or 16 of the Harbours Act 1964,
- (c) for which any provision that—
    - (i) is contained in an Act, but
    - (ii) does not form part of the enactments relating to town and country planning,

    deems permission under those enactments to have been granted,
- (d) which any such provision deems not to constitute development for the purposes of those enactments, or
- (e) for which permission is not required under the enactments relating to town and country planning by reason only of Crown immunity,

and that fact is stated in the notice.]

CASE C

Not more than six months before the giving of the notice to quit, the Tribunal granted a certificate under paragraph 9 of Part II of this Schedule that the tenant of the holding was not fulfilling his responsibilities to farm in accordance with the rules of good husbandry, and that fact is stated in the notice.

CASE D

At the date of the giving of the notice to quit the tenant had failed to comply with a notice in writing served on him by the landlord, being either—

- (a) notice requiring him within two months from the service of the notice to pay any rent due in respect of the agricultural holding to which the notice to quit relates, or
- (b) a notice requiring him within a reasonable period specified in the notice to remedy any breach by the tenant that was capable of being remedied of any term or condition of his tenancy which was not inconsistent with his responsibilities to farm in accordance with the rules of good husbandry,

and it is stated in the notice to quit that it is given by reason of the said matter.

CASE E

At the date of the giving of the notice to quit the interest of the landlord in the agricultural holding had been materially prejudiced by the commission by the tenant of a breach, which was not capable of being remedied, of any term or condition of the tenancy that was not inconsistent with the tenant's responsibilities to farm in accordance with the rules of good husbandry, and it is stated in the notice that it is given by reason of the said matter.

CASE F

At the date of the giving of the notice to quit the tenant was a person who had become insolvent, and it is stated in the notice that it is given by reason of the said matter.

CASE G

The notice to quit is given—

- (a) following the death of a person who immediately before his death was the sole (or sole surviving) tenant under the contract of tenancy, and
- (b) not later than the end of the period of three months beginning with the date of any relevant notice,

and it is stated in the notice to quit that it is given by reason of that person's death.

CASE H

The notice to quit is given by the Minister and—

- (a) the Minister certifies in writing that the notice to quit is given in order to enable him to use or dispose of the land for the purpose of effecting any amalgamation (within the meaning of section 26(1) of the Agriculture Act 1967) or the reshaping of any agricultural unit, and
- (b) the instrument under which the tenancy was granted contains an acknowledgement signed by the tenant that the tenancy is subject to the provisions of this Case (or to those of Case H in section 2(3) of the Agricultural Holdings (Notices to Quit) Act 1977 or of section 29 of the Agriculture Act 1967).

[512]

NOTES

Case B: substituted by the Agricultural Holdings (Amendment) Act 1990, s 1(1), (2).
Transfer of functions: see the note at the beginning of this Act.

PART II
SUPPLEMENTARY PROVISIONS APPLICABLE TO CASES A, B, C, D, E AND G

Provisions applicable to Case A

1. Paragraphs 2 to 7 below have effect for determining whether, for the purposes of paragraph (b) of Case A, suitable alternative accommodation is or will be available for the tenant.

2. For the purposes of paragraph (b) of Case A, a certificate of the housing authority for the district in which the living accommodation in question is situated, certifying that the authority will provide suitable alternative accommodation for the tenant by a date specified in the certificate, shall be conclusive evidence that suitable alternative accommodation will be available for him by that date.

3. Where no such certificate as is mentioned in paragraph 2 above has been issued, accommodation shall be deemed to be suitable for the purposes of paragraph (b) of Case A if it consists of either—

- (a) premises which are to be let as a separate dwelling such that they will then be let on a protected tenancy (within the meaning of the Rent Act 1977), or
- (b) premises to be let as a separate dwelling on terms which will afford to the tenant security of tenure reasonably equivalent to the security afforded by Part VII of that Act in the case of a protected tenancy, [or
- (c) premises which are to be let as a separate dwelling such that they will then be let on an assured tenancy which is not an assured shorthold tenancy (construing those terms in accordance with Part I of the Housing Act 1988), or
- (d) premises to be let as a separate dwelling on terms which will afford to the tenant security of tenure reasonably equivalent to the security afforded by Chapter I of Part I of that Act in the case of an assured tenancy which is not an assured shorthold tenancy]

and the accommodation fulfils the conditions in paragraph 4 below.

[(2) Any reference in sub-paragraph (1) above to an assured tenancy does not include a reference to a tenancy in respect of which possession might be recovered on any of Grounds 1 to 5 in Schedule 2 to the Housing Act 1988.]

4.—(1) The accommodation must be reasonably suitable to the needs of the tenant's family as regards proximity to place of work and either—

- (a) similar as regards rental and extent to the accommodation afforded by dwelling-houses provided in the neighbourhood by any housing authority for persons whose needs as regards extent are similar to those of the tenant and his family, or
- (b) reasonably suitable to the means of the tenant and to the needs of the tenant and his family as regards extent and character.

(2) For the purposes of sub-paragraph (1)(a) above, a certificate of a housing authority stating—

    (a)   the extent of the accommodation afforded by dwelling-houses provided by the authority to meet the needs of tenants with families of such number as may be specified in the certificate, and

    (b)   the amount of the rent charged by the authority for dwelling-houses affording accommodation of that extent,

shall be conclusive evidence of the facts so stated.

(3)   If any furniture was provided by the landlord for use under the tenancy in question, furniture must be provided for use in the alternative accommodation which is either—

    (a)   similar to that so provided, or

    (b)   reasonably suitable to the needs of the tenant and his family.

5.   Accommodation shall not be deemed to be suitable to the needs of the tenant and his family if the result of their occupation of the accommodation would be that it would be an overcrowded dwelling-house for the purposes of Part X of the Housing Act 1985.

6.   Any document purporting—

    (a)   to be a certificate of a housing authority named in it issued for the purposes of this Schedule, and

    (b)   to be signed by the proper officer of the authority,

shall be received in evidence and, unless the contrary is shown, shall be deemed to be such a certificate without further proof.

7.—(1)   In paragraphs 2, 4 and 6 above "housing authority", and "district" in relation to such an authority, mean a local housing authority and their district within the meaning of the Housing Act 1985.

(2)   For the purposes of paragraphs 4 and 5 a dwelling-house may be a house or part of a house.

Provisions applicable to Case B

8.—(1)   For the purposes of Case B no account shall be taken of any permission granted as mentioned in paragraph (a) of that Case if the permission—

    (a)   ...

    (b)   relates to the working of coal by opencast operations, and

    (c)   was granted subject to a restoration condition and to an aftercare condition in which the use specified is use for agriculture or use for forestry.

(2)   In this paragraph "restoration condition" and "aftercare condition" have the meaning given by [section 336(1) of the Town and Country Planning Act 1990].

[8A.—(1)   For the purposes of Case B—

    (a)   "general development order" means an order under section 59 of the Town and Country Planning Act 1990 which is made as a general order, and

    (b)   "the enactments relating to town and country planning" means the planning Acts (as defined in section 336(1) of the Town and Country Planning Act 1990) and any enactment amending or replacing any of those Acts.

(2)   In relation to any time before the commencement of Part III of the Town and Country Planning Act 1990, sub-paragraph (1) above shall have effect as if—

    (a)   in paragraph (a), for "59" there were substituted "24" and for "1990" there were substituted "1971", and

    (b)   in paragraph (b), for the words from "planning Acts" onwards there were substituted "repealed enactments (as defined in section 1(1) of the Planning (Consequential Provisions) Act 1990)".]

Provisions applicable to Case C

9.—(1)   For the purposes of Case C the landlord of an agricultural holding may apply to the Tribunal for a certificate that the tenant is not fulfilling his responsibilities to farm in accordance with the rules of good husbandry; and the Tribunal, if satisfied that the tenant is not fulfilling his said responsibilities, shall grant such a certificate.

(2)   In determining whether to grant a certificate under this paragraph the Tribunal shall disregard any practice adopted by the tenant in pursuance of any provision of the contract of tenancy, or of any other agreement with the landlord, which indicates (in whatever terms) that its object is the furtherance of one or more of the following purposes, namely—

(a)   the conservation of flora or fauna or of geological or physiographical features of special interest;

(b)   the protection of buildings or other objects of archaeological, architectural or historic interest;

(c)   the conservation or enhancement of the natural beauty or amenity of the countryside or the promotion of its enjoyment by the public.

[(3)   In determining whether to grant a certificate under this paragraph, the Tribunal shall disregard any practice adopted by the tenant in compliance with any obligation accepted by or imposed on the tenant under [section 94 or 95 of the Water Resources Act 1991].]

Provisions applicable to Case D

10.—(1)   For the purposes of Case D—

(a)   a notice such as that mentioned in paragraph (a) or (b) of that Case must be in the prescribed form,

(b)   where such a notice in the prescribed form requires the doing of any work of repair, maintenance or replacement, any further notice requiring the doing of any such work which is served on the tenant less than twelve months after the earlier notice shall be disregarded unless the earlier notice was withdrawn with his agreement in writing,

(c)   a period of less than six months shall not be treated as a reasonable period within which to do any such work, and

(d)   any provision such as is mentioned in paragraph 9(2) above shall (if it would not otherwise be so regarded) be regarded as a term or condition of the tenancy which is not inconsistent with the tenant's responsibilities to farm in accordance with the rules of good husbandry.

(2)   Different forms may be prescribed for the purpose of paragraph (b) of Case D in relation to different circumstances.

[(3)   For the purposes of that Case compliance with any obligation accepted by or imposed on the tenant under [section 94 or 95 of the Water Resources Act 1991] shall not be capable of constituting a breach by the tenant of the terms or conditions of his tenancy.]

Provisions applicable to Case E

11.—(1)   Where—

(a)   the landlord is a smallholdings authority, or

(b)   the landlord is the Minister and the holding is on land held by him for the purposes of smallholdings,

then, in considering whether the interest of the landlord has been materially prejudiced as mentioned in Case E, regard shall be had to the effect of the breach in question not only on the holding itself but also on the carrying out of the arrangements made by the smallholdings authority or the Minister (as the case may be) for the letting and conduct of smallholdings.

(2)   For the purposes of Case E any provision such as is mentioned in paragraph 9(2) above shall (if it would not otherwise be so regarded) be regarded as a term or condition of the tenancy which is not inconsistent with the tenant's responsibilities to farm in accordance with the rules of good husbandry.

[(3)   For the purposes of that Case compliance with any obligation accepted by or imposed on the tenant under [section 94 or 95 of the Water Resources Act 1991] shall not be capable of constituting a breach by the tenant of the terms or conditions of his tenancy.]

Provisions applicable to Case G

12.   For the purposes of Case G—

(a)   "tenant" does not include an executor, administrator, trustee in bankruptcy or other person deriving title from a tenant by operation of law, and

(b)   the reference to the date of any relevant notice shall be construed as a reference—

      (i)   to the date on which a notice in writing was served on the landlord by or on behalf of an executor or administrator of the tenant's estate informing the landlord of the tenant's death or the date on which the landlord was given notice by virtue of section 40(5) of this Act of any application with respect to the holding under section 39 or 41, or

      (ii) where both of those events occur, to the date of whichever of them occurs first.

[513]

NOTES

Para 3: sub-para (2) added by the Housing Act 1988, s 140(1), Sch 17, Pt II, para 69.

Para 8: in sub-para (1) words omitted repealed by the Coal Industry Act 1994, s 67(1), (8), Sch 9, para 35, Sch 11, Pt II; in sub-para (2) words in square brackets substituted by the Planning (Consequential Provisions) Act 1990, s 4, Sch 2, para 72.

Para 8A: inserted by the Agricultural Holdings (Amendment) Act 1990, s 1(1), (3).

Paras 9–11: sub-para (3) added by the Water Act 1989, s 190(1), Sch 25, para 75, words in square brackets therein substituted by the Water Consolidation (Consequential Provisions) Act 1991, s 2(1), Sch 1, para 43.

Transfer of functions: see the note at the beginning of this Act.

Regulations: the Agricultural Holdings (Forms of Notice to Pay Rent or to Remedy) Regulations 1987, SI 1987/711 at **[1160]**.

SCHEDULE 4
MATTERS FOR WHICH PROVISION MAY BE MADE BY ORDER UNDER
SECTION 29

Section 29

1.   Requiring any question arising under the provisions of section 26(2) of, and Schedule 3 to, this Act to be determined by arbitration under this Act.

2.   Limiting the time within which any such arbitration may be required or within which an arbitrator may be appointed by agreement between the parties, or (in default of such agreement) an application may be made under [section 84(2) of] this Act for the appointment of an arbitrator, for the purposes of any such arbitration.

3.   Extending the period within which a counter-notice may be given by the tenant under section 26(1) of this Act where any such arbitration is required.

4.   Suspending the operation of notices to quit until the expiry of any time fixed in pursuance of paragraph 2 above for the making of any such appointment by agreement or application as is there mentioned or, where any such appointment or application has been duly made, until the termination of any such arbitration.

5.   Postponing the date at which a tenancy is to be terminated by a notice to quit which has effect in consequence of any such arbitration or of an application under section 26(1) or 28(2) of this Act or under provisions made by virtue of paragraph 12 below.

6.   Excluding the application of section 26(1) of this Act in relation to sub-tenancies in such cases as may be specified in the order.

7.   Making such provision as appears to the Lord Chancellor expedient for the purpose of safeguarding the interests of sub-tenants including provision enabling the Tribunal, where the interest of a tenant is terminated by notice to quit, to secure that a sub-tenant will hold from the landlord on the like terms as he held from the tenant.

8.   The determination by arbitration under this Act of any question arising under such a notice as is mentioned in paragraph (b) of Case D, being a notice requiring the doing of any work of repair, maintenance or replacement (including the question whether the notice is capable of having effect for the purposes of that Case).

9.   Enabling the arbitrator, on an arbitration under this Act relating to such a notice as is mentioned in paragraph 8 above, to modify the notice—

    (a)   by deleting any item or part of an item of work specified in the notice as to which, having due regard to the interests of good husbandry as respects the agricultural holding to which the notice relates and of sound management of the estate of which that holding forms part or which that holding constitutes, the arbitrator is satisfied that it is unnecessary or unjustified, or

(b) by substituting, in the case of any item or part of an item of work so specified, a different method or material for the method or material which the notice would otherwise require to be followed or used where, having regard to the purpose which that item or part is intended to achieve, the arbitrator is satisfied that—

    (i) the last-mentioned method or material would involve undue difficulty or expense,

    (ii) the first-mentioned method or material would be substantially as effective for the purpose, and

    (iii) in all the circumstances the substitution is justified.

10. Enabling the time within which anything is to be done in pursuance of such a notice as is mentioned in paragraph (b) of Case D to be extended or to be treated as having been extended.

11. Enabling a tenancy, in a case where that time is extended, to be terminated either by a notice to quit served less than twelve months before the date on which it is to be terminated, or at a date other than the end of a year of the tenancy, or both by such a notice and at such a date.

12. Securing that, where a subsequent notice to quit is given in accordance with provisions made by virtue of paragraph 11 above in a case where the original notice to quit fell within section 28(1) of this Act, then, if the tenant serves on the landlord a counter-notice in writing within one month after the giving of the subsequent notice to quit (or, if the date specified in that notice for the termination of the tenancy is earlier, before that date), the subsequent notice to quit shall not have effect unless the Tribunal consent to its operation, and applying section 28(5) of this Act as regards the giving of that consent.

13. The recovery by a tenant of the cost of any work which is done by him in compliance with a notice requiring him to do it, but which is found by arbitration under this Act to be work which he was not under an obligation to do.

[514]

NOTES

Para 2: words in square brackets substituted by the Regulatory Reform (Agricultural Tenancies) (England and Wales) Order 2006, SI 2006/2805, arts 2, 7(5), subject to transitional provisions in art 10 thereof.

Orders: the Agricultural Holdings (Arbitration on Notices) Order 1987, SI 1987/710 at **[1142]**.

SCHEDULE 5
NOTICE TO QUIT WHERE TENANT IS A SERVICE MAN

Section 30

1. In this Schedule—

"the 1951 Act" means the Reserve and Auxiliary Forces (Protection of Civil Interests) Act 1951;

"period of residence protection" in the case of a service man who performs a period of relevant service, other than a short period of training, means the period comprising that period of service and the four months immediately following the date on which it ends;

"relevant service" means service (as defined in section 64(1) of the 1951 Act) of a description specified in Schedule 1 to that Act;

"service man" means a man or woman who performs a period of relevant service;

"short period of training" has the meaning given by section 64(1) of the 1951 Act.

2.—(1) Paragraph 3 below shall have effect where—

(a) the tenant of an agricultural holding to which this Schedule applies performs a period of relevant service, other than a short period of training, and

(b) during his period of residence protection there is given to him—

    (i) notice to quit the holding, or

    (ii) notice to quit a part of it to which this Schedule applies.

(2) This Schedule applies to—

(a) any agricultural holding which comprises such a dwelling-house as is mentioned in section 10 of the Rent Act 1977 [or paragraph 7 of Schedule 1 to the Housing Act 1988], that is to say a dwelling-house occupied by the person responsible for the control (whether as tenant or as servant or agent of the tenant) of the farming of the holding, and

(b) any part of an agricultural holding, being a part which consists of or comprises such a dwelling-house.

3.—(1) Section 26(1) of this Act shall apply notwithstanding the existence of any such circumstances as are mentioned in Cases B to G; but where the Tribunal are satisfied that such circumstances exist, then, subject to sub-paragraph (2) below, the Tribunal shall not be required to withhold their consent to the operation of the notice to quit by reason only that they are not satisfied that circumstances exist such as are mentioned in paragraphs (a) to (f) of section 27(3) of this Act.

(2) In determining whether to give or withhold their consent under section 26 of this Act the Tribunal—

(a) if satisfied that circumstances exist such as are mentioned in Cases B to G or in section 27(3) of this Act, shall consider to what extent (if at all) the existence of those circumstances is directly or indirectly attributable to the service man's performing or having performed the period of service in question, and

(b) in any case, shall consider to what extent (if at all) the giving of such consent at a time during the period of protection would cause special hardship in view of circumstances directly or indirectly attributable to the service man's performing or having performed that period of service,

and the Tribunal shall withhold their consent to the operation of the notice to quit unless in all the circumstances they consider it reasonable to give their consent.

4. Where the tenant of an agricultural holding to which this Schedule applies performs a period of relevant service, other than a short period of training, and—

(a) a notice to quit the holding, or a part of it to which this Schedule applies, is given to him before the beginning of his period of residence protection, and

(b) the tenant duly serves a counter-notice under section 26(1) of this Act, and

(c) the Tribunal have not before the beginning of his period of residence protection decided whether to give or withhold consent to the operation of the notice to quit,

paragraph 3(2) above shall (with the necessary modifications) apply in relation to the giving or withholding of consent to the operation of the notice to quit as it applies in relation to the giving or withholding of consent to the operation of a notice to quit given in the circumstances mentioned in paragraph 2(1) above.

5. The Lord Chancellor's power under section 29 of this Act to provide for the matters specified in paragraphs 1 to 7 of Schedule 4 to this Act shall apply in relation to the provisions of sections 26 and 27 of this Act as modified by the preceding provisions of this Schedule as they apply in relation to the provisions of those sections apart from this Schedule.

6.—(1) The Lord Chancellor may make regulations—

(a) for enabling a counter-notice under section 26(1) of this Act to be served on behalf of a service man at a time when he is serving abroad, in a case where a notice to quit is given to him as mentioned in paragraph 2(1) above, and

(b) for enabling an act or proceedings consequential upon the service of a counter-notice under section 26(1) to be performed or conducted on behalf of a service man at a time when he is serving abroad, either in such a case as is mentioned in paragraph (a) above or in a case where paragraph 4 above applies in relation to him.

(2) References in sub-paragraph (1) above to a time when a service man is serving abroad are references to a time when he is performing a period of relevant service and is outside the United Kingdom.

(3) Regulations under this paragraph may contain such incidental and consequential provisions as appear to the Lord Chancellor to be necessary or expedient for the purposes of the regulations.

[515]

NOTES

Para 2: words in square brackets inserted by the Housing Act 1988, s 140(1), Sch 17, Pt I, para 70.
Orders: the Agricultural Holdings (Arbitration on Notices) Order 1987, SI 1987/710 at **[1142]**.

Regulations: the Reserve and Auxiliary Forces (Agricultural Tenants) Regulations 1959, SI 1959/84 at **[1022]** (having effect as if made under para 6 by virtue of the Interpretation Act 1978, s 17(2)(b)).

SCHEDULE 6
ELIGIBILITY TO APPLY FOR NEW TENANCY UNDER PART IV OF THIS ACT
Sections 36, 50

PART I
"ELIGIBLE PERSON": SUPPLEMENTARY PROVISIONS

Preliminary

1.—(1)   In this Schedule—
"the livelihood condition" means paragraph (a) of the definition of "eligible person" in section 36(3) of this Act;
"the occupancy condition" means paragraph (b) of that definition.

(2)   For the purposes of this Schedule a body corporate is controlled by a close relative of the deceased if he or his spouse [or his civil partner], or he and his spouse together [or he and his civil partner together], have the power to secure—
(a)   by means of the holding of shares or the possession of voting power in or in relation to that or any other body corporate, or
(b)   by virtue of any powers conferred by the articles of association or other document regulating that or any other body corporate,
that the affairs of that body corporate are conducted in accordance with his, her or their wishes, respectively.

(3)   Any reference in this Schedule to the spouse of a close relative of the deceased does not apply in relation to any time *when the relative's marriage is the subject of a decree of judicial separation or a decree nisi of divorce or of nullity of marriage.*

[(4)   Any reference in this Schedule to the civil partner of a close relative of the deceased does not apply in relation to any time when the relative's civil partnership is subject to—
(a)   a separation order under Chapter 2 of Part 2 of the Civil Partnership Act 2004, or
(b)   a dissolution order, nullity order or presumption of death order that is a conditional order under that Chapter.]

The livelihood condition

2.   For the purposes of the livelihood condition, any period during which a close relative of the deceased was, in the period of seven years mentioned in that condition, attending a full-time course at a university, college or other [establishment of higher or further education] shall be treated as a period throughout which his only or principal source of livelihood derived from his agricultural work on the holding; but not more than three years in all shall be so treated by virtue of this paragraph.

Commercial unit of agricultural land

3.—(1)   In the occupancy condition "commercial unit of agricultural land" means a unit of agricultural land which is capable, when farmed under competent management, of producing a net annual income of an amount not less than the aggregate of the average annual earnings of two full-time, male agricultural workers aged twenty or over.

(2)   In so far as any units of production for the time being prescribed by an order under paragraph 4 below are relevant to the assessment of the productive capacity of a unit of agricultural land when farmed as aforesaid, the net annual income which that unit is capable of producing for the purposes of this paragraph shall be ascertained by reference to the provisions of that order.

4.   The Minister shall by order—
(a)   prescribe such units of production relating to agricultural land as he considers appropriate, being units framed by reference to any circumstances whatever and designed for the assessment of the productive capacity of such land, and

(b)   for any period of twelve months specified in the order, determine in relation to any unit of production so prescribed the amount which is to be regraded for the purposes of paragraph 3 above as the net annual income from that unit in that period.

Ministerial statements as to net annual income of land

5.—(1)   For the purposes of any proceedings under sections 36 to 48 of this Act in relation to the holding, the Minister shall—

(a)   at the request of any of the following persons, namely any close relative of the deceased, the landlord or the secretary of the Tribunal, and

(b)   in relation to any relevant land,

determine by reference to the provisions of any order for the time being in force under paragraph 4 above the net annual income which, in his view, the land is capable of producing for the purposes of paragraph 3 above, and shall issue a written statement of his view and the grounds for it to the person making the request.

(2)   In sub-paragraph (1) above "relevant land" means agricultural land which is—

(a)   occupied (or, by virtue of section 58 of this Act or this Part of this Schedule, deemed to be occupied) by any close relative of the deceased (whether he is, where the request is made by such a relative, the person making the request or not), or

(b)   the subject of an application made under section 39 of this Act by any such relative.

(3)   Where—

(a)   for the purposes of any proceedings under sections 36 to 48 of this Act the Minister has issued a statement to any person containing a determination under sub-paragraph (1) above made by reference to the provisions of an order under paragraph 4 above, and

(b)   before any hearing by the Tribunal in those proceedings is due to begin it appears to him that any subsequent order under that paragraph has affected any matter on which that determination was based,

he shall make a revised determination under sub-paragraph (1) above and shall issue a written statement of his view and the grounds for it to the person in question.

(4)   Any statement issued by the Minister in pursuance of this paragraph shall be evidence of any facts stated in it as facts on which his view is based.

(5)   Any document purporting to be a statement issued by the Minister in pursuance of this paragraph and to be signed for or on behalf of the Minister shall be taken to be such a statement unless the contrary is shown.

Occupation to be disregarded for purposes of occupancy condition

6.—(1)   Occupation by a close relative of the deceased of any agricultural land shall be disregarded for the purposes of the occupancy condition if he occupies it only—

(a)   under a tenancy approved by the Minister under subsection (1) of section 2 of this Act or under a tenancy falling within subsection (3)(a) of that section,

(b)   under a tenancy for more than one year but less than two years,

(c)   under a tenancy not falling within paragraph (a) or (b) above and not having effect as a contract of tenancy,

(d)   under a tenancy to which section 3 of this Act does not apply by virtue of section 5 of this Act,

[(dd)   under a farm business tenancy, within the meaning of the Agricultural Tenancies Act 1995, for less than five years (including a farm business tenancy which is a periodic tenancy),]

(e)   as a licensee, or

(f)   as an executor, administrator, trustee in bankruptcy or person otherwise deriving title from another person by operation of law.

(2)   Paragraphs (a) to (e) of sub-paragraph (1) above do not apply in the case of a tenancy or licence granted to a close relative of the deceased by his spouse [or civil partner] or by a body corporate controlled by him.

(3)   References in the following provisions of this Schedule to the occupation of land by any person do not include occupation under a tenancy, or in a capacity, falling within paragraphs (a) to (f) of that sub-paragraph.

Joint occupation

7.—(1)   Where any agricultural land is jointly occupied by a close relative of the deceased and one or more other persons as—

(a)   beneficial joint tenants,
(b)   tenants in common,
(c)   joint tenants under a tenancy, or
(d)   joint licensees,

the relative shall be treated for the purposes of the occupancy condition as occupying the whole of the land.

(2)   If, however, the Tribunal in proceedings under section 39 of this Act determine on the application of the close relative that his appropriate share of the net annual income which the land is, or was at any time, capable of producing for the purposes of paragraph 3 above is or was then less than the aggregate of the earnings referred to in that paragraph, then, for the purpose of determining whether the occupancy condition is or was then satisfied in his case, the net annual income which the land is, or (as the case may be) was, capable of so producing shall be treated as limited to his appropriate share.

(3)   For the purposes of sub-paragraph (2) above the appropriate share of the close relative shall be ascertained—

(a)   where he is a beneficial or other joint tenant or a joint licensee, by dividing the net annual income which the land is or was at the time in question capable of producing for the purposes of paragraph 3 above by the total number of joint tenants or joint licensees for the time being,

(b)   where he is a tenant in common, by dividing the said net annual income in such a way as to attribute to him and to the other tenant or tenants in common shares of the income proportionate to the extent for the time being of their respective undivided shares in the land.

Deemed occupation in case of Tribunal direction

8.—(1)   Where a close relative of the deceased is, by virtue of a direction of the Tribunal under section 39 of this Act, for the time being entitled (whether or not with any other person) to a tenancy of the whole or part of any agricultural holding held by the deceased at the date of death other than the holding, he shall, for the purposes of the occupancy condition, be deemed to be in occupation of the land comprised in that holding or (as the case may be) in that part of that holding.

(2)   Where by virtue of sub-paragraph (1) above any land is deemed to be occupied by each of two or more close relatives of the deceased as a result of a direction entitling them to a joint tenancy of the land, the provisions of paragraph 7 above shall apply to each of the relatives as if the land were jointly occupied by him and the other relative or relatives as joint tenants under that tenancy.

Occupation by spouse[, civil partner] or controlled company

9.—(1)   For the purposes of the occupancy condition and of paragraph 7 above, occupation—

(a)   by the spouse[, or civil partner,] of a close relative of the deceased, or
(b)   by a body corporate controlled by a close relative of the deceased,

shall be treated as occupation by the relative.

(2)   Where, in accordance with sub-paragraph (1) above, paragraph 7 above applies to a close relative of the deceased in relation to any time by virtue of the [joint occupation of land by—

(a)   his spouse or civil partner or a body corporate, and
(b)   any other person or persons,

297

sub-paragraphs] (2) and (3) of that paragraph shall apply to the relative as if he were the holder of the interest in the land for the time being held by his spouse [or civil partner] or the body corporate, as the case may be.

Deemed occupation in case of tenancy or licence granted by close relative, spouse[, civil partner] or controlled company

10.—(1)   Where—
  (a)   any agricultural land is occupied by any person under such a tenancy as is mentioned in paragraphs (a) to (d) of paragraph 6(1) above or as a licensee and,
  (b)   that tenancy or licence was granted by a close relative of the deceased or a connected person (or both), being at the time it was granted a person or persons entitled to occupy the land otherwise than under a tenancy, or in a capacity, falling within paragraphs (a) to (f) of paragraph 6(1),

then, unless sub-paragraph (2) below applies, the close relative shall, for the purposes of the occupancy condition, be deemed to be in occupation of the whole of the land.

   (2)   Where the tenancy or licence referred to in sub-paragraph (1) above was granted by the person or persons there referred to and one or more other persons who were at the time it was granted entitled to occupy the land as mentioned in paragraph (b) of that sub-paragraph, sub-paragraphs (2) and (3) of paragraph 7 above shall apply to the close relative as if the land were jointly occupied by him and the said other person or persons as holders of their respective interests for the time being in the land.

   (3)   In this paragraph "connected person", in relation to a close relative of the deceased, means—
  (a)   the relative's spouse [or civil partner], or
  (b)   a body corporate controlled by the relative;

and for the purposes of sub-paragraph (2) above and the provisions of paragraph 7 there mentioned any interest in the land for the time being held by a connected person by whom the tenancy or licence was granted shall be attributed to the relative.

[516]

NOTES

  Para 1: in sub-para (2) words in square brackets inserted, and sub-para (4) added, by the Civil Partnership Act 2004, s 81, Sch 8, para 39(1)–(3); in sub-para (3) for the words in italics there are substituted, with savings, the words "when a separation order or a divorce order under the Family Law Act 1996 is in force in relation to the relative's marriage or that marriage is the subject of a decree nisi of nullity" by the Family Law Act 1996, s 66(1), Sch 8, para 36, as from a day to be appointed; for savings see s 66(2) of, Sch 9, para 5 to, the 1996 Act.
  Para 2: words in square brackets substituted by the Education Reform Act 1988, s 237, Sch 12, para 96.
  Para 6: sub-para (1)(dd) inserted by the Agricultural Tenancies Act 1995, s 40, Schedule, para 32; in sub-para (2) words in square brackets inserted by the Civil Partnership Act 2004, s 81, Sch 8, para 39(1), (4).
  Para 9: in the cross-heading immediately preceding this para and in sub-para (1) words in square brackets inserted and in sub-para (2) words in first pair of square brackets substituted and words in second pair of square brackets inserted by the Civil Partnership Act 2004, s 81, Sch 8, para 39(1), (5), (6), (8).
  Para 10: in the cross-heading immediately preceding this para and in sub-para (3) words in square brackets inserted by the Civil Partnership Act 2004, s 81, Sch 8, para 39(1), (7), (8).
  Transfer of functions: see the note at the beginning of this Act.
  Orders: the Agricultural Holdings (Units of Production) (England) Order 2006, SI 2006/2628; the Agricultural Holdings (Units of Production) (Wales) Order 2006, SI 2006/2796.

PART II
MODIFICATIONS OF PART I OF THIS SCHEDULE IN ITS APPLICATION TO
SUCCESSION ON RETIREMENT

11.   The modifications of Part I of this Schedule referred to in section 50(4) of this Act are as follows.

12.   The reference in paragraph 1(1) to section 36(3) of this Act shall be read as a reference to section 50(2) of this Act.

13.   References to a close relative of the deceased shall be read as references to the nominated successor.

14.   In paragraph 5—
(a)   references to sections 36 to 48 of this Act shall be read as references to sections 50 to 58 of this Act,
(b)   the reference in sub-paragraph (1) to any close relative of the deceased shall be read as a reference to the nominated successor, and
(c)   for sub-paragraph (2) there shall be substituted—

"(2)   In sub-paragraph (1) above "relevant land" means agricultural land which is occupied (or, by virtue of this Part of this Schedule, is deemed to be occupied) by the nominated successor.".

15.   The reference in paragraph 7(2) to section 39 of this Act shall be read as a reference to section 53 of this Act.

16.   For paragraph 8 there shall be substituted—

"8.   Where the nominated successor is, by virtue of a direction of the Tribunal under section 53(7) of this Act, for the time being entitled to a tenancy of any agricultural holding held by the retiring tenant other than the holding he shall, for the purposes of the occupancy condition, be deemed to be in occupation of that holding.".

[517]

SCHEDULE 7
LONG-TERM IMPROVEMENTS BEGUN ON OR AFTER 1ST MARCH 1948 FOR WHICH COMPENSATION IS PAYABLE
Sections 64, 66 etc

PART I
IMPROVEMENTS TO WHICH CONSENT OF LANDLORD REQUIRED

1.   Making or planting of osier beds.

2.   Making of water meadows.

3.   Making of watercress beds.

4.   Planting of hops.

5.   Planting of orchards or fruit bushes.

6.   Warping or weiring of land.

7.   Making of gardens.

8.   Provision of underground tanks.

[518]

PART II
IMPROVEMENTS TO WHICH CONSENT OF LANDLORD OR APPROVAL OF TRIBUNAL REQUIRED

9.   Erection, alteration or enlargement of buildings, and making or improvement of permanent yards.

10.   Carrying out works in compliance with an improvement notice served, or an undertaking accepted, under Part VII of the Housing Act 1985 or Part VIII of the Housing Act 1974.

11.   Erection or construction of loading platforms, ramps, hard standings for vehicles or other similar facilities.

12.   Construction of silos.

13. Claying of land.

14. Marling of land.

15. Making or improvement of roads or bridges.

16. Making or improvement of water courses, culverts, ponds, wells or reservoirs, or of works for the application of water power for agricultural or domestic purposes or of works for the supply, distribution or use of water for such purposes (including the erection or installation of any structures or equipment which form part of or are to be used for or in connection with operating any such works).

17. Making or removal of permanent fences.

18. Reclaiming of waste land.

19. Making or improvement of embankments or sluices.

20. Erection of wirework for hop gardens.

21. Provision of permanent sheep-dipping accommodation.

22. Removal of bracken, gorse, tree roots, boulders or other like obstructions to cultivation.

23. Land drainage (other than improvements falling within paragraph 1 of Schedule 8 to this Act).

24. Provision or laying-on of electric light or power.

25. Provision of facilities for the storage or disposal of sewage or farm waste.

26. Repairs to fixed equipment, being equipment reasonably required for the proper farming of the holding, other than repairs which the tenant is under an obligation to carry out.

27. The grubbing up of orchards or fruit bushes.

28. Planting trees otherwise than as an orchard and bushes other than fruit bushes.

[519]

SCHEDULE 8
SHORT-TERM IMPROVEMENTS BEGUN ON OR AFTER 1ST MARCH 1948, AND
OTHER MATTERS, FOR WHICH COMPENSATION IS PAYABLE
Sections 64, 65, etc

PART I
IMPROVEMENTS (TO WHICH NO CONSENT REQUIRED)

1. Mole drainage and works carried out to secure its efficient functioning.

2. Protection of fruit trees against animals.

3. Clay burning.

4. Liming (including chalking) of land.

5. Application to land of purchased manure and fertiliser, whether organic or inorganic.

6. Consumption on the holding of corn (whether produced on the holding or not) or of cake or other feeding stuff not produced on the holding, by horses, cattle, sheep, pigs or poultry.

[520]

PART II
TENANT-RIGHT MATTERS

7.   Growing crops and severed or harvested crops and produce, being in either case crops or produce grown on the holding in the last year of tenancy, but not including crops or produce which the tenant has a right to sell or remove from the holding.

8.   Seeds sown and cultivations, fallows and acts of husbandry performed on the holding at the expense of the tenant (including the growing of herbage crops for commercial seed production).

9.   Pasture laid down with clover, grass, lucerne, sainfoin or other seeds, being either—
   (a)   pasture laid down at the expense of the tenant otherwise than in compliance with an obligation imposed on him by an agreement in writing to lay it down to replace temporary pasture comprised in the holding when the tenant entered on the holding which was not paid for by him, or
   (b)   pasture paid for by the tenant on entering on the holding.

10.—(1)   Acclimatisation, hefting or settlement of hill sheep on hill land.

   (2)   In this paragraph—
   "hill sheep" means sheep which—
      (a)   have been reared and managed on a particular hill or mountain,
      (b)   have developed an instinct not to stray from the hill or mountain,
      (c)   are able to withstand the climatic conditions typical of the hill or mountain, and
      (d)   have developed resistance to diseases which are likely to occur in the area in which the hill or mountain is situated;
   "hill land" means any hill or mountain where only hill sheep are likely to thrive throughout the year.

11.—(1)   In areas of the country where arable crops can be grown in an unbroken series of not less than six years and it is reasonable that they should be grown on the holding or part of it, the residual fertility value of the sod of the excess qualifying leys on the holding, if any.

   (2)   For the purposes of this paragraph—
   (a)   the growing of an arable crop includes the growing of clover, grass, lucerne, sainfoin or other seeds grown for a period of less than one year but does not include the laying down of a ley continuously maintained as such for more than one year,
   (b)   the qualifying leys comprising the excess qualifying leys shall be those indicated to be such by the tenant, and
   (c)   qualifying leys laid down at the expense of the landlord without reimbursement by the tenant or any previous tenant of the holding or laid down by and at the expense of the tenant pursuant to agreement by him with the landlord for the establishment of a specified area of leys on the holding as a condition of the landlord giving consent to the ploughing or other destruction of permanent pasture or pursuant to a direction given by an arbitrator on a reference under section 14(2) of this Act, shall not be included in the excess qualifying leys.

   (3)   In this paragraph—
   "leys" means land laid down with clover, grass, lucerne, sainfoin or other seeds, but does not include permanent pasture;
   "qualifying leys" means—
      (a)   leys continuously maintained as such for a period of three or more growing seasons since being laid down excluding, if the leys were undersown or autumn-sown, the calendar year in which the sowing took place, and
      (b)   arable land which within the three growing seasons immediately preceding the termination of the tenancy was ley continously maintained as aforesaid before being destroyed by ploughing or some other means for the production of a tillage crop or crops;
   and for the purpose of paragraph (a) above the destruction of a ley (by ploughing or some other means) followed as soon as practicable by re-seeding to a ley without sowing a crop in the interval between such destruction and such re-seeding shall be treated as not constituting a break in the continuity of the maintenance of the ley;

"the excess qualifying leys" means the area of qualifying leys on the holding at the termination of the tenancy which is equal to the area (if any) by which one-third of the aggregate of the areas of leys on the holding on the following dates, namely,

(a)   at the termination of the tenancy,

(b)   on the date one year prior to such termination, and

(c)   on the date two years prior to such termination,

exceeds the accepted proportion at the termination of the tenancy;

"the accepted proportion" means the area which represents the proportion which the total area of the leys on the holding would, taking into account the capability of the holding, be expected to bear to the area of the holding, excluding the permanent pasture on the holding, or, if a greater proportion is provided for by or under the terms of the tenancy, that proportion.

[521]

SCHEDULE 9
COMPENSATION TO TENANT FOR IMPROVEMENTS BEGUN BEFORE 1ST MARCH 1948

Sections 64, 79

PART I
TENANT'S RIGHT TO COMPENSATION FOR OLD IMPROVEMENTS

1.—(1)   The tenant of an agricultural holding shall, subject to the provisions of this Act, be entitled on the termination of the tenancy, on quitting the holding, to obtain from his landlord compensation for an improvement specified in Part II of this Schedule carried out on the holding by the tenant, being an improvement begun before 1st March 1948.

(2)   Improvements falling within sub-paragraph (1) above are in this Schedule referred to as "old improvements".

(3)   The tenant of an agricultural holding shall not be entitled to compensation under this Schedule for an improvement which he was required to carry out by the terms of his tenancy where the contract of tenancy was made before 1st January 1921.

(4)   Nothing in this Schedule shall prejudice the right of a tenant to claim any compensation to which he may be entitled under custom or agreement, or otherwise, in lieu of any compensation provided by this Schedule.

(5)   The tenant of an agricultural holding shall not be entitled to compensation under this Schedule for an old improvement made on land which, at the time when the improvement was begun, was not a holding within the meaning of the Agricultural Holdings Act 1923, as originally enacted, and would not have fallen to be treated as such a holding by virtue of section 33 of that Act.

2.—(1)   The amount of any compensation under this Schedule for an old improvement shall be an amount equal to the increase attributable to the improvement in the value of the agricultural holding as a holding, having regard to the character and situation of the holding and the average requirements of tenants reasonably skilled in husbandry.

(2)   In the ascertainment of the amount of the compensation payable under this Schedule to the tenant of an agricultural holding in respect of an old improvement, there shall be taken into account any benefit which the landlord has given or allowed to the tenant in consideration of the tenant's executing the improvement, whether expressly stated in the contract of tenancy to be so given or allowed or not.

3.—(1)   Compensation under this Schedule shall not be payable for an old improvement specified in any of paragraphs 1 to 15 of Part II of this Schedule unless, before the execution of the improvement, the landlord consented in writing (whether unconditionally or upon terms as to compensation or otherwise agreed between him and the tenant) to the execution of the improvement.

(2)   Where the consent was given upon agreed terms as to compensation, compensation payable under the agreement shall be substituted for compensation under this Schedule.

4.—(1)   Compensation under this Schedule shall not be payable for an old improvement consisting of that specified in paragraph 16 of Part II of this Schedule unless the tenant gave to the landlord, not more than three or less than two months before beginning to execute the improvement, notice in writing under section 3 of the Agricultural Holdings Act 1923 of his intention to execute the improvement and of the manner in which he proposed to execute it, and—

(a) the landlord and tenant agreed on the terms on which the improvement was to be executed, or

(b) in a case where no agreement was reached and the tenant did not withdraw the notice, the landlord failed to exercise the right conferred on him by that section to execute the improvement himself within a reasonable time.

(2) Subsection (1) above shall not have effect if the landlord and tenant agreed, by the contract of tenancy or otherwise, to dispense with notice under the said section 3.

(3) If the landlord and tenant agreed (whether after notice was given under the said section 3 or by an agreement to dispense with notice under that section) upon terms as to compensation upon which the improvement was to be executed, compensation payable under the agreement shall be substituted for compensation under this Schedule.

5.—(1) Where the tenant of an agricultural holding has remained in the holding[, or in any agricultural holding which comprised the whole or a substantial part of the land comprised in the holding,] during two or more tenancies, he shall not be deprived of his right to compensation under this Schedule in respect of old improvements by reason only that the improvements were made during a tenancy other than the one at the termination of which he quits the holding.

[(1A) Where this Act applies in relation to any tenancy referred to in sub-paragraph (1) above by virtue of section 4(1)(g) of the Agricultural Tenancies Act 1995, the reference in that sub-paragraph to a substantial part of the land comprised in the holding means a substantial part determined by reference to either area or value.]

(2) Where, on entering into occupation of an agricultural holding, the tenant, with the consent in writing of his landlord, paid to an outgoing tenant any compensation payable under or in pursuance of this Schedule (or the Agricultural Holdings Act 1948 or the Agricultural Holdings Act 1923) in respect of the whole or part of an old improvement, he shall be entitled, on quitting the holding, to claim compensation for the improvement or part in the same manner, if at all, as the outgoing tenant would have been entitled if the outgoing tenant had remained tenant of the holding and quitted it at the time at which the tenant quits it.

[522]

NOTES

Para 5: words in square brackets in sub-para (1) inserted and sub-para (1A) inserted, except in relation to compensation payable on termination of a tenancy where that tenancy was granted before 19 October 2006, by the Regulatory Reform (Agricultural Tenancies) (England and Wales) Order 2006, SI 2006/2805, arts 2, 6(6)–(8).

PART II
OLD IMPROVEMENTS FOR WHICH COMPENSATION IS PAYABLE

1. Erection, alteration or enlargement of buildings.

2. Formation of silos.

3. Making and planting of osier beds.

4. Making of water meadows or works or irrigation.

5. Making of gardens.

6. Making or improvement of roads or bridges.

7. Making or improvement of watercourses, ponds, wells or reservoirs or of works for the application of water power or for supply of water for agricultural or domestic purposes.

8. Making or removal of permanent fences.

9. Planting of hops.

10. Planting of orchards or fruit bushes.

11. Reclaiming of waste land.

12. Warping or weiring of land.

13. Embankments and sluices against floods.

14. Erection of wirework in hop gardens.

15. Provision of permanent sheep-dipping accommodation.

16. Drainage.

[523]

SCHEDULE 10
MARKET GARDEN IMPROVEMENTS
Sections 79, 80

1. Planting of standard or other fruit trees permanently set out.

2. Planting of fruit bushes permanently set out.

3. Planting of strawberry plants.

4. Planting of asparagus, rhubarb and other vegetable crops which continue productive for two or more years.

5. Erection, alteration or enlargement of buildings for the purpose of the trade or business of a market gardener.

[524]–[525]

(*Sch 11 repealed by the Regulatory Reform (Agricultural Tenancies) (England and Wales) Order 2006, SI 2006/2805, arts 2, 9(1), 18, Sch 2, subject to transitional provisions in art 10 thereof.*)

SCHEDULE 12
MODIFICATIONS APPLICABLE TO OLD TENANCIES AND OTHER SIMILAR CASES
Sections 65, 70, 76, 77, 78, 98

General

1. Section 2 of this Act shall not apply to an agreement made before 1st March 1948.

2. Section 3 of this Act shall not apply to a tenancy granted or agreed to be granted before 1st January 1921.

Right to remove fixtures

3. A tenant shall not be entitled by virtue of section 10(1) or 79 of this Act (or the said section 79 as applied by paragraph 10 below) to remove a fixture or building acquired by him before 1st January 1901.

Notices to quit

4.—(1) Where a tenancy of an agricultural holding subsists under an agreement entered into before 25th March 1947, section 25(1) of this Act does not apply—

(a) to a notice given by or on behalf of the Secretary of State under the provisions of any agreement of tenancy, where possession of the land is required for naval, military or air force purposes, or

(b) to a notice given by a corporation carrying on a railway, dock, canal, water or other undertaking in respect of land acquired by the corporation for the purposes of their undertaking or by a government department or local authority, where possession of the land is required by the corporation, government department or authority for the purpose (not being the use of the land for agriculture) for which it was acquired by the corporation, department or authority or appropriated under any statutory provision.

(2) In the application of sub-paragraph (1)(b) above to a Board, the reference to land acquired by the corporation for the purposes of their undertaking shall be construed as including a reference to land transferred to that Board by section 31 of the Transport Act 1962 or, in the case of [Transport for London, transferred to the London Transport Executive], by section 16 of the Transport (London) Act 1969, being land—

(a) acquired, for the purpose of an undertaking vested in the British Transport Commission by Part II of the Transport Act 1947, by the body carrying on that undertaking, or

(b) acquired by a body carrying on an undertaking vested in any such undertaking as is mentioned in paragraph (a) above by virtue of an amalgamation or absorption scheme under the Railways Act 1921, being a scheme that came into operation on or after 7th July 1923,

and the reference to the purpose for which the land was acquired or appropriated by the corporation shall be construed accordingly.

(3) In sub-paragraph (2) above "a Board" means any of the following, namely—
Associated British Ports,
the British Railways Board,
the British Waterways Board, and
[Transport for London].

[(4) Sub-paragraph (2) above shall have effect in relation to a company which is a subsidiary (within the meaning of the Greater London Authority Act 1999) of Transport for London as it has effect in relation to Transport for London, so far as relates to land transferred to the London Transport Executive as there mentioned and subsequently transferred to the company (whether before or after it became a subsidiary of Transport for London).]

(5) Where by a scheme under section 7 of the Transport Act 1968 relevant land has been transferred by the British Railways Board to another body, sub-paragraph (2) above shall (so far as relates to relevant land so transferred) have effect in relation to that body as it has effect in relation to the British Railways Board; and in this sub-paragraph "relevant land" means land falling within paragraph (a) or (b) of sub-paragraph (2) above and transferred to the British Railways Board as there mentioned.

(6) Where, by virtue of an Act (whether public, general or local) passed, or an instrument having effect under an Act made, after 7th July 1923 and before 30th July 1948, any right of a corporation carrying on a water undertaking or of a local authority to avail itself of the benefit conferred by section 25(2)(b) of the Agricultural Holdings Act 1923 was transferred to some other person, that other person shall have the same right to avail himself of the benefit conferred by sub-paragraph (1)(b) above as the corporation or authority would have had if the Act or instrument by virtue of which the transfer was effected had not been passed or made.

Compensation for improvements

5. The tenant of an agricultural holding shall not be entitled to compensation under section 64(1) of this Act for an improvement which he was required to carry out by the terms of his tenancy where the contract of tenancy was made before 1st January 1921.

Compensation for tenant-right matters

6.—(1) Where the tenant of an agricultural holding entered into occupation of the holding before 1st March 1948, section 65(1) of this Act shall not apply to him as regards the matters specified in paragraphs 7 to 10 of Part II of Schedule 8 to this Act, unless, before the termination of the tenancy, he gives notice in writing to the landlord stating that he elects that it is to apply to him as regards those matters.

(2)   Where the tenancy terminates by reason of a notice to quit and at any time while the notice to quit is current the landlord gives notice in writing to the tenant requiring him to elect whether section 65(1) of this Act is to apply to him as regards the matters specified in paragraphs 7 to 10 of Part II of Schedule 8 to this Act, the tenant shall not be entitled to give a notice under sub-paragraph (1) above after the expiry of—

(a)   one month from the giving of the notice under this sub-paragraph, or

(b)   if the operation of the notice to quit depends upon any proceedings under section 26 or 27 of this Act (including any proceedings under Schedule 3 to this Act), one month from the termination of those proceedings.

7.—(1)   This paragraph applies where the tenant of an agricultural holding entered into occupation of the holding before 31st December 1951 and immediately before that date subsection (1) of section 47 of the Agricultural Holdings Act 1948 applied to him as regards the matters now specified in paragraphs 7 to 9 of Part II of Schedule 8 to this Act (whether by virtue of his having entered into occupation of the holding on or after 1st March 1948 or by virtue of a notice having been given under paragraph (c) of the proviso to subsection (1) of the said section 47).

(2)   Where this paragraph applies, section 65(1) of this Act shall not apply to the tenant as regards the matters specified in paragraph 10 of Part II of Schedule 8 to this Act unless, before the termination of the tenancy, he gives notice in writing to the landlord that it is to apply to him as regards those matters.

(3)   Paragraph 6(2) above shall have effect in relation to a notice under this paragraph as if in that provision there were substituted—

(a)   for the reference to the matters specified in paragraphs 7 to 10 of Part II of Schedule 8 to this Act a reference to the matters specified in paragraph 10 of Part II of that Schedule, and

(b)   for the reference to a notice under paragraph 6(1) above, a reference to a notice under this paragraph.

8.—(1)   In a case where, by virtue of paragraph 6 or 7 above, section 65(1) above does not apply to a tenant as regards all or any of the matters specified in paragraphs 7 to 10 of Part II of Schedule 8 to this Act—

(a)   sections 70(4) and (5) and 76(3) of this Act shall have effect with the omission of references to the excluded matters,

(b)   section 77(1) of this Act shall not apply to compensation to the tenant for the excluded matters, and

(c)   section 78(3) of this Act, in so far as it provides that a claim for compensation in a case for which the provisions of this Act do not provide for compensation shall not be enforceable except under an agreement in writing, shall not apply to a claim by a tenant for compensation for the excluded matters.

(2)   In this paragraph "the excluded matters" means, in relation to a case to which this paragraph applies, the matters as regards which section 65(1) does not apply to the tenant.

9.   The Minister may revoke or vary the provisions of paragraphs 6 to 8 above so far as they relate to the matters specified in paragraph 10 of Part II of Schedule 8 to this Act as if those provisions were contained in an order made under section 91 of this Act.

Market gardens

10.—(1)   Except as provided by this paragraph, subsections (2) to (5) of section 79 of this Act shall not apply unless the agreement in writing mentioned in subsection (1) of that section was made on or after 1st January 1896.

(2)   Where—

(a)   under a contract of tenancy current on 1st January 1896 an agricultural holding was at that date in use or cultivation as a market garden with the knowledge of the landlord, and

(b)   the tenant had then executed on the holding, without having received before the execution a written notice of dissent by the landlord, an improvement of a kind specified in Schedule 10 to this Act (other than one consisting of such an alteration of a building as did not constitute an enlargement of it),

subsections (2) to (5) of section 79 (and section 81) of this Act shall apply in respect of the holding as if it had been agreed in writing after that date that the holding should be let or treated as a market garden.

(3) The improvements in respect of which compensation is payable under subsections (2) to (5) of section 79 of this Act as applied by this paragraph shall include improvements executed before, as well as improvements executed after, 1st January 1896.

(4) Where the land used and cultivated as mentioned in sub-paragraph (2) above consists of part of an agricultural holding only, this paragraph shall apply as if that part were a separate holding.

[526]

NOTES
Para 4: words in square brackets substituted by the Transport for London (Consequential Provisions) Order 2003, SI 2003/1615, art 2, Sch 1, Pt 1, para 13.
Transfer of functions: see the note at the beginning of this Act.

SCHEDULE 13
TRANSITIONAL PROVISIONS AND SAVINGS

Section 99

Construction of references to old and new law

1.—(1) Any reference, whether express or implied, in any enactment, instrument or document (including this Act and any enactment amended by Schedule 14 to this Act), to, or to things done or falling to be done under or for the purposes of, any provision of this Act shall, if and so far as the nature of the reference permits, be construed as including, in relation to the times, circumstances or purposes in relation to which the corresponding provision repealed by this Act has or had effect, a reference to, or as the case may be, to things done or falling to be done under or for the purposes of, that corresponding provision.

(2) Any reference, whether express or implied, in any enactment, instrument or document (including the enactments repealed by this Act and enactments, instruments and documents passed or made after the passing of this Act) to, or to things done or falling to be done under or for the purposes of, any provision repealed by this Act shall, if and so far as the nature of the reference permits, be construed as including, in relation to the times, circumstances or purposes in relation to which the corresponding provision of this Act has effect, a reference to, or as the case may be, to things done or falling to be done under or for the purposes of, that corresponding provision.

(3) In this paragraph references to any provision repealed by this Act include references to any earlier provision, corresponding to a provision so repealed, which was repealed by the Agricultural Holdings (Notices to Quit) Act 1977, the Agricultural Holdings Act 1948, the Agricultural Holdings Act 1923 or the Agricultural Holdings Act 1908.

2. References, in whatever terms, in any enactment to a holding within the meaning of the Agricultural Holdings Act 1923 shall be construed as references to an agricultural holding within the meaning of this Act.

Continuation of old law for certain pending cases

3.—(1) Nothing in this Act shall apply in relation to—
    (a) a notice to quit an agricultural holding or part of an agricultural holding—
        (i) given before the commencement of this Act, or
        (ii) in the case of a notice to quit given after that time which includes a statement that it is given by reason of the death of a former tenant, where the date of death was before that time,
    (b) an agricultural holding—
        (i) the tenancy of which terminated before the commencement of this Act, or

        (ii)   the tenant of which quitted the holding before the commencement of this Act or quitted after that time in consequence of a notice to quit falling within paragraph (a) above,

(c)   an arbitration where the arbitrator was appointed under the Agricultural Holdings Act 1948 before the commencement of this Act,

(d)   an application made before the commencement of this Act to the Tribunal under any of the enactments repealed by this Act, or

(e)   an application made after the commencement of this Act to the Tribunal for a direction entitling the applicant to a tenancy of an agricultural holding on the death or retirement of the tenant where the date of death or the date of the giving of the retirement notice was before that time;

and accordingly the enactments repealed or amended by this Act shall in relation to any such notice to quit, agricultural holding, arbitration (including an award made in such an arbitration) or application (including any proceedings arising out of any such application or any direction given in any such proceedings) continue to have effect as if this Act had not been passed.

(2)   This paragraph shall have effect subject to paragraph 1 above and paragraph 11 below.

Periods of time

4.   Where a period of time specified in any enactment repealed by this Act is current at the commencement of this Act, this Act shall have effect as if the corresponding provision of this Act had been in force when the period began to run.

Transfer of functions

5.   Any reference, whether express or implied, in this Act (or any enactment amended by Schedule 14 to this Act) to, or to anything done by, the Minister, the Tribunal, an arbitrator or the President of the Royal Institution of Chartered Surveyors shall where the relevant function has been transferred to that person be construed, in relation to any time before the transfer, as including a reference to, or to the corresponding thing done by, the person by whom the function was then exercisable.

6.   Section 22 of this Act shall have effect in relation to the appointment of a person in pursuance of an application made before 1st January 1986 under section 16(2) of the Agricultural Holdings Act 1948 as if for references to the President of the Royal Institution of Chartered Surveyors there were substituted references to the Minister and as if subsections (4) and (5) were omitted.

7.   ...

Compensation

8.   Notwithstanding section 16 of the Interpretation Act 1978, rights to compensation conferred by this Act shall be in lieu of rights to compensation conferred by any enactment repealed by this Act.

Rights to remove fixtures

9.   Sections 13 and 67 of the Agricultural Holdings Act 1948 shall continue to have effect (to the exclusion of sections 10 and 79 of this Act) in relation to an agricultural holding in a case where the tenant gave notice under subsection (2)(b) of the said section 13 before 12th September 1984 as the said sections 13 and 67 had effect before that date.

Compensation for damage by game

10.   Section 14 of the Agricultural Holdings Act 1948 shall continue to have effect (to the exclusion of section 20 of this Act) in relation to an agricultural holding in a case where a

PART I
STATUTES

notice was given to the landlord under paragraph (a) of the proviso to subsection (1) of the said section 14 before 12th September 1984 as the said section 14 had effect before that date.

Succession on death or retirement

11.—(1)   Where Part IV of this Act has effect in relation to an application under that Part, references in that Part to notices to quit shall include references to notices to quit given before the commencement of this Act and, in particular, section 54 of this Act shall apply (to the exclusion of paragraph 4 of Schedule 2 to the Agricultural Holdings Act 1984) in relation to a notice to quit given before the commencement of this Act as it applies in relation to a notice to quit given after that time.

(2)   Where, by virtue of paragraph 3(1) above, Part II of the Agriculture (Miscellaneous Provisions) Act 1976 or Schedule 2 to the Agricultural Holdings Act 1984 has effect in relation to an application under the said Part II or, as the case may be, under the said Schedule 2, references in the said Part II or the said Schedule 2 to notices to quit shall include references to notices to quit given after the commencement of this Act and, in particular, paragraph 4 of the said Schedule 2 shall apply (to the exclusion of section 54 of this Act) in relation to a notice to quit given after the commencement of this Act as it applies in relation to a notice to quit given before that time.

(3)   This paragraph is without prejudice to the generality of paragraph 1 above.

12.   Without prejudice to the generality of section 34(1)(b)(iii) of this Act, a written contract of tenancy which grants the tenancy of an agricultural holding and indicates (in whatever terms) that section 2(1) of the Agricultural Holdings Act 1984 is not to apply in relation to the tenancy shall be taken to be such a contract of tenancy as is mentioned in that section.

Record of condition of holding

13.—(1)   In section 70(2)(b) of this Act the reference to a record made under section 22 of this Act shall include a reference to a record made before 12th September 1984 under section 16 of the Agricultural Holdings Act 1948 as it had effect before that date.

(2)   Sub-paragraph (1) above is without prejudice to the generality of paragraph 1 above.

Insolvency

14.   Sections 80(9) and 96(2) of this Act shall have effect—
   (a)   until the date on which Part III of the Insolvency Act 1985 comes into force, and
   (b)   on or after that date, in any case in which a petition of bankruptcy was presented, or a receiving order or adjudication in bankruptcy was made, before that date,
as if for paragraph (a) of section 96(2) there were substituted—
   "(a)   he has become bankrupt or has made a composition or arrangement with his creditors or a receiving order is made against him".

15.   …

Notices to quit

16   Paragraphs 10(1)(d) and 11(2) of Part II of Schedule 3 to this Act shall not apply in relation to any act or omission by a tenant which occurred before 12th September 1984.

[527]

NOTES

   Paras 7, 15: repealed the Regulatory Reform (Agricultural Tenancies) (England and Wales) Order 2006, SI 2006/2805, arts 2, 9(2), 18, Sch 2, subject to transitional provisions in art 10 thereof.

(Schs 14, 15 contain consequential amendments and repeals outside the scope of this work.)

INSOLVENCY ACT 1986

(1986 c 45)

ARRANGEMENT OF SECTIONS

THE FIRST GROUP OF PARTS
COMPANY INSOLVENCY; COMPANIES WINDING UP

PART II
ADMINISTRATION

PART IV
WINDING UP OF COMPANIES REGISTERED UNDER THE COMPANIES ACTS

CHAPTER VI
WINDING UP BY THE COURT

Grounds and effect of winding-up petition

Commencement of winding-up

CHAPTER VIII
PROVISIONS OF GENERAL APPLICATION IN WINDING UP

Preferential debts

Property subject to floating charge

Disclaimer (England and Wales only)

PART VII
INTERPRETATION FOR FIRST GROUP OF PARTS

THE THIRD GROUP OF PARTS
MISCELLANEOUS MATTERS BEARING ON BOTH COMPANY AND INDIVIDUAL
INSOLVENCY; GENERAL INTERPRETATION; FINAL PROVISIONS

PART XII
PREFERENTIAL DEBTS IN COMPANY AND INDIVIDUAL INSOLVENCY

PART XVIII
INTERPRETATION

PART XIX
FINAL PROVISIONS

An Act to consolidate the enactments relating to company insolvency and winding up (including the winding up of companies that are not insolvent, and of unregistered companies); enactments relating to the insolvency and bankruptcy of individuals; and other enactments bearing on those two subject matters, including the functions and qualification of insolvency practitioners, the public administration of insolvency, the penalisation and redress of malpractice and wrongdoing, and the avoidance of certain transactions at an undervalue

[25 July 1986]

NOTES

Modification: any reference to solicitor(s) etc, except in s 413 and Sch 7 of this Act, modified to include references to bodies recognised under the Administration of Justice Act 1985, s 9 by virtue of the Solicitors' Incorporated Practices Order 1991, SI 1991/2684, arts 4, 5, Sch 1.

Insolvent partnerships: this Act is extensively applied and modified in relation to insolvent partnerships by the Insolvent Partnerships Order 1994, SI 1994/2421 (as amended).

Official Receiver: as to the contracting out of functions of the Official Receiver conferred by or under this Act, see the Contracting Out (Functions of the Official Receiver) Order 1995, SI 1995/1386.

THE FIRST GROUP OF PARTS
COMPANY INSOLVENCY; COMPANIES WINDING UP

1–7B   *((Pt I) Outside the scope of this work.)*

[PART II
ADMINISTRATION

8 Administration

Schedule B1 to this Act (which makes provision about the administration of companies) shall have effect.]

[528]

NOTES

Pt II substituted, for Pt II as originally enacted (ss 8–27), by the Enterprise Act 2002, s 248(1), subject to savings and transitional provisions in s 249 of, Sch 17, para 1 to, the 2002 Act, and the Enterprise Act 2002 (Commencement No 4 and Transitional Provisions and Savings) Order 2003, SI 2003/2093, art 3(1), (2)(a), (3).

28–72H   (*(Pt III) Outside the scope of this work.*)

PART IV
WINDING UP OF COMPANIES REGISTERED UNDER THE COMPANIES ACTS

NOTES

Building Societies: as to the application, with modifications, of this Part to the winding up of building societies, see the Building Societies Act 1986, s 90, Sch 15, Pts I, II.

Friendly Societies: as to the application, with modifications, of this Part to the winding up of incorporated friendly societies by virtue of the Friendly Societies Act 1992, s 21(1) or 22(2), see s 23 of, and Sch 10 to, that Act.

73–116   (*Outside the scope of this work.*)

CHAPTER VI
WINDING UP BY THE COURT

117–121   (*Outside the scope of this work.*)

Grounds and effect of winding-up petition

122–125   (*Outside the scope of this work.*)

126   Power to stay or restrain proceedings against company

(1)   At any time after the presentation of a winding-up petition, and before a winding-up order has been made, the company, or any creditor or contributory, may—

(a)   where any action or proceeding against the company is pending in the High Court or Court of Appeal in England and Wales or Northern Ireland, apply to the court in which the action or proceeding is pending for a stay of proceedings therein, and

(b)   where any other action or proceeding is pending against the company, apply to the court having jurisdiction to wind up the company to restrain further proceedings in the action or proceeding;

and the court to which application is so made may (as the case may be) stay, sist or restrain the proceedings accordingly on such terms as it thinks fit.

(2)   In the case of a company registered under section 680 of the Companies Act (pre-1862 companies; companies formed under legislation other than the Companies Acts) or the previous corresponding legislation, where the application to stay, sist or restrain is by a creditor, this section extends to actions and proceedings against any contributory of the company.

[529]

127   (*Outside the scope of this work.*)

128   Avoidance of attachments, etc

(1)   Where a company registered in England and Wales is being wound up by the court, any attachment, sequestration, distress or execution put in force against the estate or effects of the company after the commencement of the winding up is void.

(2)   This section, so far as relates to any estate or effects of the company situated in England and Wales, applies in the case of a company registered in Scotland as it applies in the case of a company registered in England and Wales.

[530]

Commencement of winding up

129   (*Outside the scope of this work.*)

130 Consequences of winding-up order

(1)   On the making of a winding-up order, a copy of the order must forthwith be forwarded by the company (or otherwise as may be prescribed) to the registrar of companies, who shall enter it in his records relating to the company.

(2)   When a winding-up order has been made or a provisional liquidator has been appointed, no action or proceeding shall be proceeded with or commenced against the company or its property, except by leave of the court and subject to such terms as the court may impose.

(3)   When an order has been made for winding up a company registered under section 680 of the Companies Act, no action or proceeding shall be commenced or proceeded with against the company or its property or any contributory of the company, in respect of any debt of the company, except by leave of the court, and subject to such terms as the court may impose.

(4)   An order for winding up a company operates in favour of all the creditors and of all contributories of the company as if made on the joint petition of a creditor and of a contributory.

[531]

131–174   (*Outside the scope of this work.*)

CHAPTER VIII
PROVISIONS OF GENERAL APPLICATION IN WINDING UP

Preferential debts

175 Preferential debts (general provision)

(1)   In a winding up the company's preferential debts (within the meaning given by section 386 in Part XII) shall be paid in priority to all other debts.

(2)   Preferential debts—
-   (a)   rank equally among themselves after the expenses of the winding up and shall be paid in full, unless the assets are insufficient to meet them, in which case they abate in equal proportions; and
-   (b)   so far as the assets of the company available for payment of general creditors are insufficient to meet them, have priority over the claims of holders of debentures secured by, or holders of, any floating charge created by the company, and shall be paid accordingly out of any property comprised in or subject to that charge.

[532]

176 Preferential charge on goods distrained

(1)   This section applies where a company is being wound up by the court in England and Wales, and is without prejudice to section 128 (avoidance of attachments, etc).

(2)   Where any person (whether or not a landlord or person entitled to rent) has distrained upon the goods or effects of the company in the period of 3 months ending with the date of the winding-up order, those goods or effects, or the proceeds of their sale, shall be charged for the benefit of the company with the preferential debts of the company to the extent that the company's property is for the time being insufficient for meeting them.

(3)   Where by virtue of a charge under subsection (2) any person surrenders any goods or effects to a company or makes a payment to a company, that person ranks, in respect of the amount of the proceeds of sale of those goods or effects by the liquidator or (as the case may be) the amount of the payment, as a preferential creditor of the company, except as against so much of the company's property as is available for the payment of preferential creditors by virtue of the surrender or payment.

[533]

[Property subject to floating charge]

NOTES
Cross-heading: inserted by the Enterprise Act 2002, s 252.

[176ZA   Payment of expenses of winding up (England and Wales)

(1)   The expenses of winding up in England and Wales, so far as the assets of the company available for payment of general creditors are insufficient to meet them, have priority over any claims to property comprised in or subject to any floating charge created by the company and shall be paid out of any such property accordingly.

(2)   In subsection (1)—
   (a)   the reference to assets of the company available for payment of general creditors does not include any amount made available under section 176A(2)(a);
   (b)   the reference to claims to property comprised in or subject to a floating charge is to the claims of—
      (i)   the holders of debentures secured by, or holders of, the floating charge, and
      (ii)   any preferential creditors entitled to be paid out of that property in priority to them.

(3)   Provision may be made by rules restricting the application of subsection (1), in such circumstances as may be prescribed, to expenses authorised or approved—
   (a)   by the holders of debentures secured by, or holders of, the floating charge and by any preferential creditors entitled to be paid in priority to them, or
   (b)   by the court.

(4)   References in this section to the expenses of the winding up are to all expenses properly incurred in the winding up, including the remuneration of the liquidator.]

[533A]

NOTES
Commencement: 20 January 2007 (certain purposes); to be appointed (otherwise).
Inserted by the Companies Act 2006, s 1282(1), partly as from 20 January 2007, and fully as from a day to be appointed.

176A, 177   (*Outside the scope of this work.*)

Disclaimer (England and Wales only)

178   Power to disclaim onerous property

(1)   This and the next two sections apply to a company that is being wound up in England and Wales.

(2)   Subject as follows, the liquidator may, by the giving of the prescribed notice, disclaim any onerous property and may do so notwithstanding that he has taken possession of it, endeavoured to sell it, or otherwise exercised rights of ownership in relation to it.

(3)   The following is onerous property for the purposes of this section—
   (a)   any unprofitable contract, and
   (b)   any other property of the company which is unsaleable or not readily saleable or is such that it may give rise to a liability to pay money or perform any other onerous act.

(4)   A disclaimer under this section—
   (a)   operates so as to determine, as from the date of the disclaimer, the rights, interests and liabilities of the company in or in respect of the property disclaimed; but
   (b)   does not, except so far as is necessary for the purpose of releasing the company from any liability, affect the rights or liabilities of any other person.

(5)   A notice of disclaimer shall not be given under this section in respect of any property if—
   (a)   a person interested in the property has applied in writing to the liquidator or one of his predecessors as liquidator requiring the liquidator or that predecessor to decide whether he will disclaim or not, and

(b)   the period of 28 days beginning with the day on which that application was made, or such longer period as the court may allow, has expired without a notice of disclaimer having been given under this section in respect of that property.

(6)   Any person sustaining loss or damage in consequence of the operation of a disclaimer under this section is deemed a creditor of the company to the extent of the loss or damage and accordingly may prove for the loss or damage in the winding up.

[534]

179   Disclaimer of leaseholds

(1)   The disclaimer under section 178 of any property of a leasehold nature does not take effect unless a copy of the disclaimer has been served (so far as the liquidator is aware of their addresses) on every person claiming under the company as underlessee or mortgagee and either—
(a)   no application under section 181 below is made with respect to that property before the end of the period of 14 days beginning with the day on which the last notice served under this subsection was served; or
(b)   where such an application has been made, the court directs that the disclaimer shall take effect.

(2)   Where the court gives a direction under subsection (1)(b) it may also, instead of or in addition to any order it makes under section 181, make such orders with respect to fixtures, tenant's improvements and other matters arising out of the lease as it thinks fit.

[535]

180   Land subject to rentcharge

(1)   The following applies where, in consequence of the disclaimer under section 178 of any land subject to a rentcharge, that land vests by operation of law in the Crown or any other person (referred to in the next subsection as "the proprietor").

(2)   The proprietor and the successors in title of the proprietor are not subject to any personal liability in respect of any sums becoming due under the rentcharge except sums becoming due after the proprietor, or some person claiming under or through the proprietor, has taken possession or control of the land or has entered into occupation of it.

[536]

181   Powers of court (general)

(1)   This section and the next apply where the liquidator has disclaimed property under section 178.

(2)   An application under this section may be made to the court by—
(a)   any person who claims an interest in the disclaimed property, or
(b)   any person who is under any liability in respect of the disclaimed property, not being a liability discharged by the disclaimer.

(3)   Subject as follows, the court may on the application make an order, on such terms as it thinks fit, for the vesting of the disclaimed property in, or for its delivery to—
(a)   a person entitled to it or a trustee for such a person, or
(b)   a person subject to such a liability as is mentioned in subsection (2)(b) or a trustee for such a person.

(4)   The court shall not make an order under subsection (3)(b) except where it appears to the court that it would be just to do so for the purpose of compensating the person subject to the liability in respect of the disclaimer.

(5)   The effect of any order under this section shall be taken into account in assessing for the purpose of section 178(6) the extent of any loss or damage sustained by any person in consequence of the disclaimer.

(6)   An order under this section vesting property in any person need not be completed by conveyance, assignment or transfer.

[537]

182   Powers of court (leaseholds)

(1)   The court shall not make an order under section 181 vesting property of a leasehold nature in any person claiming under the company as underlessee or mortgagee except on terms making that person—

(a) subject to the same liabilities and obligations as the company was subject to under the lease at the commencement of the winding up, or

(b) if the court thinks fit, subject to the same liabilities and obligations as that person would be subject to if the lease had been assigned to him at the commencement of the winding up.

(2) For the purposes of an order under section 181 relating to only part of any property comprised in a lease, the requirements of subsection (1) apply as if the lease comprised only the property to which the order relates.

(3) Where subsection (1) applies and no person claiming under the company as underlessee or mortgagee is willing to accept an order under section 181 on the terms required by virtue of that subsection, the court may, by order under that section, vest the company's estate or interest in the property in any person who is liable (whether personally or in a representative capacity, and whether alone or jointly with the company) to perform the lessee's covenants in the lease.

The court may vest that estate and interest in such a person freed and discharged from all estates, incumbrances and interests created by the company.

(4) Where subsection (1) applies and a person claiming under the company as underlessee or mortgagee declines to accept an order under section 181, that person is excluded from all interest in the property.

[538]

183–246 (*Outside the scope of this work.*)

PART VII
INTERPRETATION FOR FIRST GROUP OF PARTS

NOTES

Building Societies: as to the application, with modifications, of this Part to the winding up of building societies, see the Building Societies Act 1986, s 90, Sch 15, Pt I.

Friendly Societies: as to the application, with modifications, of this Part to the winding up of incorporated friendly societies by virtue of the Friendly Societies Act 1992, s 21(1) or 22(2), see s 23 of, and Sch 10 to, that Act.

247 "Insolvency" and "go into liquidation"

(1) In this Group of Parts, except in so far as the context otherwise requires, "insolvency", in relation to a company, includes the approval of a voluntary arrangement under Part I, [or the appointment of an administrator or an administrative receiver].

(2) For the purposes of any provision in this Group of Parts, a company goes into liquidation if it passes a resolution for voluntary winding up or an order for its winding up is made by the court at a time when it has not already gone into liquidation by passing such a resolution.

[(3) The reference to a resolution for voluntary winding up in subsection (2) includes a reference to a resolution which is deemed to occur by virtue of—

(a) paragraph 83(6)(b) of Schedule B1, or

(b) an order made following conversion of administration or a voluntary arrangement into winding up by virtue of Article 37 of the EC Regulation.]

[539]

NOTES

Sub-s (1): words in square brackets substituted by the Enterprise Act 2002, s 248(3), Sch 17, paras 9, 33(1), (2), subject to savings and transitional provisions (i) in a case where a petition for an administration order has been presented before 15 September 2003 (see the Enterprise Act 2002 (Commencement No 4 and Transitional Provisions and Savings) Order 2003, SI 2003/2093, art 3), and (ii) in relation to special administration regimes (see s 249 of the 2002 Act).

Sub-s (3): (originally added by the Insolvency Act 1986 (Amendment) (No 2) Regulations 2002, SI 2002/1240, regs 3, 12) substituted by the Enterprise Act 2002, s 248(3), Sch 17, paras 9, 33(1), (3), subject to savings as noted to sub-s (1) above.

248 "Secured creditor", etc

In this Group of Parts, except in so far as the context otherwise requires—

(a)　"secured creditor", in relation to a company, means a creditor of the company who holds in respect of his debt a security over property of the company, and "unsecured creditor" is to be read accordingly; and

(b)　"security" means—
　　(i)　in relation to England and Wales, any mortgage, charge, lien or other security, and
　　(ii)　in relation to Scotland, any security (whether heritable or moveable), any floating charge and any right of lien or preference and any right of retention (other than a right of compensation or set off).

[540]

249　"Connected" with a company

For the purposes of any provision in this Group of Parts, a person is connected with a company if—

(a)　he is a director or shadow director of the company or an associate of such a director or shadow director, or

(b)　he is an associate of the company;

and "associate" has the meaning given by section 435 in Part XVIII of this Act.

[541]

250　"Member" of a company

For the purposes of any provision in this Group of Parts, a person who is not a member of a company but to whom shares in the company have been transferred, or transmitted by operation of law, is to be regarded as a member of the company, and references to a member or members are to be read accordingly.

[542]

251　Expressions used generally

In this Group of Parts, except in so far as the context otherwise requires—

"administrative receiver" means—
　　(a)　an administrative receiver as defined by section 29(2) in Chapter I of Part III, or
　　(b)　a receiver appointed under section 51 in Chapter II of that Part in a case where the whole (or substantially the whole) of the company's property is attached by the floating charge;

"business day" means any day other than a Saturday, a Sunday, Christmas Day, Good Friday or a day which is a bank holiday in any part of Great Britain;

"chattel leasing agreement" means an agreement for the bailment or, in Scotland, the hiring of goods which is capable of subsisting for more than 3 months;

"contributory" has the meaning given by section 79;

"director" includes any person occupying the position of director, by whatever name called;

"floating charge" means a charge which, as created, was a floating charge and includes a floating charge within section 462 of the Companies Act (Scottish floating charges);

"office copy", in relation to Scotland, means a copy certified by the clerk of court;

"the official rate", in relation to interest, means the rate payable under section 189(4);

"prescribed" means prescribed by the rules;

"receiver", in the expression "receiver or manager", does not include a receiver appointed under section 51 in Chapter II of Part III;

"retention of title agreement" means an agreement for the sale of goods to a company, being an agreement—
　　(a)　which does not constitute a charge on the goods, but
　　(b)　under which, if the seller is not paid and the company is wound up, the seller will have priority over all other creditors of the company as respects the goods or any property representing the goods;

"the rules" means rules under section 411 in Part XV; and

"shadow director", in relation to a company, means a person in accordance with whose directions or instructions the directors of the company are accustomed to act (but so that a person is not deemed a shadow director by reason only that the directors act on advice given by him in a professional capacity);

and any expression for whose interpretation provision is made by Part XXVI of the Companies Act, other than an expression defined above in this section, is to be construed in accordance with that provision.

[543]

THE SECOND GROUP OF PARTS
INSOLVENCY OF INDIVIDUALS; BANKRUPTCY

252–263G ((*Pt VIII*) *outside the scope of this work.*)

PART IX
BANKRUPTCY

264–282 (*Ss 264–274, 276, 278–282 outside the scope of this work; s 275 repealed by the Enterprise Act 2002, ss 269, 278(2), Sch 23, paras 1, 2, Sch 26, subject to transitional provisions; s 277 repealed by the Criminal Justice Act 1988, s 170(2), Sch 16, as from a day to be appointed.*)

CHAPTER II
PROTECTION OF BANKRUPT'S ESTATE AND INVESTIGATION OF HIS AFFAIRS

283 Definition of bankrupt's estate

(1) Subject as follows, a bankrupt's estate for the purposes of any of this Group of Parts comprises—
  (a) all property belonging to or vested in the bankrupt at the commencement of the bankruptcy, and
  (b) any property which by virtue of any of the following provisions of this Part is comprised in that estate or is treated as falling within the preceding paragraph.

(2) Subsection (1) does not apply to—
  (a) such tools, books, vehicles and other items of equipment as are necessary to the bankrupt for use personally by him in his employment, business or vocation;
  (b) such clothing, bedding, furniture, household equipment and provisions as are necessary for satisfying the basic domestic needs of the bankrupt and his family.

This subsection is subject to section 308 in Chapter IV (certain excluded property reclaimable by trustee).

(3) Subsection (1) does not apply to—
  (a) property held by the bankrupt on trust for any other person, or
  (b) the right of nomination to a vacant ecclesiastical benefice.

[(3A) Subject to section 308A in Chapter IV, subsection (1) does not apply to—
  (a) a tenancy which is an assured tenancy or an assured agricultural occupancy, within the meaning of Part I of the Housing Act 1988, and the terms of which inhibit an assignment as mentioned in section 127(5) of the Rent Act 1977, or
  (b) a protected tenancy, within the meaning of the Rent Act 1977, in respect of which, by virtue of any provision of Part IX of that Act, no premium can lawfully be required as a condition of assignment, or
  (c) a tenancy of a dwelling-house by virtue of which the bankrupt is, within the meaning of the Rent (Agriculture) Act 1976, a protected occupier of the dwelling-house, and the terms of which inhibit an assignment as mentioned in section 127(5) of the Rent Act 1977, or
  (d) a secure tenancy, within the meaning of Part IV of the Housing Act 1985, which is not capable of being assigned, except in the cases mentioned in section 91(3) of that Act.]

(4) References in any of this Group of Parts to property, in relation to a bankrupt, include references to any power exercisable by him over or in respect of property except in so far as the power is exercisable over or in respect of property not for the time being comprised in the bankrupt's estate and—
  (a) is so exercisable at a time after either the official receiver has had his release in respect of that estate under section 299(2) in Chapter III or a meeting summoned by the trustee of that estate under section 331 in Chapter IV has been held, or
  (b) cannot be so exercised for the benefit of the bankrupt;

and a power exercisable over or in respect of property is deemed for the purposes of any of this Group of Parts to vest in the person entitled to exercise it at the time of the transaction or event by virtue of which it is exercisable by that person (whether or not it becomes so exercisable at that time).

(5)   For the purposes of any such provision in this Group of Parts, property comprised in a bankrupt's estate is so comprised subject to the rights of any person other than the bankrupt (whether as a secured creditor of the bankrupt or otherwise) in relation thereto, but disregarding—

(a)   any rights in relation to which a statement such as is required by section 269(1)(a) was made in the petition on which the bankrupt was adjudged bankrupt, and

(b)   any rights which have been otherwise given up in accordance with the rules.

(6)   This section has effect subject to the provisions of any enactment not contained in this Act under which any property is to be excluded from a bankrupt's estate.

[544]

NOTES

Sub-s (3A): inserted by the Housing Act 1988, s 117(1).

283A   (*Outside the scope of this work.*)

284   Restrictions on dispositions of property

(1)   Where a person is adjudged bankrupt, any disposition of property made by that person in the period to which this section applies is void except to the extent that it is or was made with the consent of the court, or is or was subsequently ratified by the court.

(2)   Subsection (1) applies to a payment (whether in cash or otherwise) as it applies to a disposition of property and, accordingly, where any payment is void by virtue of that subsection, the person paid shall hold the sum paid for the bankrupt as part of his estate.

(3)   This section applies to the period beginning with the day of the presentation of the petition for the bankruptcy order and ending with the vesting, under Chapter IV of this Part, of the bankrupt's estate in a trustee.

(4)   The preceding provisions of this section do not give a remedy against any person—

(a)   in respect of any property or payment which he received before the commencement of the bankruptcy in good faith, for value and without notice that the petition had been presented, or

(b)   in respect of any interest in property which derives from an interest in respect of which there is, by virtue of this subsection, no remedy.

(5)   Where after the commencement of his bankruptcy the bankrupt has incurred a debt to a banker or other person by reason of the making of a payment which is void under this section, that debt is deemed for the purposes of any of this Group of Parts to have been incurred before the commencement of the bankruptcy unless—

(a)   that banker or person had notice of the bankruptcy before the debt was incurred, or

(b)   it is not reasonably practicable for the amount of the payment to be recovered from the person to whom it was made.

(6)   A disposition of property is void under this section notwithstanding that the property is not or, as the case may be, would not be comprised in the bankrupt's estate; but nothing in this section affects any disposition made by a person of property held by him on trust for any other person.

[545]

285   Restriction on proceedings and remedies

(1)   At any time when proceedings on a bankruptcy petition are pending or an individual has been adjudged bankrupt the court may stay any action, execution or other legal process against the property or person of the debtor or, as the case may be, of the bankrupt.

(2)   Any court in which proceedings are pending against any individual may, on proof that a bankruptcy petition has been presented in respect of that individual or that he is an undischarged bankrupt, either stay the proceedings or allow them to continue on such terms as it thinks fit.

(3)   After the making of a bankruptcy order no person who is a creditor of the bankrupt in respect of a debt provable in the bankruptcy shall—

   (a)   have any remedy against the property or person of the bankrupt in respect of that debt, or

   (b)   before the discharge of the bankrupt, commence any action or other legal proceedings against the bankrupt except with the leave of the court and on such terms as the court may impose.

This is subject to sections 346 (enforcement procedures) and 347 (limited right to distress).

(4)   Subject as follows, subsection (3) does not affect the right of a secured creditor of the bankrupt to enforce his security.

(5)   Where any goods of an undischarged bankrupt are held by any person by way of pledge, pawn or other security, the official receiver may, after giving notice in writing of his intention to do so, inspect the goods.

Where such a notice has been given to any person, that person is not entitled, without leave of the court, to realise his security unless he has given the trustee of the bankrupt's estate a reasonable opportunity of inspecting the goods and of exercising the bankrupt's right of redemption.

(6)   References in this section to the property or goods of the bankrupt are to any of his property or goods, whether or not comprised in his estate.

[546]

286–304   (*Outside the scope of this work.*)

CHAPTER IV
ADMINISTRATION BY TRUSTEE

Preliminary

305   General functions of trustee

(1)   This Chapter applies in relation to any bankruptcy where either—

   (a)   the appointment of a person as trustee of a bankrupt's estate takes effect, or

   (b)   the official receiver becomes trustee of a bankrupt's estate.

(2)   The function of the trustee is to get in, realise and distribute the bankrupt's estate in accordance with the following provisions of this Chapter; and in the carrying out of that function and in the management of the bankrupt's estate the trustee is entitled, subject to those provisions, to use his own discretion.

(3)   It is the duty of the trustee, if he is not the official receiver—

   (a)   to furnish the official receiver with such information,

   (b)   to produce to the official receiver, and permit inspection by the official receiver of, such books, papers and other records, and

   (c)   to give the official receiver such other assistance,

as the official receiver may reasonably require for the purpose of enabling him to carry out his functions in relation to the bankruptcy.

(4)   The official name of the trustee shall be "the trustee of the estate of ..., a bankrupt" (inserting the name of the bankrupt); be he may be referred to as "the trustee in bankruptcy" of the particular bankrupt.

[547]

Acquisition, control and realisation of bankrupt's estate

306   Vesting of bankrupt's estate in trustee

(1)   The bankrupt's estate shall vest in the trustee immediately on his appointment taking effect or, in the case of the official receiver, on his becoming trustee.

(2)   Where any property which is, or is to be, comprised in the bankrupt's estate vests in the trustee (whether under this section or under any other provision of this Part), it shall so vest without any conveyance, assignment or transfer.

[548]

[306A   Property subject to restraint order

(1)   This section applies where—
  (a)   property is excluded from the bankrupt's estate by virtue of section 417(2)(a) of the Proceeds of Crime Act 2002 (property subject to a restraint order),
  (b)   an order under section 50, 52, 128, 198 or 200 of that Act has not been made in respect of the property, and
  (c)   the restraint order is discharged.

(2)   On the discharge of the restraint order the property vests in the trustee as part of the bankrupt's estate.

(3)   But subsection (2) does not apply to the proceeds of property realised by a management receiver under section 49(2)(d) or 197(2)(d) of that Act (realisation of property to meet receiver's remuneration and expenses).]

[548A]

NOTES
Commencement: 24 March 2003.
Inserted, together with ss 306B, 306C, by the Proceeds of Crime Act 2002, s 456, Sch 11, paras 1, 16(1), (3).

[306B   Property in respect of which receivership or administration order made

(1)   This section applies where—
  (a)   property is excluded from the bankrupt's estate by virtue of section 417(2)(b), (c) or (d) of the Proceeds of Crime Act 2002 (property in respect of which an order for the appointment of a receiver or administrator under certain provisions of that Act is in force),
  (b)   a confiscation order is made under section 6, 92 or 156 of that Act,
  (c)   the amount payable under the confiscation order is fully paid, and
  (d)   any of the property remains in the hands of the receiver or administrator (as the case may be).

(2)   The property vests in the trustee as part of the bankrupt's estate.]

[548B]

NOTES
Commencement: 24 March 2003.
Inserted as noted to s 306A at **[548A]**.

[306C   Property subject to certain orders where confiscation order discharged or quashed

(1)   This section applies where—
  (a)   property is excluded from the bankrupt's estate by virtue of section 417(2)(a), (b), (c) or (d) of the Proceeds of Crime Act 2002 (property in respect of which a restraint order or an order for the appointment of a receiver or administrator under that Act is in force),
  (b)   a confiscation order is made under section 6, 92 or 156 of that Act, and
  (c)   the confiscation order is discharged under section 30, 114 or 180 of that Act (as the case may be) or quashed under that Act or in pursuance of any enactment relating to appeals against conviction or sentence.

(2)   Any such property in the hands of a receiver appointed under Part 2 or 4 of that Act or an administrator appointed under Part 3 of that Act vests in the trustee as part of the bankrupt's estate.

(3)   But subsection (2) does not apply to the proceeds of property realised by a management receiver under section 49(2)(d) or 197(2)(d) of that Act (realisation of property to meet receiver's remuneration and expenses).]

[548C]

NOTES
Commencement: 24 March 2003.
Inserted as noted to s 306A at **[548A]**.

307–308 (*Outside the scope of this work.*)

[308A Vesting in trustee of certain tenancies

Upon the service on the bankrupt by the trustee of a notice in writing under this section, any tenancy—
    (a)   which is excluded by virtue of section 283(3A) from the bankrupt's estate, and
    (b)   to which the notice relates,
vests in the trustee as part of the bankrupt's estate; and, except against a purchaser in good faith, for value and without notice of the bankruptcy, the trustee's title to that tenancy has relation back to the commencement of the bankruptcy.]

[549]

NOTES
Inserted by the Housing Act 1988, s 117(2).

309   Time-limit for notice under s 307 or 308

(1)   Except with the leave of the court, a notice shall not be served—
    (a)   under section 307, after the end of the period of 42 days beginning with the day on which it first came to the knowledge of the trustee that the property in question had been acquired by, or had devolved upon, the bankrupt;
    (b)   under section 308 [or section 308A], after the end of the period of 42 days beginning with the day on which the property [or tenancy] in question first came to the knowledge of the trustee.

(2)   For the purposes of this section—
    (a)   anything which comes to the knowledge of the trustee is deemed in relation to any successor of his as trustee to have come to the knowledge of the successor at the same time; and
    (b)   anything which comes (otherwise than under paragraph (a)) to the knowledge of a person before he is the trustee is deemed to come to his knowledge on his appointment taking effect or, in the case of the official receiver, on his becoming trustee.

[550]

NOTES
Sub-s (1): words in square brackets inserted by the Housing Act 1988, s 117(3).

310–314   (*Outside the scope of this work.*)

Disclaimer of onerous property

315   Disclaimer (general power)

(1)   Subject as follows, the trustee may, by the giving of the prescribed notice, disclaim any onerous property and may do so notwithstanding that he has taken possession of it, endeavoured to sell it or otherwise exercised rights of ownership in relation to it.

(2)   The following is onerous property for the purposes of this section, that is to say—
    (a)   any unprofitable contract, and
    (b)   any other property comprised in the bankrupt's estate which is unsaleable or not readily saleable, or is such that it may give rise to a liability to pay money or perform any other onerous act.

(3)   A disclaimer under this section—
    (a)   operates so as to determine, as from the date of the disclaimer, the rights, interests and liabilities of the bankrupt and his estate in or in respect of the property disclaimed, and
    (b)   discharges the trustee from all personal liability in respect of that property as from the commencement of his trusteeship,
but does not, except so far as is necessary for the purpose of releasing the bankrupt, the bankrupt's estate and the trustee from any liability, affect the rights or liabilities of any other person.

(4)   A notice of disclaimer shall not be given under this section in respect of any property that has been claimed for the estate under section 307 (after-acquired property) or 308 (personal property of bankrupt exceeding reasonable replacement value) [or 308A], except with the leave of the court.

(5)   Any person sustaining loss or damage in consequence of the operation of a disclaimer under this section is deemed to be a creditor of the bankrupt to the extent of the loss or damage and accordingly may prove for the loss or damage as a bankruptcy debt.

[551]

NOTES
Sub-s (4): words in square brackets inserted by the Housing Act 1988, s 117(4).

316   Notice requiring trustee's decision

(1)   Notice of disclaimer shall not be given under section 315 in respect of any property if—
   (a)   a person interested in the property has applied in writing to the trustee or one of his predecessors as trustee requiring the trustee or that predecessor to decide whether he will disclaim or not, and
   (b)   the period of 28 days beginning with the day on which that application was made has expired without a notice of disclaimer having been given under section 315 in respect of that property.

(2)   The trustee is deemed to have adopted any contract which by virtue of this section he is not entitled to disclaim.

[552]

317   Disclaimer of leaseholds

(1)   The disclaimer of any property of a leasehold nature does not take effect unless a copy of the disclaimer has been served (so far as the trustee is aware of their addresses) on every person claiming under the bankrupt as underlessee or mortgagee and either—
   (a)   no application under section 320 below is made with respect to the property before the end of the period of 14 days beginning with the day on which the last notice served under this subsection was served, or
   (b)   where such an application has been made, the court directs that the disclaimer is to take effect.

(2)   Where the court gives a direction under subsection (1)(b) it may also, instead of or in addition to any order it makes under section 320, make such orders with respect to fixtures, tenant's improvements and other matters arising out of the lease as it thinks fit.

[553]

318   Disclaimer of dwelling house

Without prejudice to section 317, the disclaimer of any property in a dwelling house does not take effect unless a copy of the disclaimer has been served (so far as the trustee is aware of their addresses) on every person in occupation of or claiming a right to occupy the dwelling house and either—
   (a)   no application under section 320 is made with respect to the property before the end of the period of 14 days beginning with the day on which the last notice served under this section was served, or
   (b)   where such an application has been made, the court directs that the disclaimer is to take effect.

[554]

319   Disclaimer of land subject to rentcharge

(1)   The following applies where, in consequence of the disclaimer under section 315 of any land subject to a rentcharge, that land vests by operation of law in the Crown or any other person (referred to in the next subsection as "the proprietor").

(2)   The proprietor, and the successors in title of the proprietor, are not subject to any personal liability in respect of any sums becoming due under the rentcharge, except sums becoming due after the proprietor, or some person claiming under or through the proprietor, has taken possession or control of the land or has entered into occupation of it.

[555]

320 Court order vesting disclaimed property

(1)   This section and the next apply where the trustee has disclaimed property under section 315.

(2)   An application may be made to the court under this section by—
(a)   any person who claims an interest in the disclaimed property,
(b)   any person who is under any liability in respect of the disclaimed property, not being a liability discharged by the disclaimer, or
(c)   where the disclaimed property is property in a dwelling-house, any person who at the time when the bankruptcy petition was presented was in occupation of or entitled to occupy the dwelling house.

(3)   Subject as follows in this section and the next, the court may, on an application under this section, make an order on such terms as it thinks fit for the vesting of the disclaimed property in, or for its delivery to—
(a)   a person entitled to it or a trustee for such a person,
(b)   a person subject to such a liability as is mentioned in subsection (2)(b) or a trustee for such a person, or
(c)   where the disclaimed property is property in a dwelling-house, any person who at the time when the bankruptcy petition was presented was in occupation of or entitled to occupy the dwelling house.

(4)   The court shall not make an order by virtue of subsection (3)(b) except where it appears to the court that it would be just to do so for the purpose of compensating the person subject to the liability in respect of the disclaimer.

(5)   The effect of any order under this section shall be taken into account in assessing for the purposes of section 315(5) the extent of any loss or damage sustained by any person in consequence of the disclaimer.

(6)   An order under this section vesting property in any person need not be completed by any conveyance, assignment or transfer.

[556]

321 Order under s 320 in respect of leaseholds

(1)   The court shall not make an order under section 320 vesting property of a leasehold nature in any person, except on terms making that person—
(a)   subject to the same liabilities and obligations as the bankrupt was subject to under the lease on the day the bankruptcy petition was presented, or
(b)   if the court thinks fit, subject to the same liabilities and obligations as that person would be subject to if the lease had been assigned to him on that day.

(2)   For the purposes of an order under section 320 relating to only part of any property comprised in a lease, the requirements of subsection (1) apply as if the lease comprised only the property to which the order relates.

(3)   Where subsection (1) applies and no person is willing to accept an order under section 320 on the terms required by that subsection, the court may (by order under section 320) vest the estate or interest of the bankrupt in the property in any person who is liable (whether personally or in a representative capacity and whether alone or jointly with the bankrupt) to perform the lessee's covenants in the lease.

The court may by virtue of this subsection vest that estate and interest in such a person freed and discharged from all estates, incumbrances and interests created by the bankrupt.

(4)   Where subsection (1) applies and a person declines to accept any order under section 320, that person shall be excluded from all interest in the property.

[557]

322–335   (*Ss 322–326, 328–335 outside the scope of this work; s 327 repealed by the Criminal Justice Act 1988, s 170(2), Sch 16, as from a day to be appointed.*)

CHAPTER V
EFFECT OF BANKRUPTCY ON CERTAIN RIGHTS, TRANSACTIONS, ETC

335A–338   (*Outside the scope of this work.*)

Adjustment of prior transactions, etc

339–346   (*Outside the scope of this work.*)

347   Distress, etc

(1)   The right of any landlord or other person to whom rent is payable to distrain upon the goods and effects of an undischarged bankrupt for rent due to him from the bankrupt is available (subject to [sections 252(2)(b) and 254(1) above and] subsection (5) below) against goods and effects comprised in the bankrupt's estate, but only for 6 months' rent accrued due before the commencement of the bankruptcy.

(2)   Where a landlord or other person to whom rent is payable has distrained for rent upon the goods and effects of an individual to whom a bankruptcy petition relates and a bankruptcy order is subsequently made on that petition, any amount recovered by way of that distress which—

(a)   is in excess of the amount which by virtue of subsection (1) would have been recoverable after the commencement of the bankruptcy, or

(b)   is in respect of rent for a period or part of a period after the distress was levied,

shall be held for the bankrupt as part of his estate.

(3)   Where any person (whether or not a landlord or person entitled to rent) has distrained upon the goods or effects of an individual who is adjudged bankrupt before the end of the period of 3 months beginning with the distraint, so much of those goods or effects, or of the proceeds of their sale, as is not held for the bankrupt under subsection (2) shall be charged for the benefit of the bankrupt's estate with the preferential debts of the bankrupt to the extent that the bankrupt's estate is for the time being insufficient for meeting those debts.

(4)   Where by virtue of any charge under subsection (3) any person surrenders any goods or effects to the trustee of a bankrupt's estate or makes a payment to such a trustee, that person ranks, in respect of the amount of the proceeds of the sale of those goods or effects by the trustee or, as the case may be, the amount of the payment, as a preferential creditor of the bankrupt, except as against so much of the bankrupt's estate as is available for the payment of preferential creditors by virtue of the surrender or payment.

(5)   A landlord or other person to whom rent is payable is not at any time after the discharge of a bankrupt entitled to distrain upon any goods or effects comprised in the bankrupt's estate.

(6)   Where in the case of any execution—

(a)   a landlord is (apart from this section) entitled under section 1 of the Landlord and Tenant Act 1709 or section 102 of the County Courts Act 1984 (claims for rent where goods seized in execution) to claim for an amount not exceeding one year's rent, and

(b)   the person against whom the execution is levied is adjudged bankrupt before the notice of claim is served on the [enforcement officer,] or other officer charged with the execution,

the right of the landlord to claim under that section is restricted to a right to claim for an amount not exceeding 6 months' rent and does not extend to any rent payable in respect of a period after the notice of claim is so served.

(7)   Nothing in subsection (6) imposes any liability on [an enforcement officer] or other officer charged with an execution to account to the official receiver or the trustee of a bankrupt's estate for any sums paid by him to a landlord at any time before [the enforcement officer] or other officer was served with notice of the bankruptcy order in question.

But this subsection is without prejudice to the liability of the landlord.

(8)   [Subject to sections 252(2)(b) and 254(1) above] nothing in this Group of Parts affects any right to distrain otherwise than for rent; and any such right is at any time exercisable without restriction against property comprised in a bankrupt's estate, even if that right is expressed by any enactment to be exercisable in like manner as a right to distrain for rent.

(9)   Any right to distrain against property comprised in a bankrupt's estate is exercisable notwithstanding that the property has vested in the trustee.

(10)   The provisions of this section are without prejudice to a landlord's right in a bankruptcy to prove for any bankruptcy debt in respect of rent.

[(11)   In this section "enforcement officer" means an individual who is authorised to act as an enforcement officer under the Courts Act 2003.]

[558]

NOTES
Sub-ss (1), (8): words in square brackets inserted by the Insolvency Act 2000, s 3, Sch 3, paras 1, 14, subject to transitional provisions in SI 2002/2711, art 4.
Sub-ss (6), (7): words in square brackets substituted by the Courts Act 2003, s 109(1), Sch 8, para 298(1)–(3).
Sub-s (11): added by the Courts Act 2003, s 109(1), Sch 8, para 298(1), (4).

348–379   (*Ss 348–360, 363–379 outside the scope of this work; ss 361, 362 repealed by the Enterprise Act 2002, ss 263, 278(2), Sch 26.*)

PART XI
INTERPRETATION FOR SECOND GROUP OF PARTS

380   Introductory

The next five sections have effect for the interpretation of the provisions of this Act which are comprised in this Group of Parts; and where a definition is provided for a particular expression, it applies except so far as the context otherwise requires.

[559]

381   "Bankrupt" and associated terminology

(1)   "Bankrupt" means an individual who has been adjudged bankrupt and, in relation to a bankruptcy order, it means the individual adjudged bankrupt by that order.

(2)   "Bankruptcy order" means an order adjudging an individual bankrupt.

(3)   "Bankruptcy petition" means a petition to the court for a bankruptcy order.

[560]

382   "Bankruptcy debt", etc

(1)   "Bankruptcy debt", in relation to a bankrupt, means (subject to the next subsection) any of the following—
   (a)   any debt or liability to which he is subject at the commencement of the bankruptcy,
   (b)   any debt or liability to which he may become subject after the commencement of the bankruptcy (including after his discharge from bankruptcy) by reason of any obligation incurred before the commencement of the bankruptcy,
   (c)   *any amount specified in pursuance of section 39(3)(c) of the Powers of Criminal Courts Act 1973 in any criminal bankruptcy order made against him before the commencement of the bankruptcy, and*
   (d)   any interest provable as mentioned in section 322(2) in Chapter IV of Part IX.

(2)   In determining for the purposes of any provision in this Group of Parts whether any liability in tort is a bankruptcy debt, the bankrupt is deemed to become subject to that liability by reason of an obligation incurred at the time when the cause of action accrued.

(3)   For the purposes of references in this Group of Parts to a debt or liability, it is immaterial whether the debt or liability is present or future, whether it is certain or contingent or whether its amount is fixed or liquidated, or is capable of being ascertained by fixed rules or as a matter of opinion; and references in this Group of Parts to owing a debt are to be read accordingly.

(4)   In this Group of Parts, except in so far as the context otherwise requires, "liability" means (subject to subsection (3) above) a liability to pay money or money's worth, including any liability under an enactment, any liability for breach of trust, any liability in contract, tort or bailment and any liability arising out of an obligation to make restitution.

[561]

NOTES
Sub-s (1): para (c) repealed by the Criminal Justice Act 1988, s 170(2), Sch 16, as from a day to be appointed.

383 "Creditor", "security", etc

(1) "Creditor"—
   (a) in relation to a bankrupt, means a person to whom any of the bankruptcy debts is owed (*being, in the case of an amount falling within paragraph (c) of the definition in section 382(1) of "bankruptcy debt", the person in respect of whom that amount is specified in the criminal bankruptcy order in question*), and
   (b) in relation to an individual to whom a bankruptcy petition relates, means a person who would be a creditor in the bankruptcy if a bankruptcy order were made on that petition.

(2) Subject to the next two subsections and any provision of the rules requiring a creditor to give up his security for the purposes of proving a debt, a debt is secured for the purposes of this Group of Parts to the extent that the person to whom the debt is owed holds any security for the debt (whether a mortgage, charge, lien or other security) over any property of the person by whom the debt is owed.

(3) Where a statement such as is mentioned in section 269(1)(a) in Chapter I of Part IX has been made by a secured creditor for the purposes of any bankruptcy petition and a bankruptcy order is subsequently made on that petition, the creditor is deemed for the purposes of the Parts in this Group to have given up the security specified in the statement.

(4) In subsection (2) the reference to a security does not include a lien on books, papers or other records, except to the extent that they consist of documents which give a title to property and are held as such.

[562]

NOTES

Sub-s (1): words in italics in para (a) repealed by the Criminal Justice Act 1988, s 170(2), Sch 16, as from a day to be appointed.

384 "Prescribed" and "the rules"

(1) Subject to the next subsection [and sections 342C(7) and 342F(9) in Chapter V of Part IX], "prescribed" means prescribed by the rules; and "the rules" means rules made under section 412 in Part XV.

(2) References in this Group of Parts to the amount prescribed for the purposes of any of the following provisions—
   section 273;
   [section 313A;]
   section 346(3);
   section 354(1) and (2);
   section 358;
   section 360(1);
   section 361(2); and
   section 364(2)(d),
and references in those provisions to the prescribed amount are to be read in accordance with section 418 in Part XV and orders made under that section.

[563]

NOTES

Sub-s (1): words in square brackets inserted by the Welfare Reform and Pensions Act 1999, s 84(1), Sch 12, Pt II, paras 70, 72.
Sub-s (2): words in square brackets inserted by the Enterprise Act 2002, s 261(5).

385 Miscellaneous definitions

(1) The following definitions have effect—
   "the court", in relation to any matter, means the court to which, in accordance with section 373 in Part X and the rules, proceedings with respect to that matter are allocated or transferred;
   "creditor's petition" means a bankruptcy petition under section 264(1)(a);
   "criminal bankruptcy order" means an order under section 39(1) of the Powers of Criminal Courts Act 1973;
   "debt" is to be construed in accordance with section 382(3);

"the debtor"—

    (a)   in relation to a proposal for the purposes of Part VIII, means the individual making or intending to make that proposal, and

    (b)   in relation to a bankruptcy petition, means the individual to whom the petition relates;

"debtor's petition" means a bankruptcy petition presented by the debtor himself under section 264(1)(b);

"dwelling house" includes any building or part of a building which is occupied as a dwelling and any yard, garden, garage or outhouse belonging to the dwelling house and occupied with it;

"estate", in relation to a bankrupt is to be construed in accordance with section 283 in Chapter II of Part IX;

"family", in relation to a bankrupt, means the persons (if any) who are living with him and are dependent on him;

["insolvency administration order" means an order for the administration in bankruptcy of the insolvent estate of a deceased debtor (being an individual at the date of his death);

"insolvency administration petition" means a petition for an insolvency administration order;

"the Rules" means the Insolvency Rules 1986.]

"secured" and related expressions are to be construed in accordance with section 383; and

"the trustee", in relation to a bankruptcy and the bankrupt, means the trustee of the bankrupt's estate.

(2)   References in this Group of Parts to a person's affairs include his business, if any.

[564]

NOTES

Definition "criminal bankruptcy order" repealed by the Criminal Justice Act 1988, s 170(2), Sch 16, as from a day to be appointed; definitions "insolvency administration order", "insolvency administration petition" and "the Rules" inserted by the Administration of Insolvent Estates of Deceased Persons Order 1986, SI 1986/1999, art 6.

THE THIRD GROUP OF PARTS

MISCELLANEOUS MATTERS BEARING ON BOTH COMPANY AND INDIVIDUAL
INSOLVENCY; GENERAL INTERPRETATION; FINAL PROVISIONS

PART XII

PREFERENTIAL DEBTS IN COMPANY AND INDIVIDUAL INSOLVENCY

NOTES

Building Societies: as to the application, with modifications, of this Part to the winding up of building societies, see the Building Societies Act 1986, s 90, Sch 15, Pts I, II.

Friendly Societies: as to the application, with modifications, of this Part to the winding up of incorporated friendly societies by virtue of the Friendly Societies Act 1992, s 21(1) or 22(2), see s 23 of, and Sch 10 to, that Act.

386 Categories of preferential debts

(1)   A reference in this Act to the preferential debts of a company or an individual is to the debts listed in Schedule 6 to this Act [(contributions to occupational pension schemes; remuneration, &c of employees; levies on coal and steel production)]; and references to preferential creditors are to be read accordingly.

(2)   In that Schedule "the debtor" means the company or the individual concerned.

(3)   Schedule 6 is to be read with [Schedule 4 to the Pension Schemes Act 1993] (occupational pension scheme contributions).

[565]

NOTES

Sub-s (1): words in square brackets substituted by the Enterprise Act 2002, s 251(3), subject to transitional provisions in relation to the abolition of preferential status for Crown debts in cases which were started before 15 September 2003 (see the Enterprise Act 2002 (Commencement No 4 and Transitional Provisions and Savings) Order 2003, SI 2003/2093, art 4).

Sub-s (3): words in square brackets substituted by the Pension Schemes Act 1993, s 190, Sch 8, para 18.

387 "The relevant date"

(1) This section explains references in Schedule 6 to the relevant date (being the date which determines the existence and amount of a preferential debt).

(2) For the purposes of section 4 in Part I (meetings to consider company voluntary arrangement), the relevant date in relation to a company which is not being wound up is—

> [(a) if the company is in administration, the date on which it entered administration, and

> (b) if the company is not in administration, the date on which the voluntary arrangement takes effect.]

[(2A) For the purposes of paragraph 31 of Schedule A1 (meetings to consider company voluntary arrangement where a moratorium under section 1A is in force), the relevant date in relation to a company is the date of filing.]

(3) In relation to a company which is being wound up, the following applies—

> (a) if the winding up is by the court, and the winding-up order was made immediately upon the discharge of an administration order, the relevant date is [the date on which the company entered administration];

> [(aa) if the winding up is by the court and the winding-up order was made following conversion of administration into winding up by virtue of Article 37 of the EC Regulation, the relevant date is [the date on which the company entered administration];

> (ab) if the company is deemed to have passed a resolution for voluntary winding up by virtue of an order following conversion of administration into winding up under Article 37 of the EC Regulation, the relevant date is [the date on which the company entered administration];]

> (b) if the case does not fall within paragraph (a)[, (aa) or (ab)] and the company—
> > (i) is being wound up by the court, and
> > (ii) had not commenced to be wound up voluntarily before the date of the making of the winding-up order,
>
> the relevant date is the date of the appointment (or first appointment) of a provisional liquidator or, if no such appointment has been made, the date of the winding-up order;

> [(ba) if the case does not fall within paragraph (a), (aa), (ab) or (b) and the company is being wound up following administration pursuant to paragraph 83 of Schedule B1, the relevant date is the date on which the company entered administration;]

> (c) if the case does not fall within either [paragraph (a), (aa), (ab), (b) or (ba)], the relevant date is the date of the passing of the resolution for the winding up of the company.

[(3A) In relation to a company which is in administration (and to which no other provision of this section applies) the relevant date is the date on which the company enters administration.]

(4) In relation to a company in receivership (where section 40 or, as the case may be, section 59 applies), the relevant date is—

> (a) in England and Wales, the date of the appointment of the receiver by debenture-holders, and

> (b) in Scotland, the date of the appointment of the receiver under section 53(6) or (as the case may be) 54(5).

(5) For the purposes of section 258 in Part VIII (individual voluntary arrangements), the relevant date is, in relation to a debtor who is not an undischarged bankrupt—

> [(a) where an interim order has been made under section 252 with respect to his proposal, the date of that order, and

> (b) in any other case, the date on which the voluntary arrangement takes effect.]

(6) In relation to a bankrupt, the following applies—

(a)   where at the time the bankruptcy order was made there was an interim receiver appointed under section 286, the relevant date is the date on which the interim receiver was first appointed after the presentation of the bankruptcy petition;

(b)   otherwise, the relevant date is the date of the making of the bankruptcy order.

[566]

NOTES

Sub-s (2): paras (a), (b) substituted by the Enterprise Act 2002, s 248(3), Sch 17, paras 9, 34(1), (2), subject to savings and transitional provisions (i) in a case where a petition for an administration order has been presented before 15 September 2003 (see the Enterprise Act 2002 (Commencement No 4 and Transitional Provisions and Savings) Order 2003, SI 2003/2093, art 3), and (ii) in relation to special administration regimes (see s 249 of the 2002 Act).

Sub-s (2A): inserted by the Insolvency Act 2000, s 1, Sch 1, paras 1, 9.

Sub-s (3): paras (aa), (ab) and words in square brackets in para (b) inserted by the Insolvency Act 1986 (Amendment) (No 2) Regulations 2002, SI 2002/1240, regs 3, 16; words in square brackets in paras (a), (aa), (ab), (c) substituted and para (ba) inserted by the Enterprise Act 2002, s 248(3), Sch 17, paras 9, 34(1), (3), subject to savings as noted to sub-s (2) above.

Sub-s (3A): inserted by the Enterprise Act 2002, s 248(3), Sch 17, paras 9, 34(1), (4), subject to savings as noted to sub-s (2) above.

Sub-s (5): words in square brackets substituted by the Insolvency Act 2000, s 3, Sch 3, paras 1, 15, subject to transitional provisions in SI 2002/2711, art 4.

388–434   (*Ss 388–401, 403, 404, 406–434 outside the scope of this work; s 402 repealed by the Criminal Justice Act 1988, s 170(2), Sch 16, as from a day to be appointed; s 405 repealed by the Enterprise Act 2002, ss 272(1), 278(2), Sch 26.*)

PART XVIII
INTERPRETATION

435   Meaning of "associate"

(1)   For the purposes of this Act any question whether a person is an associate of another person is to be determined in accordance with the following provisions of this section (any provision that a person is an associate of another person being taken to mean that they are associates of each other).

[(2)   A person is an associate of an individual if that person is—
(a)   the individual's husband or wife or civil partner, or
(b)   a relative of—
(i)   the individual, or
(ii)   the individual's husband or wife or civil partner, or
(c)   the husband or wife or civil partner of a relative of—
(i)   the individual, or
(ii)   the individual's husband or wife or civil partner.]

(3)   A person is an associate of any person with whom he is in partnership, and of the husband or wife [or civil partner] or a relative of any individual with whom he is in partnership; and a Scottish firm is an associate of any person who is a member of the firm.

(4)   A person is an associate of any person whom he employs or by whom he is employed.

(5)   A person in his capacity as trustee of a trust other than—
(a)   a trust arising under any of the second Group of Parts or the Bankruptcy (Scotland) Act 1985, or
(b)   a pension scheme or an employees' share scheme (within the meaning of the Companies Act),
is an associate of another person if the beneficiaries of the trust include, or the terms of the trust confer a power that may be exercised for the benefit of, that other person or an associate of that other person.

(6)   A company is an associate of another company—
(a)   if the same person has control of both, or a person has control of one and persons who are his associates, or he and persons who are his associates, have control of the other, or
(b)   if a group of two or more persons has control of each company, and the groups

either consist of the same persons or could be regarded as consisting of the same persons by treating (in one or more cases) a member of either group as replaced by a person of whom he is an associate.

(7)   A company is an associate of another person if that person has control of it or if that person and persons who are his associates together have control of it.

(8)   For the purposes of this section a person is a relative of an individual if he is that individual's brother, sister, uncle, aunt, nephew, niece, lineal ancestor or lineal descendant, treating—

(a)   any relationship of the half blood as a relationship of the whole blood and the stepchild or adopted child of any person as his child, and

(b)   an illegitimate child as the legitimate child of his mother and reputed father;

and references in this section to a husband or wife include a former husband or wife and a reputed husband or wife [and references to a civil partner include a former civil partner [and a reputed civil partner]].

(9)   For the purposes of this section any director or other officer of a company is to be treated as employed by that company.

(10)   For the purposes of this section a person is to be taken as having control of a company if—

(a)   the directors of the company or of another company which has control of it (or any of them) are accustomed to act in accordance with his directions or instructions, or

(b)   he is entitled to exercise, or control the exercise of, one third or more of the voting power at any general meeting of the company or of another company which has control of it;

and where two or more persons together satisfy either of the above conditions, they are to be taken as having control of the company.

(11)   In this section "company" includes any body corporate (whether incorporated in Great Britain or elsewhere); and references to directors and other officers of a company and to voting power at any general meeting of a company have effect with any necessary modifications.

[567]

NOTES

Sub-s (2): substituted by the Civil Partnership Act 2004, s 261(1), Sch 27, para 122(1), (2).

Sub-s (3): words in square brackets inserted by the Civil Partnership Act 2004, s 261(1), Sch 27, para 122(1), (3).

Sub-s (8): words in first (outer) pair of square brackets added by the Civil Partnership Act 2004, s 261(1), Sch 27, para 122(1), (4); words in second (inner) pair of square brackets added by the Civil Partnership Act 2004 (Overseas Relationships and Consequential, etc Amendments) Order 2005, SI 2005/3129, art 4(4), Sch 4, para 8.

436   Expressions used generally

In this Act, except in so far as the context otherwise requires (and subject to Parts VII and XI)—

"the appointed day" means the day on which this Act comes into force under section 443;

"associate" has the meaning given by section 435;

"business" includes a trade or profession;

"the Companies Act" means the Companies Act 1985;

"conditional sale agreement" and "hire-purchase agreement" have the same meanings as in the Consumer Credit Act 1974;

["the EC Regulation" means Council Regulation (EC) No 1346/2000;]

["EEA State" means a state that is a Contracting Party to the Agreement on the European Economic Area signed at Oporto on 2nd May 1992 as adjusted by the Protocol signed at Brussels on 17th March 1993;]

"modifications" includes additions, alterations and omissions and cognate expressions shall be construed accordingly;

"property" includes money, goods, things in action, land and every description of property wherever situated and also obligations and every description of interest, whether present or future or vested or contingent, arising out of, or incidental to, property;

"records" includes computer records and other non-documentary records;

"subordinate legislation" has the same meaning as in the Interpretation Act 1978; and "transaction" includes a gift, agreement or arrangement, and references to entering into a transaction shall be construed accordingly.

[568]

PART I
STATUTES

NOTES

Definition "the EC Regulation" inserted by the Insolvency Act 1986 (Amendment) Regulations 2002, SI 2002/1037, regs 2, 4; definition "EEA State" inserted by the Insolvency Act 1986 (Amendment) Regulations 2005, SI 2005/879, reg 2(1), (3), for effect see reg 3 thereof.

436A   (*Outside the scope of this work.*)

PART XIX
FINAL PROVISIONS

437–442   (*Ss 437–439, 442 outside the scope of this work; ss 440, 441 apply only to Scotland and Northern Ireland respectively.*)

443   Commencement

This Act comes into force on the day appointed under section 236(2) of the Insolvency Act 1985 for the coming into force of Part III of that Act (individual insolvency and bankruptcy), immediately after that Part of that Act comes into force for England and Wales.

[569]

444   Citation

This Act may be cited as the Insolvency Act 1986.

[570]

SCHEDULES

(*Sch A1 outside the scope of this work.*)

[SCHEDULE B1
ADMINISTRATION

Section 8

1.–39.   …

EFFECT OF ADMINISTRATION

Dismissal of pending winding-up petition

40.—(1)   A petition for the winding up of a company—
  (a)   shall be dismissed on the making of an administration order in respect of the company, and
  (b)   shall be suspended while the company is in administration following an appointment under paragraph 14.

  (2)   Sub-paragraph (1)(b) does not apply to a petition presented under—
  (a)   section 124A (public interest), or
  [(aa)   section 124B (Ses),]
  (b)   section 367 of the Financial Services and Markets Act 2000 (c 8) (petition by Financial Services Authority).

  (3)   Where an administrator becomes aware that a petition was presented under a provision referred to in sub-paragraph (2) before his appointment, he shall apply to the court for directions under paragraph 63.

Dismissal of administrative or other receiver

41.—(1)   When an administration order takes effect in respect of a company any administrative receiver of the company shall vacate office.

(2)   Where a company is in administration, any receiver of part of the company's property shall vacate office if the administrator requires him to.

(3)   Where an administrative receiver or receiver vacates office under sub-paragraph (1) or (2)—

    (a)   his remuneration shall be charged on and paid out of any property of the company which was in his custody or under his control immediately before he vacated office, and

    (b)   he need not take any further steps under section 40 or 59.

(4)   In the application of sub-paragraph (3)(a)—

    (a)   "remuneration" includes expenses properly incurred and any indemnity to which the administrative receiver or receiver is entitled out of the assets of the company,

    (b)   the charge imposed takes priority over security held by the person by whom or on whose behalf the administrative receiver or receiver was appointed, and

    (c)   the provision for payment is subject to paragraph 43.

Moratorium on insolvency proceedings

42.—(1)   This paragraph applies to a company in administration.

(2)   No resolution may be passed for the winding up of the company.

(3)   No order may be made for the winding up of the company.

(4)   Sub-paragraph (3) does not apply to an order made on a petition presented under—

    (a)   section 124A (public interest), or

    [(aa)   section 124B (Ses),]

    (b)   section 367 of the Financial Services and Markets Act 2000 (c 8) (petition by Financial Services Authority).

(5)   If a petition presented under a provision referred to in sub-paragraph (4) comes to the attention of the administrator, he shall apply to the court for directions under paragraph 63.

Moratorium on other legal process

43.—(1)   This paragraph applies to a company in administration.

(2)   No step may be taken to enforce security over the company's property except—

    (a)   with the consent of the administrator, or

    (b)   with the permission of the court.

(3)   No step may be taken to repossess goods in the company's possession under a hire-purchase agreement except—

    (a)   with the consent of the administrator, or

    (b)   with the permission of the court.

(4)   A landlord may not exercise a right of forfeiture by peaceable re-entry in relation to premises let to the company except—

    (a)   with the consent of the administrator, or

    (b)   with the permission of the court.

(5)   In Scotland, a landlord may not exercise a right of irritancy in relation to premises let to the company except—

    (a)   with the consent of the administrator, or

    (b)   with the permission of the court.

(6)   No legal process (including legal proceedings, execution, distress and diligence) may be instituted or continued against the company or property of the company except—

    (a)   with the consent of the administrator, or

    (b)   with the permission of the court.

(7)   Where the court gives permission for a transaction under this paragraph it may impose a condition on or a requirement in connection with the transaction.

(8)   In this paragraph "landlord" includes a person to whom rent is payable.

Interim moratorium

44.—(1)   This paragraph applies where an administration application in respect of a company has been made and—
  (a)   the application has not yet been granted or dismissed, or
  (b)   the application has been granted but the administration order has not yet taken effect.

(2)   This paragraph also applies from the time when a copy of notice of intention to appoint an administrator under paragraph 14 is filed with the court until—
  (a)   the appointment of the administrator takes effect, or
  (b)   the period of five business days beginning with the date of filing expires without an administrator having been appointed.

(3)   Sub-paragraph (2) has effect in relation to a notice of intention to appoint only if it is in the prescribed form.

(4)   This paragraph also applies from the time when a copy of notice of intention to appoint an administrator is filed with the court under paragraph 27(1) until—
  (a)   the appointment of the administrator takes effect, or
  (b)   the period specified in paragraph 28(2) expires without an administrator having been appointed.

(5)   The provisions of paragraphs 42 and 43 shall apply (ignoring any reference to the consent of the administrator).

(6)   If there is an administrative receiver of the company when the administration application is made, the provisions of paragraphs 42 and 43 shall not begin to apply by virtue of this paragraph until the person by or on behalf of whom the receiver was appointed consents to the making of the administration order.

(7)   This paragraph does not prevent or require the permission of the court for—
  (a)   the presentation of a petition for the winding up of the company under a provision mentioned in paragraph 42(4),
  (b)   the appointment of an administrator under paragraph 14,
  (c)   the appointment of an administrative receiver of the company, or
  (d)   the carrying out by an administrative receiver (whenever appointed) of his functions.

Publicity

45.—(1)   While a company is in administration every business document issued by or on behalf of the company or the administrator must state—
  (a)   the name of the administrator, and
  (b)   that the affairs, business and property of the company are being managed by him.

(2)   Any of the following commits an offence if without reasonable excuse he authorises or permits a contravention of sub-paragraph (1)—
  (a)   the administrator,
  (b)   an officer of the company, and
  (c)   the company.

(3)   In sub-paragraph (1) "business document" means—
  (a)   an invoice,
  (b)   an order for goods or services, and
  (c)   a business letter.

46.–116.   ...]

[571]

NOTES

Commencement: 15 September 2003.

Inserted by the Enterprise Act 2002, s 248(2), Sch 16, subject to savings and transitional provisions in s 249 of the 2002 Act, and the Enterprise Act 2002 (Commencement No 4 and Transitional Provisions and Savings) Order 2003, SI 2003/2093, art 3.

Paras 1–39: outside the scope of this work.

Para 40: sub-para (2)(aa) inserted by the European Public Limited-Liability Company Regulations 2004, SI 2004/2326, reg 73(4)(c).

Para 42: sub-para (4)(aa) inserted by SI 2004/2326, reg 73(4)(c).
Paras 46–116: outside the scope of this work.

(Schs 1–5 outside the scope of this work.)

SCHEDULE 6
THE CATEGORIES OF PREFERENTIAL DEBTS
Section 386

1.–7.   ...

Category 4: Contributions to occupational pension schemes, etc

8.   Any sum which is owed by the debtor and is a sum to which [Schedule 4 to the Pension Schemes Act 1993] applies (contributions to occupational pension schemes and state scheme premiums).

Category 5: Remuneration, etc, of employees

9.   So much of any amount which—
   (a)   is owed by the debtor to a person who is or has been an employee of the debtor, and
   (b)   is payable by way of remuneration in respect of the whole or any part of the period of 4 months next before the relevant date,
as does not exceed so much as may be prescribed by order made by the Secretary of State.

10.   An amount owed by way of accrued holiday remuneration, in respect of any period of employment before the relevant date, to a person whose employment by the debtor has been terminated, whether before, on or after that date.

11.   So much of any sum owed in respect of money advanced for the purpose as has been applied for the payment of a debt which, if it had not been paid, would have been a debt falling within paragraph 9 or 10.

12.   So much of any amount which—
   (a)   is ordered (whether before or after the relevant date) to be paid by the debtor under the Reserve Forces (Safeguard of Employment) Act 1985, and
   (b)   is so ordered in respect of a default made by the debtor before that date in the discharge of his obligations under that Act,
as does no exceed such amount as may be prescribed by order made by the Secretary of State.

Interpretation for Category 5

13.—(1)   For the purposes of paragraphs 9 to 12, a sum is payable by the debtor to a person by way of remuneration in respect of any period if—
   (a)   it is paid as wages or salary (whether payable for time or for piece work or earned wholly or partly by way of commission) in respect of services rendered to the debtor in that period, or
   (b)   it is an amount falling within the following sub-paragraph and is payable by the debtor in respect of that period.

   [(2)   An amount falls within this sub-paragraph if it is—
   (a)   a guarantee payment under Part III of the Employment Rights Act 1996 (employee without work to do);
   (b)   any payment for time off under section 53 (time off to look for work or arrange training) or section 56 (time off for ante-natal care) of that Act or under section 169 of the Trade Union and Labour Relations (Consolidation) Act 1992 (time off for carrying out trade union duties etc);
   (c)   remuneration on suspension on medical grounds, or on maternity grounds, under Part VII of the Employment Rights Act 1996; or

(d)   remuneration under a protective award under section 189 of the Trade Union and Labour Relations (Consolidation) Act 1992 (redundancy dismissal with compensation).]

14.—(1)   This paragraph relates to a case in which a person's employment has been terminated by or in consequence of his employer going into liquidation or being adjudged bankrupt or (his employer being a company not in liquidation) by or in consequence of—

(a)   a receiver being appointed as mentioned in section 40 of this Act (debenture-holders secured by floating charge), or

(b)   the appointment of a receiver under section 53(6) or 54(5) of this Act (Scottish company with property subject to floating charge), or

(c)   the taking of possession by debenture-holders (so secured), as mentioned in section 196 of the Companies Act.

(2)   For the purposes of paragraphs 9 to 12, holiday remuneration is deemed to have accrued to that person in respect of any period of employment if, by virtue of his contract of employment or of any enactment that remuneration would have accrued in respect of that period if his employment had continued until he became entitled to be allowed the holiday.

(3)   The reference in sub-paragraph (2) to any enactment includes an order or direction made under an enactment.

15.   Without prejudice to paragraphs 13 and 14—

(a)   any remuneration payable by the debtor to a person in respect of a period of holiday or of absence from work through sickness or other good cause is deemed to be wages or (as the case may be) salary in respect of services rendered to the debtor in that period, and

(b)   references here and in those paragraphs to remuneration in respect of a period of holiday include any sums which, if they had been paid, would have been treated for the purposes of the enactments to social security as earnings in respect of that period.

[Category 6: Levies on coal and steel production

15A.   Any sums due at the relevant date from the debtor in respect of—

(a)   the levies on the production of coal and steel referred to in Articles 49 and 50 of the ECSC Treaty, or

(b)   any surcharge for delay provided for in Article 50(3) of that Treaty and Article 6 of Decision 3/52 of the High Authority of the Coal and Steel Community.]

Orders

16.   An order under paragraph 9 or 12—

(a)   may contain such transitional provisions as may appear to the Secretary of State necessary or expedient;

(b)   shall be made by statutory instrument subject to annulment in pursuance of a resolution of either House of Parliament.

[572]

NOTES

Paras 1–7: repealed by the Enterprise Act 2002, ss 251(1), 278(2), Sch 26, subject to transitional provisions in relation to the abolition of preferential status for Crown debts in cases which were started before 15 September 2003 (see the Enterprise Act 2002 (Commencement No 4 and Transitional Provisions and Savings) Order 2003, SI 2003/2093, art 4).

Para 8: words in square brackets substituted by the Pension Schemes Act 1993, s 190, Sch 8, para 18.
Para 13: sub-para (2) substituted by the Employment Rights Act 1996, s 240, Sch 1, para 29.
Para 15A: inserted by the Insolvency (ECSC Levy Debts) Regulations 1987, SI 1987/2093, reg 2.
Order: the Insolvency Proceedings (Monetary Limits) Order 1986, SI 1986/1996.

(Schs 7–14 outside the scope of this work.)

AGRICULTURE ACT 1986

(1986 c 49)

An Act to make further provision relating to agriculture and agricultural and other food products, horticulture and the countryside; and for connected matters

[25 July 1986]

1–12 *(Outside the scope of this work.)*

Compensation to tenants for milk quotas

13 Compensation to outgoing tenants for milk quota

Schedule 1 to this Act shall have effect in connection with the payment to certain agricultural tenants on the termination of their tenancies of compensation in respect of milk quota (within the meaning of that Schedule).

[573]

NOTES

As to the disapplication of this section to a farm business tenancy, see the Agricultural Tenancies Act 1995, s 16(3) at **[651]**.

---

14 *(Applies to Scotland only.)*

15 Rent arbitrations: milk quotas

(1) Where there is a reference under section 12 of the Agricultural Holdings Act 1986 (arbitration of rent) in respect of land which comprises or is part of a holding in relation to which quota is registered under the Dairy Produce Quotas Regulations 1986 which was transferred to the tenant by virtue of a transaction the cost of which was borne wholly or partly by him, the arbitrator shall (subject to any agreement between the landlord and tenant to the contrary) disregard—

    (a) in a case where the land comprises the holding, any increase in the rental value of the land which is due to that quota (or, as the case may be, the corresponding part of that quota); or

    (b) in a case where the land is part of the holding, any increase in that value which is due to so much of that quota (or part) as would fall to be apportioned to the land under those Regulations on a change of occupation of the land.

(2) In determining for the purposes of this section whether quota was transferred to a tenant by virtue of a transaction the cost of which was borne wholly or partly by him—

    (a) any payment made by the tenant in consideration for the grant or assignment to him of the tenancy or any previous tenancy of any land comprised in the holding, shall be disregarded;

    (b) any person who would be treated under paragraph 2, 3 or 4 of Schedule 1 to this Act as having had quota transferred to him or having paid the whole or part of the cost of any transaction for the purposes of a claim under that Schedule shall be so treated for the purposes of this section; and

    (c) any person who would be so treated under paragraph 4 of that Schedule if a sub-tenancy to which his tenancy is subject had terminated, shall be so treated for the purposes of this section.

(3) In this section—

    "quota" and "holding" have the same meanings as in the Dairy Produce Quotas Regulations 1986;

    "tenant" and "tenancy" have the same meanings as in the Agricultural Holdings Act 1986.

(4) Section 95 of that Act (Crown land) applies to this section as it applies to the provisions of that Act.

[574]

16–22 *(Ss 16, 19 apply to Scotland only; ss 17, 18, 20, 22 outside the scope of this work; s 21 repealed by the Rights of Way Act 1990, s 6.)*

Supplemental

23, 23A   (*Outside the scope of this work.*)

24   Short title, commencement, consequential amendments, repeals and extent

(1)   This Act may be cited as the Agriculture Act 1986.

(2)   Sections 8 ... above and the repeals consequential on sections 8 ... above shall come into force on such date as the Ministers acting jointly may by order made by statutory instrument appoint ...; and in this subsection "the Ministers" means the Ministers responsible for agriculture in the parts of the United Kingdom to which the provision in question extends.

(3)   An order under subsection (2) above may appoint different dates for the coming into force of different provisions.

(4)   The provisions mentioned in Schedule 3 to this Act shall have effect subject to the amendments there specified (being amendments consequential on the provisions of this Act).

(5)   The enactments mentioned in Schedule 4 to this Act (which include some spent provisions) are hereby repealed to the extent specified in the third column of that Schedule.

(6)   Sections 1, 13, 15, 18(7) ... above and Schedule 1 to this Act do not extend to Scotland.

(7)   The provisions of this Act do not extend to Northern Ireland except for sections 4 to 6, 8, ... 11, 18(13) and 22, this section and the provisions of Schedules 3 and 4 which affect enactments extending there.

[575]

NOTES

Sub-s (2): words omitted repealed by the Statute Law (Repeals) Act 2004.
Sub-s (6): words omitted repealed by the Statute Law (Repeals) Act 2004.
Sub-s (7): references omitted repealed by the Statute Law (Repeals) Act 2004.
Transfer of functions: Functions of the Minister, so far as exercisable in relation to Wales, are transferred to the National Assembly for Wales, by the National Assembly for Wales (Transfer of Functions) Order 1999, SI 1999/672, art 2, Sch 1.
Orders: the Agriculture Act 1986 (Commencement No 1) Order 1986, SI 1986/1484; the Agriculture Act 1986 (Commencement No 2) (Scotland) Order 1986, SI 1986/1485; the Agriculture Act 1986 (Commencement No 3) Order 1986, SI 1986/1596; the Agriculture Act 1986 (Commencement No 4) Order 1986, SI 1986/2301; the Agriculture Act 1986 (Commencement No 5) Order 1991, SI 1991/2635; the Agriculture Act 1986 (Commencement No 6) Order 1998, SI 1998/879.

SCHEDULE 1
TENANTS' COMPENSATION FOR MILK QUOTA

Section 13

PART I
RIGHT TO COMPENSATION

Tenants' rights to compensation

1.—(1)   Subject to the following provisions of this Schedule, where on the termination of the tenancy of any land the tenant has milk quota registered as his in relation to a holding consisting of or including the land, the tenant shall be entitled, on quitting the land, to obtain from his landlord a payment—

   (a)   if the tenant had milk quota allocated to him in relation to land comprised in the holding ("allocated quota"), in respect of so much of the relevant quota as consists of allocated quota; and

   (b)   if the tenant had milk quota allocated to him as aforesaid or was in occupation of the land as a tenant on 2nd April 1984 (whether or not under the tenancy which is terminating), in respect of so much of the relevant quota as consists of transferred quota transferred to him by virtue of a transaction the cost of which was borne wholly or partly by him.

(2)   In sub-paragraph (1) above—
   "the relevant quota" means—

(a)   in a case where the holding mentioned in sub-paragraph (1) above consists only of the land subject to the tenancy, the milk quota registered in relation to the holding; and

(b)   otherwise, such part of that milk quota as falls to be apportioned to that land on the termination of the tenancy;

"transferred quota" means milk quota transferred to the tenant by virtue of the transfer to him of the whole or part of a holding.

(3)   A tenant shall not be entitled to more than one payment under this paragraph in respect of the same land.

Succession on death or retirement of tenant

2.—(1)   This paragraph applies where on the termination of the tenancy of any land after 2nd April 1984 a new tenancy of the land or part of the land has been granted to a different tenant ("the new tenant") and that tenancy—

(a)   was obtained by virtue of a direction under section 39 or 53 of the Agricultural Holdings Act 1986 (direction for grant of tenancy to successor on death or retirement of previous tenant);

(b)   was granted (following a direction under section 39 of that Act) in circumstances within section 45(6) of that Act (new tenancy granted by agreement to persons entitled to tenancy under direction); or

(c)   is such a tenancy as is mentioned in section 37(1)(b) or (2) of that Act (tenancy granted by agreement to close relative).

(2)   Where this paragraph applies—

(a)   any milk quota allocated or transferred to the former tenant (or treated as having been allocated or transferred to him) in respect of the land which is subject to the new tenancy shall be treated as if it had instead been allocated or transferred to the new tenant; and

(b)   in a case where milk quota is treated under paragraph (a) above as having been transferred to the new tenant, he shall be treated for the purposes of any claim in respect of that quota—

    (i)   as if he had paid so much of the cost of the transaction by virtue of which the milk quota was transferred as the former tenant bore (or is treated as having borne); and

    (ii)   in a case where the former tenant was in occupation of the land on 2nd April 1984 (or is treated as having been in occupation of the land on that date), as if he had been in occupation of it on that date.

(3)   Sub-paragraph (1) above applies in relation to the grant of a new tenancy before the date on which the Agricultural Holdings Act 1986 comes into force as if the references in that sub-paragraph to sections 39, 53 and 45(6) of that Act were references to section 20 of the Agriculture (Miscellaneous Provisions) Act 1976, paragraph 5 of Schedule 2 to the Agricultural Holdings Act 1984 and section 23(6) of the said Act of 1976 respectively.

Assignments

3.   Where the tenancy of any land has been assigned after 2nd April 1984 (whether by deed or by operation of law)—

(a)   any milk quota allocated or transferred to the assignor (or treated as having been allocated or transferred to him) in respect of the land shall be treated as if it had instead been allocated or transferred to the assignee; and

(b)   in a case where milk quota is treated under paragraph (a) above as having been transferred to the assignee, he shall be treated for the purposes of any claim in respect of that quota—

    (i)   as if he had paid so much of the cost of the transaction by virtue of which the milk quota was transferred as the assignor bore (or is treated as having borne); and

    (ii)   in a case where the assignor was in occupation of the land on 2nd April 1984 (or is treated as having been in occupation of the land on that date), as if he had been in occupation of it on that date;

and accordingly the assignor shall not be entitled to a payment under paragraph 1 above in respect of that land.

Sub-tenancies

4.   Where the sub-tenancy of any land terminates after 2nd April 1984 then, for the purposes of determining the sub-landlord's entitlement under paragraph 1 above—

    (a)   any milk quota allocated or transferred to the sub-tenant (or treated as having been allocated or transferred to him) in respect of the land shall be treated as if it had instead been allocated or transferred to the sub-landlord;

    (b)   in a case where milk quota is treated under paragraph (a) above as having been transferred to the sub-landlord, he shall be treated for the purposes of any claim in respect of that quota—

        (i)   as if he had paid so much of the cost of the transaction by virtue of which the milk quota was transferred as the sub-tenant bore (or is treated as having borne); and

        (ii)   in a case where the sub-tenant was in occupation of the land on 2nd April 1984 (or is treated as having been in occupation of the land on that date), as if he had been in occupation of it on that date;

    (c)   if the sub-landlord does not occupy the land after the sub-tenancy has ended and the sub-tenant has quitted the land, the sub-landlord shall be taken to have quitted the land when the sub-tenant quitted it.

[576]

NOTES

As to the disapplication of this Schedule to a farm business tenancy, see the Agricultural Tenancies Act 1995, s 16(3) at **[651]**.

PART II
AMOUNT OF COMPENSATION PAYABLE

Calculation of payment

5.—(1)   The amount of the payment to which the tenant of any land is entitled under paragraph 1 above on the termination of his tenancy shall be determined in accordance with the following provisions of this paragraph.

(2)   The amount of the payment to which the tenant is entitled under paragraph 1 above in respect of allocated quota shall be an amount equal—

    (a)   in a case where the allocated quota exceeds the standard quota for the land, to the value of the sum of—

        (i)   the tenant's fraction of the standard quota, and

        (ii)   the amount of the excess;

    (b)   in a case where the allocated quota is equal to the standard quota, to the value of the tenant's fraction of the allocated quota; and

    (c)   in a case where the allocated quota is less than the standard quota, to the value of such proportion of the tenant's fraction of the allocated quota as the allocated quota bears to the standard quota.

(3)   The amount of the payment the tenant is entitled to under paragraph 1 above in respect of transferred quota shall be an amount equal—

    (a)   in a case where the tenant bore the whole of the cost of the transaction by virtue of which the transferred quota was transferred to him, to the value of the transferred quota; and

    (b)   in a case where the tenant bore only part of that cost, to the value of the corresponding part of the transferred quota.

"Standard quota"

6.—(1)   Subject to the following provisions of this paragraph the standard quota for any land for the purposes of this Schedule shall be calculated by multiplying the relevant number of hectares by the prescribed quota per hectare; and for the purposes of this paragraph—

    (a)   "the relevant number of hectares" means the average number of hectares of the land in question used during the relevant period for the feeding of dairy cows kept on the land or, if different, the average number of hectares of the land which could

341

reasonably be expected to have been so used (having regard to the number of grazing animals other than dairy cows kept on the land during that period); and
(b)   "the prescribed quota per hectare" means such number of litres as the Minister may from time to time by order prescribe for the purposes of this sub-paragraph.

(2)   Where by virtue of the quality of the land in question or climatic conditions in the area the amount of milk which could reasonably be expected to have been produced from one hectare of the land during the relevant period ("the reasonable amount") is greater or less than the prescribed average yield per hectare, then sub-paragraph (1) above shall not apply and the standard quota shall be calculated by multiplying the relevant number of hectares by such proportion of the prescribed quota per hectare as the reasonable amount bears to the prescribed average yield per hectare; and the Minister shall by order prescribe the amount of milk to be taken as the average yield per hectare for the purposes of this sub-paragraph.

(3)   Where the relevant quota of the land includes milk quota allocated in pursuance of an award of quota made by the Dairy Produce Quota Tribunal for England and Wales[, or by the Secretary of State or the National Assembly for Wales following the appeals procedure,] which has not been allocated in full, the standard quota for the land shall be reduced by the amount by which the milk quota allocated in pursuance of the award falls short of the amount awarded (or, in a case where only part of the milk quota allocated in pursuance of the award is included in the relevant quota, by the corresponding proportion of that shortfall).

[(3A)   In sub-paragraph (3) above "the appeals procedure" means—
(a)   in England, the appeals procedure established under the Common Agricultural Policy Non-IACS Support Schemes (Appeals) (England) Regulations 2004 (SI 2004/590); and
(b)   in Wales, the appeals procedure established under the Common Agricultural Policy Non-IACS Support Schemes (Appeals) (Wales) Regulations 2004 (SI 2004/685 (W73)).]

(4)   In sub-paragraph (3) above the references to milk quota allocated in pursuance of an award of quota include references to quota allocated by virtue of the amount awarded not originally having been allocated in full.

(5)   In this paragraph—
(a)   references to land used for the feeding of dairy cows kept on the land do not include land used for growing cereal crops for feeding to dairy cows in the form of loose grain; and
(b)   references to dairy cows are to cows kept for milk production (other than uncalved heifers).

(6)   An order under this paragraph may make different provision for different cases.

(7)   The power to make an order under this paragraph shall be exercisable by statutory instrument and any instrument containing such an order shall be subject to annulment in pursuance of a resolution of either House of Parliament.

"Tenant's fraction"

7.—(1)   For the purposes of this Schedule "the tenant's fraction" means the fraction of which—
(a)   the numerator is the annual rental value at the end of the relevant period of the tenant's dairy improvements and fixed equipment; and
(b)   the denominator is the sum of that value and such part of the rent payable by the tenant in respect of the relevant period as is attributable to the land used in that period for the feeding, accommodation or milking of dairy cows kept on the land.

(2)   For the purposes of sub-paragraph (1)(a) above the rental value of the tenant's dairy improvements and fixed equipment shall be taken to be the amount which would fall to be disregarded under paragraph 2(1) of Schedule 2 to the Agricultural Holdings Act 1986 on a reference made in respect of the land in question under section 12 of that Act (arbitration of rent), so far as that amount is attributable to tenant's improvements to, or tenant's fixed equipment on, land used for the feeding, accommodation or milking of dairy cows kept on the land in question.

(3)   Where—
(a)   the relevant period is less than or greater than 12 months; or
(b)   rent was only payable by the tenant in respect of part of the relevant period,

the average rent payable in respect of one month in the relevant period or, as the case may be, in that part shall be determined and the rent referred to in sub-paragraph (1)(b) above shall be taken to be the corresponding annual amount.

(4)   For the purposes of sub-paragraph (2) above "tenant's improvements" and "tenant's fixed equipment" have the same meanings as in paragraph 2 of Schedule 2 to the 1986 Act, except that—

    (a)   any allowance made or benefit given by the landlord after the end of the relevant period in consideration of the execution of improvements wholly or partly at the expense of the tenant shall be disregarded for the purposes of sub-paragraph (2)(a) of that paragraph;

    (b)   any compensation received by the tenant after the end of the relevant period in respect of any improvement or fixed equipment shall be disregarded for the purposes of sub-paragraph (3) of that paragraph; and

    (c)   where paragraph 2 above applies in respect of any land, improvements or equipment which would be regarded as tenant's improvements or equipment on the termination of the former tenant's tenancy (if he were entitled to a payment under this Schedule in respect of that land) shall be regarded as the new tenant's improvements or equipment.

"Relevant period"

8.   In this Schedule "the relevant period" means—

    (a)   the period in relation to which the allocated quota was determined; or

    (b)   where it was determined in relation to more than one period, the period in relation to which the majority was determined or, if equal amounts were determined in relation to different periods, the later of those periods.

Valuation of milk quota

9.   The value of milk quota to be taken into account for the purposes of paragraph 5 above is the value of the milk quota at the time of the termination of the tenancy in question and in determining that value at that time there shall be taken into account such evidence as is available, including evidence as to the sums being paid for interests in land—

    (a)   in cases where milk quota is registered in relation to the land; and

    (b)   in cases where no milk quota is so registered.

[577]

NOTES
   Para 6: in sub-para (3) words in square brackets inserted, and sub-para (3A) inserted, by the Dairy Produce (Miscellaneous Provisions) Regulations 2007, SI 2007/477, reg 4(1), (2).
   Disapplication: see the note to Pt I of this Schedule at **[576]**.
   Transfer of functions: Functions of the Minister, so far as exercisable in relation to Wales, are transferred to the National Assembly for Wales, by the National Assembly for Wales (Transfer of Functions) Order 1999, SI 1999/672, art 2, Sch 1.
   Orders: the Milk Quota (Calculation of Standard Quota) Order 1986, SI 1986/1530 at **[1098]**.

PART III
SUPPLEMENTAL PROVISIONS

Determination of standard quota and tenant's fraction before end of tenancy

10.—(1)   Where, on the termination of a tenancy of any land, the tenant may be entitled to a payment under paragraph 1 above, the landlord or tenant may at any time before the termination of the tenancy by notice in writing served on the other demand that the determination of the standard quota for the land or the tenant's fraction shall be referred to arbitration.

(2)   On a reference under this paragraph the arbitrator shall determine the standard quota for the land or, as the case may be, the tenant's fraction (so far as determinable at the date of the reference).

(3)   Section 84 of the Agricultural Holdings Act 1986 (arbitrations) shall apply as if the matters mentioned in this paragraph were required by that Act to be determined by arbitration under that Act.

Settlement of tenant's claim on termination of tenancy

11.—(1)   Subject to the provisions of this paragraph, any claim arising under paragraph 1 above shall be determined by arbitration under the Agricultural Holdings Act 1986 and no such claim shall be enforceable unless before the expiry of the period of two months from the termination of the tenancy the tenant serves notice in writing on his landlord of his intention to make the claim.

(2)   The landlord and tenant may within the period of eight months from the arbitration of the tenancy by agreement in writing settle the claim but where the claim has not been settled during that period it shall be determined by arbitration under the Agricultural Holdings Act 1986.

(3)   In any case where on the termination of the tenancy in question a new tenancy of the land or part of the land may be granted to a different tenant by virtue of a direction under section 39 of the Agricultural Holdings Act 1986 then, as respects any claim in respect of that land or part, references in sub-paragraphs (1) and (2) above to the termination of the tenancy shall be construed as references to the following time, namely—

   (a)   in a case where no application is made under that section within the period within which such an application may be made, the expiry of that period;
   (b)   in a case where every such application made within that period is withdrawn, the expiry of that period or the time when the last outstanding application is withdrawn (whichever is the later);
   (c)   in a case where the Agricultural Land Tribunal refuse every such application for a direction under that section, the time when the last outstanding application is refused; and
   (d)   in a case where the Tribunal give such a direction, the relevant time for the purposes of section 46 of that Act;

and no notice may be served under sub-paragraph (1) above before that time.

(4)   Where a tenant lawfully remains in occupation of part of the land subject to the tenancy after the termination of the tenancy or, in a case where sub-paragraph (3) above applies, after the time substituted for the termination of the tenancy by virtue of that sub-paragraph, the references in sub-paragraphs (1) and (2) above to the termination of the tenancy shall be construed as references to the termination of the occupation.

(5)   Section 84 of the Agricultural Holdings Act 1986 (arbitrations) shall apply as if the requirements of this paragraph were requirements of that Act, …

(6)   Where—
   (a)   before the termination of the tenancy of any land the landlord and tenant have agreed in writing the amount of the standard quota for the land or the tenant's fraction or the value of milk quota which is to be used for the purpose of calculating the payment to which the tenant will be entitled under this Schedule on the termination of the tenancy; or
   (b)   the standard quota or the tenant's fraction has been determined by arbitration in pursuance of paragraph 10 above,

the arbitrator determining the claim under this paragraph shall, subject to sub-paragraph (7) below, award payment in accordance with that agreement or determination.

(7)   Where it appears to the arbitrator that any circumstances relevant to the agreement or determination mentioned in sub-paragraph (6) above were materially different at the time of the termination of the tenancy from those at the time the agreement or determination was made, he shall disregard so much of the agreement or determination as appears to him to be affected by the change in circumstances.

Enforcement

12.   Section 85 of the Agricultural Holdings Act 1986 (enforcement) and section 86(1), (3) and (4) of that Act (power of landlord to obtain charge on holding) shall apply to any sum which becomes due to a tenant by virtue of this Schedule as they apply to the sums mentioned in those sections.

Termination of tenancy of part of tenanted land

13.   References in this Schedule to the termination of a tenancy of land include references to the resumption of possession of part of the land subject to the tenancy—
    (a)   by the landlord by virtue of section 31 or 43(2) of the Agricultural Holdings Act 1986 (notice to quit part);
    (b)   by the landlord in pursuance of a provision in the contract of tenancy; or
    (c)   by a person entitled to a severed part of the reversionary estate in the land by virtue of a notice to quit that part given to the tenant by virtue of section 140 of the Law of Property Act 1925;
and in the case mentioned in paragraph (c) above this Schedule shall apply as if the person resuming possession were the landlord of the land of which he resumes possession.

Severing of reversionary estate

14.—(1)   Where the reversionary estate in the land is for the time being vested in more than one person in several parts, the tenant shall be entitled, on quitting all the land, to require that any amount payable to him under this Schedule shall be determined as if the reversionary estate were not so severed.

(2)   Where sub-paragraph (1) above applies, the arbitrator shall, where necessary, apportion the amount awarded between the persons who for the purposes of this Schedule together constitute the landlord of the land, and any additional costs of the award caused by the apportionment shall be paid by those persons in such proportions as the arbitrator may determine.

Powers of limited owners

15.   Notwithstanding that a landlord of any land is not the owner in fee simple of the land or, in a case where his interest is an interest in a leasehold, that he is not absolutely entitled to the leasehold, he may for the purposes of this Schedule do anything which he might do if he were such an owner or, as the case may be, were so entitled.

Notices

16.—(1)   Any notice under this Schedule shall be duly served on the person on whom it is to be served if it is delivered to him, or left at his proper address, or sent to him by post in a registered letter or by the recorded delivery service.

(2)   Any such notice shall be duly served on an incorporated company or body if it is served on the secretary or clerk of the company or body.

(3)   Any such notice to be served on a landlord or tenant of any land shall, where an agent or servant is responsible for the control of the management or farming, as the case may be, of the land, be duly served if served on that agent or servant.

(4)   For the purposes of this paragraph and of section 7 of the Interpretation Act 1978 (service by post), the proper address of any person on whom any such notice is to be served shall, in the case of the secretary or clerk of an incorporated company or body, be that of the registered or principal office of the company or body, and in any other case be the last known address of the person in question.

(5)   Unless or until the tenant of any land has received—
    (a)   notice that the person who before that time was entitled to receive the rents and profits of the land ("the original landlord") has ceased to be so entitled; and
    (b)   notice of the name and address of the person who has become entitled to receive the rents and profits,
any notice served on the original landlord by the tenant shall be deemed for the purposes of this Schedule to have been served on the landlord of the land.

Crown land

17.—(1)   The provisions of this Schedule shall apply to land which belongs to Her Majesty in right of the Crown or to the Duchy of Lancaster, the Duchy of Cornwall or a Government department or which is held in trust for Her Majesty for the purposes of a Government department, subject in each case to such modifications as the Minister may by regulations prescribe.

(2) For the purposes of this Schedule—
   (a)   as respects land belonging to Her Majesty in right of the Crown, the Crown Estate Commissioners or the proper officer or body having charge of the land for the time being, or, if there is no such officer or body, such person as Her Majesty may appoint in writing under the Royal Sign Manual, shall represent Her Majesty and shall be deemed to be the landlord,
   (b)   as respects land belonging to Her Majesty in right of the Duchy of Lancaster, the Chancellor of the Duchy shall represent Her Majesty and shall be deemed to be the landlord;
   (c)   as respects land belonging to the Duchy of Cornwall, such person as the Duke of Cornwall or the possessor for the time being of the Duchy of Cornwall appoints shall represent the Duchy and shall be deemed to be the landlord and may do any act or thing which a landlord is authorised or required to do under this Act.

(3) Any sum payable under this Schedule by the Duke of Cornwall (or any other possessor for the time being of the Duchy of Cornwall) may be raised and paid as if it were an expense incurred in permanently improving the possessions of the Duchy as mentioned in section 8 of the Duchy of Cornwall Management Act 1863.

(4) Any sum payable under this Schedule by the Chancellor of the Duchy of Lancaster may—
   (a)   be raised and paid as if it were an expense incurred in the improvement of land belonging to Her Majesty in right of the Duchy within section 25 of the Duchy of Lancaster Act 1817; or
   (b)   be paid out of the annual revenues of the Duchy.

(5) The power to make regulations under this paragraph shall be exercisable by statutory instrument and any statutory instrument containing such regulations shall be subject to annulment in pursuance of a resolution of either House of Parliament.

Interpretation

18.—(1) In this Schedule—
   "allocated quota" has the meaning given in paragraph 1(1) above;
   "holding" has the same meaning as in the 1986 Regulations;
   "landlord" means any person for the time being entitled to receive the rents and profits of any land and "sub-landlord" shall be construed accordingly;
   "milk quota" means—
      (a)   in the case of a tenant registered in the direct sales register maintained under the 1986 Regulations, a direct sales quota (within the meaning of the 1986 Regulations); and
      (b)   in the case of a tenant registered in the wholesale register maintained under those Regulations, a wholesale quota (within the meaning of those Regulations);
   "the Minister" means—
      (a)   in the case of land in England, the [Secretary of State]; and
      (b)   in the case of land in Wales, the Secretary of State;
   "registered", in relation to milk quota, means—
      (a)   in the case of direct sales quota (within the meaning of the 1986 Regulations) registered in the direct sales register maintained under those Regulations; and
      (b)   in the case of a wholesale quota (within the meaning of those Regulations) registered in a wholesale register maintained under those Regulations;
   "relevant quota" has the meaning given in paragraph 1(2) above;
   "standard quota" has the meaning given in paragraph 6 above;
   "the 1986 Regulations" means the Dairy Produce Quotas Regulations 1986;
   "tenancy" means a tenancy from year to year (including any arrangement which would have effect as if it were such a tenancy by virtue of section 2 of the Agricultural Holdings Act 1986 if it had not been approved by the Minister) or a tenancy to which section 3 of that Act applies (or would apply apart from section 5 of that Act); and "tenant" and "sub-tenant" shall be construed accordingly;
   "tenant's fraction" has the meaning given in paragraph 7 above;

"termination", in relation to a tenancy, means the cesser of the letting of the land in question or the agreement for letting the land, by reason of effluxion of time or from any other cause;

"transferred quota" has the meaning given in paragraph 1(2) above.

(2)   In this Schedule references to land used for the feeding of dairy cows kept on the land and to dairy cows have the same meaning as in paragraph 6 above.

(3)   The designations of landlord and tenant shall continue to apply to the parties until the conclusion of any proceedings taken under or in pursuance of this Schedule.

[578]

NOTES

Para 11: in sub-para (5) words omitted repealed by the Regulatory Reform (Agricultural Tenancies) (England and Wales) Order 2006, SI 2006/2805, art 18, Sch 2.

Para 18: words in square brackets in definition "the Minister" substituted by the Ministry of Agriculture, Fisheries and Food (Dissolution) Order 2002, SI 2002/794, art 5(1), Sch 1, para 30.

Disapplication: see the note to Pt I of this Schedule at **[576]**.

Transfer of functions: Functions of the Minister, so far as exercisable in relation to Wales, are transferred to the National Assembly for Wales, by the National Assembly for Wales (Transfer of Functions) Order 1999, SI 1999/672, art 2, Sch 1.

(Sch 2 applies to Scotland only; Schs 3, 4, in so far as unrepealed, outside the scope of this work.)

LANDLORD AND TENANT ACT 1987

(1987 c 31)

An Act to confer on tenants of flats rights with respect to the acquisition by them of their landlord's reversion; to make provision for the appointment of a manager at the instance of such tenants and for the variation of long leases held by such tenants; to make further provision with respect to service charges payable by tenants of flats and other dwellings; to make other provision with respect to such tenants; to make further provision with respect to permissible purposes and objects of registered housing associations as regards the management of leasehold property; and for connected purposes

[15 May 1987]

1–45   *(Outside the scope of this work.)*

PART VI
INFORMATION TO BE FURNISHED TO TENANTS

46   Application of Part VI, etc

(1)   This Part applies to premises which consist of or include a dwelling and are not held under a tenancy to which Part II of the Landlord and Tenant Act 1954 applies.

(2)   In this Part "service charge" has the meaning given by section 18(1) of the 1985 Act.

[(3)   In this Part "administration charge" has the meaning given by paragraph 1 of Schedule 11 to the Commonhold and Leasehold Reform Act 2002.]

[578A]

NOTES

Sub-s (3): inserted by the Commonhold and Leasehold Reform Act 2002, s 158, Sch 11, Pt 2, paras 7, 9.

47   Landlord's name and address to be contained in demands for rent etc

(1)   Where any written demand is given to a tenant of premises to which this Part applies, the demand must contain the following information, namely—

(a)   the name and address of the Landlord, and

    (b)   if that address is not in England and Wales, an address in England and Wales at which notices (including notices in proceedings) may be served on the landlord by the tenant.

(2)   Where—

    (a)   a tenant of any such premises is given such a demand, but

    (b)   it does not contain any information required to be contained in it by virtue of subsection (1),

then (subject to subsection (3)) any part of the amount demanded which consists of a service charge [or an administration charge] ("the relevant amount") shall be treated for all purposes as not being due from the tenant to the landlord at any time before that information is furnished by the landlord by notice given to the tenant.

(3)   The relevant amount shall not be so treated in relation to any time when, by virtue of an order of any court [or tribunal], there is in force an appointment of a receiver or manager whose functions include the receiving of service charges [or (as the case may be) administration charges] from the tenant.

(4)   In this section "demand" means a demand for rent or other sums payable to the landlord under the terms of the tenancy.

[578B]

NOTES

Sub-s (2): words in square brackets inserted by the Commonhold and Leasehold Reform Act 2002, s 158, Sch 11, Pt 2, paras 7, 10(1), (2).

Sub-s (3): words in first pair of square brackets inserted, except in relation to any application made to an LVT or any proceedings transferred to an LVT by a county court before 30 September 2003 in relation to England and before 30 March 2004 in relation to Wales, and words in second pair of square brackets inserted by the Commonhold and Leasehold Reform Act 2002, ss 158, 176, Sch 11, Pt 2, paras 7, 10(1), (3), Sch 13, paras 8, 10.

Modified, where the RTM company has acquired the right to manage, by the Commonhold and Leasehold Reform Act 2002, s 102, Sch 7, para 12.

---

48   Notification by landlord of address for service of notices

(1)   A landlord of premises to which this Part applies shall by notice furnish the tenant with an address in England and Wales at which notices (including notices in proceedings) may be served on him by the tenant.

(2)   Where a landlord of any such premises fails to comply with subsection (1), any rent[, service charge or administration charge] otherwise due from the tenant to the landlord shall (subject to subsection (3)) be treated for all purposes as not being due from the tenant to the landlord at any time before the landlord does comply with that subsection.

(3)   Any such rent[, service charge or administration charge] shall not be so treated in relation to any time when, by virtue of an order of any court [or tribunal], there is in force an appointment of a receiver or manager whose functions include the receiving of rent[, service charges or (as the case may be) administration charges] from the tenant.

[578C]

NOTES

Sub-s (2): words in square brackets substituted by the Commonhold and Leasehold Reform Act 2002, s 158, Sch 11, Pt 2, paras 7, 11(1), (2).

Sub-s (3): words in first and third pairs of square brackets substituted, and words in second pair of square brackets inserted, except in relation to any application made to an LVT or any proceedings transferred to an LVT by a county court before 30 September 2003 in relation to England and before 30 March 2004 in relation to Wales, by the Commonhold and Leasehold Reform Act 2002, ss 158, 176, Sch 11, Pt 2, paras 7, 11(1), (3), Sch 13, paras 8, 11.

Modified, where the RTM company has acquired the right to manage, by the Commonhold and Leasehold Reform Act 2002, s 102, Sch 7, para 12.

49–51   (*Outside the scope of this work.*)

PART VII
GENERAL

52–61   (*Outside the scope of this work.*)

62 Short title, commencement and extent

(1) This Act may be cited as the Landlord and Tenant Act 1987.

(2) This Act shall come into force on such day as the Secretary of State may by order appoint.

(3) An order under subsection (2)—
  (a) may appoint different days for different provisions or for different purposes; and
  (b) may make such transitional, incidental, supplemental or consequential provision or saving as the Secretary of State considers necessary or expedient in connection with the coming into force of any provision of this Act or the operation of any enactment which is repealed or amended by a provision of this Act during any period when the repeal or amendment is not wholly in force.

(4) This Act extends to England and Wales only.

[578D]

(*Schs 1–5 outside the scope of this work.*)

LANDLORD AND TENANT ACT 1988

(1988 c 26)

ARRANGEMENT OF SECTIONS

An Act to make new provision for imposing statutory duties in connection with covenants in tenancies against assigning, underletting, charging or parting with the possession of premises without consent

[29 July 1988]

1 Qualified duty to consent to assigning, underletting etc of premises

(1) This section applies in any case where—
  (a) a tenancy includes a covenant on the part of the tenant not to enter into one or more of the following transactions, that is—
    (i) assigning,
    (ii) underletting,
    (iii) charging, or
    (iv) parting with the possession of,
  the premises comprised in the tenancy or any part of the premises without the consent of the landlord or some other person, but
  (b) the covenant is subject to the qualification that the consent is not to be unreasonably withheld (whether or not it is also subject to any other qualification).

(2) In this section and section 2 of this Act—
  (a) references to a proposed transaction are to any assignment, underletting, charging or parting with possession to which the covenant relates, and
  (b) references to the person who may consent to such a transaction are to the person who under the covenant may consent to the tenant entering into the proposed transaction.

(3) Where there is served on the person who may consent to a proposed transaction a written application by the tenant for consent to the transaction, he owes a duty to the tenant within a reasonable time—
  (a) to give consent, except in a case where it is reasonable not to give consent,

349

(b)   to serve on the tenant written notice of his decision whether or not to give consent specifying in addition—
  (i)   if the consent is given subject to conditions, the conditions,
  (ii)   if the consent is withheld, the reasons for withholding it.

(4)   Giving consent subject to any condition that is not a reasonable condition does not satisfy the duty under subsection (3)(a) above.

(5)   For the purposes of this Act it is reasonable for a person not to give consent to a proposed transaction only in a case where, if he withheld consent and the tenant completed the transaction, the tenant would be in breach of a covenant.

(6)   It is for the person who owed any duty under subsection (3) above—
  (a)   if he gave consent and the question arises whether he gave it within a reasonable time, to show that he did,
  (b)   if he gave consent subject to any condition and the question arises whether the condition was a reasonable condition, to show that it was,
  (c)   if he did not give consent and the question arises whether it was reasonable for him not to do so, to show that it was reasonable,

and, if the question arises whether he served notice under that subsection within a reasonable time, to show that he did.

[579]

NOTES
Modification: this section is modified where the RTM company has acquired the right to manage, by the Commonhold and Leasehold Reform Act 2002, s 102, Sch 7, para 13(1), (2).

2 Duty to pass on applications

(1)   If, in a case where section 1 of this Act applies, any person receives a written application by the tenant for consent to a proposed transaction and that person—
  (a)   is a person who may consent to the transaction or (though not such a person) is the landlord, and
  (b)   believes that another person, other than a person who he believes has received the application or a copy of it, is a person who may consent to the transaction,

he owes a duty to the tenant (whether or not he owes him any duty under section 1 of this Act) to take such steps as are reasonable to secure the receipt within a reasonable time by the other person of a copy of the application.

(2)   The reference in section 1(3) of this Act to the service of an application on a person who may consent to a proposed transaction includes a reference to the receipt by him of an application or a copy of an application (whether it is for his consent or that of another).

[580]

3 Qualified duty to approve consent by another

(1)   This section applies in any case where—
  (a)   a tenancy includes a covenant on the part of the tenant not without the approval of the landlord to consent to the sub-tenant—
    (i)   assigning,
    (ii)   underletting,
    (iii)   charging, or
    (iv)   parting with the possession of,
  the premises comprised in the sub-tenancy or any part of the premises, but
  (b)   the covenant is subject to the qualification that the approval is not to be unreasonably withheld (whether or not it is also subject to any other qualification).

(2)   Where there is served on the landlord a written application by the tenant for approval or a copy of a written application to the tenant by the sub-tenant for consent to a transaction to which the covenant relates the landlord owes a duty to the sub-tenant within a reasonable time—
  (a)   to give approval, except in a case where it is reasonable not to give approval,
  (b)   to serve on the tenant and the sub-tenant written notice of his decision whether or not to give approval specifying in addition—
    (i)   if approval is given subject to conditions, the conditions,
    (ii)   if approval is withheld, the reasons for withholding it.

(3)   Giving approval subject to any condition that is not a reasonable condition does not satisfy the duty under subsection (2)(a) above.

(4)   For the purposes of this section it is reasonable for the landlord not to give approval only in a case where, if he withheld approval and the tenant gave his consent, the tenant would be in breach of covenant.

(5)   It is for a landlord who owed any duty under subsection (2) above—
  (a)   if he gave approval and the question arises whether he gave it within a reasonable time, to show that he did,
  (b)   if he gave approval subject to any condition and the question arises whether the condition was a reasonable condition, to show that it was,
  (c)   if he did not give approval and the question arises whether it was reasonable for him not to do so, to show that it was reasonable,

and, if the question arises whether he served notice under that subsection within a reasonable time, to show that he did.

[581]

NOTES
Modification: sub-ss (2), (4), (5) are modified where the RTM company has acquired the right to manage, by the Commonhold and Leasehold Reform Act 2002, s 102, Sch 7, para 13(1), (3).

4   Breach of duty

A claim that a person has broken any duty under this Act may be made the subject of civil proceedings in like manner as any other claim in tort for breach of statutory duty.

[582]

5   Interpretation

(1)   In this Act—
  "covenant" includes condition and agreement,
  "consent" includes licence,
  "landlord" includes any superior landlord from whom the tenant's immediate landlord directly or indirectly holds,
  "tenancy", subject to subsection (3) below, means any lease or other tenancy (whether made before or after the coming into force of this Act) and includes—
    (a)   a sub-tenancy, and
    (b)   an agreement for a tenancy
  and references in this Act to the landlord and to the tenant are to be interpreted accordingly, and
  "tenant", where the tenancy is affected by a mortgage (within the meaning of the Law of Property Act 1925) and the mortgagee proposes to exercise his statutory or express power of sale, includes the mortgagee.

(2)   An application or notice is to be treated as served for the purposes of this Act if—
  (a)   served in any manner provided in the tenancy, and
  (b)   in respect of any matter for which the tenancy makes no provision, served in any manner provided by section 23 of the Landlord and Tenant Act 1927.

(3)   This Act does not apply to a secure tenancy (defined in section 79 of the Housing Act 1985) [or to an introductory tenancy (within the meaning of Chapter I of Part V of the Housing Act 1996)].

(4)   This Act applies only to applications for consent or approval served after its coming into force.

[583]

NOTES
Sub-s (3): words in square brackets added by the Housing Act 1996 (Consequential Amendments) Order 1997, SI 1997/74, art 2, Schedule, para 5.

6   Application to Crown

This Act binds the Crown; but as regards the Crown's liability in tort shall not bind the Crown further than the Crown is made liable in tort by the Crown Proceedings Act 1947.

[584]

7 Short title, commencement and extent

(1)   This Act may be cited as the Landlord and Tenant Act 1988.

(2)   This Act shall come into force at the end of the period of two months beginning with the day on which it is passed.

(3)   This Act extends to England and Wales only.

[585]

LOCAL GOVERNMENT FINANCE ACT 1988

(1988 c 41)

An Act to create community charges in favour of certain authorities, to create new rating systems, to provide for precepting by certain authorities and levying by certain bodies, to make provision about the payment of grants to certain authorities, to require certain authorities to maintain certain funds, to make provision about the capital expenditure and the administration of the financial affairs of certain authorities, to abolish existing rates, precepts and similar rights, to abolish rate support grants and supplementary grants for transport purposes, to make amendments as to rates and certain grants, to make certain amendments to the law of Scotland as regards community charges, rating and valuation, to provide for the establishment of valuation and community charge tribunals, and for connected purposes

[29 July 1988]

1–40   *((Pts I, II) repealed, subject to savings, by the Local Government Finance Act 1992, ss 117(2), 118(1), Sch 14.)*

PART III
NON-DOMESTIC RATING

41–63   *(Outside the scope of this work.)*

Interpretation

64   Hereditaments

(1)   A hereditament is anything which, by virtue of the definition of hereditament in section 115(1) of the 1967 Act, would have been a hereditament for the purposes of that Act had this Act not been passed.

(2)   In addition, a right is a hereditament if it is a right to use any land for the purpose of exhibiting advertisements and—
- (a)   the right is let out or reserved to any person other than the occupier of the land, or
- (b)   where the land is not occupied for any other purpose, the right is let out or reserved to any person other than the owner of the land.

[(2A)   In addition, a right is a hereditament if—
- (a)   it is a right to use any land for the purpose of operating a meter to measure a supply of gas or electricity or such other service as—
  - (i)   the Secretary of State in relation to England, or
  - (ii)   the National Assembly for Wales in relation to Wales,
  may by order specify, and
- (b)   the meter is owned by a person other than the consumer of the service.]

(3)   The Secretary of State may make regulations providing that in prescribed cases—
- (a)   anything which would (apart from the regulations) be one hereditament shall be treated as more than one hereditament;
- (b)   anything which would (apart from the regulations) be more than one hereditament shall be treated as one hereditament.

[(3A)   The Secretary of State may make regulations providing that where on any land there are two or more moorings which—

(a) are owned by the same person,

(b) are not domestic property, and

(c) are separately occupied, or available for separate occupation, by persons other than that person,

a valuation officer may determine that, for the purposes of the compilation or alteration of a local non-domestic rating list, all or any of the moorings, or all or any of them together with any adjacent moorings or land owned and occupied by that person, shall be treated as one hereditament.

(3B) Regulations under subsection (3A) above may provide that—

(a) where a valuation officer makes a determination as mentioned in that subsection, he shall, if prescribed conditions are fulfilled, supply prescribed persons with prescribed information;

(b) while such a determination is in force—

(i) the person who on any day is the owner of the moorings (or the moorings and land) which constitute the hereditament shall be treated for the purposes of sections 43, 44A and 45 above as being in occupation of all of the hereditament on that day; and

(ii) no other person shall be treated for those purposes as being in occupation of all or any part of the hereditament on that day.]

(4) A hereditament is a relevant hereditament if it consists of property of any of the following descriptions—

(a) lands;

(b) coal mines;

(c) mines of any other description, other than a mine of which the royalty or dues are for the time being wholly reserved in kind;

(d) ...

(e) any right which is a hereditament by virtue of subsection (2) [or (2A)] above.

(5)–(7) ...

[(7A)–(7D)] ...

(8) A hereditament is non-domestic if either—

(a) it consists entirely of property which is not domestic, or

(b) it is a composite hereditament.

(9) A hereditament is composite if part only of it consists of domestic property.

(10) A hereditament shall be treated as wholly or mainly used for charitable purposes at any time if at the time it is wholly or mainly used for the sale of goods donated to a charity and the proceeds of sale of the goods (after any deduction of expenses) are applied for the purposes of a charity.

(11) In subsection (2) above "land" includes a wall or other part of a building and a sign, hoarding, frame, post or other structure erected or to be erected on land.

[(11A) The Secretary of State in relation to England, and the National Assembly in relation to Wales, may by regulations make provision as to what is to be regarded as being a meter for the purposes of subsection (2A) above.

(11B) In subsection (2A) above "land" includes a wall or other part of a building.]

[(12) In subsections (3A) and (3B) above 'owner', in relation to a mooring, means the person who (if the mooring is let) is entitled to receive rent, whether on his own account or as agent or trustee for any other person, or (if the mooring is not let) would be so entitled if the mooring were let, and 'owned' shall be construed accordingly.]

[586]

NOTES

Sub-s (2A): inserted by the Local Government Act 2003, s 66(1).

Sub-ss (3A), (3B): inserted by the Local Government Finance Act 1992, s 104, Sch 10, Pt I, para 2.

Sub-s (4): para (d) repealed by the Local Government and Rating Act 1997, ss 2(2), 33(2), Sch 4; words in square brackets in para (e) inserted by the Local Government Act 2003, s 66(2).

Sub-ss (5)–(7): repealed by the Local Government and Rating Act 1997, s 33, Sch 3, para 25, Sch 4.

Sub-ss (7A)–(7D): inserted by the Local Government and Housing Act 1989, s 139, Sch 5, paras 1, 33, 79(3), and repealed by the Local Government and Rating Act 1997, s 33, Sch 3, para 25, Sch 4.

Sub-ss (11A), (11B): inserted by the Local Government Act 2003, s 66(3).

Sub-s (12): added by the Local Government Finance Act 1992, s 104, Sch 10, Pt I, para 2.

1967 Act: General Rate Act 1967.

Transfer of functions: functions of the Secretary of State, so far as exercisable in relation to Wales, are transferred to the National Assembly for Wales, by the National Assembly for Wales (Transfer of Functions) Order 1999, SI 1999/672, art 2, Sch 1.

Regulations: the Non-Domestic Rating (Miscellaneous Provisions) Regulations 1989, SI 1989/1060; the Non-Domestic Rating (Miscellaneous Provisions) (No 2) Regulations 1989, SI 1989/2303; the Non-Domestic Rating (Caravan Sites) Regulations 1990, SI 1990/673; the Non-Domestic Rating (Electricity Generators) Regulations 1991, SI 1991/475; the Non-Domestic Rating (Ports of London and Tilbury) Regulations 1991, SI 1991/2906; the Non-Domestic Rating (Multiple Moorings) Regulations 1992, SI 1992/557; the Non-Domestic Rating (Telecommunications Apparatus) (England) Regulations 2000, SI 2000/2421; the Non-Domestic Rating (Telecommunications Apparatus) (Wales) Regulations 2000, SI 2000/3383; the Central Rating List (Wales) Regulations 2005, SI 2005/422; the Non-Domestic Rating (Communications and Light Railways) (England) Regulations 2005, SI 2005/549; the Central Rating List (England) Regulations 2005, SI 2005/551.

65 Owners and occupiers

(1) The owner of a hereditament or land is the person entitled to possession of it.

(2) Whether a hereditament or land is occupied, and who is the occupier, shall be determined by reference to the rules which would have applied for the purposes of the 1967 Act had this Act not been passed (ignoring any express statutory rules such as those in sections 24 and 46A of that Act).

(3) Subsections (1) and (2) above shall have effect subject to [the following provisions of this section].

(4) Regulations under section 64(3) above may include rules for ascertaining—
    (a)   whether the different hereditaments or the one hereditament (as the case may be) shall be treated as occupied or unoccupied;
    (b)   who shall be treated as the owner or occupier of the different hereditaments or the one hereditament (as the case may be).

(5) A hereditament which is not in use shall be treated as unoccupied if (apart from this subsection) it would be treated as occupied by reason only of there being kept in or on the hereditament plant, machinery or equipment—
    (a)   which was used in or on the hereditament when it was last in use, or
    (b)   which is intended for use in or on the hereditament.

(6) A hereditament shall be treated as unoccupied if (apart from this subsection) it would be treated as occupied by reason only of—
    (a)   the use of it for the holding of public meetings in furtherance of a person's candidature at a parliamentary or local government election, or
    (b)   if it is a house, the use of a room in it by a returning officer for the purpose of taking the poll in a parliamentary or local government election.

(7) In subsection (6) above "returning officer" shall be construed in accordance with section 24 or 35 of the Representation of the People Act 1983 (as the case may be).

(8) A right which is a hereditament by virtue of section 64(2) above shall be treated as occupied by the person for the time being entitled to the right.

[(8A) In a case where—
    (a)   land consisting of a hereditament is used (permanently or temporarily) for the exhibition of advertisements or for the erection of a structure used for the exhibition of advertisements,
    (b)   section 64(2) above does not apply, and
    (c)   apart from this subsection, the hereditament is not occupied,
the hereditament shall be treated as occupied by the person permitting it to be so used or, if that person cannot be ascertained, its owner.]

(9) ...

[587]

NOTES

Sub-s (3): words in square brackets substituted by the Local Government and Rating Act 1997, s 2(1), (3)(a).

Sub-s (8A): inserted with retrospective effect, by the Local Government and Housing Act 1989, s 139, Sch 5, paras 1, 34, 79(3).

Sub-s (9): repealed by the Local Government and Rating Act 1997, ss 2(1), (3)(b), 33(2), Sch 4.

1967 Act: General Rate Act 1967.

Regulations: the Non-Domestic Rating (Telecommunications Apparatus) (England) Regulations 2000, SI 2000/2421; the Non-Domestic Rating (Telecommunications Apparatus) (Wales) Regulations 2000, SI 2000/3383; the Central Rating List (Wales) Regulations 2005, SI 2005/422; the Non-Domestic Rating (Communications and Light Railways) (England) Regulations 2005, SI 2005/549; the Central Rating List (England) Regulations 2005, SI 2005/551.

[65A Crown property

(1) This Part applies to the Crown as it applies to other persons.

(2) Accordingly, liability to a non-domestic rate in respect of a hereditament is not affected by the fact that—
  (a) the hereditament is occupied by the Crown or by a person acting on behalf of the Crown or is used for Crown purposes, or
  (b) the Crown or a person acting on behalf of the Crown is the owner of the hereditament.

(3) If (apart from this subsection) any property would consist of two or more Crown hereditaments, the property is to be treated for the purposes of this Part as if it were a single hereditament occupied by such one of the occupiers as appears to the billing authority to occupy the largest part of the property.

(4) In this section, "Crown hereditament" means a hereditament which—
  (a) is occupied by a Minister of the Crown or Government department or by any officer or body exercising functions on behalf of the Crown, but
  (b) is not provided or maintained by a local authority [or by a police authority established under section 3 of the Police Act 1996].

(5) In this section—
  (a) references to this Part include any subordinate legislation (within the meaning of the Interpretation Act 1978) made under it, and
  (b) "local authority" has the same meaning as in the Local Government Act 1972, and includes the Common Council of the City of London.

(6) The Secretary of State may by order amend subsection (4)(b) above so as to alter the persons for the time being referred to there.

(7) Subsection (3) above does not affect the power conferred by section 64(3) above.]

[588]

NOTES

Inserted by the Local Government and Rating Act 1997, s 3.

Sub-s (4): words in square brackets substituted by the Criminal Justice and Police Act 2001, s 128(1), Sch 6, Pt 3, para 73.

66 Domestic property

(1) [Subject to subsections (2), (2B) and (2E) below,] property is domestic if—
  (a) it is used wholly for the purposes of living accommodation,
  (b) it is a yard, garden, outhouse or other appurtenance belonging to or enjoyed with property falling within paragraph (a) above,
  (c) it is a private garage [which either has a floor area of 25 square metres or less or is] used wholly or mainly for the accommodation of a private motor vehicle, or
  (d) it is private storage premises used wholly or mainly for the storage of articles of domestic use.

[(2) Property is not domestic property if it is wholly or mainly used in the course of a business for the provision of short-stay accommodation, that is to say accommodation—
  (a) which is provided for short periods to individuals whose sole or main residence is elsewhere, and
  (b) which is not self-contained self-catering accommodation provided commercially.

[(2A) Subsection (2) above does not apply if—
  (a) it is intended that within the year beginning with the end of the day in relation to which the question is being considered, short-stay accommodation will not be provided within the hereditament for more than six persons simultaneously; and
  (b) the person intending to provide such accommodation intends to have his sole or

main residence within that hereditament throughout any period when such accommodation is to be provided, and that any use of living accommodation within the hereditament which would, apart from this subsection, cause any part of it to be treated as non-domestic, will be subsidiary to the use of the hereditament for, or in connection with, his sole or main residence.]

(2B)   A building or self-contained part of a building is not domestic property if—

    (a)   the relevant person intends that, in the year beginning with the end of the day in relation to which the question is being considered, the whole of the building or self-contained part will be available for letting commercially, as self-catering accommodation, for short periods totalling 140 days or more, and

    (b)   on that day his interest in the building or part is such as to enable him to let it for such periods.

(2C)   For the purposes of subsection (2B) the relevant person is—

    (a)   where the property in question is a building and is not subject as a whole to a relevant leasehold interest, the person having the freehold interest in the whole of the building; and

    (b)   in any other case, any person having a relevant leasehold interest in the building or self-contained part which is not subject (as a whole) to a single relevant leasehold interest inferior to his interest.

(2D)   Subsection (2B) above does not apply where the building or self-contained part is used as the sole or main residence of any person …]

[(2E)   Property is not domestic property if it is timeshare accommodation within the meaning of the Timeshare Act 1992.]

[(3)   Subsection (1) above does not apply in the case of a pitch occupied by a caravan, but if in such a case the caravan is the sole or main residence of an individual, the pitch and the caravan, together with any garden, yard, outhouse or other appurtenance belonging to or enjoyed with them, are domestic property].

[(4)   Subsection (1) above does not apply in the case of a mooring occupied by a boat, but if in such a case the boat is the sole or main residence of an individual, the mooring and the boat, together with any garden, yard, outhouse or other appurtenance belonging to or enjoyed with them, are domestic property.

(4A)   Subsection (3) or (4) above does not have effect in the case of a pitch occupied by a caravan, or a mooring occupied by a boat, which is an appurtenance enjoyed with other property to which subsection (1)(a) above applies.]

(5)   Property not in use is domestic if it appears that when next in use it will be domestic.

(6)   …

(7)   Whether anything is a caravan shall be construed in accordance with Part I of the Caravan Sites and Control of Development Act 1960.

(8)   …

[(8A)   In this section—

    "business" includes—

        (a)   any activity carried on by a body of persons, whether corporate or unincorporate, and

        (b)   any activity carried on by a charity;

    "commercially" means on a commercial basis, and with a view to the realisation of profits; and

    "relevant leasehold interest" means an interest under a lease or underlease which was granted for a term of 6 months or more and conferred the right to exclusive possession throughout the term.]

(9)   The Secretary of State may by order amend, or substitute another definition for, any definition of domestic property for the time being effective for the purposes of this Part.

[589]

NOTES

Sub-s (1): words in first pair of square brackets, as inserted by the Standard Community Charge and Non-Domestic Rating (Definition of Domestic Property) Order 1990, SI 1990/162, art 3(1), (2)(a), substituted by the Non-Domestic Rating (Definition of Domestic Property) Order 1993, SI 1993/542, art 2(a); words in second pair of square brackets inserted by SI 1990/162, art 3(1), (2)(b).

Sub-ss (2), (2B), (2C): substituted, together with sub-ss (2A), (2D), for sub-s (2) as originally enacted, by SI 1990/162, art 3(1), (3).

Sub-s (2A): substituted, together with sub-ss (2), (2B)–(2D), for sub-s (2) as originally enacted, by SI 1990/162, art 3(1), (3); substituted by the Standard Community Charge and Non-Domestic Rating (Definition of Domestic Property) (Amendment) Order 1991, SI 1991/474, art 3(1).

Sub-s (2D): substituted, together with sub-ss (2), (2A)–(2C), for sub-s (2) as originally enacted, by SI 1990/162, art 3(1), (3); words omitted repealed, subject to a saving, by the Local Government Finance Act 1992, ss 117(1), (2), 118(1), Sch 13, para 70(1), Sch 14.

Sub-s (2E): inserted by SI 1993/542, art 2(b).

Sub-s (3): substituted by the Rating (Caravans and Boats) Act 1996, s 1(1), (2).

Sub-ss (4), (4A): substituted, for original sub-s (4), by the Ratings (Caravans and Boats) Act 1996, s 1(1), (3).

Sub-ss (6), (8): repealed with retrospective effect, by the Caravans (Standard Community Charge and Rating) Act 1991, s 1(2), (3).

Sub-s (8A): inserted by SI 1990/162, art 3(1), (4).

Transfer of functions: functions of the Secretary of State, so far as exercisable in relation to Wales, are transferred to the National Assembly for Wales, by the National Assembly for Wales (Transfer of Functions) Order 1999, SI 1999/672, art 2, Sch 1.

Orders: the Standard Community Charge and Non-Domestic Rating (Definition of Domestic Property) Order 1990, SI 1990/162; the Non-Domestic Rating (Definition of Domestic Property) Order 1993, SI 1993/542.

67–129   (*In so far as unrepealed, outside the scope of this work.*)

PART XI
MISCELLANEOUS AND GENERAL

130–137   (*Ss 130–132 repealed by the Local Government and Housing Act 1989, s 194(2), Sch 12, Pt I; ss 133, 134 repealed, subject to a saving, by the Local Government Finance Act 1992, ss 117(2), 118(1), Sch 14; ss 135–137 outside the scope of this work.*)

General

138–151   (*Ss 138–149, 151 in so far as unrepealed, outside the scope of this work; s 150 applies to Scotland only.*)

152   Citation

This Act may be cited as the Local Government Finance Act 1988.

[590]

(*Schs 1–13 in so far as unrepealed are outside the scope of this work or apply to Scotland only.*)

LAW OF PROPERTY (MISCELLANEOUS PROVISIONS) ACT 1989

(1989 c 34)

An Act to make new provision with respect to deeds and their execution and contracts for the sale or other disposition of interests in land; and to abolish the rule of law known as the rule in Bain v Fothergill

[27 July 1989]

1   Deeds and their execution

(1)   Any rule of law which—
    (a)   restricts the substances on which a deed may be written;
    (b)   requires a seal for the valid execution of an instrument as a deed by an individual; or
    (c)   requires authority by one person to another to deliver an instrument as a deed on his behalf to be given by deed,
is abolished.

(2)   An instrument shall not be a deed unless—
    (a)   it makes it clear on its face that it is intended to be a deed by the person making it or, as the case may be, by the parties to it (whether by describing itself as a deed or expressing itself to be executed or signed as a deed or otherwise); and
    (b)   it is validly executed as a deed—
        [(i)   by that person or a person authorised to execute it in the name or on behalf of that person, or
        (ii)   by one or more of those parties or a person authorised to execute it in the name or on behalf of one or more of those parties.]

[(2A)   For the purposes of subsection (2)(a) above, an instrument shall not be taken to make it clear on its face that it is intended to be a deed merely because it is executed under seal.]

(3)   An instrument is validly executed as a deed by an individual if, and only if—
    (a)   it is signed—
        (i)   by him in the presence of a witness who attests the signature; or
        (ii)   at his direction and in his presence and the presence of two witnesses who each attest the signature; and
    (b)   it is delivered as a deed ...

(4)   In subsections (2) and (3) above "sign", in relation to an instrument, includes—
    [(a)   an individual signing the name of the person or party on whose behalf he executes the instrument; and
    (b)   making one's mark on the instrument,
and "signature" is to be construed accordingly.]

[(4A)   Subsection (3) above applies in the case of an instrument executed by an individual in the name or on behalf of another person whether or not that person is also an individual.]

(5)   Where a solicitor[, duly certificated notary public] or licensed conveyancer, or an agent or employee of a solicitor[, duly certificated notary public] or licensed conveyancer, in the course of or in connection with a transaction ..., purports to deliver an instrument as a deed on behalf of a party to the instrument, it shall be conclusively presumed in favour of a purchaser that he is authorised so to deliver the instrument.

(6)   In subsection (5) above—
    ["purchaser" has the same meaning] as in the Law of Property Act 1925;
    ["duly certificated notary public" has the same meaning as it has in the Solicitors Act 1974 by virtue of section 87 of that Act;] ...

         .....

(7)   Where an instrument under seal that constitutes a deed is required for the purposes of an Act passed before this section comes into force, this section shall have effect as to signing, sealing or delivery of an instrument by an individual in place of any provision of that Act as to signing, sealing or delivery.

(8)   The enactments mentioned in Schedule 1 to this Act (which in consequence of this section require amendments other than those provided by subsection (7) above) shall have effect with the amendments specified in that Schedule.

(9)   Nothing in subsection (1)(b), (2), (3), (7) or (8) above applies in relation to deeds required or authorised to be made under—
    (a)   the seal of the county palatine of Lancaster;
    (b)   the seal of the Duchy of Lancaster; or
    (c)   the seal of the Duchy of Cornwall.

(10)   The references in this section to the execution of a deed by an individual do not include execution by a corporation sole and the reference in subsection (7) above to signing, sealing or delivery by an individual does not include signing, sealing or delivery by such a corporation.

(11)   Nothing in this section applies in relation to instruments delivered as deeds before this section comes into force.

[591]

NOTES

Sub-s (2): words in square brackets substituted, except in relation to any instrument executed before 15 September 2005, by the Regulatory Reform (Execution of Deeds and Documents) Order 2005, SI 2005/1906, art 7(3).

Sub-s (2A): inserted, except in relation to any instrument executed before 15 September 2005, by SI 2005/1906, art 8.

Sub-s (3): words omitted repealed, except in relation to any instrument executed before 15 September 2005, by SI 2005/1906, art 10(2), Sch 2.

Sub-s (4): words in square brackets substituted, except in relation to any instrument executed before 15 September 2005, by SI 2005/1906, art 10(1), Sch 1, paras 13, 14.

Sub-s (4A): inserted, except in relation to any instrument executed before 15 September 2005, by SI 2005/1906, art 7(4).

Sub-s (5): words in square brackets inserted by the Courts and Legal Services Act 1990, s 125(2), Sch 17, para 20; words omitted repealed, except in relation to any instrument executed before 15 September 2005, by SI 2005/1906, arts 9, 10(2), Sch 2.

Sub-s (6): in definition "purchaser" words in square brackets substituted and definition "interest of land" (omitted) and immediately preceding word omitted repealed, except in relation to any instrument executed before 15 September 2005, by SI 2005/1906, art 10, Sch 1, paras 13, 15, Sch 2; definition "duly certificated notary public" inserted by the Courts and Legal Services Act 1990, s 125(2), Sch 17, para 20.

PART I
STATUTES

2   Contracts for sale etc of land to be made by signed writing

(1)   A contract for the sale or other disposition of an interest in land can only be made in writing and only by incorporating all the terms which the parties have expressly agreed in one document or, where contracts are exchanged, in each.

(2)   The terms may be incorporated in a document either by being set out in it or by reference to some other document.

(3)   The document incorporating the terms or, where contracts are exchanged, one of the documents incorporating them (but not necessarily the same one) must be signed by or on behalf of each party to the contract.

(4)   Where a contract for the sale or other disposition of an interest in land satisfies the conditions of this section by reason only of the rectification of one or more documents in pursuance of an order of a court, the contract shall come into being, or be deemed to have come into being, at such time as may be specified in the order.

(5)   This section does not apply in relation to—
   (a)   a contract to grant such a lease as is mentioned in section 54(2) of the Law of Property Act 1925 (short leases);
   (b)   a contract made in the course of a public auction; or
   [(c)   a contract regulated under the Financial Services and Markets Act 2000, other than a regulated mortgage contract[, a regulated home reversion plan or a regulated home purchase plan];]

and nothing in this section affects the creation or operation of resulting, implied or constructive trusts.

(6)   In this section—
   "disposition" has the same meaning as in the Law of Property Act 1925;
   "interest in land" means any estate, interest or charge in or over land *or in or over the proceeds of sale of land.*
   ["regulated mortgage contract"[, "regulated home reversion plan" and "regulated home purchase plan"] must be read with—
      (a)   section 22 of the Financial Services and Markets Act 2000,
      (b)   any relevant order under that section, and
      (c)   Schedule 22 to that Act.]

(7)   Nothing in this section shall apply in relation to contracts made before this section comes into force.

(8)   ...

[592]

NOTES

Sub-s (5): para (c) substituted by the Financial Services and Markets Act 2000 (Consequential Amendments and Repeals) Order 2001, SI 2001/3649, art 317(1), (2), words in square brackets substituted by the Financial Services and Markets Act 2000 (Regulated Activities) (Amendment) (No 2) Order 2006, SI 2006/2383, art 27(2)(a), subject to savings in arts 37–39 thereof.

Sub-s (6): in definition "interest in land" words in italics repealed by the Trusts of Land and Appointment of Trustees Act 1996, s 25(2), Sch 4 (for savings in connection with the abolition of the doctrine of conversion, see ss 3, 18(3), 25(5) of the 1996 Act); definition "regulated mortgage contract" inserted by SI 2001/3649, art 317(1), (3), words in square brackets substituted by SI 2006/2383, art 27(2)(b), subject to savings in art 25(4), (5) thereof.

Sub-s (8): repeals the Law of Property Act 1925, s 40.

3 Abolition of rule in Bain v Fothergill

The rule of law known as the rule in Bain v Fothergill is abolished in relation to contracts made after this section comes into force.

[593]

4 Repeals

The enactments mentioned in Schedule 2 to this Act are repealed to the extent specified in the third column of that Schedule.

[594]

5 Commencement

(1)   The provisions of this Act to which this subsection applies shall come into force on such day as the Lord Chancellor may by order made by statutory instrument appoint.

(2)   The provisions to which subsection (1) above applies are—
  (a)   section 1 above; and
  (b)   section 4 above, except so far as it relates to section 40 of the Law of Property Act 1925.

(3)   The provisions of this Act to which this subsection applies shall come into force at the end of the period of two months beginning with the day on which this Act is passed.

(4)   The provisions of this Act to which subsection (3) above applies are—
  (a)   sections 2 and 3 above; and
  (b)   section 4 above, so far as it relates to section 40 of the Law of Property Act 1925.

[595]

NOTES
Order: the Law of Property (Miscellaneous Provisions) Act 1989 (Commencement) Order 1990, SI 1990/1175.

6 Citation

(1)   This Act may be cited as the Law of Property (Miscellaneous Provisions) Act 1989.

(2)   This Act extends to England and Wales only.

[596]

(Schs 1, 2 contain amendments and repeals which, in so far as they relate to provisions in this work have been incorporated.)

LOCAL GOVERNMENT AND HOUSING ACT 1989

(1989 c 42)

ARRANGEMENT OF SECTIONS

PART IX
MISCELLANEOUS AND GENERAL

Local Government Finance Act 1988

Supplementary

An Act to make provision with respect to the members, officers and other staff and the procedure of local authorities; to amend Part III of the Local Government Act 1974 and Part II of the Local Government (Scotland) Act 1975 and to provide for a national code of local government conduct; to make further provision about the finances and expenditure of local authorities (including provision with respect to housing subsidies) and about companies in which local authorities have interests; to make provision for and in connection with renewal areas, grants towards the cost of improvement and repair of housing accommodation and the carrying out of works of maintenance, repair and improvement; to amend the Housing Act 1985 and Part III of the Local Government Finance Act 1982; to make amendments of and consequential upon Parts I, II and IV of the Housing Act 1988; to amend the Local Government Finance Act 1988 and the Abolition of Domestic Rates Etc (Scotland) Act 1987 and certain enactments relating, as respects Scotland, to rating and valuation, and to provide for the making of grants; to make provision with respect to the imposition of charges by local authorities; to make further provision about certain existing grants and about financial assistance to and planning by local authorities in respect of emergencies; to amend sections 102 and 211 of the Local Government (Scotland) Act 1973; to amend the Local Land Charges Act 1975; to enable local authorities in Wales to be known solely by Welsh language names; to provide for the transfer of new town housing stock; to amend certain of the provisions of the Housing (Scotland) Act 1987 relating to a secure tenant's right to purchase his house; to amend section 47 of the Race Relations Act 1976; to confer certain powers on the Housing Corporation, Housing for Wales and Scottish Homes; to make provision about security of tenure for certain tenants under long tenancies; to provide for the making of grants and giving of guarantees in respect of certain activities carried on in relation to the construction industry; to provide for the repeal of certain enactments relating to improvement notices, town development and education support grants; to make, as respects Scotland, further provision in relation to the phasing of progression to registered rent for houses let by housing associations or Scottish Homes and in relation to the circumstances in which rent increases under assured tenancies may be secured; and for connected purposes

[16 November 1989]

1–138   ((*Pts I–VIII*) *outside the scope of this work.*)

PART IX
MISCELLANEOUS AND GENERAL

Local Government Finance Act 1988 ...

NOTES
Words omitted from cross heading outside the scope of the work.

139–148   (*Ss 139, 147, 148 outside the scope of this work; ss 142–145 apply to Scotland only; ss 140, 141, 146 repealed, subject to savings by the Local Government Finance Act 1992, ss 117(2), 118, Sch 14.*)

149   Statutory references to rating

(1)–(5)   ...

(6)   Without prejudice to the generality of the powers conferred by this section, section 37 of the Landlord and Tenant Act 1954 (which provides for compensation by reference to rateable values) shall be amended in accordance with Schedule 7 to this Act.

[597]

NOTES
Sub-ss (1)–(5): outside the scope of this work.

150–189   (*Ss 150–158, 160, 161(1), 162–169, 171–175, 180, 182–184, 186–89 outside the scope of this work; ss 159, 161(2), 170, 176–179, 181, 185 apply to Scotland only.*)

Supplementary

190   Regulations

(1)   Under any power to make regulations conferred by any provision of this Act, different provision may be made for different cases and different descriptions of cases (including different provision for different areas).

(2)   Any power to make regulations conferred by any provision of this Act shall be exercisable by statutory instrument which, except in the case of a statutory instrument containing regulations under section 150 or section 151 of Schedule 10, shall be subject to annulment in pursuance of a resolution of either House of Parliament.

[598]

191   Separate provisions for Wales

(1)   Where any provision of this Act which extends to England and Wales confers (directly or by amendment of another Act) a power on the Secretary of State to make regulations, orders, rules or determinations or to give directions or specify any matter, the power may be exercised differently for England and Wales, whether or not it is exercised separately.

(2)   This section is without prejudice to section 190(1) above and to any other provision of this Act or of any Act amended by this Act by virtue of which powers may be exercised differently in different cases or in any other circumstances.

[599]

NOTES

Transfer of functions: Functions of the Secretary of State, so far as exercisable in relation to Wales, are transferred to the National Assembly for Wales, by the National Assembly for Wales (Transfer of Functions) Order 1999, SI 1999/672, art 2, Sch 1.

192   (*Outside the scope of this work.*)

193   Application to Isles of Scilly

(1)   This Act applies to the Isles of Scilly subject to such exceptions, adaptations and modifications as the Secretary of State may by order direct.

(2)   The power to make an order under this section shall be exercisable by statutory instrument which shall be subject to annulment in pursuance of a resolution of either House of Parliament.

[600]

194   (*Outside the scope of this work.*)

195   Short title, commencement and extent

(1)   This Act may be cited as the Local Government and Housing Act 1989.

(2)   The provisions of sections 1 and 2, 9, 10, 13 to 20 above, Parts II to V (with the exception in Part II of section 24), VII and VIII and (in this Part) sections 140 to 145, 156, 159, 160, 162, 164, 165, [168] to 173, 175 to 180, 182 and 183, 185, 186 and 194, except in so far as it relates to paragraphs 104 to 106 of Schedule 11, shall come into force on such day as the Secretary of State may by order made by statutory instrument appoint, and different days may be so appointed for different provisions or for different purposes.

(3)   An order under subsection (2) above may contain such transitional provisions and savings (whether or not involving the modification of any statutory provision) as appear to the Secretary of State necessary or expedient in connection with the provisions brought into force by the order.

(4)   Subject to subsection (5) below, this Act, except Parts I and II and sections 36(9), 140 to 145, 150 to 152, 153, 155, 157, 159, 161, 166, 168, 170, 171, 176 to 182, 185, 190, 192, 194(1), 194(4) and this section, extends to England and Wales only.

(5)   Notwithstanding anything in subsection (4) above, any provision of Schedule 11 or Part II of Schedule 12 to this Act which amends or repeals any provision of the following enactments does not extend to Scotland—

    (a)   the Military Lands Act 1892;

    (b)   the Local Authorities (Expenditure Powers) Act 1983.

(6)   This Act does not extend to Northern Ireland.

[601]

PART I
STATUTES

NOTES

Sub-s (2): number in square brackets substituted by the Housing Act 2004, s 265(1), Sch 15, para 35. Orders: none of the commencement orders made under this section are relevant to the provisions of the Act reproduced in this work.

SCHEDULES

(Schs 1–5 outside the scope of this work; Sch 6 applies to Scotland only.)

SCHEDULE 7
COMPENSATION PROVISIONS OF LANDLORD AND TENANT ACT 1954, PART II
Section 149

1.   Any reference in this Schedule to a section which is not otherwise identified is a reference to that section of the Landlord and Tenant Act 1954, Part II of which relates to security of tenure for business, professional and other tenants.

2.   ...

3.   The amendments made by paragraph 2 above do not have effect unless the date which, apart from paragraph 4 below, is relevant for determining the rateable value of the holding under subsection (5) of section 37 is on or after 1st April 1990.

4.—(1)   Subject to paragraph 3 above and paragraph 5 below, in any case where—

    (a)   the tenancy concerned was entered into before 1st April 1990 or was entered into on or after that date in pursuance of a contract made before that date, and

    (b)   the landlord's notice under section 25 or, as the case may be, section 26(6) is given before 1st April 2000, and

    (c)   within the period referred to in section 29(3) for the making of an application under section 24(1), the tenant gives notice to the landlord that he wants the special basis of compensation provided for by this paragraph,

the amendments made by paragraph 2 above shall not have effect and section 37 shall, instead, have effect with the modification specified in sub-paragraph (2) below.

(2)   The modification referred to in sub-paragraph (1) above is that the date which is relevant for the purposes of determining the rateable value of the holding under subsection (5) of section 37 shall be 31st March 1990 instead of the date on which the landlord's notice is given.

5.   In any case where—

    (a)   paragraph 4(1)(a) above applies, and

    (b)   on 31st March 1990, the rateable value of the holding could be determined only in accordance with paragraph (c) of subsection (5) of section 37,

no notice may be given under paragraph 4(1)(b) above.

[602]

NOTES

Para 2: amends the Landlord and Tenant Act 1954, s 37 at **[262]**.

(Sch 8 spent; Schs 9–12 in so far as unrepealed outside the scope of this work.)

LANDLORD AND TENANT (LICENSED PREMISES) ACT 1990

(1990 c 39)

An Act to repeal section 43(1)(d) of the Landlord and Tenant Act 1954; and for connected purposes

[1 November 1990]

1 Licensed premises: application of Landlord and Tenant Act 1954, Part II

(1)   In the Landlord and Tenant Act 1954 (in this section referred to as "the 1954 Act"), in section 43 (tenancies excluded from Part II), paragraph (d) of subsection (1) (which excludes tenancies of premises licensed for the sale of intoxicating liquor for consumption on the premises) shall cease to have effect in relation to any tenancy entered into on or after 11th July 1989, otherwise than in pursuance of a contract made before that date.

(2)   If a tenancy—
  (a)   is of a description mentioned in paragraph (d) of subsection (1) of section 43 of the 1954 Act, and
  (b)   is in existence on 11th July 1992, and
  (c)   does not fall within subsection (1) above,
that paragraph shall cease to have effect in relation to the tenancy on and after 11th July 1992; and section 24(3)(b) of the 1954 Act (which, in certain cases, preserves the effect of a notice to quit given in respect of a tenancy which becomes one to which Part II of the 1954 Act applies) shall not have effect in the case of a tenancy which becomes one to which that Part applies by virtue of this subsection.

(3)   In relation to a tenancy falling within subsection (2) above, before 11th July 1992 the following notices may be given and any steps may be taken in consequence thereof as if section 43(1)(d) of the 1954 Act had already ceased to have effect—
  (a)   a notice under section 25 of the 1954 Act (termination of tenancy by landlord) specifying as the date of termination 11th July 1992 or any later date;
  (b)   a notice under section 26 of the 1954 Act (tenant's request for a new tenancy) requesting a new tenancy beginning not earlier than that date; and
  (c)   a notice under section 27(1) of the 1954 Act (termination by tenant of tenancy for fixed term) stating that the tenant does not desire his tenancy to be continued.

(4)   In this section "tenancy" has the same meaning as in Part II of the 1954 Act.

[603]

2 Short title, repeal, commencement and extent

(1)   This Act may be cited as the Landlord and Tenant (Licensed Premises) Act 1990.

(2)   Subject to subsections (1) and (2) of section 1 of this Act,—
  (a)   section 43(1)(d) of the Landlord and Tenant Act 1954, and
  (b)   paragraph 5 of Schedule 2 to the Finance Act 1959 (which amended section 43 by substituting the present subsection (1)(d)),
are hereby repealed.

(3)   This Act shall come into force at the end of the period of two months beginning with the day on which it is passed.

(4)   This Act does not extend to Scotland or Northern Ireland.

[604]

CHARITIES ACT 1993

(1993 c 10)

An Act to consolidate the Charitable Trustees Incorporation Act 1872 and, except for certain spent or transitional provisions, the Charities Act 1960 and Part I of the Charities Act 1992

[27 May 1993]

1–35 *((Pts I–IV) Outside the scope of this work.)*

PART V
CHARITY LAND

36 Restrictions on dispositions

(1) Subject to the following provisions of this section and section 40 below, no land held by or in trust for a charity shall be [conveyed, transferred], leased or otherwise disposed of without an order of the court or of [the Commission].

(2) Subsection (1) above shall not apply to a disposition of such land if—
    (a)   the disposition is made to a person who is not—
        (i)   a connected person (as defined in Schedule 5 to this Act), or
        (ii)   a trustee for, or nominee of, a connected person; and
    (b)   the requirements of subsection (3) or (5) below have been complied with in relation to it.

(3) Except where the proposed disposition is the granting of such a lease as is mentioned in subsection (5) below [the requirements mentioned in subsection (2)(b) above are that], the charity trustees must, before entering into an agreement for the sale, or (as the case may be) for a lease or other disposition, of the land—
    (a)   obtain and consider a written report on the proposed disposition from a qualified surveyor instructed by the trustees and acting exclusively for the charity;
    (b)   advertise the proposed disposition for such period and in such manner as the surveyor has advised in his report (unless he has there advised that it would not be in the best interests of the charity to advertise the proposed disposition); and
    (c)   decide that they are satisfied, having considered the surveyor's report, that the terms on which the disposition is proposed to be made are the best that can reasonably be obtained for the charity.

(4) For the purposes of subsection (3) above a person is a qualified surveyor if—
    (a)   he is a fellow or professional associate of the Royal Institution of Chartered Surveyors or of the Incorporated Society of Valuers and Auctioneers or satisfies such other requirement or requirements as may be prescribed by regulations made by the [Minister]; and
    (b)   he is reasonably believed by the charity trustees to have ability in, and experience of, the valuation of land of the particular kind, and in the particular area, in question;
and any report prepared for the purposes of that subsection shall contain such information, and deal with such matters, as may be prescribed by regulations so made.

(5) Where the proposed disposition is the granting of a lease for a term ending not more than seven years after it is granted (other than one granted wholly or partly in consideration of a fine), [the requirements mentioned in subsection (2)(b) above are that] the charity trustees must, before entering into an agreement for the lease—
    (a)   obtain and consider the advice on the proposed disposition of a person who is reasonably believed by the trustees to have the requisite ability and practical experience to provide them with competent advice on the proposed disposition; and
    (b)   decide that they are satisfied, having considered that person's advice, that the terms on which the disposition is proposed to be made are the best that can reasonably be obtained for the charity.

(6) Where—
    (a)   any land is held by or in trust for a charity, and
    (b)   the trusts on which it is so held stipulate that it is to be used for the purposes, or any particular purposes, of the charity,
then (subject to subsections (7) and (8) below and without prejudice to the operation of the preceding provisions of this section) the land shall not be *sold*, leased or otherwise disposed of unless the charity trustees have *previously*—
    (i)   given public notice of the proposed disposition, inviting representations to be made to them within a time specified in the notice, being not less than one month from the date of the notice; and
    (ii)   taken into consideration any representations made to them within that time about the proposed disposition.

[(6A)   In subsection (6) above "the relevant time" means—
    (a)   where the charity trustees enter into an agreement for the sale, or (as the case may be) for the lease or other disposition, the time when they enter into that agreement, and
    (b)   in any other case, the time of the disposition.]

(7)   Subsection (6) above shall not apply to any such disposition of land as is there mentioned if—
    (a)   the disposition is to be effected with a view to acquiring by way of replacement other property which is to be held on the trusts referred to in paragraph (b) of that subsection; or
    (b)   the disposition is the granting of a lease for a term ending not more than two years after it is granted (other than one granted wholly or partly in consideration of a fine).

(8)   [The Commission] may direct—
    (a)   that subsection (6) above shall not apply to dispositions of land held by or in trust for a charity or class of charities (whether generally or only in the case of a specified class of dispositions or land, or otherwise as may be provided in the direction), or
    (b)   that that subsection shall not apply to a particular disposition of land held by or in trust for a charity,

if, on an application made to them in writing by or on behalf of the charity or charities in question, [the Commission is satisfied] that it would be in the interests of the charity or charities [for the Commission] to give the direction.

(9)   The restrictions on disposition imposed by this section apply notwithstanding anything in the trusts of a charity; but nothing in this section applies—
    (a)   to any disposition for which general or special authority is expressly given (without the authority being made subject to the sanction of an order of the court) by any statutory provision contained in or having effect under an Act of Parliament or by any scheme legally established; or
    (b)   to any disposition of land held by or in trust for a charity which—
        (i)   is made to another charity otherwise than for the best price that can reasonably be obtained, and
        (ii)   is authorised to be so made by the trusts of the first-mentioned charity; or
    (c)   to the granting, by or on behalf of a charity and in accordance with its trusts, of a lease to any beneficiary under those trusts where the lease—
        (i)   is granted otherwise than for the best rent that can reasonably be obtained; and
        (ii)   is intended to enable the demised premises to be occupied for the purposes, or any particular purposes, of the charity.

(10)   Nothing in this section applies—
    (a)   to any disposition of land held by or in trust for an exempt charity;
    (b)   to any disposition of land by way of mortgage or other security; or
    (c)   to any disposition of an advowson.

(11)   In this section "land" means land in England or Wales.

[605]

NOTES

Sub-ss (1), (8): words in square brackets substituted by the Charities Act 2006, s 75(1), Sch 8, paras 96, 128(1), (2), (7).

Sub-ss (3), (5): words in square brackets inserted by the Charities Act 2006, s 75(1), Sch 8, paras 96, 128(1), (3), (4).

Sub-s (4): word in square brackets in para (a) substituted by the Transfer of Functions (Third Sector, Communities and Equality) Order 2006, SI 2006/2951, art 6, Schedule, para 4(o).

Sub-s (6): words in square brackets substituted for the word "sold" by the Charities Act 2006, s 75(1), Sch 8, paras 96, 128(1), (5), except in relation to any sale, lease or other disposition where before 27 February 2007 the charity trustees have entered into an agreement for the disposition; see the Charities Act 2006 (Commencement No 1, Transitional Provisions and Savings) Order 2007, SI 2007/309, art 6(1).

Sub-s (6A): inserted by the Charities Act 2006, s 75(1), Sch 8, paras 96, 128(1), (6), except in relation to any sale, lease or other disposition where before 27 February 2007 the charity trustees have entered into an agreement for the disposition; see the Charities Act 2006 (Commencement No 1, Transitional Provisions and Savings) Order 2007, SI 2007/309, art 6(1).

Regulations: the Charities (Qualified Surveyors' Reports) Regulations 1992, SI 1992/2980 (having effect as if made hereunder by virtue of the Interpretation Act 1978, s 17(2)(b)).

---

37 Supplementary provisions relating to dispositions

(1)   Any of the following instruments, namely—

(a)   any contract for the sale, or for a lease or other disposition, of land which is held by or in trust for a charity, and

(b)   any conveyance, transfer, lease or other instrument effecting a disposition of such land,

shall state—

(i)   that the land is held by or in trust for a charity,

(ii)   whether the charity is an exempt charity and whether the disposition is one falling within paragraph (a), (b) or (c) of subsection (9) of section 36 above, and

(iii)   if it is not an exempt charity and the disposition is not one falling within any of those paragraphs, that the land is land to which the restrictions on disposition imposed by that section apply.

(2)   Where any land held by or in trust for a charity is [conveyed, transferred], leased or otherwise disposed of by a disposition to which subsection (1) or (2) of section 36 above applies, the charity trustees shall certify in the instrument by which the disposition is effected—

(a)   (where subsection (1) of that section applies) that the disposition has been sanctioned by an order of the court or of [the Commission] (as the case may be), or

(b)   (where subsection (2) of that section applies) that the charity trustees have power under the trusts of the charity to effect the disposition, and that they have complied with the provisions of that section so far as applicable to it.

(3)   Where subsection (2) above has been complied with in relation to any disposition of land, then in favour of a person who (whether under the disposition or afterwards) acquires an interest in the land for money or money's worth, it shall be conclusively presumed that the facts were as stated in the certificate.

(4)   Where—

(a)   any land held by or in trust for a charity is [conveyed, transferred], leased or otherwise disposed of by a disposition to which subsection (1) or (2) of section 36 above applies, but

(b)   subsection (2) above has not been complied with in relation to the disposition,

then in favour of a person who (whether under the disposition or afterwards) in good faith acquires an interest in the land for money or money's worth, the disposition shall be valid whether or not—

(i)   the disposition has been sanctioned by an order of the court or of [the Commission], or

(ii)   the charity trustees have power under the trusts of the charity to effect the disposition and have complied with the provisions of that section so far as applicable to it.

(5)   Any of the following instruments, namely—

(a)   any contract for the sale, or for a lease or other disposition, of land which will, as a result of the disposition, be held by or in trust for a charity, and

(b)   any conveyance, transfer, lease or other instrument effecting a disposition of such land,

shall state—

(i)   that the land will, as a result of the disposition, be held by or in trust for a charity,

(ii)   whether the charity is an exempt charity, and

(iii)   if it is not an exempt charity, that the restrictions on disposition imposed by section 36 above will apply to the land (subject to subsection (9) of that section).

(6)   *In section 29(1) of the Settled Land Act 1925 (charitable and public trusts)*—

(a)   *the requirement for a conveyance of land held on charitable, ecclesiastical or public trusts to state that it is held on such trusts shall not apply to any instrument to which subsection (1) above applies; and*

(b)   *the requirement imposed on a purchaser, in the circumstances mentioned in section 29(1) of that Act, to see that any consents or orders requisite for authorising a transaction have been obtained shall not apply in relation to any disposition in relation to which subsection (2) above has been complied with;*

and expressions used in this subsection which are also used in that Act have the same meaning as in that Act.

[(7)   Where the disposition to be effected by any such instrument as is mentioned in subsection (1)(b) or (5)(b) above will be—
  (a)   a registrable disposition, or
  (b)   a disposition which triggers the requirement of registration,
the statement which, by virtue of subsection (1) or (5) above, is to be contained in the instrument shall be in such form as may be prescribed by land registration rules.

(8)   Where the registrar approves an application for registration of—
  (a)   a disposition of registered land, or
  (b)   a person's title under a disposition of unregistered land,
and the instrument effecting the disposition contains a statement complying with subsections (5) and (7) above, he shall enter in the register a restriction reflecting the limitation under section 36 above on subsequent disposal.]

(9)   Where—
  (a)   any such restriction is entered in the register in respect of any land, and
  (b)   the charity by or in trust for which the land is held becomes an exempt charity,
the charity trustees shall apply to the registrar for [the removal of the entry]; and on receiving any application duly made under this subsection the registrar shall [remove the entry].

(10)   Where—
  (a)   any registered land is held by or in trust for an exempt charity and the charity ceases to be an exempt charity, or
  (b)   any registered land becomes, as a result of a declaration of trust by the registered proprietor, land held in trust for a charity (other than an exempt charity),
the charity trustees shall apply to the registrar for such a restriction as is mentioned in subsection (8) above to be entered in the register in respect of the land; and on receiving any application duly made under this subsection the registrar shall enter such a restriction in the register in respect of the land.

(11)   In this section—
  (a)   references to a disposition of land do not include references to—
      (i)   a disposition of land by way of mortgage or other security,
      (ii)   any disposition of an advowson, or
      (iii)   any release of a rentcharge failing within section 40(1) below; and
  (b)   "land" means land in England or Wales;
and subsections (7) to (10) above shall be construed as one with the [Land Registration Act 2002].

[606]

NOTES
  Sub-ss (2), (4): words in square brackets substituted by the Charities Act 2006, s 75(1), Sch 8, paras 96, 129.
  Sub-s (6): repealed by the Trusts of Land and Appointment of Trustees Act 1996, s 25(2), Sch 4; the original wording is reproduced here for reasons of historical interest or in view of the savings contained in ss 3, 18(3), 25(5) of the 1996 Act.
  Sub-ss (7), (8): substituted by the Land Registration Act 2002, s 133, Sch 11, para 29(1), (2).
  Sub-ss (9), (11): words in square brackets substituted by the Land Registration Act 2002, s 133, Sch 11, para 29(1), (3), (4).
  Rules: the Land Registration Rules 2003, SI 2003/1417.

38–83   (*Outside the scope of this work.*)

PART X
SUPPLEMENTARY

84–95   (*Outside the scope of this work.*)

96   Construction of references to a "charity" or to particular classes of charity

  (1)   In this Act, except in so far as the context otherwise requires—
    "charity" means any institution, corporate or not, which is established for charitable purposes and is subject to the control of the High Court in the exercise of the court's jurisdiction with respect to charities;
    "ecclesiastical charity" has the same meaning as in the Local Government Act 1894;

"exempt charity" means (*subject to section 24(8) above*) a charity comprised in Schedule 2 to this Act;

"local charity" means, in relation to any area, a charity established for purposes which are by their nature or by the trusts of the charity directed wholly or mainly to the benefit of that area or of part of it;

"parochial charity" means, in relation to any parish or (in Wales) community, a charity the benefits of which are, or the separate distribution of the benefits of which is, confined to inhabitants of the parish or community, or of a single ancient ecclesiastical parish which included that parish or community or part of it, or of an area consisting of that parish or community with not more than four neighbouring parishes or communities.

(2) The expression "charity" is not in this Act applicable—

    (a) to any ecclesiastical corporation (that is to say, any corporation in the Church of England, whether sole or aggregate, which is established for spiritual purposes) in respect of the corporate property of the corporation, except to a corporation aggregate having some purposes which are not ecclesiastical in respect of its corporate property held for those purposes; or

    (b) to any Diocesan Board of Finance [(or any subsidiary thereof)] within the meaning of the Endowments and Glebe Measure 1976 for any diocese in respect of the diocesan glebe land of that diocese within the meaning of that Measure; or

    (c) to any trust of property for purposes for which the property has been consecrated.

(3) A charity shall be deemed for the purposes of this Act to have a permanent endowment unless all property held for the purposes of the charity may be expended for those purposes without distinction between capital and income, and in this Act "permanent endowment" means, in relation to any charity, property held subject to a restriction on its being expended for the purposes of the charity.

(4) *References in this Act to a charity whose income from all sources does not in aggregate amount to more than a specified amount shall be construed—*

    (a) *by reference to the gross revenues of the charity, or*

    (b) *if the Commissioners so determine, by reference to the amount which they estimate to be the likely amount of those revenues,*

but without (in either case) bringing into account anything for the yearly value of land occupied by the charity apart from the pecuniary income (if any) received from that land; and any question as to the application of any such reference to a charity shall be determined by the Commissioners, whose decision shall be final.

(5) [The Commission] may direct that for all or any of the purposes of this Act an institution established for any special purposes of or in connection with a charity (being charitable purposes) shall be treated as forming part of that charity or as forming a distinct charity.

[(6) [The Commission] may direct that for all or any of the purposes of this Act two or more charities having the same charity trustees shall be treated as a single charity.]

[607]

NOTES

Sub-s (1): definition "charity" substituted as follows—

""charity" has the meaning given by section 1(1) of the Charities Act 2006;", and

in definition "exempt charity" words in italics repealed by the Charities Act 2006, s 75(1), (2), Sch 8, paras 96, 173(1), (2), (3)(a), Sch 9, as from a day to be appointed.

Sub-s (2): in para (b) words in square brackets inserted by the Church of England (Miscellaneous Provisions) Measure 2000, s 11, subject to transitional provisions in s 19 of, and Sch 7 to, that Measure.

Sub-s (4): repealed by the Charities Act 2006, s 75(1), (2), Sch 8, paras 96, 173(1), (3)(b), Sch 9, as from a day to be appointed.

Sub-s (5): words in square brackets substituted by the Charities Act 2006, s 75(1), Sch 8, paras 96, 173(1), (4).

Sub-s (6): added by the Charities (Amendment) Act 1995, s 1; words in square brackets substituted by the Charities Act 2006, s 75(1), Sch 8, paras 96, 173(1), (4).

---

97 General interpretation

(1) In this Act, except in so far as the context otherwise requires—

"charitable purposes" means purposes which are exclusively *charitable according to the law of England and Wales;*

"charity trustees" means the persons having the general control and management of the administration of a charity;

["CIO" means charitable incorporated organisation;]

["the Commission" means the Charity Commission;]

"company" means a company formed and registered under the Companies Act 1985 or to which the provisions of that Act apply as they apply to such a company;

"the court" means the High Court and, within the limits of its jurisdiction, any other court in England and Wales having a jurisdiction in respect of charities concurrent (within any limit of area or amount) with that of the High Court, and includes any judge or officer of the court exercising the jurisdiction of the court;

"financial year"—

    (a)   in relation to a charity which is a company, shall be construed in accordance with section 223 of the Companies Act 1985; and

    (b)   in relation to any other charity, shall be construed in accordance with regulations made by virtue of section 42(2) above;

but this definition is subject to the transitional provisions in section 99(4) below and Part II of Schedule 8 to this Act;

"gross income", in relation to charity, means its gross recorded income from all sources including special trusts;

"independent examiner", in relation to a charity, means such a person as is mentioned in section 43(3)(a) above;

"institution" [means an institution whether incorporated or not, and] includes any trust or undertaking;

["members", in relation to a charity with a body of members distinct from the charity trustees, means any of those members;]

["the Minister" means the Minister for the Cabinet Office;]

"the official custodian" means the official custodian for charities;

"permanent endowment" shall be construed in accordance with section 96(3) above;

["principal regulator", in relation to an exempt charity, means the charity's principal regulator within the meaning of section 13 of the Charities Act 2006;]

"the register" means the register of charities kept under section 3 above and "registered" shall be construed accordingly;

"special trust" means property which is held and administered by or on behalf of a charity for any special purposes of the charity, and is so held and administered on separate trusts relating only to that property but a special trust shall not, by itself, constitute a charity for the purposes of Part VI of this Act;

["the Tribunal" means the Charity Tribunal;]

"trusts" in relation to a charity, means the provisions establishing it as a charity and regulating its purposes and administration, whether those provisions take effect by way of trust or not, and in relation to other institutions has a corresponding meaning.

(2)   In this Act, except in so far as the context otherwise requires, "document" includes information recorded in any form, and, in relation to information recorded otherwise than in legible form—

    (a)   any reference to its production shall be construed as a reference to the furnishing of a copy of it in legible form; and

    (b)   any reference to the furnishing of a copy of, or extract from, it shall accordingly be construed as a reference to the furnishing of a copy of, or extract from, it in legible form.

(3)   No vesting or transfer of any property in pursuance of any provision of [Part 4, 7, 8A or 9] of this Act shall operate as a breach of a covenant or condition against alienation or give rise to a forfeiture.

[608]–[609]

NOTES

Sub-s (1): in definition "charitable purpose" for the words in italics there are substituted the words "charitable purposes as defined by section 2(1) of the Charities Act 2006;" and definition "CIO" inserted by the Charities Act 2006, ss 34, 75(1), Sch 7, Pt 2, paras 3, 7, Sch 8, paras 96, 174(a), as from a day to be appointed under s 79(2) of that Act, and definition "the Commissioners" substituted, in definition "institution" words in square brackets inserted and definitions "members", "the Minister", "principal regulator" and "the Tribunal" inserted by s 75(1) of, and Sch 8, paras 96, 174(b)–(d) to, that Act.

Sub-s (3): words in square brackets substituted, except in so far as they refer to Part 8A, for the words "Part IV or IX" by the Charities Act 2006, s 75(1), Sch 8, paras 96, 175.

98, 99 (*S 98 outside the scope of this work, s 99 repealed by the Statute Law (Repeals) Act 2004.*)

100 Short title and extent

(1)   This Act may be cited as the Charities Act 1993.

(2)   Subject to subsection (3) to (6) below, this Act extends only to England and Wales.

(3)   [Sections 10 to 10C] above and this section extend to the whole of the United Kingdom.

(4)   Section 15(2) [and sections 24 to 25A extend] also to Northern Ireland.

(5)   ...

(6)   The amendments in Schedule 6 and the repeals in Schedule 7 have the same extent as the enactments to which they refer and section 98 above extends accordingly.

[610]

NOTES
Sub-s (3): words in square brackets substituted, except in so far as they refer to s 10B, for the words "Section 10" by the Charities Act 2006, s 75(1), Sch 8, paras 96, 176.
Sub-s (4): words in square brackets substituted by the Charities Act 2006, s 23(5).
Sub-s (5): repealed by the Charities and Investment (Scotland) Act 2005, s 95, Sch 3, para 9.

(*Sch 1 repealed by the Charities Act 2006, ss 6(6), 75(2), Sch 9; Schs 1A–1D, 2–8 outside the scope of this work.*)

SUNDAY TRADING ACT 1994

(1994 c 20)

An Act to reform the law of England and Wales relating to Sunday trading; to make provision as to the rights of shop workers under the law of England and Wales in relation to Sunday working; and for connected purposes

[5 July 1994]

1 Reform of law relating to Sunday trading

(1)   Schedules 1 and 2 to this Act shall come into force on such day as the Secretary of State may by order made by statutory instrument appoint (in this section referred to as "the appointed day").

(2)   ...

[611]

NOTES
Sub-s (2): repeals the Shops Act 1950, ss 47–66, Schs 5–7.
Orders: the Sunday Trading Act 1994 Appointed Day Order 1994, SI 1994/1841, appointing 26 August 1994 as the day on which Schs 1, 2 come into force.

2   (*Outside the scope of this work.*)

3 Construction of certain leases and agreements

(1)   Where any lease or agreement (however worded) entered into before the commencement of this section has the effect of requiring the occupier of a shop to keep the shop open for the serving of retail customers—
    (a)   during normal business hours, or
    (b)   during hours to be determined otherwise than by or with the consent of the occupier,
that lease or agreement shall not be regarded as requiring, or as enabling any person to require, the occupier to open the shop on Sunday for the serving of retail customers.

(2)   Subsection (1) above shall not affect any lease or agreement—

(a)   to the extent that it relates specifically to Sunday and would (apart from this section) have the effect of requiring Sunday trading of a kind which before the commencement of this section would have been lawful by virtue of any provision of Part IV of the Shops Act 1950, or

(b)   to the extent that it is varied by agreement after the commencement of this section.

(3)   In this section "retail customer" and "shop" have the same meaning as in Schedule 1 to this Act.

[612]

4–8   (*Ss 4, 6–8 outside the scope of this work; s 5 repealed by the Deregulation and Contracting Out Act 1994, s 81(1), Sch 17.*)

9   Short title, repeals, commencement and extent

(1)   This Act may be cited as the Sunday Trading Act 1994.

(2)   The enactments mentioned in Schedule 5 to this Act are hereby repealed to the extent specified in the third column of that Schedule.

(3)   The following provisions of this Act—

sections 2 to 5,

subsection (2) of this section, and

Schedules 3, 4 and 5,

shall not come into force until the appointed day (as defined in section 1 above).

(4)   This Act extends to England and Wales only.

[613]

SCHEDULES

SCHEDULE 1
RESTRICTIONS ON SUNDAY OPENING OF LARGE SHOPS

Section 1(1)

Interpretation

1.   In this Schedule—

["alcohol" has the same meaning as in the Licensing Act 2003,]

"large shop" means a shop which has a relevant floor area exceeding 280 square metres,

"medicinal product" and "registered pharmacy" have the same meaning as in the Medicines Act 1968,

"relevant floor area", in relation to a shop, means the internal floor area of so much of the shop as consists of or is comprised in a building, but excluding any part of the shop which, throughout the week ending with the Sunday in question, is used neither for the serving of customers in connection with the sale of goods nor for the display of goods,

"retail customer" means a person who purchases goods retail,

"retail sale" means any sale other than a sale for use or resale in the course of a trade or business, and references to retail purchase shall be construed accordingly,

"sale of goods" does not include—

(a)   the sale of meals, refreshments or [alcohol] for consumption on the premises on which they are sold, or

(b)   the sale of meals or refreshments prepared to order for immediate consumption off those premises,

"shop" means any premises where there is carried on a trade or business consisting wholly or mainly of the sale of goods, and

"stand", in relation to an exhibition, means any platform, structure, space or other area provided for exhibition purposes,

["veterinary medicinal product" has the same meaning as in regulation 2 of the Veterinary Medicines Regulations 2006.]

2.–9.   ...

[614]

NOTES

Para 1: definition "alcohol" substituted for definition "intoxicating liquor" and in definition "sale of goods" word in square brackets substituted by the Licensing Act 2003, s 198(1), Sch 6, para 110(1), (2); definition "veterinary medicinal product" inserted by the Veterinary Medicines Regulations 2006, SI 2006/2407, reg 44(3), Sch 9, Pt 1, para 9(a).

Paras 2–9: outside the scope of this work.

(Schs 2–5 outside the scope of this work.)

LAW OF PROPERTY (MISCELLANEOUS PROVISIONS) ACT 1994

(1994 c 36)

ARRANGEMENT OF SECTIONS

PART I
IMPLIED COVENANTS FOR TITLE

The covenants

Effect of covenants

Transitional provisions

PART II
MATTERS ARISING IN CONNECTION WITH DEATH

PART III
GENERAL PROVISIONS

An Act to provide for new covenants for title to be implied on dispositions of property; to amend the law with respect to certain matters arising in connection with the death of the owner of property; and for connected purposes

[3 November 1994]

PART I
IMPLIED COVENANTS FOR TITLE

The covenants

1 Covenants to be implied on a disposition of property

(1)   In an instrument effecting or purporting to effect a disposition of property there shall be implied on the part of the person making the disposition, whether or not the disposition is for valuable consideration, such of the covenants specified in sections 2 to 5 as are applicable to the disposition.

(2)   Of those sections—
  (a)   sections 2, 3(1) and (2), 4 and 5 apply where dispositions are expressed to be made with full title guarantee; and
  (b)   sections 2, 3(3), 4 and 5 apply where dispositions are expressed to be made with limited title guarantee.

(3)   Sections 2 to 4 have effect subject to section 6 (no liability under covenants in certain cases); and sections 2 to 5 have effect subject to section 8(1) (limitation or extension of covenants by instrument effecting the disposition).

(4)   In this Part—
  "disposition" includes the creation of a term of years;
  "instrument" includes an instrument which is not a deed; and
  "property" includes a thing in action, and any interest in real or personal property.

[615]

2 Right to dispose and further assurance

(1)   If the disposition is expressed to be made with full title guarantee or with limited title guarantee there shall be implied the following covenants—
  (a)   that the person making the disposition has the right (with the concurrence of any other person conveying the property) to dispose of the property as he purports to, and
  (b)   that that person will at his own cost do all that he reasonably can to give the person to whom he disposes of the property the title he purports to give.

(2)   The latter obligation includes—
  (a)   in relation to a disposition of an interest in land the title to which is registered, doing all that he reasonably can to ensure that the person to whom the disposition is made is entitled to be registered as proprietor with at least the class of title registered immediately before the disposition; and
  (b)   in relation to a disposition of an interest in land the title to which is required to be registered by virtue of the disposition, giving all reasonable assistance fully to establish to the satisfaction of the Chief Land Registrar the right of the person to whom the disposition is made to registration as proprietor.

(3)   In the case of a disposition of an existing legal interest in land, the following presumptions apply, subject to the terms of the instrument, in ascertaining for the purposes of the covenants implied by this section what the person making the disposition purports to dispose of—
  (a)   where the title to the interest is registered, it shall be presumed that the disposition is of the whole of that interest;
  (b)   where the title to the interest is not registered, then—
    (i)   if it appears from the instrument that the interest is a leasehold interest, it shall be presumed that the disposition is of the property for the unexpired portion of the term of years created by the lease; and
    (ii)   in any other case, it shall be presumed that what is disposed of is the fee simple.

[616]

3 Charges, incumbrances and third party rights

(1)   If the disposition is expressed to be made with full title guarantee there shall be implied a covenant that the person making the disposition is disposing of the property free—

(a)   from all charges and incumbrances (whether monetary or not), and

(b)   from all other rights exercisable by third parties,

other than any charges, incumbrances or rights which that person does not and could not reasonably be expected to know about.

(2)   In its application to charges, incumbrances and other third party rights subsection (1) extends to liabilities imposed and rights conferred by or under any enactment, except to the extent that such liabilities and rights are, by reason of—

(a)   being, at the time of the disposition, only potential liabilities and rights in relation to the property, or

(b)   being liabilities and rights imposed or conferred in relation to property generally,

not such as to constitute defects in title.

(3)   If the disposition is expressed to be made with limited title guarantee there shall be implied a covenant that the person making the disposition has not since the last disposition for value—

(a)   charged or incumbered the property by means of any charge or incumbrance which subsists at the time when the disposition is made, or granted third party rights in relation to the property which so subsist, or

(b)   suffered the property to be so charged or incumbered or subjected to any such rights,

and that he is not aware that anyone else has done so since the last disposition for value.

[617]

4 Validity of lease

(1)   Where the disposition is of leasehold land and is expressed to be made with full title guarantee or with limited title guarantee, the following covenants shall also be implied—

(a)   that the lease is subsisting at the time of the disposition, and

(b)   that there is no subsisting breach of a condition or tenant's obligation, and nothing which at that time would render the lease liable to forfeiture.

(2)   If the disposition is the grant of an underlease, the references to "the lease" in subsection (1) are references to the lease out of which the underlease is created.

[618]

5 Discharge of obligations where property subject to rentcharge or leasehold land

(1)   Where the disposition is a mortgage of property subject to a rentcharge, [of leasehold land or of a commonhold unit], and is expressed to be made with full title guarantee or with limited title guarantee, the following covenants shall also be implied.

(2)   If the property is subject to a rentcharge, there shall be implied a covenant that the mortgagor will fully and promptly observe and perform all the obligations under the instrument creating the rentcharge that are for the time being enforceable with respect to the property by the owner of the rentcharge in his capacity as such.

(3)   If the property is leasehold land, there shall be implied a covenant that the mortgagor will fully and promptly observe and perform all the obligations under the lease subject to the mortgage that are for the time being imposed on him in his capacity as tenant under the lease.

[(3A   If the property is a commonhold unit, there shall be implied a covenant that the mortgagor will fully and promptly observe and perform all the obligations under the commonhold community statement that are for the time being imposed on him in his capacity as a unit-holder or as a joint unit-holder.]

[(4)   In this section—

(a)   "commonhold community statement", "commonhold unit", "joint unit-holder" and "unit-holder" have the same meanings as in the Commonhold and Leasehold Reform Act 2002, and

(b)   "mortgage" includes charge, and "mortgagor" shall be construed accordingly.]

[619]

NOTES

Sub-s (1): words in square brackets substituted by the Commonhold and Leasehold Reform Act 2002, s 68, Sch 5, para 7(1), (2).

Sub-s (3A): inserted by the Commonhold and Leasehold Reform Act 2002, s 68, Sch 5, para 7(1), (3).

Sub-s (4): substituted by the Commonhold and Leasehold Reform Act 2002, s 68, Sch 5, para 7(1), (4).

Effect of covenants

6   No liability under covenants in certain cases

(1)   The person making the disposition is not liable under the covenants implied by virtue of—

(a)   section 2(1)(a) (right to dispose),

(b)   section 3 (charges, incumbrances and third party rights), or

(c)   section 4 (validity of lease),

in respect of any particular matter to which the disposition is expressly made subject.

(2)   Furthermore that person is not liable under any of those covenants for anything (not falling within subsection (1))—

(a)   which at the time of the disposition is within the actual knowledge, or

(b)   which is a necessary consequence of facts that are then within the actual knowledge,

of the person to whom the disposition is made.

(3)   For this purpose section 198 of the Law of Property Act 1925 (deemed notice by virtue of registration) shall be disregarded.

[(4)   Moreover, where the disposition is of an interest the title to which is registered under the Land Registration Act 2002, that person is not liable under any of those covenants for anything (not falling within subsection (1) or (2)) which at the time of the disposition was entered in relation to that interest in the register of title under that Act.]

[620]

NOTES

Sub-s (4): added by the Land Registration Act 2002, s 133, Sch 11, para 31(1), (2).

7   Annexation of benefit of covenants

The benefit of a covenant implied by virtue of this Part shall be annexed and incident to, and shall go with, the estate or interest of the person to whom the disposition is made, and shall be capable of being enforced by every person in whom that estate or interest is (in whole or in part) for the time being vested.

[621]

8   Supplementary provisions

(1)   The operation of any covenant implied in an instrument by virtue of this Part may be limited or extended by a term of that instrument.

(2)   Sections 81 and 83 of the Law of Property Act 1925 (effect of covenant with two or more jointly; construction of implied covenants) apply to a covenant implied by virtue of this Part as they apply to a covenant implied by virtue of that Act.

(3)   Where in an instrument effecting or purporting to effect a disposition of property a person is expressed to direct the disposition, this Part applies to him as if he were the person making the disposition.

(4)   This Part has effect—

(a)   where "gyda gwarant teitl llawn" is used instead of "with full title guarantee", and

(b)   where "gyda gwarant teitl cyfyngedig" is used instead of "with limited title guarantee",

as it has effect where the English words are used.

[622]

9 Modifications of statutory forms

(1) Where a form set out in an enactment, or in an instrument made under an enactment, includes words which (in an appropriate case) would have resulted in the implication of a covenant by virtue of section 76 of the Law of Property Act 1925, the form shall be taken to authorise instead the use of the words "with full title guarantee" or "with limited title guarantee" or their Welsh equivalent given in section 8(4).

(2) This applies in particular to the forms set out in ... Schedules 4 ... to the Law of Property Act 1925.

[623]

NOTES
Sub-s (2): words omitted repealed by the Statute Law (Repeals) Act 2004.

Transitional provisions

10 General saving for covenants in old form

(1) Except as provided by section 11 below (cases in which covenants in old form implied on disposition after commencement), ... as regards dispositions of property made after the commencement of this Part.

(2) The repeal of those provisions by this Act accordingly does not affect the enforcement of a covenant implied by virtue of either of them on a disposition before the commencement of this Part.

[624]

NOTES
Sub-s (1): words omitted repeal the Law of Property Act 1925, s 76, and the Land Registration Act 1925, s 24(1)(a).

11 Covenants in old form implied in certain cases

(1) Section 76 of the Law of Property Act 1925 applies in relation to a disposition of property made after the commencement of this Part in pursuance of a contract entered into before commencement where—
  (a) the contract contains a term providing for a disposition to which that section would have applied if the disposition had been made before commencement, and
  (b) the existence of the contract and of that term is apparent on the face of the instrument effecting the disposition,
unless there has been an intervening disposition of the property expressed, in accordance with this Part, to be made with full title guarantee.

(2) Section 24(1)(a) of the Land Registration Act 1925 applies in relation to a disposition of a leasehold interest in land made after the commencement of this Part in pursuance of a contract entered into before commencement where—
  (a) the covenant specified in that provision would have been implied on the disposition if it had been made before commencement, and
  (b) the existence of the contract is apparent on the face of the instrument effecting the disposition,
unless there has been an intervening disposition of the leasehold interest expressed, in accordance with this Part, to be made with full title guarantee.

(3) In subsections (1) and (2) an "intervening disposition" means a disposition after the commencement of this Part to, or to a predecessor in title of, the person by whom the disposition in question is made.

(4) Where in order for subsection (1) or (2) to apply it is necessary for certain matters to be apparent on the face of the instrument effecting the disposition, the contract shall be deemed to contain an implied term that they should so appear.

[625]

12 Covenants in new form to be implied in other cases

(1) This section applies to a contract for the disposition of property entered into before the commencement of this Part where the disposition is made after commencement and

section 11 (cases in which covenants in old form to be implied) does not apply because there has been an intervening disposition expressed, in accordance with this Part, to be with full title guarantee.

(2) A contract which contains a term that the person making the disposition shall do so as beneficial owner shall be construed as requiring that person to do so by an instrument expressed to be made with full title guarantee.

(3) A contract which contains a term that the person making the disposition shall do so—

(a) as settlor, or

(b) as trustee or mortgagee or personal representative,

shall be construed as requiring that person to do so by an instrument expressed to be made with limited title guarantee.

(4) A contract for the disposition of a leasehold interest in land entered into at a date when the title to the leasehold interest was registered shall be construed as requiring the person making the disposition for which it provides to do so by an instrument expressed to be made with full title guarantee.

(5) Where this section applies and the contract provides that any of the covenants to be implied by virtue of section 76 of the Law of Property Act 1925 or section 24(1)(a) of the Land Registration Act 1925 shall be implied in a modified form, the contract shall be construed as requiring a corresponding modification of the covenants implied by virtue of this Part.

[626]

13 Application of transitional provisions in relation to options

For the purposes of sections 11 and 12 (transitional provisions, implication of covenants in old form in certain cases and new form in others) as they apply in relation to a disposition of property in accordance with an option granted before the commencement of this Part and exercised after commencement, the contract for the disposition shall be deemed to have been entered into on the grant of the option.

[627]

PART II
MATTERS ARISING IN CONNECTION WITH DEATH

14–16 (*Outside the scope of this work.*)

17 Notices affecting land: absence of knowledge of intended recipient's death

(1) Service of a notice affecting land which would be effective but for the death of the intended recipient is effective despite his death if the person serving the notice has no reason to believe that he has died.

(2) Where the person serving a notice affecting land has no reason to believe that the intended recipient has died, the proper address for the purposes of section 7 of the Interpretation Act 1978 (service of documents by post) shall be what would be the proper address apart from his death.

(3) The above provisions do not apply to a notice authorised or required to be served for the purposes of proceedings before—

(a) any court,

(b) any tribunal specified in Schedule 1 to the Tribunals and Inquiries Act 1992 (tribunals within general supervision of Council on Tribunals), or

(c) the Chief Land Registrar or [the Adjudicator to Her Majesty's Land Registry];

but this is without prejudice to the power to make provision in relation to such proceedings by rules of court, procedural rules within the meaning of section 8 of the Tribunals and Inquiries Act 1992 or rules under section 144 of [the Land Registration Act 2002].

[628]

NOTES

Sub-s (3): words in square brackets substituted by the Land Registration Act 2002, s 133, Sch 11, para 31(1), (3).

18   Notices affecting land: service on personal representatives before filing of grant

(1)   A notice affecting land which would have been authorised or required to be served on a person but for his death shall be sufficiently served before a grant of representation has been filed if—

(a)   it is addressed to "The Personal Representatives of" the deceased (naming him) and left at or sent by post to his last known place of residence or business in the United Kingdom, and

(b)   a copy of it, similarly addressed, is served on the Public Trustee.

(2)   The reference in subsection (1) to the filing of a grant of representation is to the filing at the Principal Registry of the Family Division of the High Court of a copy of a grant of representation in respect of the deceased's estate or, as the case may be, the part of his estate which includes the land in question.

(3)   The method of service provided for by this section is not available where provision is made—

(a)   by or under any enactment, or

(b)   by an agreement in writing,

requiring a different method of service, or expressly prohibiting the method of service provided for by this section, in the circumstances.

[629]

19   Functions of Public Trustee in relation to notices, etc

(1)   The Public Trustee may give directions as to the office or offices at which documents may be served on him—

(a)   by virtue of section 9 of the Administration of Estates Act 1925 (as substituted by section 14(1) above), or

(b)   in pursuance of section 18(1)(b) above (service on Public Trustee of copy of certain notices affecting land);

and he shall publish such directions in such manner as he considers appropriate.

(2)   The Lord Chancellor may by regulations make provision with respect to the functions of the Public Trustee in relation to such documents; and the regulations may make different provision in relation to different descriptions of document or different circumstances.

(3)   The regulations may, in particular, make provision requiring the Public Trustee—

(a)   to keep such documents for a specified period and thereafter to keep a copy or record of their contents in such form as may be specified;

(b)   to keep such documents, copies and records available for inspection at such reasonable hours as may be specified; and

(c)   to supply copies to any person on request.

In this subsection "specified" means specified by or under the regulations.

(4)   Regulations under this section shall be made by statutory instrument which shall be subject to annulment in pursuance of a resolution of either House of Parliament.

(5)   The following provisions of the Public Trustee Act 1906, namely—

(a)   section 8(5) (payment of expenses out of money provided by Parliament), and

(b)   section 9(1) [and (3)] (provisions as to fees),

apply in relation to the functions of the Public Trustee in relation to documents to which this section applies as in relation to his functions under that Act.

[630]

NOTES

Sub-s (5): words in square brackets substituted by the Public Trustee (Liability and Fees) Act 2002, s 2(4).

Regulations: the Public Trustee (Notices Affecting Land) (Title on Death) Regulations 1995, SI 1995/1330.

PART III
GENERAL PROVISIONS

20 Crown application

This Act binds the Crown.

[631]

21 Consequential amendments and repeals

(1)   The enactments specified in Schedule 1 are amended in accordance with that Schedule, the amendments being consequential on the provisions of this Act.

(2)   The enactments specified in Schedule 2 are repealed to the extent specified.

(3)   In the case of section 76 of the Law of Property Act 1925 and section 24(1)(a) of the Land Registration Act 1925, those provisions are repealed in accordance with section 10(1) above (general saving for covenants in old form).

(4)   The amendments consequential on Part I of this Act (namely those in paragraphs 1, 2, 3, 5, 7, 9 and 12 of Schedule 1) shall not have effect in relation to any disposition of property to which, by virtue of section 10(1) or 11 above (transitional provisions), section 76 of the Law of Property Act 1925 or section 24(1)(a) of the Land Registration Act 1925 continues to apply.

[632]

22 Extent

(1)   The provisions of this Act extend to England and Wales.

(2)   In addition—
   (a)   the provisions of Schedules 1 and 2 (consequential amendments and repeals) extend to Scotland so far as they relate to enactments which so extend; and
   (b)   the provisions of Schedule 1 extend to Northern Ireland so far as they relate to enactments which so extend.

[633]

23 Commencement

(1)   The provisions of this Act come into force on such day as the Lord Chancellor may appoint by order made by statutory instrument.

(2)   Different days may be appointed for different provisions and for different purposes.

[634]

NOTES

Orders: the Law of Property (Miscellaneous Provisions) Act 1994 (Commencement No 1) Order 1995, SI 1995/145; the Law of Property (Miscellaneous Provisions) Act 1994 (Commencement No 2) Order 1995, SI 1995/1317.

---

24 Short title

This Act may be cited as the Law of Property (Miscellaneous Provisions) Act 1994.

[635]

(Schs 1, 2 outside the scope of this work.)

AGRICULTURAL TENANCIES ACT 1995

(1995 c 8)

ARRANGEMENT OF SECTIONS

PART I
GENERAL PROVISIONS

Farm business tenancies

PART II
RENT REVIEW UNDER FARM BUSINESS TENANCY

PART III
COMPENSATION ON TERMINATION OF FARM BUSINESS TENANCY

Tenant's entitlement to compensation

PART IV
MISCELLANEOUS AND SUPPLEMENTAL

Resolution of disputes

Miscellaneous

Supplemental

An Act to make further provision with respect to tenancies which include agricultural land.
[9 May 1995]

PART I
GENERAL PROVISIONS

Farm business tenancies

1 Meaning of "farm business tenancy"

(1)   A tenancy is a "farm business tenancy" for the purposes of this Act if—
    (a)   it meets the business conditions together with either the agriculture condition or the notice conditions, and
    (b)   it is not a tenancy which, by virtue of section 2 of this Act, cannot be a farm business tenancy.

(2)   The business conditions are—
    (a)   that all or part of the land comprised in the tenancy is farmed for the purposes of a trade or business, and
    (b)   that, since the beginning of the tenancy, all or part of the land so comprised has been so farmed.

(3)   The agriculture condition is that, having regard to—
    (a)   the terms of the tenancy,
    (b)   the use of the land comprised in the tenancy,
    (c)   the nature of any commercial activities carried on on that land, and
    (d)   any other relevant circumstances,
the character of the tenancy is primarily or wholly agricultural.

(4)   The notice conditions are—
    (a)   that, on or before the relevant day, the landlord and the tenant each gave the other a written notice—
        (i)   identifying (by name or otherwise) the land to be comprised in the tenancy or proposed tenancy, and
        (ii)   containing a statement to the effect that the person giving the notice intends that the tenancy or proposed tenancy is to be, and remain, a farm business tenancy, and

(b) that, at the beginning of the tenancy, having regard to the terms of the tenancy and any other relevant circumstances, the character of the tenancy was primarily or wholly agricultural.

(5) In subsection (4) above "the relevant day" means whichever is the earlier of the following—

(a) the day on which the parties enter into any instrument creating the tenancy, other than an agreement to enter into a tenancy on a future date, or

(b) the beginning of the tenancy.

(6) The written notice referred to in subsection (4) above must not be included in any instrument creating the tenancy.

(7) If in any proceedings—

(a) any question arises as to whether a tenancy was a farm business tenancy at any time, and

(b) it is proved that all or part of the land comprised in the tenancy was farmed for the purposes of a trade or business at that time,

it shall be presumed, unless the contrary is proved, that all or part of the land so comprised has been so farmed since the beginning of the tenancy.

(8) Any use of land in breach of the terms of the tenancy, any commercial activities carried on in breach of those terms, and any cessation of such activities in breach of those terms, shall be disregarded in determining whether at any time the tenancy meets the business conditions or the agriculture condition, unless the landlord or his predecessor in title has consented to the breach or the landlord has acquiesced in the breach.

[636]

2 Tenancies which cannot be farm business tenancies

(1) A tenancy cannot be a farm business tenancy for the purposes of this Act if—

(a) the tenancy begins before 1st September 1995, or

(b) it is a tenancy of an agricultural holding beginning on or after that date with respect to which, by virtue of section 4 of this Act, the Agricultural Holdings Act 1986 applies.

(2) In this section "agricultural holding" has the same meaning as in the Agricultural Holdings Act 1986.

[637]

3 Compliance with notice conditions in cases of surrender and re-grant

(1) This section applies where—

(a) a tenancy ("the new tenancy") is granted to a person who, immediately before the grant, was the tenant under a farm business tenancy ("the old tenancy") which met the notice conditions specified in section 1(4) of this Act,

(b) the condition in subsection (2) below or the condition in subsection (3) below is met, and

(c) except as respects the matters mentioned in subsections (2) and (3) below and matters consequential on them, the terms of the new tenancy are substantially the same as the terms of the old tenancy.

(2) The first condition referred to in subsection (1)(b) above is that the land comprised in the new tenancy is the same as the land comprised in the old tenancy, apart from any changes in area which are small in relation to the size of the holding and do not affect the character of the holding.

(3) The second condition referred to in subsection (1)(b) above is that the old tenancy and the new tenancy are both fixed term tenancies, but the term date under the new tenancy is earlier than the term date under the old tenancy.

(4) Where this section applies, the new tenancy shall be taken for the purposes of this Act to meet the notice conditions specified in section 1(4) of this Act.

(5) In subsection (3) above, "the term date", in relation to a fixed term tenancy, means the date fixed for the expiry of the term.

[638]

Exclusion of Agricultural Holdings Act 1986

4 Agricultural Holdings Act 1986 not to apply in relation to new tenancies except in special cases

(1) The Agricultural Holdings Act 1986 (in this section referred to as "the 1986 Act") shall not apply in relation to any tenancy beginning on or after 1st September 1995 (including any agreement to which section 2 of that Act would otherwise apply beginning on or after that date), except [(subject to subsection (2B) below)] any tenancy of an agricultural holding which—

(a)   is granted by a written contract of tenancy entered into before 1st September 1995 and indicating (in whatever terms) that the 1986 Act is to apply in relation to the tenancy,

(b)   is obtained by virtue of a direction of an Agricultural Land Tribunal under section 39 or 53 of the 1986 Act,

(c)   is granted (following a direction under section 39 of that Act) in circumstances falling within section 45(6) of that Act,

(d)   is granted on an agree of the 1986 Act is to apply in relation to the tenancy, d succession by a written contract of tenancy indicating (in whatever terms) that Part IV,

(e)   is created by the acceptance of a tenant, in accordance with the provisions as to compensation known as the "Evesham custom" and set out in subsections (3) to (5) of section 80 of the 1986 Act, on the terms and conditions of the previous tenancy, …

(f)   is granted to a person who, immediately before the grant of the tenancy, was the tenant of the holding, or of any agricultural holding which comprised the whole or a substantial part of the land comprised in the holding, under a tenancy in relation to which the 1986 Act applied[, and is so granted because an agreement between the parties (not being an agreement expressed to take effect as a new tenancy between the parties) has effect as an implied surrender followed by the grant of the tenancy, or]

[(g)   is granted to a person who, immediately before the grant of the tenancy, was the tenant of the holding, or of any agricultural holding which comprised the whole or a substantial part of the land comprised in the holding, under a tenancy in relation to which the 1986 Act applied, and is so granted by a written contract of tenancy indicating (in whatever terms) that the 1986 Act is to apply in relation to the tenancy.]

(2) For the purposes of subsection (1)(d) above, a tenancy ("the current tenancy") is granted on an agreed succession if, and only if,—

(a)   the previous tenancy of the holding or a related holding was a tenancy in relation to which Part IV of the 1986 Act applied, …

[(b)   the current tenancy is granted to a person (alone or jointly with other persons) who, if the tenant under that previous tenancy ("the previous tenant") had died immediately before the grant, would have been his close relative, and

·(c)   either of the conditions in subsection (2A) below is satisfied.]

[(2A)   The conditions referred to in subsection (2)(c) above are—

(a)   the current tenancy is granted to a person (alone or jointly with other persons) who was or had become the sole or sole remaining applicant for a direction of an Agricultural Land Tribunal for a tenancy, and

(b)   the current tenancy—

(i)   is granted as a result of an agreement between the landlord and the previous tenant, and

(ii)   is granted, and begins, before the date of the giving of any retirement notice by the previous tenant, or if no retirement notice is given, before the date of death of the previous tenant.]

[(2B)   The 1986 Act shall not apply by virtue of subsection (1)(f) or (g) above in relation to the tenancy of an agricultural holding ("the current holding") where—

(a)   the whole or a substantial part of the land comprised in the current holding was comprised in an agricultural holding ("the previous holding") which was subject to a tenancy granted after the commencement of this subsection in relation to which the 1986 Act applied by virtue of subsection (1)(f) or (g) above;

(b)   the whole or a substantial part of the land comprised in the previous holding was comprised in an agricultural holding ("the original holding") which was at the commencement of this subsection subject to a tenancy in relation to which the 1986 Act applied; and

(c)   the land comprised in the original holding does not, on the date of the grant of the tenancy of the current holding, comprise the whole or a substantial part of the land comprised in the current holding.]

[(2C)   The references in subsections (1)(g) and (2B) above to a substantial part of the land comprised in the holding mean a substantial part determined by reference to either area or value.]

(3)   In this section—
   (a)   "agricultural holding" and "contract of tenancy" have the same meaning as in the 1986 Act, …
   (b)   "close relative" and "related holding" have the meaning given by section 35(2) of that Act[, and
   (c)   "retirement notice" has the meaning given by section 49(3) of that Act.]

[639]

PART I STATUTES

NOTES

Sub-s (1): words in first pair of square brackets inserted, word omitted from para (e) repealed, words in square brackets in para (f) substituted and para (g) added, except in relation to any tenancy granted before 19 October 2006, by the Regulatory Reform (Agricultural Tenancies) (England and Wales) Order 2006, SI 2006/2805, arts 11, 12(1)–(5), (12), 18, Sch 2.

Sub-s (2): word omitted repealed and paras (b), (c) substituted for para (b) as originally enacted, except in relation to any tenancy granted before 19 October 2006, by SI 2006/2805, arts 11, 12(1), (6), (7), (12), 18, Sch 2.

Sub-ss (2A)–(2C): inserted, except in relation to any tenancy granted before 19 October 2006, by SI 2006/2805, arts 11, 12(1), (8)–(10), (12).

Sub-s (3): word omitted repealed and para (c) and immediately preceding word added, except in relation to any tenancy granted before 19 October 2006, by SI 2006/2805, arts 11, 12(1), (11), (12), 18, Sch 2.

Termination of the tenancy

5   Tenancies for more than two years to continue from year to year unless terminated by notice

(1)   A farm business tenancy for a term of more than two years shall, instead of terminating on the term date, continue (as from that date) as a tenancy from year to year, but otherwise on the terms of the original tenancy so far as applicable, unless at least twelve months … before the term date a written notice has been given by either party to the other of his intention to terminate the tenancy.

(2)   In subsection (1) above "the term date", in relation to a fixed term tenancy, means the date fixed for the expiry of the term.

(3)   For the purposes of section 140 of the Law of Property Act 1925 (apportionment of conditions on severance of reversion), a notice under subsection (1) above shall be taken to be a notice to quit.

(4)   This section has effect notwithstanding any agreement to the contrary.

[640]

NOTES

Sub-s (1): words omitted repealed the Regulatory Reform (Agricultural Tenancies) (England and Wales) Order 2006, SI 2006/2805, arts 11, 13, 18, Sch 2.

---

6   Length of notice to quit

(1)   Where a farm business tenancy is a tenancy from year to year, a notice to quit the holding or part of the holding shall (notwithstanding any provision to the contrary in the tenancy) be invalid unless—
   (a)   it is in writing,
   (b)   it is to take effect at the end of a year of the tenancy, and
   (c)   it is given at least twelve months … before the date on which it is to take effect.

(2) Where, by virtue of section 5(1) of this Act, a farm business tenancy for a term of more than two years is to continue (as from the term date) as a tenancy from year to year, a notice to quit which complies with subsection (1) above and which is to take effect on the first anniversary of the term date shall not be invalid merely because it is given before the term date; and in this subsection "the term date" has the meaning given by section 5(2) of this Act.

(3) Subsection (1) above does not apply in relation to a counter-notice given by the tenant by virtue of subsection (2) of section 140 of the Law of Property Act 1925 (apportionment of conditions on severance of reversion).

[641]

NOTES

Sub-s (1): words omitted repealed the Regulatory Reform (Agricultural Tenancies) (England and Wales) Order 2006, SI 2006/2805, arts 11, 13, 18, Sch 2.

7 Notice required for exercise of option to terminate tenancy or resume possession of part

(1) Where a farm business tenancy is a tenancy for a term of more than two years, any notice to quit the holding or part of the holding given in pursuance of any provision of the tenancy shall (notwithstanding any provision to the contrary in the tenancy) be invalid unless it is in writing and is given at least twelve months ... before the date on which it is to take effect.

(2) Subsection (1) above does not apply in relation to a counter-notice given by the tenant by virtue of subsection (2) of section 140 of the Law of Property Act 1925 (apportionment of conditions on severance of reversion).

(3) Subsection (1) above does not apply to a tenancy which, by virtue of subsection (6) of section 149 of the Law of Property Act 1925 (lease for life or lives or for a term determinable with life or lives or on the marriage of[, or formation of a civil partnership by,] the lessee), takes effect as such a term of years as is mentioned in that subsection.

[642]

NOTES

Sub-s (1): words omitted repealed by the Regulatory Reform (Agricultural Tenancies) (England and Wales) Order 2006, SI 2006/2805, arts 11, 13, 18, Sch 2.
Sub-s (3): words in square brackets inserted by the Civil Partnership Act 2004, s 81, Sch 8, para 49.

Tenant's right to remove fixtures and buildings

8 Tenant's right to remove fixtures and buildings

(1) Subject to the provisions of this section—
  (a) any fixture (of whatever description) affixed, whether for the purposes of agriculture or not, to the holding by the tenant under a farm business tenancy, and
  (b) any building erected by him on the holding,
may be removed by the tenant at any time during the continuance of the tenancy or at any time after the termination of the tenancy when he remains in possession as tenant (whether or not under a new tenancy), and shall remain his property so long as he may remove it by virtue of this subsection.

(2) Subsection (1) above shall not apply—
  (a) to a fixture affixed or a building erected in pursuance of some obligation,
  (b) to a fixture affixed or a building erected instead of some fixture or building belonging to the landlord,
  (c) to a fixture or building in respect of which the tenant has obtained compensation under section 16 of this Act or otherwise, or
  (d) to a fixture or building in respect of which the landlord has given his consent under section 17 of this Act on condition that the tenant agrees not to remove it and which the tenant has agreed not to remove.

(3) In the removal of a fixture or building by virtue of subsection (1) above, the tenant shall not do any avoidable damage to the holding.

(4)   Immediately after removing a fixture or building by virtue of subsection (1) above, the tenant shall make good all damage to the holding that is occasioned by the removal.

(5)   This section applies to a fixture or building acquired by a tenant as it applies to a fixture or building affixed or erected by him.

(6)   Except as provided by subsection (2)(d) above, this section has effect notwithstanding any agreement or custom to the contrary.

(7)   No right to remove fixtures that subsists otherwise than by virtue of this section shall be exercisable by the tenant under a farm business tenancy.

[643]

PART II
RENT REVIEW UNDER FARM BUSINESS TENANCY

9   Application of Part II

This Part of this Act applies in relation to a farm business tenancy (notwithstanding any agreement to the contrary) unless the tenancy is created by an instrument which—
  (a)   expressly states that the rent is not to be reviewed during the tenancy, ...
  (b)   provides that the rent is to be varied, at a specified time or times during the tenancy—
      (i)   by or to a specified amount, or
      (ii)   in accordance with a specified formula which does not preclude a reduction and which does not require or permit the exercise by any person of any judgment or discretion in relation to the determination of the rent of the holding,
but otherwise is to remain fixed[, or
  (c)   does not contain any provision which precludes a reduction in the rent during the tenancy, and—
      (i)   expressly states that this Part of this Act does not apply, or
      (ii)   makes provision for the reference of rent reviews to an independent expert whose decision is final.]

[644]

NOTES

Word omitted from para (a) repealed and para (c) and word "or" immediately preceding it added by the Regulatory Reform (Agricultural Tenancies) (England and Wales) Order 2006, SI 2006/2805, arts 11, 14(1), 18, Sch 2; for effect see art 14(3) thereof.

10   Notice requiring statutory rent review

(1)   The landlord or tenant under a farm business tenancy in relation to which this Part of this Act applies may by notice in writing given to the other (in this Part of this Act referred to as a "statutory review notice") require that the rent to be payable in respect of the holding as from the review date shall be referred to arbitration in accordance with this Act.

(2)   In this Part of this Act "the review date", in relation to a statutory review notice, means a date which—
  (a)   is specified in the notice, and
  (b)   complies with subsections (3) to (6) below.

(3)   The review date must be at least twelve months but less than twenty-four months after the day on which the statutory review notice is given.

(4)   If the parties have agreed in writing that the rent is to be, or may be, varied as from a specified date or dates, or at specified intervals, the review date must be a date as from which the rent could be varied under the agreement.

(5)   If the parties have agreed in writing that the review date for the purposes of this Part of this Act is to be a specified date or dates, the review date must be that date or one of those dates.

(6)   If the parties have not agreed as mentioned in subsection (4) or (5) above, the review date—
  (a)   must be an anniversary of the beginning of the tenancy or, where the landlord and

the tenant have agreed in writing that the review date for the purposes of this Act is to be some other day of the year, that day of the year, and

(b) must not fall before the end of the period of three years beginning with the latest of any of the following dates—

    (i) the beginning of the tenancy,

    (ii) any date as from which there took effect a previous direction of an arbitrator as to the amount of the rent,

    (iii) any date as from which there took effect a previous determination as to the amount of the rent made, otherwise than as arbitrator, by a person appointed under an agreement between the landlord and the tenant, and

    (iv) any date as from which there took effect a previous agreement in writing between the landlord and the tenant, entered into since the grant of the tenancy, as to the amount of the rent.

[645]

11 Review date where new tenancy of severed part of reversion

(1) This section applies in any case where a farm business tenancy ("the new tenancy") arises between—

(a) a person who immediately before the date of the beginning of the tenancy was entitled to a severed part of the reversionary estate in the land comprised in a farm business tenancy ("the original tenancy") in which the land to which the new tenancy relates was then comprised, and

(b) the person who immediately before that date was the tenant under the original tenancy,

and the rent payable under the new tenancy at its beginning represents merely the appropriate portion of the rent payable under the original tenancy immediately before the beginning of the new tenancy.

(2) In any case where this section applies—

(a) references to the beginning of the tenancy in subsection (6) of section 10 of this Act shall be taken to be references to the beginning of the original tenancy, and

(b) references to rent in that subsection shall be taken to be references to the rent payable under the original tenancy,

until the first occasion following the beginning of the new tenancy on which any such direction, determination or agreement with respect to the rent of the new holding as is mentioned in that subsection takes effect.

[646]

12 Appointment of arbitrator

Where a statutory review notice has been given in relation to a farm business tenancy, but—

(a) no arbitrator has been appointed under an agreement made since the notice was given, and

(b) no person has been appointed under such an agreement to determine the question of the rent (otherwise than as arbitrator) on a basis agreed by the parties,

either party may, at any time during the period of six months ending with the review date, apply to the President of the Royal Institution of Chartered Surveyors (in this Act referred to as "the RICS") for the appointment of an arbitrator by him.

[647]

13 Amount of rent

(1) On any reference made in pursuance of a statutory review notice, the arbitrator shall determine the rent properly payable in respect of the holding at the review date and accordingly shall, with effect from that date, increase or reduce the rent previously payable or direct that it shall continue unchanged.

(2) For the purposes of subsection (1) above, the rent properly payable in respect of a holding is the rent at which the holding might reasonably be expected to be let on the open market by a willing landlord to a willing tenant, taking into account (subject to subsections (3) and (4) below) all relevant factors, including (in every case) the terms of the tenancy (including those which are relevant for the purposes of section 10(4) to (6) of this Act, but not those [which (apart from this section) preclude a reduction in the rent during the tenancy)].

(3)   The arbitrator shall disregard any increase in the rental value of the holding which is due to tenant's improvements other than—

    (a)   any tenant's improvement provided under an obligation which was imposed on the tenant by the terms of his tenancy or any previous tenancy and which arose on or before the beginning of the tenancy in question,

    (b)   any tenant's improvement to the extent that any allowance or benefit has been made or given by the landlord in consideration of its provision, and

    (c)   any tenant's improvement to the extent that the tenant has received any compensation from the landlord in respect of it.

(4)   The arbitrator—

    (a)   shall disregard any effect on the rent of the fact that the tenant who is a party to the arbitration is in occupation of the holding, and

    (b)   shall not fix the rent at a lower amount by reason of any dilapidation or deterioration of, or damage to, buildings or land caused or permitted by the tenant.

(5)   In this section "tenant's improvement", and references to the provision of such an improvement, have the meaning given by section 15 of this Act.

[648]

NOTES

Sub-s (2): words in square brackets substituted by the Regulatory Reform (Agricultural Tenancies) (England and Wales) Order 2006, SI 2006/2805, arts 11, 15.

---

14   Interpretation of Part II

In this Part of this Act, unless the context otherwise requires—

    "the review date", in relation to a statutory review notice, has the meaning given by section 10(2) of this Act;

    "statutory review notice" has the meaning given by section 10(1) of this Act.

[649]

PART III

COMPENSATION ON TERMINATION OF FARM BUSINESS TENANCY

Tenant's entitlement to compensation

15   Meaning of "tenant's improvement"

For the purposes of this Part of this Act a "tenant's improvement", in relation to any farm business tenancy, means—

    (a)   any physical improvement which is made on the holding by the tenant by his own effort or wholly or partly at his own expense, or

    (b)   any intangible advantage which—

        (i)   is obtained for the holding by the tenant by his own effort or wholly or partly at his own expense, and

        (ii)   becomes attached to the holding,

and references to the provision of a tenant's improvement are references to the making by the tenant of any physical improvement falling within paragraph (a) above or the obtaining by the tenant of any intangible advantage falling within paragraph (b) above.

[650]

16   Tenant's right to compensation for tenant's improvement

(1)   The tenant under a farm business tenancy shall, subject to the provisions of this Part of this Act, be entitled on the termination of the tenancy, on quitting the holding, to obtain from his landlord compensation in respect of any tenant's improvement.

(2)   A tenant shall not be entitled to compensation under this section in respect of—

    (a)   any physical improvement which is removed from the holding, or

    (b)   any intangible advantage which does not remain attached to the holding.

(3)   Section 13 of, and Schedule 1 to, the Agriculture Act 1986 (compensation to outgoing tenants for milk quota) shall not apply in relation to a farm business tenancy.

[651]

Conditions of eligibility

17 Consent of landlord as condition of compensation for tenant's improvement

(1) A tenant shall not be entitled to compensation under section 16 of this Act in respect of any tenant's improvement unless the landlord has given his consent in writing to the provision of the tenant's improvement.

(2) Any such consent may be given in the instrument creating the tenancy or elsewhere.

(3) Any such consent may be given either unconditionally or on condition that the tenant agrees to a specified variation in the terms of the tenancy.

(4) The variation referred to in subsection (3) above must be related to the tenant's improvement in question.

(5) This section does not apply in any case where the tenant's improvement consists of planning permission.

[652]

18 Conditions in relation to compensation for planning permission

(1) A tenant shall not be entitled to compensation under section 16 of this Act in respect of a tenant's improvement which consists of planning permission unless—

    (a) the landlord has given his consent in writing to the making of the application for planning permission,

    (b) that consent is expressed to be given for the purpose—

        (i) of enabling a specified physical improvement falling within paragraph (a) of section 15 of this Act lawfully to be provided by the tenant, or

        (ii) of enabling the tenant lawfully to effect a specified change of use, and

    (c) on the termination of the tenancy, the specified physical improvement has not been completed or the specified change of use has not been effected.

(2) Any such consent may be given either unconditionally or on condition that the tenant agrees to a specified variation in the terms of the tenancy.

(3) The variation referred to in subsection (2) above must be related to the physical improvement or change of use in question.

[653]

19 Reference to arbitration of refusal or failure to give consent or of condition attached to consent

(1) Where, in relation to any tenant's improvement, the tenant under a farm business tenancy is aggrieved by—

    (a) the refusal of his landlord to give his consent under section 17(1) of this Act,

    (b) the failure of his landlord to give such consent within two months of a written request by the tenant for such consent, or

    (c) any variation in the terms of the tenancy required by the landlord as a condition of giving such consent,

the tenant may by notice in writing given to the landlord demand that the question shall be referred to arbitration under this section; but this subsection has effect subject to subsections (2) and (3) below.

(2) No notice under subsection (1) above may be given in relation to any tenant's improvement which the tenant has already provided or begun to provide, unless that improvement is a routine improvement.

(3) No notice under subsection (1) above may be given—

    (a) in a case falling within paragraph (a) or (c) of that subsection, after the end of the period of two months beginning with the day on which notice of the refusal or variation referred to in that paragraph was given to the tenant, or

    (b) in a case falling within paragraph (b) of that subsection, after the end of the period of four months beginning with the day on which the written request referred to in that paragraph was given to the landlord.

(4) Where the tenant has given notice under subsection (1) above but no arbitrator has been appointed under an agreement made since the notice was given, the tenant or the landlord may apply to the President of the RICS, subject to subsection (9) below, for the appointment of an arbitrator by him.

(5)   The arbitrator shall consider whether, having regard to the terms of the tenancy and any other relevant circumstances (including the circumstances of the tenant and the landlord), it is reasonable for the tenant to provide the tenant's improvement.

(6)   Subject to subsection (9) below, the arbitrator may unconditionally approve the provision of the tenant's improvement or may withhold his approval, but may not give his approval subject to any condition or vary any condition required by the landlord under section 17(3) of this Act.

(7)   If the arbitrator gives his approval, that approval shall have effect for the purposes of this Part of this Act and for the purposes of the terms of the farm business tenancy as if it were the consent of the landlord.

(8)   In a case falling within subsection (1)(c) above, the withholding by the arbitrator of his approval shall not affect the validity of the landlord's consent or of the condition subject to which it was given.

(9)   Where, at any time after giving a notice under subsection (1) above in relation to any tenant's improvement which is not a routine improvement, the tenant begins to provide the improvement—

  (a)   no application may be made under subsection (4) above after that time,
  (b)   where such an application has been made but no arbitrator has been appointed before that time, the application shall be ineffective, and
  (c)   no award may be made by virtue of subsection (6) above after that time except as to the costs of the reference and award in a case where the arbitrator was appointed before that time.

(10)   For the purposes of this section—

"fixed equipment" includes any building or structure affixed to land and any works constructed on, in, over or under land, and also includes anything grown on land for a purpose other than use after severance from the land, consumption of the thing grown or its produce, or amenity;

"routine improvement", in relation to a farm business tenancy, means any tenant's improvement which—

  (a)   is a physical improvement made in the normal course of farming the holding or any part of the holding, and
  (b)   does not consist of fixed equipment or an improvement to fixed equipment,

but does not include any improvement whose provision is prohibited by the terms of the tenancy.

[654]

Amount of compensation

20   Amount of compensation for tenant's improvement not consisting of planning permission

(1)   [Subject to subsection (4A) below,] the amount of compensation payable to the tenant under section 16 of this Act in respect of any tenant's improvement shall be an amount equal to the increase attributable to the improvement in the value of the holding at the termination of the tenancy as land comprised in a tenancy.

(2)   Where the landlord and the tenant have entered into an agreement in writing whereby any benefit is given or allowed to the tenant in consideration of the provision of a tenant's improvement, the amount of compensation otherwise payable in respect of that improvement shall be reduced by the proportion which the value of the benefit bears to the amount of the total cost of providing the improvement.

(3)   Where a grant has been or will be made to the tenant out of public money in respect of a tenant's improvement, the amount of compensation otherwise payable in respect of that improvement shall be reduced by the proportion which the amount of the grant bears to the amount of the total cost of providing the improvement.

(4)   Where a physical improvement which has been completed or a change of use which has been effected is authorised by any planning permission granted on an application made by the tenant, section 18 of this Act does not prevent any value attributable to the fact that the physical improvement or change of use is so authorised from being taken into account under

391

this section in determining the amount of compensation payable in respect of the physical improvement or in respect of any intangible advantage obtained as a result of the change of use.

[(4A)   Where the landlord and the tenant have agreed in writing, after the commencement of this subsection, to limit the amount of compensation payable under section 16 of this Act in respect of any tenant's improvement, that amount shall be the lesser of—

    (a)   the amount determined in accordance with subsections (1) to (4) above, and

    (b)   the compensation limit.

(4B)   In subsection (4A) above, "the compensation limit" means—

    (a)   an amount agreed by the parties in writing, or

    (b)   where the parties are unable to agree on an amount, an amount equal to the cost to the tenant of making the improvement.]

(5)   This section does not apply where the tenant's improvement consists of planning permission.

[655]

NOTES

  Sub-s (1): words in square brackets inserted by the Regulatory Reform (Agricultural Tenancies) (England and Wales) Order 2006, SI 2006/2805, arts 11, 16(1).

  Sub-ss (4A), (4B): inserted by SI 2006/2805, arts 11, 16(2).

---

21   Amount of compensation for planning permission

(1)   The amount of compensation payable to the tenant under section 16 of this Act in respect of a tenant's improvement which consists of planning permission shall be an amount equal to the increase attributable to the fact that the relevant development is authorised by the planning permission in the value of the holding at the termination of the tenancy as land comprised in a tenancy.

(2)   In subsection (1) above, "the relevant development" means the physical improvement or change of use specified in the landlord's consent under section 18 of this Act in accordance with subsection (1)(b) of that section.

(3)   Where the landlord and the tenant have entered into an agreement in writing whereby any benefit is given or allowed to the tenant in consideration of the obtaining of planning permission by the tenant, the amount of compensation otherwise payable in respect of that permission shall be reduced by the proportion which the value of the benefit bears to the amount of the total cost of obtaining the permission.

[656]

22   Settlement of claims for compensation

(1)   Any claim by the tenant under a farm business tenancy for compensation under section 16 of this Act shall, subject to the provisions of this section, be determined by arbitration under this section.

(2)   No such claim for compensation shall be enforceable unless before the end of the period of two months beginning with the date of the termination of the tenancy the tenant has given notice in writing to his landlord of his intention to make the claim and of the nature of the claim.

(3)   Where—

    (a)   the landlord and the tenant have not settled the claim by agreement in writing, and

    (b)   no arbitrator has been appointed under an agreement made since the notice under subsection (2) above was given,

either party may, after the end of the period of four months beginning with the date of the termination of the tenancy, apply to the President of the RICS for the appointment of an arbitrator by him.

(4)   Where—

    (a)   an application under subsection (3) above relates wholly or partly to compensation in respect of a routine improvement (within the meaning of section 19 of this Act) which the tenant has provided or has begun to provide, and

    (b)   that application is made at the same time as an application under section 19(4) of this Act relating to the provision of that improvement, the President of the RICS shall appoint the same arbitrator on both applications and, if both applications are made by the same person, only one fee shall be payable by virtue of section 30(2) of this Act in respect of them.

(5)   Where a tenant lawfully remains in occupation of part of the holding after the termination of a farm business tenancy, references in subsections (2) and (3) above to the termination of the tenancy shall, in the case of a claim relating to that part of the holding, be construed as references to the termination of the occupation.

[657]

Supplementary provisions with respect to compensation

23   Successive tenancies

(1)   Where the tenant under a farm business tenancy has remained in the holding during two or more such tenancies, he shall not be deprived of his right to compensation under section 16 of this Act by reason only that any tenant's improvement was provided during a tenancy other than the one at the termination of which he quits the holding.

(2)   The landlord and tenant under a farm business tenancy may agree that the tenant is to be entitled to compensation under section 16 of this Act on the termination of the tenancy even though at that termination the tenant remains in the holding under a new tenancy.

(3)   Where the landlord and the tenant have agreed as mentioned in subsection (2) above in relation to any tenancy ("the earlier tenancy"), the tenant shall not be entitled to compensation at the end of any subsequent tenancy in respect of any tenant's improvement provided during the earlier tenancy in relation to the land comprised in the earlier tenancy.

[658]

24   Resumption of possession of part of holding

(1)   Where—
   (a)   the landlord under a farm business tenancy resumes possession of part of the holding in pursuance of any provision of the tenancy, or
   (b)   a person entitled to a severed part of the reversionary estate in a holding held under a farm business tenancy resumes possession of part of the holding by virtue of a notice to quit that part given to the tenant by virtue of section 140 of the Law of Property Act 1925,

the provisions of this Part of this Act shall, subject to subsections (2) and (3) below, apply to that part of the holding (in this section referred to as "the relevant part") as if it were a separate holding which the tenant had quitted in consequence of a notice to quit and, in a case falling within paragraph (b) above, as if the person resuming possession were the landlord of that separate holding.

(2)   The amount of compensation payable to the tenant under section 16 of this Act in respect of any tenant's improvement provided for the relevant part by the tenant and not consisting of planning permission shall, subject to section 20(2) to [(4A)] of this Act, be an amount equal to the increase attributable to the tenant's improvement in the value of the original holding on the termination date as land comprised in a tenancy.

(3)   The amount of compensation payable to the tenant under section 16 of this Act in respect of any tenant's improvement which consists of planning permission relating to the relevant part shall, subject to section 21(3) of this Act, be an amount equal to the increase attributable to the fact that the relevant development is authorised by the planning permission in the value of the original holding on the termination date as land comprised in a tenancy.

(4)   In a case falling within paragraph (a) or (b) of subsection (1) above, sections 20 and 21 of this Act shall apply [(subject to subsection (4A) below)] on the termination of the tenancy, in relation to the land then comprised in the tenancy, as if the reference in subsection (1) of each of those sections to the holding were a reference to the original holding.

[(4A)   Where—
   (a)   the landlord and the tenant have agreed in writing, after the commencement of this subsection, to limit the amount of compensation payable under section 16 of this Act in respect of any tenant's improvement not consisting of planning permission,
   (b)   that improvement is provided for both the relevant part and the land comprised in the tenancy after the termination date, .

393

(c)   the case falls within paragraph (a) or (b) of subsection (1) above,

(d)   the tenant has already received compensation in respect of the improvement, determined in accordance with subsection (2) above, and

(e)   further compensation in respect of the improvement is payable under section 16 of this Act on termination of the tenancy,

the compensation limit referred to in section 20(4A) of this Act shall, for the purposes of determining that further compensation, be reduced by an amount equal to the amount of compensation already received by the tenant in respect of the improvement.]

(5)   In subsections (2) to [(4A)] above—

"the original holding" means the land comprised in the farm business tenancy—
(a)   on the date when the landlord gave his consent under section 17 or 18 of this Act in relation to the tenant's improvement, or
(b)   where approval in relation to the tenant's improvement was given by an arbitrator, on the date on which that approval was given,

"the relevant development", in relation to any tenant's improvement which consists of planning permission, has the meaning given by section 21(2) of this Act, and

"the termination date" means the date on which possession of the relevant part was resumed.

[659]

NOTES

Sub-ss (2), (5): numbers in square brackets substituted by the Regulatory Reform (Agricultural Tenancies) (England and Wales) Order 2006, SI 2006/2805, arts 11, 17(1), (4).
Subs (4): words in square brackets inserted by SI 2006/2805, arts 11, 17(2).
Sub-s (4A): inserted by SI 2006/2805, arts 11, 17(3).

25   Compensation where reversionary estate in holding is severed

(1)   Where the reversionary estate in the holding comprised in a farm business tenancy is for the time being vested in more than one person in several parts, the tenant shall be entitled, on quitting the entire holding, to require that any compensation payable to him under section 16 of this Act shall be determined as if the reversionary estate were not so severed.

(2)   Where subsection (1) applies, the arbitrator shall, where necessary, apportion the amount awarded between the persons who for the purposes of this Part of this Act together constitute the landlord of the holding, and any additional costs of the award caused by the apportionment shall be directed by the arbitrator to be paid by those persons in such proportions as he shall determine.

[660]

26   Extent to which compensation recoverable under agreements

(1)   In any case for which apart from this section the provisions of this Part of this Act provide for compensation, a tenant shall be entitled to compensation in accordance with those provisions and not otherwise, and shall be so entitled notwithstanding any agreement to the contrary.

(2)   Nothing in the provisions of this Part of this Act, apart from this section, shall be construed as disentitling a tenant to compensation in any case for which those provisions do not provide for compensation.

[661]

27   Interpretation of Part III

In this Part of this Act, unless the context otherwise requires—

"planning permission" has the meaning given by section 336(1) of the Town and Country Planning Act 1990;

"tenant's improvement", and references to the provision of such an improvement, have the meaning given by section 15 of this Act.

[662]

PART IV
MISCELLANEOUS AND SUPPLEMENTAL

Resolution of disputes

28 Resolution of disputes

(1)   Subject to subsections (4) and (5) below and to section 29 of this Act, any dispute between the landlord and the tenant under a farm business tenancy, being a dispute concerning their rights and obligations under this Act, under the terms of the tenancy or under any custom, shall be determined by arbitration.

(2)   Where such a dispute has arisen, the landlord or the tenant may give notice in writing to the other specifying the dispute and stating that, unless before the end of the period of two months beginning with the day on which the notice is given the parties have appointed an arbitrator by agreement, he proposes to apply to the President of the RICS for the appointment of an arbitrator by him.

(3)   Where a notice has been given under subsection (2) above, but no arbitrator has been appointed by agreement, either party may, after the end of the period of two months referred to in that subsection, apply to the President of the RICS for the appointment of an arbitrator by him.

(4)   ...

(5)   Subsections (1) to (3) above do not apply in relation to—
   (a)   the determination of rent in pursuance of a statutory review notice (as defined in section 10(1) of this Act),
   (b)   any case falling within section 19(1) of this Act, ...
   (c)   any claim for compensation under Part III of this Act[, or
   (d)   any dispute relating to rent review, in any case where Part II of this Act is excluded by virtue of section 9(c)(ii) of this Act.]

[663]

NOTES

Sub-s (4): repealed by the Arbitration Act 1996, s 107(2), Sch 4.

Sub-s (5): word omitted repealed and para (d) and word "or" immediately preceding it added by the Regulatory Reform (Agricultural Tenancies) (England and Wales) Order 2006, SI 2006/2805, arts 11, 14(2), 18, Sch 2; for effect see art 14(3) thereof.

29 Cases where right to refer claim to arbitration under section 28 does not apply

(1)   Section 28 of this Act does not apply in relation to any dispute if—
   (a)   the tenancy is created by an instrument which includes provision for disputes to be resolved by any person other than—
      (i)   the landlord or the tenant, or
      (ii)   a third party appointed by either of them without the consent or concurrence of the other, and
   (b)   either of the following has occurred—
      (i)   the landlord and the tenant have jointly referred the dispute to the third party under the provision, or
      (ii)   the landlord or the tenant has referred the dispute to the third party under the provision and notified the other in writing of the making of the reference, the period of four weeks beginning with the date on which the other was so notified has expired and the other has not given a notice under section 28(2) of this Act in relation to the dispute before the end of that period.

(2)   For the purposes of subsection (1) above, a term of the tenancy does not provide for disputes to be "resolved" by any person unless that person (whether or not acting as arbitrator) is enabled under the terms of the tenancy to give a decision which is binding in law on both parties.

[664]

30 General provisions applying to arbitrations under Act

(1)   Any matter which is required to be determined by arbitration under this Act shall be determined by the arbitration of a sole arbitrator.

(2)   Any application under this Act to the President of the RICS for the appointment of an arbitrator by him must be made in writing and must be accompanied by such reasonable fee as the President may determine in respect of the costs of making the appointment.

(3)   Where an arbitrator appointed for the purposes of this Act dies or is incapable of acting and no new arbitrator has been appointed by agreement, either party may apply to the President of the RICS for the appointment of a new arbitrator by him.

[665]

Miscellaneous

31   (*Amends the Law of Property Act 1925, s 99(13), adds s 99(13A), (13B) thereof, and repeals the Agricultural Holdings Act 1986, Sch 14, para 12.*)

32   Power of limited owners to give consents etc

The landlord under a farm business tenancy, whatever his estate or interest in the holding, may, for the purposes of this Act, give any consent, make any agreement or do or have done to him any other act which he might give, make, do or have done to him if he were owner in fee simple or, if his interest is an interest in a leasehold, were absolutely entitled to that leasehold.

[666]

33   Power to apply and raise capital money

(1)   The purposes authorised by section 73 of the Settled Land Act 1925 (*either as originally enacted or as applied in relation to trusts for sale by section 28 of the Law of Property Act 1925*) or section 26 of the Universities and College Estates Act 1925 for the application of capital money shall include—

   (a)   the payment of expenses incurred by a landlord under a farm business tenancy in, or in connection with, the making of any physical improvement on the holding,

   (b)   the payment of compensation under section 16 of this Act, and

   (c)   the payment of the costs, charges and expenses incurred by him on a reference to arbitration under section 19 or 22 of this Act.

(2)   The purposes authorised by section 71 of the Settled Land Act 1925 (*either as originally enacted or as applied in relation to trusts for sale by section 28 of the Law of Property Act 1925*) as purposes for which money may be raised by mortgage shall include the payment of compensation under section 16 of this Act.

(3)   Where the landlord under a farm business tenancy—

   (a)   is a tenant for life or in a fiduciary position, and

   (b)   is liable to pay compensation under section 16 of this Act,

he may require the sum payable as compensation and any costs, charges and expenses incurred by him in connection with the tenant's claim under that section to be paid out of any capital money held on the same trusts as the settled land.

(4)   In subsection (3) above—

"capital money" includes any personal estate held on the same trusts as the land; *and*

"settled land" includes land held on trust for sale or vested in a personal representative.

[667]

NOTES

Sub-s (1), (2), (4): words in italics repealed by the Trusts of Land and Appointment of Trustees Act 1996, s 25(2), Sch 4; the original wording is reproduced here for reasons of historical interest and in view of the savings contained in ss 3, 18(3), 25(5) of the 1996 Act.

---

34   Estimation of best rent for purposes of Acts and other instruments

(1)   In estimating the best rent or reservation in the nature of rent of land comprised in a farm business tenancy for the purposes of a relevant instrument, it shall not be necessary to take into account against the tenant any increase in the value of that land arising from any tenant's improvements.

(2)   In subsection (1) above—

"a relevant instrument" means any Act of Parliament, deed or other instrument which authorises a lease to be made on the condition that the best rent or reservation in the nature of rent is reserved;

"tenant's improvement" has the meaning given by section 15 of this Act.

[668]

35   *(Amends the Solicitors Act 1974, s 22(2), (3A).)*

Supplemental

36   Service of notices

(1)   This section applies to any notice or other document required or authorised to be given under this Act.

(2)   A notice or other document to which this section applies is duly given to a person if—

   (a)   it is delivered to him,

   (b)   it is left at his proper address, or

   (c)   it is given to him in a manner authorised by a written agreement made, at any time before the giving of the notice, between him and the person giving the notice.

(3)   A notice or other document to which this section applies is not duly given to a person if its text is transmitted to him by facsimile or other electronic means otherwise than by virtue of subsection (2)(c) above.

(4)   Where a notice or other document to which this section applies is to be given to a body corporate, the notice or document is duly given if it is given to the secretary or clerk of that body.

(5)   Where—

   (a)   a notice or other document to which this section applies is to be given to a landlord under a farm business tenancy and an agent or servant of his is responsible for the control of the management of the holding, or

   (b)   such a document is to be given to a tenant under a farm business tenancy and an agent or servant of his is responsible for the carrying on of a business on the holding,

the notice or document is duly given if it is given to that agent or servant.

(6)   For the purposes of this section, the proper address of any person to whom a notice or other document to which this section applies is to be given is—

   (a)   in the case of the secretary or clerk of a body corporate, the registered or principal office of that body, and

   (b)   in any other case, the last known address of the person in question.

(7)   Unless or until the tenant under a farm business tenancy has received—

   (a)   notice that the person who before that time was entitled to receive the rents and profits of the holding ("the original landlord") has ceased to be so entitled, and

   (b)   notice of the name and address of the person who has become entitled to receive the rents and profits,

any notice or other document given to the original landlord by the tenant shall be deemed for the purposes of this Act to have been given to the landlord under the tenancy.

[669]

37   Crown land

(1)   This Act shall apply in relation to land in which there subsists, or has at any material time subsisted, a Crown interest as it applies in relation to land in which no such interest subsists or has ever subsisted.

(2)   For the purposes of this Act—

   (a)   where an interest belongs to Her Majesty in right of the Crown and forms part of the Crown Estate, the Crown Estate Commissioners shall be treated as the owner of the interest,

   (b)   where an interest belongs to Her Majesty in right of the Crown and does not form part of the Crown Estate, the government department having the management of the land or, if there is no such department, such person as Her Majesty may appoint in writing under the Royal Sign Manual shall be treated as the owner of the interest,

(c)   where an interest belongs to Her Majesty in right of the Duchy of Lancaster, the Chancellor of the Duchy shall be treated as the owner of the interest,

(d)   where an interest belongs to a government department or is held in trust for Her Majesty for the purposes of a government department, that department shall be treated as the owner of the interest, and

(e)   where an interest belongs to the Duchy of Cornwall, such person as the Duke of Cornwall or the possessor for the time being of the Duchy of Cornwall appoints shall be treated as the owner of the interest and, in the case where the interest is that of landlord, may do any act or thing which a landlord is authorised or required to do under this Act.

(3)   If any question arises as to who is to be treated as the owner of a Crown interest, that question shall be referred to the Treasury, whose decision shall be final.

(4)   In subsections (1) and (3) above "Crown interest" means an interest which belongs to Her Majesty in right of the Crown or of the Duchy of Lancaster or to the Duchy of Cornwall, or to a government department, or which is held in trust for Her Majesty for the purposes of a government department.

(5)   Any compensation payable under section 16 of this Act by the Chancellor of the Duchy of Lancaster may be raised and paid under section 25 of the Duchy of Lancaster Act 1817 (application of monies) as an expense incurred in improvement of land belonging to Her Majesty in right of the Duchy.

(6)   In the case of land belonging to the Duchy of Cornwall, the purposes authorised by section 8 of the Duchy of Cornwall Management Act 1863 (application of monies) for the advancement of parts of such gross sums as are there mentioned shall include the payment of compensation under section 16 of this Act.

(7)   Nothing in subsection (6) above shall be taken as prejudicing the operation of the Duchy of Cornwall Management Act 1982.

[670]

38   Interpretation

(1)   In this Act, unless the context otherwise requires—
"agriculture" includes horticulture, fruit growing, seed growing, dairy farming and livestock breeding and keeping, the use of land as grazing land, meadow land, osier land, market gardens and nursery grounds, and the use of land for woodlands where that use is ancillary to the farming of land for other agricultural purposes, and "agricultural" shall be construed accordingly;
"building" includes any part of a building;
"fixed term tenancy" means any tenancy other than a periodic tenancy;
"holding", in relation to a farm business tenancy, means the aggregate of the land comprised in the tenancy;
"landlord" includes any person from time to time deriving title from the original landlord;
"livestock" includes any creature kept for the production of food, wool, skins or fur or for the purpose of its use in the farming of land;
"the RICS" means the Royal Institution of Chartered Surveyors;
"tenancy" means any tenancy other than a tenancy at will, and includes a sub-tenancy and an agreement for a tenancy or sub-tenancy;
"tenant" includes a sub-tenant and any person deriving title from the original tenant or sub-tenant;
"termination", in relation to a tenancy, means the cesser of the tenancy by reason of effluxion of time or from any other cause.

(2)   References in this Act to the farming of land include references to the carrying on in relation to land of any agricultural activity.

(3)   A tenancy granted pursuant to a contract shall be taken for the purposes of this Act to have been granted when the contract was entered into.

(4)   For the purposes of this Act a tenancy begins on the day on which, under the terms of the tenancy, the tenant is entitled to possession under that tenancy; and references in this Act to the beginning of the tenancy are references to that day.

(5)   The designations of landlord and tenant shall continue to apply until the conclusion of any proceedings taken under this Act in respect of compensation.

[671]

39   Index of defined expressions

In this Act the expressions listed below are defined by or otherwise fall to be construed in accordance with the provisions indicated—

agriculture, agricultural	section 38(1)
begins, beginning (in relation to a tenancy)	section 38(4)
building	section 38(1)
farm business tenancy	section 1
farming (of land)	section 38(2)
fixed term tenancy	section 38(1)
grant (of a tenancy)	section 38(3)
holding (in relation to a farm business tenancy)	section 38(1)
landlord	section 38(1) and (5)
livestock	section 38(1)
planning permission (in Part III)	section 27
provision (of a tenant's improvement) (in Part III)	section 15
the review date (in Part II)	section 10(2)
the RICS	section 38(1)
statutory review notice (in Part II)	section 10(1)
tenancy	section 38(1)
tenant	section 38(1) and (5)
tenant's improvement (in Part III)	section 15
termination (of a tenancy)	section 38(1).

[672]

40   Consequential amendments

The Schedule to this Act (which contains consequential amendments) shall have effect.

[673]

41   Short title, commencement and extent

(1)   This Act may be cited as the Agricultural Tenancies Act 1995.

(2)   This Act shall come into force on 1st September 1995.

(3)   Subject to subsection (4) below, this Act extends to England and Wales only.

(4)   The amendment by a provision of the Schedule to this Act of an enactment which extends to Scotland or Northern Ireland also extends there, except that paragraph 9 of the Schedule does not extend to Northern Ireland.

[674]

(*Schedule outside the scope of this work.*)

LANDLORD AND TENANT (COVENANTS) ACT 1995

(1995 c 30)

ARRANGEMENT OF SECTIONS

An Act to make provision for persons bound by covenants of a tenancy to be released from such covenants on the assignment of the tenancy, and to make other provision with respect to rights and liabilities arising under such covenants; to restrict in certain circumstances the operation of rights of re-entry, forfeiture and disclaimer; and for connected purposes.

[19 July 1995]

Preliminary

1   Tenancies to which the Act applies

(1)   Sections 3 to 16 and 21 apply only to new tenancies.

(2)   Sections 17 to 20 apply to both new and other tenancies.

(3)   For the purposes of this section a tenancy is a new tenancy if it is granted on or after the date on which this Act comes into force otherwise than in pursuance of—
   (a)   an agreement entered into before that date, or
   (b)   an order of a court made before that date.

(4)   Subsection (3) has effect subject to section 20(1) in the case of overriding leases granted under section 19.

(5)   Without prejudice to the generality of subsection (3), that subsection applies to the grant of a tenancy where by virtue of any variation of a tenancy there is a deemed surrender and regrant as it applies to any other grant of a tenancy.

(6)   Where a tenancy granted on or after the date on which this Act comes into force is so granted in pursuance of an option granted before that date, the tenancy shall be regarded for the purposes of subsection (3) as granted in pursuance of an agreement entered into before that date (and accordingly is not a new tenancy), whether or not the option was exercised before that date.

(7)   In subsection (6) "option" includes right of first refusal.

[675]

2   Covenants to which the Act applies

(1)   This Act applies to a landlord covenant or a tenant covenant of a tenancy—
   (a)   whether or not the covenant has reference to the subject matter of the tenancy, and
   (b)   whether the covenant is express, implied or imposed by law,
but does not apply to a covenant falling within subsection (2).

(2)   Nothing in this Act affects any covenant imposed in pursuance of—
   (a)   section 35 or 155 of the Housing Act 1985 (covenants for repayment of discount on early disposals);
   (b)   paragraph 1 of Schedule 6A to that Act (covenants requiring redemption of landlord's share); or

(c)   [section 11 or 13 of the Housing Act 1996 or] paragraph 1 or 3 of Schedule 2 to the Housing Associations Act 1985 (covenants for repayment of discount on early disposals or for restricting disposals).

[676]

NOTES
Sub-s (2): words in square brackets in para (c) inserted by the Housing Act 1996 (Consequential Provisions) Order 1996, SI 1996/2325, art 5, Sch 2, para 22.

Transmission of covenants

3 Transmission of benefit and burden of covenants

(1)   The benefit and burden of all landlord and tenant covenants of a tenancy—
    (a)   shall be annexed and incident to the whole, and to each and every part, of the premises demised by the tenancy and of the reversion in them, and
    (b)   shall in accordance with this section pass on an assignment of the whole or any part of those premises or of the reversion in them.

(2)   Where the assignment is by the tenant under the tenancy, then as from the assignment the assignee—
    (a)   becomes bound by the tenant covenants of the tenancy except to the extent that—
        (i)   immediately before the assignment they did not bind the assignor, or
        (ii)   they fall to be complied with in relation to any demised premises not comprised in the assignment; and
    (b)   becomes entitled to the benefit of the landlord covenants of the tenancy except to the extent that they fall to be complied with in relation to any such premises.

(3)   Where the assignment is by the landlord under the tenancy, then as from the assignment the assignee—
    (a)   becomes bound by the landlord covenants of the tenancy except to the extent that—
        (i)   immediately before the assignment they did not bind the assignor, or
        (ii)   they fall to be complied with in relation to any demised premises not comprised in the assignment; and
    (b)   becomes entitled to the benefit of the tenant covenants of the tenancy except to the extent that they fall to be complied with in relation to any such premises.

(4)   In determining for the purposes of subsection (2) or (3) whether any covenant bound the assignor immediately before the assignment, any waiver or release of the covenant which (in whatever terms) is expressed to be personal to the assignor shall be disregarded.

(5)   Any landlord or tenant covenant of a tenancy which is restrictive of the user of land shall, as well as being capable of enforcement against an assignee, be capable of being enforced against any other person who is the owner or occupier of any demised premises to which the covenant relates, even though there is no express provision in the tenancy to that effect.

(6)   Nothing in this section shall operate—
    (a)   in the case of a covenant which (in whatever terms) is expressed to be personal to any person, to make the covenant enforceable by or (as the case may be) against any other person; or
    (b)   to make a covenant enforceable against any person if, apart from this section, it would not be enforceable against him by reason of its not having been registered under the [Land Registration Act 2002] or the Land Charges Act 1972.

(7)   To the extent that there remains in force any rule of law by virtue of which the burden of a covenant whose subject matter is not in existence at the time when it is made does not run with the land affected unless the covenantor covenants on behalf of himself and his assigns, that rule of law is hereby abolished in relation to tenancies.

[677]

NOTES
Sub-s (6): words in square brackets substituted by the Land Registration Act 2002, s 133, Sch 11, para 33(1), (2).

4 Transmission of rights of re-entry

The benefit of a landlord's right of re-entry under a tenancy—
  (a) shall be annexed and incident to the whole, and to each and every part, of the reversion in the premises demised by the tenancy, and
  (b) shall pass on an assignment of the whole or any part of the reversion in those premises.

[678]

Release of covenants on assignment

5 Tenant released from covenants on assignment of tenancy

  (1) This section applies where a tenant assigns premises demised to him under a tenancy.

  (2) If the tenant assigns the whole of the premises demised to him, he—
  (a) is released from the tenant covenants of the tenancy, and
  (b) ceases to be entitled to the benefit of the landlord covenants of the tenancy,
as from the assignment.

  (3) If the tenant assigns part only of the premises demised to him, then as from the assignment he—
  (a) is released from the tenant covenants of the tenancy, and
  (b) ceases to be entitled to the benefit of the landlord covenants of the tenancy,
only to the extent that those covenants fall to be complied with in relation to that part of the demised premises.

  (4) This section applies as mentioned in subsection (1) whether or not the tenant is tenant of the whole of the premises comprised in the tenancy.

[679]

6 Landlord may be released from covenants on assignment of reversion

  (1) This section applies where a landlord assigns the reversion in premises of which he is the landlord under a tenancy.

  (2) If the landlord assigns the reversion in the whole of the premises of which he is the landlord—
  (a) he may apply to be released from the landlord covenants of the tenancy in accordance with section 8; and
  (b) if he is so released from all of those covenants, he ceases to be entitled to the benefit of the tenant covenants of the tenancy as from the assignment.

  (3) If the landlord assigns the reversion in part only of the premises of which he is the landlord—
  (a) he may apply to be so released from the landlord covenants of the tenancy to the extent that they fall to be complied with in relation to that part of those premises; and
  (b) if he is, to that extent, so released from all of those covenants, then as from the assignment he ceases to be entitled to the benefit of the tenant covenants only to the extent that they fall to be complied with in relation to that part of those premises.

  (4) This section applies as mentioned in subsection (1) whether or not the landlord is landlord of the whole of the premises comprised in the tenancy.

[680]

7 Former landlord may be released from covenants on assignment of reversion

  (1) This section applies where—
  (a) a landlord assigns the reversion in premises of which he is the landlord under a tenancy, and
  (b) immediately before the assignment a former landlord of the premises remains bound by a landlord covenant of the tenancy ("the relevant covenant").

  (2) If immediately before the assignment the former landlord does not remain the landlord of any other premises demised by the tenancy, he may apply to be released from the relevant covenant in accordance with section 8.

(3)   In any other case the former landlord may apply to be so released from the relevant covenant to the extent that it falls to be complied with in relation to any premises comprised in the assignment.

(4)   If the former landlord is so released from every landlord covenant by which he remained bound immediately before the assignment, he ceases to be entitled to the benefit of the tenant covenants of the tenancy.

(5)   If the former landlord is so released from every such landlord covenant to the extent that it falls to be complied with in relation to any premises comprised in the assignment, he ceases to be entitled to the benefit of the tenant covenants of the tenancy to the extent that they fall to be so complied with.

(6)   This section applies as mentioned in subsection (1)—
  (a)   whether or not the landlord making the assignment is landlord of the whole of the premises comprised in the tenancy; and
  (b)   whether or not the former landlord has previously applied (whether under section 6 or this section) to be released from the relevant covenant.

[681]

8   Procedure for seeking release from a covenant under section 6 or 7

(1)   For the purposes of section 6 or 7 an application for the release of a covenant to any extent is made by serving on the tenant, either before or within the period of four weeks beginning with the date of the assignment in question, a notice informing him of—
  (a)   the proposed assignment or (as the case may be) the fact that the assignment has taken place, and
  (b)   the request for the covenant to be released to that extent.

(2)   Where an application for the release of a covenant is made in accordance with subsection (1), the covenant is released to the extent mentioned in the notice if—
  (a)   the tenant does not, within the period of four weeks beginning with the day on which the notice is served, serve on the landlord or former landlord a notice in writing objecting to the release, or
  (b)   the tenant does so serve such a notice but the court, on the application of the landlord or former landlord, makes a declaration that it is reasonable for the covenant to be so released, or
  (c)   the tenant serves on the landlord or former landlord a notice in writing consenting to the release and, if he has previously served a notice objecting to it, stating that that notice is withdrawn.

(3)   Any release from a covenant in accordance with this section shall be regarded as occurring at the time when the assignment in question takes place.

(4)   In this section—
  (a)   "the tenant" means the tenant of the premises comprised in the assignment in question (or, if different parts of those premises are held under the tenancy by different tenants, each of those tenants);
  (b)   any reference to the landlord or the former landlord is a reference to the landlord referred to in section 6 or the former landlord referred to in section 7, as the case may be; and
  (c)   "the court" means a county court.

[682]

Apportionment of liability between assignor and assignee

9   Apportionment of liability under covenants binding both assignor and assignee of tenancy or reversion

(1)   This section applies where—
  (a)   a tenant assigns part only of the premises demised to him by a tenancy;
  (b)   after the assignment both the tenant and his assignee are to be bound by a non-attributable tenant covenant of the tenancy; and
  (c)   the tenant and his assignee agree that as from the assignment liability under the covenant is to be apportioned between them in such manner as is specified in the agreement.

(2)   This section also applies where—

(a)   a landlord assigns the reversion in part only of the premises of which he is the landlord under a tenancy;

(b)   after the assignment both the landlord and his assignee are to be bound by a non-attributable landlord covenant of the tenancy; and

(c)   the landlord and his assignee agree that as from the assignment liability under the covenant is to be apportioned between them in such manner as is specified in the agreement.

(3)   Any such agreement as is mentioned in subsection (1) or (2) may apportion liability in such a way that a party to the agreement is exonerated from all liability under a covenant.

(4)   In any case falling within subsection (1) or (2) the parties to the agreement may apply for the apportionment to become binding on the appropriate person in accordance with section 10.

(5)   In any such case the parties to the agreement may also apply for the apportionment to become binding on any person (other than the appropriate person) who is for the time being entitled to enforce the covenant in question; and section 10 shall apply in relation to such an application as it applies in relation to an application made with respect to the appropriate person.

(6)   For the purposes of this section a covenant is, in relation to an assignment, a "non-attributable" covenant if it does not fall to be complied with in relation to any premises comprised in the assignment.

(7)   In this section "the appropriate person" means either—

(a)   the landlord of the entire premises referred to in subsection (1)(a) (or, if different parts of those premises are held under the tenancy by different landlords, each of those landlords), or

(b)   the tenant of the entire premises referred to in subsection (2)(a) (or, if different parts of those premises are held under the tenancy by different tenants, each of those tenants),

depending on whether the agreement in question falls within subsection (1) or subsection (2).

[683]

10 Procedure for making apportionment bind other party to lease

(1)   For the purposes of section 9 the parties to an agreement falling within subsection (1) or (2) of that section apply for an apportionment to become binding on the appropriate person if, either before or within the period of four weeks beginning with the date of the assignment in question, they serve on that person a notice informing him of—

(a)   the proposed assignment or (as the case may be) the fact that the assignment has taken place;

(b)   the prescribed particulars of the agreement; and

(c)   their request that the apportionment should become binding on him.

(2)   Where an application for an apportionment to become binding has been made in accordance with subsection (1), the apportionment becomes binding on the appropriate person if—

(a)   he does not, within the period of four weeks beginning with the day on which the notice is served under subsection (1), serve on the parties to the agreement a notice in writing objecting to the apportionment becoming binding on him, or

(b)   he does so serve such a notice but the court, on the application of the parties to the agreement, makes a declaration that it is reasonable for the apportionment to become binding on him, or

(c)   he serves on the parties to the agreement a notice in writing consenting to the apportionment becoming binding on him and, if he has previously served a notice objecting thereto, stating that that notice is withdrawn.

(3)   Where any apportionment becomes binding in accordance with this section, this shall be regarded as occurring at the time when the assignment in question takes place.

(4)   In this section—

"the appropriate person" has the same meaning as in section 9;

"the court" means a county court;

"prescribed" means prescribed by virtue of section 27.

[684]

Excluded assignments

11 Assignments in breach of covenant or by operation of law

(1)   This section provides for the operation of sections 5 to 10 in relation to assignments in breach of a covenant of a tenancy or assignments by operation of law ("excluded assignments").

(2)   In the case of an excluded assignment subsection (2) or (3) of section 5—
- (a)   shall not have the effect mentioned in that subsection in relation to the tenant as from that assignment, but
- (b)   shall have that effect as from the next assignment (if any) of the premises assigned by him which is not an excluded assignment.

(3)   In the case of an excluded assignment subsection (2) or (3) of section 6 or 7—
- (a)   shall not enable the landlord or former landlord to apply for such a release as is mentioned in that subsection as from that assignment, but
- (b)   shall apply on the next assignment (if any) of the reversion assigned by the landlord which is not an excluded assignment so as to enable the landlord or former landlord to apply for any such release as from that subsequent assignment.

(4)   Where subsection (2) or (3) of section 6 or 7 does so apply—
- (a)   any reference in that section to the assignment (except where it relates to the time as from which the release takes effect) is a reference to the excluded assignment; but
- (b)   in that excepted case and in section 8 as it applies in relation to any application under that section made by virtue of subsection (3) above, any reference to the assignment or proposed assignment is a reference to any such subsequent assignment as is mentioned in that subsection.

(5)   In the case of an excluded assignment section 9—
- (a)   shall not enable the tenant or landlord and his assignee to apply for an agreed apportionment to become binding in accordance with section 10 as from that assignment, but
- (b)   shall apply on the next assignment (if any) of the premises or reversion assigned by the tenant or landlord which is not an excluded assignment so as to enable him and his assignee to apply for such an apportionment to become binding in accordance with section 10 as from that subsequent assignment.

(6)   Where section 9 does so apply—
- (a)   any reference in that section to the assignment or the assignee under it is a reference to the excluded assignment and the assignee under that assignment; but
- (b)   in section 10 as it applies in relation to any application under section 9 made by virtue of subsection (5) above, any reference to the assignment or proposed assignment is a reference to any such subsequent assignment as is mentioned in that subsection.

(7)   If any such subsequent assignment as is mentioned in subsection (2), (3) or (5) above comprises only part of the premises assigned by tenant or (as the case may be) only part of the premises the reversion in which was assigned by the landlord on the excluded assignment—
- (a)   the relevant provision or provisions of section 5, 6, 7 or 9 shall only have the effect mentioned in that subsection to the extent that the covenants or covenant in question fall or falls to be complied with in relation to that part of those premises; and
- (b)   that subsection may accordingly apply on different occasions in relation to different parts of those premises.

[685]

Third party covenants

12 Covenants with management companies etc

(1)   This section applies where—
- (a)   a person other than the landlord or tenant ("the third party") is under a covenant of a tenancy liable (as principal) to discharge any function with respect to all or any of the demised premises ("the relevant function"); and

(b)   that liability is not the liability of a guarantor or any other financial liability referable to the performance or otherwise of a covenant of the tenancy by another party to it.

(2)   To the extent that any covenant of the tenancy confers any rights against the third party with respect to the relevant function, then for the purposes of the transmission of the benefit of the covenant in accordance with this Act it shall be treated as if it were—
(a)   a tenant covenant of the tenancy to the extent that those rights are exercisable by the landlord; and
(b)   a landlord covenant of the tenancy to the extent that those rights are exercisable by the tenant.

(3)   To the extent that any covenant of the tenancy confers any rights exercisable by the third party with respect to the relevant function, then for the purposes mentioned in subsection (4), it shall be treated as if it were—
(a)   a tenant covenant of the tenancy to the extent that those rights are exercisable against the tenant; and
(b)   a landlord covenant of the tenancy to the extent that those rights are exercisable against the landlord.

(4)   The purposes mentioned in subsection (3) are—
(a)   the transmission of the burden of the covenant in accordance with this Act; and
(b)   any release from, or apportionment of liability in respect of, the covenant in accordance with this Act.

(5)   In relation to the release of the landlord from any covenant which is to be treated as a landlord covenant by virtue of subsection (3), section 8 shall apply as if any reference to the tenant were a reference to the third party

[686]

Joint liability under covenants

13   Covenants binding two or more persons

(1)   Where in consequence of this Act two or more persons are bound by the same covenant, they are so bound both jointly and severally.

(2)   Subject to section 24(2), where by virtue of this Act—
(a)   two or more persons are bound jointly and severally by the same covenant, and
(b)   any of the persons so bound is released from the covenant,
the release does not extend to any other of those persons.

(3)   For the purpose of providing for contribution between persons who, by virtue of this Act, are bound jointly and severally by a covenant, the Civil Liability (Contribution) Act 1978 shall have effect as if—
(a)   liability to a person under a covenant were liability in respect of damage suffered by that person;
(b)   references to damage accordingly included a breach of a covenant of a tenancy; and
(c)   section 7(2) of that Act were omitted.

[687]

14   *(Repeals the Law of Property Act 1925, s 77(1)(c), (d) and the Land Registration Act 1925, s 24(1)(b), (2).)*

Enforcement of covenants

15   Enforcement of covenants

(1)   Where any tenant covenant of a tenancy, or any right of re-entry contained in a tenancy, is enforceable by the reversioner in respect of any premises demised by the tenancy, it shall also be so enforceable by—
(a)   any person (other than the reversioner) who, as the holder of the immediate reversion in those premises, is for the time being entitled to the rents and profits under the tenancy in respect of those premises, or
(b)   any mortgagee in possession of the reversion in those premises who is so entitled.

(2)   Where any landlord covenant of a tenancy is enforceable against the reversioner in respect of any premises demised by the tenancy, it shall also be so enforceable against any person falling within subsection (1)(a) or (b).

(3)   Where any landlord covenant of a tenancy is enforceable by the tenant in respect of any premises demised by the tenancy, it shall also be so enforceable by any mortgagee in possession of those premises under a mortgage granted by the tenant.

(4)   Where any tenant covenant of a tenancy, or any right of re-entry contained in a tenancy, is enforceable against the tenant in respect of any premises demised by the tenancy, it shall also be so enforceable against any such mortgagee.

(5)   Nothing in this section shall operate
   (a)   in the case of a covenant which (in whatever terms) is expressed to be personal to any person, to make the covenant enforceable by or (as the case may be) against any other person; or
   (b)   to make a covenant enforceable against any person if, apart from this section, it would not be enforceable against him by reason of its not having been registered under the [Land Registration Act 2002] or the Land Charges Act 1972.

(6)   In this section—
   "mortgagee" and "mortgage" include "chargee" and "charge" respectively;
   "the reversioner", in relation to a tenancy, means the holder for the time being of the interest of the landlord under the tenancy.

[688]

NOTES
Sub-s (5): words in square brackets substituted by the Land Registration Act 2002, s 133, Sch 11, para 33(1), (2).

Liability of former tenant etc in respect of covenants

16   Tenant guaranteeing performance of covenant by assignee

(1)   Where on an assignment a tenant is to any extent released from a tenant covenant of a tenancy by virtue of this Act ("the relevant covenant"), nothing in this Act (and in particular section 25) shall preclude him from entering into an authorised guarantee agreement with respect to the performance of that covenant by the assignee.

(2)   For the purposes of this section an agreement is an authorised guarantee agreement if—
   (a)   under it the tenant guarantees the performance of the relevant covenant to any extent by the assignee; and
   (b)   it is entered into in the circumstances set out in subsection (3); and
   (c)   its provisions conform with subsections (4) and (5).

(3)   Those circumstances are as follows—
   (a)   by virtue of a covenant against assignment (whether absolute or qualified) the assignment cannot be effected without the consent of the landlord under the tenancy or some other person;
   (b)   any such consent is given subject to a condition (lawfully imposed) that the tenant is to enter into an agreement guaranteeing the performance of the covenant by the assignee; and
   (c)   the agreement is entered into by the tenant in pursuance of that condition.

(4)   An agreement is not an authorised guarantee agreement to the extent that it purports—
   (a)   to impose on the tenant any requirement to guarantee in any way the performance of the relevant covenant by any person other than the assignee; or
   (b)   to impose on the tenant any liability, restriction or other requirement (of whatever nature) in relation to any time after the assignee is released from that covenant by virtue of this Act.

(5)   Subject to subsection (4), an authorised guarantee agreement may—
   (a)   impose on the tenant any liability as sole or principal debtor in respect of any obligation owed by the assignee under the relevant covenant;
   (b)   impose on the tenant liabilities as guarantor in respect of the assignee's

performance of that covenant which are no more onerous than those to which he would be subject in the event of his being liable as sole or principal debtor in respect of any obligation owed by the assignee under that covenant;

(c)   require the tenant, in the event of the tenancy assigned by him being disclaimed, to enter into a new tenancy of the premises comprised in the assignment—

    (i)   whose term expires not later than the term of the tenancy assigned by the tenant, and

    (ii)   whose tenant covenants are no more onerous than those of that tenancy;

(d)   make provision incidental or supplementary to any provision made by virtue of any of paragraphs (a) to (c).

(6)   Where a person ("the former tenant") is to any extent released from a covenant of a tenancy by virtue of section 11(2) as from an assignment and the assignor under the assignment enters into an authorised guarantee agreement with the landlord with respect to the performance of that covenant by the assignee under the assignment—

(a)   the landlord may require the former tenant to enter into an agreement under which he guarantees, on terms corresponding to those of that authorised guarantee agreement, the performance of that covenant by the assignee under the assignment; and

(b)   if its provisions conform with subsections (4) and (5), any such agreement shall be an authorised guarantee agreement for the purposes of this section; and

(c)   in the application of this section in relation to any such agreement—

    (i)   subsections (2)(b) and (c) and (3) shall be omitted, and

    (ii)   any reference to the tenant or to the assignee shall be read as a reference to the former tenant or to the assignee under the assignment.

(7)   For the purposes of subsection (1) it is immaterial that—

(a)   the tenant has already made an authorised guarantee agreement in respect of a previous assignment by him of the tenancy referred to in that subsection, it having been subsequently revested in him following a disclaimer on behalf of the previous assignee, or

(b)   the tenancy referred to in that subsection is a new tenancy entered into by the tenant in pursuance of an authorised guarantee agreement;

and in any such case subsections (2) to (5) shall apply accordingly.

(8)   It is hereby declared that the rules of law relating to guarantees (and in particular those relating to the release of sureties) are, subject to its terms, applicable in relation to any authorised guarantee agreement as in relation to any other guarantee agreement.

[689]

17   Restriction on liability of former tenant or his guarantor for rent or service charge etc

(1)   This section applies where a person ("the former tenant") is as a result of an assignment no longer a tenant under a tenancy but—

(a)   (in the case of a tenancy which is a new tenancy) he has under an authorised guarantee agreement guaranteed the performance by his assignee of a tenant covenant of the tenancy under which any fixed charge is payable; or

(b)   (in the case of any tenancy) he remains bound by such a covenant.

(2)   The former tenant shall not be liable under that agreement or (as the case may be) the covenant to pay any amount in respect of any fixed charge payable under the covenant unless, within the period of six months beginning with the date when the charge becomes due, the landlord serves on the former tenant a notice informing him—

(a)   that the charge is now due; and

(b)   that in respect of the charge the landlord intends to recover from the former tenant such amount as is specified in the notice and (where payable) interest calculated on such basis as is so specified.

(3)   Where a person ("the guarantor") has agreed to guarantee the performance by the former tenant of such a covenant as is mentioned in subsection (1), the guarantor shall not be liable under the agreement to pay any amount in respect of any fixed charge payable under the covenant unless, within the period of six months beginning with the date when the charge becomes due, the landlord serves on the guarantor a notice informing him—

(a)   that the charge is now due; and

(b)   that in respect of the charge the landlord intends to recover from the guarantor such amount as is specified in the notice and (where payable) interest calculated on such basis as is so specified.

(4)   Where the landlord has duly served a notice under subsection (2) or (3), the amount (exclusive of interest) which the former tenant or (as the case may be) the guarantor is liable to pay in respect of the fixed charge in question shall not exceed the amount specified in the notice unless—

(a)   his liability in respect of the charge is subsequently determined to be for a greater amount,

(b)   the notice informed him of the possibility that that liability would be so determined, and

(c)   within the period of three months beginning with the date of the determination, the landlord serves on him a further notice informing him that the landlord intends to recover that greater amount from him (plus interest, where payable).

(5)   For the purposes of subsection (2) or (3) any fixed charge which has become due before the date on which this Act comes into force shall be treated as becoming due on that date; but neither of those subsections applies to any such charge if before that date proceedings have been instituted by the landlord for the recovery from the former tenant of any amount in respect of it.

(6)   In this section—

"fixed charge", in relation to tenancy, means—

(a)   rent,

(b)   any service charge as defined by section 18 of the Landlord and Tenant Act 1985 (the words "of a dwelling" being disregarded for this purpose), and

(c)   any amount payable under a tenant covenant of the tenancy providing for the payment of a liquidated sum in the event of a failure to comply with any such covenant;

"landlord", in relation to a fixed charge, includes any person who has a right to enforce payment of the charge.

[690]

18   Restriction of liability of former tenant or his guarantor where tenancy subsequently varied

(1)   This section applies where a person ("the former tenant") is as a result of an assignment no longer a tenant under a tenancy but—

(a)   (in the case of a new tenancy) he has under an authorised guarantee agreement guaranteed the performance by his assignee of any tenant covenant of the tenancy; or

(b)   (in the case of any tenancy) he remains bound by such a covenant.

(2)   The former tenant shall not be liable under the agreement or (as the case may be) the covenant to pay any amount in respect of the covenant to the extent that the amount is referable to any relevant variation of the tenant covenants of the tenancy effected after the assignment.

(3)   Where a person ("the guarantor") has agreed to guarantee the performance by the former tenant of a tenant covenant of the tenancy, the guarantor (where his liability to do so is not wholly discharged by any such variation of the tenant covenants of the tenancy) shall not be liable under the agreement to pay any amount in respect of the covenant to the extent that the amount is referable to any such variation.

(4)   For the purposes of this section a variation of the tenant covenants of a tenancy is a "relevant variation" if either—

(a)   the landlord has, at the time of the variation, an absolute right to refuse to allow it; or

(b)   the landlord would have had such a right if the variation had been sought by the former tenant immediately before the assignment by him but, between the time of that assignment and the time of the variation, the tenant covenants of the tenancy have been so varied as to deprive the landlord of such a right.

(5)   In determining whether the landlord has or would have had such a right at any particular time regard shall be had to all the circumstances (including the effect of any provision made by or under any enactment).

(6)   Nothing in this section applies to any variation of the tenant covenants of a tenancy effected before the date on which this Act comes into force.

(7)   In this section "variation" means a variation whether effected by deed or otherwise.

[691]

Overriding leases

19   Right of former tenant or his guarantor to overriding lease

(1)   Where in respect of any tenancy ("the relevant tenancy") any person ("the claimant") makes full payment of an amount which he has been duly required to pay in accordance with section 17, together with any interest payable, he shall be entitled (subject to and in accordance with this section) to have the landlord under that tenancy grant him an overriding lease of the premises demised by the tenancy.

(2)   For the purposes of this section "overriding lease" means a tenancy of the reversion expectant on the relevant tenancy which—
- (a)   is granted for a term equal to the remainder of the term of the relevant tenancy plus three days or the longest period (less than three days) that will not wholly displace the landlord's reversionary interest expectant on the relevant tenancy, as the case may require; and
- (b)   (subject to subsections (3) and (4) and to any modifications agreed to by the claimant and the landlord) otherwise contains the same covenants as the relevant tenancy, as they have effect immediately before the grant of the lease.

(3)   An overriding lease shall not be required to reproduce any covenant of the relevant tenancy to the extent that the covenant is (in whatever terms) expressed to be a personal covenant between the landlord and the tenant under that tenancy.

(4)   If any right, liability or other matter arising under a covenant of the relevant tenancy falls to be determined or otherwise operates (whether expressly or otherwise) by reference to the commencement of that tenancy—
- (a)   the corresponding covenant of the overriding lease shall be so framed that that right, liability or matter falls to be determined or otherwise operates by reference to the commencement of that tenancy; but
- (b)   the overriding lease shall not be required to reproduce any covenant of that tenancy to the extent that it has become spent by the time that that lease is granted.

(5)   A claim to exercise the right to an overriding lease under this section is made by the claimant making a request for such a lease to the landlord; and any such request—
- (a)   must be made to the landlord in writing and specify the payment by virtue of which the claimant claims to be entitled to the lease ("the qualifying payment"); and
- (b)   must be so made at the time of making the qualifying payment or within the period of 12 months beginning with the date of that payment.

(6)   Where the claimant duly makes such a request—
- (a)   the landlord shall (subject to subsection (7)) grant and deliver to the claimant an overriding lease of the demised premises within a reasonable time of the request being received by the landlord; and
- (b)   the claimant—
    - (i)   shall thereupon deliver to the landlord a counterpart of the lease duly executed by the claimant, and
    - (ii)   shall be liable for the landlord's reasonable costs of and incidental to the grant of the lease.

(7)   The landlord shall not be under any obligation to grant an overriding lease of the demised premises under this section at a time when the relevant tenancy has been determined; and a claimant shall not be entitled to the grant of such a lease if at the time when he makes his request—
- (a)   the landlord has already granted such a lease and that lease remains in force; or
- (b)   another person has already duly made a request for such a lease to the landlord and that request has been neither withdrawn nor abandoned by that person.

(8)   Where two or more requests are duly made on the same day, then for the purposes of subsection (7)—

(a)   a request made by a person who was liable for the qualifying payment as a former tenant shall be treated as made before a request made by a person who was so liable as a guarantor; and

(b)   a request made by a person whose liability in respect of the covenant in question commenced earlier than any such liability of another person shall be treated as made before a request made by that other person.

(9)   Where a claimant who has duly made a request for an overriding lease under this section subsequently withdraws or abandons the request before he is granted such a lease by the landlord, the claimant shall be liable for the landlord's reasonable costs incurred in pursuance of the request down to the time of its withdrawal or abandonment; and for the purposes of this section—

(a)   a claimant's request is withdrawn by the claimant notifying the landlord in writing that he is withdrawing his request; and

(b)   a claimant is to be regarded as having abandoned his request if—

    (i)   the landlord has requested the claimant in writing to take, within such reasonable period as is specified in the landlord's request, all or any of the remaining steps required to be taken by the claimant before the lease can be granted, and

    (ii)   the claimant fails to comply with the landlord's request,

and is accordingly to be regarded as having abandoned it at the time when that period expires.

(10)   Any request or notification under this section may be sent by post.

(11)   The preceding provisions of this section shall apply where the landlord is the tenant under an overriding lease granted under this section as they apply where no such lease has been granted; and accordingly there may be two or more such leases interposed between the first such lease and the relevant tenancy.

[692]

20 Overriding leases: supplementary provisions

(1)   For the purposes of section 1 an overriding lease shall be a new tenancy only if the relevant tenancy is a new tenancy.

(2)   Every overriding lease shall state—

(a)   that it is a lease granted under section 19, and

(b)   whether it is or is not a new tenancy for the purposes of section 1;

and any such statement shall comply with such requirements as may be prescribed by [land registration rules under the Land Registration Act 2002].

(3)   A claim that the landlord has failed to comply with subsection (6)(a) of section 19 may be made the subject of civil proceedings in like manner as any other claim in tort for breach of statutory duty; and if the claimant under that section fails to comply with subsection (6)(b)(i) of that section he shall not be entitled to exercise any of the rights otherwise exercisable by him under the overriding lease.

(4)   An overriding lease—

(a)   shall be deemed to be authorised as against the persons interested in any mortgage of the landlord's interest (however created or arising); and

(b)   shall be binding on any such persons;

and if any such person is by virtue of such a mortgage entitled to possession of the documents of title relating to the landlord's interest—

    (i)   the landlord shall within one month of the execution of the lease deliver to that person the counterpart executed in pursuance of section 19(6)(b)(i); and

    (ii)   if he fails to do so, the instrument creating or evidencing the mortgage shall apply as if the obligation to deliver a counterpart were included in the terms of the mortgage as set out in that instrument.

(5)   It is hereby declared—

(a)   that the fact that an overriding lease takes effect subject to the relevant tenancy shall not constitute a breach of any covenant of the lease against subletting or parting with possession of the premises demised by the lease or any part of them; and

(b)   that each of sections 16, 17 and 18 applies where the tenancy referred to in subsection (1) of that section is an overriding lease as it applies in other cases falling within that subsection.

(6)   No tenancy shall be registrable under the Land Charges Act 1972 or be taken to be an estate contract within the meaning of that Act by reason of any right or obligation that may arise under section 19, and any right arising from a request made under that section shall not be [capable of falling within paragraph '2 of Schedule 1 or 3 to the Land Registration Act 2002]; but any such request shall be registrable under the Land Charges Act 1972, or may be the subject of a notice [under the Land Registration Act 2002], as if it were an estate contract.

(7)   In this section—
    (a)   "mortgage" includes "charge"; and
    (b)   any expression which is also used in section 19 has the same meaning as in that section.

[693]

NOTES
Sub-ss (2), (6): words in square brackets substituted by the Land Registration Act 2002, s 133, Sch 11, para 33(1), (3), (4).

Forfeiture and disclaimer

21   Forfeiture or disclaimer limited to part only of demised premises

(1)   Where—
    (a)   as a result of one or more assignments a person is the tenant of part only of the premises demised by a tenancy, and
    (b)   under a proviso or stipulation in the tenancy there is a right of re-entry or forfeiture for a breach of a tenant covenant of the tenancy, and
    (c)   the right is (apart from this subsection) exercisable in relation to that part and other land demised by the tenancy,
the right shall nevertheless, in connection with a breach of any such covenant by that person, be taken to be a right exercisable only in relation to that part.

(2)   Where—
    (a)   a company which is being wound up, or a trustee in bankruptcy, is as a result of one or more assignments the tenant of part only of the premises demised by a tenancy, and
    (b)   the liquidator of the company exercises his power under section 178 of the Insolvency Act 1986, or the trustee in bankruptcy exercises his power under section 315 of that Act, to disclaim property demised by the tenancy,
the power is exercisable only in relation to the part of the premises referred to in paragraph (a).

[694]

Landlord's consent to assignments

22   (*Inserts the Landlord and Tenant Act 1927, s 19(1A)–(1E).*)

Supplemental

23   Effects of becoming subject to liability under, or entitled to benefit of, covenant etc

(1)   Where as a result of an assignment a person becomes, by virtue of this Act, bound by or entitled to the benefit of a covenant, he shall not by virtue of this Act have any liability or rights under the covenant in relation to any time falling before the assignment.

(2)   Subsection (1) does not preclude any such rights being expressly assigned to the person in question.

(3)   Where as a result of an assignment a person becomes, by virtue of this Act, entitled to a right of re-entry contained in a tenancy, that right shall be exercisable in relation to any breach of a covenant of the tenancy occurring before the assignment as in relation to one occurring thereafter, unless by reason of any waiver or release it was not so exercisable immediately before the assignment.

[695]

24 Effects of release from liability under, or loss of benefit of, covenant

(1)   Any release of a person from a covenant by virtue of this Act does not affect any liability of his arising from a breach of the covenant occurring before the release.

(2)   Where—
 (a)   by virtue of this Act a tenant is released from a tenant covenant of a tenancy, and
 (b)   immediately before the release another person is bound by a covenant of the tenancy imposing any liability or penalty in the event of a failure to comply with that tenant covenant,

then, as from the release of the tenant, that other person is released from the covenant mentioned in paragraph (b) to the same extent as the tenant is released from that tenant covenant.

(3)   Where a person bound by a landlord or tenant covenant of a tenancy—
 (a)   assigns the whole or part of his interest in the premises demised by the tenancy, but
 (b)   is not released by virtue of this Act from the covenant (with the result that subsection (1) does not apply),

the assignment does not affect any liability of his arising from a breach of the covenant occurring before the assignment.

(4)   Where by virtue of this Act a person ceases to be entitled to the benefit of a covenant, this does not affect any rights of his arising from a breach of the covenant occurring before he ceases to be so entitled.

[696]

25 Agreement void if it restricts operation of the Act

(1)   Any agreement relating to a tenancy is void to the extent that—
 (a)   it would apart from this section have effect to exclude, modify or otherwise frustrate the operation of any provision of this Act, or
 (b)   it provides for—
  (i)   the termination or surrender of the tenancy, or
  (ii)   the imposition on the tenant of any penalty, disability or liability,
 in the event of the operation of any provision of this Act, or
 (c)   it provides for any of the matters referred to in paragraph (b)(i) or (ii) and does so (whether expressly or otherwise) in connection with, or in consequence of, the operation of any provision of this Act.

(2)   To the extent that an agreement relating to a tenancy constitutes a covenant (whether absolute or qualified) against the assignment, or parting with the possession, of the premises demised by the tenancy or any part of them—
 (a)   the agreement is not void by virtue of subsection (1) by reason only of the fact that as such the covenant prohibits or restricts any such assignment or parting with possession; but
 (b)   paragraph (a) above does not otherwise affect the operation of that subsection in relation to the agreement (and in particular does not preclude its application to the agreement to the extent that it purports to regulate the giving of, or the making of any application for, consent to any such assignment or parting with possession).

(3)   In accordance with section 16(1) nothing in this section applies to any agreement to the extent that it is an authorised guarantee agreement; but (without prejudice to the generality of subsection (1) above) an agreement is void to the extent that it is one falling within section 16(4)(a) or (b).

(4)   This section applies to an agreement relating to a tenancy whether or not the agreement is—
 (a)   contained in the instrument creating the tenancy; or
 (b)   made before the creation of the tenancy.

[697]

26 Miscellaneous savings etc

(1)   Nothing in this Act is to be read as preventing—
 (a)   a party to a tenancy from releasing a person from a landlord covenant or a tenant covenant of the tenancy; or

(b)   the parties to a tenancy from agreeing to an apportionment of liability under such a covenant.

(2)   Nothing in this Act affects the operation of section 3(3A) of the Landlord and Tenant Act 1985 (preservation of former landlord's liability until tenant notified of new landlord).

(3)   No apportionment which has become binding in accordance with section 10 shall be affected by any order or decision made under or by virtue of any enactment not contained in this Act which relates to apportionment.

[698]

27   Notices for the purposes of the Act

(1)   The form of any notice to be served for the purposes of section 8, 10 or 17 shall be prescribed by regulations made by the Lord Chancellor by statutory instrument.

(2)   The regulations shall require any notice served for the purposes of section 8(1) or 10(1) ("the initial notice") to include
(a)   an explanation of the significance of the notice and the options available to the person on whom it is served;
(b)   a statement that any objections to the proposed release, or (as the case may be) to the proposed binding effect of the apportionment, must be made by notice in writing served on the person or persons by whom the initial notice is served within the period of four weeks beginning with the day on which the initial notice is served; and
(c)   an address in England and Wales to which any such objections may be sent.

(3)   The regulations shall require any notice served for the purposes of section 17 to include an explanation of the significance of the notice.

(4)   If any notice purporting to be served for the purposes of section 8(1), 10(1) or 17 is not in the prescribed form, or in a form substantially to the same effect, the notice shall not be effective for the purposes of section 8, section 10 or section 17 (as the case may be).

(5)   Section 23 of the Landlord and Tenant Act 1927 shall apply in relation to the service of notices for the purposes of section 8, 10 or 17.

(6)   Any statutory instrument made under this section shall be subject to annulment in pursuance of a resolution of either House of Parliament.

[699]

NOTES

Regulations: the Landlord and Tenant (Covenants) Act 1995 (Notices) Regulations 1995, SI 1995/2964 at **[1239]**.

28   Interpretation

(1)   In this Act (unless the context otherwise requires—
"assignment" includes equitable assignment and in addition (subject to section 11) assignment in breach of a covenant of a tenancy or by operation of law;
"authorised guarantee agreement" means an agreement which is an authorised guarantee agreement for the purposes of section 16;
"collateral agreement", in relation to a tenancy, means any agreement collateral to the tenancy, whether made before or after its creation;
"consent" includes licence;
"covenant" includes term, condition and obligation, and references to a covenant (or any description of covenant) of a tenancy include a covenant (or a covenant of that description) contained in a collateral agreement;
"landlord" and "tenant", in relation to a tenancy, mean the person for the time being entitled to the reversion expectant on the term of the tenancy and the person so entitled to that term respectively;
"landlord covenant", in relation to a tenancy, means a covenant falling to be complied with by the landlord of premises demised by the tenancy;
"new tenancy" means a tenancy which is a new tenancy for the purposes of section 1;
"reversion" means the interest expectant on the termination of a tenancy;
"tenancy" means any lease or other tenancy and includes—
(a)   a sub-tenancy, and
(b)   an agreement for a tenancy,

but does not include a mortgage term;

"tenant covenant", in relation to a tenancy, means a covenant falling to be complied with by the tenant of premises demised by the tenancy.

(2)   For the purposes of any reference in this Act to a covenant falling to be complied with in relation to a particular part of the premises demised by a tenancy, a covenant falls to be so complied with if—

(a)   it in terms applies to that part of the premises, or

(b)   in its practical application it can be attributed to that part of the premises (whether or not it can also be so attributed to other individual parts of those premises).

(3)   Subsection (2) does not apply in relation to covenants to pay money; and, for the purposes of any reference in this Act to a covenant falling to be complied with in relation to a particular part of the premises demised by a tenancy, a covenant of a tenancy which is a covenant to pay money falls to be so complied with if—

(a)   the covenant in terms applies to that part; or

(b)   the amount of the payment is determinable specifically by reference—

(i)   to that part, or

(ii)   to anything falling to be done by or for a person as tenant or occupier of that part (if it is a tenant covenant), or

(iii)   to anything falling to be done by or for a person as landlord of that part (if it is a landlord covenant).

(4)   Where two or more persons jointly constitute either the landlord or the tenant in relation to a tenancy, any reference in this Act to the landlord or the tenant is a reference to both or all of the persons who jointly constitute the landlord or the tenant, as the case may be (and accordingly nothing in section 13 applies in relation to the rights and liabilities of such persons between themselves).

(5)   References in this Act to the assignment by a landlord of the reversion in the whole or part of the premises demised by a tenancy are to the assignment by him of the whole of his interest (as owner of the reversion) in the whole or part of those premises.

(6)   For the purposes of this Act—

(a)   any assignment (however effected) consisting in the transfer of the whole of the landlord's interest (as owner of the reversion) in any premises demised by a tenancy shall be treated as an assignment by the landlord of the reversion in those premises even if it is not effected by him; and

(b)   any assignment (however effected) consisting in the transfer of the whole of the tenant's interest in any premises demised by a tenancy shall be treated as an assignment by the tenant of those premises even if it is not effected by him.

[700]

29   Crown application

This Act binds the Crown.

[701]

30   Consequential amendments and repeals

(1)   The enactments specified in Schedule 1 are amended in accordance with that Schedule, the amendments being consequential on the provisions of this Act.

(2)   The enactments specified in Schedule 2 are repealed to the extent specified.

(3)   Subsections (1) and (2) do not affect the operation of—

(a)   section 77 of, or Part IX or X of Schedule 2 to, the Law of Property Act 1925, or

(b)   section 24(1)(b) or (2) of the Land Registration Act 1925,

in relation to tenancies which are not new tenancies.

(4)   In consequence of this Act nothing in the following provisions, namely—

(a)   sections 78 and 79 of the Law of Property Act 1925 (benefit and burden of covenants relating to land), and

(b)   sections 141 and 142 of that Act (running of benefit and burden of covenants with reversion),

shall apply in relation to new tenancies.

(5)   The Lord Chancellor may by order made by statutory instrument make, in the case of such enactments as may be specified in the order, such amendments or repeals in, or such modifications of, those enactments as appear to him to be necessary or expedient in consequence of any provision of this Act.

(6)   Any statutory instrument made under subsection (5) shall be subject to annulment in pursuance of a resolution of either House of Parliament.

[702]

31   Commencement

(1)   The provisions of this Act come into force on such day as the Lord Chancellor may appoint by order made by statutory instrument.

(2)   An order under this section may contain such transitional provisions and savings (whether or not involving the modification of any enactment) as appear to the Lord Chancellor necessary or expedient in connection with the provisions brought into force by the order.

[703]

NOTES

Orders: the Landlord and Tenant (Covenants) Act 1995 (Commencement) Order 1995, SI 1995/2963.

32   Short title and extent

(1)   This Act may be cited as the Landlord and Tenant (Covenants) Act 1995.

(2)   This Act extends to England and Wales only.

[704]

(Schs 1, 2 contain amendments and repeals which, in so far as they relate to provisions in this work have been incorporated.)

DISABILITY DISCRIMINATION ACT 1995

(1995 c 50)

ARRANGEMENT OF SECTIONS

PART I
DISABILITY

PART II
THE EMPLOYMENT FIELD AND MEMBERS
OF LOCALLY-ELECTABLE AUTHORITIES

Employment

Office-holders

*An Act to make it unlawful to discriminate against disabled persons in connection with
employment, the provision of goods, facilities and services or the disposal or management
of premises; to make provision about the employment of disabled persons; and to establish
a National Disability Council*

[8 November 1995]

NOTES

Note that amendments made to this Act by the Special Educational Needs and Disability (Northern
Ireland) Order 2005, SI 2005/1117 (NI 6) and the Disability Discrimination (Northern Ireland)
Order 2006, SI 2006/312 (NI 1) that apply to Northern Ireland only are not reproduced.

PART I
DISABILITY

1   Meaning of "disability" and "disabled person"

(1)   Subject to the provisions of Schedule 1, a person has a disability for the purposes of
this Act if he has a physical or mental impairment which has a substantial and long-term
adverse effect on his ability to carry out normal day-to-day activities.

(2)   In this Act "disabled person" means a person who has a disability.

[705]

2, 3   (*Outside the scope of this work.*)

PART II
[THE EMPLOYMENT FIELD] [AND MEMBERS OF LOCALLY-ELECTABLE
AUTHORITIES]

NOTES

Words in first pair of square brackets substituted by the Disability Discrimination Act 1995
(Amendment) Regulations 2003, SI 2003/1673, regs 3(1), 4(1); words in second pair of square brackets
added by the Disability Discrimination Act 2005, s 19(1), Sch 1, Pt 1, paras 1, 4.

3A, 3B   (*Outside the scope of this work.*)

[Employment]

NOTES

Heading substituted by the Disability Discrimination Act 1995 (Amendment) Regulations 2003,
SI 2003/1673, regs 3(1), 5.

4   (*Outside the scope of this work.*)

[4A   Employers: duty to make adjustments

(1)   Where—
  (a)   a provision, criterion or practice applied by or on behalf of an employer, or
  (b)   any physical feature of premises occupied by the employer,

places the disabled person concerned at a substantial disadvantage in comparison with
persons who are not disabled, it is the duty of the employer to take such steps as it is
reasonable, in all the circumstances of the case, for him to have to take in order to prevent the
provision, criterion or practice, or feature, having that effect.

(2)   In subsection (1), "the disabled person concerned" means—

419

(a)   in the case of a provision, criterion or practice for determining to whom employment should be offered, any disabled person who is, or has notified the employer that he may be, an applicant for that employment;

(b)   in any other case, a disabled person who is—

    (i)   an applicant for the employment concerned, or

    (ii)   an employee of the employer concerned.

(3)   Nothing in this section imposes any duty on an employer in relation to a disabled person if the employer does not know, and could not reasonably be expected to know—

(a)   in the case of an applicant or potential applicant, that the disabled person concerned is, or may be, an applicant for the employment; or

(b)   in any case, that that person has a disability and is likely to be affected in the way mentioned in subsection (1).]

[706]

NOTES

Commencement: 3 July 2003 (certain purposes); 1 October 2004 (otherwise).

Substituted, together with ss 4, 4B–4F, for ss 4–6 as originally enacted, by the Disability Discrimination Act 1995 (Amendment) Regulations 2003, SI 2003/1673, regs 3(1), 5.

4B   (*Outside the scope of this work.*)

[Office-holders]

NOTES

Heading substituted by the Disability Discrimination Act 1995 (Amendment) Regulations 2003, SI 2003/1673, regs 3(1), 5.

4C, 4D   (*Outside the scope of this work.*)

[4E   Office-holders: duty to make adjustments

(1)   Where—

(a)   a provision, criterion or practice applied by or on behalf of a relevant person, or

(b)   any physical feature of premises—

    (i)   under the control of a relevant person, and

    (ii)   at or from which the functions of an office or post to which this section applies are performed,

places the disabled person concerned at a substantial disadvantage in comparison with persons who are not disabled, it is the duty of the relevant person to take such steps as it is reasonable, in all the circumstances of the case, for him to have to take in order to prevent the provision, criterion or practice, or feature, having that effect.

(2)   In this section, "the disabled person concerned" means—

(a)   in the case of a provision, criterion or practice for determining who should be appointed to, or recommended or approved in relation to, an office or post to which this section applies, any disabled person who—

    (i)   is, or has notified the relevant person that he may be, seeking appointment to, or (as the case may be) seeking a recommendation or approval in relation to, that office or post, or

    (ii)   is being considered for appointment to, or (as the case may be) for a recommendation or approval in relation to, that office or post;

(b)   in any other case, a disabled person—

    (i)   who is seeking or being considered for appointment to, or a recommendation or approval in relation to, the office or post concerned, or

    (ii)   who has been appointed to the office or post concerned.

(3)   Nothing in this section imposes any duty on the relevant person in relation to a disabled person if the relevant person does not know, and could not reasonably be expected to know—

(a)   in the case of a person who is being considered for, or is or may be seeking, appointment to, or a recommendation or approval in relation to, an office or post, that the disabled person concerned—

(i) is, or may be, seeking appointment to, or (as the case may be) seeking a recommendation or approval in relation to, that office or post, or

(ii) is being considered for appointment to, or (as the case may be) for a recommendation or approval in relation to, that office or post; or

(b) in any case, that that person has a disability and is likely to be affected in the way mentioned in subsection (1).]

[707]

NOTES

Commencement: 3 July 2003 (certain purposes); 1 October 2004 (otherwise).
Substituted as noted to s 4A at **[706]**.

[4F   Office-holders: supplementary

(1)   In sections 4C to 4E, appointment to an office or post does not include election to an office or post.

(2)   In sections 4D and 4E, "relevant person" means—
   (a) in a case relating to an appointment to an office or post, the person with power to make that appointment;
   (b) in a case relating to the making of a recommendation or the giving of an approval in relation to an appointment, a person or body referred to in section 4C(3)(b) with power to make that recommendation or (as the case may be) to give that approval;
   (c) in a case relating to a term of an appointment, the person with power to determine that term;
   (d) in a case relating to a working condition afforded in relation to an appointment—
      (i) the person with power to determine that working condition; or
      (ii) where there is no such person, the person with power to make the appointment;
   (e) in a case relating to the termination of an appointment, the person with power to terminate the appointment;
   (f) in a case relating to the subjection of a disabled person to any other detriment or to harassment, any person or body falling within one or more of paragraphs (a) to (e) in relation to such cases as are there mentioned.

(3)   In subsection (2)(d), "working condition" includes—
   (a) any opportunity for promotion, a transfer, training or receiving any other benefit; and
   (b) any physical feature of premises at or from which the functions of an office or post are performed.]

[708]

NOTES

Commencement: 3 July 2003 (certain purposes); 1 October 2004 (otherwise).
Substituted as noted to s 4A at **[706]**.

4G–14   (*Outside the scope of this work.*)

[14A   Qualifications bodies: discrimination and harassment

(1)   It is unlawful for a qualifications body to discriminate against a disabled person—
   (a) in the arrangements which it makes for the purpose of determining upon whom to confer a professional or trade qualification;
   (b) in the terms on which it is prepared to confer a professional or trade qualification on him;
   (c) by refusing or deliberately omitting to grant any application by him for such a qualification; or
   (d) by withdrawing such a qualification from him or varying the terms on which he holds it.

(2)   It is also unlawful for a qualifications body, in relation to a professional or trade qualification conferred by it, to subject to harassment a disabled person who holds or applies for such a qualification.

(3)   In determining for the purposes of subsection (1) whether the application by a qualifications body of a competence standard to a disabled person constitutes discrimination

within the meaning of section 3A, the application of the standard is justified for the purposes of section 3A(1)(b) if, but only if, the qualifications body can show that—
- (a) the standard is, or would be, applied equally to persons who do not have his particular disability; and
- (b) its application is a proportionate means of achieving a legitimate aim.

(4) For the purposes of subsection (3)—
- (a) section 3A(2) (and (6)) does not apply; and
- (b) section 3A(4) has effect as if the reference to section 3A(3) were a reference to subsection (3) of this section.

(5) In this section and section 14B—
"qualifications body" means any authority or body which can confer a professional or trade qualification, but it does not include—
- (a) a responsible body (within the meaning of Chapter 1 or 2 of Part 4),
- (b) a local education authority in England or Wales, or
- (c) an education authority (within the meaning of section 135(1) of the Education (Scotland) Act 1980);

"confer" includes renew or extend;
"professional or trade qualification" means an authorisation, qualification, recognition, registration, enrolment, approval or certification which is needed for, or facilitates engagement in, a particular profession or trade;
"competence standard" means an academic, medical or other standard applied by or on behalf of a qualifications body for the purpose of determining whether or not a person has a particular level of competence or ability.]

[709]

NOTES
Commencement: 3 July 2003 (certain purposes); 1 October 2004 (otherwise).
Substituted, together with ss 13, 14, 14B–14D, for ss 13–15 as originally enacted, by the Disability Discrimination Act 1995 (Amendment) Regulations 2003, SI 2003/1673, regs 3(1), 13.

[14B Qualifications bodies: duty to make adjustments

(1) Where—
- (a) a provision, criterion or practice, other than a competence standard, applied by or on behalf of a qualifications body; or
- (b) any physical feature of premises occupied by a qualifications body,

places the disabled person concerned at a substantial disadvantage in comparison with persons who are not disabled, it is the duty of the qualifications body to take such steps as it is reasonable, in all the circumstances of the case, for it to have to take in order to prevent the provision, criterion or practice, or feature, having that effect.

(2) In this section "the disabled person concerned" means—
- (a) in the case of a provision, criterion or practice for determining on whom a professional or trade qualification is to be conferred, any disabled person who is, or has notified the qualifications body that he may be, an applicant for the conferment of that qualification;
- (b) in any other case, a disabled person who—
  - (i) holds a professional or trade qualification conferred by the qualifications body, or
  - (ii) applies for a professional or trade qualification which it confers.

(3) Nothing in this section imposes a duty on a qualifications body in relation to a disabled person if the body does not know, and could not reasonably be expected to know—
- (a) in the case of an applicant or potential applicant, that the disabled person concerned is, or may be, an applicant for the conferment of a professional or trade qualification; or
- (b) in any case, that that person has a disability and is likely to be affected in the way mentioned in subsection (1).]

[710]

NOTES
Commencement: 3 July 2003 (certain purposes); 1 October 2004 (otherwise).
Substituted as noted to s 14A at **[709]**.

[Practical work experience

14C Practical work experience: discrimination and harassment

(1)   It is unlawful, in the case of a disabled person seeking or undertaking a work placement, for a placement provider to discriminate against him—
- (a)   in the arrangements which he makes for the purpose of determining who should be offered a work placement;
- (b)   in the terms on which he affords him access to any work placement or any facilities concerned with such a placement;
- (c)   by refusing or deliberately omitting to afford him such access;
- (d)   by terminating the placement; or
- (e)   by subjecting him to any other detriment in relation to the placement.

(2)   It is also unlawful for a placement provider, in relation to a work placement, to subject to harassment—
- (a)   a disabled person to whom he is providing a placement; or
- (b)   a disabled person who has applied to him for a placement.

[(3)   This section and section 14D do not apply—
- (a)   to anything which is unlawful under any provision of section 4, sections 19 to 21A, sections 21F to 21J or Part 4; or
- (b)   to anything which would be unlawful under any such provision but for the operation of any provision in or made under this Act.]

(4)   In this section and section 14D—
  "work placement" means practical work experience undertaken for a limited period for the purposes of a person's vocational training;
  "placement provider" means any person who provides a work placement to a person whom he does not employ.

(5)   This section and section 14D do not apply to a work placement undertaken in any of the naval, military and air forces of the Crown.]

[711]

NOTES

Commencement: 3 July 2003 (certain purposes); 1 October 2004 (otherwise).
Substituted as noted to s 14A at **[709]**.
Sub-s (3): substituted by the Disability Discrimination Act 2005, s 19(1), Sch 1, Pt 1, paras 1, 6.

[14D Practical work experience: duty to make adjustments

(1)   Where—
- (a)   a provision, criterion or practice applied by or on behalf of a placement provider, or
- (b)   any physical feature of premises occupied by the placement provider,

places the disabled person concerned at a substantial disadvantage in comparison with persons who are not disabled, it is the duty of the placement provider to take such steps as it is reasonable, in all the circumstances of the case, for him to have to take in order to prevent the provision, criterion or practice, or feature, having that effect.

(2)   In this section, "the disabled person concerned" means—
- (a)   in the case of a provision, criterion or practice for determining to whom a work placement should be offered, any disabled person who is, or has notified the placement provider that he may be, an applicant for that work placement;
- (b)   in any other case, a disabled person who is—
  - (i)   an applicant for the work placement concerned, or
  - (ii)   undertaking a work placement with the placement provider.

(3)   Nothing in this section imposes any duty on a placement provider in relation to the disabled person concerned if he does not know, and could not reasonably be expected to know—
- (a)   in the case of an applicant or potential applicant, that the disabled person concerned is, or may be, an applicant for the work placement; or
- (b)   in any case, that that person has a disability and is likely to be affected in the way mentioned in subsection (1).]

[712]

NOTES
Commencement: 3 July 2003 (certain purposes); 1 October 2004 (otherwise).
Substituted as noted to s 14A at **[709]**.

15–17C   (*S 15 (together with ss 13, 14) as originally enacted, is substituted by new ss 13, 14, 14A–14D, by the Disability Discrimination Act 1995 (Amendment) Regulations 2003, SI 2003/1673, regs 3(1), 13; s 16 renumbered as s 18A at* **[713]** *by SI 2003/1673, regs 3(1), 14(2); ss 17, 17A–17C outside the scope of this work.*)

[Supplementary and general]

NOTES
Heading inserted by the Disability Discrimination Act 1995 (Amendment) Regulations 2003, SI 2003/1673, regs 3(1), 17(1).

18   (*Repealed by the Disability Discrimination Act 2005, ss 11(1), 19(2), Sch 2.*)

[18A   Alterations to premises occupied under leases

(1)   This section applies where—
   (a)   [a person to whom a duty to make reasonable adjustments applies] ("the occupier") occupies premises under a lease;
   (b)   but for this section, the occupier would not be entitled to make a particular alteration to the premises; and
   (c)   the alteration is one which the occupier proposes to make in order to comply with [that duty].

(2)   Except to the extent to which it expressly so provides, the lease shall have effect by virtue of this subsection as if it provided—
   (a)   for the occupier to be entitled to make the alteration with the written consent of the lessor;
   (b)   for the occupier to have to make a written application to the lessor for consent if he wishes to make the alteration;
   (c)   if such an application is made, for the lessor not to withhold his consent unreasonably; and
   (d)   for the lessor to be entitled to make his consent subject to reasonable conditions.

(3)   In this section—
   "lease" includes a tenancy, sub-lease or sub-tenancy and an agreement for a lease, tenancy, sub-lease or sub-tenancy; and
   "sub-lease" and "sub-tenancy" have such meaning as may be prescribed.

(4)   If the terms and conditions of a lease—
   (a)   impose conditions which are to apply if the occupier alters the premises, or
   (b)   entitle the lessor to impose conditions when consenting to the occupier's altering the premises,
the occupier is to be treated for the purposes of subsection (1) as not being entitled to make the alteration.

(5)   Part I of Schedule 4 supplements the provisions of this section.]

[713]

NOTES
Commencement: 3 July 2003 (certain purposes); 1 October 2004 (otherwise).
Originally enacted as s 16 and renumbered as s 18A by the Disability Discrimination Act 1995 (Amendment) Regulations 2003, SI 2003/1673, regs 3(1), 14(2).
Sub-s (1): words in square brackets substituted by SI 2003/1673, regs 3(1), 14(3).
Modification: Modified, in relation to any case where the occupier occupies premises under a sub-lease or sub-tenancy, by the Disability Discrimination (Employment Field) (Leasehold Premises) Regulations 2004, SI 2004/153, regs 8, 9(a), (b).
Regulations: the Disability Discrimination (Employment Field) (Leasehold Premises) Regulations 2004, SI 2004/153.

18B–18E   (*Outside the scope of this work.*)

PART III
DISCRIMINATION IN OTHER AREAS

Goods, facilities and services

19   Discrimination in relation to goods, facilities and services

(1)   It is unlawful for a provider of services to discriminate against a disabled person—

    (a)   in refusing to provide, or deliberately not providing, to the disabled person any service which he provides, or is prepared to provide, to members of the public;

    (b)   in failing to comply with any duty imposed on him by section 21 in circumstances in which the effect of that failure is to make it impossible or unreasonably difficult for the disabled person to make use of any such service;

    (c)   in the standard of service which he provides to the disabled person or the manner in which he provides it to him; or

    (d)   in the terms on which he provides a service to the disabled person.

(2)   For the purposes of this section and sections 20 [to 21ZA]—

    (a)   the provision of services includes the provision of any goods or facilities;

    (b)   a person is "a provider of services" if he is concerned with the provision, in the United Kingdom, of services to the public or to a section of the public; and

    (c)   it is irrelevant whether a service is provided on payment or without payment.

(3)   The following are examples of services to which this section and sections 20 and 21 apply—

    (a)   access to and use of any place which members of the public are permitted to enter;

    (b)   access to and use of means of communication;

    (c)   access to and use of information services;

    (d)   accommodation in a hotel, boarding house or other similar establishment;

    (e)   facilities by way of banking or insurance or for grants, loans, credit or finance;

    (f)   facilities for entertainment, recreation or refreshment;

    (g)   facilities provided by employment agencies or under section 2 of the Employment and Training Act 1973;

    (h)   the services of any profession or trade, or any local or other public authority.

(4)   In the case of an act which constitutes discrimination by virtue of section 55, this section also applies to discrimination against a person who is not disabled.

[(5)   Regulations may provide for subsection (1) and section 21(1), (2) and (4) not to apply, or to apply only to a prescribed extent, in relation to a service of a prescribed description.]

[(5A)   Nothing in this section or sections 20 to 21A applies to the provision of a service in relation to which discrimination is unlawful under Part 4.]

(6)   ...

[714]

NOTES

Sub-s (2): words in square brackets substituted by the Disability Discrimination Act 2005, s 19(1), Sch 1, Pt 1, paras 1, 13(1), (2).

Sub-s (5): substituted by the Disability Discrimination Act 2005, s 19(1), Sch 1, Pt 1, paras 1, 13(1), (3).

Sub-s (5A): inserted by the Special Educational Needs and Disability Act 2001, s 38(1), (6); substituted by the Disability Discrimination Act 2005, s 19(1), Sch 1, Pt 1, paras 1, 13(1), (4).

Sub-s (6): repealed by the Special Educational Needs and Disability Act 2001, ss 38(1), (5)(b), 42(6), Sch 9.

Regulations: the Disability Discrimination (Services and Premises) Regulations (Northern Ireland) 1996, SR 1996/557.

20   Meaning of "discrimination"

(1)   For the purposes of section 19, a provider of services discriminates against a disabled person if—

(a)   for a reason which relates to the disabled person's disability, he treats him less favourably than he treats or would treat others to whom that reason does not or would not apply; and

(b)   he cannot show that the treatment in question is justified.

(2)   For the purposes of section 19, a providers of services also discriminates against a disabled person if—

(a)   he fails to comply with a section 21 duty imposed on him in relation to the disabled person; and

(b)   he cannot show that his failure to comply with that duty is justified.

(3)   For the purposes of this section, treatment is justified only if—

(a)   in the opinion of the provider of services, one or more of the conditions mentioned in subsection (4) are satisfied; and

(b)   it is reasonable, in all the circumstances of the case, for him to hold that opinion.

(4)   The conditions are that—

(a)   in any case, the treatment is necessary in order not to endanger the health or safety of any person (which may include that of the disabled person);

(b)   in any case, the disabled person is incapable of entering into an enforceable agreement, or of giving an informed consent, and for that reason the treatment is reasonable in that case;

(c)   in a case falling within section 19(1)(a), the treatment is necessary because the provider of services would otherwise be unable to provide the service to members of the public;

(d)   in a case falling within section 19(1)(c) or (d), the treatment is necessary in order for the provider of services to be able to provide the service to the disabled person or to other members of the public;

(e)   in a case falling within section 19(1)(d), the difference in the terms on which the service is provided to the disabled person and those on which it is provided to other members of the public reflects the greater cost to the provider of services in providing the service to the disabled person.

(5)   Any increase in the cost of providing a service to a disabled person which results from compliance by a provider of services with a section 21 duty shall be disregarded for the purposes of subsection (4)(e).

(6)   Regulations may make provision, for purposes of this section, as to circumstances in which—

(a)   it is reasonable for a provider of services to hold the opinion mentioned in subsection (3)(a);

(b)   it is not reasonable for a provider of services to hold that opinion.

(7)   Regulations may make provision for subsection (4)(b) not to apply in prescribed circumstances where—

(a)   a person is acting for a disabled person under a power of attorney;

(b)   functions conferred by or under *Part VII of the Mental Health Act 1983* are exercisable in relation to a disabled person's property or affairs; or

[(c)   powers are exercisable in relation to a disabled person's property or affairs in consequence of the appointment, under the law of Scotland, of a guardian, tutor or judicial factor.]

(8)   Regulations may make provision, for purposes of this section, as to circumstances (other than those mentioned in subsection (4)) in which treatment is to be taken to be justified.

(9)   In subsections (3), (4) and (8) "treatment" includes failure to comply with a section 21 duty.

[715]

NOTES

Sub-s (7): for the words in italics in para (b) there are substituted the words "the Mental Capacity Act 2005" by the Mental Capacity Act 2005, s 67(1), Sch 6, para 41, as from a day to be appointed; para (c) substituted by the Disability Discrimination Act 2005, s 19(1), Sch 1, Pt 1, paras 1, 14.

Regulations: the Disability Discrimination (Services and Premises) Regulations (Northern Ireland) 1996, SR 1996/557; the Disability Discrimination (Service Providers and Public Authorities Carrying Out Functions) Regulations 2005, SI 2005/2901.

---

21 Duty of providers of services to make adjustments

(1) Where a provider of services has a practice, policy or procedure which makes it impossible or unreasonably difficult for disabled persons to make use of a service which he provides, or is prepared to provide, to other members of the public, it is his duty to take such steps as it is reasonable, in all the circumstances of the case, for him to have to take in order to change that practice, policy or procedure so that it no longer has that effect.

(2) Where a physical feature (for example, one arising from the design or construction of a building or the approach or access to premises) makes it impossible or unreasonably difficult for disabled persons to make use of such a service, it is the duty of the provider of that service to take such steps as it is reasonable, in all the circumstances of the case, for him to have to take in order to—

   (a) remove the feature;

   (b) alter it so that it no longer has that effect;

   (c) provide a reasonable means of avoiding the feature; or

   (d) provide a reasonable alternative method of making the service in question available to disabled persons.

(3) Regulations may prescribe—

   (a) matters which are to be taken into account in determining whether any provision of a kind mentioned in subsection (2)(c) or (d) is reasonable; and

   (b) categories of providers of services to whom subsection (2) does not apply.

(4) Where an auxiliary aid or service (for example, the provision of information on audio tape or of a sign language interpreter) would—

   (a) enable disabled persons to make use of a service which a provider of services provides, or is prepared to provide, to members of the public, or

   (b) facilitate the use by disabled persons of such a service,

it is the duty of the provider of that service to take such steps as it is reasonable, in all the circumstances of the case, for him to have to take in order to provide that auxiliary aid or service.

(5) Regulations may make provision, for the purposes of this section—

   (a) as to circumstances in which it is reasonable for a provider of services to have to take steps of a prescribed description;

   (b) as to circumstances in which it is not reasonable for a provider of services to have to take steps of a prescribed description;

   (c) as to what is to be included within the meaning of "practice, policy or procedure";

   (d) as to what is not to be included within the meaning of that expression;

   (e) as to things which are to be treated as physical features;

   (f) as to things which are not to be treated as such features;

   (g) as to things which are to be treated as auxiliary aids or services;

   (h) as to things which are not to be treated as auxiliary aids or services.

(6) Nothing in this section requires a provider of services to take any steps which would fundamentally alter the nature of the service in question or the nature of his trade, profession or business.

(7) Nothing in this section requires a provider of services to take any steps which would cause him to incur expenditure exceeding the prescribed maximum.

(8) Regulations under subsection (7) may provide for the prescribed maximum to be calculated by reference to—

   (a) aggregate amounts of expenditure incurred in relation to different cases;

   (b) prescribed periods;

   (c) services of a prescribed description;

   (d) premises of a prescribed description; or

   (e) such other criteria as may be prescribed.

(9) Regulations may provide, for the purposes of subsection (7), for expenditure incurred by one provider of services to be treated as incurred by another.

(10) This section imposes duties only for the purpose of determining whether a provider of services has discriminated against a disabled person; and accordingly a breach of any such duty is not actionable as such.

[716]

NOTES

Commencement: 26 April 1999 (sub-ss (3), (5)); 1 October 1999 (sub-ss (1), (2)(d), (4), (6), (10)); 1 October 2004 (sub-s (2)(a)–(c)); to be appointed (otherwise).

Regulations: the Disability Discrimination (Services and Premises) Regulations 1999, SI 1999/1191; the Disability Discrimination (Providers of Services) (Adjustment of Premises) Regulations 2001, SI 2001/3253; the Disability Discrimination (Service Providers and Public Authorities Carrying Out Functions) Regulations 2005, SI 2005/2901; the Disability Discrimination (Transport Vehicles) Regulations 2005, SI 2005/3190.

21ZA, 21A–21M   (*Outside the scope of this work.*)

Premises

22   Discrimination in relation to premises

(1)   It is unlawful for a person with power to dispose of any premises to discriminate against a disabled person—

    (a)   in the terms on which he offers to dispose of those premises to the disabled person;

    (b)   by refusing to dispose of those premises to the disabled person; or

    (c)   in his treatment of the disabled person in relation to any list of persons in need of premises of that description.

(2)   Subsection (1) does not apply to a person who owns an estate or interest in the premises and wholly occupies them unless, for the purpose of disposing of the premises, he—

    (a)   uses the services of an estate agent, or

    (b)   publishes an advertisement or causes an advertisement to be published.

(3)   It is unlawful for a person managing any premises to discriminate against a disabled person occupying those premises—

    (a)   in the way he permits the disabled person to make use of any benefits or facilities;

    (b)   by refusing or deliberately omitting to permit the disabled person to make use of any benefits or facilities; or

    (c)   by evicting the disabled person, or subjecting him to any other detriment.

[(3A)   Regulations may make provision, for purposes of subsection (3)—

    (a)   as to who is to be treated as being, or as to who is to be treated as not being, a person who manages premises;

    (b)   as to who is to be treated as being, or as to who is to be treated as not being, a person occupying premises.]

(4)   It is unlawful for any person whose licence or consent is required for the disposal of any premises comprised in, or (in Scotland) the subject of, a tenancy to discriminate against a disabled person by withholding his licence or consent for the disposal of the premises to the disabled person.

(5)   Subsection (4) applies to tenancies created before as well as after the passing of this Act.

(6)   In this section—

"advertisement" includes every form of advertisement or notice, whether to the public or not;

"dispose", in relation to premises, includes granting a right to occupy the premises, and, in relation to premises comprised in, or (in Scotland) the subject of, a tenancy, includes—

    (a)   assigning the tenancy, and

    (b)   sub-letting or parting with possession of the premises or any part of the premises;

and "disposal" shall be construed accordingly;

"estate agent" means a person who, by way of profession or trade, provides services for the purpose of finding premises for persons seeking to acquire them or assisting in the disposal of premises; and

"tenancy" means a tenancy created—

    (a)   by a lease or sub-lease,

    (b)   by an agreement for a lease or sub-lease,

    (c)   by a tenancy agreement, or

    (d)   in pursuance of any enactment.

(7)   In the case of an act which constitutes discrimination by virtue of section 55, this section also applies to discrimination against a person who is not disabled.

(8)   This section applies only in relation to premises in the United Kingdom.

[717]

NOTES

Sub-s (3A): inserted by the Disability Discrimination Act 2005, s 19(1), Sch 1, Pt 1, paras 1, 16.
Regulations: the Disability Discrimination (Premises) Regulations 2006, SI 2006/887.

22A   (*Outside the scope of this work.*)

23 Exemption for small dwellings

(1)   Where the conditions mentioned in subsection (2) are satisfied, subsection (1), (3) or (as the case may be) (4) of section 22 does not apply.

(2)   The conditions are that—
    (a)   the relevant occupier resides, and intends to continue to reside, on the premises;
    (b)   the relevant occupier shares accommodation on the premises with persons who reside on the premises and are not members of his household;
    (c)   the shared accommodation is not storage accommodation or a means of access; and
    (d)   the premises are small premises.

(3)   For the purposes of this section, premises are "small premises" if they fall within subsection (4) or (5).

(4)   Premises fall within this subsection if—
    (a)   only the relevant occupier and members of his household reside in the accommodation occupied by him;
    (b)   the premises comprise, in addition to the accommodation occupied by the relevant occupier, residential accommodation for at least one other household;
    (c)   the residential accommodation for each other household is let, or available for letting, on a separate tenancy or similar agreement; and
    (d)   there are not normally more than two such other households.

(5)   Premises fall within this subsection if there is not normally residential accommodation on the premises for more than six persons in addition to the relevant occupier and any members of his household.

(6)   For the purposes of this section "the relevant occupier" means—
    (a)   in a case falling within section 22(1), the person with power to dispose of the premises, or a near relative of his;
    [(aa) in a case falling within section 22(3), the person managing the premises, or a near relative of his;]
    (b)   in a case falling within section 22(4), the person whose licence or consent is required for the disposal of the premises, or a near relative of his.

(7)   For the purposes of this section—
    "near relative" means a person's spouse [or civil partner], partner, parent, child, grandparent, grandchild, or brother or sister (whether of full or half blood or [by marriage or civil partnership)]; and
    ["partner" means the other member of a couple consisting of—
    (a)   a man and a woman who are not married to each other but are living together as husband and wife, or
    (b)   two people of the same sex who are not civil partners of each other but are living together as if they were civil partners.]

[718]

NOTES

Sub-s (6): para (aa) inserted by the Disability Discrimination Act 2005, s 19(1), Sch 1, Pt 1, paras 1, 18.
Sub-s (7): in definition "near relative" words in first pair of square brackets inserted and words in second pair of square brackets substituted, and definition "partner" substituted, by the Civil Partnership Act 2004, s 261(1), Sch 27, para 150.

24   Meaning of "discrimination"

(1)   For the purposes of [sections 22 and 22A], a person ("A") discriminates against a disabled person if—

(a)   for a reason which relates to the disabled person's disability, he treats him less favourably than he treats or would treat others to whom that reason does not or would not apply; and

(b)   he cannot show that the treatment in question is justified.

(2)   For the purposes of this section, treatment is justified only if—

(a)   in A's opinion, one or more of the conditions mentioned in subsection (3) are satisfied; and

(b)   it is reasonable, in all the circumstances of the case, for him to hold that opinion.

(3)   The conditions are that—

(a)   in any case, the treatment is necessary in order not to endanger the health or safety of any person (which may include that of the disabled person);

(b)   in any case, the disabled person is incapable of entering into an enforceable agreement, or of giving an informed consent, and for that reason the treatment is reasonable in that case;

(c)   in a case falling within section 22(3)(a), the treatment is necessary in order for the disabled person or the occupiers of other premises forming part of the building to make use of the benefit or facility;

(d)   in a case falling within section 22(3)(b), the treatment is necessary in order for the occupiers of other premises forming part of the building to make use of the benefit or facility;

[(e)   in a case to which subsection (3A) applies, the terms are less favourable in order to recover costs which—

(i)   as a result of the disabled person having a disability, are incurred in connection with the disposal of the premises, and

(ii)   are not costs incurred in connection with taking steps to avoid liability under section 24G(1);

(f)   in a case to which subsection (3B) applies, the disabled person is subjected to the detriment in order to recover costs which—

(i)   as a result of the disabled person having a disability, are incurred in connection with the management of the premises, and

(ii)   are not costs incurred in connection with taking steps to avoid liability under section 24A(1) or 24G(1)].

[(3A)   This subsection applies to a case if—

(a)   the case falls within section 22(1)(a);

(b)   the premises are to let;

(c)   the person with power to dispose of the premises is a controller of them; and

(d)   the proposed disposal of the premises would involve the disabled person becoming a person to whom they are let.

(3B)   This subsection applies to a case if-

(a)   the case falls within section 22(3)(c);

(b)   the detriment is not eviction;

(c)   the premises are let premises;

(d)   the person managing the premises is a controller of them; and

(e)   the disabled person is a person to whom the premises are let or, although not a person to whom they are let, is lawfully under the letting an occupier of them.

(3C)   Section 24G(3) and (4) apply for the purposes of subsection (3A) as for those of section 24G; and section 24A(3) and (4) apply for the purposes of subsection (3B) as for those of section 24A.]

(4)   Regulations may make provision, for purposes of this section, as to circumstances in which—

(a)   it is reasonable for a person to hold the opinion mentioned in subsection 2(a);

(b)   it is not reasonable for a person to hold that opinion.

[(4A)   Regulations may make provision for the condition specified in subsection (3)(b) not to apply in prescribed circumstances.]

(5)   Regulations may make provision, for purposes of this section, as to circumstances (other than those mentioned in subsection (3)) in which treatment is to be taken to be justified.

[719]

PART I
STATUTES

NOTES

Sub-s (2): words in square brackets substituted by the Disability Discrimination Act 2005, s 19(1), Sch 1, Pt 1, paras 1, 19(1), (2).

Sub-s (3): paras (e), (f) added by the Disability Discrimination Act 2005, s 19(1), Sch 1, Pt 1, paras 1, 19(1), (3).

Sub-ss (3A)–(3C), (4A): inserted by the Disability Discrimination Act 2005, s 19(1), Sch 1, Pt 1, paras 1, 19(1), (4), (5).

See further, in relation to circumstances in which mental incapacity justification does not apply: the Disability Discrimination (Premises) Regulations 2006, SI 2006/887, reg 2.

Regulations: the Disability Discrimination (Services and Premises) Regulations (Northern Ireland) 1996, SR 1996/557; the Disability Discrimination (Premises) Regulations 2006, SI 2006/887.

Enforcement, etc

[24A   Let premises: discrimination in failing to comply with duty

(1)   It is unlawful for a controller of let premises to discriminate against a disabled person—

    (a)   who is a person to whom the premises are let; or

    (b)   who, although not a person to whom the premises are let, is lawfully under the letting an occupier of the premises.

(2)   For the purposes of subsection (1), a controller of let premises discriminates against a disabled person if—

    (a)   he fails to comply with a duty under section 24C or 24D imposed on him by reference to the disabled person; and

    (b)   he cannot show that failure to comply with the duty is justified (see section 24K).

(3)   For the purposes of this section and sections 24B to 24F, a person is a controller of let premises if he is—

    (a)   a person by whom the premises are let; or

    (b)   a person who manages the premises.

(4)   For the purposes of this section and sections 24B to 24F—

    (a)   "let" includes sub-let; and

    (b)   premises shall be treated as let by a person to another where a person has granted another a contractual licence to occupy them.

(5)   This section applies only in relation to premises in the United Kingdom.]

[719A]

NOTES

Commencement: 4 December 2006.

Inserted, together with ss 24B–24H, 24J–24L, by the Disability Discrimination Act 2005, s 13.

[24B   Exceptions to section 24A(1)

(1)   Section 24A(1) does not apply if—

    (a)   the premises are, or have at any time been, the only or principal home of an individual who is a person by whom they are let; and

    (b)   since entering into the letting—

        (i)   the individual has not, and

        (ii)   where he is not the sole person by whom the premises are let, no other person by whom they are let has,

used for the purpose of managing the premises the services of a person who, by profession or trade, manages let premises.

(2)   Section 24A(1) does not apply if the premises are of a prescribed description.

(3)   Where the conditions mentioned in section 23(2) are satisfied, section 24A(1) does not apply.

(4)   For the purposes of section 23 "the relevant occupier" means, in a case falling within section 24A(1), a controller of the let premises, or a near relative of his; and "near relative" has here the same meaning as in section 23.]

[719B]

NOTES
Commencement: 4 December 2006.
Inserted as noted to s 24A at **[719A]**.

[24C Duty for purposes of section 24A(2) to provide auxiliary aid or service

(1)   Subsection (2) applies where—

    (a)   a controller of let premises receives a request made by or on behalf of a person to whom the premises are let;

    (b)   it is reasonable to regard the request as a request that the controller take steps in order to provide an auxiliary aid or service; and

    (c)   either the first condition, or the second condition, is satisfied.

(2)   It is the duty of the controller to take such steps as it is reasonable, in all the circumstances of the case, for him to have to take in order to provide the auxiliary aid or service (but see section 24E(1)).

(3)   The first condition is that—

    (a)   the auxiliary aid or service—

        (i)   would enable a relevant disabled person to enjoy, or facilitate such a person's enjoyment of, the premises, but

        (ii)   would be of little or no practical use to the relevant disabled person concerned if he were neither a person to whom the premises are let nor an occupier of them; and

    (b)   it would, were the auxiliary aid or service not to be provided, be impossible or unreasonably difficult for the relevant disabled person concerned to enjoy the premises.

(4)   The second condition is that—

    (a)   the auxiliary aid or service—

        (i)   would enable a relevant disabled person to make use, or facilitate such a person's making use, of any benefit, or facility, which by reason of the letting is one of which he is entitled to make use, but

        (ii)   would be of little or no practical use to the relevant disabled person concerned if he were neither a person to whom the premises are let nor an occupier of them; and

    (b)   it would, were the auxiliary aid or service not to be provided, be impossible or unreasonably difficult for the relevant disabled person concerned to make use of any benefit, or facility, which by reason of the letting is one of which he is entitled to make use.]

[719C]

NOTES
Commencement: 4 December 2006.
Inserted as noted to s 24A at **[719A]**.

[24D Duty for purposes of section 24A(2) to change practices, terms etc

(1)   Subsection (3) applies where—

    (a)   a controller of let premises has a practice, policy or procedure which has the effect of making it impossible, or unreasonably difficult, for a relevant disabled person—

        (i)   to enjoy the premises, or

        (ii)   to make use of any benefit, or facility, which by reason of the letting is one of which he is entitled to make use, or

    (b)   a term of the letting has that effect,

and (in either case) the conditions specified in subsection (2) are satisfied.

(2)   Those conditions are—

    (a)   that the practice, policy, procedure or term would not have that effect if the relevant disabled person concerned did not have a disability;

    (b)   that the controller receives a request made by or on behalf of a person to whom the premises are let; and

(c) that it is reasonable to regard the request as a request that the controller take steps in order to change the practice, policy, procedure or term so as to stop it having that effect.

(3) It is the duty of the controller to take such steps as it is reasonable, in all the circumstances of the case, for him to have to take in order to change the practice, policy, procedure or term so as to stop it having that effect (but see section 24E(1)).]

[719D]

NOTES
Commencement: 4 December 2006.
Inserted as noted to s 24A at **[719A]**.

[24E Sections 24C and 24D: supplementary and interpretation

(1) For the purposes of sections 24C and 24D, it is never reasonable for a controller of let premises to have to take steps consisting of, or including, the removal or alteration of a physical feature.

(2) Sections 24C and 24D impose duties only for the purpose of determining whether a person has, for the purposes of section 24A, discriminated against another; and accordingly a breach of any such duty is not actionable as such.

(3) In sections 24C and 24D "relevant disabled person", in relation to let premises, means a particular disabled person—
(a) who is a person to whom the premises are let; or
(b) who, although not a person to whom the premises are let, is lawfully under the letting an occupier of the premises.

(4) For the purposes of sections 24C and 24D, the terms of a letting of premises include the terms of any agreement which relates to the letting of the premises.]

[719E]

NOTES
Commencement: 4 December 2006.
Inserted as noted to s 24A at **[719A]**.

[24F Let premises: victimisation of persons to whom premises are let

(1) Where a duty under section 24C or 24D is imposed on a controller of let premises by reference to a person who, although not a person to whom the premises are let, is lawfully under the letting an occupier of the premises, it is unlawful for a controller of the let premises to discriminate against a person to whom the premises are let.

(2) For the purposes of subsection (1), a controller of the let premises discriminates against a person to whom the premises are let if—
(a) the controller treats that person ("T") less favourably than he treats or would treat other persons whose circumstances are the same as T's; and
(b) he does so because of costs incurred in connection with taking steps to avoid liability under section 24A(1) for failure to comply with the duty.

(3) In comparing T's circumstances with those of any other person for the purposes of subsection (2)(a), the following (as well as the costs' having been incurred) shall be disregarded—
(a) the making of the request that gave rise to the imposition of the duty; and
(b) the disability of each person who—
(i) is a disabled person or a person who has had a disability, and
(ii) is a person to whom the premises are let or, although not a person to whom the premises are let, is lawfully under the letting an occupier of the premises.]

[719F]

NOTES
Commencement: 4 December 2006.
Inserted as noted to s 24A at **[719A]**.

[24G Premises that are to let: discrimination in failing to comply with duty

(1)   Where—
   (a)   a person has premises to let, and
   (b)   a disabled person is considering taking a letting of the premises,
it is unlawful for a controller of the premises to discriminate against the disabled person.

(2)   For the purposes of subsection (1), a controller of premises that are to let discriminates against a disabled person if—
   (a)   he fails to comply with a duty under section 24J imposed on him by reference to the disabled person; and
   (b)   he cannot show that failure to comply with the duty is justified (see section 24K).

(3)   For the purposes of this section and sections 24H and 24J, a person is a controller of premises that are to let if he is—
   (a)   a person who has the premises to let; or
   (b)   a person who manages the premises.

(4)   For the purposes of this section and sections 24H and 24J—
   (a)   "let" includes sub-let;
   (b)   premises shall be treated as to let by a person to another where a person proposes to grant another a contractual licence to occupy them;
and references to a person considering taking a letting of premises shall be construed accordingly.

(5)   This section applies only in relation to premises in the United Kingdom.]

[719G]

NOTES
Commencement: 4 December 2006.
Inserted as noted to s 24A at **[719A]**.

[24H   Exceptions to section 24G(1)

(1)   Section 24G(1) does not apply in relation to premises that are to let if the premises are, or have at any time been, the only or principal home of an individual who is a person who has them to let and—
   (a)   the individual does not use, and
   (b)   where he is not the sole person who has the premises to let, no other person who has the premises to let uses,
the services of an estate agent (within the meaning given by section 22(6)) for the purposes of letting the premises.

(2)   Section 24G(1) does not apply if the premises are of a prescribed description.

(3)   Where the conditions mentioned in section 23(2) are satisfied, section 24G(1) does not apply.

(4)   For the purposes of section 23 "the relevant occupier" means, in a case falling within section 24G(1), a controller of the premises that are to let, or a near relative of his; and "near relative" has here the same meaning as in section 23.]

[719H]

NOTES
Commencement: 4 December 2006.
Inserted as noted to s 24A at **[719A]**.

[24J   Duties for purposes of section 24G(2)

(1)   Subsection (2) applies where—
   (a)   a controller of premises that are to let receives a request made by or on behalf of a relevant disabled person;
   (b)   it is reasonable to regard the request as a request that the controller take steps in order to provide an auxiliary aid or service;
   (c)   the auxiliary aid or service—
      (i)   would enable the relevant disabled person to become, or facilitate his becoming, a person to whom the premises are let, but

(ii)   would be of little or no practical use to him if he were not considering taking a letting of the premises; and

(d)   it would, were the auxiliary aid or service not to be provided, be impossible or unreasonably difficult for the relevant disabled person to become a person to whom the premises are let.

(2)   It is the duty of the controller to take such steps as it is reasonable, in all the circumstances of the case, for the controller to have to take in order to provide the auxiliary aid or service (but see subsection (5)).

(3)   Subsection (4) applies where—

(a)   a controller of premises that are to let has a practice, policy or procedure which has the effect of making it impossible, or unreasonably difficult, for a relevant disabled person to become a person to whom the premises are let;

(b)   the practice, policy or procedure would not have that effect if the relevant disabled person did not have a disability;

(c)   the controller receives a request made by or on behalf of the relevant disabled person; and

(d)   it is reasonable to regard the request as a request that the controller take steps in order to change the practice, policy or procedure so as to stop it having that effect.

(4)   It is the duty of the controller to take such steps as it is reasonable, in all the circumstances of the case, for him to have to take in order to change the practice, policy or procedure so as to stop it having that effect (but see subsection (5)).

(5)   For the purposes of this section, it is never reasonable for a controller of premises that are to let to have to take steps consisting of, or including, the removal or alteration of a physical feature.

(6)   In this section "relevant disabled person", in relation to premises that are to let, means a particular disabled person who is considering taking a letting of the premises.

(7)   This section imposes duties only for the purpose of determining whether a person has, for the purposes of section 24G, discriminated against another; and accordingly a breach of any such duty is not actionable as such.]

[**719J**]

NOTES

Commencement: 4 December 2006.
Inserted as noted to s 24A at [**719A**].

[24K   Let premises and premises that are to let: justification

(1)   For the purposes of sections 24A(2) and 24G(2), a person's failure to comply with a duty is justified only if—

(a)   in his opinion, a condition mentioned in subsection (2) is satisfied; and

(b)   it is reasonable, in all the circumstances of the case, for him to hold that opinion.

(2)   The conditions are—

(a)   that it is necessary to refrain from complying with the duty in order not to endanger the health or safety of any person (which may include that of the disabled person concerned);

(b)   that the disabled person concerned is incapable of entering into an enforceable agreement, or of giving informed consent, and for that reason the failure is reasonable.

(3)   Regulations may—

(a)   make provision, for purposes of this section, as to circumstances in which it is, or as to circumstances in which it is not, reasonable for a person to hold the opinion mentioned in subsection (1)(a);

(b)   amend or omit a condition specified in subsection (2) or make provision for it not to apply in prescribed circumstances;

(c)   make provision, for purposes of this section, as to circumstances (other than any for the time being mentioned in subsection (2)) in which a failure is to be taken to be justified.]

[**719K**]

NOTES

Commencement: 30 Jun 2005 (for the purpose of exercising any power to make regulations, orders or rules of court); 4 December 2006 (otherwise).

Inserted as noted to s 24A at **[719A]**.

See further, in relation to circumstances in which mental incapacity justification does not apply: the Disability Discrimination (Premises) Regulations 2006, SI 2006/887, reg 2.

Regulations: the Disability Discrimination (Premises) Regulations 2006, SI 2006/887.

[24L Sections 24 to 24K: power to make supplementary provision

(1) Regulations may make provision, for purposes of sections 24(3A) and (3B) and 24A to 24K—

    (a) as to circumstances in which premises are to be treated as let to a person;

    (b) as to circumstances in which premises are to be treated as not let to a person;

    (c) as to circumstances in which premises are to be treated as being, or as not being, to let;

    (d) as to who is to be treated as being, or as to who is to be treated as not being, a person who, although not a person to whom let premises are let, is lawfully under the letting an occupier of the premises;

    (e) as to who is to be treated as being, or as to who is to be treated as not being, a person by whom premises are let;

    (f) as to who is to be treated as having, or as to who is to be treated as not having, premises to let;

    (g) as to who is to be treated as being, or as to who is to be treated as not being, a person who manages premises;

    (h) as to things which are, or as to things which are not, to be treated as auxiliary aids or services;

    (i) as to what is, or as to what is not, to be included within the meaning of "practice, policy or procedure";

    (j) as to circumstances in which it is, or as to circumstances in which it is not, reasonable for a person to have to take steps of a prescribed description;

    (k) as to steps which it is always, or as to steps which it is never, reasonable for a person to have to take;

    (l) as to circumstances in which it is, or as to circumstances in which it is not, reasonable to regard a request as being of a particular kind;

    (m) as to things which are, or as to things which are not, to be treated as physical features;

    (n) as to things which are, or as to things which are not, to be treated as alterations of physical features.

(2) Regulations under subsection (1)(a) may (in particular) provide for premises to be treated as let to a person where they are a commonhold unit of which he is a unit-holder; and "commonhold unit", and "unit-holder" in relation to such a unit, have here the same meaning as in Part 1 of the Commonhold and Leasehold Reform Act 2002.

(3) The powers under subsections (1)(j) and (k) are subject to sections 24E(1) and 24J(5).]

[719L]

NOTES

Commencement: 30 Jun 2005 (for the purpose of exercising any power to make regulations, orders or rules of court); 4 December 2006 (otherwise).

Inserted as noted to s 24A at **[719A]**.

Regulations: the Disability Discrimination (Premises) Regulations 2006, SI 2006/887.

[24M Premises provisions do not apply where other provisions operate

(1) Sections 22 to 24L do not apply—

    (a) in relation to the provision of premises by a provider of services where he provides the premises in providing services to members of the public;

    (b) in relation to the provision, in the course of a Part 2 relationship, of premises by the regulated party to the other party;

    (c) in relation to the provision of premises to a student or prospective student—

        (i) by a responsible body within the meaning of Chapter 1 or 2 of Part 4, or

      (ii)   by an authority in discharging any functions mentioned in section 28F(1); or

    (d)   to anything which is unlawful under section 21F or which would be unlawful under that section but for the operation of any provision in or made under this Act.

(2)   Subsection (1)(a) has effect subject to any prescribed exceptions.

(3)   In subsection (1)(a) "provider of services", and providing services, have the same meaning as in section 19.

(4)   For the purposes of subsection (1)(b)—

    (a)   "Part 2 relationship" means a relationship during the course of which an act of discrimination against, or harassment of, one party to the relationship by the other party to it is unlawful under sections 4 to 15C; and

    (b)   in relation to a Part 2 relationship, "regulated party" means the party whose acts of discrimination, or harassment, are made unlawful by sections 4 to 15C.

(5)   In subsection (1)(c) "student" includes pupil.]

[719M]

NOTES

Commencement: 4 December 2006.

Inserted by the Disability Discrimination Act 2005, s 19(1), Sch 1, Pt 1, paras 1, 20.

25 Enforcement, remedies and procedure

(1)   A claim by any person that another person—

    (a)   has discriminated against him in a way which is unlawful under this Part; or

    (b)   is by virtue of section 57 or 58 to be treated as having discriminated against him in such a way,

may be made the subject of civil proceedings in the same way as any other claim in tort or (in Scotland) in reparation for breach of statutory duty.

(2)   For the avoidance of doubt it is hereby declared that damages in respect of discrimination in a way which is unlawful under this Part may include compensation for injury to feelings whether or not they include compensation under any other head.

(3)   Proceedings in England and Wales shall be brought only in a county court.

(4)   Proceedings in Scotland shall be brought only in a sheriff court.

(5)   The remedies available in such proceedings are those which are available in the High Court or (as the case may be) the Court of Session.

(6)   Part II of Schedule 3 makes further provision about the enforcement of this Part and about procedure.

[(6A)   Subsection (1) does not apply in relation to a claim by a person that another person—

    (a)   has discriminated against him in relation to the provision under a group insurance arrangement of facilities by way of insurance; or

    (b)   is by virtue of section 57 or 58 to be treated as having discriminated against him in relation to the provision under such an arrangement of such facilities.]

[[(7)   Subsection (1) does not apply in relation to a claim by a person that another person—

    (a)   has discriminated against him in relation to the provision of employment services; or

    (b)   is by virtue of section 57 or 58 to be treated as having discriminated against him in relation to the provision of employment services.

(8)   A claim—

    (a)   of the kind referred to in subsection (6A) or (7), or

    (b)   by a person that another

        (i)   has subjected him to harassment in a way which is unlawful under section 21A(2), or

        (ii)   is by virtue of section 57 or 58 to be treated as having subjected him to harassment in such a way,

may be presented as a complaint to an employment tribunal.]

(9)   Section 17A(1A) to (7) and paragraphs 3 and 4 of Schedule 3 apply in relation to a complaint under subsection (8) as if it were a complaint under section 17A(1) (and paragraphs 6 to 8 of Schedule 3 do not apply in relation to such a complaint).]

[720]

NOTES
Sub-s (6A): inserted by the Disability Discrimination Act 2005, s 11(2).
Sub-ss (7), (8): added, together with sub-s (9), by the Disability Discrimination Act 1995 (Amendment) Regulations 2003, SI 2003/1673, regs 3(1), 19(2); substituted by the Disability Discrimination Act 2005, s 19(1), Sch 1, Pt 1, paras 1, 21.
Sub-s (9): added, together with sub-ss (7), (8), by SI 2003/1673, regs 3(1), 19(2).

26   Validity and revision of certain agreements

(1)   Any term in a contract for the provision of goods, facilities or services or in any other agreement is void so far as it purports to—

(a)   require a person to do anything which would contravene any provision of, or made under, this Part,

(b)   exclude or limit the operation of any provision of this Part, or

(c)   prevent any person from making a claim under this Part.

[(1A)   Subsection (1) does not apply to—

(a)   any term in a contract for the provision of employment services;

(b)   any term in a contract which is a group insurance arrangement; or

(c)   a term which—

(i)   is in an agreement which is not a contract of either of those kinds, and

(ii)   relates to the provision of employment services or the provision under a group insurance arrangement of facilities by way of insurance.]

(2)   Paragraphs (b) and (c) of subsection (1) do not apply to an agreement settling a claim to which section 25 applies.

(3)   On the application of any person interested in an agreement to which subsection (1) applies, a county court or a sheriff court may make such order as it thinks just for modifying the agreement to take account of the effect of subsection (1).

(4)   No such order shall be made unless all persons affected have been—

(a)   given notice of the application; and

(b)   afforded an opportunity to make representations to the court.

(5)   Subsection (4) applies subject to any rules of court providing for that notice to be dispensed with.

(6)   An order under subsection (3) may include provision as respects any period before the making of the order.

[721]

NOTES
Sub-s (1A): inserted by the Disability Discrimination Act 1995 (Amendment) Regulations 2003, SI 2003/1673, regs 3(1), 19(3); substituted by the Disability Discrimination Act 2005, s 19(1), Sch 1, Pt 1, paras 1, 22.

27   Alterations to premises occupied under leases

(1)   This section applies where—

(a)   a provider of services[,a public authority (within the meaning given by section 21B) or an association to which section 21F applies] ("the occupier") occupies premises under a lease;

(b)   but for this section, [the occupier] would not be entitled to make a particular alteration to the premises; and

(c)   the alteration is one which the occupier proposes to make in order to comply with a section 21 duty [or a duty imposed under section 21E or 21H].

(2)   Except to the extent to which it expressly so provides, the lease shall have effect by virtue of this subsection as if it provided—

(a)   for the occupier to be entitled to make the alteration with the written consent of the lessor;

PART I
STATUTES

(b)   for the occupier to have to make a written application to the lessor for consent if he wishes to make the alteration;

(c)   if such an application is made, for the lessor not to withhold his consent unreasonably; and

(d)   for the lessor to be entitled to make his consent subject to reasonable conditions.

(3)   In this section—

"lease" includes a tenancy, sub-lease or sub-tenancy and an agreement for a lease, tenancy, sub-lease or sub-tenancy; and

"sub-lease" and "sub-tenancy" have such meaning as may be prescribed.

(4)   If the terms and conditions of a lease—

(a)   impose conditions which are to apply if the occupier alters the premises, or

(b)   entitle the lessor to impose conditions when consenting to the occupier's altering the premises,

the occupier is to be treated for the purposes of subsection (1) as not being entitled to make the alteration.

(5)   Part II of Schedule 4 supplements the provisions of this section.

[722]

NOTES

Commencement: 9 May 2001 (sub-ss (3), (5) (certain purposes)); 1 October 2004 (sub-ss (1), (2), (4), (5) (otherwise)).

Sub-s (1): words in first pair of square brackets inserted, words in second pair of square brackets substituted and words in third pair of square brackets added by the Disability Discrimination Act 2005, s 19(1), Sch 1, Pt 1, paras 1, 23.

Modification: the Disability Discrimination (Providers of Services) (Adjustment of Premises) Regulations 2001, SI 2001/3253, reg 9(1)–(3), provides for the modification of this section in relation to any case where the occupier occupies premises under a sub-lease or sub-tenancy.

Regulations: the Disability Discrimination (Providers of Services) (Adjustment of Premises) Regulations 2001, SI 2001/3253; the Disability Discrimination (Service Providers and Public Authorities Carrying Out Functions) Regulations 2005, SI 2005/2901.

28–31C   (*Outside the scope of this work.*)

PART V
PUBLIC TRANSPORT

32–47   (*Outside the scope of this work.*)

Supplemental

48   Offences by bodies corporate etc

(1)   Where an offence under section 40 *or 46* committed by a body corporate is committed with the consent or connivance of, or is attributable to any neglect on the part of, a director, manager, secretary or other similar officer of the body, or a person purporting to act in such a capacity, he as well as the body corporate is guilty of the offence.

(2)   In subsection (1) "director", in relation to a body corporate whose affairs are managed by its members, means a member of the body corporate.

(3)   Where, in Scotland, an offence under section 40 *or 46* committed by a partnership or by an unincorporated association other than a partnership is committed with the consent or connivance of, or is attributable to any neglect on the part of, a partner in the partnership or (as the case may be) a person concerned in the management or control of the association, he, as well as the partnership or association, is guilty of the offence.

[723]

NOTES

Sub-ss (1), (3): words in italics repealed by the Disability Discrimination Act 2005, s 19(2), Sch 2, as from a day to be appointed.

49   Forgery and false statements[, and impersonation]

(1)   In this section "relevant document" means—

(a)   a certificate of exemption issued under [section 36, 37 or 37A];

(b)   a notice of a kind mentioned in [section 36(9)(b), 37(8)(b) or 37A(8)(b)];

(c)   an accessibility certificate; *or*

(d)   an approval certificate[; or

(e)   a rail vehicle accessibility compliance certificate.]

(2)   A person is guilty of an offence if, with intent to deceive, he—

(a)   forges, alters or uses a relevant document;

(b)   lends a relevant document to any other person;

(c)   allows a relevant document to be used by any other person; or

(d)   makes or has in his possession any document which closely resembles a relevant document.

(3)   A person who is guilty of an offence under subsection (2) is liable—

(a)   on summary conviction, to a fine not exceeding the statutory maximum;

(b)   on conviction on indictment, to imprisonment for a term not exceeding two years or to a fine or to both.

(4)   A person who knowingly makes a false statement for the purpose of obtaining an accessibility certificate *or an approval certificate* is guilty of an offence and liable on summary conviction to a fine not exceeding level 4 on the standard scale.

[(5)   A person who falsely pretends to be a person authorised to exercise power under section 47G is guilty of an offence and liable on summary conviction to a fine not exceeding level 4 on the standard scale.]

[724]

NOTES

Commencement: 6 April 2005 (certain purposes); to be appointed (otherwise).

Section heading: words in square brackets added by the Disability Discrimination Act 2005, s 8(2), as from a day to be appointed.

Sub-s (1): words in square brackets in paras (a), (b) substituted by the Private Hire Vehicles (Carriage of Guide Dogs etc) Act 2002, s 4; word in italics in para (c) repealed, and para (e) and word "or" immediately preceding it added by the Disability Discrimination Act 2005, ss 7(2)(a), 19(2), Sch 2, as from a day to be appointed.

Sub-s (4): for the words in italics there are substituted the words ", an approval certificate or a rail vehicle accessibility compliance certificate" by the Disability Discrimination Act 2005, s 7(2)(b), as from a day to be appointed.

Sub-s (5): added by the Disability Discrimination Act 2005, s 8(2), as from a day to be appointed.

49A–49I, 50–52   (*Outside the scope of this work.*)

PART VII
SUPPLEMENTAL

53A–58   (*Outside the scope of this work.*)

59 Statutory authority and national security etc

(1)   Nothing in this Act makes unlawful any act done—

(a)   in pursuance of any enactment; or

[(b)   in pursuance of any instrument made under any enactment by—

(i)   a Minister of the Crown,

(ii)   imposed by a member of the Scottish Executive, ...

(iii)   the National Assembly for Wales [constituted by the Government of Wales Act 1998, or

(iv)   the Welsh Ministers, the First Minister for Wales or the Counsel General to the Welsh Assembly Government]; or

(c)   to comply with any condition or requirement—

(i)   imposed by a Minister of the Crown (whether before or after the passing of this Act) by virtue of any enactment, ...

(ii)   imposed by a member of the Scottish Executive (whether before or after the coming into force of this sub-paragraph) by virtue of any enactment, ...

(iii)   imposed by the National Assembly for Wales [constituted by the Government of Wales Act 1998] (whether before or after the coming into force of this sub-paragraph) by virtue of any enactment][, or

> (iv)   imposed by the Welsh Ministers, the First Minister for Wales or the Counsel General to the Welsh Assembly Government].

(2)   In subsection (1) "enactment" includes one passed or made after the date on which this Act is passed and "instrument" includes one made after that date.

[(2A)   Nothing in—
   (a)   Part 2 of this Act, or
   (b)   Part 3 of this Act to the extent that it relates to the provision of employment services,
makes unlawful any act done for the purpose of safeguarding national security if the doing of the act was justified by that purpose.]

(3)   Nothing in [any other provision of] this Act makes unlawful any act done for the purpose of safeguarding national security.

[725]

NOTES

Sub-s (1): paras (b), (c) substituted by the Disability Discrimination Act 2005, s 19(1), Sch 1, Pt 1, paras 1, 30; word omitted from para (b)(ii), (c)(ii) repealed, words in square brackets in paras (b), (c) inserted, and para (c)(iv) and word "or" immediately preceding it added by the Government of Wales Act 2006 (Consequential Modifications and Transitional Provisions) Order 2007, SI 2007/1388, art 3, Sch 1, paras 47, 61.

Sub-s (2A): inserted by the Disability Discrimination Act 1995 (Amendment) Regulations 2003, SI 2003/1673, regs 3(1), 23(a).

Sub-s (3): words in square brackets inserted by SI 2003/1673, regs 3(1), 23(b).

PART VIII
MISCELLANEOUS

59A–63   (*Ss 59A, 60, 61 outside the scope of this work; ss 62, 63 repealed by the Employment Tribunals Act 1996, s 45, Sch 3, Pt I.*)

64   Application to Crown etc

[(A1)   The following provisions bind the Crown—
   (a)   sections 21B to 21E and Part 5A, and
   (b)   the other provisions of this Act so far as applying for the purposes of provisions mentioned in paragraph (a);
and sections 57 and 58 shall apply for purposes of provisions mentioned in paragraph (a) as if service as a Crown servant were employment by the Crown.]

(1)   This Act[, other than the provisions mentioned in paragraphs (a) and (b) of subsection (A1),] applies—
   (a)   to an act done by or for purposes of a Minister of the Crown or government department, or
   (b)   to an act done on behalf of the Crown by a statutory body, or a person holding a statutory office,
as it applies to an act done by a private person.

(2)–(8)   …

[726]

NOTES

Sub-s (A1): inserted by the Disability Discrimination Act 2005, s 19(1), Sch 1, Pt 1, paras 1, 31(1), (2).

Sub-s (1): words in square brackets inserted by the Disability Discrimination Act 2005, s 19(1), Sch 1, Pt 1, paras 1, 31(1), (3).

Sub-ss (2)–(8): outside the scope of this work.

64A–69   (*Outside the scope of this work.*)

70   Short title, commencement, extent etc

(1)   This Act may be cited as the Disability Discrimination Act 1995.

(2)   This section (apart from subsections (4), (5) and (7)) comes into force on the passing of this Act.

(3)   The other provisions of this Act come into force on such day as the Secretary of State may by order appoint and different days may be appointed for different purposes.

(4), (5), (5A), (5B) ...

(6)   [Subject to subsections (5A) and (5B), this Act extends to England and Wales, Scotland and Northern Ireland;] but in their application to Northern Ireland the provisions of this Act mentioned in Schedule 8 shall have effect subject to the modifications set out in that Schedule.

(7)   ...

(8)   Consultations which are required by any provision of this Act to be held by the Secretary of State may be held by him before the coming into force of that provision.

[727]

NOTES

Sub-ss (4), (5), (5A), (5B): outside the scope of this work.

Sub-s (6): words in square brackets substituted by the Disability Discrimination Act 1995 (Amendment) Regulations 2003, SI 2003/1673, regs 3(1), 28(b).

Sub-s (7): amends the House of Commons Disqualification Act 1975, Sch 1, Pt II and the Northern Ireland Assembly Disqualification Act 1975, Sch 1, Pt II.

Orders: the Disability Discrimination Act 1995 (Commencement No 1) Order 1995, SI 1995/3330; the Disability Discrimination Act 1995 (Commencement No 1) Order (Northern Ireland) 1996, SR 1996/1; the Disability Discrimination Act 1995 (Commencement No 2) Order 1996, SI 1996/1336; the Disability Discrimination Act 1995 (Commencement No 2) Order (Northern Ireland) 1996, SR 1996/219; the Disability Discrimination Act 1995 (Commencement No 3 and Saving and Transitional Provisions) Order 1996, SI 1996/1474; the Disability Discrimination Act 1995 (Commencement No 3 and Saving and Transitional Provisions) Order (Northern Ireland) 1996, SR 1996/280; the Disability Discrimination Act 1995 (Commencement No 4) Order (Northern Ireland) 1996, SR 1996/560; the Disability Discrimination Act 1995 (Commencement No 4) Order 1996, SI 1996/3003; the Disability Discrimination Act 1995 (Commencement No 5) Order 1998, SI 1998/1282; the Disability Discrimination Act 1995 (Commencement No 5) Order (Northern Ireland) 1998, SR 1998/183; the Disability Discrimination Act 1995 (Commencement Order No 6) Order 1999, SI 1999/1190; the Disability Discrimination Act 1995 (Commencement No 7) Order 2000, SI 2000/1969; the Disability Discrimination Act 1995 (Commencement No 8) Order 2000, SI 2000/2989; the Disability Discrimination Act 1995 (Commencement No 9) Order 2001, SI 2001/2030; the Disability Discrimination Act 1995 (Commencement No 10) (Scotland) Order 2003, SI 2003/215; the Disability Discrimination Act 1995 (Commencement No 11) Order 2005, SI 2005/1122.

(Schs 1–3A outside the scope of this work.)

SCHEDULE 4
PREMISES OCCUPIED UNDER LEASES
Sections [18A(5)], 27(5)

PART I
OCCUPATION BY [EMPLOYER ETC]

Failure to obtain consent to alteration

1.   If any question arises as to whether the occupier has failed to comply with [any duty to make reasonable adjustments], by failing to make a particular alteration to the premises, any constraint attributable to the fact that he occupies the premises under a lease is to be ignored unless he has applied to the lessor in writing for consent to the making of the alteration.

Joining lessors in proceedings under [section 17A ...]

2.—(1)   In any proceedings [on a complaint under section 17A], in a case to which [section 18A] applies, the complainant or the occupier may ask the tribunal hearing the complaint to direct that the lessor be joined or sisted as a party to the proceedings.

(2)   The request shall be granted if it is made before the hearing of the complaint begins.

(3)   The tribunal may refuse the request if it is made after the hearing of the complaint begins.

(4)   The request may not be granted if it is made after the tribunal has determined the complaint.

(5)   Where a lessor has been so joined or sisted as a party to the proceedings, the tribunal may determine—
- (a)   whether the lessor has—
  - (i)   refused consent to the alteration, or
  - (ii)   consented subject to one or more conditions, and
- (b)   if so, whether the refusal or any of the conditions was unreasonable.

(6)   If, under sub-paragraph (5), the tribunal determines that the refusal or any of the conditions was unreasonable it may take one or more of the following steps—
- (a)   make such declaration as it considers appropriate;
- (b)   make an order authorising the occupier to make the alteration specified in the order;
- (c)   order the lessor to pay compensation to the complainant.

(7)   An order under sub-paragraph (6)(b) may require the occupier to comply with conditions specified in the order.

(8)   Any step taken by the tribunal under sub-paragraph (6) may be in substitution for, or in addition to, any step taken by the tribunal under [section 17A(2)].

(9)   If the tribunal orders the lessor to pay compensation it may not make an order under [section 17A(2)] ordering the occupier to do so.

Regulations

3.   Regulations may make provision as to circumstances in which—
- (a)   a lessor is to be taken, for the purposes of [section 18A] and this Part of this Schedule to have—
  - (i)   withheld his consent;
  - (ii)   withheld his consent unreasonably;
  - (iii)   acted reasonably in withholding his consent;
- (b)   a condition subject to which a lessor has given his consent is to be taken to be reasonable;
- (c)   a condition subject to which a lessor has given his consent is to be taken to be unreasonable.

Sub-leases etc

4.   The Secretary of State may by regulations make provision supplementing, or modifying, the provision made by [section 18A] or any provision made by or under this Part of this Schedule in relation to cases where the occupier occupies premises under a sub-lease or sub-tenancy.

[728]

NOTES

Part heading, paras 1, 3, 4: words in square brackets substituted by the Disability Discrimination Act 1995 (Amendment) Regulations 2003, SI 2003/1673, regs 3(1), 29(3).

Para 2: words in square brackets in cross-heading preceding this para, words in second pair of square brackets in sub-para (1), and words in square brackets in sub-paras (8), (9) substituted by SI 2003/1673, regs 3(1), 29(3); words omitted from cross-heading preceding this para repealed and words in first pair of square brackets in sub-para (1) substituted by the Disability Discrimination Act 2005, s 19(1), Sch 1, Pt 1, paras 1, 40(1), (2).

Modification: paras 1–3 are modified in relation to cases where the occupier occupies premises under a sub-lease or sub-tenancy by the Disability Discrimination (Sub-leases and Sub-tenancies) Regulations 1996, SI 1996/1333, reg 4; para 2 is modified in relation to any case where the occupier occupies premises under a sub-lease or sub-tenancy, by the Disability Discrimination (Employment Field) (Leasehold Premises) Regulations 2004, SI 2004/153, regs 8, 9(c).

Regulations: the Disability Discrimination (Employment) Regulations (Northern Ireland) 1996, SR 1996/419; the Disability Discrimination (Sub-leases and Sub-tenancies) Regulations (Northern Ireland) 1996, SR 1996/420; the Disability Discrimination (Employment Field) (Leasehold Premises) Regulations 2004, SI 2004/153.

PART II
OCCUPATION BY [PERSONS SUBJECT TO A DUTY UNDER SECTION 21, 21E OR 21H]

Failure to obtain consent to alteration

5. If any question arises as to whether the occupier has failed to comply with the section 21 duty [or a duty imposed under section 21E or 21H], by failing to make a particular alteration to premises, any constraint attributable to the fact that he occupies the premises under a lease is to be ignored unless he has applied to the lessor in writing for consent to the making of the alteration.

Reference to court

6.—(1) If the occupier has applied in writing to the lessor for consent to the alteration and—
    (a)   that consent has been refused, or
    (b)   the lessor has made his consent subject to one or more conditions,
the occupier or a disabled person who has an interest in the proposed alteration to the premises being made, may refer the matter to a county court or, in Scotland, to the sheriff.

(2) In the following provisions of this Schedule "court" includes "sheriff".

(3) On such a reference the court shall determine whether the lessor's refusal was unreasonable or (as the case may be) whether the condition is, or any of the conditions are, unreasonable.

(4) If the court determines—
    (a)   that the lessor's refusal was unreasonable, or
    (b)   that the condition is, or any of the conditions are, unreasonable,
it may make such declaration as it considers appropriate or an order authorising the occupier to make the alteration specified in the order.

(5) An order under sub-paragraph (4) may require the occupier to comply with conditions specified in the order.

Joining lessors in proceedings under section 25

7.—(1) In any proceedings on a claim [under section 25 in a case to which section 27 applies, other than a claim presented as a complaint under section 25(8),] the plaintiff, the pursuer or the occupier concerned may ask the court to direct that the lessor be joined or sisted as a party to the proceedings.

(2) The request shall be granted if it is made before the hearing of the claim begins.

(3) The court may refuse the request if it is made after the hearing of the claim begins.

(4) The request may not be granted if it is made after the court has determined the claim.

(5) Where a lessor has been so joined or sisted as a party to the proceedings, the court may determine—
    (a)   whether the lessor has—
        (i)   refused consent to the alteration, or
        (ii)   consented subject to one or more conditions, and
    (b)   if so, whether the refusal or any of the conditions was unreasonable.

(6) If, under sub-paragraph (5), the court determines that the refusal or any of the conditions was unreasonable it may take one or more of the following steps—
    (a)   make such declaration as it considers appropriate;
    (b)   make an order authorising the occupier to make the alteration specified in the order;
    (c)   order the lessor to pay compensation to the complainant.

(7) An order under sub-paragraph (6)(b) may require the occupier to comply with conditions specified in the order.

(8)   If the court orders the lessor to pay compensation it may not order the occupier to do so.

[Joining lessors in proceedings relating to group insurance or employment services

7A.—(1)   In any proceedings on a complaint under section 25(8) in a case to which section 27 applies, the complainant or the occupier may ask the tribunal hearing the complaint to direct that the lessor be joined or sisted as a party to the proceedings.

(2)   The request shall be granted if it is made before the hearing of the complaint begins.

(3)   The tribunal may refuse the request if it is made after the hearing of the complaint begins.

(4)   The request may not be granted if it is made after the tribunal has determined the complaint.

(5)   Where a lessor has been so joined or sisted as a party to the proceedings, the tribunal may determine—
   (a)   whether the lessor has—
      (i)   refused consent to the alteration, or
      (ii)   consented subject to one or more conditions; and
   (b)   if so, whether the refusal or any of the conditions was unreasonable.

(6)   If, under sub-paragraph (5), the tribunal determines that the refusal or any of the conditions was unreasonable it may take one or more of the following steps—
   (a)   make such declaration as it considers appropriate;
   (b)   make an order authorising the occupier to make the alteration specified in the order;
   (c)   order the lessor to pay compensation to the complainant.

(7)   An order under sub-paragraph (6)(b) may require the occupier to comply with conditions specified in the order.

(8)   Any step taken by the tribunal under sub-paragraph (6) may be in substitution for, or in addition to, any step taken by the tribunal under section 17A(2).

(9)   If the tribunal orders the lessor to pay compensation it may not make an order under section 17A(2) ordering the occupier to do so.]

Regulations

8.   Regulations may make provision as to circumstances in which—
   (a)   a lessor is to be taken, for the purposes of section 27 and this Part of this Schedule to have—
      (i)   withheld his consent;
      (ii)   withheld his consent unreasonably;
      (iii)   acted reasonably in withholding his consent;
   (b)   a condition subject to which a lessor has given his consent is to be taken to be reasonable;
   (c)   a condition subject to which a lessor has given his consent is to be taken to be unreasonable.

Sub-leases etc

9.   The Secretary of State may by regulations make provision supplementing, or modifying, the provision made by section 27 or any provision made by or under this Part of this Schedule in relation to cases where the occupier occupies premises under a sub-lease or sub-tenancy.

[729]

NOTES

Commencement: 9 May 2001 (paras 8, 9); 1 October 2004 (paras 5–7).

Part heading: words in square brackets substituted by the Disability Discrimination Act 2005, s 19(1), Sch 1, Pt 1, paras 1, 40(1), (3).

Para 5: words in square brackets inserted by the Disability Discrimination Act 2005, s 19(1), Sch 1, Pt 1, paras 1, 40(1), (4).

Para 7: words in square brackets in sub-para (1) substituted by the Disability Discrimination Act 2005, s 19(1), Sch 1, Pt 1, paras 1, 40(1), (5).

Para 7A: inserted, together with immediately preceding cross-heading, by the Disability Discrimination Act 2005, s 19(1), Sch 1, Pt 1, paras 1, 40(1), (6).

Modification: the Disability Discrimination (Providers of Services) (Adjustment of Premises) Regulations 2001, SI 2001/3253, reg 9, provides for the modification of this Part in relation to any case where the occupier occupies premises under a sub-lease or sub-tenancy.

Regulations: the Disability Discrimination (Providers of Services) (Adjustment of Premises) Regulations 2001, SI 2001/3253; the Disability Discrimination (Service Providers and Public Authorities Carrying Out Functions) Regulations 2005, SI 2005/2901.

(Pt 3 and Schs 4A–8 outside the scope of this work.)

ARBITRATION ACT 1996

(1996 c 23)

An Act to restate and improve the law relating to arbitration pursuant to an arbitration agreement; to make other provision relating to arbitration and arbitration awards; and for connected purposes

[17 June 1996]

PART I
ARBITRATION PURSUANT TO AN ARBITRATION AGREEMENT

Introductory

1–4   *(Outside the scope of this work.)*

5 Agreements to be in writing

(1)   The provisions of this Part apply only where the arbitration agreement is in writing, and any other agreement between the parties as to any matter is effective for the purposes of this Part only if in writing.

The expressions "agreement", "agree" and "agreed" shall be construed accordingly.

(2)   There is an agreement in writing—
   (a)   if the agreement is made in writing (whether or not it is signed by the parties),
   (b)   if the agreement is made by exchange of communications in writing, or
   (c)   if the agreement is evidenced in writing.

(3)   Where parties agree otherwise than in writing by reference to terms which are in writing, they make an agreement in writing.

(4)   An agreement is evidenced in writing if an agreement made otherwise than in writing is recorded by one of the parties, or by a third party, with the authority of the parties to the agreement.

(5)   An exchange of written submissions in arbitral or legal proceedings in which the existence of an agreement otherwise than in writing is alleged by one party against another party and not denied by the other party in his response constitutes as between those parties an agreement in writing to the effect alleged.

(6)   References in this Part to anything being written or in writing include its being recorded by any means.

[730]

6–104   *(Outside the scope of this work.)*

PART IV
GENERAL PROVISIONS

105–109   *(Outside the scope of this work.)*

110 Short title

This Act may be cited as the Arbitration Act 1996.

[731]

(Schs 1–4 outside the scope of this work.)

HUMAN RIGHTS ACT 1998

(1998 c 42)

ARRANGEMENT OF SECTIONS

Introduction

An Act to give further effect to rights and freedoms guaranteed under the European Convention on Human Rights; to make provision with respect to holders of certain judicial offices who become judges of the European Court of Human Rights; and for connected purposes

[9 November 1998]

Introduction

1 The Convention Rights

(1)   In this Act "the Convention rights" means the rights and fundamental freedoms set out in—
    (a)   Articles 2 to 12 and 14 of the Convention,
    (b)   Articles 1 to 3 of the First Protocol, and
    (c)   [Article 1 of the Thirteenth Protocol],
as read with Articles 16 to 18 of the Convention.

(2)   Those Articles are to have effect for the purposes of this Act subject to any designated derogation or reservation (as to which see sections 14 and 15).

(3)   The Articles are set out in Schedule 1.

(4)   The [Secretary of State] may by order make such amendments to this Act as he considers appropriate to reflect the effect, in relation to the United Kingdom, of a protocol.

(5)   In subsection (4) "protocol" means a protocol to the Convention—
  (a)   which the United Kingdom has ratified; or
  (b)   which the United Kingdom has signed with a view to ratification.

(6)   No amendment may be made by an order under subsection (4) so as to come into force before the protocol concerned is in force in relation to the United Kingdom.

[732]

NOTES
  Sub-s (1): words in square brackets substituted by the Human Rights Act 1998 (Amendment) Order 2004, SI 2004/1574, art 2(1).
  Sub-s (4): words in square brackets substituted by the Secretary of State for Constitutional Affairs Order 2003, SI 2003/1887, art 9, Sch 2, para 10(1).

2   Interpretation of Convention rights

(1)   A court or tribunal determining a question which has arisen in connection with a Convention right must take into account any—
  (a)   judgment, decision, declaration or advisory opinion of the European Court of Human Rights,
  (b)   opinion of the Commission given in a report adopted under Article 31 of the Convention,
  (c)   decision of the Commission in connection with Article 26 or 27(2) of the Convention, or
  (d)   decision of the Committee of Ministers taken under Article 46 of the Convention, whenever made or given, so far as, in the opinion of the court or tribunal, it is relevant to the proceedings in which that question has arisen.

(2)   Evidence of any judgment, decision, declaration or opinion of which account may have to be taken under this section is to be given in proceedings before any court or tribunal in such manner as may be provided by rules.

(3)   In this section "rules" means rules of court or, in the case of proceedings before a tribunal, rules made for the purposes of this section—
  (a)   by ... [the Lord Chancellor or] the Secretary of State, in relation to any proceedings outside Scotland;
  (b)   by the Secretary of State, in relation to proceedings in Scotland; or
  (c)   by a Northern Ireland department, in relation to proceedings before a tribunal in Northern Ireland—
    (i)   which deals with transferred matters; and
    (ii)   for which no rules made under paragraph (a) are in force.

[733]

NOTES
  Sub-s (3): words omitted from para (a) repealed by the Secretary of State for Constitutional Affairs Order 2003, SI 2003/1887, art 9, Sch 2, para 10(2); words in square brackets in para (a) inserted by the Transfer of Functions (Lord Chancellor and Secretary of State) Order 2005, SI 2005/3429, art 8, Schedule, para 3.
  By the Transfer of Functions (Lord Chancellor and Secretary of State) Order 2005, SI 2005/3429, art 3(2), the functions of the Secretary of State under sub-s (3)(a) are to be exercisable concurrently with the Lord Chancellor.

Legislation

3   Interpretation of legislation

(1)   So far as it is possible to do so, primary legislation and subordinate legislation must be read and given effect in a way which is compatible with the Convention rights.

(2)   This section—
  (a)   applies to primary legislation and subordinate legislation whenever enacted;
  (b)   does not affect the validity, continuing operation or enforcement of any incompatible primary legislation; and

(c)   does not affect the validity, continuing operation or enforcement of any incompatible subordinate legislation if (disregarding any possibility of revocation) primary legislation prevents removal of the incompatibility.

[734]

4, 5   (*Outside the scope of this work.*)

Public authorities

6   Acts of public authorities

(1)   It is unlawful for a public authority to act in a way which is incompatible with a Convention right.

(2)   Subsection (1) does not apply to an act if—
(a)   as the result of one or more provisions of primary legislation, the authority could not have acted differently; or
(b)   in the case of one or more provisions of, or made under, primary legislation which cannot be read or given effect in a way which is compatible with the Convention rights, the authority was acting so as to give effect to or enforce those provisions.

(3)   In this section "public authority" includes—
(a)   a court or tribunal, and
(b)   any person certain of whose functions are functions of a public nature,

but does not include either House of Parliament or a person exercising functions in connection with proceedings in Parliament.

(4)   *In subsection (3) "Parliament" does not include the House of Lords in its judicial capacity.*

(5)   In relation to a particular act, a person is not a public authority by virtue only of subsection (3)(b) if the nature of the act is private.

(6)   "An act" includes a failure to act but does not include a failure to—
(a)   introduce in, or lay before, Parliament a proposal for legislation; or
(b)   make any primary legislation or remedial order.

[735]

NOTES

Sub-s (4): repealed by the Constitutional Reform Act 2005, ss 40(4), 146, Sch 9, Pt 1, para 66(1), (4), Sch 18, Pt 5, as from a day to be appointed.

7   Proceedings

(1)   A person who claims that a public authority has acted (or proposes to act) in a way which is made unlawful by section 6(1) may—
(a)   bring proceedings against the authority under this Act in the appropriate court or tribunal, or
(b)   rely on the Convention right or rights concerned in any legal proceedings,

but only if he is (or would be) a victim of the unlawful act.

(2)   In subsection (1)(a) "appropriate court or tribunal" means such court or tribunal as may be determined in accordance with rules; and proceedings against an authority include a counterclaim or similar proceeding.

(3)   If the proceedings are brought on an application for judicial review, the applicant is to be taken to have a sufficient interest in relation to the unlawful act only if he is, or would be, a victim of that act.

(4)   If the proceedings are made by way of a petition for judicial review in Scotland, the applicant shall be taken to have title and interest to sue in relation to the unlawful act only if he is, or would be, a victim of that act.

(5)   Proceedings under subsection (1)(a) must be brought before the end of—
(a)   the period of one year beginning with the date on which the act complained of took place; or

(b)   such longer period as the court or tribunal considers equitable having regard to all the circumstances,

but that is subject to any rule imposing a stricter time limit in relation to the procedure in question.

(6)   In subsection (1)(b) "legal proceedings" includes—

(a)   proceedings brought by or at the instigation of a public authority; and

(b)   an appeal against the decision of a court or tribunal.

(7)   For the purposes of this section, a person is a victim of an unlawful act only if he would be a victim for the purposes of Article 34 of the Convention if proceedings were brought in the European Court of Human Rights in respect of that act.

(8)   Nothing in this Act creates a criminal offence.

(9)   In this section "rules" means—

(a)   in relation to proceedings before a court or tribunal outside Scotland, rules made by ... [the Lord Chancellor or] the Secretary of State for the purposes of this section or rules of court,

(b)   in relation to proceedings before a court or tribunal in Scotland, rules made by the Secretary of State for those purposes,

(c)   in relation to proceedings before a tribunal in Northern Ireland—

(i)   which deals with transferred matters; and

(ii)   for which no rules made under paragraph (a) are in force,

rules made by a Northern Ireland department for those purposes,

and includes provision made by order under section 1 of the Courts and Legal Services Act 1990.

(10)   In making rules, regard must be had to section 9.

(11)   The Minister who has power to make rules in relation to a particular tribunal may, to the extent he considers it necessary to ensure that the tribunal can provide an appropriate remedy in relation to an act (or proposed act) of a public authority which is (or would be) unlawful as a result of section 6(1), by order add to—

(a)   the relief or remedies which the tribunal may grant; or

(b)   the grounds on which it may grant any of them.

(12)   An order made under subsection (11) may contain such incidental, supplemental, consequential or transitional provision as the Minister making it considers appropriate.

(13)   "The Minister" includes the Northern Ireland department concerned.

[736]

NOTES

Sub-s (9): words omitted from para (a) repealed by the Secretary of State for Constitutional Affairs Order 2003, SI 2003/1887, art 9, Sch 2, para 10(2); words in square brackets inserted by the Transfer of Functions (Lord Chancellor and Secretary of State) Order 2005, SI 2005/3429, art 8, Schedule, para 3.

By the Transfer of Functions (Lord Chancellor and Secretary of State) Order 2005, SI 2005/3429, art 3(2), the functions of the Secretary of State under sub-s (9)(a), and under sub-s (11) by virtue thereof, are to be exercisable concurrently with the Lord Chancellor.

Rules: the Human Rights Act 1998 (Jurisdiction) (Scotland) Rules 2000, SSI 2000/301; the Proscribed Organisations Appeal Commission (Human Rights Act 1998 Proceedings) Rules 2006, SI 2006/2290.

---

8 Judicial remedies

(1)   In relation to any act (or proposed act) of a public authority which the court finds is (or would be) unlawful, it may grant such relief or remedy, or make such order, within its powers as it considers just and appropriate.

(2)   But damages may be awarded only by a court which has power to award damages, or to order the payment of compensation, in civil proceedings.

(3)   No award of damages is to be made unless, taking account of all the circumstances of the case, including—

(a)   any other relief or remedy granted, or order made, in relation to the act in question (by that or any other court), and

(b)   the consequences of any decision (of that or any other court) in respect of that act,

the court is satisfied that the award is necessary to afford just satisfaction to the person in whose favour it is made.

(4)   In determining—
  (a)   whether to award damages, or
  (b)   the amount of an award,
the court must take into account the principles applied by the European Court of Human Rights in relation to the award of compensation under Article 41 of the Convention.

(5)   A public authority against which damages are awarded is to be treated—
  (a)   in Scotland, for the purposes of section 3 of the Law Reform (Miscellaneous Provisions) (Scotland) Act 1940 as if the award were made in an action of damages in which the authority has been found liable in respect of loss or damage to the person to whom the award is made;
  (b)   for the purposes of the Civil Liability (Contribution) Act 1978 as liable in respect of damage suffered by the person to whom the award is made.

(6)   In this section—
  "court" includes a tribunal;
  "damages" means damages for an unlawful act of a public authority; and
  "unlawful" means unlawful under section 6(1).

[737]

9   Judicial acts

(1)   Proceedings under section 7(1)(a) in respect of a judicial act may be brought only—
  (a)   by exercising a right of appeal;
  (b)   on an application (in Scotland a petition) for judicial review; or
  (c)   in such other forum as may be prescribed by rules.

(2)   That does not affect any rule of law which prevents a court from being the subject of judicial review.

(3)   In proceedings under this Act in respect of a judicial act done in good faith, damages may not be awarded otherwise than to compensate a person to the extent required by Article 5(5) of the Convention.

(4)   An award of damages permitted by subsection (3) is to be made against the Crown; but no award may be made unless the appropriate person, if not a party to the proceedings, is joined.

(5)   In this section—
  "appropriate person" means the Minister responsible for the court concerned, or a person or government department nominated by him;
  "court" includes a tribunal;
  "judge" includes a member of a tribunal, a justice of the peace [(or, in Northern Ireland, a lay magistrate)] and a clerk or other officer entitled to exercise the jurisdiction of a court;
  "judicial act" means a judicial act of a court and includes an act done on the instructions, or on behalf, of a judge; and
  "rules" has the same meaning as in section 7(9).

[738]

NOTES
Sub-s (5): in definition "judge", words in square brackets inserted by the Justice (Northern Ireland) Act 2002, s 10(6), Sch 4, para 39.

10–19   (*Outside the scope of this work.*)

Supplemental

20   (*Outside the scope of this work.*)

21   Interpretation, etc

(1)   In this Act—
  "amend" includes repeal and apply (with or without modifications);

"the appropriate Minister" means the Minister of the Crown having charge of the appropriate authorised government department (within the meaning of the Crown Proceedings Act 1947);

"the Commission" means the European Commission of Human Rights;

"the Convention" means the Convention for the Protection of Human Rights and Fundamental Freedoms, agreed by the Council of Europe at Rome on 4th November 1950 as it has effect for the time being in relation to the United Kingdom;

"declaration of incompatibility" means a declaration under section 4;

"Minister of the Crown" has the same meaning as in the Ministers of the Crown Act 1975;

"Northern Ireland Minister" includes the First Minister and the deputy First Minister in Northern Ireland;

"primary legislation" means any—

(a)   public general Act;

(b)   local and personal Act;

(c)   private Act;

(d)   Measure of the Church Assembly;

(e)   Measure of the General Synod of the Church of England;

(f)   Order in Council—

     (i)   made in exercise of Her Majesty's Royal Prerogative;

     (ii) made under section 38(1)(a) of the Northern Ireland Constitution Act 1973 or the corresponding provision of the Northern Ireland Act 1998; or

     (iii) amending an Act of a kind mentioned in paragraph (a), (b) or (c);

and includes an order or other instrument made under primary legislation (otherwise than by the [Welsh Ministers, the First Minister for Wales, the Counsel General to the Welsh Assembly Government], a member of the Scottish Executive, a Northern Ireland Minister or a Northern Ireland department) to the extent to which it operates to bring one or more provisions of that legislation into force or amends any primary legislation;

"the First Protocol" means the protocol to the Convention agreed at Paris on 20th March 1952;

.....

"the Eleventh Protocol" means the protocol to the Convention (restructuring the control machinery established by the Convention) agreed at Strasbourg on 11th May 1994;

["the Thirteenth Protocol" means the protocol to the Convention (concerning the abolition of the death penalty in all circumstances) agreed at Vilnius on 3rd May 2002;]

"remedial order" means an order under section 10;

"subordinate legislation" means any—

(a)   Order in Council other than one—

     (i)   made in exercise of Her Majesty's Royal Prerogative;

     (ii) made under section 38(1)(a) of the Northern Ireland Constitution Act 1973 or the corresponding provision of the Northern Ireland Act 1998; or

     (iii) amending an Act of a kind mentioned in the definition of primary legislation;

[(ba) Measure of the National Assembly for Wales;

(bb) Act of the National Assembly for Wales;]

(b)   Act of the Scottish Parliament;

(c)   Act of the Parliament of Northern Ireland;

(d)   Measure of the Assembly established under section 1 of the Northern Ireland Assembly Act 1973;

(e)   Act of the Northern Ireland Assembly;

(f)   order, rules, regulations, scheme, warrant, byelaw or other instrument made under primary legislation (except to the extent to which it operates to bring one or more provisions of that legislation into force or amends any primary legislation);

(g)   order, rules, regulations, scheme, warrant, byelaw or other instrument made under legislation mentioned in paragraph (b), (c), (d) or (e) or made under an Order in Council applying only to Northern Ireland;

(h)   order, rules, regulations, scheme, warrant, byelaw or other instrument made by a member of the Scottish Executive[, Welsh Ministers, the First Minister for Wales, the Counsel General to the Welsh Assembly Government], a Northern Ireland Minister or a Northern Ireland department in exercise of prerogative or other executive functions of Her Majesty which are exercisable by such a person on behalf of Her Majesty;

"transferred matters" has the same meaning as in the Northern Ireland Act 1998; and

"tribunal" means any tribunal in which legal proceedings may be brought.

(2) The references in paragraphs (b) and (c) of section 2(1) to Articles are to Articles of the Convention as they had effect immediately before the coming into force of the Eleventh Protocol.

(3) The reference in paragraph (d) of section 2(1) to Article 46 includes a reference to Articles 32 and 54 of the Convention as they had effect immediately before the coming into force of the Eleventh Protocol.

(4) The references in section 2(1) to a report or decision of the Commission or a decision of the Committee of Ministers include references to a report or decision made as provided by paragraphs 3, 4 and 6 of Article 5 of the Eleventh Protocol (transitional provisions).

(5) *Any liability under the Army Act 1955, the Air Force Act 1955 or the Naval Discipline Act 1957 to suffer death for an offence is replaced by a liability to imprisonment for life or any less punishment authorised by those Acts; and those Acts shall accordingly have effect with the necessary modifications.*

[739]

NOTES

Sub-s (1): in definition "primary legislation" words in square brackets substituted, in definition "subordinate legislation" paras (ba), (bb) inserted and words in square brackets in para (h) inserted, by the Government of Wales Act 2006, s 160(1), Sch 10, para 56(1), (2); definition "the Sixth Protocol" omitted repealed and definition "the Thirteenth Protocol" inserted by the Human Rights Act 1998 (Amendment) Order 2004, SI 2004/1574, art 2(2).

Sub-s (5): repealed by the Armed Forces Act 2006, s 378(2), Sch 17, as from a day to be appointed.

Emergency regulations made under the Civil Contingencies Act 2004, s 20 are to be treated as subordinate legislation and not primary legislation for the purposes of this Act: see s 30(2) of the 2004 Act.

22 Short title, commencement, application and extent

(1) This Act may be cited as the Human Rights Act 1998.

(2) Sections 18, 20 and 21(5) and this section come into force on the passing of this Act.

(3) The other provisions of this Act come into force on such day as the Secretary of State may by order appoint; and different days may be appointed for different purposes.

(4) Paragraph (b) of subsection (1) of section 7 applies to proceedings brought by or at the instigation of a public authority whenever the act in question took place; but otherwise that subsection does not apply to an act taking place before the coming into force of that section.

(5) This Act binds the Crown.

(6) This Act extends to Northern Ireland.

(7) *Section 21(5), so far as it relates to any provision contained in the Army Act 1955, the Air Force Act 1955 or the Naval Discipline Act 1957, extends to any place to which that provision extends.*

[740]

NOTES

Sub-s (7): repealed by the Armed Forces Act 2006, s 378(2), Sch 17, as from a day to be appointed.

Orders: the Human Rights Act 1998 (Commencement) Order 1998, SI 1998/2882; the Human Rights Act 1998 (Commencement No 2) Order 2000, SI 2000/1851.

SCHEDULE 1
THE ARTICLES

Section 1(3)

PART I
THE CONVENTION
RIGHTS AND FREEDOMS

...

Article 6
Right to a fair trial

1.   In the determination of his civil rights and obligations or of any criminal charge against him, everyone is entitled to a fair and public hearing within a reasonable time by an independent and impartial tribunal established by law. Judgment shall be pronounced publicly but the press and public may be excluded from all or part of the trial in the interest of morals, public order or national security in a democratic society, where the interests of juveniles or the protection of the private life of the parties so require, or to the extent strictly necessary in the opinion of the court in special circumstances where publicity would prejudice the interests of justice.

2.   ...

3.   ...

...

Article 8
Right to respect for private and family life

1.   Everyone has the right to respect for his private and family life, his home and his correspondence.

2.   There shall be no interference by a public authority with the exercise of this right except such as is in accordance with the law and is necessary in a democratic society in the interests of national security, public safety or the economic well-being of the country, for the prevention of disorder or crime, for the protection of health or morals, or for the protection of the rights and freedoms of others.

...

[741]

NOTES

Articles 2–5, 6(2), (3), 7, 9–12, 14, 16–18: outside the scope of this work.

PART II
THE FIRST PROTOCOL

Article 1
Protection of property

Every natural or legal person is entitled to the peaceful enjoyment of his possessions. No one shall be deprived of his possessions except in the public interest and subject to the conditions provided for by law and by the general principles of international law.

The preceding provisions shall not, however, in any way impair the right of a State to enforce such laws as it deems necessary to control the use of property in accordance with the general interest or to secure the payment of taxes or other contributions or penalties.

...

[742]

NOTES
Articles 2, 3: outside the scope of this work.

(Pt III and Schs 2–4 outside the scope of this work.)

CONTRACTS (RIGHTS OF THIRD PARTIES) ACT 1999

(1999 c 31)

ARRANGEMENT OF SECTIONS

An Act to make provision for the enforcement of contractual terms by third parties
[11 November 1999]

1 Right of third party to enforce contractual term

(1) Subject to the provisions of this Act, a person who is not a party to a contract (a "third party") may in his own right enforce a term of the contract if—
    (a)   the contract expressly provides that he may, or
    (b)   subject to subsection (2), the term purports to confer a benefit on him.

(2) Subsection (1)(b) does not apply if on a proper construction of the contract it appears that the parties did not intend the term to be enforceable by the third party.

(3) The third party must be expressly identified in the contract by name, as a member of a class or as answering a particular description but need not be in existence when the contract is entered into.

(4) This section does not confer a right on a third party to enforce a term of a contract otherwise than subject to and in accordance with any other relevant terms of the contract.

(5) For the purpose of exercising his right to enforce a term of the contract, there shall be available to the third party any remedy that would have been available to him in an action for breach of contract if he had been a party to the contract (and the rules relating to damages, injunctions, specific performance and other relief shall apply accordingly).

(6) Where a term of a contract excludes or limits liability in relation to any matter references in this Act to the third party enforcing the term shall be construed as references to his availing himself of the exclusion or limitation.

(7) In this Act, in relation to a term of a contract which is enforceable by a third party—
    "the promisor" means the party to the contract against whom the term is enforceable by the third party, and
    "the promisee" means the party to the contract by whom the term is enforceable against the promisor.

[743]

2 Variation and rescission of contract

(1) Subject to the provisions of this section, where a third party has a right under section 1 to enforce a term of the contract, the parties to the contract may not, by agreement, rescind the contract, or vary it in such a way as to extinguish or alter his entitlement under that right, without his consent if—

(a)   the third party has communicated his assent to the term to the promisor,

(b)   the promisor is aware that the third party has relied on the term, or

(c)   the promisor can reasonably be expected to have foreseen that the third party would rely on the term and the third party has in fact relied on it.

(2)   The assent referred to in subsection (1)(a)—

(a)   may be by words or conduct, and

(b)   if sent to the promisor by post or other means, shall not be regarded as communicated to the promisor until received by him.

(3)   Subsection (1) is subject to any express term of the contract under which—

(a)   the parties to the contract may by agreement rescind or vary the contract without the consent of the third party, or

(b)   the consent of the third party is required in circumstances specified in the contract instead of those set out in subsection (1)(a) to (c).

(4)   Where the consent of a third party is required under subsection (1) or (3), the court or arbitral tribunal may, on the application of the parties to the contract, dispense with his consent if satisfied—

(a)   that his consent cannot be obtained because his whereabouts cannot reasonably be ascertained, or

(b)   that he is mentally incapable of giving his consent.

(5)   The court or arbitral tribunal may, on the application of the parties to a contract, dispense with any consent that may be required under subsection (1)(c) if satisfied that it cannot reasonably be ascertained whether or not the third party has in fact relied on the term.

(6)   If the court or arbitral tribunal dispenses with a third party's consent, it may impose such conditions as it thinks fit, including a condition requiring the payment of compensation to the third party.

(7)   The jurisdiction conferred on the court by subsections (4) to (6) is exercisable by both the High Court and a county court.

[744]

3 Defences etc available to promisor

(1)   Subsections (2) to (5) apply where, in reliance on section 1, proceedings for the enforcement of a term of a contract are brought by a third party.

(2)   The promisor shall have available to him by way of defence or set-off any matter that—

(a)   arises from or in connection with the contract and is relevant to the term, and

(b)   would have been available to him by way of defence or set-off if the proceedings had been brought by the promisee.

(3)   The promisor shall also have available to him by way of defence or set-off any matter if—

(a)   an express term of the contract provides for it to be available to him in proceedings brought by the third party, and

(b)   it would have been available to him by way of defence or set-off if the proceedings had been brought by the promisee.

(4)   The promisor shall also have available to him—

(a)   by way of defence or set-off any matter, and

(b)   by way of counterclaim any matter not arising from the contract,

that would have been available to him by way of defence or set-off or, as the case may be, by way of counterclaim against the third party if the third party had been a party to the contract.

(5)   Subsections (2) and (4) are subject to any express term of the contract as to the matters that are not to be available to the promisor by way of defence, set-off or counterclaim.

(6)   Where in any proceedings brought against him a third party seeks in reliance on section 1 to enforce a term of a contract (including, in particular, a term purporting to exclude or limit liability), he may not do so if he could not have done so (whether by reason of any particular circumstances relating to him or otherwise) had he been a party to the contract.

[745]

4   Enforcement of contract by promisee

Section 1 does not affect any right of the promisee to enforce any term of the contract.

[746]

5   Protection of party promisor from double liability

Where under section 1 a term of a contract is enforceable by a third party, and the promisee has recovered from the promisor a sum in respect of—

    (a)   the third party's loss in respect of the term, or

    (b)   the expense to the promisee of making good to the third party the default of the promisor,

then, in any proceedings brought in reliance on that section by the third party, the court or arbitral tribunal shall reduce any award to the third party to such extent as it thinks appropriate to take account of the sum recovered by the promisee.

[747]

6   Exceptions

(1)   Section 1 confers no rights on a third party in the case of a contract on a bill of exchange, promissory note or other negotiable instrument.

(2)   Section 1 confers no rights on a third party in the case of any contract binding on a company and its members under section 14 of the Companies Act 1985.

[(2A)   Section 1 confers no rights on a third party in the case of any incorporation document of a limited liability partnership or any limited liability partnership agreement as defined in the Limited Liability Partnerships Regulations 2001 (SI No 2001/1090).]

(3)   Section 1 confers no right on a third party to enforce—

    (a)   any term of a contract of employment against an employee,

    (b)   any term of a worker's contract against a worker (including a home worker), or

    (c)   any term of a relevant contract against an agency worker.

(4)   In subsection (3)—

    (a)   "contract of employment", "employee", "worker's contract", and "worker" have the meaning given by section 54 of the National Minimum Wage Act 1998,

    (b)   "home worker" has the meaning given by section 35(2) of that Act,

    (c)   "agency worker" has the same meaning as in section 34(1) of that Act, and

    (d)   "relevant contract" means a contract entered into, in a case where section 34 of that Act applies, by the agency worker as respects work falling within subsection (1)(a) of that section.

(5)   Section 1 confers no rights on a third party in the case of—

    (a)   a contract for the carriage of goods by sea, or

    (b)   a contract for the carriage of goods by rail or road, or for the carriage of cargo by air, which is subject to the rules of the appropriate international transport convention,

except that a third party may in reliance on that section avail himself of an exclusion or limitation of liability in such a contract.

(6)   In subsection (5) "contract for the carriage of goods by sea" means a contract of carriage—

    (a)   contained in or evidenced by a bill of lading, sea waybill or a corresponding electronic transaction, or

    (b)   under or for the purposes of which there is given an undertaking which is contained in a ship's delivery order or a corresponding electronic transaction.

(7)   For the purposes of subsection (6)—

    (a)   "bill of lading", "sea waybill" and "ship's delivery order" have the same meaning as in the Carriage of Goods by Sea Act 1992, and

    (b)   a corresponding electronic transaction is a transaction within section 1(5) of that Act which corresponds to the issue, indorsement, delivery or transfer of a bill of lading, sea waybill or ship's delivery order.

(8)   In subsection (5) "the appropriate international transport convention" means—

    (a)   in relation to a contract for the carriage of goods by rail, the Convention which has the force of law in the United Kingdom under [regulation 3 of the Railways (Convention on International Carriage by Rail) Regulations 2005],

   (b)   in relation to a contract for the carriage of goods by road, the Convention which has the force of law in the United Kingdom under section 1 of the Carriage of Goods by Road Act 1965, and

   (c)   in relation to a contract for the carriage of cargo by air—

       (i)   the Convention which has the force of law in the United Kingdom under section 1 of the Carriage by Air Act 1961, or

      (ii)   the Convention which has the force of law under section 1 of the Carriage by Air (Supplementary Provisions) Act 1962, or

     (iii)   either of the amended Conventions set out in Part B of Schedule 2 or 3 to the Carriage by Air Acts (Application of Provisions) Order 1967.

[748]

NOTES

Sub-s (2A): inserted by the Limited Liability Partnerships Regulations 2001, SI 2001/1090, reg 9(1), Sch 5, para 20.

Sub-s (8): in para (a) words in square brackets substituted by the Railways (Convention on International Carriage by Rail) Regulations 2005, SI 2005/2092, reg 9(2), Sch 3, para 3.

---

7 Supplementary provisions relating to third party

(1)   Section 1 does not affect any right or remedy of a third party that exists or is available apart from this Act.

(2)   Section 2(2) of the Unfair Contract Terms Act 1977 (restriction on exclusion etc of liability for negligence) shall not apply where the negligence consists of the breach of an obligation arising from a term of a contract and the person seeking to enforce it is a third party acting in reliance on section 1.

(3)   In sections 5 and 8 of the Limitation Act 1980 the references to an action founded on a simple contract and an action upon a specialty shall respectively include references to an action brought in reliance on section 1 relating to a simple contract and an action brought in reliance on that section relating to a specialty.

(4)   A third party shall not, by virtue of section 1(5) or 3(4) or (6), be treated as a party to the contract for the purposes of any other Act (or any instrument made under any other Act).

[749]

8 Arbitration provisions

(1)   Where—

   (a)   a right under section 1 to enforce a term ("the substantive term") is subject to a term providing for the submission of disputes to arbitration ("the arbitration agreement"), and

   (b)   the arbitration agreement is an agreement in writing for the purposes of Part I of the Arbitration Act 1996,

the third party shall be treated for the purposes of that Act as a party to the arbitration agreement as regards disputes between himself and the promisor relating to the enforcement of the substantive term by the third party.

(2)   Where—

   (a)   a third party has a right under section 1 to enforce a term providing for one or more descriptions of dispute between the third party and the promisor to be submitted to arbitration ("the arbitration agreement"),

   (b)   the arbitration agreement is an agreement in writing for the purposes of Part I of the Arbitration Act 1996, and

   (c)   the third party does not fall to be treated under subsection (1) as a party to the arbitration agreement,

the third party shall, if he exercises the right, be treated for the purposes of that Act as a party to the arbitration agreement in relation to the matter with respect to which the right is exercised, and be treated as having been so immediately before the exercise of the right.

[750]

9 Northern Ireland

(1)   In its application to Northern Ireland, this Act has effect with the modifications specified in subsections (2) and (3).

(2)   In section 6(2), for "section 14 of the Companies Act 1985" there is substituted "Article 25 of the Companies (Northern Ireland) Order 1986".

(3)   In section 7, for subsection (3) there is substituted—

"(3)   In Articles 4(a) and 15 of the Limitation (Northern Ireland) Order 1989, the references to an action founded on a simple contract and an action upon an instrument under seal shall respectively include references to an action brought in reliance on section 1 relating to a simple contract and an action brought in reliance on that section relating to a contract under seal.".

(4)   ...

[751]

NOTES

Sub-s (4): repeals the Law Reform (Husband and Wife) (Northern Ireland) Act 1964, s 5 and amends s 6 thereof.

---

10   Short title, commencement and extent

(1)   This Act may be cited as the Contracts (Rights of Third Parties) Act 1999.

(2)   This Act comes into force on the day on which it is passed but, subject to subsection (3), does not apply in relation to a contract entered into before the end of the period of six months beginning with that day.

(3)   The restriction in subsection (2) does not apply in relation to a contract which—
  (a)   is entered into on or after the day on which this Act is passed, and
  (b)   expressly provides for the application of this Act.

(4)   This Act extends as follows—
  (a)   section 9 extends to Northern Ireland only;
  (b)   the remaining provisions extend to England and Wales and Northern Ireland only.

[752]

TERRORISM ACT 2000

(2000 c 11)

An Act to make provision about terrorism; and to make temporary provision for Northern Ireland about the prosecution and punishment of certain offences, the preservation of peace and the maintenance of order

[20 July 2000]

PART I
INTRODUCTORY

1   Terrorism: interpretation

(1)   In this Act "terrorism" means the use or threat of action where—
  (a)   the action falls within subsection (2),
  (b)   the use or threat is designed to influence the government [or an international governmental organisation] or to intimidate the public or a section of the public, and
  (c)   the use or threat is made for the purpose of advancing a political, religious or ideological cause.

(2)   Action falls within this subsection if it—
  (a)   involves serious violence against a person,
  (b)   involves serious damage to property,
  (c)   endangers a person's life, other than that of the person committing the action,
  (d)   creates a serious risk to the health or safety of the public or a section of the public, or
  (e)   is designed seriously to interfere with or seriously to disrupt an electronic system.

(3)   The use or threat of action falling within subsection (2) which involves the use of firearms or explosives is terrorism whether or not subsection (1)(b) is satisfied.

(4)   In this section—
  (a)   "action" includes action outside the United Kingdom,
  (b)   a reference to any person or to property is a reference to any person, or to property, wherever situated,
  (c)   a reference to the public includes a reference to the public of a country other than the United Kingdom, and
  (d)   "the government" means the government of the United Kingdom, of a Part of the United Kingdom or of a country other than the United Kingdom.

(5)   In this Act a reference to action taken for the purposes of terrorism includes a reference to action taken for the benefit of a proscribed organisation.

[753]

NOTES
Sub-s (1): words in square brackets inserted by the Terrorism Act 2006, s 34(a).

2–113   (*Outside the scope of this work.*)

PART VIII
GENERAL

114–127   (*Outside the scope of this work.*)

128   Commencement

The preceding provisions of this Act, apart from sections 2(1)(b) and (2) and 118 and Schedule 1, shall come into force in accordance with provision made by the Secretary of State by order.

[754]

NOTES
Orders: the commencement order relevant to the provisions of this Act printed in this title is the Terrorism Act 2000 (Commencement No 3) Order 2001, SI 2001/421.

129   (*Outside the scope of this work.*)

130   Extent

(1)   Subject to subsections (2) to (6), this Act extends to the whole of the United Kingdom.

(2)   Section 59 shall extend to England and Wales only.

(3)   The following shall extend to Northern Ireland only—
  (a)   section 60, and
  (b)   Part VII.

(4)   Section 61 shall extend to Scotland only.

(5)   In Schedule 5—
  (a)   Part I shall extend to England and Wales and Northern Ireland only, and
  (b)   Part II shall extend to Scotland only.

(6)   The amendments and repeals in Schedules 15 and 16 shall have the same extent as the enactments to which they relate.

[755]

131   Short title

This Act may be cited as the Terrorism Act 2000.

[756]

(*Schs 1–16 outside the scope of this work.*)

COMMONHOLD AND LEASEHOLD REFORM ACT 2002

(2002 c 15)

An Act to make provision about commonhold land and to amend the law about leasehold property

[1 May 2002]

ARRANGEMENT OF SECTIONS

PART 1
COMMONHOLD

Nature of commonhold

Commonhold unit

Common parts

Commonhold community statement

Operation of commonhold

PART 3
SUPPLEMENTARY

PART 1
COMMONHOLD

Nature of commonhold

1 Commonhold land

(1) Land is commonhold land if—

(a) the freehold estate in the land is registered as a freehold estate in commonhold land,

(b) the land is specified in the memorandum of association of a commonhold association as the land in relation to which the association is to exercise functions, and

(c) a commonhold community statement makes provision for rights and duties of the commonhold association and unit-holders (whether or not the statement has come into force).

(2) In this Part a reference to a commonhold is a reference to land in relation to which a commonhold association exercises functions.

(3) In this Part—
"commonhold association" has the meaning given by section 34,
"commonhold community statement" has the meaning given by section 31,
"commonhold unit" has the meaning given by section 11,
"common parts" has the meaning given by section 25, and
"unit-holder" has the meaning given by sections 12 and 13.

(4) Sections 7 and 9 make provision for the vesting in the commonhold association of the fee simple in possession in the common parts of a commonhold.

[757]

NOTES
Commencement: 27 September 2004.

2–10 (*Outside the scope of this work.*)

Commonhold unit

11 Definition

(1) In this Part "commonhold unit" means a commonhold unit specified in a commonhold community statement in accordance with this section.

(2) A commonhold community statement must—
(a) specify at least two parcels of land as commonhold units, and
(b) define the extent of each commonhold unit.

(3) In defining the extent of a commonhold unit a commonhold community statement—
(a) must refer to a plan which is included in the statement and which complies with prescribed requirements,
(b) may refer to an area subject to the exclusion of specified structures, fittings, apparatus or appurtenances within the area,
(c) may exclude the structures which delineate an area referred to, and
(d) may refer to two or more areas (whether or not contiguous).

(4) A commonhold unit need not contain all or any part of a building.

[758]

NOTES
Commencement: 27 September 2004.
Regulations: the Commonhold Regulations 2004, SI 2004/1829.

12–16 (*Outside the scope of this work.*)

17 Leasing: residential

(1)–(4) ...

(5) A commonhold unit is residential if provision made in the commonhold community statement by virtue of section 14(1) requires it to be used only—
(a) for residential purposes, or
(b) for residential and other incidental purposes.

[759]

PART I
STATUTES

NOTES

Commencement: 27 September 2004.

Sub-ss (1)–(4): outside the scope of this work.

18 Leasing: non-residential

An instrument or agreement which creates a term of years absolute in a commonhold unit which is not residential (within the meaning of section 17) shall have effect subject to any provision of the commonhold community statement.

[760]

NOTES

Commencement: 27 September 2004.

19 Leasing: supplementary

(1) Regulations may—

    (a)   impose obligations on a tenant of a commonhold unit;

    (b)   enable a commonhold community statement to impose obligations on a tenant of a commonhold unit.

(2) Regulations under subsection (1) may, in particular, require a tenant of a commonhold unit to make payments to the commonhold association or a unit-holder in discharge of payments which—

    (a)   are due in accordance with the commonhold community statement to be made by the unit-holder, or

    (b)   are due in accordance with the commonhold community statement to be made by another tenant of the unit.

(3) Regulations under subsection (1) may, in particular, provide—

    (a)   for the amount of payments under subsection (2) to be set against sums owed by the tenant (whether to the person by whom the payments were due to be made or to some other person);

    (b)   for the amount of payments under subsection (2) to be recovered from the unit-holder or another tenant of the unit.

(4) Regulations may modify a rule of law about leasehold estates (whether deriving from the common law or from an enactment) in its application to a term of years in a commonhold unit.

(5) Regulations under this section—

    (a)   may make provision generally or in relation to specified circumstances, and

    (b)   may make different provision for different descriptions of commonhold land or commonhold unit.

[761]

NOTES

Commencement: 27 September 2004.

Regulations: the Commonhold Regulations 2004, SI 2004/1829.

20 Other transactions

(1) A commonhold community statement may not prevent or restrict the creation, grant or transfer by a unit-holder of—

    (a)   an interest in the whole or part of his unit, or

    (b)   a charge over his unit.

(2) Subsection (1) is subject to sections 17 to 19 (which impose restrictions about leases).

(3) It shall not be possible to create an interest of a prescribed kind in a commonhold unit unless the commonhold association—

    (a)   is a party to the creation of the interest, or

    (b)   consents in writing to the creation of the interest.

(4)   A commonhold association may act as described in subsection (3)(a) or (b) only if—
(a)   the association passes a resolution to take the action, and
(b)   at least 75 per cent of those who vote on the resolution vote in favour.

(5)   An instrument or agreement shall be of no effect to the extent that it purports to create an interest in contravention of subsection (3).

(6)   In this section "interest" does not include—
(a)   a charge, or
(b)   an interest which arises by virtue of a charge.

[762]

NOTES
Commencement: 27 September 2004.

21   Part-unit: interests

(1)   It shall not be possible to create an interest in part only of a commonhold unit.

(2)   But subsection (1) shall not prevent—
(a)   the creation of a term of years absolute in part only of a residential commonhold unit where the term satisfies prescribed conditions,
(b)   the creation of a term of years absolute in part only of a non-residential commonhold unit, or
(c)   the transfer of the freehold estate in part only of a commonhold unit where the commonhold association consents in writing to the transfer.

(3)   An instrument or agreement shall be of no effect to the extent that it purports to create an interest in contravention of subsection (1).

(4)   Subsection (5) applies where—
(a)   land becomes commonhold land or is added to a commonhold unit, and
(b)   immediately before that event there is an interest in the land which could not be created after that event by reason of subsection (1).

(5)   The interest shall be extinguished by virtue of this subsection to the extent that it could not be created by reason of subsection (1).

(6)   Section 17(2) and (4) shall apply (with any necessary modifications) in relation to subsection (2)(a) and (b) above.

(7)   Where part only of a unit is held under a lease, regulations may modify the application of a provision which—
(a)   is made by or by virtue of this Part, and
(b)   applies to a unit-holder or a tenant or both.

(8)   Section 20(4) shall apply in relation to subsection (2)(c) above.

(9)   Where the freehold interest in part only of a commonhold unit is transferred, the part transferred—
(a)   becomes a new commonhold unit by virtue of this subsection, or
(b)   in a case where the request for consent under subsection (2)(c) states that this paragraph is to apply, becomes part of a commonhold unit specified in the request.

(10)   Regulations may make provision, or may require a commonhold community statement to make provision, about—
(a)   registration of units created by virtue of subsection (9);
(b)   the adaptation of provision made by or by virtue of this Part or by or by virtue of a commonhold community statement to a case where units are created or modified by virtue of subsection (9).

[763]

NOTES
Commencement: 27 September 2004 (sub-ss (1)–(3), (6)–(10)); to be appointed (otherwise).
Regulations: the Commonhold Regulations 2004, SI 2004/1829.

22   Part-unit: charging

(1)   It shall not be possible to create a charge over part only of an interest in a commonhold unit.

(2)   An instrument or agreement shall be of no effect to the extent that it purports to create a charge in contravention of subsection (1).

(3)   Subsection (4) applies where—
   (a)   land becomes commonhold land or is added to a commonhold unit, and
   (b)   immediately before that event there is a charge over the land which could not be created after that event by reason of subsection (1).

(4)   The charge shall be extinguished by virtue of this subsection to the extent that it could not be created by reason of subsection (1).

[764]

NOTES
Commencement: 27 September 2004.

23   Changing size

(1)   An amendment of a commonhold community statement which redefines the extent of a commonhold unit may not be made unless the unit-holder consents—
   (a)   in writing, and
   (b)   before the amendment is made.

(2)   But regulations may enable a court to dispense with the requirement for consent on the application of a commonhold association in prescribed circumstances.

[765]

NOTES
Commencement: 27 September 2004.

24   Changing size: charged unit

(1)   This section applies to an amendment of a commonhold community statement which redefines the extent of a commonhold unit over which there is a registered charge.

(2)   The amendment may not be made unless the registered proprietor of the charge consents—
   (a)   in writing, and
   (b)   before the amendment is made.

(3)   But regulations may enable a court to dispense with the requirement for consent on the application of a commonhold association in prescribed circumstances.

(4)   If the amendment removes land from the commonhold unit, the charge shall by virtue of this subsection be extinguished to the extent that it relates to the land which is removed.

(5)   If the amendment adds land to the unit, the charge shall by virtue of this subsection be extended so as to relate to the land which is added.

(6)   Regulations may make provision—
   (a)   requiring notice to be given to the Registrar in circumstances to which this section applies;
   (b)   requiring the Registrar to alter the register to reflect the application of subsection (4) or (5).

[766]

NOTES
Commencement: 27 September 2004.
Regulations: the Commonhold Regulations 2004, SI 2004/1829.

Common parts

25   Definition

(1)   In this Part "common parts" in relation to a commonhold means every part of the commonhold which is not for the time being a commonhold unit in accordance with the commonhold community statement.

(2)   A commonhold community statement may make provision in respect of a specified part of the common parts (a "limited use area") restricting—
    (a)   the classes of person who may use it;
    (b)   the kind of use to which it may be put.

(3)   A commonhold community statement—
    (a)   may make provision which has effect only in relation to a limited use area, and
    (b)   may make different provision for different limited use areas.

[767]

NOTES
Commencement: 27 September 2004.

26   Use and maintenance

A commonhold community statement must make provision—
    (a)   regulating the use of the common parts;
    (b)   requiring the commonhold association to insure the common parts;
    (c)   requiring the commonhold association to repair and maintain the common parts.

[768]

NOTES
Commencement: 27 September 2004.

27   Transactions

(1)   Nothing in a commonhold community statement shall prevent or restrict—
    (a)   the transfer by the commonhold association of its freehold estate in any part of the common parts, or
    (b)   the creation by the commonhold association of an interest in any part of the common parts.

(2)   In this section "interest" does not include—
    (a)   a charge, or
    (b)   an interest which arises by virtue of a charge.

[769]

NOTES
Commencement: 27 September 2004.

28   Charges: general prohibition

(1)   It shall not be possible to create a charge over common parts.

(2)   An instrument or agreement shall be of no effect to the extent that it purports to create a charge over common parts.

(3)   Where by virtue of section 7 or 9 a commonhold association is registered as the proprietor of common parts, a charge which relates wholly or partly to the common parts shall be extinguished by virtue of this subsection to the extent that it relates to the common parts.

(4)   Where by virtue of section 30 land vests in a commonhold association following an amendment to a commonhold community statement which has the effect of adding land to the common parts, a charge which relates wholly or partly to the land added shall be extinguished by virtue of this subsection to the extent that it relates to that land.

(5)   This section is subject to section 29 (which permits certain mortgages).

[770]

NOTES
Commencement: 27 September 2004.

29   New legal mortgages

(1)   Section 28 shall not apply in relation to a legal mortgage if the creation of the mortgage is approved by a resolution of the commonhold association.

(2) A resolution for the purposes of subsection (1) must be passed—
  (a) before the mortgage is created, and
  (b) unanimously.

(3) In this section "legal mortgage" has the meaning given by section 205(1)(xvi) of the Law of Property Act 1925 (c 20) (interpretation).

[771]

NOTES
Commencement: 27 September 2004.

30 Additions to common parts

(1) This section applies where an amendment of a commonhold community statement—
  (a) specifies land which forms part of a commonhold unit, and
  (b) provides for that land (the "added land") to be added to the common parts.

(2) The amendment may not be made unless the registered proprietor of any charge over the added land consents—
  (a) in writing, and
  (b) before the amendment is made.

(3) But regulations may enable a court to dispense with the requirement for consent on the application of a commonhold association in specified circumstances.

(4) On the filing of the amended statement under section 33—
  (a) the commonhold association shall be entitled to be registered as the proprietor of the freehold estate in the added land, and
  (b) the Registrar shall register the commonhold association in accordance with paragraph (a) (without an application being made).

[772]

NOTES
Commencement: 27 September 2004.

Commonhold community statement

31 Form and content: general

(1) A commonhold community statement is a document which makes provision in relation to specified land for—
  (a) the rights and duties of the commonhold association, and
  (b) the rights and duties of the unit-holders.

(2) A commonhold community statement must be in the prescribed form.

(3) A commonhold community statement may—
  (a) impose a duty on the commonhold association;
  (b) impose a duty on a unit-holder;
  (c) make provision about the taking of decisions in connection with the management of the commonhold or any other matter concerning it.

(4) Subsection (3) is subject to—
  (a) any provision made by or by virtue of this Part, and
  (b) any provision of the memorandum or articles of the commonhold association.

(5) In subsection (3)(a) and (b) "duty" includes, in particular, a duty—
  (a) to pay money;
  (b) to undertake works;
  (c) to grant access;
  (d) to give notice;
  (e) to refrain from entering into transactions of a specified kind in relation to a commonhold unit;
  (f) to refrain from using the whole or part of a commonhold unit for a specified purpose or for anything other than a specified purpose;
  (g) to refrain from undertaking works (including alterations) of a specified kind;

(h)   to refrain from causing nuisance or annoyance;

(i)   to refrain from specified behaviour;

(j)   to indemnify the commonhold association or a unit-holder in respect of costs arising from the breach of a statutory requirement.

(6)   Provision in a commonhold community statement imposing a duty to pay money (whether in pursuance of subsection (5)(a) or any other provision made by or by virtue of this Part) may include provision for the payment of interest in the case of late payment.

(7)   A duty conferred by a commonhold community statement on a commonhold association or a unit-holder shall not require any other formality.

(8)   A commonhold community statement may not provide for the transfer or loss of an interest in land on the occurrence or non-occurrence of a specified event.

(9)   Provision made by a commonhold community statement shall be of no effect to the extent that—

(a)   it is prohibited by virtue of section 32,

(b)   it is inconsistent with any provision made by or by virtue of this Part,

(c)   it is inconsistent with anything which is treated as included in the statement by virtue of section 32, or

(d)   it is inconsistent with the memorandum or articles of association of the commonhold association.

[773]

NOTES
Commencement: 27 September 2004.
Regulations: the Commonhold Regulations 2004, SI 2004/1829.

32   Regulations

(1)   Regulations shall make provision about the content of a commonhold community statement.

(2)   The regulations may permit, require or prohibit the inclusion in a statement of—

(a)   specified provision, or

(b)   provision of a specified kind, for a specified purpose or about a specified matter.

(3)   The regulations may—

(a)   provide for a statement to be treated as including provision prescribed by or determined in accordance with the regulations;

(b)   permit a statement to make provision in place of provision which would otherwise be treated as included by virtue of paragraph (a).

(4)   The regulations may—

(a)   make different provision for different descriptions of commonhold association or unit-holder;

(b)   make different provision for different circumstances;

(c)   make provision about the extent to which a commonhold community statement may make different provision for different descriptions of unit-holder or common parts.

(5)   The matters to which regulations under this section may relate include, but are not limited to—

(a)   the matters mentioned in sections 11, 14, 15, 20, 21, 25, 26, 27, 38, 39 and 58, and

(b)   any matter for which regulations under section 37 may make provision.

[774]

NOTES
Commencement: 27 September 2004.
Regulations: the Commonhold Regulations 2004, SI 2004/1829.

33   Amendment

(1)   Regulations under section 32 shall require a commonhold community statement to make provision about how it can be amended.

(2)   The regulations shall, in particular, make provision under section 32(3)(a) (whether or not subject to provision under section 32(3)(b)).

(3)   An amendment of a commonhold community statement shall have no effect unless and until the amended statement is registered in accordance with this section.

(4)   If the commonhold association makes an application under this subsection the Registrar shall arrange for an amended commonhold community statement to be kept in his custody, and referred to in the register, in place of the unamended statement.

(5)   An application under subsection (4) must be accompanied by a certificate given by the directors of the commonhold association that the amended commonhold community statement satisfies the requirements of this Part.

(6)   Where an amendment of a commonhold community statement redefines the extent of a commonhold unit, an application under subsection (4) must be accompanied by any consent required by section 23(1) or 24(2) (or an order of a court dispensing with consent).

(7)   Where an amendment of a commonhold community statement has the effect of changing the extent of the common parts, an application under subsection (4) must be accompanied by any consent required by section 30(2) (or an order of a court dispensing with consent).

(8)   Where the Registrar amends the register on an application under subsection (4) he shall make any consequential amendments to the register which he thinks appropriate.

[775]

NOTES

Commencement: 27 September 2004.

34–36   (*Outside the scope of this work.*)

Operation of commonhold

37, 38   (*Outside the scope of this work.*)

39   Reserve fund

(1)   Regulations under section 32 may, in particular, require a commonhold community statement to make provision—

    (a)   requiring the directors of the commonhold association to establish and maintain one or more funds to finance the repair and maintenance of common parts;

    (b)   requiring the directors of the commonhold association to establish and maintain one or more funds to finance the repair and maintenance of commonhold units.

(2)   Where a commonhold community statement provides for the establishment and maintenance of a fund in accordance with subsection (1) it must also make provision—

    (a)   requiring or enabling the directors of the commonhold association to set a levy from time to time,

    (b)   specifying the percentage of any levy set under paragraph (a) which is to be allocated to each unit,

    (c)   requiring each unit-holder to make payments in respect of the percentage of any levy set under paragraph (a) which is allocated to his unit, and

    (d)   requiring the directors of the commonhold association to serve notices on unit-holders specifying payments required to be made by them and the date on which each payment is due.

(3)   For the purpose of subsection (2)(b)—

    (a)   the percentages allocated by a commonhold community statement to the commonhold units must amount in aggregate to 100;

    (b)   a commonhold community statement may specify 0 per cent in relation to a unit.

(4)   The assets of a fund established and maintained by virtue of this section shall not be used for the purpose of enforcement of any debt except a judgment debt referable to a reserve fund activity.

(5)   For the purpose of subsection (4)—

(a) "reserve fund activity" means an activity which in accordance with the commonhold community statement can or may be financed from a fund established and maintained by virtue of this section,

(b) assets are used for the purpose of enforcement of a debt if, in particular, they are taken in execution or are made the subject of a charging order under section 1 of the Charging Orders Act 1979 (c 53), and

(c) the reference to a judgment debt includes a reference to any interest payable on a judgment debt.

[776]

NOTES

Commencement: 27 September 2004.

40–179 (*Outside the scope of this work.*)

PART 3
SUPPLEMENTARY

180 (*Outside the scope of this work.*)

181 Commencement etc

(1) Apart from section 104 and sections 177 to 179, the preceding provisions (and the Schedules) come into force in accordance with provision made by order made by the appropriate authority.

(2) The appropriate authority may by order make any transitional provisions or savings in connection with the coming into force of any provision in accordance with an order under subsection (1).

(3) The power to make orders under subsections (1) and (2) is exercisable by statutory instrument.

(4) In this section "the appropriate authority" means—

(a) in relation to any provision of Part 1 or section 180 and Schedule 14 so far as relating to section 104, the Lord Chancellor, and

(b) in relation to any provision of Part 2 or section 180 and Schedule 14 so far as otherwise relating, the Secretary of State (as respects England) and the National Assembly for Wales (as respects Wales).

[777]

NOTES

Orders: the Commonhold and Leasehold Reform Act 2002 (Commencement No 1, Savings and Transitional Provisions) (Wales) Order 2002, SI 2002/3012; the Commonhold and Leasehold Reform Act 2002 (Commencement No 2 and Savings) (England) Order 2003, SI 2003/1986; the Commonhold and Leasehold Reform Act 2002 (Commencement No 3) Order 2003, SI 2003/2377; the Commonhold and Leasehold Reform Act 2002 (Commencement No 2 and Savings) (Wales) Order 2004, SI 2004/669; the Commonhold and Leasehold Reform Act 2002 (Commencement No 4) Order 2004, SI 2004/1832; the Commonhold and Leasehold Reform Act 2002 (Commencement No 5 and Saving and Transitional Provision) Order 2004, SI 2004/3056; the Commonhold and Leasehold Reform Act 2002 (Commencement No 5 and Saving and Transitional Provision) (Amendment) (England) Order 2005, SI 2005/193; the Commonhold and Leasehold Reform Act 2002 (Commencement No 3 and Saving and Transitional Provision) (Wales) Order 2005, SI 2005/1353; the Commonhold and Leasehold Reform Act 2002 (Commencement No 6) (England) Order 2007, SI 2007/1256.

182 Extent

This Act extends to England and Wales only.

[778]

183 Short title

This Act may be cited as the Commonhold and Leasehold Reform Act 2002.

[779]

(*Schs 1–14 outside the scope of this work.*)

PART II
STATUTORY INSTRUMENTS

RENEWABLE LEASEHOLDS REGULATIONS 1925

(SR & O 1925/857)

NOTES
Made: 24 August 1925.
Authority: Law of Property Act 1922, Sch 15.
Transfer of functions: by virtue of the Transfer of Functions (Ministry of Food) Order 1955, SI 1955/554, the style and title of the Minister of Agriculture and Fisheries was changed to "the Minister of Agriculture, Fisheries and Food". Subsequently, the Ministry of Agriculture, Fisheries and Food was dissolved by the Ministry of Agriculture, Fisheries and Food (Dissolution) Order 2002, SI 2002/794. Subject to specific provision to the contrary, the functions of the Minister were transferred to the Secretary of State, and the property, rights and liabilities of the Minister were transferred to the Secretary of State for Environment, Food and Rural Affairs.

1   For the purposes of paragraph 12(6) of the Fifteenth Schedule to the Law of Property Act 1922, as amended by the Law of Property (Amendment) Act 1924, five per cent shall be the prescribed percentage applicable generally except where the Minister in any particular instance with a view to maintaining any existing practice prescribed any other percentage.

[1001]

2—(1)   Where any question or dispute is under paragraph 16 of the Fifteenth Schedule to the Law of Property Act 1922, submitted to the Minister of Agriculture and Fisheries for determination, the matter shall be determined under and in accordance with the provisions of the Arbitration Act 1889, and—

(a)   unless either party to the arbitration shall, within seven days after receipt of a written notice by the Minister that he proposes that a person to be appointed by him shall act as arbitrator, give notice in writing to the Minister that he objects to such proposal, the Minister may appoint an officer of the Ministry of Agriculture and Fisheries or other person to act as the arbitrator, in which case the award made by the person so appointed shall be deemed to be an award by the Minister; or

(b)   the Minister may appoint any officer of the Ministry or other person to hear on his behalf the parties or their solicitors or counsel and the witnesses in the arbitration and to report thereon to the Minister to enable him to make an award, and for the purposes of or in connection with such hearing the person appointed shall have all the powers of an arbitrator.

(2)   If any person appointed to act under this Regulation shall die or in the judgment of the Minister become incapable or unfit the Minister may appoint another person to act in his place.

(3)   The remuneration of any person, other than an officer of the Ministry, who is appointed to act under this Regulation shall be fixed by the Minister.

(4)   The submission of any question or dispute to the Minister for determination shall be in writing signed by or on behalf of the party submitting the same and shall set out the question or dispute to be determined. Provided that the submission may, with the sanction of the Minister or any person appointed by him to act under this Regulation, be amended or varied on such terms as to payment of costs or otherwise as the Minister or such person as aforesaid may determine.

(5)   These Regulations shall come into operation on the first day of January, nineteen hundred and twenty-six, and may be cited as the Renewable Leaseholds Regulations 1925.

(6)   These Regulations do not extend to Scotland or Ireland.

[1002]

NOTES
Modification: any reference to solicitor(s) etc modified to include references to bodies recognised under the Administration of Justice Act 1985, s 9, by the Solicitors' Incorporated Practices Order 1991, SI 1991/2684, arts 4, 5, Sch 1.
Arbitration Act 1889: see now the Arbitration Act 1996.

FILING OF LEASES RULES 1925

(SR & O 1925/1128)

NOTES
Made: 11 November 1925.
Authority: Administration of Justice Acts 1920 and 1925 (repealed) and the Law of Property Act 1922, Sch 15, para 20.
Modification: any reference to solicitor(s) etc modified to include references to bodies recognised under the Administration of Justice Act 1985, s 9, by the Solicitors' Incorporated Practices Order 1991, SI 1991/2684, arts 4, 5, Sch 1.

ARRANGEMENT OF RULES

1 Deposit and index of instruments

(1)   Any person may, subject to the payment of the prescribed fee, deposit at the Central Office of the Supreme Court the original or counterpart of any instrument to which these Rules apply.

(2)   There shall be deposited, together with any such instrument, a short description of the instrument in Form No 1 in the Schedule to these Rules.

(3)   An alphabetical index of the name of each lessee, lessor, or underlessee under any deposited instrument, and of the names of the assignors or assignees under any such instrument shall be kept in the Filing Department of the Central Office.

(4)   The instruments to which these Rules apply are leases, underleases, and assignments of leases and underleases, and office copies of any such lease, underlease, or assignment.

[1003]

2 Requisition for search

Any person who desires—

    (a)   to search the alphabetical index or the file of instruments; or

    (b)   to inspect any deposited instrument

shall deliver at the Filing Department a requisition for that purpose signed by himself or by his solicitor, together with the prescribed fee.

[1004]

3 Form and contents of requisition

(1)   The requisition shall be in Form No 2 in the Schedule to these Rules and shall state—

    (a)   the name, address and description of the applicant and, where a solicitor is acting on behalf of the applicant, the name and address of that solicitor, and

    (b)   the purpose for which the search and inspection are required, and

    (c)   the interest which the applicant has or claims to have under the instrument or in any reversion expectant upon the term implied therein by operation of law,

and shall contain a declaration that the statements made in the requisition are true.

(2)   Where the requisition is signed by a solicitor, it shall state that he is duly authorised to act on behalf of the applicant.

(3)   The requisition shall be filed in the Central Office.

[1005]

4 Acceptance or refusal of requisition

If the requisition complies with these Rules and the applicant appears to have an interest (whether or not being a charge) either beneficial or in a fiduciary capacity under the instrument or any reversion expectant upon the term implied therein by operation of law, the applicant shall be allowed to search for and inspect the instrument. Any doubt arising under this rule shall be referred to the Senior Master of the Supreme Court who shall decide whether the search and inspection shall be allowed.

[1006]

5 Office copies

(1) When a search has been authorised, the applicant may require an office copy of the deposited instrument or any part thereof to be issued to him with or without any endorsements thereon or with or without any plan.

(2) The request for the issue of an office copy shall be in Form No 3 in the Schedule to these Rules and shall contain an undertaking to pay the prescribed fee when ascertained.

(3) When the office copy is ready for issue, notification thereof shall be sent by post to the applicant or his solicitor, with a memorandum of the amount of the fee payable.

(4) The applicant or his solicitor shall, after the payment of the prescribed fee, apply for the office copy to be delivered to the bearer of the request or to be sent by post, at the risk of the applicant, to the applicant or his solicitor. Any such application shall be in the Form No 4 in the Schedule to these Rules and, where it includes a request that the office copy shall be sent by post, shall be accompanied by a stamped envelope (draft size) addressed to the person to whom the copy is to be sent.

[1007]

6 Conversion of copies into office copies

(1) On presentation at the Filing Department of a copy of any deposited instrument for the purpose of having it stamped as an office copy, the copy shall be examined and, if found correct, shall, subject to the payment of the prescribed fee, be stamped as an office copy.

(2) Where the instrument to which any copy so presented has annexed to it or endorsed upon it any plan or endorsements, the copy presented shall be accompanied by a tracing of the plan and a copy of the endorsements.

[1008]

7 Notes authorised on a search

No copies of or extracts from any deposited instrument shall be made except as provided in the foregoing provisions of these Rules, and no person authorised to inspect an instrument under these Rules shall be allowed to use any ink when inspecting a deposited instrument, but any person so authorised shall be entitled in the course of inspection to take a note in pencil of—

(a) the date of the instrument,
(b) the parties to the instrument,
(c) the parcels, plan and rent,
(d) the nature of the covenants, and
(e) the endorsements, if any, upon the instrument.

[1009]

8 Application forms

(1) Copies of the Forms prescribed under these Rules will be supplied free of cost on application at the Central Office Filing Department.

(2) The forms shall be adhered to with such modifications only as the circumstances of each case may render necessary.

[1010]

9 Short title, commencement

(1) These Rules may be cited as the Filing of Leases Rules 1925.

(2) These Rules shall come into operation on the first day of January, nineteen hundred and twenty-six.

[1011]

PART II
STATUTORY INSTRUMENTS

SCHEDULE

NOTES
This Schedule contains forms which are not themselves reproduced in this work, but their numbers and titles are listed below.

Form No	Title
1	Application under the Fifteenth Schedule to the Law of Property Act 1922 for deposit of an instrument
2	Requisition under the Fifteenth Schedule to the Law of Property Act 1922 for a search
3	Request for Office copy to be prepared
4	Request for Office copy to be delivered or sent by post

LANDLORD AND TENANT (DETERMINATION OF RATEABLE VALUE PROCEDURE) RULES 1954

(SI 1954/1255)

NOTES
Made: 24 September 1954.
Authority: Landlord and Tenant Act 1954, s 37(6).

1   These Rules may be cited as the Landlord and Tenant (Determination of Rateable Value Procedure) Rules 1954, and shall come into operation on the first day of October, 1954.

[1012]

2—(1)   In these Rules—
"The Commissioners" means the Commissioners of Inland Revenue;
"The Act" means the Landlord and Tenant Act 1954, and other expressions have the same meaning as in that Act.

(2)   The Interpretation Act 1889 shall apply to these Rules as it applies to an Act of Parliament.

[1013]

NOTES
Interpretation Act 1889: see now the Interpretation Act 1978.

3—(1)   Any reference to the Commissioners of a dispute arising as to the determination of the rateable value of any holding for the purposes of Sections 37(2) and 63(2) of the Act, shall be in the form "A" in the Schedule hereto, or in a form substantially to the like effect. A separate form shall be completed in respect of each holding.

(2)   The said reference may be made either:—
(a)   by one of the parties, or
(b)   jointly by two or more of the parties to the dispute:

Provided that, where the said reference is not made by all the parties jointly, the party or parties making the reference shall, on the same day as the reference is made, send a copy thereof to the other party, or parties, to the dispute.

[1014]

4   The Commissioners shall, so soon as may be after the receipt of a reference, send a copy thereof to the Valuation Officer.

[1015]

5   The Valuation Officer shall, upon receipt of the copy of the reference, inform the parties that the dispute has been referred to him for determination and that they may make representations to him on the matter in writing within twenty-eight days, or such longer time as he may in a particular case allow.

[1016]

6   The Valuation Officer may require the parties to furnish him with such information as he may reasonably require for the proper determination of the rateable value of the holding.

[1017]

7   The Valuation Officer may, before making his determination, invite all the parties to a meeting at his office or at such other place as he may think convenient.

[1018]

8   The Valuation Officer shall so soon as may be determine the rateable value of the holding and shall send a notification of his determination to the Commissioners and to each of the parties together with a statement of their right of appeal to the Lands Tribunal under Section 37(5) of the Act. The notification of such determination shall be in the form "B" in the Schedule hereto, and a separate notification shall be sent in respect of each holding.

[1019]

SCHEDULE

Regulations 3, 8

FORM "A"

Landlord and Tenant Act, 1954

Re

ference of a dispute arising as to the determination of the Rateable Value of any holding for the purposes of Section 37(2) or of Section 63(2).

To:—The Commissioners of Inland Revenue,
Somerset House,
London, WC2.

PART I (*Applicable to all references*).

*I/We being *a party/parties to a dispute which has arisen as to the determination for the purposes of Section *[37(2)/63(2)] of the rateable value of a holding known as†
.... hereby
refer the dispute for decision by a Valuation Officer.

	‡(1)	‡(2)	‡(3)
Signed	....	....	....
Capacity in which reference made (e g Tenant, Landlord, etc)	....	....	....
Address	....	....	....
	....	....	....
	....	....	....
Date	....	....	....

*Delete as appropriate
†Insert here address or situation, and such further particulars as may be necessary for the identification of the holding.
‡See headnote to Part II of form.

PART II (*Applicable where the reference is not made by all the parties to the dispute*).

Note.—Where the reference is not made by all the parties, the party or parties making the reference should sign and complete the form in Part I above, and should give below the name or names of the other party or parties to the dispute, and should send a copy of this form, as completed, to the other party or parties.

Name(s) and address(es) of other party(ies)

	(A)	(B)
Name	....	....
Address	....	....
	....	....
	....	....

[1020]

FORM "B"

Landlord and Tenant Act, 1954

Determination of Rateable Value

Whereas a dispute has arisen as to the determination for the purposes of Section *[37(2)/ 63(2)] of the rateable value of the holding described in the first column of the Schedule hereto.

Now I the undersigned being the Valuation Officer to whom the Commissioners of Inland Revenue have pursuant to Section 37(5) referred the dispute for determination hereby determine that for the said purposes the rateable value of the said holding shall be the amount set out in the second column of the said Schedule.

*Delete as appropriate

THE SCHEDULE above referred to

†Description of Holding	Rateable Value as Determined

†The description will follow that in A

Dated this .... day of .... ,   19 ....

Signed   ....

Valuation Officer

for ....

Official Address   ....

....

....

To:—The Commissioners of Inland Revenue

and to:—[The Parties to the Dispute]

....

....

....

Any party who is dissatisfied with the foregoing determination may appeal to the Lands Tribunal by giving written notice of such appeal to the Registrar of the Lands Tribunal within 21 days from the date hereof.

[1021]

RESERVE AND AUXILIARY FORCES (AGRICULTURAL TENANTS) REGULATIONS 1959

(SI 1959/84)

NOTES

Made: 15 January 1959.

Authority: Reserve and Auxiliary Forces (Protection of Civil Interests) Act 1951, s 22 (see now the Agricultural Holdings Act 1986, ss 30, 94, Sch 5, para 6).

1   These Regulations, which may be cited as the Reserve and Auxiliary Forces (Agricultural Tenants) Regulations, 1959, shall come into operation on the 26th day of January, 1959.

[1022]

2   The Reserve and Auxiliary Forces (Protection of Civil Interests) (Agricultural Tenants' Representation) Regulations, 1951, are hereby revoked, so however that any direction given under those Regulations shall have effect as if it had been given under these Regulations.

[1023]

3   In these Regulations, unless the context otherwise requires—

"1948 Act" means the Agricultural Holdings Act, 1948, as amended;

"1951 Act" means the Reserve and Auxiliary Forces (Protection of Civil Interests) Act, 1951, as amended;

"chairman" means the chairman of an Agricultural Land Tribunal established under section 73 of the Agriculture Act, 1947, for the area in which the holding which is the subject of a notice to quit or of proceedings to which these Regulations apply is wholly or in the greater part situate, or a person nominated under paragraph 16(1)(a) or appointed under paragraph 16A of the Ninth Schedule to that Act to act as chairman in that area, and "secretary" means the secretary of that tribunal.

[1024]

NOTES

Agricultural Holdings Act 1948: see now the Agricultural Holdings Act 1986.

Reserve and Auxiliary Forces (Protection of Civil Interests) Act 1951: see now the Agricultural Holdings Act 1986.

4   The Interpretation Act 1889, shall apply to the interpretation of these Regulations as it applies to the interpretation of an Act of Parliament.

[1025]

NOTES

Interpretation Act 1889: see now the Interpretation Act 1978.

5   Where the chairman is satisfied on an application by any person that—

(a)   a notice to quit has been given to a service man as mentioned in subsection (1) of section 21 of the 1951 Act,

(b)   the service man is serving abroad,

(c)   the applicant is a fit person to serve a counter-notice under subsection (1) of section 24 of the 1948 Act on the service man's behalf but is not duly authorised to do so, and

(d)   the application is made in good faith in the interests of the service man, the chairman may direct that the applicant be deemed to be duly authorised to serve the counter-notice on the service man's behalf.

[1026]

NOTES

Reserve and Auxiliary Forces (Protection of Civil Interests) Act 1951, s 21: see now the Agricultural Holdings Act 1986, Sch 5.

Agricultural Holdings Act 1948, s 24(1): see now the Agricultural Holdings Act 1986, s 26.

PART II
STATUTORY INSTRUMENTS

6 Where a counter-notice under subsection (1) of section 24 of the 1948 Act has been served—

(a) in a case where a notice to quit has been given to a service man as mentioned in subsection (1) of section 21 of the 1951 Act, or

(b) in a case where subsection (5) of the said section 21 applies in relation to a service man,

and it appears to the chairman that—

(i) it is necessary for any act or proceedings consequential upon the service of the counter-notice to be performed or conducted by the service man;

(ii) the service man is serving abroad, and

(iii) no person has been duly authorised to perform the act or conduct the proceedings on the service man's behalf,

the chairman may, whether on an application by any person or otherwise, direct that some fit person who is willing to perform the act or conduct the proceedings shall be deemed to be authorised for that purpose and to take all such steps as may be necessary or incidental thereto.

[1027]

NOTES
Agricultural Holdings Act 1948, s 24(1): see now the Agricultural Holdings Act 1986, s 26.
Reserve and Auxiliary Forces (Protection of Civil Interests) Act 1951, s 21: see now the Agricultural Holdings Act 1986, Sch 5.

7—(1) An application to the chairman for a direction under these Regulations shall be made in writing and delivered or sent to the secretary.

(2) The chairman may, for the purpose of deciding whether to give the direction, require the applicant to furnish such testimonial or other evidence in support of his application as the chairman may think fit.

[1028]

AGRICULTURE (MISCELLANEOUS TIME-LIMITS) REGULATIONS 1959

(SI 1959/171)

NOTES
Made: 29 January 1959.
Authority: Agricultural Holdings Act 1948, ss 7(1), (2), 30(2), 94(1) (see now the Agricultural Holdings Act 1986, ss 9(1), (3), 94, 96(1)).

1—(1) These regulations may be cited as the Agriculture (Miscellaneous Time-Limits) Regulations, 1959, and shall come into operation on the 4th day of February, 1959.

(2) ...

(3) In these regulations the expression "the Act" means the Agricultural Holdings Act, 1948.

(4) The Interpretation Act 1889 shall apply to the interpretation of these Regulations as it applies to the interpretation of an Act of Parliament.

[1029]

NOTES
Para (2): revokes the Agriculture (Miscellaneous Time-Limits) Regulations 1948, SI 1948/188.
Agricultural Holdings Act 1948: see now the Agricultural Holdings Act 1986.
Interpretation Act 1889: see now the Interpretation Act 1978.

2—(1) ...

(2) The time within which a landlord may, pursuant to sub-section (1) of section 7 of the Act, require that there shall be determined by arbitration and paid by the tenant the amount of

any compensation referred to in the said sub-section, shall be one month from the date on which there takes effect by virtue of section 5 or section 6 of the Act any transfer from the tenant to the landlord of liability for the maintenance or repair of any item of fixed equipment.

(3)   The time within which a tenant may, pursuant to sub-section (2) of section 7 of the Act, require that any claim in respect of a previous failure by the landlord to discharge a liability for the maintenance or repair of any item of fixed equipment shall be determined by arbitration, shall be one month from the date on which there takes effect by virtue of section 5 or section 6 of the Act any transfer from the landlord to the tenant of the said liability for the maintenance or repair of any item of fixed equipment.

[1030]

NOTES
Para (1): spent on the repeal of the Agricultural Holdings Act 1948, s 30.
Agricultural Holdings Act 1948, ss 5, 6, 7: see now the Agricultural Holdings Act 1986, ss 6, 7, 8, 9.

SMALLHOLDINGS (FULL-TIME EMPLOYMENT) REGULATIONS 1970

(SI 1970/1050)

NOTES
Made: 14 July 1970.
Authority: Agriculture Act 1970, ss 39(2), 63.

1   Citation and commencement

These regulations may be cited as the Smallholdings (Full-Time Employment) Regulations 1970, and shall come into operation on 1st August 1970.

[1031]

2   Interpretation

(1)   In these regulations, unless the context otherwise requires—
"the Act" means the Agriculture Act 1970;
"the appropriate Minister" means in relation to England, except Monmouthshire, the Minister of Agriculture, Fisheries and Food and, in relation to Wales, including Monmouthshire, the Minister of Agriculture Fisheries and Food and the Secretary of State for Wales acting jointly.

(2)   The Interpretation Act 1889 applies for the interpretation of these regulations as it applies for the interpretation of an Act of Parliament.

[1032]

NOTES
Interpretation Act 1889: see now the Interpretation Act 1978.
Ministry of Agriculture, Fisheries and Food: the Ministry of Agriculture, Fisheries and Food was dissolved by the Ministry of Agriculture, Fisheries and Food (Dissolution) Order 2002, SI 2002/794. Subject to specific provision to the contrary, the functions of the Minister were transferred to the Secretary of State, and the property, rights and liabilities of the Minister were transferred to the Secretary of State for Environment, Food and Rural Affairs. Functions of the Minister of Agriculture, Fisheries and Food, so far as exercisable in relation to Wales, are transferred to the National Assembly for Wales, by the National Assembly for Wales (Transfer of Functions) Order 1999, SI 1999/672, art 2, Sch 1.

3   Estimate of full-time employment capability

(1)   For the purposes of section 39(2) of the Act (which relates to a holding which shall be treated as falling within the upper limit for a small-holding) the number of men for whom a holding is capable when farmed under reasonably skilled management, of providing full-time employment shall be estimated by reference to the standard labour requirements of the holding in accordance with the Schedule to these regulations it being assumed that a system of husbandry suitable for the district is followed and that the greater part of the feeding stuffs required by any livestock kept on the holding is grown there.

(2)   A holding shall be treated as being capable of providing full-time employment for not more than two men (including the person to whom it is let) with or without additional part-time employment for another man if its standard labour requirements are less than 900 standard man-days in aggregate in a year on average.

[1033]

SCHEDULE

Regulation 3

In this Schedule—

"existing smallholding" means a holding which, being a holding held by a smallholdings authority for the purposes of smallholdings, is let as a small-holding at the time when the authority submit proposals, in which that holding is included, to the appropriate Minister under the provisions of section 40, section 42 or section 43 of the Act or, if the holding is not at that time let as a smallholding and is not being used for any purpose, is a holding which, when it was last let, was let as a smallholding; and

"proposed smallholding" means a holding which a smallholdings authority, in any proposals submitted by them to the appropriate Minister under the provisions of section 40, section 42 or section 43 of the Act propose to form by carrying out any such transaction as is mentioned in paragraph (a) or paragraph (c) of section 40.

1.   The standard labour requirements of an existing smallholding shall be expressed in standard man-days estimated, except as is otherwise provided in paragraphs 3 to 6 of this Schedule, by multiplying respectively the number of standard man-days set out in the table below in relation to any kind of crop or livestock therein mentioned by the total number of [hectares] (or other units to which the standard man-days are related in the table) of that kind of crop, or the average of the numbers of that kind of livestock, shown to the satisfaction of the appropriate Minister to be comprised in the agricultural operations carried on on the holding in the course of an average period of twelve months, adding together the results so obtained and increasing the total by 15 per cent.

2.   The standard labour requirements of a proposed smallholding shall be expressed in standard man-days estimated, except as is otherwise provided in paragraphs 5 and 6 of this Schedule, by multiplying respectively the number of standard man-days set out in the table below in relation to any kind of crop or livestock therein mentioned by the total number of [hectares] (or other units to which the standard man-days are related in the table) of that kind of crop, or the average of the numbers of that kind of livestock, which are shown to the satisfaction of the appropriate Minister to be capable of being comprised in the agricultural operations carried on on the holding, when it is farmed under reasonably skilled management, in the course of an average period of twelve months, adding together the results so obtained and increasing the total by 15 per cent.

3.   Where double cropping is practised on land forming part of an existing smallholding the area of both crops shall be included in the estimate.

4.   Agisted livestock shall be deemed to be on an existing smallholding while they are on land forming part of the holding and not otherwise.

5.   A cow of a dairy type which suckles calves shall be classified as a beef cow.

6.   Calves less than seven days old, unweaned piglets, and unweaned lambs shall not be included in the estimate.

[Table

Crops	Standard man-days (per hectare)
Wheat	4.9
Barley	4.9
Oats	7.4
Mixed corn	7.4

Rye for threshing	6.2
Potatoes, first early	37.1
main crop and second early	37.1
Beans for stockfeeding	7.4
Turnips, swedes and fodder beet for stockfeeding	22.2
Mangolds	27.2
Rape or cole for stockfeeding	2.5
Kale for stockfeeding	3.7
Cabbage, savoys and kohlrabi for stockfeeding	12.4
Mustard for seed, fodder or ploughing-in	7.4
Other crops for stockfeeding (inc vetches and tares but not lucerne and grasses)	7.4
Sugar beet	24.7
Hops	173
Orchards grown commercially	56.8
Orchards not grown commercially	2.5
Small fruit:	
Strawberries	173
Raspberries	197.7
Currants, black	98.8
Gooseberries	98.8
Other small fruit	148.3
All brassicas	49.4
Carrots, earlies	148.3
Carrots, main crop	24.7
Parsnips	61.8
Turnips and swedes	49.4
Beetroot (red beet)	74.1
Onions, salad	247.1
Onions, harvesting dry	61.8
Beans, broad	74.1
Beans, runner:	
bush	74.1
climbing	197.7
Beans, French	61.8
Peas, green for market	74.1
Peas, all others for processing	7.4
Celery	98.8
Lettuce, not under glass	74.1
Other vegetables and mixed areas	123.6
Hardy nursery stock	123.6
Bulbs	247.1
Other flowers not under glass	617.8
Crops under glass or sheds	3212.3
Other crops not for feeding to farm livestock	7.4

PART II
STATUTORY INSTRUMENTS

Bare fallow	1.2
Lucerne	3.1
Clover, sainfoin and temporary grasses	1.9
Permanent grass	1.2

Livestock	Standard man-days (per head per annum)
Dairy cows in milk or in calf and heifers in milk	10
Dairy heifers in calf	3.5
Beef cows in milk or in calf and heifers in milk	3
Bulls being used for service	6
All other cattle	2.5
Ewes	0.7
Rams	0.7
Wethers and other sheep 1 year old and over	0.2
Breeding sows and gilts	4
Boars	4
Other pigs over 2 months old	1
Poultry — Hens and pullets (other than growing pullets), geese and turkeys	0.1
— Fowls for breeding	0.2
— Ducks	0.2
— Broilers, growing pullets and other table fowl	0.1]

[1034]

NOTES

Paras 1, 2: words in square brackets substituted by the Smallholdings (Full-Time Employment) (Amendment) Regulations 1992, SI 1992/2816, regs 2, 3.
Table: substituted by SI 1992/2816, regs 2, 3.

AGRICULTURE (MAINTENANCE, REPAIR AND INSURANCE OF FIXED EQUIPMENT) REGULATIONS 1973

(SI 1973/1473)

NOTES

Made: 17 August 1973.
Authority: Agricultural Holdings Act 1948, s 6(1), as read with the Agriculture (Miscellaneous Provisions) Act 1972, s 15(2) (see now the Agricultural Holdings Act 1986, ss 7, 94).

1 Citation and commencement

These regulations may be cited as the Agriculture (Maintenance, Repair and Insurance of Fixed Equipment) Regulations 1973, and shall come into operation on 29th September 1974.

[1035]

2 Interpretation

The Interpretation Act 1889 shall apply for the interpretation of these regulations as it applies for the interpretation of an Act of Parliament and as if these regulations and the regulations hereby revoked were Acts of Parliament.

[1036]

3 Incorporation of provisions in tenancy agreements

The provisions set forth in the Schedule hereto relating to the maintenance, repair and insurance of fixed equipment shall be deemed to be incorporated in every contract of tenancy of an agricultural holding, whether made before or after the commencement of the Agricultural Holdings Act 1948, except in so far as they would impose on one of the parties to an agreement in writing a liability which under the agreement is imposed on the other:

Provided that where the interest of the landlord is held for the purposes of a Government department, or where a person representing Her Majesty or the Duke of Cornwall under section 87 of the Agricultural Holdings Act 1948 is deemed to be the landlord, or where the landlord has made provision approved by the Minister for defraying the cost of any such works of repair or replacement as are referred to in sub-paragraph (1)(b) of paragraph 2 of the Schedule hereto, the provision of sub-paragraph (1)(a) of the said paragraph 2 requiring the landlord to insure against loss or damage by fire shall not apply.

[1037]

4 (*Revokes the Agriculture* (*Maintenance, Repair and Insurance of Fixed Equipment*) *Regulations 1948, SI 1948/184.*)

SCHEDULE
MAINTENANCE, REPAIR AND INSURANCE OF THE FIXED EQUIPMENT OF
A HOLDING

Regulation 3

PART I

Rights and liabilities of the landlord

1.—(1) To execute all repairs and replacements to the under-mentioned parts of the farmhouse, cottages and farm buildings, namely:—roofs, including chimney stacks, chimney pots, eaves-guttering and downpipes, main walls and exterior walls, howsoever constructed, including walls and fences of open and covered yards and garden walls, together with any interior repair or decoration made necessary as a result of structural defect to such roofs or walls, floors, floor joists, ceiling joists and timbers, exterior and interior staircases and fixed ladders (including banisters or handrails) of the farmhouse and cottages, and doors, windows and skylights, including the frames of such doors, windows and skylights (but excepting glass or glass substitute, sashcords, locks and fastenings): provided that in the case of repairs and replacements to floor-boards, interior staircases and fixed ladders (including banisters or handrails), doors and windows and opening skylights (including frames), eaves-guttering and downpipes, the landlord may recover one-half of the reasonable cost thereof from the tenant.

(2) To execute all repairs and replacements to underground water supply pipes, wells, bore-holes and reservoirs and all underground installations connected therewith, and to sewage disposal systems, including septic tanks, filtering media and cesspools (but excluding covers and tops).

(3) Except as provided by paragraph 8, to replace anything mentioned in paragraph 5(1) which has worn out or otherwise become incapable of further repair unless the tenant is himself liable to replace it under paragraph 6.

2.—(1)
    (a)   To keep the farmhouse, cottages and farm buildings insured to their full value against loss or damage by fire; and
    (b)   as often as the farmhouse, cottages and farm buildings or any, or any part, of them shall be destroyed or damaged by fire, to execute all works of repair or

replacement thereto necessary to make good damage by fire and to cause all money received in respect of such destruction or damage by virtue of such insurance to be laid out in the execution of such works.

(2)   The proviso to paragraph 1(1) shall not apply to works falling within sub-paragraph (1)(b) of this paragraph.

3.—(1)   As often as may be necessary in order to prevent deterioration, and in any case at intervals of not more than five years, properly to paint with at least two coats of a suitable quality or properly and adequately to gas-tar, creosote or otherwise effectively treat with a preservative material all outside wood and ironwork of the farmhouse, cottages and farm buildings, the inside wood and ironwork of all external outward opening doors and windows of farm buildings (but not of the farmhouse or cottages), and the interior structural steelwork of open-sided farm buildings which have been previously painted, gas-tarred, creosoted or otherwise treated with preservative material or which it is necessary in order to prevent deterioration of the same so to paint, gas-tar, creosote or treat with preservative material: provided that in respect of doors, windows, eaves-guttering and downpipes the landlord may recover one-half of the reasonable cost of such work from the tenant, but if any such work to any of those items is completed before the commencement of the fifth year of the tenancy the sum which the landlord may so recover from the tenant shall be restricted to an amount equal to the aggregate of one-tenth part of such reasonable cost in respect of each year that has elapsed between the commencement of the tenancy and the completion of such work.

(2)   In the last foregoing sub-paragraph "open-sided" means having the whole or the greater part of at least one side or end permanently open, apart from roof supports, if any.

4.—(1)   The landlord shall be under no liability—
   (a)   to execute repairs or replacements or to insure buildings or fixtures which are the property of the tenant, or
   (b)   subject to paragraph 2(1)(b), to execute repairs or replacements rendered necessary by the wilful act or the negligence of the tenant or any members of his household or his employees.

(2)   If the tenant does not start work on the repairs or replacements for which he is liable under paragraphs 5, 6, 7 and 8 within two months, or if he fails to complete them within three months of receiving from the landlord a written notice (not being a notice to remedy breach of tenancy agreement by doing work of repair, maintenance or replacement in a form prescribed under section 19(1) and (3) of the Agriculture (Miscellaneous Provisions) Act 1963) specifying the necessary repairs or replacements and calling on him to execute them the landlord may enter and execute such repairs or replacements and recover the reasonable cost from the tenant forthwith.

(3)
   (a)   If the tenant wishes to contest his liability to execute any repairs or replacements specified in a notice served upon him by the landlord under the last foregoing sub-paragraph he shall within one month serve a counter-notice in writing upon the landlord specifying the grounds on which and the items of repair or replacement in respect of which he denies liability and requiring the question of liability in respect thereof to be determined by arbitration under the Act.
   (b)   Upon service of the counter-notice on the landlord, the operation of the notice (including the running of time thereunder) shall be suspended, in so far as it relates to the items specified in the counter-notice, until the termination of an arbitration determining the question of liability in respect of those items.
   (c)   In this sub-paragraph, "termination", in relation to an arbitration, means the date on which the arbitrator's award is delivered to the tenant.

[1038]

NOTES

Agriculture (Miscellaneous Provisions) Act 1963: see now the Agricultural Holdings Act 1986.

PART II

Rights and liabilities of the tenant

Except in so far as such liabilities fall to be undertaken by the landlord under Part I hereof:

5.—(1)   To repair and to keep and leave clean and in good tenantable repair, order and condition the farmhouse, cottages and farm buildings together with all fixtures and fittings, boilers, ranges and grates, drains, sewers, gulleys, grease-traps, manholes and inspection chambers, electrical supply systems and fittings, water supply systems and fittings in so far as they are situated above ground, including pipes, tanks, cisterns, sanitary fittings, drinking troughs and pumping equipment, hydraulic rams (whether situated above or below ground), fences, hedges, field walls, stiles, gates and posts, cattle grids, bridges, culverts, ponds, watercourses, sluices, ditches, roads and yards in and upon the holding, or which during the tenancy may be erected or provided thereon.

(2)   To repair or replace all removable covers to manholes, to inspection chambers and to sewage disposal systems.

(3)   To keep clean and in good working order all roof valleys, eaves-guttering and downpipes, wells, septic tanks, cesspools and sewage disposal systems.

(4)   To use carefully so as to protect from wilful, reckless or negligent damage all items for the repair or replacement of which the landlord is responsible under paragraph 1; and also to report in writing immediately to the landlord any damage, however caused, to items for the repair or replacement of which the landlord is responsible.

6.   Subject to paragraph 2(1)(b)—

(1)   to replace or repair and, upon replacement or repair, adequately to paint, gas-tar, creosote or otherwise treat with effective preservative material as may be proper, all items of fixed equipment, and to do any work, where such replacement, repair or work is rendered necessary by the wilful act or negligence of the tenant or any members of his household or his employees; and

(2)   to replace anything mentioned in paragraph 5(1) which has worn out or otherwise become incapable of repair if its condition has been brought about by or is substantially due to the tenant's failure to repair it.

7.   As often as may be necessary, and in any case at intervals of not more than seven years, properly to clean, colour, whiten, paper, paint, limewash or otherwise treat with materials of suitable quality the inside of the farmhouse, cottages and farm buildings, including the interior of outward opening doors and windows of the farmhouse and cottages, which have been previously so treated and in the last year of the tenancy to limewash the inside of all buildings which previously have been limewashed.

[8.—(1)   Notwithstanding the general liability of the landlord for repairs and replacements, to renew all broken or cracked tiles or slates and to replace all slipped tiles or slates from time to time as the damage occurs, but so that the cost shall not exceed £100 in any one year of the tenancy.

(2)   This paragraph shall not have effect so as to render a tenant liable for the cost of any renewals or replacement of tiles in excess of £25 which have been carried out by the landlord prior to 24th March 1988.]

9.   To cut, trim or lay a proper proportion of the hedges in each year of the tenancy so as to maintain them in good and sound condition.

10.   To dig out, scour and cleanse all ponds, watercourses, ditches and grips, as may be necessary to maintain them at sufficient width and depth, and to keep clear from obstruction all field drains and their outlets.

11.—(1)   If the last year of the tenancy is not a year in which such cleaning, colouring, whitening, papering, painting, limewashing or other treatment as is mentioned in paragraph 7 is due to be carried out, the tenant shall pay to the landlord at the end of such last year either the estimated reasonable cost thereof or a sum equal to the aggregate of one-seventh part of that cost in respect of each year that has elapsed since such last cleaning, colouring, whitening, papering, painting, limewashing or other treatment as aforesaid, was completed, whichever is the less.

(2)   If the last year of the tenancy is not a year in which the landlord is liable, under paragraph 3, to paint, gas-tar, creosote or otherwise treat the doors, windows, eaves-guttering and downpipes of buildings, the tenant shall pay to the landlord at the end of such last year either one-half of the estimated reasonable cost thereof or a sum equal to the aggregate of

one-tenth part of that cost in respect of each year that has elapsed since such last painting, gas-tarring, creosoting or other treatment as aforesaid, was completed, whichever is the less.

(3)   In the assessment of any compensation payable by the tenant on the termination of the tenancy in respect of dilapidation, any accrued liability under the two preceding sub-paragraphs shall be taken into account.

[12.—(1)   If thc landlord fails to execute repairs other than repairs to an underground waterpipe which are his liability within three months of receiving from the tenant a written notice specifying the necessary repairs and calling on him to execute them, the tenant may execute such repairs and, except to the extent to which under the terms of Part I hereof the tenant is liable to bear the cost, recover (subject to the landlord's right to require arbitration under sub-paragraph (5) below) the reasonable cost from the landlord forthwith.

(2)   If the landlord fails to execute any repairs which are his liability to an underground waterpipe within one week of receiving from the tenant a written notice specifying the necessary repairs and calling on him to execute them, the tenant may execute such repairs and, except to the extent to which under the terms of Part I hereof the tenant is liable to bear the cost, recover (subject to the landlord's right to require arbitration under sub-paragraph (5) below) the reasonable cost from the landlord upon the expiry of a period of one month from the execution of the repairs.

(3)   Subject to sub-paragraph (4) below, if the landlord fails to execute any replacements which are his liability within three months of receiving from the tenant a written notice specifying the necessary replacements and calling on him to execute them, the tenant may execute such replacements and, except to the extent to which under the terms of Part I hereof the tenant is liable to bear the cost, recover (subject to the landlord's rights to require arbitration under sub-paragraph (5) below) the reasonable cost from the landlord forthwith.

(4)   The tenant shall not be entitled to recover, in respect of the aggregate of the replacements executed by him after being specified in a notice given in pursuance of sub-paragraph (3) above, in any year of the tenancy any sum in excess of whichever of the following sums is hereinafter specified in relation to the replacements so executed, that is to say—

    (a)   in relation to replacements executed in any year of the tenancy terminating on or before 24th March 1988, a sum equal to the rent of the holding for that year or £500, whichever is the smaller, or

    (b)   in relation to replacements executed in any year of the tenancy terminating after 24th March 1988, a sum equal to the rent of the holding for that year or £2,000, whichever is the smaller.

(5)

    (a)   If the landlord wishes to contest his liability to execute any repairs or replacements specified in a notice served upon him by the tenant under sub-paragraph (1), (2) or (3) above he shall within one month of the service of that notice serve a counter-notice in writing upon the tenant specifying the grounds on which and the items of repair or replacement in respect of which he denies liability and requiring the question of liability in respect thereof to be determined by arbitration under the Act.

    (b)   Upon service of a counter-notice on the tenant which relates to a notice served on the landlord under sub-paragraph (1) or (3) above, the operation of the notice so served upon sub-paragraph (1) or (3) (including the running of time thereunder) shall be suspended, in so far as it relates to the items specified in the counter-notice, until the termination of an arbitration determining the question of liability in respect of those items.

    (c)   Upon service of a counter-notice on the tenant which relates to a notice served on the landlord under sub-paragraph (2) above, the tenant's right under that sub-paragraph to recover the reasonable cost of the repairs specified in the counter-notice shall not arise unless the question of liability to execute those repairs is first determined by arbitration in favour of the tenant, and shall thereupon arise from the termination of the arbitration.

    (d)   In this sub-paragraph "termination" in relation to an arbitration means the date on which the arbitrator's award is delivered to the landlord.]

[1039]

NOTES

Paras 8, 12: substituted by the Agriculture (Maintenance, Repair and Insurance of Fixed Equipment) (Amendment) Regulations 1988, SI 1988/281, reg 2.

PART III

General provisions

13.—(1)   If at any time and from time to time the landlord or the tenant shall be of opinion that any item of fixed equipment is, or before the same was damaged or destroyed by fire was, redundant to the farming of the holding, the landlord or the tenant may by giving two months' notice in writing to the other of them require that the question whether such item of fixed equipment is, or before such damage or destruction was, so redundant shall be determined, in default of agreement, by arbitration under the Act, and if the arbitrator shall award that the said item of fixed equipment is, or before such damage or destruction by fire was, redundant to the farming of the holding then, as from the date of such award, paragraph 14(1) shall apply to that item and both the landlord and the tenant shall be relieved from all liability in respect of any antecedent breach of any obligation to maintain, repair or replace the item of fixed equipment so awarded to be redundant and the landlord shall be entitled to demolish and remove such item of fixed equipment and to enter upon the holding for those purposes.

(2)   In any arbitration to which sub-paragraph (1) of this paragraph applies, no item of fixed equipment shall be determined to be, or to have been before damage or destruction by fire, as the case may be, redundant to the farming of the holding, unless the arbitrator shall be satisfied that the repair or replacement of such item is or, as the case may be, was, not reasonably required having regard to—

  (a)
      (i)   the landlord's responsibilities to manage the holding in accordance with the rules of good estate management; and
      (ii)   the period for which the holding may reasonably be expected to remain a separate holding; and
  (b)   the character and situation of the holding and the average requirements of a tenant reasonably skilled in husbandry.

14.   Nothing contained in Part I or Part II hereof shall create any liability on the part of either landlord or tenant:

(1)   to maintain, repair, replace or insure any item of fixed equipment which the landlord and the tenant agree in writing to be obsolete or redundant to the farming of the holding or which in the event of any dispute between them as to whether it is, or before the same was damaged or destroyed by fire was, redundant to the farming of the holding, shall be awarded to be so redundant by an arbitrator in an arbitration as mentioned in paragraph 13; or

(2)   to execute any work if and so far as the execution of such work is rendered impossible (except at prohibitive or unreasonable expense) by reason of subsidence of any land or the blocking of outfalls which are not under the control of either the landlord or the tenant.

15.   If any claim, question or difference shall arise between the landlord and the tenant under the foregoing provisions hereof, not being a matter which, otherwise than under the provisions of this paragraph, is required by or by virtue of the Act or section 19 of the Agriculture (Miscellaneous Provisions) Act 1963 (notice to remedy breach of tenancy agreement) or regulations or orders made thereunder or the foregoing provisions hereof to be determined by arbitration under the Act, such claim, question or difference shall be determined, in default of agreement, by arbitration under the Act.

Interpretation

16.—(1)   In this Schedule, unless the context otherwise requires, "the Act" means the Agricultural Holdings Act 1948 as amended by any other enactment.

(2)   Any reference in this Schedule to a numbered paragraph is a reference to the paragraph bearing that number in this Schedule.

[1040]

NOTES

Agriculture (Miscellaneous Provisions) Act 1963: see now the Agricultural Holdings Act 1986.
Agricultural Holdings Act 1948: see now the Agricultural Holdings Act 1986.

AGRICULTURE (MISCELLANEOUS PROVISIONS) ACT 1976 (APPLICATION OF PROVISIONS) REGULATIONS 1977

(SI 1977/1215)

NOTES
Made: 21 July 1977.
Authority: Agriculture (Miscellaneous Provisions) Act 1976, s 23(8) (see now the Agricultural Holdings Act 1986, ss 45(8), 94).

1 Citation, commencement and interpretation

(1) These Regulations may be cited as the Agriculture (Miscellaneous Provisions) Act 1976 (Application of Provisions) Regulations 1977 and shall come into operation on 23rd August 1977.

(2) In these Regulations "the Act" means the Agriculture (Miscellaneous Provisions) Act 1976.

(3) The Interpretation Act 1889 shall apply to the interpretation of these Regulations as it applies to the interpretation of an Act of Parliament.

[1041]

NOTES
Interpretation Act 1889: see now the Interpretation Act 1978.

2 Application of the Act in cases of death before succession

(1) Where a person entitled to a joint tenancy of an agricultural holding by virtue of a direction under section 20(9) of the Act dies before the relevant time (as defined in section 23(2) of the Act) without having become the tenant or a joint tenant of that holding, that direction shall from the date of his death cease to have effect in relation to that person if he is survived by any other person jointly entitled under the direction; but the direction shall continue to have effect (subject to the provisions of the Act) in relation to the other person or persons as if the dead person had not been named therein; and the provisions of Part II of the Act, so far as relevant, shall apply accordingly.

(2) Where—
   (a) a person entitled to a tenancy of an agricultural holding by virtue of a direction under section 20(5) or (6) of the Act; or
   (b) the sole survivor of two or more persons entitled to a joint tenancy of an agricultural holding by virtue of a direction under section 20(9) of the Act

dies before the relevant time (as defined in section 23(2) of the Act) without having become the tenant or joint tenant of that holding, the provisions of Part II of the Act, except section 23(8), shall apply in accordance with the provisions of the Schedule to these Regulations subject to the exceptions, additions and modifications set out therein.

(3) Where two or more persons who are jointly entitled to a tenancy of the holding by virtue of a direction under section 20(9) of the Act have died in circumstances rendering it uncertain which of them survived the other, such deaths shall for the purposes of these Regulations be presumed to have occurred in order of seniority, and accordingly the younger shall be deemed to have survived the elder.

[1042]

SCHEDULE
APPLICATION OF PART II OF THE ACT
Article 2

1. Sections 16 and 17 shall not apply.

2. Section 18 shall apply—
   (a) with the addition of the following subsection after subsection (1):—

   "(1A) In subsection (1) and in the definition of "the deceased" in sub-section (2), the expression "tenant" includes a person who is—

      (i)   entitled to a tenancy of an agricultural holding by virtue of a direction by the Tribunal under section 20(5) or (6) of this Act; or

    (ii)   the sole survivor of two or more persons entitled to a joint tenancy of an agricultural holding by virtue of such a direction under section 20(9) of this Act,

and who dies before the time at which, had he survived, he would have been deemed to have been granted and to have accepted that tenancy or joint tenancy";

(b)   with the addition in subsection (4) of the words "(except section 19A)" after the words "this Part of this Act";

(c)   as if the reference in subsection (4)(e) to subsection (1) included a reference to subsection (1A);

(d)   with the exception of subsection (5).

3.   Section 19 shall not apply, but instead the following section shall be added:—

"19A—   (1)   Where at the date of death of the deceased the holding is the subject of a relevant notice to quit, the operation of that notice shall, subject to subsection (2) below and notwithstanding any provision of this Act having effect prior to the death of the deceased, take effect at the date specified in the notice for the termination of the tenancy to which it relates:

Provided that where, in the case of a relevant notice to quit, there remains at the date of death of the deceased a period of less than twelve months before the date specified in the notice for the termination of the tenancy of the holding, the operation of the notice shall be postponed for a period of twelve months.

    (2)   A relevant notice to quit shall not have effect unless either—

(a)   no application to become the tenant of the holding is made under section 20 of this Act within the relevant period; or

(b)   one or more such applications having been made within that period, either—

    (i)   none of the applicants is determined by the Tribunal to be in their opinion a suitable person to become the tenant of the holding; or

   (ii)   the Tribunal consent under section 22 of this Act to the operation of the notice to quit.

    (3)   In this section "relevant notice to quit" means a notice to quit the holding falling within section 24(2)(g) of the 1948 Act.".

4.   Sections 20 and 21 shall apply.

5.   Section 22 shall apply as if the references to section 19 of the Act were references to section 19A.

6.   Section 23 shall apply:—

(a)   as if, in subsection (1), for the words "the date of death", there were substituted the words "the date when the original tenant died";

(b)   as if for subsection (2) there were substituted the following subsection:—

"(2A)   In this and the following section "the relevant time" means the end of the twelve months immediately following the end of the year of tenancy in which the deceased died.";

(c)   as if, in subsection (3), for the words "on the date of death the holding was held by the deceased" there were substituted the words "immediately before the death of the original tenant he held the holding";

(d)   as if the following subsection were added:—

"(9)   In this and the next following section "the original tenant" means the tenant of the holding to whose tenancy the deceased would have succeeded, had he survived, by virtue of the provisions of this Part of this Act.".

7.   Section 24 shall apply as if in subsection (5)(a) for the word "deceased's" there were substituted the words "the original tenant's".

[1043]

NOTES
1948 Act: Agricultural Holdings Act 1948.

AGRICULTURAL LAND TRIBUNALS (RULES) ORDER 1978

(SI 1978/259)

NOTES
Made: 27 February 1978.
Authority: Agriculture Act 1947, s 73(3), (4), the Agricultural Holdings Act 1948, s 50(3) and the Agriculture (Miscellaneous Provisions) Act 1954, s 6(4), (6) (in so far as was made under the 1948 Act, see now the Agricultural Holdings Act 1986, ss 67(5), (7), (4)).

1 Citation, commencement and interpretation

(1)   This Order may be cited as the Agricultural Land Tribunals (Rules) Order 1978 and shall come into operation on 7th April 1978.

(2)   The Interpretation Act 1889 shall apply to the interpretation of this Order as it applies to the interpretation of an Act of Parliament.

[1044]

NOTES
Interpretation Act 1889: see now the Interpretation Act 1978.

2 Rules of procedure

The Rules set out in Schedule 1 to this Order shall apply for the purposes of proceedings before Agricultural Land Tribunals other than proceedings arising from any application made under Part II of the Agriculture (Miscellaneous Provisions) Act 1976 [or under Schedule 2 to the Agricultural Holdings Act 1984].

[1045]

NOTES
Words in square brackets added by the Agricultural Land Tribunals (Succession to Agricultural Tenancies) Order 1984, SI 1984/1301, art 3.

3   (*Spent on the revocation of the Agricultural Land Tribunals (Succession to Agricultural Tenancies) Order 1976, SI 1976/2183 by the Agricultural Land Tribunals (Succession to Agricultural Tenancies) Order 1984, SI 1984/1301.*)

4 Revocation of orders

(1)   The Agricultural Land Tribunals and Notices to Quit Order 1959,
the Agricultural Land Tribunals (Amendment) Order 1959,
the Agricultural Land Tribunals (Amendment) Order 1961, and
the Agricultural Land Tribunals (Amendment) Order 1974
are hereby revoked except to such extent as may be necessary for the disposal of an application pending at the commencement of this Order.

(2)   The Agriculture (Procedure of Agricultural Land Tribunals) Order 1954 (which was revoked with a saving in 1959) shall continue to have effect for the purpose of references to an Agricultural Land Tribunal under section 86 of the Agriculture Act 1947.

[1046]

SCHEDULES

SCHEDULE 1
RULES OF PROCEDURE FOR AGRICULTURAL LAND TRIBUNALS
Article 2

PRELIMINARY

1 Citation and interpretation

(1)   These Rules may be cited as the Agricultural Land Tribunals Rules 1978.

(2)   In these Rules, unless the context otherwise requires—

"the 1948 Act" means the Agricultural Holdings Act 1948;

"the 1977 Act" means the Agricultural Holdings (Notices to Quit) Act 1977;

"chairman" means the chairman of the tribunal or a person nominated under paragraph 16(1)(a) or appointed under paragraph 16A of the Ninth Schedule to the Agriculture Act 1947 to act as chairman;

"drainage case" means proceedings on an application under section 40 or 41 of the Land Drainage Act 1976;

"secretary" means the secretary of the tribunal;

"tribunal" means the Agricultural Land Tribunal for the area in which the agricultural holding which is the subject of an application, or the greater part of that holding, is situate.

(3)　A form referred to by number means the form so numbered in the Appendix to these Rules, or a form substantially to the like effect, with such variations as the circumstances may require.

(4)　Any reference in these Rules to any rule or enactment shall, unless the context otherwise requires, be construed as a reference to that rule or enactment as amended, extended or applied by any other rule or enactment.

(5)　Expressions defined in or used for the purposes of the 1977 Act have the same meaning in these Rules.

FORM OF APPLICATION

2　Consent to operation of notice to quit

(1)　An application for the tribunal's consent to the operation of a notice to quit under section 2(1) of the 1977 Act which is made by the landlord before the giving of the said notice shall be made not more than twelve months and not less than three months before the commencement of the period at the expiration of which the notice to quit is intended to have effect.

(2)　An application for the tribunal's consent to the operation of a notice to quit under section 2(1) or 4(2) or (3) of the 1977 Act which is made by the landlord after service upon him by the tenant of a counter-notice shall be made within one month of the service of the counter-notice.

(3)　An application under this rule shall be made in form 1.

3　Postponement of operation of notice to quit

An application under Article 12(1) of the Agricultural Holdings (Arbitration on Notices) Order 1978 to postpone the termination of a tenancy shall, unless made at the hearing of the proceedings before the tribunal on an application under the 1977 Act, be made in form 2.

4　Certificate of bad husbandry (Case C)

An application under section 2(4) of the 1977 Act shall be made in form 3.

5　Variation or revocation of conditions

An application under section 3(5) of the 1977 Act shall be made in form 4.

6　Directions relating to fixed equipment

(1)　An application under section 4(1) of the Agriculture Act 1958 for a direction for the provision, alteration or repair of fixed equipment shall be made in form 5.

(2)　An application under section 4(4) of the Agriculture Act 1958 for the extension of the period specified in a direction under section 4(1) shall be made in writing and shall state the grounds of the application.

7　Approval of long-term improvements

(1)　An application under section 50(1) of the 1948 Act for the tribunal's approval of the carrying out of a long-term improvement shall be made in form 6.

(2)　The time within which a landlord may serve a notice under section 50(3) of the 1948 Act that he proposes himself to carry out an improvement shall be one month from the date on which he receives notice in writing of the tribunal's approval of the carrying out of the improvement.

PART II

STATUTORY INSTRUMENTS

(3)   An application under section 50(4)(b) of the 1948 Act for a determination that the landlord has failed to carry out an improvement within a reasonable time shall be made in form 7.

8   Treating agricultural holding as market garden

An application under section 68 of the 1948 Act for a direction that an agricultural holding shall be treated as a market garden shall be made in form 8.

9   Restrictions on burning of heather or grass

An application under section 21 of the Hill Farming Act 1946 for a direction shall be made in form 9.

10   Section 20(5) of the Mineral Workings Act 1951

(1)   An application under section 21(2)(b) of the Agriculture Act 1947 as it applies for the purposes of section 20(5) of the Mineral Workings Act 1951 for a determination that some person should be treated as owner of the land other than the person who would be so treated apart from the determination shall be made in form 10.

(2)   Any person who is specified in an application under paragraph (1) as being affected by the determination shall be a party to the proceedings on the application for the purposes of these Rules.

11   Applications under Land Drainage Act 1976

(1)   An application under section 40 or 41 of the Land Drainage Act 1976 for an order requiring the carrying out of work for putting a ditch in proper order or authorising the applicant to carry out drainage work on land shall be made in form 11.

(2)   Without prejudice to rule 12(1), on any application under section 40 of the Land Drainage Act 1976, the occupier of any land which may be entered in pursuance of the order shall be a party to the application.

(3)   Without prejudice to rule 12(1), on any application under section 41 of the Land Drainage Act 1976, the owner of any land on which it is proposed that any work should be carried out and the occupier of any land which may be entered in pursuance of the order shall be parties to the application.

(4)   Where, on the hearing of an application under section 40, the applicant states that he desires also to apply under section 41 for an order authorising him to carry out the same or substantially the same work as that referred to in his application, the tribunal may, if they think fit, deal with the application as if it had been made under section 41 as well as under section 40.

PARTIES ETC

12   Persons affected to be parties

(1)   Without prejudice to rule 10(2), any person against whom any relief is sought on an application under rules 2 to 11 (or on an application by the Crown under section 6 of the 1977 Act) shall be a party to the proceedings on that application.

(2)   Any authority having power to enforce the statutory requirement specified in an application under rule 6(1) shall be entitled to be heard on the proceedings on an application under that paragraph, and shall be treated as a party thereto except for the purposes of rule 15.

13   Sub-tenancies

(1)   Where an application is made to the tribunal in respect of an agricultural holding the whole or any part of which has been sublet, every landlord, tenant and sub-tenant of that holding shall be a party to the proceedings on that application.

(2)   Paragraph (1) shall not apply in a drainage case.

14   Joinder of parties

If it appears to the chairman or to the tribunal, whether on the application of a party or otherwise, that it is desirable to join any person as a party to the proceedings, the chairman or the tribunal, as the case may be, may order such person to be joined and may give such consequential directions as may be just, including directions as to the service of documents on any person so joined and as to the time within which he may reply to the application.

FORM OF REPLY

15 Reply

(1) Any party who intends to oppose the whole or any part of an application to the tribunal shall, within one month of a copy of the application being served on him under rule 17 (or, in a drainage case, within the time allowed by rule 21(5)), reply thereto in the form appended to the copy of the application served on him.

(2) Where no reply is received by the secretary within the time allowed by paragraph (1), the tribunal may decide to make an order in the terms of the application without a formal hearing.

(3) Paragraph (1) does not apply to an application under rule 5 or to an application by the Crown under section 6 of the 1977 Act, and paragraph (2) does not apply in a drainage case.

GENERAL PROVISIONS AS TO APPLICATIONS AND REPLIES

16 Application, reply and supporting documents

(1) Every application and reply shall be signed by the party making it or by some person authorised to do so on his behalf, and shall be delivered or sent in duplicate to the secretary.

(2) Every application shall be accompanied by two copies of a map of the land which is the subject of the application on a scale of 6" to one mile or 1/10,000 or larger.

(3) Where a party intends to give evidence about any land which is not shown on the map referred to in paragraph (2), his application or reply shall be accompanied by two copies of a map of that land on a scale of 6" to one mile or 1/10,000 or larger.

(4) Every application and reply shall be accompanied by two copies of any plan or other document which the party making the application or reply intends to adduce in support of his case.

(5) Where there are more than two parties to proceedings, the party making an application or reply, as the case may be, shall deliver or send to the secretary one additional copy thereof, and of any map, plan or other document accompanying the application or reply, for service on each additional party.

(6) The chairman may, on such terms as he thinks fit, dispense with any map, plan or other document required to be furnished by any party under this rule where it appears to him that the map, plan or other document, or a copy thereof, is already in the possession of the tribunal or of some other party to the proceedings, or that to require it to be furnished would be unreasonable on the ground of expense or otherwise.

(7) A request for the chairman's direction under this rule shall be made in writing and shall be delivered or sent to the secretary on or before the delivery of the application or reply of the party making the request.

17 Service of documents by secretary

On receiving from any party an application, reply or other document referred to in rule 16, the secretary shall forthwith serve one copy thereof on every other party to the proceedings.

18 Withdrawal of application or reply

(1) A party may withdraw his application or reply by giving notice in writing to the secretary at any time before the hearing and on receipt of such a notice the secretary shall forthwith notify all other parties.

(2) Where a reply is withdrawn the tribunal may, except in a drainage case, decide to make an order in the terms of the application without a formal hearing.

(3) If, on the withdrawal of an application or reply, it appears to the chairman that the case is a proper one for the award of costs under the power conferred by section 5 of the Agriculture (Miscellaneous Provisions) Act 1954, he shall cause the tribunal to be convened

for the purpose of determining whether costs should be awarded, and the secretary shall give to all parties not less than seven days' notice of the date, time and place appointed for that purpose.

PREPARATION FOR HEARING

19 Interlocutory applications

Unless the chairman otherwise orders, an application for directions on any matter which the chairman has power to determine under these Rules shall be made in writing stating the grounds of the application and shall be delivered or sent to the secretary together with a sufficient number of copies for service on the other party or parties.

20 Disclosure of documents

(1) A party shall furnish to the secretary on his request any document or other information which the tribunal may require and which it is in the power of that party to furnish, and shall afford to all other parties an opportunity to inspect such document or a copy of such document, and to take copies thereof.

(2) Nothing in paragraph (1) shall require the furnishing of any information which it would be contrary to the public interest to disclose.

21 Minister's report in drainage cases

(1) On receipt of an application in a drainage case, the tribunal shall call on the Minister of Agriculture, Fisheries and Food to provide a report on the matters to which the application relates, and for that purpose the tribunal may authorise any officer of the Minister to enter and inspect any land specified by the tribunal.

(2) A report made under paragraph (1) may recommend that no order or that an order in the terms set out in the report be made by the tribunal.

(3) On receipt of the report the secretary shall serve a copy thereof on every party.

(4) Within one month of a copy of the report being served on him the applicant shall serve a notice on the tribunal in form 12 stating whether or not he agrees with the facts stated and the recommendations made in the report; and rules 16(1) and (5) and 17 shall apply to the notice as if it were an application.

(5) The time within which a party is required by rule 15 to reply to the application shall, in a drainage case, run from the date of the service on him of the notice under paragraph (4).

(6) A report under this rule shall be prima facie evidence of the facts set out therein, but the maker of the report shall, unless the tribunal otherwise direct, attend any formal hearing of the application for the purpose of being examined and cross-examined on the contents of the report.

22 Summary determination in drainage cases

Where, in a drainage case,—
    (a)   the report received under rule 21—
        (i)   recommends that an order be made and
        (ii)   in the case of an application under section 40 of the Land Drainage Act 1976 names a party to the application as the person whom it recommends should be required to carry out any work; and
    (b)   the applicant has notified the tribunal of his acceptance of the recommendation, and
    (c)   every other party has either—
        (i)   notified the tribunal of his acceptance of the recommendation, or
        (ii)   failed to reply to the application within the time allowed by rule 21(5), or
        (iii)   withdrawn his reply,

the tribunal may decide to make an order on the application substantially in the terms of the recommendation without a formal hearing.

23 Notice of hearing

(1) As soon as practicable after receipt of the reply or, as the case may be, after the time for replying has expired, the chairman shall fix a date, time and place for the hearing of the application.

(2)   Where rule 15(1) does not apply, the chairman shall fix a date, time and place for the hearing as soon as practicable after receipt of the application.

(3)   The chairman may alter the date, time or place fixed for any hearing if it appears to him necessary or desirable to do so to avoid hardship to the parties or for other good cause.

(4)   The secretary shall send to every party notice in form 13 of the date, time and place of any hearing which, except with the consent of the parties, shall not be earlier than fourteen days after the date on which the notice is sent.

THE HEARING

24   Tribunal to sit in public

The tribunal shall sit in public unless it appears to them that there are exceptional reasons which make it desirable that the hearing or some part of it should take place in private:

Provided that where a hearing or part of a hearing takes place in private, a member of the Council on Tribunals in his capacity as such shall be entitled to attend.

25   Right of audience

Any party may appear and be heard in person or by counsel or solicitor or by a representative appointed in writing.

26   Procedure at hearing

(1)   At the hearing the party making the application shall begin and other parties shall be heard in such order as the tribunal may determine.

(2)   Subject to the provisions of these Rules and to any direction given by the chairman, the procedure at the hearing shall be such as the tribunal may direct.

(3)   The tribunal may adjourn the hearing from time to time if for any reason it appears to them necessary or desirable to do so.

27   Default of appearance

If a party fails to appear at the time fixed for the hearing, the tribunal, if they are satisfied that the party has been afforded an adequate opportunity of attending, may—
    (a)   where the party failing to appear is the applicant, dismiss the application, or
    (b)   in any other case, proceed to determine the application in the absence of that party.

EVIDENCE

28   Evidence

(1)   The tribunal may admit evidence notwithstanding that it would not be admissible in a court of law.

(2)   Evidence before the tribunal may be given—
    (a)   orally, on oath or on affirmation or otherwise,
    (b)   by affidavit, if the parties consent, or
    (c)   by means of written statements produced by the maker when giving evidence or, if the tribunal consent, by another witness.

(3)   At any stage of the proceedings the tribunal may, of their own motion or on the application of any party, order the personal attendance of a deponent or of the maker of any written statement for examination and cross-examination, or admit any map, plan or other document in evidence.

29   Witnesses

(1)   The tribunal shall give each party an opportunity to call witnesses and to cross-examine any witness called by or on behalf of any other party and to re-examine his own witnesses after cross-examination, and a party may, if he so desires, give evidence as a witness on his own behalf.

(2)   The tribunal may call a witness who may, after giving evidence, be cross-examined by any party.

PART II
STATUTORY INSTRUMENTS

(3)   The tribunal may require any witness to give evidence on oath or affirmation.

(4)   The provisions of the County Court Rules 1936 as to the issuing of witness summonses shall apply for the purposes of any proceedings before the tribunal as they apply for the purposes of an arbitration under the 1948 Act.

30   Inspection of land

(1)   The tribunal may enter on and inspect an agricultural holding owned or occupied by any party (whether the holding is the subject of the proceedings or not) and inspect any fixed or other equipment, produce or livestock thereon.

(2)   Notice of the tribunal's intention to inspect a holding shall be given by the secretary to all parties and to any other occupier of the holding and, unless given orally at the hearing, shall be given in writing at least twenty-four hours before the intended entry.

(3)   The parties, their representatives and expert witnesses and any other occupier of the holding may attend the inspection.

THE DECISION

31   Decision of the tribunal

(1)   The decision of the tribunal, which in the event of disagreement between the members shall be the decision of the majority, shall be given in writing, together with a statement of the tribunal's reasons for their decision.

(2)   The chairman may correct any clerical mistake in the written record of the tribunal's decision.

(3)   The secretary shall send to each party a copy of the tribunal's decision and reasons.

(4)   The secretary may supply a further copy of the tribunal's decision and reasons or any part thereof to any party who appears reasonably to require it.

(5)   A copy issued under paragraph (3) or (4) shall be certified by the secretary as a true copy and shall be prima facie evidence of the matters contained therein.

32   Variation of order in drainage cases

Any order made following a decision of the tribunal in a drainage case may be varied whether as to the time within which any work is to be carried out or otherwise and on an application to vary the order which shall be made in form 14 the chairman may give all such directions as may be just.

REFERENCE TO HIGH COURT

33   Request under section 6 of Agriculture (Miscellaneous Provisions) Act 1954

(1)   A request for the reference to the High Court of a question of law arising in the course of proceedings before the tribunal shall, unless made at the hearing, be made in writing to the secretary not later than fourteen days from the date on which a copy of the tribunal's decision was sent to the party making the request and shall be accompanied by as many copies of the request as there are other parties; and the secretary shall thereupon serve a copy of the request on every such party.

(2)   If the tribunal refuse the request, the secretary shall, not later than fourteen days from the date of his receipt of the request, notify all parties of the refusal; and if the party making the request, being aggrieved by the refusal, intends to apply for an order directing the tribunal to refer the question of law to the High Court, he shall, within seven days after receiving notice of the refusal, serve on the secretary notice in writing of the intended application accompanied by as many copies of the notice as there are other parties; and the secretary shall thereupon serve a copy of the notice on every such party.

(3)   A case stated on a question of law for the decision of the High Court shall set out the question of law and the facts found by the tribunal and shall be signed by the chairman and sent to the party who requested the reference within two months after the date of the request or, as the case may be, within two months after the making of an order by the High Court directing the reference.

34 Modification of tribunal's decision following High Court proceedings

(1)   The powers of the tribunal under section 6(5) of the Agriculture (Miscellaneous Provisions) Act 1954 may be exercised by the chairman in any case where he does not consider it necessary to convene the tribunal for that purpose; but if it appears to the chairman that there should be a further hearing before the tribunal, he shall fix a date, time and place for the hearing.

(2)   Where a further hearing consequent on the reference to the High Court cannot conveniently take place before the tribunal as originally constituted, the chairman shall cause a fresh tribunal to be constituted for that purpose.

SUPPLEMENTAL

35   Mode of service

(1)   Every application, reply or other document required or authorised by these Rules to be served on any person shall be deemed to have been duly served if it is delivered to him or left at his proper address, or sent to him by post in a registered letter or by recorded delivery.

(2)   Any such document required or authorised to be given to, or served on, an incorporated company or body shall be duly given or served if given to or served on the secretary or clerk of the company or body.

(3)   The proper address of any person to or on whom any such document is to be given or served shall, in the case of a secretary or clerk of any incorporated company or body, be that of the registered or principal office of the company or body and, in any other case, be the last known address of the person in question.

(4)   Where any such document is to be given to, or served on, any person as being the owner of land and the land belongs to an ecclesiastical benefice, a copy thereof shall be served on the Church Commissioners.

36   Substituted service

If any person on whom any document is required to be served for the purpose of these Rules cannot be found, or has died and has no known personal representative, or is out of the United Kingdom, or if for any other reason service on him cannot be readily effected, the chairman may dispense with service on such person or may make an order for substituted service on such other person or in such other form (whether by advertisement in a newspaper or otherwise) as the chairman may think fit.

37   Extension of time

The time appointed by or under these Rules for doing any act or taking any step in connection with any proceedings may be extended by the chairman on such terms and conditions, if any, as appear to him just.

38   Failure to comply with rules

Any failure on the part of any person to comply with the provisions of these Rules shall not render the proceedings, or anything done in pursuance thereof, invalid unless the chairman or the tribunal so direct.

[1047]

NOTES

Agricultural Holdings Act 1948: see now the Agricultural Holdings Act 1986.
Agricultural Holdings (Notices to Quit) Act 1977: see now the Agricultural Holdings Act 1986.
Land Drainage Act 1976, ss 40, 41: see now the Land Drainage Act 1991, ss 28–30.
Agriculture Act 1958, s 4(1), (4): see now the Agricultural Holdings Act 1986, s 11(1), (2), (7).
County Court Rules 1936: the 1936 Rules were revoked and replaced by the County Court Rules 1981, SI 1981/1687. The 1981 Rules were subsequently replaced by the Civil Procedure Rules 1998, SI 1998/3132, except to the extent that provision was made by practice direction for the 1981 Rules to continue to apply to proceedings issued before 26 April 1999. Note also that r 2.1(2) of the 1998 Rules (as amended) also provides that those Rules do not apply to the following kinds of proceedings: insolvency proceedings, non-contentious or common form probate proceedings, proceedings in the High Court when acting as a Prize Court, proceedings before the judge within the meaning of the Mental Health Act 1983, Pt VII, family proceedings, and election proceedings in the High Court. As to witness summonses generally, see now rr 34.2–34.6 of the 1998 Rules.

Minister of Agriculture, Fisheries and Food: the Ministry of Agriculture, Fisheries and Food was dissolved by the Ministry of Agriculture, Fisheries and Food (Dissolution) Order 2002, SI 2002/794. Subject to specific provision to the contrary, the functions of the Minister were transferred to the Secretary of State, and the property, rights and liabilities of the Minister were transferred to the Secretary of State for Environment, Food and Rural Affairs. Functions of the Minister of Agriculture, Fisheries and Food, so far as exercisable in relation to Wales, are transferred to the National Assembly for Wales, by the National Assembly for Wales (Transfer of Functions) Order 1999, SI 1999/672, art 2, Sch 1.

APPENDIX
rule 2(3)

FORM 1
Ref No
To be inserted by the Secretary.

Agricultural Land Tribunal

Application for Consent to Operation of Notice to Quit
To the Secretary of the Agricultural Land Tribunal
for the .... Area.

   1.   I, ... [*block capitals*]

of .... [*address*],

hereby apply under—

        *(a) Section 2(1),

        *(b) Section 4(2),

        *(c) Section 4(3),

of the Agricultural Holdings (Notices to Quit) Act 1977 for the consent of the Tribunal to the operation of a notice to quit which I *propose to give/have given to my tenant,

.... [*block capitals*]

of .... [*address*]

   2.

        *(a) I propose to serve the notice before the .... day of .... , 19   .

        *(b) The notice was served on the .... day of .... , 19 , and a counter-notice was served by the tenant on the .... day of .... 19 .

   3.   The holding in respect of which the notice *will be/has been given is known as .... and consists of:—

        (a) ... . hectares of arable land (including temporary grass)

        (Ordnance Survey Field Nos ....);

        (b) ... . hectares of permanent pasture

        (Ordnance Survey Field Nos ....);

        (c) ... . hectares of rough grazing

        (Ordnance Survey Field Nos ....);

        (d) ... . hectares of other land (including orchards)

        (Ordnance Survey Field Nos ....);

Total .... hectares.   ANNUAL RENT £

   4.   The holding includes the following buildings [*give a general description*]:—

   †5.   I apply for the Tribunal's consent to the operation of the notice to quit on the following ground(s) provided in paragraph(s) .... of section 3(3) of the Agricultural Holdings (Notices to Quit) Act 1977[1]. [*This paragraph is relevant to an application under section 2(1) of the Act, in which case it is important to refer to footnote (1). In other cases the paragraph should be struck out.*]

6.   The main facts on which I will base my case are (*give a brief outline*):—[2]

7.   If I obtain possession of the land I intend:—

   *(a) to farm it myself;

   *(b) to let it to another tenant (*state name and address if known*).

8.   I/The future tenant*[3] at present farm(s) other land consisting of:—

   (a)   .... hectares of arable land (including temporary grass)

   (Ordnance Survey Field Nos ....);

   (b)   ... . hectares of permanent pasture

   (Ordnance Survey Field Nos ....);

   (c)   .... hectares of rough grazing

   (Ordnance Survey Field Nos ....);

   (d)   ... . hectares of other land (including orchards)

   (Ordnance Survey Field Nos ....);

Total .... hectares.

9.   I attach the following documents which I intend to produce in support of my case:—

   (a)   two[4] copies of a 6" to one mile or 1/10,000[5] map of the holding described in paragraph 3 above (and of the other land referred to in paragraph 8)†[6];

   (b)   two[4] copies of[7]:—

Date .... Signed[8] ....
*Strike out whichever is inapplicable.
†Strike out if inapplicable.

PART II
STATUTORY INSTRUMENTS

---

[1]   The applicant must state on which paragraph or paragraphs of the subsection he intends to rely. The five paragraphs, as amended, are as follows:
   (a)   that the carrying out of the purpose for which the landlord proposes to terminate the tenancy is desirable in the interests of good husbandry as respects the land to which the notice relates, treated as a separate unit; or
   (b)   that the carrying out thereof is desirable in the interests of sound management of the estate of which the land to which the notice relates forms part or which that land constitutes (*see footnote 6 below*); or
   (c)   that the carrying out thereof is desirable for the purposes of agricultural research, education, experiment or demonstration, or for the purposes of the enactments relating to small-holdings or allotments; or
   (d)   that greater hardship would be caused by withholding than by giving consent to the operation of the notice; or
   (e)   that the landlord proposes to terminate the tenancy for the purpose of the land's being used for a use, other than for agriculture, not falling within Case B (i e in section 2(3) of the Agricultural Holdings (Notices to Quit) Act 1977).
[2]   Where the tenant is a serviceman within the meaning of section 11 of the Agricultural Holdings (Notices to Quit) Act 1977, and the notice to quit is given for one or more of the reasons specified in Case B, D or E, the reasons for the giving of the notice must be stated and, if any question arising out of them has been determined by arbitration, the determination should also be stated.
[3]   Paragraph 8 need not be completed if the name of the future tenant is unknown. Where land is described, a map should be provided (*footnote 6 below*).
[4]   Two copies of the application and of any map and document must be sent to the Secretary, and if there are more than two parties (e g if the holding or part of it is sublet), an additional copy of the application, etc, must be supplied for, and the Secretary must be informed of the name and address of, each additional party.
[5]   A larger scale map may be used if preferred. Ordnance Survey Field Numbers must be marked on the map.
[6]   Where it is intended to give evidence about any land other than that which is the subject of the notice to quit, it must be shown either on the map produced or on a separate map of a scale of 6" to one mile or 1/10,000 or larger.
[7]   Mention any other document which is attached to this application.
[8]   If signed by any person other than the applicant himself, he should state in what capacity or by what authority he signs.

[1048]

FORM 1R

Ref No

To be inserted by the Secretary.

Agricultural Land Tribunal

Reply to Application for Consent to Operation of Notice to Quit

To the Secretary of the Agricultural Land Tribunal

for the .... Area.

I, ... [*block capitals*]

of .... [*address*],

tenant[1] of .. .. [*name or description of holding*],

having received a copy of the application (bearing the above reference number) for the Tribunal's consent to the operation of a notice to quit, reply as follows:

1. The facts stated in the first four paragraphs of the application are correct except that:—

2. In addition to the land which is the subject of the application, I farm the following land[2]:—

which includes the following buildings (*give a general description*):—

3. My main reasons for resisting the application are:—

4. My landlord is not acting fairly and reasonably because[3]:—

5. I attach copies of the following relevant documents[4]:—

Date .... Signed[5] ....

---

[1]
- (a) If this form is completed by a sub-tenant, he should state whether he is sub-tenant of the whole or part of the holding; if of part, he should describe the part with reference to paragraphs 3 and 4 of the application and should state Ordnance Survey Field Numbers.
- (b) If this form is completed by a superior landlord, he should omit paragraph 2.

[2]
- (a) If you farm other land as part of the same unit with that which is the subject of the application, give a description, stating the area (in hectares) which is arable (including temporary grass), pasture (including rough grazing) and other land (including orchards) and giving the Ordnance Survey Field Numbers. If the land is farmed separately, give a general description, stating area, kind of farming and approximate distance from the holding in question.
- (b) If the other land is not shown on the map produced by the landlord, you should produce a map of it of a scale of 6" to one mile or 1/10,000 (or larger) and giving the Ordnance Survey Field Numbers. If the land is not farmed as part of the same unit, or for any other good reason, you may, before or at the time of sending your reply, apply to the Secretary of the Tribunal in writing for the Chairman to dispense with the map.

[3] The Tribunal will not give consent if, in all the circumstances, it appears to them that a fair and reasonable landlord would not insist on possession. If you have any special reasons for saying your landlord is acting unfairly or unreasonably which do not appear under paragraph 3, you should state them under paragraph 4.

[4]
- (a) Two copies of the reply and of any document which you wish to submit to the Tribunal must be sent to the Secretary, and, if there are more than two parties (eg, if holding or part of it is sublet), an additional copy of each must be supplied for each additional party.
- (b) If you disagree with any map or plan attached to the application, your reply should be accompanied by two copies of a 6" to one mile or 1/10,000 (or larger) map showing what you consider to be the true position and marking the Ordnance Survey Field Numbers.

[5] If signed by any person other than the tenant himself, he should state in what capacity or by what authority he signs.

[1049]

FORM 2

rule 3
Ref No
To be inserted by the Secretary.

Agricultural Land Tribunal

Application to Postpone Operation of Notice to Quit

To the Secretary of the Agricultural Land Tribunal
for the .... Area.

1.   I, ... [*block capitals*]

of .... [*address*],

hereby apply under Article 12(1) of the Agricultural Holdings (Arbitration on Notices) Order 1978 for the Tribunal to postpone the operation of the Notice to Quit served on me by my landlord:—

.... [*block capitals*]

of .... [*address*],

in respect of: .... [*name or description of holding*].

2.   The Tribunal consented on the .... day of .... , 19   , to the operation of the said notice on the application of my landlord bearing reference number ....

3.   If its operation is not postponed the Notice will expire on the .... day of 19   .

4.   My main reasons for this application are:—

5.   I attach two[1] copies of a 6" to one mile or 1/10,000[2] map of the land which was the subject of the notice to quit[3] and of the following documents which I intend to produce in support of my case:—

Date .... Signed[4] ....

---

[1]   Two copies of the application and any map or document must be sent to the Secretary, and if there are more than two parties (eg, if the land is held under a sub-tenancy) an additional copy of the application etc, must be supplied for, and the Secretary must be informed of the name and address of, each additional party. A written notice is required (by Article 12(2) of the 1978 Order referred to above) to be given at the same time to the landlord.

[2]   A larger scale map may be used if preferred. Ordnance Survey Field Numbers must be marked on the map.

[3]   The Chairman of the Tribunal has power in all cases to dispense with maps, etc. A request for a direction on this subject should be made in writing before or at the time of sending the application.

[4]   If signed by any person other than the applicant himself, he should state in what capacity or by what authority he signs.

[1050]

FORM 2R

Ref No
To be inserted by the Secretary.

Agricultural Land Tribunal

Reply to Application to Postpone Operation of Notice to Quit

To the Secretary of the Agricultural Land Tribunal
for the .... Area.

I, ... [*block capitals*]

of .... [*address*],

landlord of .... [*name or description of holding*],

having received a copy of the application (bearing the above reference number) for the Tribunal to postpone the operation of the notice to quit the above named holding, reply as follows:—

PART II
STATUTORY INSTRUMENTS

503

1. The facts stated in the first three paragraphs of the application are correct except that:—

2.

   *(a) I request that there should be no postponement.

   *(b) I would agree to postponement up to the .... day of .... ,
   19 .

3. My main reasons for resisting the application are:—

4. I attach copies of the following relevant documents[1]:—

Date .... Signed[2] ....

*Strike out whichever is inapplicable.

---

[1]

   (a) Two copies of the reply and of any document which you wish to submit to the Tribunal must be sent to the Secretary, and, if there are more than two parties (eg, if the land is sub-let), an additional copy of each must be supplied for each additional party.

   (b) If you disagree with any map or plan attached to the application, your reply should be accompanied by two copies of a 6" to one mile or 1/10,000 (or larger) map showing what you consider to be the true position and marking the Ordnance Survey Field Numbers.

[2] If signed by any person other than the landlord himself, he should state in what capacity or by what authority he signs.

[1051]

FORM 3

rule 4
Ref No
To be inserted by the Secretary.

Agricultural Land Tribunal

Application for Certificate of Bad Husbandry

To the Secretary of the Agricultural Land Tribunal
for the .... Area.

1. I, ... [*block capitals*]

of .... [*address*],

hereby apply under section 2(4) of the Agricultural Holdings (Notices to Quit) Act 1977 for a certificate that my tenant, ... [*block capitals*]

of .... [*address*]

is not fulfilling his responsibility to farm .... [*name or description of holding*]

in accordance with the rules of good husbandry.

2. The land consists of:—

   (a) ... . hectares of arable land (including temporary grass)

   (Ordnance Survey Field Nos ....);

   (b) ... . hectares of permanent pasture

   (Ordnance Survey Field Nos ....);

   (c) ... . hectares of rough grazing

   (Ordnance Survey Field Nos ....);

   (d) ... . hectares of other land (including orchards)

   (Ordnance Survey Field Nos ....);

Total .... hectares.

3. The holding includes the following buildings [*give a general description*]:—

4. If a certificate of bad husbandry is granted I propose to serve a notice to quit.

5. The main grounds on which I allege bad husbandry are:—

6. I attach the following documents which I intend to produce in support of my case:—

    (a) two[1] copies of a 6" to one mile or 1/10,000[2] map of the holding described in paragraph 3 above;

    (b) two[1] copies of[3]:—

Date .... Signed[4] ....

---

[1] Two copies of the application and of any map and document must be sent to the Secretary, and if there are more than two parties (eg, if the holding or part of it is sub-let), an additional copy of the application, etc, must be supplied for, and the Secretary must be informed of the name and address of, each additional party.

[2] A larger scale map may be used if preferred. Ordnance Survey Field Numbers must be marked on the map.

[3] Mention any other document which is attached to this application.

[4] If signed by any person other than the applicant himself, he should state in what capacity or by what authority he signs.

[1052]

FORM 3R

Ref No
To be inserted by the Secretary.

Agricultural Land Tribunal

Reply to Application for Certificate of Bad Husbandry

To the Secretary of the Agricultural Land Tribunal
for the .... Area.
I, ... [*block capitals*]
of .... [*address*],
tenant[1] of .... [*name or description of holding*],
having received a copy of the application (bearing the above reference number) for the Tribunal's certificate of bad husbandry, reply as follows:

1. The facts stated in the first three paragraphs of the application are correct except that:—

2. My main reasons for resisting the application are:—

3. I attach copies of the following relevant documents[2]

Date .... Signed[3] ....

---

[1] If this form is completed by a sub-tenant, he should state whether he is sub-tenant of the whole or part of the holding; if of part, he should describe the part with reference to paragraph 2 and 3 of the application and should state Ordnance Survey Field Numbers.

[2]

    (a) Two copies of the reply and of any document which you wish to submit to the Tribunal must be sent to the Secretary, and, if there are more than two parties (eg, if holding or part of it is sub-let), an additional copy of each must be supplied for each additional party.

    (b) If you disagree with any map or plan attached to the application, your reply should be accompanied by two copies of a 6" to one mile or 1/10,000 (or larger) map showing what you consider to be the true position and marking the Ordnance Survey Field Numbers.

[3] If signed by any person other than the tenant himself, he should state in what capacity or by what authority he signs.

[1053]

FORM 4

rule 5
Ref No
To be inserted by the Secretary.

Agricultural Land Tribunal

Application for Variation or Revocation of Condition Imposed by the Tribunal

To the Secretary of the Agricultural Land Tribunal
for the .... Area.

1.   I, ... [*block capitals*]

of .... [*address*],

hereby apply under section 3(5) of the Agricultural Holdings (Notices to Quit) Act 1977 for the Tribunal to vary or revoke the condition imposed by them under section 3(4) thereof on granting my application bearing the reference number ....

2.

    *(a) I wish the Tribunal to revoke the condition.

    *(b) I wish the Tribunal to revoke the condition; but if they are unwilling to do so, I request them to make the following variation:—

    *(c) I do not wish the Tribunal to revoke the condition, but only to make the following variation:—

3.   The main reasons for my application are:—

4.   I attach two[1] copies of a 6" to one mile or 1/10,000[2] map of the holding which was the subject of the notice to quit[3] and of the following documents which I intend to produce in support of my case[4]:—

Date .... Signed[5] ....
*Strike out whichever is inapplicable.

---

[1]   Two copies of the application and of any map and document must be sent to the Secretary.
[2]   A larger scale map may be used if preferred. Ordnance Survey Field Number must be marked on the map.
[3]   The Chairman of the Tribunal has power in all cases to dispense with maps, etc (eg, if they are already in the possession of the Tribunal). A request for a direction on this subject should be made in writing before or at the time of sending the application.
[4]   Mention any other document which is attached to the application.
[5]   If signed by any person other than the applicant himself, he should state in what capacity or by what authority he signs.

[1054]

FORM 5

rule 6(1)
Ref No
To be inserted by the Secretary.

Agricultural Land Tribunal

Application for Direction to Provide Fixed Equipment

To the Secretary of the Agricultural Land Tribunal
for the .... Area.

1.   I, ... [*block capitals*]

of .... [*address*],

tenant of .... [*name or description of holding*],

hereby apply under section 4 of the Agriculture Act 1958 for the Tribunal to direct my landlord .... [*block capitals*]

of .... [*address*]

to carry out the following work on the said holding:—

2.

   (a)   On the .... day of .... , 19   , I requested my landlord in writing to carry out the said work and he *refused on the .... day of .... , 19   /has had reasonable time to agree but has not done so.

   (b)   No term in my contract of tenancy or in any other agreement binds me or my landlord to carry out the said work.

   (c)   My landlord is not bound by any enactment to carry out the said work.

3.   The holding consists of:—

   (a)   ... . hectares of arable land (including temporary grass)

   (Ordnance Survey Field Nos ....);

   (b)   ... . hectares of permanent pasture

   (Ordnance Survey Field Nos ....);

   (c)   ... . hectares of rough grazing

   (Ordnance Survey Field Nos ....);

   (d)   ... . hectares of other land (including orchards)

   (Ordnance Survey Field Nos ....);

Total .... hectares.

4.   The holding includes the following buildings:—

5.   The type of farming carried on the holding is[1]:—

6.   I wish to carry on the following agricultural activity on the said holding to the extent and in the manner specified, viz:—

7.   If I were to do so without the said work being carried out, I should contravene the following statutory requirements in the following respects:—

8.   I attach the following documents which I intend to produce in support of my case:—

   (a)   two[2] copies of a 6" to one mile or 1/10,000[3] map of the holding described in paragraph 3 above,

   (b)   two[2] copies of the following plan:—

   (c)   two[2] copies of my contract of tenancy and any other document[4]:—

Date .... Signed[5] ....

*Strike out whichever is inapplicable.

---

[1]   Under section 4(1) of the Agriculture Act 1958 the Tribunal cannot direct a landlord to carry out work in connection with an agricultural activity specified in the tenant's application where the activity has not been carried on on the holding for a period of at least three years immediately preceding the making of the application unless they are satisfied that the starting of the activity did not or, where it has not yet been started, will not constitute or form part of a substantial alteration of the type of farming carried on on the holding.

[2]   Two copies of the application and of any map and document must be sent to the Secretary, and if there are more than two parties (eg, if the land is held under a sub-tenancy), an additional copy of the contract of tenancy and of the application, etc, must be supplied for, and the Secretary must be informed of the name and address of, each additional party.

[3]   A larger scale map may be used if preferred. Ordnance Survey Field Numbers must be marked on the map.

[4]   Mention any other document which is attached to this application. The Chairman of the Tribunal has power in all cases to dispense with maps or other documents (eg, where the landlord already has a copy of the contract of tenancy). A request for a direction on this subject should be made in writing before or at the time of sending the application.

[5]   If signed by any person other than the applicant himself, he should state in what capacity or by what authority he signs.

[1055]

FORM 5R

Ref No
To be inserted by the Secretary.

Agricultural Land Tribunal

Reply to Application for Direction to Provide Fixed Equipment

To the Secretary of the Agricultural Land Tribunal
for the .... Area.
I, ... [*block capitals*]
of .... [*address*],
landlord[1] of .... [*name or description of holding*],
having received a copy of the application (bearing the above reference number) for the
Tribunal's direction to me to carry out certain work on the said holding, reply as follows:—

1. With regard to paragraph 2(a) of the application, I—

 *(a) agree that the request was made and refused;

 *(b) agree that the request was made, but

  *(i) deny that it was refused,

  *(ii) say that I have not yet had reasonable time to agree to it;

 *(c) deny that the request was made.

2. The other facts stated in the first four paragraphs of the application are correct, except that:—

3. My main reasons for resisting the application are:—

 *(a) that the carrying on of the activity specified in paragraph 6 of the application to the extent and in the manner specified therein—

  *(i) will not involve the contravention of any statutory requirement even if the said work is not carried out;

  *(ii) would be unreasonable having regard to the tenant's responsibilities to farm the holding in accordance with the rules of good husbandry;

 *(b) that the activity specified in paragraph 6 of the application has not been carried on on the holding for a period of at least three years immediately preceding the making of the application and that the starting of the activity *constitutes/forms part of a substantial alteration of the type of farming carried on on the holding;

 *(c) that the direction asked for would be unreasonable having regard to—

  *(i) my responsibilities to manage the land comprised in the holding in accordance with the rules of good estate management;

  *(ii) the period for which the holding may be expected to remain a separate holding;

  *(iii) [*any other reasons*].

4. I attach copies of the following relevant documents[2]:—
Date .... Signed[3] ....
*Strike out whichever is inapplicable.

---

[1] If this form is completed by a superior landlord he should omit paragraph 1.
[2]

 (a) Two copies of the reply and of any document which you wish to submit to the Tribunal must be sent to the Secretary, and, if there are more than two parties (eg, if the holding is sublet), an additional copy of each must be supplied for each additional party.
 (b) If you disagree with any map or plan attached to the application, your reply should be accompanied by two copies of a 6" to one mile or 1/10,000 (or larger) map showing what you consider to be the true position and marking the Ordnance Survey Field Numbers.
[3] If signed by any person other than the landlord himself, he should state in what capacity or by what authority he signs.

[1056]

FORM 6

rule 7(1)
Ref No
To be inserted by the Secretary.

Agricultural Land Tribunal

Application for Approval of Long-Term Improvement

To the Secretary of the Agricultural Land Tribunal
for the .... .Area.

1. I, ... [*block capitals*]

of .... [*address*],

tenant of .... [*name or description of holding*],

hereby apply for the Tribunal's approval under section 50 of the Agricultural Holdings Act 1948 (as amended by the Agriculture Act 1958) of the carrying out of the following improvement(s) on the said holding:—

2. My landlord is .... [*block capitals*]

of .... [*address*].

3. The holding consists of:—

 (a) ... . hectares of arable land (including temporary grass)

 (Ordnance Survey Field Nos ....);

 (b) ... . hectares of permanent pasture

 (Ordnance Survey Field Nos ....);

 (c) ... . hectares of rough grazing

 (Ordnance Survey Field Nos ....);

 (d) ... . hectares of other land (including orchards)

 (Ordnance Survey Field Nos ....);

Total .... hectares.

4. The holding includes the following buildings:— [*give a general description*]

5. I requested my landlord on the .... day of .... , 19.... , to consent in writing to the carrying out of the said improvement(s), but he—

 *(a) refuses to give his consent.

 *(b) will only consent subject to the following terms to which I am unwilling to agree:— [*state the terms and your reason for not agreeing*]

6. My main reasons for wishing for the improvements to be carried out are:—

7. I attach the following documents which I intend to produce in support of my case:—

 (a) two[1] copies of a 6" to one mile or 1/10,000[2] map of the holding described in paragraph 4 above;

 (b) two[1] copies of the following plan:—

 (c) two[1] copies of[3]:—

Date .... Signed[4] ....
*Strike out whichever is inapplicable.

---

[1] Two copies of the application and of any map and document must be sent to the Secretary, and if there are more than two parties (eg, if the holding is held under a sub-tenancy), an additional copy of the application, etc, must be supplied for, and the Secretary must be informed of the name and address of, each additional party.
[2] A larger scale map may be used if preferred. Ordnance Survey Field Numbers must be marked on the map.
[3] Mention any other document which is attached to this application.

⁴   If signed by any person other than the applicant himself, he should state in what capacity or by
      what authority he signs.

[1057]

FORM 6R

Ref No
To be inserted by the Secretary.

Agricultural Land Tribunal

Reply to Application for Approval of Long-Term Improvement

To the Secretary of the Agricultural Land Tribunal
for the .... Area.
I, ... [*block capitals*]
of .... [*address*],
landlord of .... [*name or description of holding*],
having received a copy of the application (bearing the above reference number) for the
Tribunal's approval under section 50 of the Agricultural Holdings Act 1948 (as amended) of
the carrying out on the said holding of the improvement(s) specified therein, reply as follows:

1.   The facts stated in the first four paragraphs of the application are correct except
      that:—

2.

      *(a) I deny that the request referred to in paragraph 5 of the application was
            made.

      *(b) I do not wish the improvements to be carried out because:—

      *(c) I agree the improvements being carried out subject to the following
            terms:— [*state terms and any special reasons*]

3.   My main reasons for resisting the application are:—

4.   I attach copies of the following relevant documents¹:—

Date .... Signed² ....
*Strike out whichever is inapplicable.

¹

      (a)   Two copies of the reply and of any document which you wish to submit to the Tribunal
             should be sent to the Secretary, and, if there are more than two parties (eg, if the holding
             is sublet), an additional copy of each must be supplied for each additional party.
      (b)   If you disagree with any map or plan attached to the application your reply should be
             accompanied by two copies of a 6" to one mile or 1/10,000 (or larger) map or plan
             showing what you consider to be the true position and marking the Ordnance Survey
             Field Numbers.
²   If signed by any person other than the landlord himself, he should state in what capacity or by
     what authority he signs.

[1058]

FORM 7

rule 7(3)
Ref No
To be inserted by the Secretary.

Agricultural Land Tribunal

Application for Determination that Landlord has Failed to carry out Improvement within a Reasonable Time

To the Secretary of the Agricultural Land Tribunal
for the .... Area.

1.   I, ... [*block
      capitals*]

      of .... [*address*],

      tenant of .... [*name or description of holding*], hereby apply to the Tribunal in pursuance of section 50(4)(b) of the Agricultural Holdings Act 1948 (as amended by the Agriculture Act 1958) to determine that my landlord:

.... [*block capitals*]

of .... [*address*]

has failed within a reasonable time to carry out the following improvements to the said holding:—

2. The said improvement was approved by the Tribunal on my application bearing reference number ....

3. The Tribunal's decision was dated .... day of .... , 19   , and my landlord notified me of his proposal to carry out the said improvement himself on the .... day of .... , 19   .

4. My landlord has failed to carry out the said improvements:— [*if he has done any part of them, give particulars*]

5. My main reasons for saying that the delay is unreasonable are:—

6. I attach two[1] copies each of—

    (a) a 6" to one mile or 1/10,000[2] map of the holding[3];

    (b) the following plan showing the intended improvement(s):—

    (c) the following other documents[4]:—

Date .... Signed[5] ....

---

[1]   Two copies of the application and of any map and document must be sent to the Secretary, and if there are more than two parties (eg, if the holding is held under a sub-tenancy), an additional copy of the application, etc, must be supplied for, and the Secretary must be informed of the name and address of, each additional party.

[2]   A larger scale map may be used if preferred. Ordnance Survey Field Numbers must be marked on the map.

[3]   The Chairman of the Tribunal has power in all cases to dispense with maps, etc (eg, if they are already in the possession of the Tribunal or the other parties). A request for a direction on this subject should be made in writing before or at the time of sending the application.

[4]   Mention any other documents which are attached to the application.

[5]   If signed by any person other than the applicant himself, he should state in what capacity or by what authority he signs.

[1059]

FORM 7R

Ref No
To be inserted by the Secretary.

Agricultural Land Tribunal

Reply to Application for Determination that Landlord has Failed to carry out Improvement within a Reasonable Time

To the Secretary of the Agricultural Land Tribunal
for the .... Area.
I, ... [*block capitals*]
of .... [*address*],
landlord of .... [*name or description of holding*],
having received a copy of the application (bearing the above reference number) for the Tribunal's determination that I have failed within a reasonable time to carry out on the said holding the improvement(s) specified therein, reply as follows:—

1. The facts stated in the first three paragraphs of the application are correct except that:—

2. My main reasons for resisting the application are:—

    *(a) I have adequately carried out the said improvement(s);

*(b) I intend to carry out the said improvement(s) but have not yet had reasonable time to do so for the following reasons:—
[*give particulars*]

*(c) [*any other reasons*]

3.   I attach copies of the following relevant documents[1]:—

Date .... Signed[2] ....

*Strike out whichever is inapplicable.

---

[1]

    (a)   Two copies of the reply and of any document which you wish to submit to the Tribunal must be sent to the Secretary, and, if there are more than two parties (eg, if the holding is sub-let) an additional copy of each must be supplied for each additional party.

    (b)   If you disagree with any map or plan attached to the application your reply should be accompanied by two copies of a 6" to one mile to 1/10,000 (or larger) map or plan showing what you consider to be the true position and marking the Ordnance Survey Field Numbers.

[2]   If signed by any person other than the landlord himself he should state in what capacity or by what authority he signs.

[1060]

FORM 8

rule 8
Ref No
To be inserted by the Secretary.

Agricultural Land Tribunal

Application for Direction to Treat an Agricultural Holding as a Market Garden

To the Secretary of the Agricultural Land Tribunal
for the .... Area.

1.   I, ... [*block capitals*]

of .... [*address*],

tenant of .... [*name or description of holding*],

hereby apply to the Tribunal to direct under section 68 of the Agricultural Holdings Act 1948 (as amended by the Agriculture Act 1958) that *the said holding/the part of the said holding specified in paragraph 6 below shall be treated as a market garden so that section 67 of the said Act shall apply.

2.   My landlord is .... [*block capitals*]

of .... [*address*].

3.   I requested him on the .... day of 19   , to agree in writing to the (part of the) holding being so treated, but he *refused on the .... day of .... 19.... /has had reasonable time but has failed to do so.

4.   The holding consists of:—

    (a)   .... hectares of arable land (including temporary grass)

    (Ordnance Survey Field Nos ....);

    (b)   .... hectares of permanent pasture

    (Ordnance Survey Field Nos ....);

    (c)   .... hectares of rough grazing

    (Ordnance Survey Field Nos ....);

    (d)   .... hectares of other land (including orchards)

    (Ordnance Survey Field Nos ....);

Total .... hectares.

5.   The holding includes the following buildings:— [*give a general description*]

6.   I wish to make the following improvements:—

Ordnance Survey Field Nos .... Improvements

7.   For the following main reasons I request the Tribunal to direct that the *holding/part of the holding described in paragraph 6 above be treated as a market garden:—

8.   I attach the following documents which I intend to produce in support of my case:—

      (a)   two[1] copies of a 6" to one mile or 1/10,000[2] map of the holding described in paragraph 4 above;

      (b)   two[1] copies of the following plan:—

      (c)   two[1] copies of[3]:—

Date .... Signed[4] ....

*Strike out whichever is inapplicable.

---

[1]   Two copies of the application and of any map and document must be sent to the Secretary, and if there are more than two parties (eg, if the holding is held under a sub-tenancy), an additional copy of the application, etc, must be supplied for, and the Secretary must be informed of the name and address of, each additional party.

[2]   A larger scale map may be used if preferred. Ordnance Survey Field Numbers must be marked on the map.

[3]   Mention any other document which is attached to this application.

[4]   If signed by any person other than the applicant himself, he should state in what capacity or by what authority he signs.

[1061]

FORM 8R

Ref No

To be inserted by the Secretary.

Agricultural Land Tribunal

Reply to Application for Direction to Treat an Agricultural Holding as a Market Garden

To the Secretary of the Agricultural Land Tribunal

for the .... Area.

I, ... [*block capitals*]

of .... [*address*],

landlord[1] of .... [*name or description of holding*],

having received a copy of the application (bearing the above reference number) for the Tribunal's direction under section 68 of the Agricultural Holdings Act 1948 (as amended) that the said holding or part thereof should be treated as a market garden in respect of the improvement(s) specified therein, reply as follows):—

1.   With regard to paragraph 3 of the application, I—

    *(a) agree that the request was made and refused;

    *(b) agree that the request was made, but say that

        *(i) I did agree to it in writing on the .... day of 19

        *(ii) I have not yet had reasonable time to agree to it;

    (c)   deny that the request was made.

2.   The other facts stated in the application are correct except that:—

3.   My main reasons for resisting the application are:—

    (a)   the land is unsuitable for market gardening for the following reasons:—

    (b)   [*any other reasons*]

4.

    (1)   If the Tribunal decide to give the direction applied for, I request them to limit its effect to the following improvement(s):—

(2)　My main reasons for this would be:—

5.　I attach copies of the following relevant documents[2]:—

Date .... Signed[3] ....

*Strike out whichever is inapplicable.

---

[1]　If this form is completed by a superior landlord, he should omit paragraph 1.

[2]

(a)　Two copies of the reply and of any document you wish to submit to the Tribunal must be sent to the Secretary, and, if there are more than two parties (eg, if the holding is sublet), an additional copy of each must be supplied for each additional party.

(b)　If you disagree with any map or plan attached to the application your reply should be accompanied by two copies of a 6" to one mile or 1/10,000 (or larger) map or plan showing what you consider to be the true position and marking the Ordnance Survey Field Numbers.

[3]　If signed by any person other than the landlord himself he should state in what capacity or by what authority he signs.

[1062]

FORM 9

rule 9
Ref No
To be inserted by the Secretary.

Agricultural Land Tribunal

Application for Direction to Avoid or Relax Covenant against the Burning of Heather or Grass

To the Secretary of the Agricultural Land Tribunal
for the .... Area.

1.　I, ... [*block capitals*]

of .... [*address*],

tenant of .... [*name or description of holding*],

hereby apply under section 21 of the Hill Farming Act 1946 (as amended by the Agriculture Act 1958) for the Tribunal's direction that the covenants, conditions or agreements contained in my lease and specified in paragraph 3 below be avoided or relaxed.

2.　My landlord is .... [*block capitals*]

of .... [*address*].

3.　The *covenant(s)/condition(s)/agreement(s) to which I refer is (are) numbered .... in my lease and I ask the Tribunal to direct that it (they) be—

　　*(a)　avoided completely;

　　*(b)　relaxed in the following way:—

　　　　*(i)　permanently;

　　　　*(ii)　for the following period:—

4.　The holding consists of:—

　　(a)　... ...... hectares of arable land (including temporary grass)

　　(Ordnance Survey Field Nos.................................);

　　(b)　... ...... hectares of permanent pasture

　　(Ordnance Survey Field Nos.................................);

　　(c)　... ...... hectares of rough grazing

　　(Ordnance Survey Field Nos.................................);

　　(d)　... ...... hectares of other land (including orchards)

　　(Ordnance Survey Field Nos.............................);

Total .... hectares.

5.   The *covenant(s)/condition(s)/agreement(s) mentioned in paragraph 3 above is (are) *impeding/preventing the proper use of the land for agricultural purposes in the following way:—

and I wish it (them) to be *avoided/relaxed so as to allow me to burn .... hectares of *heather/grass.

6.   I attach:—

(a)   two[1] copies of my lease[2];

(b)   two[1] copies of a 6" to one mile or 1/10,000[3] map of the land described in paragraph 4 above;

(c)   two[1] copies each of the following other documents[4]:—

Date .... Signed[5] ....
*Strike out whichever is inapplicable.

---

[1]   Two copies of the application and of any map and document must be sent to the Secretary, and if there are more than two parties (eg, if the land is held under a sub-tenancy), an additional copy of the application, etc, must be supplied for, and the Secretary must be informed of the name and address of, each additional party.

[2]   The Chairman of the Tribunal has power in all cases to dispense with maps or other documents (eg, where the landlord already has a copy of the lease). A request for a direction on this subject should be made in writing before or at the time of sending the application.

[3]   A larger scale map may be used if preferred. Ordnance Survey Field Numbers must be marked on the map.

[4]   Mention any other document which is attached to this application.

[5]   If signed by any person other than the applicant himself, he should state in what capacity or by what authority he signs.

[1063]

FORM 9R

Ref No
To be inserted by the Secretary.

Agricultural Land Tribunal

Reply to Application for Direction to Avoid or Relax Covenant against the Burning of Heather or Grass

To the Secretary of the Agricultural Land Tribunal

for the .... Area.

I, ... [*block capitals*]
of .... [*address*],
landlord of .... [*name or description of holding*],

having received a copy of the application (bearing the above reference number) for the Tribunal's direction that certain covenants, conditions or agreements in the applicant's lease should be avoided or relaxed, reply as follows:—

1.   The facts contained in the first four paragraphs of the application are correct except that:—

2.

*(a)   I do not wish any covenant, condition or agreement to be avoided or relaxed in any way.

*(b)   I would agree to the following *covenant(s)/condition(s)/agreement(s) being *avoided/relaxed as follows:—

3.   For the following main reasons I do not agree that the *covenant(s)/condition(s)/ agreement(s) is (are) impeding or preventing the proper use of the land for agricultural purposes or that (except as agreed in paragraph (2)(b) above) it would be expedient to relax or avoid it (them):—

4.   I attach copies of the following relevant documents[1]:—

Date .... Signed[2] ....
*Strike out whichever is inapplicable.

1

    (a)   Two copies of the reply and of any document which you wish to submit to the Tribunal must be sent to the Secretary, and, if there are more than two parties (eg, if the holding is sublet), an additional copy of each must be supplied for each additional party.

    (b)   If you disagree with any map or plan attached to the application, your reply should be accompanied by two copies of a 6" to one mile or 1/10,000 (or larger) map showing what you consider to be the true position and marking the Ordnance Survey Field Numbers.

2   If signed by any person other than the landlord himself, he should state in what capacity or by what authority he signs.

[1064]

FORM 10

rule 10(1)
Ref No
To be inserted by the Secretary.

Agricultural Land Tribunal

Application for Determination that a Person be Treated as Owner of Land

To the Secretary of the Agricultural Land Tribunal
for the .... Area.

1.   I, ... [*block capitals*]

of .... [*address*],

hereby apply to the Tribunal to determine under section 21 of the Agriculture Act 1947 that—

    *(a)   .... [*block capitals*]

of .... [*address*]

    *(b) I

be treated for the purposes of section 20 of the Mineral Workings Act 1951 as the owner of the land known as:— .... [*name or description*].

2.   My own interest in the land is:—

3.   The following person(s) would be affected by the granting of this application[1]:—

4.   The land consists of:—

    (a)   ... . hectares of arable land (including temporary grass)

    (Ordnance Survey Field Nos..................................);

    (b)   ... . hectares of permanent pasture

    (Ordnance Survey Field Nos..................................);

    (c)   ... . hectares of rough grazing

    (Ordnance Survey Field Nos..................................);

    (d)   ... . hectares of other land (including orchards)

    (Ordnance Survey Field Nos..............................);

Total .... hectares.

5.   The land includes the following buildings:— [*give a general description*]

6.   The Minister of Agriculture, Fisheries and Food proposes to make the following arrangements for the purpose of taking the following special steps (as referred to in the said section 20):— [*describe briefly*]

7.   My main reasons for this application are:—

8.   I attach the following documents which I intend to produce in support of my case:—

(a)   two[2] copies of a 6" to one mile or $1/10,000$[3] map of the land described in paragraph 4 above;

(b)   two[2] copies of[4]:—

Date .... Signed[5] ....
*Strike out whichever is inapplicable.

---

[1]   State name and address of any person mentioned and whether he is owner or occupier or what other interest he has in the land.
[2]   Two copies of the application and of any map and document must be sent to the Secretary, and if there is more than one party named in paragraph 3, an additional copy of the application, etc, must be supplied for each additional party.
[3]   A larger scale map may be used if preferred. Ordnance Survey Field Numbers must be marked on the map.
[4]   Mention any other document which is attached to the application.
[5]   If signed by any person other than the applicant himself, he should state in what capacity or by what authority he signs.

[1065]

NOTES

Minister of Agriculture, Fisheries and Food: the Ministry of Agriculture, Fisheries and Food was dissolved by the Ministry of Agriculture, Fisheries and Food (Dissolution) Order 2002, SI 2002/794. Subject to specific provision to the contrary, the functions of the Minister were transferred to the Secretary of State, and the property, rights and liabilities of the Minister were transferred to the Secretary of State for Environment, Food and Rural Affairs.

FORM 10R

Ref No
To be inserted by the Secretary.

Agricultural Land Tribunal

Reply to Application for Determination that a Person be Treated as Owner of Land

To the Secretary of the Agricultural Land Tribunal
for the .... Area.
I, ... [*block capitals*]
of .... [*address*],
having received a copy of the application (bearing the above reference number), reply as follows:—

1.   The facts stated in the first five paragraphs of the application are correct except that:—

2.   My main reasons for resisting the application are:

3.   I attach copies of the following relevant documents[1]—

Date .... Signed[2] ....

---

[1]

(a)   Two copies of the reply and of any document which you wish to submit to the Tribunal must be sent to the Secretary, and, if there are more than two parties, an additional copy of each must be supplied for each additional party.

(b)   If you disagree with any map or plan attached to the application, your reply should be accompanied by two copies of a 6" to one mile or $1/10,000$ (or larger) map showing what you consider to be the true position and marking the Ordnance Survey Field Numbers.

[2]   If signed by any person other than the party himself, he should state in what capacity or by what authority he signs.

[1066]

FORM 11

rule 11(1)
Ref No
To be inserted by the Secretary.

Agricultural Land Tribunal

Application Under Land Drainage Act 1976

To the Secretary of the Agricultural Land Tribunal
for the .... Area.

*1. I, ... [*block capitals*]

of .... [*address*],

hereby apply to the Tribunal for an order under section 40 of the Land Drainage
Act 1976 requiring .... [*state name(s) of
person(s) against whom order is sought*][1] to carry out the work mentioned in
paragraph 6 on the ground that [the land mentioned in paragraph 3, of which I am the
†owner/occupier, is being injured] [*or* the improvement of the drainage of the land
mentioned in paragraph 3, of which I am the †owner/occupier, is being prevented] by
the condition of the ditch mentioned in paragraph 4.

*   To be used for application under s 40.

†   Strike out whichever is inapplicable.

‡ [In the event of the Tribunal deciding not to make such an order I hereby apply in the
alternative under section 41 of the said Act for an order authorising me to carry out the
said work.]

‡   Strike out if inapplicable.

OR

*[1. I, ... [*block capitals*]

of .... [*address*],

hereby apply to the Tribunal under section 41 of the Land Drainage Act 1976 for an
order authorising me to carry out the work mentioned in paragraph 6 on the ground that
the drainage of the land mentioned in paragraph 3, of which I am the †owner/occupier,
requires the carrying out of such work.]

*   To be used for application under s 41.

†   Strike out whichever is inapplicable.

*[2. I ask that the said order should authorise me [*or* the person required to carry out
the said work] to enter on the land mentioned in paragraph 4 [and paragraph 7]
so far as may be necessary for the carrying out of the said work.]

*   To be used for application under s 40 or s 41: strike out if no such authority is
asked for.

3.   I am the *owner/occupier of [*describe the land affected by application and give
Ordnance Survey Field Numbers*].

*   Strike out whichever is inapplicable.

*4.   Injury to my said land is being caused [and/or the improvement of the drainage
of my said land is being prevented] by the condition of the under-mentioned
ditch [*specify ditch, stating land through which it passes and if possible the
Ordnance Survey Field Numbers of that land*].

*   To be used for application under s 40.

OR

*[4.   The drainage of my said land requires:—

†(a) the carrying out of work in connection with the under-mentioned ditch:

†(b) and/or the replacement or construction of the under-mentioned ditch:

†(c) and/or the alteration or removal of drainage work in connection with the under-mentioned ditch:

[*specify ditch, stating land through which it passes and if possible the Ordnance Survey Field Numbers of that land*] ....].

*   To be used for application under s 41.

†   Strike out whichever is inapplicable.

5.   The condition of the said ditch and its effect on my land is as follows [and/or the construction of the said ditch is required for the following reason]:

6.   The work which is required to be carried out is as follows:—

*[7.   For the purpose of carrying out the said work it will be necessary to enter the under-mentioned land in addition to that mentioned in paragraph 4 [*describe land, stating Ordnance Survey Field Numbers if possible*].   ]

*   Strike out if inapplicable.

8.   This application affects the interests of the following persons:[2]

(a)   .... [*block capitals*]

of .... [*address*]

who is the *owner/occupier of [the following part of] the land mentioned in paragraph 4 [*or* 7] of this application [*or as the case may be*][3]

(b)   .... [*block capitals*]

of .... [*address*]

who is the *owner/occupier of [the following part of] the land mentioned in paragraph 4 [*or* 7] of this application [*or as the case may be*].[3]

*   Strike out whichever is inapplicable.

*[9.   To the best of my information and belief the following persons in addition to those named in paragraph 8 have rights in or over the said ditch and the land through which it passes:

(a)   .... [*block capitals*]

of .... [*address*]

who is ....]

(b)   .... [*block capitals*]

of .... [*address*]

who is ....]

*   Strike out if inapplicable.

10.   I attach the following documents which I intend to produce in support of my case:—

(a)   two[4] copies of a 6" to one mile or 1/10,000[5] map of the land described in paragraphs 3 and 4 [and 7] above;

(b)   two[4] copies of[6]:—

Date .... Signed[7] ....

---

[1]   Section 40 enables an order to be made against the owner or occupier of land through which the ditch passes or which abuts on the ditch or against any person who, although not such an owner or occupier, has a right to carry out the work specified in the order.

[2]   State the names of all persons who are to be parties to the proceedings. These must include any person against whom an order is applied for under section 40 as well as the name of the occupier of any land on which entry may be necessary for carrying out work under section 40 or 41 and, in the case of an application under section 41, the name of the owner of any land on which it is proposed that any work should be carried out. If more than two persons are named, continue on separate sheet.

[3]   State whether owner or occupier of the land or persons having a right to carry out the proposed work on the ditch mentioned in paragraph 4.

 4 Two copies of the application and of any map and document must be sent to the Secretary, and if there are more than two parties, an additional copy of the application, etc, must be supplied for each additional party.

5 A larger scale map may be used if preferred. Ordnance Survey Field Numbers must be marked on the map where required.

6 Mention any other document which is attached to this application.

7 If signed by any person other than the applicant himself, he should state in what capacity or by what authority he signs.

[1067]

FORM 11R

Ref No
To be inserted by the Secretary.

Agricultural Land Tribunal

Reply to Application Under Land Drainage Act 1976

To the Secretary of the Agricultural Land Tribunal
for the .... Area.
I, ... [*block capitals*]
of .... [*address*],
having received a copy of the application (bearing the above reference number) and of the
report provided by the Minister of Agriculture, Fisheries and Food for the purpose thereof and
of the applicant's notice in Form 12 reply as follows:—

  1. The facts stated in the said application and in the said report are correct except that:—

  2.

    *(a) I agree to an order being made

      *(i) in the terms of the recommendation in the report; or

      *(ii) in the terms asked for in the application [*if different from those recommended in the report*]; or

      *(iii) in the terms stated in the applicant's notice.

    *(b) I resist the application

    *   Strike out whichever is inapplicable.

  3. *My main reasons for resisting the application are:—

  *   Strike out if inapplicable.

  4. I attach copies of the following relevant documents[1]:—
Date .... Signed[2] ....

1

  (a) Two copies of the reply and of any document which you wish to submit to the Tribunal must be sent to the Secretary, and, if there are more than two parties, an additional copy of each must be supplied for each additional party.

  (b) If you disagree with any map or plan attached to the application or if, in your reply, you mention any land not shown thereon, your reply should be accompanied by two copies of a 6" to one mile or 1/10,000 (or larger) map showing what you consider to be the true position or showing the other land mentioned in your reply, as the case may be, and marking the Ordnance Survey Field Numbers.

2 If signed by any person other than the party himself, he should state in what capacity or by what authority he signs.

[1068]

NOTES

Minister of Agriculture, Fisheries and Food: the Ministry of Agriculture, Fisheries and Food was dissolved by the Ministry of Agriculture, Fisheries and Food (Dissolution) Order 2002, SI 2002/794. Subject to specific provision to the contrary, the functions of the Minister were transferred to the Secretary of State, and the property, rights and liabilities of the Minister were transferred to the Secretary of State for Environment, Food and Rural Affairs.

FORM 12

rule 21(4)
Ref No
To be inserted by the Secretary.

Agricultural Land Tribunal

Land Drainage Act 1976 Notice by Applicant under Rule 21(4) of the Agricultural Land Tribunals Rules 1978

To the Secretary of the Agricultural Land Tribunal
for the .... Area.
I, ... [*block capitals*]
of .... [*address*],
having applied to the Tribunal on the   day of   19   (under reference number
..........................) for an order under section 40 [and/or section 41]* of the Land Drainage
Act 1976, and having received a copy of the report provided by the Minister of Agriculture,
Fisheries and Food for the purpose of my application, state as follows:
*Strike out whichever is inapplicable.

1.   I accept the facts stated in the report with the exception of:

2.

*(a)   I accept the recommendation made in the report and hereby request the Tribunal to make an order on my application in the terms of the recommendation.

*(b)   I do not accept the recommendation made in the report and I request the Tribunal to make an order on my application in the terms asked for therein [*or* in the following modified terms].

*   Strike out whichever is inapplicable.

3.   I attach the following documents which I intend to produce in support of my case:—[1]

Date .... Signed[2] ....

---

[1]   Two copies of this notice must be sent to the Secretary together with two copies of any map or document which you wish to submit to the Tribunal and which has not already been submitted with the application. If there are more than two parties, an additional copy of the notice, etc, must be supplied for each additional party.
[2]   If signed by any person other than the applicant himself, he should state in what capacity or by what authority he signs.

[1069]

NOTES
   Minister of Agriculture, Fisheries and Food: the Ministry of Agriculture, Fisheries and Food was dissolved by the Ministry of Agriculture, Fisheries and Food (Dissolution) Order 2002, SI 2002/794. Subject to specific provision to the contrary, the functions of the Minister were transferred to the Secretary of State, and the property, rights and liabilities of the Minister were transferred to the Secretary of State for Environment, Food and Rural Affairs.

FORM 13

rule 23(4)
Ref No
To be inserted by the Secretary.

Agricultural Land Tribunal

Notice of Hearing

Land at:
Applicant/s:
Respondent/s:
TAKE NOTICE that the HEARING of the APPLICATION in respect of the above named
Holding will be held on   at   commencing at
Dated .... 197........ Signed ....
(Secretary of the Tribunal)

NOTE TO PARTIES

You may find of assistance the following note of rules of evidence and procedure, which apply to this hearing and which are contained in the Agricultural Land Tribunals Rules 1978.

1. *Rules of Evidence*

   (a) Any evidence may be admitted by the tribunal, including evidence that would not be admissible in a court of law.

   (b) Evidence before the tribunal may be given—

       (i) orally, on oath or on affirmation or otherwise,

       (ii) by affidavit, if the parties consent, or

       (iii) by means of written statements produced by the maker when giving evidence or, if the tribunal consent, by another witness.

   If evidence is tendered in the form of a written statement, four copies of the statement should be available at the hearing for the tribunal and two copies for the other parties.

   (c) At any stage of the proceedings the tribunal may, of their own motion or on the application of any party, order the personal attendance of the maker of any written statement for examination and cross-examination.

   (d) The secretary may require a party to give to the tribunal documents or other information, and to afford to all other parties an opportunity to inspect such documents, or copies of them, and to take copies of them.

   If the parties intend to produce documents at the hearing, they should if possible agree them beforehand, list them in order and put them into one agreed bundle. Four copies of this bundle should be available if possible for the use of the tribunal.

   (e) The tribunal may, after giving notice to all parties and to any other occupier of the land, enter and inspect any agricultural holding owned or occupied by any party, whether the holding is the subject of the proceedings or not, and may inspect any fixed or other equipment, produce or livestock thereon.

2. *Procedure at the Hearing*

   (a) The tribunal sit in public unless exceptional circumstances make it desirable that the hearing, or some part of it, should take place in private.

   (b) A party may appear and be heard in person or by counsel or solicitor or by a representative appointed in writing.

   (c) The party making the application will begin and the other parties will be heard in such order as the tribunal may determine.

3. *Witnesses*

   (a) Each party will be given an opportunity to call and cross-examine witnesses, and a party may if he wishes give evidence as a witness on his own behalf.

   (b) The tribunal may call witnesses, who may after giving evidence be cross-examined by any party.

   (c) The provisions of the County Court Rules 1936, as amended, as to the issue of witness summonses (Order 20, rule 8) apply for the purposes of any proceedings before the tribunal. Under these Rules, a party desiring a person to be summoned as a witness must apply to the [district judge] by filling in the prescribed form in the county court office.

4. *Default of Appearance*

   If a party fails to appear at the time fixed for the hearing, the tribunal may—

       (i) dismiss the application where the party failing to appear is the applicant, or

> (ii) proceed in any other case to determine the application in the party's absence, if satisfied that the party failing to appear has been afforded an adequate opportunity of attending.

[1070]

NOTES

Para 3(c): words in square brackets substituted by virtue of the Courts and Legal Services Act 1990, s 74(1)(a), (3).

County Court Rules 1936: the 1936 Rules were revoked and replaced by the County Court Rules 1981, SI 1981/1687. The 1981 Rules were subsequently replaced by the Civil Procedure Rules 1998, SI 1998/3132, except to the extent that provision was made by practice direction for the 1981 Rules to continue to apply to proceedings issued before 26 April 1999. Note also that r 2.1(2) of the 1998 Rules (as amended) also provides that those Rules do not apply to the following kinds of proceedings: insolvency proceedings, non-contentious or common form probate proceedings, proceedings in the High Court when acting as a Prize Court, proceedings before the judge within the meaning of the Mental Health Act 1983, Pt VII, family proceedings, and election proceedings in the High Court. As to witness summonses generally, see now rr 34.2–34.6 of the 1998 Rules.

FORM 14

rule 32
Ref No
To be inserted by the Secretary.

Agricultural Land Tribunal

Application for Variation of Order made under Land Drainage Act 1976

To the Secretary of the Agricultural Land Tribunal

for the .... .Area.

1.   I, ... [*block capitals*]

of .... [*address*],

hereby apply to the Tribunal to vary its order dated   the day of   19 .

2.   The order was made on *[my application] [the application of ....

.... [*block capitals*]

of .... [*address*]]

bearing the reference number ....

*   Strike out whichever is inapplicable.

3.   The variation for which I apply is:—

4.   My main reasons for making this application are:—

5.   I attach copies of the following documents which I intend to produce in support of my case[1]:—

Date .... Signed[2] ....

---

[1]   Two copies of this application and of any document which you wish to submit to the Tribunal must be sent to the Secretary, and, if there are more than two parties, an additional copy of each must be supplied for each additional party.

[2]   If signed by any person other than the applicant himself, he should state in what capacity or by what authority he signs.

[1071]

NOTES

See further, in relation to references to orders made under the Land Drainage Act 1976: the Water Consolidation (Consequential Provisions) Act 1991, Sch 2, para 15(2).

(Sch 2 spent on the revocation of the Agricultural Land Tribunals (Succession to Agricultural Tenancies) Order 1976, SI 1976/2183 by the Agricultural Land Tribunals (Succession to Agricultural Tenancies) Order 1984, SI 1984/1301.)

PART II
STATUTORY INSTRUMENTS

AGRICULTURE (CALCULATION OF VALUE FOR COMPENSATION) REGULATIONS 1978

(SI 1978/809)

NOTES
Made: 25 May 1978.
Authority: Agricultural Holdings Act 1948, s 51(1) (see now the Agricultural Holdings Act 1986, ss 66(2), 94, 96(1)).

1 Citation and commencement

These regulations may be cited as the Agriculture (Calculation of Value for Compensation) Regulations 1978, and shall come into operation on 1st July 1978.

[1072]

2 Interpretation

(1)   In these regulations, unless the context otherwise requires,—
"the Act" means the Agricultural Holdings Act 1948;
"roots" means the produce of any root crop of a kind normally grown for consumption on the holding;
"tenant" means the outgoing tenant;
"year" means a period of twelve consecutive calendar months.

(2)   The Interpretation Act 1889 applies for the interpretation of these regulations as it applies for the interpretation of an Act of Parliament and as if these regulations and the regulations hereby revoked were Acts of Parliament.

(3)   Any reference in these regulations to any enactment shall be construed as a reference to that enactment as amended, varied or extended under that enactment or by or under any other enactment.

[1073]

NOTES
Interpretation Act 1889: see now the Interpretation Act 1978.

3 Compensation for improvements and other matters

Subject to subsections (2) and (3) of section 51 of the Act and to regulation 4 below, the compensation for any improvement or other matter specified in a numbered paragraph of the Fourth Schedule to the Act shall, where the tenancy of the tenant claiming such compensation terminates on or after the coming into operation of these regulations, be calculated in accordance with the paragraph so numbered in Schedule 1 to these regulations.

[1074]

4 Reduction of compensation

(1)   Where any work in relation to an improvement or other matter has not been carried out in the most efficient and economical manner practicable in the circumstances, or any improvement or other matter has been adversely affected by—
   (a)   any breach by the tenant of the rules of good husbandry, or
   (b)   any other act or omission of the tenant, whether intentional or negligent,
and the compensation for that improvement or other matter calculated pursuant to regulation 3 above exceeds the actual value to an incoming tenant, the compensation shall be reduced so as not to exceed such actual value, but no reduction shall be made for any adverse effects of seasonal conditions which the tenant could not reasonably have been expected to guard against or mitigate.

(2)   Where—
   (a)   any hay, fodder crops, straw, roots, manure or compost are destroyed by fire or otherwise or, after the giving of a notice to quit by the tenant or the landlord and without the landlord's written consent, are sold by the tenant or removed by him from the holding, and

(b)   but for the destruction, sale or removal, compensation would have been payable to the tenant under paragraph 8 of the Fourth Schedule to the Act in respect of the produce destroyed, sold or removed,

the compensation which would otherwise be payable to the tenant under these regulations shall be reduced by an amount equal to the reasonable cost to an incoming tenant of replacing on the holding produce similar in all respects to that which has been destroyed, sold or removed, less the value of the replaced produce itself, calculated under these regulations as if it had been on the holding when the tenant quitted at the termination of the tenancy.

(3)   Paragraphs 8 to 10 of Part II of Schedule 1 to these regulations do not apply to crops or produce grown, seeds sown, cultivations, fallows or acts of husbandry performed or pasture laid down in contravention of the terms of a written contract of tenancy unless either—

(a)   the tenant shows that the terms contravened were inconsistent with the fulfilment of the tenant's responsibilities to farm the holding in accordance with the rules of good husbandry, or

(b)   the contravention was reasonably necessary in consequence of the giving of a direction by the Minister under the Agriculture Act 1947 or by the Secretary of State for Wales under that Act as read with the Transfer of Functions (Wales) (No 1) Order 1978.

[1075]

5   Revocations

The instruments mentioned in Schedule 2 to these regulations are hereby revoked, but without prejudice to their application in relation to tenancies terminating before the coming into operation of these regulations.

[1076]

SCHEDULES

SCHEDULE 1

Regulation 3

PART I

1   Mole drainage and works carried out to secure the efficient functioning thereof

(1)

(a)   Where the moles discharge into a piped main drain, the value shall (subject to sub-paragraph (2) below) be the reasonable cost of the work less one-sixth for each year since the work was completed;

(b)   Where the moles discharge direct into an open ditch (whether the outfalls are piped or not), the value shall (subject to sub-paragraph (2) below) be the reasonable cost of the work less one-third for each year since the work was completed.

(2)   If the value of any work, calculated in accordance with sub-paragraph (1) above, exceeds the actual value to an incoming tenant, in any case where—

(a)   plans on a suitable scale, made at the time when the work was done, and showing the position of all moles, mains and outfalls, are not made available to the landlord; or

(b)   moles were not drawn at a proper depth, having regard to the nature of the soil and subsoil; or

(c)   any ditches into which the outfalls discharge have not been maintained clean, free from obstruction and at a proper depth since the work was done; or

(d)   deep cultivation or other work interfering with the efficient functioning of the drains has been done on the land since the drainage work was completed; or

(e)   the land is not of consistently suitable slope or soil texture for mole drainage to be effective; or

(f)   the drainage scheme was not a proper one, having regard to all the conditions, or was not efficiently carried out; or

(g)   for any other reason, the drainage system does not function efficiently,

the value so calculated shall be reduced so as not to exceed such actual value.

2 Protection of fruit trees against animals

The value shall be the reasonable cost of the protection, whether around each tree or around the perimeter of the orchard or both, reduced where necessary according to—
  (a)   the existing condition of the protection;
  (b)   the existing condition of the fruit trees;
  (c)   the further period for which protection is likely to be necessary.

3 —

4 Clay burning

The value shall be the reasonable cost of the work, less one-quarter for each growing season since the work was completed.

[5 Liming (including chalking) of land

  (1)   Subject to sub-paragraph (2), the value shall be, for a period of one year following the application of lime to the land, the reasonable cost of the lime so applied and shall thereafter reduce by equal annual depreciation of such an amount that, at the end of a period of years calculated from the date of such application in accordance with Table 1 by reference to mean annual excess winter rainfall in respect of the land and to type of land and rate of application to the land (subsequent to the application of lime) of nitrogenous fertiliser, the value shall be nil.

  (2)   For the purposes of sub-paragraph (1), the cost shall not be regarded as reasonable to the extent that it exceeds the higher of—
  (a)   the cost (calculated as at the time when lime was applied to the land) of the quantity of ground limestone or chalk (whichever is the cheaper) which would have been used in the application to the land of calcium oxide at a rate of 7.5 tonnes per hectare, and
  (b)   the cost (calculated as at the time when lime was applied to the land) of lime recommended for application to the land in scientific advice relating to the condition of the soil.

  (3)   In this paragraph and Table 1—
  "cost" includes the cost of delivery and application;
  "lime" includes chalk;
  "mean annual excess winter rainfall" means the mean annual amount of rain falling between the date in autumn when the soil reaches field capacity and the end of March in the following year, less the amount of evapotranspiration from the soil during that period, as is indicated by the data on such rainfall in relation to different areas of England and Wales produced by the Meteorological Office for the period commencing with the winter of 1940–1941 and finishing with the winter of 1969–1970 and contained in Ministry of Agriculture, Fisheries and Food Technical Bulletins 34 ("Climate and Drainage") and 35 ("The Agricultural Climate of England and Wales"), both published in 1976 by Her Majesty's Stationery Office, and the map "Mean Annual Excess Winter Rainfall" published in 1979 by the Ministry of Agriculture, Fisheries and Food.]

TABLE 1
DEPRECIATION OF VALUE OF LIME

Mean annual excess winter rainfall (millimetres)	Where the land comprises permanent pasture or long-term leys with more than 250 kilogrammes per hectare of nitrogen applied annually, or arable or mixed ley and arable land Value of lime to be depreciated over:—	Where the land comprises permanent pasture or long-term leys with up to 250 kilogrammes per hectare or nitrogen applied annually Value of lime to be depreciated over:—
Less than 250	8 years	9 years
250 to 500	6 years	7 years
More than 500	4 years	5 years

6 Application to land of purchased manure and fertiliser, whether organic or inorganic

A. Purchased fertilisers containing nitrogen, phosphate or potash:

I. Fertilisers other than bulky organic manures:

(1)   Where no crop has been taken from the land since the fertiliser was applied, the value shall be the reasonable cost of the fertiliser as applied to the land (including the cost of delivery and application).

(2)   Where one crop or more has been taken from the land since the fertiliser was applied, the value shall be,—

    (a)   for nitrogen contained in the fertiliser, nil;

    (b)   subject as provided below, for each Unit of phosphoric acid (as P_2O_5) contained in the fertiliser, the amount calculated in accordance with Table 2 below: Provided that—

        (i)   where a phosphatic fertiliser contains less than one-tenth of its total phosphoric acid content in an insoluble form, as indicated by the solubility test appropriate to that fertiliser, its total phosphoric acid content shall be treated as soluble;

        (ii)   where a phosphatic fertiliser other than a fertiliser specified and applied as described in items 2(a), 2(b)(i) or 3(a) in Table 2 contains more than one-tenth of its total phosphoric acid content in an insoluble form, the value shall be restricted to and determined only for each Unit of phosphoric acid in soluble form in that fertiliser;

        (iii)   for the purpose of this sub-paragraph, permanent grassland shall be taken to mean grassland which at the termination of the tenancy has been established for five or more years;

        (iv)   in the case of land situated in an area in which rapid fixation of phosphate occurs, the foregoing provisions of this sub-paragraph shall not apply and the value for each Unit of phosphoric acid contained in fertiliser applied to that land shall be the residual value (if any) determined in accordance with scientific evidence and by reference to the reasonable cost of the fertiliser as applied to the land (including the cost of delivery and application);

    (c)   for each Unit of potash (K_2O) contained in the fertiliser, the amount calculated in accordance with Table 3 below: Provided that—

        (i)   where a vegetable crop has been produced from the land following the application of the fertiliser and the majority of the stem and leaf was removed, the value shall be nil, but where the said majority was left on the land, the value shall be calculated in accordance with item 1 in Table 3, and where an intermediate proportion of stem and leaf was removed, the value shall be calculated in accordance with such proportion;

        (ii)   in the case of land comprised in holdings which are entirely or mainly horticultural holdings, the value shall be calculated in accordance with item 1 in Table 3.

(3)   For the purposes of sub-paragraph (2) above, a Unit of nutrient (phosphoric acid (as P_2O_5) or, as the case may be, potash (K_2O)) is the amount of nutrient contained in one per cent of a tonne of fertiliser calculated on the basis of the percentage content of the nutrient in the fertiliser as stated in the relevant statutory statement given in relation to the fertiliser under section 68 of the Agriculture Act 1970.

[TABLE 2
UNIT VALUE OF PHOSPHORIC ACID (AS P_2O_5) IN ONE PER CENT OF A TONNE OF FERTILISER

		After		
		One	Two Growing Seasons	Three
	Nature of Fertiliser	p	p	p
1.	Organic forms and inorganic forms (including basic slag) but excluding rock phosphates and calcined aluminium calcium phosphate	158	79	39
2.	Soft ground rock phosphates[1] applied in—			
	(a) areas with a mean annual excess winter rainfall[2] of 450 mm or more	158	79	79
	(b) areas with a mean annual excess winter rainfall[2] of less than 450 mm			
	(i) Permanent grassland	158	79	79
	(ii) Other crops	nil	nil	nil
3.	Other ground rock phosphates applied in—			
	(a) areas with a mean annual excess winter rainfall[2] of 450 mm or more	39	39	39
	(b) areas with a means annual excess winter rainfall[2] of less than 450 mm	nil	nil	nil
4.	Calcined aluminium calcium phosphate	The value, if any, shall be such as may be determined in accordance with scientific evidence		

Notes:

[1] "Soft" ground rock phosphates in this Table means the material of that name described in Group 2 in Section A of Schedule 1 to the Fertilisers Regulations 1977.

[2] "Mean annual excess winter rainfall" in this Table has the same meaning as in paragraph 5(3).]

II. Bulky organic manures brought on to the holding:

Subject to sub-paragraphs (3) and (4) below, the values of bulky organic manures brought on and applied to the holding shall be in accordance with the provisions of sub-paragraphs (1) and (2) below:—

   (1) Farmyard manure:

      (a) Where no payment was made for the manure and—

         (i) no crop has been taken from the land since the manure was applied, the value shall be the cost of delivery and application;

         (ii) one crop or more has been taken from the land since the manure was applied, the value shall be, after the first growing season, one-half, and after the second growing season, one-quarter, of the cost of delivery and application, and thereafter, nil;

[TABLE 3
UNIT VALUE OF POTASH (K₂O) IN ONE PER CENT OF A TONNE OF FERTILISER

	After		
Type of crops to which fertiliser is applied	One Growing Season	Two Growing Seasons	Three Growing Seasons
	p	p	p
1. Applied to arable crops (except forage crops) and all root crops where tops are left on the land, except potatoes (see also 4 below)	92	46	nil
2. Applied to leys, permanent grassland or forage crops which are grazed or the product cut and fed on the holding	92	46	nil
3. Applied to leys and permanent grassland the product of which is cut and removed from the holding	nil	nil	nil
4. Applied to roots (including potatoes) and forage crops which are removed from the holding	nil	nil	nil]

(b)   Where payment was made for the manure and—
    (i)   no crop has been taken from the land since the manure was applied, the value shall be the cost of the manure as applied to the land (including the cost of delivery and application);
    (ii)   one crop or more has been taken from the land since the manure was applied, the value shall be, after the first growing season, one-half, and after the second growing season, one-quarter, of the said cost, and thereafter, nil:

Provided that the value of any type of manure specified in Table 4 below shall not exceed the value specified in relation to that type in the appropriate circumstances set out in that Table.

[TABLE 4
VALUE PER TONNE OF PURCHASED FARMYARD

Type of manure	No crop off	After one growing season	After two growing seasons	After three growing seasons
	p	p	p	p
Cattle (farmyard manure)	735	368	184	nil
Horse (stable manure)	800	400	200	nil
Pig (farmyard manure)	770	385	193	nil
Poultry (deep litter)	1380	690	345	nil
Poultry (broiler manure)	1625	813	406	nil]

(2)   Slurry:

Where manure is brought on and applied to the land in the form of slurry, the value shall be the reasonable cost of cartage (if any) and application.

(3)   No compensation shall be payable under sub-paragraph (1) or (2) above in respect of the excess (if any) of the rates of application set out in the second column below in relation to the type of bulky organic manure specified in the first column below:—

Bulky Organic Manure

(1)	(2)
Type applied	*Application per hectare per annum*
Cattle, horse or pig manure	50 tonnes
Deep litter poultry manure	18 tonnes
Broiler poultry manure	12.5 tonnes

(4)   No value shall be given to, and no compensation shall be payable in respect of, any purchased manure applied to land during the last year of the tenancy after the last crop was removed from that land unless such application was made at the written request, or with the written consent, of the landlord.

B. Magnesium and copper:

(1)—

  (a)

   (i)   Subject to sub-paragraph (b) of this paragraph, where magnesium (in whatever chemical compound form) has been applied to land following and in accordance with scientific advice, the value of the magnesium so applied shall be taken to be the amount (if any) by which the net cost (including the cost of delivery and application) of the quantity of calcined magnesite required to provide the same quantity of magnesium as was actually applied (such net cost being calculated by reference to average prices and costs prevailing at the time of the purchase, delivery and application respectively, of the magnesium) exceeds the net cost (including, and calculated, as aforesaid) of the quantity of calcined magnesite which would provide 60 kilogrammes of magnesium per hectare.

   (ii)   After the first, second and third growing seasons following application of the magnesium, the value calculated in accordance with sub-paragraph (a)(i) above shall be reduced to three-quarters, one-half and one-quarter, respectively, and to nil thereafter.

  (b)   Sub-paragraph (a) above shall not apply to magnesium applied to land in the form of a magnesian fertiliser specified in Group 5 of Section A of Schedule 1 to the Fertilisers Regulations 1977.

(2)—

  (a)   Subject to sub-paragraph (b) below, where copper (in whatever chemical compound form) has been applied to land following and in accordance with scientific advice, the value of the copper so applied shall be taken to be the amount (if any) by which the net cost (including the cost of delivery and application) of the quantity of hydrated copper sulphate required to provide the same quantity of copper as was actually applied (such net cost being calculated by reference to average prices and costs prevailing at the time of the purchase, delivery and application, respectively, of the copper) exceeds the net cost (including, and calculated, as aforesaid) of the quantity of hydrated copper sulphate which would provide six kilogrammes of copper per hectare;

  (b)   The value of copper applied calculated in accordance with sub-paragraph (a) above shall be reduced by one-eighth for each year following application of the copper.

[7   Consumption on the holding of corn (whether produced on the holding or not) or of cake or other feeding stuffs not produced on the holding by horses, cattle, sheep, pigs or poultry

(1)   The values per tonne of feeding stuff consumed on the holding set out in Tables 5(a) and (b) in Part I of this Schedule shall apply in all cases where feeding stuffs are fed to the animals and poultry specified in those Tables in buildings or open yards and the open slurry is stored under average conditions.

(2)   Where the conditions of storage of the open slurry are other than average, for closed slurry or farm yard manure or where the feeding stuffs are fed directly on the land the values set out in the said Tables 5(a) and (b) shall be adjusted in accordance with Table 6 set out below.

(3)   For the purpose of sub-paragraph (2) above and the said Table 6, the expression "closed slurry" means slurry stored under slats or in a covered container.]

[TABLE 5(A)
UNEXHAUSTED MANURIAL VALUES OF FEEDING STUFFS PER TONNE:
CATTLE, SHEEP AND PIGS—OPEN SLURRY

Feeding Stuff	No crop off	After one growing season		After two growing seasons	
		of arable crops (except forage crops) or of leys, permanent grassland or forage crops grazed or the product cut and fed on the holding or of root crops the tops of which are left on the land	of leys, permanent grassland, roots or forage crops where the product is removed from the holding	of arable crops (except forage crops) or of leys, permanent grassland or forage crops grazed or the product cut and fed on the holding or of root crops the tops of which are left on the land	of leys, permanent grassland, roots or forage crops where the product is removed from the holding
	p	p	p	p	p
1. Grass hay	395	197	53	84	12
2. Clover hay	470	235	78	96	18
3. Dried grass	523	262	88	106	20
4. Dried lucerne	532	266	92	106	19
5. Straw	133	66	26	25	5
6. Mangels	63	31	8	14	3
7. Swedes	47	23	8	10	2
8. Turnips	47	23	8	10	2
9. Potatoes	89	44	13	19	3
10. Sugar beet pulp (dried-molasses)	309	155	40	61	4
11. Sugar beet pulp (wet-double pressed 18% DM)	62	31	8	12	1
12. Brewers grains (wet)	67	34	33	10	9
13. Field beans	407	204	139	69	37
14. Field peas	310	155	103	51	25
15. Barley	204	102	67	37	20
16. Wheat	185	92	70	33	22
17. Oats	190	95	71	32	21
18. Maize	145	72	52	25	15

PART II
STATUTORY INSTRUMENTS

19. Rice meal	203	101	80	37	26
20. Middlings/Bran	411	205	148	80	52
21. Cassava (Manioc)	70	33	21	14	7
22. Hominy chop	277	139	97	53	32
23. Locust beans	137	68	32	25	7
24. Citrus pulp	158	79	40	27	8
25. Fish meal	1422	711	642	287	252
26. Soya bean meal	615	308	184	105	43
27. Decorticated cotton cake	685	342	267	123	85
28. Undecorticated cotton cake	563	281	206	108	70
29. Linseed cake/meal	524	262	180	93	52
30. Palm kernel cake/meal	265	133	107	45	32
31. Coconut cake/meal	521	261	135	103	41
32. Decorticated groundnut cake	502	251	173	76	37
33. Rapeseed cake/meal	607	303	222	108	67
34. Meat meal	1325	663	628	276	259
35. Meat and bone meal	1711	855	768	368	324
36. Dried skimmed milk	601	300	196	117	65
37. Skimmed milk (liquid)	59	29	19	11	6
38. Liquid whey	29	14	7	6	3
39. Liquid urea	452	226	70	81	3
40. Urea	1014	507	507	0	0
41. Compounded cake: for each 1% CP	20	10	8	4	3

TABLE 5(B)
UNEXHAUSTED MANURIAL VALUES OF FEEDING STUFFS PER TONNE:
POULTRY—OPEN SLURRY

Feeding Stuff	No crop off	*After one growing season*		*After two growing seasons*	
		of arable crops (except forage crops) or of leys, permanent grassland or forage crops grazed or the product cut and fed on the holding or of root crops the tops of which are left on the land	of leys, permanent grassland, roots or forage crops where the product is removed from the holding	of arable crops (except forage crops) or of leys, permanent grassland or forage crops grazed or the product cut and fed on the holding or of root crops the tops of which are left on the land	of leys, permanent grassland, roots or forage crops where the product is removed from the holding
	p	p	p	p	p
1. Dried grass	493	213	39	106	20
2. Field beans	371	138	74	69	37
3. Field peas	284	102	50	51	25
4. Barley	189	75	40	37	20
5. Wheat	171	66	44	33	22
6. Oats	173	65	41	32	21
7. Maize	133	51	30	25	15
8. Rice meal	188	73	52	37	26
9. Middlings/Bran	384	161	104	80	52
10. Cassava (Manioc)	65	28	13	14	7
11. Fish meal	1360	574	505	287	252
12. Soya bean meal	570	210	87	105	43
13. Decorticated cotton cake	637	246	171	123	85
14. Undecorticated cotton cake	526	216	141	108	70
15. Linseed cake/meal	486	186	104	93	52
16. Palm Kernel cake/meal	245	89	63	45	32
17. Decorticated groundnut	456	152	74	76	37
18. Rapeseed cake/meal	561	215	134	108	67
19. Meat meal	1280	552	518	276	259

PART II
STATUTORY INSTRUMENTS

| 20. Meat and bone meal | 1643 | 735 | 648 | 368 | 324 |
| 21. Compounded cake: for each 1% CP | 19 | 8 | 5 | 4 | 3 |

TABLE 6
ADJUSTMENTS FOR PREPARATION AND STORAGE OF EFFLUENT

Method of preparation and storage	Adjustment to open slurry (average conditions) tables
Closed slurry under average conditions	Add 20 per cent
Closed slurry under ideal conditions	Add 30 per cent
Farmyard manure under average conditions	Add 40 per cent
Farmyard manure under ideal conditions	Add 50 per cent
Slurry under adverse conditions	Subtract up to 50 per cent depending on conditions
Farmyard manure under adverse conditions	Add up to 30 per cent depending on conditions
Feedingstuffs fed directly on the land	Add 35 per cent]

[1077]

NOTES
Para 3: appears as in the Queen's Printer's copy.
Para 5 and Table 1: substituted by the Agriculture (Calculation of Value for Compensation) (Amendment) Regulations 1981, SI 1981/822, reg 3(1), Schedule.
Tables 2–4, 5(a), 5(b), 6: substituted for original Tables 2–4, 5(a)–(h), (j), 6 by the Agriculture (Calculation of Value for Compensation) (Amendment) Regulations 1983, SI 1983/1475, reg 3(1), Schedule, Pt II.
Para 7: substituted by SI 1983/1475, reg 3(1), Schedule, Pt I.

PART II

8 Growing crops and severed or harvested crops and produce, being in either case crops or produce grown on the holding in the last year of the tenancy, but not including crops or produce which the tenant has a right to sell or remove from the holding

   (1)   Growing crops:—
      (a)   The value of growing crops, except root and green crops of a kind normally grown on a holding held under an autumn tenancy, shall be the reasonable cost of seeds sown, and cultivations, fallows and acts of husbandry performed, calculated in accordance with the provisions of paragraph 9 below;
      (b)   The value of growing root and green crops of a kind normally grown on a holding held under an autumn tenancy shall be the average market value on the holding of good quality crops, less the manurial value thereof calculated in accordance with [Tables 5(a) and (b)] above on the basis of 'no crop off':
   Provided that if the value so calculated exceeds the actual value to an incoming tenant in any case where—
      (i)   the crops are of inferior quality, or
      (ii)   the quantity of any kind of crops exceeds the quantity reasonably required for the system of farming practised on the holding,
   the value so calculated shall be reduced so as not to exceed such actual value;
      (c)   In the case of—
         (i)   autumn-sown crops where the land was held under a spring tenancy, and

      (ii)   grass and clover seeds sown on land held under a spring or autumn tenancy from which no crop has been taken before termination of the tenancy,

the value shall be increased by an additional amount representing the enhancement of the value to an incoming tenant of the growing crop, but such additional amount shall not in any case exceed the rental value, at the termination of the tenancy, of the land sown to the crop, such rental value to be calculated by reference to the same matters and criteria as are by section 8 of the Act required to be taken into consideration or applied for the determination of the rent of a holding pursuant to that enactment:

Provided that if the area of any such crop exceeds the area of such crop which would normally be grown on the holding, having regard to the character and type of the holding and the terms of the tenancy (hereinafter referred to as "the normal area") the foregoing provisions of this sub-paragraph shall apply only to the normal area of such crop.

(2)   For the purposes of sub-paragraph (1) above "spring tenancy" means a yearly tenancy the last yearly term of which commenced between 1st January and 30th June inclusive, and "autumn tenancy" means a yearly tenancy the last yearly term of which commenced between 1st September and 31st December inclusive.

(3)   Severed or harvested crops and produce:—

The value shall be the market value for consumption by agricultural livestock on the holding of hay, fodder crops, straw, roots and other crops or produce of good quality less the manurial value thereof calculated in accordance with [Tables 5(a) and (b)] above on the basis of 'no crop off': Provided that if the value so calculated exceeds the actual value to an incoming tenant in any case where—

    (a)   the crops or produce are of inferior quality; or
    (b)   the quantity of any kind of crops or produce exceeds the quantity reasonably required for the system of farming practised on the holding; or
    (c)   the crops or produce are not left in convenient or proper places on the farm; or
    (d)   any hay or straw is not properly stacked and thatched or otherwise protected, the value so calculated shall be reduced so as not to exceed such actual value.

9 Seeds sown and cultivations, fallows and acts of husbandry performed on the holding at the expense of the tenant

(1)   The value shall be the reasonable cost of seeds sown and of cultivations, fallows and acts of husbandry performed, taking into account—

    (a)   normal current costs, having regard to the current agricultural wage, the cost of horse and tractor operations, the size and shape of the fields, and other relevant conditions;
    (b)   reasonable costs of hired tractor cultivations;
    (c)   increased costs over normal tractor rates, where owing to the size of the farm or fields, the shape of the fields, or to other special circumstances, it was reasonable to use horse labour;

but leaving out of account any expenditure incurred by the tenant up to and including the removal from the land of the last preceding crop and any rent paid by the tenant.

(2)   For the purposes of sub-paragraph (1) above, the reasonable cost shall not be regarded as reduced merely because more than one operation was carried out by the tenant at the same time.

(3)   Nothing in sub-paragraph (1) above shall be taken to limit the operation of this paragraph to any particular method of sowing nor to cultivations, fallows or acts of husbandry performed in any particular way.

10 Pasture laid down with clover, grass, lucerne, sainfoin or other seeds, being either—

    (a)   pasture laid down at the expense of the tenant otherwise than in compliance with an obligation imposed on him by an agreement in writing to lay it down to replace temporary pasture comprised in the holding when the tenant entered thereon which was not paid for by him; or
    (b)   pasture paid for by the tenant on entering on the holding.

(1)   Where no crop has been removed either by mowing or by grazing, the value shall be the reasonable cost of seeds sown, and cultivations, fallows and acts of husbandry performed, calculated in accordance with paragraph 9 above, but also taking into account any expenditure incurred solely for the benefit of the pasture before the removal of any crop in or with which the pasture was sown.

(2)   Where one crop or more has been removed either by mowing or by grazing, the value shall be the face value of the pasture, taking into account—
- (a)   present condition;
- (b)   management since sowing;
- (c)   situation on the holding;
- (d)   fencing;
- (e)   water supply;
- (f)   any other circumstances appearing to be relevant.

11   Acclimatisation, hefting or settlement of hill sheep on hill land

(1)   The value of hill sheep on hill land shall include such amount (if any) as represents the value attributable to the acclimatisation, hefting or settlement of the sheep on such land, but the said amount shall not [exceed a sum of eight pounds per sheep plus ten per cent of the market value of each sheep].

(2)   Any amount which may be included in the value of hill sheep under the provisions of the last foregoing sub-paragraph shall be apportioned and separately shown by the person carrying out the valuation as being attributable to the value of acclimatisation, hefting or settlement of such sheep.

12   Residual sod fertility value in certain districts

(1)   In this paragraph—
["arable crop" does not include a ley of more than one years duration;]
"leys" means land laid down with clover, grass, lucerne, sainfoin or other seeds, but does not include permanent pasture;
"continuously maintained leys" means leys continuously maintained as such for a period of three or more growing seasons since being laid down excluding, if the leys were undersown or autumn-sown, the calendar year in which the sowing took place; and, for the purpose of this definition, the destruction of a ley (by ploughing or some other means) followed as soon as practicable by re-seeding to a ley without sowing a crop in the interval between such destruction and such re-seeding shall be treated as not constituting a break in the continuity of the maintenance of the ley;
"former leys" means arable land which within the three growing seasons immediately preceding the termination of the tenancy was ley which was continuously maintained ley before being destroyed by ploughing or some other means for the production of a tillage crop or crops;
"qualifying leys" means continuously maintained leys and former leys or either of them;
"the excess qualifying leys" means, subject as provided below, the area of qualifying leys on the holding at the termination of the tenancy which is equal to the area (if any) by which one-third of the aggregate of the areas of leys on the holding on the following dates, namely,—
- (a)   at the termination of the tenancy,
- (b)   on the date one year prior to such termination, and
- (c)   on the date two years prior to such termination

exceeds the accepted proportion at the termination of the tenancy: Provided that for the purpose of this definition qualifying leys laid down at the expense of the landlord without reimbursement by the tenant or any previous tenant of the holding or laid down by and at the expense of the tenant pursuant to agreement by him with the landlord for the establishment of a specified area of leys on the holding as a condition of the landlord giving consent to the ploughing or other destruction of permanent pasture or pursuant to a direction given by an arbitrator on a reference under section 10(1) of the Act shall not be included in the area of qualifying leys on the holding at the termination of the tenancy;
["the accepted proportion" means the area which represents the proportion which the total area of the leys on the holding would, taking into account the capability of the holding, be expected to bear to the area of the holding, excluding the permanent pasture thereon, or, if a greater proportion is provided for by or under the terms of the tenancy, that proportion.]

(2)   [In areas of the country where arable crops can be grown in an unbroken series of not less than six years, and it is reasonable that they should be grown on the holding or part thereof, the residual fertility value of the sod of the excess qualifying leys shall be calculated (subject to sub-paragraph (3) below) as follows—]
- (a)   in respect of continuously maintained leys, [£24 per hectare] if any herbage has

been cut and removed in the last growing season before the termination of the tenancy and [£40 per hectare] if the sward was, during such last growing season, grazed only;

[(b)   in respect of continuously maintained leys, the values specified in sub-paragraph (a) above shall be increased by £8 per hectare for each additional growing season over three growing seasons for which the leys have been established, but such increase shall not exceed a total of £48 per hectare if any herbage was cut and removed during the last growing season before the termination of the tenancy and shall not exceed £64 per hectare if the herbage was, during such last growing season, grazed only;

(c)   in respect of any former ley where the first crop which has been sown in the last growing season before the termination of the tenancy has not been removed from the ground, the value shall be the value specified in sub-paragraphs (a) and (b) above according to the period for which the ley had been established before it was ploughed or otherwise destroyed and to whether the herbage was cut and removed, or grazed only, in the last growing season before the ley was ploughed or otherwise destroyed;]

(d)   in respect of any former ley to which sub-paragraph (c) above does not apply,—
(i)

(aa)   if only one arable crop was removed from the land following ploughing or other destruction of the ley, the value shall be two-thirds of the value specified in sub-paragraphs (a) and (b), and

(bb)   if only two arable crops were removed from the land following ploughing or other destruction of the ley, the value shall be one-third of the value specified in sub-paragraphs (a) and (b),

according, in each case, to the period for which the ley had been established before it was ploughed or otherwise destroyed and to whether the herbage was cut and removed, or grazed only, in the last growing season before the ley was ploughed or otherwise destroyed; and

(ii)   if more than two arable crops were removed from the land following ploughing or other destruction of the ley, the value shall be nil.

(3)   Where the tenant is entitled to compensation in respect of a ley both under sub-paragraph (2) of paragraph 10 above and under sub-paragraph (2)(a) and, if applicable, sub-paragraph (2)(b) of this paragraph, the aggregate of the respective values per hectare thereunder, taken together, shall not exceed [£164 per hectare].

[1078]

NOTES

Paras 8, 11: words in square brackets substituted by the Agriculture (Calculation of Value for Compensation) (Amendment) Regulations 1983, SI 1983/1475, reg 3(2)(a), (b).

Para 12: in sub-para (1) definition "arable crop" inserted and definition "the accepted proportion" substituted by SI 1983/1475, reg 3(2)(c); in sub-para (2) words in first pair of square brackets and paras (b), (c) substituted by SI 1983/1475, reg 3(2)(d), words in second and third pairs of square brackets substituted by the Agriculture (Calculation of Value for Compensation) (Amendment) Regulations 1980, SI 1980/751, reg 3(2)(b); in sub-para (3) words in square brackets substituted by SI 1980/751, reg 3(2)(d).

AGRICULTURAL LAND TRIBUNALS (AREAS) ORDER 1982

(SI 1982/97)

NOTES

Made: 29 January 1982.
Authority: Agriculture Act 1947, s 73.

---

1   This Order may be cited as the Agricultural Land Tribunals (Areas) Order 1982 and shall come into operation on 2nd March 1982.

[1079]

2—(1)   For the purposes of section 73 of the Agriculture Act 1947 there shall be eight areas as specified in column 1 of the Schedule to this Order.

(2)   Each area shall comprise the counties and the London Boroughs which are set out in respect of it in column 2 of the said Schedule.

(3)   For the purposes of the preceding paragraph and of the said Schedule the Isles of Scilly shall be treated as if they were a county.

[1080]

3   Any proceedings which on the coming into operation of this Order are pending before an Agricultural Land Tribunal may thereafter be continued before the Agricultural Land Tribunal for the area in which the whole or the greater part of the agricultural holding to which the proceedings relate is situate, and that tribunal shall have power to hear and determine them.

[1081]

SCHEDULE

Article 2

Column 1 *Areas*	Column 2 *Counties and London Boroughs*
Northern	Cleveland
	Cumbria
	Durham
	Northumberland
	Tyne and Wear
Yorkshire and Humberside	Humberside
	North Yorkshire
	South Yorkshire
	West Yorkshire
Eastern	Bedfordshire
	Cambridgeshire
	Essex
	Hertfordshire
	Lincolnshire
	Norfolk
	Northamptonshire
	Suffolk
	London Boroughs north of the river Thames except Richmond upon Thames
Midlands	Derbyshire
	Herefordshire and Worcestershire
	Leicestershire
	Nottinghamshire
	Warwickshire
	West Midlands
Western	Cheshire
	Greater Manchester
	Lancashire
	Merseyside
	Shropshire
	Staffordshire
South Western	Avon
	Cornwall

	Devon
	Dorset
	Gloucestershire
	Somerset
	Wiltshire
	Isles of Scilly
South Eastern	Berkshire
	Buckinghamshire
	East Sussex
	Hampshire
	Isle of Wight
	Kent
	Oxfordshire
	Surrey
	West Sussex
	London Boroughs south of the river Thames including Richmond upon Thames
Welsh	Clwyd
	Dyfed
	Gwent
	Gwynedd
	Mid Glamorgan
	Powys
	South Glamorgan
	West Glamorgan

[1082]

AGRICULTURAL LAND TRIBUNALS (SUCCESSION TO AGRICULTURAL TENANCIES) ORDER 1984

(SI 1984/1301)

NOTES
Made: 26 July 1984.
Authority: Agriculture Act 1947, ss 73(3), (4), 108(3).

ARRANGEMENT OF ARTICLES

PART II
STATUTORY INSTRUMENTS

NOTES

Agriculture (Miscellaneous Provisions) Act 1976: see now the Agricultural Holdings Act 1986.
Agricultural Holdings Act 1984: see now the Agricultural Holdings Act 1986.

1 Citation and commencement

This Order may be cited as the Agricultural Land Tribunals (Succession to Agricultural Tenancies) Order 1984 and shall come into operation on 12th September 1984.

[1083]

2 Rules of procedure

The rules set out in the Schedule to this Order shall apply to any proceedings before Agricultural Land Tribunals arising from any application made after the commencement of this Order under Part II of the Agriculture (Miscellaneous Provisions) Act 1976 or under Schedule 2 to the Agricultural Holdings Act 1984.

[1084]

3 (*Amends the Agricultural Land Tribunals (Rules) Order 1978, SI 1978/259, art 2.*)

4 Revocation

The Agricultural Land Tribunals (Succession to Agricultural Tenancies) Order 1976 is hereby revoked except to such extent as may be necessary for the disposal of an application pending at the commencement of this Order.

[1085]

SCHEDULE
RULES OF PROCEDURE FOR AGRICULTURAL LAND TRIBUNALS UNDER
PART II OF THE AGRICULTURAL (MISCELLANEOUS PROVISIONS) ACT 1976
AND SCHEDULE 2 TO THE AGRICULTURAL HOLDINGS ACT 1984
Article 2

PART I
PRELIMINARY

1 Citation and interpretation

(1)   These rules may be cited as the Agricultural Land Tribunals (Succession) Rules 1984.

(2)   In these rules "the principal rules" means the Agricultural Land Tribunals Rules 1978 and expressions defined in the principal rules have the same meaning in these rules.

(3)   Unless the context otherwise requires, any reference in these rules—

    (a)   to a numbered rule shall be construed as a reference to the rule bearing that number in these rules; or

    (b)   to a numbered form shall be construed as a reference to the form bearing that number in the Appendix to these rules, or a form substantially to the like effect with such variations as the circumstances may require.

[1086]

PART II
APPLICATION FOR SUCCESSION ON DEATH OF TENANT UNDER PART II OF THE AGRICULTURE (MISCELLANEOUS PROVISIONS) ACT 1976

2   Interpretation of Part II

(1)   In this Part of these rules, unless the context otherwise requires—
"the 1976 Act" means the Agriculture (Miscellaneous Provisions) Act 1976;
"applicant" means a person who has made an application under rule 3(1);
"designated applicant" means an applicant who has been validly designated by the deceased in his will in accordance with section 20(10) of the 1976 Act;
"holding" means a holding in respect of which an application under rule 3(1) is made;
"landlord" means the landlord of the holding;
"the relevant period" means the period of three months beginning with day after the date of death.

(2)   Other expressions defined for the purposes of, or of any provision in, sections 18 to 23 of the 1976 Act (notably in sections 18(1), (2) and (7), 20(10), 22(6) and 23(2) have the same meaning in this Part of these rules.

FORMS OF APPLICATION AND REPLY

3   Application by eligible person wishing to be treated as eligible person

(1)   An application to the tribunal under section 21 of the 1976 Act for a direction entitling the applicant to a tenancy of an agricultural holding shall be made in Form 1.

(2)   An application to the tribunal under section 2 of the 1976 Act for a determination that the applicant is to be treated as an eligible person shall be made in Form 1 and if the applicant also makes an application under section 20 of that Act, both applications shall be made at the same time and in the same Form.

(3)   An application made under this rule shall not be entertained by the tribunal if it is not made within the relevant period.

4   Landlord's application for consent to operation of notice to quit

(1)   An application by the landlord under section 22 of the 1976 Act for the tribunal's consent to the operation of a notice to quit shall be in Form 2 and, subject to paragraphs (3) and (4), may be made at any time after the landlord receives notice of an application under rule 3(1).

(2)   Where the landlord bases his application under section 22 of the 1976 Act on the ground of hardship to a person or persons other than himself, he shall give particulars in his application of that person or those persons and of the hardship on which he relies.

(3)   Where, at the expiry of the relevant period, only one application under rule 3(1) in respect of the holding is pending, any application by the landlord shall be made within four months after a copy of the application under rule 3(1) is served on him.

(4)   Where, at the expiry of the relevant period, more than one application under rule 3(1) in respect of the holding is pending, any application by the landlord shall be made—
   (a)   within four months after a copy of the first application under rule 3(1) is served on him, or
   (b)   within one month after the date on which the number of applications under rule 3(1) which are pending is reduced to one or within one month after such earlier date as the tribunal may direct,
whichever of those periods expires last.

(5)   The secretary shall forthwith inform the landlord of the start of any period of four months under paragraph (3) or paragraph (4) and any period of one month under paragraph (4).

5   Notice of application

(1)   An applicant shall at the time of making his application serve notice of the application in Form 3 on the landlord and on any person who, to the knowledge of the applicant, has made or may be able to make an application under rule 3(1), and shall inform the tribunal in his application of the name and address of every person to be notified by him.

(2)   The applicant shall also inform the tribunal in his application of the name and address of—

(a)   the personal representatives of the deceased, or, if a grant of probate or of letters of administration has not been made, any person who appears to be responsible for the management of the holding on behalf of the deceased's estate;

(b)   any other person who to the knowledge of the applicant may be interested in the outcome of the application,

and in each case shall give the tribunal an indication of the nature of that person's interest in the outcome of the application.

6   Landlord's reply

A landlord who intends to oppose the whole or any part of an application under rule 3(1) shall, within one month after a copy of the application has been served on him, reply thereto in Form 1R (which is the form appended to the copy of the application served on him).

7   Applicant's reply to landlord's application

An applicant who intends to oppose an application to the tribunal under rule 4 shall, within one month after a copy of the application has been served on him, reply thereto in Form 2R (which is the form appended to the copy of the application served on him).

8   Applicant's reply to other applications under rule 3(1)

(1)   An applicant who intends to oppose any application under rule 3(1) by any other person shall, within one month after the expiry of the relevant period, reply to that application in Form 4.

(2)   Any request by two, three or four applicants for the consent of the landlord to a direction entitling them to a joint tenancy of the holding under section 20(9) of the 1976 Act may be made in the reply of each of them under this rule.

PARTIES

9   Applications to be heard together, and parties

Subject to the following provision of these rules, all applications under rule 3(1) or (2) in respect of any particular holding which are made within the relevant period, and any applications in respect thereof by the landlord, shall be heard and determined together as if each of them other than the first had been made by a party in the course of the proceedings on the first of them to be made, and, accordingly, there shall be parties to the proceedings on each application by an applicant—

(a)   that applicant,

(b)   the landlord, and

(c)   any other applicant whose application was made within the relevant period and is still pending.

GENERAL PROVISIONS AS TO APPLICATIONS AND REPLIES

10   Service of documents by secretary

(1)   As soon as possible after receiving from any person any document under rule 3, 4, 6, 7 or 8 the secretary shall serve one copy thereof on every other person who, in accordance with rule 9, is a party to the proceedings on that application.

(2)   As soon as possible after any fresh application under rule 3(1) is made in respect of a holding, the secretary shall serve on the fresh applicant one copy of every document which has not already been served on him but which would have been served on him had he been a party from the outset to the proceedings.

(3)   As soon as possible after the expiry of the relevant period, the secretary shall serve on all those persons whose names and addresses were supplied under rule 5(2) by an applicant notice of the existence of the proceedings in respect of the holding and of the names and addresses of the parties thereto, and shall inform each of those persons that, if he so requests in writing, a copy of the eventual decision of the tribunal will be sent to him by the secretary.

11   Application of principal rules relating to applications and replies

(1)   Rules 16 (except for paragraph (5)) and 18 (except for paragraph (2)) of the principal rules shall apply to applications and replies under this Part of these rules.

(2)   Rule 15(2) of the principal rules shall apply in the case of an application by the landlord under this Part of these rules.

(3)   Rule 18(2) of the principal rules shall apply to a reply under rule 7 of these rules if the relevant period has expired and, following the withdrawal of the reply, there is no other outstanding reply to the application by the landlord.

HEARINGS

12   Date and place of hearing

As soon as practicable the chairman shall fix a date, time and place for the hearing of all applications made in the proceedings under this Part of these rules.

13   Duty to adjourn part of hearing

(1)   Where on the date of the hearing the landlord has not made an application under rule 4(3) but the time allowed for him to do so has not expired, the tribunal shall not proceed to give a direction under section 20 of the 1976 Act except with the consent of the landlord.

(2)   Where on the date of the hearing the time allowed for a reply under rule 7 has not expired, or has not started to run, the tribunal shall not proceed to hear the application of the landlord except with the consent of every applicant who has not yet replied thereto.

(3)   Where under this rule consent is required but is not given the tribunal shall adjourn the proceedings and the chairman shall give such directions as he thinks fit for the further hearing of the proceedings.

14   Application of principal rules relating to preparation for hearing and to hearing

Rules 19, 20, 23(3) and (4), 24, 25, 26(2) and (3) and 27 of the principal rules shall apply with the necessary modifications to applications under this Part of these rules.

FURTHER PROVISIONS RELATING TO HEARINGS

15   Sanctions for failure to reply

(1)   If no reply to an application under rule 3(1) is received from the landlord by the secretary within the time allowed by rule 6, then, subject to section 20(7) of the 1976 Act, the landlord shall not be entitled to dispute any matter alleged in that application, but this paragraph does not affect any right of the landlord to rely upon his own application under rule 4.

(2)   Where pursuant to rule 15(2) or 18(2) of the principal rules (as applied by rule 11(2) and (3) of these rules), the tribunal decide to make an order in the terms of the application by the landlord without a formal hearing, any application under rule 3(1) in respect of the holding shall be dismissed.

(3)   If no reply to an application under rule 3(1) is received from an applicant by the secretary within the time allowed by rule 8(1), the applicant who has not replied shall not be entitled to dispute any matter alleged in the application, but this paragraph does not affect the right of that applicant to claim before the tribunal that he is more suitable than the other applicant.

16   Procedure at hearing in case of sole applicant

Where on the date of the hearing only one application under rule 3(1) is pending before the tribunal, the applicant shall begin, and the order of proceedings shall be the same as in civil proceedings in the High Court as if the application were an action begun by writ and as if any application by the landlord were a counterclaim.

17   Procedure at hearing in case of multiple accidents where designation is claimed

(1)   Where any applicant under rule 3(1) claims to be a designated applicant the tribunal shall first hear him as to the validity of his claim to be a designated applicant (and if more than one applicant so claims, the tribunal shall hear them on those respective claims in the order determined by the tribunal), and shall then afford any other applicant (including any applicant who himself so claims) an opportunity to reply to that claim.

(2)   The tribunal shall thereupon determine the validity of each claim to be a designated applicant.

(3)   If the tribunal determine that an applicant under rule 3(1) is a designated applicant, they shall then hear that person's application as if he were the only applicant.

(4)   If under paragraph (3) the tribunal determine that the designated applicant is a suitable person to become the tenant of the holding, they—
- (a)   shall dismiss all other applications under rule 3(1), and
- (b)   shall, subject to rule 13, hear any application by the landlord.

(5)   If under paragraph (3) the tribunal determine that the designated applicant is not a suitable person to become the tenant of the holding, they—
- (a)   shall dismiss his application, and
- (b)   shall, unless there is any remaining issue to be determined under paragraph (2) above, hear the remaining applications under rule 3(1) in accordance with rules 13 and 16 (or, in the case of two or more such applications, under rule 18) as if no applicant had claimed to be a designated applicant.

(6)   If under paragraphs (1) and (2) the tribunal determine that there is no designated applicant, rule 18 shall apply.

18   Procedure at hearing is ease of multiple applicants where designation is not claimed

(1)   Where the tribunal have to hear more than one application under rule 3(1) and no applicant claims or has been determined to be a designated applicant, then, subject to any direction by the chairman, the tribunal shall—

- (a)   dispose of the various matters before them in the following order, that is to say—
    - (i)   any determination as to eligibility under section 21(3) of the 1976 Act;
    - (ii)   any remaining issue as to eligibility under section 20(3) of the 1976 Act;
    - (iii)   any determination as to suitability under section 20(3) of the 1976 Act;
    - (iv)   any question of exercising the discretion conferred by section 20(9) of the 1976 Act;
    - (v)   any determination as to relative suitability under section 20(6) of the 1976 Act;
    - (vi)   any question arising under section 20(9A) of the 1976 Act;
    - (vii)   subject to rule 13, any question arising on an application by the landlord under section 22 of the 1976 Act, and
- (b)   hear the person who is in the position of applicant in respect of any of the matters referred to in subparagraph (a) above and then the other parties in such order as the tribunal may determine, and, for the purpose of this subparagraph, any request for the landlord's consent made under rule 8(2) or at the hearing shall be treated as if it were an application.

(2)   Where, under paragraph (1)(a)(iii), two or more applicants are determined to be suitable persons to become the tenant of the holding, then—

- (a)   the tribunal shall ask the landlord if he will consent to the giving of a direction in accordance with section 20(9) of the 1976 Act specifying any two, any three, or any four of the suitable applicants and entitling them to a joint tenancy of the holding, and if the landlord then consents the tribunal may (after hearing such of the suitable applicants as wish to be heard) give a direction specifying the applicants in respect of whom the landlord's consent is given, and entitling them to a joint tenancy of the holding;
- (b)   the tribunal may give the landlord an opportunity to consent within such time as they may allow, and may regard his consent as refused if not given within that time.

(3)   Where the tribunal dispose of any matter under paragraph (1)(a)(i), (ii), (iii), (v) or (vii) in such a way that any particular application can no longer succeed, that application shall be dismissed.

19   Further provisions relating to notice to quit

Where the proceedings are adjourned under rule 13(1) and the landlord then fails to make an application under rule 4 within the time allowed by that rule, the tribunal may, without a formal hearing, give a direction under section 20(5) or 20(6) of the 1976 Act (as the case may be) entitling the suitable applicant to a tenancy of the holding.

20   Application of principal rules relating to evidence, decisions, etc

(1)   Rules 28 to 31 and 33 to 38 of the principal rules shall apply with the necessary modifications to proceedings under this Part of these rules as they apply to other proceedings before the tribunal.

(2)   For the purposes of rules 31, 33 and 34 of the principal rules, any dismissal of an application under these rules shall be a decision, and all such decisions, and the reasons for them, may be given in a single document at the conclusion of the proceedings unless the chairman otherwise decides.

21   Postponement of operation of notice to quit or direction

(1)   Where the tribunal give their consent to the operation of a notice to quit under section 22 of the 1976 Act within the period of three months ending with the original operative date or at any time after that date, any application by the tenant under subsection (6) of that section for the notice to have effect from a later date shall be made in writing to the secretary before the hearing or verbally at the hearing.

(2)   Where the tribunal give a direction under section 20(5), (6) or (9) of the 1976 Act within the period of three months ending with the relevant time apart from section 23 (2A) of that Act, any application by the tenant under that subsection for the direction to have effect from a later time shall be made in writing to the secretary before the hearing or verbally at the hearing.

[1087]

PART III
APPLICATION FOR SUCCESSION BY PERSON NOMINATED BY RETIRING
TENANT UNDER SCHEDULE 2 TO THE AGRICULTURAL HOLDINGS ACT 1984

22   Interpretation of Part III

(1)   In this Part of these rules "the 1984 Act" means the Agricultural Holdings Act 1984.

(2)   Expressions defined for the purposes of, or of any provision in, paragraphs 1 to 6 of Schedule 2 to the 1984 Act (notably in paragraphs 1 (1) and (2) and 6(7), have the same meaning in this Part of these rules.

FORM OF APPLICATION AND REPLY

23   Application by nominated successor

(1)   An application by the nominated successor to the tribunal under paragraph 5(1) of Schedule 2 to the 1984 Act for a direction entitling him to a tenancy of an agricultural holding shall be made in Form 5.

(2)   An application made under this rule shall not be entertained by the tribunal if it is not made within the relevant period.

24   Notice of application

The nominated successor shall at the time of making his application serve notice of the application in Form 6 on the landlord.

25   Landlord's reply

A landlord who intends to oppose the whole or any part of an application under rule 23(1) shall, within one month after a copy of the application has been served on him, reply thereto in Form 5R (which is the form appended on the copy of the application served on him).

PARTIES

26   Parties

There shall be parties to the proceedings on an application by the nominated successor—
    (a)   the nominated successor,
    (b)   the landlord, and
    (c)   the retiring tenant or (in the case of a joint tenancy) all the retiring tenants.

GENERAL PROVISIONS AS TO APPLICATIONS AND REPLIES

27 Service of documents by secretary

As soon as possible after receiving from any person any document under rule 23 or 25 the secretary shall serve one copy thereof on every other person who, in accordance with rule 26, is a party to the proceedings on that application.

28 Application of principal rules relating to applications and replies under this Part of these rules

Rules 16 (except for paragraph (5)) and 18 (except for paragraph (2)) of the principal rules shall apply to applications and replies under this Part of these rules.

HEARINGS

29 Date and place of hearing

As soon as practicable the chairman shall fix a date, time and place for the hearing of an application made under this Part of these rules.

30 Application of principal rules relating to preparation for hearing and to hearing

Rules 19, 20, 23(3) and (4), 24, 25, 26(2) and (3) and 27 of the principal rules shall apply with the necessary modifications to applications under this Part of these rules.

FURTHER PROVISIONS RELATING TO HEARINGS

31 Sanctions for failure to reply

If no reply to an application under rule 23(1) is received from the landlord by the secretary within the time allowed by rule 25, then, subject to paragraph 5(5) of Schedule 2 to the 1984 Act, the landlord shall not be entitled to dispute any matter alleged in that application.

32 Procedure at hearing

(1) Subject to paragraph (2), at the hearing the nominated successor shall begin and the other parties shall be heard in such order as the tribunal may determine.

(2) Where the retirement notice to which the nominated successor's application relates includes a statement in accordance with paragraph 2(3) of Schedule 2 to the 1984 Act that the notice is given on the grounds mentioned in that provision, the tribunal shall first consider whether the conditions specified in paragraph 5(3)(a) and (b) of that Schedule are satisfied and, if the tribunal determine that those conditions are not satisfied, they shall dismiss the nominated successor's application.

33 Application of principal rules relating to evidence, decisions etc

(1) Rules 28 to 31 and 33 to 38 of the principal rules shall apply with the necessary modifications to proceedings under this Part of these rules as they apply to other proceedings before the tribunal.

(2) For the purposes of rules 31, 33 and 34 of the principal rules, any dismissal of an application under these rules shall be a decision, and all such decisions, and the reasons for them, may be given in a single document at the conclusion of the proceedings unless the chairman otherwise decides.

34 Postponement of operation of direction

Where the tribunal give a direction under paragraph 5(6) of Schedule 2 to the 1984 Act within the period of three months ending with the retirement date, any application by the tenant under paragraph 6(7) of that Schedule for the direction to have effect from a later time shall be made in writing to the secretary before the hearing or verbally at the hearing.

[1088]

APPENDIX
FORMS

Rule 1(3)(b)

FORM 1 (SUCCESSION ON DEATH)

Rule 3(1) and (2)
Ref No
To be inserted by the secretary.

AGRICULTURAL LAND TRIBUNAL

Application for Direction giving Entitlement to Tenancy of Agricultural Holding

Application for Determination that Applicant be Treated as an Eligible Person

[In completing this form it is important to refer to the notes]

PART A—To be completed by all applicants

To the secretary of the Agricultural Land Tribunal
for the   Area.

1.   I,   *[block capitals]*

of   *[address]*

hereby apply under section 20(1) of the Agriculture (Miscellaneous Provisions) Act 1976 for a direction entitling me to a tenancy of the holding specified in paragraph 2 below.

2.   The holding in respect of which the application is made as known as and consists of:—

(a)   hectares of arable land (including temporary grass)

(Ordnance Survey Field Nos   );

(b)   hectares of permanent pasture

(Ordnance Survey Field Nos   );

(c)   hectares of rough grazing

(Ordnance Survey Field Nos   );

(d)   hectares of other land (including orchards)

(Ordnance Survey Field Nos   );

Total   hectares.   ANNUAL RENT £

3.   The current year of the tenancy of the holding expires on

4.   The holding includes the following buildings [*give a general description*]:—

†5.   The holding forms part of a larger agricultural unit known as and consisting of [*give a general description*]:—

6.   The application arises on the death of   formerly the tenant of the holding referred to in paragraph 2, who died on[1]

His/her tenancy was—

*(a)   granted before 12th July 1984.

*(b)   obtained on or after 12th July 1984 by virtue of a direction of the Agricultural Land Tribunal under section 20 of the 1976 Act.

*(c)   granted on or after 12th July 1984 following a direction of the Agricultural Land Tribunal under section 20 of the 1976 Act but commenced before the relevant time for the purposes of section 23 of that Act.

*(d)   granted on or after 12th July 1984 by a written contract of tenancy indicating that the succession provisions in Part II of the 1976 Act should apply.

*(e)   granted on or after 12th July 1984 to a person who, immediately before that date, was a tenant of the holding or of any agricultural holding which comprised the whole or a substantial part of the land comprised in the holding.

7.   The landlord of the holding is

of   [address].

†8.   I am the sole person validly designated by the deceased tenant of the holding in

PART II
STATUTORY INSTRUMENTS

547

his will as the person he wished to succeed him as tenant of the holding. A copy of the relevant part of the will in which I am designated is attached [*attach a copy of or extract from the will marking the relevant passage*][2].

9.

†(a) I am the *wife/*husband/*brother/*sister/*child of the deceased tenant[3].

†(b) I was treated by the deceased tenant as a child of the family in relation to his marriage to   4

on   [*give date of marriage*].

†10.

(a) During the seven years ending with the date of death of the deceased tenant my only or my principal source of livelihood was derived from—

*(i) my agricultural work on the holding, or on an agricultural unit of which the holding forms a part;

*(ii) his/his and my agricultural work on the holding, or on an agricultural unit of which the holding forms a part;

during the following period(s) and in the following manner [*give details of the way livelihood derived from agricultural work on the holding*][5]:—

*(b) During the period(s) specified in paragraph 10(a) I had the following source(s) of livelihood other than those derived from the holding or from an agricultural unit of which the holding forms a part [*give details of other sources of livelihood*]:—

*(c) During the period(s) specified in paragraph 10(a) I had no other source of livelihood.

†11. During the seven years ending with the date of death of the deceased tenant I attended a full-time course at   [*name of university, college or other establishment of further education*] during the following period(s) [*give details of time spent at university, etc*][5],[6]:—

During this period/these periods I studied the following subjects and obtained the following qualifications [*give details of subjects studied and any qualifications obtained*]:—

†12.

(a) The following agricultural land is occupied by me, my spouse or a company under my control, the control of my spouse or our joint control as owner-occupier/tenant/licensee, whether alone or jointly with others [*give particulars of any land occupied, including area and any land occupied jointly with others*][7]:—

†(b) The following agricultural land is occupied by a person under a licence or such a tenancy as is mentioned in paragraph 2(1)(a) to (d) of Schedule 3A to the 1976 Act [8] granted by *me and/or *my spouse and/or *a company controlled by me and/or my spouse †together with one or more other persons, being at the time it was granted a person or persons entitled to occupy the land otherwise than under a tenancy, or in a capacity, falling within paragraph 2(1)(a) to (f) of that Schedule[8] [*give particulars of any land occupied, including area*]:—

†(c) I apply under paragraph 4(2) of Schedule 3A to the 1976 Act for the net annual income from the following agricultural land which is—

*(i) jointly occupied;

*(ii) deemed by virtue of paragraph 6(2) of that Schedule to be jointly occupied;

by me and one or more other persons (not being only my spouse or a company under my control, the control of my spouse or our joint control) to be treated as limited to my appropriate share of that net annual income [*give particulars of any land in joint occupation or deemed joint occupation*][9]:—

13.   I was born on

14.   I claim to be a suitable person to receive the tenancy of this holding because[10]:—

PART B—To be completed if you think that you may not fully satisfy the requirements of paragraph 10(a)

15.   Further to the application set out in the preceding paragraphs of this Form,

I,   [*block capitals*]

of the above address also apply under section 21(2) of the 1976 Act for a determination that I am to be treated as an eligible person for the purposes of Part II of that Act[11].

16.

(a)   During the seven years ending with the date of death of the deceased tenant my livelihood was derived from—

*(i)   my agricultural work on the holding referred to in paragraph 2, or on an agricultural unit of which the holding forms a part;

*(ii)   his/his and my agricultural work on the holding referred to in paragraph 2, or on an agricultural unit of which the holding forms a part;

to a material extent during the following period(s) and in the following manner [*give details of the extent to which livelihood was derived from agricultural work on the holding*][12]:—

†(b)   During the period(s) specified in paragraph 16(a) I had the following source(s) of livelihood other than those derived from the holding or from an agricultural unit of which the holding forms a part [*give details of other sources of livelihood*]:—

†(c)   During the period(s) specified in paragraph 16(a) I had no other source of livelihood.

†17.   During the seven years ending with the date of death of the deceased tenant I attended a full-time course at   [*name of university, college or other establishment of further education*] during the following period(s) [*give details of time spent at university, etc*][6]:—

During this period/these periods I studied the following subjects and obtained the following qualifications [*give details of subjects studied and any qualifications obtained*]:—

†18.   I claim that, because of the following circumstances, it is fair and reasonable for me to be able to apply under section 20 of the 1976 Act for a direction entitling me to a tenancy of the holding referred to in paragraph 21[3]:—

PART C—To be completed by all applicants

19.   I attach the following documents which I intend to produce in support of my case:—

(a)   two[14] copies of a 6" to one mile or 1/10,000[15] map of the holding described in paragraph 2 above (and of the other land referred to in paragraph 5);

(b)   two[14] copies of [16]:—

20.   The persons whom I shall notify of this application/these applications are[17]:—

(a)   the landlord of the holding whose name and address are:—

(b)

(c)

(d)

21.

(a)   The following is/are the personal representative(s) of the deceased tenant or [*if there are no personal representatives*] the person or persons responsible for the management of the holding on behalf of the deceased's estate[18]:—

Name(s)   ....

Address(es)   ....

....

....

....

(b) The following person(s) is/are or my be interested in the outcome of this application[18]:—

Name(s)   ....

Address(es)   ....

....

....

....

Nature of   ....

interest   ....

Date   ....   Signed[19]   ....

*Strike out whichever is inapplicable.
†Strike out if inapplicable.

Notes:

[1] Formal proof of the date of death will be required at the hearing.

[2] This paragraph should be completed only if the applicant received a specific bequest of the deceased's tenancy under his will or is specifically named in the will as the person whom the deceased tenant wished to succeed him as tenant of the holding. It will be necessary for a grant of probate or administration to be obtained from the Family Division of the High Court in respect of the will before the tribunal can hear any claim to be a designated applicant. Where an applicant establishes that he is so designated under the deceased tenant's will, no other application will be considered unless the tribunal determine that the designated applicant is not an eligible person or is not a suitable person to become the tenant of the holding.

[3] Formal proof of the relationship to the deceased, eg, by production of marriage or birth certificates, may be required at the hearing. Adopted children should complete this sub-paragraph, and not paragraph 9(b) following.

[4] Paragraph 9(b) may apply where the applicant was the step-child or foster child or the deceased or was otherwise treated by him as his child. An outline should be given of the circumstances relied on as establishing that the applicant was treated by the deceased as his child in relation to the marriage. Production of the relevant marriage certificate and any relevant birth certificate may be required at the hearing.

[5] To qualify under paragraph 10(a)(i) the applicant should have derived his only or principal source of livelihood from his agricultural work on the holding (or on a larger unit of which the holding forms part) during a total of five years of the seven years ending with the death of the deceased tenant. Paragraph 10(a)(ii) is available only to a widow of the deceased tenant. The total of five years may be made up of one continuous period, or one or more separate periods. A period of full-time education at a university etc, may, in the circumstances set out in note [6], count towards the five-year period of earning a livelihood from the holding, and reference should be made to paragraph 11 and note[6] in deciding whether the requirements of this paragraph can be satisfied.

An applicant who cannot satisfy the requirements of paragraph 10(a) fully but who believes he can satisfy them to a material extent should not complete paragraphs 10 and 11 but should complete instead paragraph 15, together with paragraphs 16, 17 (if relevant) and 18 in Part B of the Form. The Notes to those paragraphs should also be consulted. Where an applicant is in any doubt as to whether or not he can satisfy the requirements of paragraph 10 fully, he is advised to complete paragraphs 10 and 11 (if relevant) and Part B of the Form.

[6] Any period or periods (up to an aggregate total of three years) during the seven years ending with the date of death of the deceased tenant during which the applicant was attending a full-time course at a university, college or other establishment of further education will be treated as a period throughout which his only or principal source of livelihood was derived from his agricultural work on the holding. Any subject may have been studied.

[7] Land occupied by the applicant's spouse or by a company controlled by that person or jointly by that person and the applicant should not be included in paragraph 12 where either of the parties has obtained a decree of judicial separation or a decree nisi of divorce or of nullity of marriage

and in each case that decree remains unrescinded. In addition, land should not be included in paragraph 12 if it is occupied by the applicant, his spouse or a controlled company—

(a)   under a tenancy approved under section 2(1) of the Agricultural Holdings Act 1948 or under such a tenancy relating to the use of land for grazing or mowing as is referred to in the proviso to that provision;

(b)   under a tenancy for more than one year but less than two years;

(c)   under a tenancy not falling within (a) or (b) above and not having effect as a contract of tenancy;

(d)   under a tenancy to which section 3 of the 1948 Act does not apply by virtue of section 3B of that Act;

(e)   as a licensee; or

(f)   as an executor, administrator, trustee in bankruptcy or person otherwise deriving title from another person by operation of law.

However, where the applicant occupies land in accordance with (a) to (e) above under a licence or tenancy granted to him by his spouse or by a body corporate controlled by him, that land should be included in paragraph 12.

8   Paragraph 2(1)(a) to (f) of Schedule 3A to the Agriculture (Miscellaneous Provisions) Act 1976 is set out in note[7].

9   If the applicant occupies land jointly with one or more other persons (not being only his spouse or a company under the control of the applicant or his spouse or under their joint control), or if the applicant is deemed to occupy land jointly with one or more such persons, he may in either case complete the application set out in paragraph 12(c) of the Form for the net annual income which the land is or was capable of producing to be treated as limited to his appropriate share.

10   All matters relied on as supporting the claim to be a suitable person to become the tenant of the holding should be summarised. These should include details of the applicant's training and practical experience of agriculture, physical health, financial standing and any educational qualifications not already listed in paragraph 11 or 17.

11   This paragraph should be completed (together with paragraphs 16, 17 (if relevant) and 18) in any case where the applicant, while otherwise meeting the conditions contained in paragraphs (a) and (c) of the definition of "eligible person" in section 18(2) of the 1976 Act cannot fully satisfy the conditions as to deriving his principal or main source of livelihood from the holding contained in paragraph (b) of that subsection. (It is also necessary for the application set out in paragraph 1 of the Form to be completed in addition to completing this paragraph.) An applicant who fully satisfies the requirements of paragraph 10(a) need not complete this paragraph or paragraphs 16, 17 and 18.

12   The applicant should state to what extent he has derived his livelihood from his agricultural work on the holding (or on a larger unit of which the holding forms part) during a total of five years of the seven years ending with the death of the deceased tenant. Paragraph 16(a)(ii) applies only to a widow of the deceased tenant. The total of five years may be made up of one continuous period, or one or more separate periods. A period of full-time education at a university, etc, may in certain circumstances count in relation to the five year period as a period in which a livelihood was derived from agricultural work on the holding, and paragraph 17 should also be completed where relevant.

13   A summary should be given of matters relied on as establishing that it is fair and reasonable that the applicant should be entitled to apply under section 20 of the 1976 Act for a tenancy of the holding, though not fully satisfying the conditions specified in paragraph (b) of the definition of "eligible person" in section 18(2) of that Act. The length of time the applicant has lived on the holding, details of work done by him on the holding (apart from those already given in paragraph 16) and any special circumstances which have prevented him from qualifying in full as an eligible person under paragraph (b) of the definition of "eligible person" should be given. (Note [5] describes the requirements needed to qualify fully under paragraph (b) of the definition.)

14   By virtue of rule 11(1) of the Agricultural Land Tribunals (Succession) Rules 1984 two copies of the application and of any map and document must be sent to the secretary.

15   A larger scale map may be used if preferred. Ordnance Survey Field Numbers must be marked on the map.

16   Mention any other document which is attached to this application.

17   The applicant is required to send to the landlord of the holding, and to every other person who to his knowledge has made or may be able to make an application for a tenancy of the holding, notice of this application in Form 3 (Succession on Death) which is set out in the Appendix to the Agricultural Land Tribunals (Succession) Rules 1984. The applicant should enter the name and address of the landlord at (a) and the names and addresses of appropriate other persons (if any) respectively at (b), (c) and (d), etc.

18   This information is required by rule 5(2) of those Rules.

19   If signed by any person other than the applicant himself, he should state in what capacity or by what authority he signs.

[1089]

FORM 1R (SUCCESSION ON DEATH)

Rule 6

Ref No

To be inserted by the secretary.

AGRICULTURAL LAND TRIBUNAL

Reply to Application for Direction giving Entitlement to Tenancy of Agricultural Holding

Reply to Application for Determination that Applicant be Treated as an Eligible Person

To the secretary of the Agricultural Land Tribunal
for the   Area.
I,   *[block capitals]*
of   *[address]*
landlord of   ₑ   *[name or description of holding]*
having received a copy of the application bearing the above reference number reply as
follows:—

    1.   The facts stated in paragraphs 1, 2, 4 and 7 of the application are, to the best of any knowledge, information and belief, correct †except that:—

   †2.   I dispute the claim of the applicant to be an eligible person[1] on the following grounds:—

   †3.   I dispute the claim of the applicant to be treated as an eligible person[2] on the following grounds:—

    4.   I have the following comments on the suitability of the applicant to become the tenant of the above holding:—

    5.   I attach two copies of the following relevant documents[3]:—

    6.   I consider the application to be invalid by reason of[4]:—
Date ....   Signed[5] ....
†Strike out if inapplicable.
TAKE NOTICE THAT IF YOU DO NOT REPLY IN THIS FORM WITHIN ONE MONTH OF THE DATE OF SERVICE ON YOU OF THE ATTACHED APPLICATION, THEN, SUBJECT TO SECTION 20(7) OF THE AGRICULTURE (MISCELLANEOUS PROVISIONS) ACT 1976, YOU WILL NOT BE ENTITLED AT THE HEARING OF THE APPLICATION TO DISPUTE ANY MATTER ALLEGED IN IT.

Notes:
[1]   The paragraphs of the application which (where completed) will be relevant to the applicant's claim to be an eligible person are paragraphs 9, 10, 11 and 12.
[2]   The paragraphs of the application which (where completed) will be relevant to the applicant's claim to be treated as an eligible person are paragraphs 15, 16, 17 and 18.
[3]   By virtue of rule 11(1) of the Agricultural Land Tribunals (Succession) Rules 1984 two copies of this reply and of any document which you wish to submit to the tribunal must be sent to the secretary. If you disagree with any map or plan attached to the application, your reply should be accompanied by two copies of a 6" to one mile or 1/10,000 (or larger) map showing what you consider to be the true position and marking the Ordnance Survey Field Numbers.
[4]   If you consider that, for any reason, the applicant is not legally entitled to make his application, you should state succinctly the grounds on which you rely.
[5]   If signed by any person other than the landlord himself, he should state in what capacity or by what authority he signs.

[1090]

FORM 2 (SUCCESSION ON DEATH)
Rule 4(1)
Ref No
To be inserted by the secretary.

AGRICULTURAL LAND TRIBUNAL

Application for Consent to Operation of Notice to Quit

To the secretary of the Agricultural Land Tribunal
for the   Area.

    1.   I,   *[block capitals]*

       of   *[address]*

hereby apply under section 22(1) of the Agriculture (Miscellaneous Provisions) Act 1976 for the consent of the tribunal to the operation of a notice to quit which I gave to   and   being the personal representative(s) of   [*block capitals*] deceased, formerly of   [*address*].

I was officially notified of his/her death by   on

2.   The notice to quit was served on [*insert date*]

in respect of the holding known as

3.   An application (bearing reference number ....) to the tribunal under Part II of the 1976 Act or a tenancy of this holding was made on

Full particulars of the holding are set out in that application †(as amended in reply to that application dated   ).

4.   I apply for the tribunal's consent to the operation of the notice to quit in the event of an applicant under the application referred to in paragraph 3, or any other such applicant, being determined by the tribunal to be a suitable person to become the tenant of the holding.

5.   The grounds upon which I make this application are those provided by paragraphs(s)   of section 3(3) of the Agricultural Holdings (Notices to Quit) Act 1977 as read with section 22(2) of the 1976 Act, as amended. [*It is important to refer to note* [1].]

6.   The main facts on which I will base my case are:—

7.   If I obtain possession of the land I intend:—

         *(a) to farm it myself.

         *(b) to let it to another tenant [*state name and address if known*].

         *(c) [*state any other intention*]

†8.   The future tenant referred to in paragraph 7(b)[2] at present farms other land consisting of:—

         (a)   hectares of arable land (including temporary grass)

         (Ordnance Survey Field Nos   );

         (b)   hectares of permanent pasture

         (Ordnance Survey Field Nos   );

         (c)   hectares of rough grazing

         (Ordnance Survey Field Nos   );

         (d)   hectares of other land (including orchards)

         (Ordnance Survey Field Nos   );

TOTAL   hectares

9.   I attach the following documents which I intend to produce in support of my case:—

         (a)   two copies[3] of a 6" to one mile or 1/10,000[4] map of the land described in paragraph 8[5] above;

         (b)   two copies[3] of[6]:—

Date.......................................   Signed[7].......................................
*Strike out whichever is inapplicable.
†Strike out if inapplicable.

Notes:
[1]   The applicant must state on which paragraph or paragraphs of the subsection he intends to rely. The five paragraphs state as follows:—
         (a)   that the carrying out of the purpose for which the landlord proposes to terminate the tenancy is desirable in the interests of good husbandry as respects the land to which the notice relates, treated as a separate unit;

PART II
STATUTORY INSTRUMENTS

(b)   that the carrying out thereof is desirable in the interests of sound management of the estate of which the land to which the notice relates forms part or which that land constitutes (see note [5] below);

(c)   that the carrying out thereof is desirable for the purposes of agricultural research, education, experiment or demonstration, or for the purposes of the enactments relating to smallholdings or allotments;

(d)   that greater hardship would be caused by withholding than by giving consent to the operation of the notice;

(e)   that the landlord proposes to terminate the tenancy for the purpose of the land's being used for a use, other than for agriculture, not falling within Case B in section 2(3) of the Agricultural Holdings (Notices to Quit) Act 1977.

        If, under paragraph (d) above, the applicant intends to rely on hardship to a person or persons other than himself, he should set out in paragraph 6 the name of every person who will be so affected, and the relationship of that person to himself, and should state the nature of the hardship on which he relies.

[2]   Paragraph 8 need not be completed if the name of the future tenant is unknown. Where land is described, a map should be provided (see note [5] below).

[3]   By virtue of rule 11(1) of the Agricultural Land Tribunals (Succession) Rules 1984 two copies of the application and of any map and document must be sent to the secretary.

[4]   A larger scale map may be used if preferred. Ordnance Survey Field Numbers must be marked on the map.

[5]   Where it is intended to give evidence about any land other than that which is the subject of the notice to quit, it must be shown either on the map produced or on a separate map of a scale of 6" to one mile or 1/10,000 (or larger).

[6]   Mention any other document which is attached to this application.

[7]   If signed by any person other than the applicant himself, he should state in what capacity or by what authority he signs.

[1091]

FORM 2R (SUCCESSION ON DEATH)

Rule 7
Ref No
To be inserted by the secretary.

AGRICULTURAL LAND TRIBUNAL

Reply to Application for Consent to Operation of Notice to Quit

To the secretary of the Agricultural Land Tribunal
for the   Area.
I,   *[block capitals]*
of   *[address]*
having applied to the tribunal on   for a direction
entitling me to a tenancy of   and having received a copy
of the application (bearing the above reference number) for the tribunal's consent to the operation of a notice to quit, reply as follows:—

1.   The facts stated in the first three paragraphs of the application are correct †except that:—

2.   My main reasons for resisting the application are:—

†3.   The landlord is not acting fairly and reasonably because[1]:—

4.   I attach copies of the following relevant documents[2]:—

Date.....................................   Signed[3] ....

TAKE NOTICE THAT IF YOU DO NOT REPLY IN THIS FORM WITHIN ONE MONTH OF THE DATE OF SERVICE ON YOU OF THE ATTACHED APPLICATION BY THE LANDLORD OF THE HOLDING FOR THE TRIBUNAL'S CONSENT TO THE OPERATION OF THE LANDLORD'S NOTICE TO QUIT, THE TRIBUNAL MAY GIVE THAT CONSENT SUMMARILY AND SUMMARILY DISMISS YOUR OWN APPLICATION TO BE GRANTED A TENANCY OF THE HOLDING, WITHOUT HEARING YOUR CASE.

†Strike out if inapplicable.

Notes:

[1]   The tribunal must withhold consent if, in all the circumstances, it appears that a fair and reasonable landlord would not insist on possession. If you have any special reasons for saying the landlord is acting unfairly or unreasonably which do not appear under paragraph 2, you should state them under paragraph 3.

[2]   By virtue of rule 11(1) of the Agricultural Land Tribunals (Succession) Rules 1984 two copies of

the reply and of any document which you wish to submit to the tribunal must be sent to the secretary.

If you disagree with any map or plan attached to the application, your reply should be accompanied by two copies of a 6" to one mile or 1/10,000 (or larger) map showing what you consider to be the true position and marking the Ordnance Survey Field Numbers.

3   If signed by any person other than the applicant himself, he should state in what capacity or by what authority he signs.

[1092]

FORM 3 (SUCCESSION ON DEATH)

Rule 5(1)

Ref No

To be inserted by the secretary.

AGRICULTURAL LAND TRIBUNAL

Notice of Application for Entitlement to Tenancy under Part II of the Agriculture (Miscellaneous Provisions) Act 1976

To: *[name]*
of   *[address]*
I,   *[block capitals]*
of   *[address]*
hereby give you notice that I applied on   *[date of application]*
under Part II of the above-named Act for a direction entitling me to a tenancy of the agricultural holding known as
[address or brief description of holding] in succession to
[name of deceased tenant of the holding] who died on
Dated .... Signed ....
A copy of the full application will in due course be sent to the landlord and any other applicants by the secretary to the tribunal.

[1093]

FORM 4 (SUCCESSION ON DEATH)

Rule 8
Ref No
To be inserted by the secretary.

AGRICULTURAL LAND TRIBUNAL

Reply to Application for Direction giving Entitlement to Tenancy of Agricultural Holding

To the secretary of the Agricultural Land Tribunal
for the   Area.
I,   *[block capitals]*
of   *[address]*
having received a copy of the application of   (hereinafter
called "the applicant") bearing the above reference number, reply as follows:—

1.   The facts stated in the first seven paragraphs of the application are correct †except that:—

2.   *I accept the applicant's claim to be a designated applicant, as stated in paragraph 8 of the application.

OR

*I dispute the applicant's claim to be designated applicant, as stated in paragraph 8 of the application, on the following grounds:—

3.   I do not dispute any of the matters stated in paragraphs 9–13, 16 and 17 of the application †except that:—

4.   I claim to be a more suitable person than the applicant to be granted a tenancy of the holding; and I base this claim on the following grounds:—

†5.   The applicant and I †(and)   have agreed to request the landlord's consent to a direction entitling us to a joint tenancy of the holding.

Date .... Signed ....

PART II
STATUTORY INSTRUMENTS

†Strike out if inapplicable
*Strike out whichever is inapplicable.

[1094]

FORM 5 (SUCCESSION ON RETIREMENT)
Rule 23(1)
Ref No
To be inserted by the secretary.

AGRICULTURAL LAND TRIBUNAL

Application for Direction giving Entitlement to Tenancy of Agricultural Holding
[In completing this form it is important to refer to the notes]
To the secretary of the Agricultural Land Tribunal
for the   Area.

1. I,   *[block capitals]*

of   *[address]*

hereby apply under paragraph 5(1) of Schedule 2 to the Agricultural Holdings Act 1984 for a direction entitling me to a tenancy of the holding specified in paragraph 2 below.

2. The holding in respect of which the application is made is known as and consists of:—

    (a)   hectares of arable land (including temporary grass)

    (Ordnance Survey Field Nos   );

    (b)   hectares of permanent pasture

    (Ordnance Survey Field Nos   );

    (c)   hectares of rough grazing

    (Ordnance Survey Field Nos   );

    (d)   hectares of other land (including orchards)

    (Ordnance Survey Field Nos   );

TOTAL   hectares   ANNUAL RENT £   .

3. The current year of the tenancy of the holding expires on

4. The holding includes the following buildings [*give a general description*]:—

†5. The holding forms part of a larger agricultural unit known as and consisting of [*give general description*]:—

6. The landlord of the holding is

of   *[address]*

The tenant(s) of the holding is/are

of   *[address(es)]*.

7. This application arises as a result of a retirement notice given by the tenant(s) to the landlord on

8. I am the nominated successor.

9.

    †(a) I am the *wife/*husband/*brother/*sister/*child of the tenant [*where there is more than one tenant, specify which*][1].

    †(b) I am treated by the tenant [*where there is more than one tenant, specify which*] as a child of the family in relation to his marriage to [2] on   [*give date of marriage*].

10.

(a) During the seven years ending with the date on which the tenant(s) gave the retirement notice to the landlord my only or principal source of livelihood was derived from—

*(i) my agricultural work on the holding, or on an agricultural unit of which the holding forms a part;

*(ii) the tenant's/the tenant's and my [*where there is more than one tenant, specify which*] agricultural work on the holding, or on an agricultural unit of which the holding forms a part;

during the following period(s) and in the following manner [*give details of the way livelihood derived from agricultural work on the holding*][3]:—

*(b) During the period(s) specified in paragraph 10(a) I had the following source(s) of livelihood other than those derived from the holding or from an agricultural unit of which the holding forms a part [*give details of other sources of livelihood*]:—

*(c) During the period(s) specified in paragraph 10(a) I had no other source of livelihood.

†11. During the seven years ending with the date on which the tenant(s) gave the retirement notice to the landlord I attended a full-time course at [*name of university, college or other establishment of further education*] during the following period(s) [*give details of time spent at university, etc*][4]:—

During this period/these periods I studied the following subjects and obtained the following qualifications [*give details of subjects studied and any qualifications obtained*]:—

†12.

(a) The following agricultural land is occupied by me, my spouse or a company under my control, the control of my spouse or our joint control as owner-occupier/tenant/licensee, whether alone or jointly with others [*give particulars of any land occupied, including area and any land occupied jointly with others*][5]:—

†(b) The following agricultural land is occupied by a person under a licence or such a tenancy as is mentioned in paragraph 2(1)(a) to (d) of Schedule 3A to the Agriculture (Miscellaneous Provisions) Act 1976[6] granted by *me and/or *my spouse and/or *a company controlled by me and/or my spouse† together with one or more other persons, being at the time it was granted a person or persons entitled to occupy the land otherwise than under a tenancy, or in a capacity, falling within paragraph 2(1)(a) to (f) of that Schedule[6] [*give particulars of any land occupied including area*]:—

†(c) I apply under paragraph 4(2) of Schedule 3A to the 1976 Act, as applied by paragraph 1(4)(b) of Schedule 2 to the 1984 Act, for the net annual income from the following agricultural land which is—

*(i) jointly occupied;

*(ii) deemed by virtue of paragraph 6(2) of the said Schedule 3A, as applied by the said paragraph 1(4)(b), to be jointly occupied;

by me and one or more other persons (not being only my spouse or a company under my control, the control of my spouse or our joint control) to be treated as limited to my appropriate share of that net annual income [*give particulars of any land in joint occupation or deemed joint occupation*][7]:—

13. I was born on

14. I claim to be a suitable person to receive the tenancy of this holding because[8]:—

15. I attach the following documents which I intend to produce in support of my case:—

(a) two[9] copies of a 6" to one mile or 1/10,000[10] map of the holding described in paragraph 2 above (and of the other land referred to in paragraph 5);

(b) two[9] copies of the retirement notice;

(c) two[9] copies of[11]:—

16. I shall notify the landlord of this application[12].

Date... Signed[13]...

Signature of retiring tenant(s)

....

....

....

....

*Strike out whichever is inapplicable.
†Strike out if inapplicable.

Notes:

1   Formal proof of the relationship to the tenant, eg, by production of marriage or birth certificates, may be required at the hearing. Adopted children should complete this sub-paragraph, and not paragraph 9(b) following.

2   Paragraph 9(b) may apply where the applicant is the step-child or foster child of the tenant or is otherwise treated by him as his child. An outline should be given of the circumstances relied on as establishing that the applicant is treated by the tenant as his child in relation to the marriage. Production of the relevant marriage certificate and any relevant birth certificate may be required at the hearing.

3   To qualify under paragraph 10(a)(i) the applicant should have derived his only or principal source of livelihood from his agricultural work on the holding (or on a larger unit of which the holding forms part) during a total of five years of the seven years ending with the date on which the tenant(s) gave the landlord the retirement notice. Paragraph 10(a)(ii) is available only to a tenant's wife. The total of five years may be made up of one continuous period, or one or more separate periods. A period of full-time education at a university etc, may, in the circumstances set out in note [4], count towards the five-year period of earning a livelihood from the holding, and reference should be made to paragraph 11 and note [4] in deciding whether the requirements of this paragraph can be satisfied.

4   Any period or periods (up to an aggregate total of three years) during the seven years ending with the date on which the tenant(s) gave the retirement notice to the landlord during which the applicant was attending a full-time course at a university, college or other establishment of further education will be treated as a period throughout which his only or principal source of livelihood was derived from his agricultural work on the holding. Any subject may have been studied.

5   Land occupied by the applicant's spouse or by a company controlled by that person or jointly by that person and the applicant should not be included in paragraph 12 where either of the parties has obtained a decree of judicial separation or a decree nisi of divorce or of nullity of marriage and in each case that decree remains unrescinded. In addition, land should not be included in paragraph 12 if it is occupied by the applicant, his spouse or a controlled company—

(a)   under a tenancy approved under section 2(1) of the Agricultural Holdings Act 1948 or under such a tenancy relating to the use of land for grazing or mowing as is referred to in the proviso to that provision;

(b)   under a tenancy for more than one year but less than two years;

(c)   under a tenancy not falling within (a) or (b) above and not having effect as a contract of tenancy;

(d)   under a tenancy to which section 3 of the 1948 Act does not apply by virtue of section 3B of that Act;

(e)   as a licensee; or

(f)   as an executor, administrator, trustee in bankruptcy or person otherwise deriving title from another person by operation of law.

However, where the applicant occupies land in accordance with (a) to (e) above under a licence or tenancy granted to him by his spouse or by a body corporate controlled by him, that land should be included in paragraph 12.

6   Paragraph 2(1)(a) to (f) of Schedule 3A to the Agriculture (Miscellaneous Provisions) Act 1976 is set out in note[5].

7   If the applicant occupies land jointly with one or more other persons (not being only his spouse or a company under the control of the applicant or his spouse or under their joint control), or if the applicant is deemed to occupy land jointly with one or more such persons, he may in either case complete the application set out in paragraph 12(c) of the Form for the net annual income which the land is or was capable of producing to be treated as limited to his appropriate share.

8   All matters relied on as supporting the claim to be a suitable person to become the tenant of the holding should be summarised. These should include details of the applicant's training and practical experience of agriculture, physical health, financial standing and any educational qualifications not already listed in paragraph 11.

9   By virtue of rule 28 of the Agricultural Land Tribunals (Succession) Rules 1984 two copies of the application and of any map and document must be sent to the secretary.

10   A larger scale map may be used if preferred. Ordnance Survey Field Numbers must be marked on the map.

11   Mention any other document which is attached to this application.

¹² The applicant is required to send to the landlord of the holding notice of this application in Form 6 (Succession on Retirement) which is set out in the Appendix to the Agricultural Land Tribunals (Succession) Rules 1984.

¹³ If signed by any person other than the applicant himself, he should state in what capacity or by what authority he signs.

[1095]

FORM 5R (SUCCESSION ON RETIREMENT)

Rule 25
Ref No
To be inserted by the secretary.

AGRICULTURAL LAND TRIBUNAL

Reply to Application for Direction giving Entitlement to Tenancy of Agricultural Holding

To the secretary of the Agricultural Land Tribunal
for the   Area.
I,   [*block capitals*]
of   [*address*]
landlord of   [*name or description of holding*]
having received a copy of the application bearing the above reference number reply as
follows:—

1. The facts stated in paragraphs 1, 2, 4, 6 and 7 of the application are, to the best of my knowledge, information and belief, correct †except that:—

†2. I dispute the claim of the applicant to be an eligible person1 on the following grounds:—

3. I have the following comments on the suitability of the applicant to become the tenant of the above holding:—

†4. I claim that greater hardship would be caused by the tribunal giving the direction sought by the applicant than by refusing his application and my reasons for this claim are:—

†5. The tenancy is the subject of a notice to quit Case *B/*C/*D/*E/*F served on [*date*].

†[*For Case C only*] The notice to quit is founded on a certificate granted in accordance with an application made on [*date*].

†[*For Case D only*] The notice to quit is founded on a notice given for the purposes of that Case on [*date*].

6. I attach two copies of the following relevant documents²:—

7. I consider the application to be invalid by reason of³:—

Date.......................................   Signed⁴...
*Strike out whichever is inapplicable.
†Strike out if inapplicable.
TAKE NOTICE THAT IF YOU DO NOT REPLY IN THIS FORM WITHIN ONE MONTH OF THE DATE OF SERVICE ON YOU OF THE ATTACHED APPLICATION, THEN, SUBJECT TO PARAGRAPH 5(5) OF SCHEDULE 2 TO THE AGRICULTURAL HOLDINGS ACT 1984, YOU WILL NOT BE ENTITLED AT THE HEARING OF THE APPLICATION TO DISPUTE ANY MATTER ALLEGED IN IT.

Notes:
¹ The paragraphs of the application which (where completed) will be relevant to the applicant's claim to be an eligible person are paragraphs 9, 10, 11 and 12.
² By virtue of rule 28 of the Agricultural Land Tribunals (Succession) Rules 1984 two copies of this reply and of any document which you wish to submit to the tribunal must be sent to the secretary. If you disagree with any map or plan attached to the application, your reply should be accompanied by two copies of a 6" to one mile or 1/10,000 (or larger) map showing what you consider to be the true position and marking the Ordnance Survey Field Numbers.
³ If you consider that, for any reason, the applicant is not legally entitled to make his application, you should state succinctly the grounds on which you rely.

⁴   If signed by any person other than the landlord himself, he should state in what capacity or by
what authority he signs.

[1096]

FORM 6 (SUCCESSION ON RETIREMENT)

Rule 24
Ref No
To be inserted by the secretary.

AGRICULTURAL LAND TRIBUNAL

**Notice of Application for Entitlement to Tenancy under Schedule 2 to the Agricultural
Holdings Act 1984**

To: [*name*]
of   [*address*]
I,   [*block capitals*]
of   [*address*]
hereby give you notice that I applied on   [*date of application*]
under Schedule 2 to the above-named Act for a direction entitling me to a tenancy of the
agricultural holding known as   [*address or brief
description of holding*] in succession to   [*name of present
tenant(s) of the holding*]
who served on you his/their retirement notice on
Dated.................................   Signed..
A copy of the full application will in due course be sent to you by the secretary to the tribunal.

[1097]

MILK QUOTA (CALCULATION OF STANDARD QUOTA)
ORDER 1986

(SI 1986/1530)

NOTES
   Made: 27 August 1986.
   Authority: Agriculture Act 1986, Sch 1, para 6.

1   Application, title and commencement

This order, which applies to land in England and Wales, may be cited as the Milk Quota
(Calculation of Standard Quota) Order 1986 and shall come into operation on 25th September
1986.

[1098]

[2   Interpretation

In this Order, the expressions "disadvantaged land" and "severely disadvantaged land" have
the same meaning as in the Hill Livestock (Compensatory Allowances) Regulations 1992.]

[1099]

NOTES
   Substituted by the Milk Quota (Calculation of Standard Quota) (Amendment) Order 1992,
SI 1992/1225, art 2.

3   Prescribed quota

The number of litres prescribed for the purposes of sub-paragraph 6(1)(b) of Schedule 1 to the
Agriculture Act 1986 (calculation of standard quota) in respect of each of the breeds shown in
Column 1 of the Schedule to this order is the number shown opposite that breed in—
   (a)   column 2(a) in relation to severely disadvantaged land;
   (b)   column 3(a) in relation to disadvantaged land; and
   (c)   column 4(a) in relation to any other land.

[1100]

4 Average yield per hectare

The amount of milk to be taken as the average yield per hectare for the purposes of sub-paragraph 6(2) of Schedule 1 to the Agriculture Act 1986 (calculation of standard quota in exceptional cases) in respect of each of the breeds shown in Column 1 of the Schedule to this order is the amount shown opposite that breed in—

    (a)   column 2(b) in relation to severely disadvantaged land;

    (b)   column 3(b) in relation to disadvantaged land; and

    (c)   column 4(b) in relation to any other land.

[1101]

[SCHEDULE

Articles 3, 4

(1)	(2) Severely disadvantaged land		(3) Disadvantaged land		(4) Other land	
Breed	*(a) Quota/ Hectare*	*(b) Average Yield/ Hectare*	*(a) Quota/ Hectare*	*(b) Average Yield/ Hectare*	*(a) Quota/ Hectare*	*(b) Average Yield/ Hectare*
	Litres	Litres	Litres	Litres	Litres	Litres
Channel Island and South Devon and breeds with similar characteristics	4,550	5,737	5,310	6,694	6,070	7,650
Ayrshire and Dairy Shorthorn and breeds with similar characteristics	5,205	6,562	6,075	7,656	6,940	8,750
Other	5,355	6,750	6,250	7,875	7,140	9,000]

[1102]

NOTES

Substituted by the Milk Quota (Calculation of Standard Quota) (Amendment) Order 1992, SI 1992/1225, art 2, Schedule.

INSOLVENCY RULES 1986

(SI 1986/1925)

NOTES

Made: 10 November 1986.
Authority: Insolvency Act 1986, ss 411, 412.

ARRANGEMENT OF RULES

INTRODUCTORY PROVISIONS

THE FIRST GROUP OF PARTS
COMPANY INSOLVENCY; COMPANIES WINDING UP

PART 4
COMPANIES WINDING UP

CHAPTER 15
DISCLAIMER

THE SECOND GROUP OF PARTS
INDIVIDUAL INSOLVENCY; BANKRUPTCY

PART 6
BANKRUPTCY

CHAPTER 14
DISCLAIMER

THE THIRD GROUP OF PARTS

PART 13
INTERPRETATION AND APPLICATION

NOTES

Modification: any reference to solicitor(s) etc modified to include references to bodies recognised under the Administration of Justice Act 1985, s 9, by the Solicitors' Incorporated Practices Order 1991, SI 1991/2684, arts 4, 5, Sch 1.

INTRODUCTORY PROVISIONS

0.1 Citation and commencement

These Rules may be cited as the Insolvency Rules 1986 and shall come into force on 29th December 1986.

[1103]

[0.2 Construction and interpretation

(1) In these Rules—

"the Act" means the Insolvency Act 1986 (any reference to a numbered section being to a section of that Act);

"the Companies Act" means the Companies Act 1985;

"CPR" means the Civil Procedure Rules 1998 and "CPR" followed by a Part or rule by number means the Part or rule with that number in those Rules;

"RSC" followed by an Order by number means the Order with that number set out in Schedule 1 to the CPR; and

"the Rules" means the Insolvency Rules 1986.

(2) References in the Rules to *ex parte* hearings shall be construed as references to hearings without notice being served on any other party; references to applications made *ex parte* as references to applications made without notice being served on any other party and other references which include the expression "*ex parte*" shall be similarly construed.

(3) Subject to paragraphs (1) and (2), Part 13 of the Rules has effect for their interpretation and application.]

[1104]

NOTES

Substituted by the Insolvency (Amendment) (No 2) Rules 1999, SI 1999/1022, r 3, Schedule, para 1.

0.3 Extent

(1) Parts 1, 2 and 4 of the Rules, and Parts 7 to 13 as they relate to company insolvency, apply in relation to companies which the courts in England and Wales have jurisdiction to wind up.

[(2) Rule 3.1 applies to all receivers to whom Part III of the Act applies, Rule 3.39 and 3.40 apply to all receivers who are not administrative receivers, and the remainder of Part 3 of the Rules applies to administrative receivers appointed otherwise than under section 51 (Scottish Receivership).]

(3) Parts 5 and 6 of the Rules, and Parts 7 to 13 as they relate to individual insolvency, extend to England and Wales only.

[1105]

NOTES

Para (2): substituted by the Insolvency (Amendment) Rules 2003, SI 2003/1730, r 3.

THE FIRST GROUP OF PARTS
COMPANY INSOLVENCY; COMPANIES WINDING UP

1.1–3.40   ((*Pts 1–3*) *Outside the scope of this work.*)

PART 4
COMPANIES WINDING UP

4.1–4.186   (*Outside the scope of this work.*)

CHAPTER 15
DISCLAIMER

4.187 Liquidator's notice of disclaimer

(1)   Where the liquidator disclaims property under section 178, the notice of disclaimer shall contain such particulars of the property disclaimed as enable it to be easily identified.

(2)   The notice shall be signed by the liquidator and filed in court, with a copy. The court shall secure that both the notice and the copy are sealed and endorsed with the date of filing.

(3)   The copy notice, so sealed and endorsed, shall be returned by the court to the liquidator as follows—
  (a)   if the notice has been delivered at the offices of the court by the liquidator in person, it shall be handed to him,
  (b)   if it has been delivered by some person acting on the liquidator's behalf, it shall be handed to that person, for immediate transmission to the liquidator, and
  (c)   otherwise, it shall be sent to the liquidator by first class post.

The court shall cause to be endorsed on the original notice, or otherwise recorded on the file, the manner in which the copy notice was returned to the liquidator.

(4)   For the purposes of section 178, the date of the prescribed notice is that which is endorsed on it, and on the copy, in accordance with this Rule.

[1106]

4.188 Communication of disclaimer to persons interested

(1)   Within 7 days after the day on which the copy of the notice of disclaimer is returned to him under Rule 4.187, the liquidator shall send or give copies of the notice (showing the date endorsed as required by that Rule) to the persons mentioned in paragraphs (2) to (4) below.

(2)   Where the property disclaimed is of a leasehold nature, he shall send or give a copy to every person who (to his knowledge) claims under the company as underlessee or mortgagee.

(3)   He shall in any case send or give a copy of the notice to every person who (to his knowledge)—
  (a)   claims an interest in the disclaimed property, or
  (b)   is under any liability in respect of the property, not being a liability discharged by the disclaimer.

(4)   If the disclaimer is of an unprofitable contract, he shall send or give copies of the notice to all such persons as, to his knowledge, are parties to the contract or have interests under it.

(5) If subsequently it comes to the liquidator's knowledge, in the case of any person, that he has such an interest in the disclaimed property as would have entitled him to receive a copy of the notice of disclaimer in pursuance of paragraphs (2) to (4), the liquidator shall then forthwith send or give to that person a copy of the notice.

But compliance with this paragraph is not required if—
  (a)   the liquidator is satisfied that the person has already been made aware of the disclaimer and its date, or
  (b)   the court, on the liquidator's application, orders that compliance is not required in that particular case.

[1107]

4.189   Additional notices

The liquidator disclaiming property may, without prejudice to his obligations under sections 178 to 180 and Rules 4.187 and 4.188, at any time give notice of the disclaimer to any persons who in his opinion ought, in the public interest or otherwise, to be informed of it.

[1108]

4.190   Duty to keep court informed

The liquidator shall notify the court from time to time as to the persons to whom he has sent or given copies of the notice of disclaimer under the two preceding Rules, giving their names and addresses, and the nature of their respective interests.

[1109]

4.191   Application by interested party under s 178(5)

Where, in the case of any property, application is made to the liquidator by an interested party under section 178(5) (request for decision whether the property is to be disclaimed or not), the application—

    (a)   shall be delivered to the liquidator personally or by registered post, and

    (b)   shall be made in the form known as "notice to elect", or a substantially similar form.

[1110]

4.192   Interest in property to be declared on request

    (1)   If, in the case of property which the liquidator has the right to disclaim, it appears to him that there is some person who claims, or may claim, to have an interest in the property, he may give notice to that person calling on him to declare within 14 days whether he claims any such interest and, if so, the nature and extent of it.

    (2)   Failing compliance with the notice, the liquidator is entitled to assume that the person concerned has no such interest in the property as will prevent or impede its disclaimer.

[1111]

4.193   Disclaimer presumed valid and effective

Any disclaimer of property by the liquidator is presumed valid and effective, unless it is proved that he has been in breach of his duty with respect to the giving of notice of disclaimer, or otherwise under sections 178 to 180, or under this Chapter of the Rules.

[1112]

4.194   Application for exercise of court's powers under s 181

    (1)   This Rule applies with respect to an application by any person under section 181 for an order of the court to vest or deliver disclaimed property.

    (2)   The application must be made within 3 months of the applicant becoming aware of the disclaimer, or of his receiving a copy of the liquidator's notice of disclaimer sent under Rule 4.188, whichever is the earlier.

    (3)   The applicant shall with his application file in court an affidavit—

    (a)   stating whether he applies under paragraph (a) of section 181(2) (claim of interest in the property) or under paragraph (b) (liability not discharged);

    (b)   specifying the date on which he received a copy of the liquidator's notice of disclaimer, or otherwise became aware of the disclaimer; and

    (c)   specifying the grounds of his application and the order which he desires the court to make under section 181.

    (4)   The court shall fix a venue for the hearing of the application; and the applicant shall, not later than 7 days before the date fixed, give to the liquidator notice of the venue, accompanied by copies of the application and the affidavit under paragraph (3).

    (5)   On the hearing of the application, the court may give directions as to other persons (if any) who should be sent or given notice of the application and the grounds on which it is made.

    (6)   Sealed copies of any order made on the application shall be sent by the court to the applicant and the liquidator.

(7)   In a case where the property disclaimed is of a leasehold nature, and section 179 applies to suspend the effect of the disclaimer, there shall be included in the court's order a direction giving effect to the disclaimer.

This paragraph does not apply if, at the time when the order is issued, other applications under section 181 are pending in respect of the same property.

[1113]

4.195–4.231   (*Outside the scope of this work.*)

THE SECOND GROUP OF PARTS
INDIVIDUAL INSOLVENCY; BANKRUPTCY

5.1–5.65   ((*Pt 5*) *Outside the scope of this work.*)

PART 6
BANKRUPTCY

6.1–6.177   (*Outside the scope of this work.*)

CHAPTER 14
DISCLAIMER

6.178   Trustee's notice of disclaimer

(1)   Where the trustee disclaims property under section 315, the notice of disclaimer shall contain such particulars of the property disclaimed as enable it to be easily identified.

(2)   The notice shall be signed by the trustee and filed in court, with a copy. The court shall secure that both the notice and the copy are sealed and endorsed with the date of filing.

(3)   The copy notice, so sealed and endorsed, shall be returned by the court to the trustee as follows—
    (a)   if the notice has been delivered at the offices of the court by the trustee in person, it shall be handed to him,
    (b)   if it has been delivered by some person acting on the trustee's behalf, it shall be handed to that person, for immediate transmission to the trustee, and
    (c)   otherwise, it shall be sent to the trustee by first class post.

The court shall cause to be endorsed on the original notice, or otherwise recorded on the file, the manner in which the copy notice was returned to the trustee.

(4)   For the purposes of section 315, the date of the prescribed notice is that which is endorsed on it, and on the copy, in accordance with this Rule.

[1114]

6.179   Communication of disclaimer to persons interested

(1)   Within 7 days after the day on which a copy of the notice of disclaimer is returned to him, the trustee shall send or give copies of the notice (showing the date endorsed as required by Rule 6.178) to the persons mentioned in paragraphs (2) to (5) below.

(2)   Where the property disclaimed is of a leasehold nature, he shall send or give a copy to every person who (to his knowledge) claims under the bankrupt as underlessee or mortgagee.

(3)   Where the disclaimer is of property in a dwelling-house, he shall send or give a copy to every person who (to his knowledge) is in occupation of, or claims a right to occupy, the house.

(4)   He shall in any case send or give a copy of the notice to every person who (to his knowledge)—
    (a)   claims an interest in the disclaimed property, or
    (b)   is under any liability in respect of the property, not being a liability discharged by the disclaimer.

(5)   If the disclaimer is of an unprofitable contract, he shall send or give copies of the notice to all such persons, as, to his knowledge, are parties to the contract or have interests under it.

(6)   If subsequently it comes to the trustee's knowledge, in the case of any person, that he has such an interest in the disclaimed property as would have entitled him to receive a copy of the notice of disclaimer in pursuance of paragraphs (2) to (5), the trustee shall then forthwith send or give to that person a copy of the notice.

But compliance with this paragraph is not required if—
  (a)   the trustee is satisfied that the person has already been made aware of the disclaimer and its date, or
  (b)   the court, on the trustee's application, orders that compliance is not required in that particular case.

[(7)   A notice or copy notice to be served on any person under the age of 18 in relation to the disclaimer of property in a dwelling-house is sufficiently served if sent or given to the parent or guardian of that person.]

[1115]

NOTES
Para (7): added by the Insolvency (Amendment) Rules 1987, SI 1987/1919, r 3(1), Schedule, Pt 1, para 120.

6.180   Additional notices

The trustee disclaiming property may, without prejudice to his obligations under sections 315 to 319 and Rules 6.178 and 6.179, at any time give notice of the disclaimer to any persons who in his opinion ought, in the public interest or otherwise, to be informed of it.

[1116]

6.181   Duty to keep court informed

The trustee shall notify the court from time to time as to the persons to whom he has sent or given copies of the notice of disclaimer under the two preceding Rules, giving their names and addresses, and the nature of their respective interests.

[1117]

6.182   Application for leave to disclaim

(1)   Where under section 315(4) the trustee requires the leave of the court to disclaim property claimed for the bankrupt's estate under section 307 or 308, he may apply for that leave *ex parte*.

(2)   The application must be accompanied by a report—
  (a)   giving such particulars of the property proposed to be disclaimed as enable it to be easily identified,
  (b)   setting out the reasons why, the property having been claimed for the estate, the court's leave to disclaim is now applied for, and
  (c)   specifying the persons (if any) who have been informed of the trustee's intention to make the application.

(3)   If it is stated in the report that any person's consent to the disclaimer has been signified, a copy of that consent must be annexed to the report.

(4)   The court may, on consideration of the application, grant the leave applied for; and it may, before granting leave—
  (a)   order that notice of the application be given to all such persons who, if the property is disclaimed, will be entitled to apply for a vesting or other order under section 320, and
  (b)   fix a venue for the hearing of the application under section 315(4).

[1118]

6.183   Application by interested party under s 316

(1)   The following applies where, in the case of any property, application is made to the trustee by an interested party under section 316 (request for decision whether the property is to be disclaimed or not).

(2)   The application—
  (a)   shall be delivered to the trustee personally or by registered post, and

(b) shall be made in the form known as "notice to elect", or a substantially similar form.

(3) This paragraph applies in a case where the property concerned cannot be disclaimed by the trustee without the leave of the court.

If within the period of 28 days mentioned in section 316(1) the trustee applies to the court for leave to disclaim, the court shall extend the time allowed by that section for giving notice of disclaimer to a date not earlier than the date fixed for the hearing of the application.

[1119]

6.184 Interest in property to be declared on request

(1) If, in the case of property which the trustee has the right to disclaim, it appears to him that there is some person who claims, or may claim, to have an interest in the property, he may give notice to that person calling on him to declare within 14 days whether he claims any such interest and, if so, the nature and extent of it.

(2) Failing compliance with the notice, the trustee is entitled to assume that the person concerned has no such interest in the property as will prevent or impede its disclaimer.

[1120]

6.185 Disclaimer presumed valid and effective

Any disclaimer of property by the trustee is presumed valid and effective, unless it is proved that he has been in breach of his duty with respect to the giving of notice of disclaimer, or otherwise under sections 315 to 319, or under this Chapter of the Rules.

[1121]

6.186 Application for exercise of court's powers under s 320

(1) This Rule applies with respect to an application by any person under section 320 for an order of the court to vest or deliver disclaimed property.

(2) The application must be made within 3 months of the applicant becoming aware of the disclaimer, or of his receiving a copy of the trustee's notice of disclaimer sent under Rule 6.179, whichever is the earlier.

(3) The applicant shall with his application file an affidavit—

(a) stating whether he applies under paragraph (a) of section 320(2) (claim of interest in the property), under paragraph (b) (liability not discharged) or under paragraph (c) (occupation of dwelling-house);

(b) specifying the date on which he received a copy of the trustee's notice of disclaimer, or otherwise became aware of the disclaimer; and

(c) specifying the grounds of his application and the order which he desires the court to make under section 320.

(4) The court shall fix a venue for the hearing of the application; and the applicant shall, not later than 7 days before the date fixed, give to the trustee notice of the venue, accompanied by copies of the application and the affidavit under paragraph (3).

(5) On the hearing of the application, the court may give directions as to other persons (if any) who should be sent or given notice of the application and the grounds on which it is made.

(6) Sealed copies of any order made on the application shall be sent by the court to the applicant and the trustee.

(7) In a case where the property disclaimed is of a leasehold nature, or is property in a dwelling-house, and section 317 or (as the case may be) section 318 applies to suspend the effect of the disclaimer, there shall be included in the court's order a direction giving effect to the disclaimer.

This paragraph does not apply if, at the time when the order is issued, other applications under section 320 are pending in respect of the same property.

[1122]

6.187–6A.8 (*Outside the scope of this work.*)

THE THIRD GROUP OF PARTS

7.1–12.22   *((Pts 7–12) Outside the scope of this work.)*

PART 13
INTERPRETATION AND APPLICATION

13.1 Introductory

This Part of the Rules has effect for their interpretation and application; and any definition given in this Part applies except, and in so far as, the context otherwise requires.

[1123]

13.2 "The court"; "the registrar"

(1)   Anything to be done under or by virtue of the Act or the Rules by, to or before the court may be done by, to or before a judge or the registrar.

(2)   The registrar may authorise any act of a formal or administrative character which is not by statute his responsibility to be carried out by the chief clerk or any other officer of the court acting on his behalf, in accordance with directions given by the Lord Chancellor.

(3)   In individual insolvency proceedings, "the registrar" means a Registrar in Bankruptcy of the High Court, or the [district judge or deputy district judge] of a county court.

(4)   In company insolvency proceedings in the High Court, "the registrar" means—
    (a)   subject to the following paragraph, a Registrar in Bankruptcy of the High Court;
    (b)   where the proceedings are in the District Registry of Birmingham, Bristol, Cardiff, Leeds, Liverpool, Manchester, Newcastle-upon-Tyne or Preston, the [District Judge].

(5)   In company insolvency proceedings in a county court, "the [district judge]" means the officer of the court whose duty it is to exercise the functions which in the High Court are exercised by a [district judge].

[1124]

NOTES

Paras (3)–(5): words in square brackets substituted by virtue of the Courts and Legal Services Act 1990, s 74(1), (3).

13.3 "Give notice", etc

(1)   A reference in the Rules to giving notice, or to delivering, sending or serving any document, means that the notice or document may be sent by post, unless under a particular Rule personal service is expressly required.

(2)   Any form of post may be used, unless under a particular Rule a specified form is expressly required.

(3)   Personal service of a document is permissible in all cases.

(4)   Notice of the venue fixed for an application may be given by service of the sealed copy of the application under Rule 7.4(3).

[1125]

13.4 Notice, etc to solicitors

Where under the Act or the Rules a notice or other document is required or authorised to be given to a person, it may, if he has indicated that his solicitor is authorised to accept service on his behalf, be given instead to the solicitor.

[1126]

13.5 Notice to joint liquidators, joint trustees, etc

Where two or more persons are acting jointly as the responsible insolvency practitioner in any proceedings, delivery of a document to one of them is to be treated as delivery to them all.

[1127]

13.6 "Venue"

References to the "venue" for any proceeding or attendance before the court, or for a meeting, are to the time, date and place for the proceeding, attendance or meeting.

[1128]

**PART II
STATUTORY INSTRUMENTS**

13.7 "Insolvency proceedings"

"Insolvency proceedings" means any proceedings under the Act or the Rules.

[1129]

13.8 "Insolvent estate"

References to "the insolvent estate" are—
- (a) in relation to a company insolvency, the company's assets, and
- (b) in relation to an individual insolvency, the bankrupt's estate or (as the case may be) the debtor's property.

[1130]

13.9 "Responsible insolvency practitioner", etc

(1) In relation to any insolvency proceedings, "the responsible insolvency practitioner" means—
- (a) the person acting in a company insolvency, as supervisor of a voluntary arrangement under Part I of the Act, or as administrator, administrative receiver, liquidator or provisional liquidator;
- (b) the person acting in an individual insolvency, as the supervisor of a voluntary arrangement under Part VIII of the Act, or as trustee or interim receiver;
- (c) the official receiver acting as receiver and manager of a bankrupt's estate.

(2) Any reference to the liquidator, provisional liquidator, trustee or interim receiver includes the official receiver when acting in the relevant capacity.

[(3) A reference to an "authorised person" is a reference to a person who is authorised pursuant to section 389A of the Act to act as nominee or supervisor of a voluntary arrangement proposed or approved under Part I or Part VIII of the Act.]

[1131]

NOTES

Para (3): added by the Insolvency (Amendment) (No 2) Rules 2002, SI 2002/2712, r 7.

13.10 "Petitioner"

In winding-up and bankruptcy, references to "the petitioner" or "the petitioning creditor" include any person who has been substituted as such, or been given carriage of the petition.

[1132]

13.11 *(Outside the scope of this work.)*

[13.12 "Debt", "liability" (winding up)

(1) "Debt", in relation to the winding up of a company, means (subject to the next paragraph) any of the following—
- (a) any debt or liability to which the company is subject at the date on which it goes into liquidation;
- (b) any debt or liability to which the company may become subject after that date by reason of any obligation incurred before that date; and
- (c) any interest provable as mentioned in Rule 4.93(1).

(2) For the purposes of any provision of the Act or the Rules about winding up, any liability in tort is a debt provable in the winding up, if either—
- (a) the cause of action has accrued at the date on which the company goes into liquidation; or
- (b) all the elements necessary to establish the cause of action exist at that date except for actionable damage.

(3) For the purposes of references in any provision of the Act or the Rules about winding up to a debt or liability, it is immaterial whether the debt or liability is present or future, whether it is certain or contingent, or whether its amount is fixed or liquidated, or is capable of being ascertained by fixed rules or as a matter of opinion; and references in any such provision to owing a debt are to be read accordingly.

(4) In any provision of the Act or the Rules about winding up, except in so far as the context otherwise requires, "liability" means (subject to paragraph (3) above) a liability to pay

money or money's worth, including any liability under an enactment, any liability for breach of trust, any liability in contract, tort or bailment, and any liability arising out of an obligation to make restitution.

(5)   This Rule shall apply where a company is in administration and shall be read as if references to winding-up were a reference to administration.]

[1133]

NOTES

Commencement: 1 June 2006.

Substituted by the Insolvency (Amendment) Rules 2006, SI 2006/1272, r 4, subject to transitional provisions and savings in r 3 thereof.

[13.12A   "Authorised deposit-taker and former authorised deposit-taker"

(1)   "Authorised deposit-taker" means a person with permission under Part 4 of the Financial Services and Markets Act 2000 to accept deposits.

(2)   "Former authorised deposit-taker" means a person who—
   (a)   is not an authorised deposit-taker,
   (b)   was formerly an authorised institution under the Banking Act 1987, or a recognised bank or a licensed institution under the Banking Act 1979, and
   (c)   continues to have liability in respect of any deposit for which it had a liability at a time when it was an authorised institution, recognised bank or licensed institution.

(3)   Paragraphs (1) and (2) must be read with—
   (a)   section 22 of the Financial Services and Markets Act 2000;
   (b)   any relevant order under that section; and
   (c)   Schedule 22 to that Act.]

[1133A]

NOTES

Inserted by the Financial Services and Markets Act 2000 (Consequential Amendments and Repeals) Order 2001, SI 2001/3649, art 381.

13.13   Expressions used generally

(1)   "Business day" means any day other than a Saturday, a Sunday, Christmas Day, Good Friday or a day which is a bank holiday in any part of Great Britain under or by virtue of the Banking and Financial Dealings Act 1971 except in Rules 1.7, 4.10, 4.11, 4.16, 4.20, 5.10 and 6.23 where "business day" shall include any day which is a bank holiday in Scotland but not in England and Wales.]

(2)   "The Department" means the Department of Trade and Industry.

(3)   "File in court" [and file with the court] means deliver to the court for filing.

(4)   "The Gazette" means the London Gazette.

(5)   "General regulations" means regulations made by the Secretary of State under Rule 12.1.

[(6)   "Practice direction" means a direction as to the practice and procedure of any court within the scope of the CPR.

(7)   "Prescribed order of priority" means the order of priority of payments laid down by Chapter 20 of Part 4 of the Rules, or Chapter 23 of Part 6.]

[(8)   "Centre of main interests" has the same meaning as in the EC Regulation.

(9)   "Establishment" has the meaning given by Article 2(h) of the EC Regulation.

(10)   "Main proceedings" means proceedings opened in accordance with Article 3(1) of the EC Regulation and falling within the definition of insolvency proceedings in Article 2(a) of the EC Regulation and
   (a)   in relation to England and Wales and Scotland set out in Annex A to the EC Regulation under the heading "United Kingdom", and
   (b)   in relation to another member State, set out in Annex A to the EC Regulation under the heading relating to that member State.

(11) "Member State liquidator" means a person falling within the definition of liquidator in Article 2(b) of the EC Regulation appointed in proceedings to which it applies in a member State other than the United Kingdom.

(12) "Secondary proceedings" means proceedings opened in accordance with Articles 3(2) and 3(3) of the EC Regulation and falling within the definition of winding-up proceedings in Article 2(c) of the EC Regulation, and

    (a)   in relation to England and Wales and Scotland, set out in Annex B to the EC Regulation under the heading "United Kingdom", and

    (b)   in relation to another member State, set out in Annex B to the EC Regulation under the heading relating to that member State.

(13) "Temporary administrator" means a temporary administrator referred to by Article 38 of the EC Regulation.

(14) "Territorial proceedings" means proceedings opened in accordance with Articles 3(2) and 3(4) of the EC Regulation and falling within the definition of insolvency proceedings in Article 2(a) of the EC Regulation, and

    (a)   in relation to England and Wales and Scotland, set out in Annex A to the EC Regulation under the heading "United Kingdom", and

    (b)   in relation to another member State, set out in Annex A to the EC Regulation under the heading relating to that member State.]

[(15) "Prescribed part" has the same meaning as it does in section 176A(2)(a).]

[1134]

NOTES

Para (1): substituted by the Insolvency (Amendment) (No 2) Rules 1999, SI 1999/1022, r 3, Schedule, para 14(a).

Para (3): words in square brackets inserted by the Insolvency (Amendment) Rules 2003, SI 2003/1730, r 13, Sch 1, Pt 10, para 66(a), subject to transitional provisions and savings in r 5 thereof.

Paras (6), (7): substituted, for original para (6), by SI 1999/1022, r 3, Schedule, para 14(b).

Paras (8)–(14): added by the Insolvency (Amendment) Rules 2002, SI 2002/1307, rr 3, 10(7), subject to savings in relation to anything done under, or for the purposes of, this provision before 31 May 2002.

Para (15): added by SI 2003/1730, r 13, Sch 1, Pt 10, para 66(b), subject to transitional provisions and savings in r 5 thereof.

13.14 Application

(1) Subject to paragraph (2) of this Rule, and save where otherwise expressly provided, the Rules apply—

    (a)   to … receivers appointed on or after the day on which the Rules come into force,

    (b)   to bankruptcy proceedings where the bankruptcy petition is presented on or after the day on which the Rules come into force, and

    (c)   to all other insolvency proceedings commenced on or after that day.

(2) The Rules also apply to winding-up and bankruptcy proceedings commenced before that day to which provisions of the Act are applied by Schedule 11 to the Act, to the extent necessary to give effect to those provisions.

[1135]

NOTES

Para (1): word omitted from sub-para (a) revoked by the Insolvency (Amendment) Rules 1987, SI 1987/1919, r 3(1), Schedule, Pt 1, para 152.

SCHEDULES

(Schs 1, 2 outside the scope of this work; Sch 3 revoked by SI 1993/602, r 3, Schedule, para 4.)

SCHEDULE 4
FORMS

(Pts 1–3 outside the scope of this work.)

PART 4
COMPANIES WINDING UP

(Forms 4.1–4.52 outside the scope of this work.)

[FORM 4.53

Rule 4.187, 4.188, 4.189

Notice of Disclaimer under Section 178 of the Insolvency Act 1986

(Title)

Part 1

(a) Insert name of liquidator

I, (a) _____ the liquidator of the above-named company, disclaim all the company's interest in:

(b) Insert full particulars of property*

(b)

Dated _____

Signed _____

Name in BLOCK LETTERS _____

Address _____

Part 2

NOTE:

(c) Insert name of court

This is a copy of a notice filed at (c)
Court

(d) Insert date that notice filed in court

on (d)

Seal of the Court

Part 3

(e) Insert name and address of person to be sent copy notice under Rule 4.188 or 4.189

To: (e) _____

_____

_____

This is a copy of a notice of disclaimer filed by the liquidator in the above matter at (c)   Court.

NOTE: 1.   Part 1 is to be completed by the liquidator and filed in court with a copy

Part 2 is to be completed by the court and returned to the liquidator

Part 3 is to be completed by or on behalf of the liquidator when sending out copy notice under Rule 4.188 or 4.189.

2.   The attention of a recipient of this notice is drawn to sections 178–182 of the Insolvency Act 1986.

3. Where the property concerned consists of land or buildings the nature of the interest should also be stated (e g whether leasehold, freehold, etc).

[1136]

NOTES

Substituted by the Insolvency (Amendment) Rules 1987, SI 1987/1919, r 3(1), Schedule, Pt 2, para 158(1), Pt 5.

FORM 4.54

Rule 4.191

Notice to Elect

(Title)

(a) Insert name, address and particulars of interest in property (e g landlord etc)

I (a)

(b) Insert details

of property comprising (b)

require the liquidator to decide within 28 days of receiving this notice whether he will disclaim the above property or not and to notify me of his decision.

Dated _____

Signed _____

Name in BLOCK LETTERS _____

To the liquidator of the above-named company.

Address

[1137]

FORM 4.55

Rule 4.192

Notice of Intended Disclaimer to Interested Party

(Title)

(a) Insert full particulars of property

I intend to disclaim (a)

If you claim an interest in this property, you must declare to me the nature and extent of your claim within 14 days of receiving this notice

If you fail to do so, I am entitled to assume that you do not have any interest in the property which will prevent or impede my disclaimer

Dated _____

Signed _____

Liquidator

Name in BLOCK LETTERS _____

[1138]

(Forms 4.56–4.72 and Pt 5 outside the scope of this work.)

PART 6
BANKRUPTCY

(*Forms 6.1–6.60 outside the scope of this work.*)

[FORM 6.61

Rule 6.178, 6.179, 6.180

Notice of disclaimer under section 315 of the Insolvency Act 1986

(Title)

Part 1

(a) Insert
name of
trustee

I, (a) _____ the trustee of the above-named bankrupt's estate
disclaim all my interest in:

(b) Insert full
particulars of
property*

(b)

Dated _____

Signed _____

Name in BLOCK LETTERS _____

Address _____

Part 2

(c) Insert
name of court

NOTE:

This is a copy of a notice filed at
(c)   Court

(d) Insert date
that notice
filed in court

on (d)

Seal of the Court

Part 3

(e) Insert
name and
address of
person to be
sent copy
notice under
Rule 6.179 or
6.180

To: (e) _____
_____
_____

This is a copy of a notice of disclaimer filed by the trustee in the above
matter at (c)   Court.

NOTE: 1.   Part 1 is to be completed by the trustee and filed in court
with a copy

Part 2 is to be completed by the court and returned to the
trustee

Part 3 is to be completed by or on behalf of the trustee
when sending out copy notice under Rule 6.179 or 6.180

2.   The attention of a recipient of this notice is drawn to
sections 315–321 of the Insolvency Act 1986.

3.   Where the property concerned consists of land or buildings
the nature of the interest should also be stated (e g whether
leasehold, freehold, etc).]

[1139]

NOTES
Substituted by the Insolvency (Amendment) Rules 1987, SI 1987/1919, r 3(1), Schedule, Pt 2, para 158(1), Pt 5.

FORM 6.62

Rule 6.183

Notice to Elect

(Title)

(a) Insert
name, address
and particulars
of interest in
property
(eg landlord
etc)

I (a) _____

(b) Insert
details

of property comprising (b)

Dated _____

Signed _____

Name in BLOCK LETTERS _____

To the trustee of the above-named bankrupt's estate.

Address

[1140]

FORM 6.63

Rule 6.184

Notice of Intended Disclaimer to Interested Party

(TITLE)

(Title)

(a) Insert full
particulars of
property

I intend to disclaim (a) _____

If you claim an interest in this property, you must declare to me the
nature and extent of your claim within 14 days of receiving this notice

If you fail to do so, I am entitled to assume that you do not have any
interest in the property which will prevent or impede my disclaimer

Dated _____

Signed _____

Trustee

Address _____

Name in BLOCK LETTERS _____

[1141]

(Forms 6.64–6.84, Pts 7–9 and Schs 5, 6 outside the scope of this work.)

AGRICULTURAL HOLDINGS (ARBITRATION ON NOTICES) ORDER 1987

(SI 1987/710)

NOTES

Made: 8 April 1987.
Authority: Agricultural Holdings Act 1986, s 29, Sch 4, paras 1–6, 8–13, Sch 5, para 5.

ARRANGEMENT OF ARTICLES

PART I
PRELIMINARY

PART II
NOTICES TO DO WORK

Notices requiring arbitration

Powers of arbitrator

Supplementary

PART III
NOTICES TO QUIT

Arbitration concerning notices to quit

Postponement of operation of notice to quit

Extension of time under notice to remedy after notice to quit

Supplementary

577

PART IV
REVOCATION

PART I
PRELIMINARY

1 Citation and commencement

This Order may be cited as the Agricultural Holdings (Arbitration on Notices) Order 1987 and shall come into force on 12th May 1987.

[1142]

2 Interpretation

(1)   In this Order, unless the context otherwise requires—
"the 1986 Act" means the Agricultural Holdings Act 1986;
"notice to remedy" means a notice served on the tenant of an agricultural holding for the purposes of Case D requiring him to remedy a breach of a term or condition of his tenancy;
"notice to do work" means a notice to remedy which requires the doing of any work of repair, maintenance or replacement;
"termination", in relation to an arbitration, means the date on which the arbitrator's award is delivered to the tenant.

(2)   Any reference in this Order to a numbered article shall be construed as a reference to the article bearing that number in this Order.

[1143]

PART II
NOTICES TO DO WORK

Notices requiring arbitration

3 Notice where arbitration is available at the notice to remedy stage only

(1)   Where a tenant on whom a notice to do work has been served wishes to have determined by arbitration under the 1986 Act any of the following questions, namely—
(a)   his liability under the terms or conditions of his tenancy to any of the work specified in the notice,
(b)   the deletion from the notice of any item or part of an item of work on the ground that it is unnecessary or unjustified, or
(c)   the substitution, in the case of any item or part of an item of work, of a different method or material for the method or material which the notice would otherwise required to be followed or used,
he shall do so by service of a notice requiring the question or questions to be determined by arbitration under the 1986 Act.

(2)   A notice under paragraph (1) above shall be in writing, and shall be served on the landlord within one month after the service on the tenant of the notice to do work.

(3)   A notice under paragraph (1) above shall specify, as the case may be—
(a)   any items in respect of which the tenant denies liability,
(b)   any items or parts of items which the tenant claims to be unnecessary or unjustified, and
(c)   any method or material in respect of which the tenant desires a substitution to be made.

[1144]

4 Notice on other questions or in other cases

(1)   Where the tenant on whom a notice to do work has been served wishes to have determined by arbitration under the 1986 Act in addition to a question specified in article 3(1) any other question arising under that notice which is not a question so specified, he shall do so

by serving on the landlord within one month after the service of the notice to do work a notice in writing requiring the question to be so determined.

(2)   Where the tenant on whom a notice to do work has been served does not wish any question specified in article 3(1) to be determined by arbitration under the 1986 Act but wishes to have determined by such arbitration any other question arising under that notice, he shall do so—

(a)   by serving on the landlord within one month after the service of the notice to do work a notice in writing requiring the question to be so determined, or

(b)   by serving a notice in accordance with article 9.

(3)   Nothing in this article shall preclude a tenant who has required arbitration under this article and who has been found liable to comply with a notice to do work or with any part of it from subsequently requiring arbitration under article 9 on the ground that, in consequence of anything happening before the expiration of the time for doing the work as extended by the arbitrator in pursuance of article 6(2), if would have been unreasonable to require the tenant to do the work within that time.

[1145]

Powers of arbitrator

5   Power to modify notice

In addition to any powers otherwise available to him, an arbitrator may—

(a)   in relation to any question specified in article 3(1)(b), modify, a notice to do work by deleting any item or part of an item of work specified in the notice as to which, having due regard to the interests of good husbandry as respects the agricultural holding to which the notice relates and of sound management of the estate of which that holding forms part or which that holding constitutes, the arbitrator is satisfied that it is unnecessary or unjustified, and

(b)   in relation to a question specified in article 3(1)(c) modify a notice to do work by substituting, in the case of any item or part of an item of work specified in the notice, a different method or material for the method or material which the notice would otherwise require to be followed or used where, having regard to the purpose which that item or part is intended to achieve, the arbitrator is satisfied that—

(i)   the last-mentioned method or material would involve undue difficulty or expense,

(ii)   the first-mentioned method or material would be substantially as effective for that purpose, and

(iii)   in all the circumstances the substitution is justified.

[1146]

Supplementary

6   Extension of time for doing work

(1)   Where a tenant requires any question to be determined by arbitration under article 3 or 4, the time specified for doing the work which is the subject of the arbitration shall be extended until the termination of the arbitration.

(2)   Where the arbitrator finds that the tenant is liable to comply with a notice to do work or with any part of it, he shall extend the time for doing that work by such further period as he thinks fit.

[1147]

7   Date of termination of tenancy on failure to do work

(1)   Where the time specified for doing any work is extended under article 6(2), the arbitrator may, either of his own motion or on the application of the landlord made not later than fourteen days after the termination of the arbitration, specify a date for the termination of the tenancy by notice to quit in the event of the tenant's failure to do the work within the extended time.

(2)   A date specified under paragraph (1) above shall not be earlier than—

(a)   the date on which the tenancy could have been terminated by notice to quit served on the expiration of the time originally specified in the notice to do work, or

(b)   six months after the expiration of the extended time,

whichever is the later.

(3)   Where the landlord applies to the arbitrator under paragraph (1) above, he shall at the same time give written notice of the application to the tenant (except where the application is made at the arbitration) and the tenant shall be entitled to be heard on the application.

(4)   A notice to quit on a date specified under paragraph (1) above shall be served on the tenant within one month after the expiration of the extended time, and shall (subject to any right to contest its effectiveness available to the tenant) be valid notwithstanding that it is served less than twelve months before the date on which the tenancy is to be terminated or that that date is not the end of a year of the tenancy.

[1148]

8   Recovery of cost of work

Where, on an arbitration relating to whole or in part to the question specified in article 3(1)(a), it appears to the arbitrator that the tenant has done work required by a notice to do work which he was under no obligation to do, the arbitrator shall determine the reasonable cost of such work, which shall be recoverable from the landlord by the tenant in accordance with section 85(1) of the 1986 Act.

[1149]

PART III
NOTICES TO QUIT

Arbitration concerning notices to quit

9   Notice requiring arbitration

Where it is stated in a notice to quit an agricultural holding or part thereof that the notice is given for one or more of the reasons specified in Case A, B, D or E and the tenant wishes to contest any question arising under the provisions of section 26(2) of, and Schedule 3 to, the 1986 Act relating to any of the reasons so stated, he shall within one month after the service of the notice serve on the landlord notice in writing requiring the question to be determined by arbitration under the 1986 Act.

[1150]

10   Appointment of arbitrator

A notice under article 9 requiring arbitration under the 1986 Act shall cease to be effective three months after the date of the service of that notice unless before the expiry of those three months—

(a)   an arbitrator has been appointed by agreement between the parties, or

(b)   (in default of such agreement) an application has been made by the tenant or the landlord under [section 84(2) of] that Act for the appointment of an arbitrator,

for the purposes of that arbitration.

[1151]

NOTES
Words in square brackets in para (b) substituted by the Regulatory Reform (Agricultural Tenancies) (England and Wales) Order 2006, SI 2006/2805, art 18, Sch 1, Pt 2, para 2.

11   Service of counter-notice

Where—

(1)   an arbitration is required under article 9 in respect of a notice to quit which is capable of taking effect either as notice to quit to which section 26(2) of the 1986 Act applies or in the alternative as a notice to quit to which section 26(1) of that Act applies, and

(2)   in consequence of the arbitration that notice takes effect as a notice to quit to which section 26(1) applies,

the time within which a counter-notice may be served by the tenant on the landlord under section 26(1) of the 1986 Act shall be one month from the termination of the arbitration.

[1152]

Postponement of operation of notice to quit

12   During arbitration

Where a tenant requires a question arising out of a notice to quit to be determined by arbitration under article 9, the operation of the notice shall be suspended until—

(a)   the expiry of the time fixed in article 10 for appointing an arbitrator by agreement or for making an application under [section 84(2) of] the 1986 Act, or

(b)   where any such appointment or application has been duly made, the termination of the arbitration.

[1153]

NOTES

Words in square brackets in para (a) substituted by the Regulatory Reform (Agricultural Tenancies) (England and Wales) Order 2006, SI 2006/2805, art 18, Sch 1, Pt 2, para 2.

13   After arbitration or proceedings

(1)   Where—

(a)   a notice to quit has effect in consequence of an arbitration under article 9, or the Tribunal have consented to the operation of the notice under section 26(1) or 28(2) of the 1986 Act or article 15(5), and

(b)   the notice would, but for the provisions of this article, come into operation on or within six months fatter the termination of the arbitration, or the giving of the consent,

the arbitrator or the Tribunal may, either of his or their own motion or on the application of the tenant made not later than fourteen days after the termination of the arbitration or the giving of the consent, postpone the termination of the tenancy for a period not exceeding twelve months.

(2)   Where the tenant applies to the arbitrator or the Tribunal under paragraph (1) above, he shall at the same time give written notice of the application to the landlord (except where the application is made at the arbitration or at the hearing before the Tribunal) and the landlord shall be entitled to be heard on the application.

[1154]

Extension of time under notice to remedy after notice to quit

14   Extension by arbitrator

Where—

(a)   notice to quit is stated to be given by reason of the tenant's failure to remedy a breach of any term or condition of his tenancy—

(i)   within the time specified in a notice to remedy, or

(ii)   within that time as extended by the landlord, or in pursuance of article 6 or of this article, and

(b)   it appears to the arbitrator on an arbitration under article 9 that, notwithstanding that the time originally specified or extended was reasonable, it would, in consequence of anything happening before the expiration of that time, have been unreasonable to require the tenant to remedy the breach within that time,

the arbitrator may treat the time as having been extended, or further extended, and may make his award as if the time had not expired; and where the breach has not been remedied at the date of the award, the arbitrator may extend the time by such period as he considers reasonable, having regard to the length of time which has elapsed since the service of the notice to remedy.

[1155]

15   Termination of tenancy following extension

(1)   Where the time specified for doing any work is extended under article 14, the arbitrator may, either of his own motion or on the application of the landlord made not later

than fourteen days after the termination of the arbitration, specify a date for the termination of the tenancy by a subsequent notice to quit in the event of the tenant's failure to do the work within the extended time.

(2)   A date specified under paragraph (1) above shall not be earlier than—

(a)   the date on which the tenancy could have been terminated by the original notice to quit (that is, the notice which was the subject of the arbitration), or

(b)   six months after the expiration of the extended time,

whichever is the later.

(3)   Where the landlord applies to the arbitrator under paragraph (1) above, he shall at the same time give written notice of the application to the tenant (except where the application is made at the arbitration) and the tenant shall be entitled to be heard on the application.

(4)   A notice to quit on a date specified under paragraph (1) above shall be served on the tenant within one month after the expiration of the extended time, and, subject to paragraph (5) below, shall be valid notwithstanding it is served less than twelve months before the date on which the tenancy is to be terminated or that that date is not the end of a year of the tenancy.

(5)   Where a subsequent notice to quit is given in accordance with paragraph (1) above in a case where the original notice to quit included a statement in accordance with Case D to the effect that it was given by reason of the tenant's failure to comply with a notice to do work, then, if the tenant serves on the landlord a counter-notice in writing within one month after the giving of the subsequent notice to quit (or, if the date specified in that notice for the termination of the tenancy is earlier, before that date), the subsequent notice to quit shall not have effect unless the Tribunal consent to its operation.

(6)   On an application made for the consent of the Tribunal under paragraph (5) above on the part of the landlord, the Tribunal shall consent to the operation of the notice to quit unless it appears to them, having regard—

(a)   to the extent to which the tenant has failed to comply with the notice to do work,

(b)   to the consequences of his failure to comply with it in any respect, and

(c)   to the circumstances surrounding any such failure,

that a fair and reasonable landlord would not insist on possession.

[1156]

Supplementary

16   Notice to sub-tenants

(1)   Section 26(1) of the 1986 Act shall not apply where notice to quit an agricultural holding or part thereof is given to a sub-tenant by a tenant who has himself been given notice to quit that holding or part thereof and the fact that the tenant has been given such notice is stated in the notice given to the sub-tenant.

(2)   Such a notice given to a sub-tenant shall have effect only if the notice to quit given to the tenant by the landlord itself has effect.

(3)   Where a tenant accepts notice to quit part of a holding as notice to quit the whole under section 32 of the 1986 Act, then, for the purpose of this article, the notice given by him shall be deemed to be a notice to quit the entire holding.

[1157]

17   Service men

(1)   In any case to which, notwithstanding the existence of any such circumstances as are mentioned in Cases B to G, section 26(1) of the 1986 Act applies by virtue of the modification of that section by paragraph 3 of Schedule 5 to that Act, paragraphs (2) to (4) below shall have effect.

(2)   Where, on an application by the landlord for the consent of the Tribunal to the operation of a notice to quit, it appears to the Tribunal that the notice to quit was given for one or more of the reasons specified in Case B, D or E, and that it is expedient that any question arising under the provisions of section 26(2) of, and Schedule 3 to, the 1986 Act relating to any of the reasons so stated should be determined by arbitration between the landlord and tenant under that Act before the Tribunal consider whether to grant or withhold consent to the operation of the notice to quit, they may require that the question be determined accordingly.

(3)   Article 9 shall apply with the addition of the following words—

"so, however, that the tenant's failure to serve such a notice shall not affect his right to contest the question in proceedings before the Tribunal consequent upon the service of a counter-notice under section 26(1) of the 1986 Act or in any arbitration by which the Tribunal may require any such question to be determined".

(4)   Article 11 shall not apply, but where a tenant requires a question to be determined by arbitration in pursuance of article 9, the time within which a counter-notice under section 26(1) of the 1986 Act may be served by the tenant on the landlord under that subsection shall be one month from the termination of the arbitration.

[1158]

PART IV
REVOCATION

18   Revocation

The Agricultural Holdings (Arbitration on Notices) Order 1978 and the Agricultural Holdings (Arbitration on Notices) (Variation) Order 1984 are hereby revoked, but without prejudice to their application in relation to notices to do work and notices to quit which have been served before the commencement of this Order, and to any proceedings relating to or consequent upon any such notices.

[1159]

AGRICULTURAL HOLDINGS (FORMS OF NOTICE TO PAY RENT OR TO REMEDY) REGULATIONS 1987

(SI 1987/711)

NOTES
Made: 7 April 1987.
Authority: Agricultural Holdings Act 1986, Sch 3, Pt II, para 10(1)(a), (2).

1   Citation and commencement

These Regulations may be cited as the Agricultural Holdings (Forms of Notice to Pay Rent or to Remedy) Regulations 1987 and shall come into force on 12th May 1987.

[1160]

2   Interpretation

(1)   In these Regulations—
"the 1986 Act" means the Agricultural Holdings Act 1986;
"notice to pay rent" means a notice served on the tenant of an agricultural holding for the purposes of Case D requiring him to pay rent due;
"notice to remedy" means a notice served on the tenant of an agricultural holding for the purposes of Case D requiring him to remedy a breach of a term or condition of his tenancy.

(2)   A form referred to by number in these Regulations means the form so numbered in the Schedule to these Regulations or a form substantially to the same effect.

[1161]

3   Form of notice to pay rent

A notice to pay rent shall be in Form 1.

[1162]

4   Forms of notice to remedy

A notice to remedy which requires the doing of any work of repair, maintenance or replacement shall be in Form 2 and any other notice to remedy shall be in Form 3.

[1163]

5 Revocation

The Agricultural Holdings (Forms of Notice to Pay Rent or to Remedy) Regulations 1984 are hereby revoked, but without prejudice to their application in relation to any notice served before the coming into operation of these Regulations.

[1164]

SCHEDULE

Regulations 2(2), 3, 4

FORM 1

Agricultural Holdings Act 1986

Schedule 3, Part I, Case D

Notice to tenant to pay rent due

Re: the holding known as ....

To ....

....

(Name and address of tenant)

> IMPORTANT— FAILURE TO COMPLY WITH THIS NOTICE MAY BE RELIED ON AS REASON FOR A NOTICE TO QUIT UNDER CASE D. IF YOU WANT YOUR TENANCY TO CONTINUE YOU MUST ACT QUICKLY. READ THE NOTICE AND ALL THE NOTES CAREFULLY. IF YOU ARE IN ANY DOUBT ABOUT THE ACTION YOU SHOULD TAKE, GET ADVICE IMMEDIATELY, e g FROM A SOLICITOR, SURVEYOR OR CITIZENS ADVICE BUREAU.

1.   I hereby give you notice that I require you to pay within two months from the date of service of this Notice* the rent due in respect of the above holding as set out below:

*Note: This Notice may not be served before the rent is due.

Particulars of rent not paid

Date when due	*Amount due*
....	....

2.   This Notice is given in accordance with Case D in Part I of Schedule 3 to the Agricultural Holdings Act 1986, and failure to comply with it within the period specified above may be relied on as a reason for a notice to quit under Case D.

3.   Your attention is drawn to the Notes following the signature to this Notice.

Signed .... Date ....

(If signed by any person other than the landlord of the holding, state in what capacity or by what authority the signature is affixed.)

Address..

....

....

....

Notes

1.   You cannot at this stage refer to arbitration either your liability to comply with this Notice to pay rent or any other question as to the validity of the Notice. You will, however, be entitled to do so later if a notice to quit is served on you on the ground that you have failed to comply with this Notice to pay rent. That is the *only* opportunity you will have to challenge this Notice.

2.   At that stage under article 9 of the Agricultural Holdings (Arbitration on Notices) Order 1987 (SI 1987/710) you have one month after the service of the notice to quit within which you can serve on your landlord a notice in writing requiring the question to be determined by arbitration under the Agricultural Holdings Act 1986 (c 5).

3. You will then have three months from the date of service of that notice in which to appoint an arbitrator by agreement or (in default of such agreement) to make an application under paragraph 1 of Schedule 11 to that Act for the appointment of an arbitrator. If this is not done by you or your landlord your notice requiring arbitration ceases to be effective (see article 10 of that Order).

[1165]

FORM 2

Agricultural Holdings Act 1986

Schedule 3, Part I, Case D

Notice to tenant to remedy breach of tenancy by doing work of repair, maintenance or replacement

Re: the holding known as ....

To ....

....

(Name and address of tenant)

IMPORTANT — FAILURE TO COMPLY WITH THIS NOTICE MAY BE RELIED ON AS REASON FOR A NOTICE TO QUIT UNDER CASE D. IF YOU WANT YOUR TENANCY TO CONTINUE YOU MUST ACT QUICKLY. READ THE NOTICE AND ALL THE NOTES CAREFULLY. IF YOU ARE IN ANY DOUBT ABOUT THE ACTION YOU SHOULD TAKE, GET ADVICE IMMEDIATELY, e g FROM A SOLICITOR, SURVEYOR OR CITIZENS ADVICE BUREAU.

---

1. I hereby give you notice that I require you to remedy within .... months* from the date of service of this Notice the breaches, set out below, of the terms or conditions of your tenancy, being breaches which are capable of being remedied of terms or conditions which are not inconsistent with your responsibilities to farm the holding in accordance with the rules of good husbandry.

* Note: This period must be a reasonable period for the tenant to remedy the breaches and must in any event be not less than six months.

2. This Notice requires the doing of the work of repair, maintenance or replacement specified below.

Particulars of breaches of terms or conditions of tenancy

Term or condition of tenancy	*Particulars of breach and work required to remedy it*
....	....
....	....

3. This Notice is given in accordance with Case D in Part I of Schedule 3 to the Agricultural Holdings Act 1986, and failure to comply with it within the period specified above may be relied on as a reason for a notice to quit under Case D.

4. Your attention is drawn to the Notes following the signature to this Notice.

Signed .... Date ....

(If signed by any person other than the landlord of the holding, state in what capacity or by what authority the signature is affixed.)

Address..

....

....

....

Notes

In these Notes "the Order" means the Agricultural Holdings (Arbitration on Notices) Order 1987 (SI 1987/710).

What to do if you wish—

(a) *to contest your liability to do the work, required by this notice to remedy (Question (a)); or*

    (b)   *to request the deletion from this Notice to remedy of any item or part of an item of work on the ground that it is unnecessary or unjustified (Question (b)); or*

    (c)   *to request the substitution in the case of any item or part of an item of a different method or material for the method or material for the method which this Notice to remedy would otherwise require to be followed or used (Question (c)).*

1.   Questions (a), (b) and (c) mentioned in the heading to these Notes can be referred to arbitration under article 3(1) of the Order. To do so you *must* serve a notice in writing upon your landlord *within one month* of the service upon you of this Notice to remedy. The notice you serve upon your landlord should specify—

    (a)   if you are referring Question (a), the items for which you deny liability,

    (b)   if you are referring Question (b), the items you wish to be deleted,

    (c)   if you are referring Question (c), the different methods or materials you wish to be substituted,

and in each case should require the matter to be determined by arbitration under the Agricultural Holdings Act 1986 (c 5). You will not be able to refer Question (a), (b) or (c) to arbitration later, on receipt of a notice to quit. This action does not prevent you settling the matter in writing by agreement with your landlord.

Carrying out the work

2.   If you refer any of these Questions (a), (b) and (c) to arbitration, you are not obliged to carry out the work which is the subject of the reference to arbitration unless and until the arbitrator decides that you are liable to do it; but you *must* carry out any work which you are not referring to arbitration.

3.   If you are referring Question (a) to arbitration you may if you wish carry out any of the work which is the subject of that reference to arbitration without waiting for the arbitrator's award. If you do this and the arbitrator finds that you have carried out any such work which you were under no obligation to do, he will determine at the time he makes his award the reasonable cost of any such work which you have done and you will be entitled to recover this from your landlord (see article 8 of the Order). This provision does *not* apply in the case of work referred to arbitration under Question (b) or Question (c).

What to do if you wish to contest any other question arising under this Notice to remedy

4.   If you wish to contest any other question arising under this Notice other than Question (a), (b) or (c), such as whether the time specified in the Notice to do work is a reasonable period in which to carry out the work, you should refer the question to arbitration in either of the following ways, according to whether or not you are also at the same time referring Question (a), (b) or (c) to arbitration—

    (a)   If you are referring Question (a), (b) or (c) to arbitration, then you *must* also refer to arbitration at the same time any other questions relevant to this Notice which you may wish to dispute.

To do this, you should include in the Notice to your landlord referred to in Note 1 above a statement of the other questions which you require to be determined by arbitration under the Agricultural Holdings Act 1986 (see article 4(1) of the Order).

    (b)   If you are not referring Question (a), (b) or (c) to arbitration, but wish to contest some other question arising under this Notice to remedy, you may refer that question to arbitration either now, on receipt of this Notice, or later, if you get a notice to quit.

To refer the question to arbitration now, you should serve on your landlord *within one month* after the service of this Notice to remedy a notice in writing setting out what it is you require to be determined by arbitration under the Agricultural Holdings Act 1986 (see article 4(2)(a) of the Order).

Alternatively, you have one month after the service of the notice to quit within which you can serve on your landlord a notice in writing requiring the question to be determined by arbitration under the 1986 Act (see article 9 of the Order). You will then have three months from the date of service of service of that notice in which to appoint an arbitrator by agreement or (in default of such agreement) to make an application under paragraph 1 of Schedule 11 to that Act for the appointment of an arbitrator. If this is not done by you or your landlord your notice requiring arbitration ceases to be effective (see article 10 of the Order).

Warning

5.   Notes 1 to 4 above outline the *only* opportunities you have to challenge this Notice to remedy.

Extensions of time allowed for complying with this Notice to remedy

6.   If you refer to arbitration now any question arising from this Notice to remedy, the time allowed for complying with the Notice will be extended until the termination of the arbitration. If the arbitrator decides that you are liable to do any of the work specified in this Notice to remedy, he will extend the time in which the work is to be done by such period as he thinks fit (see article 6(2) of the Order).

Warning as to the effect which any extension of the time allowed for complying with this Notice to remedy may have upon a subsequent notice to quit

7.   If your time for doing the work is extended as mentioned in note 6 above, the arbitrator can specify a date for the termination of your tenancy should you fail to complete the work you are liable to do within the extended time. Then, if you did fail to complete that work within the extended time, your landlord could serve a notice to quit upon you expiring on the date which the arbitrator had specified, and the notice would be valid even though that date might be less than twelve months after the next term date, and might not expire on a term date. The arbitrator cannot, however, specify a termination date which is less than six months after the expiry of the extended time to do the work. Nor can he specify a date which is earlier than would have been possible if you had not required arbitration on this Notice to remedy and had failed to do the work (see article 7 of the Order).

[1166]

FORM 3

Agricultural Holdings Act 1986

Schedule 3, Part I, Case D

Notice to tenant to remedy breach of tenancy (not being a notice requiring the doing of any work of repair, maintenance or replacement)

Re: the holding known as ....

To ....

....

(Name and address of tenant)

IMPORTANT — FAILURE TO COMPLY WITH THIS NOTICE MAY BE RELIED ON AS REASON FOR A NOTICE TO QUIT UNDER CASE D. IF YOU WANT YOUR TENANCY TO CONTINUE YOU MUST ACT QUICKLY. READ THE NOTICE AND ALL THE NOTES CAREFULLY. IF YOU ARE IN ANY DOUBT ABOUT THE ACTION YOU SHOULD TAKE, GET ADVICE IMMEDIATELY, e g FROM A SOLICITOR, SURVEYOR OR CITIZENS ADVICE BUREAU.

---

1.   I hereby give you notice that I require you to remedy within .... months from the date of service of this Notice the breaches, set out below, of the terms or conditions of your tenancy, being breaches which are capable of being remedied of terms or conditions which are not inconsistent with your responsibilities to farm the holding in accordance with the rules of good husbandry.

PART II
STATUTORY INSTRUMENTS

Particulars of breaches of terms or conditions of tenancy

Term or condition of tenancy   *Particulars of breach*

....

....

   2.   This Notice is given in accordance with Case D in Part I of Schedule 3 to the Agricultural Holdings Act 1986 and failure to comply with it within the period specified may be relied on as a reason for a notice to quit under Case D.

   3.   Your attention is drawn to the Notes following the signature to this Notice.

Signed ....   Date ....
(If signed by any person other than the landlord of the holding, state in what capacity or by what authority the signature is affixed).
Address...
....
....
....

Notes

   1.   You cannot at this stage refer to arbitration either your liability to comply with this Notice to remedy or any other question as to the validity of the Notice. You will, however, be entitled to do so later if a notice to quit is served on you on the ground that you have failed to comply with this Notice to remedy. That is the *only* opportunity you will have to challenge this Notice.

   2.   At that stage under article 9 of the Agricultural Holdings (Arbitration on Notices) Order 1987 (SI 1987/710), you have one month after the service of the notice to quit within which you can serve on your landlord a notice in writing requiring the question to be determined by arbitration under the Agricultural Holdings Act 1986 (c 5).

   3.   You will then have three months from the date of service of that notice in which to appoint an arbitrator by agreement or (in default of such agreement) to make an application under paragraph 1 of Schedule 11 to that Act for the appointment of an arbitrator. If this is not done by you or your landlord your notice requiring arbitration ceases to be effective (see article 10 of that Order).

[1167]

TOWN & COUNTRY PLANNING (USE CLASSES) ORDER 1987

(SI 1987/764)

NOTES

Made: 28 April 1987.
Authority: Town and Country Planning Act 1990, ss 55(2)(f), 333(7).

ARRANGEMENT OF ARTICLES

1 Citation and commencement

This Order may be cited as the Town and Country Planning (Use Classes) Order 1987 and shall come into force on 1st June 1987.

[1167A]

2 Interpretation

In this Order, unless the context otherwise requires:—

"care" means personal care for people in need of such care by reason of old age, disablement, past or present dependence on alcohol or drugs or past or present mental disorder, and in class C2 also includes the personal care of children and medical care and treatment;

"day centre" means premises which are visited during the day for social or recreational purposes or for the purposes of rehabilitation or occupational training, at which care is also provided;

.....

"industrial process" means a process for or incidental to any of the following purposes:—

- (a) the making of any article or part of any article (including a ship or vessel, or a film, video or sound recording);
- (b) the altering, repairing, maintaining, ornamenting, finishing, cleaning, washing, packing, canning, adapting for sale, breaking up or demolition of any article; or
- (c) the getting, dressing or treatment of minerals;

in the course of any trade or business other than agriculture, and other than a use carried out in or adjacent to a mine or quarry;

"Schedule" means the Schedule to this Order;

"site" means the whole area of land within a single unit of occupation.

[1167B]

NOTES

Definitions omitted revoked by SI 1992/657, art 2(1).

3 Use Classes

(1) Subject to the provisions of this Order, where a building or other land is used for a purpose of any class specified in the Schedule, the use of that building or that other land for any other purpose of the same class shall not be taken to involve development of the land.

(2) References in paragraph (1) to a building include references to land occupied with the building and used for the same purposes.

(3) A use which is included in and ordinarily incidental to any use in a class specified in the Schedule is not excluded from the use to which it is incidental merely because it is specified in the Schedule as a separate use.

(4) Where land on a single site or on adjacent sites used as parts of a single undertaking is used for purposes consisting of or including purposes falling [within classes B1 and B2] in the Schedule, those classes may be treated as a single class in considering the use of that land for the purposes of this Order, so long as the area used for a purpose falling [within class B2] is not substantially increased as a result.

(5) ...

(6) No class specified in the Schedule includes use—

- (a) as a theatre,
- (b) as an amusement arcade or centre, or a funfair,
- [(c) as a launderette,]
- (d) for the sale of fuel for motor vehicles,
- (e) for the sale or display for sale of motor vehicles,
- (f) for a taxi business or business for the hire of motor vehicles,
- (g) as a scrapyard, or a yard for the storage or distribution of minerals or the breaking of motor vehicles,
- [(h) for any work registrable under the Alkali, etc. Works Regulation Act 1906],
- [(i) as a hostel]

PART II
STATUTORY INSTRUMENTS

[(j)   as a waste disposal installation for the incineration, chemical treatment (as defined in Annex IIA to Directive 75/442/EEC under heading D9), or landfill of waste to which Directive 91/689/EEC applies],

[(k)   as a retail warehouse club being a retail club where goods are sold, or displayed for sale, only to persons who are members of that club;

(l)   as a night-club],

[(m)   as a casino].

[(7)   Where a building or other land is situated in Wales, class B8 (storage or distribution) does not include use of that building or land for the storage of, or as a distribution centre for, radioactive material or radioactive waste.

(8)   For the purpose of paragraph (7), "radioactive material" and "radioactive waste" have the meanings assigned to those terms in the Radioactive Substances Act 1993.]

[1167C]

NOTES
Para (4): words in square brackets substituted by the Town and Country Planning (Use Classes) (Amendment) Order 1995, SI 1995/297, art 2(1).
Para (5): revoked by the Town and Country Planning (Use Classes) (Amendment) (No 2) Order 1992, SI 1992/657, art 2(2).
Para (6): sub-para (c) substituted by the Town and Country Planning (Use Classes) (Amendment) Order 1991, SI 1991/1567, art 2(1); sub-para (h) inserted by the Town and Country Planning (Use Classes) (Amendment) Order 1992, SI 1992/610, art 2(1)(b); sub-para (i) inserted by the Town and Country Planning (Use Classes) (Amendment) Order 1994, SI 1994/724, art 2(1); sub-para (j) inserted by the Town and Country Planning (Environmental Impact Assessment) (England and Wales) Regulations 1999, SI 1999/293, reg 35(2); sub-paras (k), (l) inserted, in relation to England, by the Town and Country Planning (Use Classes) (Amendment) (England) Order 2005, SI 2005/84, art 2(1); sub-para (m) inserted, in relation to England, by the Town and Country Planning (Use Classes) (Amendment) (England) Order 2006, SI 2006/220, art 2(1), (2).
Paras (7), (8): inserted, in relation to Wales, by the Town and Country Planning (Use Classes) (Amendment) (Wales) Order 2002, SI 2002/1875, art 2.

4   Change of use of part of building or land

In the case of a building for a purpose within class C3 (dwellinghouses) in the Schedule, the use as a separate dwellinghouse of any part of the building or of any land occupied with and used for the same purposes as the building is not, by virtue of this Order, to be taken as not amounting to development.

[1167D]

5   (*Revokes the Town and Country Planning (Use Classes) Order 1972, SI 1972/1385 and the Town and Country Planning (Use Classes) (Amendment) Order 1983, SI 1983/1614.*)

SCHEDULE

Articles 3, 4

PART A

Class A1. Shops

Use for all or any of the following purposes—
(a)   for the retail sale of goods other than hot food,
(b)   as a post office,
(c)   for the sale of tickets or as a travel agency,
(d)   for the sale of sandwiches or other cold food for consumption off the premises,
(e)   for hairdressing,
(f)   for the direction of funerals,
(g)   for the display of goods for sale,
(h)   for the hiring out of domestic or personal goods or articles,
[(i)   for the washing or cleaning of clothes or fabrics on the premises,
(j)   for the reception of goods to be washed, cleaned or repaired,]
[(k)   as an internet café; where the primary purpose of the premises is to provide facilities for enabling members of the public to access the internet,]
where the sale, display or service is to visiting members of the public.

Class A2. Financial and professional services

Use for the provision of—
  (a)   financial services, or
  (b)   professional services (other than health or medical services), or
  (c)   any other services (including use as a betting office) which it is appropriate to
        provide in a shopping area,
where the services are provided principally to visiting members of the public.

Class A3. Food and drink

Use for the sale of food and drink for consumption on the premises or of hot food for
consumption off the premises.

[Class A3. Restaurants and cafes

Use for the sale of food and drink for consumption on the premises.

Class A4. Drinking establishments

Use as a public house, wine-bar or other drinking establishment

Class A5. Hot food takeaways

Use for the sale of hot food for consumption off the premises.]

[1167E]

NOTES

Class A1: paras (i), (j) substituted by the Town and Country Planning (Use Classes) (Amendment)
Order 1991, SI 1991/1567, art 2(2); para (k) inserted, in relation to England, by the Town and Country
Planning (Use Classes) (Amendment) (England) Order 2005, SI 2005/84, art 2(2)(a).
    Classes A3–A5: substituted, for Class A3 as originally enacted, in relation to England, by SI 2005/84,
art 2(2)(b).

PART B

Class B1. Business

Use for all or any of the following purposes—
  (a)   as an office other than a use within class A2 (financial and professional services),
  (b)   for research and development of products or processes, or
  (c)   for any industrial process,
being a use which can be carried out in any residential area without detriment to the amenity
of that area by reason of noise, vibration, smell, fumes, smoke, soot, ash, dust or grit.

Class B2. General industrial

Use for the carrying on of an industrial process other than one falling within Class B1 above
…

Class B3.

…

Class B4–Class B7.

…

Class B8. Storage or distribution.

Use for storage or as a distribution centre.

[1167F]

NOTES

Class B2: words omitted revoked by the Town and Country Planning (Use Classes) (Amendment)
Order 1995, SI 1995/297, art 2(2)(a).

Class B3: revoked by the Town and Country Planning (Use Classes) (Amendment) Order 1992, SI 1992/610, art 2(b).

Classes B4–B7 revoked by SI 1995/297, art 2(2)(b).

PART C

[Class C1. Hotels

Use as a hotel or as a boarding or guest house where, in each case, no significant element of care is provided.]

Class C2. Residential institutions

Use for the provision of residential accommodation and care to people in need of care (other than a use within Class C3 (dwelling houses)).

Use as a hospital or nursing home.

Use as a residential school, college or training centre.

[Class C2A. Secure residential institutions

Use for the provision of secure residential accommodation, including use as a prison, young offenders institution, detention centre, secure training centre, custody centre, short-term holding centre, secure hospital, secure local authority accommodation or use as military barracks.]

Class C3. Dwellinghouses

Use as a dwellinghouse (whether or not as a sole or main residence)—
  (a) by a single person or by people living together as a family, or
  (b) by not more than 6 residents living together as a single household (including a household where care is provided for residents).

[1167G]

NOTES

Class C1: substituted by the Town and Country Planning (Use Classes) (Amendment) Order 1994, SI 1994/724, art 2(2).

Class C2A: inserted in relation to England by the Town and Country Planning (Application of Subordinate Legislation to the Crown) Order 2006, SI 2006/1282, art 5(1), (2) and in relation to Wales by the Town and Country Planning (Miscellaneous Amendments and Modifications relating to Crown Land) (Wales) Order 2006, SI 2006/1386, art 2(1), (2).

PART D

Class D1. Non-residential institutions

Any use not including a residential use—
  (a) for the provision of any medical or health services except the use of premises attached to the residence of the consultant or practitioner,
  (b) as a creche, day nursery or day centre,
  (c) for the provision of education,
  (d) for the display of works of art (otherwise than for sale or hire),
  (e) as a museum,
  (f) as a public library or public reading room,
  (g) as a public hall or exhibition hall,
  (h) for, or in connection with, public worship or religious instruction,
  [(i) as a law court].

Class D2. Assembly and leisure

Use as—
  (a) a cinema,
  (b) a concert hall,
  (c) a bingo hall *or casino*,
  (d) a dance hall,

(e)   a swimming bath, skating rink, gymnasium or area for other indoor or outdoor sports or recreations, not involving motorised vehicles or firearms.

[1167H]

NOTES

Class D1: para (i) inserted in relation to England by the Town and Country Planning (Application of Subordinate Legislation to the Crown) Order 2006, SI 2006/1282, art 5(1), (3) and in relation to Wales by SI 2006/1386, art 2(1), (3).

Class D2: in para (c) words in italics revoked, in relation to England, by the Town and Country Planning (Use Classes) (Amendment) (England) Order 2006, SI 2006/220, art 2(1), (3).

AGRICULTURE (TIME-LIMIT) REGULATIONS 1988

(SI 1988/282)

NOTES

Made: 17 February 1988.
Authority: Agricultural Holdings Act 1986, s 9(4).

1   Citation and commencement

These Regulations may be cited as the Agriculture (Time-Limit) Regulations 1988, and shall come into force on 24th March 1988.

[1168]

2   Time limit

The prescribed period after the coming into force of the Agriculture (Maintenance, Repair and Insurance of Fixed Equipment) (Amendment) Regulations 1988 (which vary the model terms of a tenancy of an agricultural holding as to maintenance, repair and insurance established by the operation of regulations under section 7 of the Agricultural Holdings Act 1986) within which an arbitrator shall for the purposes of specifying the terms of a tenancy of an agricultural holding pursuant to section 6(2) of that Act disregard the variation effected by the said Agriculture (Maintenance, Repair and Insurance of Fixed Equipment) (Amendment) Regulations 1988 shall be three months from the date of the coming into force of those Regulations.

[1169]

SET-ASIDE REGULATIONS 1988

(SI 1988/1352)

NOTES

Made: 28 July 1988.
Authority: European Communities Act 1972, s 2(2).

ARRANGEMENT OF REGULATIONS

1   Citation, commencement and extent

(1)   These Regulations may be cited as the Set-Aside Regulations 1988 and shall come into force on the day after the day on which these Regulations are made.

(2)   These Regulations shall apply to Great Britain.

[1170]

2   Interpretation

(1)   In these Regulations, unless the context otherwise requires—

["Agricultural Land Tribunal" means an Agricultural Land Tribunal established under Part V of the Agriculture Act 1947;]

"agriculture" includes horticulture, fruit growing, seed growing, dairy farming, livestock breeding and keeping and freshwater fish farming, the use of land as grazing land, meadow land, osier land, reed beds, market gardens and nursery grounds, and "agricultural" shall be construed accordingly;

"application" means an application for aid under regulation 5 and "applicant" and "apply" shall be construed accordingly;

"the appropriate Minister" means—

    (a)   in relation to England, the Minister of Agriculture, Fisheries and Food;

    (b)   in relation to Scotland or Wales, the Secretary of State;

"arable crops" means crops of a type listed in Schedule 1;

"arable land" means land used for the production of arable crops [or for rotational fallow];

"beneficiary" means—

    (a)   a person whose application has been accepted; or

    (b)   a person who occupies a holding or part of a holding following a change of occupation of that holding or part and who has given an undertaking to comply with set-aside obligations relating to that holding or part assumed by the previous occupier;

"the Broads" shall have the same meaning as in section 2(3) of the Norfolk and Suffolk Broads Act 1988;

["designated maps" means—

    (a)   in relation to England, the 3 volumes of maps numbered 1 to 3, each such volume being marked "volume of maps of less-favoured farming areas in England" and with the number of the volume, dated 20th May 1991, signed and sealed by the Minister of Agriculture, Fisheries and Food and deposited at the offices of the Ministry of Agriculture, Fisheries and Food at Nobel House, 17 Smith Square, London SW1P 3JR;

    (b)   in relation to Wales, the 2 volumes of maps numbered 1 and 2, both volumes being marked "volume of maps of less-favoured farming areas in Wales" and with the number of the volume, dated 20th May 1991, signed by the Secretary of State for Wales and deposited at the offices of the Welsh Office Agriculture Department at Trawsgoed, Aberystwyth, Dyfed SY23 4HT;

    (c)   *(applies to Scotland only.)*]

"eligible person" means a person who on the date of the submission of his application occupies a holding ... as an owner or tenant and who at the commencement of the set-aside period will have so occupied that holding for a period of at least twelve months;

["fallow land" means permanent fallow or rotational fallow;

"grazed fallow" means fallow land grazed extensively by livestock;]

["grazing land" does not include land grazed by horses unless they are kept for food or use in the farming of land;]

"holding" means land which is occupied as a unit for agricultural purposes;

"landlord" means—

    (a)   in England and Wales, in relation to the tenant of a holding or part of a holding, any person who either solely or jointly owns or has a superior tenancy of that holding or part;

    (b)   *(applies to Scotland only.)*

and, where appropriate, includes a head tenant;

"less-favoured area" means land—

    [(a)   which is situated in an area included in the list of less-favoured farming areas adopted by the Council or the Commission of the European Communities under Article 2(2) of Council Directive 75/268/EEC on mountain and hill farming and farming in certain less-favoured areas, as amended by Council Directive 80/666/EEC, which list is contained in Council Directive 84/169/EEC, as amended by Commission Decision 91/25/EEC, and]

    (b)   which—

        (i)   is, in the opinion of the appropriate Minister, inherently suitable for extensive livestock production but not for the production of crops in quantity materially greater than that necessary to feed such livestock as are capable of being maintained on such land, and whose agricultural production is, in the opinion of the appropriate Minister, restricted in its range by, or by any combination of, soil, relief, aspect or climate, or

        (ii)   is situated in the Isles of Scilly,

which land is within the area shaded blue or pink on the designated maps;

["livestock" includes any creature kept for the production of food, wool, skins, or fur or for the purpose of its use in farming the land or in the carrying on in relation to land of any agricultural activity;]

"National Park Authority" means a special planning board or a joint planning board or a National Park Committee constituted or re-constituted in accordance with Part I of Schedule 17 to the Local Government Act 1972;

"permanent fallow" means land which fallowed for the whole of the set-aside period;

"reference period" means the period commencing on 1st July 1987 and ending on 30th June 1988;

"relevant arable crops" means crops of a type listed in List A in Schedule 1;

"relevant arable land" means land used for the production of relevant arable crops;

"rotational fallow" means land fallowed as part of the arable rotation;

"the set-aside area" means the area of … land which a beneficiary undertakes to set aside under the provisions of these Regulations;

"set-aside land" means any land forming part of the set-aside area;

"the set-aside obligations" means—

    (a)   the obligations assumed by a beneficiary by virtue of the undertakings referred to in regulation 3 [or 12]; and

    (b)   (where these apply) the requirements laid down in regulations 4, (1), [7(2),] 8 and 9(1) and (2);

"the set-aside period" means—

    (a)   in relation to an application accepted by the appropriate Minister in 1988, the period commencing on the date of acceptance of that application or 1st October 1988, whichever is later, and ending on 30th September 1993;

    (b)   in relation to an application accepted by the appropriate Minister in a year subsequent to 1988, the period of five consecutive years from 1st October in that year;

["to set aside" means in relation to land, to withdraw it from agricultural production;]

"Site of Special Scientific Interest" means any area of land notified by the Nature Conservancy Council under the provisions of section 28(1) of the Wildlife and Countryside Act 1981;

"tenant" means—

    (a)   in England and Wales, a person who occupies a holding or part of a holding either—

        (i)   under an agreement for the letting of land for a tenancy from year to year; or

        (ii)   under an agreement which has effect by virtue of section 2(1) [or section 3(1)] of the Agricultural Holdings Act 1986 as an agreement for the letting of land for a tenancy from year to year; or

    (iii)   under a contract of tenancy for a fixed term of years of which at least five years remain unexpired at the commencement of the set-aside period;

  (b)   *(applies to Scotland only.)*

and, where appropriate, includes a sub-tenant;

["vernacular buildings" means buildings traditionally found in the locality;]

"the Woodland Grant Scheme" means the scheme made by the Forestry Commissioners and published in June 1988 under which the Forestry Commissioners enter into agreements to make grants pursuant to section 1 of the Forestry Act 1979 for and in connection with the use and management of land for forestry purposes.

["year" means, except for the purposes of the definitions of "the set-aside period" and "tenant", a period of 12 months commencing on 1st October.]

(2)   Any reference in these Regulations to a numbered regulation or Schedule shall be construed as a reference to the regulation or Schedule bearing that number in these Regulations.

[1171]

NOTES

Para (1): definitions "Agricultural Land Tribunal", "fallow land", "grazed fallow", "livestock", "vernacular buildings" and "year" inserted, in definition "the set-aside obligations" figure in second pair of square brackets inserted, and in definition "tenant" words in square brackets inserted, by the Set-Aside (Amendment) Regulations 1990, SI 1990/1716, reg 4; in definition "arable land" words in square brackets inserted, definition "grazing land" inserted, in definition "the set-aside obligations" figure in first pair of square brackets inserted, in definitions "eligible person" and "the set-aside area" words omitted revoked, and definition "to set aside" substituted, by the Set-Aside (Amendment) Regulations 1989, SI 1989/1042, reg 3; definition "designated maps" substituted, and in definition "less-favoured area" sub-para (a) substituted, by the Set-Aside (Amendment) Regulations 1991, SI 1991/1993, reg 3.

Modification: sub-s (1) is modified in relation to a National Park authority in Wales by the National Park Authorities (Wales) Order 1995, SI 1995/2803, art 18, Sch 5, para 14, as amended by SI 1996/534, art 3, Schedule, and in relation to a National Park authority in England by the National Park Authorities (England) Order 1996, SI 1996/1243, art 18, Sch 5, para 11.

Minister of Agriculture, Fisheries and Food: the Ministry of Agriculture, Fisheries and Food was dissolved by the Ministry of Agriculture, Fisheries and Food (Dissolution) Order 2002, SI 2002/794. Subject to specific provision to the contrary, the functions of the Minister were transferred to the Secretary of State, and the property, rights and liabilities of the Minister were transferred to the Secretary of State for Environment, Food and Rural Affairs.

Ministry of Agriculture, Fisheries and Food: see the note Minister of Agriculture, Fisheries and Food, above.

---

3 Aid for set aside of arable land

(1)   Subject to the provisions of these Regulations, the appropriate Minister may make payments of aid to any eligible person who undertakes for the duration of the set-aside period—

  [(a)   to set aside on his holding an area of land which—

    (i)   is arable land or temporary grassland at the time the undertaking is given;

    (ii)   was arable land in the reference period; and

    (iii)   is equal in size to at least 20 per cent of the relevant arable land on that holding in the reference period but does not exceed an area equal in size to such relevant arable land; and]

  [(b)   to use the set-aside area for one of the following—

    (i)   permanent fallow;

    (ii)   rotational fallow;

    (iii)   grazed fallow (subject to regulation 7A);

    (iv)   woodland;

    (v)   non-agricultural purposes;

    (vi)   a combination of any two or more of (iii), (iv) and (v);

    (vii)   a combination of any two or more of (i), (ii), (iv) and (v); and]

  (c)   to ensure that the area of relevant arable land on his holding shall not exceed the area of relevant arable land on his holding in the reference period, less an area equal in size to the set-aside area.

(2)   Subject to the provisions of these Regulations, the appropriate Minister may make payments of aid to any beneficiary who, within three years from the date of acceptance of his original application, undertakes for the remainder of the set-aside period—

(a)   to set aside an additional area of the arable land [or temporary grassland] on his holding which was arable land in the reference period; and

[(b)   to use that additional set-aside area for one of the purposes set out in paragraph (1)(b)(ii)–(vi) above or a combination of any two or more of (ii), (iv) and (v), provided that—

   (i)   if he has undertaken to use any land for either of the purposes set out in paragraph 1(b)(i) or (ii) he shall undertake not to use that additional set-aside area for the purposes set out in paragraph 1(b)(iii) or (vi);

   (ii)   if he has undertaken to use any land for the purpose set out in paragraph 1(b)(iii) he shall undertake not to use that additional set-aside area for the purposes set out in paragraph 1(b)(i) or (ii), or a combination of (ii) and (iv), (ii) and (v) or (ii), (iv) and (v); and]

(c)   to ensure that the area of relevant arable land on his holding shall not exceed the area of relevant arable land on his holding in the reference period, less an area equal in size to the sum of the original set-aside area and the additional set-aside area.

(3)   Subject to the provisions of these Regulations, the appropriate Minister may make payments of aid to any beneficiary who enlarges his holding by the acquisition of arable land [or temporary grassland] which was arable land in the reference period and who, within four years from the date of acceptance of his original application, undertakes for the remainder of the set-aside period—

(a)   to set aside an area of that acquired ... land; and

[(b)   to use that additional set-aside area for one of the purposes set out in paragraph (1)(b)(ii)–(vi) above or a combination of any two or more of (ii), (iv) and (v), provided that—

   (i)   if he has undertaken to use any land for either of the purposes set out in paragraph 1(b)(i) or (ii) he shall undertake not to use that additional set-aside area for the purposes set out in paragraph 1(b)(iii) or (vi);

   (ii)   if he has undertaken to use any land for the purpose set out in paragraph 1(b)(iii) he shall undertake not to use that additional set-aside area for the purposes set out in paragraph 1(b)(i) or (ii), or a combination of (ii) and (iv), (ii) and (v) or (ii), (iv) and (v); and]

(c)   to ensure that the area of relevant arable land on his enlarged holding shall not exceed the sum of the area of relevant arable land on his holding in the reference period and the area of relevant arable land comprised in [that acquired land] in the reference period, less an area equal in size to the sum of the original set-aside area and the additional set-aside area.

(4)   In determining whether any arable land was arable land in the reference period for the purposes of paragraphs (1) to (3) above, no account shall be taken of any land which was converted to the production of arable crops in the period commencing on 1st January 1988 and ending on 30th June 1988.

[1172]

NOTES

Para (1): sub-para (a) substituted by the Set-Aside (Amendment) Regulations 1989, SI 1989/1042, reg 4(a); sub-para (b) substituted by the Set-Aside (Amendment) Regulations 1990, SI 1990/1716, reg 5(a).

Para (2): words in square brackets in sub-para (a) inserted by SI 1989/1042, reg 4(b)(i); sub-para (b) substituted by SI 1990/1716, reg 5(b).

Para (3): words in first pair of square brackets inserted, word omitted from sub-para (a) revoked, and words in square brackets in sub-para (c) substituted, by SI 1989/1042, reg 4(c); sub-para (b) substituted by SI 1990/1716, reg 5(b).

---

4   Requirements in relation to the set-aside area

(1)   The set-aside area shall include either—

(a)   one whole field amounting to at least one hectare; or

(b)   an area consisting of adjacent whole fields and amounting to at least one hectare.

(2)   Where any set-aside land consists of a strip of land, that strip shall be at least 15 metres wide.

[1173]

5 Applications for aid

(1)   An application for aid under these regulations shall be made at such time and in such form as the appropriate Minister reasonably may require and shall include—

(a)   a map of the applicant's holding showing—
  (i)   the boundaries of the holding and internal field boundaries;
  (ii)   the area of land which the applicant proposes to set aside;
  (iii)   the area of land on which the applicant intends to continue production of relevant arable crops;

(b)   details of the type of production carried out or to be carried out on each individual field during the reference period and during the period of twelve months immediately preceding the commencement of the set-aside period;

(c)   a description of the intended use or uses of the proposed set-aside area;

(d)   if required by the appropriate Minister, documentary evidence showing the nature of the applicant's estate or interest in the holding; [and

(e)   where an applicant proposes to use set-aside land for grazed fallow, details of the number of each type of livestock kept in the reference period on the holding of which the land he proposes to set aside for grazed fallow formed part and the amount of feed required by them in the reference period.]

(2)   An application by a beneficiary who proposes to set aside additional areas of ... land under the provisions of regulation 3(2) or (3) shall contain such information and shall be made at such time and in such form as the appropriate Minister reasonably may require.

[1174]

NOTES
Para (1): words in square brackets added by the Set-Aside (Amendment) Regulations 1990, SI 1990/1716, reg 6.
Para (2): word omitted revoked by the Set-Aside (Amendment) Regulations 1989, SI 1989/1042, reg 5.

6 Restrictions on acceptance of applications for aid

(1)   The appropriate Minister shall not accept an application from a tenant who proposes to use any set-aside land for woodland or for non-agricultural purposes unless he is satisfied that that tenant has obtained the consent in writing of the landlord of that land to the making of the application.

(2)   The appropriate Minister shall not accept an application from a tenant who proposes to use any set-aside land for permanent fallow[, rotational fallow or grazed fallow] unless he is satisfied that that tenant has notified the landlord of that land in writing of his intention to make the application.

(3)   The appropriate Minister shall not accept an application from any person who proposes to set aside land within a Site of Special Scientific Interest, a National Park or the Broads, unless he is satisfied that that person has notified the Nature Conservancy Council, the National Park Authority or the Broads Authority, respectively, in writing of his intention to make the application.

(4)   The appropriate Minister shall not accept an application from any person who proposes to use more than 0.25 hectares of set-aside land for woodland unless that person either—

(a)   has submitted an application to the Forestry Commissioners under the Woodland Grant Scheme for a grant for the planting of woodland on that land; or

(b)   has submitted an application to the appropriate Minister for grant in relation to that land under the Farm Woodland Scheme 1988.

(5)   The appropriate Minister may refuse to accept an application where he is satisfied that—

(a)   the set aside of any land or the use of any set-aside land in accordance with the proposals contained in that application would frustrate the purposes of any assistance previously given or to be given out of money provided by Parliament or by the European Economic Community;

(b)   payment of aid under these Regulations in respect of any land which an applicant proposes to set aside would duplicate any assistance previously given or to be given out of money provided by Parliament or by the European Economic Community.

[1175]

PART II
STATUTORY INSTRUMENTS

NOTES
Para (2): words in square brackets substituted by the Set-Aside (Amendment) Regulations 1990, SI 1990/1716, reg 7.

[7 Requirements in relation to use for fallow

(1)   A beneficiary whose undertaking takes effect on or after 1st October 1990 or who, in accordance with regulation 10, terminates part of the undertakings given by him shall observe in relation to any land which he has undertaken to set aside for permanent fallow or rotational fallow the requirements set out in paragraphs (1)(a), 2, 3, 4(a) and 5 to 14 of Schedule 2.

(2)   A beneficiary whose undertaking takes effect before 1st October 1990 may elect before 1st October 1990 to observe in relation to any land which he has undertaken to set aside for permanent fallow or rotational fallow the requirements set out in paragraphs 1(a), 2, 3, 4(a) and 5 to 14 of Schedule 2 but shall, if he does not so elect, observe in relation to that land the requirements set out in paragraphs 1(b), 2, 3, 4(b), 5 to 12, 13 in so far as it relates to the features listed in sub-paragraphs (a) and (b), and 14 of Schedule 2.

(3)   Where any set-aside land is used for rotational fallow, the beneficiary shall, before 1st October in each year of the set-aside period, notify the appropriate Minister of the location of the area of set-aside land to be used for that purpose in that year.

(4)   Where a beneficiary has undertaken to use any set-aside land for rotational fallow, and provided that he observes the requirements set out in paragraphs 1(a), 2, 3, 4(a) and 5 to 14 of Schedule 2—
   (a)   subject to sub-paragraph (b), he may in any year alter the area of the land which he undertook to set aside for rotational fallow if the amount by which he increases or reduces that area does not;
      (i)   exceed 10 per cent of the area of land which he undertook to set aside for rotational fallow, or
      (ii)   reduce the area of set-aside land below 20 per cent of the relevant arable land on the holding in the reference period or increase the said area above that which is equal in size to such relevant arable land; and
   (b)   he may only reduce the area of the land which he undertook to set aside for rotational fallow if he has in any previous year increased the area of land which he undertook to set aside for rotational fallow by at least that same amount.

(5)   Where any set-aside land is used for grazed fallow, the beneficiary shall observe in relation to that land the requirements set out in Schedule 3.]

[1176]

NOTES
Substituted by the Set-Aside (Amendment) Regulations 1990, SI 1990/1716, reg 8.

[7A—(1)   Subject to paragraph (4) below, where a beneficiary uses set-aside land for grazed fallow he shall not allow the number of livestock units on his holding to exceed the maximum number of livestock units in the reference period on the holding of which the set-aside land formed part.

(2)   Subject to paragraph (4) below, where livestock were not kept in the reference period on the holding of which the set-aside land formed part, the beneficiary shall only use the fallow land on that set-aside land for grazed fallow for deer or goats, and he shall not allow the number of livestock units on his holding to exceed the number of livestock units representing one livestock unit per hectare of the forage area of his holding.

(3)   Subject to paragraph (4) below, except where the beneficiary's holding is identical to that of which the set-aside land referred to in paragraph (1) above formed part, where that holding comprises a greater or lesser forage area than the forage area of the holding referred to in that paragraph, for the purposes of paragraph (1) above, the maximum number of livestock units in the reference period on the holding of which the set-aside land formed part shall be deemed to bear the same proportion to the total number of livestock units on that holding in the reference period as the forage area of the beneficiary's holding at the time he gives his undertaking to set aside land for grazed fallow bears to the forage area in the reference period of the holding of which the set-aside land formed part.

(4)   Where a beneficiary enlarges his holding by the acquisition of arable land or temporary grassland which was arable land in the reference period, and

(a)

    (i)   already uses for grazed fallow set-aside land forming part or all of a holding on which livestock were kept in the reference period; and

    (ii) undertakes to set aside an area of that acquired land for grazed fallow, where such land forms part or all of a holding on which no livestock were kept in the reference period; or

(b)

    (i)   already uses for grazed fallow set-aside land forming part or all of a holding on which no livestock were kept in the reference period; and

    (ii) undertakes to set aside an area of that acquired land for grazed fallow, where such land forms part or all of a holding on which livestock were kept in the reference period,

if he uses his holding for the grazing of only deer or goats, he shall not allow to be grazed on that holding more than the sum of:

    (i)   the number of livestock units in the reference period on the holding of which the set-aside land formed part; and

    (ii) the number of livestock units representing one livestock unit per hectare of the forage area of the acquired land; but

if he uses his holding for the grazing of livestock (other than exclusively deer or goats), he shall not allow to be grazed on that holding more than the number of livestock units in the reference period on the land forming part or all of the holding on which livestock were kept in the reference period.

(5) For the purposes of this regulation—

(a) "his holding" means all the land occupied by the beneficiary as a unit at the time he gave his undertaking to set aside land for grazed fallow, together with any land subsequently acquired by him; and

(b) the equivalent in livestock units of an animal of the type described in the first column of Schedule 4 shall be the number specified in the second column of that Schedule.]

[1177]

NOTES

Inserted by the Set-Aside (Amendment) Regulations 1990, SI 1990/1716, reg 9.

8 Requirements in relation to use for woodland

[(1) Where a beneficiary has undertaken to use any set-aside land for woodland, that beneficiary shall, until planting commences, undertake to use that set-aside land for permanent fallow and shall observe in relation to it the relevant requirements set out in Schedule 2.]

(2) Where a beneficiary has submitted an application to the Forestry Commissioners under the Woodland Grant Scheme for a grant for the planting of woodland on any set-aside land, he shall not commence planting on that land until his application has been approved in accordance with the provisions of that Scheme.

(3) Where a beneficiary has submitted an application to the appropriate Minister under the Farm Woodland Scheme for grant in relation to any set-aside land, he shall not commence planting on that land until his application has been approved in accordance with the provisions of that Scheme.

(4) Where a beneficiary has submitted an application for grant in relation to the planting of woodlands on any set-aside land under the Woodland Grant Scheme or the Farm Woodland Scheme, and that application is not approved, that beneficiary shall, subject to regulations 10 and 11, use that land for permanent fallow for the remainder of the set-aside period.

[1178]

NOTES

Para (1): substituted by the Set-Aside (Amendment) Regulations 1990, SI 1990/1716, reg 10.

9 Requirements in relation to use for non-agricultural purposes

[(1) Where a beneficiary has undertaken to use any set-aside land for woodland, that beneficiary shall, until planting commences, undertake to use that set-aside land for permanent fallow and shall observe in relation to it the relevant requirements set out in Schedule 2.]

(2) Where a beneficiary has undertaken to use any set-aside land for non-agricultural purposes, that beneficiary shall not use that land for—

(a) the extraction of minerals; or

(b) the erection of any building or other permanent structure with a view to the use of such building or structure for any of the following purposes—
    (i) the carrying of any industrial process;
    (ii) the retail or wholesale sale of goods;
    (iii) use as a dwellinghouse, hotel or lodging house or for the purposes of a residential institution of any description;
    (iv) use for office accommodation;
    (v) use as a storage or distribution centre.

(3) Notwithstanding paragraph (2) above, a beneficiary may use set-aside land for the erection of any building or other permanent structure with a view to the use of that building or structure for the purposes of any business of a type specified in the Schedule to the Farm Business Specification Order 1987 where that business is carried on by a person also carrying on a business consisting in or partly in the pursuit of agriculture on the same or adjacent land.

[1179]

NOTES

Para (1): substituted by the Set-Aside (Amendment) Regulations 1990, SI 1990/1716, reg 11.

10 Termination of undertakings

(1) Within a period of three years from the commencement of the set-aside period, a beneficiary may terminate the undertakings given by him under regulations 3 or 12 in relation to all [or part of] the land on his holding to which those undertakings relate, provided that the termination shall not take effect before the expiry of that three-year period [and provided that, if he terminates those undertakings in relation to only part of that land, he does not thereby reduce the area of land set aside below 20 per cent of the relevant arable land on the holding in the reference period].

(2) A beneficiary shall notify the appropriate Minister at least three months before the expiry of the three-year period referred to in paragraph (1) of his intention to terminate the undertakings and the notification shall be made in such form and shall contain such information relating to the termination as that Minister reasonably may require.

(3) In paragraphs (1) and (2) above, references to the beneficiary shall include the personal representatives of that beneficiary where he has died.

(4) Where a beneficiary has terminated his undertakings under the provisions of paragraph (1) above [or has been notified that his undertakings are treated as terminated by the appropriate Minister under the provisions of Regulation 16(3A)], the appropriate Minister shall not, within two years of the termination, accept an application from that beneficiary for aid under these Regulations in relation to any land to which those undertakings relate.

[1180]

NOTES

Paras (1), (4): words in square brackets added and inserted by the Set-Aside (Amendment) Regulations 1990, SI 1990/1716, reg 12.

11 Change of use of set-aside land

(1) Subject to the provisions of this regulation, a beneficiary may, within three years of the commencement of the set-aside period, change the use of any set-aside land, with the exception of land on which woodlands have been planted, from the use to which he has undertaken to put that land [if he undertakes to put that land to one of the other uses specified in regulation 3(1)(b)(ii)–(iv) or a combination of the uses specified in (ii), (iv) and (v)].

(2)   The beneficiary shall notify the [appropriate] Minister of an intended change of use and the notification shall be in such form and shall contain such information relating to the intended change of use as that Minister reasonably may require.

[(2A)   Subject to regulation 13(2)(b), (3)(b) and (4)(b) where, on or after 1st October 1990, a beneficiary changes the use of set-aside land in any year he shall receive payment at the rate payable in respect of the use made by him of that land in that year which attracts the lowest rate of payment as set out in the table in regulation 13.]

(3)   ...

[(4)   Except where a beneficiary receives the rate for permanent fallow in accordance with the provisions of regulation 13(2), (3) or (4), where he changes the use of any set-aside land from use for permanent fallow to any other use, the appropriate Minister shall recover or withhold from that beneficiary the difference between any payments made or due to him under these Regulations on the basis of the use of that land for permanent fallow and payments made or due to him on the basis of the use of that land for rotational fallow.]

(5)   Where a beneficiary notifies the appropriate Minister that he intends to change the use of any set-aside land which he occupies as a tenant from use for permanent [fallow, rotational fallow or grazed fallow] to use for woodland or non-agricultural purposes, the appropriate Minister shall not approve that change of use unless he is satisfied that that beneficiary has obtained the consent in writing of the landlord of that land to that change of use.

[1181]

NOTES
   Paras (1), (5): words in square brackets substituted by the Set-Aside (Amendment) Regulations 1990, SI 1990/1716, reg 13(a), (f).
   Para (2): word in square brackets inserted by SI 1990/1716, reg 13(b).
   Para (2A): inserted by SI 1990/1716, reg 13(c).
   Para (3): revoked by SI 1990/1716, reg 13(d).
   Para (4): substituted by SI 1990/1716, reg 13(e).

12   Change of occupation

(1)   Where there is a change of occupation of the entirety or any part of a beneficiary's holding during the course of the set-aside period by reason of the devolution of that holding or part on the death of the beneficiary, or otherwise—

(a)   the beneficiary (or, if he has died, his personal representatives) shall notify the appropriate Minister in writing of the change of occupation within three months of its occurrence and shall supply to that Minister such information relating to that change of occupation in such form and within such period as that Minister reasonably may determine;

(b)   the new occupier of that holding or part may give an undertaking to the appropriate Minister to comply with the set-aside obligations relating to that holding or part for the remainder of the set-aside period.

(2)   Where there is a change of occupation of part of a holding, the appropriate Minister shall determine the extent to which the set-aside obligations assumed by the original occupier relate to that part having regard to—

(a)   the area of arable land [or temporary grassland] comprised in that part, and

(b)   the area of set-aside land (if any) comprised in that part and the use or uses to which that land is put.

(3)   The appropriate Minister shall not accept an undertaking from a new occupier of a holding or part of a holding to comply with set-aside obligations assumed by the original occupier unless that minister is satisfied that that new occupier occupies that holding or part as an owner or tenant or as the personal representative of the original occupier.

(4)   Any undertaking given by a new occupier to comply with set-aside obligations shall contain such information and shall be given in such form and within such period following the change of occupation as the appropriate Minister reasonably may determine.

(5)   Where the appropriate Minister has accepted an undertaking from a new occupier to comply with set-aside obligations—

(a)   the new occupier shall be deemed to be an eligible person who has applied for aid under the provisions of these Regulations; and

    (b)   the undertaking to comply with set-aside obligations shall be deemed to take effect on the date of the acceptance by that Minister of that undertaking.

(6)   Where within a period of three months from the date of change of occupation a new occupier has not given an undertaking to comply with set-aside obligations assumed by the original occupier, the appropriate Minister may—

    (a)   withhold the whole or any part of any payments due to the original occupier; and

    (b)   recover from that original occupier or his personal representatives the whole or any part of any payments of aid already made to him.

(7)   Paragraph (6) above shall not apply where the change of occupation of a holding or part of a holding is the result of—

    (a)   the compulsory purchase of that holding or part; ...

    (b)   the death of the original occupier, and
        (i)   that original occupier occupied that holding or part as a tenant; and
        (ii)   following the death of that original occupier the tenancy or lease under which he occupied that holding or part was terminated by the landlord[; or]

    [(c)   in England and Wales, the termination of a tenancy following the operation of a notice to quit to which the Agricultural Land Tribunal has consented under section 26(1) of the Agricultural Holdings Act 1986 having been satisfied as to any of the matters specified in section 27(3) of that Act, or the termination of a tenancy following the service of a notice to quit stating that the circumstances in Case A, B, G or H of Schedule 3 to that Act apply; or

    (d)   *(applies to Scotland only.)*]

[1182]

NOTES

Para (2): words in square brackets in sub-para (a) inserted by the Set-Aside (Amendment) Regulations 1989, SI 1989/1042, reg 7.

Para (7): word omitted from sub-para (a) revoked, word in square brackets in sub-para (b), and sub-paras (c), (d), added, by the Set-Aside (Amendment) Regulations 1990, SI 1990/1716, reg 14.

---

13 Amounts and payment of aid

(1)   Subject to the provisions of this regulation and to regulations 10 and 16, payment of aid shall be by way of five payments made annually in arrears in relation to the use of set-aside land specified in column 1 of the table in this regulation at the rate per hectare of such land specified in column 2.

[(1)	(2)	
Use of set-aside land	*Amount of annual payment per hectare of set-aside land*	
	Less-favoured area	Other
	£	£
1. Permanent fallow		
(a) Subject to paragraph 1(b) below where the beneficiary is required under regulation 7(1) to observe the requirements set out in paragraphs (a), 2, 3, 4(a) and 5 to 14 of Schedule 2—		

PART II
STATUTORY INSTRUMENTS

[(1) Use of set-aside land			(2) Amount of annual payment per hectare of set-aside land	
			Less-favoured area	Other
			£	£
	(i)	where the beneficiary has undertaken to set aside for permanent fallow or rotational fallow more than 100 hectares, and more than 75 per cent, of the land which was relevant arable land in the reference period, each hectare of set-aside land used for permanent fallow in excess of the first 100 hectares of permanent fallow and rotational fallow	152	172
	(ii)	each hectare to which (i) above does not apply	202	222
(b)	where the beneficiary elects under regulation 7(2) to observe the requirements set out in paragraphs 1(a), 2, 3, 4(a) and 5 to 14 of Schedule 2, or where the beneficiary entered into an undertaking which took effect before 1st October 1990 and enters into another undertaking which takes effect on or after that date, or in accordance with regulation 10, terminates part of the undertakings given by him—			
	(i)	where the beneficiary has undertaken to set aside for permanent fallow or rotational fallow more than 100 hectares, and more than 75 per cent, of the land which was relevant arable land in the reference period, each hectare of set-aside land used for permanent fallow in excess of the first 100 hectares of permanent fallow and rotational fallow	140	160
	(ii)	each hectare to which (i) above does not apply	190	210
(c)	where the beneficiary is required under regulation 7(2) to observe the requirements set out in paragraphs 1(b), 2, 3, 4(b), 5 to 12, 13 in so far as it relates to the features listed in sub-paragraphs (a) and (b), and 14 of Schedule 2		180	200
2.	Rotational fallow			
(a)	Subject to paragraph 2(b) below where the beneficiary is required under regulation 7(1) to observe the requirements set out in paragraphs 1(a), 2, 3, 4(a) and 5 to 14 of Schedule 2—			
	(i)	where the beneficiary has undertaken to set aside for permanent fallow or rotational fallow more than 100 hectares, and more than 75 per cent, of the land which was relevant arable land in the reference period, each hectare of set-aside land used for rotational fallow in excess of the first 100 hectares of permanent fallow and rotational fallow	132	152

[(1) Use of set-aside land	(2) Amount of annual payment per hectare of set-aside land	
	Less-favoured area £	Other £
(ii) each hectare to which (i) above does not apply	182	202
where the beneficiary elects under regulation 7(2) to observe the requirements set out in paragraphs 1(a), 2, 3, 4(a) and 5 to 14 of Schedule 2, or		
where the beneficiary entered into an undertaking which took effect before 1st October 1990 and enters into another undertaking which takes effect on or after that date, or		
in accordance with regulation 10, terminates part of the undertakings given by him—		
(i) where the beneficiary has undertaken to set aside for permanent fallow or rotational fallow more than 100 hectares, and more than 75 per cent, of the land which was relevant arable land in the reference period, each hectare of set-aside land used for rotational fallow in excess of the first 100 hectares of permanent fallow and rotational fallow	120	140
(ii) each hectare to which (i) above does not apply	170	190
(c) where the beneficiary is required under regulation 7(2) to observe the requirements set out in paragraphs 1(b), 2, 3, 4(b), 5 to 12, 13 in so far as it relates to the features listed in sub-paragraphs (a) and (b), and 14 of Schedule 2.	160	180
3. Grazed fallow	100	110
4. Non-agricultural purposes	130	150
5. Woodland (other than under the provisions of the Farm Woodland Scheme)	180	200]

[(1A)   Where the set-aside land has been used for both permanent fallow and rotational fallow, in calculating for the purposes of paragraphs 1 and 2 of the table referred to in paragraph (1) at which rate per hectare payments should be made, the number of hectares of set-aside land used for rotational fallow shall be counted before counting the number of hectares used for permanent fallow.]

(2)   Where a beneficiary uses any set-aside land for woodland under the provisions of the Farm Woodland Scheme, he shall receive in relation to that land—

    (a)   in respect of the year in which planting commences and any subsequent year in the set-aside period, the same rate as under the provisions of that Scheme;

    (b)   in respect of any year in the set-aside period prior to that in which planting commences, the rate for permanent fallow[, having regard to regulation 7(1) and (2),] specified in the table in this regulation.

(3)   Where a beneficiary uses any set-aside land for woodland otherwise than under the provisions of the Farm Woodland Scheme, he shall receive in relation that land—

(a)   in respect of the year in which planting commences and any subsequent year in the set-aside period, the rate for woodland specified in the table in this regulation;

(b)   in respect of any year in the set-aside period prior to that in which planting commences, the rate for permanent fallow[, having regard to regulation 7(1) and (2),] specified in the table in this regulation.

(4)   Where a beneficiary uses any set-aside for non-agricultural purposes, he shall receive in relation to that land—

(a)   in respect of the year in which the conversion to use for non-agricultural purposes commences and any subsequent year in the set-aside period, the rate for non-agricultural purposes specified in the table in this regulation;

(b)   in respect of any year in the set-aside period prior to that in which conversion to use for non-agricultural purposes commences, the rate for permanent fallow[, having regard to regulation 7(1) and (2),] specified in the table in this regulation.

(5)   The appropriate Minister may deduct from the annual payments payable to a beneficiary in respect of any set-aside land under these Regulations the whole or any part of any annual payments made to that beneficiary in respect of that land under an agreement made with the appropriate Minister under section 18(3) of the Agriculture Act 1986.

[1183]

NOTES

Para (1): table substituted by the Set-Aside (Amendment) Regulations 1990, SI 1990/1716, reg 15(a), Sch 1.

Para (1A): inserted by SI 1990/1716, reg 15(b).

Paras (2)–(4): words in square brackets inserted by SI 1990/1716, reg 15(c).

14   Claims for aid

Any claim for the payment of aid under these Regulations shall be made at such time and in such form and shall contain such information as the appropriate Minister reasonably may require.

[1184]

15   Obligation to permit entry and inspection

(1)   A beneficiary shall permit any officer duly authorised by the appropriate Minister, accompanied by such persons acting under his instructions as appear to that officer to be necessary for the purpose, at all reasonable times and on production of his authority on demand, to enter upon that beneficiary's holding in order to inspect any land, document or record with a view to verifying—

(a)   the accuracy of any particulars given in any application or claim for aid or in any undertaking made by a new occupier to comply with set-aside obligations, or in any notification made under the provisions of regulations [7(3)] or 11(2); and

(b)   compliance with the set aside obligations.

(2)   A beneficiary shall render all reasonable assistance to the authorised officer in relation to the matters mentioned in paragraph (1), and in particular shall—

(a)   produce such document or record as may be required by that officer for inspection; and

(b)   at the request of that officer, accompany him in making the inspection of any land and identify any area of land which is concerned in any application or claim for aid or in any undertaking made by a new occupier to comply with set-aside obligations, or in any notification made under the provisions of regulations [7(3)] or 11(2).

[1185]

NOTES

Paras (1), (2): number in square brackets substituted by the Set-Aside (Amendment) Regulations 1990, SI 1990/1716, reg 16.

16   Withholding and recovery of aid

(1)   Where any person with a view to obtaining the payment of aid to himself or any other person, makes any statement or furnishes any information which is false or misleading in a material respect, the appropriate Minister may withhold the whole or any part of any aid

payable to that person or to such other person, and may recover the whole or any part of any aid already paid to that person or to such other person.

(2)   Where a beneficiary—

  (a)   fails to comply with any of the set-aside obligations; or

  (b)   fails without reasonable excuse to comply with the requirements as to notification in regulations [7(3)], 10(2) or 11(2); or

  (c)   fails without reasonable excuse to permit entry and inspection by an authorised officer or to render all reasonable assistance to such authorised officer as required by regulation 15,

the appropriate Minister may withhold the whole or any part of any aid payable to that beneficiary, and may recover the whole or any part of any aid already paid to him.

(3)   Where it appears to the appropriate Minister that a beneficiary who has planted woodland on set-aside land in accordance with the provisions of the Woodland Grant Scheme, has failed to comply with the requirements of that Scheme, that Minister may withhold the whole or any part of any aid payable to that beneficiary under these Regulations and may recover from that beneficiary the whole or any part of any aid already paid to him under these Regulations.

[(3A)   In addition to withholding or recovering aid under paragraphs (1), (2) or (3) the Minister may treat as terminated all the undertakings given by the beneficiary under these Regulations.]

(4)   Where the appropriate Minister recovers from a beneficiary the whole of any aid already paid to him, that Minister may in addition require from that beneficiary payment of interest on that aid at a rate to be determined annually by that Minister and calculated on the basis of the period of time elapsed between the payment of the aid and recovery from the beneficiary.

(5)   Before withholding or recovering any aid under paragraph (2)(a), the appropriate Minister shall—

  (a)   give to the beneficiary a written explanation of the reasons for the proposed withholding or recovery; and

  (b)   afford the beneficiary an opportunity of appearing before and being heard by a person appointed for that purpose by the appropriate Minister; and

  (c)   consider the report by the person so appointed and supply a copy of the report to the beneficiary.

[1186]

NOTES
Para (2): figure in square brackets substituted by the Set-Aside (Amendment) Regulations 1990, SI 1990/1716, reg 17(a).
Para (3A): inserted by SI 1990/1716, reg 17(b).

17   False statements

If any person, for the purposes of obtaining for himself or any other person any aid under these Regulations, knowingly or recklessly makes a statement which is false in a material particular, that person shall be guilty of an offence and liable, on summary conviction, to a fine not exceeding [level 5 on the standard scale].

[1187]

NOTES
Reference to level 5 on the standard scale substituted by virtue of the Criminal Justice Act 1988, s 52.

PART II
STATUTORY INSTRUMENTS

SCHEDULES

SCHEDULE 1
ARABLE CROPS

Regulation 2(1)

List A   *List B*

Common wheat   Potatoes

Durum wheat   …

Rye

Barley

Oats

Grain maize

Bucklewheat

Millet

Canary seed

Triticale

Fresh vegetables

Peas and beans harvested in dried form for human or animal consumption

Sugar beet

Hops

Oilseed rape

Linseed

Castor seed

Safflower

Sunflower seed

Flax

[Forage roots and tubers, except potatoes

Lucerne/alfalfa, except when grown as part of a grass mixture

Sainfoin, except when grown as part of a grass mixture

Clover, except when grown as part of a grass mixture

Lupins

Vetches, except when grown as part of a grass mixture

Fodder kale

Fodder rape

Fodder maize

Seed of a kind listed under the heading Gramine (Grasses) in Schedule 1
to the Fodder Plant Seeds Regulations 1985 where the crop from which
the seed is obtained has been the subject of an official examination within
the meaning of those Regulations]

[1188]

NOTES

Entries in square brackets added, and entries omitted revoked, by the Set-Aside (Amendment)
Regulations 1989, SI 1989/1042, reg 8.

SCHEDULE 2
REQUIREMENTS RELATING TO THE MANAGEMENT OF [PERMANENT FALLOW
OR ROTATIONAL FALLOW]
Regulations 7(1) [and (2)], 8(1), 9(1)

Establishment and retention of plant cover

[1.(a)   The beneficiary shall sow a plant cover immediately after the commencement of
the set-aside period unless the crop or plant cover on the land immediately prior to
the commencement of the set-aside period consisted of one or more of the
following: common wheat, durum wheat, rye, barley, oats, buckwheat, millet,
canary seed, triticale, lucerne/alfalfa, sainfoin, clover, vetches, grass (whether for
grazing or for herbage seed), mustard. If the beneficiary is prevented from
establishing a plant cover by exceptional weather conditions, he shall do so as
soon as practicable; or

(b)   the beneficiary shall establish a plant cover immediately after the commencement
of the set-aside period. If the crop planted in the year prior to the commencement
of the set-aside period has not yet been harvested, the plant cover shall be
established immediately after the harvest. If the beneficiary is prevented from
establishing a plant cover by exceptional weather conditions, he shall do so as
soon as practicable. The establishment of a plant cover may take the form of the
regeneration of naturally-occurring vegetation.]

2.   The beneficiary shall retain the plant cover throughout the period in which the
requirements in this Schedule apply to the land.

3.   Notwithstanding the requirement in paragraph 2 above, the beneficiary may destroy the
plant cover by cultivation where this is necessary—

(a)   in order to prepare for the production of a crop, provided that the destruction of
the plant cover does not take place before 1st August preceding the establishment
of that crop; or

(b)   in order to control the spread of weeds, provided that where plant cover is
destroyed for this purpose it shall be re-established [by sowing or plant cover] as
soon as practicable thereafter; or

(c)   in order to prepare for the establishment of an alternative plant cover, provided
that that alternative cover is established [by sowing a plant cover] as soon as
practicable after the destruction of the previous cover.

[4.(a)   The beneficiary shall cut the plant cover at least twice in every year, such cuts to
be taken at intervals of at least 1 month and one such cut to be taken in the period
between 30th June and 1st September; or

(b)   the beneficiary shall cut the plant cover at least once in every year; and shall not in
either case sell cuttings or use them for feeding livestock.]

5.   Notwithstanding the requirement in paragraph 4 above, the appropriate Minister may
authorise a beneficiary not to cut plant cover on any land to which the requirements in this
Schedule apply where that beneficiary has submitted to that Minister written proposals for the
creation or maintenance of a wildlife habitat on that land.

Use of fertilisers and waste materials

6.   The beneficiary shall not apply any inorganic fertiliser which contains nitrogen at any
time between the end of the previous harvest and the establishment of a subsequent crop.

7.   The beneficiary shall not apply any inorganic fertiliser which does not contain nitrogen
(other than lime) before 1st August in the year in which a crop is to be established.

[7A.   Notwithstanding the requirements in paragraphs 6 and 7 above, the appropriate
Minister may authorise a beneficiary to apply an inorganic fertiliser to any land to which the
requirements in this Schedule apply where he is satisfied that the land is located in an area
normally used as a feeding-ground by over-wintering migratory geese. The beneficiary shall
manage any land to which an inorganic fertiliser is applied pursuant to such authorisation in
such a way as to provide a feeding-ground for such geese.]

PART II
STATUTORY INSTRUMENTS

8. The beneficiary shall not apply any organic fertiliser at any time between the end of the previous harvest and the establishment of a subsequent crop. The appropriate Minister may authorise a beneficiary to apply slurry or manure where that Minister is satisfied that the application is necessary in order to prevent soil erosion.

9. The beneficiary shall not use the land as a dumping ground for any type of organic or inorganic material.

Use of pesticides

10. The beneficiary shall not apply pesticides.

11. Notwithstanding the requirement in paragraph 10 above, the appropriate Minister may authorise a beneficiary to apply herbicides provided that any herbicide used is of a type which is absorbed into the plant primarily through the leaves and the stem and which has little or no persistence in water and in the soil.

12. The beneficiary shall make a written record of the type, quantity, date and method of application of any herbicide used and of the reason for such use and shall keep the written record for the duration of the set-aside period.

Maintenance of environmental features

13. The beneficiary shall maintain—

    (a)   all existing hedges and rows of trees (including hedgerow trees), ...

    (b)   all existing lakes, lochs, watercourses, ponds and pools,

    [(c)   all existing unimproved grassland, moorland and heath; and

    (d)   all existing vernacular buildings and stone walls,]

which he is entitled to maintain and which are situated on or adjacent to any land to which the requirements in this Schedule apply.

Land improvement works

14. The beneficiary shall not install any new drainage system, nor substantially modify any existing drainage system.

[1189]

NOTES

    Heading: words in square brackets substituted, and figure in square brackets in enabling regulation inserted, by the Set-Aside (Amendment) Regulations 1990, SI 1990/1716, regs 18, 19(a).

    Paras 1, 4: substituted by SI 1990/1716, reg 19(b), (e).

    Para 3: words in square brackets in sub-paras (b), (c) inserted by SI 1990/1716, reg 19(c), (d).

    Para 7A: inserted by the Set-Aside (Amendment) Regulations 1989, SI 1989/1042, reg 9.

    Para 13: word omitted from sub-para (a) revoked, and sub-paras (c), (d) inserted, by SI 1990/1716, reg 19(f).

[SCHEDULE 3
REQUIREMENTS RELATING TO THE MANAGEMENT OF GRAZED FALLOW
Regulation 7(5)

1. The beneficiary shall sow with grass the area to be grazed by livestock and shall retain that grassland throughout the period during which the requirements in this Schedule apply to the land.

2. The beneficiary shall not sow an area of grassland using a seeds mixture which contains clover, other than a seeds mixture with a white clover content by weight of no more than 5 per cent or of 1.5 kilograms per hectare, whichever is the lesser.

3. The beneficiary shall not irrigate the land.

4. Except during the period of 12 months from the date of sowing the grass the beneficiary shall not apply to it any organic or inorganic fertiliser, other than manure produced by livestock whilst grazing the land.

5. Except during the period of 12 months from the date of sowing the grass the beneficiary shall not apply pesticides or herbicides.

6. The beneficiary shall not cut the grass more than once in every year following the commencement of the set-aside period. The beneficiary shall not sell cuttings but may use them to feed his livestock.

7. The beneficiary shall maintain—
    (a)   all existing hedges and rows of trees (including hedgerow trees),
    (b)   all existing lakes, lochs, watercourses, ponds and pools,
    (c)   all existing unimproved grassland, moorland and heath, and
    (d)   all existing vernacular buildings and stone walls,
which he is entitled to maintain and which are situated on or adjacent to any land to which the requirements in this Schedule apply.

8. The beneficiary shall not install any new drainage system, nor substantially modify any existing drainage system.]

[1190]

NOTES
    Added by the Set-Aside (Amendment) Regulations 1990, SI 1990/1716, reg 20, Sch 2.

[SCHEDULE 4

Regulation 7A(5)

Livestock	*Livestock Units*
Bull, cow or other bovine animal over 2 years or equine animal over 6 months	1.00
Bovine animal 6 months to 2 years	0.60
Sheep	0.15
Goat or deer	0.15]

[1191]

NOTES
    Added by the Set-Aside (Amendment) Regulations 1990, SI 1990/1716, reg 20, Sch 3.

DISTRESS FOR RENT RULES 1988

(SI 1988/2050)

NOTES
    Made: 21 November 1988.
    Authority: Law of Distress Amendment Act 1888, s 8; Law of Distress Amendment Act 1895, s 3.

ARRANGEMENT OF RULES

1 Citation and Commencement

These Rules may be cited as the Distress for Rent Rules 1988 and shall come into operation on 1st February 1989.

[1192]

2 Interpretation

(1)   In these Rules—
    "Judge" means a Judge of a county court;
    "certificate" means a certificate to act as a bailiff granted under the Law of Distress Amendment Act 1888, as amended by the Law of Distress Amendment Act 1895;
    "Registrar" means a Registrar of a county court;
    ["court officer" has the meaning given in the Civil Procedure Rules 1998;]
    "lodge in court" shall have the meaning given in the Court Funds Rules 1987;
    "Court Funds Rules" means the Court Funds Rules 1987;
    ["Table" means the table set out in Appendix 3 to these Rules;
    "home county court" means, in relation to any person, the county court in whose district that person has his principal place of business or his main residence;
    "issuing county court" means a county court whose name appears in column 2 of the Table; and "the applicant's issuing county court" means, in relation to an applicant, the county court whose name appears in column 2 of the Table opposite the name of his home county court;
    "issuing area" means, in relation to an issuing county court, the area constituted by the district of that issuing county court and the districts of any other county courts whose names appear in column 1 of the Table opposite the name of that issuing county court;
    "appropriate newspaper" means a local newspaper appearing in a list of local newspapers approved by the court officer of the issuing county court for the purpose of publication of notices under rule 5(5).]

(2)   A Form referred to by number in these Rules means the Form so numbered in Appendix 2 to these Rules and shall be used with such variations as the circumstances may require.

[1193]

NOTES

Para (1): definition in first pair of square brackets substituted and definitions in second pair of square brackets inserted by the Distress for Rent (Amendment) Rules 1999, SI 1999/2360, r 5.

3 Forms of Certificate

(1)   A [certificate] in Form 1 may be granted only by a Judge and shall authorise the bailiff named in it to levy at any place in England and Wales.

(2) ...

[1194]

NOTES
Para (1): word in square brackets substituted by the Distress for Rent (Amendment) Rules 1999, SI 1999/2360, r 4(a).
Para (2): revoked by SI 1999/2360, r 6.

4 Applications for Certificates

[(1) An application for the grant of a certificate shall be made in Form 3.]

(2), (3) ...

(4) Applications under this rule shall be filed in the office of [the applicant's issuing county court], accompanied by the fee prescribed by the [County Court Fees Order 1999] for the "commencement of [originating] proceedings for any other remedy or relief", and shall be lodged together with—

    (a) ... two references, one of which may be from the applicant's employer or an approved officer of the Certificated Bailiffs' Association of England and Wales and shall deal with the applicant's knowledge of the law of distress and his previous experience of levying distress, and

    (b) ... a certified copy not more than one month old of the result of a search of the Register of County Court Judgments against the applicant's full name and his home and business addresses for the last six years, and

    (c) ... two passport sized photographs of the applicant, and

    (d) ... copies of the Forms 7, 8 and 9 intended to be used by the applicant when levying distress, which shall conform to the design and layout prescribed in Appendix 2, shall be on paper of durable quality and of the size A4 as specified by the International Standards Organisation, and shall be in a clear and legible printed or type-written form.

(5) The statements in an application under this rule shall be verified on oath.

(6) The applicant shall, if so directed, lodge such further evidence as the Judge ... may reasonably require in support of his application.

[1195]

NOTES
Para (1): substituted by the Distress for Rent (Amendment) Rules 1999, SI 1999/2360, r 7(1).
Paras (2), (3): revoked by SI 1999/2360, r 7(2).
Para (4): words in first and second pairs of square brackets substituted, words in third pair of square brackets inserted and words omitted revoked by SI 1999/2360, r 7(3).
Para (6): words omitted revoked by SI 1999/2360, r 8.

5 Granting of Certificates

(1) The Judge ... shall not grant a certificate to any applicant—

    (a) who fails to satisfy the Judge ... , as the case may be, that—

        (i) he is a fit and proper person to hold a certificate, and

        (ii) he possesses a sufficient knowledge of the law of distress; or,

    (b) who carries on or will be employed in any business which includes buying debts.

(2) [No application for a certificate shall be granted] except on the personal attendance of the applicant and his examination on oath at the hearing of the application.

(3) No certificate shall be granted to any officer of a county court.

(4) The name and address of all applicants for a [certificate] shall be exhibited in the public area of the court office for the 60 days prior to the hearing of the application.

[(5) The applicant shall cause to be published in an appropriate newspaper a notice in the form set out in paragraph (7) so that the notice appears in three separate editions of that newspaper during the 60 days prior to the hearing of the application.

(6) The applicant shall, not less than three days before the hearing of the application, file with the court the editions of the appropriate newspaper (or extracts from it) showing the notices referred to in paragraph (5).

PART II
STATUTORY INSTRUMENTS

(7)   The form of the notice to be published by the applicant shall be:

Notice is hereby given that [name] *of* [business name and address] *has applied to the Judge at* [   ] *county court for a Bailiff's Certificate. Any person who knows of a reason why* [name] *is not a fit and proper person to be granted a certificate should write to the Court Manager at* [name and address of county court] *before* [date of hearing of application].

(8)   Each issuing county court shall compile and maintain a list of appropriate newspapers published within its issuing area and copies of the list shall be:
- (a)   exhibited in the public area of the court office of each county court in the issuing area; and
- (b)   given to members of the public on request.]

[1196]

NOTES
Para (1): words omitted revoked by the Distress for Rent (Amendment) Rules 1999, SI 1999/2360, r 8.
Paras (2), (4): words in square brackets substituted by SI 1999/2360, rr 4(a), 9(1).
Paras (5)–(8): added by SI 1999/2360, r 9(2).

6   Security

(1)   The applicant shall be required to—
- (a)   lodge in court by way of bond or deposit, or
- (b)   satisfy the Judge ... that there is subsisting by way of bond or deposit,

security totalling £10,000 ...

(2)   The security referred to in paragraph (1) above shall be for the due performance of the bailiff's duties and for any reasonable costs, fees and expenses incurred in the investigation of any complaint lodged against the bailiff, or in the cancellation of his certificate, and shall be applied in accordance with rules 8 and 9.

[(2A)   The bailiff shall maintain the security referred to in paragraph (1) above throughout the duration of the certificate.

(2B)   If, at any time during the duration of the certificate, for any reason (other than where rule 9(2) applies), the security referred to in paragraph (1) above no longer exists, or is reduced in value so that it amounts to less than £10,000, the bailiff shall provide fresh security under this rule to the satisfaction of the court.]

(3)   Where a deposit is lodged in court under paragraph (1) above, the provisions of the Court Funds Rules shall apply.

[1197]

NOTES
Para (1): words omitted revoked by the Distress for Rent (Amendment) Rules 1999, SI 1999/2360, rr 8, 10(1).
Paras (2A), (2B): inserted by SI 1999/2360, r 10(2).

7   Duration of Certificates

(1)   A [certificate] shall, unless cancelled, have effect for the period of two years from the date of its grant.

(2)   ...

[1198]

NOTES
Para (1): word in square brackets substituted by the Distress for Rent (Amendment) Rules 1999, SI 1999/2360, r 4(a).
Para (2): revoked by SI 1999/2360, r 11.

[7A   Change of bailiff's name, address, etc

(1)   In this rule "relevant details" means a bailiff's name, address or other written information appearing on the certificate.

(2)   If there is any change in the relevant details, the bailiff shall without delay give written notice of the change to the issuing county court and produce his certificate ("the old certificate") to the court officer of the issuing county court.

(3) When a bailiff gives notice and produces the old certificate in accordance with paragraph (2) above, the Judge of the issuing county court shall issue to the bailiff a replacement certificate reflecting the change in the relevant details but in all other respects (including, without limitation, the date of expiry of the certificate) the same as the old certificate.

(4) When a replacement certificate is issued in accordance with paragraph (3) above, the court officer shall retain and cancel the old certificate.

(5) No fee shall be payable for the issue of a replacement certificate in accordance with this rule.]

[1199]

NOTES
Inserted by the Distress for Rent (Amendment) Rules 1999, SI 1999/2360, r 12.

8 Complaints as to fitness to hold a certificate

(1) Any complaint as to the conduct or fitness of any bailiff who holds a certificate shall be made [in Form 4 or, where the complainant has conducted a formal investigation into a complaint by a third party against the bailiff, in Form 5] to the court from which the certificate issued.

(2) Upon receipt of any such complaint as is referred to in paragraph (1), the [court officer] shall send written details of the complaint to the bailiff and require him to deliver a written reply to the court office within 14 days thereafter or within such longer time as the court may specify.

(3) If the bailiff fails to deliver the reply within the time specified, or if upon reading the reply the Judge is unsatisfied as to the bailiff's fitness to hold a certificate, the [court officer] shall issue a Notice summoning the bailiff to appear before the Judge on a specified date and show cause why his certificate should not be cancelled.

[(3A) If upon reading the reply the Judge is satisfied as to the bailiff's fitness to hold a certificate, the court officer shall issue a notice to the bailiff to that effect and no further action shall be taken in respect of that complaint.]

(4) The [court officer] shall send a copy of the Notice [under paragraph (3) or (as the case may be) (3A) above] to the complainant and any other interested party.

[(4A) If, after a notice has been issued under paragraph (3) above, the complainant so applies in writing, and the application is received by the court not later than the date 14 days before the date set for the hearing, the court officer of the court receiving the complaint shall order that the complaint be heard in the issuing county court whose name appears in column 2 of the Table opposite the name of the complainant's home county court.

(4B) In the event of an order being made under paragraph (4A) above, the court officer of the court receiving the complaint shall forthwith send:
  (a)   to the court officer of the court hearing the complaint:
    (i)   certified copies of any relevant entries in the records of the court receiving the complaint; and
    (ii)   copies of all other documents in his custody relating to the bailiff's certificate and to the complaint; and
  (b)   to the bailiff and any other interested party, notice of the order made under paragraph (4A) above.]

(5) At the hearing—
  (i)   the bailiff shall attend for examination and may make representations, and
  (ii)   the complainant may attend and make representations.

(6) The procedure to be followed at the hearing, including the calling of evidence, shall be such as the Judge considers just, and he may proceed with the hearing notwithstanding that the bailiff has failed to attend.

[(7) If an order is made under paragraph (4A) above, the court officer of the court hearing the complaint shall, following the hearing, send to the court officer of the court which received the complaint certified copies of the order and all other documents in his custody relating to the bailiff's certificate and to the complaint, including the certified copies and copies sent under paragraph (4B)(a) above.]

[1200]

NOTES

Para (1): words in square brackets inserted by the Distress for Rent (Amendment) Rules 1999, SI 1999/2360, r 13(1).

Paras (2), (3): words in square brackets substituted by SI 1999/2360, r 4(b).

Paras (3A), (4A), (4B), (7): inserted by SI 1999/2360, r 13(2), (4), (5).

Para (4): words in first pair of square brackets substituted and words in second pair of square brackets inserted by SI 1999/2360, rr 4(b), 13(3).

9 Cancellation of Certificates

(1)   Following the hearing of any complaint under rule 8 the Judge may, whether he cancels the certificate or not, order that the security shall be forfeited either wholly or in part, and that the amount or amounts directed to be forfeited shall be paid to any complainant by way of compensation for failure in due performance of the bailiff's duties, costs or expenses or, where costs, fees and expenses have been incurred by the court, to Her Majesty's Paymaster General.

(2)   Where an order for the forfeiture of the security, either wholly or in part, is made but the certificate is not cancelled, the Judge may direct that fresh security under rule 6 shall be provided.

(3)   Where a certificate is cancelled, the order of the Judge shall be in Form 6 and, subject to the provisions of this rule, the security shall be cancelled and the balance of the deposit returned to the bailiff.

(4)   When a certificate is cancelled or expires it shall nevertheless continue to have effect for the purpose of any distress where the bailiff has entered into possession before the date of cancellation or expiry, unless the Judge otherwise directs.

(5)   When a [certificate] is cancelled or expires it shall be surrendered to the Judge, unless he otherwise directs.

[(5A   When a bailiff holding a certificate ceases, for any reason, to carry on business as a bailiff he shall forthwith surrender his certificate to the Judge at the county court which issued the certificate, unless the Judge otherwise directs, and as from the date of the surrender the certificate shall be treated as if it had expired on that date.]

(6)   When a certificate is cancelled the [court officer] shall publish a Notice [to that effect in an appropriate newspaper, and the costs of the notice] shall be deducted from the security.

[(7)   References, in this rule, to the cancellation of a certificate shall not include the cancellation of a certificate upon the issue of a duplicate certificate, in accordance with rule 7A(4).]

[1201]

NOTES

Paras (5), (6): words in square brackets substituted by SI 1999/2360, rr 4, 14(2).

Paras (5A), (7): inserted by the Distress for Rent (Amendment) Rules 1999, SI 1999/2360, r 14(1), (3).

10 Fees, Charges and Expenses

No person shall be entitled to charge, or recover from, a tenant any fees, charges or expenses for levying a distress, or for doing any act or thing in relation thereto, other than those authorised by the tables in Appendix 1 to these Rules.

[1202]

11—(1)   In the case of any difference as to fees, charges and expenses between any of the parties, the fees, charges and expenses shall upon application be [assessed, by way of detailed assessment under Part 47 of the Civil Procedure Rules 1998,] by the Registrar of the county court of the district where the distress is levied, and he may make such order as he thinks fit as to the costs of the [detailed assessment].

(2)   Where the court in which the [detailed assessment] is conducted is not the court in which the bailiff was granted his certificate and the Registrar is of opinion on the [detailed assessment] that there has been overcharging of such magnitude as to call into question the fitness of a bailiff to hold a certificate, the [court officer] shall send to the court in which the bailiff was granted his certificate a copy of the [completed bill] endorsed with a Note of the Registrar's opinion.

(3)   The receipt of a bill under paragraph (2), shall be treated as a complaint under rule 8(1).

[1203]

NOTES

Paras (1), (2): words in square brackets substituted by the Distress for Rent (Amendment) Rules 1999, SI 1999/2360, rr 4(b), 15.

12   Levy and Removal

(1)   Every bailiff levying a distress shall produce his certificate to the tenant if he is present or, in the absence of the tenant, to such other person present as appears to be in control of the premises.

(2)   A bailiff levying distress shall deliver to the tenant, or leave on the premises where distress is levied, a memorandum in Form 7 identifying the bailiff and specifying in an Inventory the goods distrained on and setting out the amounts for which the distress is levied and the fees, charges and expenses authorised by these Rules and being actually and necessarily incurred under them.

(3)   A bailiff or his agent attending to remove goods from the premises or withdrawing from possession prior to sale of the distrained goods shall deliver to the tenant or leave on the premises where distress is levied a memorandum in Form 9 setting out the expenses of removal authorised by and incurred under these Rules.

[1204]

13   List of Certificates

[(1)   Each issuing county court shall compile a list of bailiffs carrying on business within that court's issuing area and holding certificates as at 1st February every year, and the list shall be exhibited in the public area of the court office of each county court in the issuing area.]

(2)   When a certificate is cancelled the list shall be amended to include that fact.

[1205]

NOTES

Para (1): substituted by the Distress for Rent (Amendment) Rules 1999, SI 1999/2360, r 16.

14   Repeal

On the coming into operation of these Rules:—

(a)   the Distress for Rent Rules 1983 shall be revoked save with respect to distresses levied before these Rules come into operation; and

(b)   any certificate granted or renewed before these Rules come into operation shall continue to have effect for the period for which it was granted as if it were a certificate granted under these Rules for all purposes except the application of rule 4; and

(c)   any certificate granted or renewed before these Rules come into operation and expressed to expire between 31st January 1989 and 30th April 1989 shall continue to have effect until 30th April 1989 as if it were a certificate granted under these Rules for all purposes except the application of rule 4.

[1206]

APPENDICES

APPENDIX 1
TABLE OF FEES, CHARGES AND EXPENSES

[1.   For levying distress—

(i) on any debt up to and including £100 a fixed fee of   £21.65

(ii) on any debt which exceeds £100 a scale fee calculated as follows:

on the first £100 of that debt	£21.65
on the next £100	12½%
on the next £400	4%
on the next £1,500	2½%
on the next £8,000	1%
and on any additional sum	¼%.]

2.   For attending to levy distress where the levy is not made, the reasonable costs and charges for attending to levy, not exceeding the fees which would have been due under paragraph 1 if the distress had been levied; the costs and charges are subject to [detailed assessment] under rule 11.

3.   For taking possession—

(i)   where a [person] is left in physical possession, [£7.80] per day

(ii)   where walking possession is taken, [80p] per day

Note: The charge for walking possession is payable only if a walking possession agreement in Form 8 has been concluded.

A [person] left in possession must provide his own board in every case.

The possession fee is payable in respect of the day on which the distress is levied, but a fee for physical possession must not be charged where a walking possession agreement is signed at the time when the distress is levied.

4.   For appraisement, at the request in writing of the tenant, the reasonable fees, charges and expenses of the broker, subject to [detailed assessment] under rule 11.

5.   For attending to remove, the reasonable costs and charges attending the removal; the costs and charges are subject to [detailed assessment] under rule 11.

6.   For sale—

(i)   where the sale is held on the auctioneer's premises, for commission to the auctioneer, an inclusive charge to include all out-of-pocket expenses of 15% on the sum realised, and the reasonable cost of advertising, removal and storage.

(ii)   where the sale is held on the debtor's premises, for commission to the auctioneer, in addition to out-of-pocket expenses actually and reasonably incurred, 7½% on the sum realised.

7.   Reasonable fees, charges and expenses where distress is withdrawn or where no sale takes place, and for negotiations between landlord and tenant respecting the distress, subject to [detailed assessment] under rule 11.

8.   For the purpose of calculating any percentage charges a fraction of £1 is to be reckoned as £1 but any fraction of a penny in the total amount of the fee so calculated is to be disregarded.

9.   In addition to any amount authorised by this Table in respect of the supply of goods or services on which value added tax is chargeable there may be added a sum equivalent to value added tax at the appropriate rate on that amount.

[1207]

NOTES

Para 1: substituted by the Distress for Rent (Amendment No 2) Rules 2003, SI 2003/2141, r 2.

Paras 2–5, 7: words in square brackets substituted by the Distress for Rent (Amendment) Rules 2003, SI 2003/1858, r 2(b), (c).

APPENDIX 2
FORMS

Form 1
[Bailiff's Certificate]

In the .... County Court

PHOTO

Mr/Mrs/Miss/Ms ....

of ....

Tel No ....

Signature .... Dated ....

is authorised to levy distress in England and Wales (In accordance with Section 7 of the Law of Distress Amendment Act 1888 and Section 3 of the Law of Distress Amendment Act 1895 and the Rules made thereunder)

Signed ....

Judge .... of the .... County Court

Date .... 19 ....

The court office is at

Tel No

. Rent 1

[1208]–[1209]

NOTES

Table above Form 1 substituted by the Distress for Rent (Amendment) Rules 1999, SI 1999/2360, r 17(a).

Heading: words in square brackets substituted by SI 1999/2360, r 17(b).

(Form 2 substituted by new Forms 3–5 by the Distress for Rent (Amendment) Rules 1999, SI 1999/2360, r 17(c), Sch 1.)

[Form 3
Application for Certificate to Levy Distress

Please complete this form in BLOCK CAPITALS

In the .... County Court

Are you applying for

    A first general certificate to levy distress [ ]

    A renewal of a general bailiff's certificate [ ]

Part 1

1.	Full name	Date of Birth	
2a.	Home address	Telephone No	
2b.	Business address	Telephone No	
2c.	Which address is to be used for the purposes of this application?	Business [ ]	Home [ ]
2d.	Does your area of business extend beyond the district of the court at which the application was made?	Yes [ ]	No [ ]
3a.	Have you ever applied for and been refused or had cancelled a general or special certificate?	Yes [ ]	No [ ]
3b.	If YES, please answer the following questions		

Court to which the application was made ....

date the application was refused ....

or Court at which the certificate was cancelled ....

date of the cancellation ....

4.   Are you

	a.	In business alone, (i e a sole trader)	Yes [ ]	No [ ]
	b.	partner in a firm?	Yes [ ]	No [ ]

        If YES please give

        Full names of all partners...

        Principal place of business...

	c.	employed by a firm or a company?	Yes [ ]	No [ ]

        If YES, please state

        Full names of all principals or directors ....

        ....

        Full name of secretary ....

        Business office and registered office address(es), where appropriate

        ....

	d.	employed or self-employed as an agent in any other type of organisation? (e g Local Authority)	Yes [ ]	No [ ]

        If YES, please give

full names of persons responsible for management of levying distress for rent	*full name(s) and address(es) for all persons authorised to accept notices*
Levy distress	Notices

5.		Do you hold a licence under the Consumer Credit Act 1974?	Yes [ ]	No [ ]

        If YES, give reference number of licence ....

. 6.   A certificate cannot be issued to any person who carries on the business of buying debts. If the business in which you would be employed is in the business of buying debts, give full details here.

....

....

....

7.   What is the nature, and the general purpose, of the business in which you are engaged.

....

....

....

Part 2

8.   Have you been convicted of any offence involving   Yes [ ]   No [ ]
        fraud or other dishonesty or violence? (The
        Rehabilitation of Offenders Act 1974 applies to
        this question)

        If YES, please state

        Date of conviction ....

        Place of conviction or order ....

...

9.   Have you as an individual or a partner of a firm
        had

        —a statutory demand served upon you under the
        Insolvency Act 1986?

        —a bankruptcy order made against you?

        —an order made against you and not been
        discharged from bankruptcy?

        Tick the appropriate box   Yes [ ]   No [ ]

        If YES, give full details below

        ....

        ....

        ....

10.   Have you, as a director or secretary of a company
        or when responsible for the management of affairs
        of any organisation, within the last 3 years, had an
        administrator or administrative receiver or manager
        appointed, had a winding up petition presented to a
        court, or passed a resolution for voluntary winding
        up?

        Yes [ ]   No [ ]   N/A [ ]

        If YES, give full details below

        ....

        ....

        ....

11.   Have you ever had judgment entered or order   Yes [ ]   No [ ]
        made against you either in the High Court or in a
        county court?

> In support of your answer (Yes OR No) you must exhibit a certified copy, not more than one month old, of a search of the Register of County Court Judgments against your full name and your home and business addresses for the last six years.

Part 3

The judge can only grant a certificate if satisfied that you are a fit and proper person and have a sufficient knowledge of the law of distress.

12.   Please give any information below which may assist the judge in considering your case, for example:

—evidence of knowledge of the law of distress. The successful completion of the examination of the Certified Bailiffs' Association will be accepted as evidence here.*

—previous employment record*

—educational or professional qualifications*

enclose certified copies of these qualifications or any other documents which may assist the judge.

....

....

....

13.   You must also give two referees one of whom may be your employer or an approved officer of the Certificated Bailiffs' Association of England and Wales, one of whom must know of your knowledge of the law of distress and previous experience of the levying of distress. Details should be given below or, if in confidence, be sent to the District Judge of the county court dealing with this application.

First referee   *Second referee*

Name   Name

Address   Address

> The applicant must ensure that the two references are sent to the court; the application will not be considered until both references are received. When the references are received the court will exhibit a notice of your application. Your application can be heard 60 days after the notice is exhibited.

Part 4

I apply for a general certificate	Yes [ ]	No [ ]
I apply to renew a general certificate	Yes [ ]	No [ ]
I enclose	Yes [ ]	No [ ]
a. certified copy of search of Register of County Court Judgments	Yes [ ]	No [ ]
b. two references	Yes [ ]	No [ ]
c. two passport size photographs of myself	Yes [ ]	No [ ]
d. the fees of £	Yes [ ]	No [ ]
e. copies of the prescribed forms which I intend to use when levying distress	Yes [ ]	No [ ]
EITHER I enclose a bond and/or deposit totalling £10,000	Yes [ ]	No [ ]

OR There is a subsisting bond and/or deposit totalling   Yes [ ]   No [ ]
£10,000 lodged in court

Part 5
I will not levy distress at any premises in respect of which I am regularly employed to collect rent.
I, (name) .... make oath/affirm* and say that to the best of my knowledge the particulars contained in this application and the above statements are true.
Signed ....
Sworn or affirmed at .... in the county of ....
This .... day of .... [19.........] [20.........]
Before me ....
Proper Officer appointed by the judge to take affidavits
delete as preferred
Part 6
To be completed by the court
Two references received Yes [ ] ...... No [ ]
Notice of this application displayed on ....
You must attend when the Judge will hear your application
at .... County Court
on (date) .... at .... am/pm (delete as appropriate)]

[1210]

NOTES
   Forms 3–5 substituted for original Forms 2–5 by the Distress for Rent (Amendment) Rules 1999, SI 1999/2360, r 17(c), Sch 1.
   Words omitted from Question 8 revoked by the Distress for Rent (Amendment) Rules 2000, SI 2000/1481, r 3.

[Form 4
Complaint Against A Certificated Bailiff
(Distress for Rent Rules 1988 Rule 8)
This page should be completed by the person making the complaint. When you have done so, send it to the county court where the bailiff obtained his/her certificate. If you do not know which court this is, please telephone the Court Service Headquarters, Civil and Family Business Branch, on **020 7210 1883**, where staff will be able to tell you.
Name of bailiff ....
Name of his/her firm/company ....
Address .... Postcode ....
Type of debt bailiff was trying to enforce (council tax, fine, child support, maintenance, road traffic, rent arrears etc)
....
Who is the debt owed to? (the name of the local authority, the magistrates' court, the CSA office, etc)
....
Any reference number used by the bailiff ....
Your name ....
Your address ....
Postcode ....
Your signature ....
Date ....
Details of the complaint (please include details of when and where the action(s) complained of took place).
[Please continue on an additional page if necessary]
....
....]

[1211]

NOTES
   Substituted as noted to Form 3 above.

[Form 5
Notification to the County Court of a Complaint Upheld Against a Certificated Bailiff
(Distress for Rent Rules 1988 Rule 8)

This page should be completed by the appropriate organisation. When you have done so, send it to the county court where the bailiff obtained his/her certificate. If you do not know which court this is, please telephone the Court Service Headquarters, Civil and Family Business Branch, on **020 7210 1883**, where staff will be able to tell you.

Name of bailiff ....

Name and address of bailiff firm/company ....

.... Postcode ....

Nature of complaint (please indicate what type of debt the bailiff was enforcing)

....

Action taken

....

To your knowledge, has this complaint been investigated by any other organisation?

....

Is the bailiff still enforcing your warrants? ....

If so, please state whether it was the bailiff's employer, the creditor, a trade association or professional body, or any other body (state which)

....

Signature ....

Name ....

Date ....

Tel/Fax number ....

Address .... Postcode ....]

[1212]

NOTES

Substituted as noted to Form 3 above.

Form 6

Cancellation of bailiff's certificate

In the .... County Court

Please complete this form in BLOCK CAPITALS

(*Full name of Bailiff*) **The certificate granted to** ....

(*Bailiff's address*) of ....

Tel No ....

to act as a bailiff levying distress for rent in England and Wales is cancelled.

This cancellation does not affect any distress where he or she entered into possession before today's date.

SEAL

Signed ....

Judge

Date .... 19 ....

Rent 6

[1213]

Form 7

Notice of Seizure of Goods and Inventory

Distress for Rent Rules 1988: Rule 12

The following information must be typed or printed on this form

Where the bailiff is **in business alone i e a sole trader:**	Where the bailiff is a **partner in a firm of bailiffs**:	Where the bailiff is **employed by a firm or company**:
• full name;	• firm's name;	• firm's or company's name;
• business address;	• business address;	• business address;
• telephone number;	• telephone number;	• telephone number;
• VAT registration number;	• names of all the partners;	• names of all the partners or directors;
• consumer credit licence, if any.	• VAT registration number;	• registered office and company registration number, if a company;

• consumer credit licence, if any.	• VAT registration number;
	• consumer credit licence, if any.

Complete this form in BLOCK CAPITALS

(*Name of tenant*)	To ....
(*Address of tenant*)	of ....
	....
	and all others it may concern
(*Bailiff's full name*)	I ....
(*Address & Tel No*)	of ....
	.... Tel No.........................
	acting on a certificate granted to me at .... County Court
Name of person authorising seizure of goods	and with authority of ....
	have seized the goods specified in the inventory below
	for the sum of £ ....
	which is the rent owed to ....
	up to (date) ....
Description & full address of premises	for ....

THE GOODS WILL BE SOLD unless the Rent, together with the expenses of the seizure, is paid to me at my above address within five days of this notice. **Note**: the person who may be left in possession of the seized goods is NOT authorised to receive the payment.

Inventory

1	11 ....
2	12 ....
3	13 ....
4	14 ....
5	15 ....
6	16 ....
7	17 ....
8	18 ....
9	19 ....
10	20 ....

Any person removing these goods may be liable to penalties

Amount owing:	
Rent total sum (excluding costs)	£ ....
Costs (see scale below)	£ ....
TOTAL amount if paid today	£ ....

PART II STATUTORY INSTRUMENTS

Additional days possession at .... a day until distress
is fully paid (maximum £..................)   £ ....

TOTAL (including additional days possession fees (if any))   £ ....

Additional costs, for which you may be liable, will be incurred under the scale of fees below
in the event of further action being taken.
The fees, charges and expenses in connection with this seizure may be taxed (independently
assessed) on application to the local county court in the event of any dispute.
Signed .... dated .... 19 ....
By Bailiff

```
┌─────────────────────┐
│                     │
│                     │
│                     │
│   Scale of Fees     │
│                     │
│                     │
│                     │
└─────────────────────┘
```

Rent 7

[1214]

Form 8
Form of walking-possession agreement
(Request not to remove goods)

Distress for Rent Rules 1988
Complete this form in BLOCK CAPITALS

(Bailiff's full   **To** ....
name)

(Address of firm   **Bailiff of** ....
of certificated
bailiff)

                        .... Tel No ....

                        For my convenience and in consideration of your not leaving a [person]
                        in close possession of the goods upon which you have levied distress at

(Address of   ....
tenant)

                        ....

                        in the position which they now occupy, I agree:

                        1. To pay the lawful fees for the [person] in walking possession.

                        2. That you and the [person] in walking possession may re-enter the
                        premises at any time while the distress is in force.

                        3. That I will not remove or sell the goods or any part of them or allow
                        any other person to do so without your permission.

                        4. That the goods on which distress is levied are impounded on the
                        premises.

                        5. That I will show this form to any other person who may call with the
                        intention of levying on the goods and tell you of their visit at once.

                        6. You may remove and sell the goods at any time after .... if I
                        have not by then paid the sum due and your fees, charges and
                        expenses.

7. I certify that a copy of this agreement and the Notice of Seizure have been handed to me.

Signed ....

Date ....

Rent 8

[1215]

NOTES

Word "person" in square brackets in each place it occurs substituted by the Distress for Rent (Amendment) Rules 2003, SI 2003/1858, r 3.

Form 9
Removal expenses

Please complete this form in BLOCK CAPITALS

The following information must be typed or printed on this form

Where the bailiff is **in business alone i e a sole trader:**	Where the bailiff is a **partner in a firm of bailiffs:**	Where the bailiff is **employed by a firm or company**:
• full name;	• firm's name;	• firm's or company's name;
• business address;	• business address;	• business address;
• telephone number;	• telephone number;	• telephone number;
• VAT registration number;	• names of all the partners;	• names of all the partners or directors;
• consumer credit licence, if any.	• VAT registration number;	• registered office and company registration number, if a company;
	• consumer credit licence, if any.	• VAT registration number;
		• consumer credit licence, if any.

To ....

(Address of Tenant from which removal takes place)

of ....

....

and all others it may concern

The cost of removing/attending to remove (*delete as appropriate*) goods on .... for the purpose of sale/safe keeping is calculated as follows:

• Number and type of vehicles used for removal: ....

Basis of charge and total cost: ....   £ _____

• Number of men employed: ....

Basis of charge and total cost: ....   £ _____

• Number and type of special removal machines: ....

Basis of charge and total cost: ....   £ _____

VAT .... £ ....

Total cost (including VAT as appropriate):   £ _____

Time attended .... left ....

Total time at premises ....

Estimated return and off-loading time ....

Total time ....

The fees, charges and expenses in connection with this removal may be taxed (independently assessed) on application to the local county court in the event of any dispute.

Delete as appropriate	Memorandum handed to tenant or his representative or left on his premises at .... am/pm
(Bailiff's full name)	
(Address and telephone no)	of .... Tel No ....

Name of authorised person attending to remove ....

Signed ....   Date ....

Rent 9

[1216]

[APPENDIX 3
TABLE OF ISSUING COUNTY COURTS

Column 1 COUNTY COURT	**Column 2** ISSUING COUNTY COURT
Aberdare	Merthyr Tydfil
Aberystwyth	Aberystwyth
Accrington	Burnley
Aldershot & Farnham	Aldershot & Farnham
Altrincham	Altrincham
Ashford	Canterbury
Aylesbury	Milton Keynes
Banbury	Oxford
Barnet	Edmonton
Barnsley	Doncaster
Barnstaple	Exeter
Barrow-in-Furness	Kendal
Basildon	Southend
Basingstoke	Aldershot & Farnham
Bath	Bristol
Bedford	Bedford
...	...
Birkenhead	Birkenhead
Birmingham	Birmingham

Column 1 COUNTY COURT	Column 2 ISSUING COUNTY COURT
Bishop Auckland	Middlesbrough
Blackburn	Burnley
Blackpool	Preston
Blackwood	Newport (Gwent)
Bodmin	Truro
Bolton	Manchester
Boston	Lincoln
Bournemouth	Bournemouth
Bow	Shoreditch
Bradford	Bradford
Brecknock	Merthyr Tydfil
Brentford	Brentford
Bridgend	Cardiff
…	…
Brighton	[Brighton]
Bristol	Bristol
Bromley	Bromley
Burnley	Burnley
Burton-upon-Trent	Derby
Bury	Oldham
Bury St Edmunds	Bury St Edmunds
Buxton	Chesterfield
Caernarfon	Caernarfon
…	…
Cambridge	Cambridge
Canterbury	Canterbury
Cardiff	Cardiff
Carlisle	Carlisle
Carmarthen	Haverfordwest
Central London	Shoreditch
Chelmsford	Chelmsford
Cheltenham	Bristol
…	…
Chester	Chester
Chesterfield	Nottingham
Chichester	Chichester
Chorley	Preston
Clerkenwell	Shoreditch
Colchester	Colchester
Consett	Gateshead
Conwy & Colwyn	Caernarfon
Coventry	Coventry

Column 1 COUNTY COURT	Column 2 ISSUING COUNTY COURT
Crewe	Macclesfield
Croydon	Croydon
Darlington	Middlesbrough
Dartford	Dartford
Derby	Derby
Dewsbury	Huddersfield
Doncaster	Doncaster
Dudley	Birmingham
Durham	Gateshead
Eastbourne	Brighton
Edmonton	Edmonton
Epsom	Epsom
Evesham	Worcester
Exeter	Exeter
Gateshead	Gateshead
Gloucester	Bristol
Grantham	Lincoln
Gravesend	Dartford
...	...
Great Grimsby	Great Grimsby
...	...
Guildford	Epsom
Halifax	Huddersfield
Harlow	Cambridge
Harrogate	Harrogate
Hartlepool	Middlesbrough
Hastings	Brighton
Haverfordwest	Haverfordwest
Haywards Heath	Chichester
Hereford	Worcester
Hertford	St Albans
High Wycombe	Slough
Hitchin	Luton
Horsham	Chichester
Hove	Brighton
Huddersfield	Huddersfield
Huntingdon	Peterborough
Ilford	Romford
Ipswich	Ipswich
Keighley	Bradford
Kendal	Kendal
Kettering	Northampton

Column 1 COUNTY COURT	Column 2 ISSUING COUNTY COURT
Kidderminster	Birmingham
King's Lynn	King's Lynn
Kingston-upon-Hull	Kingston-upon-Hull
Kingston-upon-Thames	Staines
Lambeth	Lambeth
Lancaster	Lancaster
Leeds	Leeds
Leicester	Leicester
Leigh	Wigan
Lewes	Brighton
…	…
Lincoln	Lincoln
Liverpool	Liverpool
Llanelli	Swansea
Llangefni	Caernarfon
Lowestoft	Norwich
Ludlow	Telford
Luton	Luton
Macclesfield	Macclesfield
Maidstone	Medway
Manchester	Manchester
Mansfield	Nottingham
Mayor's & City of London	Shoreditch
Medway	Medway
Melton Mowbray	Leicester
Merthyr Tydfil	Merthyr Tydfil
Middlesbrough	Middlesbrough
Milton Keynes	Milton Keynes
Mold	Chester
…	…
[Morpeth & Berwick	Morpeth & Berwick]
Neath & Port Talbot	Swansea
Nelson	Burnley
Newark	Lincoln
Newbury	Reading
Newcastle-upon-Tyne	Gateshead
Newport (Isle of Wight)	Portsmouth
Newport (Gwent)	Newport (Gwent)
Northampton	Northampton
North Shields	Gateshead
Northwich	Macclesfield
Norwich	Norwich

Column 1 COUNTY COURT	Column 2 ISSUING COUNTY COURT
Nottingham	Nottingham
Nuneaton	Coventry
Oldham	Oldham
Oswestry	Telford
Oxford	Oxford
Penrith	Carlisle
Penzance	Truro
Peterborough	Peterborough
Plymouth	Plymouth
Pontefract	Leeds
Pontypool	Newport (Gwent)
Pontypridd	Merthyr Tydfil
Poole	Bournemouth
Portsmouth	Portsmouth
Preston	Preston
Rawtenstall	Burnley
Reading	Reading
Redditch	Redditch
Reigate	Epsom
Rhyl	Caernarfon
Romford	Romford
Rotherham	Sheffield
Rugby	Coventry
Runcorn	Macclesfield
St Albans	St Albans
St Helens	Liverpool
Salford	Manchester
Salisbury	Salisbury
Scarborough	Scarborough
Scunthorpe	Grimsby
Sheffield	Sheffield
Shoreditch	Shoreditch
Shrewsbury	Telford
Skegness & Spilsby	Lincoln
Skipton	Bradford
Slough	Slough
Southampton	Southampton
Southend	Southend
Southport	Liverpool
South Shields	Gateshead
Stafford	Stafford
Staines	Staines

Column 1 COUNTY COURT	Column 2 ISSUING COUNTY COURT
Stockport	Altrincham
Stoke-on-Trent	Stafford
Stourbridge	Birmingham
Stratford-upon-Avon	Coventry
Sunderland	Gateshead
Swansea	Swansea
Swindon	Bristol
Tameside	Oldham
Tamworth	Stafford
Taunton	Taunton
Telford	Telford
Thanet	Canterbury
Torquay & Newton Abbot	Torquay & Newton Abbot
Trowbridge	Bristol
Truro	Truro
Tunbridge Wells	Tunbridge Wells
Uxbridge	Uxbridge
Wakefield	Leeds
Walsall	Wolverhampton
Wandsworth	Lambeth
Warrington	Macclesfield
Warwick	Coventry
Watford	Watford
Wellingborough	Northampton
Welshpool & Newton	Welshpool & Newton
West London	Brentford
Weston-Super-Mare	Bristol
Weymouth & Dorchester	Bournemouth
Whitehaven	Whitehaven
Wigan	Wigan
Willesden	Brentford
Winchester	Southampton
Wolverhampton	Wolverhampton
Woolwich	Lambeth
Worcester	Worcester
...	...
Worksop	Lincoln
Worthing	Chichester
Wrexham	Chester
Yeovil	Taunton
York	York]

PART II
STATUTORY INSTRUMENTS

[1217]

NOTES

Inserted by the Distress for Rent (Amendment) Rules 1999, SI 1999/2360, r 18, Sch 2.

First entry omitted revoked, word in square brackets in entry "Brighton" substituted and entry "Morpeth & Berwick" inserted by the Distress for Rent (Amendment) (No 2) Rules 1999, SI 1999/2564, r 2; second, fifth and sixth entries omitted revoked by Distress for Rent (Amendment) (No 3) Rules 1999, SI 1999/3186, r 2; third entry omitted revoked by the Distress for Rent (Amendment No 2) Rules 2000, SI 2000/2737, r 2; fourth and eighth entries omitted revoked by the Distress for Rent (Amendment) Rules 2001, SI 2001/4026, r 2; seventh and ninth entries omitted revoked by the Distress for Rent (Amendment) Rules 2000, SI 2000/1481, r 2.

LANDLORD AND TENANT ACT 1954 (APPROPRIATE MULTIPLIER) ORDER 1990

(SI 1990/363)

NOTES

Made: 26 February 1990.

Authority: Landlord and Tenant Act 1954, s 37(8).

1   This Order may be cited as the Landlord and Tenant Act 1954 (Appropriate Multiplier) Order 1990 and shall come into force on 1st April 1990.

[1218]

2   In this Order references to section 37 are references to section 37 of the Landlord and Tenant Act 1954 and references to the 1989 Act are to the Local Government and Housing Act 1989.

[1219]

3   Where the date which (apart from paragraph 4 of Schedule 7 to the 1989 Act) is relevant for determining the rateable value of the holding under section 37(5) is before 1st April 1990, the appropriate multiplier for the purposes of section 37(2) is 3.

[1220]

4   Where the date which (apart from paragraph 4 of Schedule 7 to the 1989 Act) is relevant for determining the rateable value of the holding under section 37(5) is on or after 1st April 1990, the appropriate multiplier for the purposes of section 37(2) is—

(a)   1, except in a case specified in (b) below, and

(b)   8 in a case where section 37 has effect with the modification specified in paragraph 4(2) of Schedule 7 to the 1989 Act.

[1221]–[1225]

5   (*Revokes the Landlord and Tenant Act 1954 (Appropriate Multiplier) Order 1984, SI 1984/1932.*)

HIGH COURT AND COUNTY COURTS JURISDICTION ORDER 1991

(SI 1991/724)

NOTES

Made: 19 March 1991.

Authority: Courts and Legal Services Act 1990, ss 1, 120.

ARRANGEMENT OF ARTICLES

1 Title and commencement

This Order may be cited as the High Court and County Courts Jurisdiction Order 1991 and shall come into force on 1st July 1991.

[1226]

2 Jurisdiction

(1) A county court shall have jurisdiction under—
- (a)   sections ... , 146 and 147 of the Law of Property Act 1925,
- (b)   ...
- (c)   section 26 of the Arbitration Act 1950,
- (d)   section 63(2) of the Landlord and Tenant Act 1954,
- (e)   section 28(3) of the Mines and Quarries (Tips) Act 1969,
- (f)   section 66 of the Taxes Management Act 1970,
- (g)   section 41 of the Administration of Justice Act 1970,
- (h)   section 139(5)(b) of the Consumer Credit Act 1974,
- (i)   section 13 of the Torts (Interference with Goods) Act 1977,
- (j)   section 87 of the Magistrates' Courts Act 1980,
- [(k)   sections 17 and 18 of the Audit Commission Act 1998,]
- (l)   sections 15, 16, 21, 25 and 139 of the County Courts Act 1984,
- (m)   section 39(4) of, and paragraph 3(1) of Schedule 3 to, the Legal Aid Act 1988,
- (n)   sections 99, 102(5), 114, 195, 204, 230, 231 and 235(5) of the Copyright, Designs and Patents Act 1988, ...
- (o)   section 40 of the Housing Act 1988, [and
- (p)   sections 13 and 14 of the Trusts of Land and Appointment of Trustees Act 1996,]

whatever the amount involved in the proceedings and whatever the value of any fund or asset connected with the proceedings.

(2) A county court shall have jurisdiction under—
- (a)   section 10 of the Local Land Charges Act 1975, and
- (b)   section 10(4) of the Rentcharges Act 1977,

where the sum concerned or amount claimed does not exceed £5,000.

(3) A county court shall have jurisdiction under the following provisions of the Law of Property Act 1925 where the capital value of the land or interest in land which is to be dealt with does not exceed £30,000:
- (a)   sections 3, 49, 66, 181, and 188;
- (b)   proviso (iii) to paragraph 3 of Part III of Schedule 1;
- (c)   proviso (v) to paragraph 1(3) of Part IV of Schedule 1;
- (d)   provisos (iii) and (iv) to paragraph 1(4) of Part IV of Schedule 1.

(4) A county court shall have jurisdiction under sections 89, 90, 91 and 92 of the Law of Property Act 1925 where the amount owing in respect of the mortgage or charge at the commencement of the proceedings does not exceed £30,000.

(5) A county court shall have jurisdiction under the proviso to section 136(1) of the Law of Property Act 1925 where the amount or value of the debt or thing in action does not exceed £30,000.

(6) A county court shall have jurisdiction under section 1(6) of the Land Charges Act 1972—
- (a)   in the case of a land charge of Class C(i), C(ii) or D(i), if the amount does not exceed £30,000;
- (b)   in the case of a land charge of Class C(iii), if it is for a specified capital sum of money not exceeding £30,000 or, where it is not for a specified capital sum, if the capital value of the land affected does not exceed £30,000;
- (c)   in the case of a land charge of Class A, Class B, Class C(iv), Class D(ii), Class D(iii) or Class E, if the capital value of the land affected does not exceed £30,000;

    (d)   in the case of a land charge of Class F, if the land affected by it is the subject of an order made by the court under section 1 of the Matrimonial Homes Act 1983 or an application for an order under that section relating to that land has been made to the court;

    (e)   in a case where an application under section 23 of the Deeds of Arrangement Act 1914 could be entertained by the court.

(7)   A county court shall have jurisdiction under sections 69, 70 and 71 of the Solicitors Act 1974 where a bill of costs relates wholly or partly to contentious business done in a county court and the amount of the bill does not exceed £5,000.

[(7A)   A patents county court and the county courts listed in paragraph (7B) shall have jurisdiction under the following provisions of the Trade Marks Act 1994—

    (a)   sections 15, 16, 19, 23(5), 25(4)(b), 30, 31, 46, 47, 64, 73 and 74;

    (b)   paragraph 12 of Schedule 1; and

    (c)   paragraph 14 of Schedule 2,

to include jurisdiction to hear and determine any claims or matters ancillary to, or arising from proceedings brought under such provisions.

(7B)   For the purposes of paragraph (7A), the county courts at—

    (a)   Birmingham;

    (b)   Bristol;

    (c)   Cardiff;

    (d)   Leeds;

    (e)   Liverpool;

    (f)   Manchester; and

    (g)   Newcastle upon Tyne,

shall have jurisdiction.]

(8)   The enactments and statutory instruments listed in the Schedule to this Order are amended as specified therein, being amendments which are consequential on the provisions of this article.

[1227]

NOTES

Para (1): words omitted from sub-paras (a), (n) revoked, sub-para (p) and the preceding word "and" added by the High Court and County Courts Jurisdiction (Amendment) Order 1996, SI 1996/3141, art 2; sub-para (b) revoked by the High Court and County Courts Jurisdiction (Amendment) Order 2005, SI 2005/587, art 3(a); sub-para (k) substituted by virtue of the Audit Commission Act 1998, s 54(2), Sch 4, para 4(1).

Paras (7A), (7B): inserted by SI 2005/587, art 3(b).

---

3 Injunctions

The High Court shall have jurisdiction to hear an application for an injunction made in the course of or in anticipation of proceedings in a county court where a county court may not, by virtue of regulations under section 38(3)(b) of the County Courts Act 1984 or otherwise, grant such an injunction.

[1228]

4 Allocation—Commencement of proceedings

Subject to articles [4A,] 5[, 6 and 6A] proceedings in which both the county courts and the High Court have jurisdiction may be commenced either in a county court or in the High Court.

[1229]

NOTES

Number in first pair of square brackets inserted by the High Court and County Courts Jurisdiction (Amendment) Order 1999, SI 1999/1014, art 4; words in second pair of square brackets substituted by the Access to Neighbouring Land Act 1992, s 7(2).

[4A   Except for proceedings to which article 5 applies, a claim for money in which county courts have jurisdiction may only be commenced in the High Court if the financial value of the claim is more than £15,000.]

[1230]

NOTES
Inserted by the High Court and County Courts Jurisdiction (Amendment) Order 1999, SI 1999/1014, art 5.

5—[(1)   Proceedings which include a claim for damages in respect of personal injuries may only be commenced in the High Court if the financial value of the claim is £50,000 or more.]

(2)   In this article "personal injuries" means personal injuries to the [claimant] or any other person, and includes disease, impairment of physical or mental condition, and death.

[(3)   This article does not apply to proceedings which include a claim for damages in respect of an alleged breach of duty of care committed in the course of the provision of clinical or medical services (including dental or nursing services).]

[1231]

NOTES
Para (1): substituted by the High Court and County Courts Jurisdiction (Amendment) Order 1999, SI 1999/1014, art 6(a).
Para (2): word in square brackets substituted by SI 1999/1014, art 3.
Para (3): added by SI 1999/1014, art 6(b).

6   Applications [and appeals] under [section 17 of the Audit Commission Act 1998] and appeals under [section 18] of that Act shall be commenced in the High Court.

[1232]

NOTES
Words in first pair of square brackets inserted by the High Court and County Courts Jurisdiction (Amendment) Order 1993, SI 1993/1407, art 3; words in second and third pairs of square brackets substituted by virtue of the Audit Commission Act 1998, s 54(2), Sch 4, para 4(1).

[6A   Applications under section 1 of the Access to Neighbouring Land Act 1992 shall be commenced in a county court.]

[1233]

NOTES
Inserted by the Access to Neighbouring Land Act 1992, s 7(2).

7   (*Revoked by the High Court and County Courts Jurisdiction* (*Amendment*) *Order 1999, SI 1999/1014, art 7.*)

8   Enforcement
(1)   [Subject to paragraph (1A)] a judgment or order of a county court for the payment of a sum of money which it is sought to enforce wholly or partially by execution against goods—

[(a)   ... shall be enforced only in the High Court where the sum which it is sought to enforce is £5,000 or more;]

[(b)   shall be enforced only in a county court where the sum which it is sought to enforce is less than [£600];]

(c)   in any other case may be enforced in either the High Court or a county court.

[(1A)   A judgment or order of a county court for the payment of a sum of money in proceedings arising out of an agreement regulated by the Consumer Credit Act 1974 shall be enforced only in a county court.]

(2)   ...

[1234]

NOTES
Para (1): words in first pair of square brackets inserted, words omitted from para (a) revoked and para (b) substituted by the High Court and County Courts Jurisdiction (Amendment) Order 1995, SI 1995/205, art 5(a)–(c); words in second pair of square brackets substituted by the High Court and

County Courts Jurisdiction (Amendment) Order 1993, SI 1993/1407, art 4; sum in square brackets in para (b) substituted by the High Court and County Courts Jurisdiction (Amendment) Order 1999, SI 1999/1014, art 8.

Para (1A): inserted by SI 1995/205, art 5(d).

Para (2): amends the County Courts Act 1984, s 85(1).

[8A (*Inserted by the High Court and County Courts Jurisdiction (Amendment) Order 1993, SI 1993/1407, art 5, and outside the scope of this work.*)

[8B Enforcement of possession orders against trespassers

(1)   A judgment or order of a county court for possession of land made in a possession claim against trespassers may be enforced in the High Court or a county court.

(2)   In this article "a possession claim against trespassers" has the same meaning as in Part 55 of the Civil Procedure Rules 1998.]

[1235]

NOTES

Inserted by the High Court and County Courts Jurisdiction (Amendment No 2) Order 2001, SI 2001/2685, art 2.

[9   Financial value of claim

For the purposes of Articles 4A and 5, the financial value of the claim shall be calculated in accordance with rule 16.3(6) of the Civil Procedure Rules 1998.]

[1236]

NOTES

Substituted by the High Court and County Courts Jurisdiction (Amendment) Order 1999, SI 1999/1014, art 9.

10   (*Revoked by the High Court and County Courts Jurisdiction (Amendment) Order 1999, SI 1999/1014, art 10.*)

11   Crown proceedings—Transitional provisions

For a period of two years from the date upon which this Order comes into force no order shall be made transferring proceedings in the High Court to which the Crown is a party to a county court, except—

(a)   when the proceedings are set down to be tried or heard; or

(b)   with the consent of the Crown.

[1237]

12   Savings

This Order shall not apply to:

(a)   family proceedings within the meaning of Part V of the Matrimonial and Family Proceedings Act 1984;

(b)   ...

[1238]

NOTES

Para (b) revoked by the High Court and County Courts Jurisdiction (Amendment) Order 1999, SI 1999/1014, art 11.

(*Schedule contains repeals and revocations.*)

LANDLORD AND TENANT (COVENANTS) ACT 1995 (NOTICES) REGULATIONS 1995

(SI 1995/2964)

NOTES
Made: 9 November 1995.
Authority: Landlord and Tenant (Covenants) Act 1995, s 27.

1—(1)   These Regulations may be cited as the Landlord and Tenant (Covenants) Act 1995 (Notices) Regulations 1995 and shall come into force on 1st January 1996.

(2)   In these Regulations, "the Act" means the Landlord and Tenant (Covenants) Act 1995, and a form referred to by number means the form so numbered in the Schedule to these Regulations.

[1239]

2   The forms prescribed for the purposes of the Act shall be as follows, or in each case a form substantially to the like effect:

		Purpose Of Notice	Form To Be Used
(a)	(i)	Landlord informing a former tenant or guarantor of such a tenant of an amount payable in respect of a fixed charge under a covenant of the tenancy which the landlord intends to recover from that person under section 17 of the Act	Form 1
	(ii)	Landlord informing a former tenant or guarantor of such a tenant of a revised, greater amount payable in respect of a fixed charge under a covenant of the tenancy which the landlord intends to recover from that person under section 17 of the Act	Form 2
(b)	(i)	Landlord applying to be released from all the landlord covenants of the tenancy on assignment of his entire interest under sections 6 and 8 of the Act	Whole of Form 3 (landlord to complete Part I only)
	(ii)	Tenant objecting to the landlord's release under section 8 of the Act	Part II of Form 3
	(iii)	Tenant consenting to the landlord's release and withdrawing a notice objecting to such release under section 8 of the Act	Notice in writing stating that tenant is now consenting and that the notice of objection is withdrawn
(c)	(i)	Landlord applying to be released from the landlord covenants of the tenancy to the appropriate extent on assignment of part only of his interest under sections 6 and 8 of the Act	Whole of Form 4 (landlord to complete Part I only)
	(ii)	Tenant objecting to the landlord's release under section 8 of the Act	Part II of Form 4
	(iii)	Tenant consenting to the landlord's release and withdrawing a notice objecting to such release under section 8 of the Act	Notice in writing stating that tenant is now consenting and that the notice of objection is withdrawn

		Purpose Of Notice	Form To Be Used
(d)	(i)	Former landlord applying to be released from all the landlord covenants of the tenancy on a subsequent assignment of the landlord's interest under sections 7 and 8 of the Act	Whole of Form 5 (landlord to complete Part I only)
	(ii)	Tenant objecting to the former landlord's release under section 8 of the Act	Part II of Form 5
	(iii)	Tenant consenting to the former landlord's release and withdrawing a notice objecting to such release under section 8 of the Act	Notice in writing stating that tenant is now consenting and that the notice of objection is withdrawn
(e)	(i)	Former landlord who assigned part only of his interest applying to be released from the landlord covenants of the tenancy to the appropriate extent on a subsequent assignment of the landlord's interest under sections 7 and 8 of the Act	Whole of Form 6 (landlord to complete Part 1 only)
	(ii)	Tenant objecting to the former landlord's release under section 8 of the Act	Part II of Form 6
	(iii)	Tenant consenting to the former landlord's release and withdrawing a notice objecting to such release under section 8 of the Act	Notice in writing stating that tenant is now consenting and that the notice of objection is withdrawn
(f)	(i)	Tenant and tenant's assignee jointly applying for an apportionment of liability under the covenants of the tenancy to become binding on the appropriate person under sections 9 and 10 of the Act	Whole of Form 7 (tenant and assignee to complete Part 1 only)
	(ii)	Appropriate person objecting to the apportionment becoming binding on that person under section 10 of the Act	Part II of Form 7
	(iii)	Appropriate person consenting to the apportionment becoming binding on that person and withdrawing a notice objecting to the apportionment becoming so binding under section 10 of the Act	Notice in writing stating that appropriate person is now consenting and that the notice of objection is withdrawn
(g)	(i)	Landlord and landlord's assignee jointly applying for an apportionment of liability under the covenants of the tenancy to become binding on the appropriate person under sections 9 and 10 of the Act	Whole of Form 8 (landlord and assignee to complete Part 1 only)
	(ii)	Appropriate person objecting to the apportionment becoming binding on that person under section 10 of the Act	Part II of Form 8
	(iii)	Appropriate person consenting to the apportionment becoming binding on that person and withdrawing a notice objecting to the apportionment becoming so binding under section 10 of the Act	Notice in writing stating that appropriate person is now consenting and that the notice of objection is withdrawn

[1240]

SCHEDULE

FORM 1

Notice to Former Tenant or Guarantor of Intention to Recover Fixed Charge

(Landlord and Tenant (Covenants) Act 1995, section 17)
(The Act defines a fixed charge as (a) rent, (b) any service charge (as defined by section 18 of
the Landlord and Tenant Act 1985, disregarding the words "of a dwelling") and (c) any
amount payable under a tenant covenant of the tenancy providing for payment of a liquidated
sum in the event of failure to comply with the covenant)
To [name and address]:...
....

IMPORTANT—THE PERSON GIVING THIS NOTICE IS PROTECTING THE
RIGHT TO RECOVER THE AMOUNT(S) SPECIFIED FROM YOU NOW OR AT
SOME TIME IN THE FUTURE. THERE MAY BE ACTION WHICH YOU CAN
TAKE TO PROTECT YOUR POSITION. READ THE NOTICE AND ALL THE
NOTES OVERLEAF CAREFULLY. IF YOU ARE IN ANY DOUBT ABOUT THE
ACTION YOU SHOULD TAKE, SEEK ADVICE IMMEDIATELY, FOR INSTANCE
FROM A SOLICITOR OR CITIZENS ADVICE BUREAU.

---

1. This notice is given under section 17 of the Landlord and Tenant (Covenants)
    Act 1995. {*see Note 1*}

2. It relates to (address and description of property) ....

....

let under a lease dated ....and made between

....

....

[of which you were formerly tenant] [in relation to which you are liable as guarantor of
a person who was formerly tenant]. (*Delete alternative as appropriate*)

3. I/we as landlord (*"Landlord" for these purposes includes any person who has
    the right to enforce the charge*) hereby give you notice that the fixed charge(s) of
    which details are set out in the attached Schedule (*The Schedule must be in
    writing, and must indicate in relation to each item the date on which it became
    payable, the amount payable and whether it is rent, service charge or a fixed
    charge of some other kind (in which case particulars of the nature of the charge
    should be given). Charges due before 1 January 1996 are deemed to have
    become due on that date, but the actual date on which they became due should
    also be stated*) is/are now due and unpaid, and that I/we intend to recover from
    you the amount(s) specified in the Schedule [and interest from the date and
    calculated on the basis specified in the Schedule] (*Delete words in brackets if not
    applicable. If applicable, the Schedule must state the basis on which interest is
    calculated (for example, rate of interest, date from which it is payable and
    provision of Lease or other document under which it is payable)*). {*see Notes 2
    and 3*}

4. (*Delete this paragraph if not applicable. If applicable (for example, where there
    is an outstanding rent review or service charge collected on account) a further
    notice must be served on the former tenant or guarantor within three (3) months
    beginning with the date on which the greater amount is determined. If only
    applicable to one or more charge of several, the Schedule should specify which.*)

There is a possibility that your liability in respect of the fixed charge(s) detailed in the
Schedule will subsequently be determined to be for a greater amount. {*see Note 4*}

5. All correspondence about this notice should be sent to the landlord/landlord's
    agent at the address given below.

Date .... Signature of landlord/landlord's agent......................................

Name and address of landlord ....

....

....

[Name and address of agent ....

....

....]

Notes

1.   The person giving you this notice alleges that you are still liable for the performance of the tenant's obligations under the tenancy to which this notice relates, either as a previous tenant bound by privity of contract or an authorised guarantee agreement, or because you are the guarantor of a previous tenant. By giving you this notice, the landlord (or other person entitled to enforce payment, such as a management company) is protecting his right to require you to pay the amount specified in the notice. There may be other sums not covered by the notice which the landlord can also recover because they are not fixed charges (for example in respect of repairs or costs if legal proceedings have to be brought). If you pay the amount specified in this notice in full, you will have the right to call on the landlord to grant you an "overriding lease", which puts you in the position of landlord to the present tenant. There are both advantages and drawbacks to doing this, and you should take advice before coming to a decision.

Validity of notice

2.   The landlord is required to give this notice within six months of the date on which the charge or charges in question became due (or, if it became due before 1 January 1996, within six months of that date). If the notice has been given late, it is not valid and the amount in the notice cannot be recovered from you. The date of the giving of the notice may not be the date written on the notice or the date on which you actually saw it. It may, for instance, be the date on which the notice was delivered through the post to your last address known to the landlord. If you are in any doubt, you should seek advice immediately.

Interest

3.   If interest is payable on the amount due, the landlord does not have to state the precise amount of interest, but he must state the basis on which the interest is calculated to enable you to work out the likely amount, or he will not be able to claim interest at all. This does not include interest which may be payable under rules of court if legal proceedings are brought.

Change in amount due

4.   Apart from interest, the landlord is not entitled to recover an amount which is more than he has specified in the notice, with one exception. This is where the amount cannot be finally determined within six months after it is due (for example, if there is dispute concerning an outstanding rent review or if the charge is a service charge collected on account and adjusted following final determination). In such a case, if the amount due is eventually determined to be more than originally notified, the landlord may claim the larger amount *if and only if* he completes the paragraph giving notice of the possibility that the amount may change, and gives a further notice specifying the larger amount within three months of the final determination.

[1241]

FORM 2

Further Notice to Former Tenant or Guarantor of Revised Amount Due in Respect of a Fixed Charge

(Landlord and Tenant (Covenants) Act 1995, section 17)

(The Act defines a fixed charge as (a) rent, (b) any service charge (as defined by section 18 of the Landlord and Tenant Act 1985, disregarding the words "of a dwelling") and (c) any amount payable under a tenant covenant of the tenancy providing for payment of a liquidated sum in the event of failure to comply with the covenant)

To [name and address]:...

....

IMPORTANT—THE PERSON GIVING THIS NOTICE IS PROTECTING THE RIGHT TO RECOVER THE AMOUNT(S) SPECIFIED FROM YOU NOW OR AT SOME TIME IN THE FUTURE. THERE MAY BE ACTION WHICH YOU CAN TAKE TO PROTECT YOUR POSITION. READ THE NOTICE AND ALL THE NOTES OVERLEAF CAREFULLY. IF YOU ARE IN ANY DOUBT ABOUT THE ACTION YOU SHOULD TAKE, SEEK ADVICE IMMEDIATELY, FOR INSTANCE FROM A SOLICITOR OR CITIZENS ADVICE BUREAU.

---

1. This notice is given under section 17 of the Landlord and Tenant (Covenants) Act 1995. {*see Note 1*}

2. It relates to (address and description of property)...

....

let under a lease dated..................... and made between ....

....

....

[of which you were formerly tenant] [in relation to which you are liable as guarantor of a person who was formerly tenant].(*Delete alternative as appropriate*)

3. You were informed on .... (date of original notice) of the amount due in respect of a fixed charge or charges, and of the possibility that your liability in respect of the charge(s) might subsequently be determined to be for a greater amount.

4. I/we as landlord (*"Landlord" for these purposes includes any person who has the right to enforce the charge*) hereby give you notice that the fixed charge(s) of which details are set out in the attached Schedule (*The Schedule can be in any form, but must indicate in relation to each item the date on which it was revised, the revised amount payable and whether it is rent, service charge or a fixed charge of some other kind (in which case particulars of the nature of the charge should be given)*) has/have now been determined to be for a greater amount than specified in the original notice, and that I/we intend to recover from you the amount(s) specified in the Schedule [and interest from the date and calculated on the basis specified in the Schedule] (*Delete words in brackets if not applicable. If applicable, the Schedule must state the basis on which interest is calculated (for example, rate of interest, date from which it is payable and provision of Lease or other document under which it is payable)*). {*see Notes 2 and 3*}

5. All correspondence about this notice should be sent to the landlord/landlord's agent at the address given below.

Date .... Signature of landlord/landlord's agent ....

Name and address of landlord..

....

....

[Name and address of agent ....

....

....]

Notes

1. The person giving you this notice alleges that you are still liable for the performance of the tenant's obligations under the tenancy to which this notice relates, either as a previous tenant bound by privity of contract or an authorised guarantee agreement, or because you are the guarantor of a previous tenant. You

should already have been given a notice by which the landlord (or other person entitled to enforce payment, such as a management company) protected his right to require you to pay the amount specified in that notice. The purpose of this notice is to protect the landlord's right to require you to pay a larger amount, because the amount specified in the original notice could not be finally determined at the time of the original notice (for example, because there was a dispute concerning an outstanding rent review or if the charge was a service charge collected on account and adjusted following final determination).

Validity of notice

2.   The notice is not valid unless the original notice contained a warning that the amount in question might subsequently be determined to be greater. In addition, the landlord is required to give this notice within three months of the date on which the amount was finally determined. If the original notice did not include that warning, or if this notice has been given late, then this notice is not valid and the landlord cannot recover the greater amount, but only the smaller amount specified in the original notice. The date of the giving of this notice may not be the date written on the notice or the date on which you actually saw it. It may, for instance, be the date on which the notice was delivered through the post to your last address known to the person giving notice. If you are in any doubt, you should seek advice immediately.

Interest

3.   If interest is chargeable on the amount due, the landlord does not have to state the precise amount of interest, but he must have stated the basis on which the interest is calculated, or he will not be able to claim interest at all.

[1242]

FORM 3

PART I

Landlord's Notice Applying for Release from Landlord Covenants of a Tenancy on Assignment of Whole of Reversion

(Landlord and Tenant (Covenants) Act 1995, sections 6 and 8)

To [name and address]:...

....

IMPORTANT—THIS NOTICE IS INTENDED TO RELEASE YOUR LANDLORD FROM HIS OBLIGATIONS WHEN HE TRANSFERS HIS INTEREST TO A NEW LANDLORD. IF YOU CONSIDER THAT THERE IS GOOD REASON FOR YOUR LANDLORD **NOT** TO BE RELEASED, YOU MUST ACT QUICKLY. READ THE NOTICE AND ALL THE NOTES OVERLEAF CAREFULLY. IF YOU ARE IN ANY DOUBT ABOUT THE ACTION YOU SHOULD TAKE, SEEK ADVICE IMMEDIATELY, FOR INSTANCE FROM A SOLICITOR OR CITIZENS ADVICE BUREAU.

1.   This notice is given under section 8 of the Landlord and Tenant (Covenants) Act 1995. {*see Note 1*}

2.   It relates to (address and description of property)..

....

let under a lease dated..................................... and made between ....

....

....

of which you are the tenant.

3.   I/we [propose to transfer] [transferred on ......] (*Delete alternative as*

appropriate) the whole of the landlord's interest and wish to be released from the landlord's obligations under the tenancy with effect from the date of the transfer. *{see Note 2}*

4.   If you consider that it is reasonable for me/us to be released, you do not need to do anything, but it would help me/us if you notify me/us using Part II of this Form. *{see Note 3}*

5.   If you do **not** consider it reasonable for me/us to be released, you **must** notify me/us of your objection, using Part II of this Form, within the period of **FOUR WEEKS** beginning with the giving of this notice, or I/we will be released in any event. You may withdraw your objection at any time by notifying me/us in writing. *{see Notes 4–6}*

6.   All correspondence about this notice should be sent to the landlord/landlord's agent at the address given below.

Date .... Signature of landlord/landlord's agent.................................

Name and address of landlord ....

....

....

[Name and address of agent ....

....

....]

Notes to Part I

Release of landlord

1.   The landlord is about to transfer his interest to a new landlord, or has just done so, and is applying to be released from the obligations of the landlord under your tenancy. You have a number of options: you may expressly agree to the landlord's being released; you may object to his being released (with the option of withdrawing your objection later); or you may do nothing, in which case the landlord will automatically be released, with effect from the date of the transfer, once four weeks have elapsed from the date of the giving of the notice. If you choose to oppose release, you must act within four weeks of the giving of the notice.

Validity of notice

2.   The landlord must give this notice either before the transfer or within the period of four weeks beginning with the date of the transfer. If the notice has been given late, it is not valid. You should read Note 4 below concerning the date of the giving of the notice.

Agreeing to release

3.   If you are content for the landlord to be released, you may notify him of this using Part II of this Form, and the landlord will then be released as from the date of the transfer. If you do this, you may not later change your mind and object.

Objecting to release

4.   If you think that it is not reasonable for the landlord to be released, you may object to release by notifying the landlord, using Part II of this Form. You must, however, do this within four weeks of the date of the giving of the notice. The date of the giving of the notice may not be the date written on the notice or the date on which you actually saw it. It may, for instance, be the date on which the notice was delivered through the post to your last address known by the landlord. If there has been any delay in your seeing this notice you may need to act very quickly. If you are in any doubt, you should seek advice immediately. If you change your mind after objecting, you may consent instead, at any time, by notifying the landlord *in writing* that you now consent to his being released and that your objection is withdrawn.

5.   If you object within the time limit, the landlord will only be released if *either* he

applies to a court and the court decides that it is reasonable for him to be released, *or* you withdraw your objection by a notice in writing as explained in Note 4 above.

6.   In deciding whether to object, you should bear in mind that if the court finds that it is reasonable for the landlord to be released, or if you withdraw your objection late, you may have to pay costs.

[1243]

PART II

Tenant's Response to Landlord's Notice Applying for Release from Landlord Covenants of a Tenancy on Assignment of Whole of Reversion

(Landlord and Tenant (Covenants) Act 1995, section 8)

To [name and address]:...
....

1.   This notice is given under section 8 of the Landlord and Tenant (Covenants) Act 1995.

2.   It relates to (address and description of property)..
....

let under a lease dated ....and made between
....
....

⬤ of which you are the landlord or have just transferred the landlord's interest.

3.   You [propose to transfer] [transferred on ....] (*Delete alternative as appropriate*) the landlord's interest and have applied to be released from the landlord's obligations under the tenancy with effect from the date of the transfer.

4.   (*The tenant should select one version of paragraph 4 and cross out the other*)

I/we agree to your being released from the landlord's obligations with effect from the date of the transfer. {*see Note 1*}

OR

4.   I/we do **not** consider it reasonable that you should be released from the landlord's obligations, and object to the release. {*see Notes 2 and 3*}

5.   All correspondence about this notice should be sent to the tenant/tenant's agent at the address given below.

Date .... Signature of landlord/landlord's agent ....

Name and address of landlord...
....
....

[Name and address of agent ....
....
....]

Notes to Part II

Agreement to release

1.   If the tenant has indicated agreement in paragraph 4 of the notice, you will automatically be released from the landlord's obligations under the tenancy with effect from the date of your transfer of the landlord's interest.

Objection to release

2.   If the tenant has indicated an objection in paragraph 4 of the notice, you will not

be released unless either the tenant later withdraws his objection *or* you apply to the County Court to declare that it is reasonable for you to be released, and the court so declares. If you are not released, you may still apply for release when the landlord's interest, or part of it, is next transferred, and it may therefore be sensible to make arrangements for the person to whom you are making the transfer to inform you when he intends to transfer the landlord's interest in his turn.

Validity of notice of objection

3.   A notice of objection by the tenant is only valid if he has given it to you within the period of four weeks beginning with the date on which you gave him your notice applying for release. If you are in any doubt, you should seek advice before applying to the court.

[1244]

FORM 4

PART I

Landlord's Notice Applying for Release from Landlord Covenants of a Tenancy on Assignment of Part of Reversion

(Landlord and Tenant (Covenants) Act 1995, sections 6 and 8)

To [name and address]:..

....

IMPORTANT—THIS NOTICE IS INTENDED TO RELEASE YOUR LANDLORD PARTLY FROM HIS OBLIGATIONS WHEN HE TRANSFERS PART OF HIS INTEREST TO A NEW LANDLORD. IF YOU CONSIDER THAT THERE IS GOOD REASON FOR YOUR LANDLORD **NOT** TO BE RELEASED, YOU MUST ACT QUICKLY. READ THE NOTICE AND ALL THE NOTES OVERLEAF CAREFULLY. IF YOU ARE IN ANY DOUBT ABOUT THE ACTION YOU SHOULD TAKE, SEEK ADVICE IMMEDIATELY, FOR INSTANCE FROM A SOLICITOR OR CITIZENS ADVICE BUREAU.

---

1.   This notice is given under section 8 of the Landlord and Tenant (Covenants) Act 1995. *{see Note 1}*

2.   It relates to (address and description of property)..

....

let under a lease dated.. and made between ....

....

....

of which you are the tenant.

3.   I/we [propose to transfer] [transferred on] (*Delete alternative as appropriate*) part of the landlord's interest, namely ....

....

and wish to be released from the landlord's obligations under the tenancy, to the extent that they fall to be complied with in relation to that part, with effect from the date of the transfer. *{see Note 2}*

4.   If you consider that it is reasonable for me/us to be released, you do not need to do anything, but it would help me/us if you notify me/us using Part II of this Form. *{see Note 3}*

5.   If you do **not** consider it reasonable for me/us to be released, you **must** notify me/us of your objection, using Part II of this Form, within the period of **FOUR WEEKS** beginning with the giving of this notice, or I/we will be released in any event. You may withdraw your objection at any time by notifying me/us in writing. *{see Notes 4–6}*

6.   All correspondence about this notice should be sent to the landlord/landlord's agent at the address given below.

Date..................................... Signature of landlord/landlord's agent................................

Name and address of landlord...

....

....

[Name and address of agent ....

....

....]

Notes to Part I

Release of landlord

1.   The landlord is about to transfer part of his interest to a new landlord, or has just done so, and is applying to be released from the obligations of the landlord under your tenancy, to the extent that they fall to be complied with in relation to that part. You have a number of options: you may expressly agree to the landlord's being released; you may object to his being released (with the option of withdrawing your objection later); or you may do nothing, in which case the landlord will automatically be released, with effect from the date of the assignment, once four weeks have elapsed from the date of the giving of the notice. If you choose to oppose release, you must act within four weeks of the giving of the notice.

Validity of notice

2.   The landlord must give this notice either before the transfer or within the period of four weeks beginning with the date of the transfer. If the notice has been given late, it is not valid. You should read Note 4 below concerning the date of the giving of the notice.

Agreeing to release

3.   If you are content for the landlord to be released, you may notify him of this using Part II of this Form, and the landlord will then be released as from the date of the transfer. If you do this, you may not later change your mind and object.

Objecting to release

4   If you think that it is not reasonable for the landlord to be released, you may object to release by notifying the landlord, using Part II of this Form. You must, however, do this within four weeks of the date of the giving of the notice. The date of the giving of the notice may not be the date written on the notice or the date on which you actually saw it. It may, for instance, be the date on which the notice was delivered through the post to your last address known to the person giving the notice. If there has been any delay in your seeing this notice you may need to act very quickly. If you are in any doubt, you should seek advice immediately. If you change your mind after objecting, you may consent instead, at any time, by notifying the landlord *in writing* that you now consent to his being released and that your objection is withdrawn.

5.   If you object within the time limit, the landlord will only be released if *either* he applies to a court and the court decides that it is reasonable for him to be released, *or* you withdraw your objection by a notice in writing as explained in Note 4 above.

6.   In deciding whether to object, you should bear in mind that if the court finds that it is reasonable for the landlord to be released, or if you withdraw your objection late, you may have to pay costs.

[1245]

PART II

Tenant's Response to Landlord's Notice Applying for Release from Landlord Covenants of a Tenancy on Assignment of Part of Reversion

(Landlord and Tenant (Covenants) Act 1995, section 8)

To [name and address]: ....

....

1.   This notice is given under section 8 of the Landlord and Tenant (Covenants) Act 1995.

2.   It relates to (address and description of property)..

....

let under a lease dated... and made between ....

....

....

of which you are the landlord or have just transferred part of the landlord's interest.

3.   You [propose to transfer] [transferred on ....] (*Delete alternative as appropriate*) part of the landlord's interest, namely...

....

and have applied to be released from the landlord's obligations under the tenancy, to the extent that they fall to be complied with in relation to that part, with effect from the date of the transfer.

4.   (*The tenant should select one version of paragraph 4 and cross out the other*)

I/we agree to your being released from the landlord's obligations to that extent with effect from the date of the transfer. {*see Note 1*}

OR

4.   I/we do **not** consider it reasonable that you should be released from the landlord's obligations, and object to the release. {*see Notes 2 and 3*}

5.   All correspondence about this notice should be sent to the tenant/tenant's agent at the address given below.

Date..................................... Signature of landlord/landlord's agent...............................

Name and address of landlord ....

....

....

[Name and address of agent ....

....

....]

Notes to Part II

Agreement to release

1.   If the tenant has indicated agreement in paragraph 4 of the notice, you will automatically be released from the landlord's obligations under the tenancy, to the extent that they fall to be complied with in relation to the part of your interest being transferred, with effect from the date of the transfer.

Objection to release

2.   If the tenant has indicated an objection in paragraph 4 of the notice, you will not be released unless *either* the tenant later withdraws his objection *or* you apply to the County Court to declare that it is reasonable for you to be released, and the court so declares. If you are not released, you may still apply for release when the landlord's interest, or part of it, is next transferred, and it may therefore be

sensible to make arrangements for the person to whom you are making the transfer to inform you when he intends to transfer the landlord's interest in his turn.

Validity of notice of objection

3. A notice of objection by the tenant is only valid if he has given it to you within the period of four weeks beginning with the date on which you gave him your notice applying for release. If you are in any doubt, you should seek advice before applying to the court.

[1246]

FORM 5

PART I

Former Landlord's Notice Applying for Release from Landlord Covenants of a Tenancy

(Landlord and Tenant (Covenants) Act 1995, sections 7 and 8)

To [name and address]:..

....

IMPORTANT—THIS NOTICE IS INTENDED TO RELEASE THE FORMER LANDLORD OF THE PROPERTY FROM HIS OBLIGATIONS UNDER YOUR TENANCY. IF YOU CONSIDER THAT THERE IS GOOD REASON FOR THE FORMER LANDLORD **NOT** TO BE RELEASED YOU MUST ACT QUICKLY. READ THE NOTICE AND ALL THE NOTES OVERLEAF CAREFULLY. IF YOU ARE IN ANY DOUBT ABOUT THE ACTION YOU SHOULD TAKE SEEK ADVICE IMMEDIATELY FOR INSTANCE FROM A SOLICITOR OR CITIZENS ADVICE BUREAU.

---

1. This notice is given under section 8 of the Landlord and Tenant (Covenants) Act 1995. {*see Note 1*}

2. It relates to (address and description of property)..

....

let under a lease dated .... and made between ....

....

....

of which you are the tenant.

3. I/we was/were formerly landlord of the property of which you are tenant and remained bound by the landlord's obligations under the tenancy after transferring the landlord's interest. The landlord's interest, or part of it [is about to be transferred] [was transferred on ....] (*Delete alternative as appropriate*). I/we wish to be released from my/our obligations with effect from the date of that transfer. {*see Note 2*}

4. If you consider that it is reasonable for me/us to be released, you do not need to do anything, but it would help me/us if you notify me/us using Part II of this Form. {*see Note 3*}

5. If you do **not** consider it reasonable for me/us to be released, you **must** notify me/us of your objection, using Part II of this Form, within the period of **FOUR WEEKS** beginning with the giving of this notice, or I/we will be released in any event. You may withdraw your objection at any time by notifying me/us in writing. {*see Notes 4–6*}

6. All correspondence about this notice should be sent to the former landlord/former landlord's agent at the address given below.

Date.............................. Signature of former landlord/landlord's agent..........................

Name and address of former landlord ....

....

....

[Name and address of agent ....

....

....]

Notes to Part I

Release of former landlord

1.   Your landlord is about to transfer his interest, or part of it, to a new landlord, or has just done so, and a former landlord of the property is applying to be released from his obligations, from which he was not released when he transferred the landlord's interest himself. You have a number of options: you may expressly agree to the former landlord's being released; you may object to his being released (with the option of withdrawing your objection later); or you may do nothing, in which case the former landlord will automatically be released, with effect from the date of the present transfer, once four weeks have elapsed from the date of the giving of the notice. If you choose to oppose release, you must act within four weeks of the giving of the notice.

Validity of notice

2.   The former landlord is required to give this notice either before the transfer by the present landlord takes place or within the period of four weeks beginning with the date of the transfer. If the notice has been given late, it is not valid. You should read Note 4 below concerning the date of the giving of the notice.

Agreeing to release

3.   If you are content for the former landlord to be released, you may notify him of this using Part II of this Form, and the former landlord will then automatically be released as from the date of the present transfer. If you do this, you may not later change your mind and object.

Objecting to release

4.   If you think that it is not reasonable for the former landlord to be released, you may object to release by notifying the former landlord, using Part II of this Form. You must, however, do this within four weeks of the date of the giving of the notice. The date of the giving of the notice may not be the date written on the notice or the date on which you actually saw it. It may, for instance, be the date on which the notice was delivered through the post to your last address known to the person giving the notice. If there has been any delay in your seeing this notice you may need to act very quickly. If you are in any doubt, you should seek advice immediately. If you change your mind after objecting, you may consent instead, at any time, by notifying the former landlord *in writing* that you now consent to his being released and that your objection is withdrawn.

5.   If you object within the time limit, the former landlord will only be released if *either* he applies to a court and the court decides that it is reasonable for him to be released, *or* you withdraw your objection by a notice in writing as explained in Note 4 above.

6.   In deciding whether to object, you should bear in mind that if the court finds that it is reasonable for the former landlord to be released, or if you withdraw your objection late, you may have to pay costs.

[1247]

PART II

Tenant's Response to Former Landlord's Notice Applying for Release from Landlord Covenants of a Tenancy

(Landlord and Tenant (Covenants) Act 1995, section 8)

To [name and address]: ....

....

1. This notice is given under section 8 of the Landlord and Tenant (Covenants) Act 1995.

2. It relates to (address and description of property)..

let under a lease dated... and made between ....

....

....

of which you were formerly landlord.

3. You have applied to be released from the landlord's obligations under the tenancy with effect from the date of a [proposed transfer] [transfer on ....] (*Delete alternative as appropriate*) of the landlord's interest.

4. (*The tenant should select one version of paragraph 4 and cross out the other*)

I/we agree to your being released from the landlord's obligations with effect from the date of that transfer. {*see Note 1*}

OR

4. I/we do **not** consider it reasonable that you should be released from the landlord's obligations, and object to your being so released. {*see Notes 2 and 3*}

5. All correspondence about this notice should be sent to the tenant/tenant's agent at the address given below.

Date .... Signature of tenant/tenant's agent ....

Name and address of tenant..

....

....

[Name and address of agent ....

....

....]

Notes to Part II

Agreement to release

1. If the tenant has indicated agreement in paragraph 4 of the notice, you will automatically be released from the landlord's obligations under the tenancy with effect from the date of the transfer by the present landlord.

Objection to release

2. If the tenant has indicated an objection in paragraph 4 of the notice, you will not be released unless *either* the tenant later withdraws his objection *or* you apply to the County Court to declare that it is reasonable for you to be released, and the court so declares. If you are not released, you may still apply for release when the reversion, or part of it, is next assigned, and it may therefore be sensible to make arrangements for you to be informed when the present landlord's transferee intends to transfer the landlord's interest in his turn.

Validity of notice of objection

3. A notice of objection by the tenant is only valid if he has given it to you within the period of four weeks beginning with the date on which you gave him your notice applying for release. If you are in any doubt, you should seek advice before applying to the court.

[1248]

FORM 6

PART I

**Former Landlord's Notice Applying for Release from Landlord Covenants of a Tenancy
(Former Landlord Having Assigned Part of Reversion)**

(Landlord and Tenant (Covenants) Act 1995, sections 7 and 8)

To [name and address]:...

....

> IMPORTANT—THIS NOTICE IS INTENDED TO RELEASE THE FORMER
> LANDLORD OF THE PROPERTY PARTIALLY FROM HIS OBLIGATIONS
> UNDER YOUR TENANCY. IF YOU CONSIDER THAT THERE IS GOOD REASON
> FOR THE FORMER LANDLORD **NOT** TO BE RELEASED, YOU MUST ACT
> QUICKLY. READ THE NOTICE AND ALL THE NOTES OVERLEAF
> CAREFULLY. IF YOU ARE IN ANY DOUBT ABOUT THE ACTION YOU
> SHOULD TAKE, SEEK ADVICE IMMEDIATELY, FOR INSTANCE FROM A
> SOLICITOR OR CITIZENS ADVICE BUREAU.

1.   This notice is given under section 8 of the Landlord and Tenant (Covenants)
     Act 1995. {*see Note 1*}

2.   It relates to (address and description of property)...

let under a lease dated.. and made between ....

....

....

of which you are the tenant.

3.   I/we was/were formerly landlord of the property of which you are tenant and
     remained bound by all the landlord's obligations under the tenancy after
     transferring part of the landlord's interest, namely ....

....

The landlord's interest, or part of it [is about to be transferred] [was transferred on .....]
(*Delete alternative as appropriate*). I/we wish to be released from my/our obligations
with effect from the date of that transfer. {*see Note 2*}

4.   If you consider that it is reasonable for me/us to be released, you do not need to
     do anything, but it would help me/us if you notify me/us using Part II of this
     Form. {*see Note 3*}

5.   If you do **not** consider it reasonable for me/us to be released, you **must** notify
     me/us of your objection, using Part II of this Form, within the period of **FOUR
     WEEKS** beginning with the giving of this notice, or I/we will be released in any
     event. You may withdraw your objection at any time by notifying me/us in
     writing. {*see Notes 4–6*}

6.   All correspondence about this notice should be sent to the former landlord/
     former landlord's agent at the address given below.

Date .... Signature of former landlord/landlord's agent ....

Name and address of former landlord ....

....

....

[Name and address of agent ....

....

....]

Notes to Part I

Release of former landlord

1. Your landlord is about to transfer his interest, or part of it, to a new landlord, or has just done so, and a former landlord of the property is applying to be released from his obligations in relation to part of the landlord's interest, from which he was not released when he transferred that part himself. You have a number of options: you may expressly agree to the former landlord's being released; you may object to his being released (with the option of withdrawing your objection later); or you may do nothing, in which case the former landlord will automatically be released, with effect from the date of the present transfer, once four weeks have elapsed from the date of the giving of the notice. If you choose to oppose release, you must act within four weeks of the giving of the notice.

Validity of notice

2. The former landlord is required to give this notice either before the transfer by the present landlord takes place or within the period of four weeks beginning with the date of the transfer. If the notice has been given late, it is not valid. You should read Note 4 below concerning the date of the giving of the notice.

Agreeing to release

3. If you are content for the former landlord to be released, you may notify him of this using Part II of this Form, and the former landlord will then automatically be released as from the date of the present transfer. If you do this, you may not later change your mind and object.

Objecting to release

4. If you think that it is not reasonable for the former landlord to be released, you may object to release by notifying the former landlord, using Part II of this Form. You must, however, do this within four weeks of the date of the giving of the notice. The date of the giving of the notice may not be the date written on the notice or the date on which you actually saw it. It may, for instance, be the date on which the notice was delivered through the post to your last address known to the person giving the notice. If there has been any delay in your seeing this notice you may need to act very quickly. If you are in any doubt, you should seek advice immediately. If you change your mind after objecting, you may consent instead, at any time, by notifying the former landlord *in writing* that you now consent to his being released and that your objection is withdrawn.

5. If you object within the time limit, the former landlord will only be released if *either* he applies to a court and the court decides that it is reasonable for him to be released, *or* you withdraw your objection by a notice in writing as explained in Note 4 above.

6. In deciding whether to object, you should bear in mind that if the court finds that it is reasonable for the former landlord to be released, or if you withdraw your objection late, you may have to pay costs.

[1249]

PART II

Tenant's Response to Former Landlord's Notice Applying for Release from Landlord Covenants of a Tenancy (Former Landlord Having Assigned Part of Reversion)

(Landlord and Tenant (Covenants) Act 1995, section 8)

To [name and address]:..
....

1. This notice is given under section 8 of the Landlord and Tenant (Covenants) Act 1995.

2. It relates to (address and description of property)...
....

let under a lease dated.. and made between ....

....

of which you were formerly landlord.

3.   You remain bound by the landlord's obligations under the tenancy in relation to a part of the landlord's interest which you previously assigned, namely ....

....

You have applied to be released from those obligations, to the extent that they relate to that part, with effect from the date of a [proposed transfer] [transfer on...] (*Delete alternative as appropriate*) of the landlord's interest.

4.   (*The tenant should select one version of paragraph 4 and cross out the other*)

I/we agree to your being released from the landlord's obligations to that effect from the date of that transfer. {*see Note 1*}

OR

4.   I/we do **not** consider it reasonable that you should be released from the landlord's obligations, and object to your being so released. {*see Notes 2 and 3*}

5.   All correspondence about this notice should be sent to the tenant/tenant's agent at the address given below.

Date .... Signature of tenant/tenant's agent ....

Name and address of tenant...

....

....

[Name and address of agent ....

....

....]

PART II
STATUTORY INSTRUMENTS

Notes to Part II

Agreement to release

1.   If the tenant has indicated agreement in paragraph 4 of the notice, you will automatically be released from the landlord's obligations under the tenancy to the appropriate extent with effect from the date of the transfer by the present landlord.

Objection to release

2.   If the tenant has indicated an objection in paragraph 4 of the notice, you will not be released unless *either* the tenant later withdraws his objection *or* you apply to the County Court to declare that it is reasonable for you to be released, and the court so declares. If you are not released, you may still apply for release when the reversion, or part of it, is next transferred, and it may therefore be sensible to make arrangements for you to be informed when the present landlord's transferee intends to transfer the landlord's interest in his turn.

Validity of notice of objection

3.   A notice of objection by the tenant is only valid if he has given it to you within the period of four weeks beginning with the date on which you gave him your notice applying for release. If you are in any doubt, you should seek advice before applying to the court.

[1250]

FORM 7

PART I

Joint Notice by Tenant and Assignee for Binding Apportionment of Liability under Non-Attributable Tenant Covenants of a Tenancy on Assignment of Part of Property

(**Landlord and Tenant (Covenants) Act 1995, sections 9 and 10**)
To [name and address]: ....
....

> IMPORTANT—THIS NOTICE IS INTENDED TO AFFECT THE WAY IN WHICH YOU CAN ENFORCE THE TENANT'S OBLIGATIONS UNDER THE TENANCY AS BETWEEN THE TENANT AND THE NEW TENANT. IF YOU CONSIDER THAT THERE IS GOOD REASON WHY YOU SHOULD **NOT** BE BOUND BY THEIR AGREEMENT, YOU MUST ACT QUICKLY. READ THE NOTICE AND ALL THE NOTES OVERLEAF CAREFULLY. IF YOU ARE IN ANY DOUBT ABOUT THE ACTION YOU SHOULD TAKE, SEEK ADVICE IMMEDIATELY, FOR INSTANCE FROM A SOLICITOR OR CITIZENS ADVICE BUREAU.

1. This notice is given under section 10 of the Landlord and Tenant (Covenants) Act 1995. {*see Note 1*}

2. It relates to (address and description of property)..

    let under a lease dated.. and made between ....

    ....

    ....

    of which you are the landlord (*"Landlord", for these purposes, includes any person for the time being entitled to enforce the obligations in question (for example, a management company)*).

3. We are the parties to a [proposed transfer] [transfer on ....] (*Delete alternative as appropriate*) of part of the property comprised in the tenancy, namely ....

    ....

    We are jointly and severally liable to perform the obligation(s) specified in the attached Schedule, and have agreed to divide that liability between us in the manner specified in the Schedule. (*The Schedule must be in writing, and must specify the nature of the obligation, the term or condition of the Lease or other instrument under which it arises and the manner in which liability to perform it is divided under the agreement (for example, an obligation to pay service charge under a specific provision of the lease might be divided equally). It may be helpful to attach a copy of the agreement to the notice*) We wish this agreement to be binding on you as well as between us, with effect from the date of the transfer. {*see Note 2*}

4. If you consider that it is reasonable for you to be bound by this agreement, you do not need to do anything, but it would help us if you notify us using Part II of this Form. {*see Note 3*}

5. If you do **not** consider it reasonable for you to be bound by this agreement, you **must** notify both of us of your objection, using Part II of this Form, within the period of **FOUR WEEKS** beginning with the giving of this notice. You may withdraw your objection at any time by notifying us in writing. {*see Notes 4–6*}

6. All correspondence about this notice should be copied, one copy sent to each of the parties to the agreement, at the addresses given below.

    Signature of tenant/tenant's agent..

Name and address of tenant..

....

....

[Name and address of agent ....

....

....]

Signature of new tenant/agent ....

Name and address of new tenant..

....

....

[Name and address of agent ....

....

....]

Date..

Notes to Part I

Apportionment of liability

1.   The tenant is about to transfer, or has just transferred, part of his interest to a new tenant, but they are jointly and severally liable for a particular obligation or obligations covering the whole of the property. They have agreed to divide that liability between them, and are applying for you as the landlord to be bound as well, so that you can only enforce the liability against each of them as set out in their agreement. If you are bound, any subsequent landlord to whom you may transfer your interest will also be bound. You have a number of options: you may expressly agree to be bound; you may object to being bound (with the option of withdrawing your objection later); or you may do nothing, in which case you will automatically be bound, with effect from the date of the transfer, once four weeks have elapsed from the date of the giving of the notice. If you choose to object, you must act within four weeks of the giving of the notice.

Validity of notice

2.   This notice must be given either before the transfer or within the period of four weeks beginning with the date of the transfer. If the notice has been given late, it is not valid. You should read Note 4 below concerning the date of the giving of the notice.

Agreeing to be bound

3.   If you are content to be bound, you may notify the tenant and new tenant using Part II of this Form (sending a copy to each of them), and all of you will be bound with effect from the date of the transfer. If you do this, you may not later change your mind and object.

Objecting to being bound

4.   If you think that it is not reasonable for you to be bound, you may object by notifying the tenant and new tenant, using Part II of this Form (sending a copy to each of them). You must, however, do this within four weeks of the date of the giving of this notice. The date of the giving of the notice may not be the date written on the notice or the date on which you actually saw it. It may, for instance, be the date on which the notice was delivered through the post to your last address known to the person giving the notice. If there has been any delay in your seeing this notice you may need to act very quickly. If you are in any doubt, you should seek advice immediately. If you change your mind after objecting, you may consent instead, at any time, by notifying *both* the tenant and new tenant *in writing* that you now consent to be bound and that your objection is withdrawn.

5.   If you object within the time limit, the apportionment will only bind you if *either*

the tenant and new tenant apply to a court and the court decides that it is reasonable for you to be bound, *or* you withdraw your objection by notice in writing as explained in Note 4 above.

6.   In deciding whether to object, you should bear in mind that if the court finds that it is reasonable for you to be bound, *or* if you withdraw your objection late, you may have to pay costs.

[1251]

PART II

Landlord's Response to Joint Notice by Tenant and Assignee Seeking Binding Apportionment of Liability under Non-Attributable Tenant Covenants of a Tenancy on Assignment of Part of Property

(Landlord and Tenant (Covenants) Act 1995, section 10)

To [name and address]:...
....

And [name and address]: ....
....

1.   This notice is given under section 10 of the Landlord and Tenant (Covenants) Act 1995.

2.   It relates to (address and description of property)...

....

let under a lease dated....................................... and made between ....

....

....

of which I/we am/are the landlord (*"Landlord", for these purposes, includes any person for the time being entitled to enforce the obligations in question (for example, a management company)*).

3.   You have applied for me/us to be bound by your agreement to divide liability between you with effect from the [proposed transfer] [transfer on ....] (*Delete alternative as appropriate*) of part of the property comprised in the tenancy.

4.   (*The landlord should select one version of paragraph 4 and cross out the other*)

I/we agree to be bound by your agreement with effect from the date of the transfer.

{see Note 1}

OR

4.   I/we do **not** consider it reasonable that I/we should be bound by your agreement, and object to being so bound. {*see Notes 2 and 3*}

6.   All correspondence about this notice should be sent to the landlord/landlord's agent at the address given below.

Date................................ Signature of landlord/landlord's agent....................................

Name and address of landlord ....

....

....

[Name and address of agent ....

....

....]

Notes to Part II

Agreement to be bound

1.   If the landlord has indicated agreement in paragraph 3 of the notice, he will

automatically be bound by your agreement, with effect from the date of the transfer. Any subsequent landlord will also be bound.

Objection to being bound

2.   If the landlord has indicated an objection in paragraph 3 of the notice, he will not be bound by your agreement unless *either* the landlord later withdraws his objection *or* you apply to the County Court to declare that it is reasonable for him to be bound, and the court so declares.

Validity of notice of objection

3.   A notice of objection by the landlord is only valid if he has given it to each of you within the period of four weeks beginning with the date on which you gave him your notice applying for your agreement to become binding on him. If you are in any doubt, you should seek advice before applying to the court.

[1252]

FORM 8

PART I

Joint Notice by Landlord and Assignee for Binding Apportionment of Liability under Non-Attributable Landlord Covenants of a Tenancy on Assignment of Part of Reversion

(**Landlord and Tenant (Covenants) Act 1995, sections 9 and 10**)

To [name and address]:...
....

IMPORTANT—THIS NOTICE IS INTENDED TO AFFECT THE WAY IN WHICH YOU CAN ENFORCE THE LANDLORD'S OBLIGATIONS UNDER THE TENANCY AS BETWEEN THE LANDLORD AND THE NEW LANDLORD. IF YOU CONSIDER THAT THERE IS GOOD REASON WHY YOU SHOULD **NOT** BE BOUND BY THEIR AGREEMENT, YOU MUST ACT QUICKLY. READ THE NOTICE AND ALL THE NOTES OVERLEAF CAREFULLY. IF YOU ARE IN ANY DOUBT ABOUT THE ACTION YOU SHOULD TAKE, SEEK ADVICE IMMEDIATELY, FOR INSTANCE FROM A SOLICITOR OR CITIZENS ADVICE BUREAU.

1.   This notice is given under section 10 of the Landlord and Tenant (Covenants) Act 1995. {*see Note 1*}

2.   It relates to (address and description of property)...

let under a lease dated.. and made between ....
....
....

of which you are the tenant.

3.   We are the parties to a [proposed transfer] [transfer on ....] (*Delete alternative as appropriate*) of the landlord's interest in part of the property comprised in the tenancy, namely

We are jointly and severally liable to perform the obligation(s) specified in the attached Schedule, and have agreed to divide that liability between us in the manner specified in the Schedule. (*The Schedule must be in writing, and must specify the nature of the obligation, the term or condition of the Lease or other instrument under which it arises and the manner in which liability to perform it is divided under the agreement. It may be helpful to attach a copy of the agreement to the notice*) We wish this agreement to be binding on you as well as between us, with effect from the date of the transfer. {*see Note 2*}

4.   If you consider that it is reasonable for you to be bound by this agreement, you do not need to do anything, but it would help us if you notify us using Part II of this Form. {*see Note 3*}

659

5.   If you do **not** consider it reasonable for you to be bound by this agreement, you **must** notify both of us of your objection, using Part II of this Form, within the period of **FOUR WEEKS** beginning with the giving of this notice. You may withdraw your objection at any time by notifying us in writing. *[see Notes 4–6]*

6.   All correspondence about this notice should be copied, and one copy sent to each of the parties to the agreement, at the addresses given below.

Signature of landlord/landlord's agent..

Name and address of landlord ....

....

....

[Name and address of agent ....

....

....]

Signature of new landlord/agent...

Name and address of new landlord ....

....

....

[Name and address of agent ....

....

....]

Date...

Notes to Part I

Apportionment of liability

1.   The landlord is about to transfer, or has just transferred, part of his interest to a new landlord, but they are jointly and severally liable for a particular obligation or obligations covering the whole of the property. They have agreed to divide that liability between them, and are applying for you as tenant to be bound as well, so that you can only enforce the liability against each of them as set out in their agreement. If you are bound, any subsequent tenant to whom you may transfer your interest will also be bound. You have a number of options: you may expressly agree to be bound; you may object to being bound (with the option of withdrawing your objection later); or you may do nothing, in which case you will automatically be bound, with effect from the date of the transfer, once four weeks have elapsed from the date of the giving of the notice. If you choose to object, you must act within four weeks of the giving of the notice.

Validity of notice

2.   This notice must be given either before the transfer or within the period of four weeks beginning with the date of the transfer. If the notice has been given late, it is not valid. You should read Note 4 below concerning the date of the giving of the notice.

Agreeing to be bound

3.   If you are content to be bound, you may notify the landlord and new landlord using Part II of this Form (sending a copy to each of them), and all of you will be bound with effect from the date of the transfer. If you do this, you may not later change your mind and object.

Objecting to being bound

4.   If you think that it is not reasonable for you to be bound, you may object by notifying the landlord and new landlord, using Part II of this Form (sending a copy to each of them). You must, however, do this within four weeks of the date of the giving of the notice. The date of the giving of the notice may not be the date written on the notice or the date on which you actually saw it. It may, for

instance, be the date on which the notice was delivered through the post to your last address known to the person giving the notice. If there has been any delay in your seeing this notice you may need to act very quickly. If you are in any doubt, you should seek advice immediately. If you change your mind after objecting, you may consent instead, at any time, by notifying *both* the landlord and new landlord *in writing* that you now consent to be bound and that your objection is withdrawn.

5. If you object within the time limit, the apportionment will only bind you if *either* the landlord and new landlord apply to a court and the court decides that it is reasonable for you to be bound, *or* you withdraw your objection by notice in writing as explained in Note 4 above.

6. In deciding whether to object, you should bear in mind that if the court finds that it is reasonable for you to be bound, *or* if you withdraw your objection late, you may have to pay costs.

[1253]

PART II

Tenant's Response to Joint Notice by Landlord and Assignee Seeking Binding Apportionment of Liability under Non-Attributable Landlord Covenants of a Tenancy on Assignment of Part of Reversion

(Landlord and Tenant (Covenants) Act 1995, section 10)

To [name and address]: ....
....
And [name and address]: ....
....

1. This notice is given under section 10 of the Landlord and Tenant (Covenants) Act 1995.

2. It relates to (address and description of property)...

let under a lease dated.................................. and made between ....
....
....

of which I/we am/are the tenant.

3. You have applied for me/us to be bound by your agreement to divide liability between you with effect from the [proposed transfer] [transfer on ....] (*Delete alternative as appropriate*) of part of the landlord's interest in the property comprised in the tenancy.

4. (*The tenant should select one version of paragraph 4 and cross out the other*)

I/we agree to be bound by your agreement with effect from the date of the transfer.
{see Note 1}

OR

4. I/we do **not** consider it reasonable that I/we should be bound by your agreement, and object to being so bound. *{see Notes 2 and 3}*

6. All correspondence about this notice should be sent to the tenant/tenant's agent at the address given below.

Date............................ Signature of tenant/tenant's agent..

Name and address of tenant...
....
....

[Name and address of agent ....

....

....]

Notes to Part II

Agreement to be bound

1.　　If the tenant has indicated agreement in paragraph 3 of the notice, he will automatically be bound by your agreement, with effect from the date of the transfer. Any subsequent tenant will also be bound.

Objection to being bound

2.　　If the tenant has indicated an objection in paragraph 3 of the notice, he will not be bound by your agreement unless *either* the tenant later withdraws his objection *or* you apply to the County Court to declare that it is reasonable for him to be bound, and the court so declares.

Validity of notice of objection

3.　　A notice of objection by the tenant is only valid if he has given it to each of you within the period of four weeks beginning with the date on which you gave him your notice applying for your agreement to become binding on him. If you are in any doubt, you should seek advice before applying to the court.

[1254]

AGRICULTURAL HOLDINGS (FEE) REGULATIONS 1996

(SI 1996/337)

NOTES

Made: 19 February 1996.
Authority: Agricultural Holdings Act 1986, ss 22(4), 96(1), Sch 11, para 1(2).

1　Title and commencement

These Regulations may be cited as the Agricultural Holdings (Fee) Regulations 1996 and shall come into force on 1st March 1996.

[1255]

2　Prescribed fee

The fee for an application to the President of the Royal Institution of Chartered Surveyors–
　　(a)　for a person to be appointed by him under section 22(2) of the Agricultural Holdings Act 1986, or
　　(b)　for an arbitrator to be appointed by him under [section 84(2) of] that Act
is hereby increased from £70 to £115.

[1256]

NOTES

Words in square brackets in para (b) substituted by the Regulatory Reform (Agricultural Tenancies) (England and Wales) Order 2006, SI 2006/2805, art 18, Sch 1, Pt 2, para 3.

3　(*Revokes the Agricultural Holdings (Fee) Regulations 1985, SI 1985/1967.*)

CIVIL PROCEDURE RULES 1998

(SI 1998/3132)

NOTES

Made: 10 December 1998.
Authority: Civil Procedure Act 1997, ss 1, 2.

1.1–7.12   *((Pts 1–7) outside the scope of this work.)*

PART 8
ALTERNATIVE PROCEDURE FOR CLAIMS

8.1   Types of claim in which Part 8 procedure may be followed

(1)   The Part 8 procedure is the procedure set out in this Part.

(2)   A claimant may use the Part 8 procedure where—
   (a)   he seeks the court's decision on a question which is unlikely to involve a substantial dispute of fact; or
   (b)   paragraph (6) applies.

(3)   The court may at any stage order the claim to continue as if the claimant had not used the Part 8 procedure and, if it does so, the court may give any directions it considers appropriate.

(4)   Paragraph (2) does not apply if a practice direction provides that the Part 8 procedure may not be used in relation to the type of claim in question.

(5)   Where the claimant uses the Part 8 procedure he may not obtain default judgment under Part 12.

(6)   A rule or practice direction may, in relation to a specified type of proceedings—
   (a)   require or permit the use of the Part 8 procedure; and
   (b)   disapply or modify any of the rules set out in this Part as they apply to those proceedings.

(Rule 8.9 provides for other modifications to the general rules where the Part 8 procedure is being used).

[1256A]

8.2   Contents of the claim form

Where the claimant uses the Part 8 procedure the claim form must state—

    (a)   that this Part applies;

    (b)

        (i)   the question which the claimant wants the court to decide; or

        (ii)   the remedy which the claimant is seeking and the legal basis for the claim to that remedy;

    (c)   if the claim is being made under an enactment, what that enactment is;

    (d)   if the claimant is claiming in a representative capacity, what that capacity is; and

    (e)   if the defendant is sued in a representative capacity, what that capacity is.

(Part 22 provides for the claim form to be verified by a statement of truth).

(Rule 7.5 provides for service of the claim form).

[(The costs practice direction sets out the information about a funding arrangement to be provided with the claim form where the claimant intends to seek to recover an additional liability).

("Funding arrangement" and "additional liability" are defined in rule 43.2).]

            [1256B]

NOTES

Third and fourth cross-references inserted by the Civil Procedure (Amendment No 3) Rules 2000, SI 2000/1317, r 5.

[8.2A   Issue of claim form without naming defendants

    (1)   A practice direction may set out the circumstances in which a claim form may be issued under this Part without naming a defendant.

    (2)   The practice direction may set out those cases in which an application for permission must be made by application notice before the claim form is issued.]

    (3)   The application notice for permission—

    (a)   need not be served on any other person; and

    (b)   must be accompanied by a copy of the claim form that the applicant proposes to issue.

    (4)   Where the court gives permission it will give directions about the future management of the claim.]

            [1256C]

NOTES

Inserted by the Civil Procedure (Amendment) Rules 2000, SI 2000/221, r 5.

Paras (1), (2): substituted by the Civil Procedure (Amendment) Rules 2001, SI 2001/256, r 5.

8.3   Acknowledgment of service

    (1)   The defendant must—

    (a)   file an acknowledgment of service in the relevant practice form not more than 14 days after service of the claim form; and

    (b)   serve the acknowledgment of service on the claimant and any other party.

    (2)   The acknowledgment of service must state—

    (a)   whether the defendant contests the claim; and

    (b)   if the defendant seeks a different remedy from that set out in the claim form, what that remedy is.

    (3)   The following rules of Part 10 (acknowledgment of service) apply—

    (a)   rule 10.3(2) (exceptions to the period for filing an acknowledgment of service); and

    (b)   rule 10.5 (contents of acknowledgment of service).

    (4)   ...

[(The costs practice direction sets out the information about a funding arrangement to be provided with the acknowledgment of service where the defendant intends to seek to recover an additional liability).

("Funding arrangement" and "additional liability" are defined in rule 43.2).]

            [1256D]

NOTES

Para (4): revoked by The Civil Procedure (Amendment No 5) Rules 2001, SI 2001/4015, r 11.
First and second cross-references inserted by the Civil Procedure (Amendment No 3) Rules 2000, SI 2000/1317, r 6.

8.4 Consequence of not filing an acknowledgment of service

(1)   This rule applies where—
    (a)   the defendant has failed to file an acknowledgment of service; and
    (b)   the time period for doing so has expired.

(2)   The defendant may attend the hearing of the claim but may not take part in the hearing unless the court gives permission.

[1256E]

8.5 Filing and serving written evidence

(1)   The claimant must file any written evidence on which he intends to rely when he files his claim form.

(2)   The claimant's evidence must be served on the defendant with the claim form.

(3)   A defendant who wishes to rely on written evidence must file it when he files his acknowledgment of service.

(4)   If he does so, he must also, at the same time, serve a copy of his evidence on the other parties.

(5)   The claimant may, within 14 days of service of the defendant's evidence on him, file further written evidence in reply.

(6)   If he does so, he must also, within the same time limit, serve a copy of his evidence on the other parties.

(7)   The claimant may rely on the matters set out in his claim form as evidence under this rule if the claim form is verified by a statement of truth.

[1256F]

8.6 Evidence—general

(1)   No written evidence may be relied on at the hearing of the claim unless—
    (a)   it has been served in accordance with rule 8.5; or
    (b)   the court gives permission.

(2)   The court may require or permit a party to give oral evidence at the hearing.

(3)   The court may give directions requiring the attendance for cross-examination $^{(GL)}$ of a witness who has given written evidence.

(Rule 32.1 contains a general power for the court to control evidence).

[1256G]

8.7 Part 20 claims

Where the Part 8 procedure is used, Part 20 (counterclaims and other additional claims) applies except that a party may not make a Part 20 claim (as defined by rule 20.2) without the court's permission.

[1256H]

8.8 Procedure where defendant objects to use of the Part 8 procedure

(1)   Where the defendant contends that the Part 8 procedure should not be used because—
    (a)   there is a substantial dispute of fact; and
    (b)   the use of the Part 8 procedure is not required or permitted by a rule or practice direction, he must state his reasons when he files his acknowledgment of service.

(Rule 8.5 requires a defendant who wishes to rely on written evidence to file it when he files his acknowledgment of service).

(2)   When the court receives the acknowledgment of service and any written evidence it will give directions as to the future management of the case.

(Rule 8.1(3) allows the court to make an order that the claim continue as if the claimant had not used the Part 8 procedure).

[1256I]

8.9 Modifications to the general rules

Where the Part 8 procedure is followed—
  (a)   provision is made in this Part for the matters which must be stated in the claim form and the defendant is not required to file a defence and therefore—
      (i)   Part 16 (statements of case) does not apply;
      (ii)   Part 15 (defence and reply) does not apply;
      (iii) any time limit in these Rules which prevents the parties from taking a step before a defence is filed does not apply; and
      (iv)   the requirement under rule 7.8 to serve on the defendant a form for defending the claim does not apply;
  (b)   the claimant may not obtain judgment by request on an admission and therefore—
      (i)   rules 14.4 to 14.7 do not apply; and
      (ii)   the requirement under rule 7.8 to serve on the defendant a form for admitting the claim does not apply; and
  (c)   the claim shall be treated as allocated to the multi-track and therefore Part 26 does not apply.

[1256J]

9.1–55.28   (*(Pts 9–55) outside the scope of this work.*)

[PART 56
LANDLORD AND TENANT CLAIMS AND MISCELLANEOUS PROVISIONS
ABOUT LAND

I—LANDLORD AND TENANT CLAIMS

NOTES
For the Practice Directions supplementing this Part, see **[1256N]**, **[1256O]**.

56.1 Scope and interpretation

  (1)   In this Section of this Part "landlord and tenant claim" means a claim under—
  (a)   the Landlord and Tenant Act 1927;
  (b)   the Leasehold Property (Repairs) Act 1938;
  (c)   the Landlord and Tenant Act 1954;
  (d)   the Landlord and Tenant Act 1985; or
  (e)   the Landlord and Tenant Act 1987.

  (2)   A practice direction may set out special provisions with regard to any particular category of landlord and tenant claim.]

[1256K]

NOTES
This Part inserted by the Civil Procedure (Amendment) Rules 2001, SI 2001/256, r 18, Sch 2, except in relation to claim forms issued before 15 October 2001.

[56.2 Starting the claim

  (1)   The claim must be started in the county court for the district in which the land is situated unless [paragraph (2) applies] or an enactment provides otherwise.

  (2)   The claim may be started in the High Court if the claimant files with his claim form a certificate stating the reasons for bringing the claim in that court verified by a statement of truth in accordance with rule 22.1(1).

  (3)   The practice direction refers to circumstances which may justify starting the claim in the High Court.

  (4)   ...]

[1256L]

NOTES

Inserted as noted to r 56.1 at **[1256K]**.
Para (1): words in square brackets substituted by the Civil Procedure (Amendment) Rules 2004,
SI 2004/1306, r 15(a).
Para (4): revoked by SI 2004/1306, r 15(b).

[56.3 Claims for a new tenancy under section 24 and for the termination of a tenancy under section 29(2) of the Landlord and Tenant Act 1954

(1)   This rule applies to a claim for a new tenancy under section 24 and to a claim for the termination of a tenancy under section 29(2) of the 1954 Act.

(2)   In this rule—
   (a)   "the 1954 Act" means the Landlord and Tenant Act 1954;
   (b)   "an unopposed claim" means a claim for a new tenancy under section 24 of the 1954 Act in circumstances where the grant of a new tenancy is not opposed;
   (c)   "an opposed claim" means a claim for—
      (i)   a new tenancy under section 24 of the 1954 Act in circumstances where the grant of a new tenancy is opposed; or
      (ii)   the termination of a tenancy under section 29(2) of the 1954 Act.

(3)   Where the claim is an unopposed claim—
   (a)   the claimant must use the Part 8 procedure, but the following rules do not apply—
      (i)   rule 8.5; and
      (ii)   rule 8.6;
   (b)   the claim form must be served within 2 months after the date of issue and rules 7.5 and 7.6 are modified accordingly; and
   (c)   the court will give directions about the future management of the claim following receipt of the acknowledgment of service.

(4)   Where the claim is an opposed claim—
   (a)   the claimant must use the Part 7 procedure; but
   (b)   the claim form must be served within 2 months after the date of issue, and rules 7.5 and 7.6 are modified accordingly.

(The practice direction to this Part contains provisions about evidence, including expert evidence in opposed claims).]

[1256M]

NOTES

Commencement: 1 June 2004.
Inserted as noted to r 56.1 at **[1256K]**.
Substituted by the Civil Procedure (Amendment) Rules 2004, SI 2004/1306, r 16.

56.4–75.11   *((Pts 56(II)–75) outside the scope of this work.)*

PRACTICE DIRECTION—LANDLORD AND TENANT CLAIMS AND MISCELLANEOUS PROVISIONS ABOUT LAND

NOTES

This Practice Direction supplements the Civil Procedure Rules, Pt 56 at **[1256K]** et seq.

SECTION I—LANDLORD AND TENANT CLAIMS

1.1   In this section of this practice direction—
   (1)   "the 1927 Act" means the Landlord and Tenant Act 1927;
   (2)   "the 1954 Act" means the Landlord and Tenant Act 1954;
   (3)   "the 1985 Act" means the Landlord and Tenant Act 1985; and
   (4)   "the 1987 Act" means the Landlord and Tenant Act 1987.

PART II
STATUTORY INSTRUMENTS

56.2—Starting the Claim

2.1   Subject to paragraph 2.1A, the claimant in a landlord and tenant claim must use the Part 8 procedure as modified by Part 56 and this practice direction.

2.1   A   Where the landlord and tenant claim is a claim for—
(1)   a new tenancy under section 24 of the 1954 Act in circumstances where the grant of a new tenancy is opposed; or
(2)   the termination of a tenancy under section 29(2) of the 1954 Act, the claimant must use the Part 7 procedure as modified by Part 56 and this practice direction.

2.2   Except where the county court does not have jurisdiction, landlord and tenant claims should normally be brought in the county court. Only exceptional circumstances justify starting a claim in the High Court.

2.3   If a claimant starts a claim in the High Court and the court decides that it should have been started in the county court, the court will normally either strike the claim out or transfer it to the county court on its own initiative. This is likely to result in delay and the court will normally disallow the costs of starting the claim in the High Court and of any transfer.

2.4   Circumstances which may, in an appropriate case, justify starting a claim in the High Court are if—
(1)   there are complicated disputes of fact; or
(2)   there are points of law of general importance.

2.5   The value of the property and the amount of any financial claim may be relevant circumstances, but these factors alone will not normally justify starting the claim in the High Court.

2.6   A landlord and tenant claim started in the High Court must be brought in the Chancery Division.

Claims for a New Tenancy Under Section 24 and Termination of A Tenancy Under Section 29(2) of the 1954 Act

3.1   This paragraph applies to a claim for a new tenancy under section 24 and termination of a tenancy under section 29(2) of the 1954 Act where rule 56.3 applies and in this paragraph—
(1)   "an unopposed claim" means a claim for a new tenancy under section 24 of the 1954 Act in circumstances where the grant of a new tenancy is not opposed;
(2)   "an opposed claim" means a claim for—
(a)   a new tenancy under section 24 of the 1954 Act in circumstances where the grant of a new tenancy is opposed; or
(b)   the termination of a tenancy under section 29(2) of the 1954 Act; and
(3)   "grounds of opposition" means—
(a)   the grounds specified in section 30(1) of the 1954 Act on which a landlord may oppose an application for a new tenancy under section 24(1) of the 1954 Act or make an application under section 29(2) of the 1954 Act; or
(b)   any other basis on which the landlord asserts that a new tenancy ought not to be granted.

Precedence of claim forms where there is more than one application to the court under section 24(1) or section 29(2) of the 1954 Act

3.2   Where more than one application to the court under section 24(1) or section 29(2) of the 1954 Act is made, the following provisions shall apply—
(1)   once an application to the court under section 24(1) of the 1954 Act has been served on a defendant, no further application to the court in respect of the same tenancy whether under section 24(1) or section 29(2) of the 1954 Act may be served by that defendant without the permission of the court;
(2)   if more than one application to the court under section 24(1) of the 1954 Act in respect of the same tenancy is served on the same day, any landlord's application shall stand stayed until further order of the court;
(3)   if applications to the court under both section 24(1) and section 29(2) of the 1954 Act in respect of the same tenancy are served on the same day, any tenant's application shall stand stayed until further order of the court; and
(4)   if a defendant is served with an application under section 29(2) of the 1954 Act ("the section 29(2) application") which was issued at a time when an application to the court had already been made by that defendant in respect of the same tenancy under section 24(1) of the 1954 Act ("the section 24(1) application"), the service of the

section 29(2) application shall be deemed to be a notice under rule 7.7 requiring service or discontinuance of the section 24(1) application within a period of 14 days after the service of the section 29(2) application.

Defendant where the claimant is the tenant making a claim for a new tenancy under section 24 of the 1954 Act

3.3   Where a claim for a new tenancy under section 24 of the 1954 Act is made by a tenant, the person who, in relation to the claimant's current tenancy, is the landlord as defined in section 44 of the 1954 Act must be a defendant.

Contents of the claim form in all cases

3.4   The claim form must contain details of—
(1)   the property to which the claim relates;
(2)   the particulars of the current tenancy (including date, parties and duration), the current rent (if not the original rent) and the date and method of termination;
(3)   every notice or request given or made under sections 25 or 26 of the 1954 Act; and
(4)   the expiry date of—
    (a)   the statutory period under section 29A(2) of the 1954 Act; or
    (b)   any agreed extended period made under section 29B(1) or 29B(2) of the 1954 Act.

Claim form where the claimant is the tenant making a claim for a new tenancy under section 24 of the 1954 Act

3.5   Where the claimant is the tenant making a claim for a new tenancy under section 24 of the 1954 Act, in addition to the details specified in paragraph 3.4, the claim form must contain details of—
(1)   the nature of the business carried on at the property;
(2)   whether the claimant relies on section 23(1A), 41 or 42 of the 1954 Act and, if so, the basis on which he does so;
(3)   whether the claimant relies on section 31A of the 1954 Act and, if so, the basis on which he does so;
(4)   whether any, and if so what part, of the property comprised in the tenancy is occupied neither by the claimant nor by a person employed by the claimant for the purpose of the claimant's business;
(5)   the claimant's proposed terms of the new tenancy; and
(6)   the name and address of—
    (a)   anyone known to the claimant who has an interest in the reversion in the property (whether immediate or in not more than 15 years) on the termination of the claimant's current tenancy and who is likely to be affected by the grant of a new tenancy; or
    (b)   if the claimant does not know of anyone specified by sub-paragraph (6)(a), anyone who has a freehold interest in the property.

3.6   The claim form must be served on the persons referred to in paragraph 3.5(6)(a) or (b) as appropriate.

Claim form where the claimant is the landlord making a claim for a new tenancy under section 24 of the 1954 Act

3.7   Where the claimant is the landlord making a claim for a new tenancy under section 24 of the 1954 Act, in addition to the details specified in paragraph 3.4, the claim form must contain details of—
(1)   the claimant's proposed terms of the new tenancy;
(2)   whether the claimant is aware that the defendant's tenancy is one to which section 32(2) of the 1954 Act applies and, if so, whether the claimant requires that any new tenancy shall be a tenancy of the whole of the property comprised in the defendant's current tenancy or just of the holding as defined by section 23(3) of the 1954 Act; and
(3)   the name and address of—
    (a)   anyone known to the claimant who has an interest in the reversion in the property (whether immediate or in not more than 15 years) on the termination of the claimant's current tenancy and who is likely to be affected by the grant of a new tenancy; or
    (b)   if the claimant does not know of anyone specified by sub-paragraph (3)(a), anyone who has a freehold interest in the property.

PART II STATUTORY INSTRUMENTS

3.8   The claim form must be served on the persons referred to in paragraph 3.7(3)(a) or (b) as appropriate.

Claim form where the claimant is the landlord making an application for the termination of a tenancy under section 29(2) of the 1954 Act

3.9   Where the claimant is the landlord making an application for the termination of a tenancy under section 29(2) of the 1954 Act, in addition to the details specified in paragraph 3.4, the claim form must contain—
  (1)   the claimant's grounds of opposition;
  (2)   full details of those grounds of opposition; and
  (3)   the terms of a new tenancy that the claimant proposes in the event that his claim fails.

Acknowledgment of service where the claim is an unopposed claim and where the claimant is the tenant

3.10   Where the claim is an unopposed claim and the claimant is the tenant, the acknowledgment of service is to be in form N210 and must state with particulars—
  (1)   whether, if a new tenancy is granted, the defendant objects to any of the terms proposed by the claimant and if so—
      (a)   the terms to which he objects; and
      (b)   the terms that he proposes in so far as they differ from those proposed by the claimant;
  (2)   whether the defendant is a tenant under a lease having less than 15 years unexpired at the date of the termination of the claimant's current tenancy and, if so, the name and address of any person who, to the knowledge of the defendant, has an interest in the reversion in the property expectant (whether immediate or in not more than 15 years from that date) on the termination of the defendant's tenancy;
  (3)   the name and address of any person having an interest in the property who is likely to be affected by the grant of a new tenancy; and
  (4)   if the claimant's current tenancy is one to which section 32(2) of the 1954 Act applies, whether the defendant requires that any new tenancy shall be a tenancy of the whole of the property comprised in the claimant's current tenancy.

Acknowledgment of service where the claim is an unopposed claim and the claimant is the landlord

3.11   Where the claim is an unopposed claim and the claimant is the landlord, the acknowledgment of service is to be in form N210 and must state with particulars—
  (1)   the nature of the business carried on at the property;
  (2)   if the defendant relies on section 23(1A), 41 or 42 of the 1954 Act, the basis on which he does so;
  (3)   whether any, and if so what part, of the property comprised in the tenancy is occupied neither by the defendant nor by a person employed by the defendant for the purpose of the defendant's business;
  (4)   the name and address of—
      (a)   anyone known to the defendant who has an interest in the reversion in the property (whether immediate or in not more than 15 years) on the termination of the defendant's current tenancy and who is likely to be affected by the grant of a new tenancy; or
      (b)   if the defendant does not know of anyone specified by sub-paragraph (4)(a), anyone who has a freehold interest in the property; and
  (5)   whether, if a new tenancy is granted, the defendant objects to any of the terms proposed by the claimant and, if so—
      (a)   the terms to which he objects; and
      (b)   the terms that he proposes in so far as they differ from those proposed by the claimant.

Acknowledgment of service and defence where the claim is an opposed claim and where the claimant is the tenant

3.12   Where the claim is an opposed claim and the claimant is the tenant—
  (1)   the acknowledgment of service is to be in form N9; and
  (2)   in his defence the defendant must state with particulars—
      (a)   the defendant's grounds of opposition;
      (b)   full details of those grounds of opposition;
      (c)   whether, if a new tenancy is granted, the defendant objects to any of the terms proposed by the claimant and if so—

      (i)   the terms to which he objects; and

      (ii)   the terms that he proposes in so far as they differ from those proposed by the claimant;

(d)   whether the defendant is a tenant under a lease having less than 15 years unexpired at the date of the termination of the claimant's current tenancy and, if so, the name and address of any person who, to the knowledge of the defendant, has an interest in the reversion in the property expectant (whether immediately or in not more than 15 years from that date) on the termination of the defendant's tenancy;

(e)   the name and address of any person having an interest in the property who is likely to be affected by the grant of a new tenancy; and

(f)   if the claimant's current tenancy is one to which section 32(2) of the 1954 Act applies, whether the defendant requires that any new tenancy shall be a tenancy of the whole of the property comprised in the claimant's current tenancy.

Acknowledgment of service and defence where the claimant is the landlord making an application for the termination of a tenancy under section 29(2) of the 1954 Act

3.13   Where the claim is an opposed claim and the claimant is the landlord—

(1)   the acknowledgment of service is to be in form N9; and

(2)   in his defence the defendant must state with particulars—

    (a)   whether the defendant relies on section 23(1A), 41 or 42 of the 1954 Act and, if so, the basis on which he does so;

    (b)   whether the defendant relies on section 31A of the 1954 Act and, if so, the basis on which he does so; and

    (c)   the terms of the new tenancy that the defendant would propose in the event that the claimant's claim to terminate the current tenancy fails.

Evidence in an unopposed claim

3.14   Where the claim is an unopposed claim, no evidence need be filed unless and until the court directs it to be filed.

Evidence in an opposed claim

3.15   Where the claim is an opposed claim, evidence (including expert evidence) must be filed by the parties as the court directs and the landlord shall be required to file his evidence first.

Grounds of opposition to be tried as a preliminary issue

3.16   Unless in the circumstances of the case it is unreasonable to do so, any grounds of opposition shall be tried as a preliminary issue.

Applications for interim rent under section 24A to 24D of the 1954 Act

3.17   Where proceedings have already been commenced for the grant of a new tenancy or the termination of an existing tenancy, the claim for interim rent under section 24A of the 1954 Act shall be made in those proceedings by—

(1)   the claim form;

(2)   the acknowledgment of service or defence; or

(3)   an application on notice under Part 23.

3.18   Any application under section 24D(3) of the 1954 Act shall be made by an application on notice under Part 23 in the original proceedings.

3.19   Where no other proceedings have been commenced for the grant of a new tenancy or termination of an existing tenancy or where such proceedings have been disposed of, an application for interim rent under section 24A of the 1954 Act shall be made under the procedure in Part 8 and the claim form shall include details of—

(1)   the property to which the claim relates;

(2)   the particulars of the relevant tenancy (including date, parties and duration) and the current rent (if not the original rent);

(3)   every notice or request given or made under sections 25 or 26 of the 1954 Act;

(4)   if the relevant tenancy has terminated, the date and mode of termination; and

(5)   if the relevant tenancy has been terminated and the landlord has granted a new tenancy of the property to the tenant—

(a)   particulars of the new tenancy (including date, parties and duration) and the rent; and

(b)   in a case where section 24C(2) of the 1954 Act applies but the claimant seeks a different rent under section 24C(3) of that Act, particulars and matters on which the claimant relies as satisfying section 24C(3).

Other Claims Under Part II of the 1954 Act

4.1   The mesne landlord to whose consent a claim for the determination of any question arising under paragraph 4(3) of Schedule 6 to the 1954 Act shall be made a defendant to the claim.

4.2   If any dispute as to the rateable value of any holding has been referred under section 37(5) of the 1954 Act to the Commissioners of Inland Revenue for decision by a valuation officer, any document purporting to be a statement of the valuation officer of his decision is admissible as evidence of the matters contained in it.

Claim for Compensation for Improvements Under Part I of the 1927 Act

5.1   This paragraph applies to a claim under Part I of the 1927 Act.

The claim form

5.2   The claim form must include details of:
(1)   the nature of the claim or the matter to be determined;
(2)   the property to which the claim relates;
(3)   the nature of the business carried on at the property;
(4)   particulars of the lease or agreement for the tenancy including:
   (a)   the names and addresses of the parties to the lease or agreement;
   (b)   its duration;
   (c)   the rent payable;
   (d)   details of any assignment or other devolution of the lease or agreement;
(5)   the date and mode of termination of the tenancy;
(6)   if the claimant has left the property, the date on which he did so;
(7)   particulars of the improvement or proposed improvement to which the claim relates; and
(8)   if the claim is for payment of compensation, the amount claimed.

5.3   The court will fix a date for a hearing when it issues the claim form.

Defendant

5.4   The claimant's immediate landlord must be a defendant to the claim.

5.5   The defendant must immediately serve a copy of the claim form and any document served with it and of his acknowledgment of service on his immediate landlord. If the person so served is not the freeholder, he must serve a copy of these documents on his landlord and so on from landlord to landlord.

Evidence

5.6   Evidence need not be filed—with the claim form or acknowledgment of service.

Certification under section 3 of the 1927 Act

5.7   If the court intends to certify under section 3 of the 1927 Act that an improvement is a proper improvement or has been duly executed, it shall do so by way of an order.

Compensation under section 1 or 8 of the 1927 Act

5.8   A claim under section 1(1) or 8(1) of the 1927 Act must be in writing, signed by the claimant, his solicitor or agent and include details of
(1)   the name and address of the claimant and of the landlord against whom the claim is made;
(2)   the property to which the claim relates;
(3)   the nature of the business carried on at the property;
(4)   a concise statement of the nature of the claim;
(5)   particulars of the improvement, including the date when it was completed and costs; and
(6)   the amount claimed.

5.9   A mesne landlord must immediately serve a copy of the claim on his immediate superior landlord. If the person so served is not the freeholder, he must serve a copy of the document on his landlord and so on from landlord to landlord.

(Paragraphs 5.8 and 5.9 provide the procedure for making claims under section 1(1) and 8(1) of the 1927 Act—these "claims" do not, at this stage, relate to proceedings before the court)

Transfer to Leasehold Valuation Tribunal Under 1985 Act

6.1   If a question is ordered to be transferred to a leasehold valuation tribunal for determination under section 31C of the 1985 Act the court will:
   (1)   send notice of the transfer to all parties to the claim; and
   (2)   send to the leasehold valuation tribunal:
      (a)   copies certified by the district judge of all entries in the records of the court relating to the question;
      (b)   the order of transfer; and
      (c)   all documents filed in the claim relating to the question.

(Paragraph 6.1 no longer applies to proceedings in England but continues to apply to proceedings in Wales)

Claim to Enforce Obligation Under Part I of the 1987 Act

7.1   A copy of the notice served under section 19(2)(a) of the 1987 Act must accompany the claim form seeking an order under section 19(1) of that Act.

Claim for Acquisition Order Under Section 28 of the 1987 Act

8.1   This paragraph applies to a claim for an acquisition order under section 28 of the 1987 Act.

Claim form

8.2   The claim form must:
   (1)   identify the property to which the claim relates and give details to show that section 25 of the 1987 Act applies;
   (2)   give details of the claimants to show that they constitute the requisite majority of qualifying tenants;
   (3)   state the names and addresses of the claimants and of the landlord of the property, or, if the landlord cannot be found or his identity ascertained, the steps taken to find him or ascertain his identity;
   (4)   state the name and address of:
      (a)   the person nominated by the claimants for the purposes of Part III of the 1987 Act; and
      (b)   every person known to the claimants who is likely to be affected by the application, including (but not limited to), the other tenants of flats contained in the property (whether or not they could have made a claim), any mortgagee or superior landlord of the landlord, and any tenants' association (within the meaning of section 29 of the 1985 Act); and
   (5)   state the grounds of the claim.

Notice under section 27

8.3   A copy of the notice served on the landlord under section 27 of the 1987 Act must accompany the claim form unless the court has dispensed with the requirement to serve a notice under section 27(3) of the 1987 Act.

Defendants

8.4   The landlord of the property (and the nominated person, if he is not a claimant) must be defendants.

Service

8.5   A copy of the claim form must be served on each of the persons named by the claimant under paragraph 8.2(4)(b) together with a notice that he may apply to be made a party.

PART II
STATUTORY INSTRUMENTS

Payment into court by nominated person

8.6   If the nominated person pays money into court in accordance with an order under section 33(1) of the 1987 Act, he must file a copy of the certificate of the surveyor selected under section 33(2)(a) of that Act.

Claim for an Order Varying Leases Under the 1987 Act

9.1   This paragraph applies to a claim for an order under section 38 or section 40 of the 1987 Act.

Claim form

9.2   The claim form must state:
  (1)   the name and address of the claimant and of the other current parties to the lease or leases to which the claim relates;
  (2)   the date of the lease or leases, the property to which they relate, any relevant terms and the variation sought;
  (3)   the name and address of every person known to the claimant who is likely to be affected by the claim, including (but not limited to), the other tenants of flats contained in premises of which the relevant property forms a part, any previous parties to the lease, any mortgagee or superior landlord of the landlord, any mortgagee of the claimant and any tenants' association (within the meaning of section 29 of the 1985 Act); and
  (4)   the grounds of the claim.

Defendants

9.3   The other current parties to the lease must be defendants.

Service

9.4   A copy of the claim form must be served on each of the persons named under paragraph 9.2(3).

9.5   If the defendant knows of or has reason to believe that another person or persons are likely to be affected by the variation, he must serve a copy of the claim form on those persons, together with a notice that they may apply to be made a party.

Defendant's application to vary other leases

9.6   If a defendant wishes to apply to vary other leases under section 36 of the 1987 Act:
  (1)   he must make the application in his acknowledgment of service;
  (2)   paragraphs 9.2 to 9.5 apply as if the defendant were the claimant; and
  (3)   Part 20 does not apply.

(Paragraphs 9.1–9.6 no longer apply to proceedings in England but continue to apply to proceedings in Wales)

Service of Documents in Claims Under the 1987 Act

10.1   All documents must be served by the parties.

10.2   If a notice is to be served in or before a claim under the 1987 Act, it must be served—
  (1)   in accordance with section 54, and
  (2)   in the case of service on a landlord, at the address given under section 48(1).

[1256N]

SECTION II—MISCELLANEOUS PROVISIONS ABOUT LAND

Access to Neighbouring Land Act 1992

11.1   The claimant must use the Part 8 procedure.

11.2   The claim form must set out:
  (1)   details of the dominant and servient land involved and whether the dominant land includes or consists of residential property;
  (2)   the work required;
  (3)   why entry to the servient land is required with plans (if applicable);
  (4)   the names and addresses of the persons who will carry out the work;

(5)   the proposed date when the work will be carried out; and

(6)   what (if any) provision has been made by way of insurance in the event of possible injury to persons or damage to property arising out of the proposed work.

11.3   The owner and occupier of the servient land must be defendants to the claim.

Chancel Repairs Act 1932

12.1   The claimant in a claim to recover the sum required to put a chancel in proper repair must use the Part 8 procedure.

12.2   A notice to repair under section 2 of the Chancel Repairs Act 1932 must—

(1)   state—

    (a)   the responsible authority by whom the notice is given;

    (b)   the chancel alleged to be in need of repair;

    (c)   the repairs alleged to be necessary; and

    (d)   the grounds on which the person to whom the notice is addressed is alleged to be liable to repair the chancel; and

(2)   call upon the person to whom the notice is addressed to put the chancel in proper repair.

12.3   The notice must be served in accordance with Part 6.

Leasehold Reform Act 1967

13.1   In this paragraph a section or schedule referred to by number means the section or schedule so numbered in the Leasehold Reform Act 1967.

13.2   If a tenant of a house and premises wishes to pay money into court under sections 11(4), 13(1) or 13(3)—

(1)   he must file in the office of the appropriate court an application notice containing or accompanied by evidence stating—

    (a)   the reasons for the payment into court,

    (b)   the house and premises to which the payment relates;

    (c)   the name and address of the landlord; and

    (d)   so far as they are known to the tenant, the name and address of every person who is or may be interested in or entitled to the money;

(2)   on the filing of the witness statement the tenant must pay the money into court and the court will send notice of the payment to the landlord and every person whose name and address are given in the witness statement;

(3)   any subsequent payment into court by the landlord under section 11(4) must be made to the credit of the same account as the payment into court by the tenant and sub-paragraphs (1) and (2) will apply to the landlord as if he were a tenant; and

(4)   the appropriate court for the purposes of paragraph (a) is the county court for the district in which the property is situated or, if the payment into court is made by reason of a notice under section 13(3), any other county court as specified in the notice.

13.3   If an order is made transferring an application to a leasehold valuation tribunal under section 21(3), the court will:

(1)   send notice of the transfer to all parties to the application; and

(2)   send to the tribunal copies of the order of transfer and all documents filed in the proceedings.

(Paragraph 13.3 no longer applies to proceedings in England but continues to apply to proceedings in Wales)

13.4   A claim under section 17 or 18 for an order for possession of a house and premises must be made in accordance with Part 55.

13.5   In a claim under section 17 or 18, the defendant must:

(1)   immediately after being served with the claim form, serve on every person in occupation of the property or part of it under an immediate or derivative sub-tenancy, a notice informing him of the claim and of his right under paragraph 3(4) of Schedule 2 take part in the hearing of the claim with the permission of the court; and

(2)   within 14 days after being served with the claim form, file a defence stating the ground, if any, on which he intends to oppose the claim and giving particulars of every such sub-tenancy.

13.6   An application made to the High Court under section 19 or 27 shall be assigned to the Chancery Division.

[12560]–[1294]

14.1–15.1 (*Outside the scope of this work.*)

DAIRY PRODUCE QUOTAS (GENERAL PROVISIONS) REGULATIONS 2002

(SI 2002/458)

NOTES
Made: 1 March 2002.
Authority: European Communities Act 1972, s 2(2).

ARRANGEMENT OF REGULATIONS

1 Title and commencement

These Regulations may be cited as the Dairy Produce Quotas (General Provisions) Regulations 2002 and shall come into force on 31st March 2002.

[1295]

2 Interpretation

In these Regulations, unless the context otherwise requires—

"apparatus" means any drum, barrel, tank, pump, hose or any other item adapted or used for the purposes of producing or transporting milk or milk products;

"authorised officer" means a person (whether or not an officer of the relevant competent authority) who is authorised by the relevant competent authority, either generally or specifically for the purposes of these Regulations, to act under these Regulations;

["the Commission Regulation" means Commission Regulation (EC) No 595/2004 laying down detailed rules for applying Council Regulation (EC) No 1788/2003 establishing a levy in the milk and milk products sector;]

.....
.....

["the Community legislation" means the Council Regulation [and the Commission Regulation];]

"the competent authority" means,—
    (a)   in England, the Secretary of State for Environment, Food and Rural Affairs;
    (b)   in Wales, the National Assembly for Wales;
    (c)   in Scotland, the Scottish Ministers; and
    (d)   in Northern Ireland, the Department of Agriculture and Rural Development;

["the Council Regulation" means Council Regulation (EC) No 1788/2003 establishing a levy in the milk and milk products sector;]

.....

"dairy produce" means produce, expressed in kilograms or litres (one kilogram being 0.971 litres), in respect of which levy is payable;

"delivery" has the same meaning as in [Article 5(f)] of the Council Regulation, and "deliver" shall be construed accordingly;

["direct sale" has the same meaning as in Article 5(g) of the Council Regulation;]

["direct sales quota" means the quantity of dairy produce which may be sold or transferred free of charge by direct sale by a producer in a quota year without that producer being liable to pay levy;]

["direct seller" means a producer who produces milk and treats that milk or processes it into milk products on his holding and subsequently sells or transfers free of charge that milk or those milk products without their having been further treated or processed by a different undertaking which treats or processes milk or milk products;]

"holding" has the same meaning as in [Article 5(d)] of the Council Regulation;

"levy" means the levy payable under the Community legislation;

"national reserve" means the reserve described in regulation 4 of these Regulations constituted in accordance with [Article 14 of the Council Regulation];

"premises" includes any vehicle;

"producer" has the same meaning as in [Article 5(c)] of the Council Regulation;

"purchaser" means a purchaser within the meaning of [Article 5(e)] of the Council Regulation;

"quota" means direct sales quota or wholesale quota;

"quota year" means any of the periods of 12 months referred to in [Article 1(1)] of the Council Regulation (which concerns the fixing of the levy);

"relevant date", in relation to a producer, purchaser or any other person, and for the purposes of any given quota year, means the beginning of that quota year;

"relevant offence" means an offence relating to—

    (a)   any failure to comply with a requirement imposed by, or in implementation of, the Community legislation;

    (b)   the making of any statement or use of any document which is false in a material particular; or

    (c)   any disposal of incorrectly registered quota.

"relevant person" means a producer, a purchaser, any employee or agent of a producer or of a purchaser, any milk haulier, any person undertaking butterfat testing for purchasers in a laboratory, a processor of milk or milk products, or any other person involved in the buying, selling or supply of milk or milk products obtained directly from a producer or purchaser[, but does not include a consumer of milk or milk products];

"relevant proceedings" mean any criminal proceedings relating to a relevant offence;

"territory" means England, Wales, Scotland or Northern Ireland, as the case may be;

.....

.....

["wholesale quota" means the quantity of milk which may be delivered to a purchaser by a producer in a quota year without that producer being liable to pay levy;].

[1296]

NOTES

Definitions "the Commission Regulation", "the Council Regulation" substituted, definitions omitted in the first and third places revoked and in definition "the Community legislation" words in square brackets substituted by the Dairy Produce (Miscellaneous Provisions) Regulations 2007, SI 2007/477, reg 3(1), (2); definitions "the Community legislation ", "the Council Regulation", "direct sale", "direct sales quota", "direct seller", "wholesale quota" substituted, definitions omitted in the second and third places revoked, in definitions "delivery", "holding", "national reserve", "producer", "purchaser" and "quota year", words in square brackets substituted, in definition "relevant person" words in square brackets added by the Dairy Produce Quotas (General Provisions) (Amendment) Regulations 2005, SI 2005/466, reg 2(b)–(p).

---

3   Relevant competent authority

In relation to a producer, a purchaser or any other relevant person, the relevant competent authority shall be the competent authority in the territory in which the trading address, or where there is more than one such address, the principal trading address, of that producer, purchaser or other relevant person is situated at the relevant date.

[1297]

4   National reserve

There shall continue to be a national reserve comprising such wholesale and direct sales quota as is not for the time being allocated to any person, including any quota withdrawn from any producer.

[1298]

5 Powers of authorised officers

(1)   An authorised officer may, at all reasonable hours and on producing some duly authenticated document showing his authority, exercise the powers specified in this regulation for the purposes of ascertaining whether—
- (a)   a relevant person has acted, or is acting, in accordance with the Community legislation; or
- (b)   a relevant offence has been, or is being, committed.

(2)   For the purposes of this regulation, an authorised officer may enter upon a holding or any other premises of a relevant person.

(3)   An authorised officer who has entered upon a holding or any other premises of a relevant person by virtue of this regulation may—
- (a)   inspect any—
    - (i)   land, other than land used only as a dwelling;
    - (ii)   apparatus; or
    - (iii)   record or document, including any document kept by means of a computer, which relates to the allocation or transfer of quota or the trade in, or production of milk or milk products,

and
- (b)   seize and retain any such apparatus or record or document which he has reason to believe may be required as evidence in any relevant proceedings.

(4)   A relevant person shall render all reasonable assistance to the authorised officer in relation to the matters mentioned in paragraph (1) above and in particular shall produce any such record or document and supply such additional information relating to the allocation to him of quota, the transfer to or from him of quota and the trade in, or production of, milk or milk products, as the authorised officer may reasonably require.

(5)   In the case of a record or document kept by means of a computer, a relevant person shall, if so required, provide any such record or document in a form in which it may be taken away.

[1299]

6 Offences and penalties

Any person who—
- (a)   intentionally obstructs an authorised officer acting in exercise of the powers conferred on him by regulation 5(1), (2) or (3) of these Regulations; or
- (b)   fails without reasonable excuse to comply with a requirement of an authorised officer made pursuant to regulation 5(4) or (5) thereof,

shall be guilty of an offence and liable on summary conviction to a fine not exceeding level 3 on the standard scale.

[1300]–[1305]

7   (*Revoked by the Dairy Produce (Miscellaneous Provisions) Regulations 2007, SI 2007/477, reg 3(1), (3).*)

(*Schedule revoked by the Dairy Produce (Miscellaneous Provisions) Regulations 2007, SI 2007/477, reg 3(1), (4).*)

REGULATORY REFORM (BUSINESS TENANCIES) (ENGLAND AND WALES) ORDER 2003

(SI 2003/3096)

NOTES
Made: 1 December 2003.
Authority: Regulatory Reform Act 2001, ss 1, 4.

ARRANGEMENT OF ARTICLES

Introduction

Introduction

1   Citation, commencement and interpretation

(1)   This Order may be cited as the Regulatory Reform (Business Tenancies) (England and Wales) Order 2003.

(2)   This Order extends to England and Wales only.

(3)   This Order shall come into force at the end of the period of 6 months beginning with the day on which it is made.

(4)   In this Order, "the Act" means the Landlord and Tenant Act 1954.

[1306]

NOTES
Commencement: 1 June 2004.

2–20   (*Amend the Landlord and Tenant Act 1954, as follows: art 2 is introductory; art 3 amends s 24 at* **[242]***; art 4 amends s 25 at* **[247]***; art 5 substitutes s 29 at* **[251]***;art 6 amends s 30 at* **[254]***; art 7 amends s 31 at* **[255]***; art 8 amends s 31A at* **[256]***; art 9 amends s 34 at* **[259]***; art 10 inserts ss 29A, 29B at* **[252]**, **[253]***; art 11 amends s 25 at* **[247]***; art 12 amends s 26 at* **[248]***; art 13 amends s 23 at* **[241]***; art 14 amends s 30 at* **[254]***; art 15 amends s 34 at* **[259]***; art 16 amends s 42 at* **[272]***; art 17 amends s 46 at* **[276]***; art 18 substitutes ss 24A, 24B, 24C, 24D for s 24A at* **[243]**, **[244]**, **[245]**, **[246]***; art 19 amends s 37 at* **[262]***; art 20 inserts s 37A at* **[263]***.*)

Agreements to exclude security of tenure

21   (*Amends the Landlord and Tenant Act 1954, s 38 at* **[264]***.*)

22   Agreements to exclude sections 24 to 28

(1)   ...

(2)   Schedules 1 to 4 to this Order shall have effect.

[1307]

NOTES
Commencement: 1 June 2004.
Para (1): inserts the Landlord and Tenant Act 1954, s 38A at **[265]**.

23–27 (*Amend the Landlord and Tenant Act 1954, as follows: art 23 substitutes s 40 at* **[267]***; art 24 inserts ss 40A, 40B at* **[268]**, **[269]***; art 25 amends s 27 at* **[249]***; art 26 amends s 33 at* **[258]***; art 27(1), (2) amends s 44 at* **[275]***; art 27(3) amends s 35 at* **[260]**.)

Final provisions

28 Consequential amendments, repeals and subordinate provisions

(1), (2)   ...

(3) Schedules 1 to 4 to this Order are designated as subordinate provisions for the purposes of section 4 of the Regulatory Reform Act 2001.

(4) A subordinate provisions order relating to the subordinate provisions designated by paragraph (3) above shall be subject to annulment in pursuance of a resolution of either House of Parliament.

(5) The power to make a subordinate provisions order relating to those provisions is to be exercisable in relation to Wales by the National Assembly for Wales concurrently with a Minister of the Crown.

(6) Paragraph (4) above does not apply to a subordinate provisions order made by the National Assembly for Wales.

(7) The notices and statutory declarations set out in Schedules 1 to 4 to this Order shall be treated for the purposes of section 26 of the Welsh Language Act 1993 (power to prescribe Welsh forms) as if they were specified by an Act of Parliament; and accordingly the power conferred by section 26(2) of that Act may be exercised in relation to those notices and declarations.

[1308]

NOTES
Commencement: 1 June 2004.
Paras (1), (2): outside the scope of this work.

29 Transitional provisions

(1) Where, before this Order came into force—

    (a) the landlord gave the tenant notice under section 25 of the Act; or

    (b) the tenant made a request for a new tenancy in accordance with section 26 of the Act,

nothing in this Order has effect in relation to the notice or request or anything done in consequence of it.

(2) Nothing in this Order has effect in relation—

    (a) to an agreement—
        (i) for the surrender of a tenancy which was made before this Order came into force and which fell within section 24(2)(b) of the Act; or
        (ii) which was authorised by the court under section 38(4) of the Act before this Order came into force; or

    (b) to a notice under section 27(2) of the Act which was given by the tenant to the immediate landlord before this Order came into force.

(3) Any provision in a tenancy which requires an order under section 38(4) of the Act to be obtained in respect of any subtenancy shall, so far as is necessary after the coming into force of this Order, be construed as if it required the procedure mentioned in section 38A of the Act to be followed, and any related requirement shall be construed accordingly.

(4) If a person has, before the coming into force of this Order, entered into an agreement to take a tenancy, any provision in that agreement which requires an order under section 38(4) of the Act to be obtained in respect of the tenancy shall continue to be effective, notwithstanding the repeal of that provision by Article 21(2) of this Order, and the court shall retain jurisdiction to make such an order.

(5) Article 20 above does not have effect where the tenant quit the holding before this Order came into force.

(6)   Nothing in Articles 23 and 24 above applies to a notice under section 40 of the Act served before this Order came into force.

[1309]

NOTES
Commencement: 1 June 2004.

SCHEDULE 1
FORM OF NOTICE THAT SECTIONS 24 TO 28 OF THE LANDLORD AND TENANT ACT 1954 ARE NOT TO APPLY TO A BUSINESS TENANCY

Article 22(2)

To: ....

....

....*[Name and address of tenant]*

From: ....

....

....*[Name and address of landlord]*

IMPORTANT NOTICE

You are being offered a lease without security of tenure. Do not commit yourself to the lease unless you have read this message carefully and have discussed it with a professional adviser.

Business tenants normally have security of tenure – the right to stay in their business premises when the lease ends.

If you commit yourself to the lease you will be giving up these important legal rights.

—You will have **no right** to stay in the premises when the lease ends.

—Unless the landlord chooses to offer you another lease, you will need to leave the premises.

—You will be unable to claim compensation for the loss of your business premises, unless the lease specifically gives you this right.

—If the landlord offers you another lease, you will have no right to ask the court to fix the rent.

It is therefore important to get professional advice – from a qualified surveyor, lawyer or accountant – before agreeing to give up these rights.

If you want to ensure that you can stay in the same business premises when the lease ends, you should consult your adviser about another form of lease that does not exclude the protection of the Landlord and Tenant Act 1954.

If you receive this notice at least 14 days before committing yourself to the lease, you will need to sign a simple declaration that you have received this notice and have accepted its consequences, before signing the lease.

But if you do not receive at least 14 days notice, you will need to sign a "statutory" declaration. To do so, you will need to visit an independent solicitor (or someone else empowered to administer oaths).

Unless there is a special reason for committing yourself to the lease sooner, you may want to ask the landlord to let you have 14 days to consider whether you wish to give up your statutory rights. If you then decide to go ahead with the agreement to exclude the protection of the Landlord and Tenant Act 1954, you would only need to make a simple declaration, and so would not need to make a separate visit to an independent solicitor.

[1310]

NOTES
Commencement: 1 June 2004.

SCHEDULE 2
REQUIREMENTS FOR A VALID AGREEMENT THAT SECTIONS 24 TO 28 OF THE LANDLORD AND TENANT ACT 1954 ARE NOT TO APPLY TO A BUSINESS TENANCY

Article 22(2)

1.   The following are the requirements referred to in section 38A(3)(b) of the Act.

2.   Subject to paragraph 4, the notice referred to in section 38A(3)(a) of the Act must be served on the tenant not less than 14 days before the tenant enters into the tenancy to which it applies, or (if earlier) becomes contractually bound to do so.

3.   If the requirement in paragraph 2 is met, the tenant, or a person duly authorised by him to do so, must, before the tenant enters into the tenancy to which the notice applies, or (if earlier) becomes contractually bound to do so, make a declaration in the form, or substantially in the form, set out in paragraph 7.

4.   If the requirement in paragraph 2 is not met, the notice referred to in section 38A(3)(a) of the Act must be served on the tenant before the tenant enters into the tenancy to which it applies, or (if earlier) becomes contractually bound to do so, and the tenant, or a person duly authorised by him to do so, must before that time make a statutory declaration in the form, or substantially in the form, set out in paragraph 8.

5.   A reference to the notice and, where paragraph 3 applies, the declaration or, where paragraph 4 applies, the statutory declaration must be contained in or endorsed on the instrument creating the tenancy.

6.   The agreement under section 38A(1) of the Act, or a reference to the agreement, must be contained in or endorsed upon the instrument creating the tenancy.

7.   The form of declaration referred to in paragraph 3 is as follows:—
I .... (*name of declarant*) of .... (*address*) declare that—

   1.   I/ .... (*name of tenant*) propose(s) to enter into a tenancy of premises at .... (*address of premises*) for a term commencing on ....

   2.   I/The   tenant   propose(s)   to   enter   into   an   agreement   with .... (*name of landlord*) that the provisions of sections 24 to 28 of the Landlord and Tenant Act 1954 (security of tenure) shall be excluded in relation to the tenancy.

   3.   The landlord has, not less than 14 days before I/the tenant enter(s) into the tenancy, or (if earlier) become(s) contractually bound to do so served on me/the tenant a notice in the form, or substantially in the form, set out in Schedule 1 to the Regulatory Reform (Business Tenancies) (England and Wales) Order 2003. The form of notice set out in that Schedule is reproduced below.

   4.   I have/The tenant has read the notice referred to in paragraph 3 above and accept(s) the consequences of entering into the agreement referred to in paragraph 2 above.

   5.   (*as appropriate*) I am duly authorised by the tenant to make this declaration.
DECLARED this .... day of ....
To:..
....
....[*Name and address of tenant*]
From: ....
....
....[*Name and address of landlord*]

IMPORTANT NOTICE

You are being offered a lease without security of tenure. Do not commit yourself to the lease unless you have read this message carefully and have discussed it with a professional adviser.

Business tenants normally have security of tenure – the right to stay in their business premises when the lease ends.

If you commit yourself to the lease you will be giving up these important legal rights.

—You will have **no right** to stay in the premises when the lease ends.

—Unless the landlord chooses to offer you another lease, you will need to leave the premises.

—You will be unable to claim compensation for the loss of your business premises, unless the lease specifically gives you this right.

—If the landlord offers you another lease, you will have no right to ask the court to fix the rent.

It is therefore important to get professional advice – from a qualified surveyor, lawyer or accountant – before agreeing to give up these rights.

If you want to ensure that you can stay in the same business premises when the lease ends, you should consult your adviser about another form of lease that does not exclude the protection of the Landlord and Tenant Act 1954.

If you receive this notice at least 14 days before committing yourself to the lease, you will need to sign a simple declaration that you have received this notice and have accepted its consequences, before signing the lease.

But if you do not receive at least 14 days notice, you will need to sign a "statutory" declaration. To do so, you will need to visit an independent solicitor (or someone else empowered to administer oaths).

Unless there is a special reason for committing yourself to the lease sooner, you may want to ask the landlord to let you have at least 14 days to consider whether you wish to give up your statutory rights. If you then decide to go ahead with the agreement to exclude the protection of the Landlord and Tenant Act 1954, you would only need to make a simple declaration, and so would not need to make a separate visit to an independent solicitor.

8.   The form of statutory declaration referred to in paragraph 4 is as follows:—

I.. (*name of declarant*) of.. (*address*) do solemnly and sincerely declare that—

1.   I .... (*name of tenant*) propose(s) to enter into a tenancy of premises at .... (*address of premises*) for a term commencing on ....

2.   I/The tenant propose(s) to enter into an agreement with .... (name of landlord) that the provisions of sections 24 to 28 of the Landlord and Tenant Act 1954 (security of tenure) shall be excluded in relation to the tenancy.

3.   The landlord has served on me/the tenant a notice in the form, or substantially in the form, set out in Schedule 1 to the Regulatory Reform (Business Tenancies) (England and Wales) Order 2003. The form of notice set out in that Schedule is reproduced below.

4.   I have/The tenant has read the notice referred to in paragraph 3 above and accept(s) the consequences of entering into the agreement referred to in paragraph 2 above.

5.   (*as appropriate*) I am duly authorised by the tenant to make this declaration.

To: ....

....

....*[Name and address of tenant]*

From: ....

....

....*[Name and address of landlord]*

IMPORTANT NOTICE
You are being offered a lease without security of tenure. Do not commit yourself to the lease unless you have read this message carefully and have discussed it with a professional adviser.
Business tenants normally have security of tenure – the right to stay in their business premises when the lease ends.
If you commit yourself to the lease you will be giving up these important legal rights.
—You will have **no right** to stay in the premises when the lease ends.
—Unless the landlord chooses to offer you another lease, you will need to leave the premises.
—You will be unable to claim compensation for the loss of your business premises, unless the lease specifically gives you this right.
—If the landlord offers you another lease, you will have no right to ask the court to fix the rent.
It is therefore important to get professional advice – from a qualified surveyor, lawyer or accountant – before agreeing to give up these rights.
If you want to ensure that you can stay in the same business premises when the lease ends, you should consult your adviser about another form of lease that does not exclude the protection of the Landlord and Tenant Act 1954.
If you receive this notice at least 14 days before committing yourself to the lease, you will need to sign a simple declaration that you have received this notice and have accepted its consequences, before signing the lease.
But if you do not receive at least 14 days notice, you will need to sign a "statutory" declaration. To do so, you will need to visit an independent solicitor (or someone else empowered to administer oaths).
Unless there is a special reason for committing yourself to the lease sooner, you may want to ask the landlord to let you have at least 14 days to consider whether you wish to give up your statutory rights. If you then decide to go ahead with the agreement to exclude the protection of the Landlord and Tenant Act 1954, you would only need to make a simple declaration, and so would not need to make a separate visit to an independent solicitor.

AND I make this solemn declaration conscientiously believing the same to be true and by virtue of the Statutory Declaration Act 1835.
DECLARED at .... this .... day of ....
Before me   (*signature of person before whom declaration is made*)
A commissioner for oaths *or* A solicitor empowered to administer oaths or (*as appropriate*)

[1311]

NOTES
Commencement: 1 June 2004.

SCHEDULE 3
FORM OF NOTICE THAT AN AGREEMENT TO SURRENDER A BUSINESS TENANCY IS TO BE MADE
Article 22(2)
To: ....
....
....[*Name and address of tenant*]
From: ....
....
....[*Name and address of landlord*]

IMPORTANT NOTICE FOR TENANT
Do not commit yourself to any agreement to surrender your lease unless you have read this message carefully and discussed it with a professional adviser.
Normally, you have the right to renew your lease when it expires. By committing yourself to an agreement to surrender, **you will be giving up this important statutory right**.

—You will **not** be able to continue occupying the premises beyond the date provided for under the agreement for surrender, **unless** the landlord chooses to offer you a further term (in which case you would lose the right to ask the court to determine the new rent). You will need to leave the premises.

—You will be unable to claim compensation for the loss of your premises, unless the lease or agreement for surrender gives you this right.

A qualified surveyor, lawyer or accountant would be able to offer you professional advice on your options.

You do not have to commit yourself to the agreement to surrender your lease unless you want to.

If you receive this notice at least 14 days before committing yourself to the agreement to surrender, you will need to sign a simple declaration that you have received this notice and have accepted its consequences, before signing the agreement to surrender.

But if you do not receive at least 14 days notice, you will need to sign a "statutory" declaration. To do so, you will need to visit an independent solicitor (or someone else empowered to administer oaths).

Unless there is a special reason for committing yourself to the agreement to surrender sooner, you may want to ask the landlord to let you have at least 14 days to consider whether you wish to give up your statutory rights. If you then decided to go ahead with the agreement to end your lease, you would only need to make a simple declaration, and so you would not need to make a separate visit to an independent solicitor.

[1312]

NOTES

Commencement: 1 June 2004.

SCHEDULE 4
REQUIREMENTS FOR A VALID AGREEMENT TO SURRENDER A BUSINESS TENANCY

Article 22(2)

1.   The following are the requirements referred to in section 38A(4)(b) of the Act.

2.   Subject to paragraph 4, the notice referred to in section 38A(4)(a) of the Act must be served on the tenant not less than 14 days before the tenant enters into the agreement under section 38A(2) of the Act, or (if earlier) becomes contractually bound to do so.

3.   If the requirement in paragraph 2 is met, the tenant or a person duly authorised by him to do so, must, before the tenant enters into the agreement under section 38A(2) of the Act, or (if earlier) becomes contractually bound to do so, make a declaration in the form, or substantially in the form, set out in paragraph 6.

4.   If the requirement in paragraph 2 is not met, the notice referred to in section 38A(4)(a) of the Act must be served on the tenant before the tenant enters into the agreement under section 38A(2) of the Act, or (if earlier) becomes contractually bound to do so, and the tenant, or a person duly authorised by him to do so, must before that time make a statutory declaration in the form, or substantially in the form, set out in paragraph 7.

5.   A reference to the notice and, where paragraph 3 applies, the declaration or, where paragraph 4 applies, the statutory declaration must be contained in or endorsed on the instrument creating the agreement under section 38A(2).

6.   The form of declaration referred to in paragraph 3 is as follows:—

I.. (*name of declarant*) of.. (*address*) declare that—

    1.   I have/ .... (*name of tenant*) has a tenancy of premises at .... (*address of premises*) for a term commencing on ....

    2.   I/The tenant propose(s) to enter into an agreement with

.... (*name of landlord*) to surrender the tenancy on a date or in circumstances specified in the agreement.

3.   The landlord has not less than 14 days before I/the tenant enter(s) into the agreement referred to in paragraph 2 above, or (if earlier) become(s) contractually bound to do so, served on me/the tenant a notice in the form, or substantially in the form, set out in Schedule 3 to Regulatory Reform (Business Tenancies) (England and Wales) Order 2003. The form of notice set out in that Schedule is reproduced below.

4.   I have/The tenant has read the notice referred to in paragraph 3 above and accept(s) the consequences of entering into the agreement referred to in paragraph 2 above.

5.   (*as appropriate*) I am duly authorised by the tenant to make this declaration.

DECLARED this .... day of ....

To: ....

....

....*[Name and address of tenant]*

From: ....

....

....*[Name and address of landlord]*

IMPORTANT NOTICE FOR TENANT

Do not commit yourself to any agreement to surrender your lease unless you have read this message carefully and discussed it with a professional adviser.

Normally, you have the right to renew your lease when it expires. By committing yourself to an agreement to surrender, **you will be giving up this important statutory right**.

—You will **not** be able to continue occupying the premises beyond the date provided for under the agreement for surrender, **unless** the landlord chooses to offer you a further term (in which case you would lose the right to ask the court to determine the new rent). You will need to leave the premises.

—You will be unable to claim compensation for the loss of your premises, unless the lease or agreement for surrender gives you this right.

A qualified surveyor, lawyer or accountant would be able to offer you professional advice on your options.

You do not have to commit yourself to the agreement to surrender your lease unless you want to.

If you receive this notice at least 14 days before committing yourself to the agreement to surrender, you will need to sign a simple declaration that you have received this notice and have accepted its consequences, before signing the agreement to surrender. **But if you do not receive at least 14 days notice, you will need to sign a "statutory" declaration. To do so, you will need to visit an independent solicitor (or someone else empowered to administer oaths).**

Unless there is a special reason for committing yourself to the agreement to surrender sooner, you may want to ask the landlord to let you have at least 14 days to consider whether you wish to give up your statutory rights. If you then decided to go ahead with the agreement to end your lease, you would only need to make a simple declaration, and so you would not need to make a separate visit to an independent solicitor.

---

7. The form of statutory declaration referred to in paragraph 4 is as follows:—

I .... (*name of declarant*) of .... (*address*) do solemnly and sincerely declare that—

1.   I have/ .... (*name of tenant*) has a tenancy of premises at .... (*address of premises*) for a term commencing on ....

2.   I/The tenant propose(s) to enter into an agreement with .... (*name of landlord*) to surrender the tenancy on a date or in circumstances specified in the agreement.

3.   The landlord has served on me/the tenant a notice in the form, or substantially in

the form, set out in Schedule 3 to the Regulatory Reform (Business Tenancies) (England and Wales) Order 2003. The form of notice set out in that Schedule is reproduced below.

4.   I have/The tenant has read the notice referred to in paragraph 3 above and accept(s) the consequences of entering into the agreement referred to in paragraph 2 above.

5.   (*as appropriate*) I am duly authorised by the tenant to make this declaration.

To: ....

....

....*[Name and address of tenant]*

From: ....

....

....*[Name and address of landlord]*

IMPORTANT NOTICE FOR TENANT

Do not commit yourself to any agreement to surrender your lease unless you have read this message carefully and discussed it with a professional adviser.

Normally, you have the right to renew your lease when it expires. By committing yourself to an agreement to surrender, **you will be giving up this important statutory right**.

—You will **not** be able to continue occupying the premises beyond the date provided for under the agreement for surrender, **unless** the landlord chooses to offer you a further term (in which case you would lose the right to ask the court to determine the new rent). You will need to leave the premises.

—You will be unable to claim compensation for the loss of your premises, unless the lease or agreement for surrender gives you this right.

A qualified surveyor, lawyer or accountant would be able to offer you professional advice on your options.

You do not have to commit yourself to the agreement to surrender your lease unless you want to.

If you receive this notice at least 14 days before committing yourself to the agreement to surrender, you will need to sign a simple declaration that you have received this notice and have accepted its consequences, before signing the agreement to surrender. **But if you do not receive at least 14 days notice, you will need to sign a "statutory" declaration. To do so, you will need to visit an independent solicitor (or someone else empowered to administer oaths).**

Unless there is a special reason for committing yourself to the agreement to surrender sooner, you may want to ask the landlord to let you have at least 14 days to consider whether you wish to give up your statutory rights. If you then decided to go ahead with the agreement to end your lease, you would only need to make a simple declaration, and so you would not need to make a separate visit to an independent solicitor.

AND I make this solemn declaration conscientiously believing the same to be true and by virtue of the Statutory Declarations Act 1835

DECLARED this .... day of ....

Before me   (*signature of person before whom declaration is made*)

A commissioner for oaths or A solicitor empowered to administer oaths *or* (*as appropriate*)

[1313]

NOTES

Commencement: 1 June 2004.

(*Schs 5, 6 contain amendments and repeals which have been incorporated into this work where relevant.*)

DISABILITY DISCRIMINATION (EMPLOYMENT FIELD) (LEASEHOLD PREMISES) REGULATIONS 2004

(SI 2004/153)

NOTES
Made: 26 January 2004.
Authority: Disability Discrimination Act 1995, ss 5(6), (7), 6(8), (10), 12(3), 16(3), 67(3), Sch 4, paras 3, 4.

ARRANGEMENT OF REGULATIONS

1   Citation, commencement and extent

(1)   These Regulations may be cited as the Disability Discrimination (Employment Field) (Leasehold Premises) Regulations 2004 and shall come into force on 1st October 2004.

(2)   These Regulations shall not extend to Northern Ireland.

[1314]

NOTES
Commencement: 1 October 2004.

2   Interpretation

In these Regulations—
   "the Act" means the Disability Discrimination Act 1995; and
   "binding obligation" means a legally binding obligation (not contained in a lease) in
      relation to the premises whether arising from an agreement or otherwise.

[1315]

NOTES
Commencement: 1 October 2004.

3   (*Revokes the Disability Discrimination (Employment) Regulations 1996, SI 1996/1456 and the Disability Discrimination (Sub-leases and Sub-tenancies) Regulations 1996, SI 1996/1333.*)

4   Lessor withholding consent

(1)   For the purposes of section 18A of and Part I of Schedule 4 to the Act, a lessor is to be taken to have withheld his consent to an alteration where he has received a written application by or on behalf of the occupier for consent to make the alteration and has failed to meet the requirements specified in paragraph (2).

(2)   The requirements are that the lessor within a period of 21 days (beginning with the day on which he receives the application referred to in paragraph (1)) or such longer period as is reasonable—
   (a)   replies consenting to or refusing the application, or
   (b)
         (i)   replies consenting to the application subject to obtaining the consent of
               another person required under a superior lease or pursuant to a binding
               obligation, and
         (ii)   seeks that consent.

(3)   A lessor who fails to meet the requirements in paragraph (2) but who subsequently meets those requirements (except as to time)—

    (a)   shall be taken to have withheld his consent from the date of such failure, and

    (b)   shall be taken not to have withheld his consent from the time he met those requirements (except as to time).

(4)   For the purposes of this regulation, a lessor is to be treated as not having sought another person's consent unless he has applied in writing to that person indicating—

    (a)   that the lessor's consent to the alteration has been applied for in order to comply with a duty to make reasonable adjustments, and

    (b)   that he has given his consent conditionally upon obtaining the other person's consent.

[1316]

NOTES

Commencement: 1 October 2004.

5   Lessor withholding consent unreasonably

(1)   For the purposes of section 18A of and Part I of Schedule 4 to the Act, a lessor is to be taken to have withheld his consent unreasonably where paragraph (2), (3) or (4) applies.

(2)   This paragraph applies where—

    (a)   the lease provides that consent shall or will be given to an alteration of the kind in question; and

    (b)   the lessor withholds his consent to the alteration.

(3)   This paragraph applies where—

    (a)   the lease provides that consent shall or will be given to an alteration of the kind in question if it is sought in a particular way;

    (b)   it is sought in that way; and

    (c)   the lessor withholds his consent to the alteration.

(4)   This paragraph applies where the lessor is taken to have withheld his consent by virtue of regulation 4.

[1317]

NOTES

Commencement: 1 October 2004.

6   Lessor withholding consent reasonably

(1)   For the purposes of section 18A of and Part I of Schedule 4 to the Act, a lessor is to be taken to have acted reasonably in withholding his consent where—

    (a)   there is a binding obligation requiring the consent of any person to the alteration;

    (b)   he has taken steps to seek that consent; and

    (c)   that consent has not been given or has been given subject to a condition making it reasonable for him to withhold his consent.

(2)   For the purposes of section 18A of and Part I of Schedule 4 to the Act, a lessor is to be taken to have acted reasonably in withholding his consent where—

    (a)   he is bound by an agreement which allows him to consent to the alteration in question subject to a condition that he makes a payment, and

    (b)   that condition does not permit the lessor to make his own consent subject to a condition that the occupier reimburse him the payment.

[1318]

NOTES

Commencement: 1 October 2004.

7   Lessor's consent subject to conditions

(1)   For the purposes of section 18A of and Part I of Schedule 4 to the Act, a condition subject to which a lessor has given his consent is to be taken to be reasonable if it is any of the following (or a condition to similar effect)—

(a)   that the occupier must obtain any necessary planning permission and any other consent or permission required by or under any enactment;

(b)   that the occupier must submit any plans or specifications for the alteration to the lessor for approval (provided that the condition binds the lessor not to withhold approval unreasonably) and that the work is carried out in accordance with such plans or specifications;

(c)   that the lessor must be permitted a reasonable opportunity to inspect the work when completed; and

(d)   that the occupier must repay to the lessor the costs reasonably incurred in connection with the giving of his consent.

(2)   For the purposes of section 18A of and Part I of Schedule 4 to the Act, in a case where it would be reasonable for the lessor to withhold consent, a condition that upon expiry of the lease the occupier (or any assignee or successor) must reinstate any relevant part of the premises which is to be altered to its state before the alteration was made is to be taken to be reasonable.

[1319]

NOTES
Commencement: 1 October 2004.

8 Definition of sub-lease and sub-tenancy

For the purposes of section 18A of the Act—

"sub-lease" means any sub-term created out of, or deriving from, a leasehold interest; and

"sub-tenancy" means any tenancy created out of, or deriving from, a superior tenancy.

[1320]

NOTES
Commencement: 1 October 2004.

9 Modification of section 18A and Part I of Schedule 4

In relation to any case where the occupier occupies premises under a sub-lease or sub-tenancy, the provisions of section 18A of and Part I of Schedule 4 to the Act shall have effect as if they contained the following modifications—

(a)   in section 18A, for "the lessor" substitute "his immediate landlord" where it occurs in subsection (2)(a) and (b), and "the immediate landlord" where it occurs in subsection (2)(c) and (d) and subsection (4);

(b)   after section 18A(2) insert—

"(2A)   Except to the extent to which it expressly so provides, any superior lease under which the premises are held shall have effect in relation to the lessor and lessee who are parties to that superior lease as if it provided—

(a)   for the lessee to have to make a written application to the lessor for consent to the alteration;

(b)   if such an application is made, for the lessor not to withhold his consent unreasonably; and

(c)   for the lessor to be entitled to make his consent subject to reasonable conditions.";

(c)   in paragraph 2 of Schedule 4, at the end insert—

"(10)   In this paragraph and paragraph 3, references to a lessor include any superior landlord.".

[1321]

NOTES
Commencement: 1 October 2004.

LANDLORD AND TENANT ACT 1954, PART 2 (NOTICES) REGULATIONS 2004

(SI 2004/1005)

NOTES

Made: 30 March 2004.
Authority: Landlord and Tenant Act 1954, s 66.

ARRANGEMENT OF REGULATIONS

1 Citation and commencement

These Regulations may be cited as the Landlord and Tenant Act 1954, Part 2 (Notices) Regulations 2004 and shall come into force on 1st June 2004.

[1322]

NOTES

Commencement: 1 June 2004.

2 Interpretation

(1)   In these Regulations—

"the Act" means the Landlord and Tenant Act 1954; and

"the 1967 Act" means the Leasehold Reform Act 1967.

(2)   Any reference in these Regulations to a numbered form (in whatever terms) is a reference to the form bearing that number in Schedule 2 to these Regulations or a form substantially to the same effect.

[1323]

NOTES

Commencement: 1 June 2004.

3 Prescribed forms, and purposes for which they are to be used

The form with the number shown in column (1) of Schedule 1 to these Regulations is prescribed for use for the purpose shown in the corresponding entry in column (2) of that Schedule.

[1324]

NOTES

Commencement: 1 June 2004.

4 Revocation of Regulations

The Landlord and Tenant Act 1954, Part II (Notices) Regulations 1983 and the Landlord and Tenant Act 1954, Part II (Notices) (Amendment) Regulations 1989 are hereby revoked.

[1325]

NOTES

Commencement: 1 June 2004.

SCHEDULES

SCHEDULE 1
PRESCRIBED FORMS, AND PURPOSES FOR WHICH THEY ARE TO BE USED
Regulations 2(2) and 3

(1)	*(2)*
Form number	*Purpose for which to be used*
1	Ending a tenancy to which Part 2 of the Act applies, where the landlord is not opposed to the grant of a new tenancy (notice under section 25 of the Act).
2	Ending a tenancy to which Part 2 of the Act applies, where: (a) the landlord is opposed to the grant of a new tenancy (notice under section 25 of the Act); and (b) the tenant is not entitled under the 1967 Act to buy the freehold or an extended lease.
3	Tenant's request for a new tenancy of premises where Part 2 of the Act applies (notice under section 26 of the Act).
4	Landlord's notice activating tenant's duty under section 40(1) of the Act to give information as to his or her occupation of the premises and as to any sub-tenancies.
5	Tenant's notice activating duty under section 40(3) of the Act of reversioner or reversioner's mortgagee in possession to give information about his or her interest in the premises.
6	Withdrawal of notice given under section 25 of the Act ending a tenancy to which Part 2 of the Act applies (notice under section 44 of, and paragraph 6 of Schedule 6 to, the Act).
7	Ending a tenancy to which Part 2 of the Act applies, where the landlord is opposed to the grant of a new tenancy but where the tenant may be entitled under the 1967 Act to buy the freehold or an extended lease (notice under section 25 of the Act and paragraph 10 of Schedule 3 to the 1967 Act).
8	Ending a tenancy to which Part 2 of the Act applies, where: (a) the notice under section 25 of the Act contains a copy of a certificate given under section 57 of the Act that the use or occupation of the property or part of it is to be changed by a specified date; (b) the date of termination of the tenancy specified in the notice is not earlier than the date specified in the certificate; and (c) the tenant is not entitled under the 1967 Act to buy the freehold or an extended lease.
9	Ending a tenancy to which Part 2 of the Act applies, where: (a) the notice under section 25 of the Act contains a copy of a certificate given under section 57 of the Act that the use or occupation of the property or part of it is to be changed at a future date; (b) the date of termination of the tenancy specified in the notice is earlier than the date specified in the certificate; (c) the landlord opposes the grant of a new tenancy; and (d) the tenant is not entitled under the 1967 Act to buy the freehold or an extended lease.

(1)	*(2)*
Form number	*Purpose for which to be used*
10	Ending a tenancy to which Part 2 of the Act applies, where: (a) the notice under section 25 of the Act contains a copy of a certificate given under section 57 of the Act that the use or occupation of the property or part of it is to be changed at a future date; (b) the date of termination of the tenancy specified in the notice is earlier than the date specified in the certificate; (c) the landlord does not oppose the grant of a new tenancy; and (d) the tenant is not entitled under the 1967 Act to buy the freehold or an extended lease.
11	Ending a tenancy to which Part 2 of the Act applies, where the notice under section 25 of the Act contains a copy of a certificate given under section 58 of the Act that for reasons of national security it is necessary that the use or occupation of the property should be discontinued or changed.
12	Ending a tenancy to which Part 2 of the Act applies, where: (a) the notice under section 25 of the Act contains a copy of a certificate given under section 58 of the Act (as applied by section 60 of the Act) that it is necessary or expedient for achieving the purpose mentioned in section 2(1) of the Local Employment Act 1972 that the use or occupation of the property should be changed; and (b) the tenant is not entitled under the 1967 Act to buy the freehold or an extended lease.
13	Ending a tenancy to which Part 2 of the Act applies, where: (a) the notice under section 25 of the Act contains a copy of a certificate given under section 57 of the Act that the use or occupation of the property or part of it is to be changed by a specified date; and (b) the date of termination of the tenancy specified in the notice is not earlier than the date specified in the certificate; and (c) the tenant may be entitled under the 1967 Act to buy the freehold or an extended lease.
14	Ending a tenancy to which Part 2 of the Act applies, where: (a) the notice under section 25 of the Act contains a copy of a certificate given under section 57 of the Act that the use or occupation of the property or part of it is to be changed at a future date; (b) the date of termination of the tenancy specified in the notice is earlier than the date specified in the certificate; and (c) the tenant may be entitled under the 1967 Act to buy the freehold or an extended lease the landlord opposes the grant of a new tenancy.

PART II
STATUTORY INSTRUMENTS

(1)	(2)
Form number	Purpose for which to be used
15	Ending a tenancy to which Part 2 of the Act applies, where: (a) the notice under section 25 of the Act contains a copy of a certificate given under section 58 of the Act (as applied by section 60 of the Act) that it is necessary or expedient for achieving the purpose mentioned in section 2(1) of the Local Employment Act 1972 that the use or occupation of the property should be changed; and (b) the tenant may be entitled under the 1967 Act to buy the freehold or an extended lease the landlord opposes the grant of a new tenancy.
16	Ending a tenancy of Welsh Development Agency [Act 1975] premises where— (a) the notice under section 25 of the Act contains a copy of a certificate given under section 58 of the Act (as applied by section 60A of the Act) that it is necessary or expedient, for the purposes of providing employment appropriate to the needs of the area in which the premises are situated, that the use or occupation of the property should be changed; and (b) the tenant is not entitled under the 1967 Act to buy the freehold or an extended lease.
17	Ending a tenancy of Welsh Development Agency [Act 1975] premises where: (a) the notice under section 25 of the Act contains a copy of a certificate given under section 58 of the Act (as applied by section 60A of the Act) that it is necessary or expedient, for the purposes of providing employment appropriate to the needs of the area in which the premises are situated, that the use or occupation of the property should be changed; and (b) the tenant may be entitled under the 1967 Act to buy the freehold or an extended lease.

[1326]

NOTES

Commencement: 1 June 2004.

In entries relating to Forms 16, 17 in column 2, words in square brackets inserted by the Welsh Development Agency (Transfer of Functions to the National Assembly for Wales and Abolition) Order 2005, SI 2005/3226, art 7(1)(b), Sch 2, Pt 1, para 7(1), subject to transitional provisions in art 3 thereof.

SCHEDULE 2
PRESCRIBED FORMS

Regulation 2(2)

FORM 1
LANDLORD'S NOTICE ENDING A BUSINESS TENANCY WITH PROPOSALS FOR
A NEW ONE

Section 25 of the Landlord and Tenant Act 1954

IMPORTANT NOTE FOR THE LANDLORD: If you are willing to grant a new tenancy, complete this form and send it to the tenant. If you wish to oppose the grant of a new tenancy, use form 2 in Schedule 2 to the Landlord and Tenant Act 1954, Part 2 (Notices) Regulations 2004 or, where the tenant may be entitled to acquire the freehold or an extended lease, form 7 in that Schedule, instead of this form.

To: (*insert name and address of tenant*)

From: (*insert name and address of landlord*)

1.   This notice applies to the following property: (*insert address or description of property*).

2.   I am giving you notice under section 25 of the Landlord and Tenant Act 1954 to end your tenancy on (*insert date*).

3.   I am not opposed to granting you a new tenancy. You will find my proposals for the new tenancy, which we can discuss, in the Schedule to this notice.

4.   If we cannot agree on all the terms of a new tenancy, either you or I may ask the court to order the grant of a new tenancy and settle the terms on which we cannot agree.

5.   If you wish to ask the court for a new tenancy you must do so by the date in paragraph 2, unless we agree in writing to a later date and do so before the date in paragraph 2.

6.   Please send all correspondence about this notice to:

Name:

Address:

Signed: Date:

*[Landlord] *[On behalf of the landlord] *[Mortgagee] *[On behalf of the mortgagee]

*(*delete if inapplicable*)

Schedule
Landlord's Proposals for a New Tenancy

(*attach or insert proposed terms of the new tenancy*)

IMPORTANT NOTE FOR THE TENANT

This Notice is intended to bring your tenancy to an end. If you want to continue to occupy your property after the date specified in paragraph 2 you must act quickly. If you are in any doubt about the action that you should take, get advice immediately from a solicitor or a surveyor.

The landlord is prepared to offer you a new tenancy and has set out proposed terms in the Schedule to this notice. You are not bound to accept these terms. They are merely suggestions as a basis for negotiation. In the event of disagreement, ultimately the court would settle the terms of the new tenancy.

It would be wise to seek professional advice before agreeing to accept the landlord's terms or putting forward your own proposals.

NOTES

The sections mentioned below are sections of the Landlord and Tenant Act 1954, as amended, (most recently by the Regulatory Reform (Business Tenancies) (England and Wales) Order 2003).

Ending of tenancy and grant of new tenancy

This notice is intended to bring your tenancy to an end on the date given in paragraph 2. Section 25 contains rules about the date that the landlord can put in that paragraph.

However, your landlord is prepared to offer you a new tenancy and has set out proposals for it in the Schedule to this notice (section 25(8)). You are not obliged to accept these proposals and may put forward your own.

PART II
STATUTORY INSTRUMENTS

If you and your landlord are unable to agree terms either one of you may apply to the court. You may not apply to the court if your landlord has already done so (section 24(2A)). If you wish to apply to the court you must do so by the date given in paragraph 2 of this notice, unless you and your landlord have agreed in writing to extend the deadline (sections 29A and 29B).

The court will settle the rent and other terms of the new tenancy or those on which you and your landlord cannot agree (sections 34 and 35). If you apply to the court your tenancy will continue after the date shown in paragraph 2 of this notice while your application is being considered (section 24).

If you are in any doubt about what action you should take, get advice immediately from a solicitor or a surveyor.

Negotiating a new tenancy

Most tenancies are renewed by negotiation. You and your landlord may agree in writing to extend the deadline for making an application to the court while negotiations continue. Either you or your landlord can ask the court to fix the rent that you will have to pay while the tenancy continues (sections 24A to 24D).

You may only stay in the property after the date in paragraph 2 (or if we have agreed in writing to a later date, that date), if by then you or the landlord has asked the court to order the grant of a new tenancy.

If you do try to agree a new tenancy with your landlord remember:

- that your present tenancy will not continue after the date in paragraph 2 of this notice without the agreement in writing mentioned above, unless you have applied to the court or your landlord has done so, and
- that you will lose your right to apply to the court once the deadline in paragraph 2 of this notice has passed, unless there is a written agreement extending the deadline.

Validity of this notice

The landlord who has given you this notice may not be the landlord to whom you pay your rent (sections 44 and 67). This does not necessarily mean that the notice is invalid.

If you have any doubts about whether this notice is valid, get advice immediately from a solicitor or a surveyor.

Further information

An explanation of the main points to consider when renewing or ending a business tenancy, "Renewing and Ending Business Leases: a Guide for Tenants and Landlords", can be found at www.odpm.gov.uk. Printed copies of the explanation, but not of this form, are available from 1st June 2004 from Free Literature, PO Box 236, Wetherby, West Yorkshire, LS23 7NB (0870 1226 236).

[1327]

FORM 2
LANDLORD'S NOTICE ENDING A BUSINESS TENANCY AND REASONS FOR
REFUSING A NEW ONE

Section 25 of the Landlord and Tenant Act 1954

IMPORTANT NOTE FOR THE LANDLORD: If you wish to oppose the grant of a new tenancy on any of the grounds in section 30(1) of the Landlord and Tenant Act 1954, complete this form and send it to the tenant. If the tenant may be entitled to acquire the freehold or an extended lease, use form 7 in Schedule 2 to the Landlord and Tenant Act 1954, Part 2 (Notices) Regulations 2004 instead of this form.

To: (*insert name and address of tenant*)

From: (*insert name and address of landlord*)

1.   This notice relates to the following property: (*insert address or description of property*)

2.   I am giving you notice under section 25 of the Landlord and Tenant Act 1954 to end your tenancy on   *(insert date)*.

3.   I am opposed to the grant of a new tenancy.

4.   You may ask the court to order the grant of a new tenancy. If you do, I will oppose your application on the ground(s) mentioned in paragraph(s)* of section 30(1) of that Act. I draw your attention to the Table in the Notes below, which sets out all the grounds of opposition.

(insert letter(s) of the paragraph(s) relied on)

5.   If you wish to ask the court for a new tenancy you must do so before the date in paragraph 2 unless, before that date, we agree in writing to a later date.

6.   I can ask the court to order the ending of your tenancy without granting you a new tenancy. I may have to pay you compensation if I have relied only on one or more of the grounds mentioned in paragraphs (e), (f) and (g) of section 30(1). If I ask the court to end your tenancy, you can challenge my application.

7.   Please send all correspondence about this notice to:

Name:

Address:

Signed: Date:

*[Landlord] *[On behalf of the landlord] *[Mortgagee] *[On behalf of the mortgagee]

(*delete if inapplicable)

IMPORTANT NOTE FOR THE TENANT

This notice is intended to bring your tenancy to an end on the date specified in paragraph 2.

Your landlord is not prepared to offer you a new tenancy. You will not get a new tenancy unless you successfully challenge in court the grounds on which your landlord opposes the grant of a new tenancy.

If you want to continue to occupy your property you must act quickly. The notes below should help you to decide what action you now need to take. If you want to challenge your landlord's refusal to renew your tenancy, get advice immediately from a solicitor or a surveyor.

NOTES

The sections mentioned below are sections of the Landlord and Tenant Act 1954, as amended, (most recently by the Regulatory Reform (Business Tenancies) (England and Wales) Order 2003)

Ending of your tenancy

This notice is intended to bring your tenancy to an end on the date given in paragraph 2. Section 25 contains rules about the date that the landlord can put in that paragraph.

Your landlord is not prepared to offer you a new tenancy. If you want a new tenancy you will need to apply to the court for a new tenancy and successfully challenge the landlord's grounds for opposition (see the section below headed "*Landlord's opposition to new tenancy*"). If you wish to apply to the court you must do so before the date given in paragraph 2 of this notice, unless you and your landlord have agreed in writing, before that date, to extend the deadline (sections 29A and 29B).

If you apply to the court your tenancy will continue after the date given in paragraph 2 of this notice while your application is being considered (section 24). You may not apply to the court if your landlord has already done so (section 24(2A) and (2B)).

You may only stay in the property after the date given in paragraph 2 (or such later date as you and the landlord may have agreed in writing) if before that date you have asked the court to order the grant of a new tenancy or the landlord has asked the court to order the ending of your tenancy without granting you a new one.

If you are in any doubt about what action you should take, get advice immediately from a solicitor or a surveyor.

Landlord's opposition to new tenancy

If you apply to the court for a new tenancy, the landlord can only oppose your application on one or more of the grounds set out in section 30(1). If you match the letter(s) specified in paragraph 4 of this notice with those in the first column in the Table below, you can see from the second column the ground(s) on which the landlord relies.

Paragraph of section 30(1)	Grounds
(a)	Where under the current tenancy the tenant has any obligations as respects the repair and maintenance of the holding, that the tenant ought not to be granted a new tenancy in view of the state of repair of the holding, being a state resulting from the tenant's failure to comply with the said obligations.
(b)	That the tenant ought not to be granted a new tenancy in view of his persistent delay in paying rent which has become due.
(c)	That the tenant ought not to be granted a new tenancy in view of other substantial breaches by him of his obligations under the current tenancy, or for any other reason connected with the tenant's use or management of the holding.
(d)	That the landlord has offered and is willing to provide or secure the provision of alternative accommodation for the tenant, that the terms on which the alternative accommodation is available are reasonable having regard to the terms of the current tenancy and to all other relevant circumstances, and that the accommodation and the time at which it will be available are suitable for the tenant's requirements (including the requirement to preserve goodwill) having regard to the nature and class of his business and to the situation and extent of, and facilities afforded by, the holding.
(e)	Where the current tenancy was created by the sub-letting of part only of the property comprised in a superior tenancy and the landlord is the owner of an interest in reversion expectant on the termination of that superior tenancy, that the aggregate of the rents reasonably obtainable on separate lettings of the holding and the remainder of that property would be substantially less than the rent reasonably obtainable on a letting of that property as a whole, that on the termination of the current tenancy the landlord requires possession of the holding for the purposes of letting or otherwise disposing of the said property as a whole, and that in view thereof the tenant ought not to be granted a new tenancy.
(f)	That on the termination of the current tenancy the landlord intends to demolish or reconstruct the premises comprised in the holding or a substantial part of those premises or to carry out substantial work of construction on the holding or part thereof and that he could not reasonably do so without obtaining possession of the holding.
(g)	On the termination of the current tenancy the landlord intends to occupy the holding for the purposes, or partly for the purposes, of a business to be carried on by him therein, or as his residence.

In this Table "the holding" means the property that is the subject of the tenancy.

In ground (e), "the landlord is the owner an interest in reversion expectant on the termination of that superior tenancy" means that the landlord has an interest in the property that will entitle him or her, when your immediate landlord's tenancy comes to an end, to exercise certain rights and obligations in relation to the property that are currently exercisable by your immediate landlord.

If the landlord relies on ground (f), the court can sometimes still grant a new tenancy if certain conditions set out in section 31A are met.

If the landlord relies on ground (g), please note that "the landlord" may have an extended meaning. Where a landlord has a controlling interest in a company then either the landlord or the company can rely on ground (g). Where the landlord is a company and a person has a controlling interest in that company then either of them can rely on ground (g) (section 30(1A) and (1B)). A person has a "controlling interest" in a company if, had he been a company, the other company would have been its subsidiary (section 46(2)).

The landlord must normally have been the landlord for at least five years before he or she can rely on ground (g).

Compensation

If you cannot get a new tenancy solely because one or more of grounds (e), (f) and (g) applies, you may be entitled to compensation under section 37. If your landlord has opposed your application on any of the other grounds as well as (e), (f) or (g) you can only get compensation if the court's refusal to grant a new tenancy is based solely on one or more of grounds (e), (f) and (g). In other words, you cannot get compensation under section 37 if the court has refused your tenancy on *other* grounds, even if one or more of grounds (e), (f) and (g) also applies.

If your landlord is an authority possessing compulsory purchase powers (such as a local authority) you may be entitled to a disturbance payment under Part 3 of the Land Compensation Act 1973.

Validity of this notice

The landlord who has given you this notice may not be the landlord to whom you pay your rent (sections 44 and 67). This does not necessarily mean that the notice is invalid.

If you have any doubts about whether this notice is valid, get advice immediately from a solicitor or a surveyor.

Further information

An explanation of the main points to consider when renewing or ending a business tenancy, "Renewing and Ending Business Leases: a Guide for Tenants and Landlords", can be found at www.odpm.gov.uk. Printed copies of the explanation, but not of this form, are available from 1st June 2004 from Free Literature, PO Box 236, Wetherby, West Yorkshire, LS23 7NB (0870 1226 236).

[1328]

FORM 3
TENANT'S REQUEST FOR A NEW BUSINESS TENANCY

Section 26 of the Landlord and Tenant Act 1954

To: (*insert name and address of landlord*)

From: (*insert name and address of tenant*)

1.   This notice relates to the following property: (*insert address or description of property*).

2.   I am giving you notice under section 26 of the Landlord and Tenant Act 1954 that I request a new tenancy beginning on   (*insert date*).

3.   You will find my proposals for the new tenancy, which we can discuss, in the Schedule to this notice.

4.   If we cannot agree on all the terms of a new tenancy, either you or I may ask the court to order the grant of a new tenancy and settle the terms on which we cannot agree.

5.   If you wish to ask the court to order the grant of a new tenancy you must do so by the date in paragraph 2, unless we agree in writing to a later date and do so before the date in paragraph 2.

6.   You may oppose my request for a new tenancy only on one or more of the grounds set out in section 30(1) of the Landlord and Tenant Act 1954. You must tell me what your grounds are within two months of receiving this notice. If you miss this deadline you will not be able to oppose renewal of my tenancy and you will have to grant me a new tenancy.

PART II
STATUTORY INSTRUMENTS

7.   Please send all correspondence about this notice to:

Name:

Address:

Signed: Date:

*[Tenant] *[On behalf of the tenant] (*delete whichever is inapplicable*)

Schedule
Tenant's Proposals For A New Tenancy

(*attach or insert proposed terms of the new tenancy*)

IMPORTANT NOTE FOR THE LANDLORD

This notice requests a new tenancy of your property or part of it. If you want to oppose this request you must act quickly.

Read the notice and all the Notes carefully. It would be wise to seek professional advice.

NOTES

The sections mentioned below are sections of the Landlord and Tenant Act 1954, as amended, (most recently by the Regulatory Reform (Business Tenancies) (England and Wales) Order 2003)

Tenant's request for a new tenancy

This request by your tenant for a new tenancy brings his or her current tenancy to an end on the day before the date mentioned in paragraph 2 of this notice. Section 26 contains rules about the date that the tenant can put in paragraph 2 of this notice.

Your tenant can apply to the court under section 24 for a new tenancy. You may apply for a new tenancy yourself, under the same section, but not if your tenant has already served an application. Once an application has been made to the court, your tenant's cur-rent tenancy will continue after the date mentioned in paragraph 2 while the application is being considered by the court. Either you or your tenant can ask the court to fix the rent which your tenant will have to pay whilst the tenancy continues (sections 24A to 24D). The court will settle any terms of a new tenancy on which you and your tenant disagree (sections 34 and 35).

Time limit for opposing your tenant's request

If you do not want to grant a new tenancy, you have <u>two months from the making of your tenant's request</u> in which to notify him or her that you will oppose any application made to the court for a new tenancy. You do not need a special form to do this, but <u>the notice must be in writing and it must state on which of the grounds set out in section 30(1) you will oppose the application.</u> If you do not use the same wording of the ground (or grounds), as set out below, your notice may be ineffective.

If there has been any delay in your seeing this notice, you may need to act very quickly. If you are in any doubt about what action you should take, get advice immediately from a solicitor or a surveyor.

Grounds for opposing tenant's application

If you wish to oppose the renewal of the tenancy, you can do so by opposing your tenant's application to the court, or by making your own application to the court for termination without renewal. However, you can only oppose your tenant's application, or apply for termination without renewal, on one or more of the grounds set out in section 30(1). These grounds are set out below. <u>You will only be able to rely on the ground(s) of opposition that you have mentioned in your written notice to your tenant.</u>

In this Table "the holding" means the property that is the subject of the tenancy.

Paragraph of section 30(1)	Grounds
(a)	Where under the current tenancy the tenant has any obligations as respects the repair and maintenance of the holding, that the tenant ought not to be granted a new tenancy in view of the state of repair of the holding, being a state resulting from the tenant's failure to comply with the said obligations.
(b)	That the tenant ought not to be granted a new tenancy in view of his persistent delay in paying rent which has become due.
(c)	That the tenant ought not to be granted a new tenancy in view of other substantial breaches by him of his obligations under the current tenancy, or for any other reason connected with the tenant's use or management of the holding.
(d)	That the landlord has offered and is willing to provide or secure the provision of alternative accommodation for the tenant, that the terms on which the alternative accommodation is available are reasonable having regard to the terms of the current tenancy and to all other relevant circumstances, and that the accommodation and the time at which it will be available are suitable for the tenant's requirements (including the requirement to preserve goodwill) having regard to the nature and class of his business and to the situation and extent of, and facilities afforded by, the holding.
(e)	Where the current tenancy was created by the sub-letting of part only of the property comprised in a superior tenancy and the landlord is the owner of an interest in reversion expectant on the termination of that superior tenancy, that the aggregate of the rents reasonably obtainable on separate lettings of the holding and the remainder of that property would be substantially less than the rent reasonably obtainable on a letting of that property as a whole, that on the termination of the current tenancy the landlord requires possession of the holding for the purposes of letting or otherwise disposing of the said property as a whole, and that in view thereof the tenant ought not to be granted a new tenancy.
(f)	That on the termination of the current tenancy the landlord intends to demolish or reconstruct the premises comprised in the holding or a substantial part of those premises or to carry out substantial work of construction on the holding or part thereof and that he could not reasonably do so without obtaining possession of the holding.
(g)	On the termination of the current tenancy the landlord intends to occupy the holding for the purposes, or partly for the purposes, of a business to be carried on by him therein, or as his residence.

PART II
STATUTORY INSTRUMENTS

Compensation

If your tenant cannot get a new tenancy solely because one or more of grounds (e), (f) and (g) applies, he or she is entitled to compensation under section 37. If you have opposed your tenant's application on any of the other grounds mentioned in section 30(1), as well as on one or more of grounds (e), (f) and (g), your tenant can only get compensation if the court's refusal to grant a new tenancy is based solely on ground (e), (f) or (g). In other words, your tenant cannot get compensation under section 37 if the court has refused the tenancy on other grounds, even if one or more of grounds (e), (f) and (g) also applies.

If you are an authority possessing compulsory purchase powers (such as a local authority), your tenant may be entitled to a disturbance payment under Part 3 of the Land Compensation Act 1973.

Negotiating a new tenancy

Most tenancies are renewed by negotiation and your tenant has set out proposals for the new tenancy in paragraph 3 of this notice. You are not obliged to accept these proposals and may put forward your own. You and your tenant may agree in writing to extend the deadline for making an application to the court while negotiations continue. Your tenant may not apply to the court for a new tenancy until two months have passed from the date of the making of the request contained in this notice, unless you have already given notice opposing your tenant's request as mentioned in paragraph 6 of this notice (section 29A(3)).

If you try to agree a new tenancy with your tenant, remember:
- that one of you will need to apply to the court before the date in paragraph 2 of this notice, unless you both agree to extend the period for making an application.
- that any such agreement must be in writing and must be made before the date in paragraph 2 (sections 29A and 29B).

Validity of this notice

The tenant who has given you this notice may not be the person from whom you receive rent (sections 44 and 67). This does not necessarily mean that the notice is invalid.

If you have any doubts about whether this notice is valid, get advice immediately from a solicitor or a surveyor.

Further information

An explanation of the main points to consider when renewing or ending a business tenancy, "Renewing and Ending Business Leases: a Guide for Tenants and Landlords", can be found at www.odpm.gov.uk. Printed copies of the explanation, but not of this form, are available from 1st June 2004 from Free Literature, PO Box 236, Wetherby, West Yorkshire, LS23 7NB (0870 1226 236).

[1329]

FORM 4
LANDLORD'S REQUEST FOR INFORMATION ABOUT OCCUPATION AND SUB-TENANCIES

Section 40(1) of the Landlord and Tenant Act 1954

To: (*insert name and address of tenant*)

From: (*insert name and address of landlord*)

1. This notice relates to the following premises: (*insert address or description of premises*)

2. I give you notice under section 40(1) of the Landlord and Tenant Act 1954 that I require you to provide information—

(a) by answering questions (1) to (3) in the Table below;

(b) if you answer "yes" to question (2), by giving me the name and address of the person or persons concerned;

(c) if you answer "yes" to question (3), by also answering questions (4) to (10) in the Table below;

(d) if you answer "no" to question (8), by giving me the name and address of the sub-tenant; and

(e) if you answer "yes" to question (10), by giving me details of the notice or request.

TABLE

(1) Do you occupy the premises or any part of them wholly or partly for the purposes of a business that is carried on by you?
(2) To the best of your knowledge and belief, does any other person own an interest in reversion in any part of the premises?
(3) Does your tenancy have effect subject to any sub-tenancy on which your tenancy is immediately expectant?
(4) What premises are comprised in the sub-tenancy?
(5) For what term does it have effect or, if it is terminable by notice, by what notice can it be terminated?

(6)   What is the rent payable under it?
(7)   Who is the sub-tenant?
(8)   To the best of your knowledge and belief, is the sub-tenant in occupation of the premises or of part of the premises comprised in the sub-tenancy?
(9)   Is an agreement in force excluding, in relation to the sub-tenancy, the provisions of sections 24 to 28 of the Landlord and Tenant Act 1954?
(10)   Has a notice been given under section 25 or 26(6) of that Act, or has a request been made under section 26 of that Act, in relation to the sub-tenancy?

3.   You must give the information concerned in writing and within the period of one month beginning with the date of service of this notice.

4.   Please send all correspondence about this notice to:

Name:

Address:

Signed: Date:

*[Landlord] *[on behalf of the landlord] *delete whichever is inapplicable*

IMPORTANT NOTE FOR THE TENANT

This notice contains some words and phrases that you may not understand. The Notes below should help you, but it would be wise to seek professional advice, for example, from a solicitor or surveyor, before responding to this notice.

Once you have provided the information required by this notice, you must correct it if you realise that it is not, or is no longer, correct. This obligation lasts for six months from the date of service of this notice, but an exception is explained in the next paragraph. If you need to correct information already given, you must do so within one month of becoming aware that the information is incorrect.

The obligation will cease if, after transferring your tenancy, you notify the landlord of the transfer and of the name and address of the person to whom your tenancy has been transferred.

If you fail to comply with the requirements of this notice, or the obligation mentioned above, you may face civil proceedings for breach of the statutory duty that arises under section 40 of the Landlord and Tenant Act 1954. In any such proceedings a court may order you to comply with that duty and may make an award of damages.

NOTES

The sections mentioned below are sections of the Landlord and Tenant Act 1954, as amended, (most recently by the Regulatory Reform (Business Tenancies) (England and Wales) Order 2003)

Purpose of this notice

Your landlord (or, if he or she is a tenant, possibly your landlord's landlord) has sent you this notice in order to obtain information about your occupation and that of any sub-tenants. This information may be relevant to the taking of steps to end or renew your business tenancy.

Time limit for replying

You must provide the relevant information within one month of the date of service of this notice (section 40(1), (2) and (5)).

Information required

You do not have to give your answers on this form; you may use a separate sheet for this purpose. The notice requires you to provide, in writing, information in the form of answers to questions (1) to (3) in the Table above and, if you answer "yes" to question (3), also to provide information in the form of answers to questions (4) to (10) in that Table. Depending on your answer to question (2) and, if applicable in your case, questions (8) and (10), you must also provide the information referred to in paragraph 2(b), (d) and (e) of this notice. Question (2) refers to a person who owns an interest in reversion. You should answer "yes" to this question if you know or believe that there is a person who receives, or is entitled to receive, rent in respect of any part of the premises (other than the landlord who served this notice).

When you answer questions about sub-tenants, please bear in mind that, for these purposes, a sub-tenant includes a person retaining possession of premises by virtue of the Rent (Agriculture) Act 1976 or the Rent Act 1977 after the coming to an end of a sub-tenancy, and "sub-tenancy" includes a right so to retain possession (section 40(8)).

You should keep a copy of your answers and of any other information provided in response to questions (2), (8) or (10) above.

If, once you have given this information, you realise that it is not, or is no longer, correct, you must give the correct information within one month of becoming aware that the previous information is incorrect. Subject to the next paragraph, your duty to correct any information that you have already given continues for six months after you receive this notice (section 40(5)). You should give the correct information to the landlord who gave you this notice unless you receive notice of the transfer of his or her interest, and of the name and address of the person to whom that interest has been transferred. In that case, the correct information must be given to that person.

If you transfer your tenancy within the period of six months referred to above, your duty to correct information already given will cease if you notify the landlord of the transfer and of the name and address of the person to whom your tenancy has been transferred.

If you do not provide the information requested, or fail to correct information that you have provided earlier, after realising that it is not, or is no longer, correct, proceedings may be taken against you and you may have to pay damages (section 40B).

If you are in any doubt about the information that you should give, get immediate advice from a solicitor or a surveyor.

Validity of this notice

The landlord who has given you this notice may not be the landlord to whom you pay your rent (sections 44 and 67). This does not necessarily mean that the notice is invalid.

If you have any doubts about whether this notice is valid, get advice immediately from a solicitor or a surveyor.

Further information

An explanation of the main points to consider when renewing or ending a business tenancy, "Renewing and Ending Business Leases: a Guide for Tenants and Landlords", can be found at www.odpm.gov.uk. Printed copies of the explanation, but not of this form, are available from 1st June 2004 from Free Literature, PO Box 236, Wetherby, West Yorkshire, LS23 7NB (0870 1226 236).

[1330]

FORM 5
TENANT'S REQUEST FOR INFORMATION FROM LANDLORD OR LANDLORD'S MORTGAGEE ABOUT LANDLORD'S INTEREST

Section 40(3) of the Landlord and Tenant Act 1954

To: *(insert name and address of reversioner or reversioner's mortgagee in possession [see the first note below])*

From: *(insert name and address of tenant)*

1. This notice relates to the following premises: *(insert address or description of premises)*

2. In accordance with section 40(3) of the Landlord and Tenant Act 1954 I require you—

(a) to state in writing whether you are the owner of the fee simple in respect of the premises or any part of them or the mortgagee in possession of such an owner,

(b) if you answer "no" to (a), to state in writing, to the best of your knowledge and belief—

(i)   the name and address of the person who is your or, as the case may be, your mortgagor's immediate landlord in respect of the premises or of the part in respect of which you are not, or your mortgagor is not, the owner in fee simple;

(ii)   for what term your or your mortgagor's tenancy has effect and what is the earliest date (if any) at which that tenancy is terminable by notice to quit given by the landlord; and

(iii)   whether a notice has been given under section 25 or 26(6) of the Landlord and Tenant Act 1954, or a request has been made under section 26 of that Act, in relation to the tenancy and, if so, details of the notice or request;

(c)   to state in writing, to the best of your knowledge and belief, the name and address of any other person who owns an interest in reversion in any part of the premises;

(d)   if you are a reversioner, to state in writing whether there is a mortgagee in possession of your interest in the premises; and

(e)   if you answer "yes" to (d), to state in writing, to the best of your knowledge and belief, the name and address of the mortgagee in possession.

3.   You must give the information concerned within the period of one month beginning with the date of service of this notice.

4.   Please send all correspondence about this notice to:

Name:

Address:

Signed: Date:

*[Tenant] *[on behalf of the tenant] (*delete whichever is inapplicable*)

IMPORTANT NOTE FOR LANDLORD OR LANDLORD'S MORTGAGEE

This notice contains some words and phrases that you may not understand. The Notes below should help you, but it would be wise to seek professional advice, for example, from a solicitor or surveyor, before responding to this notice.

Once you have provided the information required by this notice, you must correct it if you realise that it is not, or is no longer, correct. This obligation lasts for six months from the date of service of this notice, but an exception is explained in the next paragraph. If you need to correct information already given, you must do so within one month of becoming aware that the information is incorrect.

The obligation will cease if, after transferring your interest, you notify the tenant of the transfer and of the name and address of the person to whom your interest has been transferred.

If you fail to comply with the requirements of this notice, or the obligation mentioned above, you may face civil proceedings for breach of the statutory duty that arises under section 40 of the Landlord and Tenant Act 1954. In any such proceedings a court may order you to comply with that duty and may make an award of damages.

NOTES

The sections mentioned below are sections of the Landlord and Tenant Act 1954, as amended, (most recently by the Regulatory Reform (Business Tenancies) (England and Wales) Order 2003)

Terms used in this notice

The following terms, which are used in paragraph 2 of this notice, are defined in section 40(8):

"mortgagee in possession" includes a receiver appointed by the mortgagee or by the court who is in receipt of the rents and profits;

"reversioner" means any person having an interest in the premises, being an interest in reversion expectant (whether immediately or not) on the tenancy; and

"reversioner's mortgagee in possession" means any person being a mortgagee in possession in respect of such an interest.

Section 40(8) requires the reference in paragraph 2(b) of this notice to your mortgagor to be read in the light of the definition of "mortgagee in possession".

A mortgagee (mortgage lender) will be "in possession" if the mortgagor (the person who owes money to the mortgage lender) has failed to comply with the terms of the mortgage. The mortgagee may then be entitled to receive rent that would normally have been paid to the mortgagor.

The term "the owner of the fee simple" means the freehold owner.

The term "reversioner" includes the freehold owner and any intermediate landlord as well as the immediate landlord of the tenant who served this notice.

Purpose of this notice and information required

This notice requires you to provide, in writing, the information requested in paragraph 2(a) and (c) of the notice and, if applicable in your case, in paragraph 2(b), (d) and (e). You do not need to use a special form for this purpose.

If, once you have given this information, you realise that it is not, or is no longer, correct, you must give the correct information within one month of becoming aware that the previous information is incorrect. Subject to the last paragraph in this section of these Notes, your duty to correct any information that you have already given continues for six months after you receive this notice (section 40(5)).

You should give the correct information to the tenant who gave you this notice unless you receive notice of the transfer of his or her interest, and of the name and address of the person to whom that interest has been transferred. In that case, the correct information must be given to that person.

If you do not provide the information requested, or fail to correct information that you have provided earlier, after realising that it is not, or is no longer, correct, proceedings may be taken against you and you may have to pay damages (section 40B).

If you are in any doubt as to the information that you should give, get advice immediately from a solicitor or a surveyor.

If you transfer your interest within the period of six months referred to above, your duty to correct information already given will cease if you notify the tenant of that transfer and of the name and address of the person to whom your interest has been transferred.

Time limit for replying

You must provide the relevant information within one month of the date of service of this notice (section 40(3), (4) and (5)).

Validity of this notice

The tenant who has given you this notice may not be the person from whom you receive rent (sections 44 and 67). This does not necessarily mean that the notice is invalid.

If you have any doubts about the validity of the notice, get advice immediately from a solicitor or a surveyor.

Further information

An explanation of the main points to consider when renewing or ending a business tenancy, "Renewing and Ending Business Leases: a Guide for Tenants and Landlords", can be found at www.odpm.gov.uk. Printed copies of the explanation, but not of this form, are available from 1st June 2004 from Free Literature, PO Box 236, Wetherby, West Yorkshire, LS23 7NB (0870 1226 236).

[1331]

FORM 6
LANDLORD'S WITHDRAWAL OF NOTICE TERMINATING TENANCY

Section 44 of, and Paragraph 6 of Schedule 6 to, the Landlord And Tenant Act 1954

To: (*insert name and address of tenant*)

From: (*insert name and address of landlord*)

1.   This notice is given under section 44 of, and paragraph 6 of Schedule 6 to, the Landlord and Tenant Act 1954 ("the 1954 Act").

2.   It relates to the following property: (*insert address or description of property*)

3.   I have become your landlord for the purposes of the 1954 Act.

4.   I withdraw the notice given to you by (*insert name of former landlord*), terminating your tenancy on (*insert date*).

5.   Please send any correspondence about this notice to:

Name:

Address:

Signed: Date:

*[Landlord] *[on behalf of the landlord] (**delete whichever is inapplicable*)

IMPORTANT NOTE FOR THE TENANT

If you have any doubts about the validity of this notice, get advice immediately from a solicitor or a surveyor.

NOTES

The sections and Schedule mentioned below are sections of, and a Schedule to, the Landlord and Tenant Act 1954, as amended, (most recently by the Regulatory Reform (Business Tenancies) (England and Wales) Order 2003).

Purpose of this notice

You were earlier given a notice bringing your tenancy to an end, but there has now been a change of landlord. This new notice is given to you by your new landlord and withdraws the earlier notice, which now has no effect. However, the new landlord can, if he or she wishes, give you a fresh notice with the intention of bringing your tenancy to an end (section 44 and paragraph 6 of Schedule 6)

Validity of this notice

The landlord who has given you this notice may not be the landlord to whom you pay your rent (sections 44 and 67). This does not necessarily mean that the notice is invalid.

If you have any doubts about whether this notice is valid, get advice immediately from a solicitor or a surveyor. If this notice is *not* valid, the original notice will have effect. Your tenancy will end on the date given in that notice (stated in paragraph 4 of this notice).

Further information

An explanation of the main points to consider when renewing or ending a business tenancy, "Renewing and Ending Business Leases: a Guide for Tenants and Landlords", can be found at **www.odpm.gov.uk** Printed copies of the explanation, but not of this form, are available from 1st June 2004 from Free Literature, PO Box 236, Wetherby, West Yorkshire, LS23 7NB (0870 1226 236).

[1332]

FORM 7
LANDLORD'S NOTICE ENDING A BUSINESS TENANCY (WITH REASONS FOR REFUSING A NEW TENANCY) WHERE THE LEASEHOLD REFORM ACT 1967 MAY APPLY

Section 25 of the Landlord and Tenant Act 1954 and paragraph 10 of Schedule 3 to the Leasehold Reform Act 1967

IMPORTANT NOTE FOR THE LANDLORD: Use this form where you wish to oppose the grant of a new tenancy, and the tenant may be entitled to acquire the freehold or an extended lease. Complete this form and send it to the tenant. If you are opposed to the grant of a new tenancy, and the tenant is not entitled to acquire the freehold or an extended lease, use form 2 in Schedule 2 to the Landlord and Tenant Act 1954, Part 2 (Notices) Regulations 2004 instead of this form.

PART II STATUTORY INSTRUMENTS

To: (*insert name and address of tenant*)

From: (*insert name and address of landlord*)

1.   This notice relates to the following property: (*insert address or description of property*)

2.   I am giving you notice under section 25 of the Landlord and Tenant Act 1954 to end your tenancy on (*insert date*).

3.   I am opposed to the grant of a new tenancy.

4.   You may ask the court to order the grant of a new tenancy. If you do, I will oppose your application on the ground(s) mentioned in paragraph(s)* of section 30(1) of that Act. I draw your attention to the Table in the Notes below, which sets out all the grounds of opposition.

* (*insert letter(s) of the paragraph(s) relied on*)

5.   If you wish to ask the court for a new tenancy you must do so by the date in paragraph 2 unless, before that date, we agree in writing to a later date

6.   I can ask the court to order the ending of your tenancy without granting you a new tenancy. I may have to pay you compensation if I have relied only on one or more of the grounds mentioned in paragraph (e), (f) and (g) of section 30(1). If I ask the court to end your tenancy, you can challenge my application.

7.   If you have a right under Part 1 of the Leasehold Reform Act 1967 to acquire the freehold or an extended lease of property comprised in the tenancy, notice of your desire to have the freehold or an extended lease cannot be given more than two months after the service of this notice. If you have that right, and give notice of your desire to have the freehold or an extended lease within those two months, this notice will not operate, and I may take no further proceedings under Part 2 of the Landlord and Tenant Act 1954.

*8.   If you give notice of your desire to have the freehold or an extended lease, I will be entitled to apply to the court under section 17/section 18** of the Leasehold Reform Act 1967, and propose to do so. If I am successful I may have to pay you compensation. (**delete the reference to section 17 or section 18, as the circumstances require*)

OR

*8.   If you give notice of your desire to have the freehold or an extended lease, I will be entitled to apply to the court under section 17/section 18** of the Leasehold Reform Act 1967, but do not propose to do so. (**delete the reference to section 17 or section 18, as the circumstances require*)

OR

*8.   If you give notice of your desire to have the freehold or an extended lease, I will not be entitled to apply to the court under section 17 or section 18 of the Leasehold Reform Act 1967.

*DELETE TWO *versions of this paragraph, as the circumstances require*

*9.   I know or believe that the following persons have an interest superior to your tenancy or to be the agent concerned with the property on behalf of someone who has such an interest (*insert names and addresses*):

delete if inapplicable

10.   Please send all correspondence about this notice to:

Name:

Address:

Signed: Date:

*[Landlord] *[On behalf of the landlord] *[Mortgagee] *[On behalf of the mortgagee]

(**delete if inapplicable*)

IMPORTANT NOTE FOR THE TENANT

This Notice is intended to bring your tenancy to an end on the date specified in paragraph 2.

Your landlord is not prepared to offer you a new tenancy. <u>You will not get a new tenancy unless you successfully challenge in court the grounds on which your landlord opposes the grant of a new tenancy.</u>

If you want to continue to occupy your property you must act quickly. The notes below should help you to decide what action you now need to take. If you want to challenge your landlord's refusal to renew your tenancy, get advice immediately from a solicitor or a surveyor.

NOTES

Unless otherwise stated, the sections mentioned below are sections of the Landlord and Tenant Act 1954, as amended, (most recently by the Regulatory Reform (Business Tenancies) (England and Wales) Order 2003)

Ending of your tenancy

This notice is intended to bring your tenancy to an end on the date given in paragraph 2. Section 25 contains rules about the date that the landlord can put in paragraph 2 of this notice.

Your landlord is not prepared to offer you a new tenancy. If you want a new tenancy you will need to apply to the court for a new tenancy and successfully challenge the landlord's opposition (see the section below headed "*Landlord's opposition to new tenancy*"). If you wish to apply to the court you must do so before the date given in paragraph 2 of this notice, unless you and your landlord have agreed in writing, before that date, to extend the deadline (sections 29A and 29B).

If you apply to the court your tenancy will continue after the date given in paragraph 2 of this notice while your application is being considered (section 24). You may not apply to the court if your landlord has already done so (section 24(2A) and (2B)).

You may only stay in the property after the date given in paragraph 2 (or such later date as you and the landlord may have agreed in writing) if before that date you have asked the court to order the grant of a new tenancy or the landlord has asked the court to order the ending of your tenancy without granting you a new one.

If you are in any doubt about what action you should take, get advice immediately from a solicitor or a surveyor.

Landlord's opposition to new tenancy

If you apply to the court for a new tenancy, the landlord can only oppose your application on one or more of the grounds set out in section 30(1). If you match the letter(s) specified in paragraph 4 of the notice with those in the first column in the Table below, you can see from the second column the ground(s) on which the landlord relies.

Paragraph of section 30(1)	*Grounds*
(a)	Where under the current tenancy the tenant has any obligations as respects the repair and maintenance of the holding, that the tenant ought not to be granted a new tenancy in view of the state of repair of the holding, being a state resulting from the tenant's failure to comply with the said obligations.
(b)	That the tenant ought not to be granted a new tenancy in view of his persistent delay in paying rent which has become due.
(c)	That the tenant ought not to be granted a new tenancy in view of other substantial breaches by him of his obligations under the current tenancy, or for any other reason connected with the tenant's use or management of the holding.

PART II
STATUTORY INSTRUMENTS

Paragraph of section 30(1)	*Grounds*
(d)	That the landlord has offered and is willing to provide or secure the provision of alternative accommodation for the tenant, that the terms on which the alternative accommodation is available are reasonable having regard to the terms of the current tenancy and to all other relevant circumstances, and that the accommodation and the time at which it will be available are suitable for the tenant's requirements (including the requirement to preserve goodwill) having regard to the nature and class of his business and to the situation and extent of, and facilities afforded by, the holding.
(e)	Where the current tenancy was created by the sub-letting of part only of the property comprised in a superior tenancy and the landlord is the owner of an interest in reversion expectant on the termination of that superior tenancy, that the aggregate of the rents reasonably obtainable on separate lettings of the holding and the remainder of that property would be substantially less than the rent reasonably obtainable on a letting of that property as a whole, that on the termination of the current tenancy the landlord requires possession of the holding for the purposes of letting or otherwise disposing of the said property as a whole, and that in view thereof the tenant ought not to be granted a new tenancy.
(f)	That on the termination of the current tenancy the landlord intends to demolish or reconstruct the premises comprised in the holding or a substantial part of those premises or to carry out substantial work of construction on the holding or part thereof and that he could not reasonably do so without obtaining possession of the holding.
(g)	On the termination of the current tenancy the landlord intends to occupy the holding for the purposes, or partly for the purposes, of a business to be carried on by him therein, or as his residence.

In this Table "the holding" means the property that is the subject of the tenancy.

In ground (e), "the landlord is the owner an interest in reversion expectant on the termination of that superior tenancy" means that the landlord has an interest in the property that will entitle him or her, when your immediate landlord's tenancy comes to an end, to exercise certain rights and obligations in relation to the property that are currently exercisable by your immediate landlord.

If the landlord relies on ground (f), the court can sometimes still grant a new tenancy if certain conditions set out in section 31A are met.

If the landlord relies on ground (g), please note that "the landlord" may have an extended meaning. Where a landlord has a controlling interest in a company then either the landlord or the company can rely on ground (g). Where the landlord is a company and a person has a controlling interest in that company then either of them can rely on ground (g) (section 30(1A) and (1B)). A person has a "controlling interest" in a company if, had he been a company, the other company would have been its subsidiary (section 46(2)).

The landlord must normally have been the landlord for at least five years before he or she can rely on ground (g).

Rights under the Leasehold Reform Act 1967

If the property comprised in your tenancy is a house, as defined in section 2 of the Leasehold Reform Act 1967 ("the 1967 Act"), you may have the right to buy the freehold of the property or an extended lease. If the house is for the time being let under two or more tenancies, you will not have that right if your tenancy is subject to a sub-tenancy and the sub-tenant is himself or herself entitled to that right.

You will have that right if all the following conditions are met:
    (i)   your lease was originally granted for a term of more than 35 years, or was preceded by such a lease which was granted or assigned to you; and
    (ii) your lease is of the whole house; and

(iii)   your lease is at a low rent. If your tenancy was entered into before 1 April 1990 (or later if you contracted before that date to enter into the tenancy) "low rent" means that your present annual rent is less than two-thirds of the rateable value of your house as assessed either on 23 March 1965, or on the first day of the term in the case of a lease granted to commence after 23 March 1965; and the property had a rateable value other than nil when the tenancy began or at any time before 1 April 1990. If your tenancy was granted on or after 1 April 1990, "low rent" means that the present annual rent is not more than £1,000 in London or £250 elsewhere; and

(iv)   you have been occupying the house (or any part of it) as your only or main residence (whether or not it has been occupied for other purposes) either for the whole of the last two years, or for a total of two years in the last ten years; and

(v)   the rateable value of your house was at one time within certain limits.

Claiming your rights under the 1967 Act

If you have a right to buy the freehold or an extended lease and wish to exercise it you must serve the appropriate notice on the landlord. A special form is prescribed for this purpose; it is Form 1 as set out in the Schedule to the Leasehold Reform (Notices) (Amendment) (England) Regulations 2002 (SI 2002/1715) or, if the property is in Wales, the Leasehold Reform (Notices) (Amendment) (Wales) Regulations 2002 (SI 2002/3187) (W 303). Subject to the two exceptions mentioned below, you must serve the notice claiming to buy the freehold or an extended lease within two months after the date of service of this notice. The first exception is where, within that two-month period, you apply to the court to order the grant of a new tenancy. In that case your claim to buy the freehold or an extended lease must be made when you make the application to the court. The second exception is where the landlord agrees in writing to your claim being made after the date on which it should have been made.

There are special rules about the service of notices. If there has been any delay in your seeing this notice, you may need to act very quickly.

If you are in any doubt about your rights under the 1967 Act or what action you should take, get advice immediately from a solicitor or a surveyor.

Landlord's opposition to claims under the 1967 Act

If your landlord acquired his or her interest in the house not later than 18 February 1966 he or she can object to your claim to buy the freehold or an extended lease on the grounds that he or she needs to occupy the house or that the house is needed for occupation by a member of his or her family. This objection will be under section 18 of the 1967 Act.

If you claim an extended lease, your landlord can object under section 17 of the 1967 Act on the grounds that he or she wishes to redevelop the property.

You will be able to tell from paragraph 8 of this notice whether your landlord intends to apply to the court and, if so, whether for the purposes of occupation or redevelopment of the house.

Compensation

If you cannot get a new tenancy solely because one or more of grounds (e), (f) and (g) in section 30(1) applies, you may be entitled to compensation under section 37. If your landlord has opposed your application on any of the other grounds as well as (e), (f) or (g) you can only get compensation if the court's refusal to grant a new tenancy is based solely on one or more of grounds (e), (f) and (g). In other words, you cannot get compensation under section 37 if the court has refused your tenancy on other grounds, even if one or more of grounds (e), (f) and (g) also applies.

If your landlord is an authority possessing compulsory purchase powers (such as a local authority) you may be entitled to a disturbance payment under Part 3 of the Land Compensation Act 1973.

If you have a right under the 1967 Act to buy the freehold or an extended lease but the landlord is able to obtain possession of the premises, compensation is payable under section 17(2) or section 18(4) of the 1967 Act. Your solicitor or surveyor will be able to advise you about this.

Negotiations with your landlord

If you try to buy the property by agreement or negotiate an extended lease with the landlord, remember:

●   that your present tenancy will not be extended under the 1954 Act after the date in paragraph 2 of this notice unless you agree in writing to extend the deadline for applying to the court under the 1954 Act or you (or the landlord) has applied to the court before that date (sections 29, 29A and 29B), and

- that you may lose your right to serve a notice claiming to buy the freehold or an extended lease under the 1967 Act if you do not observe the two-month time limit referred to in the note headed *Claiming your rights under the 1967 Act*.

Validity of this notice

The landlord who has given you this notice may not be the landlord to whom you pay your rent (sections 44 and 67). This does not necessarily mean that the notice is invalid.

If you have any doubts about whether this notice is valid, get advice immediately from a solicitor or a surveyor

Further information

An explanation of the main points to consider when renewing or ending a business tenancy, "Renewing and Ending Business Leases: a Guide for Tenants and Landlords", can be found at www.odpm.gov.uk. Printed copies of the explanation, but not of this form, are available from 1st June 2004 from Free Literature, PO Box 236, Wetherby, West Yorkshire, LS23 7NB (0870 1226 236).

[1333]

FORM 8
NOTICE ENDING A BUSINESS TENANCY ON PUBLIC INTEREST GROUNDS

Sections 25 and 57 of the Landlord and Tenant Act 1954

IMPORTANT NOTE FOR THE LANDLORD: Use this form if you have a section 57 certificate, but where the tenant may be entitled to acquire the freehold or an extended lease, use form 13 in Schedule 2 to the Landlord and Tenant Act 1954, Part 2 (Notices) Regulations 2004 instead of this form.

To: (*insert name and address of tenant*)

From: (*insert name and address of landlord*)

1.   This notice relates to the following property: (*insert address or description of property*)

2.   I am giving you notice under section 25 of the Landlord and Tenant Act 1954 ("the 1954 Act") to end your tenancy on (*insert date*).

3.   A certificate has been given by (*state the title of the Secretary of State on whose authority the certificate was issued or, if the certificate was issued by the National Assembly for Wales, insert* "the National Assembly for Wales") under section 57 of the 1954 Act that the use or occupation of all or part of the property should be changed by (*insert date*). A copy of the certificate appears in the Schedule to this notice.

4.   Please send all correspondence about this notice to:

Name:

Address:

Signed: Date:

*[Landlord] *[On behalf of the landlord] *[Mortgagee] *[On behalf of the mortgagee]

(**delete if inapplicable*)

Schedule
Certificate under Section 57

(*attach or insert a copy of the section 57 certificate*)

IMPORTANT NOTE FOR THE TENANT

This notice is intended to bring your tenancy to an end on the date specified in paragraph 2.

The landlord is not prepared to offer you a new tenancy because it has been certified that the occupation or use of the premises should be changed no later than the date specified in paragraph 2. The date by which the change must have taken place is specified in paragraph 3.

NOTES

The sections mentioned below are sections of the Landlord and Tenant Act 1954, as amended, (most recently by the Regulatory Reform (Business Tenancies) (England and Wales) Order 2003)

Ending of your tenancy

This notice is intended to bring your tenancy to an end on the date stated in paragraph 2 of the notice.

Your landlord is both giving you notice that your current tenancy will end on the date stated in paragraph 2 of this notice and drawing attention to a certificate under section 57 that would prevent you from applying to the court for a new tenancy.

Usually, tenants who have tenancies under Part 2 of the Landlord and Tenant Act 1954 can apply to the court for a new tenancy. However, the effect of the section 57 certificate that it is requisite that the use or occupation of all or part of the property should be changed by a certain date, is to prevent the tenant from making an application to the court for a new tenancy.

Compensation

Because the court cannot order the grant of a new tenancy, you may be entitled to compensation when you leave the property (section 59). If your landlord is an authority possessing compulsory purchase powers (such as a local authority) you may also be entitled to a disturbance payment under Part 3 of the Land Compensation Act 1973.

Validity of this notice

The landlord who has given you this notice may not be the landlord to whom you pay your rent (sections 44 and 67). This does not necessarily mean that the notice is invalid.

If you have any doubts about whether this notice is valid, get advice immediately from a solicitor or a surveyor.

Further information

An explanation of the main points to consider when renewing or ending a business tenancy, "Renewing and Ending Business Leases: a Guide for Tenants and Landlords", can be found at www.odpm.gov.uk. Printed copies of the explanation, but not of this form, are available from 1st June from Free Literature, PO Box 236, Wetherby, West Yorkshire, LS23 7NB (0870 1226 236).

[1334]

FORM 9
NOTICE ENDING A BUSINESS TENANCY WHERE A CHANGE IS REQUIRED AT A FUTURE DATE AND THE LANDLORD OPPOSES A NEW TENANCY

Sections 25 and 57 of the Landlord and Tenant Act 1954

IMPORTANT NOTE FOR THE LANDLORD: Use this form if you have a section 57 certificate and you wish to oppose the grant of a new tenancy, for the period between the end of the current tenancy and the date given in the section 57 certificate, on any of the grounds in section 30(1) of the Landlord and Tenant Act 1954.

If you are willing to grant a new tenancy for that period, use form 10 in Schedule 2 to the Landlord and Tenant Act 1954, Part 2 (Notices) Regulations 2004 instead of this form.

If the tenant may be entitled to acquire the freehold or an extended lease, use form 14 in that Schedule, instead of this form or form 10.

To: (*insert name and address of tenant*)

From: (*insert name and address of landlord*)

PART II
STATUTORY INSTRUMENTS

1.   This notice relates to the following property: (*insert address or description of property*)

2.   I am giving you notice under section 25 of the Landlord and Tenant Act 1954 ("the 1954 Act") to end your tenancy on (*insert date*).

3.   A certificate has been given by (*state the title of the Secretary of State on whose authority the certificate was issued or, if the certificate was issued by the National Assembly for Wales, insert* "the National Assembly for Wales") under section 57 of the 1954 that the use or occupation of all or part of the property should be changed by (*insert date*). A copy of the certificate appears in the Schedule to this notice.

4.   I do not intend to grant you a new tenancy between the end of your current tenancy and the date specified in the section 57 certificate.

5.   You may ask the court to order the grant of a new tenancy for a term ending not later than the date specified in the section 57 certificate. If you do, I will oppose your application on the ground(s) mentioned in paragraph(s)* of section 30(1) of the Act. I draw your attention to the Table in the Notes below, which sets out all the grounds of opposition.

* (*insert letter(s) of the paragraph(s) relied on*)

6.   If you wish to ask the court for a new tenancy you must do so by the date in paragraph 2 unless, before that date, we agree in writing to a later date.

7.   I can ask the court to order the ending of your tenancy without granting you a new tenancy. If I do, you can challenge my application.

8.   Please send all correspondence about this notice to:

Name:

Address:

Signed: Date:

*[Landlord] *[On behalf of the landlord] *[Mortgagee] *[On behalf of the mortgagee]

(**delete if inapplicable*)

IMPORTANT NOTE FOR THE TENANT

This Notice is intended to bring your tenancy to an end on the date specified in paragraph 2.

A certificate has been given that it is requisite that occupation or use of the premises should be changed by the date specified in paragraph 3 of this notice.

Your landlord has indicated that he will oppose your application for a new tenancy (if you decide to make one). <u>You will not get a new tenancy unless you successfully challenge in court the grounds on which your landlord opposes the grant of a new tenancy.</u>

If you want to continue to occupy your property you must act quickly. The notes below should help you to decide what action you now need to take. If you want to challenge your landlord's refusal to renew your tenancy, get advice immediately from a solicitor or a surveyor.

NOTES

The sections mentioned below are sections of the Landlord and Tenant Act 1954, as amended, (most recently by the Regulatory Reform (Business Tenancies) (England and Wales) Order 2003)

Ending of your tenancy

This notice is intended to bring your tenancy to an end on the date specified in paragraph 2 of the notice.

Claiming a new tenancy

Your landlord is <u>not</u> prepared to offer you a new tenancy for a limited period pending the effect of the section 57 certificate (see the section below headed "*Effect of section 57 certificate*"). If you want a new tenancy for this period you will need to apply to the court for a new tenancy and successfully challenge the landlord's opposition (see the section below headed *"Landlord's opposition to new tenancy"*).

If you wish to apply to the court you must do so before the date specified in paragraph 2 of this notice, unless you and your landlord have agreed in writing, before that date, to extend the deadline (sections 29A and 29B). However, before you take that step, read carefully the section below headed *"Effect of section 57 certificate"*.

If you apply to the court your tenancy will continue after the date specified in paragraph 2 of this notice while your application is being considered (section 24).

If you are in any doubt about what action you should take, get advice immediately from a solicitor or a surveyor.

Landlord's opposition to new tenancy

If you apply to the court for a new tenancy, the landlord can only oppose your application on one or more of the grounds set out in section 30(1). If you match the letter(s) specified in paragraph 5 of the notice with those in the first column in the Table below, you can see from the second column the ground(s) on which the landlord relies.

Paragraph of section 30(1)	Grounds
(a)	Where under the current tenancy the tenant has any obligations as respects the repair and maintenance of the holding, that the tenant ought not to be granted a new tenancy in view of the state of repair of the holding, being a state resulting from the tenant's failure to comply with the said obligations.
(b)	That the tenant ought not to be granted a new tenancy in view of his persistent delay in paying rent which has become due.
(c)	That the tenant ought not to be granted a new tenancy in view of other substantial breaches by him of his obligations under the current tenancy, or for any other reason connected with the tenant's use or management of the holding.
(d)	That the landlord has offered and is willing to provide or secure the provision of alternative accommodation for the tenant, that the terms on which the alternative accommodation is available are reasonable having regard to the terms of the current tenancy and to all other relevant circumstances, and that the accommodation and the time at which it will be available are suitable for the tenant's requirements (including the requirement to preserve goodwill) having regard to the nature and class of his business and to the situation and extent of, and facilities afforded by, the holding.
(e)	Where the current tenancy was created by the sub-letting of part only of the property comprised in a superior tenancy and the landlord is the owner of an interest in reversion expectant on the termination of that superior tenancy, that the aggregate of the rents reasonably obtainable on separate lettings of the holding and the remainder of that property would be substantially less than the rent reasonably obtainable on a letting of that property as a whole, that on the termination of the current tenancy the landlord requires possession of the holding for the purposes of letting or otherwise disposing of the said property as a whole, and that in view thereof the tenant ought not to be granted a new tenancy.
(f)	That on the termination of the current tenancy the landlord intends to demolish or reconstruct the premises comprised in the holding or a substantial part of those premises or to carry out substantial work of construction on the holding or part thereof and that he could not reasonably do so without obtaining possession of the holding.

Paragraph of section 30(1)	Grounds
(g)	On the termination of the current tenancy the landlord intends to occupy the holding for the purposes, or partly for the purposes, of a business to be carried on by him therein, or as his residence.

In this Table "the holding" means the property that is the subject of the tenancy.

In ground (e), "the landlord is the owner an interest in reversion expectant on the termination of that superior tenancy" means that the landlord has an interest in the property that will entitle him, when your immediate landlord's tenancy comes to an end, to exercise certain rights and obligations in relation to the property that are currently exercisable by your immediate landlord.

If the landlord relies on ground (f), the court can sometimes still grant a new tenancy if certain conditions set out in section 31A are met.

If the landlord relies on ground (g), please note that "the landlord" may have an extended meaning. Where a landlord has a controlling interest in a company then either the landlord or the company can rely on ground (g). Where the landlord is a company and a person has a controlling interest in that company then either of them can rely on ground (g) (section 30(1A) and (1B)). A person has a "controlling interest" in a company if, had he been a company, the other company would have been its subsidiary (section 46(2)).

The landlord must normally have been the landlord for at least five years before he or she can rely on ground (g).

Effect of section 57 certificate

A copy of a certificate issued under section 57 appears in the Schedule to this notice. The effect of the certificate is that, even if you are successful in challenging your landlord's opposition to the grant of a new tenancy, and the court orders the grant of a new tenancy, the new tenancy must end not later than the date specified in the certificate (section 57(3)(b)). Any new tenancy will not be a tenancy to which Part 2 of the 1954 Act applies (section 57(3)(b)).

Compensation

If you cannot get a new tenancy solely because one or more of grounds (e), (f) and (g) applies, you may be entitled to compensation under section 37. If your landlord has opposed your application on any of the other grounds as well as (e), (f) or (g) you can only get compensation if the court's refusal to grant a new tenancy is based solely on one or more of grounds (e), (f) and (g). In other words, you cannot get compensation under section 37 if the court has refused your tenancy on other grounds, even if one or more of grounds (e), (f) and (g) also applies.

If the court orders the grant of a new tenancy, you may be entitled to compensation under section 59 when you leave the property (on or before the date specified in the section 57 certificate).

If your landlord is an authority possessing compulsory purchase powers (such as a local authority) you may be entitled to a disturbance payment under Part 3 of the Land Compensation Act 1973.

Validity of this notice

The landlord who has given you this notice may not be the landlord to whom you pay your rent (sections 44 and 67). This does not necessarily mean that the notice is invalid.

If you have any doubts about whether this notice is valid, get advice immediately from a solicitor or a surveyor.

Further information

An explanation of the main points to consider when renewing or ending a business tenancy, "Renewing and Ending Business Leases: a Guide for Tenants and Landlords", can be found at www.odpm.gov.uk. Printed copies of the explanation, but not of this form, are available from 1st June 2004 from Free Literature, PO Box 236, Wetherby, West Yorkshire, LS23 7NB (0870 1226 236).

[1335]

FORM 10
NOTICE ENDING A BUSINESS TENANCY WHERE A CHANGE IS REQUIRED AT A FUTURE DATE AND THE LANDLORD DOES NOT OPPOSE A NEW TENANCY

Sections 25 and 57 of the Landlord and Tenant Act 1954

IMPORTANT NOTE FOR THE LANDLORD: Use this form if you have a section 57 certificate and you are willing to grant a new tenancy for the period between the end of the current tenancy and the date given in the section 57 certificate.

If you wish to oppose the grant of a new tenancy for that period on any of the grounds in section 30(1) of the Landlord and Tenant Act 1954, use form 9 in Schedule 2 to the Landlord and Tenant Act 1954, Part 2 (Notices) Regulations 2004 instead of this form.

If the tenant may be entitled to acquire the freehold or an extended lease, use form 14 in that Schedule, instead of this form or form 9.

To: (*insert name and address of tenant*)

From: (*insert name and address of landlord*)

1.   This notice relates to the following property: (*insert address or description of property*)

2.   I am giving you notice under section 25 of the Landlord and Tenant Act 1954 ("the 1954 Act") to end your tenancy on (*insert date*).

3.   A certificate has been given by (*state the title of the Secretary of State, Minister or Board on whose authority the certificate was issued or, if the certificate was issued by the National Assembly for Wales, insert* "the National Assembly for Wales") under section 57 of the 1954 Act that the use or occupation of all or part of the property should be changed by (*insert date*). A copy of the certificate appears in Schedule 1 to this notice.

4.   If you apply to the court under Part 2 of the 1954 Act for the grant of a new tenancy, I will not oppose your application. However, the court can only order the grant of a new tenancy for a term ending not later than the date in paragraph 3.

5.   You will find my proposals for the new tenancy, which we can discuss, in Schedule 2 to this notice.

6.   If we cannot agree on all the terms of a new tenancy, either you or I may ask the court to order the grant of a new tenancy and settle the terms on which we cannot agree.

7.   Please send all correspondence about this notice to:

Name:

Address:

Signed: Date:

*[Landlord] *[On behalf of the landlord] *[Mortgagee] *[On behalf of the mortgagee]

(**delete if inapplicable*)

Schedule 1
Certificate Under Section 57

(*attach or insert a copy of the section 57 certificate*)

Schedule 2
Landlord's Proposals For A New Tenancy

(*attach or insert proposed terms of the new tenancy*)

IMPORTANT NOTE FOR THE TENANT

This notice is intended to bring your tenancy to an end on the date specified in paragraph 2.

A certificate has been issued that it is requisite that occupation or use of the premises should be changed by the date specified in paragraph 3.

However, the landlord is prepared to offer you a new tenancy for the whole or part of the period between the dates in paragraphs 2 and 3 of the notice. You will find his or her proposed terms in Schedule 2 to this notice. <u>You are not bound to accept these terms.</u> They are merely suggestions as a basis for negotiation. In the event of disagreement, ultimately the court would settle the terms of the new tenancy.

It would be wise to seek professional advice before agreeing to accept the landlord's terms or putting forward your own proposals.

If you want to continue to occupy your property you must act quickly. The notes below should help you to decide what action you now need to take.

NOTES

The sections mentioned below are sections of the Landlord and Tenant Act 1954, as amended, (most recently by the Regulatory Reform (Business Tenancies) (England and Wales) Order 2003)

Ending of your tenancy

This notice is intended to bring your tenancy to an end on the date specified in paragraph 2 of the notice.

A certificate has been given under section 57 and a copy appears in Schedule 1 to this notice. The certificate states that it is requisite that occupation or use of the premises should be changed by the date specified in paragraph 3 of the notice.

However, your landlord is prepared to offer you a new tenancy, for the whole or part of the period between the dates specified in paragraphs 2 and 3 of the notice. You will find his or her proposals in Schedule 2 to this notice. You are not obliged to accept these proposals and may put forward your own.

Claiming a new tenancy

If you and your landlord are unable to agree terms, you may apply to the court (unless the landlord has already made his or her own application to the court (section 24(2A)). However, before you take that step, read carefully the section below headed "*Effect of section 57 certificate*".

An application to the court must be made by the date set out in paragraph 2, unless you and your landlord have agreed in writing, before that date, to extend the deadline (sections 29A and 29B). Otherwise, you will lose the right to renew the tenancy.

If you apply to the court, your tenancy will continue after the date shown in paragraph 2 of this notice while your application is being considered (section 24). Either you or your landlord can ask the court to fix the rent that you will have to pay while the tenancy continues (section 24A and B). The terms of any new tenancy not agreed between you and the landlord will be settled by the court (section 25).

If you are in any doubt about the action that you should take, get advice immediately from a solicitor or a surveyor.

Effect of section 57 certificate

The effect of the section 57 certificate is that, if the court orders the grant of a new tenancy, the new tenancy must end not later than the date specified in the certificate (section 57(3)(b)).

Any new tenancy will not be a tenancy to which Part 2 of the 1954 Act applies (section 57(3)(b)).

Compensation

You may be entitled to compensation under section 59 when you leave the property (on or before the date specified in the section 57 certificate).

If your landlord is an authority possessing compulsory purchase powers (such as a local authority) you may be entitled to a disturbance payment under Part 3 of the Land Compensation Act 1973.

Validity of this notice

The landlord who has given you this notice may not be the landlord to whom you pay your rent (sections 44 and 67). This does not necessarily mean that the notice is invalid.

If you have any doubts about whether this notice is valid, get advice immediately from a solicitor or a surveyor.

Further information

An explanation of the main points to consider when renewing or ending a business tenancy, "Renewing and Ending Business Leases: a Guide for Tenants and Landlords", can be found at www.odpm.gov.uk. Printed copies of the explanation, but not of this form, are available from 1st June 2004 from Free Literature, PO Box 236, Wetherby, West Yorkshire, LS23 7NB (0870 1226 236).

[1336]

FORM 11
NOTICE ENDING A BUSINESS TENANCY ON GROUNDS OF NATIONAL
SECURITY AND WITHOUT THE OPTION TO RENEW

Sections 25 and 58 of the Landlord and Tenant Act 1954

To: (*insert name and address of tenant*)

From: (*insert name and address of landlord*)

1.   This notice relates to the following property: (*insert address or description of property*)

2.   I am giving you notice under section 25 of the Landlord and Tenant Act 1954 to end your tenancy on (*insert date*).

3.   A certificate has been given by (*state the title of the Secretary of State, Minister or Board on whose authority the certificate was issued or, if the certificate was issued by the National Assembly for Wales, insert* "the National Assembly for Wales") under section 58 of the 1954 Act that it is necessary for reasons of national security that the use or occupation of the property should be discontinued or changed. A copy of the certificate appears in the Schedule to this notice.

4.   The certificate prevents me from granting you a new tenancy. It also means that you will not be able to make an application to the court under section 24(1) of the Landlord and Tenant Act 1954 for the grant of a new tenancy.

5.   Please send all correspondence about this notice to:

Name:

Address:

Signed: Date:

*[Landlord] *[On behalf of the landlord] *[Mortgagee] *[On behalf of the mortgagee]

(*delete if inapplicable*)

Schedule
Certificate Under Section 58

(attach or insert a copy of the section 58 certificate)

IMPORTANT NOTE FOR THE TENANT

This notice is intended to bring your tenancy to an end on the date specified in paragraph 2.

The national security certificate referred to in paragraph 3 of this notice means that the landlord cannot grant you a new tenancy, and the court cannot order the grant of a new tenancy. You may be entitled to compensation.

You may wish to seek professional advice in connection with this notice.

NOTES

The sections mentioned below are sections of the Landlord and Tenant Act 1954, as amended, (most recently by the Regulatory Reform (Business Tenancies) (England and Wales) Order 2003)

Ending of your tenancy

This notice is intended to bring your tenancy to an end on the date shown in paragraph 2 of the notice. Section 25 contains rules about the date that the landlord can put in that paragraph.

Tenants under tenancies to which Part 2 of the Landlord and Tenant Act 1954 applies can normally apply to the court for the grant of a new tenancy. However, a certificate has been given that it is necessary for reasons of national security that the use or occupation of the property should be discontinued or changed (section 58). The combined effect of this notice and the certificate is that you will be unable to apply to the court for the grant of a new tenancy.

Compensation

You may be entitled to compensation under section 59 when you leave the property (on or before the date specified in the section 58 certificate).

You may also be entitled to a disturbance payment under Part 3 of the Land Compensation Act 1973.

Validity of notice

The landlord who has given you this notice may not be the landlord to whom you pay your rent (sections 44 and 67). This does not necessarily mean that the notice is invalid.

If you have any doubts about whether this notice is valid, get advice immediately from a solicitor or a surveyor.

Further information

An explanation of the main points to consider when renewing or ending a business tenancy, "Renewing and Ending Business Leases: a Guide for Tenants and Landlords", can be found at www.odpm.gov.uk. Printed copies of the explanation, but not of this form, are available from 1st June 2004 from Free Literature, PO Box 236, Wetherby, West Yorkshire, LS23 7NB (0870 1226 236).

[1337]

FORM 12
NOTICE ENDING A BUSINESS TENANCY WHERE THE PROPERTY IS REQUIRED
FOR REGENERATION

Sections 25, 58 and 60 of the Landlord and Tenant Act 1954

IMPORTANT NOTE FOR THE LANDLORD: Use this form if you have a certificate under section 58 (as applied by section 60), but if the tenant may be entitled to acquire the freehold or an extended lease, use form 15 in Schedule 2 to the Landlord and Tenant Act 1954, Part 2 (Notices) Regulations 2004 instead of this form.

To: (*insert name and address of tenant*)

From: (*insert name and address of landlord*)

1.   This notice relates to the following property, which is situated in an area for the time being specified as a development area or intermediate area by an order made, or having effect as if made, under section 1 of the Industrial Development Act 1982: (*insert address or description of property*)

2.   I am giving you notice under section 25 of the Landlord and Tenant Act 1954 ("the 1954 Act") to end your tenancy on (*insert date*).

3.   A certificate has been given by (*state the title of the Secretary of State, Minister or Board on whose authority the certificate was issued*) that it is necessary or expedient for the purpose mentioned in section 2(1) of the Local Employment Act 1972 that the use or occupation of the property should be changed. A copy of the certificate appears in the Schedule to this notice.

4.   The certificate prevents me from granting you a new tenancy. It also means that you will not be able to make an application to the court under section 24(1) of the 1954 Act for the grant of a new tenancy.

5.   Please send all correspondence about this notice to:

Name:

Address:

Signed: Date:

*[Landlord] *[On behalf of the landlord]

(**delete if inapplicable*)

Schedule
Certificate Under Section 58

(*attach or insert a copy of the section 58 certificate*)

IMPORTANT NOTE FOR THE TENANT

This Notice is intended to bring your tenancy to an end on the date specified in paragraph 2.

The certificate referred to in paragraph 3 of this notice means that the landlord cannot grant you a new tenancy, and the court cannot order the grant of a new tenancy.

You may wish to seek professional advice in connection with this notice.

NOTES

The sections mentioned below are sections of the Landlord and Tenant Act 1954, as amended, (most recently by the Regulatory Reform (Business Tenancies) (England and Wales) Order 2003)

Ending of your tenancy

This notice is intended to bring your tenancy to an end. Section 25 contains rules about the date that the landlord can put in paragraph 2 of this notice.

Your landlord is both giving you notice that your current tenancy will end on the date stated in paragraph 2 of this notice and drawing attention to a certificate under section 58 (as applied by section 60) that would prevent you from applying to the court for a new tenancy.

Usually, tenants who have tenancies under Part 2 of the Landlord and Tenant Act 1954 can apply to the court for a new tenancy. However, where a Government Minister has certified that it is necessary or expedient for the purpose mentioned in section 2(1) of the Local Employment Act 1972 that the use or occupation of the property should be changed, the landlord may prevent the tenant from making an application to the court for a new tenancy.

Validity of this notice

The landlord who has given you this notice may not be the landlord to whom you pay your rent (sections 44 and 67). This does not necessarily mean that the notice is invalid.

If you have any doubts about whether this notice is valid, get advice immediately from a solicitor or a surveyor.

Further information

An explanation of the main points to consider when renewing or ending a business tenancy, "Renewing and Ending Business Leases: a Guide for Tenants and Landlords", can be found at www.odpm.gov.uk. Printed copies of the explanation, but not of this form, are available from 1st June 2004 from Free Literature, PO Box 236, Wetherby, West Yorkshire, LS23 7NB (0870 1226 236).

[1338]

FORM 13
NOTICE ENDING A BUSINESS TENANCY ON PUBLIC INTEREST GROUNDS
WHERE THE LEASEHOLD REFORM ACT 1967 MAY APPLY

Sections 25 and 57 of the Landlord and Tenant Act 1954

Paragraph 10 of Schedule 3 to the Leasehold Reform Act 1967

IMPORTANT NOTE FOR THE LANDLORD

This form *must* be used (instead of Form 8 in Schedule 2 to the Landlord and Tenant Act 1954, Part 2 (Notices) Regulations 2004) if—

(a)   no previous notice terminating the tenancy has been given under section 4 or 25 of the Landlord and Tenant Act 1954 Act or under paragraph 4(1) of Schedule 10 to the Local Government and Housing Act 1989; and

(b)   the tenancy is of a house as defined for the purposes of Part 1 of the Leasehold Reform Act 1967 ("the 1967 Act"); and

(c)   the tenancy is a long tenancy at a low rent within the meaning of the 1967 Act; and

(d)   the tenant is not a company or other artificial person.

To: (*insert name and address of tenant*)

From: (*insert name and address of landlord*)

1.   This notice relates to the following property: (*insert address or description of property*)

2.   I am giving you notice under sections 25 of the Landlord and Tenant Act 1954 ("the 1954 Act") to end your tenancy on (*insert date*).

3.   A certificate has been given by (*state the title of the Secretary of State, Minister or Board on whose authority the certificate was issued or, if the certificate was issued by the National Assembly for Wales, insert* "the National Assembly for Wales") under section 57 of the 1954 Act that the use or occupation of all or part of the property should be changed by (*insert date*). A copy of the certificate appears in the Schedule to this notice.

4.   If you have a right under Part 1 of the Leasehold Reform Act 1967 to acquire the freehold or an extended lease of property comprised in the tenancy, notice of your desire to have the freehold or an extended lease cannot be given more than two months after the service of this notice. If you have that right, and give notice of your desire to have the freehold or an extended lease within those two months, this notice will not operate, and I may take no further proceedings under Part 2 of the 1954 Act.

*5.   If you give notice of your desire to have the freehold or an extended lease, I will be entitled to apply to the court under section 17 of the Leasehold Reform Act 1967, and propose to do so. If I am successful I may have to pay you compensation.

OR

*5.   If you give notice of your desire to have the freehold or an extended lease, I will be entitled to apply to the court under section 17 of the Leasehold Reform Act 1967, but do not propose to do so.

OR

*5.   If you give notice of your desire to have the freehold or an extended lease, I will not be entitled to apply to the court under section 17 of the Leasehold Reform Act 1967.

**DELETE TWO versions of this paragraph, as the circumstances require*

*6.   I know or believe that the following persons have an interest superior to your tenancy or to be the agent concerned with the property on behalf of someone who has such an interest (*insert names and addresses*):

**delete if inapplicable*

7.   Please send all correspondence about this notice to:

Name:

Address:

Signed: Date:

*[Landlord] *[On behalf of the landlord] *[Mortgagee] *[On behalf of the mortgagee]

(**delete if inapplicable*)

Schedule
Certificate Under Section 5

(*attach or insert a copy of the section 57 certificate*)

IMPORTANT NOTE FOR THE TENANT

This Notice is intended to bring your tenancy to an end on the date specified in paragraph 2.

The landlord is not prepared to offer you a new lease because it has been certified that it is requisite that occupation or use of the premises should be changed.

NOTES

Unless otherwise stated, the sections mentioned below are sections of the Landlord and Tenant Act 1954, as amended, (most recently by the Regulatory Reform (Business Tenancies) (England and Wales) Order 2003)

Ending of your tenancy

This notice is intended to bring your tenancy to an end on the date stated in paragraph 2 of the notice.

Your landlord is both giving you notice that your current tenancy will end on the date stated in paragraph 2 of this notice and drawing attention to a certificate under section 57 that would prevent you from applying to the court for a new tenancy.

Usually, tenants who have tenancies under Part 2 of the Landlord and Tenant Act 1954 can apply to the court for a new tenancy. However, it has been certified that it is requisite that the use or occupation of all or part of the property should be changed by a certain date, the landlord may prevent the tenant from making an application to the court for a new tenancy.

Rights under the Leasehold Reform Act 1967

If the property comprised in your tenancy is a house, as defined in section 2 of the Leasehold Reform Act 1967 ("the 1967 Act"), you may have the right to buy the freehold of the property or to get an extended lease. If the house is for the time being let under two or more tenancies, you will not have that right if your tenancy is subject to a sub-tenancy and the sub-tenant is himself or herself entitled to that right.

You will have that right if all the following conditions are met:

(i)   your lease was originally granted for a term of more than 35 years, or was preceded by such a lease which was granted or assigned to you; and

(ii)   your lease is of the whole house; and

(iii) your lease is at a low rent. If your tenancy was entered into before 1 April 1990 (or later if you contracted before that date to enter into the tenancy) "low rent" means that your present annual rent is less than two-thirds of the rateable value of your house as assessed either on 23 March 1965, or on the first day of the term in the case of a lease granted to commence after 23 March 1965; and the property had a rateable value other than nil when the tenancy began or at any time before 1 April 1990. If your tenancy was granted on or after 1 April 1990, "low rent" means that the present annual rent is not more than £1,000 in London or £250 elsewhere; *and*

(iv) you have been occupying the house (or any part of it) as your only or main residence (whether or not it has been occupied for other purposes) either for the whole of the last two years, or for a total of two years in the last ten years; *and*

(v) the rateable value of your house was at one time within certain limits.

However, if you have a right to buy the freehold or to get an extended lease, you will not be able to exercise it in this case because of the certificate that has been given under section 57. That is the effect of section 28 of the 1967 Act.

Compensation

Because the court cannot order the grant of a new tenancy, you are entitled to compensation when you leave the property (section 59).

If you have a right under the 1967 Act to buy the freehold or to get an extended lease but you cannot exercise that right because of the section 57 certificate, compensation will be payable under section 17(2) of the 1967 Act.

You cannot, however, get compensation under both the 1954 Act and the 1967 Act. The compensation payable under the 1967 Act is likely to be greater than that payable under the 1954 Act. In order to be able to claim compensation under the 1967 Act you must serve the appropriate notice on the landlord. A special form is prescribed for this purpose; it is Form 1 as set out in the Schedule to the Leasehold Reform (Notices) (Amendment) (England) Regulations 2002 (SI 2002/1715), or if the property is in Wales, the Leasehold Reform (Notices) (Amendment) (Wales) Regulations 2002 (SI 2002/3187) (W303). Subject to the exception mentioned below, you must serve the notice claiming to buy the freehold or to get an extended lease within two months after the date of service of this notice. The exception is where the landlord agrees in writing to your claim being made after the date on which it should have been made.

If there has been any delay in your seeing this notice you may need to act very quickly. If you are in any doubt about the action that you should take, get advice immediately from a solicitor or a surveyor.

If your landlord is an authority possessing compulsory purchase powers (such as a local authority) you may also be entitled to a disturbance payment under Part 3 of the Land Compensation Act 1973.

Validity of this notice

The landlord who has given you this notice may not be the landlord to whom you pay your rent (sections 44 and 67). This does not necessarily mean that the notice is invalid.

If you have any doubts about whether this notice is valid, get advice immediately from a solicitor or a surveyor.

Further information

An explanation of the main points to consider when renewing or ending a business tenancy, "Renewing and Ending Business Leases: a Guide for Tenants and Landlords", can be found at www.odpm.gov.uk. Printed copies of the explanation, but not of this form, are available from 1st June 2004 from Free Literature, PO Box 236, Wetherby, West Yorkshire, LS23 7NB (0870 1226 236).

An explanation of the rights of leaseholders to buy the freehold or to have an extended lease, "Residential Long Leaseholders – A Guide to Your Rights and Responsibilities", can be found at www.odpm.gov.uk. Printed copies of the explanation, but not of this form, are available from 1st June 2004 from Free Literature, PO Box 236, Wetherby, West Yorkshire, LS23 7NB (0870 1226 236).

[1339]

FORM 14
NOTICE ENDING A BUSINESS TENANCY ON PUBLIC INTEREST GROUNDS
WHERE A CHANGE IS REQUIRED AT A FUTURE DATE AND WHERE THE
LEASEHOLD REFORM ACT 1967 MAY APPLY

Sections 25 and 57 of the Landlord and Tenant Act 1954

Paragraph 10 of Schedule 3 to the Leasehold Reform Act 1967

IMPORTANT NOTE FOR THE LANDLORD

This form *must* be used (instead of Form 9 or 10 in Schedule 2 to the Landlord and Tenant Act 1954, Part 2 (Notices) Regulations 2004) if—

(a)   no previous notice terminating the tenancy has been given under section 4 or 25 of the Landlord and Tenant Act 1954 or under paragraph 4(1) of Schedule 10 to the Local Government and Housing Act 1989; and

(b)   the tenancy is of a house as defined for the purposes of Part 1 of the Leasehold Reform Act 1967 ("the 1967 Act"); and

(c)   the tenancy is a long tenancy at a low rent within the meaning of the 1967 Act; and

(d)   the tenant is not a company or other artificial person.

To: (*insert name and address of tenant*)

From: (*insert name and address of landlord*)

1.   This notice relates to the following property: (*insert address or description of property*)

2.   I am giving you notice under sections 25 of the Landlord and Tenant Act 1954 ("the 1954 Act") to end your tenancy on (*insert date*).

*3.   If you apply to the court under Part 2 of the 1954 Act for the grant of a new tenancy, I will not oppose your application.

OR* *DELETE ONE version of this paragraph, as the circumstances require.*

3.   If you apply to the court under Part 2 of the 1954 Act for the grant of a new tenancy, I will oppose your application on the ground(s) mentioned in paragraph(s) of section 30(1) of the 1954 Act. I draw your attention to the Table in the Notes below, which sets out all the grounds of opposition.

* (*insert letter(s) of the paragraph(s) relied on*)

4.   A certificate has been given by (*state the title of the Secretary of State, Minister or Board on whose authority the certificate was issued or, if the certificate was issued by the National Assembly for Wales, insert* "the National Assembly for Wales") under section 57 of the 1954 Act that the use or occupation of all or part of the property should be changed by (*insert date*). A copy of the certificate appears in the Schedule to this notice.

5.   If you have a right under Part 1 of the Leasehold Reform Act 1967 to acquire the freehold or an extended lease of property comprised in the tenancy, notice of your desire to have the freehold or an extended lease cannot be given more than two months after the service of this notice. If you have that right, and give notice of your desire to have the freehold or an extended lease within those two months, this notice will not operate, and I may take no further proceedings under Part 2 of the Landlord and Tenant Act 1954.

**6.   If you give notice of your desire to have the freehold or an extended lease, I will be entitled to apply to the court under section 17 of the Leasehold Reform Act 1967, and propose to do so. If I am successful I may have to pay you compensation.

OR

**6.   If you give notice of your desire to have the freehold or an extended lease, I will be entitled to apply to the court under section 17 of the Leasehold Reform Act 1967, but do not propose to do so.

OR

**6.   If you give notice of your desire to have the freehold or an extended lease, I will not be entitled to apply to the court under section 17 of the Leasehold Reform Act 1967.

DELETE TWO *versions of this paragraph, as the circumstances require*

*7.   I know or believe that the following persons have an interest superior to your tenancy or to be the agent concerned with the property on behalf of someone who has such an interest (*insert names and addresses*):

*(*delete if inapplicable*)

8.   Please send all correspondence about this notice to:

Name:

Address:

Signed: Date:

*[Landlord] *[On behalf of the landlord] *[Mortgagee] *[On behalf of the mortgagee]

(**delete if inapplicable*)

Schedule
Certificate Under Section 57

(*attach or insert a copy of the section 57 certificate*)

IMPORTANT NOTE FOR THE TENANT

This Notice is intended to bring your tenancy to an end on the date specified in paragraph 2.

Your landlord may have indicated in paragraph 3 that he will oppose your application for a new tenancy (if you decide to make one). You will not get a new tenancy unless you successfully challenge in court the grounds indicated in paragraph 3 on which your landlord opposes the grant of a new tenancy.

It has been certified that it is requisite that occupation or use of the premises should be changed by the date specified in paragraph 4.

If you want to continue to occupy your property you must act quickly. The notes below should help you to decide what action you now need to take. If you are unsure about what you should do, get advice immediately from a solicitor or a surveyor.

NOTES

Unless otherwise stated, the sections mentioned below are sections of the Landlord and Tenant Act 1954, as amended, (most recently by the Regulatory Reform (Business Tenancies) (England and Wales) Order 2003)

Ending of your tenancy

This notice is intended to bring your tenancy to an end on the date stated in paragraph 2 of the notice.

Claiming a new tenancy

If you wish to apply to the court for a new tenancy you must do so by the date set out in paragraph 2 of this notice, unless you and your landlord have agreed in writing, before that date, to extend the deadline (sections 29A and 29B). However, before you take that step, read carefully the section below headed "*Effect of section 57 certificate*".

If you apply to the court, your tenancy will continue after the date shown in paragraph 2 of this notice while your application is being considered (section 24).

If you are in any doubt about what action you should take, get advice immediately from a solicitor or a surveyor.

Landlord's opposition to claim for a new tenancy

If paragraph 3 of this notice indicates that your landlord is opposed to the grant of a new tenancy, you will not get a new tenancy unless you apply to the court and successfully challenge the ground(s) of your landlord's opposition.

If you apply to the court for a new tenancy, the landlord can only oppose your application on one or more of the grounds set out in section 30(1). If you match the letter(s) specified in paragraph 3 of this notice with those in the first column in the Table below, you can see from the second column the ground(s) on which the landlord relies.

Paragraph of section 30(1)	Grounds
(a)	Where under the current tenancy the tenant has any obligations as respects the repair and maintenance of the holding, that the tenant ought not to be granted a new tenancy in view of the state of repair of the holding, being a state resulting from the tenant's failure to comply with the said obligations.
(b)	That the tenant ought not to be granted a new tenancy in view of his persistent delay in paying rent which has become due.
(c)	That the tenant ought not to be granted a new tenancy in view of other substantial breaches by him of his obligations under the current tenancy, or for any other reason connected with the tenant's use or management of the holding.
(d)	That the landlord has offered and is willing to provide or secure the provision of alternative accommodation for the tenant, that the terms on which the alternative accommodation is available are reasonable having regard to the terms of the current tenancy and to all other relevant circumstances, and that the accommodation and the time at which it will be available are suitable for the tenant's requirements (including the requirement to preserve goodwill) having regard to the nature and class of his business and to the situation and extent of, and facilities afforded by, the holding.
(e)	Where the current tenancy was created by the sub-letting of part only of the property comprised in a superior tenancy and the landlord is the owner of an interest in reversion expectant on the termination of that superior tenancy, that the aggregate of the rents reasonably obtainable on separate lettings of the holding and the remainder of that property would be substantially less than the rent reasonably obtainable on a letting of that property as a whole, that on the termination of the current tenancy the landlord requires possession of the holding for the purposes of letting or otherwise disposing of the said property as a whole, and that in view thereof the tenant ought not to be granted a new tenancy.
(f)	That on the termination of the current tenancy the landlord intends to demolish or reconstruct the premises comprised in the holding or a substantial part of those premises or to carry out substantial work of construction on the holding or part thereof and that he could not reasonably do so without obtaining possession of the holding.
(g)	On the termination of the current tenancy the landlord intends to occupy the holding for the purposes, or partly for the purposes, of a business to be carried on by him therein, or as his residence.

In the Table "the holding" means the property that is the subject of the tenancy.

In ground (e), "the landlord is the owner an interest in reversion expectant on the termination of that superior tenancy" means that the landlord has an interest in the property that will entitle him, when your immediate landlord's tenancy comes to an end, to exercise certain rights and obligations in relation to the property that are currently exercisable by your immediate landlord.

If ground (f) is specified, the court can sometimes still grant a new tenancy if certain conditions set out in section 31A of the 1954 Act can be met.

If ground (g) is specified, please note that "the landlord" may have an extended meaning. Where a landlord has a controlling interest in a company then either the landlord or the company can rely on ground (g). Where the landlord is a company and a person has a controlling interest in that company then either of them can rely on ground (g) (section 30(1A) and (1B)). A person has a "controlling interest" in a company if, had he been a company, the other company would have been its subsidiary (section 46(2)).

The landlord must normally have been the landlord for at least five years before he or she can use ground (g).

Effect of section 57 certificate

A copy of a certificate issued under section 57 appears in the Schedule to this notice. The effect of the certificate is that, even if you are successful in challenging your landlord's opposition to the grant of a new tenancy, and the court orders the grant of a new tenancy, the new tenancy must end not later than the date specified in the certificate (section 57(3)(b)).

Any new tenancy will not be a tenancy to which Part 2 of the 1954 Act applies (section 57(3)(b)).

Rights under the Leasehold Reform Act 1967

If the property comprised in your tenancy is a house, as defined in section 2 of the Leasehold Reform Act 1967 ("the 1967 Act"), you may have the right to buy the freehold of the property or to get an extended lease. If the house is for the time being let under two or more tenancies, you will not have that right if your tenancy is subject to a sub-tenancy and the sub-tenant is himself or herself entitled to that right.

You will have that right if *all* the following conditions are met:
  (i)   your lease was originally granted for a term of more than 35 years, or was preceded by such a lease which was granted or assigned to you; *and*
  (ii)   your lease is of the whole house; *and*
  (iii) your lease is at a low rent. If your tenancy was entered into before 1 April 1990 (or later if you contracted before that date to enter into the tenancy) "low rent" means that your present annual rent is less than two-thirds of the rateable value of your house as assessed either on 23 March 1965, or on the first day of the term in the case of a lease granted to commence after 23 March 1965; and the property had a rateable value other than nil when the tenancy began or at any time before 1 April 1990. If your tenancy was granted on or after 1 April 1990, "low rent" means that the present annual rent is not more than £1,000 in London or £250 elsewhere; *and*
  (iv)   you have been occupying the house (or any part of it) as your only or main residence (whether or not it has been occupied for other purposes) either for the whole of the last two years, or for a total of two years in the last ten years; *and*
  (v)   the rateable value of your house was at one time within certain limits.

However, if you have a right to buy the freehold or to get an extended lease, you will not be able to exercise it in this case because of the certificate that has been given under section 57. That is the effect of section 28 of the 1967 Act.

Compensation

If you cannot get a new tenancy solely because one or more of grounds (e), (f) and (g) applies, you may be entitled to compensation under section 37. If your landlord has opposed your application on any of the other grounds as well as (e), (f) or (g) you can only get compensation if the court's refusal to grant a new tenancy is based solely on one or more of grounds (e), (f) and (g). In other words, you cannot get compensation under section 37 if the court has refused your tenancy on *other* grounds, even if one or more of grounds (e), (f) and (g) also applies.

If the court orders the grant of a new tenancy, you may be entitled to compensation under section 59.

If you have a right under the 1967 Act to buy the freehold or to get an extended lease but you cannot exercise that right because of the section 57 certificate, compensation will be payable under that Act.

You cannot, however, get compensation under both the 1954 Act and the 1967 Act. The compensation payable under the 1967 Act is likely to be greater than that payable under the 1954 Act. In order to be able to claim compensation under the 1967 Act you must serve the appropriate notice on the landlord. A special form is prescribed for this purpose; it is Form 1 as set out in the Schedule to the Leasehold Reform (Notices) (Amendment) (England) Regulations 2002 (SI 2002/1715), or if the property is in Wales, the Leasehold Reform (Notices) (Amendment) (Wales) Regulations 2002 (SI 2002/3187) (W303). Subject to the exception mentioned below, you must serve the notice claiming to buy the freehold or to get an extended lease within two months after the date of service of this notice. The exception is where the landlord agrees in writing to your claim being made after the date on which it should have been made.

If there has been any delay in your seeing this notice you may need to act very quickly. If you are in any doubt about what action you should take, get advice immediately from a solicitor or a surveyor.

If your landlord is an authority possessing compulsory purchase powers (such as a local authority) you may be entitled to a disturbance payment under Part 3 of the Land Compensation Act 1973.

Validity of this notice

The landlord who has given you this notice may not be the landlord to whom you pay your rent (sections 44 and 67). This does not necessarily mean that the notice is invalid.

If you have any doubts about whether this notice is valid, get advice immediately from a solicitor or a surveyor.

Further information

An explanation of the main points to consider when renewing or ending a business tenancy, "Renewing and Ending Business Leases: a Guide for Tenants and Landlords", can be found at www.odpm.gov.uk. Printed copies of the explanation, but not of this form, are available from 1st June 2004 from Free Literature, PO Box 236, Wetherby, West Yorkshire, LS23 7NB (0870 1226 236).

An explanation of the rights of leaseholders to buy the freehold or to have an extended lease, "Residential Long Leaseholders – A Guide to Your Rights and Responsibilities", can be found at www.odpm.gov.uk. Printed copies of the explanation, but not of this form, are available from 1st June 2004 from Free Literature, PO Box 236, Wetherby, West Yorkshire, LS23 7NB (0870 1226 236).

[1340]

FORM 15
NOTICE ENDING A BUSINESS TENANCY WHERE THE PROPERTY IS REQUIRED FOR REGENERATION AND THE LEASEHOLD REFORM ACT 1967 MAY APPLY

Sections 25, 58 and 60 of the Landlord and Tenant Act 1954

Paragraph 10 of Schedule 3 to the Leasehold Reform Act 1967

IMPORTANT NOTE FOR THE LANDLORD

This form *must* be used (instead of Form 12 in Schedule 2 to the Landlord and Tenant Act 1954, Part 2 (Notices) Regulations 2004) if—

    (a)   no previous notice terminating the tenancy has been given under section 4 or 25 of the Landlord and Tenant Act 1954 or under paragraph 4(1) of Schedule 10 to the Local Government and Housing Act 1989; and

    (b)   the tenancy is of a house as defined for the purposes of Part 1 of the Leasehold Reform Act 1967 ("the 1967 Act"); and

    (c)   the tenancy is a long tenancy at a low rent within the meaning of the 1967 Act; and

    (d)   the tenant is not a company or other artificial person.

To: (*insert name and address of tenant*)

From: (*insert name and address of landlord*)

1.   This notice relates to the following property, which is situated in an area for the time being specified as a development area or intermediate area by an order made, or having effect as if made, under section 1 of the Industrial Development Act 1982: (*insert address or description of property*)

2.   I am giving you notice under section 25 of the Landlord and Tenant Act 1954 ("the 1954 Act") to end your tenancy on (*insert date*).

3.   A certificate has been given by (*state the title of the Secretary of State, Minister or Board on whose authority the certificate was issued*) under section 58 of the 1954 Act (as applied by section 60 of that Act) that it is necessary or expedient for the purpose mentioned in section 2(1) of the Local Employment Act 1972 that the use or occupation of the property should be changed. A copy of the certificate appears in the Schedule to this notice.

4.   The certificate prevents me from granting you a new tenancy. It also means that you will not be able to make an application to the court under section 24(1) of the 1954 Act for the grant of a new tenancy.

5.   If you have a right under Part 1 of the Leasehold Reform Act 1967 to acquire the freehold or an extended lease of property comprised in the tenancy, notice of your desire to have the freehold or an extended lease cannot be given more than two months after the service of this notice. If you have that right, and give notice of your desire to have the freehold or an extended lease within those two months, this notice will not operate, and I may take no further proceedings under Part 2 of the 1954 Act.

*6.   If you give notice of your desire to have the freehold or an extended lease, I will be entitled to apply to the court under section 17 of the Leasehold Reform Act 1967, and propose to do so. If I am successful I may have to pay you compensation.

OR

*6.   If you give notice of your desire to have the freehold or an extended lease, I will be entitled to apply to the court under section 17 of the Leasehold Reform Act 1967, but do not propose to do so.   .

OR

*6.   If you give notice of your desire to have the freehold or an extended lease, I will not be entitled to apply to the court under section 17 of the Leasehold Reform Act 1967.

DELETE TWO versions of this paragraph, as the circumstances require

**7.   I know or believe that the following persons have an interest superior to your tenancy or to be the agent concerned with the property on behalf of someone who has such an interest (*insert names and addresses*):

**(*delete if inapplicable*)

8.   Please send all correspondence about this notice to:

Name:

Address:

Signed: Date:

*[Landlord] *[On behalf of the landlord] (*delete if inapplicable*)

Schedule
Certificate Under Section 58

(*attach or insert a copy of the section 58 certificate*)

IMPORTANT NOTE FOR THE TENANT

This notice is intended to bring your tenancy to an end on the date specified in paragraph 2.

A Government Minister has decided that it is necessary or expedient that occupation or use of the premises should be changed.

It would be wise to seek professional advice.

NOTES

Unless otherwise stated, the sections mentioned below are sections of the Landlord and Tenant Act 1954, as amended, (most recently by the Regulatory Reform (Business Tenancies) (England and Wales) Order 2003)

Ending of your tenancy

This notice is intended to bring your tenancy to an end on the date stated in paragraph 2 of the notice.

Your landlord is both giving you notice that your current tenancy will end on the date stated in paragraph 2 of this notice and drawing attention to a certificate under section 58 (as applied by section 60) that would prevent you from applying to the court for a new tenancy.

Usually, tenants who have tenancies under Part 2 of the Landlord and Tenant Act 1954 can apply to the court for a new tenancy. However, where a Government Minister has certified that it is necessary or expedient for the purpose mentioned in section 2(1) of the Local Employment Act 1972 that the use or occupation of the property should be changed, the landlord may prevent the tenant from making an application to the court for a new tenancy.

Rights under the Leasehold Reform Act 1967

If the property comprised in your tenancy is a house, as defined in section 2 of the Leasehold Reform Act 1967 ("the 1967 Act"), you may have the right to buy the freehold of the property or to get an extended lease. If the house is for the time being let under two or more tenancies, you will not have that right if your tenancy is subject to a sub-tenancy and the sub-tenant is himself or herself entitled to that right.

You will have that right if *all* the following conditions are met:

(i) your lease was originally granted for a term of more than 35 years, or was preceded by such a lease which was granted or assigned to you; *and*

(ii) your lease is of the whole house; *and*

(iii) your lease is at a low rent. If your tenancy was entered into before 1 April 1990 (or later if you contracted before that date to enter into the tenancy) "low rent" means that your present annual rent is less than two-thirds of the rateable value of your house as assessed either on 23 March 1965, or on the first day of the term in the case of a lease granted to commence after 23 March 1965; and the property had a rateable value other than nil when the tenancy began or at any time before 1 April 1990. If your tenancy was granted on or after 1 April 1990, "low rent" means that the present annual rent is not more than £1,000 in London or £250 elsewhere; *and*

(iv) you have been occupying the house (or any part of it) as your only or main residence (whether or not it has been occupied for other purposes) either for the whole of the last two years, or for a total of two years in the last ten years; *and*

(v) the rateable value of your house was at one time within certain limits.

However, if you have a right to buy the freehold or to get an extended lease, you will not be able to exercise it in this case because of the certificate that has been given. That is the effect of section 28 of the 1967 Act.

Compensation

If you have a right under the 1967 Act to buy the freehold or to get an extended lease but you cannot exercise that right because of the certificate, compensation will be payable under that Act.

In order to be able to claim compensation under the 1967 Act you must serve the appropriate notice on the landlord. A special form is prescribed for this purpose; it is Form 1 as set out in the Schedule to the Leasehold Reform (Notices) (Amendment) (England) Regulations 2002 (SI 2002/1715). Subject to the exception mentioned below, you must serve the notice claiming to buy the freehold or to get an extended lease within two months after the date of service of this notice. The exception is where the landlord agrees in writing to your claim being made after the date on which it should have been made.

If there has been any delay in your seeing this notice you may need to act very quickly. <u>If you are in any doubt about what steps you should take, get advice immediately from a solicitor or a surveyor.</u>

Validity of this notice

The landlord who has given you this notice may not be the landlord to whom you pay your rent (sections 44 and 67). This does not necessarily mean that the notice is invalid.

If you have any doubts about whether this notice is valid, get advice immediately from a solicitor or a surveyor.

Further information

An explanation of the main points to consider when renewing or ending a business tenancy, "Renewing and Ending Business Leases: a Guide for Tenants and Landlords", can be found at www.odpm.gov.uk. Printed copies of the explanation, but not of this form, are available from 1st June 2004 from Free Literature, PO Box 236, Wetherby, West Yorkshire, LS23 7NB (0870 1226 236).

An explanation of the rights of leaseholders to buy the freehold or to have an extended lease, "Residential Long Leaseholders – A Guide to Your Rights and Responsibilities", can be found at www.odpm.gov.uk. Printed copies of the explanation, but not of this form, are available from 1st June 2004 from Free Literature, PO Box 236, Wetherby, West Yorkshire, LS23 7NB (0870 1226 236).

[1341]

FORM 16
NOTICE ENDING A BUSINESS TENANCY OF WELSH DEVELOPMENT AGENCY [ACT 1975] PREMISES WHERE THE PROPERTY IS REQUIRED FOR EMPLOYMENT PURPOSES

Sections 25, 58 and 60A of the Landlord and Tenant Act 1954

IMPORTANT NOTE

This form must *not* be used if—

(a)   no previous notice terminating the tenancy has been given under section 4 or 25 of the Landlord and Tenant Act 1954, or under paragraph 4(1) of Schedule 10 to the Local Government and Housing Act 1989, and

(b)   the tenancy is of a house as defined for the purposes of Part 1 of the Leasehold Reform Act 1967, and

(c)   the tenancy is a long tenancy at a low rent within the meaning of that Act, and

(d)   the tenant is not a company or other artificial person.

If (a) to (d) apply, use form 17 in Schedule 2 to the Landlord and Tenant Act 1954, Part 2 (Notices) Regulations 2004 instead of this form.

To: (*insert name and address of tenant*)

From: (*insert name and address of landlord*)

1.   This notice relates to the following property, of which you are the tenant: (*insert address or description of property*)

2.   We give you notice under section 25 of the Landlord and Tenant Act 1954 ("the 1954 Act") to end your tenancy on: (*insert date*)

3.   A certificate has been given by the National Assembly for Wales under section 58 of the 1954 Act (as applied by section 60A of that Act) that it is necessary or expedient, for the purposes of providing employment appropriate to the needs of the area in which the premises are situated, that the use or occupation of the property should be changed. A copy of the certificate appears in the Schedule to this notice.

4.   The certificate prevents us from granting you a new tenancy. It also means that you will not be able to make an application to the court under section 24(1) of the 1954 Act for the grant of a new tenancy. However, you may be entitled to compensation.

5.   Please send all correspondence about this notice to:

Name:

Address:

Signed: Date:

*[Landlord] *[On behalf of the landlord]

(*delete if inapplicable*)

Schedule
Certificate Under Section 58

(attach or insert a copy of the section 58 certificate)

IMPORTANT NOTE FOR THE TENANT

This notice is intended to bring your tenancy to an end on the date specified in paragraph 2 above.

The certificate referred to in paragraph 3 above means that the landlord cannot grant you a new tenancy, and the court cannot order the grant of a new tenancy. However, you may be entitled to compensation.

It would be wise to seek professional advice immediately in connection with this notice.

NOTES

Unless otherwise stated, the sections mentioned below are sections of the Landlord and Tenant Act 1954, as amended, (most recently by the Regulatory Reform (Business Tenancies) (England and Wales) Order 2003 SI 2003/3096)

Ending of your tenancy

1.   This notice is intended to bring your tenancy to an end on the date specified in paragraph 2 of this notice. Section 25 contains rules about the date that the landlord can put in that paragraph.

2.   Your landlord is both giving you notice that your tenancy will end on the date specified in paragraph 2 of this notice and drawing attention, in paragraph 3 of this notice, to a certificate given by the National Assembly for Wales under section 58 (as applied by section 60A) that would prevent you from applying to the court for a new tenancy under Part 2 of the Landlord and Tenant Act 1954.

3.   Usually, tenants who have tenancies under Part 2 of the Landlord and Tenant Act 1954 can apply to the court for a new tenancy. However, where the National Assembly for Wales has certified that it is necessary or expedient, for the purposes of providing employment appropriate to the needs of the area in which the premises are situated, that the use or occupation of the property should be changed, the landlord may prevent the tenant from making an application to the court for a new tenancy.

Compensation

4.   You will be entitled to compensation under section 59 when you leave the property UNLESS:

   (a)   the premises vested in the Welsh Development Agency under section 7 or 8 of the Welsh Development Agency Act 1975 [and were transferred to the National Assembly for Wales by virtue of the Welsh Development Agency (Transfer of Functions to the National Assembly for Wales and Abolition) Order 2005]; *or*

   [(b)   you were not the tenant of the premises when the interest by virtue of which the certificate referred to in paragraph 3 of this notice was given was acquired by the Welsh Development Agency or, if the interest was acquired on or after 1 April 2006, by the National Assembly for Wales in exercise of functions transferred to it by the Welsh Development Agency (Transfer of Functions to the National Assembly for Wales and Abolition) Order 2005.]

5.   You may also be entitled to a disturbance payment under Part 3 of the Land Compensation Act 1973.

Validity of this notice

6.   The landlord who has given you this notice may not be the landlord to whom you pay your rent (sections 44 and 67). This does not necessarily mean that the notice is invalid.

7.   If you have any doubts about whether this notice is valid, get advice immediately from a solicitor or a surveyor.

Further information

8.   An explanation of the main points to consider when renewing or ending a business tenancy, "Renewing and Ending Business Leases: a Guide for Tenants and Landlords", can be found at www.odpm.gov.uk Printed copies of the explanation, but not of this form, are available from 1st June 2004 from Free Literature, PO Box 236, Wetherby, West Yorkshire, LS23 7NB (0870 1226 236).

[1342]

NOTES

Heading: words in square brackets inserted by the Welsh Development Agency (Transfer of Functions to the National Assembly for Wales and Abolition) Order 2005, SI 2005/3226, art 7(1)(b), Sch 2, Pt 1, para 7(2)(a), subject to art 3 thereof.

Note 4: in para (a) words in square brackets inserted and para (b) substituted by SI 2005/3226, art 7(1)(b), Sch 2, Pt 1, para 7(2)(b), (c), subject to art 3 thereof.

FORM 17

NOTICE ENDING A BUSINESS TENANCY OF WELSH DEVELOPMENT AGENCY [ACT 1975] PREMISES WHERE THE PROPERTY IS REQUIRED FOR EMPLOYMENT PURPOSES AND THE LEASEHOLD REFORM ACT 1967 MAY APPLY

Sections 25, 58 and 60A of the Landlord and Tenant Act 1954

Paragraph 10 of Schedule 3 to the Leasehold Reform Act 1967

IMPORTANT NOTE

This form *must* be used (instead of Form 16 in Schedule 2 to the Landlord and Tenant Act 1954, Part 2 (Notices) Regulations 2004) if—

(a)   no previous notice terminating the tenancy has been given under section 4 or 25 of the Landlord and Tenant Act 1954 Act or under paragraph 4(1) of Schedule 10 to the Local Government and Housing Act 1989; and

(b)   the tenancy is of a house as defined for the purposes of Part 1 of the Leasehold Reform Act 1967; and

(c)   the tenancy is a long tenancy at a low rent within the meaning of the 1967 Act; and

(d)   the tenant is not a company or other artificial person.

To: (*insert name and address of tenant*)

From: (*insert name and address of landlord*)

1.   This notice relates to the following property, of which you are the tenant: (*insert address or description of property*):

2.   We give you notice under section 25 of the Landlord and Tenant Act 1954 ("the 1954 Act") to end your tenancy on: (*insert date*)

3.   A certificate has been given by the National Assembly for Wales under section 58 of the 1954 Act (as applied by section 60A of that Act) that it is necessary or expedient, for the purposes of providing employment appropriate to the needs of the area in which the premises are situated, that the use or occupation of the property should be changed. A copy of the certificate appears in the Schedule to this notice.

4.   The certificate prevents us from granting you a new tenancy. It also means that you will not be able to make an application to the court under section 24(1) of the 1954 Act for the grant of a new tenancy. However, you may be entitled to compensation.

5.   If you have a right under Part 1 of the Leasehold Reform Act 1967 ("the 1967 Act") to acquire the freehold or to get an extended lease of property comprised in the tenancy, notice of your desire to have the freehold or an extended lease cannot be given more than two months after the service of this notice. If you have that right, and give notice of your desire to have the freehold or an extended lease within those two months, this notice will not operate, and we may take no further proceedings under Part 2 of the 1954 Act.

*6.   If you give notice of your desire to have the freehold or an extended lease, we will be entitled to apply to the court under section 17 of the 1967 Act, and propose to do so. If we are successful we may have to pay you compensation.

OR

*6.   If you give notice of your desire to have the freehold or an extended lease, we will be entitled to apply to the court under section 17 of the 1967 Act, but do not propose to do so.

OR

*6.   If you give notice of your desire to have the freehold or an extended lease, we will not be entitled to apply to the court under section 17 of the 1967 Act.

*(*DELETE TWO versions of paragraph 6, as the circumstances require*)

**7.   We know or believe that the following persons have an interest superior to your tenancy or to be the agent concerned with the property on behalf of someone who has such an interest (*insert names and addresses*):

**(*delete if inapplicable*)

8.   Please send all correspondence about this notice to:

Name:

Address:

Signed: Date:

*[Landlord] *[On behalf of the landlord]

(**delete if inapplicable*)

Schedule
Certificate Under Section 58

(*attach or insert a copy of the section 58 certificate*)

IMPORTANT NOTE FOR THE TENANT

This notice is intended to bring your tenancy to an end on the date specified in paragraph 2 above.

The National Assembly for Wales has certified that it is necessary or expedient that occupation or use of the premises should be changed.

It would be wise to seek professional advice immediately in connection with this notice.

NOTES

Unless otherwise stated, the sections mentioned below are sections of the Landlord and Tenant Act 1954, as amended, (most recently by the Regulatory Reform (Business Tenancies) (England and Wales) Order 2003 (SI 2003/3096))

Ending of your tenancy

1.   This notice is intended to bring your tenancy to an end on the date specified in paragraph 2 of this notice. Section 25 contains rules about the date that the landlord can put in that paragraph.

2.   Your landlord is both giving you notice that your tenancy will end on the date specified in paragraph 2 of this notice and drawing attention, in paragraph 3 of this notice, to a certificate given by the National Assembly for Wales under section 58 (as applied by section 60A) that would prevent you from applying to the court for a new tenancy under Part 2 of the Landlord and Tenant Act 1954.

3.   Usually, tenants who have tenancies under Part 2 of the Landlord and Tenant Act 1954 can apply to the court for a new tenancy. However, where the National Assembly for Wales has certified that it is necessary or expedient, for the purposes of providing employment appropriate to the needs of the area in which the premises are situated, that the use or occupation of the property should be changed, the landlord may prevent the tenant from making an application to the court for a new tenancy under that Part 2.

4.   However, the Leasehold Reform Act 1967 ("the 1967 Act") may also apply in your case. If it does, you may be able to buy the freehold of the property or get an extended lease under that Act (see *Rights under the 1967 Act*: notes 5 to 7 below and *Claiming your rights under the 1967 Act*: notes 8 and 9 below). If you claim an extended lease your landlord may still be able to get possession of the property (see *Landlord's opposition to claims under the 1967 Act*: note 10 below). If he does, you may be able to get compensation (see *Compensation*: notes 11 to 14 below). The amount of any compensation will depend on the steps you have taken and under which Act (it is likely to be greater under the 1967 Act). If you have any doubt about what you should do, get professional advice immediately.

Rights under the 1967 Act

5.   If the property comprised in your tenancy is a house, as defined in section 2 of the 1967 Act, you may have the right to buy the freehold of the property or to get an extended lease.

6.   If the house is for the time being let under two or more tenancies, you will not have that right if your tenancy is subject to a sub-tenancy and the sub-tenant is himself or herself entitled to that right.

7.   You will have that right if *all* the following conditions (i) – (v) are met:
   (i)   your lease was originally granted for a term of more than 35 years, or was preceded by such a lease which was granted or assigned to you; *and*
   (ii)   your lease is of the whole house; *and*
   (iii) (where applicable) your lease is at a low rent. If your tenancy was entered into before 1 April 1990 (or later if you contracted before that date to enter into the tenancy) "low rent" means that your present annual rent is less than two-thirds of the rateable value of your house as assessed either on 23 March 1965, or on the first day of the term in the case of a lease granted to commence after 23 March 1965, and the property had a rateable value other than nil when the tenancy began or any time before 1 April 1990. If your tenancy was granted on or after 1 April 1990, "low rent" means that the present annual rent is not more than £250; *and*
   (iv)   you have been occupying the house (or any part of it) as your only or main residence (whether or not it has been occupied for other purposes) either for the whole of the last two years, or for a total of two years in the last ten years; *and*
   (v)   the rateable value of your house was at one time within certain limits.

Claiming your rights under the 1967 Act

8.   If you have the right to buy the freehold or to get an extended lease and wish to exercise it, you must serve the appropriate notice on the landlord. A special form is prescribed for this purpose; it is Form 1 as set out in the Schedule to the Leasehold Reform (Notices) (Amendment) (Wales) Regulations 2002 (SI 2002/3187)(W303). Subject to the exception mentioned below, you must serve the notice claiming to buy the freehold or to get an extended lease within two months after the date of service of this notice. The exception is where the landlord agrees in writing to your claim being made after the date on which it should have been made.

9.   There are special rules about the service of notices. If there has been any delay in your seeing this notice you may need to act very quickly. If you are in any doubt about what you should do, get advice immediately from a solicitor or a surveyor.

Landlord's opposition to claims under the 1967 Act

10.   If you claim a right under the 1967 Act, your landlord can object under section 17 of the 1967 Act on the grounds that he wishes to redevelop the property. Paragraph 6 of the notice will tell you whether the landlord believes he has the right to apply to the court under section 17 and whether or not he proposes to do so.

Compensation

11.   Because the court cannot order the grant of a new tenancy under the 1954 Act in your case, you may be entitled to compensation under the 1954 Act when you leave the property. You will not be entitled to such compensation if either:
   (a)   the premises were vested in the Welsh Development Agency under section 7 or 8 of the Welsh Development Agency Act 1975 [and were transferred to the National Assembly for Wales by virtue of the Welsh Development Agency (Transfer of Functions to the National Assembly for Wales and Abolition) Order 2005]; or
   [(b)   you were not the tenant of the premises when the interest by virtue of which the certificate referred to in paragraph 3 of this notice was given was acquired by the Welsh Development Agency or, if the interest was acquired on or after 1 April 2006, by the National Assembly for Wales in exercise of functions transferred to it by the Welsh Development Agency (Transfer of Functions to the National Assembly for Wales and Abolition) Order 2005.]

12.   You may be entitled to a disturbance payment under Part 3 of the Land Compensation Act 1973.

13.   If you have a right under the 1967 Act to buy the freehold or to get an extended lease of your premises but the landlord is able to obtain possession of the premises (see *Landlord's*

opposition to claims under the 1967 Act: note 10 above), compensation under the 1967 Act is payable. This is normally higher than compensation under the 1954 Act. Your professional adviser will be able to advise you on this.

14. In order to be able to claim compensation under the 1967 Act you must serve the appropriate notice on the landlord within the stated time limit (see *Claiming your Rights under the 1967 Act*: notes 8 and 9 above).

Validity of this notice

15. The landlord who has given you this notice may not be the landlord to whom you pay your rent (sections 44 and 67). This does not necessarily mean that the notice is invalid.

16. If you have any doubts about whether this notice is valid, get advice immediately from a solicitor or a surveyor.

Further information

17. An explanation of the main points to consider when renewing or ending a business tenancy, "Renewing and Ending Business Leases: a Guide for Tenants and Landlords", can be found at www.odpm.gov.uk Printed copies of the explanation, but not of this form, are available from 1st June 2004 from Free Literature, PO Box 236, Wetherby, West Yorkshire, LS23 7NB (0870 1226 236).

18. An explanation of the rights of leaseholders to buy the freehold or to have an extended lease, "Residential Long Leaseholders – A Guide to Your Rights and Responsibilities", can be found at www.odpm.gov.uk. Printed copies of the explanation, but not of this form, are available from Free Literature, PO Box 236, Wetherby, West Yorkshire, LS23 7NB (0870 1226 236).

[1343]

NOTES
Commencement: 1 June 2004.
Heading: words in square brackets inserted by the Welsh Development Agency (Transfer of Functions to the National Assembly for Wales and Abolition) Order 2005, SI 2005/3226, art 7(1)(b), Sch 2, Pt 1, para 7(2)(a), subject to art 3 thereof.
Note 11: in para (a) words in square brackets inserted and para (b) substituted by SI 2005/3226, art 7(1)(b), Sch 2, Pt 1, para 7(2)(b), (c), subject to art 3 thereof.

REGULATORY REFORM (FIRE SAFETY) ORDER 2005

(SI 2005/1541)

NOTES
Made: 7 June 2005.
Authority: Regulatory Reform Act 2001, s 1.

ARRANGEMENT OF ARTICLES

PART 1
GENERAL

PART 2
FIRE SAFETY DUTIES

PART 1
GENERAL

1 Citation, commencement and extent

(1)   This Order may be cited as the Regulatory Reform (Fire Safety) Order 2005 and shall come into force in accordance with paragraphs (2) and (3).

(2)   This article and article 52(1)(a) shall come into force on the day after the day on which this Order is made.

(3)   The remaining provisions of this Order shall come into force on [1st October 2006].

(4)   This Order extends to England and Wales only.

[1344]

NOTES

Commencement: 8 June 2005.
Para (3): words in square brackets substituted by the Regulatory Reform (Fire Safety) Subordinate Provisions Order 2006, SI 2006/484, art 2.
Certain functions of the Secretary of State under this article, so far as they are exercisable in or as regards Wales, are transferred to the National Assembly for Wales: see the National Assembly for Wales (Transfer of Functions) Order 2006, SI 2006/1458, arts 2(b), 3.

2 Interpretation

In this Order—
"alterations notice" has the meaning given by article 29;
"approved classification and labelling guide" means the Approved Guide to the Classification and Labelling of Dangerous Substances and Dangerous Preparations (5th edition) approved by the Health and Safety Commission on 16th April 2002;
"the CHIP Regulations" means the Chemicals (Hazard Information and Packaging for Supply) Regulations 2002;
"child" means a person who is not over compulsory school age, construed in accordance with section 8 of the Education Act 1996;
"dangerous substance" means—
    (a)   a substance or preparation which meets the criteria in the approved classification and labelling guide for classification as a substance or preparation which is explosive, oxidising, extremely flammable, highly flammable or flammable, whether or not that substance or preparation is classified under the CHIP Regulations;
    (b)   a substance or preparation which because of its physico-chemical or chemical properties and the way it is used or is present in or on premises creates a risk; and
    (c)   any dust, whether in the form of solid particles or fibrous materials or otherwise, which can form an explosive mixture with air or an explosive atmosphere;
"domestic premises" means premises occupied as a private dwelling (including any garden, yard, garage, outhouse, or other appurtenance of such premises which is not used in common by the occupants of more than one such dwelling);

"employee" means a person who is or is treated as an employee for the purposes of the Health and Safety at Work etc Act 1974 and related expressions are to be construed accordingly;

"enforcement notice" has the meaning given by article 30;

"enforcing authority" has the meaning given by article 25;

"explosive atmosphere" means a mixture, under atmospheric conditions, of air and one or more dangerous substances in the form of gases, vapours, mists or dusts in which, after ignition has occurred, combustion spreads to the entire unburned mixture;

"fire and rescue authority" means a fire and rescue authority under the Fire and Rescue Services Act 2004;

"fire inspector" means an inspector or assistant inspector appointed under section 28 of the Fire and Rescue Services Act 2004;

"general fire precautions" has the meaning given by article 4;

"hazard", in relation to a dangerous substance, means the physico-chemical or chemical property of that substance which has the potential to give rise to fire affecting the safety of a person, and references in this Order to "hazardous" are to be construed accordingly;

"inspector" means an inspector appointed under article 26 or a fire inspector;

"licensing authority" has the meaning given by article 42(3);

"normal ship-board activities" include the repair of a ship, save repair when carried out in dry dock;

"owner" means the person for the time being receiving the rackrent of the premises in connection with which the word is used, whether on his own account or as agent or trustee for another person, or who would so receive the rackrent if the premises were let at a rackrent;

"personal protective equipment" means all equipment which is intended to be worn or held by a person in or on premises and which protects that person against one or more risks to his safety, and any addition or accessory designed to meet that objective;

"place of safety" in relation to premises, means a safe area beyond the premises.

"premises" includes any place and, in particular, includes—
- (a) any workplace;
- (b) any vehicle, vessel, aircraft or hovercraft;
- (c) any installation on land (including the foreshore and other land intermittently covered by water), and any other installation (whether floating, or resting on the seabed or the subsoil thereof, or resting on other land covered with water or the subsoil thereof); and
- (d) any tent or movable structure;

"preparation" means a mixture or solution of two or more substances;

"preventive and protective measures" means the measures which have been identified by the responsible person in consequence of a risk assessment as the general fire precautions he needs to take to comply with the requirements and prohibitions imposed on him by or under this Order;

"prohibition notice" has the meaning given by article 31;

"public road" means a highway maintainable at public expense within the meaning of section 329 of the Highways Act 1980;

"rackrent" in relation to premises, means a rent that is not less than two-thirds of the rent at which the property might reasonably be expected to be let from year to year, free from all usual tenant's rates and taxes, and deducting from it the probable average cost of the repairs, insurance and other expenses (if any) necessary to maintain the property in a state to command such rent;

"the relevant local authority", in relation to premises, means—
- (a) if the premises are in Greater London but are not in the City of London, the London Borough in the area of which the premises are situated;
- (b) if the premises are in the City of London, the Common Council of the City of London;
- (c) if the premises are in England in a metropolitan county, the district council in the area of which the premises are situated;
- (d) if the premises are in England but are not in Greater London or a metropolitan county—
  - (i) the county council in the area of which the premises are situated; or
  - (ii) if there is no county council in the area of which the premises are situated, the district council in that area;
- (e) if the premises are in Wales, the county council or county borough council in the area of which the premises are situated;

"relevant persons" means—

(a) any person (including the responsible person) who is or may be lawfully on the premises; and

(b) any person in the immediate vicinity of the premises who is at risk from a fire on the premises,

but does not include a fire-fighter who is carrying out his duties in relation to a function of a fire and rescue authority under section 7, 8 or 9 of the Fire and Rescue Services Act 2004 (fire-fighting, road traffic accidents and other emergencies), other than in relation to a function under section 7(2)(d), 8(2)(d) or 9(3)(d) of that Act;

"responsible person" has the meaning given by article 3;

"risk" means the risk to the safety of persons from fire;

"risk assessment" means the assessment required by article 9(1);

"safety" means the safety of persons in respect of harm caused by fire; and "safe" shall be interpreted accordingly;

"safety data sheet" means a safety data sheet within the meaning of regulation 5 of the CHIP Regulations;

"ship" includes every description of vessel used in navigation;

"special, technical and organisational measures" include—

(a) technical means of supervision;

(b) connecting devices;

(c) control and protection systems;

(d) engineering controls and solutions;

(e) equipment;

(f) materials;

(g) protective systems; and

(h) warning and other communication systems;

"substance" means any natural or artificial substance whether in solid or liquid form or in the form of a gas or vapour;

"visiting force" means any such body, contingent, or detachment of the forces of any country as is a visiting force for the purposes of any of the provisions of the Visiting Forces Act 1952;

"workplace" means any premises or parts of premises, not being domestic premises, used for the purposes of an employer's undertaking and which are made available to an employee of the employer as a place of work and includes—

(a) any place within the premises to which such employee has access while at work; and

(b) any room, lobby, corridor, staircase, road, or other place—

(i) used as a means of access to or egress from that place of work; or

(ii) where facilities are provided for use in connection with that place of work,

other than a public road;

"young person" means any person who has not attained the age of 18.

[1345]

NOTES

Commencement: 1 October 2006.

Certain functions of the Secretary of State under this article, so far as they are exercisable in or as regards Wales, are transferred to the National Assembly for Wales: see the National Assembly for Wales (Transfer of Functions) Order 2006, SI 2006/1458, arts 2(b), 3.

---

3 Meaning of "responsible person"

In this Order "responsible person" means—

(a) in relation to a workplace, the employer, if the workplace is to any extent under his control;

(b) in relation to any premises not falling within paragraph (a)—

(i) the person who has control of the premises (as occupier or otherwise) in connection with the carrying on by him of a trade, business or other undertaking (for profit or not); or

(ii) the owner, where the person in control of the premises does not have control in connection with the carrying on by that person of a trade, business or other undertaking.

[1346]

NOTES
Commencement: 1 October 2006.
Certain functions of the Secretary of State under this article, so far as they are exercisable in or as regards Wales, are transferred to the National Assembly for Wales: see the National Assembly for Wales (Transfer of Functions) Order 2006, SI 2006/1458, arts 2(b), 3.

4   Meaning of "general fire precautions"

(1)   In this Order "general fire precautions" in relation to premises means, subject to paragraph (2)—

    (a)   measures to reduce the risk of fire on the premises and the risk of the spread of fire on the premises;

    (b)   measures in relation to the means of escape from the premises;

    (c)   measures for securing that, at all material times, the means of escape can be safely and effectively used;

    (d)   measures in relation to the means for fighting fires on the premises;

    (e)   measures in relation to the means for detecting fire on the premises and giving warning in case of fire on the premises; and

    (f)   measures in relation to the arrangements for action to be taken in the event of fire on the premises, including—

        (i)   measures relating to the instruction and training of employees; and

        (ii)   measures to mitigate the effects of the fire.

(2)   The precautions referred to in paragraph (1) do not include special, technical or organisational measures required to be taken or observed in any workplace in connection with the carrying on of any work process, where those measures—

    (a)   are designed to prevent or reduce the likelihood of fire arising from such a work process or reduce its intensity; and

    (b)   are required to be taken or observed to ensure compliance with any requirement of the relevant statutory provisions within the meaning given by section 53(1) of the Health and Safety at Work etc 1974.

(3)   In paragraph (2) "work process" means all aspects of work involving, or in connection with—

    (a)   the use of plant or machinery; or

    (b)   the use or storage of any dangerous substance.

[1347]

NOTES
Commencement: 1 October 2006.
Certain functions of the Secretary of State under this article, so far as they are exercisable in or as regards Wales, are transferred to the National Assembly for Wales: see the National Assembly for Wales (Transfer of Functions) Order 2006, SI 2006/1458, arts 2(b), 3.

5   Duties under this Order

(1)   Where the premises are a workplace, the responsible person must ensure that any duty imposed by articles 8 to 22 or by regulations made under article 24 is complied with in respect of those premises.

(2)   Where the premises are not a workplace, the responsible person must ensure that any duty imposed by articles 8 to 22 or by regulations made under article 24 is complied with in respect of those premises, so far as the requirements relate to matters within his control.

(3)   Any duty imposed by articles 8 to 22 or by regulations made under article 24 on the responsible person in respect of premises shall also be imposed on every person, other than the responsible person referred to in paragraphs (1) and (2), who has, to any extent, control of those premises so far as the requirements relate to matters within his control.

(4)   Where a person has, by virtue of any contract or tenancy, an obligation of any extent in relation to—

    (a)   the maintenance or repair of any premises, including anything in or on premises; or

    (b)   the safety of any premises,

that person is to be treated, for the purposes of paragraph (3), as being a person who has control of the premises to the extent that his obligation so extends.

PART II
STATUTORY INSTRUMENTS

(5)   Articles 8 to 22 and any regulations made under article 24 only require the taking or observance of general fire precautions in respect of relevant persons.

[1348]

NOTES

Commencement: 1 October 2006.

Certain functions of the Secretary of State under this article, so far as they are exercisable in or as regards Wales, are transferred to the National Assembly for Wales: see the National Assembly for Wales (Transfer of Functions) Order 2006, SI 2006/1458, arts 2(b), 3.

6 Application to premises

(1)   This Order does not apply in relation to—

   (a)   domestic premises, except to the extent mentioned in article 31(10);

   (b)   an offshore installation within the meaning of regulation 3 of the Offshore Installation and Pipeline Works (Management and Administration) Regulations 1995;

   (c)   a ship, in respect of the normal ship-board activities of a ship's crew which are carried out solely by the crew under the direction of the master;

   (d)   fields, woods or other land forming part of an agricultural or forestry undertaking but which is not inside a building and is situated away from the undertaking's main buildings;

   (e)   an aircraft, locomotive or rolling stock, trailer or semi-trailer used as a means of transport or a vehicle for which a licence is in force under the Vehicle Excise and Registration Act 1994 or a vehicle exempted from duty under that Act;

   (f)   a mine within the meaning of section 180 of the Mines and Quarries Act 1954, other than any building on the surface at a mine;

   (g)   a borehole site to which the Borehole Sites and Operations Regulations 1995 apply.

(2)   Subject to the preceding paragraph of this article, this Order applies in relation to any premises.

[1349]

NOTES

Commencement: 1 October 2006.

Certain functions of the Secretary of State under this article, so far as they are exercisable in or as regards Wales, are transferred to the National Assembly for Wales: see the National Assembly for Wales (Transfer of Functions) Order 2006, SI 2006/1458, arts 2(b), 3.

7 Disapplication of certain provisions

(1)   Articles 9(4) and (5) and 19(2) do not apply in relation to occasional work or short-term work involving work regulated as not being harmful, damaging, or dangerous to young people in a family undertaking.

(2)   Articles 9(2), 12, 16, 19(3) and 22(2) do not apply in relation to the use of means of transport by land, water or air where the use of means of transport is regulated by international agreements and the European Community directives giving effect to them and in so far as the use of means of transport falls within the disapplication in article 1.2(e) of Council Directive 1999/92/EC on minimum requirements for improving the safety and health of workers potentially at risk from explosive atmospheres, except for any means of transport intended for use in a potentially explosive atmosphere.

(3)   Articles 19 and 21 impose duties only on responsible persons who are employers.

(4)   The requirements of articles 8 to 23, or of any regulations made under article 24, do not have effect to the extent that they would prevent any of the following from carrying out their duties—

   (a)   any member of the armed forces of the Crown or of any visiting force;

   (b)   any constable or any member of a police force not being a constable;

   (c)   any member of any emergency service.

(5)   Without prejudice to paragraph (4), article 14(2)(f) does not apply to any premises constituting, or forming part of, a prison within the meaning of the Prison Act 1952 or constituting, or forming part of, a remand centre, detention centre or youth custody centre

provided by the Secretary of State under section 43 of that Act or any part of any other premises used for keeping persons in lawful custody or detention.

(6)   Where paragraph (4) or (5) applies, the safety of relevant persons must nevertheless be ensured so far as is possible.

[1350]

NOTES

Commencement: 1 October 2006.

Certain functions of the Secretary of State under this article, so far as they are exercisable in or as regards Wales, are transferred to the National Assembly for Wales: see the National Assembly for Wales (Transfer of Functions) Order 2006, SI 2006/1458, arts 2(b), 3.

PART 2
FIRE SAFETY DUTIES

8   Duty to take general fire precautions

(1)   The responsible person must—
    (a)   take such general fire precautions as will ensure, so far as is reasonably practicable, the safety of any of his employees; and
    (b)   in relation to relevant persons who are not his employees, take such general fire precautions as may reasonably be required in the circumstances of the case to ensure that the premises are safe.

[1351]

NOTES

Commencement: 1 October 2006.

Certain functions of the Secretary of State under this article, so far as they are exercisable in or as regards Wales, are transferred to the National Assembly for Wales: see the National Assembly for Wales (Transfer of Functions) Order 2006, SI 2006/1458, arts 2(b), 3.

9   Risk assessment

(1)   The responsible person must make a suitable and sufficient assessment of the risks to which relevant persons are exposed for the purpose of identifying the general fire precautions he needs to take to comply with the requirements and prohibitions imposed on him by or under this Order.

(2)   Where a dangerous substance is or is liable to be present in or on the premises, the risk assessment must include consideration of the matters set out in Part 1 of Schedule 1.

(3)   Any such assessment must be reviewed by the responsible person regularly so as to keep it up to date and particularly if—
    (a)   there is reason to suspect that it is no longer valid; or
    (b)   there has been a significant change in the matters to which it relates including when the premises, special, technical and organisational measures, or organisation of the work undergo significant changes, extensions, or conversions,
and where changes to an assessment are required as a result of any such review, the responsible person must make them.

(4)   The responsible person must not employ a young person unless he has, in relation to risks to young persons, made or reviewed an assessment in accordance with paragraphs (1) and (5).

(5)   In making or reviewing the assessment, the responsible person who employs or is to employ a young person must take particular account of the matters set out in Part 2 of Schedule 1.

(6)   As soon as practicable after the assessment is made or reviewed, the responsible person must record the information prescribed by paragraph (7) where—
    (a)   he employs five or more employees;
    (b)   a licence under an enactment is in force in relation to the premises; or
    (c)   an alterations notice requiring this is in force in relation to the premises.

(7)   The prescribed information is—

PART II
STATUTORY INSTRUMENTS

(a)　the significant findings of the assessment, including the measures which have been or will be taken by the responsible person pursuant to this Order; and

(b)　any group of persons identified by the assessment as being especially at risk.

(8)　No new work activity involving a dangerous substance may commence unless—

(a)　the risk assessment has been made; and

(b)　the measures required by or under this Order have been implemented.

[1352]

NOTES

Commencement: 1 October 2006.

Certain functions of the Secretary of State under this article, so far as they are exercisable in or as regards Wales, are transferred to the National Assembly for Wales: see the National Assembly for Wales (Transfer of Functions) Order 2006, SI 2006/1458, arts 2(b), 3.

10　Principles of prevention to be applied

Where the responsible person implements any preventive and protective measures he must do so on the basis of the principles specified in Part 3 of Schedule 1.

[1353]

NOTES

Commencement: 1 October 2006.

Certain functions of the Secretary of State under this article, so far as they are exercisable in or as regards Wales, are transferred to the National Assembly for Wales: see the National Assembly for Wales (Transfer of Functions) Order 2006, SI 2006/1458, arts 2(b), 3.

11　Fire safety arrangements

(1)　The responsible person must make and give effect to such arrangements as are appropriate, having regard to the size of his undertaking and the nature of its activities, for the effective planning, organisation, control, monitoring and review of the preventive and protective measures.

(2)　The responsible person must record the arrangements referred to in paragraph (1) where—

(a)　he employs five or more employees;

(b)　a licence under an enactment is in force in relation to the premises; or

(c)　an alterations notice requiring a record to be made of those arrangements is in force in relation to the premises.

[1354]

NOTES

Commencement: 1 October 2006.

Certain functions of the Secretary of State under this article, so far as they are exercisable in or as regards Wales, are transferred to the National Assembly for Wales: see the National Assembly for Wales (Transfer of Functions) Order 2006, SI 2006/1458, arts 2(b), 3.

12　Elimination or reduction of risks from dangerous substances

(1)　Where a dangerous substance is present in or on the premises, the responsible person must ensure that risk to relevant persons related to the presence of the substance is either eliminated or reduced so far as is reasonably practicable.

(2)　In complying with his duty under paragraph (1), the responsible person must, so far as is reasonably practicable, replace a dangerous substance, or the use of a dangerous substance, with a substance or process which either eliminates or reduces the risk to relevant persons.

(3)　Where it is not reasonably practicable to eliminate risk pursuant to paragraphs (1) and (2), the responsible person must, so far as is reasonably practicable, apply measures consistent with the risk assessment and appropriate to the nature of the activity or operation, including the measures specified in Part 4 of Schedule 1 to this Order to—

(a)　control the risk, and

(b)　mitigate the detrimental effects of a fire.

(4)　The responsible person must—

(a) arrange for the safe handling, storage and transport of dangerous substances and waste containing dangerous substances; and

(b) ensure that any conditions necessary pursuant to this Order for ensuring the elimination or reduction of risk are maintained.

[1355]

NOTES

Commencement: 1 October 2006.

Certain functions of the Secretary of State under this article, so far as they are exercisable in or as regards Wales, are transferred to the National Assembly for Wales: see the National Assembly for Wales (Transfer of Functions) Order 2006, SI 2006/1458, arts 2(b), 3.

13 Fire-fighting and fire detection

(1) Where necessary (whether due to the features of the premises, the activity carried on there, any hazard present or any other relevant circumstances) in order to safeguard the safety of relevant persons, the responsible person must ensure that—

(a) the premises are, to the extent that it is appropriate, equipped with appropriate fire-fighting equipment and with fire detectors and alarms; and

(b) any non-automatic fire-fighting equipment so provided is easily accessible, simple to use and indicated by signs.

(2) For the purposes of paragraph (1) what is appropriate is to be determined having regard to the dimensions and use of the premises, the equipment contained on the premises, the physical and chemical properties of the substances likely to be present and the maximum number of persons who may be present at any one time.

(3) The responsible person must, where necessary—

(a) take measures for fire-fighting in the premises, adapted to the nature of the activities carried on there and the size of the undertaking and of the premises concerned;

(b) nominate competent persons to implement those measures and ensure that the number of such persons, their training and the equipment available to them are adequate, taking into account the size of, and the specific hazards involved in, the premises concerned; and

(c) arrange any necessary contacts with external emergency services, particularly as regards fire-fighting, rescue work, first-aid and emergency medical care.

(4) A person is to be regarded as competent for the purposes of paragraph (3)(b) where he has sufficient training and experience or knowledge and other qualities to enable him properly to implement the measures referred to in that paragraph.

[1356]

NOTES

Commencement: 1 October 2006.

Certain functions of the Secretary of State under this article, so far as they are exercisable in or as regards Wales, are transferred to the National Assembly for Wales: see the National Assembly for Wales (Transfer of Functions) Order 2006, SI 2006/1458, arts 2(b), 3.

14 Emergency routes and exits

(1) Where necessary in order to safeguard the safety of relevant persons, the responsible person must ensure that routes to emergency exits from premises and the exits themselves are kept clear at all times.

(2) The following requirements must be complied with in respect of premises where necessary (whether due to the features of the premises, the activity carried on there, any hazard present or any other relevant circumstances) in order to safeguard the safety of relevant persons—

(a) emergency routes and exits must lead as directly as possible to a place of safety;

(b) in the event of danger, it must be possible for persons to evacuate the premises as quickly and as safely as possible;

(c) the number, distribution and dimensions of emergency routes and exits must be adequate having regard to the use, equipment and dimensions of the premises and the maximum number of persons who may be present there at any one time;

(d) emergency doors must open in the direction of escape;

PART II
STATUTORY INSTRUMENTS

(e) sliding or revolving doors must not be used for exits specifically intended as emergency exits;

(f) emergency doors must not be so locked or fastened that they cannot be easily and immediately opened by any person who may require to use them in an emergency;

(g) emergency routes and exits must be indicated by signs; and

(h) emergency routes and exits requiring illumination must be provided with emergency lighting of adequate intensity in the case of failure of their normal lighting.

[1357]

NOTES

Commencement: 1 October 2006.

Certain functions of the Secretary of State under this article, so far as they are exercisable in or as regards Wales, are transferred to the National Assembly for Wales: see the National Assembly for Wales (Transfer of Functions) Order 2006, SI 2006/1458, arts 2(b), 3.

15 Procedures for serious and imminent danger and for danger areas

(1) The responsible person must—

(a) establish and, where necessary, give effect to appropriate procedures, including safety drills, to be followed in the event of serious and imminent danger to relevant persons;

(b) nominate a sufficient number of competent persons to implement those procedures in so far as they relate to the evacuation of relevant persons from the premises; and

(c) ensure that no relevant person has access to any area to which it is necessary to restrict access on grounds of safety, unless the person concerned has received adequate safety instruction.

(2) Without prejudice to the generality of paragraph (1)(a), the procedures referred to in that sub-paragraph must—

(a) so far as is practicable, require any relevant persons who are exposed to serious and imminent danger to be informed of the nature of the hazard and of the steps taken or to be taken to protect them from it;

(b) enable the persons concerned (if necessary by taking appropriate steps in the absence of guidance or instruction and in the light of their knowledge and the technical means at their disposal) to stop work and immediately proceed to a place of safety in the event of their being exposed to serious, imminent and unavoidable danger; and

(c) save in exceptional cases for reasons duly substantiated (which cases and reasons must be specified in those procedures), require the persons concerned to be prevented from resuming work in any situation where there is still a serious and imminent danger.

(3) A person is to be regarded as competent for the purposes of paragraph (1) where he has sufficient training and experience or knowledge and other qualities to enable him properly to implement the evacuation procedures referred to in that paragraph.

[1358]

NOTES

Commencement: 1 October 2006.

Certain functions of the Secretary of State under this article, so far as they are exercisable in or as regards Wales, are transferred to the National Assembly for Wales: see the National Assembly for Wales (Transfer of Functions) Order 2006, SI 2006/1458, arts 2(b), 3.

16 Additional emergency measures in respect of dangerous substances

(1) Subject to paragraph (4), in order to safeguard the safety of relevant persons arising from an accident, incident or emergency related to the presence of a dangerous substance in or on the premises, the responsible person must ensure that—

(a) information on emergency arrangements is available, including—

(i) details of relevant work hazards and hazard identification arrangements; and

(ii) specific hazards likely to arise at the time of an accident, incident or emergency;

(b)   suitable warning and other communication systems are established to enable an appropriate response, including remedial actions and rescue operations, to be made immediately when such an event occurs;

(c)   where necessary, before any explosion conditions are reached, visual or audible warnings are given and relevant persons withdrawn; and

(d)   where the risk assessment indicates it is necessary, escape facilities are provided and maintained to ensure that, in the event of danger, relevant persons can leave endangered places promptly and safely.

(2)   Subject to paragraph (4), the responsible person must ensure that the information required by article 15(1)(a) and paragraph (1)(a) of this article, together with information on the matters referred to in paragraph (1)(b) and (d) is—

(a)   made available to relevant accident and emergency services to enable those services, whether internal or external to the premises, to prepare their own response procedures and precautionary measures; and

(b)   displayed at the premises, unless the results of the risk assessment make this unnecessary.

(3)   Subject to paragraph (4), in the event of a fire arising from an accident, incident or emergency related to the presence of a dangerous substance in or on the premises, the responsible person must ensure that—

(a)   immediate steps are taken to—

    (i)   mitigate the effects of the fire;

    (ii)   restore the situation to normal; and

    (iii)   inform those relevant persons who may be affected; and

(b)   only those persons who are essential for the carrying out of repairs and other necessary work are permitted in the affected area and they are provided with—

    (i)   appropriate personal protective equipment and protective clothing; and

    (ii)   any necessary specialised safety equipment and plant,

which must be used until the situation is restored to normal.

(4)   Paragraphs (1) to (3) do not apply where—

(a)   the results of the risk assessment show that, because of the quantity of each dangerous substance in or on the premises, there is only a slight risk to relevant persons; and

(b)   the measures taken by the responsible person to comply with his duty under article 12 are sufficient to control that risk.

[1359]

NOTES

Commencement: 1 October 2006.

Certain functions of the Secretary of State under this article, so far as they are exercisable in or as regards Wales, are transferred to the National Assembly for Wales: see the National Assembly for Wales (Transfer of Functions) Order 2006, SI 2006/1458, arts 2(b), 3.

17 Maintenance

(1)   Where necessary in order to safeguard the safety of relevant persons the responsible person must ensure that the premises and any facilities, equipment and devices provided in respect of the premises under this Order or, subject to paragraph (6), under any other enactment, including any enactment repealed or revoked by this Order, are subject to a suitable system of maintenance and are maintained in an efficient state, in efficient working order and in good repair.

(2)   Where the premises form part of a building, the responsible person may make arrangements with the occupier of any other premises forming part of the building for the purpose of ensuring that the requirements of paragraph (1) are met.

(3)   Paragraph (2) applies even if the other premises are not premises to which this Order applies.

(4)   The occupier of the other premises must co-operate with the responsible person for the purposes of paragraph (2).

(5)   Where the occupier of the other premises is not also the owner of those premises, the references to the occupier in paragraphs (2) and (4) are to be taken to be references to both the occupier and the owner.

(6)   Paragraph (1) only applies to facilities, equipment and devices provided under other enactments where they are provided in connection with general fire precautions.

[1360]

NOTES

Commencement: 1 October 2006.

Certain functions of the Secretary of State under this article, so far as they are exercisable in or as regards Wales, are transferred to the National Assembly for Wales: see the National Assembly for Wales (Transfer of Functions) Order 2006, SI 2006/1458, arts 2(b), 3.

18   Safety assistance

(1)   The responsible person must, subject to paragraphs (6) and (7), appoint one or more competent persons to assist him in undertaking the preventive and protective measures.

(2)   Where the responsible person appoints persons in accordance with paragraph (1), he must make arrangements for ensuring adequate co-operation between them.

(3)   The responsible person must ensure that the number of persons appointed under paragraph (1), the time available for them to fulfil their functions and the means at their disposal are adequate having regard to the size of the premises, the risks to which relevant persons are exposed and the distribution of those risks throughout the premises.

(4)   The responsible person must ensure that—
    (a)   any person appointed by him in accordance with paragraph (1) who is not in his employment—
        (i)   is informed of the factors known by him to affect, or suspected by him of affecting, the safety of any other person who may be affected by the conduct of his undertaking; and
        (ii)   has access to the information referred to in article 19(3); and
    (b)   any person appointed by him in accordance with paragraph (1) is given such information about any person working in his undertaking who is—
        (i)   employed by him under a fixed-term contract of employment, or
        (ii)   employed in an employment business,
as is necessary to enable that person properly to carry out the function specified in that paragraph.

(5)   A person is to be regarded as competent for the purposes of this article where he has sufficient training and experience or knowledge and other qualities to enable him properly to assist in undertaking the preventive and protective measures.

(6)   Paragraph (1) does not apply to a self-employed employer who is not in partnership with any other person, where he has sufficient training and experience or knowledge and other qualities properly to assist in undertaking the preventive and protective measures.

(7)   Paragraph (1) does not apply to individuals who are employers and who are together carrying on business in partnership, where at least one of the individuals concerned has sufficient training and experience or knowledge and other qualities—
    (a)   properly to undertake the preventive and protective measures; and
    (b)   properly to assist his fellow partners in undertaking those measures.

(8)   Where there is a competent person in the responsible person's employment, that person must be appointed for the purposes of paragraph (1) in preference to a competent person not in his employment.

[1361]

NOTES

Commencement: 1 October 2006.

Certain functions of the Secretary of State under this article, so far as they are exercisable in or as regards Wales, are transferred to the National Assembly for Wales: see the National Assembly for Wales (Transfer of Functions) Order 2006, SI 2006/1458, arts 2(b), 3.

19   Provision of information to employees

(1)   The responsible person must provide his employees with comprehensible and relevant information on—
    (a)   the risks to them identified by the risk assessment;
    (b)   the preventive and protective measures;

(c)   the procedures and the measures referred to in article 15(1)(a);

(d)   the identities of those persons nominated by him in accordance with article 13(3)(b) or appointed in accordance with article 15(1)(b); and

(e)   the risks notified to him in accordance with article 22(1)(c).

(2)   The responsible person must, before employing a child, provide a parent of the child with comprehensible and relevant information on—

(a)   the risks to that child identified by the risk assessment;

(b)   the preventive and protective measures; and

(c)   the risks notified to him in accordance with article 22(1)(c),

and for the purposes of this paragraph, "parent of the child" includes a person who has parental responsibility, within the meaning of section 3 of the Children Act 1989, for the child.

(3)   Where a dangerous substance is present in or on the premises, the responsible person must, in addition to the information provided under paragraph (1) provide his employees with—

(a)   the details of any such substance including—

    (i)   the name of the substance and the risk which it presents;

    (ii)   access to any relevant safety data sheet; and

    (iii)   legislative provisions (concerning the hazardous properties of any such substance) which apply to the substance; and

(b)   the significant findings of the risk assessment.

(4)   The information required by paragraph (3) must be—

(a)   adapted to take account of significant changes in the activity carried out or methods or work used by the responsible person; and

(b)   provided in a manner appropriate to the risk identified by the risk assessment.

[1362]

NOTES

Commencement: 1 October 2006.

Certain functions of the Secretary of State under this article, so far as they are exercisable in or as regards Wales, are transferred to the National Assembly for Wales: see the National Assembly for Wales (Transfer of Functions) Order 2006, SI 2006/1458, arts 2(b), 3.

20 Provision of information to employers and the self-employed from outside undertakings

(1)   The responsible person must ensure that the employer of any employees from an outside undertaking who are working in or on the premises is provided with comprehensible and relevant information on—

(a)   the risks to those employees; and

(b)   the preventive and protective measures taken by the responsible person.

(2)   The responsible person must ensure that any person working in his undertaking who is not his employee is provided with appropriate instructions and comprehensible and relevant information regarding any risks to that person.

(3)   The responsible person must—

(a)   ensure that the employer of any employees from an outside undertaking who are working in or on the premises is provided with sufficient information to enable that employer to identify any person nominated by the responsible person in accordance with article 15 (1)(b) to implement evacuation procedures as far as those employees are concerned; and

(b)   take all reasonable steps to ensure that any person from an outside undertaking who is working in or on the premises receives sufficient information to enable that person to identify any person nominated by the responsible person in accordance with article 15 (1)(b) to implement evacuation procedures as far as they are concerned.

[1363]

NOTES

Commencement: 1 October 2006.

Certain functions of the Secretary of State under this article, so far as they are exercisable in or as regards Wales, are transferred to the National Assembly for Wales: see the National Assembly for Wales (Transfer of Functions) Order 2006, SI 2006/1458, arts 2(b), 3.

21 Training

(1)   The responsible person must ensure that his employees are provided with adequate safety training—

(a)   at the time when they are first employed; and

(b)   on their being exposed to new or increased risks because of—

(i)   their being transferred or given a change of responsibilities within the responsible person's undertaking;

(ii)   the introduction of new work equipment into, or a change respecting work equipment already in use within, the responsible person's undertaking;

(iii)   the introduction of new technology into the responsible person's undertaking; or

(iv)   the introduction of a new system of work into, or a change respecting a system of work already in use within, the responsible person's undertaking.

(2)   The training referred to in paragraph (1) must—

(a)   include suitable and sufficient instruction and training on the appropriate precautions and actions to be taken by the employee in order to safeguard himself and other relevant persons on the premises;

(b)   be repeated periodically where appropriate;

(c)   be adapted to take account of any new or changed risks to the safety of the employees concerned;

(d)   be provided in a manner appropriate to the risk identified by the risk assessment; and

(e)   take place during working hours.

[1364]

NOTES

Commencement: 1 October 2006.

Certain functions of the Secretary of State under this article, so far as they are exercisable in or as regards Wales, are transferred to the National Assembly for Wales: see the National Assembly for Wales (Transfer of Functions) Order 2006, SI 2006/1458, arts 2(b), 3.

22 Co-operation and co-ordination

(1)   Where two or more responsible persons share, or have duties in respect of, premises (whether on a temporary or a permanent basis) each such person must—

(a)   co-operate with the other responsible person concerned so far as is necessary to enable them to comply with the requirements and prohibitions imposed on them by or under this Order;

(b)   (taking into account the nature of his activities) take all reasonable steps to co-ordinate the measures he takes to comply with the requirements and prohibitions imposed on him by or under this Order with the measures the other responsible persons are taking to comply with the requirements and prohibitions imposed on them by or under this Order; and

(c)   take all reasonable steps to inform the other responsible persons concerned of the risks to relevant persons arising out of or in connection with the conduct by him of his undertaking.

(2)   Where two or more responsible persons share premises (whether on a temporary or a permanent basis) where an explosive atmosphere may occur, the responsible person who has overall responsibility for the premises must co-ordinate the implementation of all the measures required by this Part to be taken to protect relevant persons from any risk from the explosive atmosphere.

[1365]

NOTES

Commencement: 1 October 2006.

Certain functions of the Secretary of State under this article, so far as they are exercisable in or as regards Wales, are transferred to the National Assembly for Wales: see the National Assembly for Wales (Transfer of Functions) Order 2006, SI 2006/1458, arts 2(b), 3.

23   (*Outside the scope of this work.*)

24   Power to make regulations about fire precautions

(1)   The Secretary of State may by regulations make provision as to the precautions which are to be taken or observed in relation to the risk to relevant persons as regards premises in relation to which this Order applies.

(2)   Without prejudice to the generality of paragraph (1), regulations made by the Secretary of State may impose requirements—

(a)   as to the provision, maintenance and keeping free from obstruction of any means of escape in case of fire;

(b)   as to the provision and maintenance of means for securing that any means of escape can be safely and effectively used at all material times;

(c)   as to the provision and maintenance of means for fighting fire and means for giving warning in case of fire;

(d)   as to the internal construction of the premises and the materials used in that construction;

(e)   for prohibiting altogether the presence or use in the premises of furniture or equipment of any specified description, or prohibiting its presence or use unless specified standards or conditions are complied with;

(f)   for securing that persons employed to work in the premises receive appropriate instruction or training in what to do in case of fire;

(g)   for securing that, in specified circumstances, specified numbers of attendants are stationed in specified parts of the premises; and

(h)   as to the keeping of records of instruction or training given, or other things done, in pursuance of the regulations.

(3)   Regulations under this article—

(a)   may impose requirements on persons other than the responsible person; and

(b)   may, as regards any of their provisions, make provision as to the person or persons who is or are to be responsible for any contravention of that provision.

(4)   The Secretary of State must, before making any regulations under this article, consult with such persons or bodies of persons as appear to him to be appropriate.

(5)   The power of the Secretary of State to make regulations under this article—

(a)   is exercisable by statutory instrument, which is subject to annulment in pursuance of a resolution of either House of Parliament;

(b)   includes power to make different provision in relation to different circumstances; and

(c)   includes power to grant or provide for the granting of exemptions from any of the provisions of the regulations, either unconditionally or subject to conditions.

[1366]

NOTES

Commencement: 1 October 2006.

Certain functions of the Secretary of State under this article, so far as they are exercisable in or as regards Wales, are transferred to the National Assembly for Wales: see the National Assembly for Wales (Transfer of Functions) Order 2006, SI 2006/1458, arts 2(b), 3.

25–53   (*Outside the scope of this work.*)

(*Schs 1–5 outside the scope of this work.*)

CONTROL OF ASBESTOS REGULATIONS 2006

(SI 2006/2739)

NOTES

Made: 12 October 2006.

Authority: Health and Safety at Work etc Act 1974, ss 15(1), (2), (3), (4), (5), (6)(b), (9), 18(2), 80(1), 82(3), Sch 3, paras 1(1)–(4), 2, 3(2), 4, 6, 8–11, 13(1), (3), 14, 15(1), 16, 20; European Communities Act 1972, s 2(2).

PART 1
PRELIMINARY

1 Citation and Commencement

These Regulations may be cited as the Control of Asbestos Regulations 2006 and shall come into force on 13th November 2006, except regulation 20(4) which shall come into force on 6th April 2007.

[1367]

NOTES
Commencement: 13 November 2006.

2 Interpretation

(1) In these Regulations—

"adequate" means adequate having regard only to the nature and degree of exposure to asbestos, and "adequately" shall be construed accordingly;

"appointed doctor" means a registered medical practitioner appointed for the time being in writing by the Executive for the purpose of these Regulations;

"approved" means approved for the time being in writing by the Health and Safety Commission or the Executive as the case may be;

"asbestos" means the following fibrous silicates—

    (a)   asbestos actinolite, CAS No 77536–66–4(*);

    (b)   asbestos grunerite (amosite), CAS No 12172–73–5(*);

    (c)   asbestos anthophyllite, CAS No 77536–67–5(*);

    (d)   chrysotile, CAS No 12001–29–5;

    (e)   crocidolite, CAS No 12001–28–4(*); and

    (f)   asbestos tremolite, CAS No 77536–68–6(*),

and references to "CAS" followed by a numerical sequence are references to CAS Registry Numbers assigned to chemicals by the Chemical Abstracts Service, a division of the American Chemical Society;

"the control limit" means a concentration of asbestos in the atmosphere when measured in accordance with the 1997 WHO recommended method, or by a method giving equivalent results to that method approved by the Health and Safety Commission, of 0.1 fibres per cubic centimetre of air averaged over a continuous period of 4 hours;

"control measure" means a measure taken to prevent or reduce exposure to asbestos (including the provision of systems of work and supervision, the cleaning of workplaces, premises, plant and equipment, and the provision and use of engineering controls and personal protective equipment);

"emergency services" include—

    (a)   police, fire, rescue and ambulance services;

    (b)   Her Majesty's Coastguard;

"employment medical adviser" means an employment medical adviser appointed under section 56 of the Health and Safety at Work etc Act 1974;

"enforcing authority" means the Executive, local authority or Office of Rail Regulation, determined in accordance with the provisions of the Health and Safety (Enforcing Authority) Regulations 1998 and the provisions of the Health and Safety (Enforcing Authority for Railways and Other Guided Transport Systems) Regulations 2006;

"the Executive" means the Health and Safety Executive;

"ISO 17020" means European Standard EN ISO/IEC 17020, "General criteria for the operation of various types of bodies performing inspection" as revised or reissued from time to time and accepted by the Comité Européen de Normalisation Electrotechnique (CEN/CENELEC);

"ISO 17025" means European Standard EN ISO/IEC 17025, "General requirements for the competence of testing and calibration laboratories" as revised or reissued from time to time and accepted by the Comité Européen de Normalisation Electrotechnique (CEN/CENELEC);

"medical examination" includes any laboratory tests and X-rays that a relevant doctor may require;

"personal protective equipment" means all equipment (including clothing) which is intended to be worn or held by a person at work and which protects that person against one or more risks to his health, and any addition or accessory designed to meet that objective;

"relevant doctor" means an appointed doctor or an employment medical adviser;

"risk assessment" means the assessment of risk required by regulation 6(1)(a);

"the 1997 WHO recommended method" means the publication "Determination of airborne fibre concentrations. A recommended method, by phase-contrast optical microscopy (membrane filter method)", WHO (World Health Organisation), Geneva 1997.

(2) For the purposes of these Regulations, except in accordance with regulation 11(3) and (5), in determining whether an employee is exposed to asbestos or whether the extent of such exposure exceeds the control limit, no account shall be taken of respiratory protective equipment which, for the time being, is being worn by that employee.

(3) A reference to work with asbestos in these Regulations shall include—

    (a) work which consists of the removal, repair or disturbance of asbestos or materials containing asbestos;

    (b) work which is ancillary to such work; and

    (c) supervision of such work and such ancillary work.

[1368]

NOTES

Commencement: 13 November 2006.

3 (*Outside the scope of this work.*)

PART 2
GENERAL REQUIREMENTS

4 Duty to manage asbestos in non-domestic premises

(1) In this regulation "the dutyholder" means—

    (a) every person who has, by virtue of a contract or tenancy, an obligation of any extent in relation to the maintenance or repair of non-domestic premises or any means of access thereto or egress therefrom; or

    (b) in relation to any part of non-domestic premises where there is no such contract or tenancy, every person who has, to any extent, control of that part of those non-domestic premises or any means of access thereto or egress therefrom,

and where there is more than one such dutyholder, the relative contribution to be made by each such person in complying with the requirements of this regulation will be determined by the nature and extent of the maintenance and repair obligation owed by that person.

(2) Every person shall cooperate with the dutyholder so far as is necessary to enable the dutyholder to comply with his duties under this regulation.

(3) In order to enable him to manage the risk from asbestos in non-domestic premises, the dutyholder shall ensure that a suitable and sufficient assessment is carried out as to whether asbestos is or is liable to be present in the premises.

(4) In making the assessment—

    (a) such steps as are reasonable in the circumstances shall be taken; and

    (b) the condition of any asbestos which is, or has been assumed to be, present in the premises shall be considered.

(5) Without prejudice to the generality of paragraph (4), the dutyholder shall ensure that—

    (a) account is taken of building plans or other relevant information and of the age of the premises; and

    (b) an inspection is made of those parts of the premises which are reasonably accessible.

(6) The dutyholder shall ensure that the assessment is reviewed forthwith if—

    (a) there is reason to suspect that the assessment is no longer valid; or

    (b) there has been a significant change in the premises to which the assessment relates.

(7) The dutyholder shall ensure that the conclusions of the assessment and every review are recorded.

(8) Where the assessment shows that asbestos is or is liable to be present in any part of the premises the dutyholder shall ensure that—

    (a) a determination of the risk from that asbestos is made;

    (b) a written plan identifying those parts of the premises concerned is prepared; and

    (c) the measures which are to be taken for managing the risk are specified in the written plan.

(9) The measures to be specified in the plan for managing the risk shall include adequate measures for—

    (a) monitoring the condition of any asbestos or any substance containing or suspected of containing asbestos;

    (b) ensuring any asbestos or any such substance is properly maintained or where necessary safely removed; and

    (c) ensuring that information about the location and condition of any asbestos or any such substance is—

        (i) provided to every person liable to disturb it, and

        (ii) made available to the emergency services.

(10) The dutyholder shall ensure that—

    (a) the plan is reviewed and revised at regular intervals, and forthwith if—

        (i) there is reason to suspect that the plan is no longer valid, or

        (ii) there has been a significant change in the premises to which the plan relates;

    (b) the measures specified in the plan are implemented; and

    (c) the measures taken to implement the plan are recorded.

(11) In this regulation, a reference to—

    (a) "the assessment" is a reference to the assessment required by paragraph (3);

    (b) "the premises" is a reference to the non-domestic premises referred to in paragraph (1); and

    (c) "the plan" is a reference to the plan required by paragraph (8).

[1369]

NOTES

Commencement: 13 November 2006.

5–37 (*Outside the scope of this work.*)

(*Schs 1–5 outside the scope of this work.*)

ENERGY PERFORMANCE OF BUILDINGS (CERTIFICATES AND INSPECTIONS) (ENGLAND AND WALES) REGULATIONS 2007

(SI 2007/991)

NOTES

Made: 23 March 2007.

Authority: European Communities Act 1972, s 2(2); Building Act 1984, ss 1(1), 8(6), 35, 47, Sch 1, paras 1, 2, 4, 7, 8, 10.

ARRANGEMENT OF REGULATIONS

PART 1
INTRODUCTORY

PART 2
DUTIES RELATING TO ENERGY PERFORMANCE CERTIFICATES

PART 1
INTRODUCTORY

1   Citation, application, extent and commencement

(1)   These Regulations may be cited as the Energy Performance of Buildings (Certificates and Inspections) (England and Wales) Regulations 2007.

(2)   Subject to regulation 4, and notwithstanding section 4 of the Building Act 1984, these Regulations, other than regulation 8, apply to all buildings including buildings which are exempt from building regulations by virtue of that section.

(3)   These Regulations extend to England and Wales.

(4)   Each provision of these Regulations mentioned in column 3 of the Table in Schedule 1 shall come into force on the date mentioned in column 2 of that Table, for the purposes mentioned in column 4.

[1370]

NOTES
Commencement: 19 April 2007.

---

2   Interpretation

(1)   In these Regulations—
"accreditation scheme" means a scheme approved by the Secretary of State in accordance with—
  (a)   regulation 25; or
  (b)   regulation 17F of the Building Regulations 2000;
"advisory report" means a report issued by an energy assessor pursuant to regulation 19;
"air-conditioning system" means a combination of all the components required to provide a form of air treatment in which the temperature is controlled or can be lowered, and includes systems which combine such air treatment with the control of ventilation, humidity and air cleanliness;
"asset rating" means a numerical indicator of the amount of energy estimated to meet the different needs associated with a standardised use of a building, calculated according to the methodology approved by the Secretary of State pursuant to regulation 17A of the Building Regulations 2000;
"building" means a roofed construction having walls, for which energy is used to condition the indoor climate, and a reference to a building includes a reference to a part of building which has been designed or altered to be used separately;
"display energy certificate" means a certificate which complies with regulation 17;
"dwelling" means a building or part of a building occupied or intended to be occupied as a separate dwelling;
"energy assessor" means an individual who is a member of an accreditation scheme;
"energy performance certificate" means a certificate which complies with regulation 11(1) of these Regulations or regulation 17E of the Building Regulations 2000;

.....

"inspection report" means a report issued by an energy assessor in accordance with regulation 22(1);
"penalty charge notice" means a notice given pursuant to regulation 40;

"recommendation report" means the recommendation report required by regulation 10, and includes a report issued by an energy assessor for the purposes of regulation 17E(4) of the Building Regulations 2000 or regulation 12(4) of the Building (Approved Inspectors etc) Regulations 2000;

"relevant person" means—

    (a)   in relation to a building which is to be sold, the seller;

    (b)   in relation to a building which is to be rented out, the prospective landlord;

    (c)   in relation to a building in circumstances where regulation 9 applies, the person responsible for carrying out the construction work; and

    (d)   in relation to an air-conditioning system, the person who has control of the operation of the system.

(2)   Unless otherwise defined in these Regulations, terms used in these Regulations have the same meaning as in European Parliament and Council Directive 2002/91/EC on the energy performance of buildings.

[1371]

NOTES

Commencement: 19 April 2007.

Para (1): definition "home information pack" (omitted) revoked by the Energy Performance of Buildings (Certificates and Inspections) (England and Wales) (Amendment) Regulations 2007, SI 2007/1669, reg 3(1), (2); for transitional provisions see reg 4 thereof.

3 Meaning of "prospective buyer or tenant"

A person becomes a prospective buyer or tenant in relation to a building when he—

    (a)   requests any information about the building from the relevant person or his agent for the purpose of deciding whether to buy or rent the building;

    (b)   makes a request to view the building for the purpose of deciding whether to buy or rent the building; or

    (c)   makes an offer, whether oral or written, to buy or rent the building.

[1372]

NOTES

Commencement: 19 April 2007.

PART 2
DUTIES RELATING TO ENERGY PERFORMANCE CERTIFICATES

4 Application of Part 2

(1)   This Part does not apply to—

    (a)   buildings which are used primarily or solely as places of worship;

    (b)   temporary buildings with a planned time of use of two years or less, industrial sites, workshops and non-residential agricultural buildings with low energy demand;

    (c)   stand-alone buildings with a total useful floor area of less than 50m² which are not dwellings.

(2)   Nothing in this Part requires an energy performance certificate to be given or made available to a prospective buyer or tenant at any time before the construction of the building has been completed.

[1373]

NOTES

Commencement: 19 April 2007.

5 Energy performance certificates on sale and rent

(1)   Subject to regulation 7, this regulation applies where a building is to be sold or rented out.

(2)   The relevant person shall make available free of charge a valid energy performance certificate to any prospective buyer or tenant—

(a) at the earliest opportunity; and
(b) in any event before entering into a contract to sell or rent out the building or, if sooner, no later than whichever is the earlier of—
    (i) in the case of a person who requests information about the building, the time at which the relevant person first makes available any information in writing about the building to the person; or
    (ii) in the case of a person who makes a request to view the building, the time at which the person views the building.

(3) Paragraph (2) does not apply if the relevant person believes on reasonable grounds that the prospective buyer or tenant—
(a) is unlikely to have sufficient means to buy or rent the building;
(b) is not genuinely interested in buying or renting a building of a general description which applies to the building; or
(c) is not a person to whom the relevant person is likely to be prepared to sell or rent out the building.

(4) Nothing in paragraph (3) authorises the doing of anything which constitutes an unlawful act of discrimination.

(5) The relevant person must ensure that a valid energy performance certificate has been given free of charge to the person who ultimately becomes the buyer or tenant.

[1374]

NOTES

Commencement: 1 June 2007 (certain purposes); 1 October 2007 (certain purposes); 6 April 2008 (certain purposes); 1 October 2008 (otherwise).

6 (*Outside the scope of this work.*)

7 Buildings to be demolished

(1) Regulations 5 and 6 do not apply in relation to a dwelling which is to be sold or rented out where the relevant person can demonstrate that—
(a) the dwelling is suitable for demolition;
(b) the resulting site is suitable for redevelopment;
(c) all the relevant planning permissions, listed building consents, and conservation area consents exist in relation to the demolition; and
(d) in relation to the redevelopment—
    (i) either outline planning permission or planning permission exists, or both; and
    (ii) where relevant, listed building consent exists.

(2) Regulation 5 does not apply in relation to any prospective buyer or tenant of a building other than a dwelling which is to be sold or rented out where—
(a) the relevant person can demonstrate that—
    (i) the building is to be sold or rented out with vacant possession;
    (ii) the building is suitable for demolition; and
    (iii) the resulting site is suitable for redevelopment; and
(b) the relevant person believes on reasonable grounds that the prospective buyer or tenant intends to demolish the building.

(3) In this regulation, "outline planning permission" has the same meaning as in article 1(2) of the Town and Country Planning (General Development Procedure) Order 1995.

[1375]

NOTES

Commencement: 1 June 2007 (paras (1), (3), certain purposes); 1 October 2007 (paras (1), (3), certain purposes); 6 April 2008 (para (2), certain purposes); 1 October 2008 (otherwise).

8, 9 (*Outside the scope of this work.*)

10 Recommendation reports

(1) Where a relevant person is under a duty under regulation 5(2), 5(5) or 9(2) to make available or give an energy performance certificate to any person, the certificate must be accompanied by a recommendation report.

(2)   A recommendation report is a report containing recommendations for the improvement of the energy performance of the building issued by the energy assessor who issued the energy performance certificate.

[1376]

NOTES
Commencement: 19 April 2007.

11   Energy performance certificates

(1)   An energy performance certificate must—

    (a)   express the asset rating of the building in a way approved by the Secretary of State under regulation 17A of the Building Regulations 2000;

    (b)   include a reference value such as a current legal standard or benchmark;

    (c)   be issued by an energy assessor who is accredited to produce energy performance certificates for that category of building; and

    (d)   include the following information—

        (i)   the reference number under which the certificate has been registered in accordance with regulation 31;

        (ii)   the address of the building;

        (iii)   an estimate of the total useful floor area of the building;

        (iv)   the name of the energy assessor who issued it;

        (v)   the name and address of the energy assessor's employer, or, if he is self-employed, the name under which he trades and his address;

        (vi)   the date on which it was issued; and

        (vii)   the name of the approved accreditation scheme of which the energy assessor is a member.

(2)   A certificate which complies with regulation 17E of the Building Regulations 2000 is also an energy performance certificate.

(3)   Subject to paragraph (4), an energy performance certificate is only valid for the purposes of this Part if—

    (a)   it was issued no more than 10 years before the date on which it is made available; and

    (b)   no other energy performance certificate for the building has since been obtained by or provided to the relevant person.

(4)   If a building is to be sold or rented out in circumstances where section 155(1) or 159(2) of the Housing Act 2004 imposes a duty on any person in relation to that building, an energy performance certificate for the building is only valid for the purposes of this Part if it was issued no earlier than the date that falls [twelve months] before the first point of marketing of the building.

[(5)   For the purposes of paragraph (4), "first point of marketing" shall be construed in accordance with regulations 3, 16(3), 21(3), 22(3) and 34(5) of the Home Information Pack (No 2) Regulations 2007.]

(6)   An energy performance certificate must not contain any information or data [(except for the address of the building)] from which a living individual (other than the energy assessor or his employer) can be identified.

(7)   Certification for apartments or units designed or altered for separate use in blocks may be based—

    (a)   except in the case of a dwelling, on a common certification of the whole building for blocks with a common heating system; or

    (b)   on the assessment of another representative apartment or unit in the same block.

(8)   Where—

    (a)   a block with a common heating system is divided into parts designed or altered for separate use; and

    (b)   one or more, but not all, of the parts are dwellings,

certification for those parts which are not dwellings may be based on a common certification of all the parts which are not dwellings.

[1377]

NOTES
Commencement: 19 April 2007.
Para (4): words in square brackets substituted by the Energy Performance of Buildings (Certificates and Inspections) (England and Wales) (Amendment) Regulations 2007, SI 2007/1669, reg 3(1), (4)(a); for transitional provisions see reg 4 thereof
Para (5): substituted by SI 2007/1669, reg 3(1), (4)(b).
Para (6): words in square brackets inserted by SI 2007/1669, reg 3(1), (4)(c).

12   Production of copies of energy performance certificates

Where this Part requires a relevant person to give or make available a valid energy performance certificate to any person, it is sufficient for the relevant person to give or make available a copy of a valid certificate.

[1378]

NOTES
Commencement: 19 April 2007.

13   Electronic production of energy performance certificates

Where regulation 5(2), 5(5) or 9(2) requires a valid energy performance certificate to be given or made available to any person, the certificate may be given or made available electronically if the intended recipient consents to receiving the certificate electronically.

[1379]

NOTES
Commencement: 19 April 2007.

14   Purposes for which certificates and recommendation reports may be disclosed

(1)   Where any person has in his possession or control a document to which this regulation applies, it is an offence for that person to disclose, or permit the disclosure of, the document or any information derived from it except in the circumstances specified in paragraph (2).

(2)   Those circumstances are—
  (a)   where the disclosure is necessary to comply with—
      (i)   any duty imposed by these Regulations; or
      (ii)   any duty imposed by Part 5 of the Housing Act 2004 or any regulations made under that Part;
  (b)   where the disclosure is authorised by Part 7;
  (c)   where the disclosure is for a purpose legitimately connected with a prospective buyer's or tenant's decision whether to buy or rent the building;
  (d)   where the disclosure is by or to an accreditation scheme operator for a purpose legitimately connected to its accreditation functions;
  (e)   where the disclosure is by or to an enforcement authority for a purpose legitimately connected to their duty under regulation 38(2);
  (f)   where the disclosure is by or to the Secretary of State for—
      (i)   the purpose of enabling her to monitor the application and enforcement of, and compliance with, the duties imposed by these Regulations; or
      (ii)   statistical or research purposes,
  provided that no particular property is identifiable from the information disclosed;
  (g)   where the disclosure is for the purpose of—
      (i)   preventing or detecting crime;
      (ii)   apprehending or prosecuting offenders;
      (iii)   establishing, exercising or defending legal rights; or
      (iv)   complying with an order of a court.

(3)   Paragraph (1) does not apply to any disclosure of a document or any information derived from it by any person who, at the time of the disclosure, is, or is acting on behalf of, an owner or tenant of the building to which the document relates.

(4)   This regulation applies to the following documents—
  (a)   an energy performance certificate or a copy of such a certificate; and

(b)   a recommendation report or a copy of such a report,

and any data collected by an energy assessor for the purposes of preparing such a document shall be treated as part of that document for the purposes of this regulation.

(5)   A person guilty of an offence under this regulation is liable on summary conviction to a fine not exceeding level 5 on the standard scale.

[1380]

NOTES

Commencement: 19 April 2007.

15–50   (*Outside the scope of this work.*)

(*Schs 1, 2 outside the scope of this work.*)

Index

I

M

MANAGEMENT COMPANY
third party covenant, [686]
MARKET GARDEN
agricultural holding treated as—
Tribunal, powers—
application, form, [1047], [1061]
direction, power, [487]
reply, form, [1062]
improvements—
agricultural holding treated as,
rights, tenant, [486]
compensation, agreement, [488],
[524]
tenancy, old, [526]
MERGER
by operation of law only—
inapplicable, estate beneficial
interest in which not deemed to
be merged/extinguished in
equity, [171]
MILK QUOTA *see also* DAIRY
PRODUCE
Agriculture Act 1986, [573]–[578]
compensation, tenant—
amount, calculation, [577]
assignment, right, [576]
Crown land, [578]
enforcement, [578]
limited owners, powers, [578]
notices, [578]
reversionary estate, severance, [578]
right, [576]
standard quota, [577]
sub-tenancies, [576]
tenant's fraction, [577], [578], [579]
termination, tenancy, part of tenanted
land, [578]
transfer, right, succession,
death/retirement, tenant, [576]
Dairy Produce Quotas (General
Provisions) Regulations 2002,
[1295]–[1300]
disadvantaged/severely disadvantaged
land, [1099], [1102]
land to which applicable, [1098]
Milk Quota (Calculation of Standard
Quota) Order 1986,
[1098]–[1102]
prescribed quota, [1100]
rent arbitrations, [574]
standard quota—
average yield per hectare, [1101],
[1102]
calculation, generally, [577],
[1098]–[1102]

MILK QUOTA—*contd*
standard quota—*contd*
determination before end, tenancy,
[578]
tenant's fraction—
calculation, [577]
determination before end, tenancy,
[578]
settlement, claim on termination,
tenancy, [578]
valuation, [577]
MILITARY PURPOSES
improvements, business premises,
tenant in contravention, [192]
restrictive covenants—
operation, [154]
places in which operative, [154]
MINING PURPOSES, LEASE
mining lease, meaning—
Landlord and Tenant Act 1927, [209]
Landlord and Tenant Act 1954, [276]
Law of Property Act 1925, [175]
settled land—
tenant for life—
capitalisation, part, mining rent,
[121]
duration, [115]
mines and minerals, meaning,
[123]
provisions, [119]
variation, [120]
MINISTER OF AGRICULTURE,
FISHERIES AND FOOD *see*
AGRICULTURE, FISHERIES AND
FOOD, MINISTER
MONMOUTHSHIRE *see* WALES
MORTGAGE
commonhold land, common parts—
legal mortgage, creation—
approval, resolution, commonhold
association, [771]
conveyance by way of—
covenant for title, [150]
legal—
capable of subsisting/being
conveyed/created at law, [130]
meaning—
Landlord and Tenant Act 1954, [296]
Law of Property Act 1925, [175]
Trustee Act 1925, [127]
mortgagee in possession—
Landlord and Tenant Act 1954, [294]

N

NATIONAL PARK AUTHORITY
set-aside regulations—
meaning, [1171]

SA

346.
420
434
62
BUT